Practical GitLab Services

A Complete DevOps Guide for Developers and Administrators

Jeffrey Painter

Apress®

Practical GitLab Services: A Complete DevOps Guide for Developers and Administrators

Jeffrey Painter
Sugar Grove, IL, USA

ISBN-13 (pbk): 979-8-8688-0426-7 ISBN-13 (electronic): 979-8-8688-0427-4
https://doi.org/10.1007/979-8-8688-0427-4

Copyright © 2024 by Jeffrey Painter

This work is subject to copyright. All rights are reserved by the Publisher, whether the whole or part of the material is concerned, specifically the rights of translation, reprinting, reuse of illustrations, recitation, broadcasting, reproduction on microfilms or in any other physical way, and transmission or information storage and retrieval, electronic adaptation, computer software, or by similar or dissimilar methodology now known or hereafter developed.

Trademarked names, logos, and images may appear in this book. Rather than use a trademark symbol with every occurrence of a trademarked name, logo, or image we use the names, logos, and images only in an editorial fashion and to the benefit of the trademark owner, with no intention of infringement of the trademark.

The use in this publication of trade names, trademarks, service marks, and similar terms, even if they are not identified as such, is not to be taken as an expression of opinion as to whether or not they are subject to proprietary rights.

While the advice and information in this book are believed to be true and accurate at the date of publication, neither the authors nor the editors nor the publisher can accept any legal responsibility for any errors or omissions that may be made. The publisher makes no warranty, express or implied, with respect to the material contained herein.

> Managing Director, Apress Media LLC: Welmoed Spahr
> Acquisitions Editor: James Robinson-Prior
> Development Editor: James Markham
> Editorial Assistant: Gryffin Winkler

Cover designed by eStudioCalamar

Cover image designed by Nicola Ricca on Unsplash

Distributed to the book trade worldwide by Springer Science+Business Media New York, 1 New York Plaza, Suite 4600, New York, NY 10004-1562, USA. Phone 1-800-SPRINGER, fax (201) 348-4505, e-mail orders-ny@springer-sbm.com, or visit www.springeronline.com. Apress Media, LLC is a California LLC and the sole member (owner) is Springer Science + Business Media Finance Inc (SSBM Finance Inc). SSBM Finance Inc is a **Delaware** corporation.

For information on translations, please e-mail booktranslations@springernature.com; for reprint, paperback, or audio rights, please e-mail bookpermissions@springernature.com.

Apress titles may be purchased in bulk for academic, corporate, or promotional use. eBook versions and licenses are also available for most titles. For more information, reference our Print and eBook Bulk Sales web page at http://www.apress.com/bulk-sales.

Any source code or other supplementary material referenced by the author in this book is available to readers on GitHub. For more detailed information, please visit https://www.apress.com/gp/services/source-code.

If disposing of this product, please recycle the paper

I dedicate this book to my father, Norman, who fought a decade-long battle with dementia with a tremendous sense of humor and grace.

Table of Contents

About the Author .... **xxvii**

About the Technical Reviewer .... **xxix**

Acknowledgments .... **xxxi**

Introduction .... **xxxiii**

Chapter 1: Only the Beginning **1**

    Introducing GitLab 1

    Setting Up a GitLab Account 3

        Creating a GitLab SaaS Account 4

        Creating Your First Project 6

        A Glimpse at GitLab's Main Interface 8

    Exploring User Options 10

        Updating Your User Profile 10

        Setting Your Preferences 12

        Accessing Your Dashboard Home Page 13

    Summary 15

Chapter 2: Just the Source **17**

    Exploring the Web IDE 17

        Editing with the Web IDE 18

        Previewing Markdown Files 21

        Viewing Changes via the Source Control Panel 22

        Committing Your Changes 23

        Reviewing the Project Summary Page 25

TABLE OF CONTENTS

    Working with Branches 26
        Creating a New Branch 26
        Reviewing Project Changes After Branch Creation 29
        Committing Changes on a Branch 32
        Visualizing Branch Changes with the Repository Graph 33
        Committing Multiple Changes on a Branch 34
    Submitting Merge Requests 37
        Creating a Merge Request 37
        Viewing Merge Request Details 39
        Tracking Open Merge Requests 41
        Merging Changes from a Merge Request 43
        Reviewing Project Changes After an MR Merge 44
    Resolving Merge Conflicts 46
        Setting Up the Conditions for a Merge Conflict 47
        Generating the Merge Conflict 49
        Exploring Ways to Resolve the Merge Conflict 51
        Committing the Conflict Resolution Change 53
        Performing an MR Merge After Committing a Conflict Resolution 56
        Reviewing Project Status After Merge of Conflicting MRs 59
    Considering Branching Strategies 63
    Summary 64

Chapter 3: Working the Remote Life 65
    Installing Git 65
    Cloning with HTTPS 67
        Preparing Your Local Environment 67
        Determining the URL to Use for Cloning with HTTPS 68
        Performing the HTTPS Clone with the Git Credential Manager 69
        Performing the HTTPS Clone Using Username and Password Credentials 71
    Cloning with SSH 72
        Creating the SSH Key Pair on Your Local Environment 72
        Registering the SSH Public Key with GitLab 74

TABLE OF CONTENTS

Testing SSH Connectivity to GitLab 77
Debugging Common Issues Connecting with SSH 78
Determining the URL to Use for Cloning with SSH 79
Cloning Your Project with SSH 79
Configuring Git 80
Configuring Your Username and Email Address 81
Locating the Global Configuration File 81
Making Changes with Git 82
Creating a New Branch in GitLab for Use by Your Local Repository 83
Synchronizing the New GitLab Branch with Your Local Environment 83
Making Changes in the Local Repository 84
Staging Changes in Your Local Repository 85
Committing Changes in Your Local Repository 86
Pushing Changes Up to the GitLab Project Repository 87
Confirming Changes in the GitLab Project Repository 87
Creating the Merge Request in GitLab and Merging It 88
Cleaning Up the Local Repository 89
Summary 90

Chapter 4: Build, Test, Rinse, and Repeat 93

Introducing the GitLab Configuration File 93
General Overview of the Configuration File 94
Creating a Basic CI/CD Pipeline Configuration 94
Associating Jobs to Stages 96
Validating Account Upon First Pipeline Run 97
Restarting a Pipeline 98
Pipeline Job Execution Through the Various Stages 99
Viewing a Job's Output 102
Viewing a Project's Pipeline Status Page 104
Project Status Impacts After a Pipeline Run 105

TABLE OF CONTENTS

Working with Docker 106
    A Personal Experience with Jenkins and GitLab 106
    The Case for Docker 108
    Exploring Docker Hub 109
    Specifying a New Default Image 113
    Defining Tasks to Run by Default Before Every Job 116
    Overriding the Default Image and before_script Tasks for a Given Job 118

Introducing CI/CD Variables 120
    Defining and Using Variables Within a Configuration File 121
    Using Predefined Variables in a Configuration File 123
    Defining Variables When Manually Running a Pipeline 124
    Setting Descriptions and Default Values for "Run Pipeline" Variables 125
    Defining CI/CD Variables at the Project or Group Level 128
    Masking Secret Values for CI/CD Variables 130

Managing CI/CD Configurations 135
    Breaking a Pipeline Configuration into Multiple Files 135
    Viewing a Merged Configuration with the CI/CD Editor 139
    Additional Include Types 140
    Breaking Jobs into Reusable Pieces Using Extends 140
    Enabling Fine-Grain Reusability with Reference Tags 144

Summary 150

Chapter 5: Under One Condition 151

Following the Rules 151
    Overview of Rules 152
    Changing Rule Behavior with the When Keyword 152
    Preparing Scripts to Explore Impacts of Rules 153
    A Simple Rule Example 157
    Variable Expression Conditions 159
    Common Predefined Variables Used in Rules 161
    Example Rules with CI_PIPELINE_SOURCE 163
    Branch Pipelines vs. Merge Request Pipelines 166

Working with Workflows	168
Interactions Between Workflows and Rules	171
File-Based Rule Conditions	171
Considerations When Using File-Based Conditions	172
Example of Rules Using File-Based Conditions	173
Overriding Variables Within a Rule	175
Dealing with Failures	178
Preparing an Example to Test Job Failures	178
Ignoring a Job Failure	180
Conditionally Ignoring a Job Failure	182
Ignoring Job Failure Based on Exit Codes	184
Running a Job Based on Another Job's Failure	188
Enabling a Job to Always Run After Another Job's Failure	191
Rerunning a Job That Failed Based on External Events	192
Manually Running Jobs	192
Pausing a Job in Order to Stop a Pipeline's Execution	193
Pausing a Job Without Blocking a Pipeline's Execution	198
Impacts of Manually Running a Paused Job That Eventually Fails	201
Impacts of Canceling a Paused Job	203
Summary	204

Chapter 6: You Build It, You Keep It 205

Creating and Preserving Artifacts	205
Denoting Generated Objects As Artifacts	205
Creating and Accessing Artifacts	209
Accessing Artifacts in Jobs of Follow-On Stages	211
Downloading Artifacts from GitLab	213
Renaming the Artifacts Zip File	215
Accessing Artifacts from a Merge Request	216
Additional Artifacts Options	220

TABLE OF CONTENTS

Working with Caches 220
    Distinction in the Pipeline Handling of Artifacts and Caches 221
    A Maven Example 221
    Build Job Updates for Maven 224
    Pipeline Updates to Cache Maven Objects 227
    Accessing the Cache in the Unit Test 232
    Impact on Cache When Rerunning the Pipeline 234
    Creating Multiple Caches in a Pipeline 236
    Marking a Cache As Read-Only 243
    Clearing Caches 246

Summary 248

Chapter 7: Let's Get Organized 249

Introducing Groups 249
    Viewing Group-Specific Projects 250
    Viewing Group Activity 251
    Viewing Members of a Group 251
    Adding Members to a Group 252
    Project Impacts When Adding a Group Member 254
    Promoting a Group Member to Higher Project Role 254
    Differences Between Group and Project Change Role Lists 256

Working with Subgroups 258
    Creating a Subgroup 258
    Viewing the Subgroup Page 260
    Adding Additional Members to a Subgroup 261
    Developer-Specific Views of Groups and Subgroups 262
    Maintainer-Specific Views of Groups and Subgroups 263
    Determining Roles Allowed to Create Projects Within a Group 264
    Determining Roles Allowed to Create Subgroups Within a Group 265

Navigating Permissions via Roles 266
    Additional Roles of Guest and Reporter 266
    Overview of Permissions 267

Comparing GitLab's Permission Model with Other Models	267
Inviting GitLab Groups As Members of Other Groups and Projects	269
Importing Project Members from Another Project	270
Special Roles for Self-Managed Sites	271
Managing Group- and Project-Specific Resources	271
Managing Group- and Project-Specific Runners	272
Managing Group- and Project-Specific Packages and Registries	272
Creating Personal Projects	273
Creating a Personal Project	273
Viewing Personal Projects from the Project Summary Page	276
Special Caveats of Personal Projects	277
Reorganizing Projects and Groups	277
Renaming a Project	277
Changing a Project's URL Path Name	279
Impacts of Changing a Project's Path	280
Archiving a Project	281
Deleting a Project	282
Transferring a Project to Another Group	283
Renaming a Group	285
Changing a Group's URL	285
Deleting a Group	286
Transferring a Group to Another Group	287
Exporting and Importing Projects	287
Exporting a Project	288
Importing a Project	289
Dealing with Import Failures	291
Summary	292
Chapter 8: I Have an Issue with That	**293**
Managing Issues	293
Viewing Project-Specific Issues	294
Creating an Issue	295

TABLE OF CONTENTS

 Viewing Issue Details 297

 Editing an Issue 297

 Reacting to an Issue 298

 Viewing Issue Activity 300

 Filtering Issues 301

 Editing Multiple Issues at Once 302

Labeling Issues and MRs 303

 Viewing Labels in Issues List 303

 Filtering Issues by Label 304

 Editing Labels 305

 Prioritizing Labels 306

 Creating a New Label 308

 Promoting Labels to a Group 309

Creating MRs from Issues 311

 Creating a Merge Request from an Issue 311

 Viewing a Merge Request Generated from an Issue 312

 Viewing Labels in Merge Requests List 314

 Impact on Issue When Merging an Associated MR 314

Linking Issues 316

 Special Considerations About Linking Issues in GitLab 317

 Linking One Issue to Another 317

 Viewing Linked Items 319

 Deleting a Link 320

 Special Link Types with Paid Subscriptions 320

Summary 320

Chapter 9: The Best Laid Plans 323

Establishing Milestones 323

 Creating Milestones 324

 Viewing Milestone Details 325

 Associating Issues with Milestones 326

 Viewing Milestones from the Issue List 328

Removing an Issue from a Milestone	329
Viewing the Project's Milestone Summary	330
Promoting Milestones to the Group Level	330
Viewing Milestone Associations with MRs	331
Viewing Milestones from the Top-Level Dashboard	332
Filtering Issues by Milestones	333
Special Considerations of Milestones	333
Defining Tasks	**334**
Creating Tasks	334
Editing a Task	336
Completing a Task	336
Viewing Tasks in the Issue List	338
Associating Tasks to Milestones	338
Filtering Tasks from an Issue List	339
Converting Document List Items to Tasks	340
Planning with Boards	**341**
Exploring an Existing Issue Board	341
Creating Additional Column Lists	342
Editing an Issue Board	343
Moving Items Between Columns on an Issue Board	344
Impact of Closing an Issue from the Board	345
Moving Issues Within a Column	346
Creating and Editing a Group-Level Issue Board	347
Creating a New Project Issue Board	349
Working with Multiple Issue Boards	350
Additional Features with Paid Subscriptions	352
Integrating with Jira	**353**
Setting Up a Jira Cloud Account	353
Installing the GitLab for Jira Cloud App	354
Configuring the GitLab for Jira Cloud App	356
Authorizing the App to Connect to Your GitLab Account	358

TABLE OF CONTENTS

   Linking the App to Your GitLab Namespace 360
   Creating the Jira API Key 362
   Configuring a GitLab Project for Jira Integration 364
   Verifying the Project Is Integrated with Jira 367
   Viewing Integrated Issues from GitLab 368
   Viewing Integrated Issues from Jira 369
   Impact of Issue Changes Made from Jira 369
   Impact of Issue Changes Made from GitLab 371
   Viewing GitLab Job Information from Jira 372
   Additional Jira Integration Features with Paid Subscriptions 373
  Summary 374

Chapter 10: It's Nice to Share 375

  Managing Docker Images 375
   Considerations When Creating Our Own Docker Images 375
   Accessing the Project Container Registry 376
   Process for Creating and Storing a Docker Image 377
   Pipeline Results of Creating, Storing, and Using a Docker Image 381
   Viewing Container Registry Changes 383
   Merge Request Results of Creating and Storing a Docker Image 385
   The Problem of Unneeded Images 386
   Setting an Image Cleanup Policy 387
  Sharing Docker Images 389
   First Attempt Accessing an Image from Another Project 390
   Investigating Why Access Was Denied 391
   Enabling a Project to Access Another's Container Registry 392
   Accessing Container Registry Images Outside of GitLab 395
   Creating Personal Access Tokens 396
   Accessing Images Using Personal Access Tokens 397
   Using DOCKER_AUTH_CONFIG to Access a Project's Container Registry 399
   Determining the DOCKER_AUTH_CONFIG Authentication String 400
   Setting DOCKER_AUTH_CONFIG As a Group CI/CD Variable 400

TABLE OF CONTENTS

Security Concerns with DOCKER_AUTH_CONFIG 401

Creating Project Deploy Tokens 402

Creating Group Deploy Tokens 404

A Brief Mention of Project and Group Access Tokens 405

Working with the Package Registry 406

Accessing the Project Package Registry 406

A Maven Example of Creating and Storing a Jar File 407

Pipeline Results of Creating and Storing a Jar File 412

Viewing Package Registry Changes 413

Viewing Package Details in the Registry 413

Effects of Multiple Pipeline Runs on the Package Registry 415

Automating Cleanup of the Package Registry 416

Summary 417

Chapter 11: There's an API for That 419

Introducing the GitLab REST API 419

Differences Between GitLab UI and REST API URLs 419

Differences Between GitLab UI and REST API Responses 420

REST API Basics 421

GitLab REST API Resources 422

Restricting Resources with URL Endpoints 423

Restricting Results with URL Parameters 424

Requesting Additional Information with URL Endpoints 425

URL Endpoint Patterns 427

Paginating Responses 428

Retrieving Additional Pages 430

Standalone Resource Examples 432

RESTing with Curl 434

Setting Up Authentication to Make API Requests 435

A Simple REST API Query with Curl 436

Using jq to Manipulate JSON Responses 437

Using jq to Pretty-Print REST API Responses 438

TABLE OF CONTENTS

    Using jq to Extract Information from REST API Responses 439
    Using Programming Languages to Manipulate REST API Responses 441
    Using Curl to Manipulate Resources 441
    Creating a Resource with the REST API 441
    Deleting a Resource with the REST API 443
    Modifying Resources with the REST API 444
Exploring GraphQL 445
    Making GraphQL Requests with Curl 445
    Reading GraphQL Queries from a File 447
    A Query to Retrieve Issues Associated with a Project 449
    A Query to Retrieve One Issue Associated with a Project 451
    A Query to Return a Sorted List of Issues Associated with a Project 452
    Creating an Object with GraphQL 454
    Updating an Object with GraphQL 455
    Deleting an Object with GraphQL 457
Interacting with GraphiQL 458
    The GraphQL Explorer 458
    Getting Help Making GraphQL Requests 460
    Pagination with GraphQL 468
    Using GraphQL Introspection 470
Deciphering the GraphQL Reference 472
    Main Sections of the GraphQL Reference 473
    The Query Type Section 474
    The Scaler Types Section 475
    The Object Types Section 477
    The Enumeration Types Section 479
    The Connections Section 481
    The Mutation Type Section 485
    The Input Types Section 487
    The Abstract Types Section 488
Summary 492

TABLE OF CONTENTS

Chapter 12: Well, Isn't That Special 495
Generating Web Pages 495
Exploring Project Templates for GitLab Pages 496
Creating a Project from a Template 496
Overview of Files Generated by the Template 497
Running the GitLab Pages Pipeline 501
Accessing the Generated Web Page 502
Exploring the "Other Examples" Page 503
Previewing Example Websites Generated by GitLab Pages 504
Enabling Access to the Generate GitLab Page 505
Creating GitLab Pages Without Templates 506
Caveat to Using GitLab Pages 506
Using Alternative URLs for GitLab Pages 507
Handling Binary Files 508
The Problem of Storing Versioned Binary Files in Git 509
The Git LFS Feature 509
Prerequisites to Git LFS 510
Marking Files to Be Managed by Git LFS 510
Migrating Existing Files to Use Git LFS 511
Cases When Git LFS Should Not Be Used 512
Summary 512

Chapter 13: I Can Do This on My Own 513
Deciding on a Plan of Implementation 513
On-Premises vs. Cloud Considerations 514
Administrative Considerations 514
Architecture Considerations 515
High-Availability Considerations 516
Disaster Recovery Considerations 516
Cost Considerations 517
GitLab Support Considerations 517
Alternative Service Considerations 518

xvii

TABLE OF CONTENTS

Instantiating the AWS Account 518
    Creating an AWS Account 518
    Creating an Admin User Group with IAM 519
    Creating an Admin User for Yourself 520
    Setting Up Multifactor Authentication 521
Preparing the VPC Network 522
    Determining the AWS Region for the GitLab POC 522
    Creating a Private VPC 523
    Setting the Number of Availability Zones 524
    Setting Up Public and Private Subnets 525
    Setting Up the NAT Gateway 526
    Reviewing How the VPC Will Be Created 526
    Reviewing the Components of the VPC 527
Creating the SSH Key Pair 528
    Creating SSH Key Pairs in AWS 528
Establishing the Domain Name 531
    Registering a Domain Through AWS 531
Generating the TLS Certificate 532
    Requesting a TLS Certificate Through AWS 533
    Associating Your Domain with the Certificate 535
    Validating Domain Ownership 536
    Waiting for the Certificate to Be Approved 537
Preparing the IAM Role 538
    Creating an IAM Policy 538
    Creating the IAM Role 542
Building the ELB 545
    Creating a Classic Load Balancer 546
    Setting the ELB Name and Scheme 547
    Setting the ELB Network Mappings 548
    Creating the ELB Security Group 549
    Setting Up ELB Listeners 554

TABLE OF CONTENTS

Associating the TLS Certificate with the ELB 555

Setting Up the ELB Health Check 556

Setting ELB Special Attributes 557

Spinning Up the ELB 558

Connecting Your Domain 559

Creating a Hosted Zone Record 559

Verifying Domain Connectivity to the ELB 564

Summary 565

Chapter 14: Things That Lurk in the Background 567

Raising the RDS 567

Creating the RDS Security Group 567

Accessing RDS 569

Creating the DB Subnet Group 570

Creating the PostgreSQL Database with RDS 572

Reviewing Database Costs 588

Stopping the Database Temporarily 589

Setting Up the ElastiCache 590

Creating the Redis Security Group 591

Accessing ElastiCache 591

Creating the Redis Subnet Group 592

Creating the Redis Cluster 594

Starting the Redis Service 602

Preparing the Bastion Hosts 602

Launching the Bastion Servers 603

Testing Connectivity to the Bastion Server 608

Creating the Second Bastion Server 609

Viewing the Bastion Instances 610

Configuring SSH Forwarding 611

Summary 618

xix

Chapter 15: The Proof Is in the Cloud 619

Spinning Up a Standalone GitLab Service 619
Introduction to AMIs 619
Searching for the Official GitLab AMI 620
Creating a GitLab Instance from an Image 621
Accessing the GitLab Instance via SSH 624
Adding PostgreSQL Extensions 625
Disabling Let's Encrypt 626
Setting the External URL 627
Disabling the Internal PostgreSQL Database 628
Configuring the External PostgreSQL Database 629
Disabling the Internal Redis Database 629
Configuring the External Redis Database 630
Applying Configuration Changes 631
Checking the Status of GitLab Services 631
Investigating Nginx Service Failure 632
Connecting the GitLab Server to the ELB 633
More Investigation into nginx Server Failure 634
Configuring the nginx Reverse Proxy 635
Investigating ELB Out of Service Failure 636
Learning Through Debugging 636
Logging In to Your GitLab Standalone Service 637

Splitting Off the Gitaly Service 638
The Reason for Splitting Off the Gitaly Service 638
Locating the Generated GitLab Secrets File 638
Creating the Gitaly Security Group 639
Spinning Up the Gitaly Server 640
Installing the GitLab Package on the Gitaly Server 641
Copying the GitLab Secrets File to the Gitaly Server 642
Configuring the Standalone Gitaly Service 643
Configuring Gitaly Storage 645

TABLE OF CONTENTS

- Spinning Up the Standalone Gitaly Service 646
- Running the Gitaly Check Command 647
- Checking Gitaly Connectivity from the GitLab Server 647
- Configuring GitLab to Use the New Standalone Gitaly Service 648
- Verifying GitLab Is Using the New Gitaly Service 649
- Disabling the Internal Gitaly Service 649
- Changing Storage Allocations Through the Administrative UI 650

Configuring Server-Side SSH 654
- A Description of SSH Server Host Keys 654
- The Need for Consistent Host Keys Across Multiple GitLab Servers 654
- Bad Approaches to Man-in-the-Middle Messages 655
- The SSH-Approved Approach Using Host Certificates 655
- GitLab's Approach Using Static Host Keys 656
- Enabling Fast Lookup of Authorized SSH Keys 657

Enabling S3 Object Storage 659
- A Possible Storage Approach Using NFS 659
- Another Approach Using S3 Object Storage 659
- Creating the KMS Encryption Key 659
- Creating the S3 Buckets 664
- Setting the Server IAM Role to Allow Access to the S3 Object Store 670
- Verifying the IAM Role Is Attached to the Standalone GitLab Server 672
- Configuring GitLab to Use the S3 Object Storage 673

Scaling the GitLab Service 674
- Creating Our Own GitLab Server AMI 675
- Testing the ELB Health Check 677
- Determining the Readiness Check Access Token 678
- Resetting the ELB Health Check to Use Readiness Check with Access Token 679
- Creating the Launch Template 680
- Creating the Auto-Scaling Group 686
- Viewing EC2 List of Instances Created by the ASG 695
- Viewing ELB List of Instances Created by the ASG 696

xxi

TABLE OF CONTENTS

Testing SSH Connectivity to the Newly Spun-Up Servers... 697
Checking GitLab Service via the UI.. 698
Stopping the Standalone GitLab Server... 699
Tagging the ASG Instances 700
Reviewing the Behind-the-Scenes Scaling Rules 702
Summary... 703

Chapter 16: Working the Never-Ending Queue 705

Managing Shared Runners.. 705
The Do-Nothing Approach 705
Managing a Farm of GitLab Runners 705
Managing Auto-Scaling GitLab Runners... 706
Setting Up Auto-Scaling Shared Runners in AWS 707
Preliminary AWS Setup.. 707
Creating the Runner Manager Server.. 714
Spinning Up a Test Runner with docker-machine... 719
Creating an Instance Runner Entry from the Administrative GUI...................................... 726
Creating the register-me Script on the Runner Manager 731
Results of Running the register-me Script 732
Creating the config.toml File 732
Applying the New Gitlab-Runner Configuration 739
Checking the Gitlab-Runner Status 740
Viewing Spun-Up Runner EC2 Instances 740
Peeking Inside the Spun-Up Runner... 742
Viewing Runner Instance List from the Administrative UI 742
Testing Running Jobs with Our Shared Runner Service.. 743
Verifying the S3 Object Cache 747
Checking Docker State in the Spun-Up Runner Server 751
Summary... 752

TABLE OF CONTENTS

Chapter 17: But Wait, There's More 753
Establishing Email Connectivity 753
- Setting Up SMTP with Amazon's Simple Email Service 753
- Configuring SMTP Settings in GitLab 761
- Testing GitLab Email Settings Programmatically 762
- Changing the Admin User Email Address 764
- Setting Up Email Routing with AWS 765
- Configuring SES to Handle Email Requests 768
- Activating the SES Rule 777
- Alternatives to Using SNS with SES 778

Enabling Secondary Services 778
- Overview of Secondary Services 779
- Enabling the External Diffs Service 779
- Enabling the ci_secure_files Service 780
- Enabling the Container Registry Service 780
- Enabling the GitLab Pages Service 784
- Scaling Considerations for the Pages Service 790

Summary 790

Chapter 18: It's an Admin's Life 791
Dealing with Users 791
- Managing Users via the Administrative UI 791
- Adding a New User 792
- Resetting a User's Password 795
- Configuring Site-Wide Settings for Users 796
- Configuring Sign-Up Restrictions 797
- Setting Sign-In Restrictions 798
- Integrating with External Authentication Services 799
- Integrating with LDAP/Active Directory Authentication Service 799
- Additional LDAP Options Available for Licensed Sites 801
- Impact of Authentication Service on License Costs 802
- Blocking Users 802

xxiii

TABLE OF CONTENTS

Banning Users 803
Deactivating Users... 803
Status of GitLab Users When Removed or Disabled from Authentication Service.............. 804
Deleting Users 805
Importance of Establishing User Management Policies 805

Updating GitLab's Configuration.. 806
Restarting the Standalone GitLab Server 806
Adding the Standalone GitLab Server to the ELB 807
Optionally Spinning Down Existing ASG Servers 809
Updating the GitLab Configuration File and Creating a New AMI 811
Updating the Launch Template with the New AMI... 812
Spinning Up New ASG Servers 814
Detaching and Shutting Down the GitLab Standalone Server 815
Using the Instance Refresh Feature to Replace ASG Servers......................... 816

Upgrading to a New Release... 817
Overview of the Release Upgrade Process... 817
The Need for Doing a GitLab Service Shutdown... 818
Broadcasting System-Wide Messages 818
Pausing Shared Runners Under Your Control 820
Special Maintenance Mode for Licensed Sites.. 821
Spinning Down ASG Servers... 821
Spinning Up the Standalone GitLab Server... 822
Creating Backups of the Standalone Servers 822
Backing Up the RDS Database.. 822
Upgrading Gitaly Server to New Release.. 824
Upgrading the Standalone GitLab Server 830
Upgrading the GitLab Runner Manager 830
Completing the Release Upgrade Process 831

Summary... 832

Chapter 19: Lights, Camera, Action! 833

Planning Your Production Setup 833
- Considering Monthly Production Costs 834
- Additional Needs of a Production-Level Self-Managed Service 836
- High-Availability Needs 836
- Disaster Recovery Needs 837
- Release Upgrade Complications 839
- Reasons for a Staging Service 839
- Monitoring Needs 840

Creating Your Production Setup 840
- Deciding Where the Primary Service Should Reside 841
- Considering AWS Direct Connect 841
- Establishing a Naming Convention for Your GitLab Services 842
- Preparing Production-Level VPC Environments 843
- Establishing AWS Component Naming Conventions 844
- Preparing TLS Certificates 844
- Defining Service-Specific AWS Key Pairs 844
- Creating Independent IAM Roles and Policies per Service and Region 845
- Database Production-Level Requirements 845
- Bastion Server Considerations 846
- Creating a Provisioning Server 846
- Gitaly Cluster Considerations 847
- GitLab Application Server Considerations 847
- Preparing for Automated Configuration File Changes 848
- Instance-Level Shared Runner Considerations 848
- Planning for the Gitaly Cluster 848

Switching to Gitaly Clusters 849
- The Gitaly Sharding Option 849
- The Gitaly Cluster Option 850
- The Case for Moving to a Licensed Version of GitLab 854
- Establishing a Gitaly Cluster in AWS 854

xxv

TABLE OF CONTENTS

- Optionally Migrating Existing Git Repositories to the Gitaly Cluster 861
- Reviewing the Gitaly Troubleshooting Guide 862
- Preparing for Disaster 862
  - AWS Disaster Recovery Considerations 863
  - Mirroring Services with GitLab Geo 864
  - High-Level Steps to Setting Up GitLab Geo 865
  - Considerations When Using GitLab Geo to Perform All Replications 865
  - Using RDS and Redis Cross-Region Read Replication 866
  - Using S3 Cross-Region Replication 866
  - Synchronizing Git Repository Changes via the Geo Tracking Database 866
  - Complications with Disaster Recovery When Using AWS Replication 867
  - Establishing a Disaster Recovery Plan 867
- Automating Upgrades 868
  - The Concept of Zero-Downtime Upgrades 868
  - Order of Upgrading Components 869
  - Tools to Automate the Upgrade Process 870
  - Choosing a Source Control Management Solution for Automating Upgrades 870
  - An Example of Automating GitLab AMI Creation 871
  - Resource Management Tools 872
  - Configuration Management Tools 876
  - Automating Upgrades to the Gitaly Cluster 878
  - Automating Upgrades to Shared Runner Managers 879
  - Orchestrating the Upgrade Process 880
  - Creating a Docker Image to Support the Automation Process 880
  - Testing the Automation Process 881
- Summary 882

Index 883

About the Author

Jeffrey Painter has spent the last 45 years in software development, working as a developer in various languages ranging from Fortran, C, C++, and Java to Python and in a variety of roles from development to administration. The last seven years have been spent at HERE Technologies as a system engineer, first maintaining a farm of Jenkins servers for entire project teams and then prototyping and maintaining several self-managed GitLab servers.

About the Technical Reviewer

Balakrishnan Seetharaman has been working at HERE Technologies for over 12 years. He is currently working as a principal DevOps engineer, and his work involves the use of GitLab, AWS, and Python on a daily basis. Some of his skills include working with Python, Ansible, Kubernetes, and Helm. His expertise is in deployment automation, CI/CD, and DevSecOps methodologies. Some of his key achievements are zero-downtime deployments using Python/Ansible, orchestrating a complex CI process across multiple projects, and ensuring seamless delivery of product stack.

Seetharaman hails from Chennai, India, which is well known for its rich culture and heritage. He completed his engineering from there and is currently residing in Berlin, Germany. He is passionate about photography, traveling, coding, and reading. Books have always inspired him to gain a better perspective of life both personally and professionally.

Acknowledgments

As is typical with acknowledgments, I would like to first thank my wife, Katherine, for her infinite patience as I holed myself up in my office for the past year writing this book. I know it wasn't easy at times. I would also like to thank my daughter, Lisa, who, unbeknownst to her, encouraged me to continue writing during times when I most wanted to give up.

I would next like to thank my former manager, Brendan Fortune, who assigned me the task of setting up our company's first GitLab service. I wasn't so sure that I could do it at first, but he had faith in knowing that if anyone could get this thing working, it was me. I would also like to acknowledge my comrade in arms, Jeff Hawk, who worked with me in setting up all the behind-the-scenes automation scripts to keep the GitLab service up and running. I couldn't have done it on my own.

Of course, there were the remaining members of the team in Europe and India who helped ensure that the service kept running 24/7 and who enhanced the administration of the service with tons of metrics. It was a pleasure to work with Cosmin, Bala, and Luigi along with the many developers in India that supported the project.

I would especially like to thank my technical reviewer, Bala Seetharaman, who helped ensure the accuracy of the book even though it meant my having to retake or touch up hundreds of screenshots.

Finally, I would like to thank the many editors, Sowmya Thodur, Jim Markham, and Gryffin Winkler who guided me on my first foray into writing a book. Their advice made this a better book, IMHO. And special thanks to my acquisition editor, James Robinson-Prior, for giving me the chance to publish this book despite having no experience in doing so.

Introduction

In the early 1960s, deep inside Chicago's Museum of Science and Industry lay a secret room – well, secret to most people. As a young child, I was made aware of this room by my father who would on occasion take me with him when he worked there. To him, the room was simply known as "the computer room," but to me, it was a magical place filled with machines that somehow appeared "alive."

To the right as you entered the room was a series of three tape drives each about six feet tall and three feet wide that had spools of large magnetic tape. Unlike tape recorders or VCRs that continually spun the tape, these machines would pull the tape in starts and stops much like a heartbeat. It was mesmerizing to watch.

In the center of the room was a large console filled with lots of lights and switches, much like an airplane's cockpit. In the back of the room behind the console was the giant vacuum-filled iron machine known as the Datatron 205 that was about six feet tall and 20 feet wide. On the front were an array of lights that blinked in distinct patterns when it was working. You could tell by watching them that the computer was methodically doing something important.

And to the right was my favorite machine: the paper tape punch/reader. This took a thin strip of tickertape-like paper and either punched holes into it or read them back. The punch mode was my favorite as it furiously sprayed little dots of confetti that spattered everywhere much like popcorn popping in a movie theater popcorn machine.

What I didn't know then was that my exposure to that computer room would be the beginning of my journey through the golden age of computing. As a programmer/analyst, I would experience working on mainframes, PDP-11 and VAX mini-computers, SUN workstations, TRS-80 desktop machines, "portable" COMPAQ machines, as well as the current laptops and tablets of today. I would experience various networking setups from "sneaker nets" to the Ethernet to the Internet of today. I had a lot of positions from testing to development to management to research to architecture. It was not only intellectually stimulating living through those times, but it was also, dare I say, fun?

Fast forward to the 2010s as I was nearing the end of my career. I had taken a position as a system administrator of a corporate internal service referred to as Jenkins as a Service, a.k.a. JaaS (pronounced jazz). The concept was simple. Jenkins was one of the

INTRODUCTION

most popular tools at the time for building and testing software through a process known as continuous integration. Management wanted to get a better handle on how this tool was used, so a team was formed to provide a service to other development teams. When a team started a new project, they would make a request for a Jenkins server just for them that we would help manage. We used AWS to spin up a server with Jenkins and other useful development tools preinstalled. Given that we could spin up the server within half an hour, JaaS became quite popular.

I was happy with managing this service and was planning to sail off into retirement by training others to take over the service before I left. But, of course, corporate had other ideas. One day out of the blue, I was given the task of spinning up this new service called "GitLab." It was supposed to be a proof of concept within the company, a chance for developers to test the service out and give their feedback. The problem was, I had never heard of this tool before and had no idea what it did or why management wanted to consider switching to it.

As was typical for a boomer like me, I searched around for reading materials such as books or PDF manuals that would help me quickly learn what this tool did and how I could easily install it. There were, after all, plenty of books on Jenkins that did so. Given this tool was relatively new (it was around its sixth release at the time), there was no such material, at least none that helped me with my task. I had to rely on GitLab's online documentation, portions of which I printed out and read on the train home from work.

It was a daunting task, but with my background in using AWS to get the Jenkins service up, I was eventually able to get a proof-of-concept GitLab service up and running. Truth be told, I made a lot of mistakes along the way. Over time, I came to better understand the inner workings of GitLab and how to use it. When it was decided to go with a production-level service, I felt better about supporting it. It was especially helpful to finally get direct support from GitLab, the company. I learned a lot from them over the years.

When I did retire, I came to the realization that I had acquired a lot of knowledge as an administrator of GitLab that I thought others would find useful. I did, after all, have conference calls set up by GitLab to discuss our service architecture. Searching around for books on GitLab, I still didn't find any that would have helped me when I first started working with it. So, I decided to write the book that I wish I had.

Rather than start with getting people to install a self-managed service on their own, which can be a frustrating task if you haven't done it before, I decided to take a different approach. For this book, I'm using a technique known as gamification (where the first syllable is pronounced "game"). It is a technique used in getting people proficient in mastering a digital game. You start off with something easy that most people can do and then you keep "leveling up" as users gain more confidence in performing more difficult tasks.

To that end, I start off the book by having you sign up for the GitLab SaaS service, which is extremely easy to do and is free to boot. From there, I cover the basic functionality of GitLab: source code management. In terms of source code management, we'll begin with GitLab's simple-to-use interface which hides the gory details of managing projects with Git, the underlying SCM tool used by GitLab. Once that is mastered, we'll look at how to use Git in coordination with GitLab to remotely manage your source code.

I then introduce GitLab's concept of CI/CD pipelines, which is unique to GitLab. You'll start off learning how to create a pipeline configuration file (which, of course, is checked in as part of your source code) to run jobs that build, test, and deploy your software product. We'll then consider how to conditionally build software using rules and then end that topic with how to store artifacts and cache intermediate objects.

Next up, I will take you through how to organize your projects into groups and subgroups. It is here that we'll look at how GitLab uses this organizational structure in conjunction with roles to determine who has permission to do certain tasks such as creating projects or modifying code.

Continuing to the next level, I'll show you how to use GitLab to manage issues and plan your work. Realizing that many businesses use other tools for this, I'll show you how GitLab lets you integrate with them. I'll use the popular Jira tool as an example.

And then we level up to the more advanced features of GitLab, some of which I didn't realize existed until months after I started administering the GitLab service. We'll look at GitLab's built-in Docker container registry in addition to its built-in package registry. From there, we'll peek at GitLab's API that lets you programmatically automate common development and administrative tasks. We'll end the advanced features investigation by showing how to create static web pages for those outside of a project using the GitLab Pages feature and then how to handle binary file storage using Git LFS.

In the latter chapters of the book, we switch from development topics to administrative ones. I begin by describing how to spin up your own self-managed GitLab service in AWS, starting with a proof-of-concept service as I did when I first started working with GitLab. I'll also show you how to set up your own shared runners that your developers can use to run CI/CD jobs. I'll then show you how to enable optional services such as

INTRODUCTION

GitLab Pages and GitLab's container registry as well as how to connect your service to an external email service.

With the proof-of-concept service out of the way, I'll discuss various administrative tasks that you'll need to do on a regular basis such as updating GitLab's configuration and upgrading to a new release. I'll conclude at the final level-up position with a discussion on what you will need to do to spin up a production-level service that takes high availability and disaster recovery into account.

There is certainly a lot to cover, but I'll help guide you through it step by step. Let the journey begin.

CHAPTER 1

Only the Beginning

GitLab is a multi-tool (also known as an all-in-one tool) for software development and management. It is composed of many individual components that are integrated together to support the full life cycle of product development, from initial planning to coding and testing all the way through deployment. It supports the DevOps model of managing software products, although it doesn't require that you follow that methodology.

In this chapter, we'll start with a high-level look at the tool exploring the most basic components first and building on them from there. After that, we focus on getting access to a free-tier version of GitLab, so you can get a feel for what the product is all about and whether it is something you would like to use in your development environment. Finally, we look at how to edit your user profile and update various preferences to your liking.

Introducing GitLab

At its core, GitLab is a source code management tool that uses Git to check in and check out code, like GitHub. It also has a project management component, like Jira, which enables teams to manage tasks and issues throughout the development process along with corresponding metrics used by project managers and other pesky overseers. In addition, it has a continuous integration and deployment component, in the same vein as Jenkins, to build and test the software under development. If that were not all, there are additional nice-to-have components to perform security checks and monitor performance among other features.

Although GitLab is billed as a single DevOps platform for all your development needs, it does allow integration with other software for those cases where another tool is required by the powers that be. For example, many corporations mandate that Jira be used to track issues and manage projects to provide consistency among all software projects. For those cases, GitLab enables integration with Jira so that you can plan agile sprints and manage user issues in Jira and correlate them with development branches in GitLab. You do lose some GitLab capabilities, such as metrics reports based on GitLab's internal planning management tools, so the integration isn't totally seamless, but that is the nature of the beast. One of the nice things about GitLab is that even if you are integrating with Jira for main project development, you can still use GitLab's planning tools for one-off projects, such as those used in hackathons, where setting up a Jira project requires more effort than its worth.

As for source code management, you could theoretically use another source code manager such as GitHub in place of GitLab to store all your code base, although this type of integration is usually reserved for public open source projects. GitLab's Git manager is the primary component around which other services are built upon, so ignoring it doesn't make much sense IMHO.

In terms of build and integration tools, you could also use Jenkins as the primary tool in place of GitLab (there are Jenkins plug-ins that integrate with GitLab, for example), but this adds an additional burden in maintaining a corporate-wide Jenkins server and/or server farm. I mention this option since there are some companies, such as the ones I've worked with, that already use Jenkins as their primary build and test tool. Rather than port all builds and test suites over to GitLab in one fell swoop (an onerous task, I might add), this integration option can be used to provide an interim migration path to GitLab without disrupting all of development.

If you look at GitLab's website, you'll see that there are quite a number of features, enough to make your head spin. In addition, there are some paid tiers that control what features are available. The pricier the tier, the more features are enabled. This is unlike some other products that simply differentiate between a free (a.k.a. community edition) and paid version (a.k.a. enterprise edition) of the product. Fortunately, the most common and useful features of GitLab exist in the free and lower-priced tiers. We'll be focusing on those in this book.

So rather than blather on about the various features, I think the best approach at this point is to start experiencing GitLab firsthand.

Setting Up a GitLab Account

Assuming you have a laptop that runs either the Windows or Mac operating system, your first instinct is most likely to download the GitLab installer so that you can test the software locally. Unfortunately, GitLab (the company) does not currently, nor does it plan to, support Windows or Mac installations of GitLab (the service). The GitLab service can only be installed on Linux/Unix-based servers.[1]

If you have a laptop that runs Linux, you might be tempted to install GitLab locally. Ditto if you have Windows that has WSL (Windows Subsystem for Linux) or Mac that has VirtualBox or similar software installed on it. Personally, I would not recommend installing GitLab server software on such a setup. One reason has to do with the complexity of the software. As mentioned earlier, GitLab is composed of many components and relies on other software packages, such as Git, to be installed; this makes GitLab a bit more complicated to install on a laptop. Another reason has to do with GitLab's memory and CPU requirements that might overwhelm your machine.

At this point, you might consider installing GitLab in a cloud environment such as AWS, Azure, or Google Cloud Platform. Having personally installed and maintained GitLab in an AWS cloud environment, I can tell you that going this route is more work than it is worth, especially if your goal is to simply test GitLab out. I will talk about how to install GitLab in a cloud environment in a later chapter should you choose to go that route.

Fortunately, GitLab provides two ways of using its service:[2] a self-managed option where you install and maintain the service on your own set of servers (typically a cloud environment but could be an on-premises server farm) and a SaaS (Software as a Service) option where you use GitLab's service via its website. There are differences between the two offerings mainly dealing with administrative features, but for learning purposes, those differences aren't relevant.

---

[1] Note, however, that GitLab does support Windows and Mac binaries for its GitLab Runner software where build and test tasks are performed.

[2] At the time of this writing, there is a third option in the works called GitLab Dedicated that is a mix between the self-managed and SaaS offerings. With the dedicated offering, GitLab manages a dedicated host environment for you so that you don't have to spin up servers and databases directly.

CHAPTER 1   ONLY THE BEGINNING

Creating a GitLab SaaS Account

To create your account on the GitLab website, go to `https://gitlab.com` in your favorite browser: Mozilla Firefox, Google Chrome, Chromium, Apple Safari, or Microsoft Edge. As always, it is best to use the latest version of your preferred browser; if you haven't updated your browser in a while, this would be a good time to do so. If you haven't already created a GitLab account, this will probably redirect you to `https://about.gitlab.com` that is a promotional page. On that page should be a "Get free trial" button. When you click that, you'll be taken to a page where you can sign up as shown in Figure 1-1.

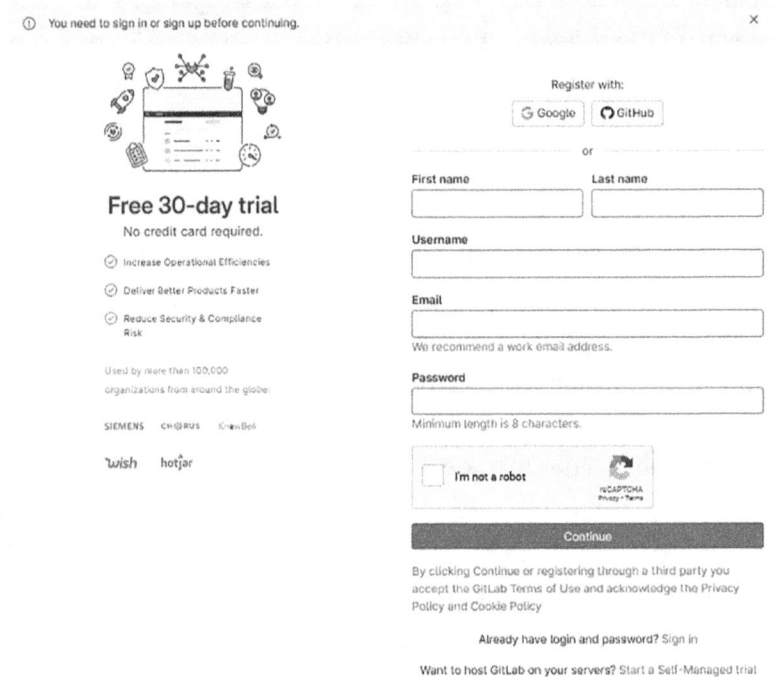

Figure 1-1.   GitLab free sign-up page

The form is self-explanatory. You get to pick your username; if it is already taken, the form will let you know so you can try a different one. Pick a name that you can easily remember as it will be your gateway to your account. For the password, I suggest using something like `www.lastpass.com` to generate it.[3] Once you enter your password, check

---

[3] For the customize your password option, I personally like to select "Easy to say" with 10 characters and then add a number and symbol for the final password.

CHAPTER 1   ONLY THE BEGINNING

the "I'm not a robot" option and select "Continue." You will be sent a confirmation email to the address supplied in this form, so make sure it is a valid one. Once you confirm the email address,[4] you will see a welcome page similar to the one in Figure 1-2.

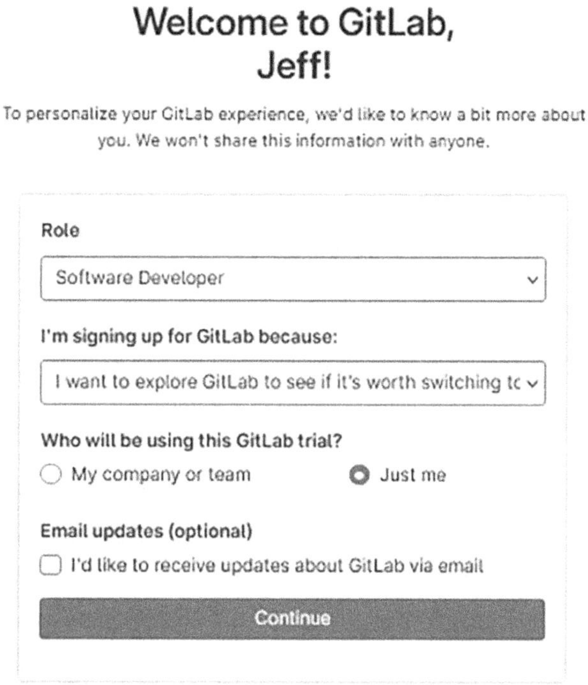

Welcome to GitLab, Jeff!

To personalize your GitLab experience, we'd like to know a bit more about you. We won't share this information with anyone.

Role

[Software Developer   v]

I'm signing up for GitLab because:

[I want to explore GitLab to see if it's worth switching to v]

Who will be using this GitLab trial?

○ My company or team   ● Just me

Email updates (optional)

☐ I'd like to receive updates about GitLab via email

[**Continue**]

Figure 1-2. *GitLab welcome page*

In this form, I selected a role as Software Developer and the "I want to explore..." option as the reason to sign up for GitLab. I also selected the "Just me" option. As you probably gathered, this information is for GitLab marketing and sales. Selecting "Continue" takes you to the "About your company" page (yes, even if you selected the "Just me" option) as shown in Figure 1-3.

---

[4] Just an FYI, I had issues with the confirmation process. It wouldn't let me log in initially. I ended up going back to the gitlab.com site and log in fresh with the credentials I just created. That worked – eventually.

5

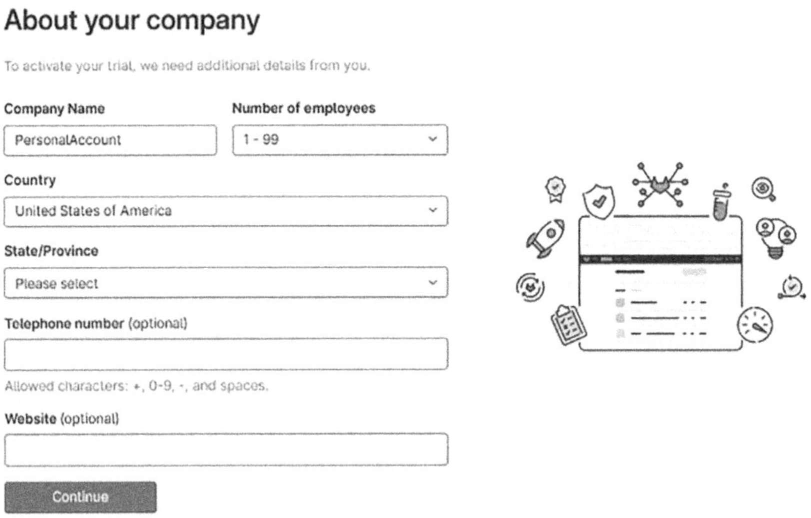

CHAPTER 1   ONLY THE BEGINNING

Figure 1-3. GitLab company info page

I used a dummy name of "PersonalAccount" as the company name with 1–99 employees. I selected the Country and State/Province and left the remaining optional items blank. Even if you are working for a company currently, I recommend just creating a personal account for yourself first so that you can explore and experiment without affecting other users in your company. You can always create an official company account later if you choose.

Creating Your First Project

Selecting Continue from the Company info page takes you to the "Create or import your first project" page as shown in Figure 1-4. I chose the group name of "PainterTraining" and a project name of "MyFirstProject." Choose names that make sense for you; note that you'll be able to create other projects and groups later, so you won't be stuck with the names you provide here. I also checked the "Include a Getting Started README" option, which, as stated, is recommended for new users. This file is indeed useful for new users.

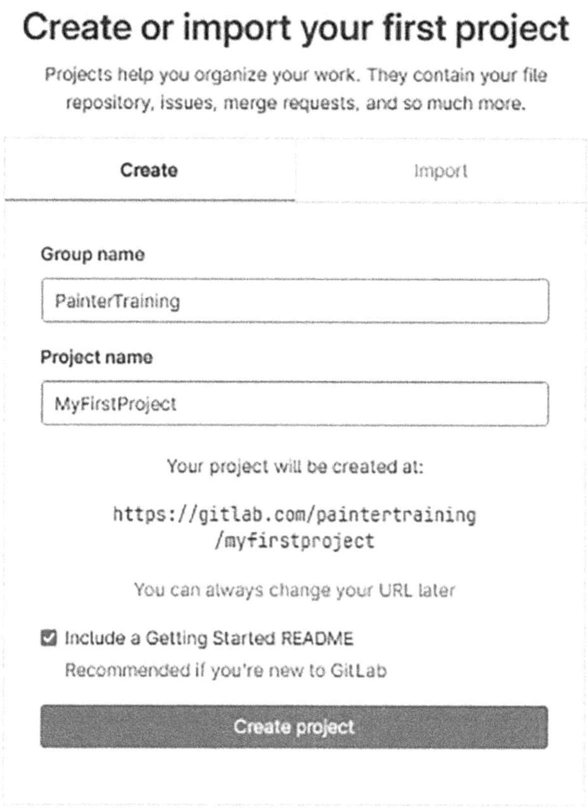

CHAPTER 1   ONLY THE BEGINNING

Create or import your first project

Projects help you organize your work. They contain your file repository, issues, merge requests, and so much more.

| Create | Import |

Group name

[PainterTraining]

Project name

[MyFirstProject]

Your project will be created at:

https://gitlab.com/paintertraining/myfirstproject

You can always change your URL later

☑ Include a Getting Started README
Recommended if you're new to GitLab

[Create project]

Figure 1-4. *First GitLab project page*

Selecting "Create project" will send you an email notifying you that the project was created. It will then take you to one more annoying page before you get to the main GitLab interface: the colleague sign-up page as shown in Figure 1-5.

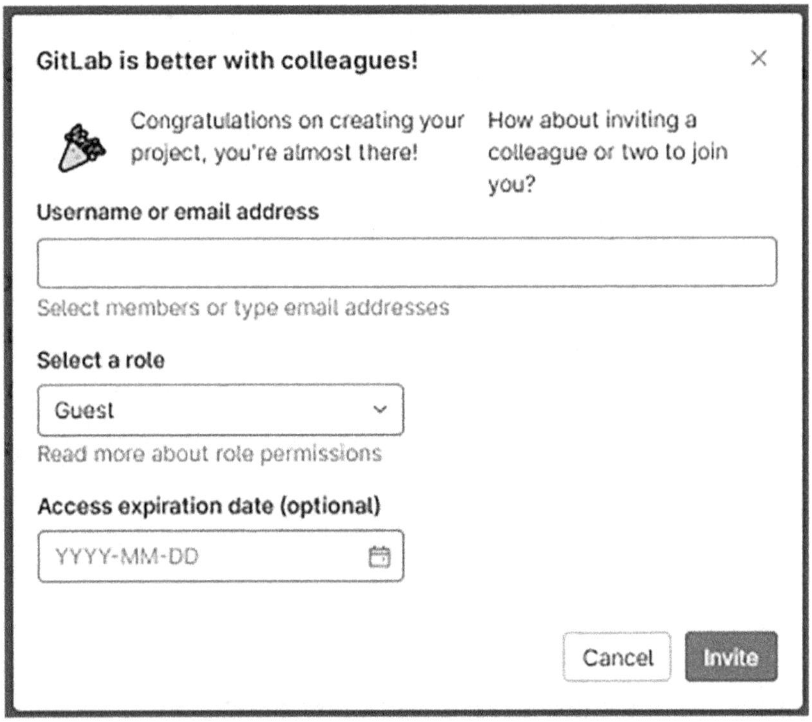

CHAPTER 1   ONLY THE BEGINNING

Figure 1-5. Colleague sign-up page

Personally, I kept this page blank and selected "Cancel" to continue on. If you have someone who may be learning this with you, feel free to add them. You can always add other users later in addition to changing their roles as needed. We'll talk about roles in a later section, so don't be too concerned about those options at this point. Again, you are not stuck with the selections you provide here.

A Glimpse at GitLab's Main Interface

Once you get past the colleague page, you are finally taken to GitLab's main interface. The good news is you only have to go through the setup sequence once. From here on out, you will be working from the main interface. Figure 1-6 shows what that interface looks like initially. Note that this may change in later versions of GitLab, so if you don't see exactly what is shown here, don't worry. It isn't important for our discussion.

CHAPTER 1 ONLY THE BEGINNING

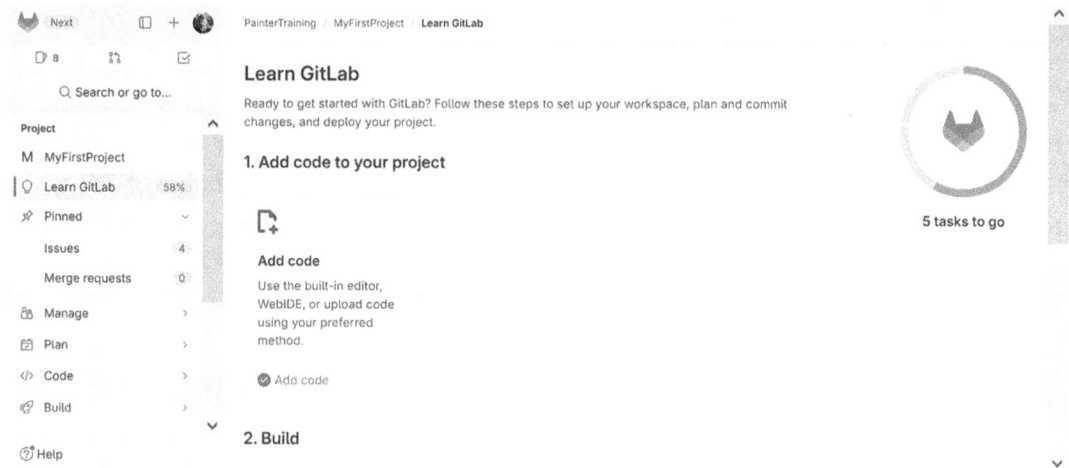

Figure 1-6. *Learn GitLab page*

The page you are initially presented with is actually a project generated by GitLab: "Learn GitLab – Ultimate trial." This is in addition to the project you created during the setup project, which in my example was called "MyFirstProject." As the name of the project implies, you are running a trial version of the ultimate tier, GitLab's highest and most expensive tier. Not to worry, you have a 30-day trial to test it out; once the trial period runs out, you'll be given the opportunity to select the tier you want to work with, including the free tier. Recall that you didn't provide a credit card number when you signed up, so you won't be automatically charged when the trial ends. Obviously, GitLab starts you with the ultimate tier to entice you into (and perhaps to become dependent on) all the features enabled by this tier.

At this point, you may want to bookmark this page so you can easily get back to it. If you don't, no worries. I'll show you how to get back to it if you end up on some other page. Feel free to test out the features of GitLab through the links and issues provided here. I don't plan on going through their tutorial since it is likely to change in the future. I'll cover the same topics in a more methodical way that does not rely on this tutorial project. We'll begin with the user profile and preferences as described in the next section.

CHAPTER 1 ONLY THE BEGINNING

Exploring User Options

If this is the first time you've seen the GitLab interface, it can be a bit overwhelming at first. There are all those funny symbols in the rightmost part of the page header and a lot of menu options in the leftmost pane of the web page that change as you navigate the interface. It is not uncommon to get lost in the GitLab universe; it happens to me all the time. No worries, we'll start with some basics to get you familiar with the interface and delve into more detailed options as we progress through this book.

Updating Your User Profile

The first thing we are going to do is set up your user profile and preferences. It's actually the first task (i.e., issue) provided in the tutorial project. Staring at the project page, you might be wondering how on earth do you get to the user options. In the left sidebar, there is an icon on the upper right-hand side that has an image initially chosen at random. If you don't see the sidebar, you may have to extend the browser window horizontally to see it. The icon you see will likely be different from the one you see in my screenshots, but rest assured, it serves the same function. If you click that icon, you'll see a drop-down menu providing a set of common user options. One of those options is "Edit profile," which we'll select next as shown in Figure 1-7.

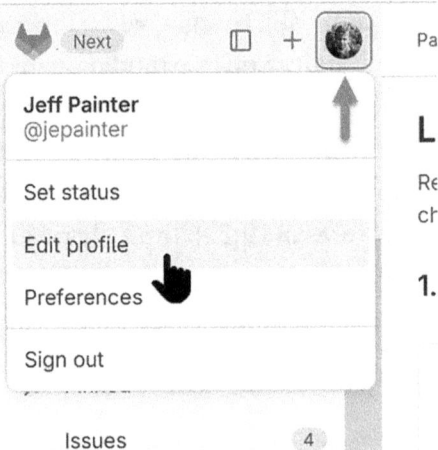

Figure 1-7. User settings edit profile selection

CHAPTER 1   ONLY THE BEGINNING

Selecting this option will take you to the "User Settings" page with the Profile option selected in the leftmost pane as shown in Figure 1-8. In this pane, you'll see the full set of user options, not just the "Edit profile" or "Preferences" options provided in the drop-down menu. Clicking any of the other items in the leftmost pane will display different pages to the right of the pane. Feel free to click through the different options to see what settings they provide. When done, click back onto the "Profile" option.

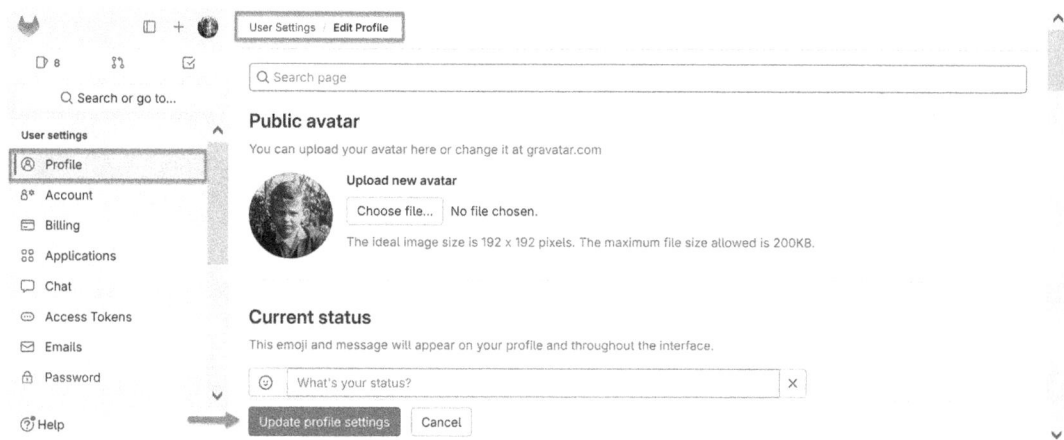

Figure 1-8. *User settings edit profile page*

The first thing you'll see is the "Public avatar" setting, which corresponds to the icon of the drop-down menu that took you here. You can make an avatar that suits you or upload a small picture that identifies you among the other users in your account. The "Current status" settings let you communicate with other users about your status, so you can let them know you are available or don't want to be disturbed. The "Time settings" section is self-explanatory.

The final "Main settings" section lets you provide personal information such as your email address and social media connections that would be useful in an open source community. You can also provide information about your job title and organization as well as your work location and a brief biography of yourself. Don't feel as if you need to fill in any of this information. Except for the email addresses, the information is not required by GitLab features as far as I know.

When you are done making changes to your profile, make sure to select the "Update profile settings" button. Otherwise, you will lose any changes just made to your profile. You can also change your mind and select the Cancel button to undo any changes you've made.

11

CHAPTER 1   ONLY THE BEGINNING

Setting Your Preferences

Now let's look at setting user preferences. There are a couple of ways to get to the preferences page. If you are already on the "User Settings" page, simply select the "Preferences" item in the leftmost pane. Alternatively, you can go to your user icon in the upper right and select "Preferences" from the drop-down menu as shown in Figure 1-9.

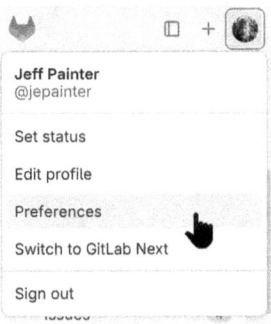

Figure 1-9. User settings preferences selection

Either method will take you to the Preferences page as shown in Figure 1-10. On this page, you'll be able to change several visual preferences such as the navigation color theme, the syntax highlighting theme, and the diff colors. It also lets you change some behaviors such as what shows up on your dashboard (which we'll get to in a minute). You can also set some localization options such as what the first day of the week should be and your language preference. Finally, there are miscellaneous options that you might find useful.

CHAPTER 1   ONLY THE BEGINNING

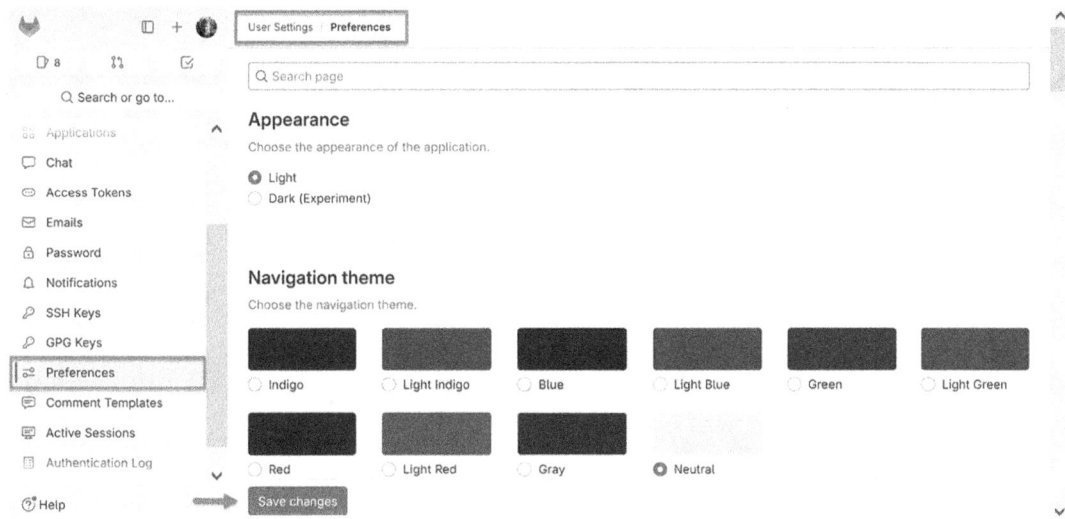

Figure 1-10. *User settings preferences page*

Except for the navigation theme being set to "Neutral," I'm going to keep with the default options to provide some consistency with screenshots in this book. Feel free to experiment with some of the preferences and set them to your liking. You can always come back and change them if you decide you don't like a particular option or get tired of what you've selected. Just remember to use the "Save changes" button when you want to preserve the changes.

Accessing Your Dashboard Home Page

We'll explore other user settings features later when we need them. At this point, we'll go to the home page (also known as the dashboard), which is where you will usually start each session. To get there, simply click the fox icon in the leftmost position of the sidebar as shown in Figure 1-11.

13

CHAPTER 1   ONLY THE BEGINNING

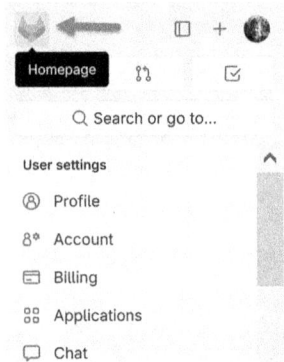

Figure 1-11.   *User dashboard option*

Assuming that your preference for the dashboard is the default "Your Projects," you'll be taken to the dashboard page that shows all your projects like the screenshot in Figure 1-12. If you've created more projects or deleted the tutorial projects, your dashboard will obviously look different.

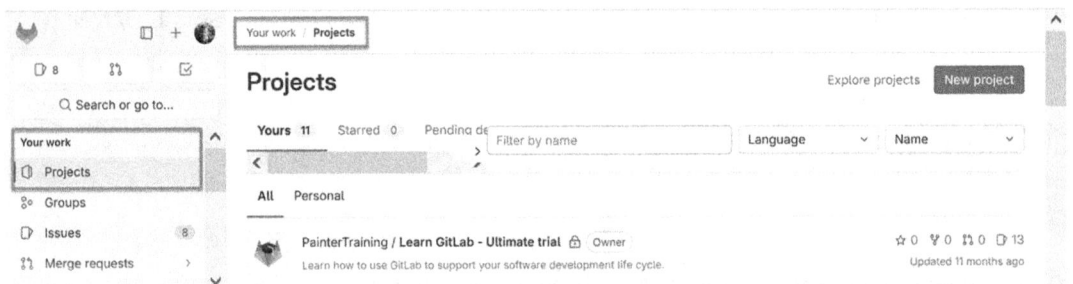

Figure 1-12.   *Initial user dashboard page*

If you changed your dashboard preference, you could still get to the projects page by selecting the fox icon in the sidebar as shown in Figure 1-13 and selecting the "Projects" menu item. This will take you to the projects page shown previously.

CHAPTER 1   ONLY THE BEGINNING

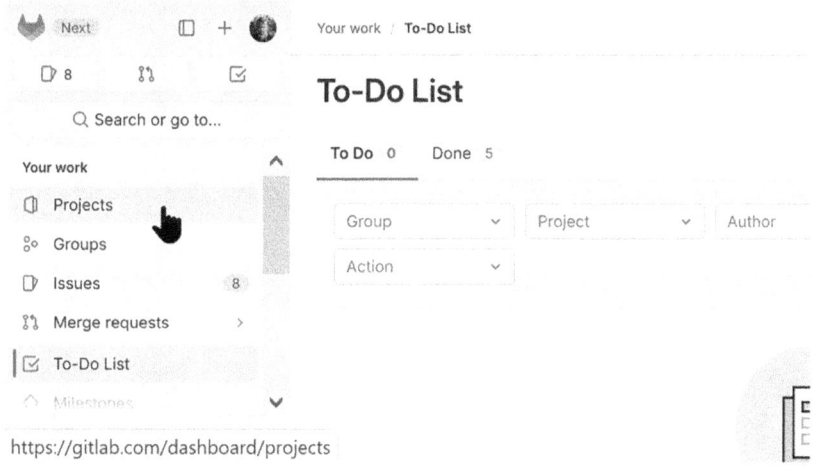

Figure 1-13. Dashboard projects selection

By the way, if you want to get back to the original tutorial (assuming you haven't deleted it), simply select the "Learn GitLab – Ultimate trial" link on the project page.

Summary

In this chapter, we covered the following items:

- Described the pros of GitLab and its architecture
- Discussed drawbacks to installing your own GitLab service
- Provided instructions on how to set up your own free account on GitLab's SaaS site
- Explored how to edit your user profile and preferences
- Reviewed the dashboard home page

Next up, we'll look into how to use GitLab to update source files and directories using GitLab's Web IDE and to manage changes made throughout the development cycle.

CHAPTER 2

Just the Source

Now that you have a GitLab account setup and tweaked your user profile and preferences, let's now look at how to manage your source code. This is, after all, the primary feature of GitLab. In this chapter, we'll first look at how to update source files and directories using GitLab's Web IDE. From there, we'll look at how we can use GitLab to manage source file changes during the normal development cycle using branches and merge requests. Since conflicting changes may arise between two or more developers, we'll also take a look at how to resolve those conflicts. We will finish off with a brief discussion on various branching strategies that different teams use.

Exploring the Web IDE

We are going to start with the first project you created during the sign-up process (which for me is the "MyFirstProject" project). The screenshot in Figure 2-1 shows what it looks like initially. You will probably see a warning message about not being able to push or pull repositories using SSH. We'll get to this later in this chapter so you can select the "Don't show again" button to dismiss that message. You are also likely shown a box asking if you want to enable Auto DevOps as shown in Figure 2-1; we do not, so simply click the x in the upper-right corner of the box to dismiss it.

CHAPTER 2   JUST THE SOURCE

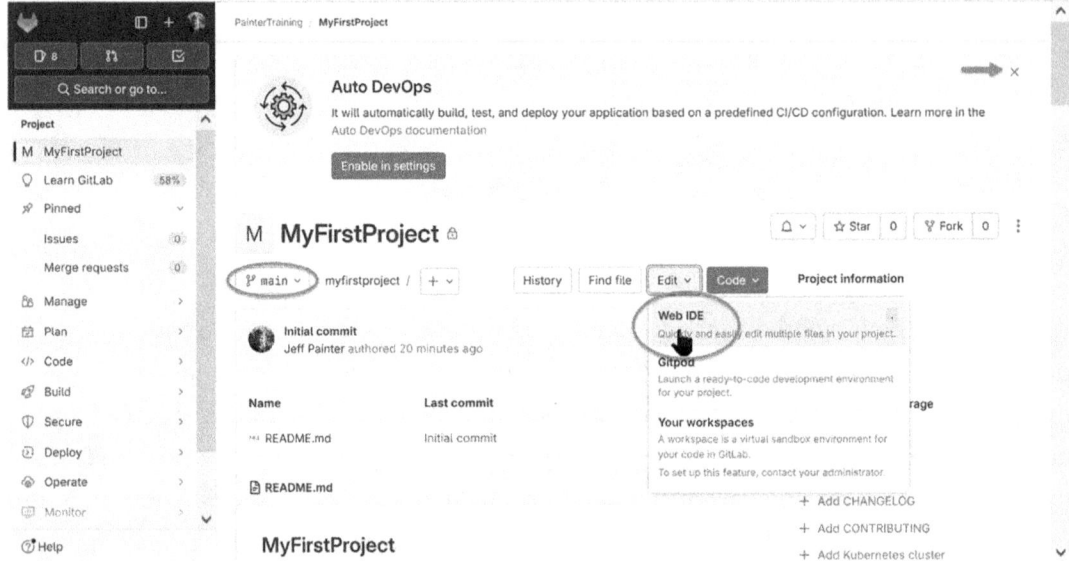

Figure 2-1. *Initial state of MyFirstProject*

What remains is a summary of your project. I highlighted the drop-down menu labeled main, which shows what branch you are currently viewing. All projects have a main branch; at this point, the project has no other branch. We'll talk about branches and the need for them later in this chapter. You'll also see a list of the files associated with this project for the given main branch. In this case, we just have the automatically generated README.md file. The md suffix indicates that this is a markdown file. If you scroll further down, you'll see a rendering of the file with the markdowns applied.

Editing with the Web IDE

One way to make changes to your existing files and to add or delete files and folders is to use GitLab's Web IDE. Select the Web IDE option from the Edit drop-down menu as highlighted in Figure 2-1. This will create a new tab or window (depending on how you have your web browser set up) with the IDE inside of it as shown in Figure 2-2. The first time you enter the IDE, you'll be presented with a "Get Started" page similar to the one shown here; this is likely to change over time, so don't be too concerned if it doesn't match what is shown here.

CHAPTER 2   JUST THE SOURCE

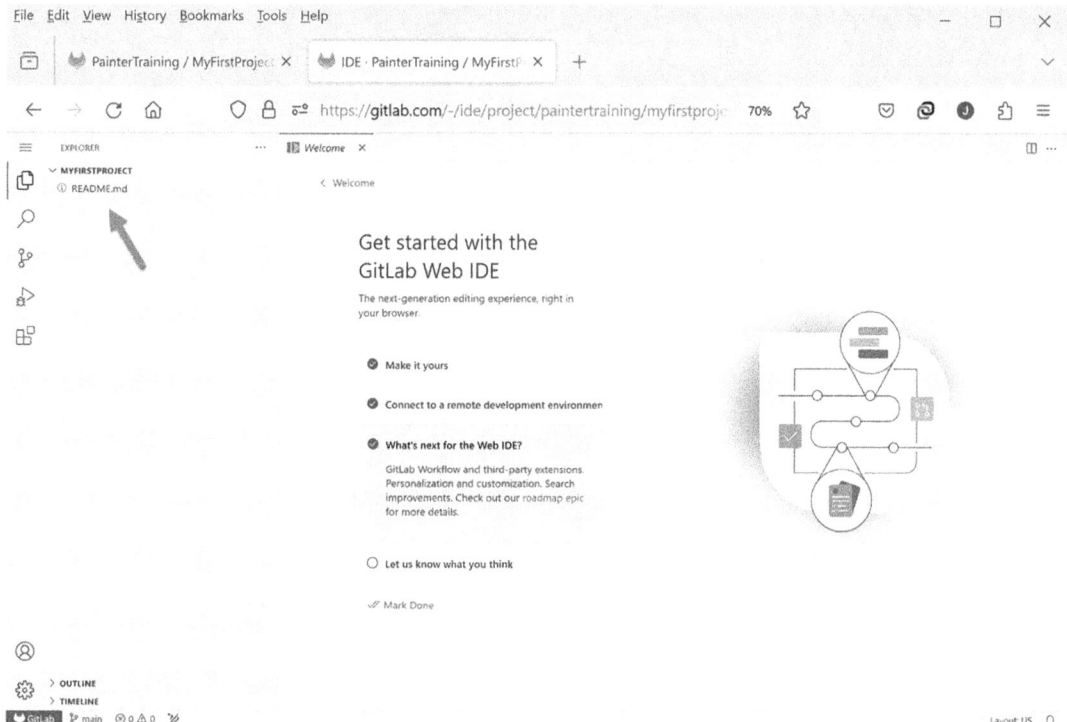

Figure 2-2. *Web IDE getting started page*

On the left-hand panel, you'll see a list of the files and folders (i.e., directories) that are contained in this project on the main branch. In this case, we only have the README.md file displayed. Clicking README.md will take you to the edit page for that file as shown in Figure 2-3. Note that what you'll see is the raw file with the markdowns exposed, not the rendered view of the markdown file.

CHAPTER 2   JUST THE SOURCE

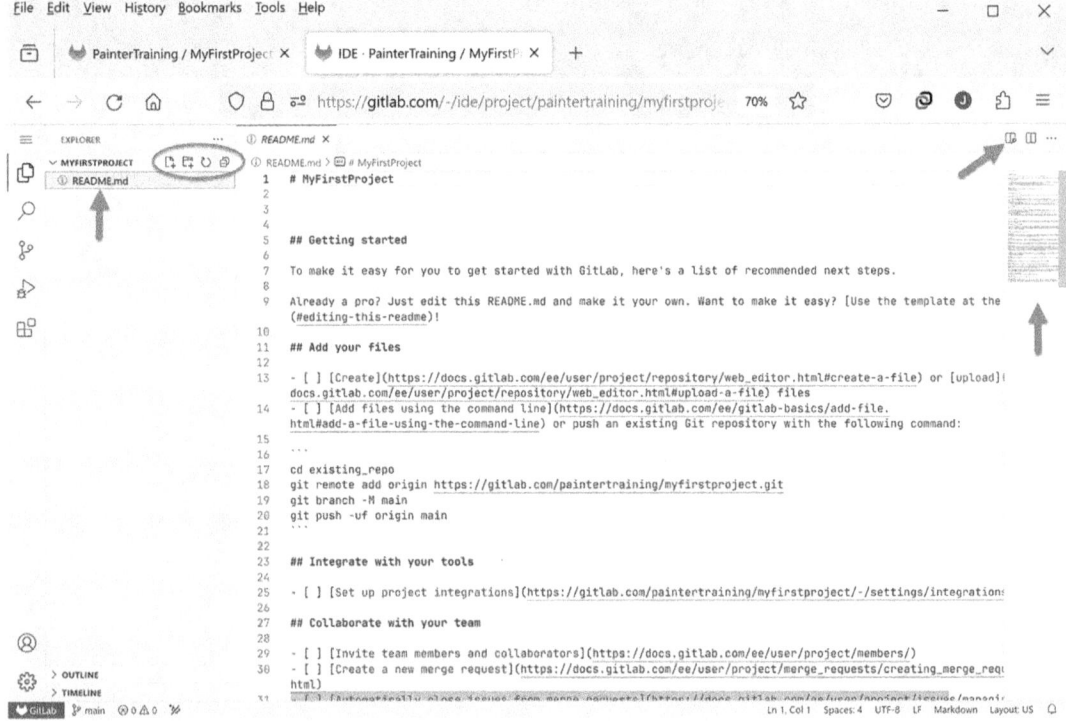

Figure 2-3. *README.md raw file edit page*

The center pane is the edit pane for the README.md file. For example, it shows the line numbers on the left to make life easier when you are presented with error messages; they are not part of the file's content. The lines of the file itself are contextually highlighted based on the type of the file being edited (md in this case). You can click anywhere within the edit pane and directly add, delete, or modify the file's content. The IDE will keep track of the changes you make. Go ahead and make some changes to the file to see how the IDE reacts.

By default, the rightmost pane is a scrolling page that lets you quickly scroll to a section of the document; simply click and hold on the box within the scrolling page to move it around. When there are errors or changes, it will also provide markers to help you move quickly to them.

If you hover your cursor in the leftmost pane, you'll see some icons appear at the top of the pane as highlighted in the previous figure. These allow you to add files or folders to your project as well as refresh the web page and collapse or expand folders. Go ahead and create a new file called file1.txt and add some text to it such as "This is my first file!" You'll see that the file is now added to the list of files in the left pane. You can add

20

directories and additional files with these controls; GitLab will keep track of them all. Note that these changes have not been committed yet, so no one else can see them from their web browser even if they are on the main branch.

Previewing Markdown Files

If you are editing the README.md file, you will see a special icon show up in the rightmost pane pointed to by the right uppermost arrow in the previous image. If you click that, you will be presented with a file preview mode so that you can easily see the effects editing the md file has on the resulting rendered view as shown in Figure 2-4. Note that you can't make changes in the preview pane itself; you'll have to make changes in the edit pane and see the effects in the preview pane.

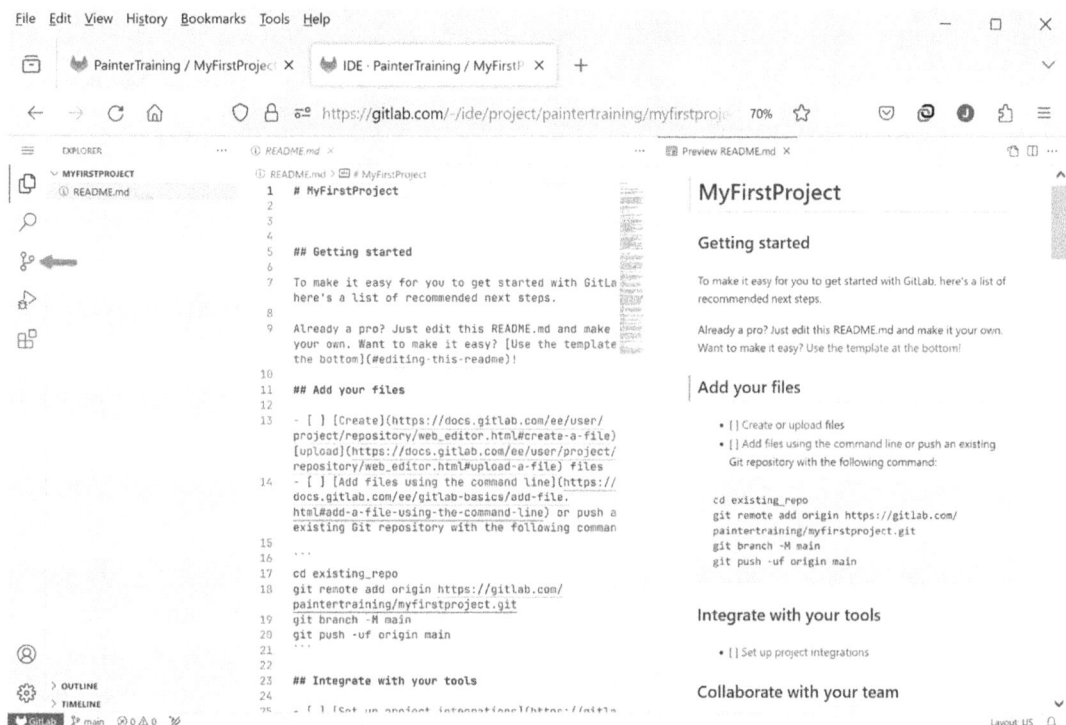

Figure 2-4. *README.md edit page with the preview pane*

CHAPTER 2   JUST THE SOURCE

Viewing Changes via the Source Control Panel

You may have noticed that as you are creating and editing files, there is an icon in the toolbar to the left that has changed; it is an icon that looks like a schematic tree, known as the source control icon, with a number next to it. The number represents the number of files that have been added, removed, or modified so far. If you click it, it will take you to the Source Control page as shown in Figure 2-5. Note that the options in the left pane have changed, and a new tab highlighting changes to the file appears.

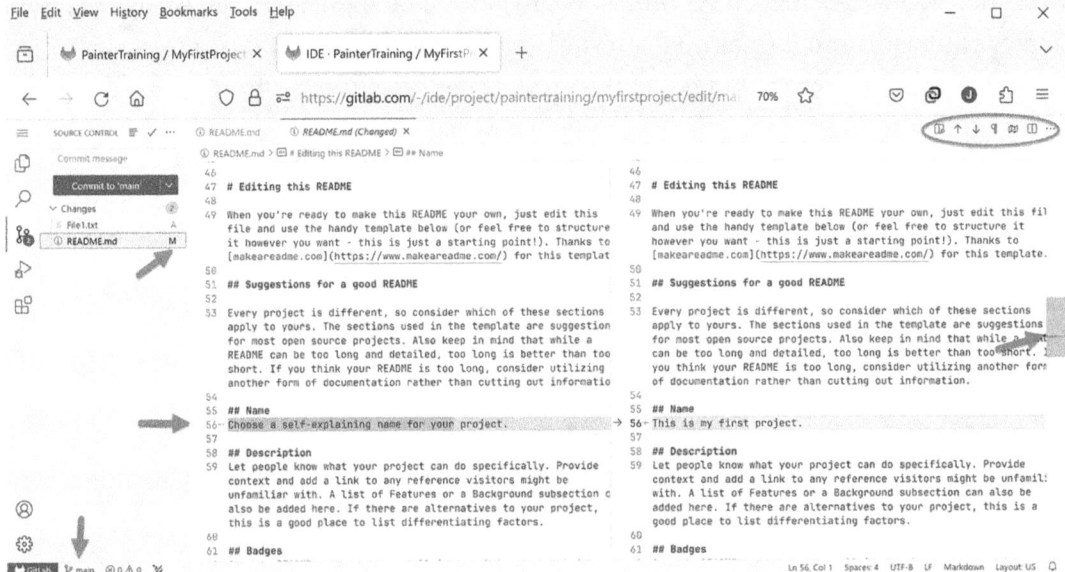

Figure 2-5. *README.md side-by-side comparison of changes*

The left pane now contains a Commit message text box, a "Commit to main" button, as well as a list of the files as before. To the right of the file may be a letter that indicates what type of change was made. For example, file1.txt has an A to indicate that it was added, and the README.md file has an M to indicate that it was modified. If you had deleted a file, it would have a D next to it. If you look at the bottom footer, you'll see that it displays the branch that is being edited, which in this case is main.

When you select the README.md file, you'll see a side-by-side display of the changes made with the left subpane showing the file before the change and the right subpane showing the file after the change. You'll also see the rightmost scrolling pane has markers indicating where changes have been made. In addition, there are new icons on the right-hand side of the header that lets you quickly move from one change to another.

CHAPTER 2   JUST THE SOURCE

Committing Your Changes

When you are done making the changes you want, you need to commit them in order for others to see them. Until you do so, you will be the only one to see the changes. To do this, enter a brief description of the change in the Commit message text box as shown in Figure 2-6. For our purposes, we'll go with the nondescript message of "My first commit"; in practice, you should enter something that is meaningful to others on your team. Make sure that the message is correctly spelled since once you've committed the change, it is difficult to edit the message.

Figure 2-6. Setting commit message with the Web IDE

Once you've entered the commit message, select the "Commit to main" button. Since we are on the main branch, we will get a pop-up message asking us if we really want to do this as shown in Figure 2-7. Normally, we would *never* make a change to the main branch like this directly; we are doing so here to illustrate the commit process. We'll go through the recommended process a little later on. If you do see this message in your real work, you should go ahead with the option of creating a branch.

CHAPTER 2 JUST THE SOURCE

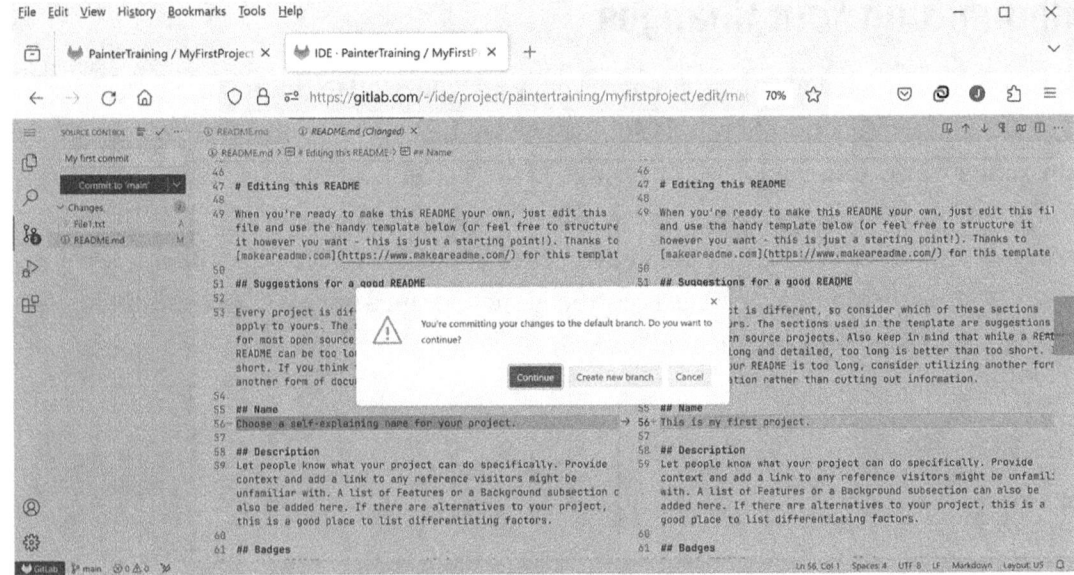

Figure 2-7. Commit to branch confirmation pop-up

Once you've selected the continue option, you'll see the commit successful message as shown in Figure 2-8. Note that this message only displays for a brief period of time; if you don't select one of the button options, it will disappear automatically. From the IDE, you'll notice that the source control icon has returned to normal and that the file change indicators are no longer visible. Note that after the commit, everyone else will be able to see the changes that were made.

CHAPTER 2   JUST THE SOURCE

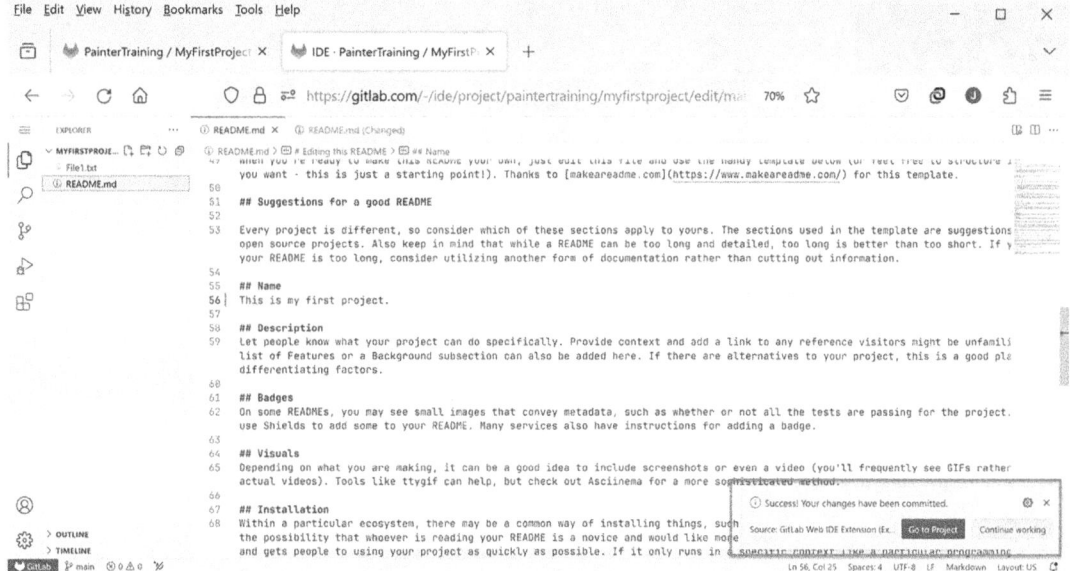

Figure 2-8. *Commit success message (transient)*

Reviewing the Project Summary Page

When you go back to the project summary page for your project, you'll notice some changes as shown in Figure 2-9. First, you'll see that the number of commits has been updated from 1 to 2. Directly underneath that, you'll see the commit message that you just entered; this will always show the latest commit message. Finally, you'll see that all files that were added are displayed in the file list (and if you deleted any files, they will no longer show up in the list). You'll also see that each file has the message from the last commit made to it. In this case, all files show "My first commit," but in general, they will have different commit messages displayed.

25

CHAPTER 2 JUST THE SOURCE

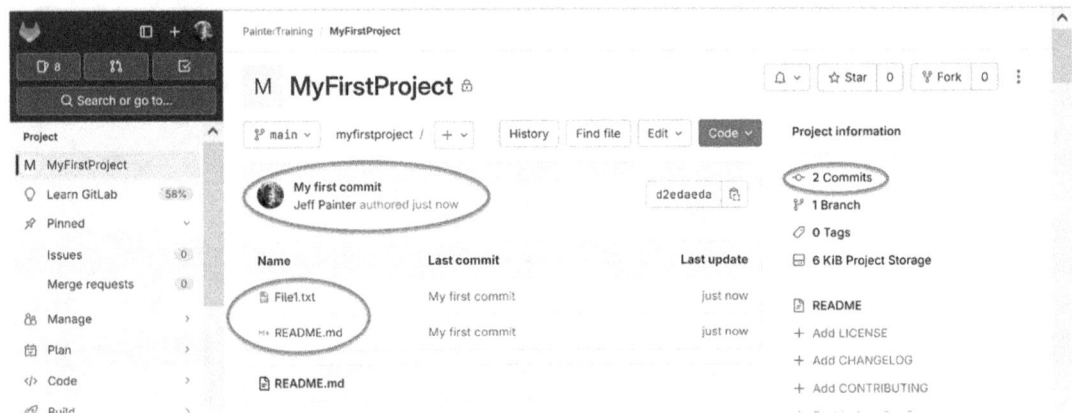

Figure 2-9. MyFirstProject after first commit

Working with Branches

If you are the only one working on a project and that project consists of mainly text and document files, then the process of editing and committing directly to the main branch might suffice for you. However, if you are part of a team or working on source code files for a website, application, or programming library, then you need to use a more robust process for managing changes to those source code files. Otherwise, you might inadvertently introduce errors that bring your website down or cause your application to misbehave unexpectedly. This immediately impacts everyone working on your project.

Creating a New Branch

This is where branches come in. You can think of a branch as a copy of all your files at a given point in time.[1] With a branch, you can then modify those files without impacting the files on the main branch. This gives you a way to commit changes and test them out prior to folding them back into the main branch, a process called merging. When there are multiple people working on a project, each one of them can create their own branch and merge their changes when completed. This allows each developer to focus on a particular task without worrying about changes made by other developers. Of

---

[1] Note that this is just a way to conceptualize branches. The exact mechanism of creating branches and keeping track of the changes made on them is much more efficient.

26

CHAPTER 2   JUST THE SOURCE

course, it is possible that two different developers make changes to the same file that will eventually conflict with each other when the changes are merged. Before we consider how those conflicts are tackled, let's first look at how the branching process works with one person.

Before you make any changes to your project files, you first create a branch where those changes will be made. There are multiple ways of creating branches. One way is to use the "+" drop-down menu from either the project summary page or the repository file page as shown in Figure 2-10.

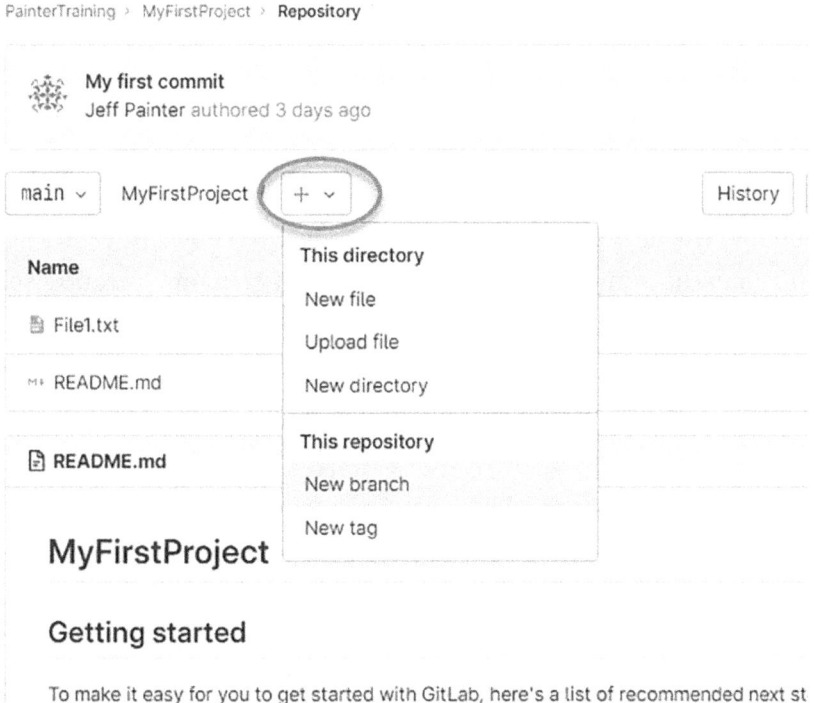

Figure 2-10. Selecting the new branch option from the project's repository page

Another way is to use the "New branch" button from the project's branches page as shown in Figure 2-11.

CHAPTER 2   JUST THE SOURCE

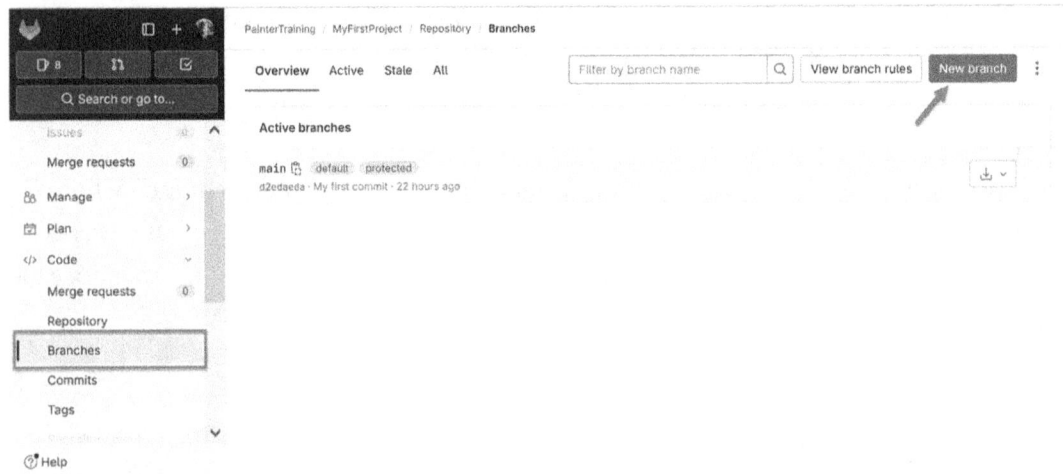

Figure 2-11. *Selecting a new branch from the project's branches page*

Either method will take you to the new branch page as shown in Figure 2-12. From this page, you enter the name of the branch in the "Branch name" text box, select which branch you are branching from (in this case, the main branch), and use the "Create branch" button to create the new branch. As you might have guessed from this form, you can create branches on top of other branches if you want. This can be used to support various branching strategies, which will be discussed later.

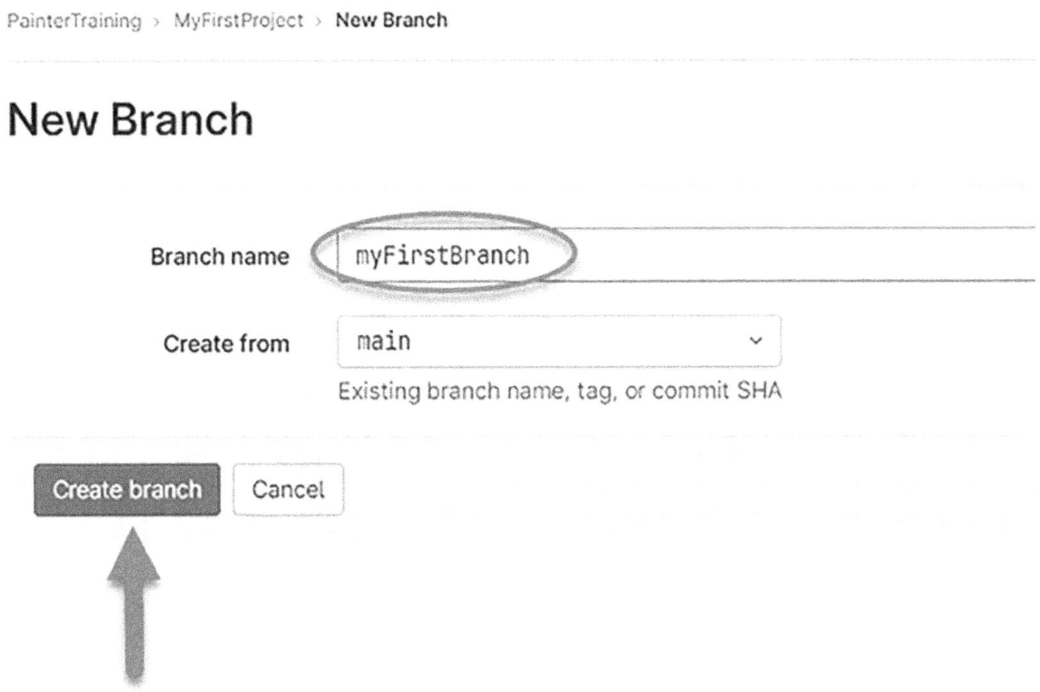

CHAPTER 2   JUST THE SOURCE

Figure 2-12. New branch creation form

Reviewing Project Changes After Branch Creation

Once you create the branch, you'll be taken to the repository file page as shown in Figure 2-13. On this page, you'll see an initial message that shows your branch has been successfully created. Also, note that the branch circled in Figure 2-13 refers to the new branch name. This lets you know that any changes you make will be applied to this branch. It should come as no surprise that the list of files for the new branch is the same as for the main branch; at this point, the two branches refer to the same set of files.

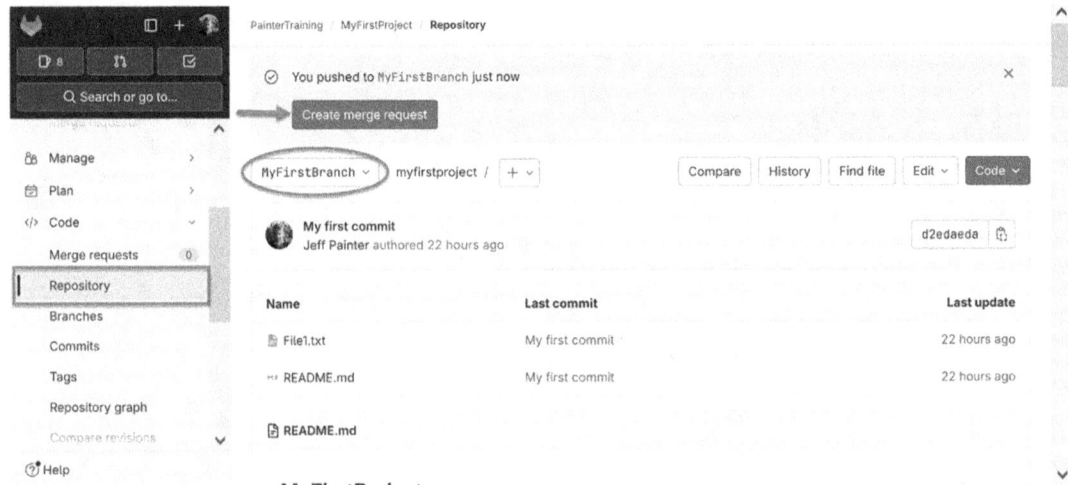

Figure 2-13. *Repository files associated with branch MyFirstBranch*

If you go to the project's branches page, you will notice that there are now two branches, each with the same commit ID as shown in Figure 2-14. Every time you commit a set of changes, a unique commit ID (called a commit hash) is generated by Git to identify it. The fact that both branches have the same commit hash indicates that they are the same. As soon as you commit changes to either branch, the commit hashes will begin to diverge.[2]

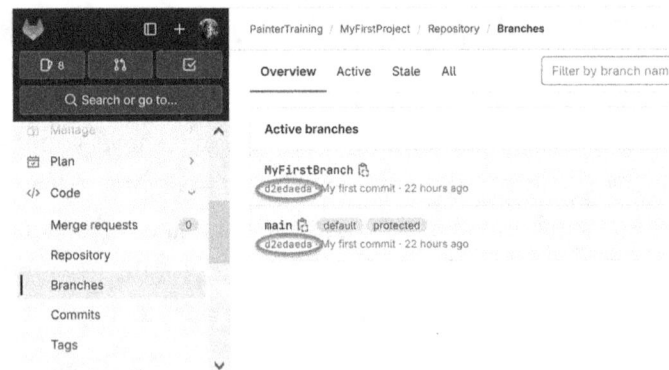

Figure 2-14. *Project branches after creation of MyFirstBranch*

---

[2] As you may have surmised, the commit hash is a hexadecimal number. The number generated is based on the contents of the changes made and are not in any particular order. Looking at any two commit hashes, you cannot tell which one came before the other.

CHAPTER 2   JUST THE SOURCE

If you go to the project's commits page, you'll see that there are two commits as shown in Figure 2-15. Commit "Initial commit" was the one created automatically when you first created the project with the initial README.md file. Commit "My first commit" is the one you made in the previous section. As you can see, the commit hash for "My first commit" matches the commit hashes of the two branches.

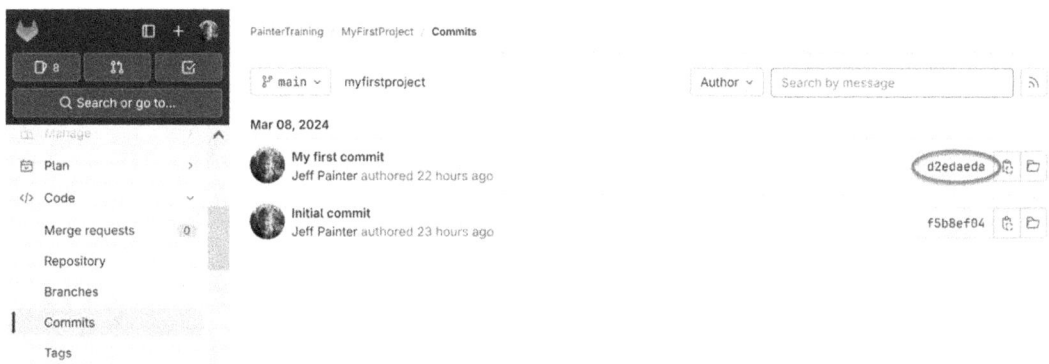

Figure 2-15.   Project commits after creation of MyFirstBranch

While we are on the topic of commit hashes, it should be noted that the numbers displayed in the previous screenshots are only the first set of digits of the hash. If you hover over the link of a commit on the repository's commits page, you'll see the full commit hash in the footer of the page as shown in Figure 2-16. As you can see, it is quite a considerable number.

Figure 2-16.   Display of full commit hash for "My first commit"

31

CHAPTER 2 JUST THE SOURCE

Committing Changes on a Branch

Using the Web IDE, I've gone ahead and made some changes by adding a File2.txt and modifying the README.md file. Figure 2-17 shows the results of committing those changes to the branch. Note that the repository file page shows the commit message and the files associated with the branch. Also, note that the branch has a drop-down menu where you can switch back to the main branch if desired. The files that were added or changed now show the last commit as "Commit 1 on MyFirstBranch."

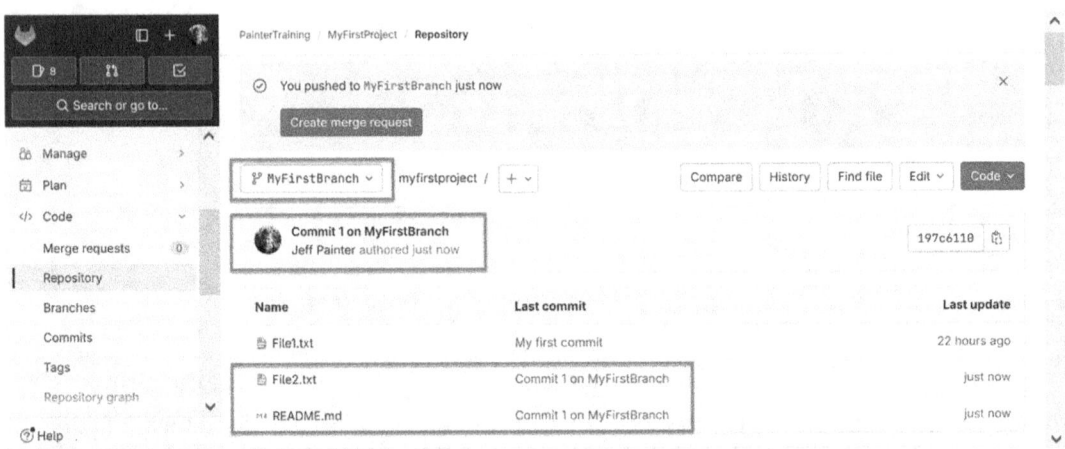

Figure 2-17. *Files associated with MyFirstBranch after commit 1 to MyFirstBranch*

Going to the project's commits page as shown in Figure 2-18 provides a list of all the commits associated with branch "MyFirstBranch." These commits are ordered from latest to earliest. Note that the branch has a drop-down menu where you can select other branches. If you select the main branch, for example, you will see that the "Commit 1 on MyFirstBranch" no longer shows up; this lets you know that changes from that commit have not been applied to the main branch.

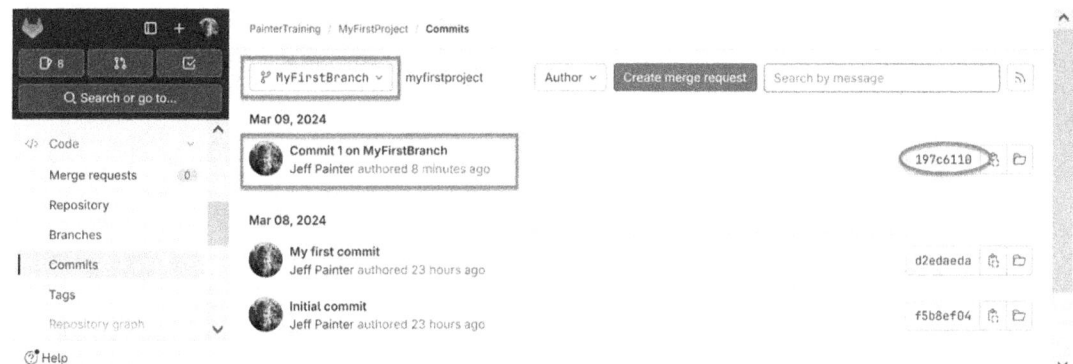

Figure 2-18. *Commits associated with MyFirstBranch after commit 1 to MyFirstBranch*

Going to the project's branches page as shown in Figure 2-19 provides a list of the two branches. Note that the commit hashes for the two branches are now different, which shows that the two branches have now diverged. Also, note that the commit hash for "MyFirstBranch" matches the commit hash for the "Commit 1 on MyFirstBranch" commit shown earlier.

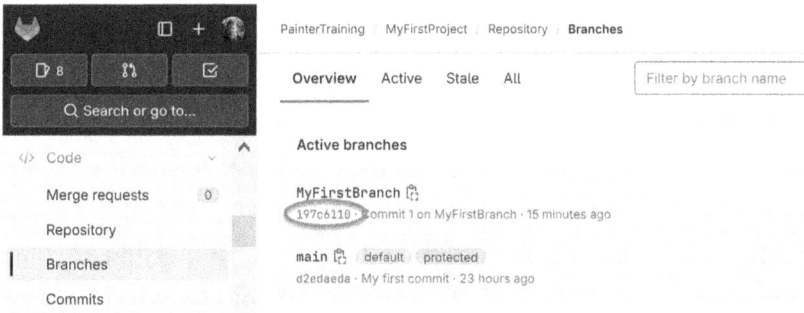

Figure 2-19. *Repository branches after commit 1 to MyFirstBranch*

Visualizing Branch Changes with the Repository Graph

You can get a visualization of the branch structures by selecting the project's repository graph page as shown in Figure 2-20. This graph shows the commits and branches from the "MyFirstBranch" perspective; the little gray arrow points to "MyFirstBranch" to reinforce this view. Using the first drop-down on the page, you can change perspectives to other branches. Feel free to switch to the main branch to see what the perspective

CHAPTER 2   JUST THE SOURCE

is from it. Given that we only have two branches so far, the perspectives aren't too interesting; the more branches you have, the more you'll appreciate the ability to switch perspectives.

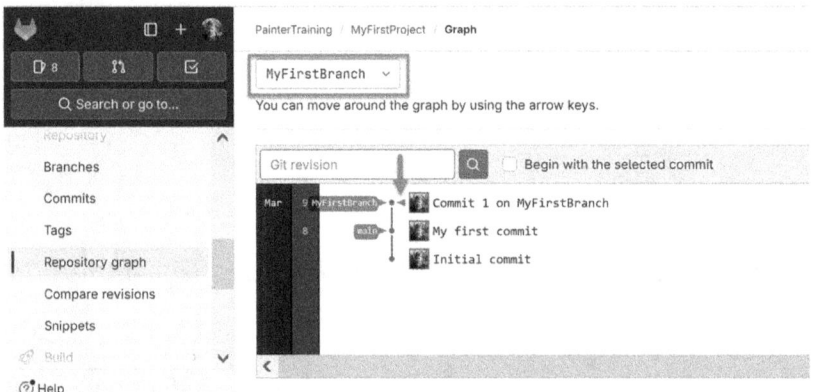

Figure 2-20. *Repository graph from the perspective of MyFirstBranch after commit 1 to MyFirstBranch*

Committing Multiple Changes on a Branch

Before we move on to the merge process, let's go ahead and commit some more changes to the branch. This is perfectly acceptable. Some people commit their changes at the end of their day to preserve them. Some people commit changes to snapshot a point in time before making significant changes; this way, they can easily go back to a working state should things get royally messed up. And then there are commits that are made to fix code that fails one or more tests. All of these are valid commit scenarios for a branch. In this project, I've created a third file and made some additional changes to the README.md file; Figure 2-21 shows the files after committing them.

34

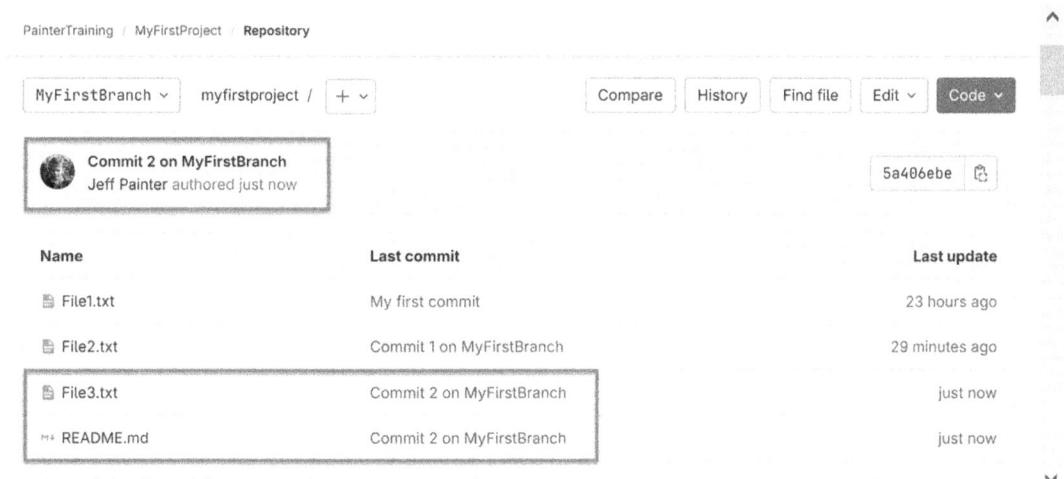

Figure 2-21. *Files associated with MyFirstBranch after commit 2 to MyFirstBranch*

Note that the commit message at the top of the page shows the latest commit message "Commit 2 on MyFirstBranch." The file list now shows the new file File3.txt and the modified file README.md with the latest commit message; file File2.txt still shows the previous commit message of "Commit 1 on MyFirstBranch."

Switching to the project's commits page, we see all the commits associated with "MyFirstBranch" as shown in Figure 2-22. You can go to the repository branches page to verify that the commit hash associated with "MyFirstBranch" matches the commit hash of the "Commit 2 on MyFirstBranch" commit.

CHAPTER 2   JUST THE SOURCE

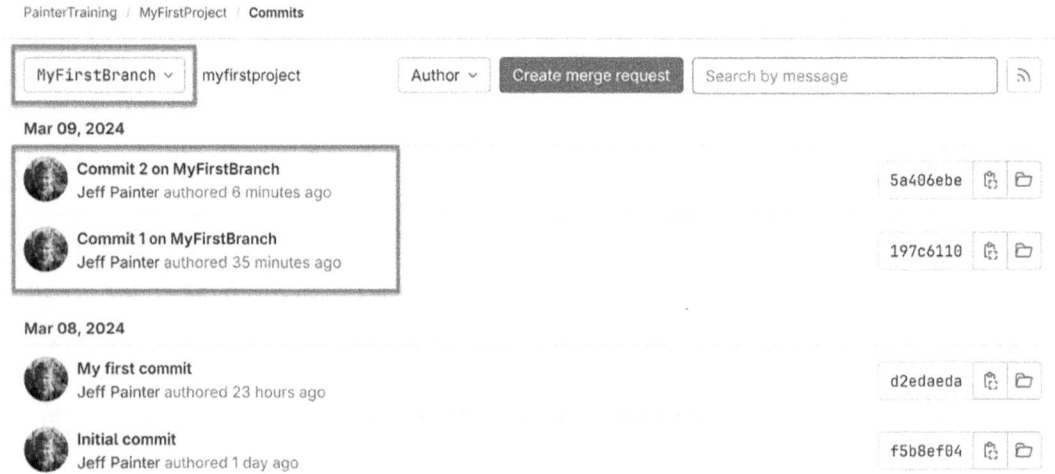

Figure 2-22. Commits associated with MyFirstBranch after commit 2 to MyFirstBranch

Switching to the repository graph, Figure 2-23 shows the graph with both commits on "MyFirstBranch." You can now see that "MyFirstBranch" is two commits away from the main branch. The graph clearly shows the order of commits made on "MyFirstBranch."

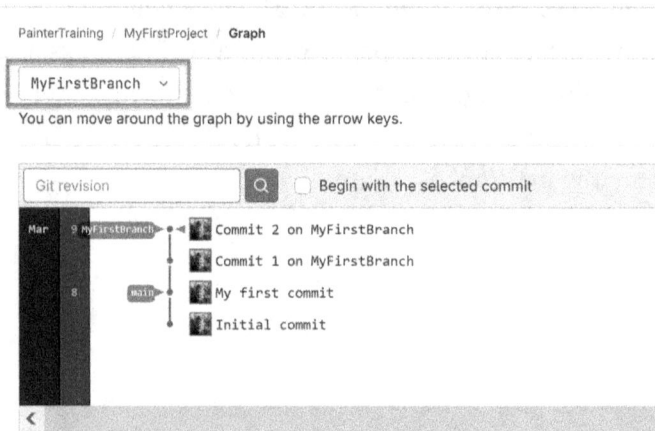

Figure 2-23. Repository graph from the perspective of MyFirstBranch after commit 2 to MyFirstBranch

CHAPTER 2 JUST THE SOURCE

Submitting Merge Requests

Now that we have some commits pushed to the new branch, we are ready to merge our changes to the main branch so that the rest of the world, or at least other developers, can use them. When we made commits directly on the main branch, pushing the commit immediately made the changes available, whether anyone was ready for them or not. As mentioned earlier, this can result in unintended consequences. To avoid this situation, GitLab introduced a feature called a merge request.

A merge request (often referred to as an MR) is an intermediate step that announces to other developers that a set of changes are ready for review and, when combined with continuous integration (which we'll talk about in a later chapter), enables tests to be run. Once the code is carefully reviewed and all tests pass, the changes can then be merged into the main branch.

Creating a Merge Request

If you check out the previous screenshots, you will notice the "Create merge request" button. This button appears in different contexts but has the same effect when you select it. Figure 2-24 shows the initial part of the new merge request page.

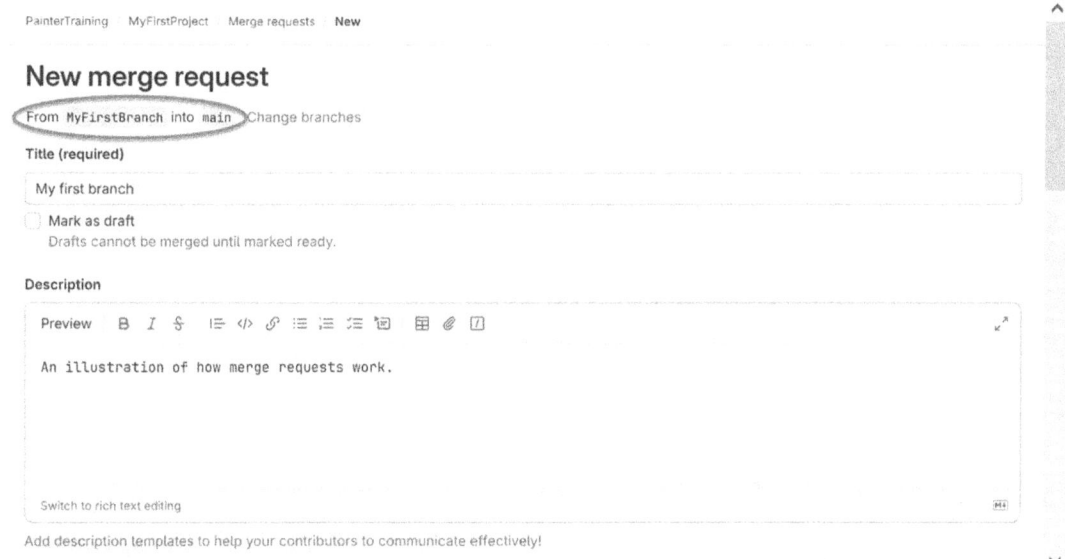

Figure 2-24. New merge request form (part 1)

37

CHAPTER 2   JUST THE SOURCE

The first item at the top of this page describes the source and target branches of the merge; in this case, the source branch is "MyFirstBranch," and the target branch is main. The title of the merge branch is derived from the name of the source branch; if that is not to your liking, you can easily change the title. The title helps other developers understand what the changes represent. You can also add a more detailed description of the changes such as what issues are addressed by the change, etc.

Figure 2-25 shows the section of the merge request page beyond the Description field. In this section, you can stipulate people who are responsible for the merge request called the assignees (which in an internal development environment will include yourself) and specify the people who you wish to review the code called the reviewers. Since we don't have any other people associated with this account yet, we will leave these fields as "Unassigned." You'll also note that there is a message letting you know that approvals are currently optional. I won't go into how to set up approval rules here, but if you are interested, expand the "Approval rules" option and select the link to GitLab's documentation that describes how to do this.

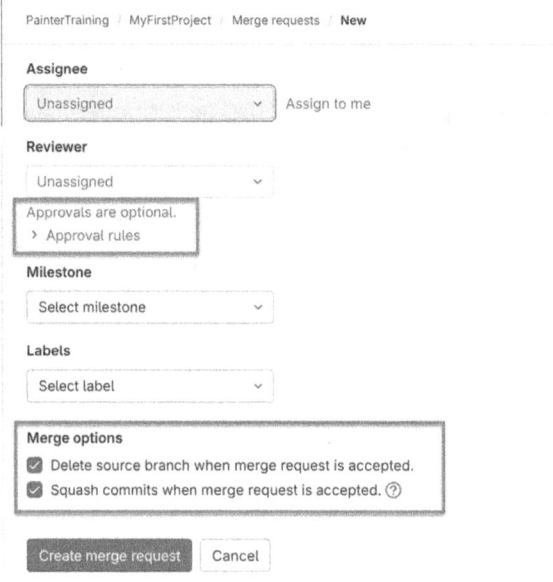

Figure 2-25. *New merge request form (part 2)*

There are other options where you can specify a milestone, define a set of labels, and identify dependent merge requests that we'll leave alone for now. The last two merge options define what happens when we finally merge the source branch into the target branch.

The "Delete source branch when merge request is accepted" option is a default option that will delete the source branch after the merge is made. This is a common way of working with developer branches. The "Squash commits when merge request is accepted" is by default turned off, but I selected it here. This option allows you to combine all the commits on the source branch into a single commit to keep the change history cleaner; this is a matter of preference. Note that you can override these options later when you do the final branch merge, so don't worry if they are not what you really intended.

At the bottom of the new merge request page following the "Create merge request" button is a tabbed subsection where you can see what commits and changes are associated with the merge request. This is shown in Figure 2-26. By the way, you may see an enabled Merge button at the end of the form. Make sure not to select this option as you will end up creating the merge request and then immediately merging it to the target branch bypassing the entire review process. This cannot be undone. Setting up approval rules helps prevent this from happening.

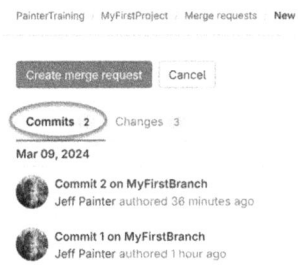

Figure 2-26. *New merge request form (part 3)*

Viewing Merge Request Details

After you create the merge request, you will be taken to the merge request detail page as shown in Figure 2-27. At the top is a feedback message that describes who created the merge request and what the source and target branches are. It should be noted that other developers associated with your account will be able to see this merge request (by design). In this case, you see the message "Ready to merge!", which indicates that there are no other requirements (such as approvals) that need to be met. We'll see in later chapters how we can require that at least one or more approvals need to be made or that all test cases must pass. For now, we are under the least restrictive set of merge policies.

CHAPTER 2   JUST THE SOURCE

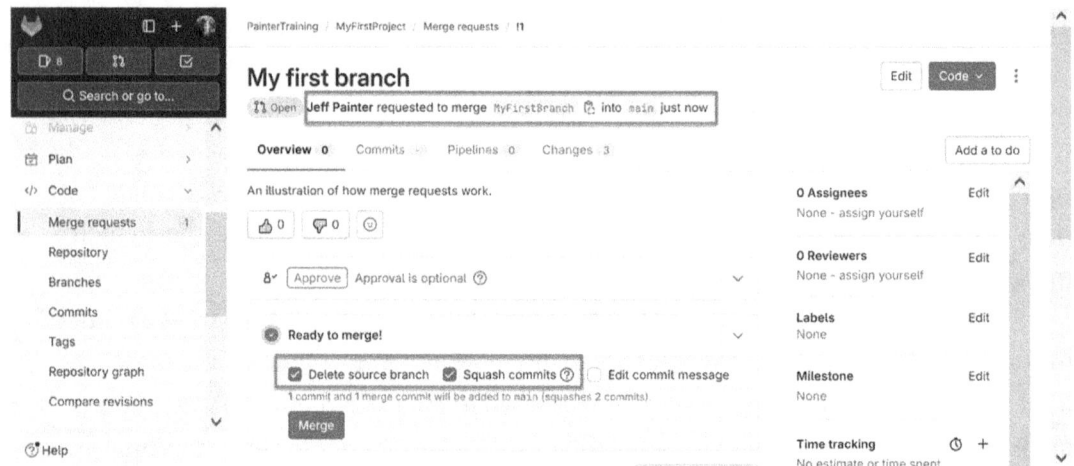

Figure 2-27. *Merge request detail page (part 1)*

You'll also see that the "Delete source branch" and "Squash commits" options are selected as requested from the new merge request page. It is here that we can override those options before we finally merge the source branch into the target branch. You'll also note there is an "Edit commit message" option that is by default unselected. If you leave this option unselected, a default message will be used based on a project template. If you select that option, you can see what the commit messages will be and edit them as shown in Figure 2-28.

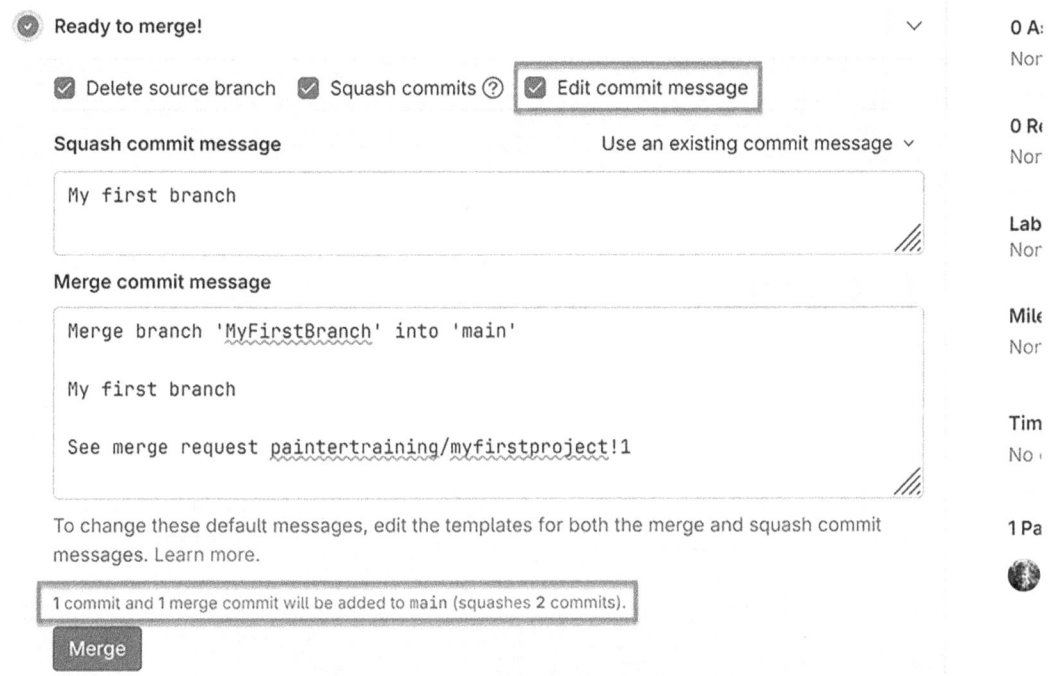

Figure 2-28. Merge request detail page (part 2)

In this example, you'll see that there are two commit messages. Because we requested to squash commits, the first commit message will be the message associated with the squash commit; any messages associated with the commits prior to being squashed will be removed. The second commit message is the merge commit message. By default, when a merge is performed, a new commit is created on the target branch itself; the squash commit (or set of original commits if commits are not squashed) will be associated with the (ghost) source branch after the merge is made. A feedback message prior to the "Merge" button lets you know that two commits will be made once the merge is complete.

Tracking Open Merge Requests

At this point, you would normally have other people review and approve the merge request. If those reviewers ask you to make changes, you will make the fixes and commit the changes to the source branch as before; this commit is automatically added to the merge request and becomes part of follow-on code reviews. Likewise, if there are tests that fail, you would commit the changes to make those tests pass, and those changes would also be added to the merge request.

CHAPTER 2   JUST THE SOURCE

In practice, there may be multiple merge requests active at any given time, especially if there is a team of developers working on different issues or tasks. You can see what merge requests are open by viewing the project's merge request summary page (select the "Merge requests" menu item from the project's page). Figure 2-29 shows the current summary page with our one open merge request. This page provides a passive way for developers and managers to review what is being worked on.

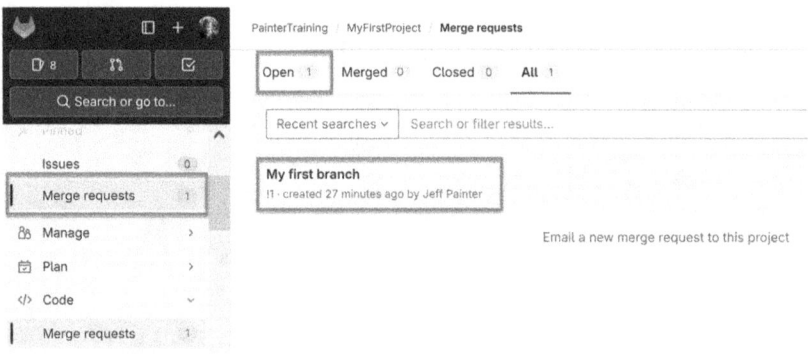

Figure 2-29.   Merge requests summary page

By the way, if you select the merge request from the summary page, you may notice an additional message about a missing pipeline as shown in Figure 2-30. Pipelines, which we discuss in a later chapter, are GitLab's method of performing continuous integration and continuous delivery/deployment (CI/CD) tasks. You can safely ignore this message for now.

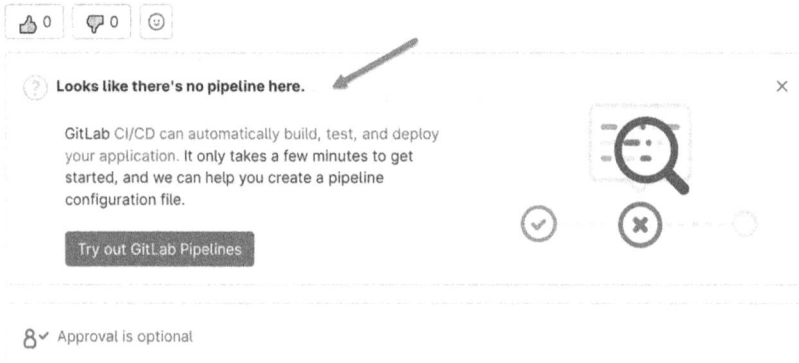

Figure 2-30.   Merge request missing pipeline message

CHAPTER 2   JUST THE SOURCE

Merging Changes from a Merge Request

Once you are happy with the state of your merge request, you can then merge the branches using the "Merge" button. Assuming the merge completes successfully, you'll see that the merge request includes additional information as shown in Figure 2-31. The merge request now provides feedback that it was merged and by whom. It also provides details of the merge noting that the commits were squashed and that the source branch was deleted. It also adds some notes in the Activity section for future reference.

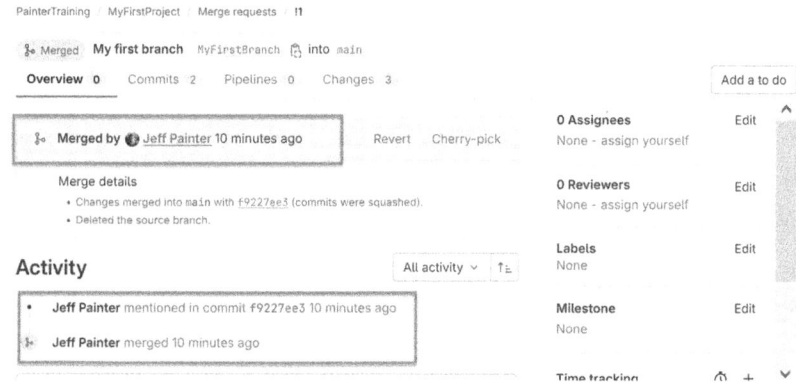

Figure 2-31. Merge request overview page after the merge of MyFirstBranch into main

If you now go back to the project's merge requests page, you'll see that the merge request has moved from Open to Merged as shown in Figure 2-32. If you are concerned that the source branch was deleted and that you may have lost the commit history associated with that branch, no worries. All of that history is now preserved as part of the merge request. Unlike branches, merge requests are always preserved unless you explicitly delete them; note that GitLab does not recommend explicitly deleting merge requests as they cannot be undone. If you created a merge request and changed your mind about merging the changes to the target branch, you can always close the merge request; this puts the merge request into the Closed state and lets others know that the request is no longer active.

43

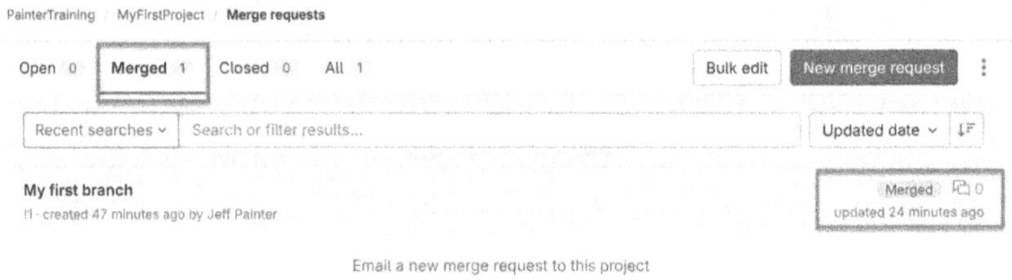

CHAPTER 2   JUST THE SOURCE

Figure 2-32. Project merge request summary

Reviewing Project Changes After an MR Merge

Now that the merge has been completed, let's take a look at the state of the project after the merge. Figure 2-33 shows that the files we created and modified on branch "MyFirstBranch" are now on the main branch. By the way, if you check the project drop-down menu (shown as main in Figure 2-33), you'll see that "MyFirstBranch" is no longer listed. You'll also note that the commit messages associated with each of the new and modified files show the squashed commit message "My first branch."

Figure 2-33. Repository files on main after merge

Switching over to the project's commits page, we see the results in Figure 2-34. For the main branch, there are now two additional commits: "My first branch" that represents the squash commit and "Merge branch 'MyFirstBranch' into 'main'" that represents the merge commit. You can drill down into each of the commits to see the differences between the two. Note that if you did not squash the commit, the original commits on "MyFirstBranch" would show up as part of the main branch.

CHAPTER 2   JUST THE SOURCE

Figure 2-34. *Commits associated with the main branch after merge*

Going to the project's branches page, we see that only the main branch appears as shown in Figure 2-35. Branch "MyFirstBranch" no longer exists, as we requested. Also, note that the commit hash for the main branch corresponds to the commit hash of the merge commit.

Figure 2-35. *Repository branches after merge*

Finally, if we go to the project's repository graph, we see the graph image as shown in Figure 2-36. The green line corresponds to what was "MyFirstBranch"; since that branch no longer exists, the green line is a ghost branch that shows the commits that were on "MyFirstBranch" prior to the merge. These ghost branches will appear whenever you merge a source branch using a merge commit. There are other methods of merging a branch, such as a fast-forward merge, which does not create merge commits and hence does not show ghost branches.

45

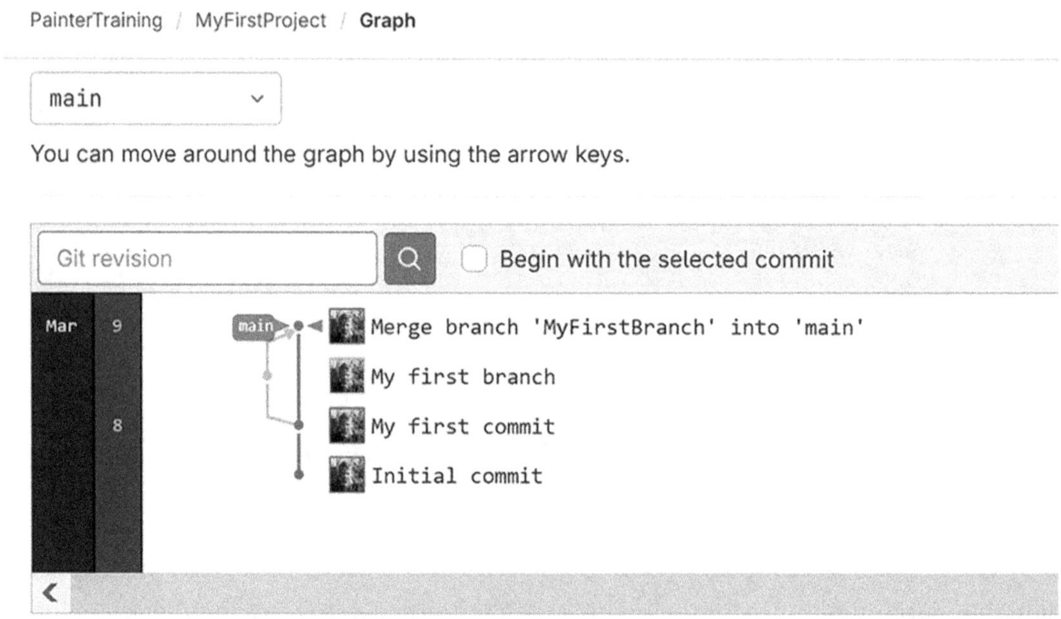

CHAPTER 2   JUST THE SOURCE

Figure 2-36. Repository graph after merge

Resolving Merge Conflicts

Let's face it, even in the best of worlds, conflicts happen. When you are working on a project with multiple developers who are making changes simultaneously, there are bound to be times when two (or more) developers make a change to a file that conflicts with each other. I should note that just because the same file is changed between two developers, it doesn't necessarily mean that a conflict will arise. One developer could make a change at the beginning of the file, while another could make a change at the end of the file; GitLab would be able to resolve the changes on its own when both changes are merged to the target branch. Conflicts arise when two developers make changes to the same line(s) of text within a file. In this case, GitLab doesn't know whose changes take precedent over the other or whether an entirely different change needs to be made. This is known as a merge conflict, and in this section, we'll look at how GitLab lets us resolve that conflict so that we can finalize the merge with the target branch and move on to other tasks.

Setting Up the Conditions for a Merge Conflict

To demonstrate merge conflicts, let's assume there are two developers A and B. Since I am the only developer associated with this account, I'm going to mimic these users by making two sets of changes simultaneously by myself. Figure 2-37 shows the set of changes made to the README.md file by developer A. Developer A created branch "devBranchA" from "main," updated the "Getting started" section by replacing "you" with "developers," and modified the License section.

Figure 2-37. *README.md inline changes made by developer A*

Figure 2-38 shows the changes made by developer B on the "devBranchB" branch created from the "main" branch shortly after the creation of branch "devBranchA." Developer B updated the "Getting started" section by replacing "you" with "users" and modified the "Project status" section.

CHAPTER 2   JUST THE SOURCE

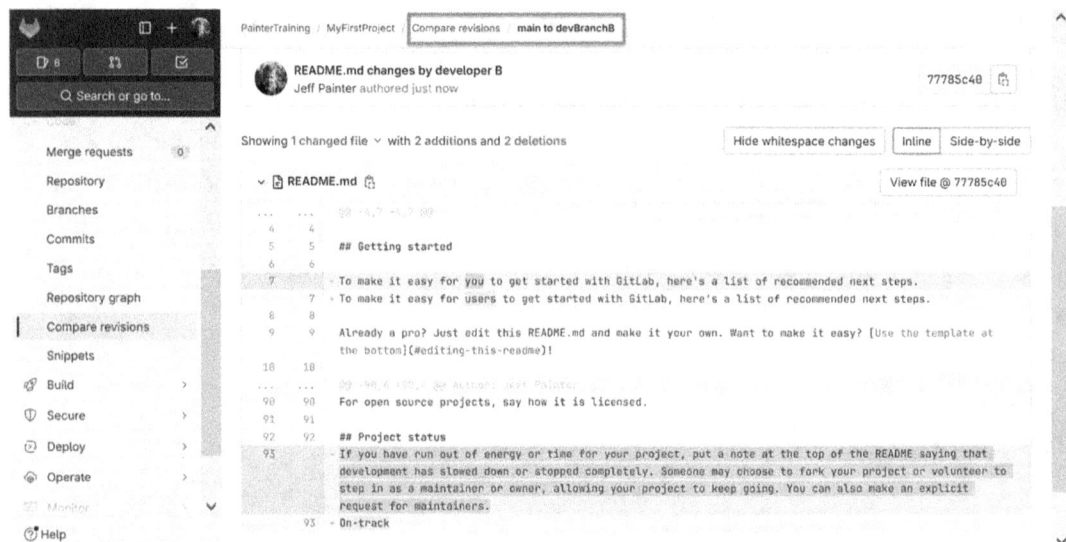

Figure 2-38. *README.md inline changes made by developer B*

Looking at the project's branches, we can see that both branches "devBranchA" and "devBranchB" are active at the same time as shown in Figure 2-39.

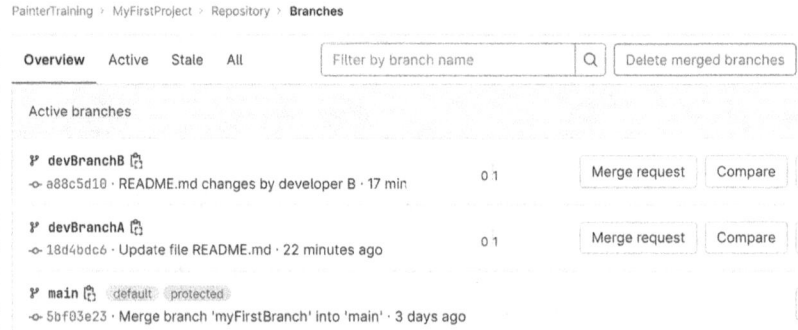

Figure 2-39. *Development branch overview*

Figure 2-40 shows the project's repository graph from the perspective of "main." Note that changes are ordered from most recent to least recent commits, so we see that developer B committed changes to "devBranchB" after developer A committed changes to "devBranchA." Had developer B made commits before developer A, the top two commits on the graph would be reversed. It doesn't matter when the branches themselves were created.

48

CHAPTER 2   JUST THE SOURCE

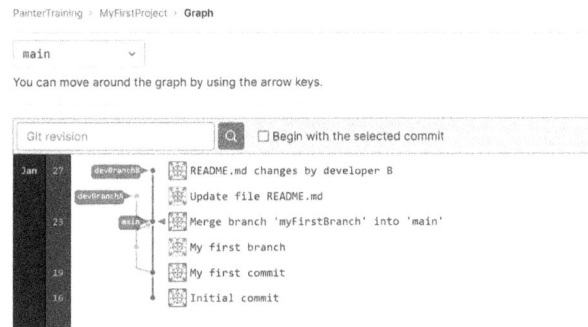

Figure 2-40. *Graph of simultaneous development branches*

Generating the Merge Conflict

Now let's assume that developer A merges their changes first. Of course, developer B could just have easily merged their changes first. Again, the order in which branches and commits are made does not influence the order in which merges are made. Figure 2-41 shows the state of the project's repository graph after the merge has been completed. From the graph, we can now see that there are two branches remaining: "main" and "devBranchB."

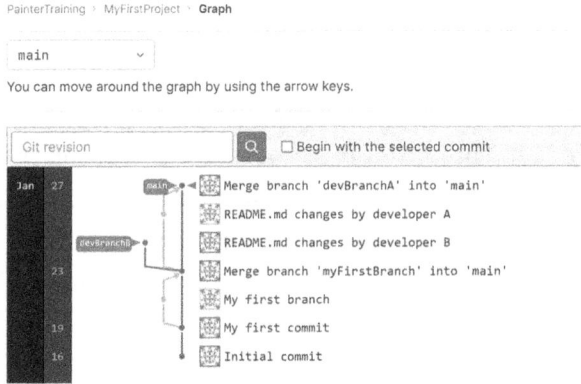

Figure 2-41. *Graph after merge made by developer A*

As soon as the merge by developer A is complete, an email is sent to developer B letting them know there is now a merge conflict on branch "devBranchB" that needs to be resolved. Even though the merge conflict existed between the two branches prior to

CHAPTER 2 JUST THE SOURCE

the merge of "devBranchA," it is not detected until after an MR has been merged. The first person to merge their changes "wins." Figure 2-42 shows what developer B sees when viewing their merge request on branch "devBranchB."

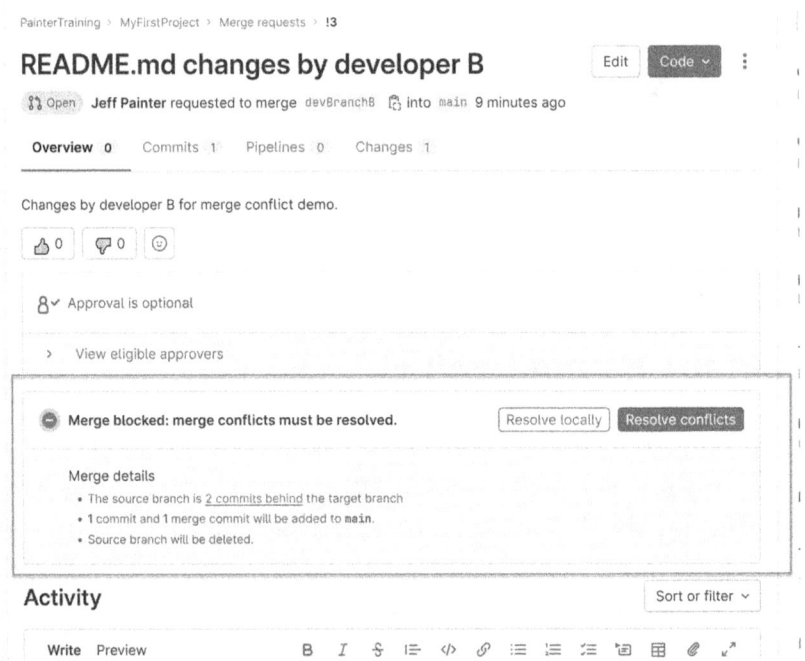

Figure 2-42. Merge conflict message for developer B

We can see that the merge request displays the "Merge blocked" message and provides us a couple ways to resolve the merge conflict. Note that the "Merge" button that usually shows up in the merge request does not appear since GitLab cannot continue until the conflict is resolved. The "Resolve locally" option can be used if you have source code on your local machine; we'll talk about how to set up a local repository on your machine in the next chapter. Clicking the "Resolve conflicts" button takes you to the page shown in Figure 2-43.

CHAPTER 2   JUST THE SOURCE

Figure 2-43. Interactive conflict resolve mode

Exploring Ways to Resolve the Merge Conflict

In interactive mode, you are given choices for each merge conflict. In this case, there is only one merge conflict identified; the other changes made by developers A and B regarding the license and project status sections are not in conflict. The upper green bar shows "our" changes with the button "Use ours," and the lower blue bar shows "their" changes with the button "Use theirs." Our change, made by developer B, was to replace "you" with "users," and their change, made by developer A, was to replace "you" with "developers." Selecting "Use theirs" changes the state as shown in Figure 2-44.

51

CHAPTER 2   JUST THE SOURCE

Figure 2-44. Conflict resolution with "use theirs"

Note that the "Use theirs" line is highlighted to show that it was the selection made. The "Use ours" line is grayed but remains so that you can change your mind later if you choose. Rest assured that when you commit the changes, only the selected change is kept. What if you don't want to use either change? You can select "Edit inline" and make the change manually as shown in Figure 2-45. In this case, you replace all the lines in the highlighted box with the text you would like in its place.

CHAPTER 2 JUST THE SOURCE

Figure 2-45. Conflict resolution using edit inline mode

Committing the Conflict Resolution Change

To resolve the conflict, I selected "Use theirs" in interactive mode and clicked the "Commit to source branch" button. This created a new commit on branch "devBranchB" with the resolved changes in place. The graph in Figure 2-46 shows the new commit with name "Merge branch 'main' into 'devBranchB.'" This seems like an odd name for the commit, but it is correct in the sense that changes made by developer A on the "main" branch have been incorporated into branch "devBranchB." By the way, this is sometimes referred to as a "reverse merge."

CHAPTER 2   JUST THE SOURCE

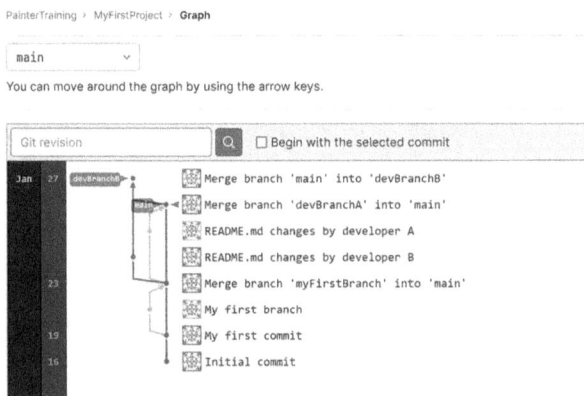

Figure 2-46. *Repository graph from the perspective of the main branch after committing conflict resolution*

Looking at the commits on "devBranchB" as shown in Figure 2-47, we see that there are four commits associated with branch "devBranchB." Note that the previous graph does not explicitly show some of the commits associated with branch "devBranchB," which can be confusing when trying to correlate it with the commits on the project's commits page. Just know that the commits page is correct; I wouldn't fret about the graph representation.

CHAPTER 2 JUST THE SOURCE

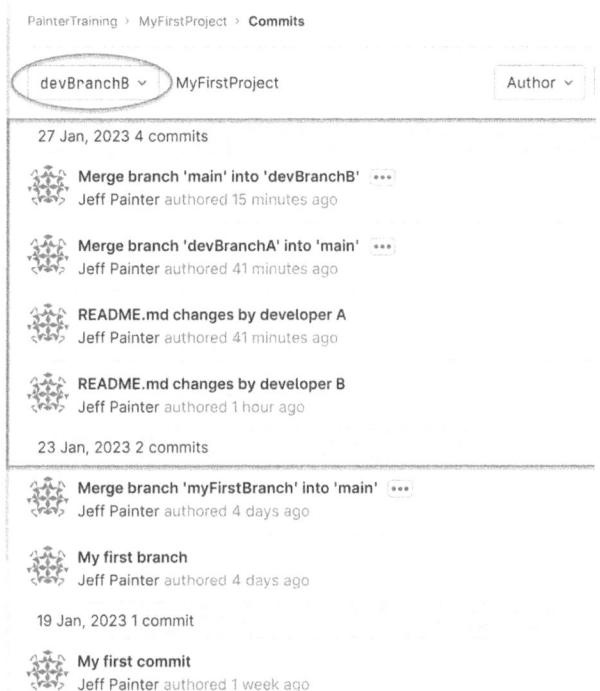

Figure 2-47. *Commits associated with devBranchB after committing conflict resolution*

Out of curiosity, let's take a look at the commit created after resolving the changes. Figure 2-48 shows the contents of that commit. What we see is that the change made by developer B to replace "you" with "users" got overridden with the change "developers" made by developer A. These changes are consistent with respect to "devBranchB" to make it consistent with the changes made by developer A.

55

CHAPTER 2   JUST THE SOURCE

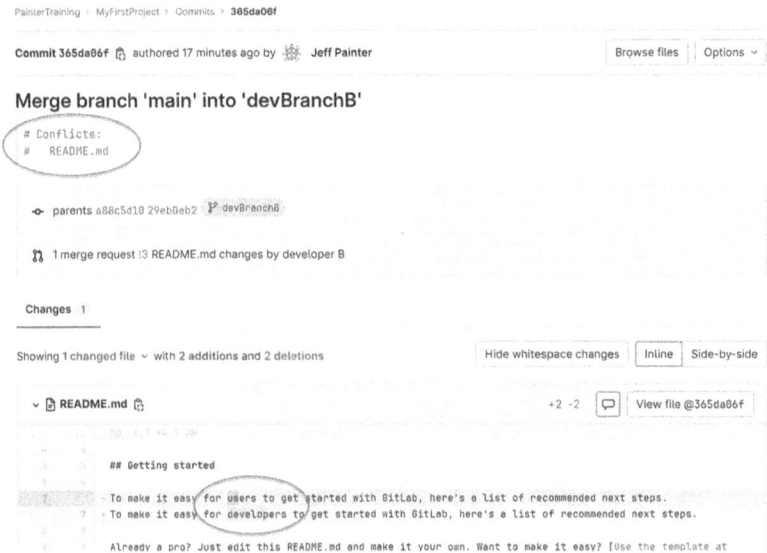

Figure 2-48. Latest commit after conflict resolution

Performing an MR Merge After Committing a Conflict Resolution

Now let's take a look at the merge request that originally alerted us to the merge conflict. Figure 2-49 shows us that the merge request is now ready to be merged. The "Merge" button is now displayed, and the activity section shows that a merge from "main" to "devBranchB" was made. We could have continued to make additional commits on branch "devBranchB" if needed, but for this example, I went ahead and performed the merge.

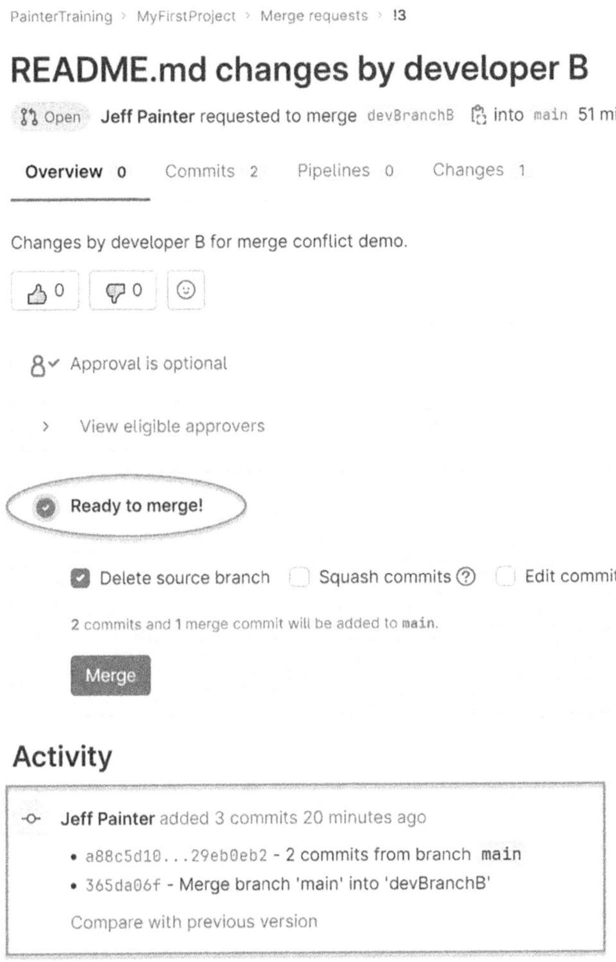

CHAPTER 2   JUST THE SOURCE

Figure 2-49. Merge request overview for developer B after committing conflict resolution

Figure 2-50 shows the graph after the last merge was made. We see branch "main" now points to the merge commit "Merge branch 'devBranchB' into 'main'" and that branch "devBranchB" no longer exists as expected. At first glance, this graph may be confusing. However, if you follow the middle green path from "Merge branch 'MyFirstBranch' into 'main'" to the final commit "Merge branch 'devBranchB' into 'main,'" you'll see that this is the old "devBranchB" branch with an injection point at "Merge branch 'devBranchA' into 'main.'"

57

CHAPTER 2   JUST THE SOURCE

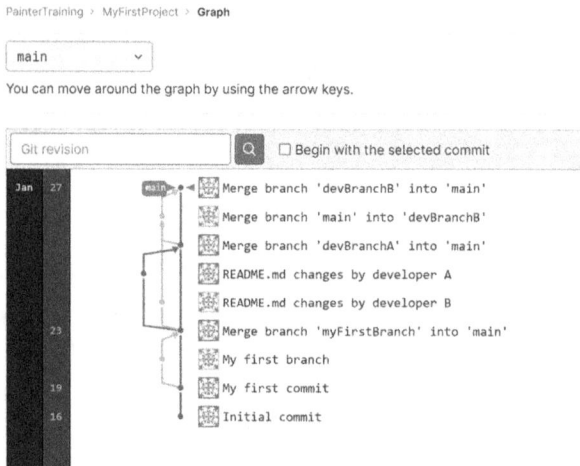

Figure 2-50. *Repository graph for the main branch after merging conflict resolution*

Switching over to the project's commits page as shown in Figure 2-51, we see that all the commits in the highlighted box are now associated with the "main" branch. Following the commits shows you that since MyFirstBranch was merged, developer B made some changes followed by changes by developer A. Developer A then merged changes into "main." This caused some merge conflicts that required developer B to resolve those conflicts, at which point developer B finally merged changes into "main." Although the commits don't explicitly tell you that there were merge conflicts, you can imply that from the reverse merge from "main" into "devBranchB."

58

CHAPTER 2 JUST THE SOURCE

Figure 2-51. *List of commits on the main branch after merging conflict resolution*

Reviewing Project Status After Merge of Conflicting MRs

Before we leave this section, let's take a look at the state of things after all these changes were made. First, if we look at the README.md file, we see in Figure 2-52 that the line that was in conflict now shows that "developers" was the final resolution. Although I don't show the remaining file, the nonconflicting changes made by both developers A and B show up in the README.md file as well.

59

CHAPTER 2   JUST THE SOURCE

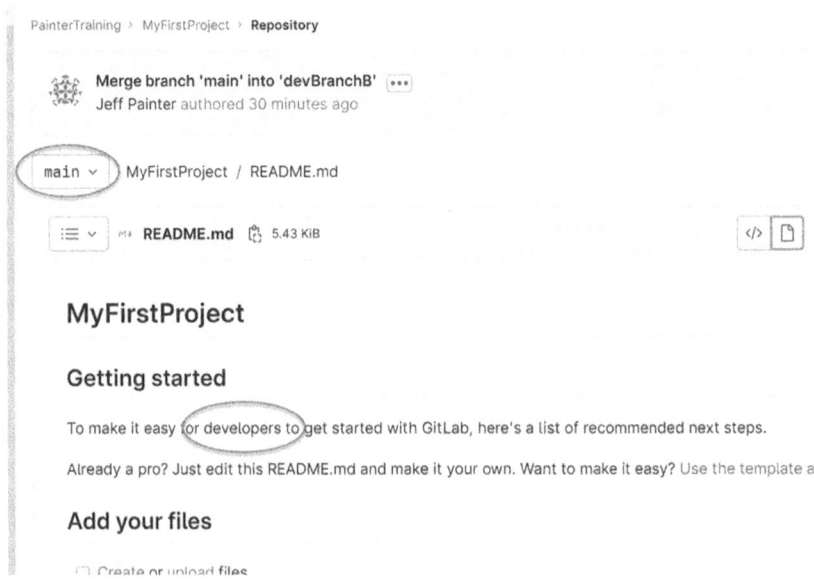

Figure 2-52. *README.md after merge by developer B*

Now let's take a look at what the project's merge requests tell us about the changes. In Figure 2-53, we see the two merge requests made by developers A and B. Given the order of these merge requests (looking from the bottom up), we can see that developer A's merge request came before developer B's merge request.

Figure 2-53. *List of merge requests that have been merged*

Figure 2-54 shows the commits associated with developer A's merge request. Here, we see that there is one commit associated with this merge commit. This commit corresponds to the README.md changes by developer A's commit.

CHAPTER 2   JUST THE SOURCE

Figure 2-54. Commits associated with developer A after conflict merge

Figure 2-55 shows the changes associated with this merge request. It shows that "you" was changed to "developers" and that the License section was updated. If you are wondering why the "Changes" count is 1 and not 2, that's because the number of changes refers to the number of files changed, not the number of individual changes.

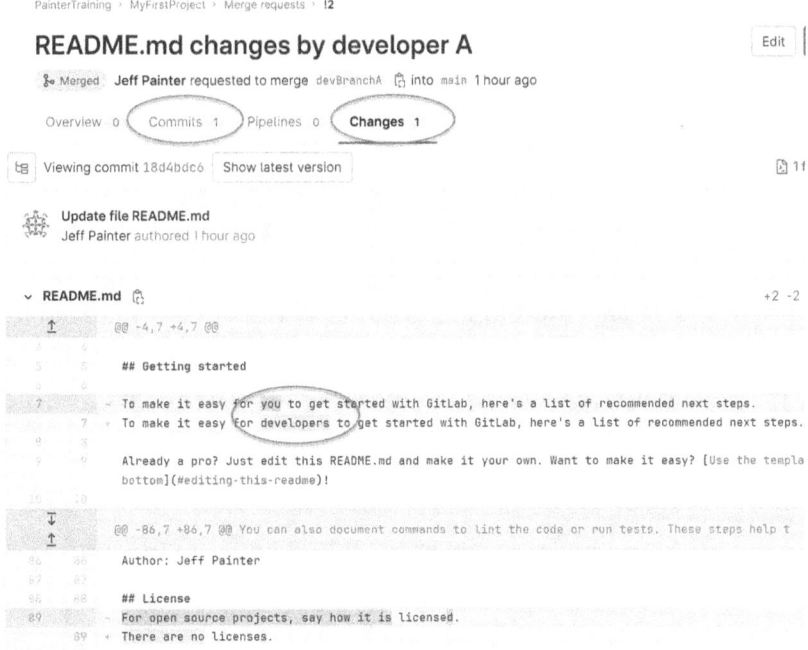

Figure 2-55. Merge request changes associated with developer A after conflict merge

61

CHAPTER 2   JUST THE SOURCE

Switching over to the merge request for developer B, we see the commits associated with that merge in Figure 2-56. Here, we see two commits. The first is the initial commit made by developer B where "you" was changed to "users" in addition to the changes made to the "Project status" section. The second is the reverse merge where the merge conflict was resolved by changing "users" to "developers."

Figure 2-56. *Commits associated with developer B after conflict merge*

Finally, Figure 2-57 shows only the "Project status" changes made by developer B. The reason you don't see the changes made to the "Getting started" section is because the two commits together nullify the change with respect to developer A's merge request. Although the first commit changed "you" to "users" and the second commit changed "users" to "developers," the final state of the "Getting started" section in developer B's merge request matches that of developer A's merge request; there is no difference to the "Getting started" section between the two merge requests. In other words, the changes reported by merge requests are, in essence, the differences between those merge requests.[3] From the context of merge requests, developer A in this example gets credited with making the change to the "Getting started" section.

---

[3] In reality, the changes are between the main branch, which at this point includes the changes made by developer A, and branch devBranchB.

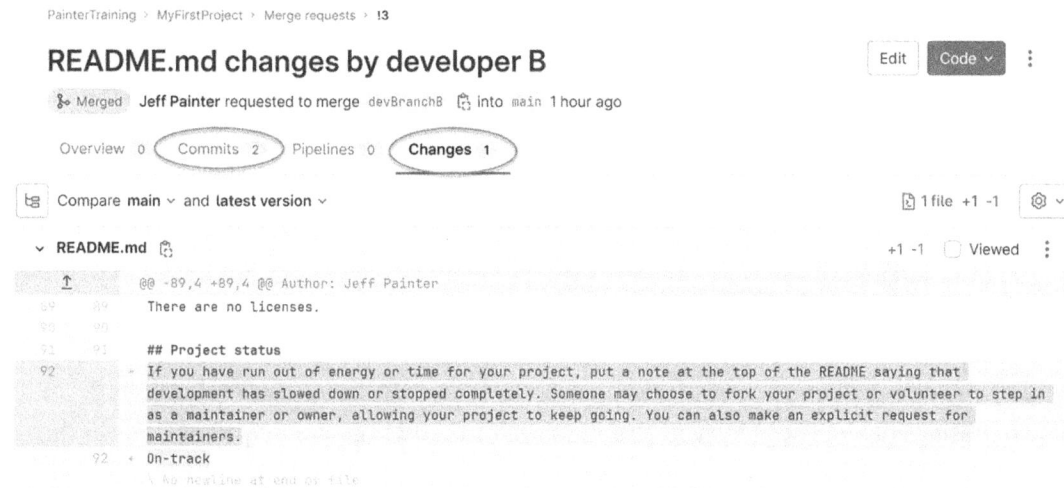

Figure 2-57. *Merge request changes associated with developer B after conflict merge*

I personally like looking at changes from the merge request perspective rather than the commit history perspective. You can easily get wrapped around an axle looking at the changes made by sequences of commits. The view of changes from merge requests is in many ways cleaner because you focus on the end results of a set of changes rather than the intermediate set of changes.

Considering Branching Strategies

So far, we've looked at one branching strategy that can be used by a development team. In this strategy, the "main" branch contains the latest code that is continuously updated and deployed. When a change needs to be made, whether that is a new feature or a bug fix, a developer creates a working branch off the "main" branch, commits the changes, creates a merge request, automatically runs tests, undergoes a code review, and then merges the working branch into the "main" branch. This strategy works well if you can continually deploy the website or application so that changes become immediately available to users or alternatively to a staging environment where users can test things out before the changes are made available in a production environment.

There are times, however, when this approach is not desired. Perhaps you are in an environment where releases are managed on a weekly, monthly, or (horror!) quarterly cadence. This is common with programming libraries, for example. You want to package a number of features and code fixes together to keep the number of releases at a manageable level for the user. A common branching strategy in this type of environment is to create a development branch off the "main" branch and have developers create and merge their working branches off the development branch. Once a release is ready, the development branch can then be merged back into the "main" branch where the product is then packaged and deployed accordingly. The cycle then repeats again with a new development branch. GitLab supports this type of strategy since it allows branches to be created from other branches.

One can imagine other branching strategies, but these two are the most common and recommended approaches. GitLab itself does not enforce or restrict the strategy you choose. Whatever strategy you choose, I recommend that you frequently look at the repository graph for your project. If it starts to look like a bowl of spaghetti or a New York City transit map, you may want to reconsider the strategy. As a former self-managed GitLab administrator, I've seen teams come across issues when merging branches because it is unclear what changes are interfering with each other across various branches. In my experience, this usually happens when there are multiple long-lived branches (we are talking months here) and changes are being maintained between them. If you hear the term "reverse merge" frequently, consider moving to another project.

Summary

To recap, we covered the following topics in this chapter:

- Described how to update files and directories using GitLab's Web IDE
- Explained how to use branches to manage changes in a multi-developer environment
- Introduced GitLab's concept of merge requests to enable reviewing changes before a merge
- Discussed how to resolve conflicts that may arise while merging code
- Considered common branching strategies that teams use during development

Next up, we'll look into how to use Git to manage changes outside of, but in cooperation with, GitLab.

CHAPTER 3

Working the Remote Life

So far, we've been making changes to our project's files using the Web IDE. It's good to know that we can do this interactively and commit our changes via the web interface. But there are risks involved with managing our code this way. For one thing, it is possible, although unlikely, that the GitLab site will become unavailable for some time, either because of a disruptive maintenance update or a denial-of-service attack against the site. More than likely, you may experience an outage with your Internet provider or company's internal network. Both have happened to me several times.

In this chapter, we'll look into how to manage source files remotely, outside of GitLab. To do this, we'll be using the Linux-based Git tool. We'll begin with how to install Git on your local computer with special consideration for the Windows OS. From there, we'll look at two ways, HTTPS and SSH, to make a copy of a GitLab project's repository on your local filesystem, a process known as cloning. Before we can make changes to the copied repository, we'll describe how to configure Git for your project. Finally, we'll discuss how to make and synchronize changes between GitLab and your local environment.

Installing Git

To edit code locally on your computer, you will need to first install the Git client software, which is a source code management (SCM) product. There are certainly other SCM products out there such as Subversion or Mercurial, but Git is a common product used by the open source community. It is also the underlying SCM used by GitLab (hence its name). GitLab does not support any other SCM product. If you already have code managed by Subversion, Mercurial, whatever, you will first need to migrate it into Git first and then manage the code thereafter using Git. How this migration is performed is beyond the scope of this book; you can easily find documentation on the Internet.[1]

Directions on how to set up Git client software for Mac, Windows, and Ubuntu Linux can be found on the GitLab documentation site here: https://docs.gitlab.com/ee/topics/git/how_to_install_git/. If the link is broken, simply do a web search for "GitLab Installing Git," and it will lead you to the documentation. Although it describes the install for Ubuntu Linux, you should be able to determine the install for other Linux distributions by using the appropriate package manager. You can also check out the Git install instructions located here: https://git-scm.com/book/en/v2/Getting-Started-Installing-Git.

I'm going to make a special note about the Windows install since it is significantly different from the Mac and Linux installs. Whereas the installs for Mac and Linux use package managers (homebrew, apt, yum, dnf, etc.) to install the software, Windows requires a binary install downloaded from the Internet that installs "Git for Windows" (which can be found at https://gitforwindows.org/). This Windows binary installs both a GUI interface and a Git bash emulator where you can use the same command-line requests on Mac or Linux terminal shells.

If you are a power developer and familiar with Linux shell commands, you could also install a Linux distribution on your Windows machine using Windows Subsystem for Linux (WSL). Instructions and requirements on how to install WSL 2 can be found here: https://learn.microsoft.com/en-us/windows/wsl/install. You get to pick the Linux distribution of your choice (Ubuntu, Debian, CentOS, Fedora, etc.). The default is Ubuntu, which is a popular distribution that does a great job at keeping the OS and all of its packages up to date (especially security updates). Once you have a Linux distribution installed, you can then use the standard Linux package manager to install Git. Note that this installs the command-line version of Git; there is no GUI component via the WSL.[2]

---

[1] As a GitLab administrator, I've performed these migrations many times for teams. Mercurial, which is a distributed SCM like Git, is the easiest to migrate. Subversion can be extremely difficult to migrate depending on the features used; there have been cases where I was unable to migrate the code. If you don't care about preserving change history, you can easily import the code base directly into GitLab and start afresh.

[2] This isn't an issue since you can either use GitLab's web interface as the GUI or install a standalone Git GUI such as Tortoise Git.

Cloning with HTTPS

Now that we have Git installed on our local machine, let's look at how we can get a copy of the files associated with a project onto it. In Git speak, this is a process known as cloning, and there are two ways to clone your code base: HTTPS and SSH. In this section, we'll focus on cloning using HTTPS and describe how to clone using SSH in the next section.

Before we proceed, I need to clarify some terminology with respect to the terms local and remote. From Git's perspective, GitLab is the remote environment, and your machine is the local environment. So, when we talk about the local repository, we mean the repository that has been copied to your local machine, and the remote repository is the project repository we copied from GitLab. The perspective from GitLab is obviously the reverse of this. From here on out, we'll be taking the perspective of Git installed on your local machine.

Preparing Your Local Environment

I've installed Git for Windows on my laptop and will use the Git bash tool to clone the project "MyFirstProject." The steps are the same if running the commands from a bash shell on your Linux, Mac, or Windows WSL environment. The first step to do is to create the directory gitlab-repos where all the Git project repositories will be stored. In Figure 3-1, I've created the gitlab-repos directory off of my home directory using the mkdir command. I then cd to that directory before cloning. The remaining commands show how to clone the repository and explore the directories and files created by the clone.

CHAPTER 3   WORKING THE REMOTE LIFE

Figure 3-1. Cloning MyFirstProject via HTTPS

Determining the URL to Use for Cloning with HTTPS

To clone the "MyFirstProject" repository, we need to determine the HTTPS URL to use. The easiest way to do this is to open the project and use the Code drop-down menu as shown in Figure 3-2. You can copy the URL to your clipboard by clicking the icon next to the "Clone with HTTPS." You could also directly select the URL text and copy it using the mechanism provided by your browser (Control-C, for example).

CHAPTER 3   WORKING THE REMOTE LIFE

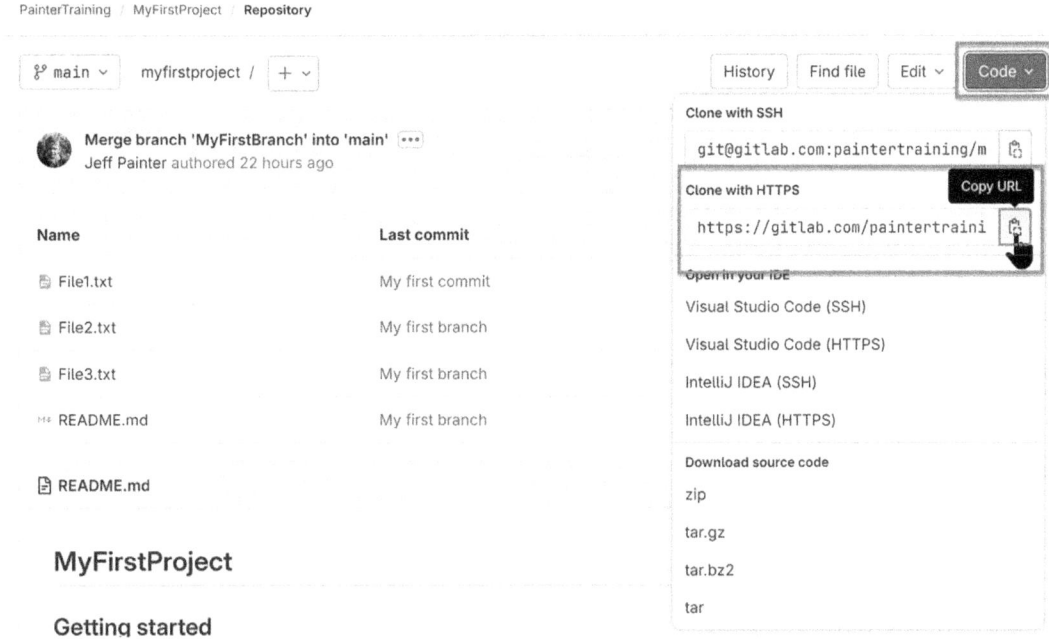

Figure 3-2. Copying the URL needed for an HTTPS clone

Performing the HTTPS Clone with the Git Credential Manager

Once you have copied the URL, go back to your bash session and type "git clone" and paste the URL using Control-V or equivalent. Hit enter and the clone process will begin. At this point, one of two things will happen. If you have the Git Credential Manager installed, which you will if you installed the Git for Windows application, you will get prompted to log in to GitLab and then authorize your manager to use your account on GitLab as shown in Figure 3-3. If you authorize it, your GitLab credentials will be stored encrypted by the Git Credential Manager on your machine. Once that is done, you will not need to provide your credentials again unless you change them.

CHAPTER 3 WORKING THE REMOTE LIFE

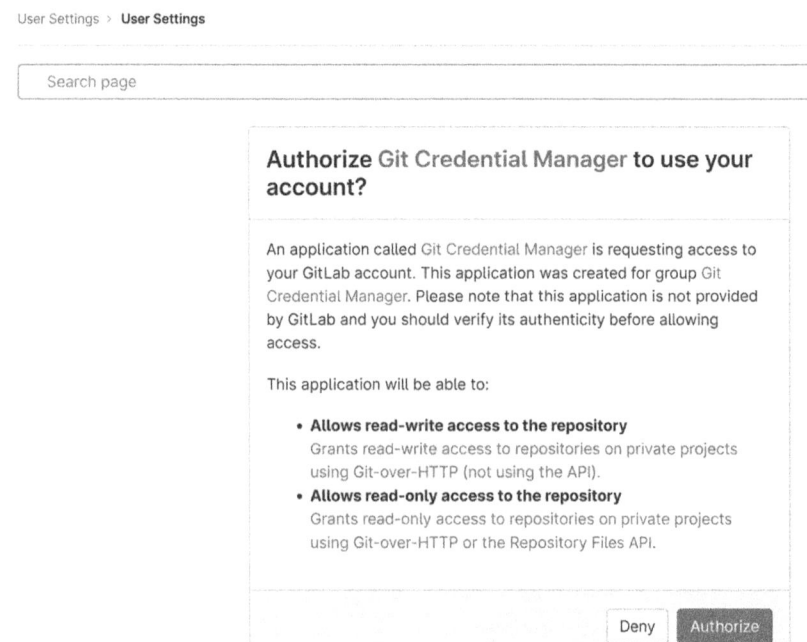

Figure 3-3. *Git Credential Manager authorization*

In case you need to, you can always revoke the authorization via GitLab's User Settings Applications as shown in Figure 3-4. This also provides a way to check that no one else has grabbed your credentials and is using Git Credential Manager to access your account.

CHAPTER 3   WORKING THE REMOTE LIFE

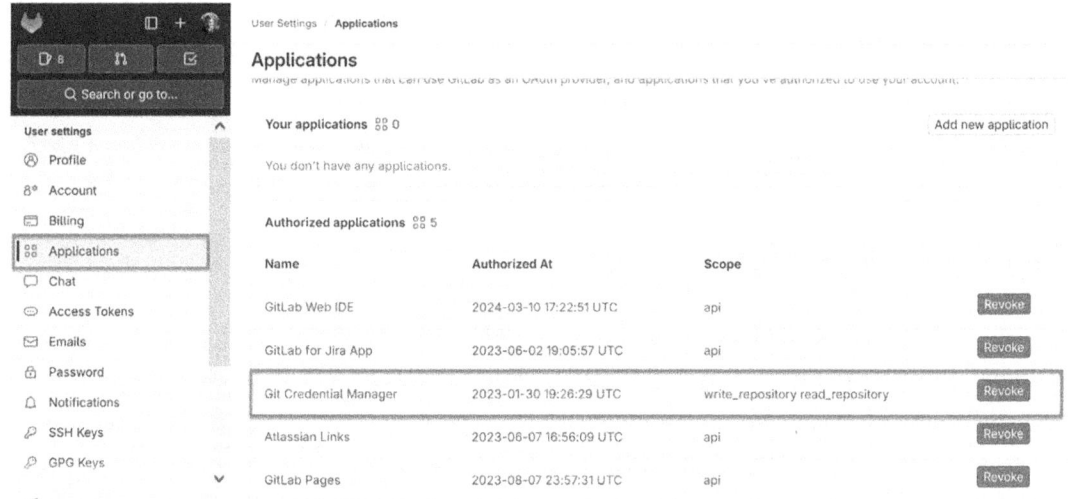

Figure 3-4. *List of user authorized applications highlighting the Git Credential Manager*

Performing the HTTPS Clone Using Username and Password Credentials

If you don't have the Git Credential Manager installed on your machine, you will instead be prompted for your GitLab username and password. If you end up using this method to authenticate, then your credentials, both username and password, will be saved on your machine in plain text. This is one of the reasons why you may see discussions in online development groups that discourage using HTTPS to clone your repository and recommend using SSH instead. The Git Credential Manager is relatively new and was developed to get around the plain text issue; however, it can be tricky to install, especially on Linux systems, so using SSH is still recommended in those cases.

Once you've gotten past authorization, the git clone operation will create a new directory with the name of the project ("MyFirstProject" in this case) and will copy all the files into that directory. It will also create a hidden directory called ".git" in your project directory that includes metadata about the project, such as commits history, branch information, etc. This directory is important for Git to function correctly; you should not mess with any of the files located under it. The various Git commands, such as git commit and git push, will make the appropriate changes to those files. Once the clone is completed, you can make changes to the files locally on your machine and push them back up at a later time. In this way, you are no longer dependent on Internet connections or website downtimes.

Before we describe how to do all that, let's first take a look at how to clone with SSH.

Cloning with SSH

The alternative to cloning a Git repository with HTTPS is to use SSH. The reason for this is that cloning with SSH is more secure than cloning with HTTPS. However, with this security comes some complexity in getting SSH to work properly, especially if you've never used SSH before. Once you have SSH set up properly on your local environment, cloning projects becomes simple. In this section, we'll go through the steps needed to successfully set up your local environment to use SSH.

Creating the SSH Key Pair on Your Local Environment

Before you can clone a project's repository using SSH, you need to have the OpenSSH client installed on your machine. For machines running Mac, Linux, and Windows 10+, this will usually be the case. In addition, if you installed Git for Windows, this would also install OpenSSH if you allowed it. Make sure that you are using a recent version of SSH; the version should at least be 6.5. You can check your version by opening a shell session (or Git bash if you are using that) and typing ssh -V as shown in Figure 3-5.

CHAPTER 3   WORKING THE REMOTE LIFE

```
jpain@LAPTOP-HRE7CTE5 MINGW64 ~
$ pwd
/c/Users/jpain

jpain@LAPTOP-HRE7CTE5 MINGW64 ~
$ ssh -V
OpenSSH_for_Windows_8.1p1, LibreSSL 3.0.2

jpain@LAPTOP-HRE7CTE5 MINGW64 ~
$ ssh-keygen -t ed25519 -f ~/.ssh/gitlab_ed25519 -C "GitLab key for me"
Generating public/private ed25519 key pair.
Your identification has been saved in C:/Users/jpain/.ssh/gitlab_ed25519.
Your public key has been saved in C:/Users/jpain/.ssh/gitlab_ed25519.pub.
The key fingerprint is:
SHA256:suYv99B1WTE46FnxB99YIt+xG/yF+ftkmjfdawQoUI4 GitLab key for me
The key's randomart image is:
+--[ED25519 256]--+
|          o.+.   |
|         o *oX*  |
|        = o *=B  |
|       E +  +"   |
|      . S . . +.o|
|       o . o o . |
|        o . . o.*|
|         o ...  O=|
|          .+... +.o|
+----[SHA256]-----+

jpain@LAPTOP-HRE7CTE5 MINGW64 ~
$ cd .ssh

jpain@LAPTOP-HRE7CTE5 MINGW64 ~/.ssh
$ ls -l
total 2
-rw-r--r-- 1 jpain 197609 411 Jan 31 11:10 gitlab_ed25519
-rw-r--r-- 1 jpain 197609 100 Jan 31 11:10 gitlab_ed25519.pub

jpain@LAPTOP-HRE7CTE5 MINGW64 ~/.ssh
$ cat gitlab_ed25519.pub
ssh-ed25519 AAAAC3NzaC1lZDI1NTE5AAAAIKOxD/M476WuJyE+NYErb2hX58mT3jtzCtC9ySAd7PBk GitLab key for me

jpain@LAPTOP-HRE7CTE5 MINGW64 ~/.ssh
$
```

Figure 3-5. *Creating an SSH key pair using OpenSSH's ssh-keygen*

You use ssh-keygen to create an SSH key pair: a public key that you'll give to GitLab and a private key that you'll keep in a special directory, .ssh, under your home directory. There are a number of SSH key types that you can use, but one of the most secure (at the time of this writing) is based on the ed25519 algorithm. I created the key pair using the following command:

```
ssh-keygen -t ed25519 -f ~/.ssh/gitlab_ed25519 -C "GitLab key for me"
```

The -t option determines the SSH key type to create. The optional -f option specifies the location and name of the key, in this case the .ssh directory under the user's home directory. The last -C option is an optional comment that will be injected into the public key to help remind you of what it is for. When the command is run, it will prompt you for an optional passphrase. If you are running Git for Windows, you will see a pop-up window where you can enter the phrase as shown in Figure 3-6. Otherwise, the prompt will appear on your terminal session. I've chosen not to use a passphrase by simply clicking the OK button in this example.

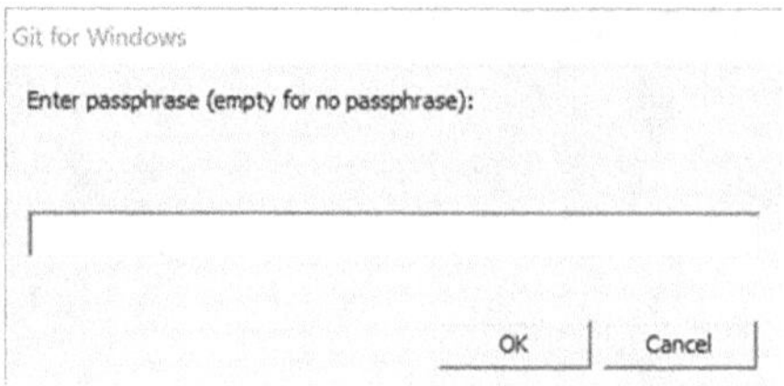

CHAPTER 3   WORKING THE REMOTE LIFE

Figure 3-6.   Git for Windows passphrase prompt

Note that if you don't have a .ssh directory, the ssh-keygen command will create it for you. In that directory, you'll see two files, which in this example are gitlab_ed25519 and gitlab_ed25519.pub. The first file is the private key that will remain in the .ssh directory. The second file is the public key. In Figure 3-5, I show the contents of the public key. It starts with the algorithm used (ssh-ed25519) followed by the key itself and ends with the comment, if any; all of that information is contained in one line of text. If you look at the contents of the private key, you'll see multiple lines in the format shown as follows:

```
-----BEGIN OPENSSH PRIVATE KEY-----
Private key contents
-----END OPENSSH PRIVATE KEY-----
```

Registering the SSH Public Key with GitLab

Now that the key pair is created, you need to add the public key to GitLab so that it will authenticate with it. To do that, go to your User Preferences and select the "SSH Keys" tab as shown in Figure 3-7. Copy the contents of the public key to the clipboard and paste them into the Key field; note that although the field shows multiple lines, it is actually just one line of text that is being wrapped around so you can see the full key. Enter a title for your key so you can identify it from GitLab[3] and leave the remaining fields at their defaults.

---

[3] You can use multiple keys with GitLab. For example, you might want to connect from multiple machines such as your home and work laptops. It is recommended that you use distinct keys for each machine in case one of them gets lost or stolen.

CHAPTER 3   WORKING THE REMOTE LIFE

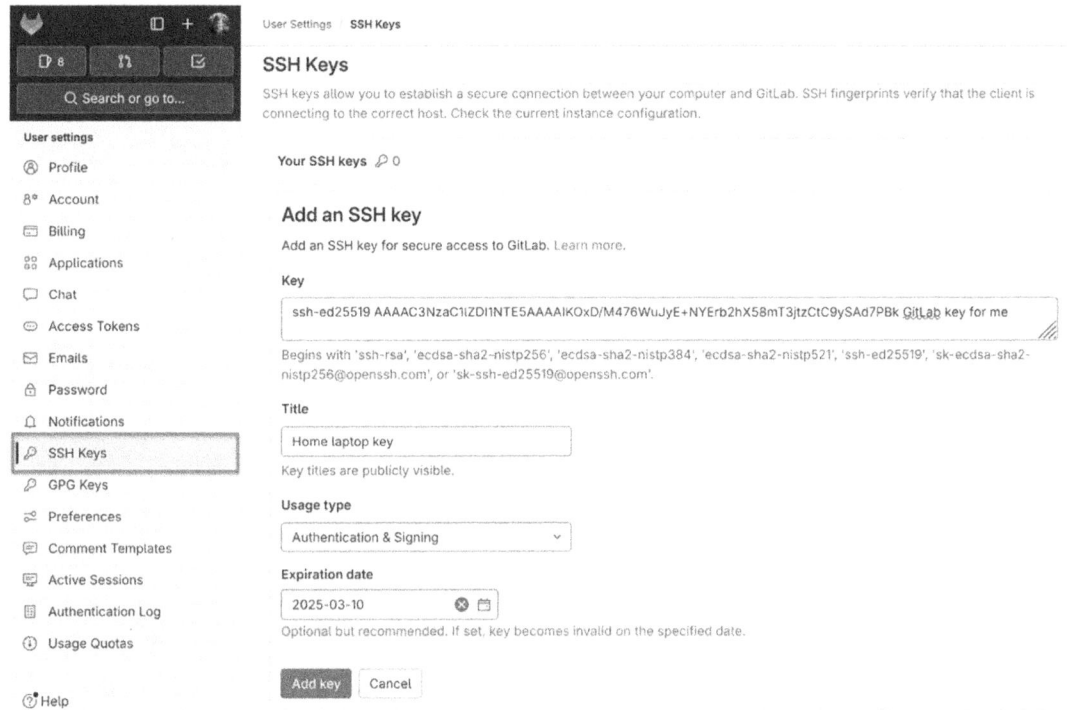

Figure 3-7. Adding an SSH key to GitLab

When you add the key, you will get a feedback page as shown in Figure 3-8. This page displays the options you've chosen along with fingerprints that uniquely identify your key pair. Note that GitLab uses the fingerprint to help look up who you are when you connect via SSH; because of this, you cannot share key pairs with another user (by design). Also, note that you will get an email alerting you to the new key being added; this is done as a security measure to ensure you are the one adding the new key.

CHAPTER 3   WORKING THE REMOTE LIFE

Figure 3-8. Response to adding an SSH key

If you go back to the User Settings SSH Keys page, you'll now see your key listed under "Your SSH Keys" as shown in Figure 3-9. In this example, it shows that I have only one key with the title "Home laptop key" along with the unique fingerprint associated with it. Note that once you add a public key, you won't be able to view it from GitLab; you'll only be presented with the fingerprint. If you discover that your private key has been compromised, you can use this page to revoke it.

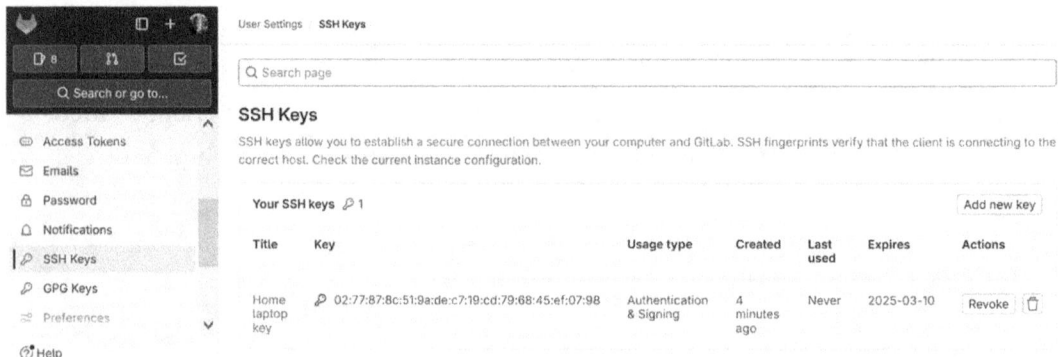

Figure 3-9. Listing of SSH keys for a given user

CHAPTER 3   WORKING THE REMOTE LIFE

Testing SSH Connectivity to GitLab

Now the moment of truth: testing SSH connectivity. To test that we can connect to gitlab.com using SSH, we run ssh -T git@gitlab.com as shown in Figure 3-10. If this is the first time running this command, you will get a prompt asking if you would like to add the host to the known_hosts file. If you are running under Git for Windows, you will get a pop-up prompt as shown in Figure 3-11. Either way, entering yes will create a known_hosts file if it does not exist and adds an entry related to the gitlab.com home site.

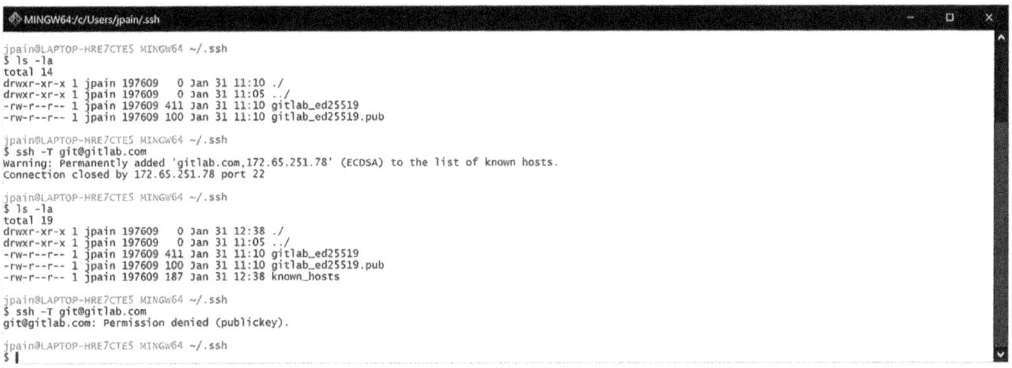

Figure 3-10. First-time test of SSH key

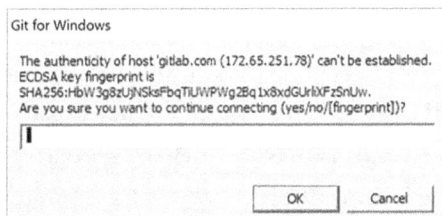

Figure 3-11. Git for Windows known host prompt

Once the known_hosts file has an entry for gitlab.com, we run the ssh -T git@gitlab.com command again to verify that GitLab accepts the connection. In my case, it did not. I knew that it wouldn't but wanted to show that this is not unusual. The ssh command is very picky about things to help ensure the highest security. For my case, I determined that I was missing the .ssh/config file that tells SSH what private key to use. Looking at Figure 3-12, I created the config file for host gitlab.com and told it to use the .ssh/gitlab_ed25519 private key. Running the ssh -T command again, I get a successful "Welcome to

77

GitLab" message that lets me know GitLab now accepts the key; it also echoes back my GitLab username to let me know that the key is correctly associated to me. Once you've passed this test, you are ready to clone a project repository using SSH.

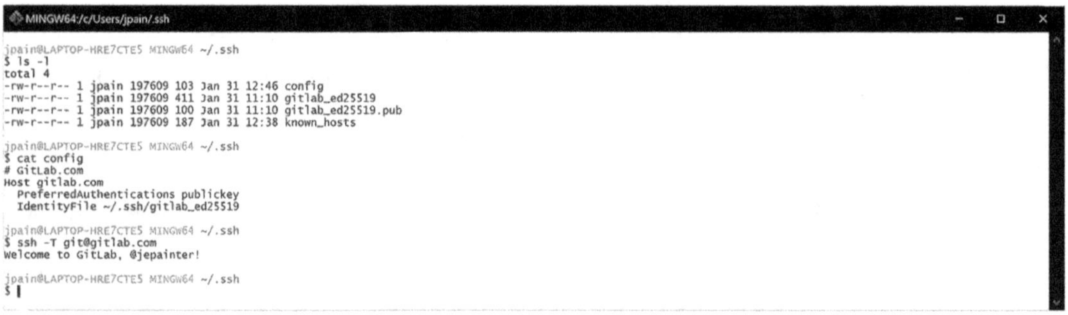

Figure 3-12. Second-time test of SSH key

Debugging Common Issues Connecting with SSH

Before we get to the cloning, I want to mention some other common issues that would cause the SSH connectivity test to fail. For Mac- and Linux-based filesystems, you need to ensure that the directory and file mode settings are correct; Windows-based filesystems are a bit looser in this since file modes are not used. First of all, you need to ensure that the .ssh directory is read-write protected only to you; when you do an ls -ld .ssh command from your home directory, you should see settings like "drwx------". If not, you need to run chmod 0700 .ssh to change the settings. Within the .ssh directory, you also need to make sure that your private SSH key is read-write protected only to you. When you do an ls -l, you should see "-rw------" associated with your private key. If not, you can change the mode settings by running chmod 0600 your_private_key_file, replacing your_private_key_file with the name of your actual file (gitlab_ed25519 in this example). Once those settings are in place, you should be able to connect successfully.

If you are still having issues, try running ssh -Tvvv git@gitlab.com to give you more verbose debug output. Running that command will usually help pinpoint the issue. Also, check out GitLab's documentation at `https://docs.gitlab.com/ee/user/ssh.html` for more detailed information about using SSH keys.

CHAPTER 3   WORKING THE REMOTE LIFE

Determining the URL to Use for Cloning with SSH

Now, to clone your project repository using SSH, go to your project page and click the Code drop-down menu and select the icon next to the "Clone with SSH" URL as shown in Figure 3-13. This will copy the SSH URL onto your clipboard. You can also select the URL text and do a Control-C (or equivalent) to copy the URL to the clipboard.

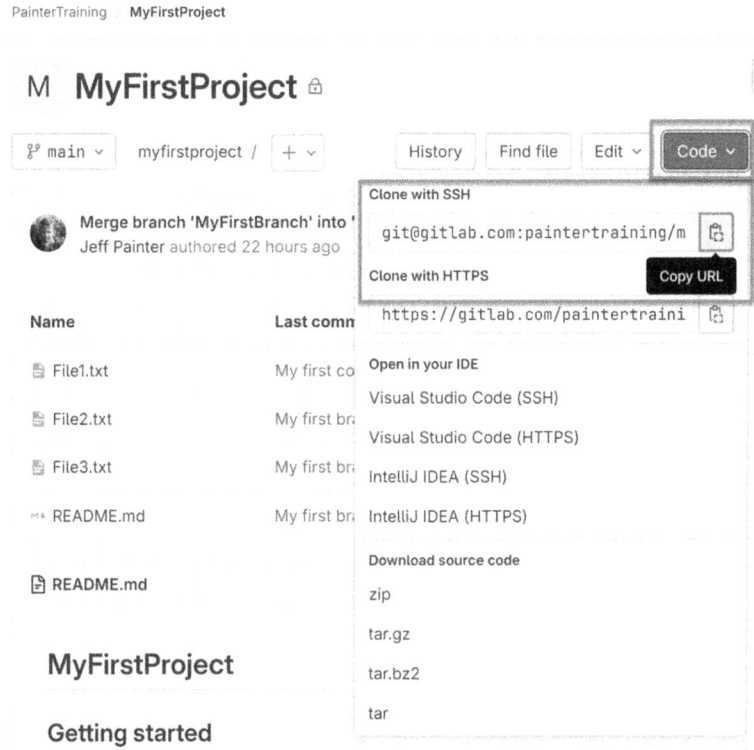

Figure 3-13.   Copying the URL needed for an SSH clone

Cloning Your Project with SSH

Now going back to your terminal or Git bash session, remove "MyFirstProject" from the gitlab-repos directory if you cloned it earlier using HTTPS and then run git clone with the copied SSH URL as shown in Figure 3-14. This will create the "MyFirstProject" directory as before with all the same files except for some minor differences in the "MyFirstProject/.git" directory. Note that when you clone with SSH, you do not get the prompt to authorize as you did when cloning with HTTPS. This is because we've already gone through the authorization checks when we tested our SSH connectivity earlier.

79

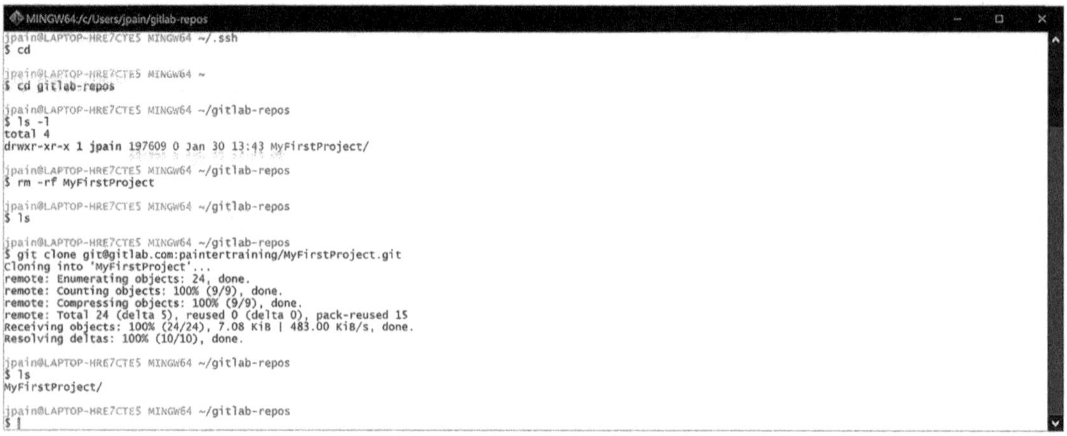

Figure 3-14. Cloning MyFirstBranch via SSH

Before we leave this section, you might be wondering why the SSH URL uses git as the user and not your GitLab username; many beginning users of GitLab incorrectly try to use my_username@gitlab.com/blah-blah, which fails when trying to do a clone. Part of the answer is that using git is more secure than using your username; once someone has your username, they have half of your credentials to begin a password-cracking attack to get into your GitLab account. Maybe they will succeed, maybe they won't, but by using git as the user, they will have a harder time breaking into your account.

So how, then, does GitLab determine that you are the user? Remember the unique fingerprint associated with your SSH key. When you use SSH, it uses your private key to generate that fingerprint and presents it to GitLab. GitLab then does a reverse lookup of that fingerprint to determine who the user is. If it can't find that fingerprint, SSH (and hence git clone) rejects the request. This is why GitLab prevents other users from using the same public key as yours; otherwise, it wouldn't know what user and account to associate the key with. You can see this in action on the Git client side by running ssh -Tvvv git@gitlab.com.

Configuring Git

Now that we've cloned "MyFirstProject" to our machine, let's look at how we would make changes locally and push them back up to our GitLab project. At this point, we have a copy of the Git repository's main branch; by default, any other branches that may exist have not been copied to our local repository. We can pull them down if we want to, but to keep things simple, we'll only bring down what we need to work on.

CHAPTER 3   WORKING THE REMOTE LIFE

Configuring Your Username and Email Address

Since this is the first time we've started working with Git on our local machine, there are a couple of settings that we should set. These settings help identify who we are to the local repository and will be used to track the changes we make. The git config command is used to set and get various configuration options that are stored on your filesystem. Configurations can be maintained globally for you or locally to a project.[4] Two options that we are going to set globally are "user.name" and "user.email" that refer to your username and email address, respectively. This is done using the git config --global command as shown in Figure 3-15. Once set, we can list them using git config --global --list as shown in the same figure.

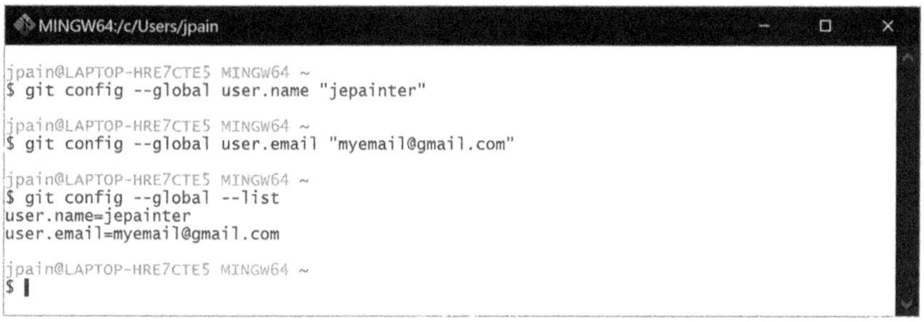

```
jpain@LAPTOP-HRE7CTE5 MINGW64 ~
$ git config --global user.name "jepainter"

jpain@LAPTOP-HRE7CTE5 MINGW64 ~
$ git config --global user.email "myemail@gmail.com"

jpain@LAPTOP-HRE7CTE5 MINGW64 ~
$ git config --global --list
user.name=jepainter
user.email=myemail@gmail.com

jpain@LAPTOP-HRE7CTE5 MINGW64 ~
$
```

Figure 3-15. *Git local configuration setup*

Locating the Global Configuration File

The global configuration file is located in your home directory as the hidden file ".gitconfig". Figure 3-16 shows the contents of this file after making the changes with git config --global made earlier. If you are wondering whether you can edit this file directly, the answer is yes, but I don't recommend it. The formatting is rather odd, especially with more complex nested configurations. To get an idea of this, compare the results of running git config --local --list with the contents of the "MyFirstProject/.git/config" file in your project.

---

[4]There are other locations where configurations can be stored, but these are the two most common ones that you will use.

CHAPTER 3   WORKING THE REMOTE LIFE

```
jpain@LAPTOP-HRE7CTE5 MINGW64 ~
$ cat ~/.gitconfig
[user]
        name = jepainter
        email = myemail@gmail.com

jpain@LAPTOP-HRE7CTE5 MINGW64 ~
$
```

Figure 3-16. *Git global configuration file contents*

Making Changes with Git

So, let's run some Git commands to get a sense of our local repository's initial state. Figure 3-17 shows some useful commands and their responses before any changes are made. The git remote -v command gives us information about the remote repository (with respect to our local repository). This was set when we did the git clone of the project. By default, the remote repository is referred to as "origin," and both fetching from and pushing to origin are to the same remote repository. The git branch -l gives a list of your local branches; in this case, there is only the main branch. The asterisk at the beginning of this branch tells us that we are currently on the main branch. Finally, git status gives us an overview of changes, if any, we've made so far; at this point, we are fully in sync with the remote main branch.

```
jpain@LAPTOP-HRE7CTE5 MINGW64 ~/gitlab-repos/MyFirstProject (main)
$ git remote -v
origin  git@gitlab.com:paintertraining/MyFirstProject.git (fetch)
origin  git@gitlab.com:paintertraining/MyFirstProject.git (push)

jpain@LAPTOP-HRE7CTE5 MINGW64 ~/gitlab-repos/MyFirstProject (main)
$ git branch -l
* main

jpain@LAPTOP-HRE7CTE5 MINGW64 ~/gitlab-repos/MyFirstProject (main)
$ git status
On branch main
Your branch is up to date with 'origin/main'.

nothing to commit, working tree clean

jpain@LAPTOP-HRE7CTE5 MINGW64 ~/gitlab-repos/MyFirstProject (main)
$
```

Figure 3-17. *Commands showing the initial state of the local Git repository*

Creating a New Branch in GitLab for Use by Your Local Repository

As we did interactively, we need to create a branch before we start to make changes. We could do this from the command line using git checkout -b demoLocalEdits, which will create the branch locally. I prefer to create the branch from GitLab first as shown in Figure 3-18. This way, I know that the name of my branch doesn't conflict with any existing branches created by other developers.

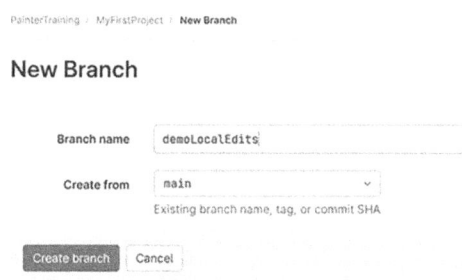

Figure 3-18. *Creating a branch in GitLab to be used in the local repository*

Synchronizing the New GitLab Branch with Your Local Environment

Once the branch is created in GitLab, we go to the "MyFirstProject" directory and pull the branch using git pull origin demoLocalEdits as shown in Figure 3-19. This creates the local branch "demoLocalEdits" that is mapped to the remote branch in GitLab. We then switch to the new branch using git checkout demoLocalEdits so that any changes will be made on this branch. For those using Git for Windows, you'll also see the branch name in parentheses at the end of the command-line prompt.

CHAPTER 3   WORKING THE REMOTE LIFE

```
jpain@LAPTOP-HRE7CTE5 MINGW64 ~/gitlab-repos/MyFirstProject (main)
$ pwd
/c/Users/jpain/gitlab-repos/MyFirstProject

jpain@LAPTOP-HRE7CTE5 MINGW64 ~/gitlab-repos/MyFirstProject (main)
$ git pull origin demoLocalEdits
From gitlab.com:paintertraining/MyFirstProject
 * branch            demoLocalEdits -> FETCH_HEAD
 * [new branch]      demoLocalEdits -> origin/demoLocalEdits
Already up to date.

jpain@LAPTOP-HRE7CTE5 MINGW64 ~/gitlab-repos/MyFirstProject (main)
$ git branch -l
* main

jpain@LAPTOP-HRE7CTE5 MINGW64 ~/gitlab-repos/MyFirstProject (main)
$ git checkout demoLocalEdits
Switched to a new branch 'demoLocalEdits'
branch 'demoLocalEdits' set up to track 'origin/demoLocalEdits'.

jpain@LAPTOP-HRE7CTE5 MINGW64 ~/gitlab-repos/MyFirstProject (demoLocalEdits)
$ git branch -l
* demoLocalEdits
  main

jpain@LAPTOP-HRE7CTE5 MINGW64 ~/gitlab-repos/MyFirstProject (demoLocalEdits)
$
```

Figure 3-19. *Commands to prepare a branch for changes in the local repository*

Making Changes in the Local Repository

I've gone ahead and made some changes to my local copy as shown in Figure 3-20. I created a new file File4.txt and updated the README.md file by removing the "Badges and Visuals" sections. I use the git diff README.md command to show the differences made in the README.md file and show the contents of the File4.txt file.

CHAPTER 3 WORKING THE REMOTE LIFE

Figure 3-20. Commands to show file changes made in the local repository

Staging Changes in Your Local Repository

I then run a git status to see what the changes are as shown in Figure 3-21. The git status shows that the README.md file has changes that have not been staged yet; in Git, files need to be staged before a commit can be made. The status command also shows that File4.txt is "untracked," meaning that it is a file not being managed yet by Git. One nice feature of Git is that it provides hints as to what to run next. In this case, I run git add README.md File4.txt to stage the files before making a commit. Running git status again, we see that the changes are staged and ready to be committed. Note that you could continue to make changes and add them before you make your final commit.

85

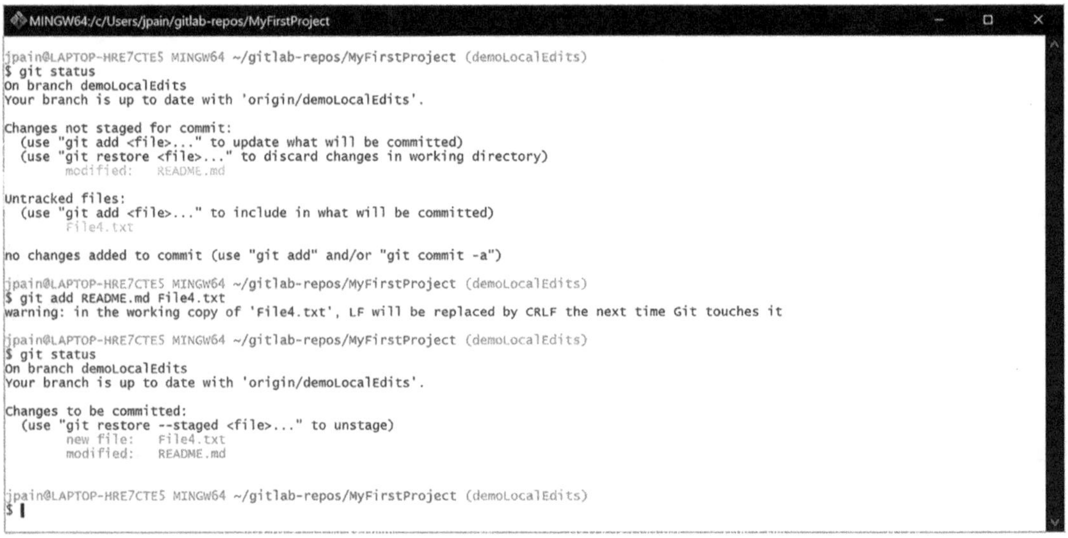
MINGW64:/c/Users/jpain/gitlab-repos/MyFirstProject
jpain@LAPTOP-HRE7CTE5 MINGW64 ~/gitlab-repos/MyFirstProject (demoLocalEdits)
$ git status
On branch demoLocalEdits
Your branch is up to date with 'origin/demoLocalEdits'.
Changes not staged for commit:
(use "git add <file>..." to update what will be committed)
(use "git restore <file>..." to discard changes in working directory)
modified: README.md
Untracked files:
(use "git add <file>..." to include in what will be committed)
File4.txt
no changes added to commit (use "git add" and/or "git commit -a")
jpain@LAPTOP-HRE7CTE5 MINGW64 ~/gitlab-repos/MyFirstProject (demoLocalEdits)
$ git add README.md File4.txt
warning: in the working copy of 'File4.txt', LF will be replaced by CRLF the next time Git touches it
jpain@LAPTOP-HRE7CTE5 MINGW64 ~/gitlab-repos/MyFirstProject (demoLocalEdits)
$ git status
On branch demoLocalEdits
Your branch is up to date with 'origin/demoLocalEdits'.
Changes to be committed:
(use "git restore --staged <file>..." to unstage)
new file: File4.txt
modified: README.md
jpain@LAPTOP-HRE7CTE5 MINGW64 ~/gitlab-repos/MyFirstProject (demoLocalEdits)
$

Figure 3-21. *Commands to stage changes in the local repository*

Committing Changes in Your Local Repository

To commit the changes, we run git commit with the -m argument that provides a description of the commit as shown in Figure 3-22. Running git status after the commit lets us know that the changes are ready to be pushed. You don't have to push the changes yet; you can continue to make additional changes and commit them if you desire. Some developers do this at the end of the day, for example, to save their changes.

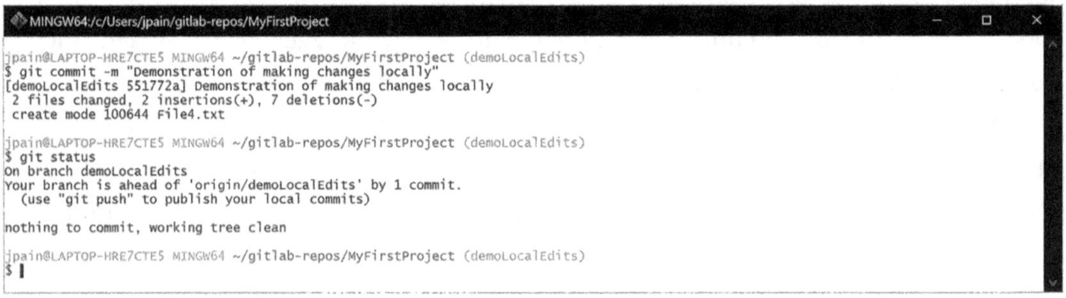
MINGW64:/c/Users/jpain/gitlab-repos/MyFirstProject
jpain@LAPTOP-HRE7CTE5 MINGW64 ~/gitlab-repos/MyFirstProject (demoLocalEdits)
$ git commit -m "Demonstration of making changes locally"
[demoLocalEdits 551772a] Demonstration of making changes locally
2 files changed, 2 insertions(+), 7 deletions(-)
create mode 100644 File4.txt
jpain@LAPTOP-HRE7CTE5 MINGW64 ~/gitlab-repos/MyFirstProject (demoLocalEdits)
$ git status
On branch demoLocalEdits
Your branch is ahead of 'origin/demoLocalEdits' by 1 commit.
(use "git push" to publish your local commits)
nothing to commit, working tree clean
jpain@LAPTOP-HRE7CTE5 MINGW64 ~/gitlab-repos/MyFirstProject (demoLocalEdits)
$

Figure 3-22. *Commands to commit changes to the local repository*

CHAPTER 3 WORKING THE REMOTE LIFE

Pushing Changes Up to the GitLab Project Repository

We then run git push origin demoLocalEdits to push the changes up to the GitLab repository as shown in Figure 3-23. Note that it returns a message from GitLab reminding us to create the merge request, even providing the URL to do so.

```
jpain@LAPTOP-HRE7CTE5 MINGW64 ~/gitlab-repos/MyFirstProject (demoLocalEdits)
$ git push origin demoLocalEdits
Enumerating objects: 6, done.
Counting objects: 100% (6/6), done.
Delta compression using up to 8 threads
Compressing objects: 100% (3/3), done.
Writing objects: 100% (4/4), 443 bytes | 221.00 KiB/s, done.
Total 4 (delta 1), reused 0 (delta 0), pack-reused 0
remote:
remote: To create a merge request for demoLocalEdits, visit:
remote:      https://gitlab.com/paintertraining/MyFirstProject/-/merge_requests/new?merge_request%5Bsource_branch%5D=demoLocalEdits
remote:
To gitlab.com:paintertraining/MyFirstProject.git
   c199320..551772a  demoLocalEdits -> demoLocalEdits

jpain@LAPTOP-HRE7CTE5 MINGW64 ~/gitlab-repos/MyFirstProject (demoLocalEdits)
$
```

Figure 3-23. *Commands to push changes up to GitLab*

Confirming Changes in the GitLab Project Repository

Figure 3-24 shows the files in GitLab after pushing to the "demoLocalEdits" branch. From here, we see the commit message that we provided with the git commit command. We also see that File4.txt now shows up, and if we viewed the README.md file, we would see that the "Badges and Visuals" section no longer exists.

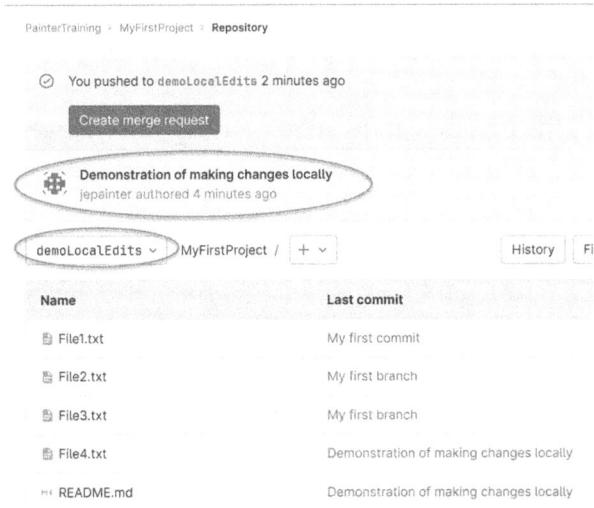

Figure 3-24. *GitLab view of project files after local push*

CHAPTER 3   WORKING THE REMOTE LIFE

Creating the Merge Request in GitLab and Merging It

Figure 3-25 shows the results of the merge request I created. It shows that the changes we made locally are now associated with the merge request as expected.

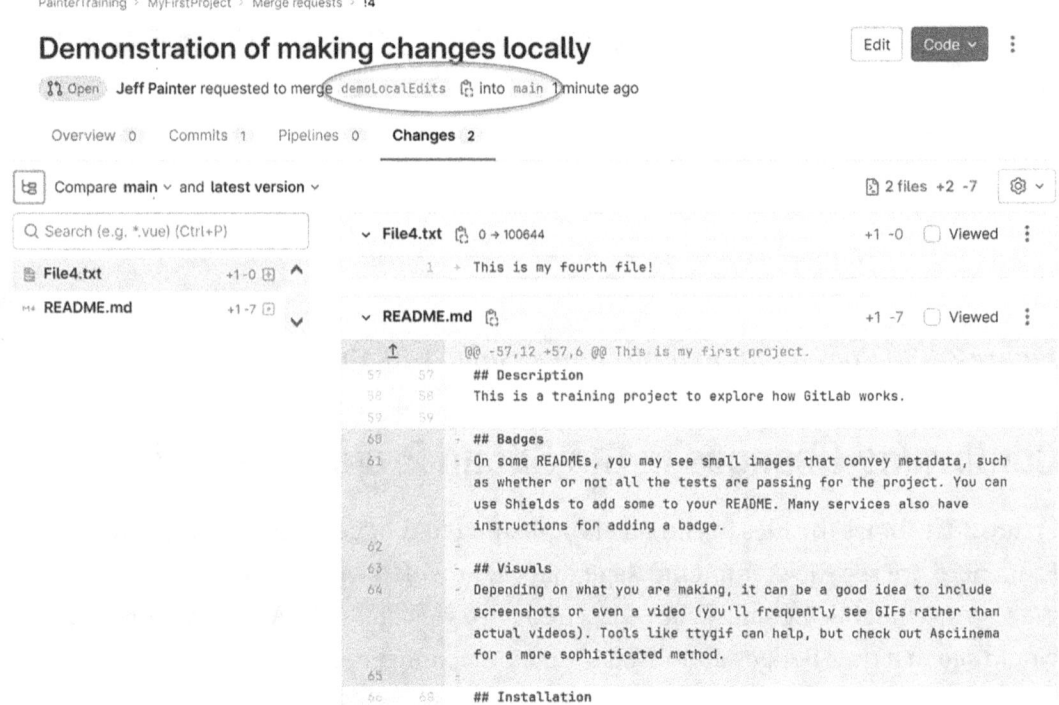

Figure 3-25. *Merge request of pushed changes in GitLab*

Figure 3-26 shows the project's graph after merging the changes onto main. Note that there is no distinction between changes made interactively via the GitLab interface or changes made via Git on our local machine. As you may have guessed, changes made interactively run Git commands "beneath the hood."

CHAPTER 3   WORKING THE REMOTE LIFE

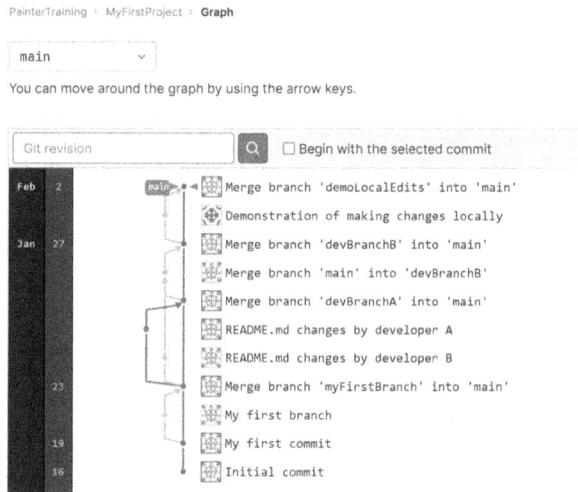

Figure 3-26. *Repository graph showing commits associated with local changes after merge*

Cleaning Up the Local Repository

At this point, we need to do some cleanup of our local repository as shown in Figure 3-27. Normally, I do a git pull while on the working branch, but in this case, I switched to the main branch using git checkout main and then deleted the local branch by running git branch -d demoLocalEdits. This gives me a warning message that I hadn't pulled the changes down from GitLab before doing this (my bad). But I can get things back to normal by running the git pull on the main branch. This syncs the main branch between my local repository and the remote GitLab repository.

89

```
jpain@LAPTOP-HRE7CTE5 MINGW64 ~/gitlab-repos/MyFirstProject (demoLocalEdits)
$ git status
On branch demoLocalEdits
Your branch is up to date with 'origin/demoLocalEdits'.

nothing to commit, working tree clean

jpain@LAPTOP-HRE7CTE5 MINGW64 ~/gitlab-repos/MyFirstProject (demoLocalEdits)
$ git checkout main
Switched to branch 'main'
Your branch is up to date with 'origin/main'.

jpain@LAPTOP-HRE7CTE5 MINGW64 ~/gitlab-repos/MyFirstProject (main)
$ git branch -l
  demoLocalEdits
* main

jpain@LAPTOP-HRE7CTE5 MINGW64 ~/gitlab-repos/MyFirstProject (main)
$ git branch -d demoLocalEdits
warning: deleting branch 'demoLocalEdits' that has been merged to
         'refs/remotes/origin/demoLocalEdits', but not yet merged to HEAD.
Deleted branch demoLocalEdits (was 551772a).

jpain@LAPTOP-HRE7CTE5 MINGW64 ~/gitlab-repos/MyFirstProject (main)
$ git branch -l
* main

jpain@LAPTOP-HRE7CTE5 MINGW64 ~/gitlab-repos/MyFirstProject (main)
$ git pull
remote: Enumerating objects: 1, done.
remote: Counting objects: 100% (1/1), done.
remote: Total 1 (delta 0), reused 0 (delta 0), pack-reused 0
Unpacking objects: 100% (1/1), 285 bytes | 40.00 KiB/s, done.
From gitlab.com:paintertraining/MyFirstProject
   c199320..74a7a34  main       -> origin/main
Updating c199320..74a7a34
Fast-forward
 File4.txt  | 1 +
 README.md  | 8 +-------
 2 files changed, 2 insertions(+), 7 deletions(-)
 create mode 100644 File4.txt

jpain@LAPTOP-HRE7CTE5 MINGW64 ~/gitlab-repos/MyFirstProject (main)
$
```

Figure 3-27. Commands to clean up the local repository after merge

This section outlined the basic commands and process used to manage your local repository and to keep it in sync with the remote GitLab repository. There are plenty of other Git commands that we have not covered that are beyond the scope of this book. No worries, there are plenty of books on Git that provide more detail on how Git manages source code via the various Git commands. If you are familiar with other SCM managers, some of the concepts in Git may seem strange. The git checkout and git add commands in particular tend to trip people up since the terms checkout and add have different meanings in other SCM managers. Fortunately, with GitLab, you have the choice of using the interactive interface, which does a good job at hiding some of Git's complexity and the Git command-line interface used on your local machine.

Summary

To recap, we covered the following topics in this chapter:

- Showed where to find instructions on how to install Git on machines running Linux or Mac

- Described how to install Git for Windows to enable using simple Linux commands including git
- Learned how to clone a GitLab repository using HTTPS
- Covered how to create an SSH key pair and register the public key with GitLab
- Learned how to clone a GitLab repository using SSH
- Discussed how to configure Git for a local repository
- Explored Git commands for synchronizing changes between GitLab and your local environment

With source change management out of the way, we'll next turn our focus on how to use GitLab to actually build something.

CHAPTER 4

Build, Test, Rinse, and Repeat

Now that we've explored how to maintain your source files both within and remotely from GitLab, let's look at another of GitLab's useful features: building products using continuous integration. In this chapter, we are going to cover the basic mechanisms of doing this. First, we will be introduced to GitLab's configuration file that defines what we wish to build and how to test it. We'll then look at how to use Docker images to simplify having to install the tools we need to build stuff. From there, we'll introduce the topic of CI/CD variables that we can use to build the same product for different environments such as development or production. Finally, we'll look at ways to split up the configuration file into smaller, more manageable pieces.

Introducing the GitLab Configuration File

If you are used to Jenkins, you are probably looking for an interactive interface where you can enter scripts, install plug-ins, send emails, and the like. GitLab doesn't work that way. Instead, you define your continuous integration environment by including a file named ".gitlab-ci.yml" (note the preceding dot). If you wondered earlier how GitLab knew you didn't have continuous integration setup, that is how.

The advantage of using a file to define your integration setup is that it is managed as part of your source code; you can determine who made changes and when they were made should something in your build or test suite start to fail. It also makes it easy to revert back to an earlier version to get things working again should you need to do so. Contrast this to Jenkins where any developer can make a change to the build or test environment via the web interface and cause things to start failing.[1] If you have auditing in place (which is optional, BTW), you will be able to trace who last changed some setting, but reverting a change can get a bit tricky.[2]

General Overview of the Configuration File

The syntax of the .gitlab-ci.yml file is YAML (YAML ain't markup language) that is a common format used in other applications; you can find more information about yaml at https://yaml.org/. Note that the file suffix is ".yml", not ".yaml"; the filename is case sensitive. Note that you can change the name of the CI/CD file in the project's CI/CD settings. A description of the keywords that may be used a .gitlab-ci.yml file can be found here: https://docs.gitlab.com/ee/ci/yaml/.

More formally, the .gitlab-ci.yml file is referred to as a CI/CD[3] pipeline configuration file. This file defines a pipeline consisting of one or more stages (build, test, deploy, etc.) that are typically run in sequence. Each stage consists of one or more jobs that are run in parallel; the number of jobs that run in simultaneously depends on the load on the GitLab runtime environment. A job defines the set of tasks to be executed such as compiling source code or running test suites. One feature of pipelines is that they are dynamic; you can place conditions on jobs that determine if they should run or not. We'll talk about this dynamic feature in more detail later on.

Creating a Basic CI/CD Pipeline Configuration

So, let's start simply and look at a very basic pipeline configuration. Fortunately, GitLab provides a lot of examples that you can use "off the shelf," so you won't have to do much editing initially. I created a new project called "MyShellPipeline" with a generated

---

[1] Some might argue that letting developers change any settings in Jenkins should be restricted, to which I agree. However, my experience as a Jenkins administrator is that most teams set up their projects so that developers can do almost anything.

[2] I realize that Jenkins introduced pipelines that store instructions in a JenkinsFile that can be managed as source code. Unfortunately, pipelines were introduced late in the game and are totally optional. To make things worse, there are two flavors of pipelines, declarative and scripted, that add complexity to those who are learning the syntax and to those who have to maintain these pipelines.

[3] CI stands for continuous integration. CD stands for either continuous delivery or continuous deployment; GitLab handles both CD scenarios.

CHAPTER 4   BUILD, TEST, RINSE, AND REPEAT

README.md file just as I did for "MyFirstProject." I wanted to keep things uncluttered for this example. Figure 4-1 shows the "Get Started" page when you select the project's CI/CD pipelines tab; at the top of the page, it prompts you to try out a "Hello world" pipeline. So, let's go ahead and select the "Try test template" button.

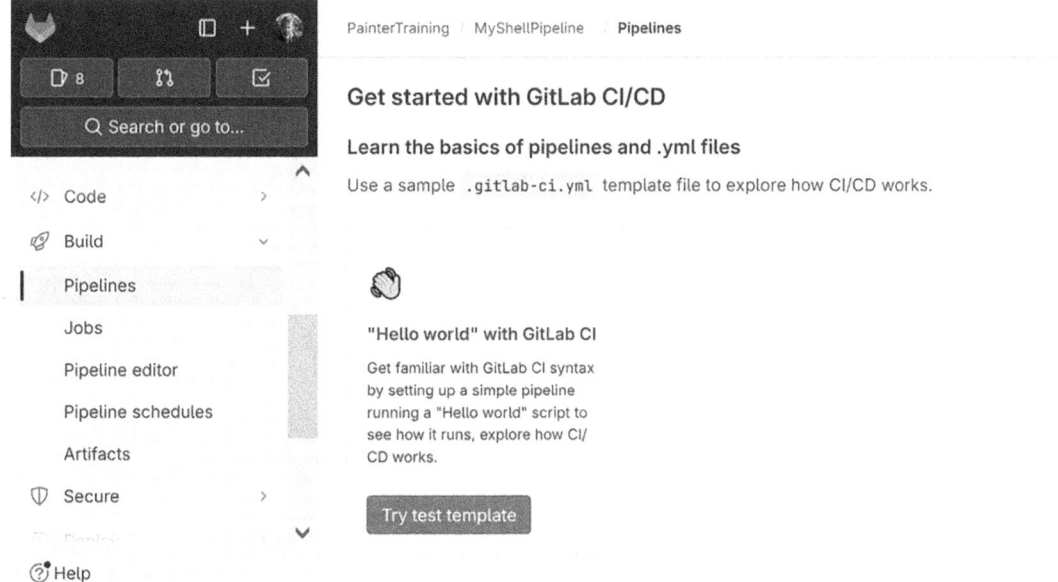

Figure 4-1.   Pipeline getting started page

At this point, a new .gitlab-ci.yml file is created in your project that you can edit and commit. Figure 4-2 shows the main contents of this file. After the comments that appear at the top of the file is the stage section as highlighted in the box. This section defines the stages that will be used by this pipeline: build, test, and deploy. The order of the stages is the order in which they are executed. If you don't explicitly define the stages, a default set of stages will be used as outlined in the .gitlab-ci.yml keyword reference documentation. Even if you use the default set of stages, I recommend that you explicitly declare them as a best practice.

95

CHAPTER 4   BUILD, TEST, RINSE, AND REPEAT

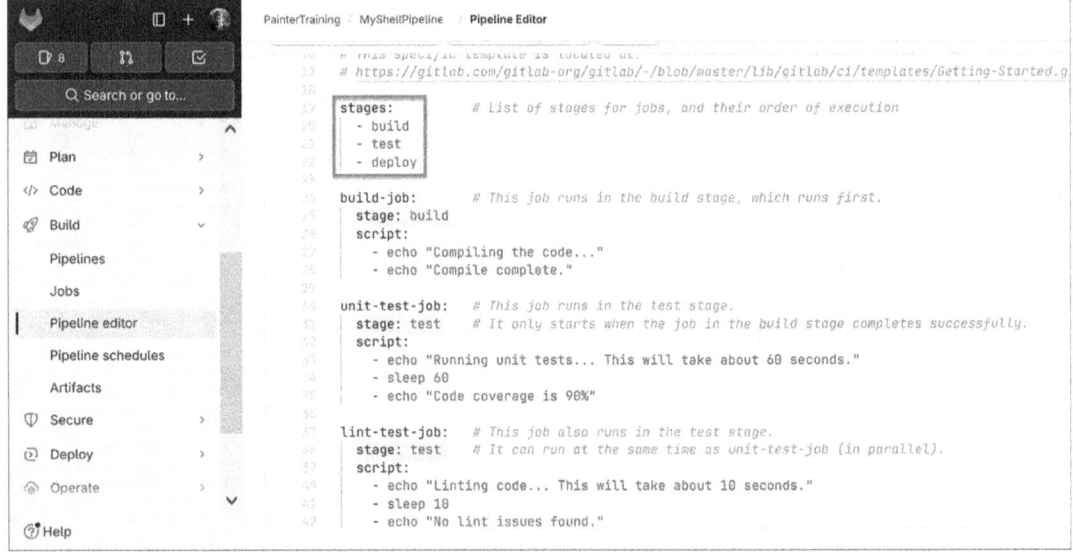

Figure 4-2. Shell pipeline example

Associating Jobs to Stages

The remainder of this file defines four jobs: build-job, unit-test-job, lint-test-job, and deploy-job. The order of these jobs is not relevant; they do not determine the order in which jobs are run, in case you are wondering. The association of jobs to stages is defined by the stage keyword within each job. In this example, build-job is associated with the build stage; unit-test-job and lint-test-job are associated with the test stage; and finally, deploy-job is associated with the deploy stage. There is no requirement that the name of the stage be included in the name of the job; this is done in this example to help you mentally map jobs to stages.

Each job in this example has a script section defined. The script sections define a sequence of shell commands that are executed in order. This example is using simple echo and sleep commands to illustrate the order of execution within a job. At the end of this page (not shown in this figure) is a text box to specify a commit message along with a "Commit" button. We'll keep the file as is and commit the changes.

CHAPTER 4   BUILD, TEST, RINSE, AND REPEAT

Validating Account Upon First Pipeline Run

Upon commit, the pipeline begins to execute; we'll discuss later how we can control this behavior. Given this is the first time we've tried to execute a pipeline, you will get feedback that the pipeline failed, both on the screen and via email. You will also be presented with a "Validate user account" form as shown in Figure 4-3. It will ask you for credit card information in order to validate your account. As mentioned at the start of the form, your card will not be charged.

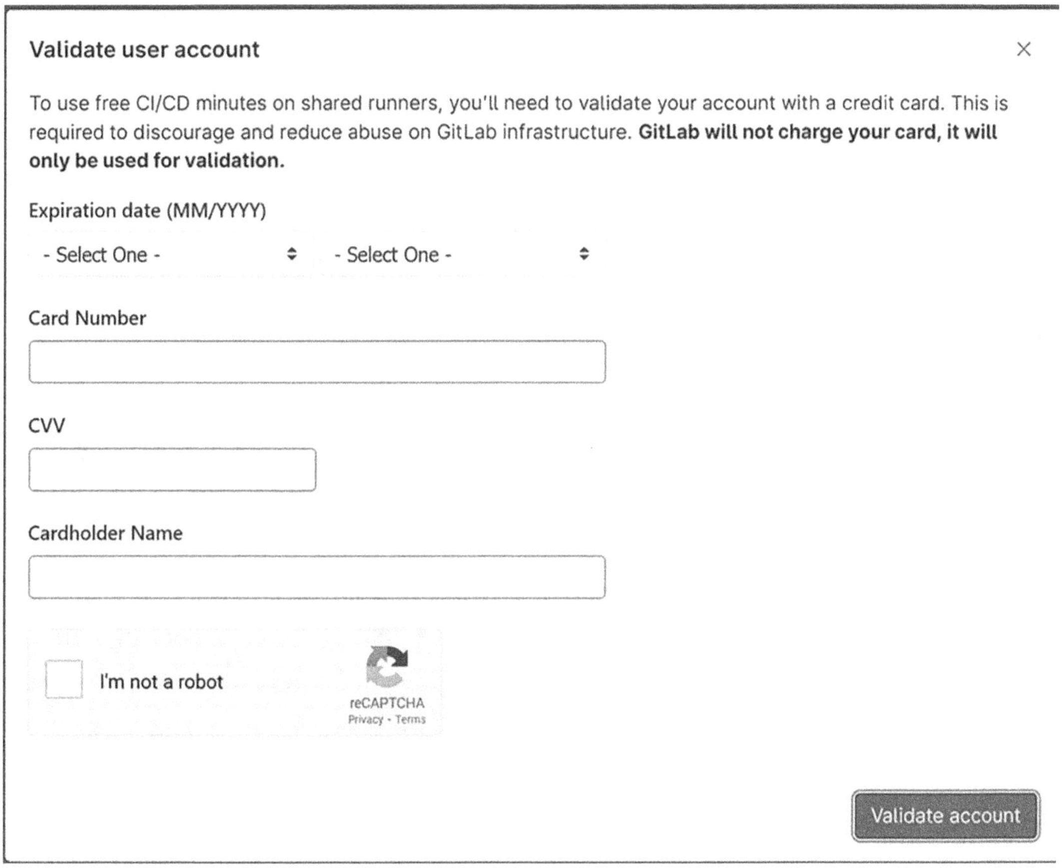

Figure 4-3. Validate user account form

   Once you validate your account, you can go to your project's pipelines page to see the failed status as shown in Figure 4-4. So why did the pipeline fail? By default, we are using shared runners hosted by GitLab to run the job. A runner is a server separate from the servers used to run the GitLab website. We'll talk later about how to set up your own

97

CHAPTER 4   BUILD, TEST, RINSE, AND REPEAT

runners, but for now, we will rely on GitLab's shared runner infrastructure. The pipeline failed because we are attempting to use the shared runner infrastructure without being authorized to do so. This is a safety mechanism on GitLab's part to prevent abuse of their infrastructure. Once you validate your account with a credit card, you'll be able to use their infrastructure (within limits set by GitLab).

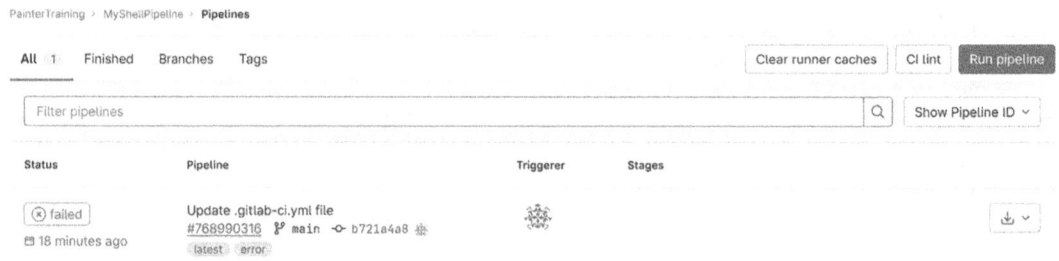

Figure 4-4. First pipeline run with error

Restarting a Pipeline

Once a pipeline fails, it will not restart on its own. You have to take some action to restart it. Now that we've validated ourselves, we can rerun the pipeline using the "Run pipeline" button located in the upper right of the project's pipelines page. This will take you to the "Run pipeline" page as shown in Figure 4-5. From this page, you can select a branch on which to run the pipeline (in this example, there is only the main branch), and you can enter values for any variables you have defined in your pipeline configuration file. Since there are no variables defined by this configuration, we simply select the "Run pipeline" button to start it.

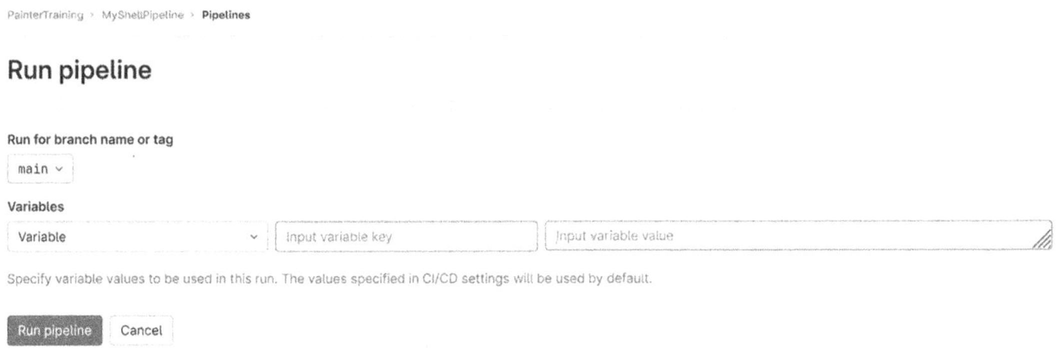

CHAPTER 4   BUILD, TEST, RINSE, AND REPEAT

Figure 4-5. Run pipeline page

Pipeline Job Execution Through the Various Stages

And with that press of a button, the action begins. Figure 4-6 shows the resulting CI/CD pipeline page with the build-job running. At the top of the page is the state of the pipeline (in this case, running); it's assigned a pipeline ID and the method in which it was triggered (in this case, triggered manually by me). The half-moon icon next to build-job in the build stage indicates that it is currently running. The remaining jobs are in a disabled state, indicated by the grayed bull's-eye icon, waiting for the build-job job to complete.

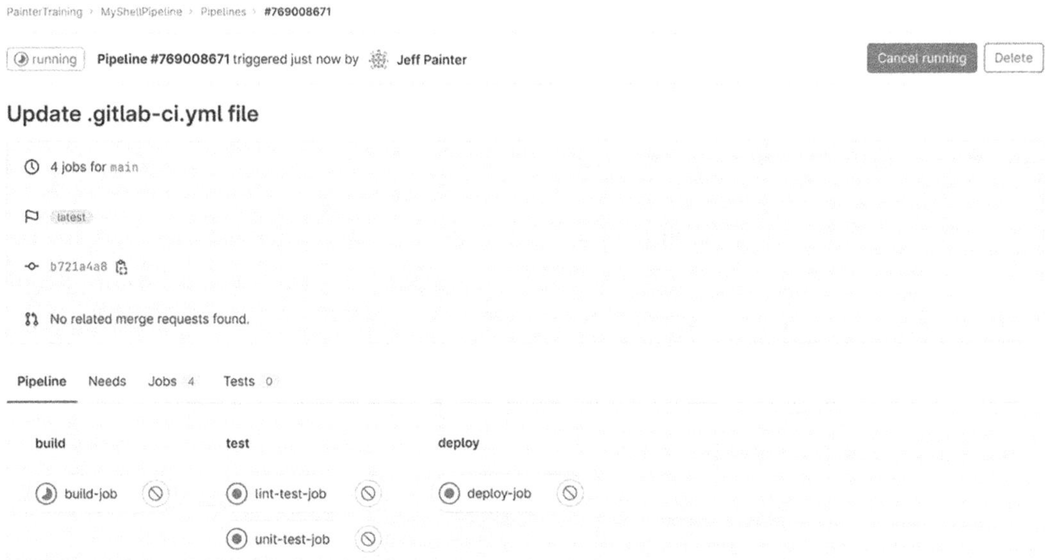

Figure 4-6. Pipeline showing build-job running

99

CHAPTER 4   BUILD, TEST, RINSE, AND REPEAT

When job build-job is completed successfully, the two jobs in the test stage begin to run as shown in Figure 4-7. Since there are available runners to run both jobs, they are run simultaneously each on their own runner. If there were not enough runners available or your account has been throttled due to too many job requests, some jobs will be put into a pending state waiting until a runner becomes available. Although the jobs under the test stage are listed in alphabetical order, there is no guarantee that the jobs will be run in that order. It should also be noted that all jobs in the test stage will be run even if any job fails. This allows you to analyze what tests are failing and make fixes to them in one commit.

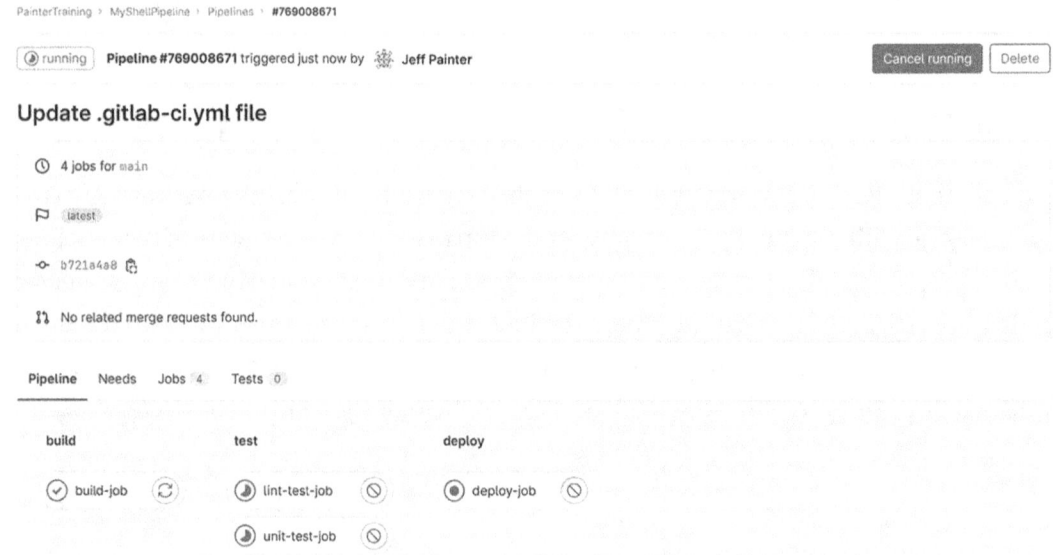

Figure 4-7. Pipeline showing test jobs running

When all tests succeed, the deploy-job is started as shown in Figure 4-8. Had any of the jobs in the test stage failed, the deploy-job would not have started. This is the default behavior of jobs in separate stages. There are ways to make exceptions to this behavior so that some jobs in later stages run despite whether a job in an earlier stage fails; we'll explore this in the next chapter. For now, the default behavior is the most common behavior people expect and rely on.

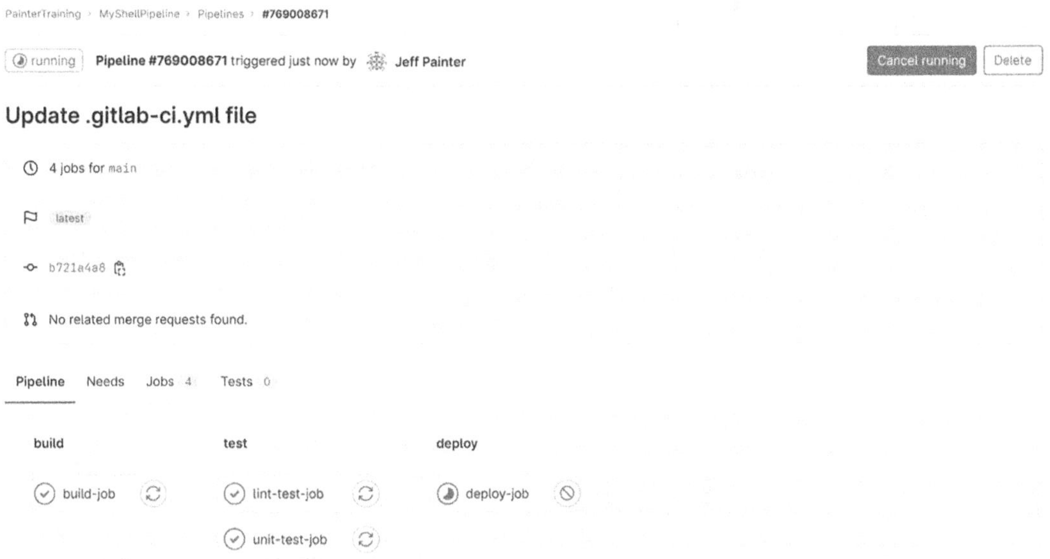

CHAPTER 4 BUILD, TEST, RINSE, AND REPEAT

Figure 4-8. Pipeline showing deploy job running

Figure 4-9 shows the pipeline status when all jobs have been completed successfully. Note that the pipeline status at the top of the page indicates that the pipeline has passed. If any of the jobs had failed, the pipeline status would be set as failed. This is the default behavior of determining the pipeline status; there are ways to ignore the status of certain jobs that we'll explore later on.

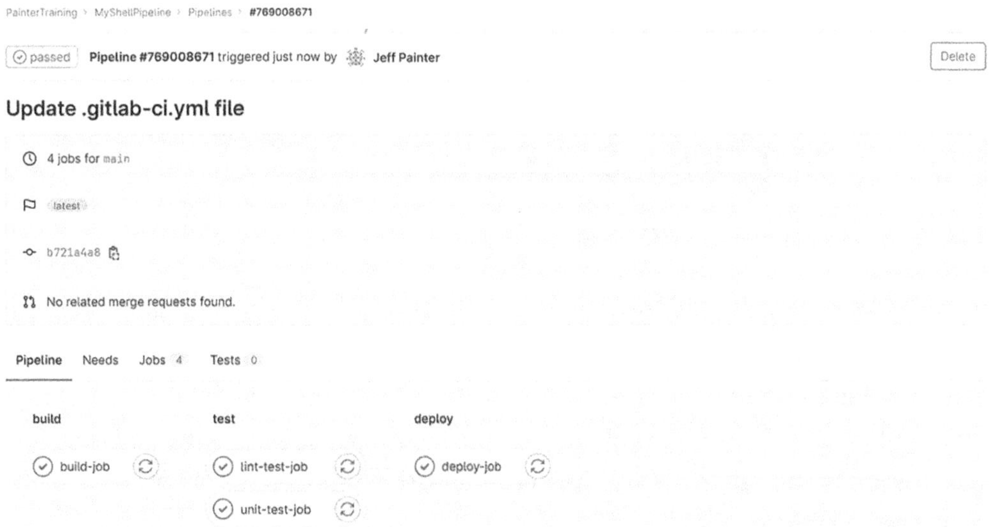

Figure 4-9. Pipeline completed with success

101

CHAPTER 4 BUILD, TEST, RINSE, AND REPEAT

Viewing a Job's Output

Now that the pipeline has been run, let's look at what a job's output looks like. You can drill down to a given job's output by clicking the job's icon in the pipeline graph. Figure 4-10 shows the output from job build-job. As you can see, it is presented as a Linux terminal screen that shows the commands that were run along with their responses. Note that it shows more than the results of your job's commands; it provides additional information about the job's environment.

Figure 4-10. Build job output

Looking at the first highlighted box, we see feedback on the runner used to execute the job. This is always the first piece of information provided in a job's output. In this case, we see that the runner is one of GitLab's shared runners. The details are not much use to us but could be helpful to GitLab's support team when debugging an issue. If you had set this job to run on one of your own runners, that information might be of use to you when debugging an issue.

102

The next highlighted box gives us an insight into how the runner is executing our script. You might have thought this would be a Linux server where we execute the commands in a shell run directly on the server. If you think about it, this would be a very dangerous thing to do security-wise as it would give you access to the server itself and possibly to other users' information. The message "Preparing the docker-machine executor" tells us that we are running our job's commands using Docker. The docker-machine part tells us that GitLab is using Docker machine to manage the GitLab runner servers. Behind the scenes, Docker machine manages a suite of servers running Docker that are dynamically spun up and down based on certain rules that we won't get into here. Suffice it to say, each job runs in its own Docker container that shields us from jobs run by other users.

What we also see is the Docker image being used to run our job: ruby:3.1. If you want more information on what this image contains, you can check it out on Docker Hub at `https://hub.docker.com/_/ruby/`. The reason our shell commands were able to run is that the ruby Docker image contains a minimal shell (not bash) running the Alpine Linux distribution. Since we didn't specify a specific Docker image to use, GitLab used a default image of ruby:3.1. This seems like an odd image to use as a default, but it makes some sense since GitLab software itself is written in Ruby. Note that this default is subject to change at any time, so best practice is to explicitly specify the Docker image(s) to use in your job. We'll see how to do this shortly.

The final highlighted box shows the output of our script, which was to echo a couple of messages. We see the command as if it were entered on a shell prompt followed by the output from that command. Note that by default, if any command fails, the job fails and no further commands in the job are executed. Like anything else, there are ways to change this behavior, but this turns out to be a very sane default to use. The job ends with some background cleanup processes to ensure no other user gets access to our job details; it also displays the job's status.

Before we leave the build-job output, note that there is meta information about the job that is shown in the upper-right highlighted box. This provides us with how long the job took to run (which includes the time to prepare the environment), how long the job was queued waiting for a runner (in this case, there was no wait), and other information such as the timeout applied to the job. All jobs have a timeout period to help protect against runaway jobs (otherwise, how would you stop it?). The default timeout period is one hour. You are also provided with a link to the commit that triggered this job as well as the pipeline that the job ran under.

Chapter 4 BUILD, TEST, RINSE, AND REPEAT

Viewing a Project's Pipeline Status Page

Figure 4-11 shows the project's pipeline status page after we've run our pipeline. It shows all attempts to run the pipeline and their status with the most recent at the top of the list. Each provides a link to the pipeline that allows us to drill down to the page we just viewed previously. It also gives us some feedback on the status of each stage (not jobs). If you hover over each stage icon, you'll see the stage name. Clicking a stage icon provides a list of the jobs run in that stage and their status; clicking a job in that drop-down list takes you directly to that job's output.

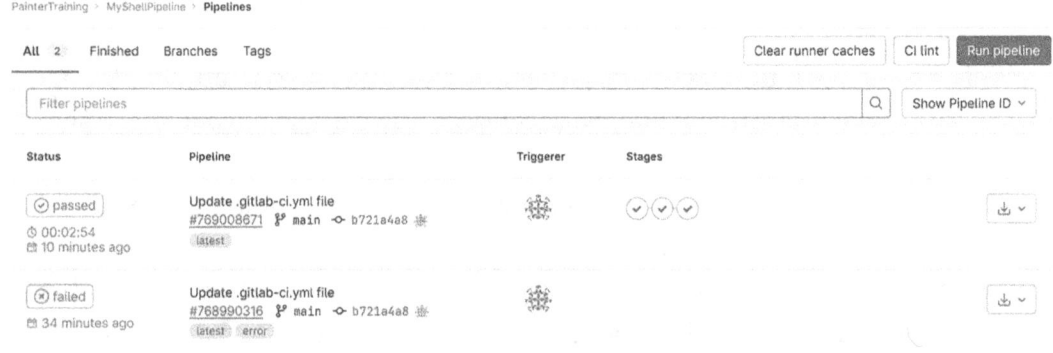

Figure 4-11. Pipeline status page

Figure 4-12 shows the output from job unit-test-job. You'll note that the output is similar to the build-job output with some minor differences. The key thing I want to point out here is that the runner used to run this job is different from the runner used to run job build-job. Although possible, it is unusual that two jobs in a given pipeline use the same runner, and even if the same runner is used, there is no sharing of information between the two jobs. The shared runner setup used by GitLab ensures that jobs are isolated from each other.

CHAPTER 4   BUILD, TEST, RINSE, AND REPEAT

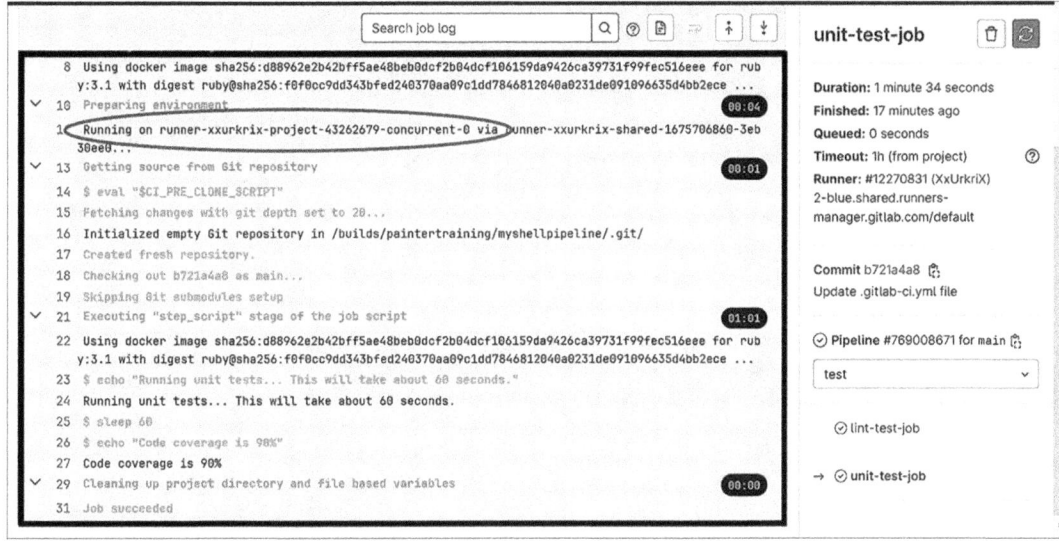

Figure 4-12.   Unit test job output

Project Status Impacts After a Pipeline Run

Before we leave this section, let's look at the project's status page to see what is different after running a pipeline. Figure 4-13 shows the status of project "MyShellPipeline." One difference is the green check mark as highlighted in the figure. This tells us that the status of the last pipeline run was successful. Clicking that check mark icon takes us to the last pipeline that was run. Also, note that the file list shows the .gitlab-ci.yml file that was created by the template for us.

Chapter 4   BUILD, TEST, RINSE, AND REPEAT

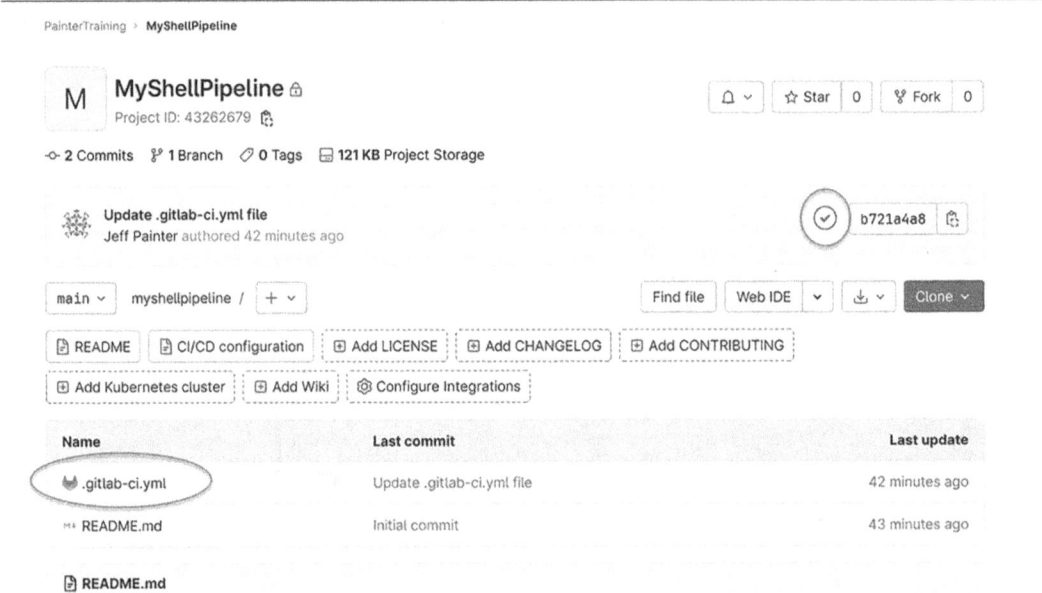

Figure 4-13. Project status page after pipeline run

Working with Docker

In the previous section, it was noted that job scripts run inside a Docker image on this thing called a runner. However, nowhere in that example pipeline configuration file was an image specified; the ruby Docker image was used by default. Obviously, that image is pretty limiting if you want a build environment using Python or similar software. So, as you may have guessed, there is a way to override this default image within the configuration file. However, before we delve into how to do that, let's consider why Docker is even used by GitLab to run pipeline jobs.

A Personal Experience with Jenkins and GitLab

A little over ten years ago, I was put in charge of creating what our company referred to as Jenkins as a Service (a.k.a. JaaS). The idea was to create a farm of Jenkins servers in Amazon's AWS, one per team, that developers could use to do their CI builds and tests. By creating Jenkins servers per team, we distributed the load of project builds across those servers. If any server failed, the downtime was restricted to just that team without impacting other teams. This also enabled us to customize Jenkins servers for a given team, which in hindsight was a bad idea.

Initially, we provided teams with a single Jenkins controller server. It was an easy configuration for us to set up and maintain.[4] The downside was that jobs were run on the controller server itself rather than delegated to agent servers; the configuration of controller and agent servers was the setup that Jenkins recommended but did not enforce. For most teams, having a single controller to both manage and run jobs was sufficient; their build and test loads did not overwhelm the server. Other teams, however, had lots of jobs running on a daily basis that required a lot of computing resources. So, for those teams, we spun up static agent servers that ran 24/7 in their AWS account tied to their controller server run in our department's account. Over time, Jenkins provided a variety of ways of managing agents dynamically, which we also helped teams use.[5]

Whether a team had a single controller server or a controller server with associated agents, we ended up installing software such as Java and Python directly on those servers as well as various Jenkins plug-ins depending on the team's needs. This, too, was a bad idea in hindsight. Eventually, there were plug-ins that enabled installing various versions of Java, for instance, but did not do the same for the commonly used Python programming language. Over time, teams needed to upgrade their versions of software on the servers themselves; this had the undesired side effect of affecting all jobs. It was not uncommon after a software update for builds and tests to start failing with no other changes to a job.

As you might have guessed, we ended up with hundreds of snowflake servers. Even with Ansible to manage the configuration of these servers, it was quite challenging for us to keep teams happy. The alternative of having a single primary controller with multiple agents for all teams to use was, in itself, a nightmare to manage. We know this because there was another team in our department that set up this configuration. Upgrading that configuration became a challenge since some updates required that the Jenkins service be brought down for maintenance, which was difficult to schedule. And if a team did not like the central service configuration, they ended up coming to us for a dedicated JaaS server.

---

[4] Can you say Amazon AMIs?

[5] We had to help teams with this task since configuring dynamic servers was tedious and more complex than it needed to be.

Looking back, the biggest issue we had with our Jenkins configurations was that the build and test environment was not controlled like the team's project code was. What you want as a developer is to set up a build and test environment that is consistent and repeatable. If you want to use Python version 3.10.8, then by golly you should be able to have an environment that specifically has that version of Python independent of any other project's requirements. With the advent of Docker, such an environment can be easily managed. By the time Jenkins provided support for Docker agents, the cat was out of the bag for us. Although some teams did convert to using Docker to control their build and test environments, most teams were unable to switch over due to already existing technical debt. If we were to start JaaS now, we would have forced teams to use Docker agents and not allow jobs to be run on the main Jenkins controller. Just saying.

So, let's switch over to GitLab. When I was tasked to set up a standalone self-managed GitLab service on Amazon AWS over six years ago, I immediately recognized the advantage of the GitLab architecture. First of all, the GitLab service runs on its own server and cannot be used to run jobs.[6] The other advantage I saw was the great support for Docker that GitLab runners enable. Although you can install the GitLab runner software on a server and run jobs "natively," this, too, is discouraged for obvious security reasons. The one exception to using Docker on GitLab runners occurs when developing software for operating systems that do not have Docker images, such as Windows or Mac OS; in this case, you need to have Windows or Mac servers with the GitLab runner software installed and have builds and tests run natively on that server.

The Case for Docker

If you are not familiar with Docker, it is a lightweight virtualization framework. It uses a special feature common in most Linux operating systems that enables running multiple virtualization environments on top of Linux. Simply stated, it allows you to run a CentOS environment on a server running Ubuntu or vice versa. This is unlike the more heavyweight virtualization frameworks that allow you to run multiple full operating systems called virtual machines (VMs) on top of a hardware interface layer. VMs are used by various cloud providers such as Amazon AWS and Google Compute Engine (GCE) to support spinning up virtual servers on demand.

---

[6] Well, technically it can be set up that way, but it is highly discouraged, especially in a moderate to large development organization.

VMs are heavyweight because they require encapsulating an entire operating system in a given image. Their advantage is that they give you full control over the environment, letting you install whatever software packages you want and saving them as a new image. Their disadvantage is that their large size requires a long time to start up (several minutes, in general).

Docker is lightweight because Docker images only include the minimum features needed by an OS relying on the existing features of the host Linux OS. Usually, this means providing at a minimum the package manager (yum, apt, etc.) used by the virtualized OS. The advantage of Docker images is their relative size compared to VMs that allow the environments to be spun up quickly (several seconds, in general). Their disadvantage is that you don't get full control of shared resources of the host server such as special GPU drivers.

The good news is there are a lot of available Docker images that you can use, most of which are free. You can find a wide range of images on Docker Hub at https://hub.docker.com/. The hard part is to determine the image you want to use. This depends on the core software you would like installed. For example, if you are developing using Python, you may want to start with one of the Python images where you get to pick the specific version of Python to use and whether you want to use a "slim" version with minimal OS packages installed or a more full version of the OS.

You can install additional software and include specific files, such as configuration files, that you need for your application by creating a Dockerfile file as defined here: https://docs.docker.com/engine/reference/builder/. This is similar to the .gitlab-ci.yml file in that it follows a particular syntax and has a variety of keywords that enable you to enhance your image. The advantage of using a Dockerfile is that it can be managed as part of your source, so you have considerable control over your build, test, and deploy environments. The other advantage for GitLab users is that it is supported by GitLab's shared runners.

Exploring Docker Hub

Let's now take a look at how to specify a specific Docker image in our .gitlab-ci.yml file. I'm going to use the Alpine Linux Docker image available from Docker Hub at https://hub.docker.com/_/alpine. Alpine is a commonly used image due to its relatively small size, which makes downloading and starting in Docker faster than other OS images. Figure 4-14 shows the initial Docker Hub page for Alpine.

CHAPTER 4   BUILD, TEST, RINSE, AND REPEAT

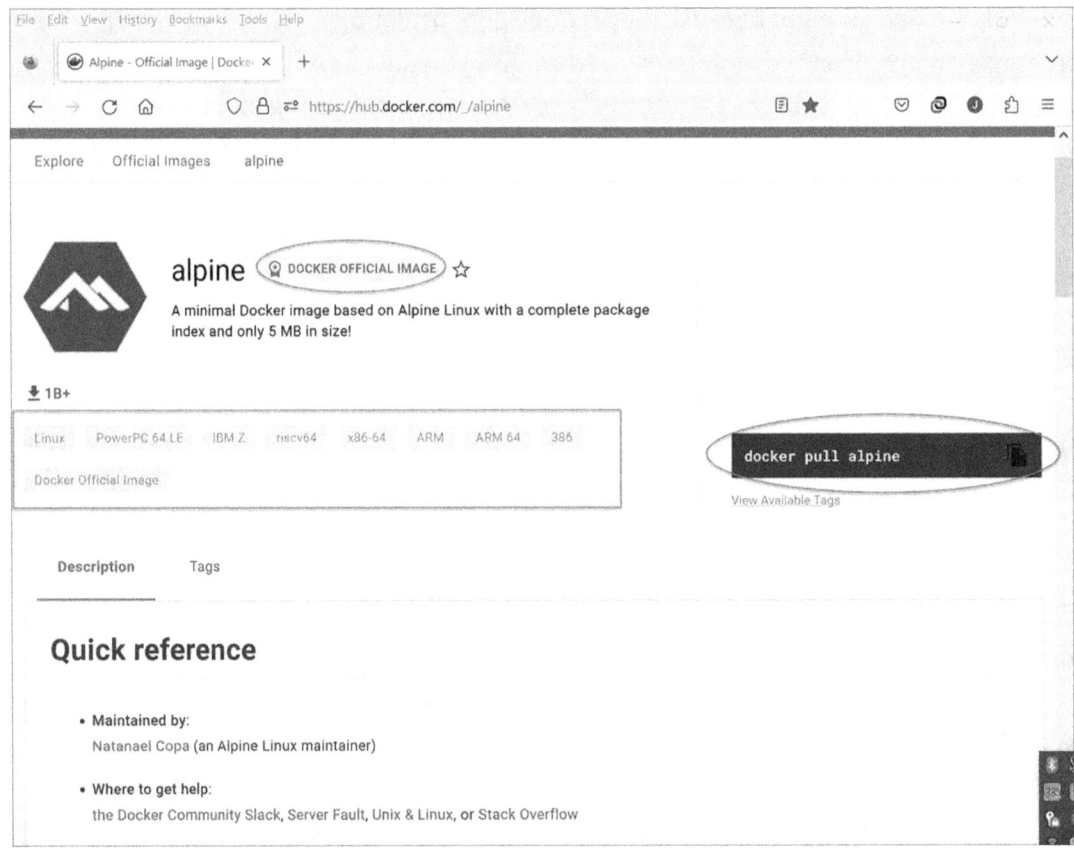

Figure 4-14. *Alpine Docker Hub page*

There are some things to note about the Alpine Docker Hub page. First, note the "Docker official image" highlighted at the top of the page. This lets you know that the image is fully supported by Docker and the people who maintain it. Not all images in Docker Hub are official images. Some may be uploaded by developers for other developers to use but are not officially supported by Docker. You can get a sense of the usefulness of an image by looking at how frequently it is downloaded as shown here below the Alpine logo. If it isn't frequently downloaded, you might be wary of using it for your own project.

Second, note the docker pull command highlighted in the figure. If you have Docker installed on your local machine, this tells you how to download the image. If you are not familiar with an image, downloading it and running it in a container locally is a good way to become familiar with it. For example, if you are not sure if a package is installed on an image, you can test it out manually before using it in a GitLab job.

CHAPTER 4   BUILD, TEST, RINSE, AND REPEAT

Third, note the list of architectures highlighted in the red box. This lets you know what host architectures support this image. This isn't something you normally have to worry about, especially with respect to GitLab. By default, GitLab shared runners use the amd64 architecture, which most Docker images support. The host architecture only becomes relevant if you are running Docker on a specialized architecture such as one used by an Android or Raspberry Pi device. You can use specialized GitLab runner tags to change the underlying architecture in certain cases. You can find out more about this in GitLab's documentation on hosted runners here: `https://docs.gitlab.com/ee/ci/runners/index.html`.

Official images provide documentation on what the image is used for and how to use it. Figure 4-15 provides a description of the Alpine image with links to how it is created along with links to more detailed documentation. Figure 4-16 shows how to use the Alpine image within a Dockerfile and install additional software packages on it. From this example, you can see that apk is the package manager for Alpine and that you use "apk add" to install a package.

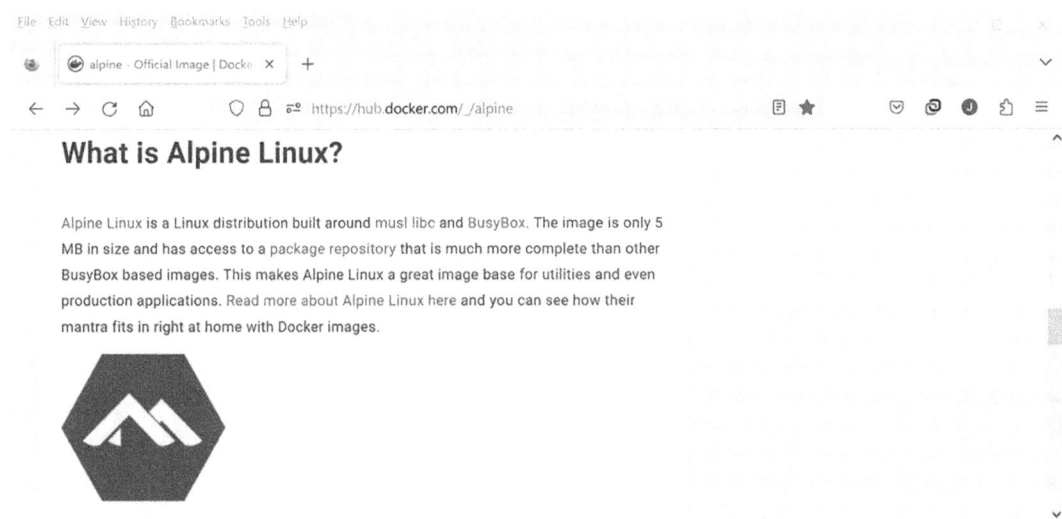

Figure 4-15. Alpine Docker Hub description

111

CHAPTER 4   BUILD, TEST, RINSE, AND REPEAT

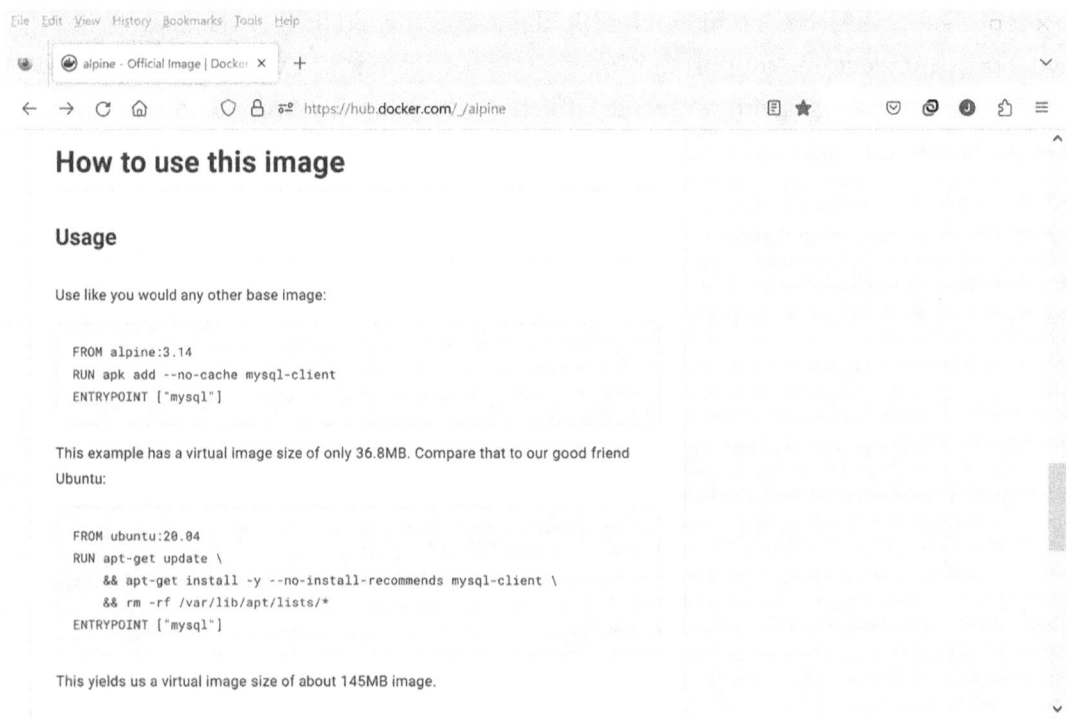

Figure 4-16. Alpine Docker Hub how-to page

The key piece of information you will need from the Docker Hub page is the tags that are available. Tags are used to identify versions and any other relevant variation provided by the image maintainers. Figure 4-17 shows the list of tags available for the Alpine image. The highlighted tags in the figure indicate tags used by the latest Alpine version supported by the image maintainers. In this case, 3.17.1 is the specific version of the latest Alpine image. If you don't care about the particular patch version of .1, .2, etc., you could use the tag 3.17. And if you only care about the major version, you could simply use the tag of 3. Finally, you could use the tag "latest" if you really don't care what version you use, but it is not recommended. When used in GitLab jobs, you should use the most specific tag required for your job. Many developers like to use the minor tag version, such as 13.7 in this example, so that they get the latest security updates but are not surprised by significant feature changes.

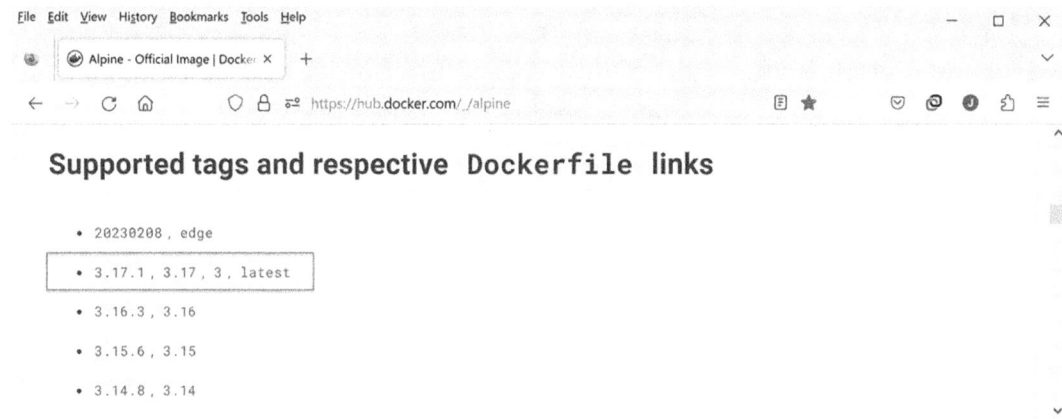

Figure 4-17. Alpine Docker Hub tags

Specifying a New Default Image

Let's update our "MyShellPipeline" to use the Alpine image by default instead of the Ruby image set by GitLab. Figure 4-18 shows the changes to our .gitlab-ci.yml file that does that. We created a default section that includes the image keyword set to alpine:3.17. As you might expect, this changes the default image for all jobs to be Alpine Linux version 3.17. GitLab knows to retrieve this image from Docker Hub. I've also updated the build-job to install bash and updated both the build-job and unit-test-job to list the available shells using /etc/shells.

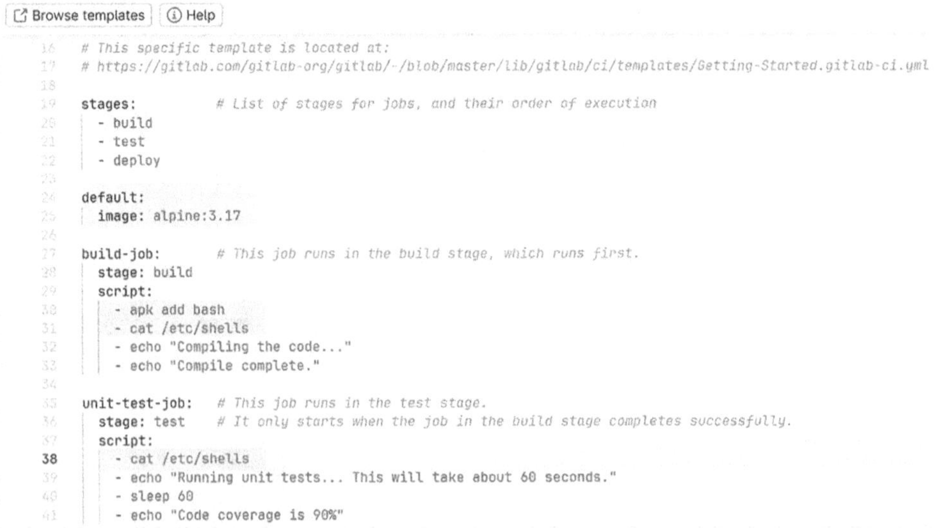

CHAPTER 4   BUILD, TEST, RINSE, AND REPEAT

```yaml
# This specific template is located at:
# https://gitlab.com/gitlab-org/gitlab/-/blob/master/lib/gitlab/ci/templates/Getting-Started.gitlab-ci.yml

stages:          # List of stages for jobs, and their order of execution
  - build
  - test
  - deploy

default:
  image: alpine:3.17

build-job:       # This job runs in the build stage, which runs first.
  stage: build
  script:
    - apk add bash
    - cat /etc/shells
    - echo "Compiling the code..."
    - echo "Compile complete."

unit-test-job:   # This job runs in the test stage.
  stage: test    # It only starts when the job in the build stage completes successfully.
  script:
    - cat /etc/shells
    - echo "Running unit tests... This will take about 60 seconds."
    - sleep 60
    - echo "Code coverage is 90%"
```

***Figure 4-18.** Docker image default set to Alpine*

When the changes are committed, a new pipeline is started. Figure 4-19 shows the resulting output of job build-job. The first highlighted area shows that the GitLab shared runner has indeed downloaded the Alpine 3.17 image instead of the Ruby image downloaded before. The second highlighted area shows the results of installing bash using the Alpine package manager apk.[7] Finally, the third highlighted area shows what shells are available; in this case, we see that bash is indeed an available shell.

---

[7] Had the image not been Alpine Linux, the apk command would have failed.

CHAPTER 4 BUILD, TEST, RINSE, AND REPEAT

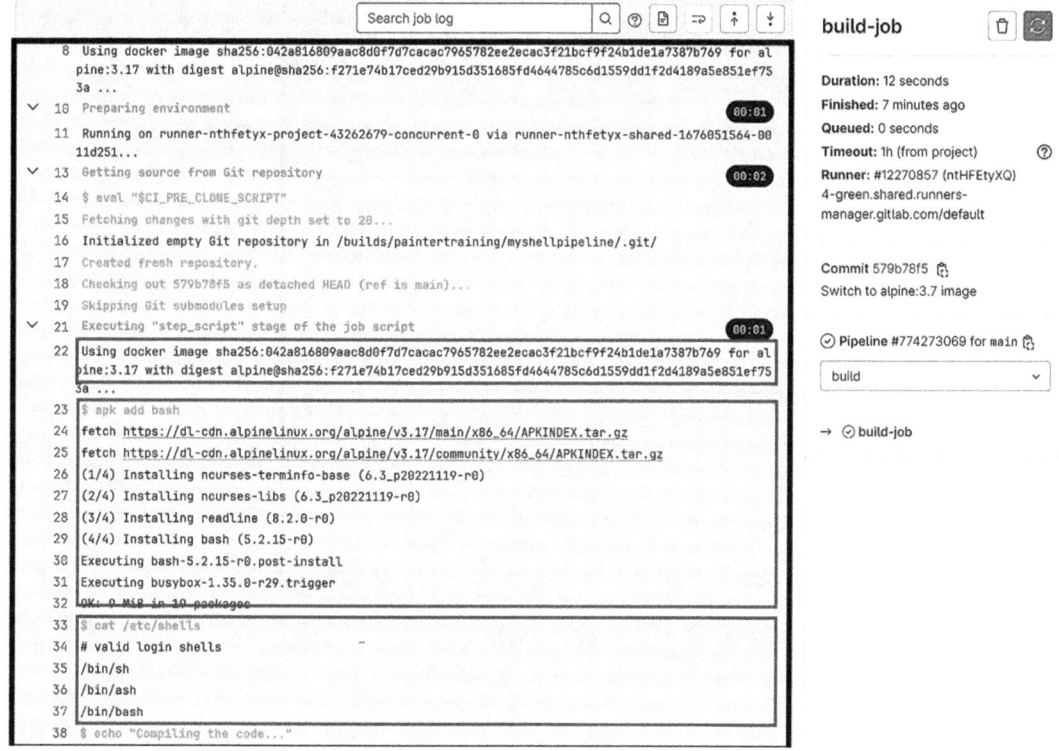

Figure 4-19. *Output of build job using Alpine*

Turning to unit-test-job, Figure 4-20 shows the output of that job. The first two highlighted areas show that the Alpine 3.17 image was used by the job. The last highlighted area shows the available shells for this job. Note that bash is not available. This shows that each job starts with the same base Alpine image; installing bash in the build job has no effect on what is installed or not in the unit test job.

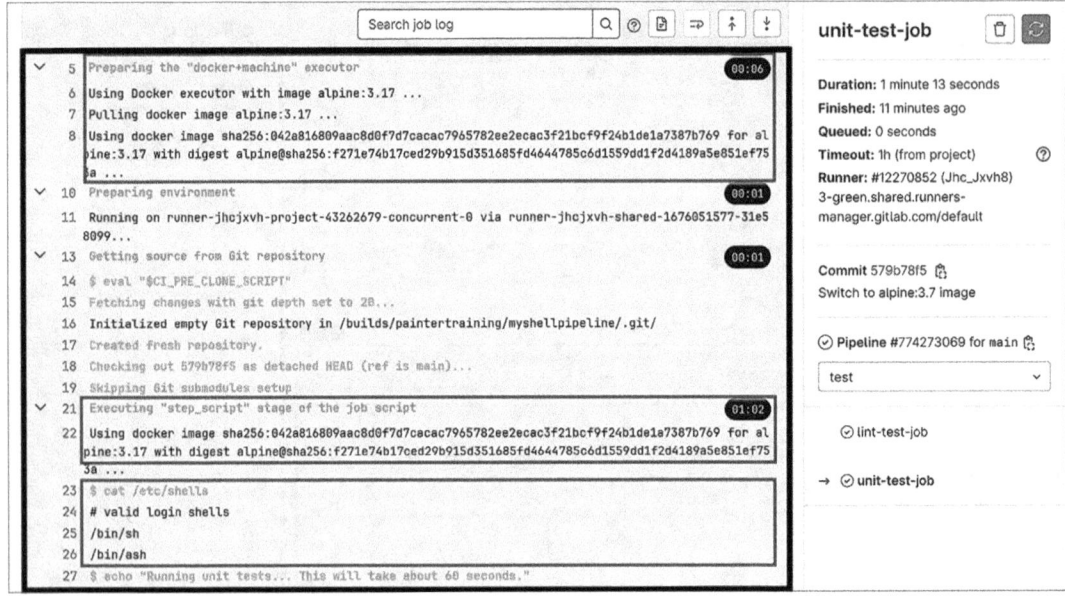

Figure 4-20. *Output of unit test using Alpine*

Defining Tasks to Run by Default Before Every Job

So, what if we wanted bash installed for every job? Does that mean we have to explicitly run apk on every job? That would be tedious to do. And if we wanted to install several packages, explicitly adding those installs on every job would make maintenance difficult, especially if we decide later to install an additional package. Figure 4-21 illustrates the before_script keyword in the default section. In this example, we moved the apk add bash line from job build-job to the default before_script section. The before_script keyword tells GitLab to run all the commands listed under that keyword for all jobs before the explicit script commands in a job are executed.

```
stages:          # List of stages for jobs, and their order of execution
  - build
  - test
  - deploy

default:
  image: alpine:3.17
  before_script:
    - apk add bash

build-job:       # This job runs in the build stage, which runs first.
  stage: build
  script:
    - cat /etc/shells
    - echo "Compiling the code..."
    - echo "Compile complete."

unit-test-job:   # This job runs in the test stage.
  stage: test    # It only starts when the job in the build stage completes successfully.
  script:
    - cat /etc/shells
    - echo "Running unit tests... This will take about 60 seconds."
    - sleep 60
    - echo "Code coverage is 90%"
```

Figure 4-21. *Adding default before_script that installs bash*

Figure 4-22 shows what effect this had on job unit-test-job. The highlighted section now shows that apk add bash was run at the start of the job before the explicit cat /etc/shells command. We see that the bash shell was indeed installed even though we did not explicitly request it as part of job unit-test-job. Also, note that from the output, you can't tell that the commands came from two different places. It is as if the before_script commands specified in the default section were prepended before the script commands of the job.[8]

---

[8] I mention this because sometimes when you are debugging a job, you might get confused why some commands not explicitly specified in the job mysteriously appear in the output.

CHAPTER 4   BUILD, TEST, RINSE, AND REPEAT

Figure 4-22. Output of the unit test with before_script

Overriding the Default Image and before_script Tasks for a Given Job

OK, so far, so good. But what happens when we need to use a different image for a specific job? For example, we might want to run a test job that requires Selenium to validate our changes. There are already images in Docker Hub that have Selenium installed, so installing it on our own would be time-consuming and not necessary given the existing image. For those cases, we can override the default image by explicitly using the image tag in the job itself. The same is true with the before_script commands; if we are using a different image, the before_script commands might not apply to the overriding image.

Figure 4-23 shows the changes made to job unit-test-job to use Ubuntu rather than the default Alpine[9] image. Since the apk add bash would fail with Ubuntu (and would be unnecessary since bash is already installed on that image), the before_script: [] line nullifies the default before_script commands. We could also, of course, specify a list of specific commands that would be used by job unit-test-job instead of the default. In either case, the default before_script commands are not used.

---

[9] This is contrived to keep the example simple. I didn't want to go through setting up a selenium test case.

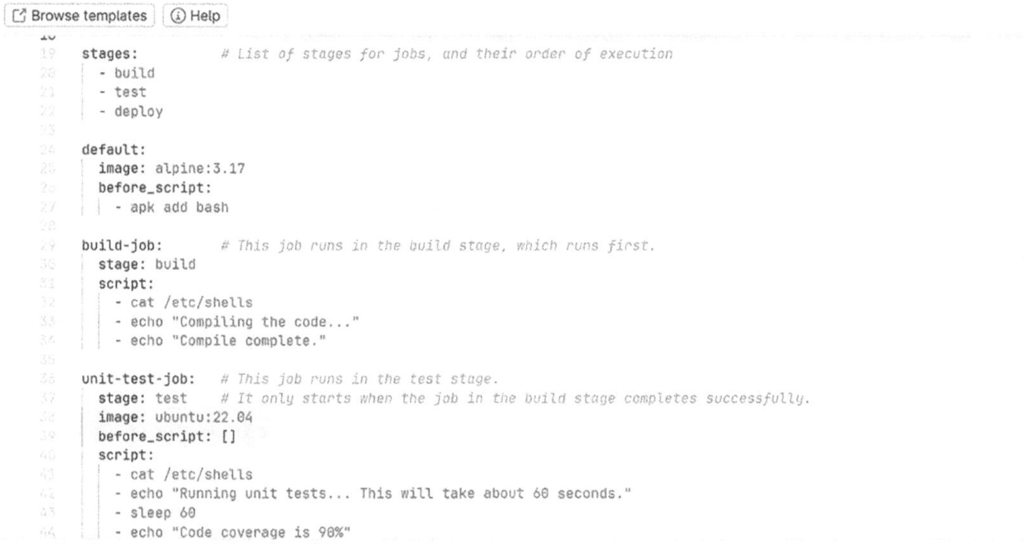

CHAPTER 4   BUILD, TEST, RINSE, AND REPEAT

```
19  stages:            # List of stages for jobs, and their order of execution
20    - build
21    - test
22    - deploy
23
24  default:
25    image: alpine:3.17
26    before_script:
27      - apk add bash
28
29  build-job:          # This job runs in the build stage, which runs first.
30    stage: build
31    script:
32      - cat /etc/shells
33      - echo "Compiling the code..."
34      - echo "Compile complete."
35
36  unit-test-job:      # This job runs in the test stage.
37    stage: test       # It only starts when the job in the build stage completes successfully.
38    image: ubuntu:22.04
39    before_script: []
40    script:
41      - cat /etc/shells
42      - echo "Running unit tests... This will take about 60 seconds."
43      - sleep 60
44      - echo "Code coverage is 90%"
```

Figure 4-23. *Unit test Docker image override*

Looking at the results of job unit-test-job in Figure 4-24, we see that the Ubuntu image was indeed used by the job and that the apk add bash command was not run, as expected. It also shows that bash, along with a number of other shells, exists on the Ubuntu image. By the way, I highlighted the prepare docker-machine section at the start of the output to illustrate that the Ubuntu image was pulled by docker-machine as well; nowhere in the execution of the unit-test-job is the Alpine image pulled or used.

CHAPTER 4   BUILD, TEST, RINSE, AND REPEAT

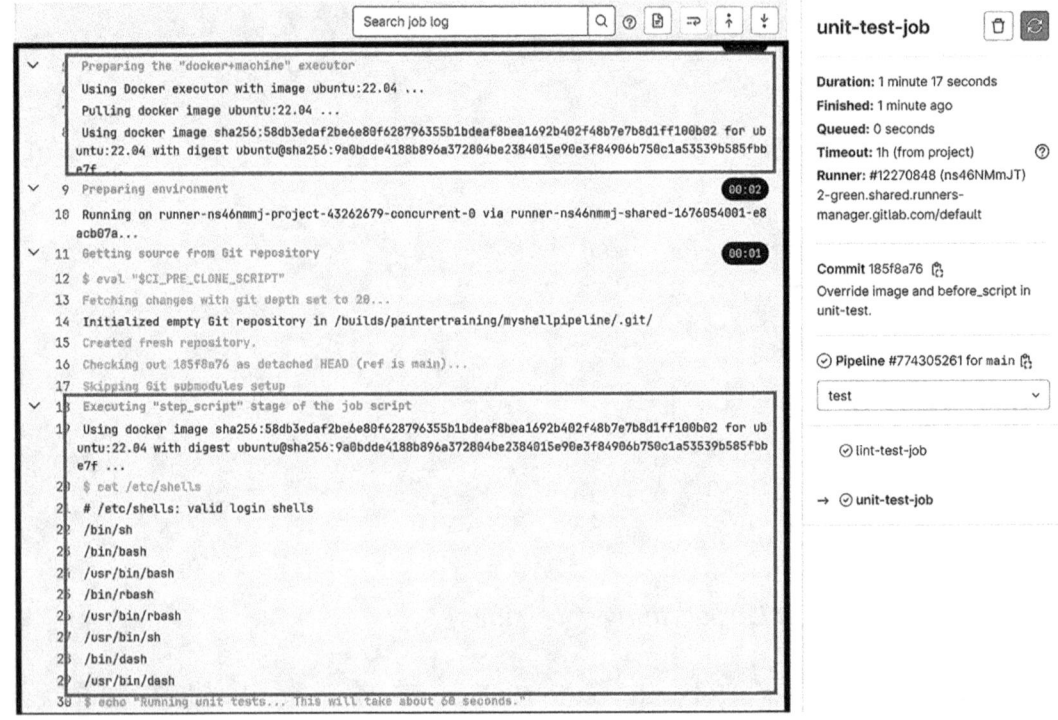

Figure 4-24. *Output of the unit test with image override*

This ends this section on using Docker images with the GitLab shared runners. You might be wondering if it is possible to create your own Docker image as a GitLab job and store it somewhere for later use. The answer is yes. In fact, you can store it in a GitLab image repository if you want; you don't have to store it in Docker Hub (although you could if you had the right permissions to do so). Using a job to create a Docker image is a bit tricky with GitLab. We'll look into this topic later after we've explored more advanced .gitlab-ci.yml keywords.

Introducing CI/CD Variables

Just as you can define and use variables in various programming languages and shell scripting environments, you can define and use variables in the CI/CD configuration file (i.e., .gitlab-ci.yml) as well. This section will look at the various ways in which variables can be defined and used within the CI/CD configuration file as well as the rules for overriding variable values.

Defining and Using Variables Within a Configuration File

Variables can be defined as key-value pairs (also known as a dictionary) using the variables keyword. Defining a variables section at the top level of a CI/CD configuration file makes those variables available to all jobs in the configuration. Defining a variables section within a job makes those variables available only within the job itself. If the same variable is defined at the top level and at the job level, the job-level value takes precedence.

The variable name should conform to shell variable syntax: only letters, numbers, and the underscore (_) character may be used as a variable name. By convention, upper-case letters are used for variable names, although it is not required; this is done to make them stand out in scripts. It is also recommended to start a variable name with a letter. The variable value is a string value. Typically, you enclose the value using single quote marks (') or double quote marks ("). Yaml will usually handle values that are not quoted; however, numeric values should always be quoted.

Within the variables section, you can define variables using the values of other variables, which is handy. In these sections, you can reference the value of a variable using one of the following forms: ${NAME}, $NAME, or %NAME%. The expansion behavior of variable references within a value does not depend on how the string is enclosed. Unlike within shell environments, variable references are expanded for strings enclosed in either single quotes or double quotes.

Within a script section, the expansion rules depend on the shell being used. For Linux shells such as bash and sh, variable references must be in the form ${NAME} or $NAME; for Windows shells, variable references must be in the form %NAME%. Also, variable expansion with script commands is different for strings enclosed in single quotes and double quotes. For strings enclosed within single quotes, variable references are not expanded, whereas for strings enclosed within double quotes, variable references are expanded.

Figure 4-25 shows these rules in action. The first highlighted section is the global variable definitions. We define three variables: MY_VAR1, MY_VAR2, and MY_VAR3 where the value for MY_VAR3 references the values of MY_VAR1 and MY_VAR2. The second highlighted area shows that build-job overrides the value of MY_VAR2. The third highlighted area shows shell statements that reference the three MY_VAR variables as well as a NOT_DEFINED_VAR reference for a variable whose value has not been defined. As an exercise, before we show the results of job build-job, try to figure out what the set of echo statements will show. Like me, you may be surprised at the results.

CHAPTER 4   BUILD, TEST, RINSE, AND REPEAT

```
24    default:
25      image: alpine:3.17
26      before_script:
27        - apk add bash
28
29    variables:
30      MY_VAR1: "global value 1"
31      MY_VAR2: "global value 2"
32      MY_VAR3: '${MY_VAR1}+${MY_VAR2}'
33
34    build-job:         # This job runs in the build stage, which runs first.
35      stage: build
36      variables:
37        MY_VAR2: local value 2
38      script:
39        - echo "MY_VAR1='${MY_VAR1}'"
40        - echo "MY_VAR2='$MY_VAR2'"
41        - echo "MY_VAR3='$MY_VAR3'"
42        - echo '$MY_VAR1+$MY_VAR2'
43        - echo "NOT_DEFINED_VAR='${NOT_DEFINED_VAR}'"
44        - cat /etc/shells
45        - echo "Compiling the code..."
46        - echo "Compile complete."
```

Figure 4-25. *Global vs. local job variable settings*

Figure 4-26 shows the output of job build-job. The section within the highlighted box is the results of each echo command. The first echo command shows that MY_VAR1 has the value defined at the global level, as expected. The second echo command shows that MY_VAR2 has the overridden value defined at the job level, as expected. The third echo command shows the result of the globally defined MY_VAR3 variable; however, note that the value of MY_VAR2 referenced within the value of MY_VAR3 resolved to the job-defined MY_VAR2 value as opposed to the globally defined MY_VAR2 value. This is interesting and probably not what you expected.[10] The fourth echo statement shows that the variables were not expanded since the value was enclosed in single quotes; this is the standard behavior of shell variables. The final echo statement shows the results of referencing a value that was not defined; this is also an expected shell behavior.

---

[10] It was definitely not what I expected. I am still trying to wrap my head around the process of variable resolution that resulted in the value that was shown by this echo statement.

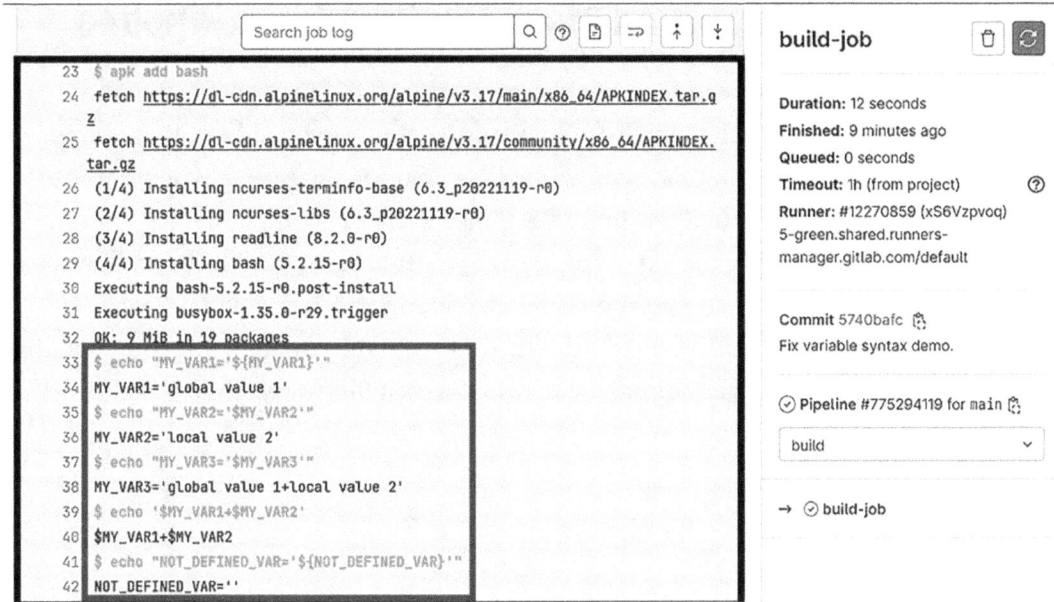

Figure 4-26. *Global vs. local job variable results*

Using Predefined Variables in a Configuration File

In addition to the variables that you define within the CI/CD configuration, there exists a whole bunch of predefined variables provided by GitLab that are available for you to use within jobs. You can find a list of these variables here: https://docs.gitlab.com/ee/ci/variables/predefined_variables.html. What you will notice is that almost all of the predefined variables begin with the prefix "CI_"; because of this, you should avoid naming any of your variables with this prefix. Also, note that some variables are only defined within a given context. For example, there are variables that are only defined during a merge request.

You should be aware that new predefined variables are created all the time. The reference list shows the GitLab version when a predefined variable was first made available. If you are using an earlier version of GitLab, the variable you wish to use might not exist yet (in which case, the value of the variable will be empty). If you are using gitlab.com as opposed to a self-managed GitLab service, this will not likely be an issue.

If you are wondering how predefined variables are useful other than to provide feedback messages in your jobs, many of these are used when defining rules. We'll discuss this use case and provide examples when we consider rules in the next chapter.

Defining Variables When Manually Running a Pipeline

There are other ways outside of the variables section in a CI/CD configuration file where variables can be defined and/or whose values can be overridden. We saw one way when we manually reran the "MyShellPipeline" earlier. Figure 4-27 shows how to specify variables when manually running the pipeline via the "Run Pipeline" option. In this example, I am setting the values of the MY_VAR1 and MY_VAR2 variables; these variables will take precedence over the values specified in both the global-level and job-level variable sections. You can also define other variables that do not appear in the variables section (perhaps variables used in a shell script file, for example).

Figure 4-27. Defining variables when explicitly running a pipeline

Figure 4-28 shows the results of job build-job when the pipeline is run with these values. As you can see, the values of MY_VAR1 and MY_VAR2 are expanded using these values. The value of MY_VAR3 is also expanded using the pipeline-supplied values as you might have expected.

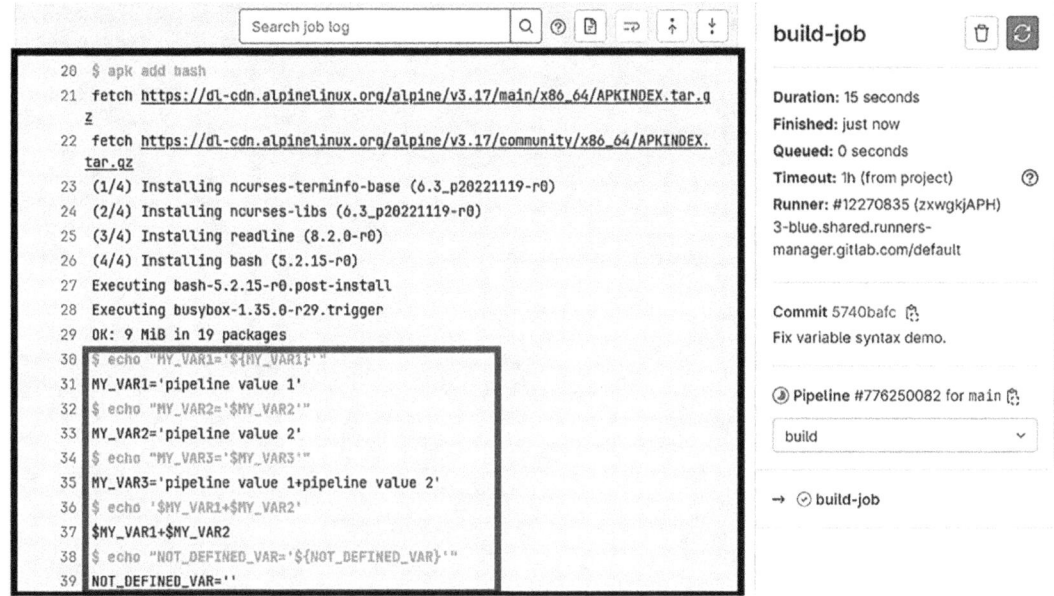

Figure 4-28. *Results of pipeline run with variable inputs*

Setting Descriptions and Default Values for "Run Pipeline" Variables

One issue that developers had with early versions of GitLab is that specifying values when running the pipeline manually required knowing the name of the variables being overridden. Also, it was easy to misspell a variable name and not get the expected value override. To combat this issue, GitLab enabled a new feature for variables defined in the global-level variables section. In the global-level variables section, you can also specify a description attribute to a given variable, in which case the variable shows up in the run pipeline form labeled with the given description text. Furthermore, a variable can have a default value that a user can override and an options section defining a list of values that may be selected using a drop-down box in the run pipeline form.

Figure 4-29 provides an example of how to define variables with descriptions. Variable MY_PIPELINE_VAR shows how to define a variable with a default value of "Some default value" that can be overridden when the pipeline is run manually; note that if you do not specify a value, the variable will have an empty value when expanded. Variable MY_PIPELINE_CHOICE shows how to define a variable that allows one of several choices with a default value of the first choice. Note that for options, a default value must be provided.

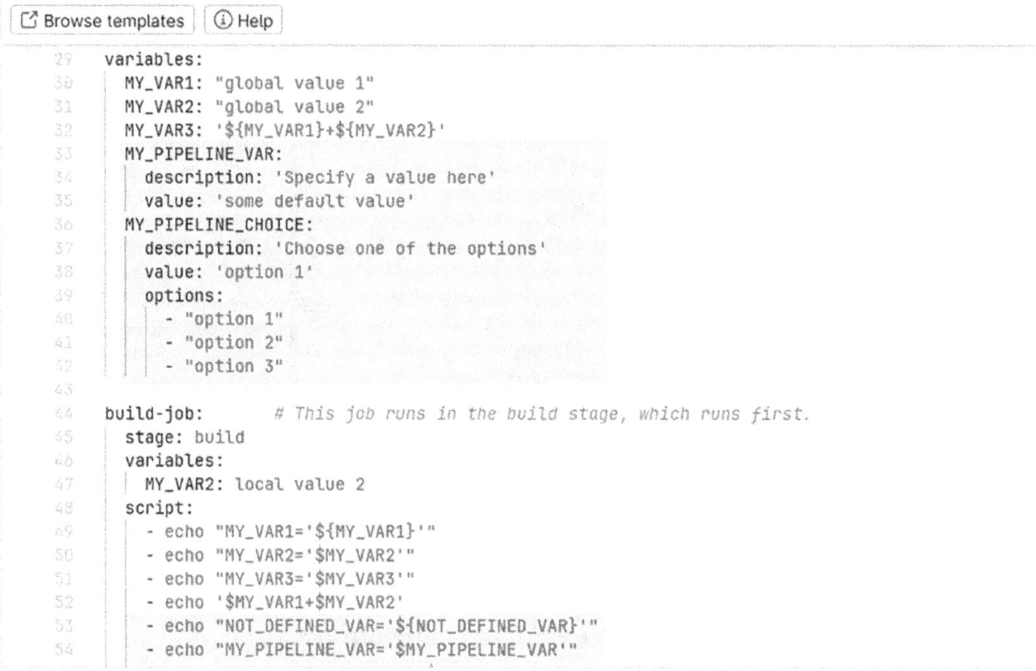

CHAPTER 4　BUILD, TEST, RINSE, AND REPEAT

```
variables:
  MY_VAR1: "global value 1"
  MY_VAR2: "global value 2"
  MY_VAR3: '${MY_VAR1}+${MY_VAR2}'
  MY_PIPELINE_VAR:
    description: 'Specify a value here'
    value: 'some default value'
  MY_PIPELINE_CHOICE:
    description: 'Choose one of the options'
    value: 'option 1'
    options:
      - "option 1"
      - "option 2"
      - "option 3"

build-job:             # This job runs in the build stage, which runs first.
  stage: build
  variables:
    MY_VAR2: local value 2
  script:
    - echo "MY_VAR1='${MY_VAR1}'"
    - echo "MY_VAR2='$MY_VAR2'"
    - echo "MY_VAR3='$MY_VAR3'"
    - echo '$MY_VAR1+$MY_VAR2'
    - echo "NOT_DEFINED_VAR='${NOT_DEFINED_VAR}'"
    - echo "MY_PIPELINE_VAR='$MY_PIPELINE_VAR'"
```

Figure 4-29. *Variable definitions with default values*

When the changes are committed, the pipeline will automatically run using the default values of MY_PIPELINE_VAR and MY_PIPELINE_CHOICE. Figure 4-30 shows what the run pipeline form looks like for variables with a description attribute. Variable MY_PIPELINE_VAR is automatically displayed in the form with the default value filled in, and variable MY_PIPELINE_CHOICE is automatically displayed with a drop-down list. In this example, I'm choosing "option 2" as the value before running the pipeline manually.

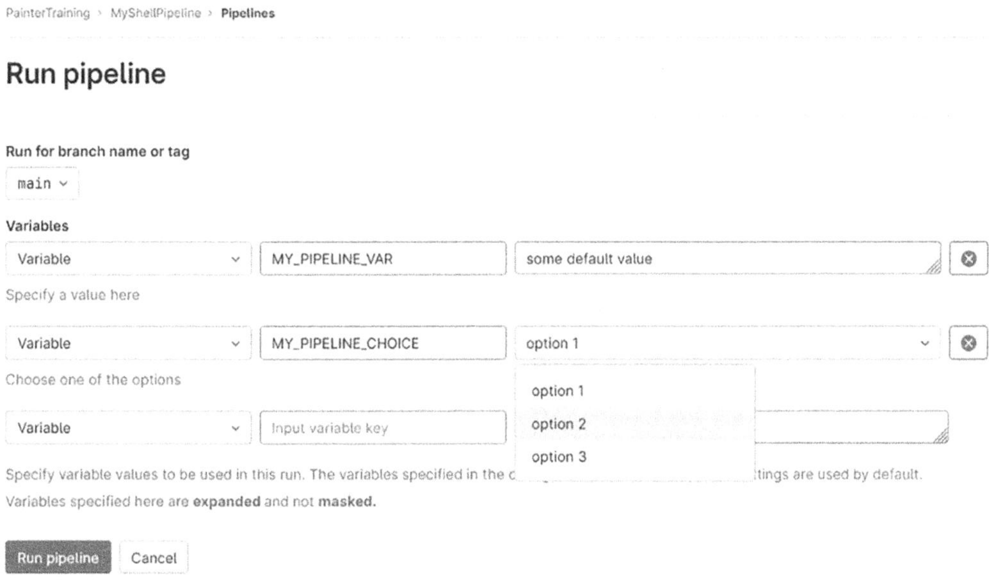

CHAPTER 4   BUILD, TEST, RINSE, AND REPEAT

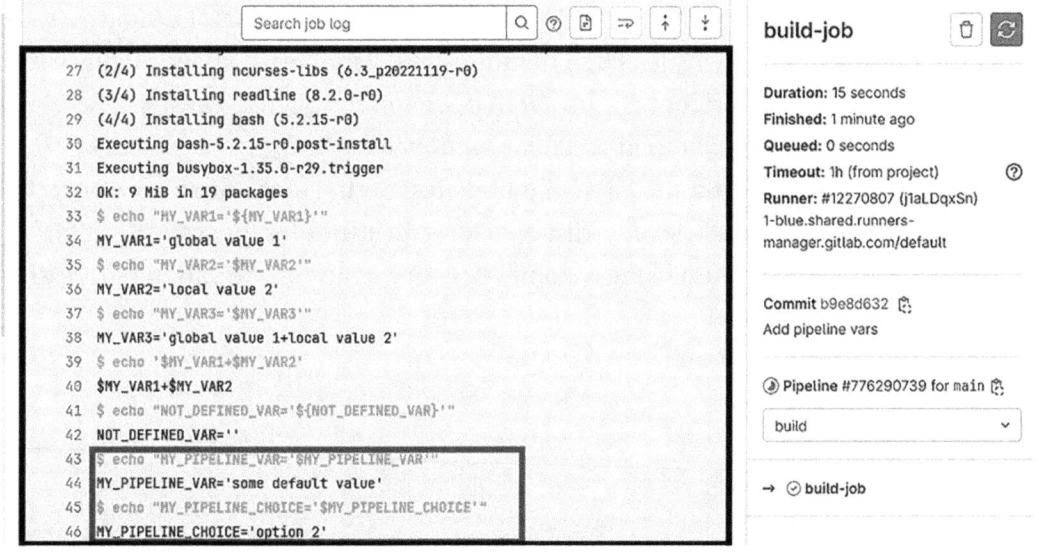

Figure 4-30.   Run pipeline form with variable descriptions, defaults, and options defined

Figure 4-31 shows the results of running the pipeline with the default value of the MY_PIPELINE_VAR variable and the value "option 2" for the MY_PIPELINE_CHOICE variable. The values shown in the echo commands return the values of these variables as entered in the run pipeline form.

Figure 4-31.   Results of pipeline run with variable defaults

127

CHAPTER 4 BUILD, TEST, RINSE, AND REPEAT

Defining CI/CD Variables at the Project or Group Level

Before we leave this section on variables, I want to discuss one more way in which variables can be defined outside of the CI/CD configuration file: via the user interface. When you are connected to the website, either the gitlab.com website or your GitLab self-managed website, you can define variables as part of your project or group settings.

One motivation for defining variables through project or group settings has to do with secrets. If you want to create a variable such as DB_PASSWORD to contain your database password, you don't want to define this as part of your checked-in CI/CD configuration file where values are visible. You also might have a set of values for the database password depending on the environment in which a database is configured. For example, you might have a development database, a staging database, and a production database each with their own passwords. Rather than defining three different variables for each environment, it would make configuration easier if you can use one variable with different values for each environment. You will also want to control who can set and change the values, especially for the tighter-controlled production environment.

Instructions on how to set variables through a project's settings can be found here: https://docs.gitlab.com/ee/ci/variables/index.html#for-a-project. Instructions on how to set variables through a group's settings can be found here: https://docs.gitlab.com/ee/ci/variables/index.html#for-a-group. The key thing to note about setting and viewing variables at the project level is that you need to have a role of Maintainer or Owner; if you have a Developer or lower role, you will not be able to see a project's variable settings (by design). For group-level variables, you need to have the role of Owner. We'll look at roles in more detail in Chapter 7.

Figure 4-32 shows the expanded variables section when you go to a project's CI/CD settings page for the first time. There is a brief description at the top about what these variables are for and a brief description of certain attributes that can be set for each variable. Near the bottom of the section is a listing of any group variables that are inherited, if any.

CHAPTER 4 BUILD, TEST, RINSE, AND REPEAT

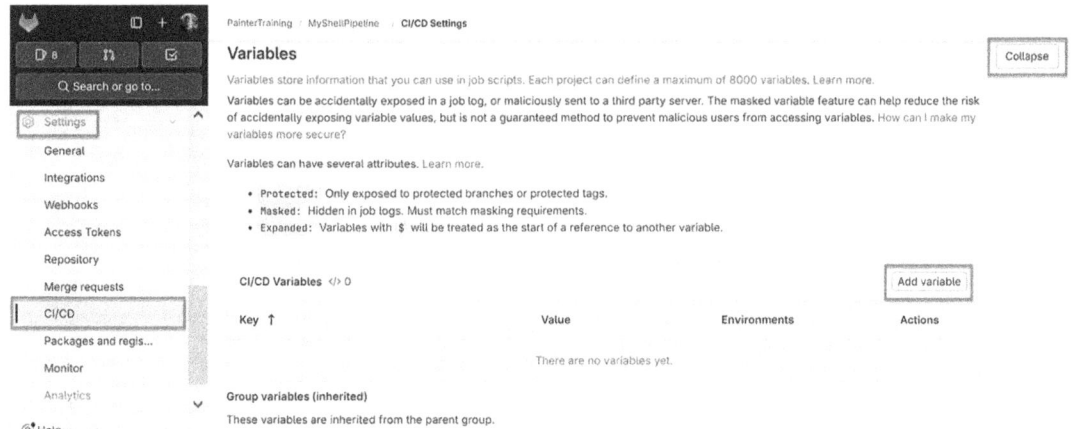

Figure 4-32. Variables section of a project's CI/CD settings page

Selecting the "Add variable" button pops up a form as shown in Figure 4-33. In this example, I've set the variable name as MY_DB_PASSWORD and its value in plain text. The type is set to "Variable" by default; you can also specify a type of "File" for file-based secrets such as private SSH keys. The environment scope is set to "All" by default; if you have multiple environments defined such as dev, stage, and production, you can set distinct values for each environment using the same key.

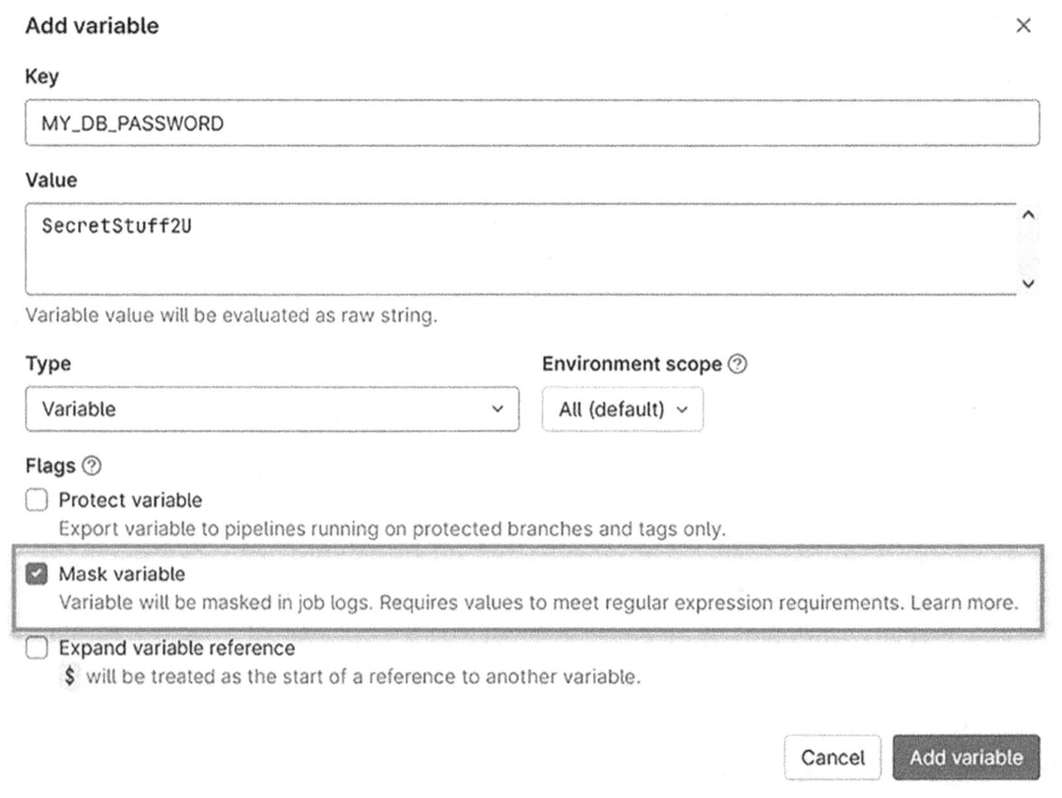

Figure 4-33. Project add variable page

Masking Secret Values for CI/CD Variables

The last section of the form includes various flag attributes that can be set. In this example, I've enabled the "Mask variable" flag that will mask the value in job log outputs, and I've disabled the "Protect variable" flag. Many first timers to GitLab assume that the "Protect variable" attribute is used to denote a variable as a secret. It is actually used to restrict its usage to protected branches (like main) and protected tags; if the variable is used in unprotected working branches, its value is undefined unless set in the "variables" section of the CI/CD configuration file.

The "Protect variable" attribute probably seems like an odd attribute to have, but it makes sense from a security viewpoint. Remember that project and group variables are restricted to those with proper permissions to view and set them. Without the "Protect variable" attribute, a developer could create a working branch and attempt to resolve the value of the variable using an echo command or by injecting the value into a file

CHAPTER 4   BUILD, TEST, RINSE, AND REPEAT

and then using cat to view it.[11] The concept of protected branches is that all changes to the branch must be peer reviewed; this makes it difficult (though not impossible) for a developer to introduce code that exposes the value of the variable.

It should be noted that the "Mask variable" attribute has severe limitations on what values can be masked. Values to be masked can only contain letters, numbers, and a small set of special characters (@, :, ., or ~). If the value entered cannot be masked, you will be notified and will not be able to save the variable with the "Mask variable" attribute set. What this means is that many passwords generated by password generators will not work when using symbols. It also means that some common secrets such as AWS secret access keys cannot be masked as is. You can work around this limitation by encoding the value in base64, but you'll have to remember to decode it before it is used.

Once you've completed the form and added the variable to the project, you will see it listed in the project's CI/CD settings summary as shown in Figure 4-34. You can continue to add up to 8000 variables.[12] You can also select the edit icon on the right of a listed variable to update or delete it.

Variables

Variables store information, like passwords and secret keys, that you can use in job scripts. Each project can define a maximum of 8000 variables. Learn more.

Variables can have several attributes. Learn more.

- **Protected:** Only exposed to protected branches or protected tags.
- **Masked:** Hidden in job logs. Must match masking requirements.
- **Expanded:** Variables with $ will be treated as the start of a reference to another variable.

Environment variables are configured by your administrator to be protected by default.

Type	↑ Key	Value	Options	Environments
Variable	MY_DB_PASSWORD	*****	Masked	All (default)

[Add variable]   [Reveal values]

Figure 4-34. *Project CI/CD variables summary page*

---

[11] Oopsie, I shouldn't have told you that!

[12] First off, 8000 seems like an odd limit to set; why not 10,000 or 5000? Secondly, I suggest keeping the number of project variables to the absolute minimum. I've seen teams go hog wild with using project and group variables creating a maintenance nightmare.

CHAPTER 4   BUILD, TEST, RINSE, AND REPEAT

Figure 4-35 shows an updated .gitlab-ci.yml file that uses the newly created MY_DB_PASSWORD variable. Note that this variable does not, nor is it required to, appear in any of the variables sections. I use the echo command to illustrate how masked variable values are marked in the job output.

```yaml
variables:
  MY_VAR1: "global value 1"
  MY_VAR2: "global value 2"
  MY_VAR3: '${MY_VAR1}+${MY_VAR2}'
  MY_PIPELINE_VAR:
    description: 'Specify a value here'
    value: 'some default value'
  MY_PIPELINE_CHOICE:
    description: 'Choose one of the options'
    value: 'option 1'
    options:
      - "option 1"
      - "option 2"
      - "option 3"

build-job:        # This job runs in the build stage, which runs first.
  stage: build
  variables:
    MY_VAR2: local value 2
  script:
    - echo "MY__DB_PASSWORD='$MY_DB_PASSWORD'"
    - echo "MY_VAR1='${MY_VAR1}'"
    - echo "MY_VAR2='$MY_VAR2'"
    - echo "MY_VAR3='$MY_VAR3'"
    - echo '$MY_VAR1+$MY_VAR2'
    - echo "NOT_DEFINED_VAR='${NOT_DEFINED_VAR}'"
```

Figure 4-35. *Updated job to display the project CI/CD variable*

The output of job build-job is shown in Figure 4-36. As you can see, the value is displayed in the job log as [MASKED].

CHAPTER 4 BUILD, TEST, RINSE, AND REPEAT

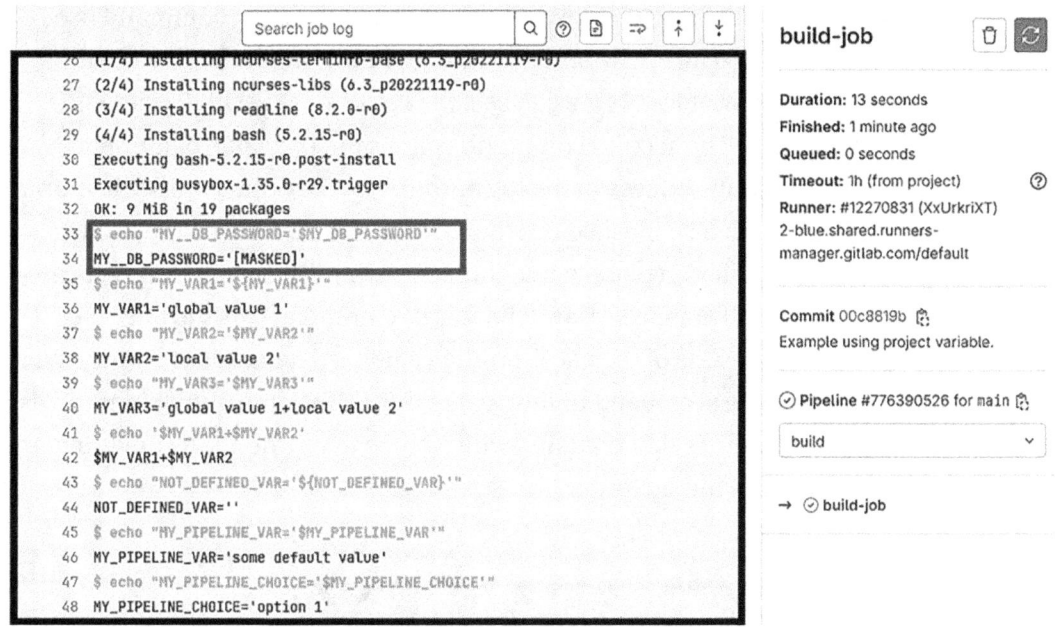

Figure 4-36. *Result showing value of the project variable*

If you are wondering how the masking feature works, I ran an experiment. In Figure 4-37, I added a few commands in job unit-test-job to illustrate masking in action with common attacks to expose the value of a masked variable. The commands I chose are based on the conjecture that masking relies on pattern matching to determine if something in the log is a masked value.

```
58          - echo "Compiling the code..."
59          - echo "Compile complete."
60
61   unit-test-job:   # This job runs in the test stage.
62     stage: test    # It only starts when the job in the build stage completes successfully.
63     image: ubuntu:22.04
64     before_script: []
65     script:
66       - printenv | grep '^MY_' | sort
67       - echo 'SecretStuff2U'
68       - echo $MY_DB_PASSWORD > ~/my_secret_file
69       - cat ~/my_secret_file
70       - grep -c 'Stuff' ~/my_secret_file
71       - cat /etc/shells
72       - echo "Running unit tests... This will take about 60 seconds."
73       - sleep 60
74       - echo "Code coverage is 90%"
75
76   lint-test-job:   # This job also runs in the test stage.
77     stage: test    # It can run at the same time as unit-test-job (in parallel).
78     script:
```

Figure 4-37. *Test of mask variable feature*

Figure 4-38 shows the log output from these commands. The first command uses the printenv command to list all environment variables known to the shell and filters out and sorts all the MY_ variables. As we can see, the value for MY_DB_PASSWORD has been properly masked. The second command echoes out the value of the secret explicitly to see how masking behaves in the log output. Not only did it mask the output of the echo command, but it also masked out the value in the command line itself. This shows that masking relies on pattern matching. The third command redirects the value of MY_DB_PASSWORD into a file, and the fourth command cats the file to see if the value is exposed. The results of the cat show the value is still masked. To verify that the file actually contains the secret and not the value [MASKED], the fifth command uses grep to return the count of lines that contain "Stuff"; since it returned 1, it shows that the file contains the contents of the secret.

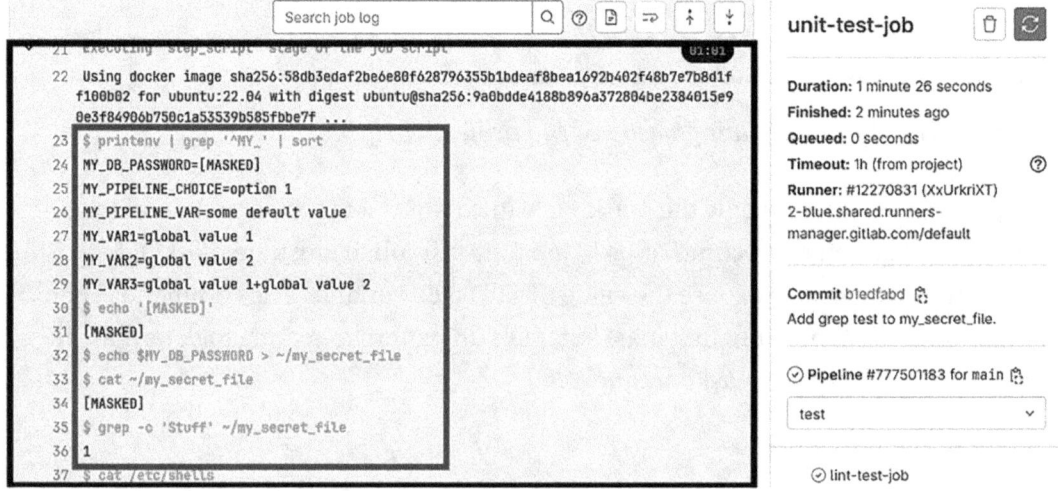

Figure 4-38. Result of mask variable test

As you can see, GitLab does a decent job of protecting masked variables in job logs. Since the masking feature relies on pattern matching the values of masked variables, you may have a better understanding of why masked values are required to follow a restricted set of rules. You should also note that a side effect of using pattern matching to mask secrets is that sometimes items in the log are replaced with [MASKED] when they don't actually refer to a secret;[13] it's just a coincidence. This doesn't happen very often, but when it does, it looks odd in the log.

Managing CI/CD Configurations

So far, we've been working with the .gitlab-ci.yml file, also referred to as a CI/CD configuration file. This file must exist in order for GitLab to define and run CI/CD pipelines. Without it, your project is simply a set of source code repository files managed by Git. However, the .gitlab-ci.yml file isn't the only CI/CD configuration file you can create to manage CI/CD pipelines. As your project gets more complex, your .gitlab-ci.yml file will quickly become unwieldy and more cumbersome to manage, especially if you have multiple developers tweaking it.

Fortunately, there are ways to break up your CI/CD configuration into multiple files as well as ways to manage reusable components to reduce duplication in your configuration. This section describes these various methods of managing your CI/CD configuration.

Breaking a Pipeline Configuration into Multiple Files

Let's first talk about how to break up your CI/CD configuration into multiple files. For this, you use the global-level include keyword. With this keyword, you can include files local to your project (the most common option), files located in another project, files available from a remote location via HTTPS, and files from predefined templates typically provided by GitLab.

I've taken the MyShellPipeline project and split out the jobs from the .gitlab-ci.yml file into separate files: .gitlab-build.yml, .gitlab-test.yml, and .gitlab-deploy.yml. Figure 4-39 shows the project files after splitting the jobs from the original .gitlab-ci.yml file. Note that the period in front of each of these filenames is a convention I use for CI/CD configuration files to differentiate them from other files; prefixing CI/CD configuration files with a period is not required.

---

[13] This could also be an indication that your secret is "weak"; for example, a secret of "password" is likely to match in many places. It is also why masked values must be at least eight characters in length; the smaller the secret, the more likely the pattern will match unrelated stuff.

CHAPTER 4   BUILD, TEST, RINSE, AND REPEAT

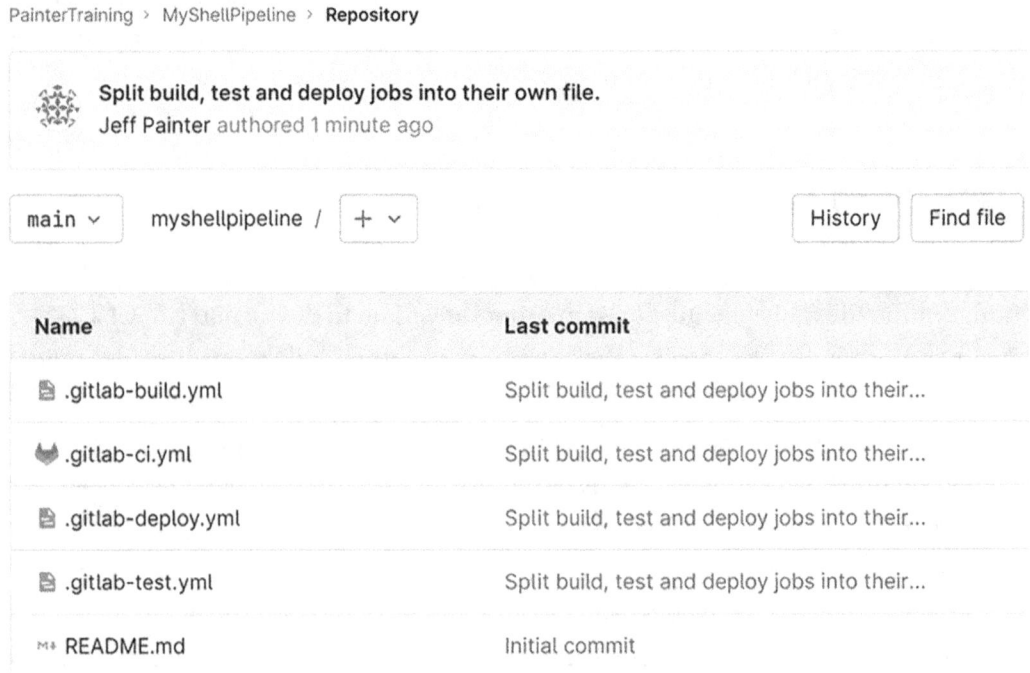

Figure 4-39. Project updated with include files

Figure 4-40 shows the contents of the .gitlab-build.yml file. It contains job build-job that was in the original .gitlab-ci.yml file. Although I don't show it here, the contents of the .gitlab-test.yml file contain the two jobs lint-test-job and unit-test-job, and the contents of the .gitlab-deploy.yml file contain job deploy-job.

CHAPTER 4 BUILD, TEST, RINSE, AND REPEAT

main ⌄   myshellpipeline / .gitlab-build.yml

📄 .gitlab-build.yml 556 bytes

```yaml
build-job:             # This job runs in the build stage, which ru
  stage: build
  variables:
    MY_VAR2: local value 2
  script:
    - echo "MY__DB_PASSWORD='$MY_DB_PASSWORD'"
    - echo "MY_VAR1='${MY_VAR1}'"
    - echo "MY_VAR2='$MY_VAR2'"
    - echo "MY_VAR3='$MY_VAR3'"
    - echo '$MY_VAR1+$MY_VAR2'
    - echo "NOT_DEFINED_VAR='${NOT_DEFINED_VAR}'"
    - echo "MY_PIPELINE_VAR='$MY_PIPELINE_VAR'"
    - echo "MY_PIPELINE_CHOICE='$MY_PIPELINE_CHOICE'"
    - cat /etc/shells
    - echo "Compiling the code..."
    - echo "Compile complete."
```

Figure 4-40. *Contents of .gitlab-build.yml file*

Figure 4-41 shows the updated .gitlab-ci.yml file with the global-level include section. This section contains a list of references to the other three CI/CD configuration files. The local keyword in each of these references is optional; the file is assumed to be local to the project if you only provide the name of the file. I included the local keyword here for clarity.

CHAPTER 4 BUILD, TEST, RINSE, AND REPEAT

```
main v    myshellpipeline / .gitlab-ci.yml

.gitlab-ci.yml   620 bytes

 1  stages:              # List of stages for jobs, and their o
 2    - build
 3    - test
 4    - deploy
 5
 6  default:
 7    image: alpine:3.17
 8    before_script:
 9      - apk add bash
10
11  variables:
12    MY_VAR1: "global value 1"
13    MY_VAR2: "global value 2"
14    MY_VAR3: '${MY_VAR1}+${MY_VAR2}'
15    MY_PIPELINE_VAR:
16      description: 'Specify a value here'
17      value: 'some default value'
18    MY_PIPELINE_CHOICE:
19      description: 'Choose one of the options'
20      value: 'option 1'
21      options:
22        - "option 1"
23        - "option 2"
24        - "option 3"
25
26  include:
27    - local: .gitlab-build.yml
28    - local: .gitlab-test.yml
29    - local: .gitlab-deploy.yml
30
```

Figure 4-41. *Job updated using include files*

Note that the "include" section can be located anywhere in the .gitlab-ci.yml file; its location is not relevant with respect to the remaining contents of the .gitlab-ci.yml file. I could have just as well placed it at the top of the file instead of the bottom. The order of the included references does matter, however. These files are included in the order in which they appear. This is important when multiple "include" files contain the same job. In this case, key-value attributes (such as variables) are merged together; if two files contain the same key, the value of the last one included is used. For sections such as before_script, no merge is taken place; the last one included is used.

Viewing a Merged Configuration with the CI/CD Editor

If you go to the project's CI/CD editor, there is a tab, Full configuration, to view the merged files as a single YAML file as highlighted in Figure 4-42. As you can see, the included file sections are shown first in the order in which they were listed followed by the rest of the .gitlab-ci.yml contents.

Figure 4-42. View of the full configuration feature

Additional Include Types

Another interesting type of include is the project include. With this type of include, you can include one or more files from another project (as long as you have permission to access that project). The project include is useful when you want to share configurations across multiple projects. This could be a set of variables to be shared or a set of common jobs to be reused. The last use case is useful for defining a common library of jobs for a given department or the whole company. The project include requires two attributes: the project name and the file to be included. You can also specify an optional ref attribute to select a given version of the file based on branch or tag. Check out the section on the include project at https://docs.gitlab.com/ee/ci/yaml/#includeproject for examples of how to use them.

The remaining types of include, remote and template, are not as common as the local and project includes. For remote includes, you specify a URL referencing a file to be downloaded. One of the things that makes the remote include less useful is its requirement that access to the website referenced by the URL must be public; you cannot specify authentication credentials to the remote site. Template includes are used to enable some GitLab features such as SAST (Static Application Software Testing) and DAST (Dynamic Application Software Testing). For these features, GitLab has provided a remote library of templates that can be included in your pipeline. You can view this library here: https://gitlab.com/gitlab-org/gitlab/-/tree/master/lib/gitlab/ci/templates.

Breaking Jobs into Reusable Pieces Using Extends

Now that we've seen how to use the include keyword to better organize our CI/CD configuration file and to reuse jobs from another project or template library, let's turn our sights on other ways we can reuse job components to reduce repeating the same configurations in multiple places.[14] There are two additional features that enable us to do that: the extends keyword and reference tags.[15]

---

[14] This is following the DRY principle: Don't Repeat Yourself.
[15] There is actually a third feature called YAML anchors that can be used but which I find nonintuitive to use. The extends keyword and reference tags provide a more elegant alternative to YAML anchors that provides the same functionality.

We saw earlier that we can use the before_script keyword to specify a common set of commands at the global level and how we could override them for a specific job. But what if we wanted to specify a common set of commands for a class of jobs such as test jobs and a different set of commands for a different class of jobs? We could, of course, use shell conditionals such as if and switch to define different sets of commands within a before_script section and use variables to determine which set to use, but this is unnecessarily complex.

Instead, we can use a feature of CI/CD configuration known as hidden jobs in conjunction with the extends keyword. A hidden job is a job whose name begins with a period; it is not included automatically in a pipeline like normal jobs are. You can then use the extends keyword in a job to "merge" the contents of the hidden job with the job being extended. Figure 4-43 illustrates how this works.

```
 1  .prep-test: # This is a hidden job; it will only be run as part of extends
 2    stage: test
 3    image: python:3.9.16-alpine3.17
 4    variables:
 5      MY_TEST_VAR1: 'prep-test-hello'
 6      MY_TEST_VAR2: 'prep-test-goodbye'
 7    before_script:
 8      - echo "Prep test before script"
 9    after_script:
10      - echo "Prep test after script"
11
12  unit-test-job:
13    extends: .prep-test
14    script:
15      - echo "MY_TEST_VAR1=$MY_TEST_VAR1"
16      - echo "MY_TEST_VAR2=$MY_TEST_VAR2"
17      - echo "Running unit tests... This will take about 60 seconds."
18      - sleep 60
19      - echo "Code coverage is 90%"
20
21  lint-test-job:
22    extends: .prep-test
23    variables:
24      MY_TEST_VAR2: 'lint-test-goodbye'
25      MY_TEST_VAR3: 'lint-test-special'
26    script:
27      - echo "MY_TEST_VAR1=$MY_TEST_VAR1"
28      - echo "MY_TEST_VAR2=$MY_TEST_VAR2"
29      - echo "MY_TEST_VAR3=$MY_TEST_VAR3"
30      - echo "Linting code... This will take about 10 seconds."
31      - sleep 10
32      - echo "No lint issues found."
33    after_script:
34      - echo "Lint test after script"
35
```

Figure 4-43. Updated test job using the extends keyword

At the top of the .gitlab-test.yml file is a definition of the .prep-test hidden job. It includes pieces of the job that we want to include in other jobs; in this case, we define the stage, an image to use for testing, some common variables for all tests, and a before_script and after_script set of commands. Note that we did not include a script section, although we could have if we wanted to. The hidden job does not have to have all the required sections of a normal job.

CHAPTER 4   BUILD, TEST, RINSE, AND REPEAT

In this example, we use the extends keyword referencing the .prep-test job for both the unit-test-job and the lint-test-job jobs. I've modified these jobs by removing the common pieces such as stage and image that are now referenced in .prep-job. In job lint-test-job, I show how to override a variable and the after_script section defined in the .prep-test job. This is similar to how defaults are overridden for specific jobs.

Figure 4-44 shows the output of job unit-test-job. From this, you can see that the Python image we specified in the .prep-test job is used in place of the default Alpine image as expected. In addition, you can see the before_script and after_script commands from the .prep-test job being executed as well as the definition of the MY_TEST_VAR1 and MY_TEST_VAR2 variables defined in .prep-test being used.

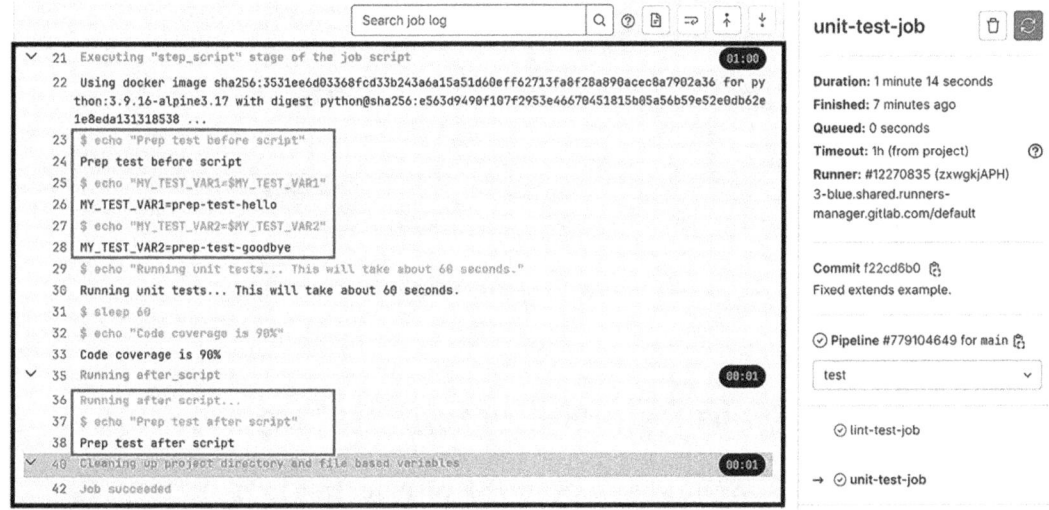

Figure 4-44. *Output of unit test using the extends feature*

We can see the results of job lint-test-job in Figure 4-45. Here, we can see the effects of overriding the MY_TEST_VAR2 variable and the after_script section. This example shows how the merging process works. For sections such as the variables section that consist of key-value pairs, all keys are merged together as a single set (MY_TEST_VAR1, MY_TEST_VAR2, and MY_TEST_VAR3); when the same key is defined in both jobs, the

143

value from the extending job (.lint-test-job in this example) is used. For sections that consist of lists, such as the after_script section containing a list of commands, only the definition in the extending job is used.[16]

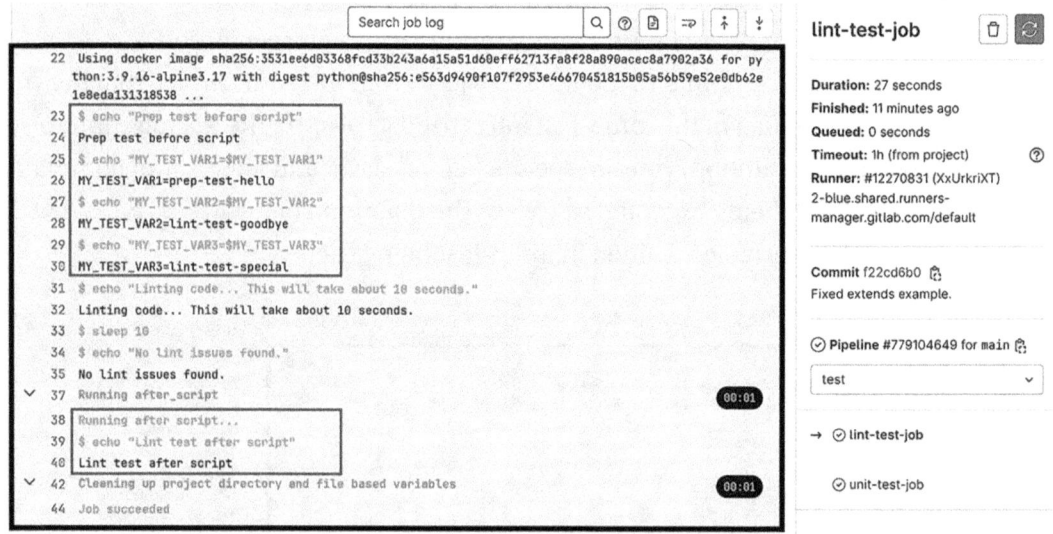

Figure 4-45. Output of lint test using the extends feature

Enabling Fine-Grain Reusability with Reference Tags

So, using the "include" keyword gives us a gross-level of reusing jobs, and the "extends" keyword gives us a more refined way of reusing portions of a job. Reference tags give us a more refined way of using specific portions of a job. As we saw, when we override certain sections, such as before_script, script, and after_script, that consist of lists of things, the extends feature requires us to discard the list from the extended job and only use the list from the extending job. But what if we wanted to use both lists?

In our previous example, suppose we still want to run the after_script commands in .prep-test in addition to steps in job .lint-test-job. We could copy the commands from the .prep-test job and include them explicitly in the after_script section of job .lint-test-job.

---

[16] The merging of dictionaries, which is an unordered set of key-value pairs, is well defined. The merging of ordered lists, on the other hand, is ambiguous in that the order in which the lists are merged matters.

But what happens later in development when we modify the commands in the .prep-test job? We would have to remember to copy the changes to job .lint-test-job.

Enter reference tags. With reference tags, we can define a hidden job with before_script, script, and/or after_script sections that we can explicitly inject into our other jobs exactly where we want them. These are custom YAML tags created by GitLab for use in CI/CD configuration files; because they are custom, YAML editors and viewers outside of the GitLab editor may not recognize them and will consider your file as invalid YAML.

Figure 4-46 illustrates the usage of reference tags. In this example, the .common-prep job contains common definitions for before_script and after_script. The .prep-test job extends .common-prep and hence inherits the before_script and after_script sections. The .common-tests job contains a script section with common commands to be used in each of the jobs; note that no job extends the .common-tests job. In the unit-test-job script section, there is a reference tag that references the script section of .common-tests; this reference allows us to merge the two echo commands with the unit-test-job script commands exactly where we want them executed – likewise for the lint-test-job script section. Since before_script and after_script sections are defined in .lint-test-job, they override the sections defined in .common-prep. Using reference tags, we can still include the before_script and after_script commands from .common-prep exactly where we need them in the corresponding sections of .lint-test-job.

```yaml
.common-prep:
  before_script:
    - echo "Common setup before test"
  after_script:
    - echo "Common teardown after test"

.prep-test:
  extends: .common-prep
  stage: test
  image: python:3.9.16-alpine3.17
  variables:
    MY_TEST_VAR1: 'prep-test-hello'
    MY_TEST_VAR2: 'prep-test-goodbye'

.common-tests:
  script:
    - echo "MY_TEST_VAR1=$MY_TEST_VAR1"
    - echo "MY_TEST_VAR2=$MY_TEST_VAR2"

unit-test-job:
  extends: .prep-test
  script:
    - echo "Running unit tests... This will take about 60 seconds."
    - !reference [.common-tests, script]
    - sleep 60
    - echo "Code coverage is 90%"

lint-test-job:
  extends: .prep-test
  variables:
    MY_TEST_VAR2: 'lint-test-goodbye'
    MY_TEST_VAR3: 'lint-test-special'
  before_script:
    - !reference [.common-prep, before_script]
    - echo 'Lint setup before test'
  script:
    - !reference [.common-tests, script]
    - echo "MY_TEST_VAR3=$MY_TEST_VAR3"
    - echo "Linting code... This will take about 10 seconds."
    - sleep 10
    - echo "No lint issues found."
  after_script:
    - echo "Lint teardown after test"
    - !reference [.common-prep, after_script]
```

Figure 4-46. *Job updated with reference tags*

Figure 4-47 shows the output of job unit-test-job. Here, we see that the before_script and after_script commands defined in .common-prep are executed as expected. In addition, we see the two echo commands from .common-tests are executed right after the echo of "Running unit test command" defined in .unit-test-job's script section.

CHAPTER 4   BUILD, TEST, RINSE, AND REPEAT

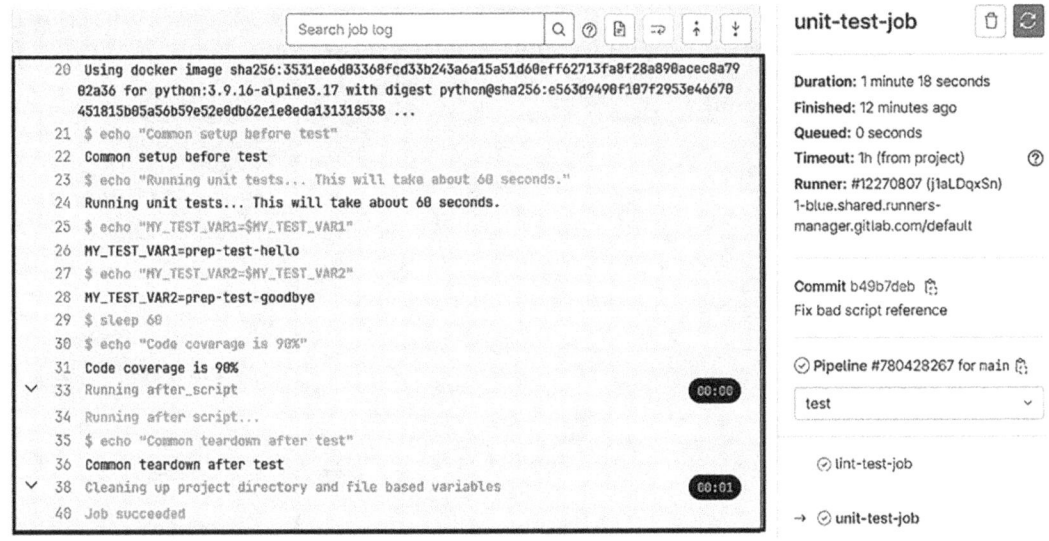

Figure 4-47. *Output of unit test with reference tags*

Figure 4-48 shows the output of lint-test-job. Here, we see that the "Common setup before test" message is displayed first followed by the "Lint setup before test" message. In addition, we see that the "Lint teardown after test" message is displayed first followed by the "Common teardown after test" message. This before_script and after_script combination illustrates how we can add additional setup and teardown sections for a test ensuring that the common setup commands are executed first, and the common teardown commands are executed last.

CHAPTER 4   BUILD, TEST, RINSE, AND REPEAT

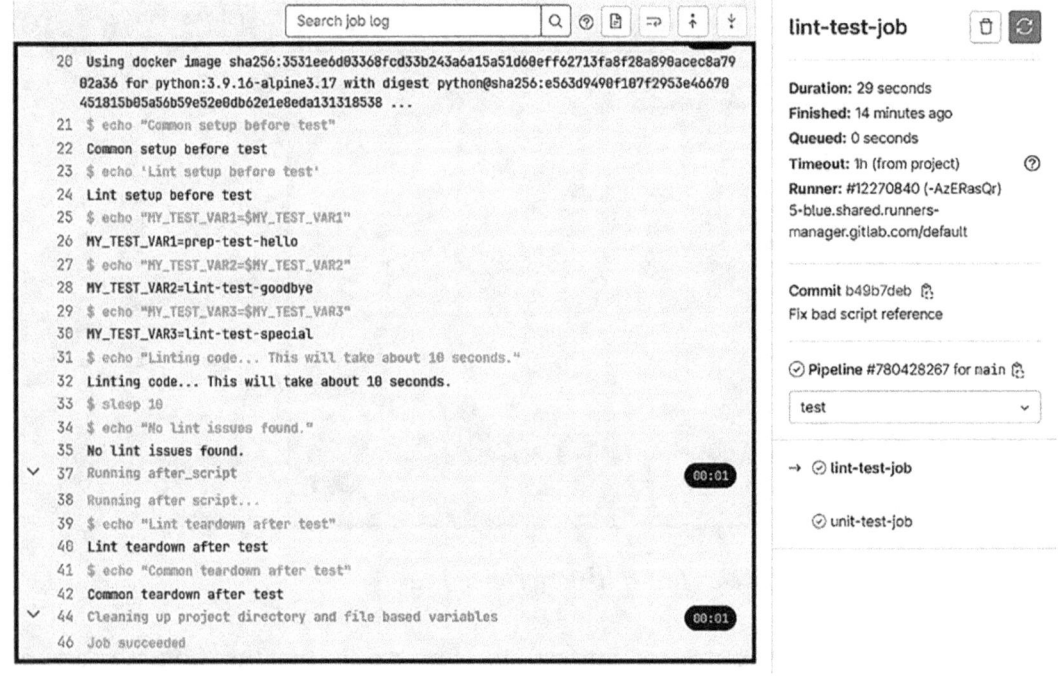

Figure 4-48. *Output of lint test with reference tags*

Finally, Figure 4-49 shows how the CI/CD editor's "Full configuration" view handles the reference tags. We see that the commands referenced by the tags are indented as sub-lists within a list. This is weird to look at but is perfectly valid YAML syntax. If you ever get confused by what commands will be executed by a job that uses extends and reference tags, the "Full configuration" view is great for clarifying things.

CHAPTER 4   BUILD, TEST, RINSE, AND REPEAT

Figure 4-49. *View of the full configuration for job with reference tags*

With the use of reference tags in this example, we see that we can easily update the common setup and teardown commands to be executed with each test and have them automatically propagate to each unit test; no copy and paste is required. Although not required here, we could have also split out the lint test setup and teardown commands into their own job similar to .common-prep and referenced them with reference tags in the same way. It's a nice way to break things down into more manageable components that can make maintenance easier.

Summary

In this chapter, we covered the basic concepts of building and testing a product that includes the following:

- Introduced the CI/CD configuration file and its overall structure
- Defined the key concepts of stages and jobs that control how a product is created as part of a build pipeline
- Learned how to use the script, before_script, and after_script keywords to specify a sequence of shell commands to be run within a job
- Covered how to use Docker images to simplify setting up a build environment with preinstalled software
- Described how to use CI/CD variables to control the building process
- Investigated different ways to modularize the CI/CD configuration file using the include and extends keywords
- Learned how to use reference tags to avoid duplicating common tasks across jobs

In the next chapter, we'll expand our discussion of CI/CD configurations by considering how to handle special conditions and failures.

CHAPTER 5

Under One Condition

So far, we've looked at how to define a pipeline via CI/CD configuration files where all jobs in all stages will be executed. There are times, however, when we may want to run a job only under certain conditions; for example, we may want to run one job when deploying to a staging environment and a different job when deploying to a production environment. Also, we may need to run cleanup jobs when a build or test failure occurs. And then there may be times when we want a job to pause awaiting some manual action to be taken, such as whether to go ahead and deploy a product to production. We'll consider all of these scenarios in this chapter.

Following the Rules

Our examples so far have dealt with static pipelines. We have defined a pipeline with four jobs: a build job, two test jobs, and a deploy job. Whenever the pipeline is triggered, either manually or when a commit is made to a branch, all jobs run in the same manner, assuming there are no failures of course. But what if we want to run the deploy job only when merged to the main branch. Or perhaps we want to run some jobs when certain files are updated; for example, if we only update the README.md file, there is no need to build code or run tests. And what if we want to override certain variables based on some condition such as running on a specific feature branch?

In other words, how do we make pipelines more dynamic? GitLab provides a number of ways to do this, some of which are deprecated.[1] In this section, we are going to focus on two of those mechanisms: rules and workflows. The basic distinction between rules and workflows is that rules control when specific jobs run and workflows control when whole pipelines run.

---

[1] Early versions of GitLab used "only" and "except" keywords to control pipelines; although these are still recognized for legacy sake, the more flexible "rules" keyword is now preferred.

CHAPTER 5   UNDER ONE CONDITION

Overview of Rules

Since workflows rely on rules, we'll consider rules first. You use the rules keyword on a job to specify a list of rules. Each rule consists of one or more conditions (with the possible exception of the last rule) along with an optional set of side effects. Conditions include the following:

- Evaluation of CI/CD variable expressions (e.g., $CI_PIPELINE_EVENT == "push")
- Changes to files
- Existence of files

The optional side effects include the following:

- Define values of one or more variables.
- Ignore job failures.

Each rule is considered in order until a match is made, at which point no further rules are considered. The conditions of each rule, if any, are evaluated to determine if the rule matches. If no rule matches, the job is "removed" from the pipeline; that is, the job will not appear in the pipeline graph and hence will not be executed.

Changing Rule Behavior with the When Keyword

So here comes the tricky part. The presence or absence of the "when" keyword in a rule determines the behavior of the rule. If the conditions of a rule are met and there is no "when" keyword associated with the rule, the job is "added" to the pipeline; that is, it will appear in the pipeline graph and will be executed at the appropriate time. If the conditions of a rule, if any, are met and there is a "when" keyword, what happens depends on the value of the keyword. Table 5-1 describes the possible values and their effects.

Table 5-1. Effects of the rule's when condition

When	Effect
on_success	Run the job if all jobs in earlier stages succeed or are allowed to fail (default)
on_failure	Run the job if at least one earlier job has failed
always	Always run the job despite the success or failures of earlier jobs
never	Never run the job; this removes the job from the pipeline
manual	Only run the job when manually triggered to do so
delayed	Special case to delay the running of a job until a later time

Note that the last rule may use the "when" keyword without any conditions. In this case, the rule acts as a catch-all rule should none of the previous rules, if any, match. If all the rules have conditions, the last rule is implicitly assumed to be when: never. If all this seems confusing to you, welcome to the club. Rules are very flexible but require some due diligence in understanding their impacts. It is not unusual to have jobs run when you did not expect them to or have jobs not run when you did expect them to.

Preparing Scripts to Explore Impacts of Rules

To help illustrate rules, I created a rule-examples branch. On that branch, I created a script directory with three bash scripts: build.sh, unit-test.sh, and deploy.sh. Figure 5-1 shows the script directory with the three files. Figure 5-2 shows the contents of the build.sh script. The other two scripts follow the same pattern replacing build references with unit-test or deploy.

CHAPTER 5 UNDER ONE CONDITION

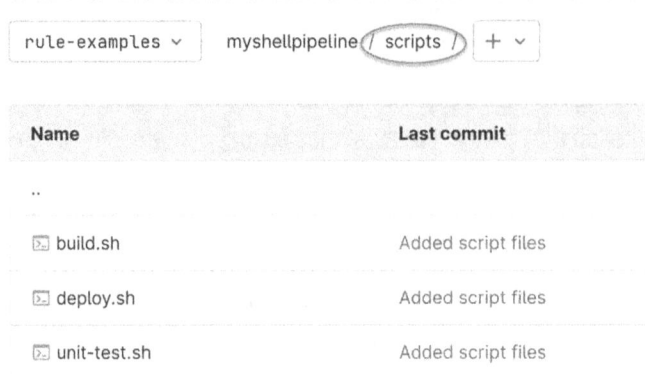

Figure 5-1. *Listing of the script directory*

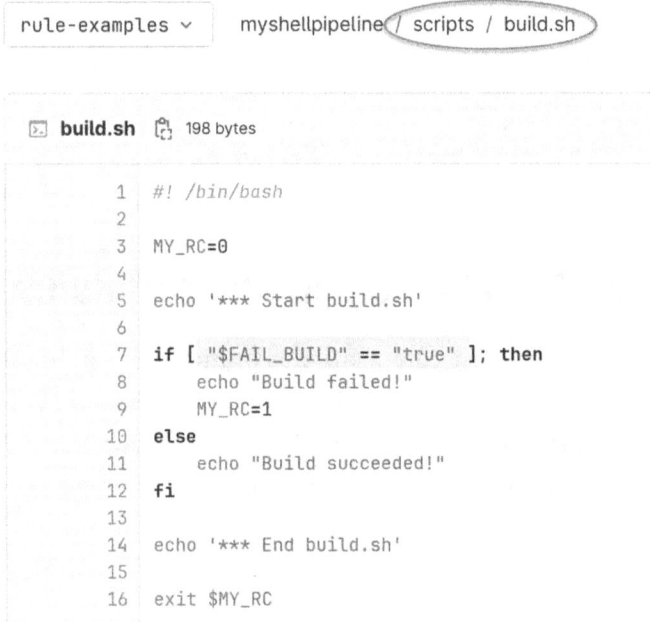

Figure 5-2. *Contents of build script*

In each of the scripts, I added a test using an environment variable to mimic success or failure of the script. The variables FAIL_BUILD, FAIL_UNIT_TEST, and FAIL_DEPLOY will be used later to test the impact of rules when jobs fail. Figure 5-3 shows the default values of these variables in the .gitlab-ci.yml file.

```
rule-examples ∨        myshellpipeline / .gitlab-ci.yml


 .gitlab-ci.yml   691 bytes
        1  stages:           # List of stages for jobs,
        2    - build
        3    - test
        4    - deploy
        5
        6  default:
        7    image: alpine:3.17
        8    before_script:
        9      - apk add bash
       10
       11  variables:
       12    FAIL_BUILD: "false"
       13    FAIL_UNIT_TEST: "false"
       14    FAIL_DEPLOY: "false"
       15    MY_VAR1: "global value 1"
       16    MY_VAR2: "global value 2"
       17    MY_VAR3: '${MY_VAR1}+${MY_VAR2}'
       18    MY_PIPELINE_VAR:
       19      description: 'Specify a value here'
```

Figure 5-3. *Updated configuration to illustrate the effect of rules*

Figure 5-4 shows the changes made to the .gitlab-build.yml file to run the scripts/build.sh file. Similar changes were made to the .gitlab-test.yml and .gitlab-deploy.yml files to run their respective scripts. Note that I marked the script files as executable[2] so that they will run in Linux without explicitly running them with bash.

---

[2] Unfortunately, it isn't possible to mark files as executable via the Web IDE. I had to create the files from a Linux command line and run chmod +x for each of them before committing and pushing the changes. If you would rather make the changes via the Web IDE, add bash before the script names in the command (e.g., bash scripts/build.sh).

CHAPTER 5   UNDER ONE CONDITION

```
rule-examples ∨    myshellpipeline / .gitlab-build.yml

 .gitlab-build.yml   580 bytes

 1   build-job:          # This job runs in the build stage, wh
 2     stage: build
 3     variables:
 4       MY_VAR2: local value 2
 5     script:
 6       - echo "MY__DB_PASSWORD='$MY_DB_PASSWORD'"
 7       - echo "MY_VAR1='${MY_VAR1}'"
 8       - echo "MY_VAR2='$MY_VAR2'"
 9       - echo "MY_VAR3='$MY_VAR3'"
10       - echo '$MY_VAR1+$MY_VAR2'
11       - echo "NOT_DEFINED_VAR='${NOT_DEFINED_VAR}'"
12       - echo "MY_PIPELINE_VAR='$MY_PIPELINE_VAR'"
13       - echo "MY_PIPELINE_CHOICE='$MY_PIPELINE_CHOICE'"
14       - cat /etc/shells
15       - echo "Compiling the code..."
16       - scripts/build.sh
17       - echo "Compile complete."
18
19
```

Figure 5-4. *Updated build job that runs the build script*

After committing and pushing these changes, Figure 5-5 shows the output of running job build-job. The unit-test-job and deploy-job jobs create similar output.

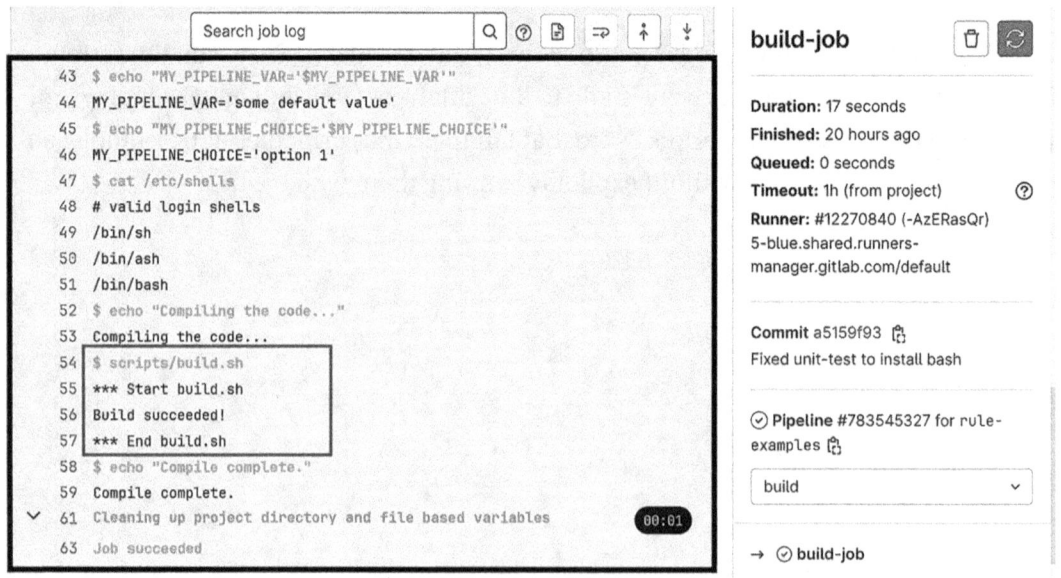

Figure 5-5. *Output of build-job running build script*

156

CHAPTER 5   UNDER ONE CONDITION

A Simple Rule Example

Before we consider rule conditions in more detail, let's create an example with a simple rule to give us a feel for how rules work. In this example, we want to change job deploy-job to only run when we are on the main branch. Figure 5-6 shows the changes needed to do that. Here, we create a condition using the predefined variable CI_COMMIT_BRANCH, which is set to the name of the branch the pipeline is running under, and the predefined variable CI_DEFAULT_BRANCH, which is set to main for our project.[3]

Figure 5-6. *Deploy job updated to only run on the main branch*

This is the simplest rule that can be created. It relies on the default when effects. If the condition is met (i.e., CI_COMMIT_BRANCH equals "main"), the default effect when: on_success is used. If the condition is not met, the default effect when: never is used. More explicitly, the rule is equivalent to the following:

```
rules:
  - if: $CI_COMMIT_BRANCH == $CI_DEFAULT_BRANCH
    when: on_success
  - when: never
```

---

[3] Older versions of GitLab used "master" as the name of the default branch. This changed around 2021 when the default branch name used by Git was switched to "main." Using CI_DEFAULT_BRANCH allows creating rules for projects that use either name. This is settable at the project level.

157

CHAPTER 5   UNDER ONE CONDITION

When we commit and push the changes on the rule-examples branch, the pipeline is run without the deploy-job as shown in the pipeline summary in Figure 5-7. Whereas before the change we had three circles for the stages of build, test, and deploy, we now only have two circles for the stages of build and test. Since deploy-job was the only job in the deploy stage and since that job was not run due to our rule, the stage itself no longer shows up in the summary.

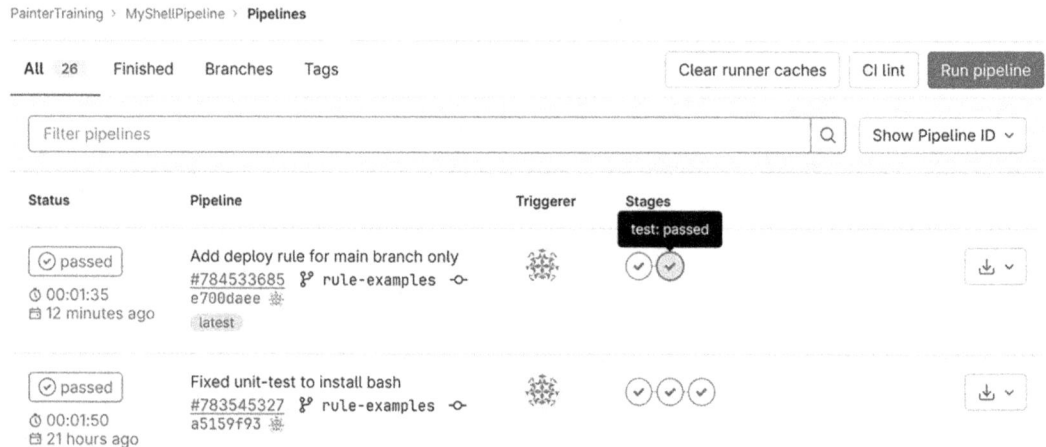

Figure 5-7. *Pipeline summary with the deploy rule in place*

We can get a clearer view of the jobs run when we switch to the pipeline's detailed view as shown in Figure 5-8. Here, we see that under the rule-examples branch, the pipeline only has three jobs. We can also see that the pipeline graph only shows the jobs run under the build and test stages; the deploy stage does not show up. This is what we mean when we say that rules make pipelines dynamic. We can determine what jobs appear and are executed based on the rules we attach to them.

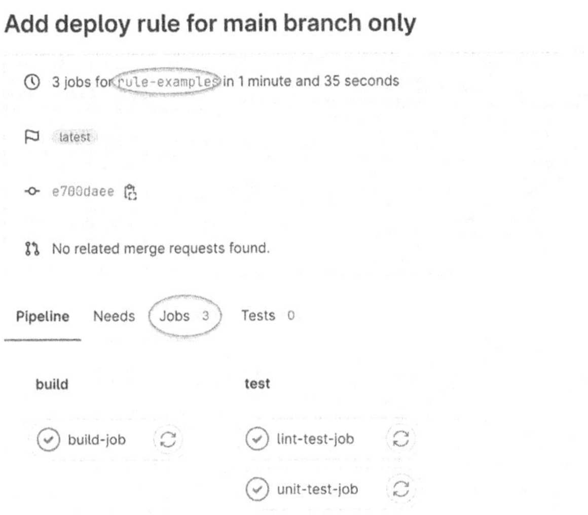

CHAPTER 5 UNDER ONE CONDITION

Figure 5-8. Pipeline detail view showing the deploy rule impact

Variable Expression Conditions

With our simple example out of the way, let's take a closer look at rule conditions, starting with the evaluation of CI/CD variable expressions. These types of expressions are pretty basic when compared to expressions in programming languages such as Python or Java since CI/CD variables only contain string values. We can group CI/CD variable expressions into the following:

- String comparisons
- Variable status tests
- Regular expression matches
- Compound expressions

String Comparisons

For string comparisons, there are only two operators: "==" and "!=". The equals operator (==) evaluates to true if both strings are the same and false otherwise. Strings must match each other by case as well, so "MyValue" and "myvalue" are not the same. The not equals operator (!=) is the opposite of the equals operator; it evaluates to true if the strings are different and false if they are equal.

159

You can specify a variable on either side (or both sides) of a string comparison. For example, $VARIABLE == "some value" and "some value" == $VARIABLE are both valid expressions. Note that the variable must be in the form $VARIABLE; you cannot use the forms ${VARIABLE} or %VARIABLE%.[4] Although the .gitlab-ci.yml reference does not state so, you can also compare two string values (e.g., "true" == "false"); however, this normally does not make much sense unless you are doing some debugging work to force the comparison to always be true or false.

Variable Status Tests

Variable status tests are used to determine if a variable is defined or not, if a variable has a value or not, and if a variable is defined and not empty. Table 5-2 describes the various status tests.

Table 5-2. Variable status tests

Status Test Expression	Meaning
$VARIABLE == null	Variable does not exist
$VARIABLE != null	Variable does exist (may or may not be empty)
$VARIABLE == ""	Variable is defined and empty
$VARIABLE != ""	Variable is defined and not empty
$VARIABLE	Variable is defined and not empty

Regular Expression Matches

Regular expression matches test the contents of a variable to see if they match (=~) or not match (!~) a regular expression (a.k.a. regex). A regular expression is enclosed in slashes (e.g., /regex/). Matches are case sensitive but may be made case insensitive by appending "i" after the regex (e.g., /regex/i). The variable to be tested must appear before the regex operator "=~" or "!~"; the regular expression must appear after the regex

---

[4] Nothing like inconsistency with variable forms. This may trip you up if you are used to using the form ${VARIABLE} elsewhere in the CI/CD configuration file.

operator. Note that the regular expression may be stored in a variable and appear after the regex operator; for example, $VARIABLE =~ $REGEX, where $REGEX is a value in the form /regex/.

Regular expression matches are commonly used with CI_COMMIT_BRANCH and CI_COMMIT_TAG variables. For example, $CI_COMMIT_BRANCH =~ /^feature.*/i will evaluate to true if a commit branch name starts with feature, Feature, FEATURE, etc. The caret character (^) at the start of the regex means that the branch must start with the value. If you remove it, feature can occur anywhere within the branch name.

Compound Expressions

Compound expressions are simply combinations of CI/CD variable expressions joined by the "and" operator (&&) or the "or" operator (||) so that multiple conditions can be evaluated. For example, $MY_VAR1 == "abc" && $MY_VAR2 == "def" evaluates to true if both MY_VAR1 has value "abc" and MY_VAR2 has value "def." If you replace && with ||, the expression evaluates to true if either MY_VAR1 has value "abc" or MY_VAR2 has value "def."

If you have a compound expression with multiple && and || operators, the && conditions are evaluated before the || conditions. For example, $MY_VAR1 == "abc" || $MY_VAR2 == "def" && $MY_VAR3 == "123" evaluates to true if MY_VAR2 is "def" and MY_VAR3 is "123" or if MY_VAR1 is "abc." You can explicitly change the order of evaluation by using parentheses. For example, ($MY_VAR1 == "abc" || $MY_VAR2 == "def") && $MY_VAR3 == "123" evaluates to true if either MY_VAR1 is "abc" or MY_VAR2 is "def" and MY_VAR3 is "123."

Common Predefined Variables Used in Rules

For CI/CD variable expressions, you can obviously test your own defined variables. More commonly, GitLab predefined variables are used with rules. The most common predefined variables used in rules are CI_COMMIT_BRANCH (as was illustrated earlier) and CI_PIPELINE_SOURCE. The CI_PIPELINE_SOURCE variable essentially tells you how the pipeline was started. It is set to one of a wide set of values. The most interesting ones for our current purposes are push, merge_request_event, and web.

The CI_PIPELINE_SOURCE is set to "push" whenever we do a git push event. When we run a pipeline manually (using the "Run pipeline" button) via the GitLab web interface, CI_PIPELINE_SOURCE is set to "web." Finally, when we create or update a

CHAPTER 5   UNDER ONE CONDITION

merge request, CI_PIPELINE_SOURCE is set to "merge_request_event." After adding some debug printout of key predefined variables, Figure 5-9 shows the results when a push was made to the rule-examples branch, and Figure 5-10 shows the results when running the pipeline manually.

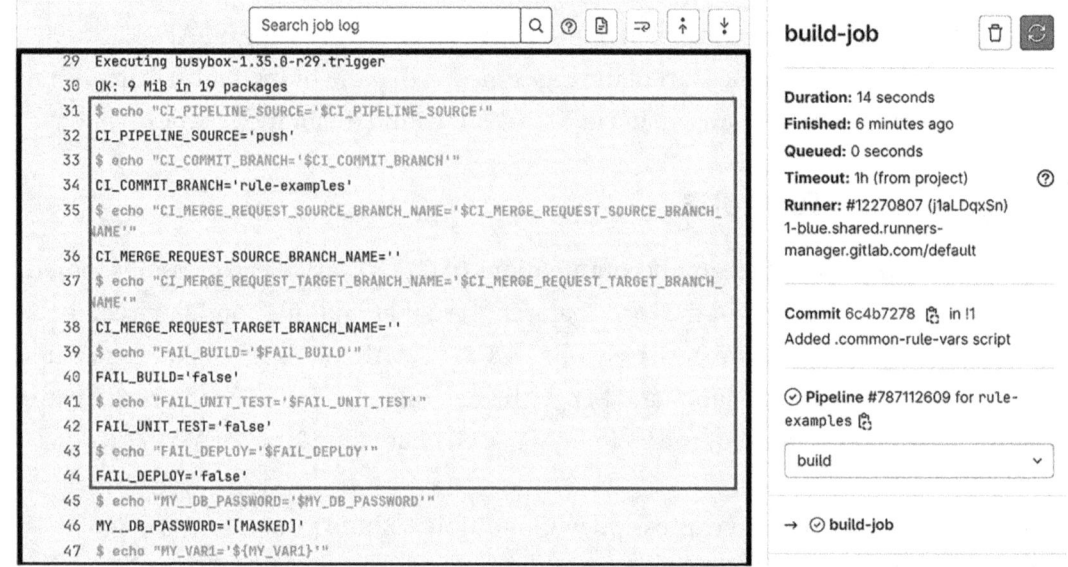

Figure 5-9. *Values of key predefined variables on push event*

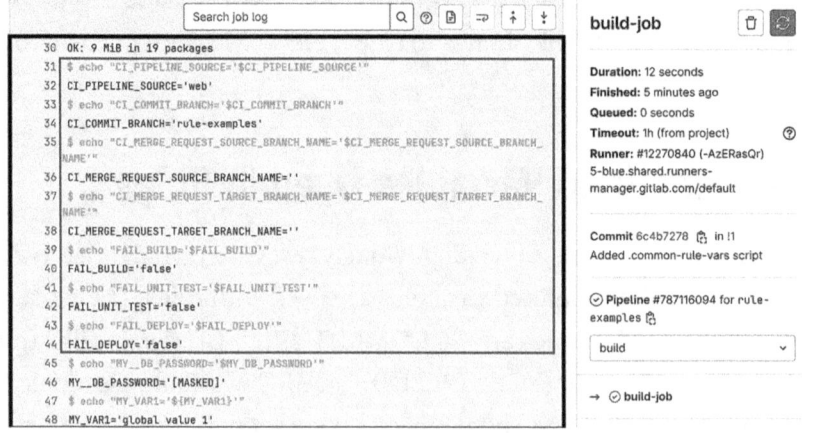

Figure 5-10. *Values of key predefined variables on web event*

CHAPTER 5　UNDER ONE CONDITION

Example Rules with CI_PIPELINE_SOURCE

To explore rules using CI_PIPELINE_SOURCE, let's create deploy-dev-job that runs in a branch that is not main. Let's also set it up so that it doesn't run when we run the pipeline manually. Figure 5-11 shows the update to the .gitlab-deploy.yml file that accomplishes that. The first rule for deploy-dev-job checks to see if we are running the pipeline manually; if so, exclude the job from the pipeline. The second rule enables the job if we are not running on the main branch.

```
    Add deploy-dev-job
    Jeff Painter authored 8 minutes ago

    .gitlab-deploy.yml    619 bytes
 1  deploy-job:
 2    stage: deploy
 3    environment: production
 4    rules:
 5      - if: $CI_COMMIT_BRANCH == $CI_DEFAULT_BRANCH
 6    script:
 7      - !reference [.common-rule-vars, script]
 8      - echo "Deploying application..."
 9      - scripts/deploy.sh
10      - echo "Application successfully deployed."
11
12  deploy-dev-job:
13    stage: deploy
14    environment: dev
15    rules:
16      - if: $CI_PIPELINE_SOURCE == "web"
17        when: never
18      - if: $CI_COMMIT_BRANCH != $CI_DEFAULT_BRANCH
19    script:
20      - !reference [.common-rule-vars, script]
21      - echo "Deploying dev application..."
22      - scripts/deploy.sh
23      - echo "Dev application successfully deployed."
24
```

Figure 5-11. *New deploy-dev-job to run only on non-main branches*

Figure 5-12 shows the pipelines created when I pushed the changes and when I ran the pipeline manually. The top pipeline shows the results when I ran the pipeline manually; it displays two circles for the build and test stages as expected. The bottom two pipelines show the results when I pushed the changes to the rule-examples branch. The bottom pipeline displays all three circles for the build, test, and deploy stages as expected. The middle pipeline, which also ran when I pushed the changes, shows one circle representing the deploy stage. That's something that was unexpected. Why did this pipeline run? The key is the "merge request" tag as highlighted in the figure.

CHAPTER 5   UNDER ONE CONDITION

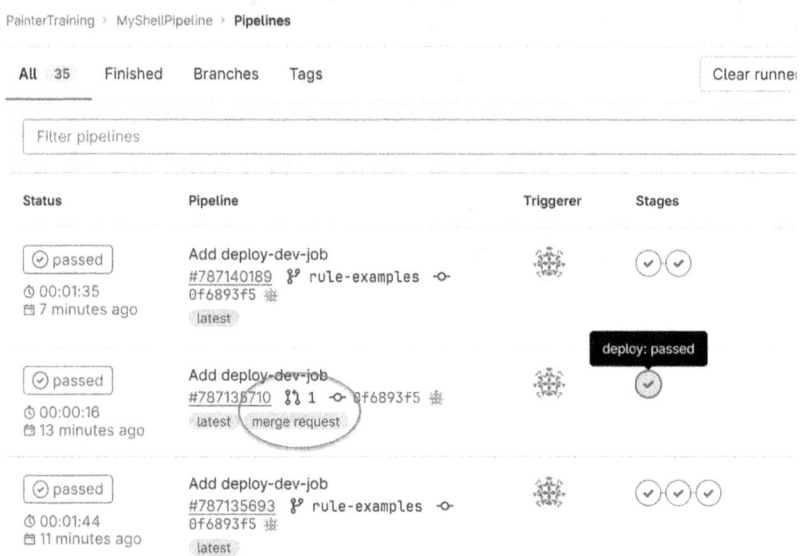

Figure 5-12.   Pipeline run summary with deploy-dev-job

So, let's do some debugging to get a better picture of what is happening. Figure 5-13 shows the results of deploy-dev-job associated with the bottom pipeline. It shows CI_PIPELINE_SOURCE as "push" and CI_COMMIT_BRANCH as "rule-examples." Given this information, we see that the second rule for deploy-dev-job enabled the running of this job; the first rule did not match since CI_PIPELINE_SOURCE is "push," not "web." So far, so good.

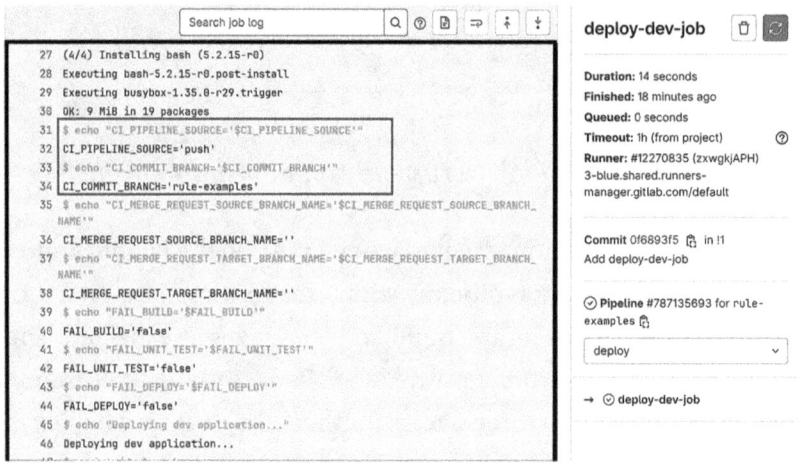

Figure 5-13.   Output of deploy-dev-job upon push event

CHAPTER 5   UNDER ONE CONDITION

Going to the manually run pipeline, Figure 5-14 shows the detailed pipeline graph. Note that the pipeline ID here matches the pipeline ID of the top pipeline in the summary page, which was the pipeline run manually. Here, we see that deploy-dev-job did not run. This is because the first rule for deploy-dev-job matched CI_PIPELINE_SOURCE of "web"; since this rule had when: never, the job was not added to the pipeline.

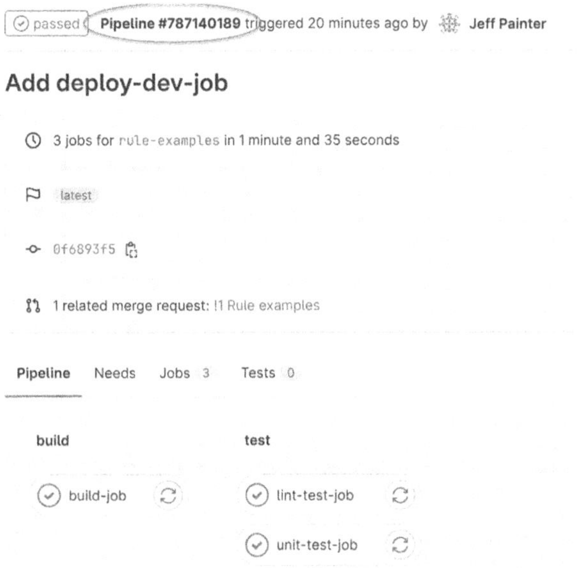

Figure 5-14. Pipeline summary of deploy-dev-job upon web event

Now to unravel the mystery of the middle pipeline. Figure 5-15 shows the output of deploy-dev-job for this pipeline. We see that CI_PIPELINE_SOURCE has the value "merge_request_event" and that CI_COMMIT_BRANCH has no value. For merge requests, there are two branches: the source and the target. We can see this in the values of CI_MERGE_REQUEST_SOURCE_BRANCH and CI_MERGE_REQUEST_TARGET_BRANCH set to rule-examples and main, respectively. The reason deploy-dev-job ran is because of its second rule: CI_COMMIT_BRANCH is not "main."

Figure 5-15. Output of deploy-dev-job upon merge request event

Branch Pipelines vs. Merge Request Pipelines

At this point, you may be thinking, OK, I see now why deploy-dev-job ran, but why didn't any of the build or test jobs run for this pipeline? This is one of the confusing things about pipelines and rules. According to the GitLab documentation, there are two types of pipelines: branch pipelines and merge request pipelines. Branch pipelines are those that respond to push events, and merge request pipelines respond to merge request events. You should only have one or the other type of pipeline for a project, but the way rules work, you actually have both simultaneously unless you define a workflow to pick the one you desire. We'll talk about workflows later in this section.

The reason the build or test jobs did not run is because they don't have any explicit rules; they rely on implicit rules. When you are on a branch that has an open merge request and you push a change, two events trigger a pipeline: push and merge_request_event. The push event triggers the branch pipeline, and the merge_request_event triggers its own merge request pipeline. Without a workflow defined, a job that does not use rules will implicitly ignore the merge request event. As soon as you set up rules for a job, the implicit rule no longer applies, and the merge_request_event can trigger a merge request pipeline unless you explicitly prevent it.

Figure 5-16 shows how to fix this problem using rules. By adding "$CI_COMMIT_BRANCH &&" to the second rule, we rule out the case when CI_COMMIT_BRANCH is empty. Figure 5-17 shows that only one pipeline is triggered as we originally expected.

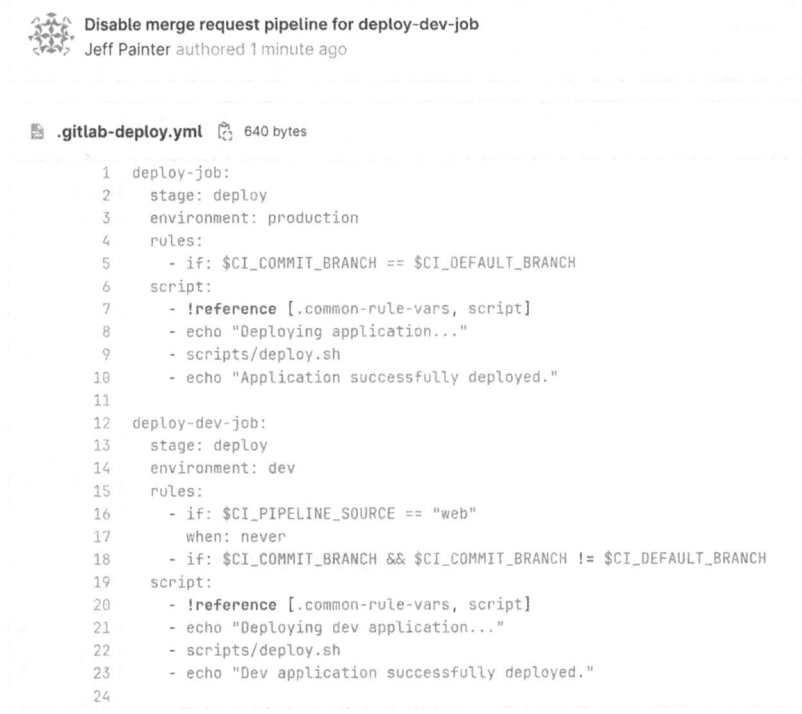

Figure 5-16. *Fix to deploy-dev-job*

Chapter 5   Under One Condition

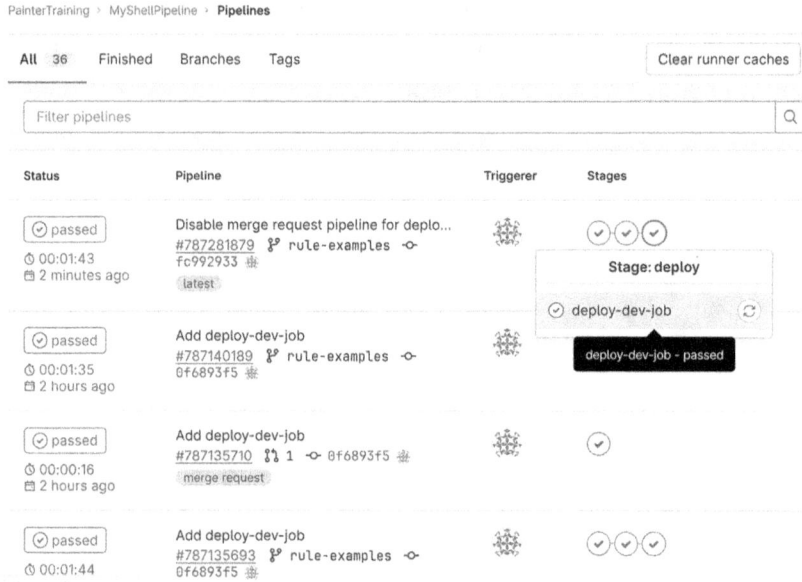

Figure 5-17.   Pipeline summary with deploy-dev-job fix in place

Working with Workflows

Before we consider the file-based rule conditions, this is a good point in time to discuss workflows. If you look into the .gitlab-ci.yml guide, you'll notice that rules are not allowed in the default section nor as a top-level section of its own as you might expect. Instead, the top-level workflow keyword is used to define a set of rules that apply to pipelines in general as opposed to specific jobs. Rules in the workflow section work in conjunction with rules defined in specific jobs; that is, rules for specific jobs do not override rules defined in the workflow section. This is one reason why rules do not appear in the default section.

A workflow can have an optional name along with a required rules section. Rules in a workflow are similar to those used in a specific job with some exceptions. The "when" option can only have the values always or never. Also, you cannot use the "allow_failure" option in a workflow rule. The main use case for a workflow is to restrict a pipeline to be either a branch pipeline or a merge request pipeline. This simplifies having to put in specific rules as we did in deploy-dev-job earlier to prevent duplicate pipelines from triggering.

GitLab has defined a couple of templates that make it easy to select a branch pipeline or a merge request pipeline. You can find the definitions for these templates here: https://gitlab.com/gitlab-org/gitlab/-/tree/master/lib/gitlab/ci/templates/ Workflows. You select the specific template using the "include" keyword. Figure 5-18 shows the changes to the .gitlab-ci.yml file that includes this template.

```
23          value: 'option 1'
24        options:
25          - "option 1"
26          - "option 2"
27          - "option 3"
28
29    .common-rule-vars:
30      script:
31        - echo "CI_PIPELINE_SOURCE='$CI_PIPELINE_SOURCE'"
32        - echo "CI_COMMIT_BRANCH='$CI_COMMIT_BRANCH'"
33        - echo "CI_MERGE_REQUEST_SOURCE_BRANCH_NAME='$CI_MERGE_REQUEST_SOURCE_BRANCH_NAME'"
34        - echo "CI_MERGE_REQUEST_TARGET_BRANCH_NAME='$CI_MERGE_REQUEST_TARGET_BRANCH_NAME'"
35        - echo "FAIL_BUILD='$FAIL_BUILD'"
36        - echo "FAIL_UNIT_TEST='$FAIL_UNIT_TEST'"
37        - echo "FAIL_DEPLOY='$FAIL_DEPLOY'"
38
39    include:
40      - template: 'Workflows/Branch-Pipelines.gitlab-ci.yml'
41      - local: .gitlab-build.yml
42      - local: .gitlab-test.yml
43      - local: .gitlab-deploy.yml
44
```

Figure 5-18. *Updated job with workflow template*

With this change in place, Figure 5-19 shows the change to deploy-dev-job that reverts the change we made earlier. Since the workflow restricts pipelines to branch pipelines and disables merge request pipelines, we no longer need the "CI_COMMIT_BRANCH &&" test. Figure 5-20 shows that after pushing the change "Use Branch Pipeline Workflow," only the branch pipeline is run. Note that with this workflow in place, we can still run the job manually as before.

CHAPTER 5   UNDER ONE CONDITION

Figure 5-19. Simplification to deploy-dev-job with workflow template in place

CHAPTER 5   UNDER ONE CONDITION

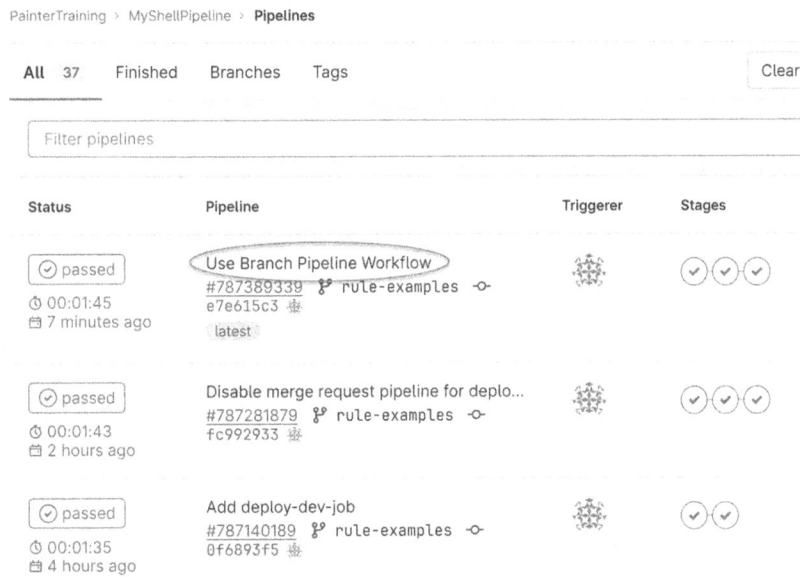

Figure 5-20.   Pipeline summary with workflow template in place

Interactions Between Workflows and Rules

You might be wondering which set of rules is applied first, the workflow rules or the job-specific rules. The answer turns out to be neither. If the workflow rules were applied first in our example, the deploy-dev-job would run on any commit, ignoring our rule to restrict it to working branches. If the job-specific rules were applied first, we would be back to running deploy-dev-job on a merge request, ignoring the workflow rule to only run when CI_COMMIT_BRANCH is defined.

So how, then, do workflow rules work with job-specific rules? The best way to explain it is that the workflow rules are applied first. When a workflow rule matches, the job-specific rules are then applied; if no workflow rule matches, the job for that pipeline type is removed. To think of it another way, both a workflow rule and a job-specific rule must match for a job to be executed.

File-Based Rule Conditions

Let's switch gears now from variable-based rule conditions to file-based rule conditions. There are two types of file-based conditions: changes and exists. You specify these conditions using the changes and exists keywords, respectively, for a given rule.

171

They are used with branch or merge request pipelines where changes are pushed (i.e., when CI_PIPELINE_SOURCE is push or merge_request_event); they are ignored for other types of pipelines such as manually run pipelines (i.e., CI_PIPELINE_SOURCE is web) or scheduled pipelines (i.e., CI_PIPELINE_SOURCE is schedule).

The changes condition, as its name implies, restricts the running of jobs based on file changes, whether a file is created or updated. This typically includes changes made in a working branch with respect to the main branch, although you can change the reference to a different branch or tag reference.

The exists condition is based on whether a file exists or not. This may seem like an odd condition to use given that you can see if a file exists, but it is useful for rules that are part of a template used by multiple projects. It is also useful for jobs that rely on generated artifacts, which we'll talk about later in this chapter.

Considerations When Using File-Based Conditions

On the surface, file-based conditions look relatively straightforward to use. You list a set of files to monitor and, based on the condition, decide whether the job should be executed or removed from the pipeline. But careful thought must be taken when considering whether file-based conditions should be used. For example, if you put some file-based conditions on the build job to only run when certain files are updated, you have to consider the implications on later stages such as test jobs. If you don't build something, what then are you testing and/or deploying?

File-based conditions are basically an optimization consideration to reduce what has to be built, tested, and/or deployed. In my experience, these are best used to weed out unnecessary tests. For example, if you know that a unit test is only useful if the test and the source files related to that test are changed, then it may be safe to not run that test. But again, you have to be careful. What if a new file comes along that would impact the test and you don't update the changes condition to run the test for that new file? You might miss an important failure had you not run the test. In other words, when using file-based conditions, you need to be due diligent every time you make changes that those conditions are still valid.

Example of Rules Using File-Based Conditions

With that said, let's look at an example using the changes condition. For this example, I went ahead and merged the changes from the rule-examples branch into main and created a new branch called file-rule-examples so that we have a clean slate in terms of file changes. Figure 5-21 shows the pipelines that ran when I did the merge followed by creating the new branch. For the merge, you'll see that the branch pipeline ran for main and executed the deploy-job as expected. For the test-rules-examples branch, you can see that the branch pipeline was run on it right away. This is the standard behavior of branch pipelines. It happened because there was a push event on the test-rule-examples pipeline.[5]

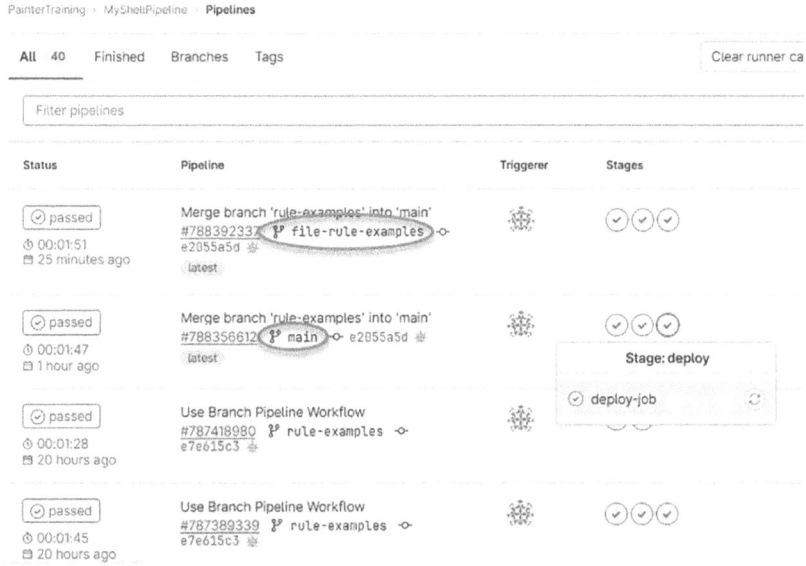

Figure 5-21. *Pipeline summary after merge followed by new branch creation*

Now suppose we want to run the unit-test-job only when there are changes to either build.sh or test.sh. Figure 5-22 shows the changes made to unit-test-job to accomplish this. Note that we only need the changes condition under rules; in this case, we did not need any variable-based conditions, although we could have if we wanted to.

---

[5] One reason teams use merge request workflows instead of branch workflows is to reduce the number of pipelines run. If you create a branch without creating a merge request, no pipeline would have run. This allows you to commit changes to the branch without triggering pipeline runs until you are ready to create the merge request.

CHAPTER 5 UNDER ONE CONDITION

```
17     script:
18       - echo "MY_TEST_VAR1=$MY_TEST_VAR1"
19       - echo "MY_TEST_VAR2=$MY_TEST_VAR2"
20
21   unit-test-job:
22     extends: .prep-test
23     rules:
24       - changes:
25           - scripts/build.sh
26           - scripts/unit-test.sh
27     script:
28       - !reference [.common-rule-vars, script]
29       - echo "Running unit tests... This will take about 60 seconds."
30       - !reference [.common-tests, script]
31       - scripts/unit-test.sh
32       - sleep 60
33       - echo "Code coverage is 90%"
34
```

Figure 5-22. *File-based rule changes for the unit test*

Figure 5-23 shows the results after pushing this change to .gitlab-test.yml. As we can see, unit-test-job was excluded from the pipeline since we did not make any changes to build.sh or test.sh. Had we made changes to either file, the unit-test-job would have been executed. I leave that up to you to verify that last statement if you want.

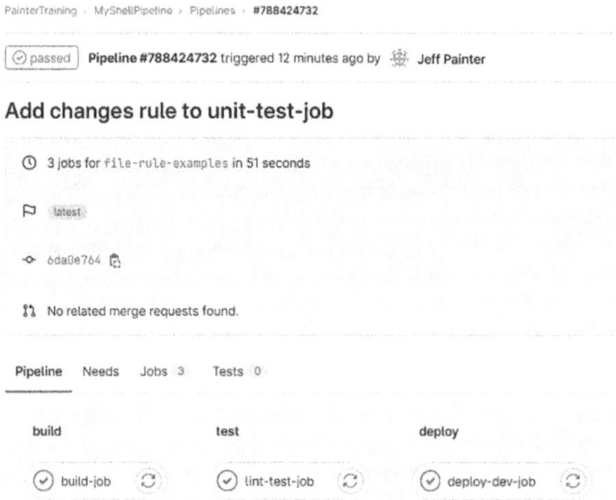

Figure 5-23. *Pipeline results with file-based rules in place*

One question you might have is "what happens when you run the pipeline manually?" Since we did not change either build.sh or test.sh, would unit-test-job still be removed from the pipeline? Figure 5-24 shows the results of manually running the pipeline after making the preceding changes. As you can see, unit-test-job did run in this case. This is what the warning in the rules:changes section (https://docs.gitlab.com/ee/ci/yaml/#ruleschanges) is trying to tell you in case you weren't quite sure what they were getting at. If you don't want unit-test-job to execute when you manually run the pipeline, you will need to put in an explicit rule before the changes rule to do that just like we did with deploy-dev-job.

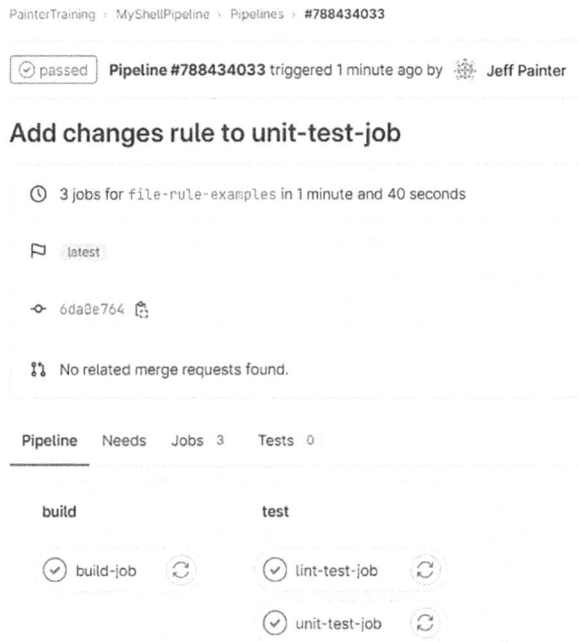

Figure 5-24. Manual run results with file-based rules in place

Overriding Variables Within a Rule

Now that we've investigated rule conditions, let's look at rule side effects, in particular the variables side effect. You use the variables keyword in rules to override a variable based on a condition, such as running a pipeline manually or running on a particular branch. Figure 5-25 shows a rule added to lint-test-job that overrides the MY_TEST_VAR3 variable when running the pipeline manually. Note the final when: on_success rule that allows other pipelines to still be enabled; without it, lint-test-job would only run for manual pipelines.

CHAPTER 5   UNDER ONE CONDITION

```
31        - scripts/unit-test.sh
32        - sleep 60
33        - echo "Code coverage is 90%"
34
35    lint-test-job:
36      extends: .prep-test
37      variables:
38        MY_TEST_VAR2: 'lint-test-goodbye'
39        MY_TEST_VAR3: 'lint-test-special'
40      rules:
41        - if: $CI_PIPELINE_SOURCE == "web"
42          variables:
43            MY_TEST_VAR3: 'lint-test-web'
44        - when: on_success
45      before_script:
46        - !reference [.common-prep, before_script]
47        - echo 'Lint setup before test'
48      script:
49        - !reference [.common-rule-vars, script]
50        - !reference [.common-tests, script]
51        - echo "MY_TEST_VAR3=$MY_TEST_VAR3"
52        - echo "Linting code... This will take about 10 seconds."
53        - sleep 10
54        - echo "No lint issues found."
55      after_script:
56        - echo "Lint teardown after test"
57        - !reference [.common-prep, after_script]
58
```

Figure 5-25. *Overriding variable values based on rules*

Figure 5-26 shows the results of running lint-test-job on a branch pipeline when a push event is received. As you can see, the value of MY_TEST_VAR3 is the job default of "lint-test-special."

CHAPTER 5   UNDER ONE CONDITION

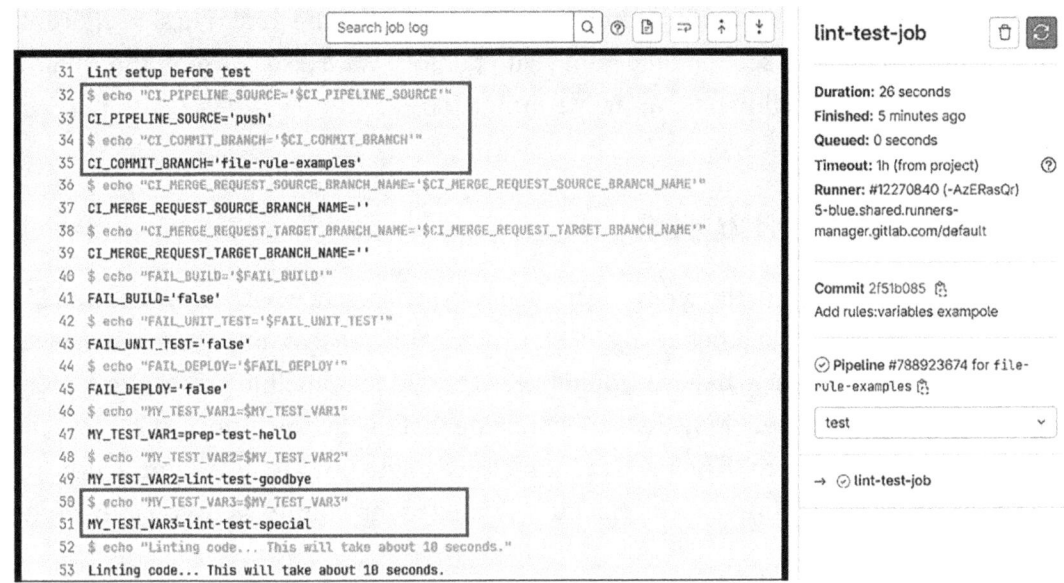

Figure 5-26. *Result of rule-based variable override after push*

Figure 5-27 shows the results of lint-test-job when the pipeline is run manually. As you can see here, MY_TEST_VAR3 is set to the rules value of lint-test-web. You can have different variables set based on different rule conditions, which is useful for debugging and such tasks as turning features on or off.

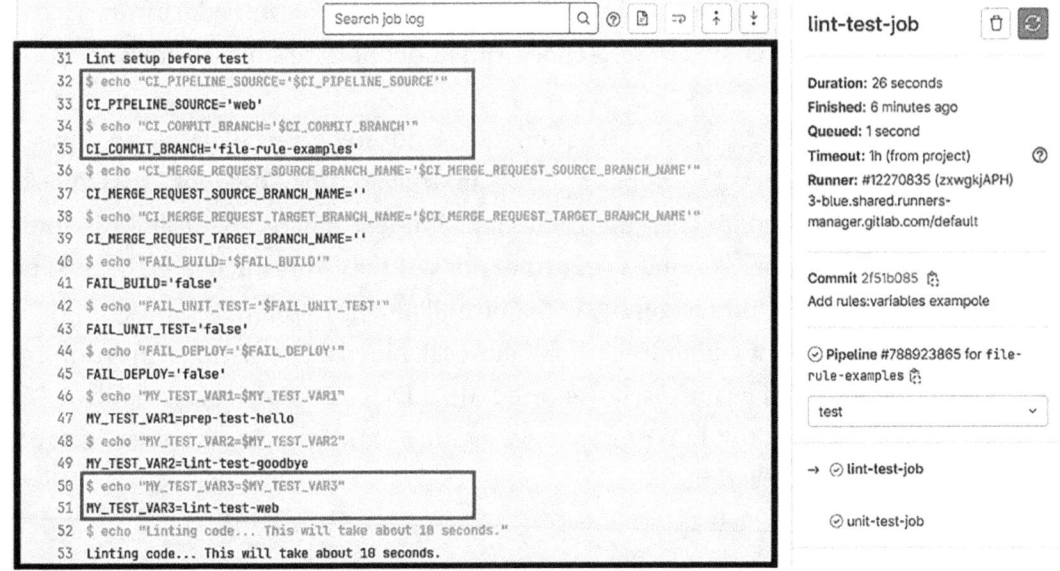

Figure 5-27. *Result of rule-based variable override running job manually*

177

This ends our current discussion on rules. We'll consider the final rule side effect of allow_failure in the next section on dealing with failures. We'll also consider the when: manual mode in the section on manually running jobs.

Dealing with Failures

When job failures happen, the typical response is to investigate what caused the issue, check in a fix, and run the pipeline again, continuing this process until the job succeeds. There are times, however, when we would like, as part of the pipeline process, to handle failures differently. In some cases, we might decide that the failure is not critical and can be safely ignored for the time being. Other times, we might need to take some action after a job failure to perform special cleanups related to the failure. We'll consider both cases in this section.

Preparing an Example to Test Job Failures

Let's first take a look at lint-test-job. For those unfamiliar with lint, it is a programming language–specific tool that performs a static analysis of your code and provides a list of warnings and errors it discovered. Some of the things a lint tool looks at are coding style violations based on a set of best-practice rules; for example, it might warn that a constant name is not in uppercase as expected. The lint tool also looks for potential errors such as code that cannot be executed or reference to an undefined variable (usually due to a misspelling of a variable name).

The lint tool for a given programming language tends to be very picky about things. It is not unusual to get tens of warnings or errors for a given run of the tool, especially for a newly written piece of code. This can result in the lint-test-job frequently failing. Some teams consider this "noise." As long as there are not serious errors uncovered by the lint tool, ignoring failure may be acceptable in the overall pipeline chain.

In order to experiment with lint-test-job failures, I added a new scripts/lint-test.sh script similar to the other scripts; it uses the FAIL_LINT_TEST variable to control whether the lint-test.sh script fails or succeeds. Figure 5-28 shows the one-line change to lint-test-job that calls the script.

CHAPTER 5　UNDER ONE CONDITION

```
35   lint-test-job:
36     extends: .prep-test
37     variables:
38       MY_TEST_VAR2: 'lint-test-goodbye'
39       MY_TEST_VAR3: 'lint-test-special'
40     rules:
41       - if: $CI_PIPELINE_SOURCE == "web"
42         variables:
43           MY_TEST_VAR3: 'lint-test-web'
44       - when: on_success
45     before_script:
46       - !reference [.common-prep, before_script]
47       - echo 'Lint setup before test'
48     script:
49       - !reference [.common-rule-vars, script]
50       - !reference [.common-tests, script]
51       - echo "MY_TEST_VAR3=$MY_TEST_VAR3"
52       - echo "Linting code... This will take about 10 seconds."
53       - scripts/lint-test.sh
54       - sleep 10
55       - echo "No lint issues found."
56     after_script:
57       - echo "Lint teardown after test"
58       - !reference [.common-prep, after_script]
59
```

Figure 5-28. *Update to lint test to illustrate failure handling*

With these changes in place, let's run the pipeline to force lint-test-job to fail to see how the pipeline normally reacts with failures. Figure 5-29 shows how to run the pipeline with FAIL_LINT_TEST set to true. Figure 5-30 shows the results of running that pipeline.

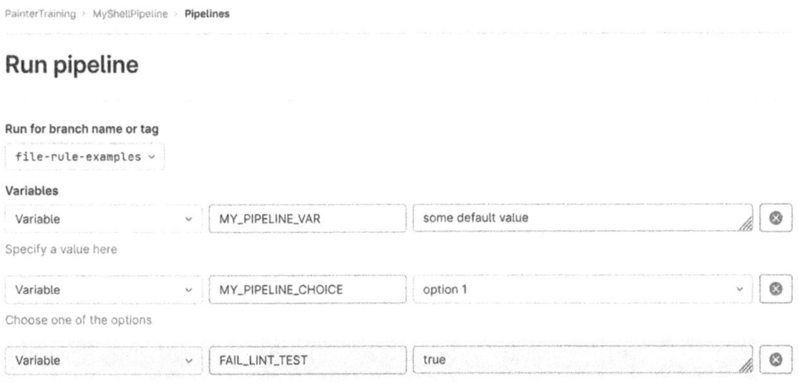

Figure 5-29. *Pipeline run to force lint test failure*

CHAPTER 5   UNDER ONE CONDITION

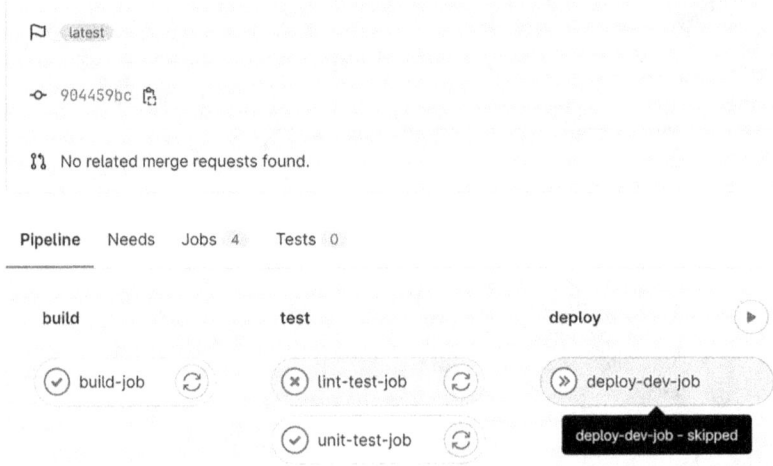

Figure 5-30. Pipeline result with lint test failure

In this pipeline, we see that the failed lint-test-job has a red circled X-icon next to it representing failure. In addition, we see that deploy-dev-job has been "skipped," letting us know that it was not able to be executed because of the failure. This is the normal behavior of failed jobs; it prevents jobs in future stages from being executed. This makes sense since we don't want to deploy if there are any outstanding errors. Because of the job failure, the pipeline itself has been marked as failed.

Ignoring a Job Failure

One reaction some teams have when confronted with persistent "noisy" failures is to remove the job or comment it out by turning it into a hidden job that never gets executed. Given that the test job has some value in running, disabling it, even temporarily to get a product deployed, is not the best option. GitLab provides an option that allows us to run the job and ignore the failure, allowing future jobs to still run. In this way, you get notified of a problem that can be investigated later, creating issues as needed to fix the problems.

Figure 5-31 shows the one-line change to enable ignoring failures. By simply adding allow_failure: true to the job, we allow the job to fail without stopping the pipeline from running future staged jobs. With this change in place, running the pipeline again with FAIL_LINT_TEST set to true results in the pipeline shown in Figure 5-32.

```
34
35  lint-test-job:
36    extends: .prep-test
37    variables:
38      MY_TEST_VAR2: 'lint-test-goodbye'
39      MY_TEST_VAR3: 'lint-test-special'
40    rules:
41      - if: $CI_PIPELINE_SOURCE == "web"
42        variables:
43          MY_TEST_VAR3: 'lint-test-web'
44      - when: on_success
45    allow_failure: true
46    before_script:
47      - !reference [.common-prep, before_script]
48      - echo 'Lint setup before test'
49    script:
50      - !reference [.common-rule-vars, script]
51      - !reference [.common-tests, script]
52      - echo "MY_TEST_VAR3=$MY_TEST_VAR3"
53      - echo "Linting code... This will take about 10 seconds."
54      - scripts/lint-test.sh
55      - sleep 10
56      - echo "No lint issues found."
57    after_script:
58      - echo "Lint teardown after test"
59      - !reference [.common-prep, after_script]
60
```

Figure 5-31. Update to lint test to ignore failure

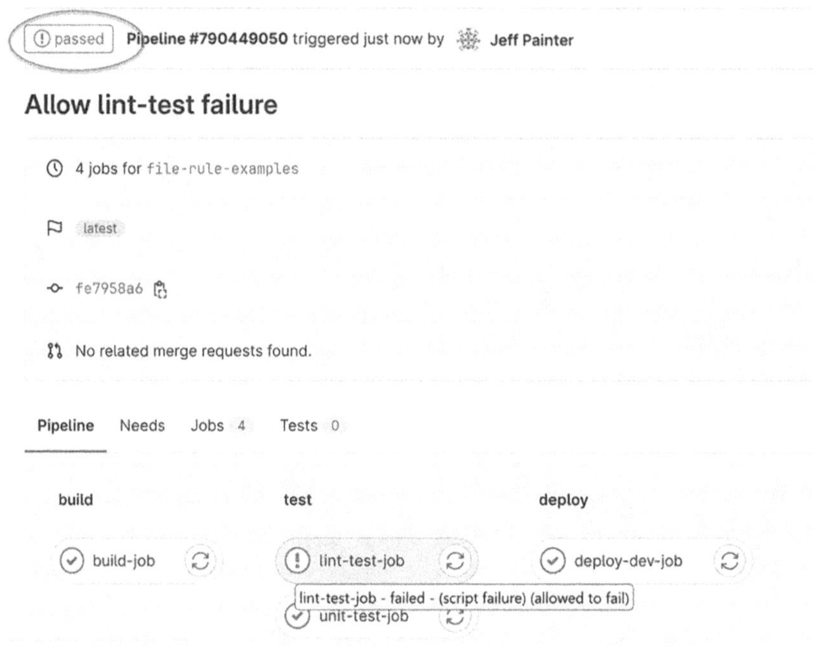

CHAPTER 5   UNDER ONE CONDITION

Figure 5-32. Pipeline result with ignore failure in place

This time, we see that lint-test-job has an exclamation icon next to it; this tells us that lint-test-job has failed but was allowed to fail, as the pop-up message indicates. Since there were no other failures in the test stage, we see that deploy-dev-job was run successfully. Also, note that the pipeline itself passed but also has the exclamation icon next to it. This lets us know when looking at the pipeline summary that something failed but was ignored and should be investigated.

Conditionally Ignoring a Job Failure

Now there may be times when we want to allow failures but under certain conditions, such as running manually. For these cases, you can use the allow_failure: keyword as part of a rule as shown in Figure 5-33. Here, we added a rule to allow failures only when we manually run the pipeline with the FAIL_UNIT_TEST variable set to true. In all other cases, if unit-test-job fails, the pipeline fails normally. Figure 5-34 shows the results of running the pipeline manually with FAIL_UNIT_TEST set to true.

CHAPTER 5 UNDER ONE CONDITION

```
17    script:
18      - echo "MY_TEST_VAR1=$MY_TEST_VAR1"
19      - echo "MY_TEST_VAR2=$MY_TEST_VAR2"
20
21  unit-test-job:
22    extends: .prep-test
23    rules:
24      - if: $CI_PIPELINE_SOURCE == "web" && $FAIL_UNIT_TEST == "true"
25        allow_failure: true
26      - when: on_success
27    script:
28      - !reference [.common-rule-vars, script]
29      - echo "Running unit tests... This will take about 60 seconds."
30      - !reference [.common-tests, script]
31      - scripts/unit-test.sh
32      - sleep 60
33      - echo "Code coverage is 90%"
34
35  lint-test-job:
36    extends: .prep-test
37    variables:
```

Figure 5-33. Unit test update to allow failure when job run manually

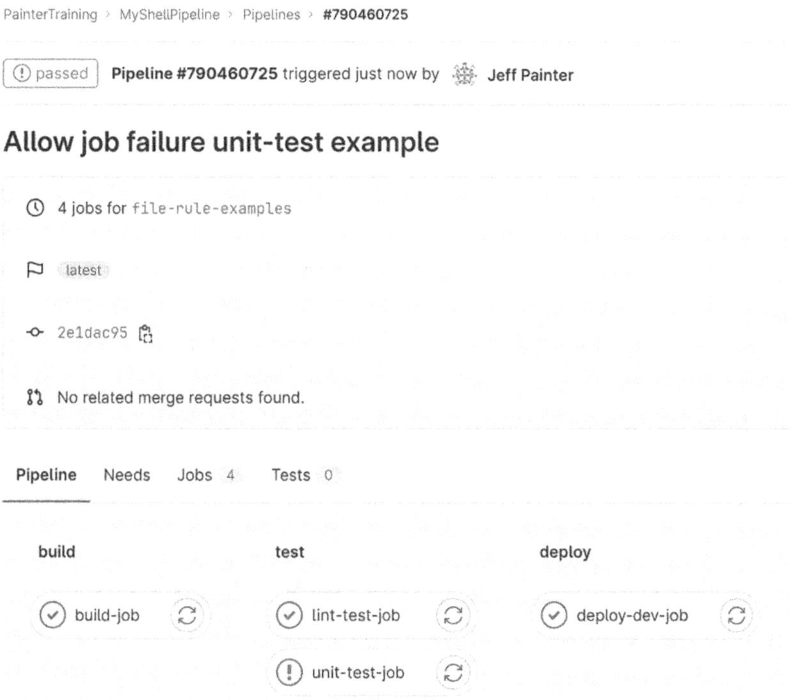

Figure 5-34. Pipeline result of manual run that allows failure

CHAPTER 5   UNDER ONE CONDITION

Ignoring Job Failure Based on Exit Codes

As mentioned earlier, lint tools typically report both errors and warnings. Warnings are minor infractions that are not likely to impact the correct running of the code. Errors, on the other hand, report major problems that are likely to impact the correct running of the code and, as a result, should be fixed right away. Is there a way to allow failures when there are just warnings and cause the job to fail if there are errors detected? It turns out that most lint tools will return different exit codes based on these conditions, such as 1 for at least one error and 2 for warnings only; if there are no issues, the lint tool returns an exit code of 0.

GitLab handles this scenario by letting us specify a set of nonzero exit codes that can be allowed to fail; all other nonzero exit codes would cause a failure that is not ignored. To illustrate this feature, I've updated the scripts/lint-test.sh script to emulate returning an exit code of 2 whenever the WARN_LINT_TEST variable is true. The new script is shown in Figure 5-35.

Figure 5-35. Lint test script update to illustrate exit code failures

Figure 5-36 shows the changes needed to lint-test-job to allow failure whenever the script returns an exit code of 2. For nonzero exit codes other than 2, the job will fail, causing the pipeline to fail. Of course, if the exit code is 0, the job succeeds.[6]

---

[6] Note that the GitLab documentation is unclear on this. It simply states that you provide a list of exit codes that are allowed to fail. It assumes without explicitly saying so that 0 represents success. I've added the distinction here that the list be nonzero exit codes.

```
34
35  lint-test-job:
36    extends: .prep-test
37    variables:
38      MY_TEST_VAR2: 'lint-test-goodbye'
39      MY_TEST_VAR3: 'lint-test-special'
40    rules:
41      - if: $CI_PIPELINE_SOURCE == "web"
42        variables:
43          MY_TEST_VAR3: 'lint-test-web'
44      - when: on_success
45    allow_failure:
46      exit_codes:
47        - 2
48    before_script:
49      - !reference [.common-prep, before_script]
50      - echo 'Lint setup before test'
51    script:
52      - !reference [.common-rule-vars, script]
53      - !reference [.common-tests, script]
54      - echo "MY_TEST_VAR3=$MY_TEST_VAR3"
55      - echo "Linting code... This will take about 10 seconds."
56      - scripts/lint-test.sh
57      - sleep 10
58      - echo "No lint issues found."
59    after_script:
60      - echo "Lint teardown after test"
61      - !reference [.common-prep, after_script]
62
```

Figure 5-36. *Lint test update to fail on specific exit codes*

Running the pipeline with WARN_LINT_TEST set to true (as opposed to FAIL_LINT_TEST set to true) results in the pipeline shown in Figure 5-37. To verify that the exit code was indeed 2, Figure 5-38 shows the output of lint-test-job for this pipeline.

CHAPTER 5   UNDER ONE CONDITION

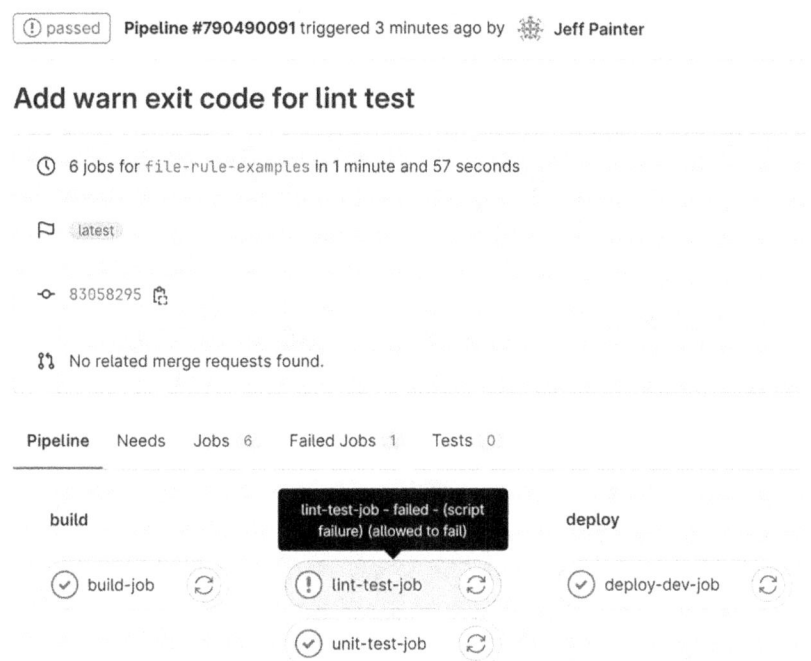

Figure 5-37.   Pipeline result when lint test returns exit code 2

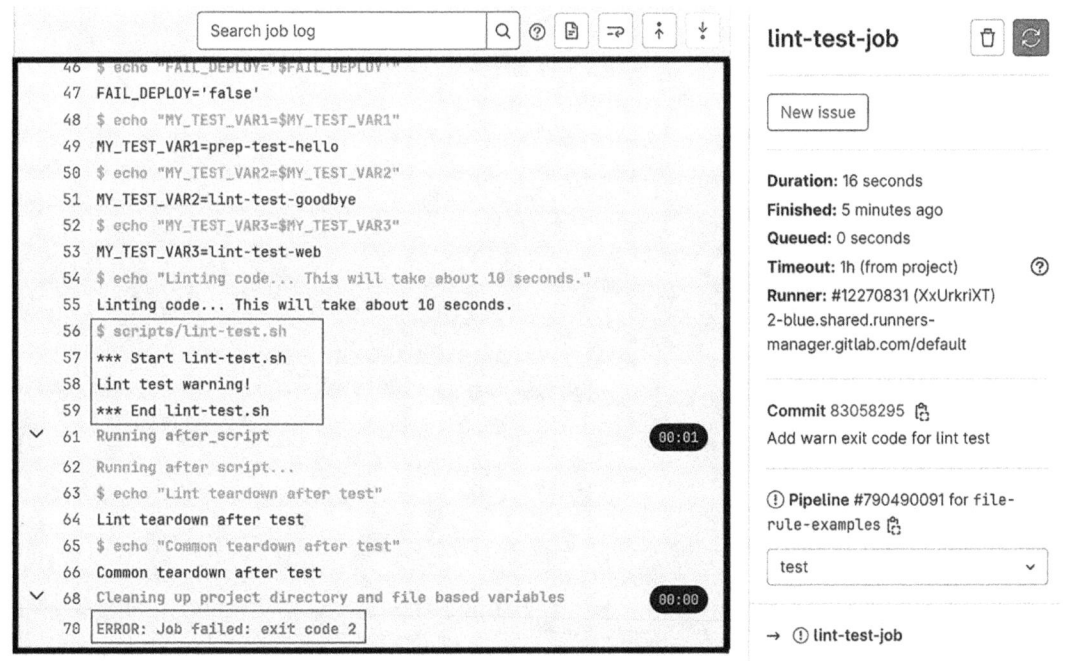

Figure 5-38.   Output of lint test job showing warning exit code

187

CHAPTER 5   UNDER ONE CONDITION

If you run the pipeline with FAIL_LINT_TEST set to true, both the job and pipeline fail. This gives you the best of both worlds. If there are errors uncovered by the lint tool, the job and pipeline will fail normally forcing you to fix the errors before proceeding. If you just have warnings, the job will fail without failing the pipeline, so you can deal with the "noise" at a later time. Note that exit codes can only be used for the job-level allow_failure keyword; it cannot be used with allow_failure inside rules.

Running a Job Based on Another Job's Failure

Allowing a job to allow a failure is one aspect of dealing with failures. But what if we want to run a job after a failure occurs? This would be useful in a scenario where we need to make some cleanups after the failure. Let's take a simple contrived example by adding a cleanup stage following our deploy stage. We'll create two jobs called cleanup-deploy and cleanup-failure. Figure 5-39 shows the changes to .gitlab-ci.yml to add the new stage following the deploy stage. Figure 5-40 shows the changes to .gitlab-deploy.yml that define the two cleanup jobs.

Figure 5-39. Update to include cleanup stage

```
16        - if: $CI_COMMIT_BRANCH != $CI_DEFAULT_BRANCH
17      script:
18        - !reference [.common-rule-vars, script]
19        - echo "Deploying dev application..."
20        - scripts/deploy.sh
21        - echo "Dev application successfully deployed."
22
23  cleanup-deploy:
24    stage: cleanup
25    script:
26      - !reference [.common-rule-vars, script]
27      - echo "Cleaning up deployment"
28      - echo "Cleanup completed."
29
30  cleanup-failure:
31    stage: cleanup
32    rules:
33      - when: on_failure
34    script:
35      - !reference [.common-rule-vars, script]
36      - echo "Cleaning up failure"
37      - echo "Failure cleanup completed."
```

Figure 5-40. Definition of cleanup jobs

When we push the changes, we see the normal pipeline flow involving the new cleanup jobs as shown in Figure 5-41. Since deploy-dev-job passed, we see that the cleanup-deploy job also ran and passed. The cleanup-failure job is marked as skipped since there were no previous jobs that failed.

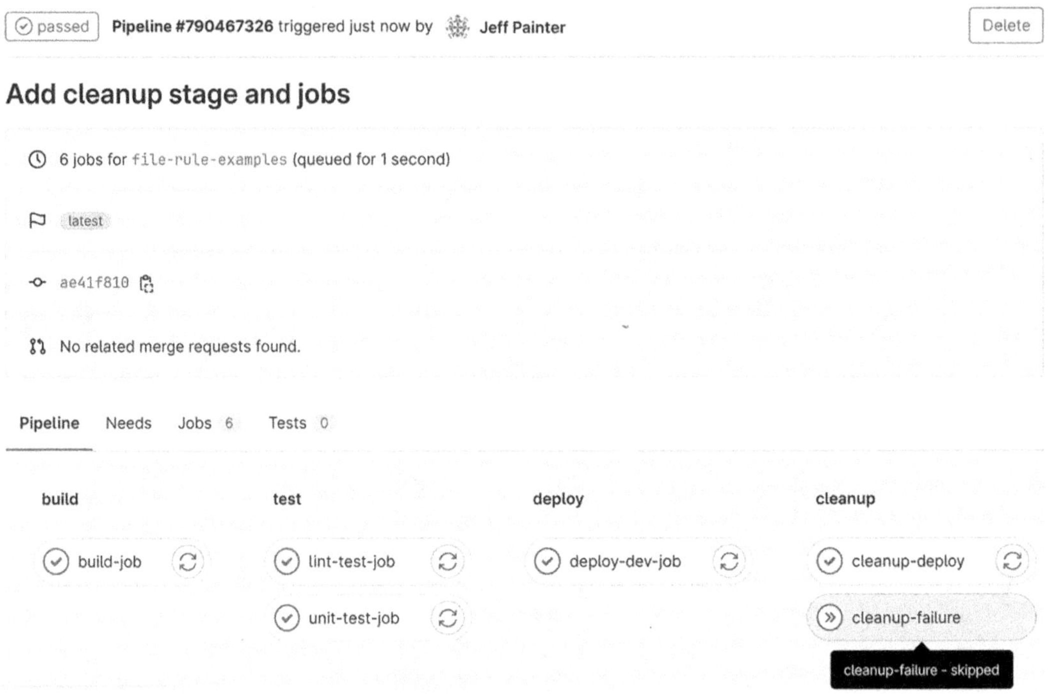

CHAPTER 5   UNDER ONE CONDITION

Figure 5-41. Pipeline run when deploy stage succeeds

When we run the job manually with FAIL_DEPLOY set to true, we see the failure pipeline flow as shown in Figure 5-42. Here, we see that deploy-dev-job failed. Because of the when: on_failure rule, we see that the cleanup-failure job ran and passed. The cleanup-deploy job was skipped due to the implicit when: on_success mode. Note that because of the deploy-dev-job failure, the pipeline itself was marked as failed even though the cleanup-failure job passed.

Figure 5-42. Pipeline run when deploy stage fails

Enabling a Job to Always Run After Another Job's Failure

For completeness, let's update the cleanup-deploy job to always run as shown in Figure 5-43. Here, we simply add the rule with when: always. Figure 5-44 shows the results of running the pipeline manually with FAIL_DEBUG set to true. In this case, we see that both jobs, cleanup-deploy and cleanup-failure, run and pass.

```
18        - !reference [.common-rule-vars, script]
19        - echo "Deploying dev application..."
20        - scripts/deploy.sh
21        - echo "Dev application successfully deployed."
22
23    cleanup-deploy:
24      stage: cleanup
25      rules:
26        - when: always
27      script:
28        - !reference [.common-rule-vars, script]
29        - echo "Cleaning up deployment"
30        - echo "Cleanup completed."
31
32    cleanup-failure:
33      stage: cleanup
34      rules:
35        - when: on_failure
36      script:
37        - !reference [.common-rule-vars, script]
38        - echo "Cleaning up failure"
39        - echo "Failure cleanup completed."
```

Figure 5-43. Update to ensure cleanup-deploy job always run

CHAPTER 5 UNDER ONE CONDITION

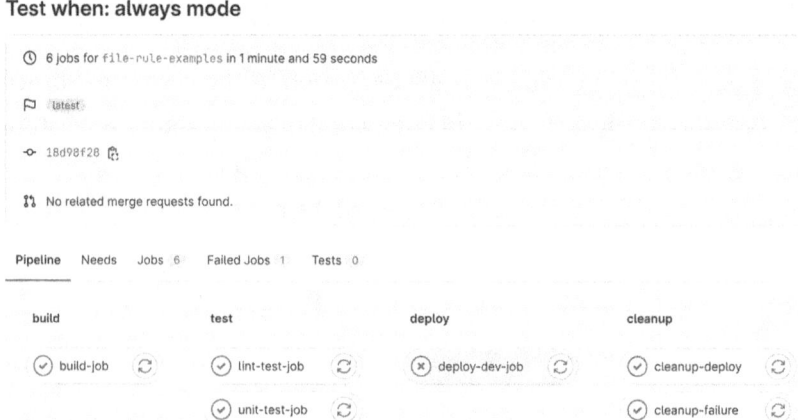

Figure 5-44. Pipeline run showing cleanup-deploy job runs after deploy stage fails

Rerunning a Job That Failed Based on External Events

One last word on failures: There may be times when a job fails because of external events rather than errors in the checked-in code base. For example, an Internet connection may have gone down during a deployment or a test that depends on an external database fails because the database went into maintenance mode. In these cases, you can simply rerun the failed job using the two arrows in a circle icon to the right of the job name in the pipeline view. Assuming that the external issue was resolved, this will restart the pipeline at the job failure rather than having to restart the pipeline from the beginning.

Manually Running Jobs

We've seen how to run a pipeline manually, but what if we want to run a single job manually? Why would we need to do this? A couple scenarios come to mind. One scenario involves making the running of a job optional; for example, there might be a test that takes a long time, and we don't want to run it every time a pipeline runs. Another scenario is when we need to introduce a decision point so that we can decide whether to proceed with running the rest of a pipeline. We'll look into this scenario first.

Pausing a Job in Order to Stop a Pipeline's Execution

When we talk about CD with respect to CI/CD, there are actually two definitions for CD: continuous deployment and continuous delivery. So far, our pipelines have used continuous deployment; that is, as soon as all tests pass, we automatically run the deployment, no questions asked. This assumes you have faith that the tests will capture any issues before deployment.

The definition of continuous delivery is slightly different. As soon as all the tests pass, we pause the pipeline workflow so that a decision by a trusted authority can be made whether to proceed or not. The software has been delivered but not deployed. You might encounter this process when creating programming libraries, for existence. Or perhaps you need to wait until a special time to release the software application with the possible intention of rolling the release back if an issue is encountered.

To enable this feature, GitLab provides the when: manual option that can be applied either at the job level or within a rule. To explore this option, let's apply this to deploy-dev-job so that we force it to pause awaiting manual input. Figure 5-45 shows deploy-dev-job updated with the when: manual option applied to the job itself.

CHAPTER 5 UNDER ONE CONDITION

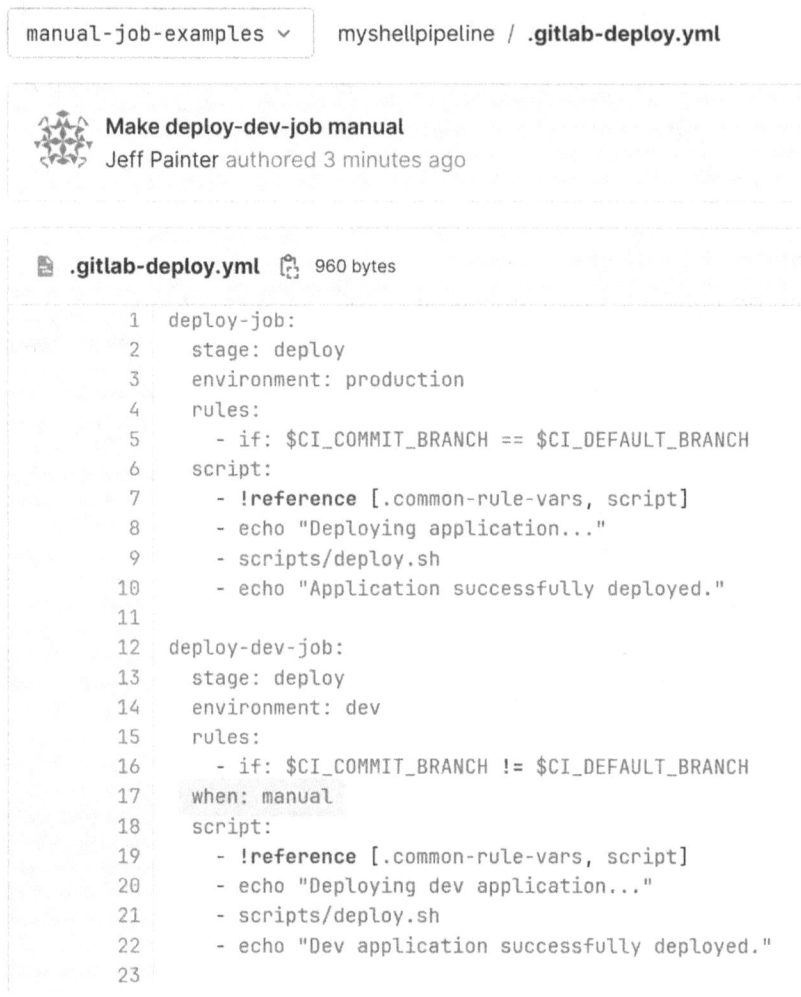

Figure 5-45. Update to require deploy-dev-job be run manually

When we check in the changes, we get the pipeline results shown in Figure 5-46. Job deploy-dev-job has a different wheel-like icon showing that the job requires manual action to run. But notice that the pipeline did not stop; the cleanup-deploy job went ahead and ran causing the pipeline to pass. This isn't exactly what we were expecting.

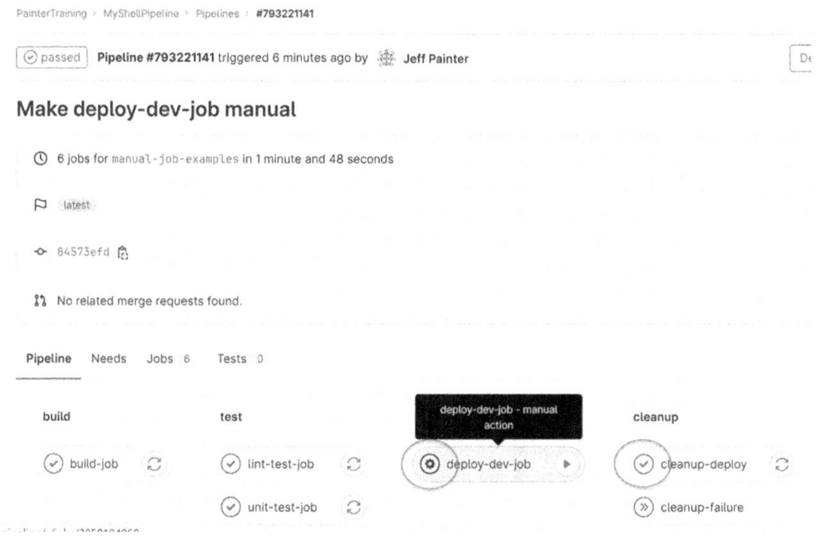

CHAPTER 5   UNDER ONE CONDITION

Figure 5-46. Pipeline result showing deploy-dev-job paused but cleanup jobs run

So why did this happen and what can we do to prevent this? It turns out that the when: manual option also depends on the allow_failure keyword. At the job level, the default value for allow_failure in this circumstance is true, which causes the pipeline to continue processing.[7] In order to put deploy-dev-job in the manual mode and cause pipeline processing to stop, the allow_failure needs to be set to false as shown in Figure 5-47.

---

[7] I personally find the combination of when: manual with allow_failure to be a bit bizarre as well as nonintuitive.

195

CHAPTER 5   UNDER ONE CONDITION

```
.gitlab-deploy.yml    983 bytes
 1   deploy-job:
 2     stage: deploy
 3     environment: production
 4     rules:
 5       - if: $CI_COMMIT_BRANCH == $CI_DEFAULT_BRANCH
 6     script:
 7       - !reference [.common-rule-vars, script]
 8       - echo "Deploying application..."
 9       - scripts/deploy.sh
10       - echo "Application successfully deployed."
11
12   deploy-dev-job:
13     stage: deploy
14     environment: dev
15     rules:
16       - if: $CI_COMMIT_BRANCH != $CI_DEFAULT_BRANCH
17     when: manual
18     allow_failure: false
19     script:
20       - !reference [.common-rule-vars, script]
21       - echo "Deploying dev application..."
22       - scripts/deploy.sh
23       - echo "Dev application successfully deployed."
24
```

Figure 5-47. *Update to deploy-dev-job to keep later stages from running*

Now when the changes are checked in, we get the pipeline results as shown in Figure 5-48. Here, we see that deploy-dev-job is put in manual mode as before. In addition, no jobs in future stages are run and the pipeline itself is marked as blocked. This is the behavior we were hoping for. Note the "Cancel running" button in the upper right. This allows us to cancel running the pipeline letting others know that we've decided not to continue with deployment.

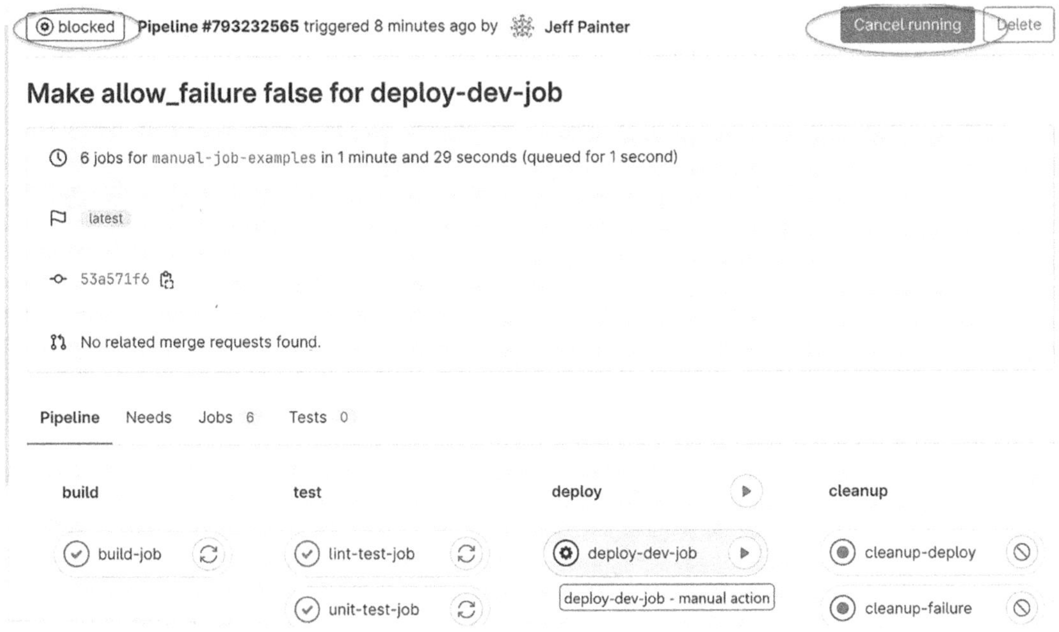

CHAPTER 5   UNDER ONE CONDITION

Make allow_failure false for deploy-dev-job

Figure 5-48. Pipeline result showing deploy-dev-job paused and cleanup jobs not run

If we decide to go ahead with deployment, clicking deploy-dev-job brings the run job page as shown in Figure 5-49. Not only does this give the "Run job" button to start the job, but it also provides a way to override variables. Unlike running the pipeline manually, it does not provide prompts for those variables with descriptions; you'll have to remember the names of those variables if you plan on overriding them.

197

CHAPTER 5   UNDER ONE CONDITION

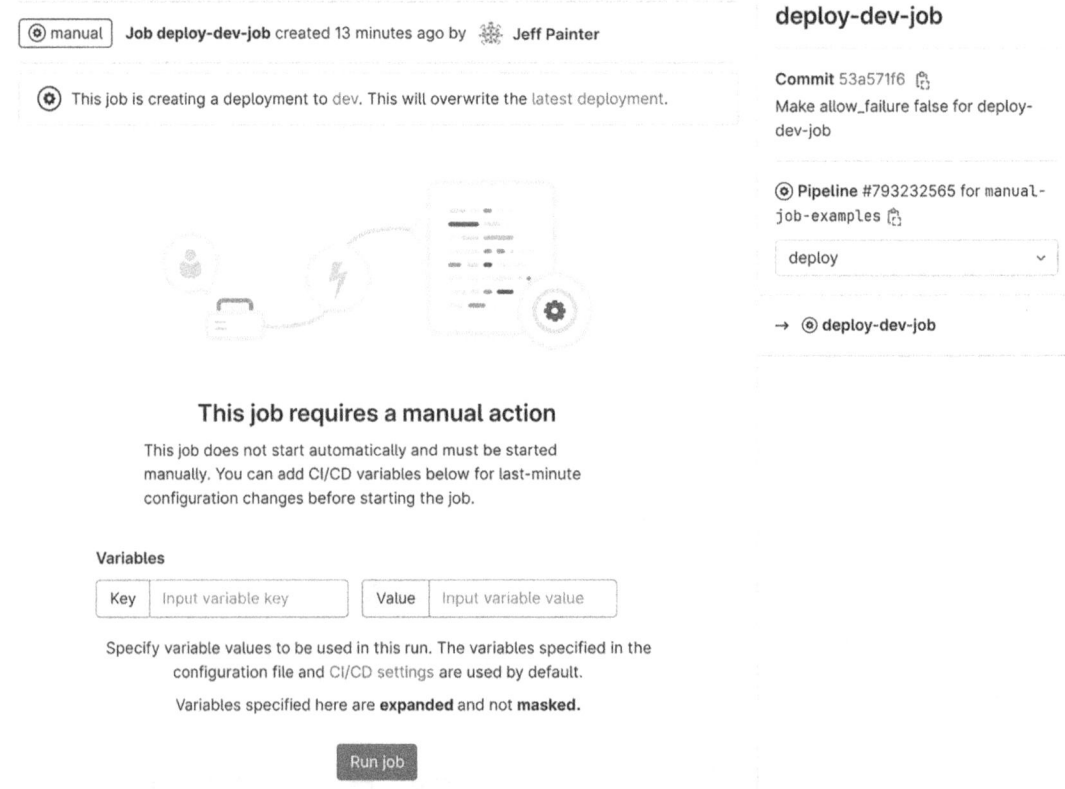

Figure 5-49. Manual run job page

Pausing a Job Without Blocking a Pipeline's Execution

Now let's look into how to make the running of a job optional without blocking the remainder of the pipeline. For this example, I added a scripts/perf-test.sh script similar to the unit-test.sh script and added a perf-test-job to the test stage. Figure 5-50 shows the new perf-test-job definition. For this example, I placed the manual action within a rule rather than at the job level. I also added a FORCE_PERF_TEST variable to force the performance test to run rather than making it optional via the when: manual rule option.

CHAPTER 5   UNDER ONE CONDITION

```
59     after_script:
60       - echo "Lint teardown after test"
61       - !reference [.common-prep, after_script]
62
63  perf-test-job:
64    extends: .prep-test
65    variables:
66      FORCE_PERF_TEST: "false"
67    rules:
68      - if: $FORCE_PERF_TEST == "true"
69      - when: manual
70    script:
71      - !reference [.common-rule-vars, script]
72      - echo "Running performance tests... This will take a long time."
73      - !reference [.common-tests, script]
74      - scripts/perf-test.sh
75      - sleep 60
76      - echo "Performance in acceptable range"
77
```

Figure 5-50. *Definition of perf-test-job to run optionally under certain conditions*

When these changes are checked in, we get the pipeline results as shown in Figure 5-51. As expected, perf-test-job is set to manual mode; however, deploy-dev-job is disabled indicating that the pipeline is blocked by perf-test-job. This forces us to run perf-test-job before we can run deploy-dev-job – not the optionality we were expecting.

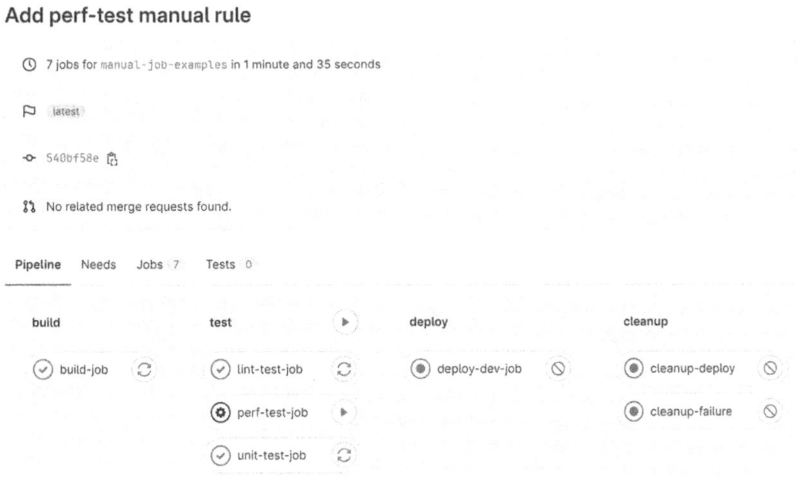

Figure 5-51. *Pipeline run with perf-test-job waiting to be run manually*

CHAPTER 5   UNDER ONE CONDITION

So why did this happen? We didn't specify allow_failure explicitly, but shouldn't it be true by default like it was at the job level? Turns out no, the default for allow_failure is false when using manual mode within a rule, opposite of the default when setting manual mode at the job level.[8] Figure 5-52 shows the change to perf-test-job to explicitly set allow_failure to true.

```
59    after_script:
60       - echo "Lint teardown after test"
61       - !reference [.common-prep, after_script]
62
63    perf-test-job:
64       extends: .prep-test
65       variables:
66          FORCE_PERF_TEST: "false"
67       rules:
68          - if: $FORCE_PERF_TEST == "true"
69            when: manual
70            allow_failure: true
71       script:
72          - !reference [.common-rule-vars, script]
73          - echo "Running performance tests... This will take a long time."
74          - !reference [.common-tests, script]
75          - scripts/perf-test.sh
76          - sleep 60
77          - echo "Performance in acceptable range"
78
```

Figure 5-52. *Fix to perf-test-job to allow further stages to run when job is paused*

Now when we check in this change, we get the pipeline results as shown in Figure 5-53. We can now go ahead and run deploy-dev-job without having to run the performance test, which is what we wanted. The pipeline is blocked because of deploy-dev-job, not because of perf-test-job.

---

[8] Arrrgh!

CHAPTER 5   UNDER ONE CONDITION

Figure 5-53.   Pipeline result with perf-test-job fix in place

Impacts of Manually Running a Paused Job That Eventually Fails

So, what happens if we run perf-test-job? If it succeeds, it is marked as passed. But what if it fails? Let's test this scenario out. Figure 5-54 shows us running perf-test-job with FAIL_PERF_TEST set to true. This will cause perf-test-job to fail.

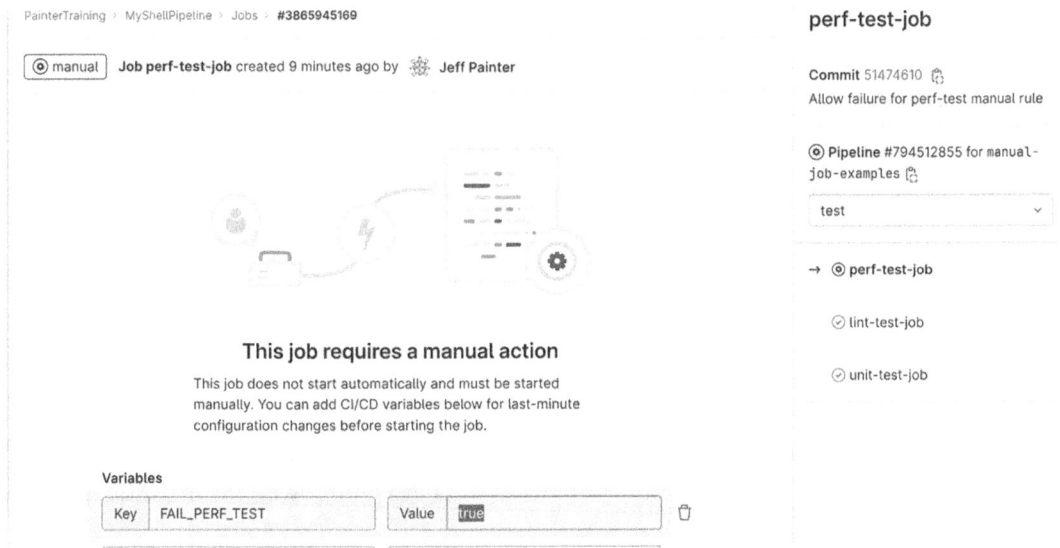

Figure 5-54.   Manual run of perf-test-job that forces it to fail

201

CHAPTER 5 UNDER ONE CONDITION

When we fail perf-test-job, we see the pipeline results as shown in Figure 5-55. Here, we see that perf-test-job failed but that it was allowed to fail. Why? Because allow_failure was set to true.[9] This might seem disturbing at first, but this is the result that makes the most sense in this scenario. We can still run deploy-dev-job if we decide to ignore the results of the performance test, perhaps because performance wasn't impacted too much.

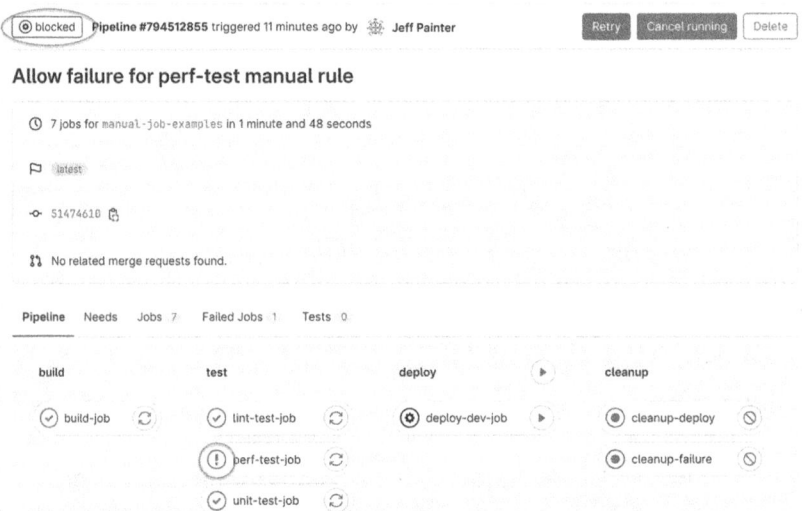

Figure 5-55. Manual run of perf-test-job that subsequently fails

At this point, you might be wondering if there is a way to have perf-test-job fail and cause it to fail the pipeline rather than allowing the pipeline to continue. Well, we already saw what happens when allow_failure is set to false; we end up blocking at perf-test-job rather than at deploy-dev-job. If we did run perf-test-job and it failed, then yes, the pipeline would fail. But that doesn't make perf-test-job optional. We might as well have set FORCE_PERF_TEST to true to automatically run perf-test-job and have it pass or fail before proceeding with deployment.

There is another weird scenario we have to consider when we make perf-test-job optional via setting allow_failure to true. Suppose we don't run perf-test-job and go ahead and run deploy-dev-job. Once deployment is complete, we can still run perf-test-job manually. Assuming that the deployment was successful and that the performance test fails, the pipeline would still show as passed but with an allowed failure. This shows

---

[9] This gives you some sense as to why allow_failure is tied to the when: manual mode.

that whether we run perf-test-job first or deploy-dev-job first, we end up in the same pipeline state. If it were possible to run perf-test-job after deploy-dev-job and perf-test-job failed, we would be misled into thinking that the pipeline failed and that the deployment was not run.[10]

Impacts of Canceling a Paused Job

Before we leave this section, let's take a look at what happens when we cancel a manual job via selecting the "Cancel running" button. In this case, when we cancel deploy-dev-job, we get the pipeline results shown in Figure 5-56. We see that the pipeline is still blocked but that all remaining jobs have been marked as canceled. If we change our minds later, the "Cancel running" button has been replaced with the "Retry" button in the upper right.

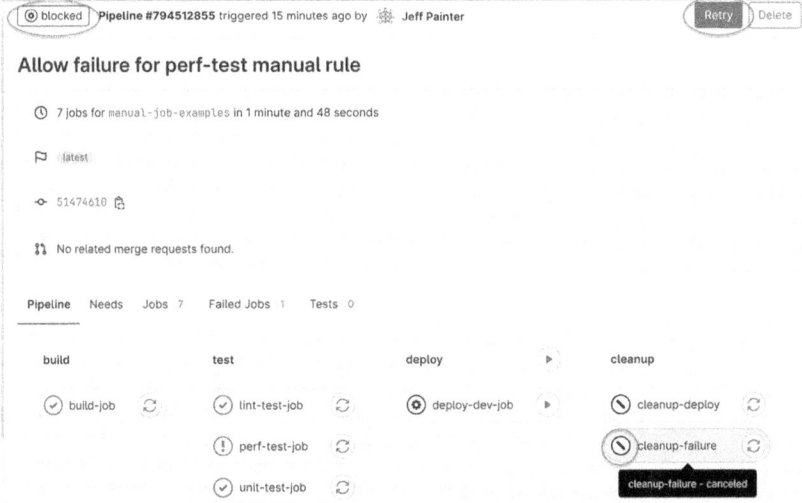

Figure 5-56. Pipeline results after canceling deploy job

---

[10] Although we could always look to the detailed pipeline graph to see that deploy-dev-job was run and passed, many people only look at the state of the pipeline itself and make the assumption that deployment failed.

Summary

In this chapter, we covered the following topics:

- Learned how to use rules to determine whether a job should run or not
- Investigated how to use variable expressions and file-based conditions in rules
- Discovered how to set variables conditionally with rules
- Determined how to ignore job failures under certain conditions
- Considered how to always run a job even after another job's failure
- Described how to pause a job to stop pipeline execution requiring manual input
- Looked into how to make a job optional without impacting a pipeline's execution

We still have one more key item to cover with respect to CI/CD pipelines: Where do we save the things that we've built as part of a pipeline process? We will cover that topic in the next chapter.

CHAPTER 6

You Build It, You Keep It

Now that we covered the basics of defining a CI/CD pipeline in GitLab, including how to control the running of jobs to handle a variety of use cases, we haven't talked yet about how to store the products that we are creating with those pipelines. In this chapter, we'll look at how to create artifacts that are the ultimate products to be deployed. In addition, we'll look at how to cache intermediate objects that are generated while creating the products to be delivered.

Creating and Preserving Artifacts

All of our examples so far have been missing one key ingredient: artifacts. Although we have build, test, and deploy stages, we haven't actually built anything to be tested or deployed. We mentioned early on that each job is independent of all other jobs, so there is the question of how can we share build artifacts between jobs if we begin each job with a fresh environment? Enter the artifacts keyword.

Denoting Generated Objects As Artifacts

Using the artifacts keyword, we let GitLab know what generated objects we want to preserve for later stages. Not everything we generate is worthy of saving. For example, many programming languages generate intermediate objects that are used to build the final product(s). Once those products are created, we no longer need the intermediate objects (or at the very least deliver those intermediate objects as part of the final deployment).

CHAPTER 6   YOU BUILD IT, YOU KEEP IT

To set up an example illustrating how to use the artifacts keyword, I updated the build.sh script to generate an index.html file. Figure 6-1 shows the changes made to the build.sh script. The script contains a simple bash function that generates a simple html file that displays the current user as well as the current date and time. We simply invoke the create_html function redirecting the output to the output/index.html file.

```bash
#! /bin/bash

MY_RC=0
MY_DIR=$( realpath $( dirname $0 ) )
MY_OUTPUT_DIR=$( realpath $MY_DIR/../output )

create_html() {
    echo '<!DOCTYPE html>'
    echo '<html>'
    echo '<body>'
    echo '<h1>My GitLab Artifact</h1>'
    echo "<p>Hello $( whoami )!</p>"
    echo "<p>Created on $( date '+%Y-%m-%d %T' ).</p>"
    echo '</body>'
    echo '</html>'
}

echo '*** Start build.sh'

if [ "$FAIL_BUILD" == "true" ]; then
    echo "Build failed!"
    MY_RC=1
else
    create_html > $MY_OUTPUT_DIR/index.html
    echo "Build succeeded!"
fi

echo '*** End build.sh'

exit $MY_RC
```

Figure 6-1. *Update to build script that creates an artifact*

I created and saved the output directory as part of the project source code. Figure 6-2 shows the initial directory contents. Inside that directory is a .gitignore file that is also saved as part of the project. There are two reasons to have that file. First of all, that file is created in order to save the directory by Git; by default, Git does not save empty directories. The second reason for .gitignore is to let Git know what files to ignore for checking in; we don't want to check in generated objects into our Git repository.

CHAPTER 6   YOU BUILD IT, YOU KEEP IT

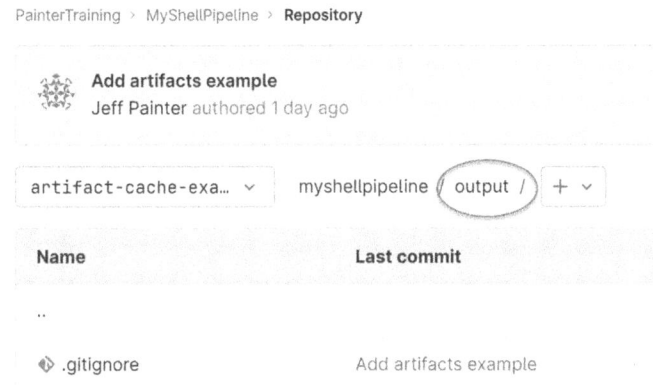

Figure 6-2. *Creation of directory to store artifacts*

Figure 6-3 shows the contents of the .gitignore file. The second line containing the asterisk (*) tells Git to ignore everything in the directory. The fourth line (!.gitignore) lets Git know that the exception to ignoring everything in the directory is the .gitignore file itself. This is a common technique for creating directories designed to hold generated objects.

Figure 6-3. *Contents of the git ignore file to prevent artifact files from getting added by Git*

With those key pieces in place, let's take a look at the .gitlab-build.yml file. Figure 6-4 shows the changes needed to preserve the file generated by the newly updated scripts/build.sh file. The artifacts section in this example uses the paths keyword to provide a list of artifacts to preserve; in this case, we preserve everything in the output directory

207

including the directory itself.[1] It also uses the exclude keyword to let GitLab know we don't want to save the .gitignore file as an artifact. For debugging, I also added a couple of lines to list all directories and files in our working directory along with a printout of the contents of the index.html file.

Figure 6-4. Update of build job to create and store artifacts

---

[1] Had we used the path output/*, only the objects within the output directory would be preserved without the output directory.

CHAPTER 6   YOU BUILD IT, YOU KEEP IT

Creating and Accessing Artifacts

When this pipeline is run, we see the output of build-job in Figure 6-5. The first highlighted section shows that index.html does exist in the output directory as expected. The second highlighted section shows the generated contents of index.html. Note that in the right-hand panel, there is a new "Job artifacts" section included as part of the job description. The "Download" button lets you download the artifacts as a zip file, which we will illustrate shortly. The "Browse" button lets you view the artifacts from the web browser.

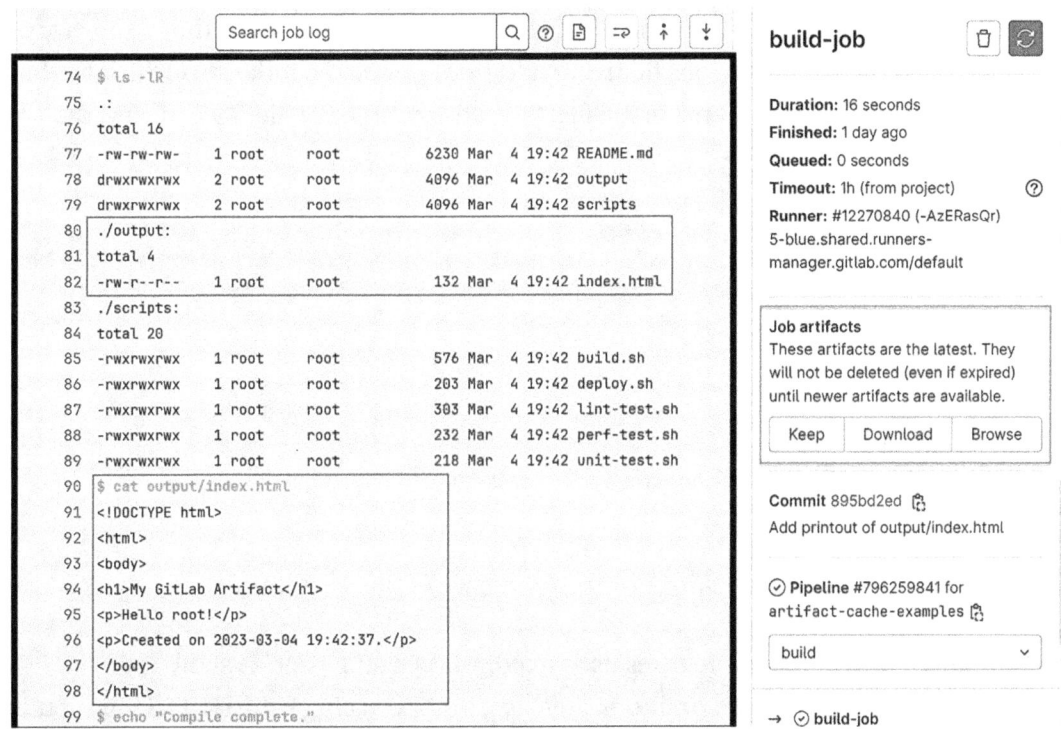

Figure 6-5. *Output of build job with artifacts*

Selecting the "Browse" button presents the artifacts web page as shown in Figure 6-6. Here, we see the output directory that we preserved via the artifacts section of the job. We can drill down into the directory by clicking the link associated with the directory name.

209

CHAPTER 6   YOU BUILD IT, YOU KEEP IT

PainterTraining > MyShellPipeline > Jobs > #3875509751 > **Artifacts**

⊘ passed   **Job** #3875509751 in pipeline #796259841 for 895bd2ed from `artifact-cache-examples` by 🎨 Jeff Painter 1 day ago

Artifacts   ⬇ Download artifacts archive

Name	Size
📁 output	

Figure 6-6.   *Artifacts web page for the given pipeline*

Figure 6-7 shows the contents of the output directory. Here, we see the ".." directory that leads us back to the previous figure. In addition, we see the index.html file icon that we can click to view the contents of the file. Since this is an html file, we can view the contents as a web page.

Figure 6-7.   *Contents of artifacts output directory*

Clicking the index.html file takes us to a redirect warning page as shown in Figure 6-8. This seems like an ominous message, but if you check the HTTPS link, you'll see that it takes you to the index.html file associated with our project's specific job. It's OK to click that link to see the resulting web page as shown in Figure 6-9. As you can see, it opened the web page in its own window/tab.

CHAPTER 6   YOU BUILD IT, YOU KEEP IT

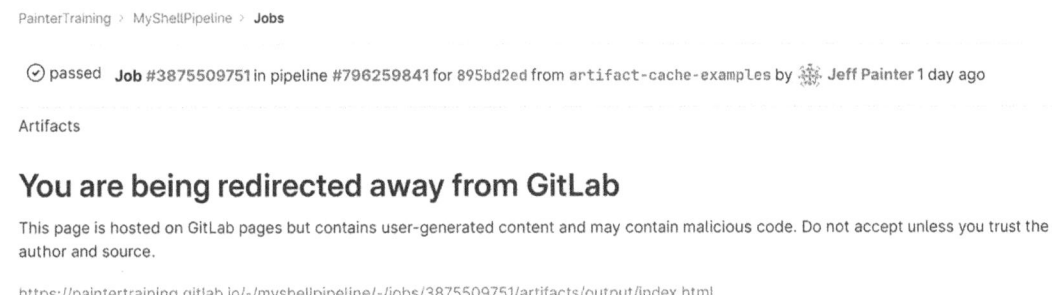

Figure 6-8.   Redirect warning when viewing an html artifact

Figure 6-9.   Web page rendering of an html artifact

Accessing Artifacts in Jobs of Follow-On Stages

So far, so good, but can we see the artifacts within other jobs? By default, artifacts are automatically copied to all jobs in follow-on stages (but not to jobs within the same stage). To see this, I updated unit-test-job to list all directories and files as well as a printout of the output/index.html file, just as I did with build-job. Figure 6-10 shows the changes I made to unit-test-job. Note that the changes were made before the call to scripts/unit-test.sh script to show that the artifacts are automatically available to the unit test.

211

```
20   unit-test-job:
21     extends: .prep-test
22     rules:
23       - if: $CI_PIPELINE_SOURCE == "web" && $FAIL_UNIT_TEST == "true"
24         allow_failure: true
25       - when: on_success
26     script:
27       - !reference [.common-rule-vars, script]
28       - echo "Running unit tests... This will take about 60 seconds."
29       - !reference [.common-tests, script]
30       - ls -lR
31       - cat output/index.html
32       - scripts/unit-test.sh
33       - sleep 60
34       - echo "Code coverage is 90%"
35
```

Figure 6-10. *Update of unit test to list artifacts generated by build job*

Figure 6-11 shows the output of unit-test-job with these changes in place. The first highlighted area shows that the output directory and the index.html file within it do indeed exist for unit-test-job. The second highlighted area shows the contents of index.html as was generated by build-job. Note that we did not need to explicitly ask for the artifacts; they were copied automatically for us. Also, note that the "Job artifacts" section that was present in the right-hand panel for build-job does not appear for unit-test-job. That section only appears for jobs that create artifacts.

CHAPTER 6   YOU BUILD IT, YOU KEEP IT

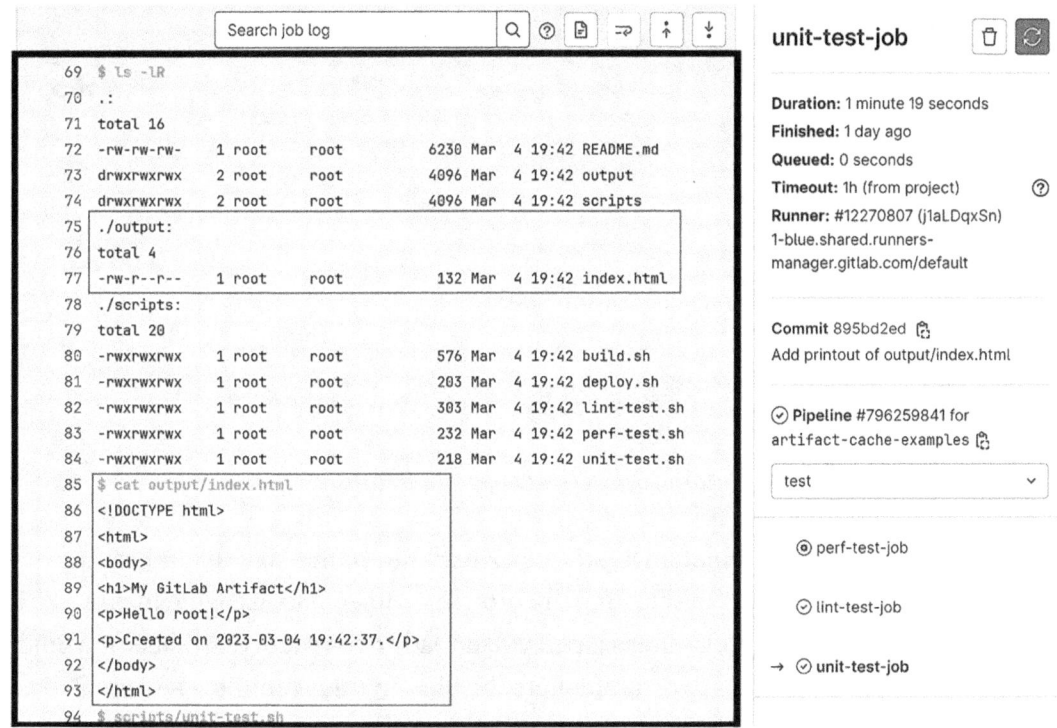

Figure 6-11.   Result of unit test listing artifacts

Downloading Artifacts from GitLab

Let's now go back and see how we can download the artifacts. In addition to downloading the artifacts using the "Download" button from the build-job view as we saw earlier, we can also download the artifacts from the pipeline summary view. Figure 6-12 shows the pipeline summary view. On the right-hand side of the pipeline, there is a download drop-down menu. When we hover over that, we see the drop-down menu, which in this case shows build-job:archive. What this tells us, by the way, is that other jobs can also have artifacts. For example, we could have created additional artifacts for unit-test-job that would then show up in the drop-down list as well.

CHAPTER 6   YOU BUILD IT, YOU KEEP IT

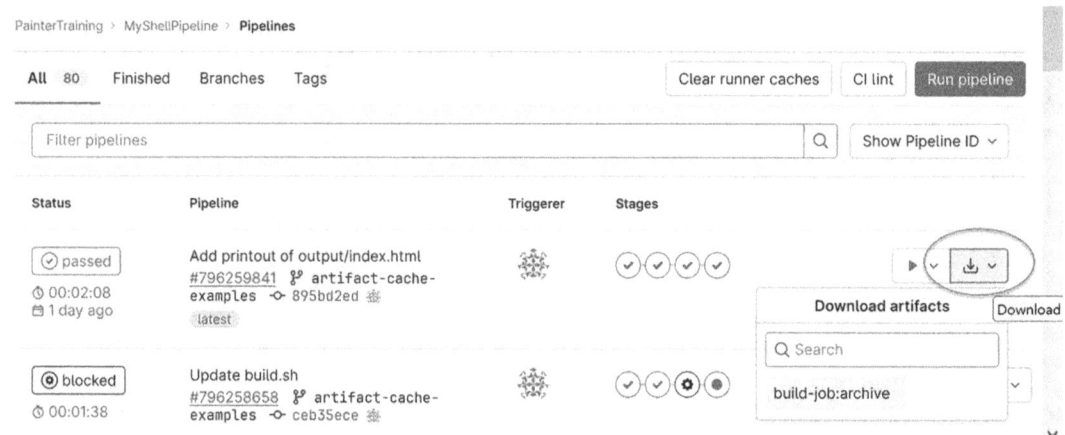

Figure 6-12. Request to download artifacts to the browser

When we select build-job:archive, we get a zip of the archive sent to our browser. Figure 6-13 shows the results of selecting the browser's download list. Note that by default GitLab uses the name artifacts.zip. If you already downloaded artifacts, it would add a number in parentheses to disambiguate the files. In this example, I had created an "artifacts(3).zip" file that I subsequently deleted.

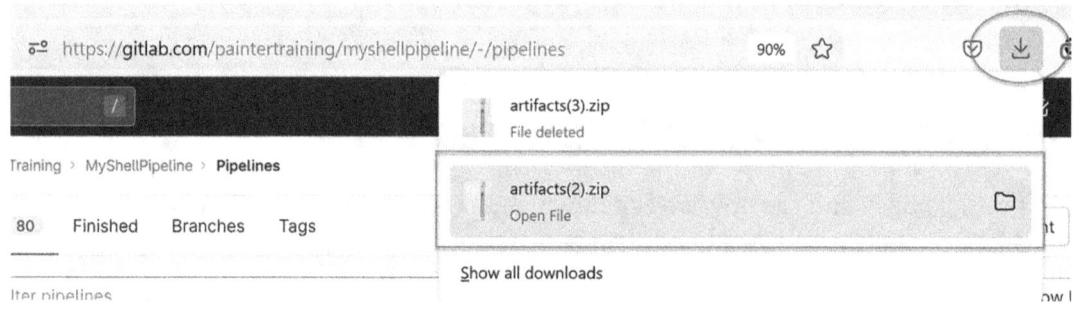

Figure 6-13. Listing of browser download (Firefox)

By the way, the artifacts.zip file gives you an insight into how artifacts are passed from the generating job to follow-on jobs. When the generating job is complete, it automatically zips the artifacts specified by the artifacts keyword into an artifacts.zip file and stores it in a known place associated with the runners. When a job in a follow-on stage starts, the runner automatically grabs the artifacts.zip file and unzips it into the working directory.

214

CHAPTER 6   YOU BUILD IT, YOU KEEP IT

Renaming the Artifacts Zip File

Since it can get really confusing if all artifact downloads were named artifacts.zip, the name keyword can be used to rename the zip filename as shown in Figure 6-14. In this example, we use a name based on the job name combined with the commit branch name. Figure 6-15 shows the new name of the downloaded zip file with this change in place.

Figure 6-14.   Update of job renaming artifact zip file

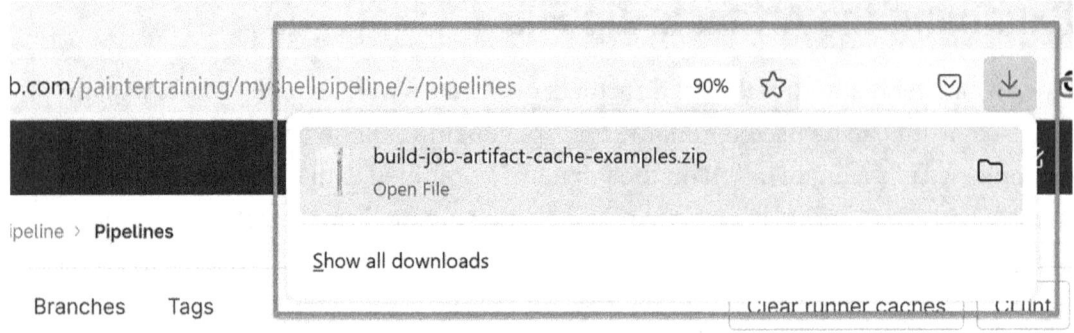

Figure 6-15. *Browser listing showing updated zip filename*

In addition to the name, an expiration time for the artifacts is specified using the expire_in keyword. In this example, we set the expiration to be one week from when the artifacts were created. On the gitlab.com site, the expiration is set by default to 30 days. Using an expiration time helps reduce the storage needed to retain old artifacts. It should be noted that the latest artifacts are always kept around indefinitely until a new pipeline is run. This is also true for pipelines that are blocked waiting for manual input, so if you have large artifacts, you should be mindful of this caveat.

Accessing Artifacts from a Merge Request

Before we turn away from the topic of artifacts, let's take a look at one more keyword: expose_as. We saw that we can download artifacts from the job that created them as well as from the pipeline. What about merge requests? Turns out we can download artifacts from there as well. Figure 6-16 shows what the default merge request looks like for a pipeline that generates artifacts. Here, we see that we have the same download dropdown options as the pipeline summary page, which behaves the same way.

CHAPTER 6   YOU BUILD IT, YOU KEEP IT

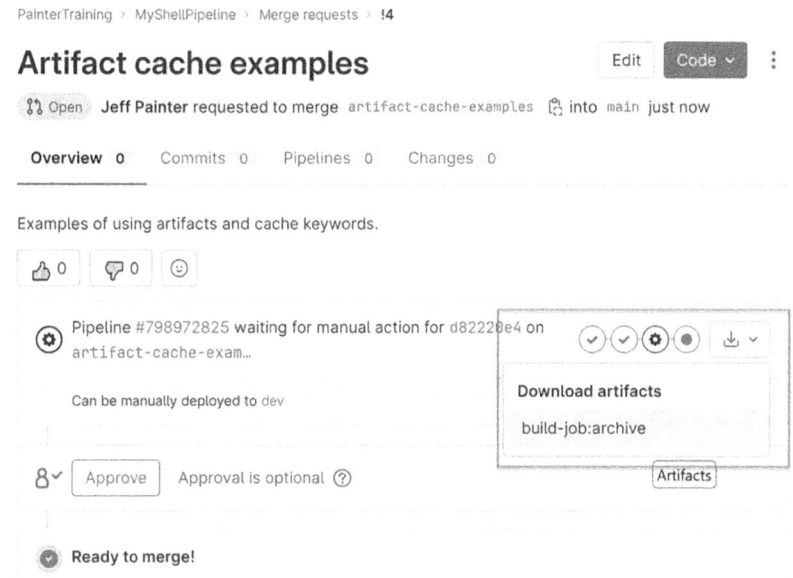

Figure 6-16. *Artifact listing related to a given merge request*

But what if we want to view the artifacts as we did with the build job via the "Browse" button? Well, we could drill down to the job and view the artifacts that way, but that requires knowing which jobs have artifacts and tediously going through each of the jobs to browse the artifacts. Wouldn't it be nice if we could do this from the merge request? Turns out the expose_as keyword will create a link in the merge request where you can browse the artifacts without having to hunt and peck for them among the jobs. Figure 6-17 illustrates how to use the expose_as keyword to generate a link in the merge request. In this example, we set the name of the link to be displayed in the merge request as build-artifacts.

CHAPTER 6 YOU BUILD IT, YOU KEEP IT

Figure 6-17. Updated build job to generate an artifact link in merge request listing

With this change in place, we can see a new section just below the pipeline in the merge request as shown in Figure 6-18. This initially appears in collapsed form with the link "View exposed artifact." When you click that link, you get the expanded form as shown in Figure 6-19. Here, we can see the build-artifacts link generated by the expose_as keyword. Clicking the browse-artifacts link takes you to the browse view we saw for build-job earlier (see Figure 6-6). If we had multiple jobs with artifacts that were also exposed, they would be listed here as well.

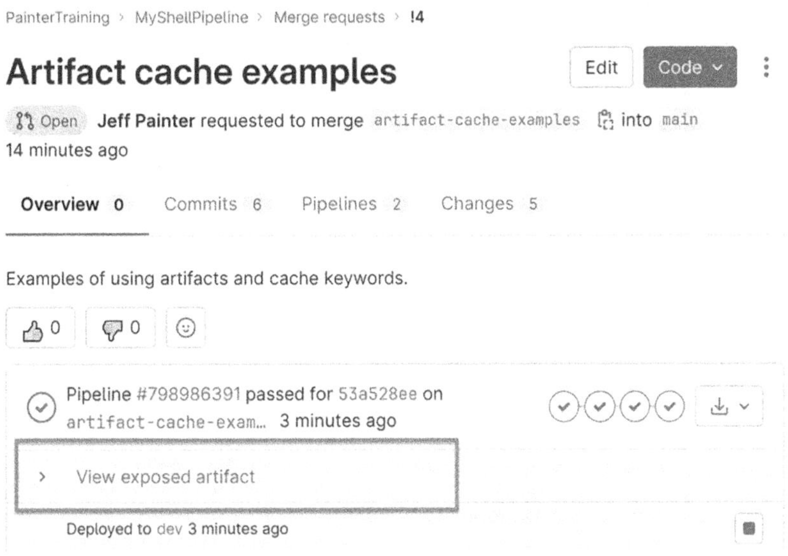

CHAPTER 6   YOU BUILD IT, YOU KEEP IT

Figure 6-18.   *Collapsed listing of artifacts for a given merge request*

Figure 6-19.   *Link to artifacts for a given merge request*

Just a word of caution: The links are generated for jobs of the last successfully completed pipeline. If you have blocked pipelines waiting for manual input or failed pipelines, those artifacts are not linked in the merge request. This makes sense since you don't want to have a mix of artifacts from different pipelines. If you want to see artifacts for failed jobs, you can use the "when" keyword to control this; this may be useful for debugging purposes.

Additional Artifacts Options

If you look at the .gitlab-ci.yml keyword reference manual, you will see a bunch of options using the reports keyword. Most of these are associated with metrics and test reports that are generated by third-party tools (such as junit). Many of them also require a paid license (premium or ultimate) to use them.

Think of reports as special artifacts to be kept separate from the artifacts being deployed. You can, of course, include reports with the rest of your artifacts, but you must do so explicitly using the paths attribute. Since there are a wide variety of reports based on the tools that create them, covering them all is beyond the scope of this book.

You can learn more about reports at `https://docs.gitlab.com/ee/ci/yaml/artifacts_reports.html`.

Working with Caches

Let's now switch to the topic of caches. Whereas artifacts are things that we generate to be deployed as part of our final product, caches are things to store intermediate objects that are used when creating an artifact (such as programming libraries) or as tools for performing some tasks (such as unit testing). If you've ever used Maven to download dependencies, you know that it can take a long time (in the order of minutes) the first time those dependencies are downloaded. Since those dependencies rarely change across builds, you would like to reuse them rather than download them each and every time.

Distinction in the Pipeline Handling of Artifacts and Caches

A big distinction between artifacts and caches is that artifacts are generated per pipeline; they are not shared across pipelines. Caches, however, can be shared across pipelines as well as jobs. They can even be shared across branches of the same type[2] (i.e., protected vs. unprotected). The overall goal of caches is to reduce the time needed to create artifacts.

Another key distinction between artifacts and caches is that artifacts are immutable, whereas caches may be updated. Once you create an artifact, you can't change it. This is an important CD principle that requires building something once and then deploying it after it has been thoroughly tested; nowhere along the pipeline should the artifact be modified. Caches, on the other hand, are temporary repositories of downloadable objects that can be updated as needed, perhaps due to version updates and the like.

A Maven Example

In order to illustrate the use of caches, I decided to use Maven. Maven is a well-known tool that downloads third-party objects into a local on-disk repository typically located in .m2/repository; it also generates intermediate objects in a target directory. To keep things simple, I installed Maven on my laptop and generated a sample application as described on Maven's website here: https://maven.apache.org/guides/getting-started/maven-in-five-minutes.html. I added the generated application in its own maven-projects directory. Figure 6-20 shows the tree structure of the generated application. App.java is the application that prints out "Hello World!" and AppTest.java contains the skeleton of a unit test.

---

[2] This didn't use to be the case in earlier versions of GitLab. You could share caches from working branches with the main branch, for example. Unfortunately, this created a security issue in that you could store an object in an unprotected cache that would expose secrets in the protected branch or otherwise inject malware into the production product.

CHAPTER 6   YOU BUILD IT, YOU KEEP IT

```
jpainter@LAPTOP-         : ~/gitlab-repos/myshellpipeline
jpainter@LAPTOP-       :                              $ tree -n maven-projects
maven-projects
└── my-app
    ├── pom.xml
    └── src
        ├── main
        │   └── java
        │       └── com
        │           └── mycompany
        │               └── app
        │                   └── App.java
        └── test
            └── java
                └── com
                    └── mycompany
                        └── app
                            └── AppTest.java

12 directories, 3 files
jpainter@LAPTOP-       :                              $
```

Figure 6-20. *Directory and file structure for the example Maven project*

The maven-projects/my-app/pom.xml file contains meta-information about the application that Maven uses to build the application. Figure 6-21 shows the top portion of the pom.xml file. One of the key pieces of metadata is the list of dependencies needed to build the application. In this example, we depend on junit 4.1 during Maven's test phase.

```
artifact-cache-exa...     myshellpipeline / maven-projects / my-app /

pom.xml   2.54 KiB

 1  <?xml version="1.0" encoding="UTF-8"?>
 2
 3  <project xmlns="http://maven.apache.org/POM/4.0.0" xmlns
 4     xsi:schemaLocation="http://maven.apache.org/POM/4.0.0
 5     <modelVersion>4.0.0</modelVersion>
 6
 7     <groupId>com.mycompany.app</groupId>
 8     <artifactId>my-app</artifactId>
 9     <version>1.0-SNAPSHOT</version>
10
11     <name>my-app</name>
12     <url>http://maen.apache.org</url>
13
14     <properties>
15        <project.build.sourceEncoding>UTF-8</project.build.s
16        <maven.compiler.source>1.7</maven.compiler.source>
17        <maven.compiler.target>1.7</maven.compiler.target>
18     </properties>
19
20     <dependencies>
21        <dependency>
22           <groupId>junit</groupId>
23           <artifactId>junit</artifactId>
24           <version>4.11</version>
25           <scope>test</scope>
26        </dependency>
27     </dependencies>
28
29     <build>
```

Figure 6-21. *Contents of the Maven pom.xml file*

Normally, these dependencies are downloaded from the Maven central repository (recently relocated to https://central.sonatype.com/?smo=true) and stored in the user home directory in the .m2/repository directory (i.e., ~/.m2/repository). If the local repository doesn't exist, it is created before the downloads take place. In our example, we want to cache the contents of this local repository to reduce the number of downloads needed each time we build the application. Note, however, that GitLab requires directories and/or files that are to be cached to be relative to the project's directory; in other words, we cannot cache the contents of ~/.m2/repository.

Fortunately, Maven allows us to specify a different location of the local Maven repository using a settings.xml file. I created the .m2 directory at the top level of our "MyShellPipeline" project and added the settings.xml file to that directory as shown in Figure 6-22. Since Maven requires that the location of the local repository be an absolute path name, I use GitLab's predefined variable CI_PROJECT_DIR to provide that. The ${env.CI_PROJECT_DIR} variable reference is Maven's way of injecting environment variables into the settings.xml file.

Figure 6-22. *Contents of the Maven settings.xml file*

CHAPTER 6   YOU BUILD IT, YOU KEEP IT

Build Job Updates for Maven

In order to build our new application, the build.sh script was updated as shown in Figure 6-23. The changes were a little bit more involved in order to run the build.sh script manually to test it out before the changes were committed. In order to run the script manually, I had to set CI_PROJECT_DIR to the parent directory since CI_PROJECT_DIR is not defined in this context; when run as part of the pipeline, this variable will already be set, so setting it to the parent directory is ignored. The mvn line in the script is what runs Maven. The -s $CI_PROJECT_DIR/.m2/settings.xml option tells Maven to use the settings file in our .m2 directory. The "clean compile" option tells Maven to clear the target directory and compile the application.[3]

```
#! /bin/bash

MY_RC=0
MY_DIR=$( realpath $( dirname $0 ) )
MY_PARENT_DIR=$( realpath $MY_DIR/.. )
MY_OUTPUT_DIR=$( realpath $MY_PARENT_DIR/output )

[[ -n $CI_PROJECT_DIR ]] || export CI_PROJECT_DIR=$MY_PARENT_DIR

create_html() {
    echo '<!DOCTYPE html>'
    echo '<html>'
    echo '<body>'
    echo '<h1>My GitLab Artifact</h1>'
    echo "<p>Hello $( whoami )!</p>"
    echo "<p>Created on $( date '+%Y-%m-%d %T' ).</p>"
    echo '</body>'
    echo '</html>'
}

echo '*** Start build.sh'

if [ "$FAIL_BUILD" == "true" ]; then
    MY_RC=1
else
    create_html > $MY_OUTPUT_DIR/index.html
    pushd $MY_PARENT_DIR/maven-projects/my-app > /dev/null
    mvn -s $CI_PROJECT_DIR/.m2/settings.xml clean compile || MY_RC=1
    popd > /dev/null
fi

[[ $MY_RC -eq 0 ]] && echo "Build succeeded!" || echo "Build failed!"

echo '*** End build.sh'

exit $MY_RC
```

Figure 6-23. Contents of the Maven build script

---

[3] Maven has additional stages (similar to GitLab) that runs tests and packages the target objects into a jar file (a glorified zip file). In this example, I stop short of running the remaining Maven stages to help illustrate the use of the cache. I don't really care about making a project at this point.

CHAPTER 6 YOU BUILD IT, YOU KEEP IT

When Maven runs, it creates a target directory under the my-app directory where the compiled objects (Java classes in this case) are stored as well as some metadata about the build. Figure 6-24 shows the structure of the target tree generated by the compile option. Note that only App.java was compiled; AppTest.java is compiled as part of Maven's test phase.

```
jpainter@                     : ~/gitlab-repos/myshellpipeline
jpainter@                     :                    $ tree -n maven-projects
maven-projects
└── my-app
    ├── pom.xml
    ├── src
    │   ├── main
    │   │   └── java
    │   │       └── com
    │   │           └── mycompany
    │   │               └── app
    │   │                   └── App.java
    │   └── test
    │       └── java
    │           └── com
    │               └── mycompany
    │                   └── app
    │                       └── AppTest.java
    └── target
        ├── classes
        │   └── com
        │       └── mycompany
        │           └── app
        │               └── App.class
        ├── generated-sources
        │   └── annotations
        └── maven-status
            └── maven-compiler-plugin
                └── compile
                    └── default-compile
                        ├── createdFiles.lst
                        └── inputFiles.lst

23 directories, 6 files
jpainter@                     :          $
```

Figure 6-24. *Directory and tree structure after manual Maven build*

For context, Figure 6-25 shows the final top-level directory of our "MyShellPipeline" project. Here, you can see the .m2 and maven-projects directories listed. The maven-projects directory has the source files checked in as shown in Figure 6-20. The .m2 directory only includes the settings.xml file. Note that we did not check in the maven-projects/my-app/target directory nor the .m2/repository directory like we did with the output directory in an earlier example. This is because Maven may delete and recreate these directories as needed; this will cause some grief to Git if this happens.

225

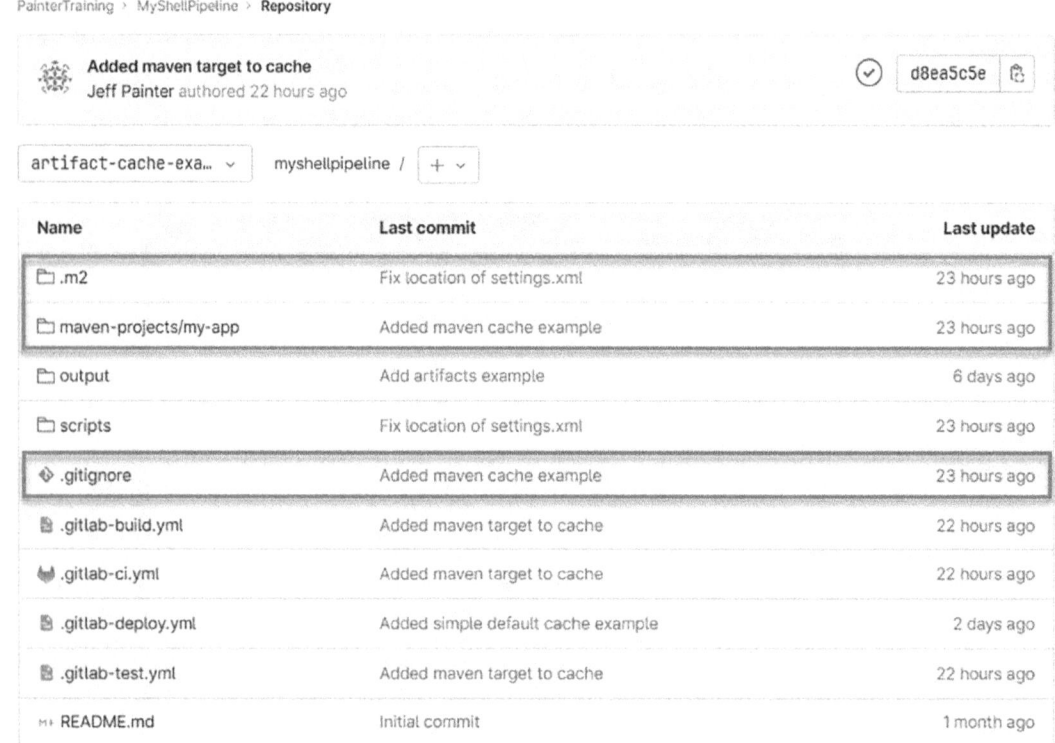

Figure 6-25. Creation of top-level cache directories in the GitLab project

Because of this behavior, the .gitignore file was added with the contents as shown in Figure 6-26. Here, we are telling Git to ignore any directory named target (wherever it occurs in the directory structure) as well as the .m2/repository directory. We didn't do this with the output directory because we control what goes in there; that is, there is no tool that would potentially delete it.

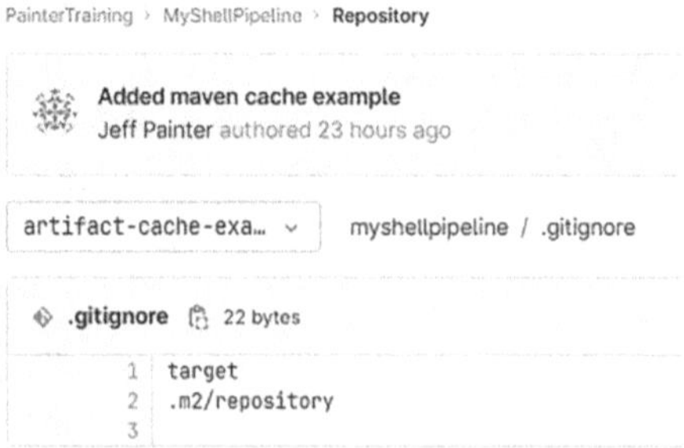

Figure 6-26. Contents of git ignore file for Maven target directories

CHAPTER 6   YOU BUILD IT, YOU KEEP IT

Pipeline Updates to Cache Maven Objects

Now that we have the preliminary Maven setup out of the way, let's look at how we can update the pipeline to cache the dependency downloads and the generated build objects. Without these changes, our build will still work, but each pipeline would download the dependencies from the Internet afresh with each run as well as regenerate the build objects at every stage. Figure 6-27 shows the changes made to the .gitlab-ci.yml file. In addition to setting the image to version 3.9.0 of Maven, we use the paths keyword in the cache section to select both the Maven repository in .m2/repository and the object directory in maven-projects/my-app/target. Everything stored in these directories will be cached. Note that the Maven Docker image we are using is based on Ubuntu, so we no longer need to install bash.

Figure 6-27. Default definition of project cache

227

To see the effects of the cache, Figure 6-28 shows the changes made to .gitlab-build.yml that prints out the two cached directories both before and after the run of scripts/build.sh. Figure 6-29 shows the changes made to .gitlab-test.yml that prints out the two cached directories before the run of scripts/unit-test.sh. Note that the explicit reference to the Python image and corresponding install of bash has been removed from this file since we are now relying on the Maven image set by default in .gitlab-ci.yml.

```
.gitlab-build.yml  909 bytes
 1  build-job:
 2    stage: build
 3    variables:
 4      MY_VAR2: local value 2
 5    artifacts:
 6      name: "$CI_JOB_NAME-$CI_COMMIT_REF_NAME"
 7      expose_as: 'build-artifacts'
 8      expire_in: 1 week
 9      paths:
10        - output/
11      exclude:
12        - output/.gitignore
13    script:
14      - !reference [.common-rule-vars, script]
15      - echo "MY_DB_PASSWORD='$MY_DB_PASSWORD'"
16      - echo '$MY_VAR1+$MY_VAR2'
17      - echo "NOT_DEFINED_VAR='${NOT_DEFINED_VAR}'"
18      - cat /etc/shells
19      - echo "Compiling the code..."
20      - if [ -d .m2/repository ]; then ls -l .m2/repository; fi
21      - if [ -d maven-projects/my-app/target ]; then ls -l maven-projects/my-app/target; fi
22      - scripts/build.sh
23      - if [ -d .m2/repository ]; then ls -l .m2/repository; fi
24      - if [ -d maven-projects/my-app/target ]; then ls -l maven-projects/my-app/target; fi
25      - if [ -f output/index.html ]; then cat output/index.html; fi
26      - echo "Compile complete."
27
```

Figure 6-28. *Update of build job to show the state of cache directories*

```yaml
.common-prep:
  before_script:
    - echo "Common setup before test"
  after_script:
    - echo "Common teardown after test"

.prep-test:
  extends: .common-prep
  stage: test
  variables:
    MY_TEST_VAR1: 'prep-test-hello'
    MY_TEST_VAR2: 'prep-test-goodbye'

.common-tests:
  script:
    - echo "MY_TEST_VAR1=$MY_TEST_VAR1"
    - echo "MY_TEST_VAR2=$MY_TEST_VAR2"

unit-test-job:
  extends: .prep-test
  rules:
    - if: $CI_PIPELINE_SOURCE == "web" && $FAIL_UNIT_TEST == "true"
      allow_failure: true
    - when: on_success
  script:
    - !reference [.common-rule-vars, script]
    - echo "Running unit tests..."
    - !reference [.common-tests, script]
    - if [ -d .m2/repository ]; then ls -l .m2/repository; fi
    - if [ -d maven-projects/my-app/target ]; then ls -l maven-projects/my-app/target; fi
    - if [ -f output/index.html ]; then cat output/index.html; fi
    - scripts/unit-test.sh
    - echo "Unit tests completed"
```

Figure 6-29. Update of unit test to show the state of cache directories

Figure 6-30 shows the results of running the pipeline for the first time with the new cache configuration. Here, we see a message warning us that the cache does not exist and hence cannot be restored. This is perfectly fine and is to be expected since we haven't cached anything yet.

CHAPTER 6   YOU BUILD IT, YOU KEEP IT

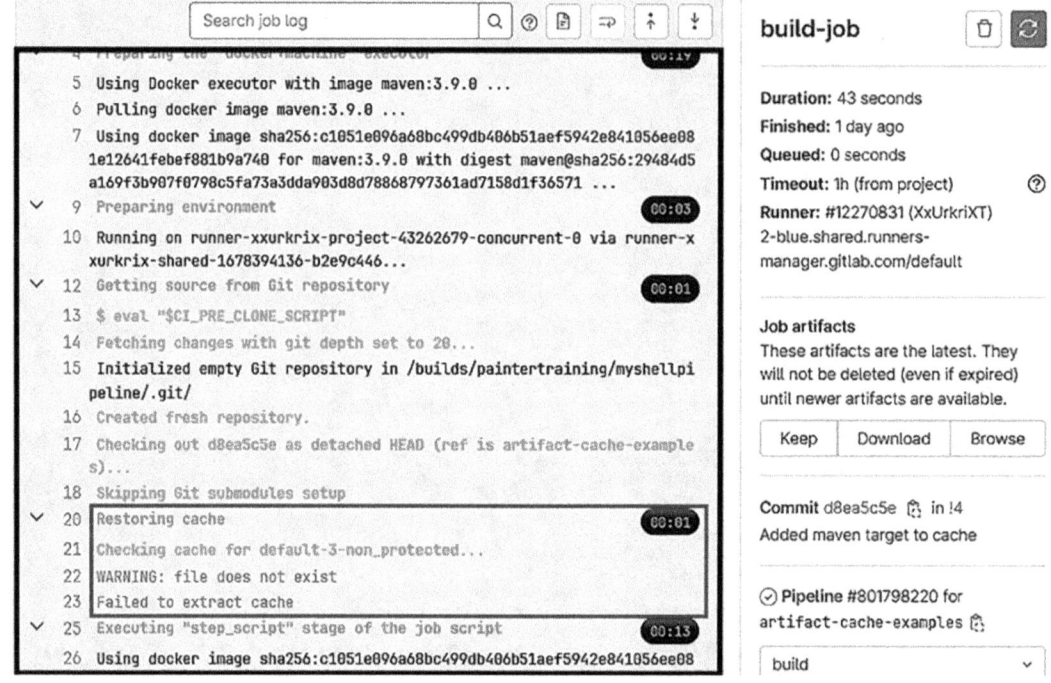

Figure 6-30. *Output of build job with cache enabled (part 1)*

Looking further down at the build job results, we see the results shown in Figure 6-31. The first highlighted area shows that neither the .m2/repository nor the maven-projects/my-app/target directories exist prior to running scripts/build.sh. The second highlighted area shows the results of running Maven within the build.sh script; here, we see that Maven is starting to download a number of dependencies into the .m2/repository directory.

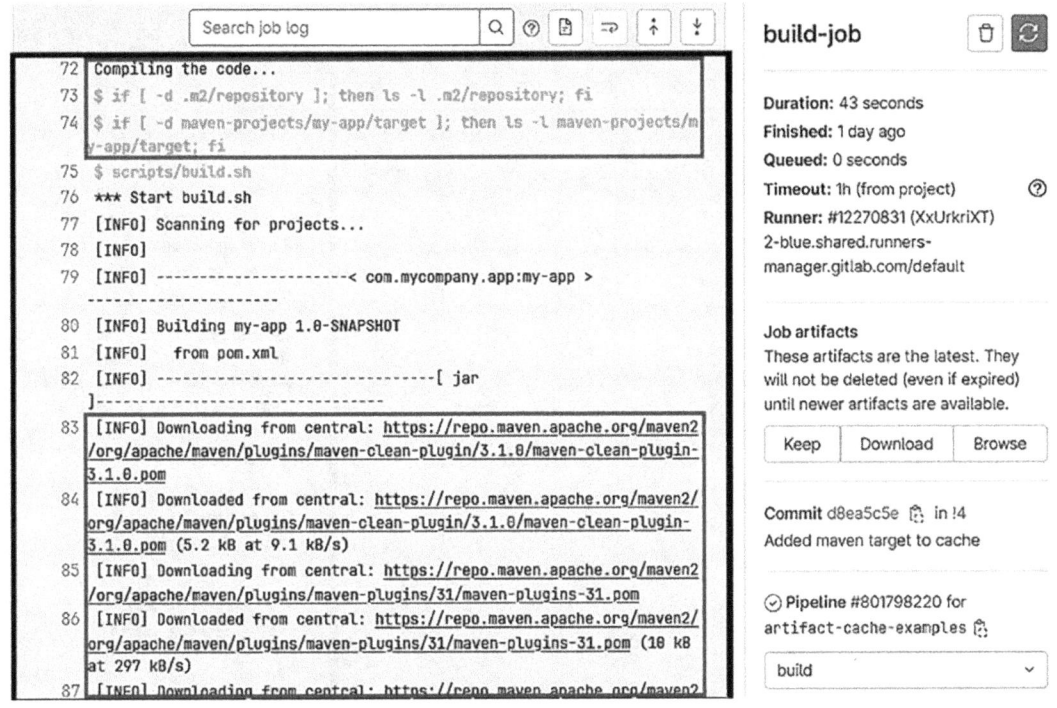

Figure 6-31. *Output of build job with cache enabled (part 2)*

Figure 6-32 shows the results near the end of the build job. After the build.sh script runs, we now see that both the .m2/repository and maven-projects/my-app/target directory have been populated.[4] At the end of the build job, we also see that the cache directories have been zipped into a cache.zip file that is then uploaded to a storage location using GCE (Google Compute Engine).[5]

---

[4] I only list the top-level directories for both of these cache directories due to the large number of files and deep subdirectory structure.

[5] You'll discover that if you try to access the provided link, you will not have proper permissions to view it. This is because this storage location is owned by GitLab. If you had any issues, the GitLab support team will be able to access this storage location for you.

CHAPTER 6   YOU BUILD IT, YOU KEEP IT

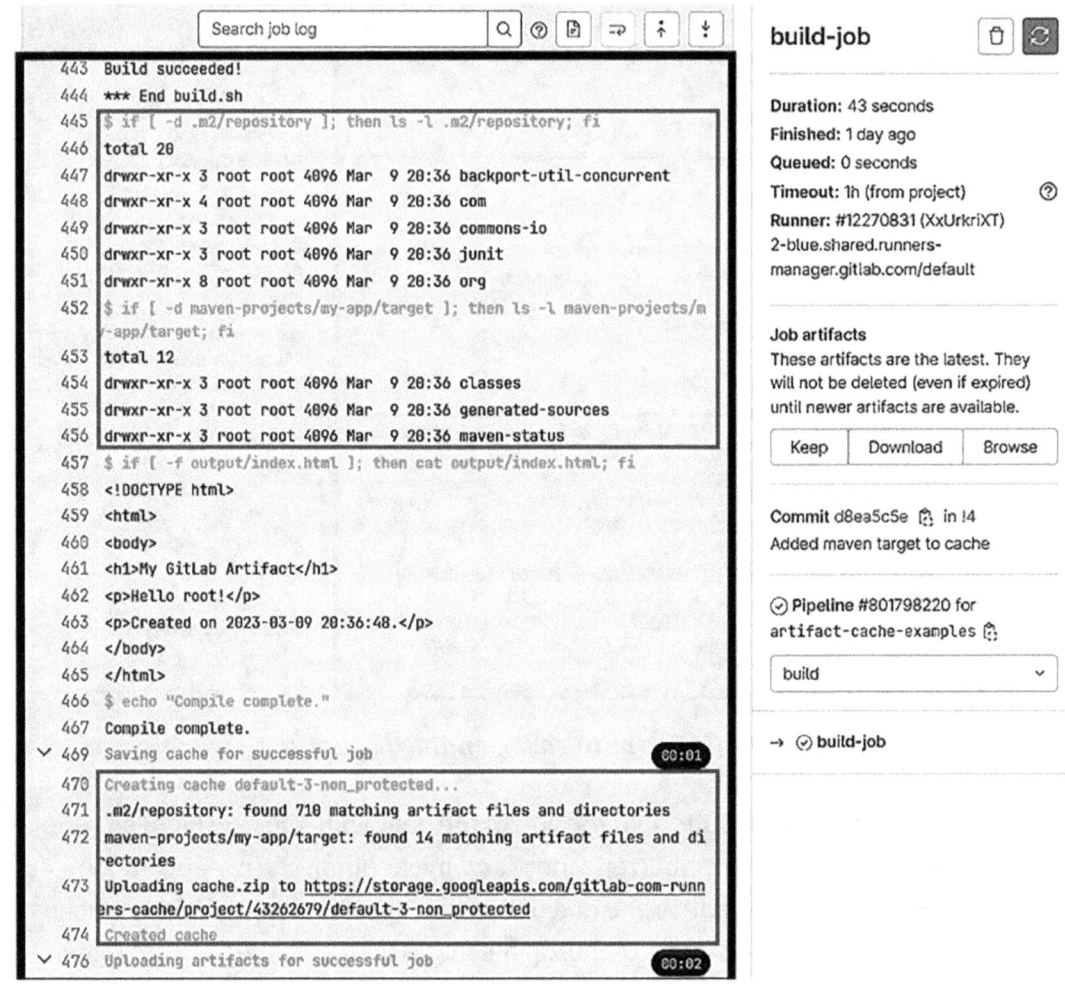

Figure 6-32. Output of build job with cache enabled (part 3)

Accessing the Cache in the Unit Test

So now that we've created the cache, let's take a look at the unit-test-job results to see how it handled the cache. Figure 6-33 shows the top of the unit-test-job results. The highlighted area indicates that cache.zip was downloaded from the same storage area used in the build job; although it doesn't state it, the cache.zip file was unzipped creating the two cache directories automatically. Note that the cache is restored before any artifacts are restored.

CHAPTER 6   YOU BUILD IT, YOU KEEP IT

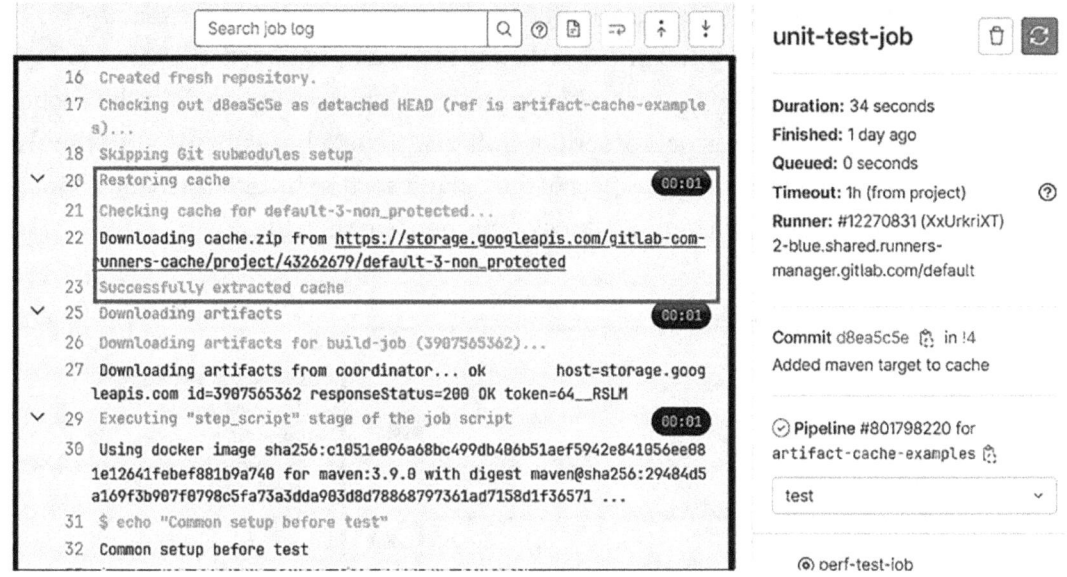

Figure 6-33. Output of unit test job with cache enabled (part 1)

Looking further down at the results of unit-test-job, we see the listing of the cache repositories prior to running scripts/unit-test.sh in Figure 6-34. Note that the date timestamps of those directories match the date timestamps shown in the earlier listing in Figure 6-31. The cache.zip file maintains those timestamps. For tools like Maven, this is useful when determining if new files need to be downloaded.

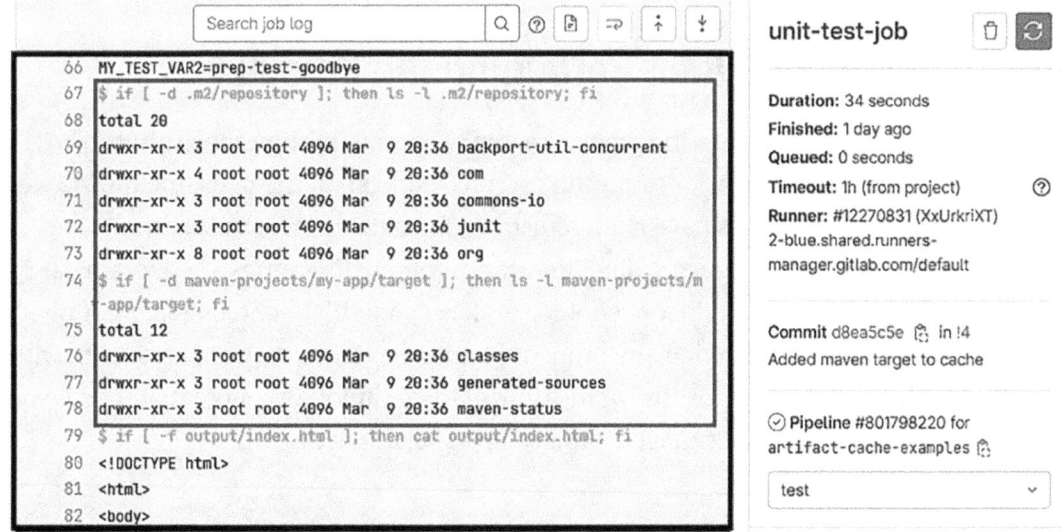

Figure 6-34. Output of unit test job with cache enabled (part 2)

233

Finally, Figure 6-35 shows the end of unit-test-job results. Here, we see that the cache directories are again zipped into a cache.zip file and uploaded to the same storage area as the build job. This happens whether or not any changes were made to the cache (which we could have made as part of scripts/unit-test.sh but chose not to at this time). In fact, since we defined the cache as part of the default section in .gitlab-ci.yml, all jobs will do this. We'll consider the ramifications of this behavior in a bit.

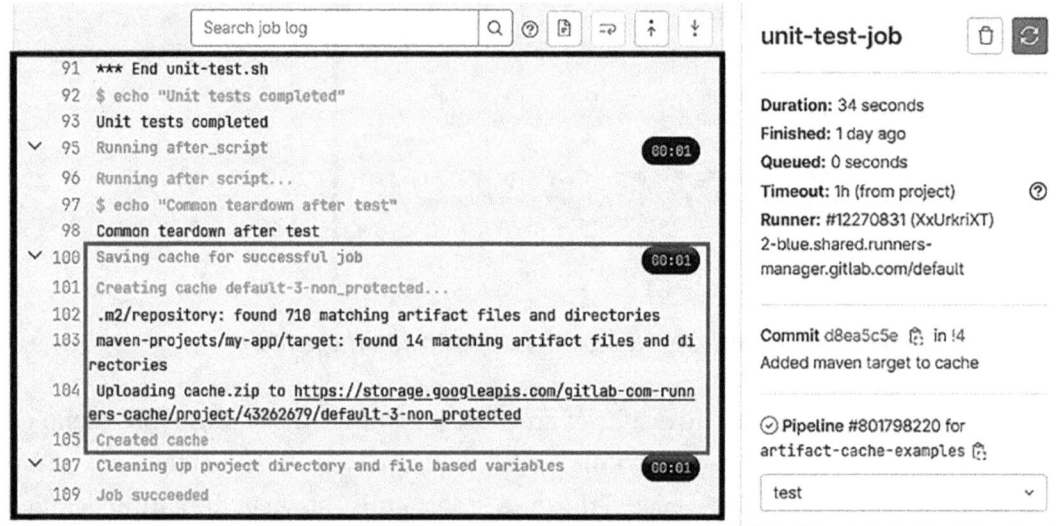

Figure 6-35. Output of unit test job with cache enabled (part 3)

Impact on Cache When Rerunning the Pipeline

So, what happens when we run the pipeline again? Figure 6-36 shows the results of listing the cache directories prior to running scripts/build.sh in the new pipeline. As we can see, the cache directories have been reinstated from the previous pipeline. As we noted with unit-test-job earlier, the date timestamps of the directories are the same as when we originally ran the build job. Looking at the second highlighted area, we now see that Maven doesn't download any more dependencies since they are up to date with the remote Maven central repository at the time of the rebuild. Also, note that the Maven clean directive has deleted the maven-project/my-app/target directory.

CHAPTER 6 YOU BUILD IT, YOU KEEP IT

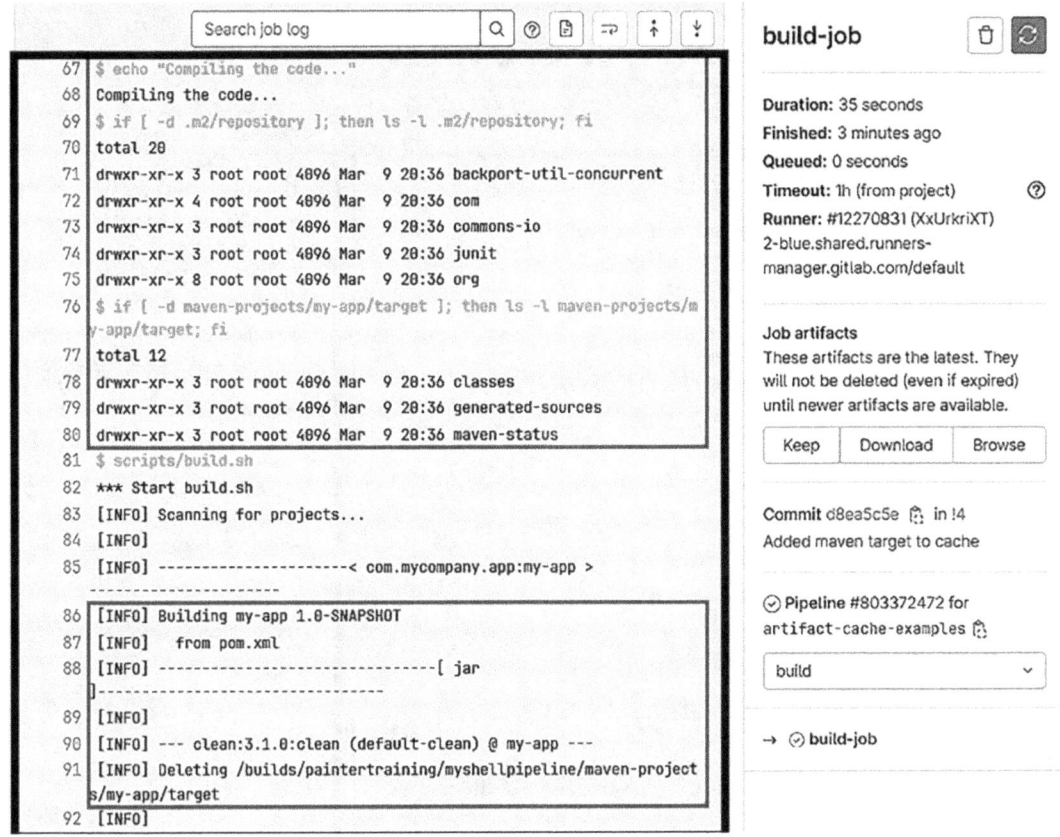

Figure 6-36. *Output of cache for the rerun of build job (part 1)*

Figure 6-37 shows the listing of the cache directories after scripts/build.sh has been run. Note that the date timestamps of the .m2/repository directories have not changed since the original build but that those of maven-projects/my-app/target have. This is a consequence of running the Maven clean directive. We forced Maven to rebuild the class objects from our source. Now when the cache.zip file is created, the new files in the target directory are preserved when uploaded to the GCE storage area. If we were to look at the unit-test-job results following this build job, we would see the new target files.

235

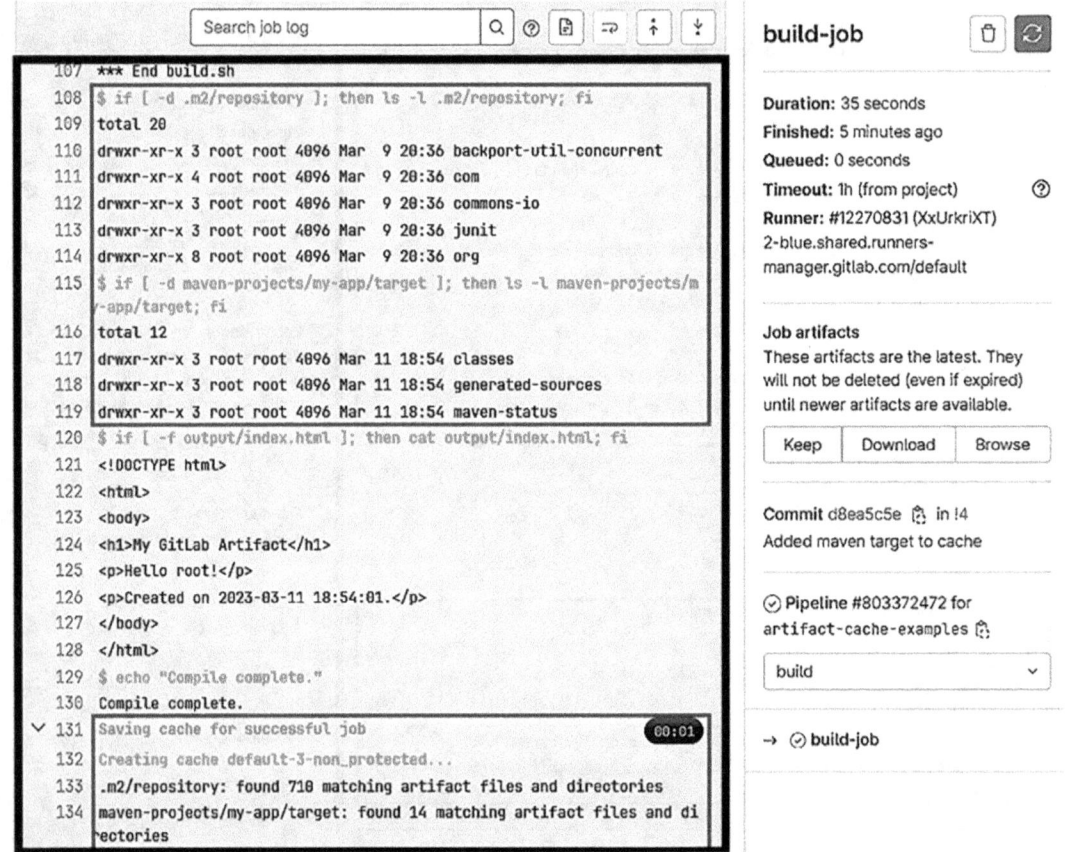

Figure 6-37. *Output of cache for the rerun of build job (part 2)*

Creating Multiple Caches in a Pipeline

So, as you may already have figured out by now, there are two main problems with the way we've set up the cache in this example. The first issue deals with the creation of cache.zip at the end of every job; it's possible that when jobs run in parallel, such as is done in the test stage, a cache.zip in one job may override a cache.zip in a parallel job. This could lead to a loss of data should one of those jobs update the cache. The second issue deals with the fact that the cache is shared across all branches of the same type. In terms of the target files, this means that one pipeline in a given branch could end up overwriting the target files in a pipeline from a different branch.

To resolve these types of issues, GitLab introduced the concept of a cache key. This key could be based on a CI/CD variable or the contents of a control file such as requirements.txt for Python or Gemfile.lock for Ruby. Using a cache key allows you to create isolated caches based on the context in which you use the cache. A common use case is to create a cache based on the branch so that two users with different working branches have their own cache. The branch cache can be further refined to caches based on job (e.g., build-job) or stage (e.g., test).

In this example, sharing the rather large Maven .m2/repository across branches isn't much of an issue since Maven can manage different download versions over time. In addition, if one job ends up overwriting the cache from another job, Maven can recover by redownloading the missing objects. The target objects, however, need to be based on the branch. We don't want to have one branch generating target objects that could be picked up by another branch accidentally.

Figure 6-38 shows the changes to the .gitlab-ci.yml file that creates two separate caches. Rather than using the default cache, two hidden jobs are used so that we can independently control what caches are used per job. We'll use the references technique to include those caches for a job. The first cache is the Maven .m2/repository cache that uses the key "m2-cache". Since the key is a static string, the cache can be shared across branches. The second cache is the target object cache. It uses the cache key $CI_COMMIT_REF_SLUG[6] to maintain caches per branch.

---

[6] Predefined variables that end in _SLUG have values that remove and/or replace special characters so that they can be used where special characters are not allowed, such as the value of the cache key.

.gitlab-ci.yml 1.60 KiB

```yaml
stages:
  - build
  - test
  - deploy
  - cleanup

default:
  image: maven:3.9.0

.cache-m2:
  cache:
    key: m2-cache
    paths:
      - .m2/repository

.cache-target:
  cache:
    key: $CI_COMMIT_REF_SLUG
    paths:
      - maven-projects/my-app/target

variables:
  FAIL_BUILD: "false"
  FAIL_UNIT_TEST: "false"
  FAIL_LINT_TEST: "false"
```

Figure 6-38. *Defining separate caches for Maven target directories using cache key*

With this change in place, Figure 6-39 shows the changes made to .gitlab-build.yml. Here, we use the list form of the cache keyword with the references to each of the caches. The order of the caches is the order in which the caches are downloaded and uploaded. Figure 6-40 shows the equivalent changes to the .gitlab-test.yml file. Note that only unit-test-job was updated; all other tests do not use the cache, so they do not need to download and reupload the cache.zip files.

.gitlab-build.yml 994 bytes

```
build-job:
  stage: build
  variables:
    MY_VAR2: local value 2
  artifacts:
    name: "$CI_JOB_NAME-$CI_COMMIT_REF_NAME"
    expose_as: 'build-artifacts'
    expire_in: 1 week
    paths:
      - output/
    exclude:
      - output/.gitignore
  cache:
    - !reference [.cache-m2, cache]
    - !reference [.cache-target, cache]
  script:
    - !reference [.common-rule-vars, script]
    - echo "MY_DB_PASSWORD='$MY_DB_PASSWORD'"
    - echo '$MY_VAR1+$MY_VAR2'
```

Figure 6-39. *Update to build job using cache keys*

```
📄 .gitlab-test.yml    2.17 KiB

 1   .common-prep:
 2     before_script:
 3       - echo "Common setup before test"
 4     after_script:
 5       - echo "Common teardown after test"
 6
 7   .prep-test:
 8     extends: .common-prep
 9     stage: test
10     variables:
11       MY_TEST_VAR1: 'prep-test-hello'
12       MY_TEST_VAR2: 'prep-test-goodbye'
13
14   .common-tests:
15     script:
16       - echo "MY_TEST_VAR1=$MY_TEST_VAR1"
17       - echo "MY_TEST_VAR2=$MY_TEST_VAR2"
18
19   unit-test-job:
20     extends: .prep-test
21     cache:
22       - !reference [.cache-m2, cache]
23       - !reference [.cache-target, cache]
24     rules:
25       - if: $CI_PIPELINE_SOURCE == "web" && $FAIL_
26         allow_failure: true
```

Figure 6-40. Update to unit test using cache keys

Figure 6-41 shows the results at the start of the build job with these changes in place. Since this is the first time we've run this pipeline with the new cache keys, we see the standard warning that the caches with those keys do not exist. The next time we run a pipeline on the same branch, we would see that both caches are downloaded. If, however, we run a pipeline on a new branch, only the .m2/repository cache would be downloaded; the target cache would report as not existing.

CHAPTER 6   YOU BUILD IT, YOU KEEP IT

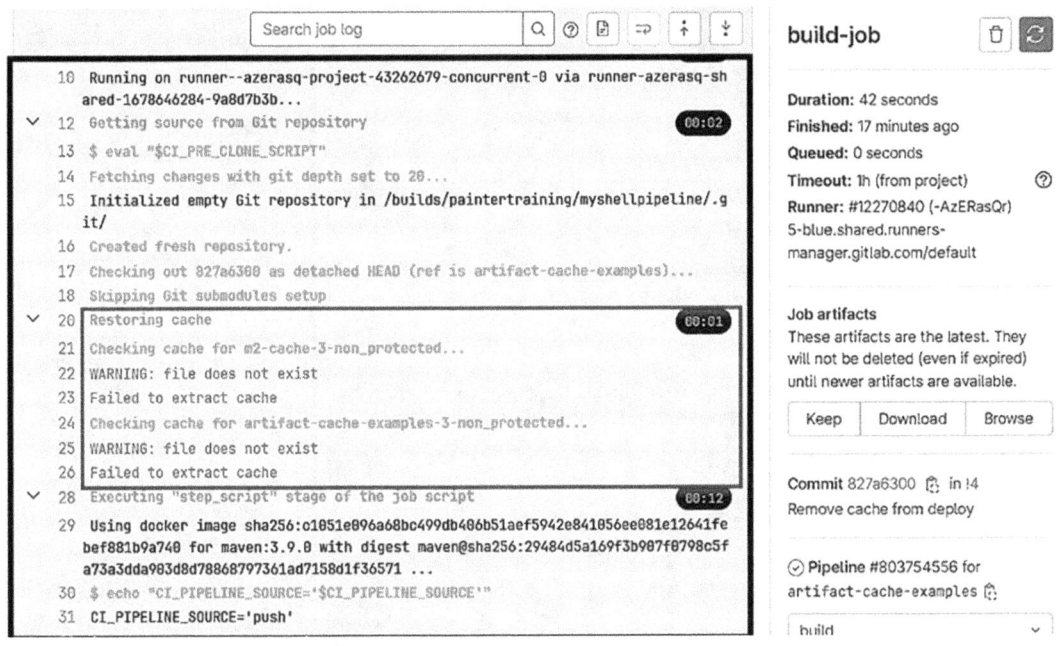

Figure 6-41.   Output of build job using cache keys (part 1)

The end of the build job is shown in Figure 6-42. Here, we see that the .m2/repository cache is zipped and uploaded first followed by the target cache. Each one is uploaded into their own GCE storage location based on the cache key and branch type (non-protected in this case).

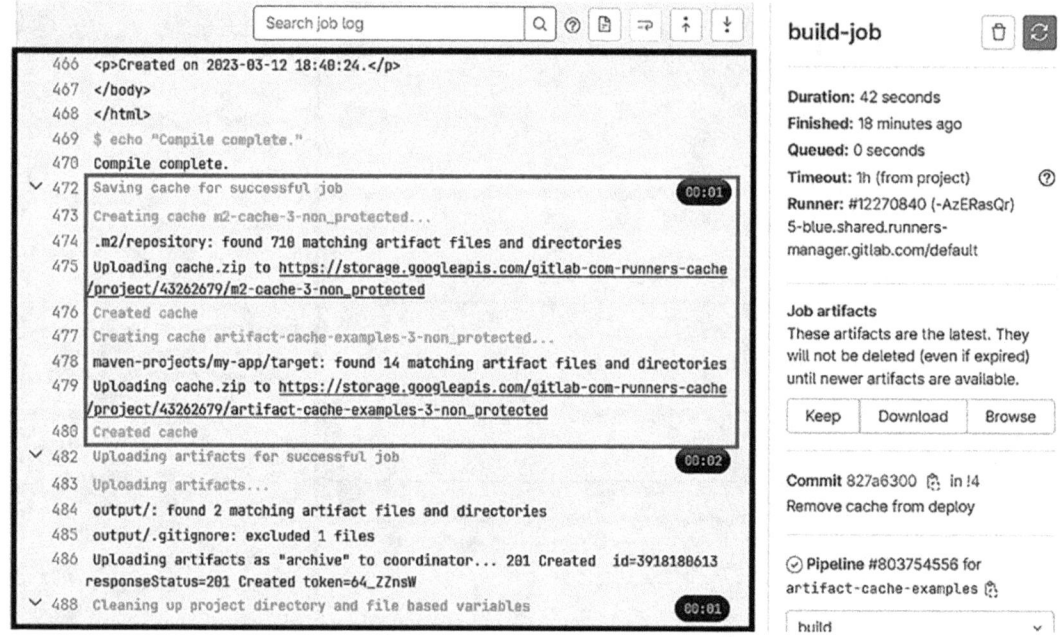

Figure 6-42. *Output of build job using cache keys (part 2)*

Figure 6-43 shows the start of unit-test-job run in the same pipeline. As expected, we see the .m2/repository cache downloaded first followed by the target cache. The end of unit-test-job uploads the caches just as they were for the build job.

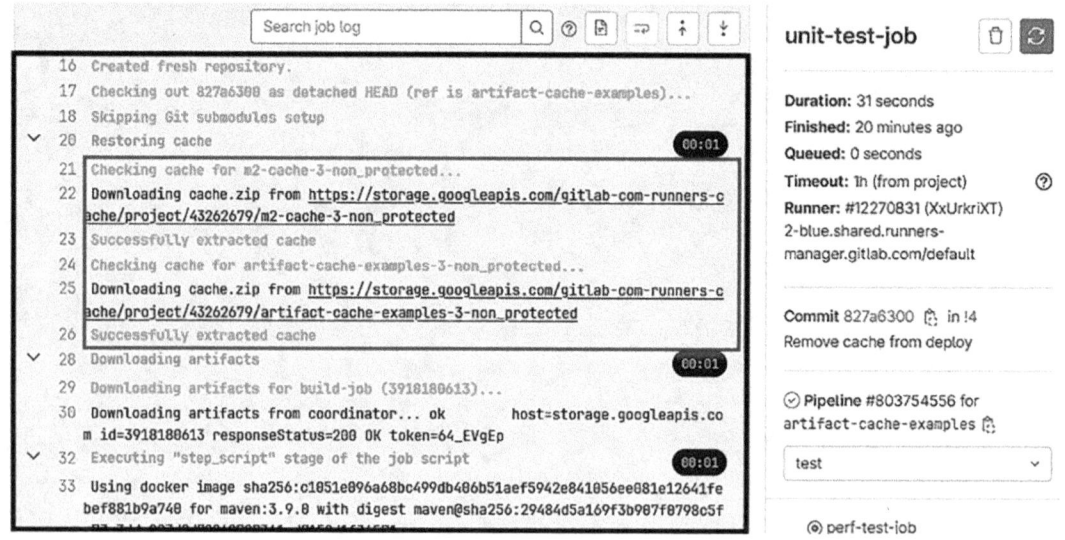

Figure 6-43. *Output of unit test using cache keys*

Marking a Cache As Read-Only

Now suppose a job uses a cache but does not change it (or changes it but does not need to save it). Is there a way to handle that scenario? Turns out we can control this using the policy keyword for caches. By default, the cache policy is pull-push (i.e., we download the cache at the start of a job and upload that cache at the end of the job). If we want to download a cache but tell GitLab not to upload it at the end (whether or not changes have been made to the cache during the job), we add policy: pull to the cache definition.[7]

To illustrate the pull policy, let's update our example so that deploy-job only downloads the target cache. Figure 6-44 shows the changes to .gitlab-ci.yml that adds a .cache-target-readonly hidden job that uses the pull policy.[8] Figure 6-45 shows the changes to the .gitlab-deploy.yml file that uses the read-only target cache.

---

[7] For completeness, you can specify policy: push to tell GitLab not to download the cache, which is a way to let people know that the cache is being created by a job.

[8] The GitLab documentation suggests using YAML anchors to modify the pull policy for an existing cache specification, but this only works if the YAML anchor and the reference to that YAML anchor are in the same configuration file.

.gitlab-ci.yml 1.72 KiB

```
stages:
  - build
  - test
  - deploy
  - cleanup

default:
  image: maven:3.9.0

.cache-m2:
  cache:
    key: m2-cache
    paths:
      - .m2/repository

.cache-target:
  cache:
    key: $CI_COMMIT_REF_SLUG
    paths:
      - maven-projects/my-app/target

.cache-target-readonly:
  cache:
    key: $CI_COMMIT_REF_SLUG
    paths:
      - maven-projects/my-app/target
    policy: pull

variables:
```

Figure 6-44. *Hidden job defining read-only caches*

```yaml
.gitlab-deploy.yml  1.04 KiB
 1  deploy-job:
 2    stage: deploy
 3    environment: production
 4    cache:
 5      - !reference [.cache-target-readonly, cache]
 6    rules:
 7      - if: $CI_COMMIT_BRANCH == $CI_DEFAULT_BRANCH
 8    script:
 9      - !reference [.common-rule-vars, script]
10      - echo "Deploying application..."
11      - scripts/deploy.sh
12      - echo "Application successfully deployed."
13
14  deploy-dev-job:
15    stage: deploy
16    environment: dev
17    cache:
18      - !reference [.cache-target-readonly, cache]
19    rules:
20      - if: $CI_COMMIT_BRANCH != $CI_DEFAULT_BRANCH
21    script:
22      - !reference [.common-rule-vars, script]
23      - echo "Deploying dev application..."
24      - scripts/deploy.sh
25      - echo "Dev application successfully deployed."
26
```

Figure 6-45. Update of deploy jobs to use read-only caches

Figure 6-46 shows the start of the deploy-job results with these changes in place. As expected, it downloaded the target cache for this run of the pipeline. What you might not have expected is the message at the end of deploy-job as shown in Figure 6-47. It provides feedback on the target cache by stating that it was not uploaded due to the policy.

CHAPTER 6   YOU BUILD IT, YOU KEEP IT

Figure 6-46. Output of deploy job using read-only caches (part 1)

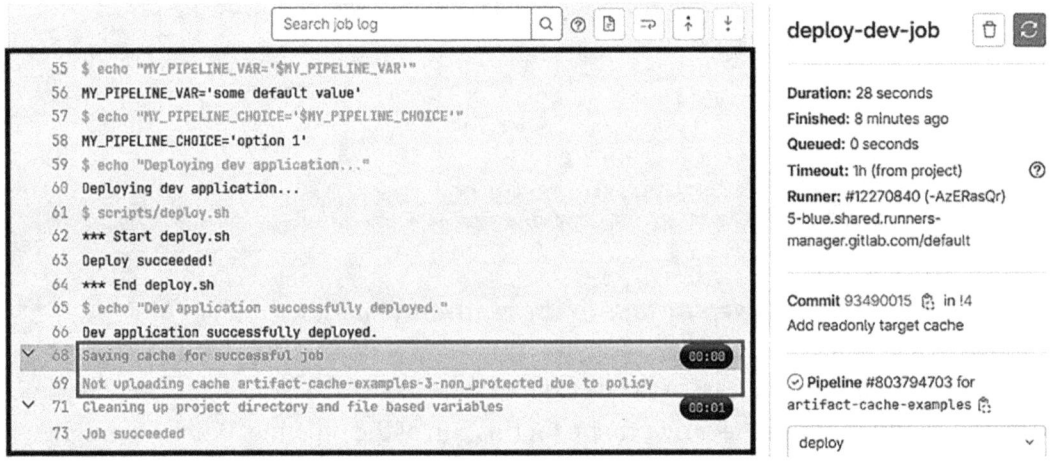

Figure 6-47. Output of deploy job using read-only caches (part 2)

Clearing Caches

We'll conclude this section by looking at how to clear caches. Sometimes, caches can get in a funky state, especially those like the Maven .m2/repository cache that are shared over time. Or perhaps they've gotten too large with objects you no longer need. For cases like these, GitLab provides a way to clear the caches, which isn't intuitively obvious. Figure 6-48 shows the pipeline summary page with the "Clear runner caches" button

CHAPTER 6   YOU BUILD IT, YOU KEEP IT

highlighted. Clicking this button will tell GitLab that any new caches should be created from scratch. It does this by incrementing an internal number associated with the project. You can see this in the name of the cache. For example, in the previous examples the .m2/repository cache is named m2-cache-3-non-protected. The 3 in the name indicates that I've cleared the cache a few times already. If I clear the cache again, that number will be incremented to 4.

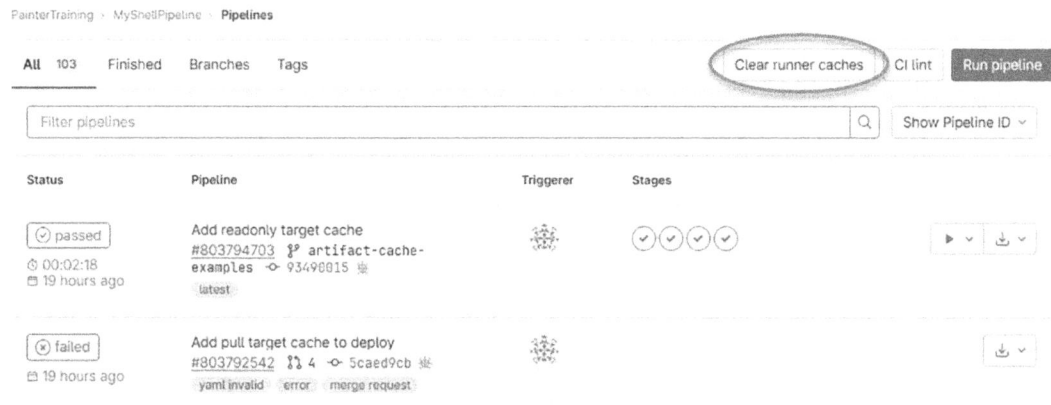

Figure 6-48. Pipeline summary with a clear cache button

So why renumber caches? It's because the old caches still remain for a period of time. If you have a pipeline where you rerun jobs or manually trigger a deployment, for example, that pipeline will still use the old cache. Any new pipeline runs will get their own set of caches.

Unlike artifacts, you can't control the expiration of caches. This is managed by GitLab itself. It will determine when a cache is no longer needed and remove it. Be forewarned, caches could be deleted even if it appears that they are still needed. The GitLab documentation warns you that caches are temporary and that you should be able to recreate them when needed. In my experience, this happens for caches that have been around for a while, such as the .m2/repository cache. This typically does not happen with newly created and/or updated caches.

CHAPTER 6   YOU BUILD IT, YOU KEEP IT

Summary

In this chapter, we covered the following items:

- Introduced the artifacts keyword to denote which generated objects are to be deployed
- Determined how to download artifacts from GitLab
- Learned how to link artifacts in merge requests
- Briefly discussed how reports are managed as special types of artifacts
- Introduced the cache keyword to stash reusable build objects across jobs and pipelines
- Described how to maintain multiple caches within a pipeline using cache keys
- Looked into how to mark a cache as read-only within a job
- Discovered how to clear caches

We've now reached the end of our discussion of GitLab's CI/CD pipelines. With everything covered here, you have enough information to create pipelines that handle most scenarios of creating products from your source code repository within GitLab. There are other optimizations and special features that we haven't explored here. And we haven't really gone into detail on how to do deployments, which is an entire topic unto itself. Some of these topics will be covered in later chapters. For now, the information in these past three chapters should get you going on creating your own pipelines.

In the next chapter, we'll switch our focus toward how to organize our projects in a multi-team environment, which includes how to set up permissions for the various members working on those teams.

CHAPTER 7

Let's Get Organized

Now that we have covered managing source code and directories within a project as well as creating pipelines to build and store artifacts for deployment, the time has come to look at how to organize our projects in a multi-team environment. In this chapter, we will cover how to manage multiple projects under a group as well as creating subgroups within groups. As part of this discussion, we'll look at how roles are used in conjunction with projects and groups to determine the permissions of team members assigned to those projects and groups.

Introducing Groups

When we signed up for our GitLab account, we created a high-level group under which all of our projects have been created. In my case, I created the "PainterTraining" group as shown in Figure 7-1. Since then, we haven't really talked much about what a group is used for other than as a place under which to collect projects. But groups play a more significant role than that. In this section, we'll explore the role that groups have in managing permissions for the projects within them as well as settings that impact those projects.

CHAPTER 7   LET'S GET ORGANIZED

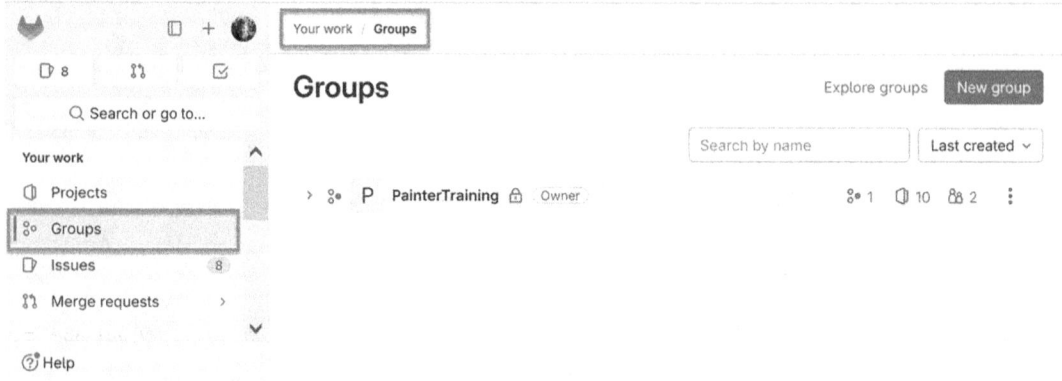

Figure 7-1. Group summary page

Viewing Group-Specific Projects

When you select the link to a group from the preceding group list, you get an overview of the group as shown in Figure 7-2. This provides a similar yet different view from the main dashboard when you select the GitLab fox icon in the upper left. On this group overview page, you get a list of projects similar to the main dashboard, but only those restricted to this group. In addition, the left-hand panel provides options that are specific to this group.

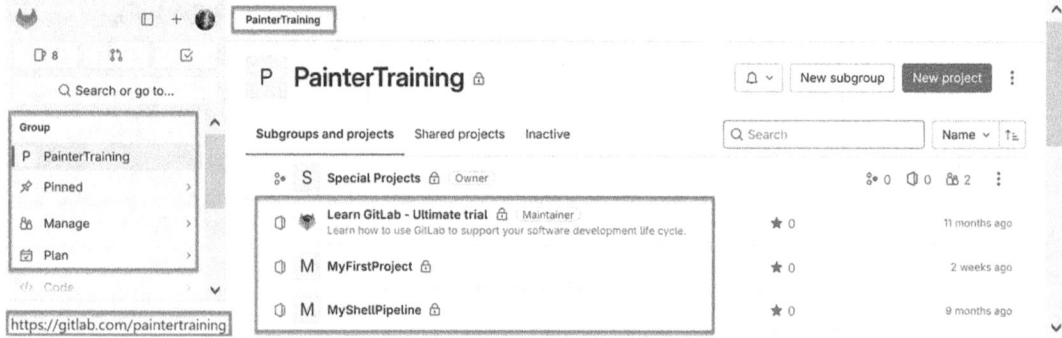

Figure 7-2. Group overview page

Viewing Group Activity

Figure 7-3 shows the activity page when we select Activity under the expanded Manage option on the left-hand side. As you can see, it shows all of the activity of users (in this case, me[1]) within this group including push and merge events. The activity list can be pretty noisy as it includes events from all projects contained in the group. GitLab itself does not provide a search capability for the activity list, but you can use the browser find feature to look for activities that match keywords should you need.

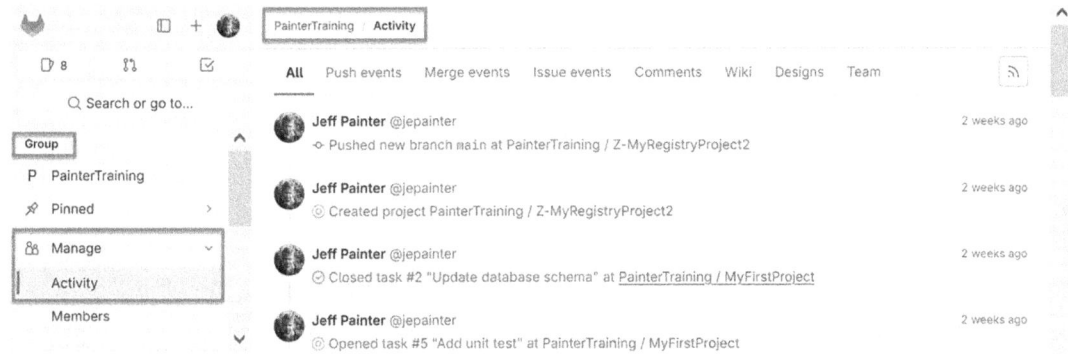

Figure 7-3. Group information activity page

Viewing Members of a Group

Let's skip down to the Group members page available under the expanded Manage option. Figure 7-4 shows the list of members currently belonging to this group along with their role. This brings us to one of the key purposes of groups: managing user permissions. Currently, I'm the only member of this group, and because I was the one to create this group when I created my GitLab account, I am also the owner of the group. This means that I have full control over the group in terms of the group's settings as well as who can join the group and what permissions they have.

---

[1] Since I will be adding other users, I updated my profile picture to more easily discern that it is me rather than use the abstract icon provided by GitLab.

CHAPTER 7   LET'S GET ORGANIZED

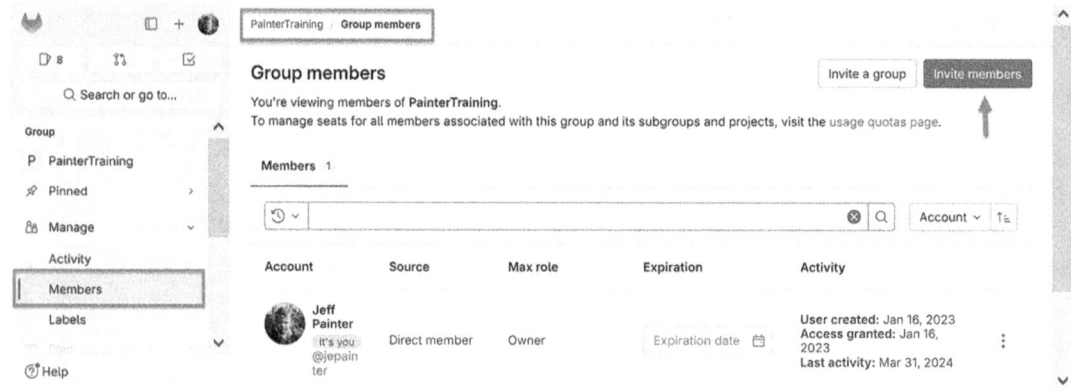

Figure 7-4. Group information members

Adding Members to a Group

So, let's add a new member to the group: my dog Heidi. Clicking the "Invite members" button brings up a pop-up dialog as shown in Figure 7-5. If the person you are inviting is not known to GitLab yet, you can enter the email address of that person; otherwise, you can add the person's GitLab username. You can also select the initial role of that person for this group. In this case, I selected Developer, which is a common role to use. Don't worry, you can change the role later if you need, but it is best to select the minimum role that that person should have.

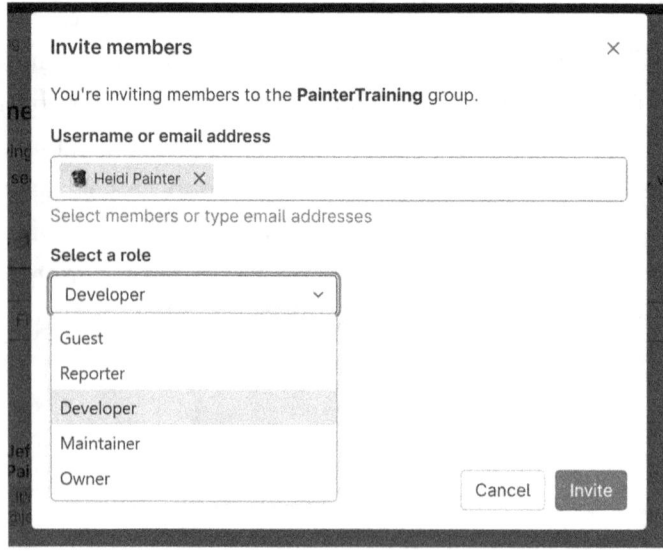

Figure 7-5. Group invite member form

CHAPTER 7 LET'S GET ORGANIZED

If you entered an email address, that person will be sent an email inviting them to join the group along with their new role (e.g., "Jeff Painter invited you to join the PainterTraining group as a developer"). That person will then go through the process of setting up their new user account similar to what you went through when you set up your own GitLab account. You will be sent an email letting you know they accepted and what their GitLab username is. If you entered that person's GitLab username on the invite, they will be sent an informational email letting them know they now have access to the group with the given role; they don't need to sign up again.

Figure 7-6 shows the group's member page after the user has accepted the invitation (in the case they were a new user) or the user was granted access (in the case they were already a user on the gitlab.com site). Note that the source for the new user indicates that the user is a direct member of the group and indicates who set up the membership. Also, note that "Max role" is a drop-down list that lets you change the role of that user for that group. You could, by the way, restrict the time the user is a member of the group by setting an expiration time; this is useful if you want to grant a user access for a brief period of time.

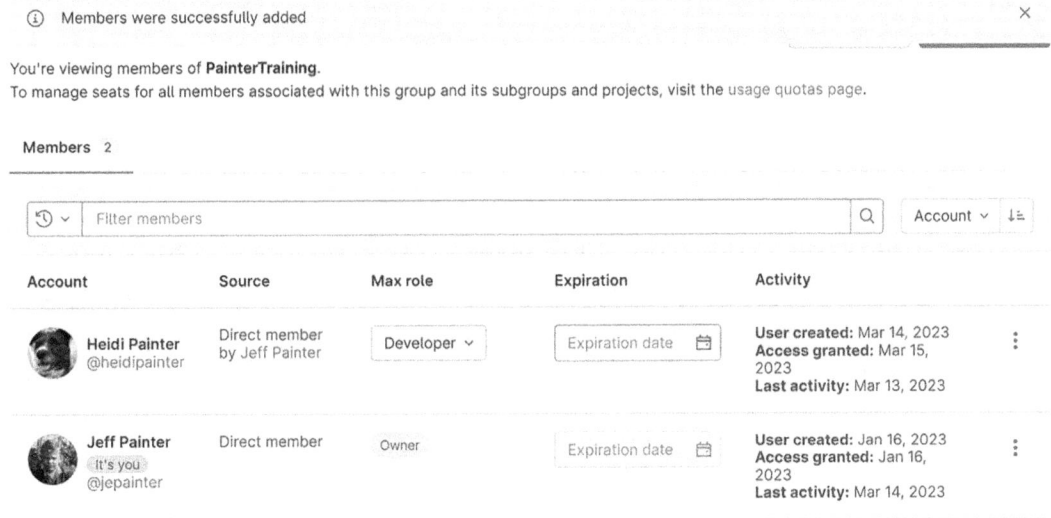

Figure 7-6. Group information with new members

253

CHAPTER 7   LET'S GET ORGANIZED

Project Impacts When Adding a Group Member

So, let's take a look at what impact this had on the projects within this group. Selecting Members under the expanded Manage option on the "MyShellPipeline" project, we see the list of project members and their roles as shown in Figure 7-7. Here, we see that the project's members and their roles are inherited from the "PainterTraining" group. This certainly makes life easier for managing users across a set of related projects in that we don't have to invite users to each and every project individually.

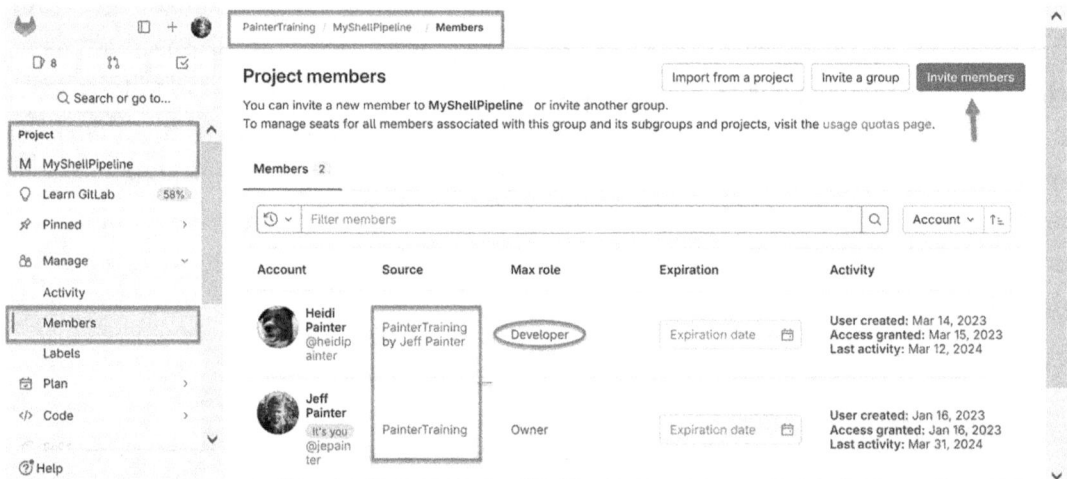

Figure 7-7. *Project information members page*

We still can, of course, add users individually to a project via the "Invite members" button for that project. For projects, maintainers and owners of the project can invite other members with the same or lower roles. For example, a maintainer can assign other members the maintainer role but not the owner role; only owners can assign other members the owner role. For groups, only the owner can invite other members to the group and set their roles; maintainers don't have the ability to invite members to a group.

Promoting a Group Member to Higher Project Role

So, what happens if we want to promote a user in a project to a higher role? For example, suppose we want to make Heidi a maintainer of the "MyShellPipeline" but remain a developer for all other projects under the "PainterTraining" group. As you can see in the previous figure, "Max role," which is inherited from the group, is not selectable as

CHAPTER 7　LET'S GET ORGANIZED

it was for the group. This seems to imply that we can't change the role, but, as it turns out, we can use the "Invite members" button. Figure 7-8 shows us inviting Heidi to be a maintainer of the "MyShellPipeline" project.

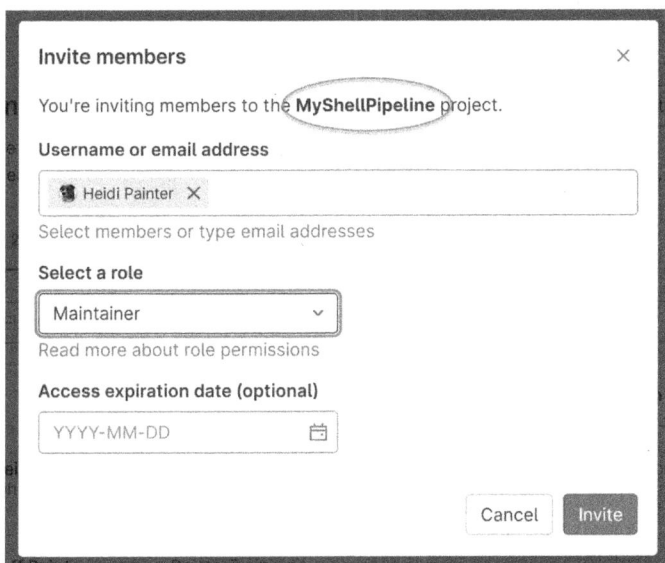

Figure 7-8. *Project invite members form with role selection*

Now when we go to the project's member page, we see that Heidi is now a maintainer of the "MyShellPipeline" project as shown in Figure 7-9. We now see from the source that Heidi is a direct member invited by me rather than an inherited member. We also see that "Max role" is now a drop-down list as we saw earlier with the group membership.

CHAPTER 7 LET'S GET ORGANIZED

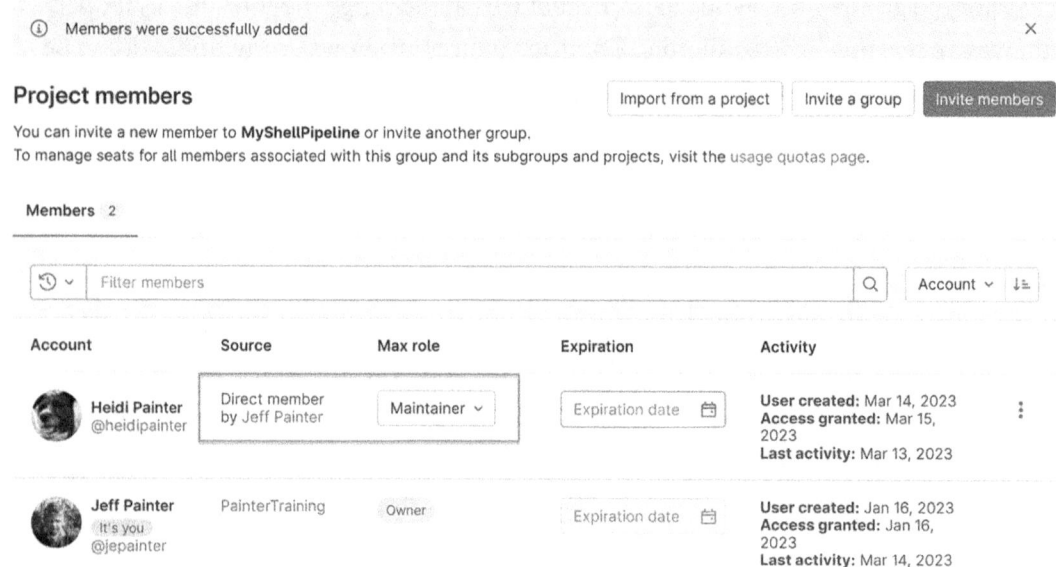

Figure 7-9. Project members after role promotion

Differences Between Group and Project Change Role Lists

There is a difference, though, between the "Max role" drop-down list for Heidi in the group's member list and the one for the project's member list. Figure 7-10 shows the list of roles available in the group's member list, and Figure 7-11 shows the list of roles available in the project's member list for Heidi. In the group's member list, we see all the roles provided from guest up to owner. However, in the project's member list, we see a smaller list of roles from developer up to owner. As it turns out, you can upgrade a project member to the same or higher role specified in the group, but you cannot downgrade them to a lower role.[2]

---

[2] If you are thinking you could get around this by using the "Invite member" button and trying to downgrade that way (since that drop-down menu provides all roles), you'll get an error message if you do.

CHAPTER 7   LET'S GET ORGANIZED

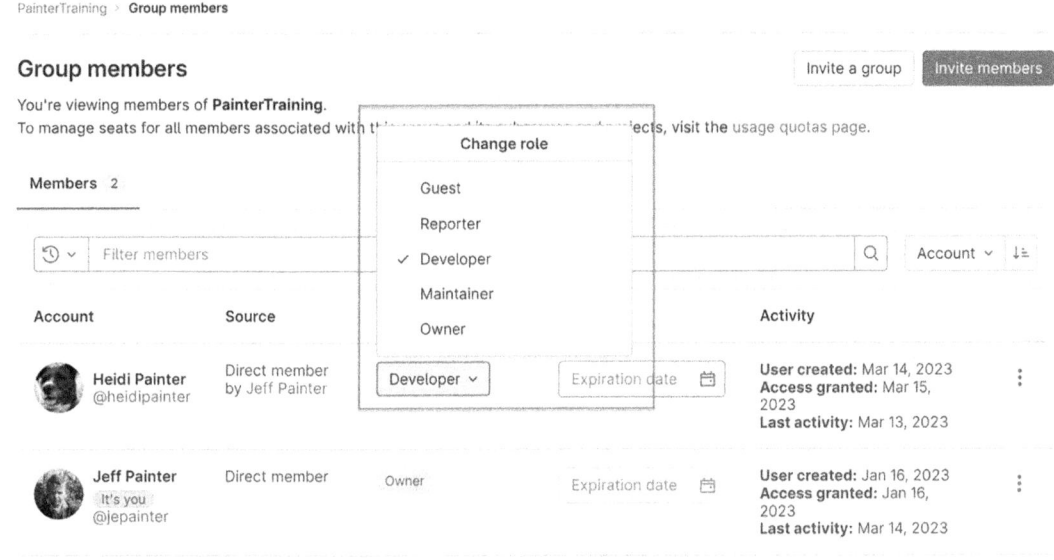

Figure 7-10.   Group member change role options

Figure 7-11.   Project member change role options

So, what happens to the project role for "MyShellPipeline" if we upgrade Heidi to the owner role in the group? In this case, Heidi would be upgraded to the owner role for the project as well even though we originally set her role to maintainer for that project.

CHAPTER 7   LET'S GET ORGANIZED

What if switching Heidi to the owner role in the group was an oopsie and you reset her back to the developer role in the group? Would you now have to go to the "MyShellPipeline" project and switch her back down to maintainer? Interestingly enough, her role in that case would automatically revert back to the maintainer role as before.

Now that we've considered groups in detail, let's look at how we can create a subgroup within a group.

Working with Subgroups

Just as most filesystems allow you to create a hierarchical directory structure to organize your files, GitLab allows you to create a hierarchical group structure to organize your projects. A group may contain a combination of projects and groups, referred to as subgroups in this context. Subgroups serve the same purpose as groups. In particular, they are used to control who can create, edit, and modify projects as well as nested subgroups.

Creating a Subgroup

To explore subgroups, let's start by creating one under our top-level group, "PainterTraining." Figure 7-12 shows the "New subgroup" button in our top-level group that lets us create a new subgroup. As we'll see later, only certain roles will be able to create subgroups.

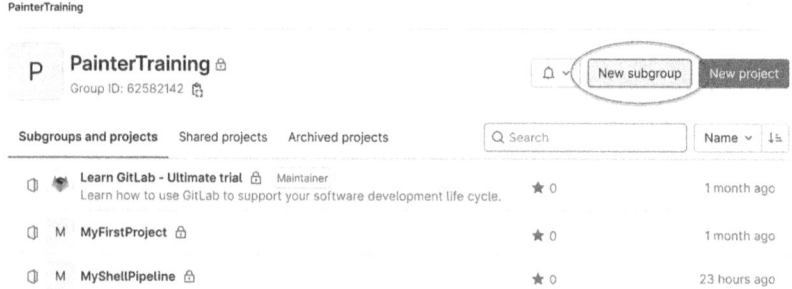

Figure 7-12. New subgroup option

Selecting the "New subgroup" button takes us to the "Create subgroup" page as shown in Figure 7-13. As you type the subgroup name, the subgroup slug is automatically displayed. As you can see, the subgroup name can have upper- and lowercase characters as well as spaces, periods, dashes, and, oddly, parentheses. The slug converts uppercase characters to their lowercase equivalents and replaces special characters with alternative characters; for example, spaces become dashes. Although you can override the subgroup slug once you've entered the subgroup name, it's best to leave the slug as is.

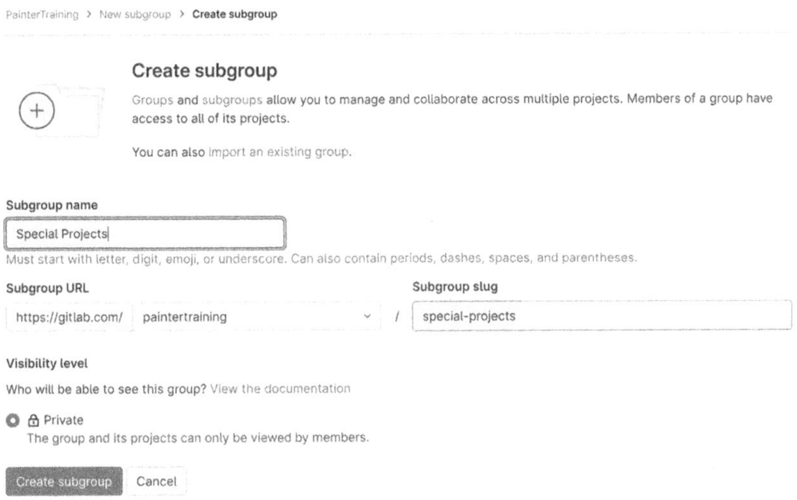

Figure 7-13. Create subgroup form

Note that the visibility level is set to "Private," which cannot be changed. This is because our top-level group was created as private as well. Once you set a group to private, all other projects and subgroups under it must be private as well. You cannot change the visibility to "Public," which on the gitlab.com site is the other alternative. If you want projects and subgroups to be public, you'll have to create a new top-level group that is public.[3] Be aware, though, that making a group or project public means that anyone on gitlab.com can view them whether or not they are authenticated.[4]

---

[3] Note that if your goal is to create a public open source project, GitLab has a special program for such projects that includes special cost benefits and features. See https://about.gitlab.com/solutions/open-source/join/ for more details.

[4] For self-managed GitLab sites, there is the "Internal" visibility option that restricts access to those who are authenticated. This option was once available for gitlab.com users but has been removed for security reasons. See https://docs.gitlab.com/ee/user/public_access.html#internal-projects-and-groups for more details.

CHAPTER 7 LET'S GET ORGANIZED

Viewing the Subgroup Page

When you create the subgroup, you are taken to the subgroup's page as shown in Figure 7-14. You'll also be sent an email notifying you that you have been granted owner access to the new subgroup. Since the newly created subgroup is empty, the page contains two panels to remind you to create a new subgroup or project. These panels only show for empty subgroups; once you've created a subgroup or project, those panels no longer show up. At that point, you'll have to use the "New subgroup" or "New project" buttons to create additional subgroups or projects.

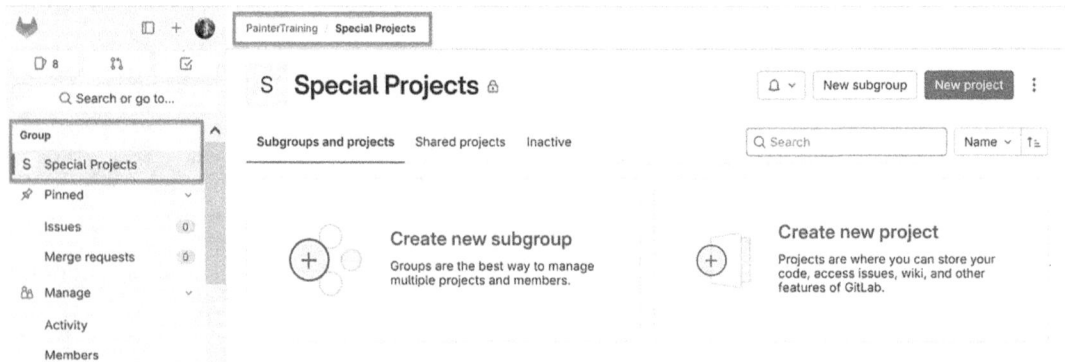

Figure 7-14. Subgroup page for Special Projects

You'll notice that the left-hand panel for the subgroup is the same as the left-hand panel for the top-level group except that the group name is replaced with the subgroup name. Otherwise, the options for the subgroup are the same as for the top-level group. Figure 7-15 shows the members page for the "Special Projects" subgroup. What this page shows is that the subgroup members and roles are inherited from the top-level "PainterTraining" group. This is the same as project member inheritance.

CHAPTER 7   LET'S GET ORGANIZED

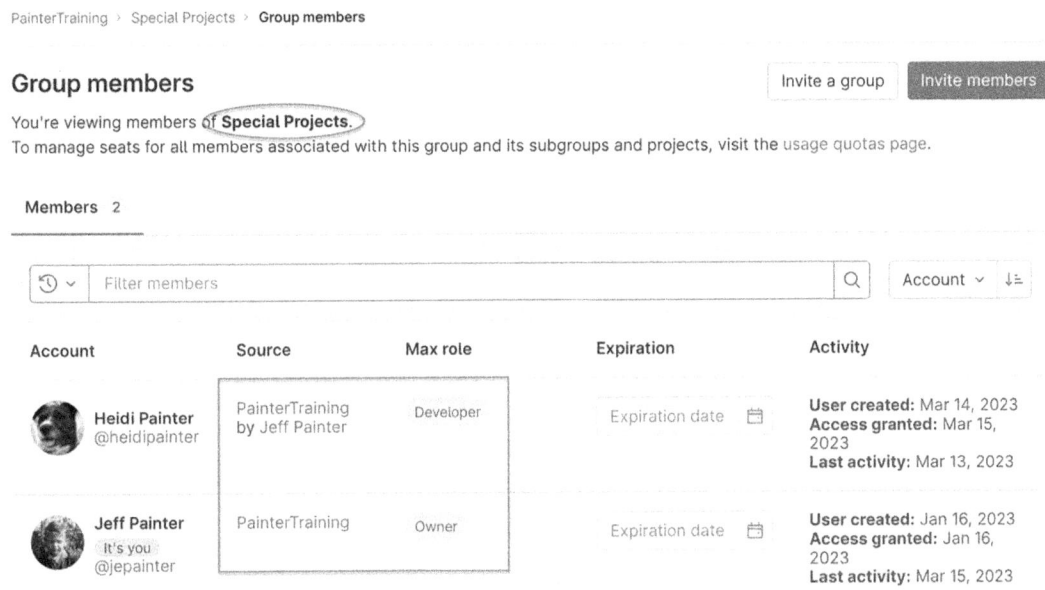

Figure 7-15.   Group members for Special Projects subgroup

Adding Additional Members to a Subgroup

Just as we can do with projects, we can invite additional members to the subgroup using the "Invite members" button. Similarly, we can promote a member's role using the "Invite members" button as well. Figure 7-16 shows the results of promoting Heidi to the maintainer role. From this point on, Heidi is a maintainer for all projects and subgroups created underneath "Special Projects."

CHAPTER 7   LET'S GET ORGANIZED

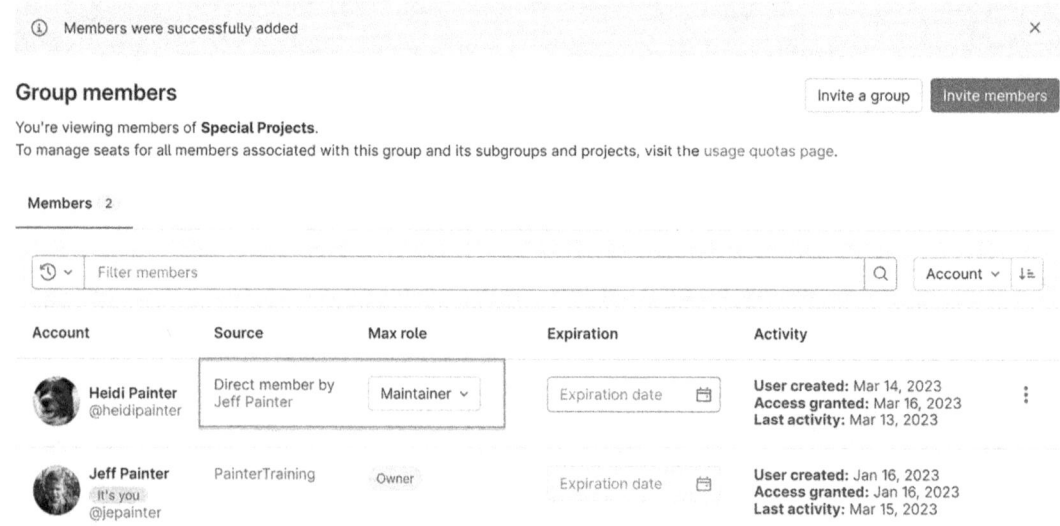

Figure 7-16.   New subgroup role for Heidi after role promotion

Developer-Specific Views of Groups and Subgroups

So now that we've given Heidi the role of developer for the "PainterTraining" group and maintainer for the "Special Projects" subgroup, let's see what impact that has from Heidi's viewpoint. After logging in as Heidi, Figure 7-17 shows Heidi's view of the top-level "PainterTraining" group; this is what a member assigned the role of developer sees. Note that some of the options in the left-hand panel for Heidi will be different; for example, some options such as "Settings" no longer appear since developers cannot change a project's settings. Also, note that as a developer, Heidi can create a new project but not a new subgroup as highlighted in the upper-right corner.

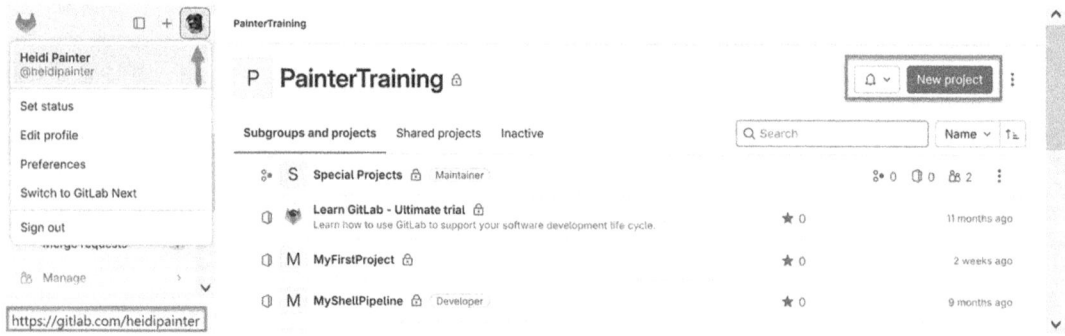

Figure 7-17.   Developer's view of top-level group view

CHAPTER 7　LET'S GET ORGANIZED

Figure 7-18 shows what a developer sees with respect to the group members page. Note that a developer can see who else is a member of the top-level group and what role they play, but cannot invite other members to the top-level group, even other developers. This is by design. Also, note that a developer can request to leave the group if they choose as highlighted for Heidi. Of course, once they've left the group, the owner would have to invite them back again.

Figure 7-18. Developer's view of top-level group members

Maintainer-Specific Views of Groups and Subgroups

Now let's take a look at what a member with maintainer role sees. Figure 7-19 shows Heidi's view of the "Special Projects" group. As with the top-level group, the left-hand panel shows the same restricted options. However, unlike the top-level group, Heidi can create both subgroups and projects under "Special Projects" as a maintainer as highlighted in the upper-right corner.

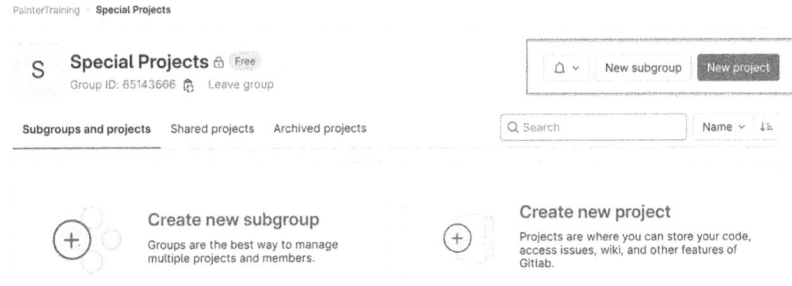

Figure 7-19. Maintainer's view of Special Projects subgroup

Figure 7-20 shows the subgroup members' view for user Heidi. As with the top-level members page, Heidi cannot invite members to the "Special Projects" subgroup even as a maintainer.[5] She still has the option to leave the subgroup if she so desires. In case you are wondering, a maintainer can invite members to projects that are under their control.

Figure 7-20. *Maintainer's view of Special Projects members*

Determining Roles Allowed to Create Projects Within a Group

For security reasons, some of you might be concerned that developers can create their own projects within a given group or subgroup. Is there a way to prevent that? Turns out that an owner of a group or subgroup can change what roles are allowed to create a project. Figure 7-21 shows the general settings for the top-level "PainterTraining" group that controls the roles allowed to create projects. By default, both developers and maintainers can create projects; this can be changed to only maintainers or set to "No one." This setting is inherited by all subgroups under this group but can be overridden for specific subgroups.

---

[5] Yes, this is a bone of contention among many maintainers. As a former administrator, one of the most frequent requests I received was to upgrade a member to owner role so that they could control member access to subgroups as well as projects.

CHAPTER 7 LET'S GET ORGANIZED

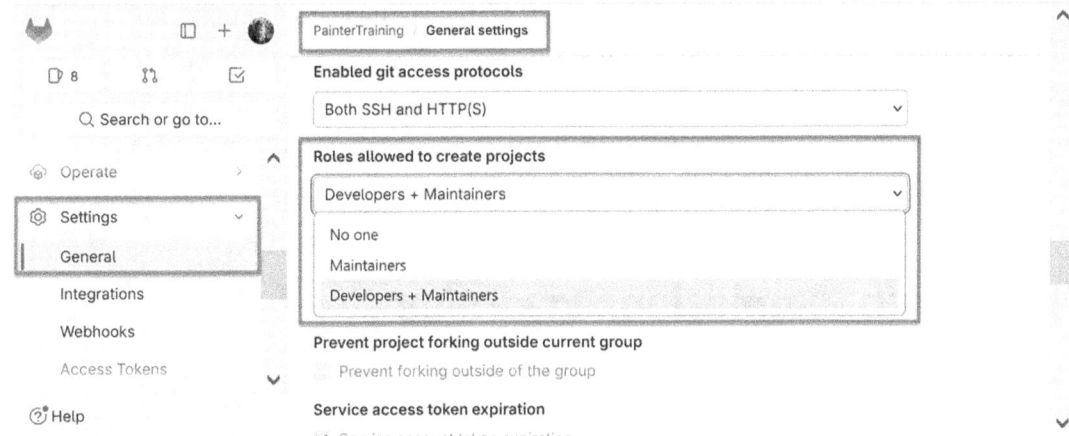

Figure 7-21. Restricting roles allowed to create projects in a group or subgroup

Determining Roles Allowed to Create Subgroups Within a Group

Likewise, if you want to end the feud between maintainers and owners regarding who can create subgroups, Figure 7-22 shows the group's general settings where this option is set. By default, maintainers are allowed to create subgroups, but this can be changed to only owners if desired. This option applies to all subgroups created under this group but can be overridden for a given subgroup by the owner if need be.

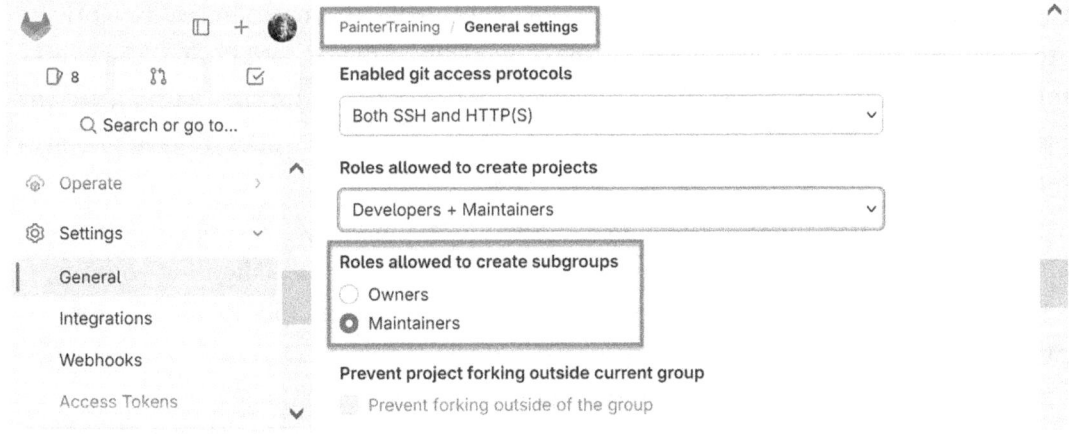

Figure 7-22. Restricting roles allowed to create subgroups by default for all groups

265

Now that we know how to assign roles to members of projects, groups, and subgroups, let's look more closely at the permissions associated with those roles. In addition, we'll look at a couple of unique, mind-boggling features of GitLab where members of a group can be assigned roles to another project or group and where members of a project can be imported to another project.

Navigating Permissions via Roles

As we've seen, roles are used to determine the permissions a member of a group or project has. In addition, we've seen that there are some group and project settings that can restrict permissions for a role. What complicates things is that a given person can have different roles depending on context. For example, Heidi is a maintainer for the "MyShellPipeline" project and the "Special Projects" group but is a developer at the top-level "PainterTraining" group and all projects other than "MyShellPipeline" under that group.

Additional Roles of Guest and Reporter

We've briefly explored the developer, maintainer, and owner roles, which correlate roughly to roles in a development team. There are two additional roles to consider: guest and reporter. At a high level, a member of a project or group with a guest role is mostly a lookie-loo, someone who can look at certain things such as source code and issues but cannot make changes to them. On gitlab.com, you can add a guest member for a private group or project so that they can access them. For self-managed GitLab sites, the guest role is only available with the ultimate license; it is not available for sites with the free or premium license. With the ultimate license, a user that only has a guest role across all of the site does not take a license seat.

The reporter role can be thought of as someone who manages issues, milestones, and the like but does not have permission to modify code. For those familiar with the agile methodology, this is roughly equivalent to a scrum master and potentially the product manager. They direct work, but do not participate in it. You can also think of a reporter as a customer service representative whose goal is to manage customer-reported incidents.

Overview of Permissions

Permissions are an ever-changing thing, especially when new features are introduced. Because of that, rather than go through all the possible roles and permissions, it is best to just point you to the sections that define them. For project permissions, check out https://docs.gitlab.com/ee/user/permissions.html#project-members-permissions. For group permissions, check out https://docs.gitlab.com/ee/user/permissions.html#group-members-permissions. To complicate matters, there are also special permissions specific to CI/CD pipelines as well as jobs, which you can find on the same document under project permissions.

Yes, the assignment of permissions to roles across various license models and SaaS vs. self-managed sites is indeed quite complex. A lot of thought went into considering security scenarios where a user could potentially circumvent access to something they should not have access to. Sometimes, this was by design, sometimes by unforeseen incidents. And sometimes the assignment of permissions to roles leads to disagreements among those assigned a given role. I mentioned this earlier with maintainers who cannot assign members to groups but can assign them to projects. Developers at times have their own beef with maintainers and owners.

I get it. People, especially developers, don't like having restrictions thrust upon them. As an administrator of my former company's Jenkins as a Service, where teams got their own Jenkins server, it was not uncommon for teams to give everyone on the team administrator access, a total libertarian view. For small tight-knit teams, this generally wasn't an issue; they tended to be careful when making changes and needed access when the team lead went on vacation, for example. For larger teams of ten or more, however, one user would end up impacting all projects on the server with some change made as an administrator, usually by upgrading a Jenkins plug-in or tweaking a global option.

Comparing GitLab's Permission Model with Other Models

Let's step back a moment here and look at how this permission model compares with other permissions models. A common permission model gives administrators the ability to create "roles" such as "Developer" or "Test Engineer" and associate permissions to them. Roles are then associated with some objects such as a project or database schema, and users or groups of users are assigned to those roles.[6] This model is quite flexible; however, the more permissions there are, the more unwieldy roles become especially when new permissions are added for new features. It can also lead to some inconsistencies where a role allows a user to create or delete an object, but not edit it.

A variation on this permission model is to have both users and groups of users where permissions are directly applied. Both users and groups of users are then associated with an object such as a filesystem directory or project.[7] Again, the more permissions there are, the more unwieldy this model becomes.

In both of these models, groups of users can be managed internally by the product or sometimes externally using an existing framework such as LDAP (Lightweight Directory Access Protocol which includes Active Directory). Using LDAP is common among organizations since it is usually set up to control access to corporate resources. In fact, LDAP can be used with self-managed GitLab sites to enable login with GitLab and to assign LDAP users and LDAP groups of users to roles associated with GitLab groups and projects.[8]

So, the key distinction between GitLab's permission model and those other models is that the association between roles and permissions with the GitLab model is fixed. In addition, the roles themselves are fixed. In terms of managing users, the GitLab permission model is simpler to maintain at the cost of flexibility. A benefit to this model is that as new permissions are introduced with new features, the GitLab permission model automatically handles them with respect to the fixed set of roles; with the other permission models, you have to go back and apply those permissions to your own set of roles, which in my experience with Jenkins is easily missed.[9] To understand the GitLab principles behind permissions, check out the link with that name available in the section: `https://docs.gitlab.com/ee/user/permissions.html#related-topics`.

---

[6] For those familiar with Jenkins, this is implemented via role-based authorization.

[7] In Jenkins, this is implemented via matrix-based authorization.

[8] In this environment, it is important to differentiate between GitLab groups and LDAP groups. They serve different purposes that are a common source of confusion among users.

[9] It's more complicated in Jenkins in that some plug-ins add their own set of permissions that appear "unexpectedly." Yes, not everyone reads or understands the documentation.

CHAPTER 7 LET'S GET ORGANIZED

Inviting GitLab Groups As Members of Other Groups and Projects

If you are using the gitlab.com site or have a self-managed service that does not use LDAP for authentication, there is one remaining aspect of GitLab groups that allows you to create your own "group of users." If you look at either a project's list of members or a group's list of members, you'll notice that in addition to inviting members, you can also invite groups as shown in Figure 7-23. As an administrator of a self-managed service that managed users via LDAP, I always found this option as an odd duck. Yet owners used this option with their own GitLab groups and projects.[10]

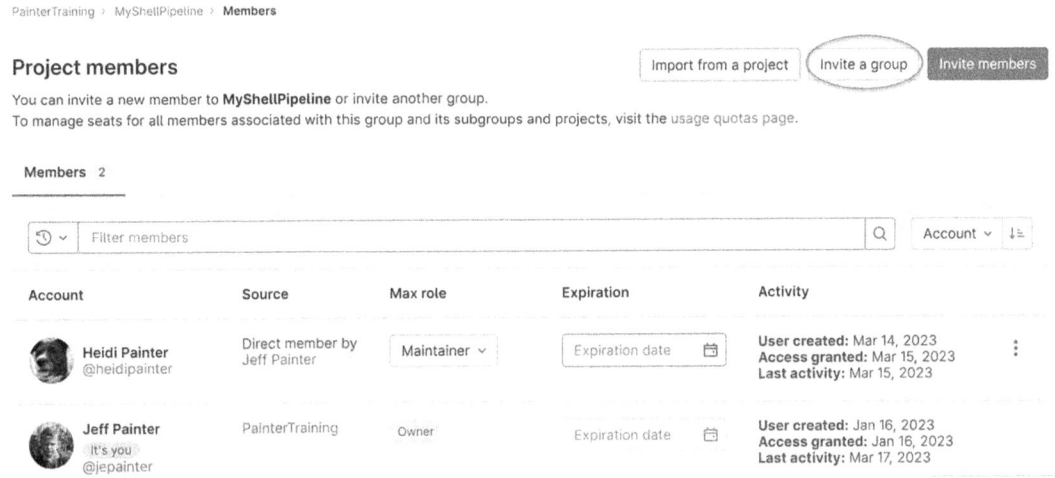

Figure 7-23. Invite group option for a project

When you select "Invite a group," you get a pop-up that is similar to Invite members, as shown in Figure 7-24. Here, you get a drop-down list of GitLab groups that are available to you[11] along with the role to give everyone in that group. If you've invited a member that is also a member of the invited group, the highest role applies. You can invite groups to groups as well as projects. What this implies, by the way, is that you can define GitLab groups that have no subgroups or projects, only members.

---

[10] Turns out that some people find the bureaucratic process of creating LDAP groups a bit too much, especially when those LDAP groups take a while to propagate to GitLab.

[11] The rules of what groups you can invite are a bit involved; they can be found here: https://docs.gitlab.com/ee/user/project/members/share_project_with_groups.html#prerequisites

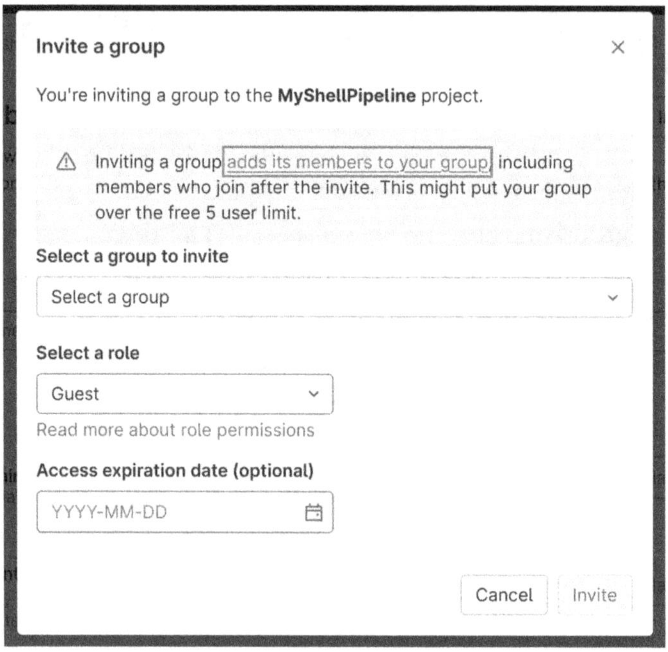

CHAPTER 7   LET'S GET ORGANIZED

Figure 7-24. Invite group form

Importing Project Members from Another Project

What if you wanted to invite members to a project from another project? This is what the "Import from a project" button in Figure 7-23 is for. When you select that button, you get the "Import members from another project" pop-up as shown in Figure 7-25. Here, you simply select the project you want to import members from. The roles of those members from the other project are maintained. If there is a duplicate, the highest role is applied.

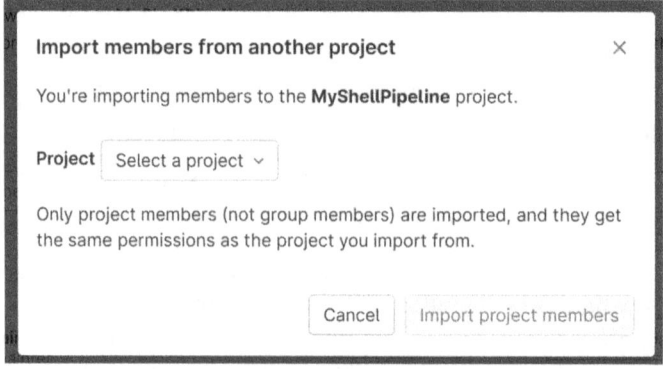

Figure 7-25. Import members from another project option

Special Roles for Self-Managed Sites

Before we leave the topic of permissions, there are two special roles that exist for self-managed sites that don't exist with the gitlab.com site, at least for you. The first special role is the administrator. Similar to Linux/Unix systems and database products, the administrator has super-user powers. An administrator is what is known as an instance-level user; the role is not based on the context of a GitLab group or project. You assign users as an admin either explicitly by another admin or, for LDAP-enabled sites, via an LDAP group.

The second special role is the auditor role. It, too, is an instance-level role but has read-only access to all groups and projects.[12] Users are assigned the auditor role by an admin. The point of an auditor is to ensure compliance of a GitLab site to corporate and/or industry standards. You can find more information about this role at `https://docs.gitlab.com/ee/administration/auditor_users.html`.

In the next section, we'll explore how to manage access to group- and project-specific resources other than subgroups and projects.

Managing Group- and Project-Specific Resources

In addition to setting permissions for users, groups are also used to manage shared resources. These resources tend to be product and/or team based. For example, we learned earlier that projects can define their own CI/CD variables, typically to store secrets or common attributes such as database names. CI/CD variables can also be defined at the group level so that they can be shared across all projects under that group. This is useful when projects under a group contribute to a joint product managed across multiple teams. In this case, some common secrets, such as database passwords, can be defined at the group level so that they are available to all supporting teams rather than be duplicated for each project.

---

[12] Prior to the introduction of this role, giving auditors access to all projects and groups, including private ones, was problematic. Admins either had to add those users explicitly to all private groups and projects or give auditors admin access. Neither option was ideal.

Managing Group- and Project-Specific Runners

Another resource managed by groups and projects is runners. Unlike the shared runners provided by gitlab.com or your self-managed site, group and project runners are specific to a given group and/or specific project. We'll talk about how to set up these runners in a future chapter, but the key takeaway is that these runners can be used to set up a pool of Windows- or Mac-specific runners needed for those types of products or simply to provide a pool of Linux-based runners available to only projects within the group. Figure 7-26 shows the section where these runners are managed for a group. Projects have a similar runner section.

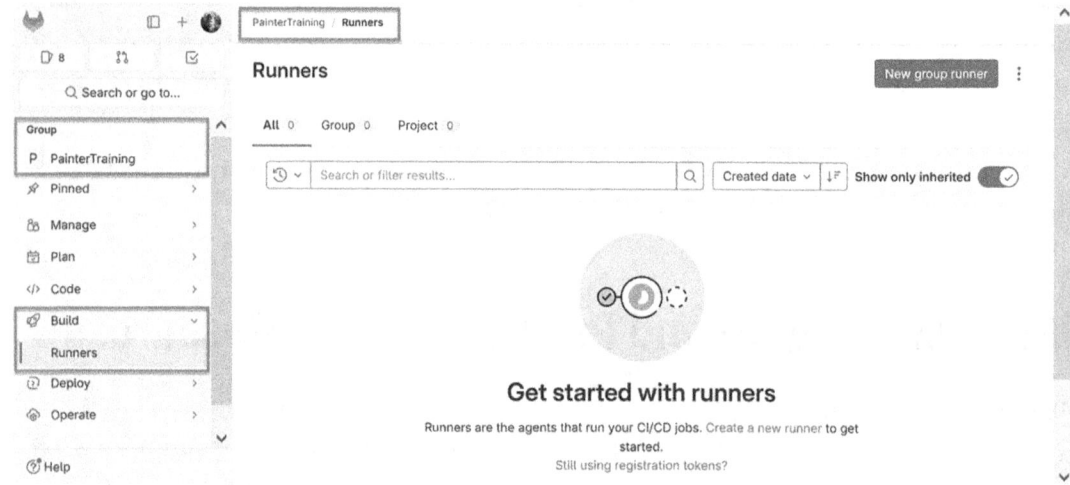

Figure 7-26. Initial group runners page

Managing Group- and Project-Specific Packages and Registries

Figure 7-27 shows the section related to packages and registries, which will be discussed in more detail in a later chapter. A package registry is a group or project shared resource used to store binary objects, such as jar or zip files, created by a project to be shared among other projects. A container registry stores Docker images created by a project for other projects to use. Finally, the dependency proxy is used to store Docker image dependencies downloaded for projects within groups that use them; this is necessary since Docker Hub puts restrictions on how many images can be downloaded in an hour.

CHAPTER 7　LET'S GET ORGANIZED

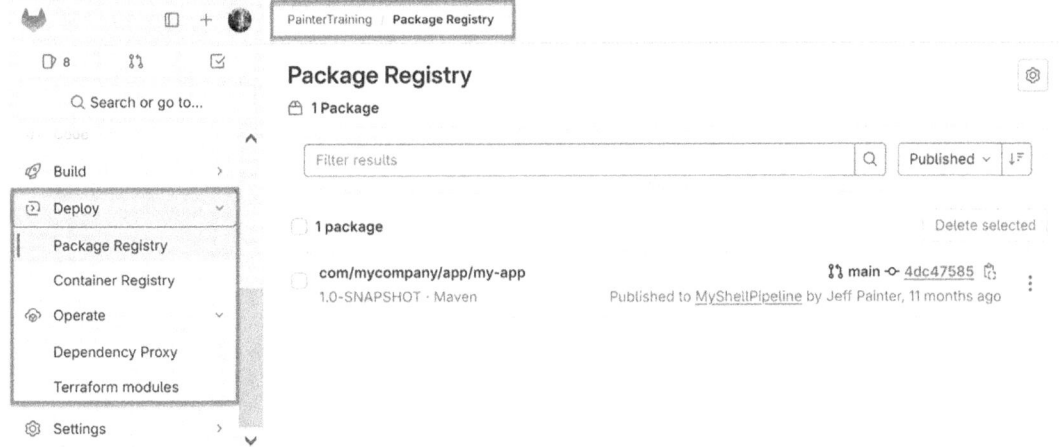

Figure 7-27. Package and registry page for a group

Now that we have considered the most common types of groups and projects, we turn our attention to a different type of project: personal ones.

Creating Personal Projects

When you are working in a corporate environment or on an open source project with other teammates, there will be times when you will want to create "sandbox" projects where you can test things out separate from the official group structure. GitLab provides a personal namespace where you can create such projects. If you haven't created one yet, it can be a little nonintuitive at first since you are normally in the top-level group or one of its subgroups where creating a new project from that group can be done directly from there. Not so with personal projects.

Creating a Personal Project

You can create a personal project by first selecting "New project" from any group. Figure 7-28 shows the initial "Create new project" page that we've seen before.

273

CHAPTER 7 LET'S GET ORGANIZED

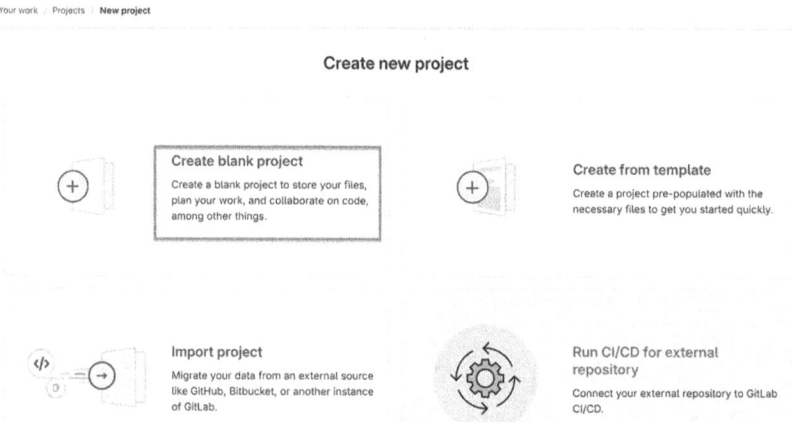

Figure 7-28. *Create new project page*

From here, we select "Create blank project," which takes you to the "Create blank project" page as shown in Figure 7-29. Here, I've entered the project name of "MySandboxProject." To make this a personal project, I selected my username "jepainter" under the Users portion of the "Pick a group or namespace" drop-down list. I kept the remaining settings of "Private" visibility level and "Initialize repository with README."

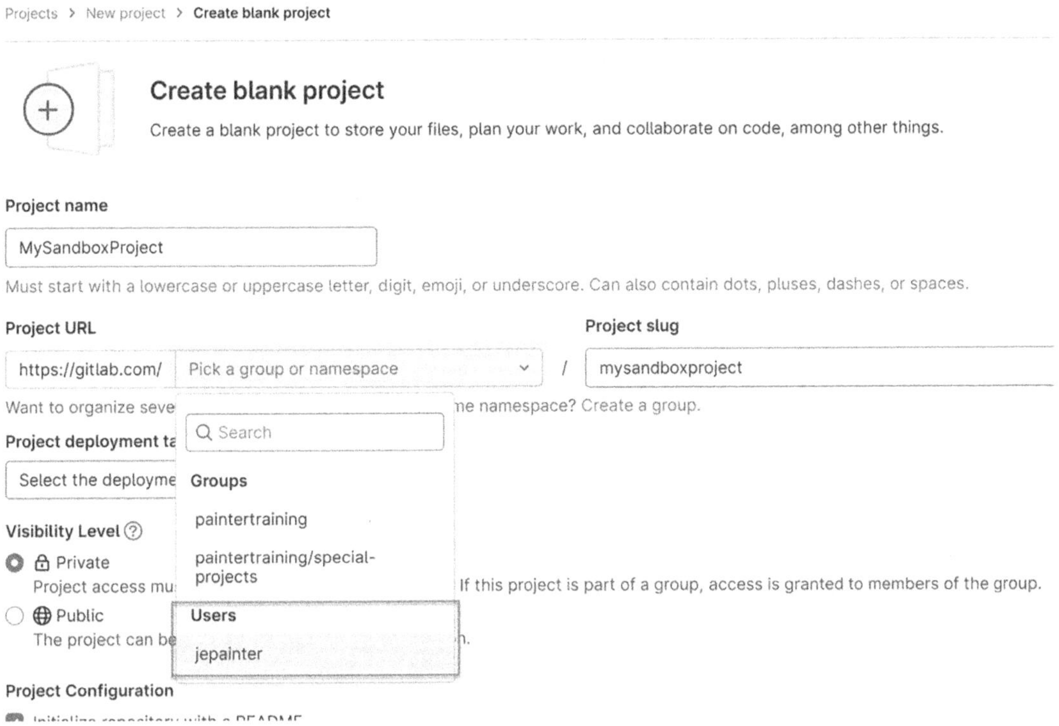

CHAPTER 7   LET'S GET ORGANIZED

Figure 7-29.   Personal project creation

Figure 7-30 shows the resulting project. Note that the URL points to my personal namespace of jepainter rather than the paintertraining URL we've seen before. Also, note that the breadcrumb at the top of the project shows my name Jeff Painter. This is how I know that this is a personal project. Other than those differences, the project looks like any other project we've created before. From here, I can add directories and files and create pipelines as I see fit. Since this is a private project, I am the only one who can see it despite whatever members are added to the top-level "PainterTraining" group. I can still add members to this group if I want, but that is generally not recommended.

275

CHAPTER 7   LET'S GET ORGANIZED

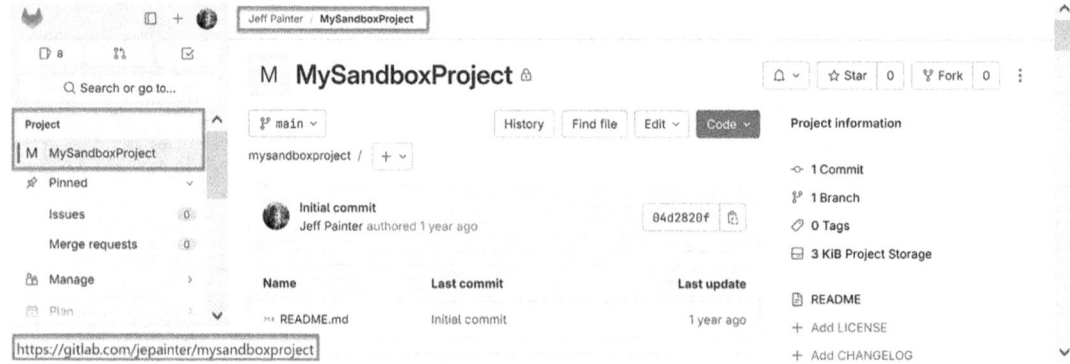

Figure 7-30.   View of personal project page

Viewing Personal Projects from the Project Summary Page

When I go to the project summary page, I can now see my project as highlighted in Figure 7-31. Here, I can see my personal project starting with "Jeff Painter" rather than "PainterTraining." In the case when there are a lot of projects, selecting the "Personal" tab will only list my personal projects. Note that when I hover over the "MySandboxProject" link, I see the URL for that project in the footer.

Figure 7-31.   Project summary with personal project

CHAPTER 7   LET'S GET ORGANIZED

Special Caveats of Personal Projects

So, you might be asking is it possible to create subgroups in my personal namespace? The answer is no. You can only create projects in your personal namespace. This is normally not an issue since you are not likely to have a lot of sandbox projects. If you need to have a sandbox area where multiple team members can participate, the best approach is to create a subgroup specifically for that purpose under which your team can create subgroups and repositories as needed.

A word of warning: Although you can add developers to your personal project, you shouldn't do this. The main issue occurs when you leave a company, and you are the sole owner of the project. Many companies remove or archive personal projects at some point after an employee leaves, affecting those other members who have been developing under the personal project. Also, since you are likely to be the only owner of the project, issues will arise when project settings need to be modified once you leave. Bottom line, a sandbox project should not be used to develop official products.

In the next section, we'll look at how to reorganize existing projects and groups including how to delete and possibly archive them.

Reorganizing Projects and Groups

Corporations change. Employees leave. Teams reorganize. Stuff happens. So, it is expected that over time, GitLab groups and projects may need to undergo changes as well. Earlier, it was mentioned that GitLab groups and projects are similar to filesystem directories and files in that they form a hierarchical structure. However, unlike filesystems where files can be easily renamed and moved around and where directories can be restructured, GitLab groups and projects are not so easily reorganized. This section deals with the various ways in which groups and projects can be changed and the implications of doing so.

Renaming a Project

We'll first focus on the types of changes that can be made to projects. The easiest and most likely type of change is renaming a project. Figure 7-32 shows the general settings page where a project's name can be changed, which occurs at the start of the section. In this example, I am changing the name of my personal project from "MySandboxProject" to "My First Sandbox Project." Note that projects are identified internally by the project's ID; this ID is unique across all projects on the given site. So, changing a project's name has no impact on references to that project.[13]

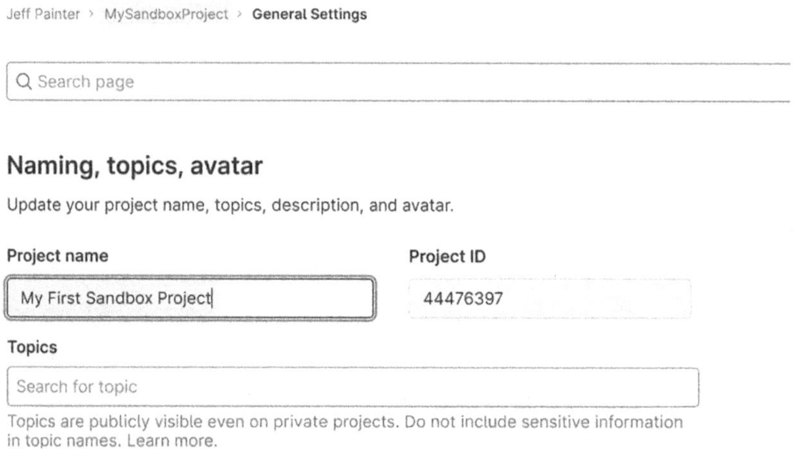

Figure 7-32. Project name change

Figure 7-33 shows the impact of renaming a project. Here, we see that my personal project has the new name of "My First Sandbox Project." But note the project's URL in the footer when I hover over the name. It has not changed. It is still referred to by its old path name of jepainter/mysandboxproject. What I changed is known as the project's "display" name. If I have a local Git clone of this project, it still refers to it by the old URL. If the change of the project's name is subtle, this probably won't cause any confusion, but if the name change is significant, it can lead to confusion later on, especially for team members that are not aware of a project's history.

---

[13] Projects are maintained in a database, so in database speak, the project ID is a primary key. The project name is simply an attribute of a project.

CHAPTER 7 LET'S GET ORGANIZED

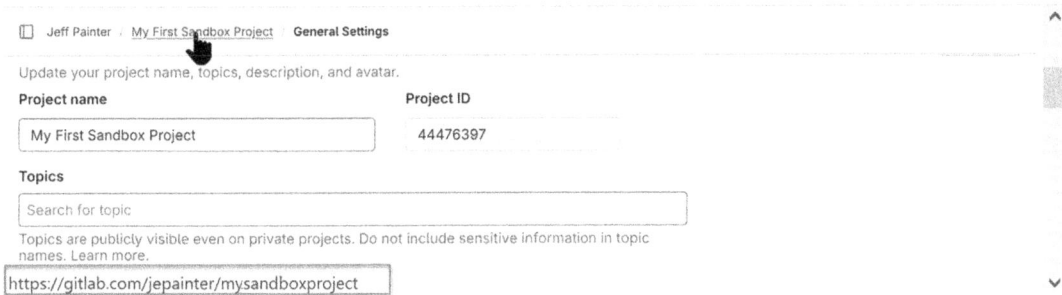

Figure 7-33. View of the project after name change

Changing a Project's URL Path Name

GitLab enables you, as the owner of a project, to also change the path name of the project. This option is provided under the "Advanced" section of a project's general settings as shown in Figure 7-34. To get to this section, you'll need to scroll to the bottom of the general settings page and select the "Expand" button to see the options. The reason that changing the path is in the "Advanced" section is that there are implications to changing a project's path unlike changing the display name.

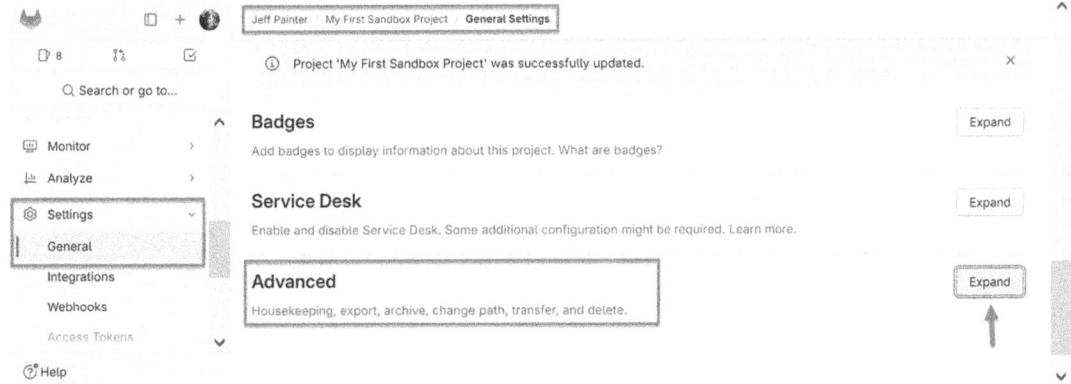

Figure 7-34. Advanced section within the project's settings

Figure 7-35 shows the "Change path" section under which a project's path can be changed. In this example, I am changing the path from mysandboxproject to myfirstsandboxproject. Note that this name is slightly different had I originally named the project "My First Sandbox Project," which would have created the project slug of "my-first-sandbox-project." This is perfectly acceptable. Also, note that only the last part

279

CHAPTER 7   LET'S GET ORGANIZED

of the URL that specifically references the project can be changed; I cannot change the jepainte portion of the URL from this setting as it would implicitly change the location of the group under which the project resides. We'll look shortly at how we can move a project from one group to another.

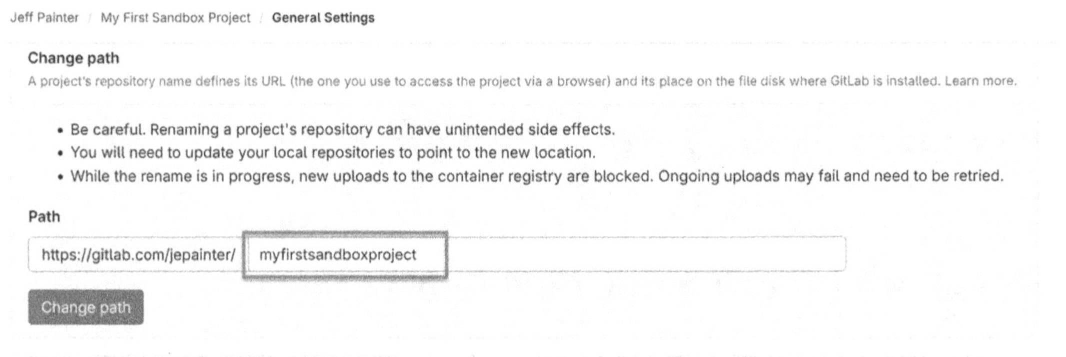

Figure 7-35.   Change path option for a given project

Impacts of Changing a Project's Path

Once I select the "Change path" button, we can see the impacts of this change in Figure 7-36. The project's name remains as "My First Sandbox Project"; changing a project's path has no impact on the project's name. Now, however, when I hover over the project's name, we see that the project URL in the footer now refers to myfirstsandboxproject as expected.

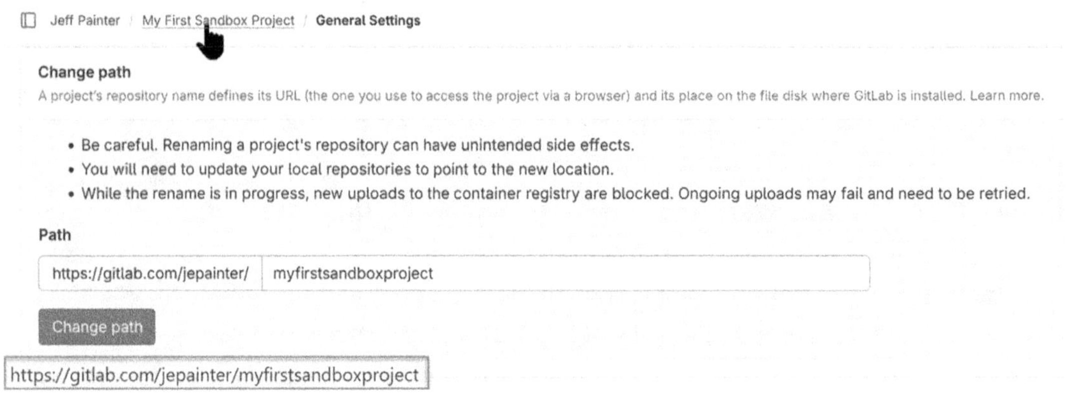

Figure 7-36.   View of the project after path change

CHAPTER 7   LET'S GET ORGANIZED

Since I just created this project and haven't done anything with it, making this change really had no impact on anything. However, if I had been working on this project for a while, there would be impacts to changing the path as noted in the warning of the "Change path" page in Figure 7-35. First of all, if anyone has a local copy of the Git repository related to this project, they will have to make changes to their local repository location[14] so that pushes, commits, and pulls still work. Also, note the phrasing "can have unintended side effects." You will see this frequently as a warning with many of the advanced settings. This is GitLab's catch-all phrase to let you know that there can be a lot of impacts too numerous to mention in a simple warning message. For example, if you have any resources such as Docker or package registries, they may no longer be accessible externally and/or you may need to recreate them. Anything that depends on the project's path will be impacted.

Archiving a Project

Now suppose you have a project that is no longer being worked on but should be kept around for historical (or legal) reasons. Figure 7-37 shows the "Archive project" section under "Advanced" settings. By selecting the "Archive project" button, this puts the project into read-only mode, meaning that it will not accept any more changes. Note that archiving a project will remove the project from most listings; in essence, it hides the project, which reduces clutter. Of course, you can unarchive a project using the "Advanced" settings section; to find it, you can use the "Archived projects" tab for a group or do a search on the name if you remember it.

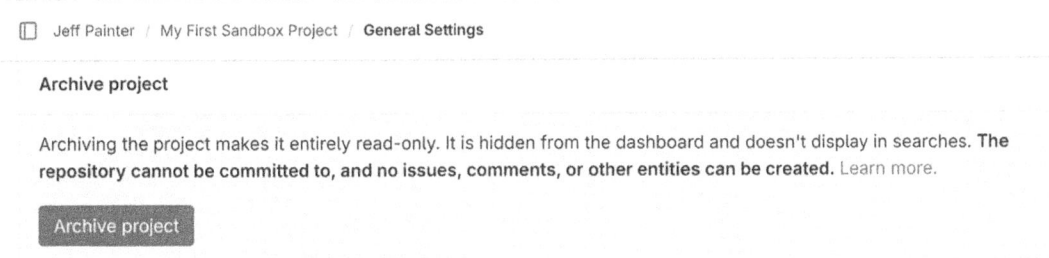

Figure 7-37. *Archive project option*

---

[14] This can be done easily by updating the remote origin setting in the .git/config file. You do not need to change the directory name containing the project, but it might help reduce confusion if you keep it around for a while.

CHAPTER 7   LET'S GET ORGANIZED

Deleting a Project

If you really don't want a project around (or you created one by mistake), you can delete the project as shown in Figure 7-38. What happens when you select the "Delete project" button depends on how the administrator of the site has configured project deletions. Most often, deleting a project will put it into a "soft" delete state, meaning that you have so many days (typically 7) to change your mind. Some administrators may increase or decrease the number of days a project can be put into a pending state.

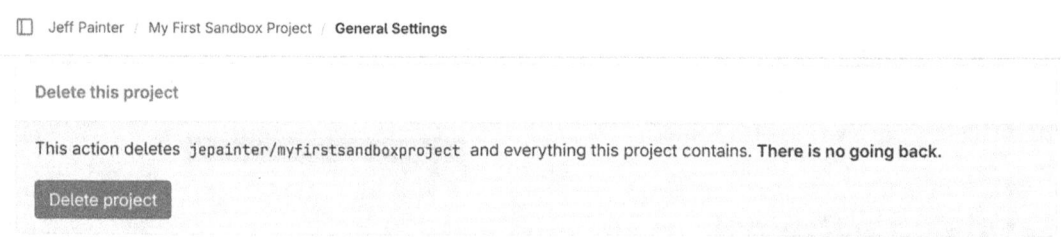

Figure 7-38.   Delete project option

Figure 7-39 shows the list of projects waiting to be "hard" deleted. From the project summary page, you can select the "Pending deletion" tab to see a list of projects that are waiting to be deleted, if any. From here, you can pick a project and undelete it from that project's advanced settings. Note the warning message from the "Delete project" section. Once a project is deleted after the pending state, it is gone and cannot be recovered.[15]

---

[15] A common request as an administrator is to recover a project that has been physically deleted. Users would ask, "can't you just recover it from backup?". The short answer is no. Deleting a project involves removing entries from various database tables and cloud storage areas in addition to the physical directories (there are multiple copies based on current GitLab architecture) where the project code was located. Backups are performed to recover from a disaster for the entire system, not to recover a specific project.

Figure 7-39. *List of projects pending deletion*

Transferring a Project to Another Group

We saw earlier that we can change a project's name and a project's final URL path. What if we want to move a project to another group, in essence changing the full project's URL path? Figure 7-40 shows the "Transfer project" section under a project's advanced settings. As you can see, the warning section is more involved than the one in the "Changing path" section. In addition to the issues that occur when changing a path, transferring a project to a new group introduces a whole slew of issues. Remember that a project inherits many things from the group and subgroups under which it is contained. There are team members, variables, runners, package registries, and Docker registries that need to be considered. The phrase "unintended side effects" incorporates all of this.

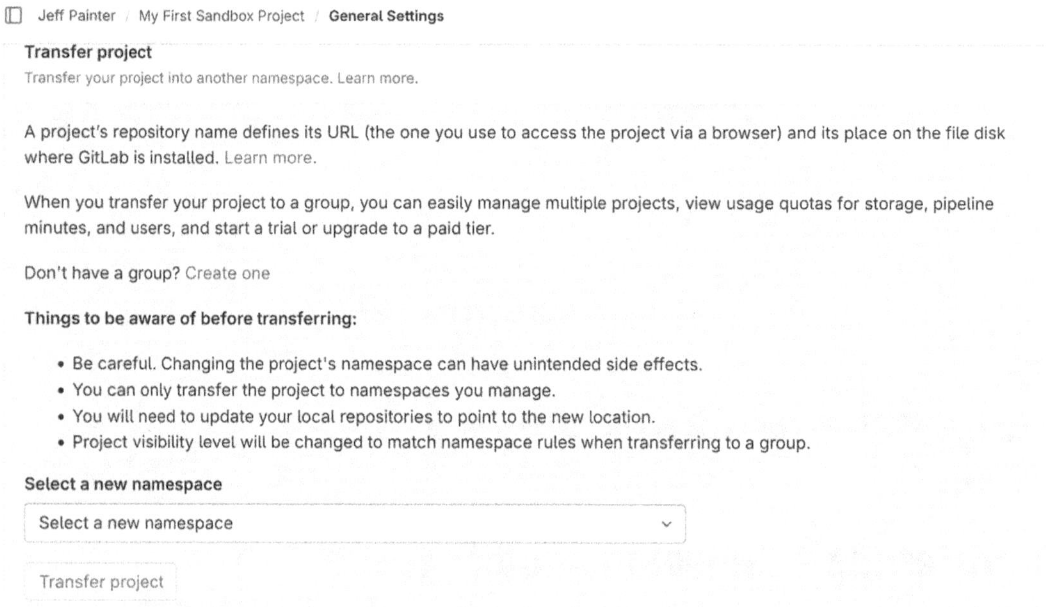

CHAPTER 7   LET'S GET ORGANIZED

Figure 7-40. Transfer project option

In addition, you can only transfer a project to a group that you manage either as a maintainer or an owner. The "Select a new namespace" will filter those groups for you. If you don't see a group name that you want to transfer a project to, then you don't have the authority to do so. You will either have to get the role set for you in the group being transferred to or add an owner of the group being transferred to as an owner of the project and have them transfer the project for you.

Because of these issues in moving projects around to different groups, one should carefully consider how groups are created and maintained in the first place. This is difficult to do, of course. We can't always see how a corporation might reorganize itself or the projects and products that it manages. Although it is easy to organize groups by department and teams, one should carefully consider whether this should be done and by how much. Organizing projects by products helps reduce the need for reorganizing but doesn't prevent it. Typically, setting up a group structure involves a mix of the two. It is definitely a balancing act.

CHAPTER 7   LET'S GET ORGANIZED

Renaming a Group

Let's now turn our attention to groups and the types of changes that can be made to them. As expected, many of the changes made to projects apply to groups as well, but not all of them. As with projects, the most basic type of change to a group is renaming it. Figure 7-41 shows how to change the name of a group. Select the group's general settings, and it appears at the top of that page. Simply change the name here and save the changes. As with projects, the group name is its display name, so there are no repercussions changing it.

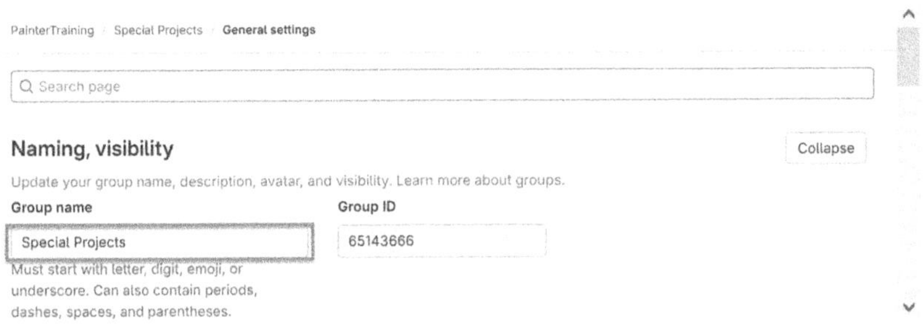

Figure 7-41. Group name change

Changing a Group's URL

Likewise, you can change the group's URL by going to the group's general settings and expanding the "Advanced" section. In that section, there is a "Change group URL" section as shown in Figure 7-42. Just as with projects, changing a group's URL has no impact on the group's name and vice versa. However, changing the group's URL will definitely have impacts on all projects contained within the group. Any local repositories of projects contained within the group will have to change their remote locations in order to continue pulling, committing, and pushing changes.

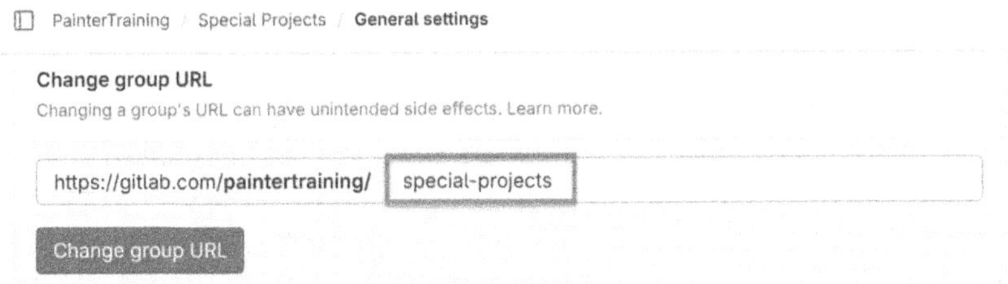

Figure 7-42. Group URL change option

285

CHAPTER 7 LET'S GET ORGANIZED

Deleting a Group

Groups can also be deleted using the advanced "Remove group" section as shown in Figure 7-43. Deleting a group is particularly dangerous as it deletes all subgroups and child projects contained under the group. As the message notes, this includes archived projects contained under that group. Since projects are "soft" deleted, you can still undelete one or more projects that were within the group, which should keep the group from being deleted.[16] However, other projects that were under the group will still be scheduled for deletion, so you will need to undelete any other projects explicitly.

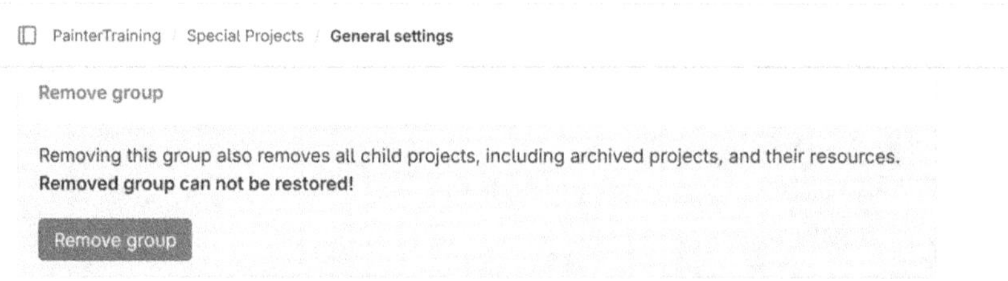

Figure 7-43. Remove group option

There is an interesting loophole that can cancel a group deletion at least in later releases of GitLab. If the user that requested the group deletion is removed from the group prior to deletion taking place, the group deletion is canceled. I suspect this is in place to deal with the "disgruntled" owner who decides to delete groups that they own in retaliation.[17]

Oddly enough, you can't archive a group like you can a project. I find this odd since this seems like the safer option to deleting a group. On the other hand, I can see the conundrum in archiving a group and then unarchiving a project under that group. Would unarchiving a project then unarchive the group and all intermediate subgroups containing that project? That seems counter to the idea of archiving the group to prevent changes to it.

---

[16] Note that I said "should." The documentation is not clear on this behavior, but I can't see that a group will be deleted if at least one project has been undeleted. Otherwise, it would create a "zombie" project. In any case, contact an administrator as soon as possible so that they can help cancel project deletions.

[17] Given how dangerous group deletion is, perhaps the solution would be to make it harder to do a deletion. Thinking in terms of a nuclear missile launch, maybe requiring at least two people to approve the deletion would make it more difficult to accidentally delete a group. It would certainly help in the retaliation scenario, unless, of course, there are two disgruntled owners.

Transferring a Group to Another Group

Finally, just as you can transfer a project to another group, you can also transfer a group to another group (as a subgroup). As Figure 7-44 shows, the "Transfer group" section in the advanced general settings allows you to make the transfer. The same implications that we encountered with transferring projects apply to transferring groups but magnified. Impacts aren't just to the group but to all subgroups and projects contained under the group being transferred.

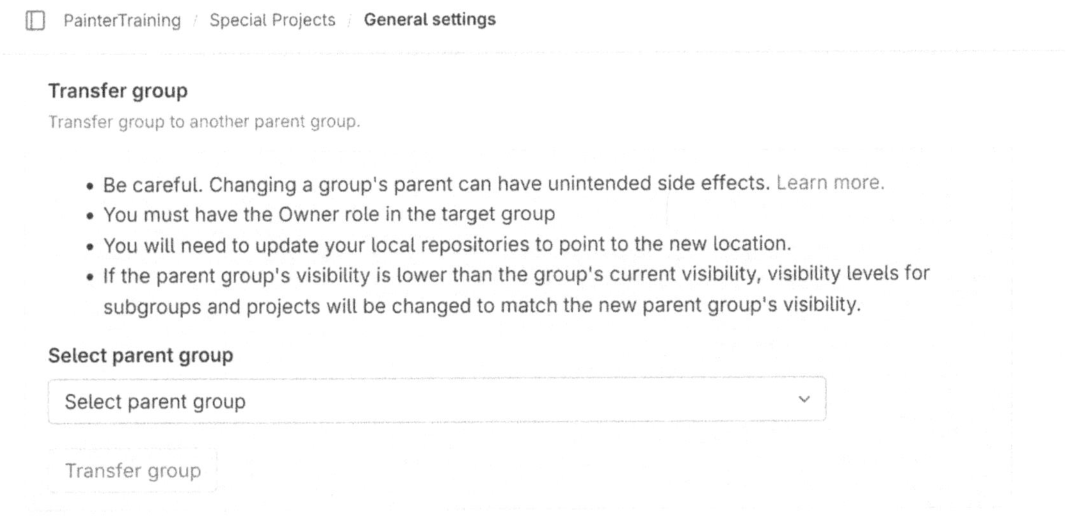

Figure 7-44. Transfer group option

Now that we've considered various ways to reorganize projects and groups within a given GitLab site, we next look at how we can export and import projects between GitLab sites.

Exporting and Importing Projects

We've talked about how to move projects around within a GitLab site, but what if we would like to copy a project between two GitLab sites. Why would we need to do this? Perhaps you have two self-managed GitLab sites, one for testing concepts out (typically referred to as staging) and one for production. Or perhaps you have been using the

CHAPTER 7   LET'S GET ORGANIZED

gitlab.com site and finally set up a self-managed site, and you want to transfer key projects from the gitlab.com site to your self-managed site. GitLab has a solution called exporting and importing a project.[18]

Exporting a Project

Figure 7-45 shows how to export a project. Like the other reorganizing tasks, it can be found under the general settings advanced section. As you can see from the description, there are some things like variables, container images, and job logs that cannot be exported. However, there are some pleasant surprises, such as issues and merge requests, which are exported.

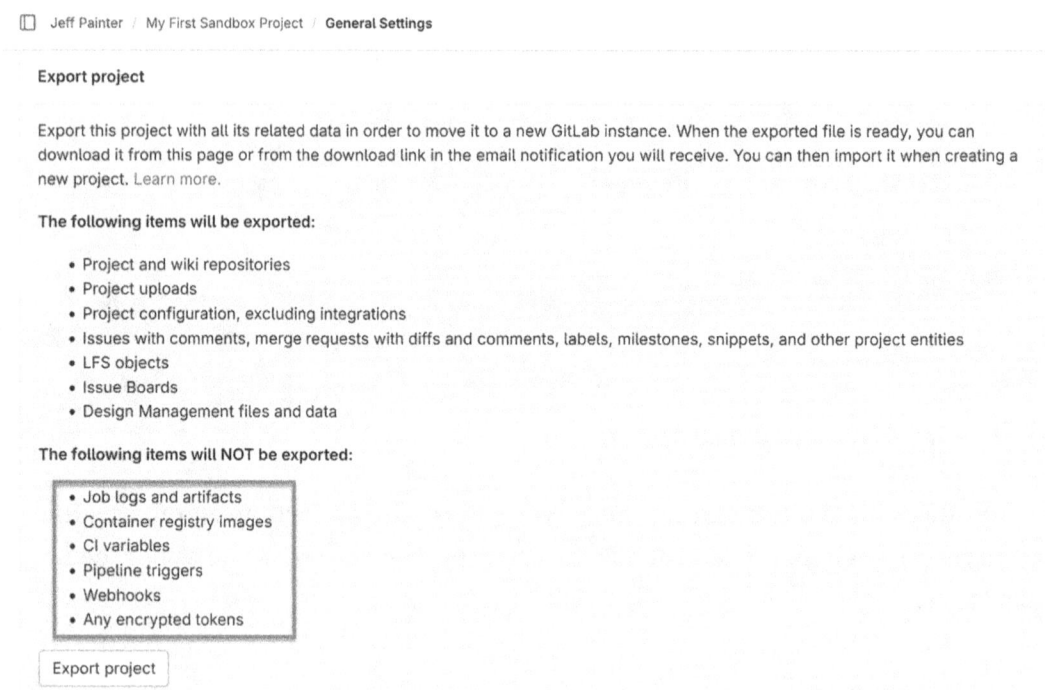

Figure 7-45. Export project option

---

[18] There used to be a group export process, but that has been deprecated. My experience with it was that exporting and importing groups was flaky and extraordinarily time-consuming. It was hard to recover from transfers where only some of the projects were recreated but not all of them were.

CHAPTER 7   LET'S GET ORGANIZED

Exporting a project is extremely easy to request. Simply select the "Export project" button, and you'll get a message that tells you the process has been started in the background and that you'll be notified by email when it has completed. When that happens, you can come back to this page, and there will be a "Download export" button that lets you download the tar.gz file as shown in Figure 7-46. You will also get a link to the downloaded file via the email message.

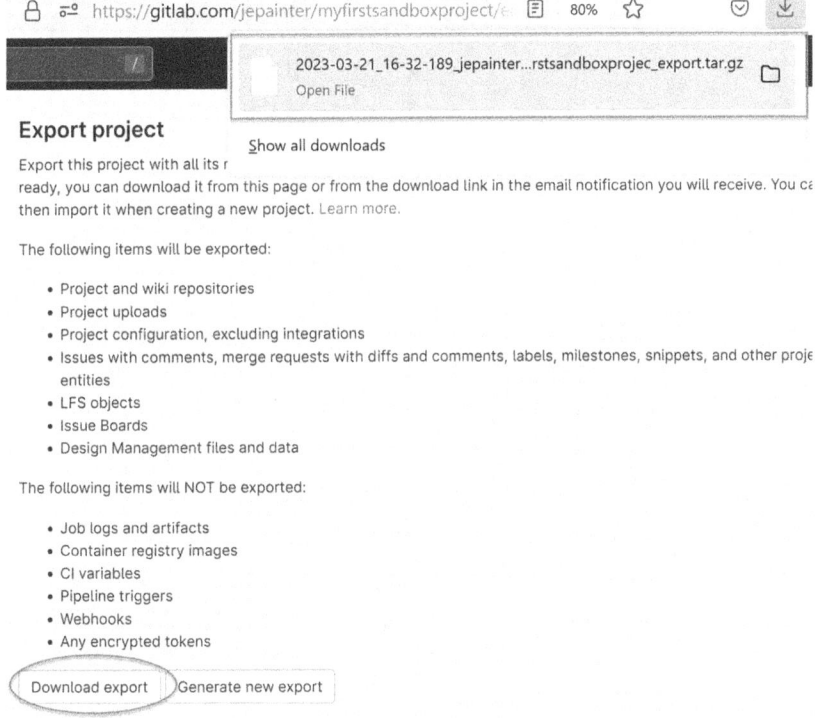

Figure 7-46. *Download export when export process completes*

Importing a Project

To import the exported project, go to the group under which you want the project to reside and select "New project" or "Create new project" if it appears. You'll be taken to the "Create new project" page as shown in Figure 7-47. From here, you want to select "Import project."

CHAPTER 7   LET'S GET ORGANIZED

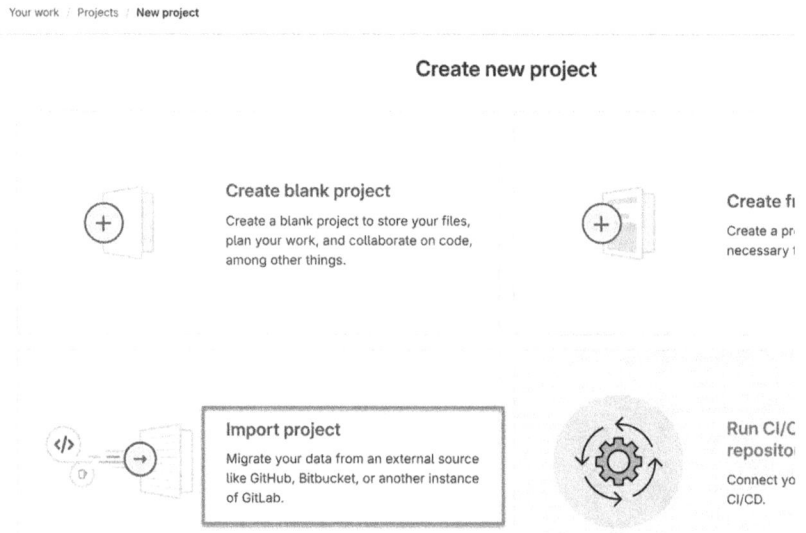

Figure 7-47. Import project selection from the new project page

Figure 7-48 shows the "Import project" page. As you can see, there are a number of ways to import a project into your GitLab group. For example, if you want to transfer a project from GitHub rather than from GitLab, you can do that here. Or if you simply have an external Git repository with source code that you want to incorporate into a GitLab project, you can do that as well. For this example, we want to select "GitLab export." Note that the import project options for a self-managed GitLab site may be different depending on what the site's administrator allows.

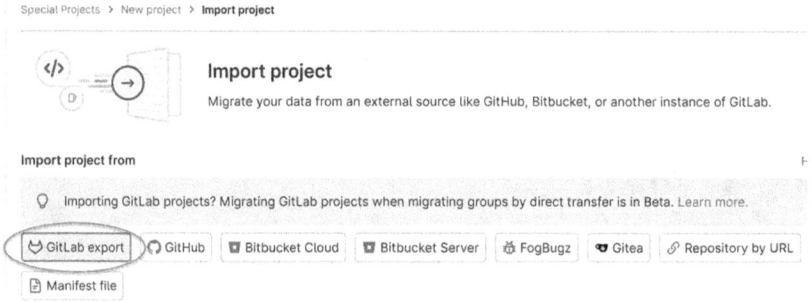

Figure 7-48. Import project page

After selecting "GitLab export," you'll be taken to the "Project import" page as shown in Figure 7-49. This page is similar to the "Create project" page in that you enter the name of the project you want to create; it doesn't need to be the same name as the exported project. The project slug is automatically generated as you enter the project name. You use the "Browse" button to find the export file that you downloaded earlier. Selecting "Import project" then recreates the project from the export file. This is done through a background process just as the export process was. Note that the import process may take some time, so you will need to come back to see when it is complete.

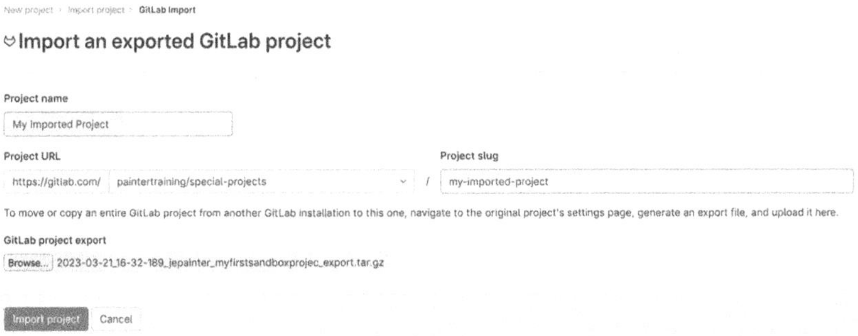

Figure 7-49. Import an exported project form

Dealing with Import Failures

It is possible that an import process fails for some reason. If this occurs, you will have what is called a "null" project, which is different from an "empty" project that exists but has no files associated with it. To understand why the import failed, you will most likely need assistance from the GitLab administrator to look into the logs to see the reason for the failure. Upon failure, you will be given the opportunity to delete the project straightaway without having to wait the seven-day pending delete period; this is because there really isn't anything to delete except an entry in the project table.

Summary

We covered the following topics in this chapter:

- Showed how to view group-specific entities such as projects, activities, and members
- Described how to add members to a group or project
- Looked at how to create subgroups within a group
- Discussed how roles are used to set permissions for members assigned to a role
- Looked into how groups can be invited as members of another project or group
- Looked into how project members can be imported as members of another project
- Considered how to control access to group- and project-specific resources such as runners
- Investigated different ways of reorganizing and deleting groups and projects
- Introduced how to export and import projects between GitLab sites

In the next chapter, we'll consider how to manage our day-to-day work using GitLab's issue feature.

CHAPTER 8

I Have an Issue with That

So, if you are like me, whenever I am doing things on my own, I like to make a to-do list to help remind me of what needs to be done. For instance, around the house, I might have a to-do list that includes "Fix the leaky faucet," or if I'm programming, I maintain a to-do list that includes things like "Create a unit test for module XYZ." This is a perfectly acceptable way of managing your time that is pretty simple to do.

However, when you get to working on a project with others, this method of keeping track of chores begins to break down, especially the larger a project team becomes. This is where having an issue tracker comes in handy. The term issue implies a problem (as in we have an issue with Johnny), but with respect to issue trackers, it has a broader meaning. Issues may be preplanned, such as creating a module for a new feature, or may be unexpected, such as when a user discovers a bug in the system.

Now that we've looked at how to organize our projects in a team environment, we'll expand our ability to work as a team by exploring GitLab's built-in issue tracker where we'll learn how to create, edit, and link issues as well as associate them with merge requests.

Managing Issues

Figure 8-1 shows the list of issues as seen from the top-level dashboard. This provides a list of all issues across all projects. One of the key things to note here is the "Select project to create issue" button in the upper right. What this tells us is that issues must be associated with projects; we just can't create an issue unattached from a project.

CHAPTER 8   I HAVE AN ISSUE WITH THAT

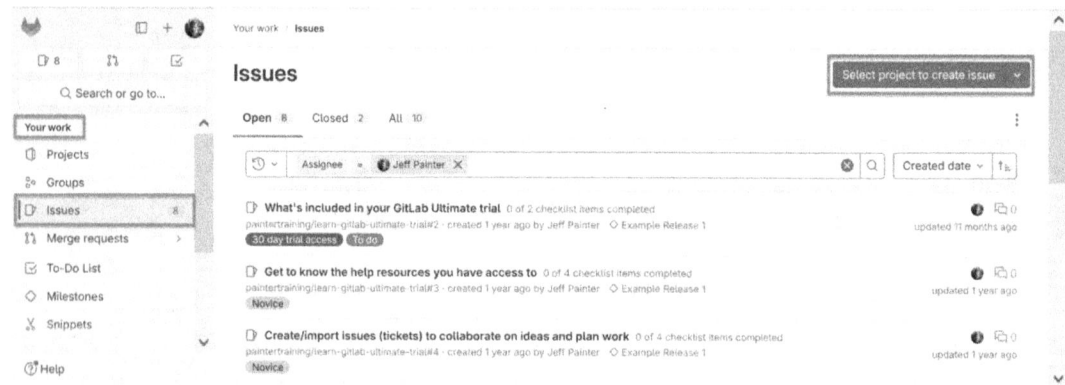

Figure 8-1. *Issues from the top-level dashboard*

Viewing Project-Specific Issues

Figure 8-2 shows what the issues page looks like for a project that does not have any issues associated with it yet. Here, I chose "MyFirstProject" as an example since I haven't created any issues for it yet. On this page, we see two options. The first is the "New issue" option that allows us to explicitly create a new issue for this project. The other is the "Import issues" option that allows us to copy issues from an external source such as a Jira project. Our focus in this section is on creating new issues explicitly.

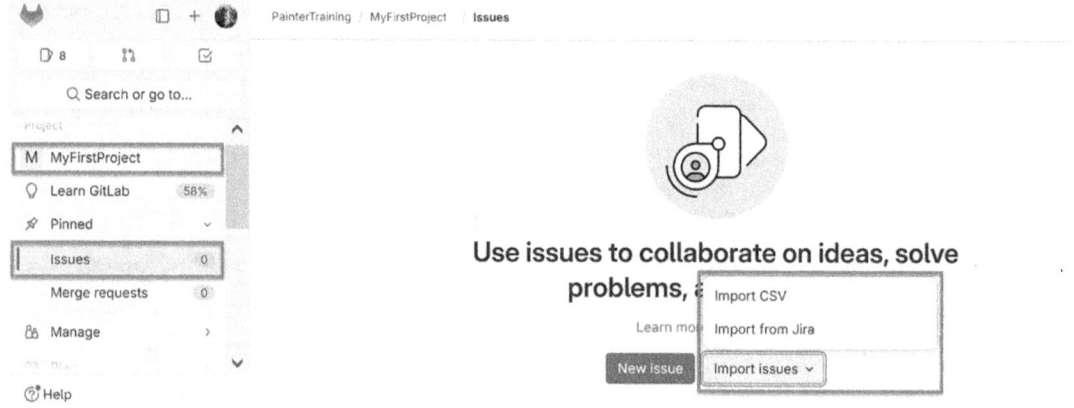

Figure 8-2. *Initial project issues list*

CHAPTER 8   I HAVE AN ISSUE WITH THAT

Looking at the "Learning GitLab" project that was created for us automatically when we signed up, we see the issues page as shown in Figure 8-3. Here, we only see the issues related to this project. The tabs at the top let us see open issues, closed issues, or all issues depending on what we are interested in finding. There is also a search where we can filter issues based on its contents or assignee, for example. The "New issue" button allows us to create a new issue explicitly. Note, however, that there is no import option as there is for newly created projects.[1]

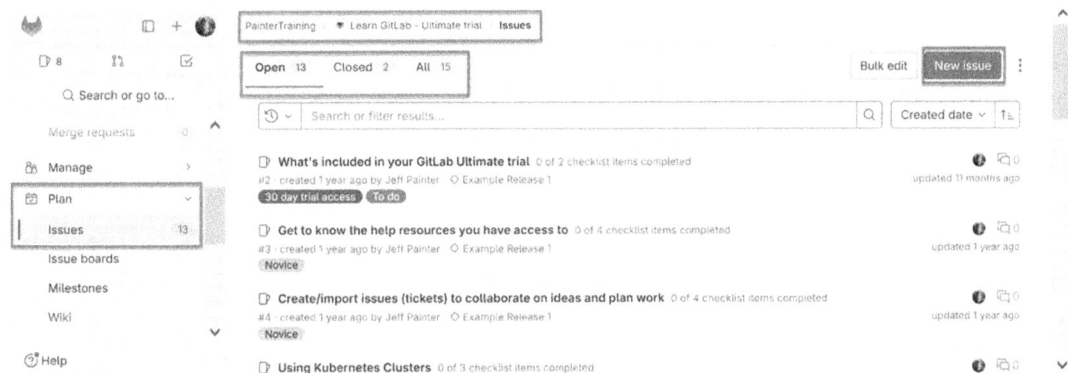

Figure 8-3. *Existing issues list for the Learn GitLab project*

Creating an Issue

When you select the "New issue" button, you are taken to the "New issue" page as partly shown in Figure 8-4. It's a big page, so I only show the top part in this figure. The form is pretty self-explanatory. You create a title for your issue that provides a brief summary of it along with a more detailed description. If you are wondering, the title does not need to be unique (although it helps within a project); each issue is given an internal number that identifies it. At the current time, the "Type" field is either "Issue," which is the most common type, or "Incident," which indicates that some operational incident, such as a service outage, has occurred.

---

[1] You might be thinking to yourself, "Well, that's inconsistent." It isn't, though. The intent with respect to issues is that you either maintain them in an external tool like Jira or you maintain them in GitLab. If you are currently maintaining them in Jira, then using the import on a project that does not have GitLab issues signals your intent to maintain those issues in GitLab from here on out. If you've already started creating issues in GitLab, then you've already signaled your intent to maintain them there regardless if there are issues in Jira.

295

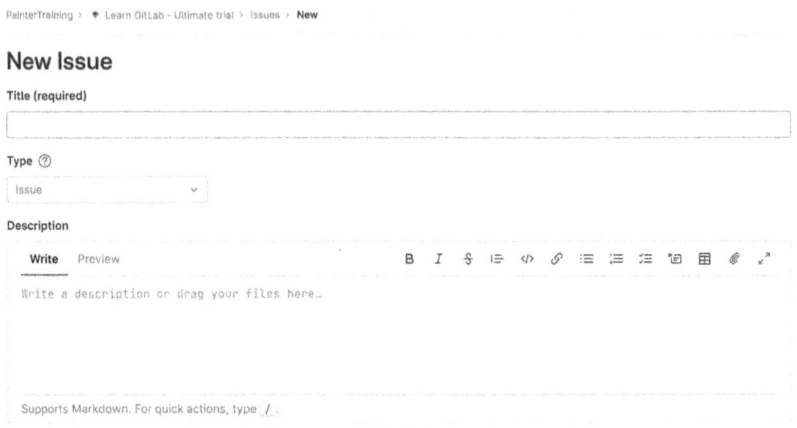

CHAPTER 8   I HAVE AN ISSUE WITH THAT

Figure 8-4. New issue form (top)

The bottom portion of the "New issue" page is shown in Figure 8-5. Here, we see some metadata about the issue that can be left as is; those fields can be set later if needed. There is a special checkbox that can make an issue only available to you and the members of the project team; this comes in handy when creating issues for the GitLab support team where you don't want it to be seen by the public at large. As you'll soon see, there is other information associated with an issue, but the "New issue" page provides the most common information likely to be known at the time of the issue's creation. When you are done filling out the form, select "Create issue" to generate a new issue for the project.

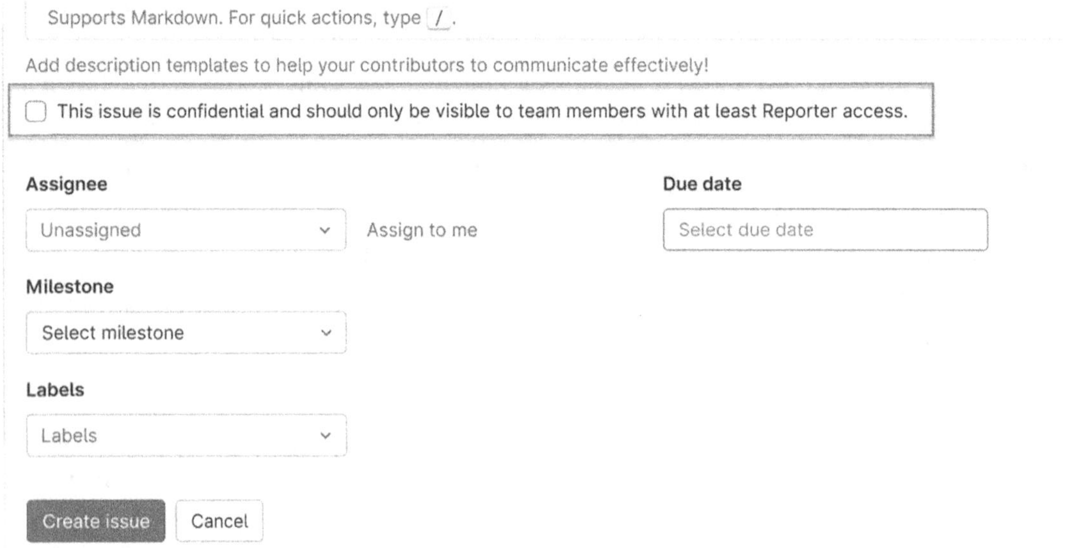

Figure 8-5. New issue form (bottom)

CHAPTER 8   I HAVE AN ISSUE WITH THAT

Viewing Issue Details

Rather than create a new issue of my own, I decided to examine an already created issue associated with the "Learning GitLab" project. For this example, I selected the last issue in the project's list as shown in Figure 8-6. As expected, the title appears at the top of the issue page, and the description directly follows it. Below the title is information about the state of the issue (open in this case), when the issue was created, and by whom. On the right-hand side is a panel containing various editable metadata associated with the issue, such as who is assigned the issue. In addition, there are various actions that can be performed on the issue, such as "Edit," "Close issue," "New related issue," or "Delete issue." The most common action shown is "Edit"; all other actions are contained in the vertical ellipses drop-down list.

Figure 8-6. *Issue detail example*

Editing an Issue

When you select "Edit," you get the "Edit issue" page similar to the one shown in Figure 8-7. The "Edit issue" page enables additional options than were available when creating the issue, which we'll discuss momentarily. In addition to editing the title, you can also update the description. Note that the description opens up in "Write" mode where you can make changes using what GitLab calls their GitLab Flavored Markdown Language (GMFL). This markdown language is similar to other markdown languages in that they use the typical hashtag (#) symbol for headings and the dash (-) symbol for list items. Some differences from other markup languages are items such as "Task Lists" and "Inline Diffs."

297

CHAPTER 8   I HAVE AN ISSUE WITH THAT

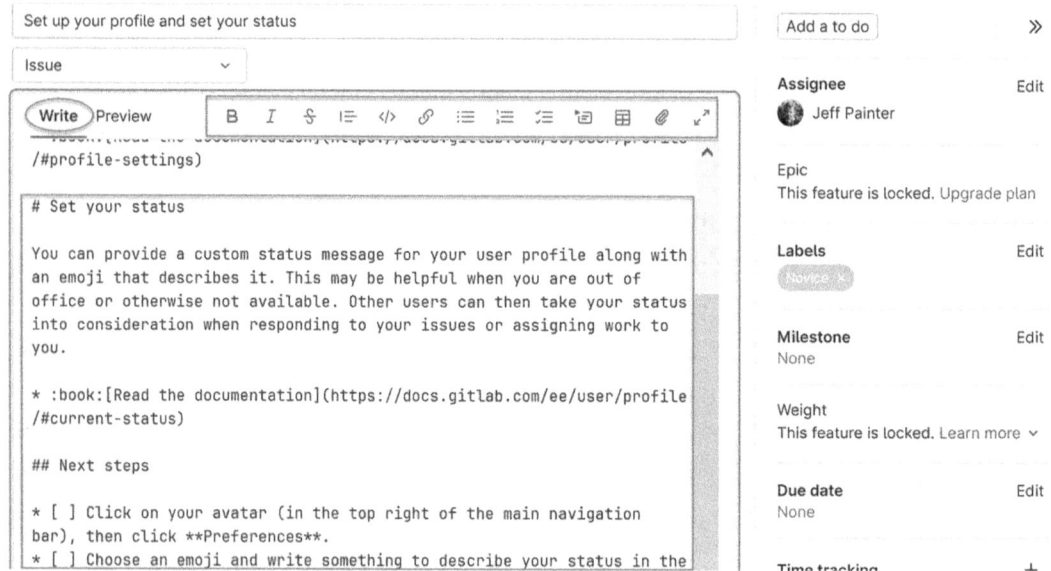

Figure 8-7. Issue edit markup

Note that this markup language is used for features other than issue descriptions; for example, it is used for comments, merge requests, milestones, etc. At the top of the edit pane is a menu bar containing common markup features such as bold text, list creation, table creation, etc. At the bottom of the description edit pane is a link to the markup language documentation that describes all the other possible markup features that can be added. The "Preview" tab is used to render your changes before saving them. As with the IDE preview mode, you cannot edit anything while in preview mode. There is a "Save changes" button following the description where you can save the changes, or you can cancel the changes if desired.

Reacting to an Issue

The section following the description is where you can provide your reaction to the issue as shown in Figure 8-8. This is one of the additional options available when you edit issues. You can click the thumbs-up or thumbs-down icon to "vote" about the issue. Voting is nonbinding but is used in cases where feedback is requested about the importance of an issue (e.g., feature request) to users. You can also add various emojis expressing your feelings about the issue. Clicking the smiley face icon brings up an extensive emoji menu from which you can choose your reaction.

CHAPTER 8   I HAVE AN ISSUE WITH THAT

Figure 8-8. *Issue reaction options*

Figure 8-9 shows how the reactions are displayed once you've finished editing the issue. Reactions are displayed after the description. Note that with the thumbs-up, thumbs-down, and emoji icons, a user can select them from here without having to edit the issue.

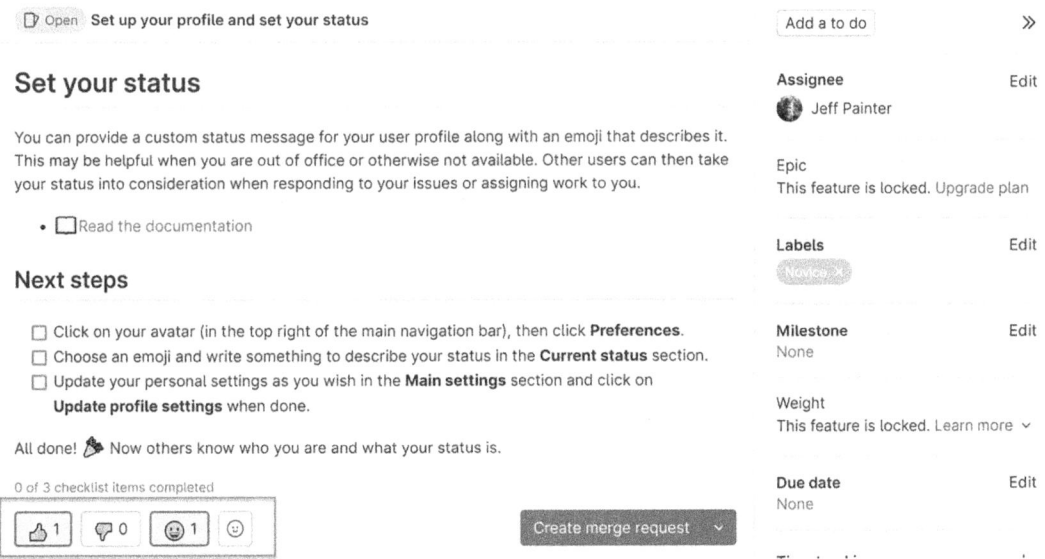

Figure 8-9. *Issue reaction view*

299

Viewing Issue Activity

At the bottom of the "Edit issue" page[2] is another feature available when editing an issue but not when creating an issue: the "Activity" section. Figure 8-10 shows what this section looks like. This is where users can make comments on the issue and/or start a thread discussion about it. Like the "Description" section, the "Activity" section uses GFML. Note that you don't have to use GFML; you can just type in plain text with no markup at all.

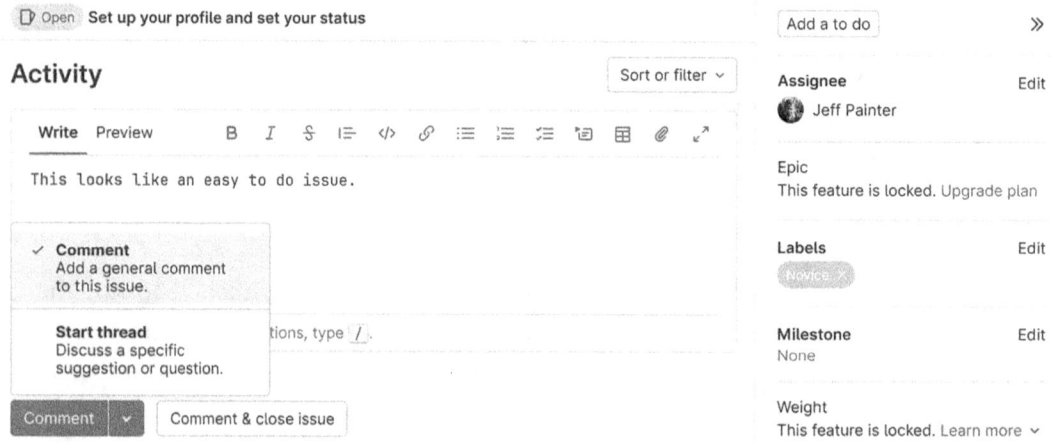

Figure 8-10. Issue activity edit section

Figure 8-11 shows how the "Activity" section looks after editing the issue. Here, you see a list of comments and threads that have already been entered. It also provides options to edit the comment (if you were the author) and reply to the comment or issue as appropriate. The "View issue" page also provides a quick way to add a comment or thread without having to edit the issue. You can also mark a comment or thread as internal to the project team.

---

[2] For now, I'm skipping the "Tasks" and "Linked items" sections, which appear before the "Activities" section. These sections will be described in the next chapter.

CHAPTER 8   I HAVE AN ISSUE WITH THAT

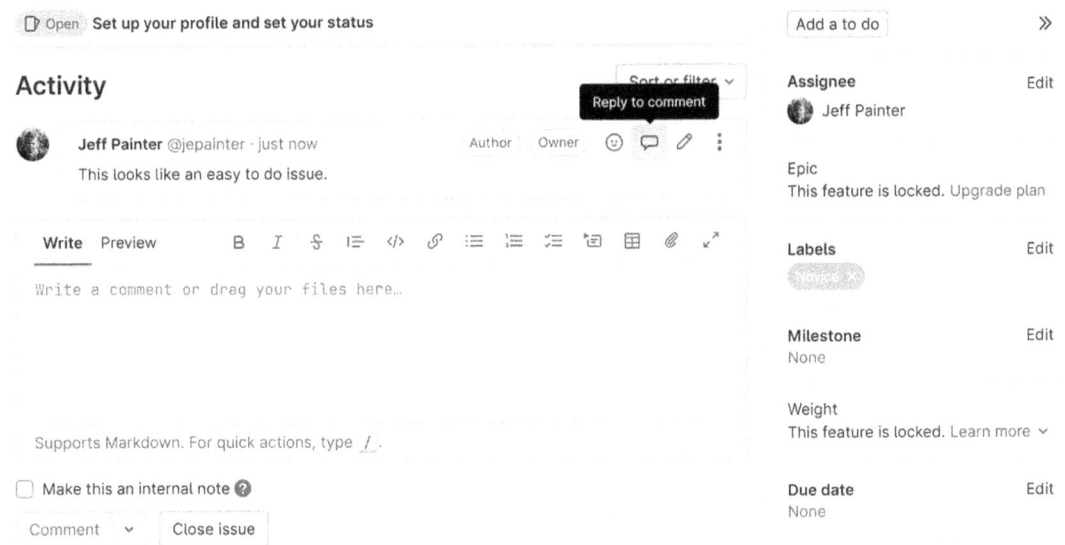

Figure 8-11. Issue activity view

Filtering Issues

When you end up with a lot of issues, paging through them can be cumbersome. From the issue list, you can filter issues by various criteria such as who was the author, etc. Figure 8-12 shows an example of filtering issues based on my positive reactions. When you click the filter box, you are given a number of possible items to filter on followed by other options to restrict what items are presented. Note the highlighted section in the lower right of the figure. This gives you a summary of reactions as well as a link to comments. You can use this to determine if anyone has commented on your issue or if there is an issue that has a lot of discussions associated with it.

301

CHAPTER 8   I HAVE AN ISSUE WITH THAT

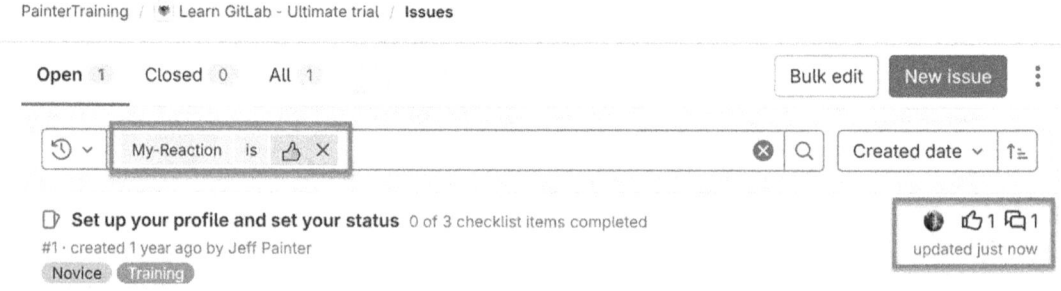

Figure 8-12. Filtered issues list

Editing Multiple Issues at Once

If you look in the upper right of the "List issues" page, you'll see a "Bulk edit" button. This is a handy way to make multiple edits to issues as shown in Figure 8-13. When you select the "Bulk edit" button, you can click individual issues or select all issues using the checkbox at the top of the section. You can then make certain changes such as who to assign the selected issues to. Clearly, not all changes make sense in a multi-edit context, for instance, description or activity changes.[3] Note that you can move the selected issues to another project using the "Move selected" button.

---

[3] However, you might argue that there are some changes, such as "Due date," that might make sense for multi-edit changes but are not enabled. If it is really important to you, you can always make a feature request with GitLab support.

CHAPTER 8   I HAVE AN ISSUE WITH THAT

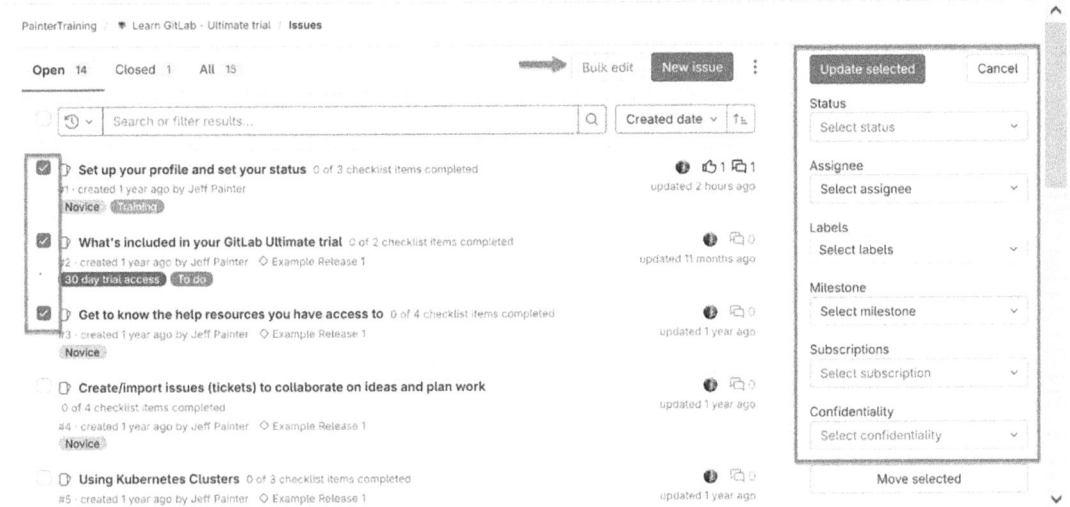

Figure 8-13. Multiple edit of issues

We'll next consider how to use labels with issues and merge requests.

Labeling Issues and MRs

Although you can filter issues by various criteria, sometimes it helps to manually mark related issues based on some common properties. For example, you might want to mark those issues related to the user interface or perhaps those related to the database. In GitLab, you can use labels to categorize issues however you like.

Viewing Labels in Issues List

Taking a look at the GitLab training project, you can see labels in action from the issues list as shown in Figure 8-14. For each of the issues listed, we see an associated list of color-coded labels. For example, the first issue listed has the labels "30 day trial access" and "To do" as highlighted in the figure. What is nice about those labels is that they are clickable.

303

CHAPTER 8   I HAVE AN ISSUE WITH THAT

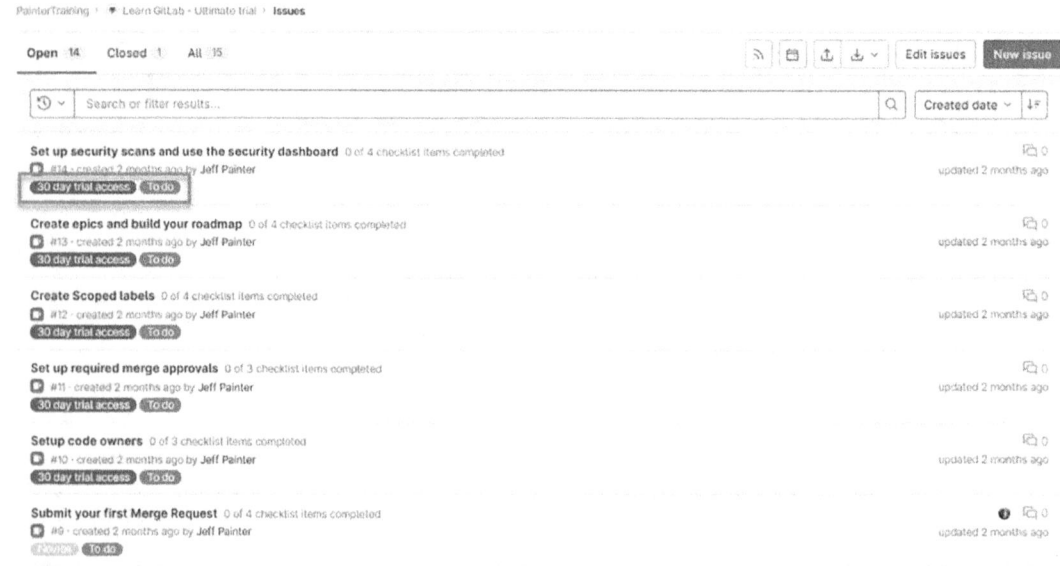

Figure 8-14. Issues list with labels

Filtering Issues by Label

Clicking a label automatically creates a list filter that only shows those issues with that label. Figure 8-15 shows what happens when the label "30 day trial access" is clicked. It automatically creates the filter "Label is 30 day trial access" and restricts the list to just those six issues. Clicking a different label replaces the filter with a new one for that label. So, if we clicked the label "To do," the filter would change to "Label is To do," and we would see all issues with the "To do" label.[4]

---

[4] If you wanted to see issues with both labels, you would have to include both filters explicitly; you can't do that just by clicking a label.

CHAPTER 8   I HAVE AN ISSUE WITH THAT

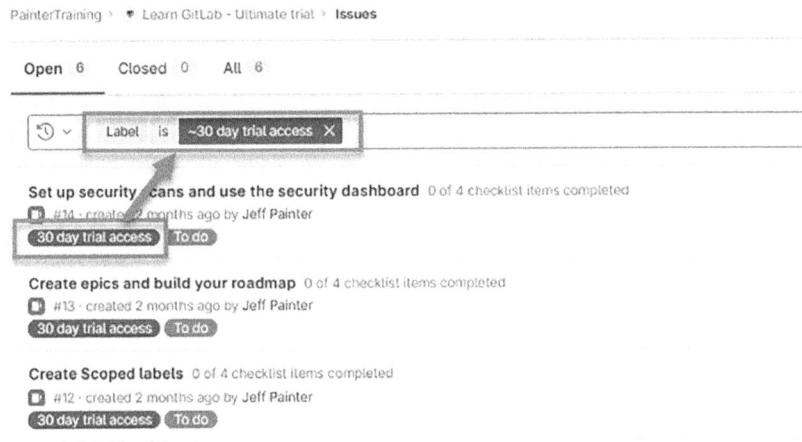

Figure 8-15. *Issues filtered by label*

Editing Labels

So, let's look at how we can edit the labels for a given issue. Figure 8-16 shows an issue where the Labels "Edit" button in the right-hand pane was selected. This shows a drop-down list of available labels. In this example, I've selected the "To do" label. I could have also deleted the "Novice" label by selecting the X located on the label. Selecting "Create project label" allows you to create a label directly from the issue page and selecting "Manage project labels" takes you to the project's "Manage ➤ Labels" page.

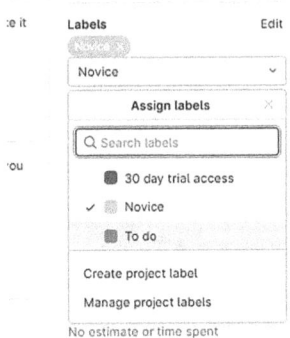

Figure 8-16. *Edit label options*

305

Figure 8-17 shows the project's "Manage ➤ Labels" page. Here, we see the list of labels available for this project.[5] On this page, we can edit the labels by changing their colors or text, or we could delete them if we so choose. The "Subscribe" option allows us to subscribe to that label so that if any issues or merge requests are tagged with that label, we would get an email notification.

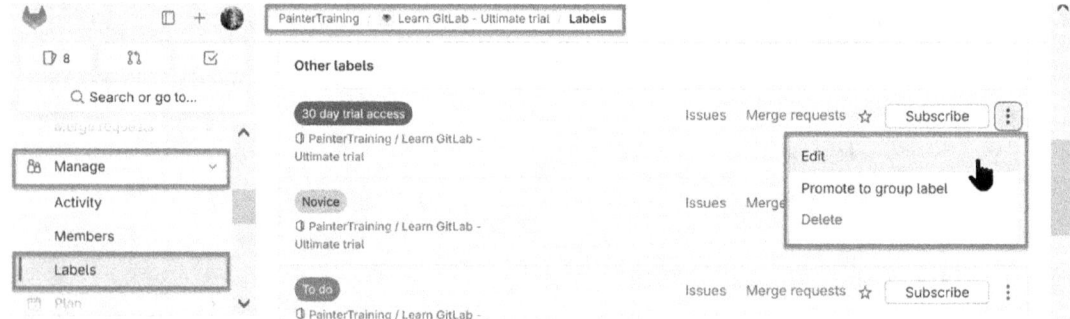

Figure 8-17. Labels list for the project

Prioritizing Labels

We can mark certain labels as higher priority by selecting the star icon for that label as shown in Figure 8-18. In this example, I've prioritized the "30 day trial access" label since that indicates issues that are time sensitive. You can also prioritize other labels and, once prioritized, change the order of their priority by dragging them to a new position.

---

[5] Note that if a project and its parent group have no labels, you can generate a default set of labels using the "Generate a default set of labels" button that would appear in this case.

CHAPTER 8   I HAVE AN ISSUE WITH THAT

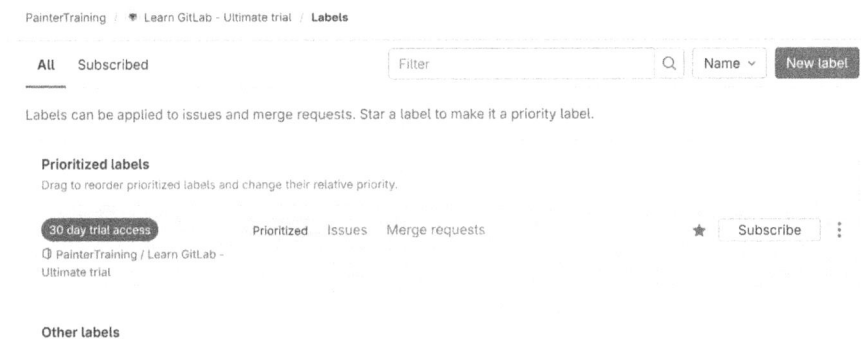

Figure 8-18. Prioritized labels list for the project

So, what do prioritizing labels buy you? Well, it comes into play when sorting issues or merge requests. In Figure 8-19, the list sort option is switched to "Label priority." This has the effect of listing issues with priority labels first. Here, we see all six issues with "30 day trial access" listed first.

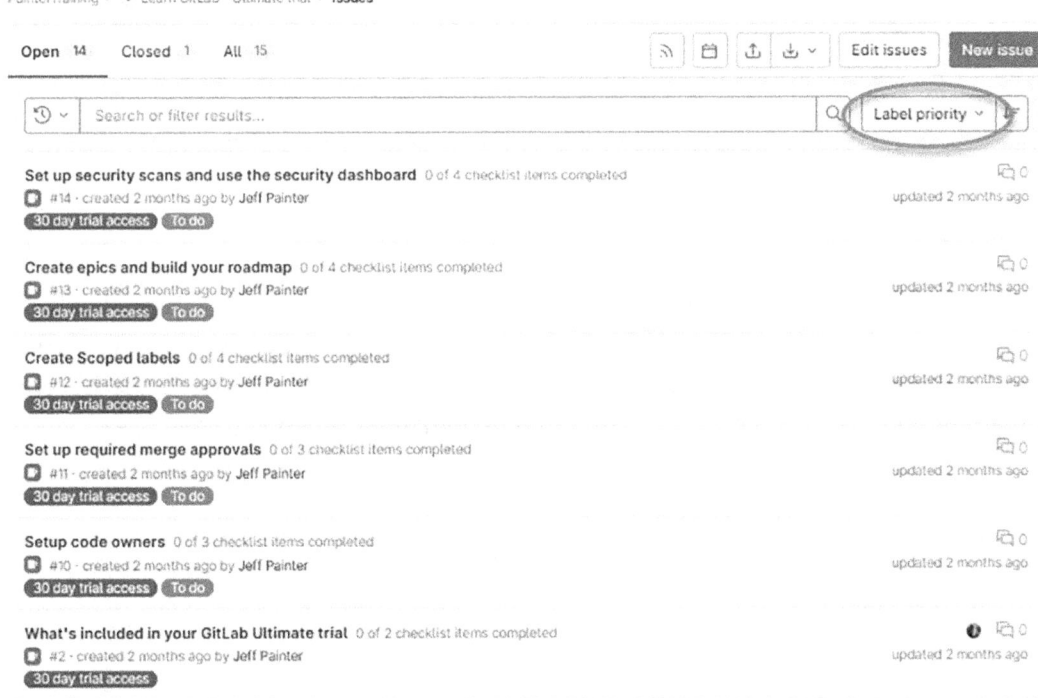

Figure 8-19. Issue priority sort

307

CHAPTER 8   I HAVE AN ISSUE WITH THAT

Creating a New Label

We can create new labels from the "Manage ➤ Labels" page by selecting the "New label" button. This takes us to the "New label" page as shown in Figure 8-20. From this page, you set the label's title, an optional description, and the background color to use when displaying the label. In this example, I created a new "Training" label with a green background color.

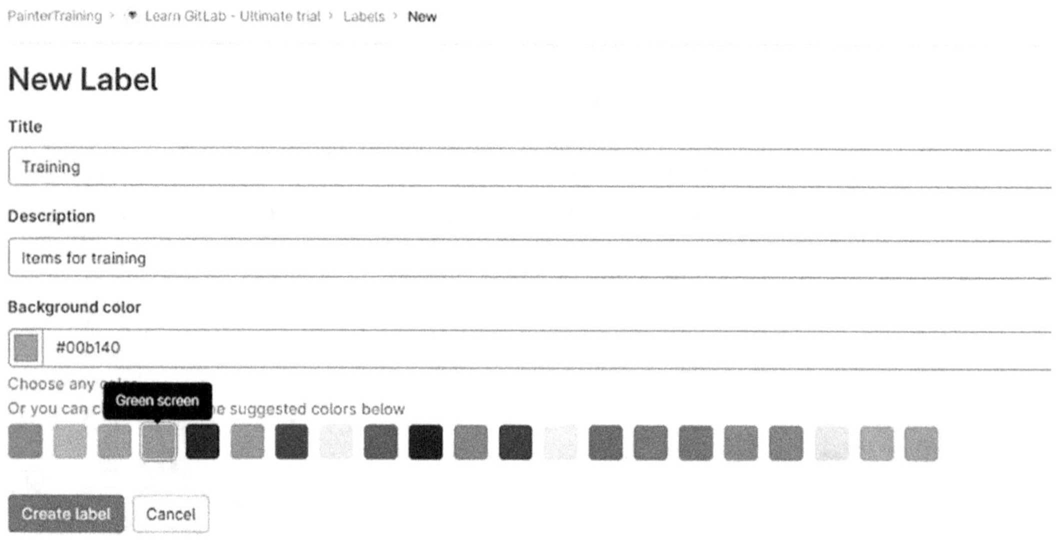

Figure 8-20. New label form

Figure 8-21 shows the result of creating the "Training" label, which is added to the bottom of the "Other labels" list. Note how the description is displayed with this label; no other labels have a description, which is why they don't show one. Once the label is created, we can use it to label issues and merge requests within the project.

CHAPTER 8   I HAVE AN ISSUE WITH THAT

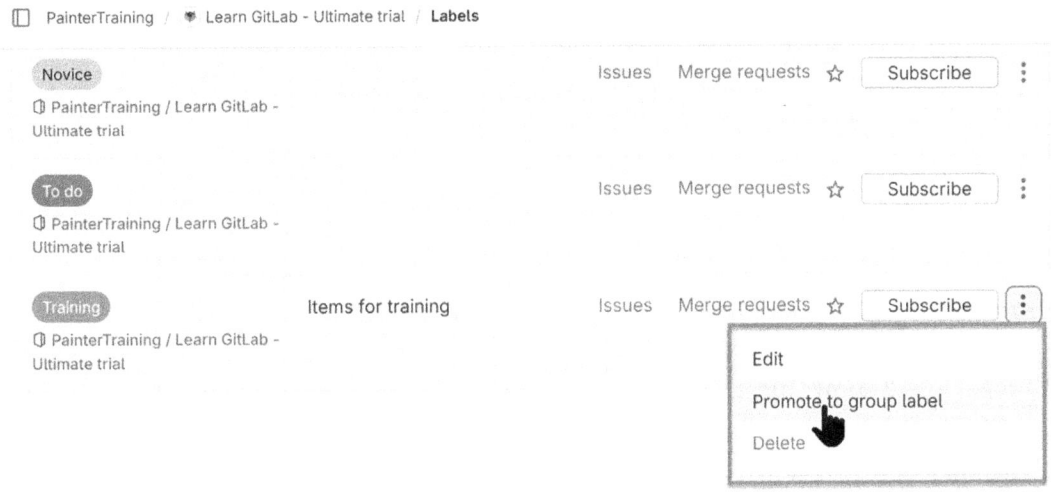

Figure 8-21. *Updated project label list*

Promoting Labels to a Group

So, what if we want to use a label across multiple projects? Do we have to create that label for each and every project? If you look at the vertical ellipses drop-down menu as shown earlier in Figure 8-21, there is the option to promote the label to the project's parent group. Clicking this option pops up the warning box as shown in Figure 8-22. This message is a warning about what will happen if other projects in the group already have that label defined; they'll be replaced with the new group label – likewise if the group label already exists. In our example, there are no other "Training" labels, so promoting simply moves the label to the group, which you can then view from the group's "Manage ➤ Labels" page.[6]

---

[6] We could also have created the "Training" label directly from the group, which is the preferred way of doing this. And yes, subgroups can define their own labels as well.

309

CHAPTER 8   I HAVE AN ISSUE WITH THAT

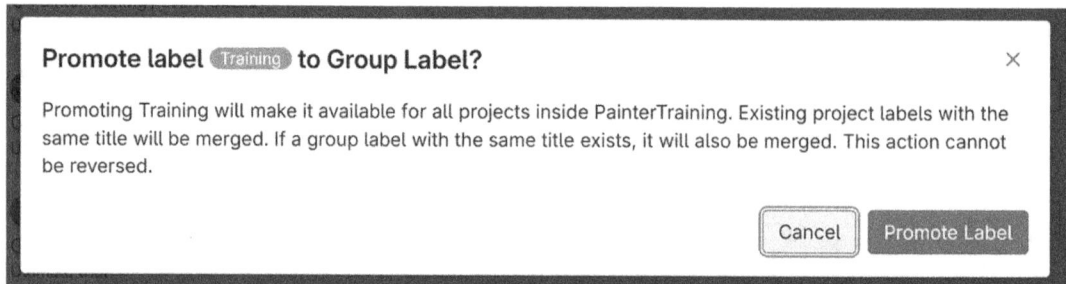

Figure 8-22. Issue label promotion from a project to a group

Figure 8-23 shows the effect of creating the "Training" label and promoting it to the project's group. It now shows up like any other label in the "Edit label" drop-down list. If we switch to any other project under "PainterTraining," we could use the "Training" label (and at this point only the "Training" label) for issues and merge requests associated with that project.

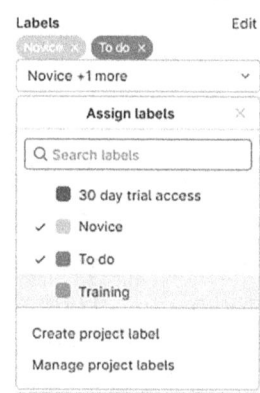

Figure 8-23. Effect of label promotion on projects

Although we can associate issues and merge requests via labels, there is a more direct way to make that association that we'll consider next.

CHAPTER 8   I HAVE AN ISSUE WITH THAT

Creating MRs from Issues

You might have noticed in some of the previous figures the "Create merge request" button. In a normal development life cycle, issues are first created to define the work to be done along with who should work on it. From there, merge requests are created, and changes are made to the code base.

Creating a Merge Request from an Issue

The "Create merge request" button in an issue helps to connect the issue to the merge request(s) that resolve it. To illustrate this, I've created an issue in the "MyShellPipeline" project as shown in Figure 8-24. This is a simple issue request to update the README file. Note that I've labeled the issue with the "Training" label that is available from the "PainterTraining" group; the activity section provides feedback on this.

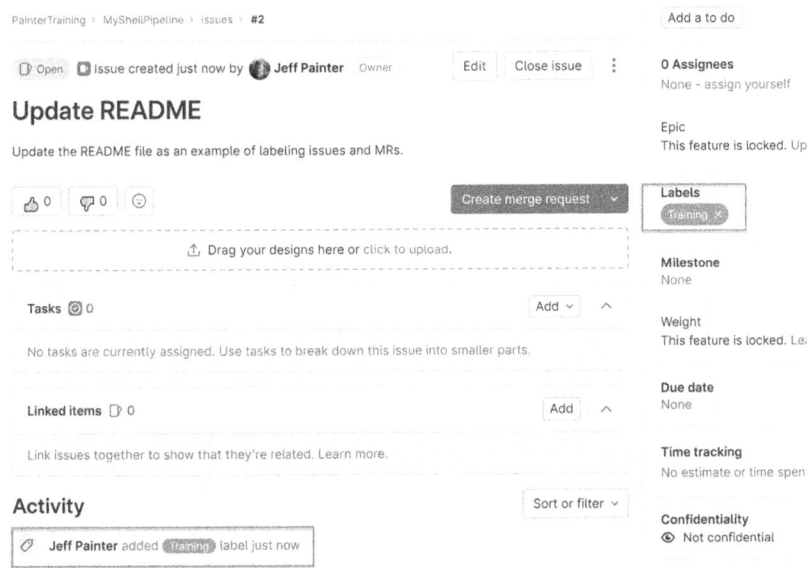

Figure 8-24.   Example MyShellPipeline issue

Figure 8-25 shows the drop-down form associated with the "Create merge request" button. In this example, I'm using the default option of creating a merge request and an associated branch. I've overwritten the default branch name to be "label-example." If I didn't overwrite this, the default would have been the issue number followed by a slug

311

CHAPTER 8   I HAVE AN ISSUE WITH THAT

created from the issue title (in this case, 2-update-readme). I mention this because if you simply selected the "Create merge request" button without going through the drop-down form, it will create that branch automatically for you, which you might not notice.[7]

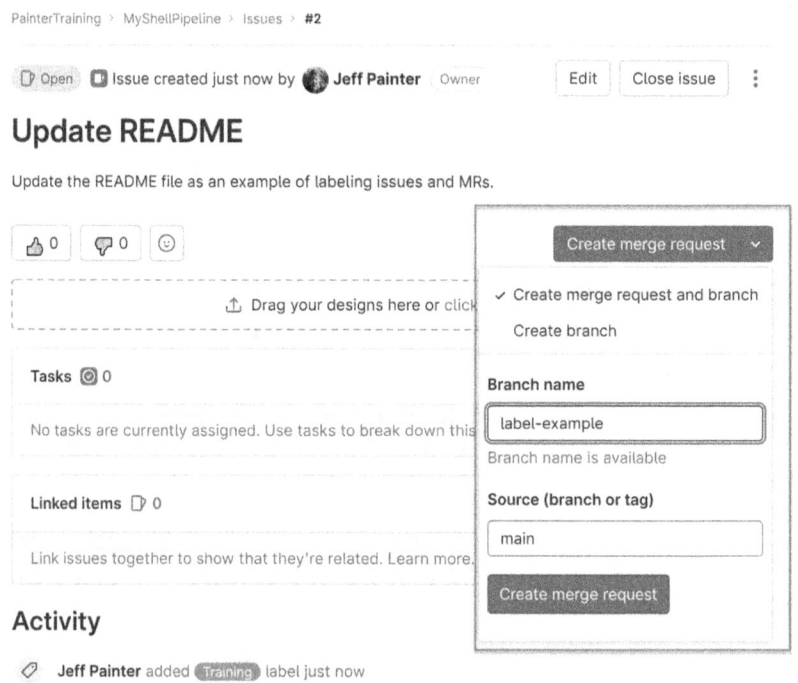

Figure 8-25. *Merge request creation from an issue*

Viewing a Merge Request Generated from an Issue

The merge request resulting from this action is shown in Figure 8-26. There are some things to note. The "Training" label from the issue is automatically copied to the merge request. Also, the default description generated for the MR is simply "Closes #2" where #2 is a link back to the issue. If you create an MR directly without going through an issue, you can still connect to an issue by adding to the description a phrase that refers to the issue number. It doesn't have to be "Closes"; you can use words like "Resolves,"

---

[7] The first time I did this, I did not realize that a branch was created for me, leading to some confusion on my part.

CHAPTER 8   I HAVE AN ISSUE WITH THAT

"Implements," "Fixes," or any variation thereof. Also, note that the MR is put into draft mode automatically, which makes sense since I haven't made any changes to be reviewed yet.

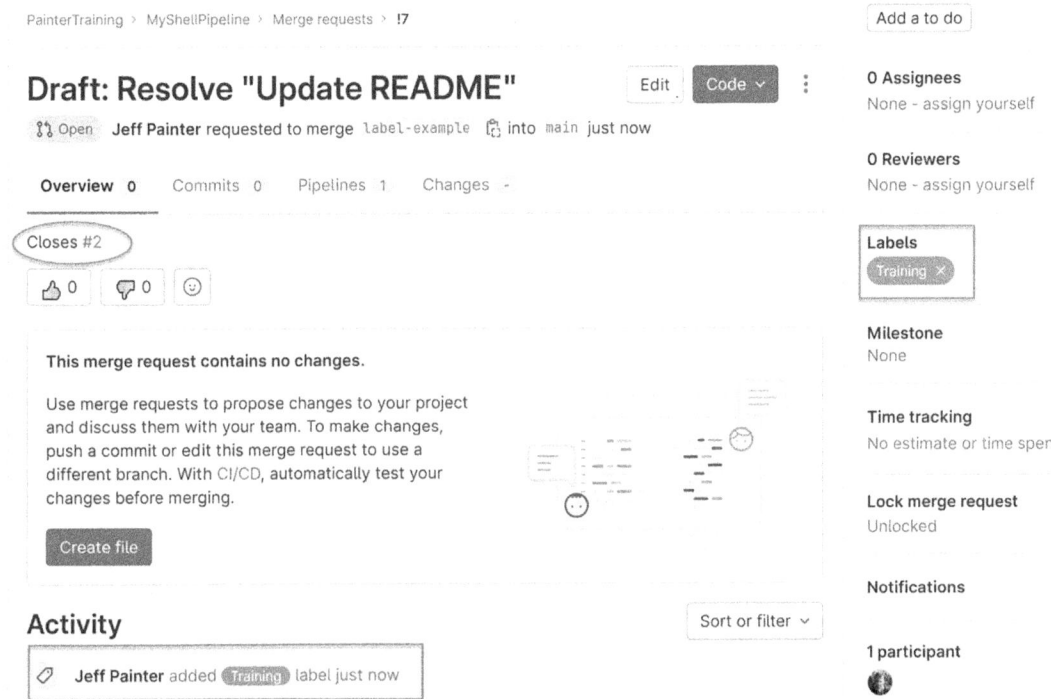

Figure 8-26. *Resulting merge request created from an issue*

In case you are wondering, you can associate an MR with more than one issue, and you can associate an issue to multiple MRs. In the latter case, you should avoid using the special closing words until the last MR since closing an MR with those words will close the issue automatically. We'll see this in action shortly. In the multiple MR case, I tend to use phrasing such as "Partial fix to #2"; adding the "to" between the closing word and the issue number will prevent the issue from being closed automatically.

313

CHAPTER 8   I HAVE AN ISSUE WITH THAT

Viewing Labels in Merge Requests List

Figure 8-27 shows what the MR list looks like after generating it from the issue. Nothing too different here except that the label inherited from the issue is shown with the MR. Also, note the icons on the right that indicate that the latest pipeline succeeded along with a warning that tells you the MR cannot be merged yet (since there are no changes and it is in draft mode).

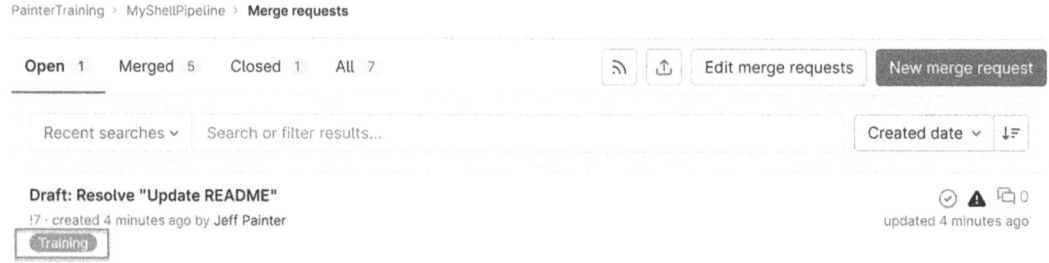

Figure 8-27. *Merge request list with issue labels*

Impact on Issue When Merging an Associated MR

For this example, I went ahead and committed some changes to the README file. Figure 8-28 shows what the MR looks like after this change. The merge changes section provides feedback on what will be done when the MR is completed; the key part here is the last statement that indicates that issue #2 will be closed. The activity section was updated to include the commit just performed. At this point, you can use the "Mark as ready" button to remove the MR from draft mode.[8]

---

[8] Alternatively, you can just remove the "Draft: " from the MR title, which is what this button does.

CHAPTER 8   I HAVE AN ISSUE WITH THAT

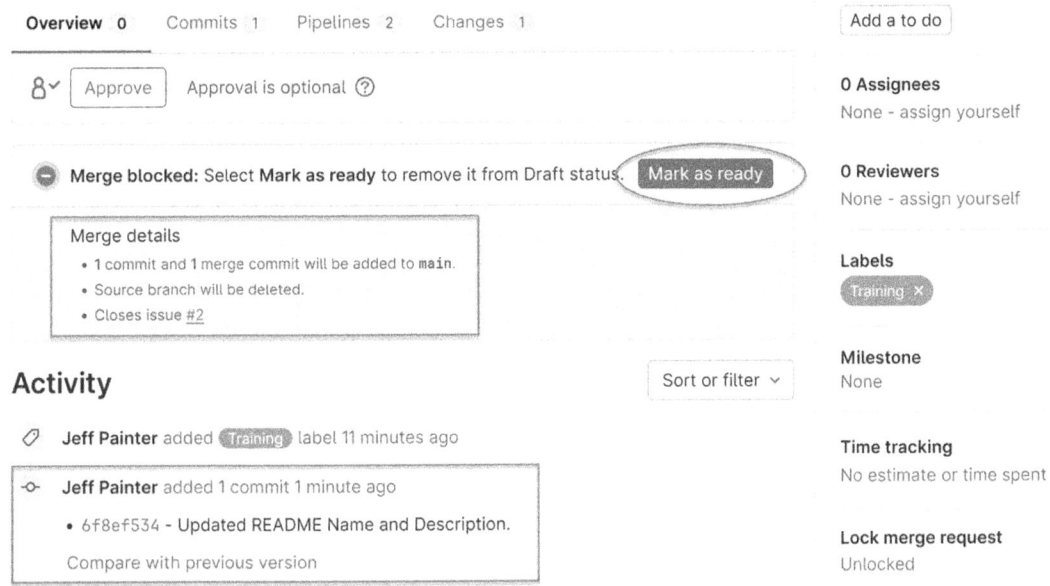

Figure 8-28. Merge request from an issue after the commit

Figure 8-29 shows the status of the MR after merging the changes. We see that the MR is now merged, as expected. We also see from the merge details that the issue was closed; this was done automatically as part of the merge.

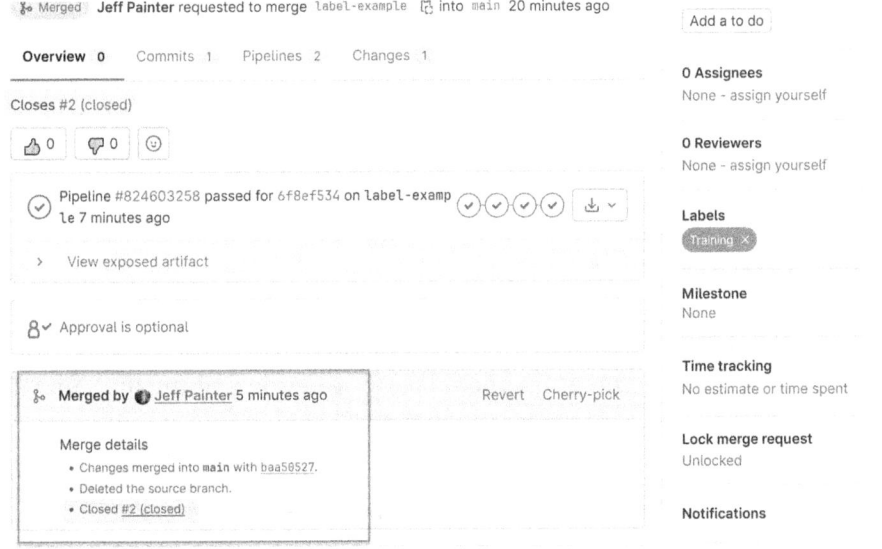

Figure 8-29. Merge request from an issue after the merge

315

CHAPTER 8   I HAVE AN ISSUE WITH THAT

Finally, Figure 8-30 shows the status of the issue after the merge. We see that the issue is indeed closed. In addition, the activity section provides feedback on how this occurred.

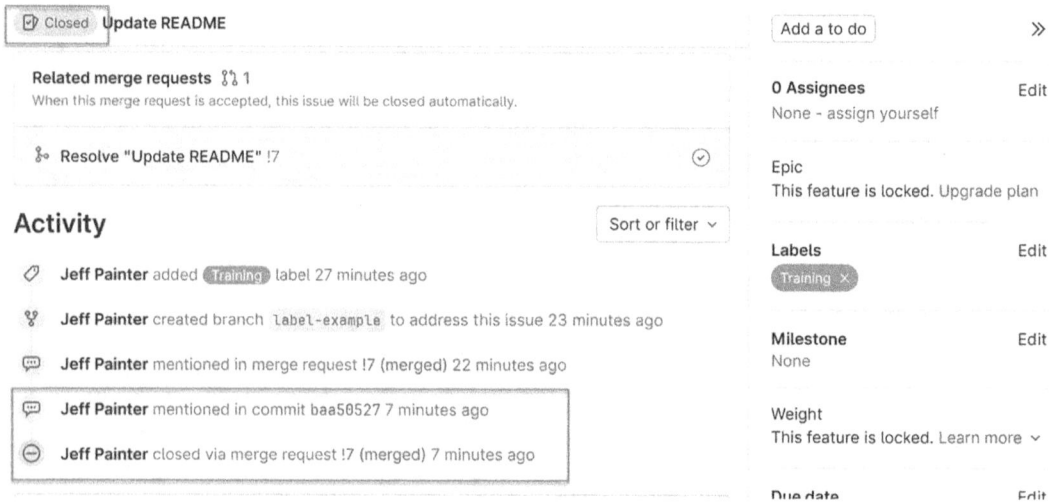

Figure 8-30. *Issue associated with the merge request after the merge*

This section describes a common workflow used by many development teams. A team member is assigned an issue and creates a merge request from that issue. The merge request is associated with a new branch. Changes are committed to that branch, and once work is completed, including code reviews if required, the merge request is closed by merging the changes into the source branch. Once the merge is completed, the associated issue is closed automatically.

In the next section, we'll look at how to link related issues.

Linking Issues

As you work with issues, you'll come to realize that issues are not always independent of each other. For example, two users might create issues describing the same problem they've discovered while using the production product. Or an issue describing a new website feature might depend on a back-end API change managed in a different project. In these cases, it helps to link these issues together so that their dependencies are clearer.

Special Considerations About Linking Issues in GitLab

Although GitLab enables linking issues together, it is a feature that isn't as rich as other issue management systems, particularly Jira. For example, with the free version of GitLab, all you can do is simply link two issues in a bidirectional "relates to" relationship even if one issue depends on another. In this case, you'll have to add descriptions to the issues to let you know what the actual relationship is and handle them explicitly.

Things are a little better with the paid subscriptions of premium and above. With these license models, GitLab adds the unidirectional "blocks" and "is blocked by" relationship. For example, if issue "A" requires issue "B" to be completed first, the two issues can be linked with issue "A" marked as "is blocked by" and issue "B" marked as "blocks." At least with the blocking relationship, you are warned when closing issue "A" while issue "B" is still open; this is not true with the simple "relates to" relationship where either issue can be closed before the other.

Some might argue that these two types of issue linking, "relates to" and "blocking," are all that is needed and actually simplify the management of links. But others argue that they help to have more semantic link types such as "duplicates" or "depends on" to convey the relationship more clearly. One factor to consider with respect to GitLab is that issues are also referenced by merge requests, where the real work is managed. So, a "duplicates" relationship can be established at the merge request level where the MR references both issues; this gets around the problem of determining what issue duplicates the other. From an MR perspective, they have the same weight.

Linking One Issue to Another

So, without further ado, let's look at how to link issues together. To illustrate, I'm just going to link together two issues in the "GitLab Learning" project, which you can also experiment with. Figure 8-31 shows a filtered list of issues in the "GitLab Learning" project. For this example, I plan to link the two highlighted issues #10 and #11.

CHAPTER 8 I HAVE AN ISSUE WITH THAT

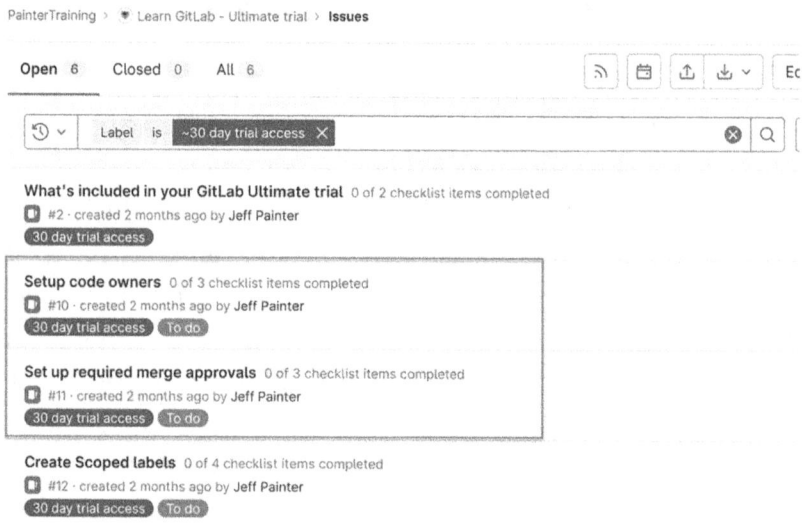

Figure 8-31. Issue list before linking

I can use either issue to link to the other, so I chose issue #10. Figure 8-32 shows the "Linked items" section in issue #10. Clicking the "Add" button brings up a text box where either the issue number beginning with # or the issue URL can be entered. Upon entering the # character in the text box, a pop-up menu of possible issues within the project shows up; this makes it easier than remembering the issue number. Selecting issue #11 from the list and hitting the "Add" button again creates the link.

CHAPTER 8   I HAVE AN ISSUE WITH THAT

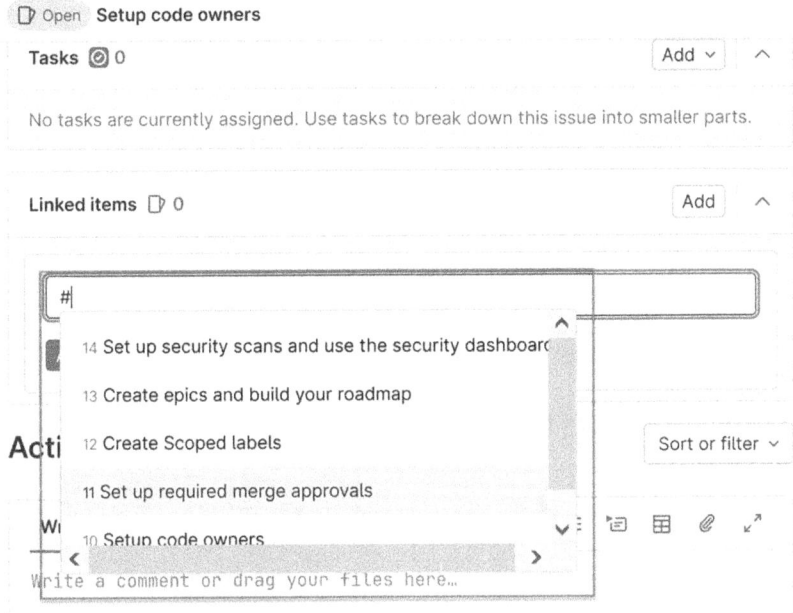

Figure 8-32. *Issue add link option*

Viewing Linked Items

Figure 8-33 shows what the "Linked items" list looks like after adding the link, and Figure 8-34 shows what the "Linked items" list in issue #11 looks like. Note that the activity section as seen in the second image describes that the issue was linked to another and by whom. Hovering over the issue title in the "Linked items" section reveals that it is a link that will take you to the related issue.

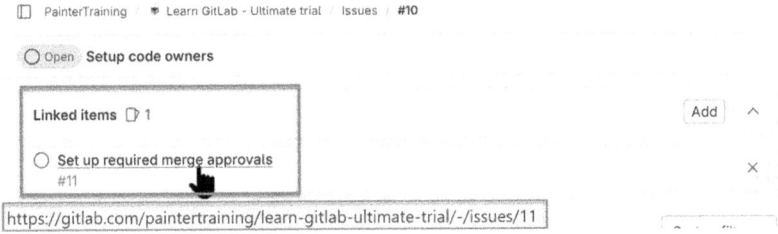

Figure 8-33. *Issue #10 list of links*

319

CHAPTER 8   I HAVE AN ISSUE WITH THAT

Figure 8-34.   Issue #11 list of links

Deleting a Link

Deleting the link is simply accomplished using the X to the right of the link title under the "Linked items" section. Obviously, deleting the link from one issue deletes the link from the related issue. Like link addition, link deletion is noted in the activities section of both issues that were linked.

Special Link Types with Paid Subscriptions

For those with a paid subscription, adding a link includes additional information in the "Add" drop-down list to set what type of relationship you are creating. To see this, go to `https://docs.gitlab.com/ee/user/project/issues/related_issues.html#add-a-linked-issue`, which shows what the drop-down list looks like in this case. By the way, with a blocking issue, you will see an additional icon in the issues list to let you know that it is blocking other issues. Otherwise, there are no indications that issues are linked when viewed from the issues list.

Summary

We covered the following topics in this chapter:

- Described how to create and edit issues
- Learned how to create and prioritize labels

- Reviewed how to use labels with issues and merge requests
- Discussed how to create a merge request from an issue
- Looked at how to link issues
- Considered different link types based on free vs. paid licenses

In the next chapter, we'll consider how to plan your work with milestones and issue boards.

CHAPTER 9

The Best Laid Plans

At this point, we shift our focus from creating and managing issues to planning using issues. For small projects with a relatively manageable number of issues, it is a pretty simple matter to plan your work. You simply pick issues off the open list, assign it to yourself or someone else, work on the issue, and close it once the work is complete. Which issue you pick usually depends on the urgency of the request or the scope of work needed to complete the task.

For larger projects or projects managed within an organization, some planning tools are required to ensure the project moves forward in a timely manner and that urgent issues are addressed. In this chapter, we'll explore GitLab's planning features of milestones, tasks, and issue boards.

As mentioned in the introductory chapter, you don't have to use GitLab's tools for everything; there are plenty of alternative tools out there instead. GitLab as a company understands this and realizes that many companies already have investments in those alternative tools. So, we'll also talk specifically about how GitLab enables integration with the commonly used Jira application.

Establishing Milestones

Many organizations use an agile or kanban methodology to plan work using short-duration iterations (2 weeks is typical). Other organizations might use a more traditional month or quarterly planning cycle to squeeze in features to be delivered at the next release point. GitLab supports both with the "Iteration" and "Milestone" features.

As it turns out, iterations are only available for paid subscriptions; this feature is not available when using the free tier. This makes some sense since the free tier is restricted to a small number of users (up to 5 users using the gitlab.com site) where iterative planning doesn't add much value.¹ Because iterations are not available with the free tier, I am not going to discuss it here. However, if you have a premium or above subscription, you can learn more about them in the GitLab documentation here: `https://docs.gitlab.com/ee/user/group/iterations/`.

Creating Milestones

Fortunately, milestones are part of the free tier, so we'll spend some time exploring them here. They are straightforward to manage. Normally, you create milestones at the project level, though you can create them at the group level as well if you have multiple projects involved in a release. Figure 9-1 shows the "Milestone" page for a project where milestones have not been created yet. Nothing too exciting here, just a splash screen, a link to the documentation, and the "New milestone" button.

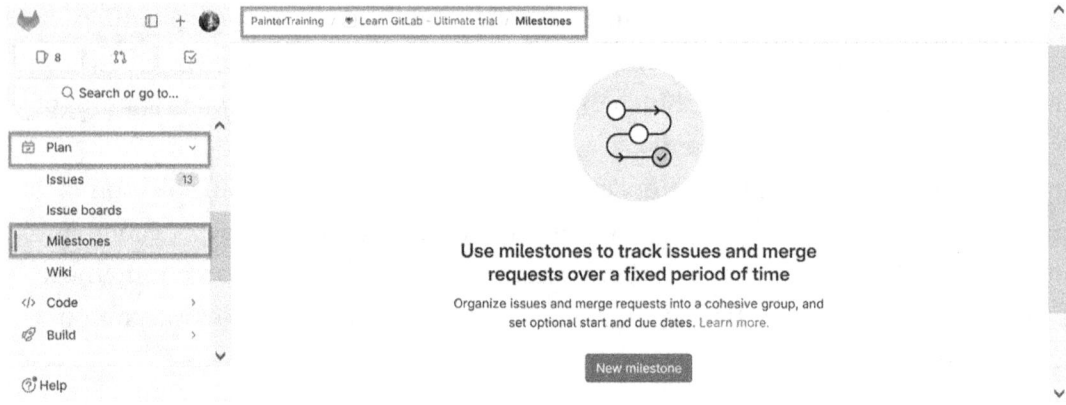

Figure 9-1. Initial project milestone page

Upon selecting the "New milestone" button, you are taken to the "New milestone" page as shown in Figure 9-2. The form is straightforward. You specify the milestone title, "Example Milestone 1" in this example. You can enter an optional start date along with the required due date. Add a description, if desired, and select the "Create milestone" button.

---

[1] If you do need an iterative planning tool with the free tier, you can use the free tier of Jira to plan your iterations instead.

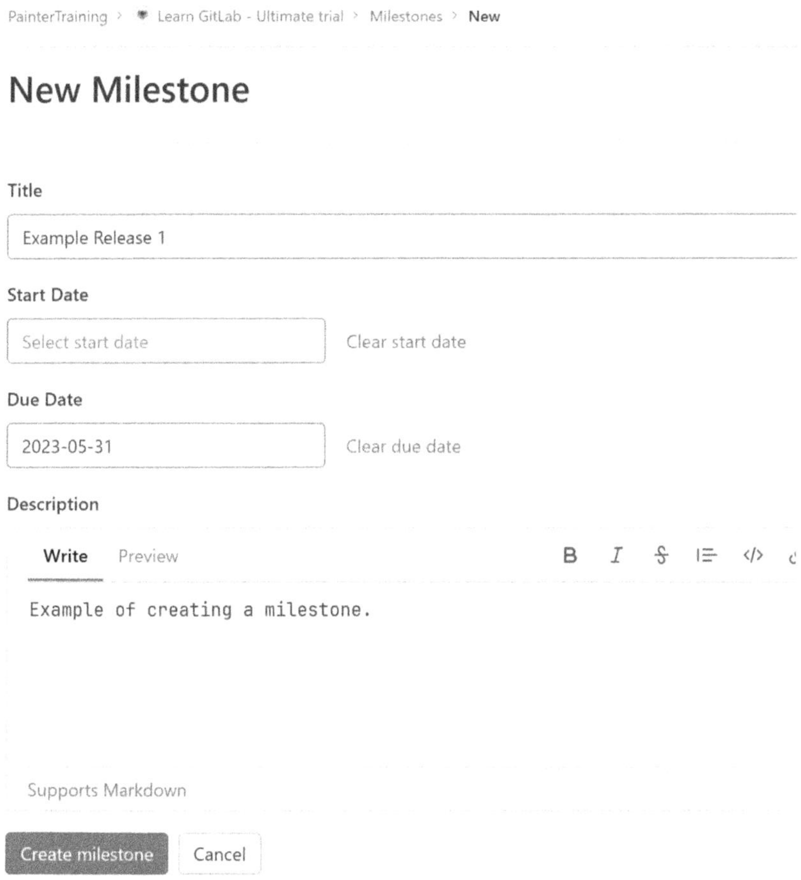

CHAPTER 9   THE BEST LAID PLANS

PainterTraining > Learn GitLab - Ultimate trial > Milestones > New

New Milestone

Title

[Example Release 1]

Start Date

[Select start date]   Clear start date

Due Date

[2023-05-31]   Clear due date

Description

Write   Preview   B I S ≡ </>

Example of creating a milestone.

Supports Markdown

[Create milestone] Cancel

Figure 9-2. *New milestone page*

Viewing Milestone Details

Once the milestone is created, we see the milestone's detail page as shown in Figure 9-3. In addition to the "Close milestone" button, we can see the options for the vertical ellipsis menu that enables us to edit, promote, and delete the milestone. At the bottom of the page are the tabs for viewing issues and merge requests assigned to the milestone, which has none when first created. The right-hand pane shows metadata for the milestone, such as the due date, as well as status summaries of issues and merge requests associated with the milestone.

325

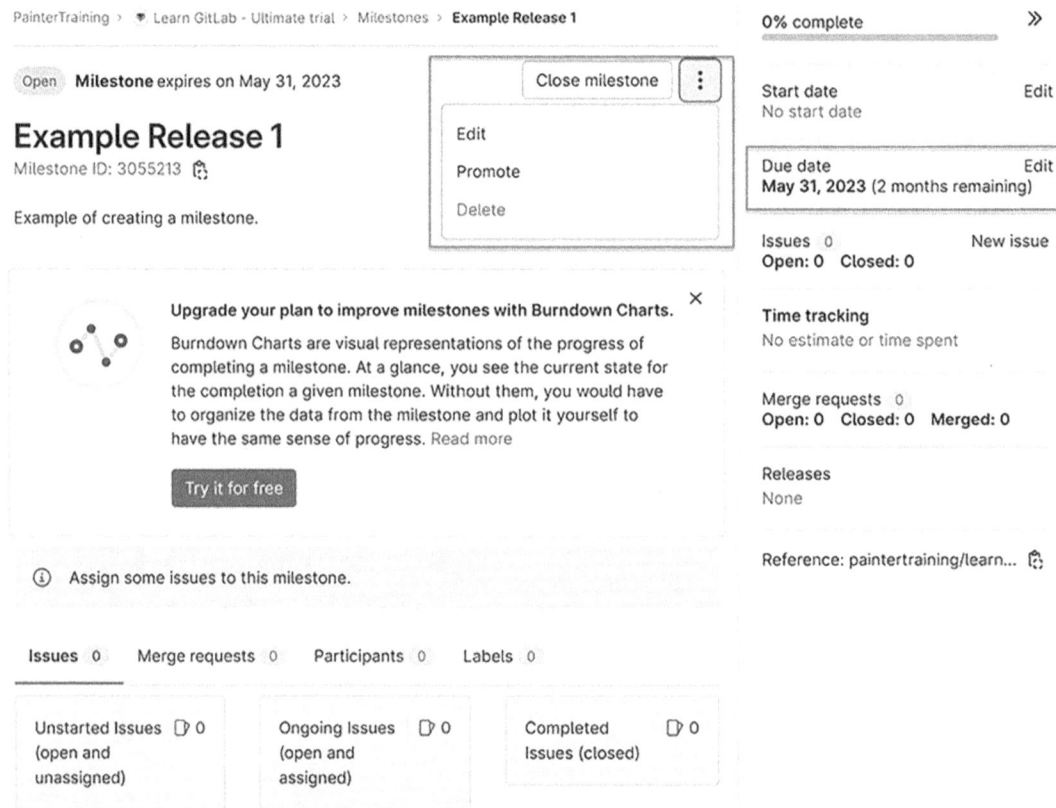

Figure 9-3. Milestone detail page

Associating Issues with Milestones

Adding issues to the milestone can be done quite simply by going to the issues page and selecting "Edit issues" as shown in Figure 9-4. Select the issues you wish to add and select the milestone from the "Assign milestone" drop-down list in the right-hand pane. You could, of course, edit each issue individually and add the milestone from there. Creating new issues allows you to select the milestone also. Adding merge requests to a milestone follows the same pattern as adding issues.

CHAPTER 9   THE BEST LAID PLANS

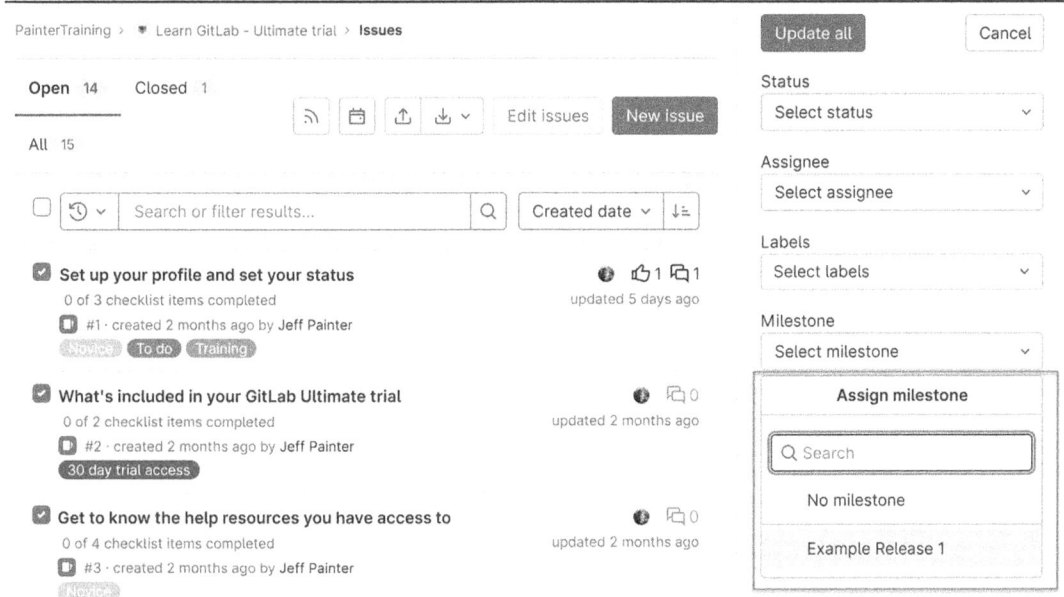

Figure 9-4. *Milestone assignment for an issue*

Figure 9-5 shows the milestone's detail page after issues have been added. The issues are separated into categories depending on their state with respect to the milestone: "Unstarted," "Ongoing," and "Completed." Note that the right-hand-side panel shows the number of issues according to the simpler "Open" and "Closed" states. In terms of the free tier subscription, this page is the best overview we can get for a milestone. For paid subscriptions, you can also view either a burn-down or burn-up chart to give you a sense of how the milestone issues are progressing over time. Check out the link `https://docs.gitlab.com/ee/user/project/milestones/burndown_and_burnup_charts.html` to explore how to use these charts.

CHAPTER 9 THE BEST LAID PLANS

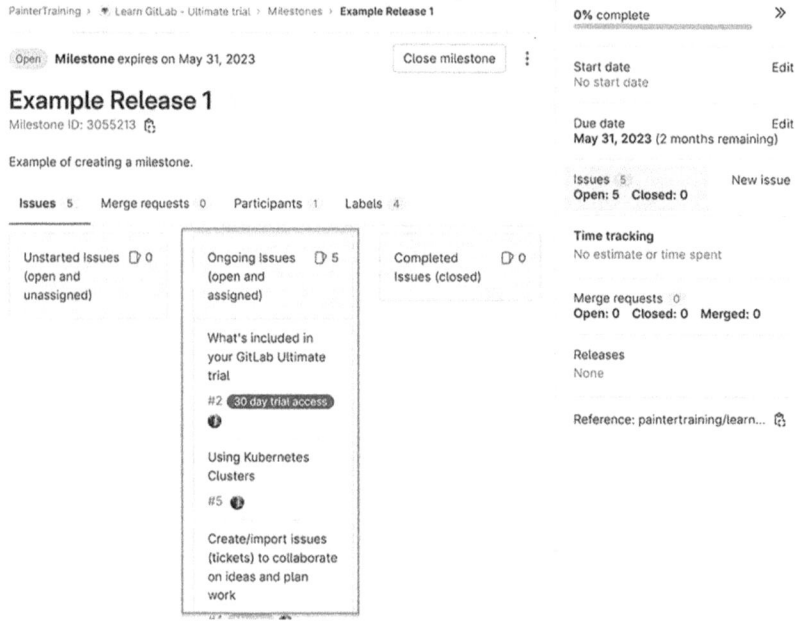

Figure 9-5. Milestone detail page after issue assignment

Viewing Milestones from the Issue List

When you go to a project's issue list, you can see which issues have a milestone based on whether they have a milestone link as shown in Figure 9-6. Clicking the link will take you directly to the milestone's detail page. In this example, the first five issues have the "Example Release 1" link; all other issues have no milestone links. As expected, issues can belong to no more than one milestone.

CHAPTER 9 THE BEST LAID PLANS

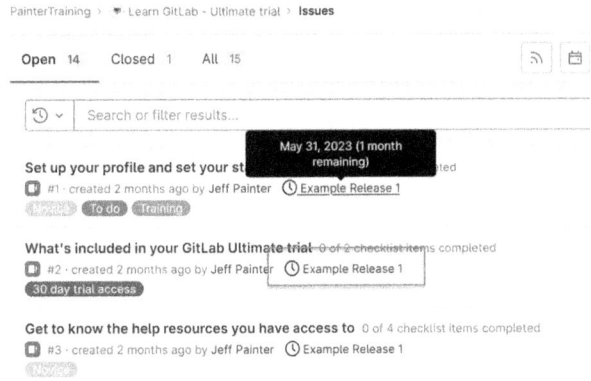

Figure 9-6. *Project list of issues with milestones*

Removing an Issue from a Milestone

You can remove an issue from a milestone (or move it to another milestone, if warranted) by editing the issue as shown in Figure 9-7. Simply select the "Edit" button next to "Milestone" in the right-hand pane and choose "No milestone" to remove it. The same process works for removing merge requests.

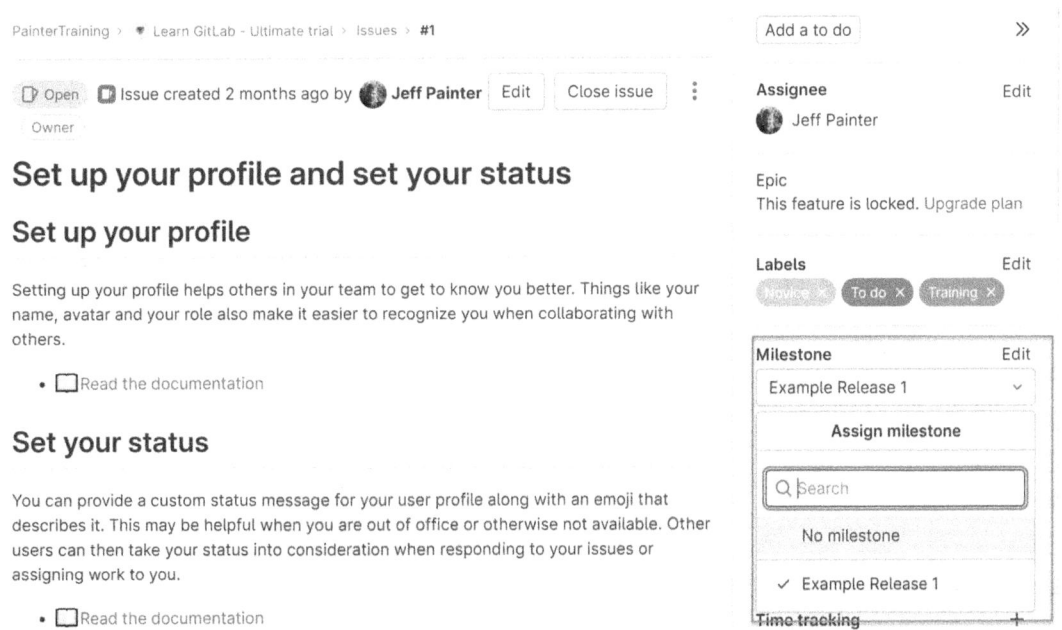

Figure 9-7. *Milestone removal from an issue*

CHAPTER 9 THE BEST LAID PLANS

Viewing the Project's Milestone Summary

Figure 9-8 shows the project's milestone summary list. In this example, we only have one milestone for this project, but it is possible to have multiple milestones listed to account for future releases. The milestone includes a brief summary of how many issues and merge requests are assigned to the milestone. It also gives a percent completion based on the total number of associated issues and merge requests.

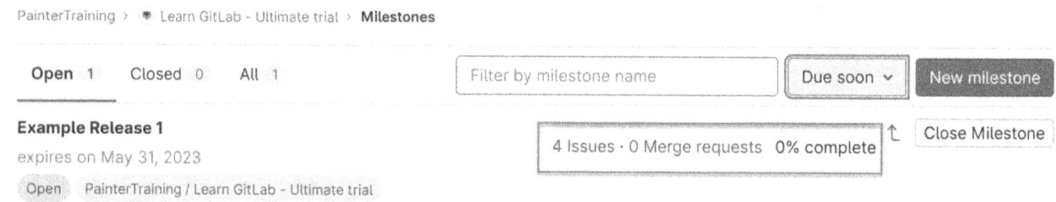

Figure 9-8. *Milestone summary list for a project*

Promoting Milestones to the Group Level

As mentioned earlier, milestones can also exist at the group level. This is convenient when many projects under a group or subgroup are part of the same release schedule. You can either create a milestone from a group directly or you can promote an existing milestone from a project to a group. In this example, we'll promote the "GitLab Learning" project milestone to its parent group. This is done using the vertical ellipsis menu as shown in Figure 9-3. Selecting the "Promote" button brings up the pop-up warning message as shown in Figure 9-9.

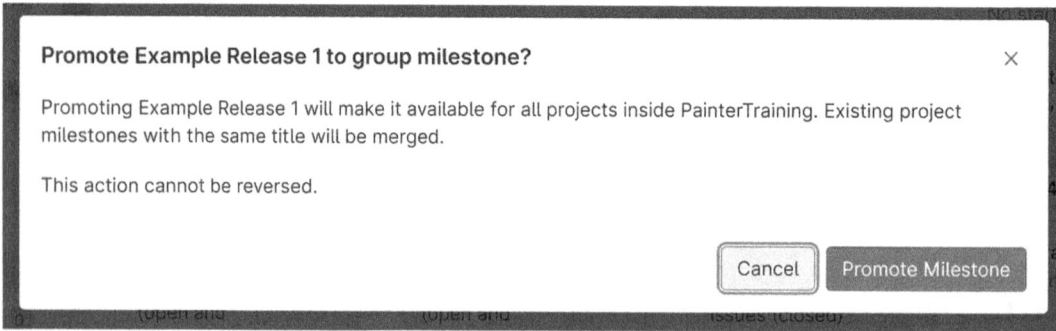

Figure 9-9. *Milestone promotion from project to group*

CHAPTER 9   THE BEST LAID PLANS

This warning is similar to the "Promote label" warning we saw in an earlier chapter. When we select the "Promote Milestone" button, we get the group milestone summary page as shown in Figure 9-10. Note that "Example Release 1" is marked as a group milestone now. Other than this, it behaves just like the project milestone except that we can now associate issues and merge requests from any of the projects under the "PainterTraining" group.

Figure 9-10. Milestone summary list for a group

Viewing Milestone Associations with MRs

To illustrate associations with merge requests, I created an issue under "MyFirstProject," which I associated with the "Example Release 1" milestone as part of the issue creation. I then generated a merge request from this issue; this automatically added the milestone to the merge request as expected. Figure 9-11 shows the milestone's detail page with merge requests highlighted. Here, we see that merge requests are split into one of four categories: "Work in progress," "Waiting for merge," "Rejected," and "Merged." We also see in the right-hand panel a count of merge requests broken down by "Open," "Closed," and "Merged."

331

CHAPTER 9   THE BEST LAID PLANS

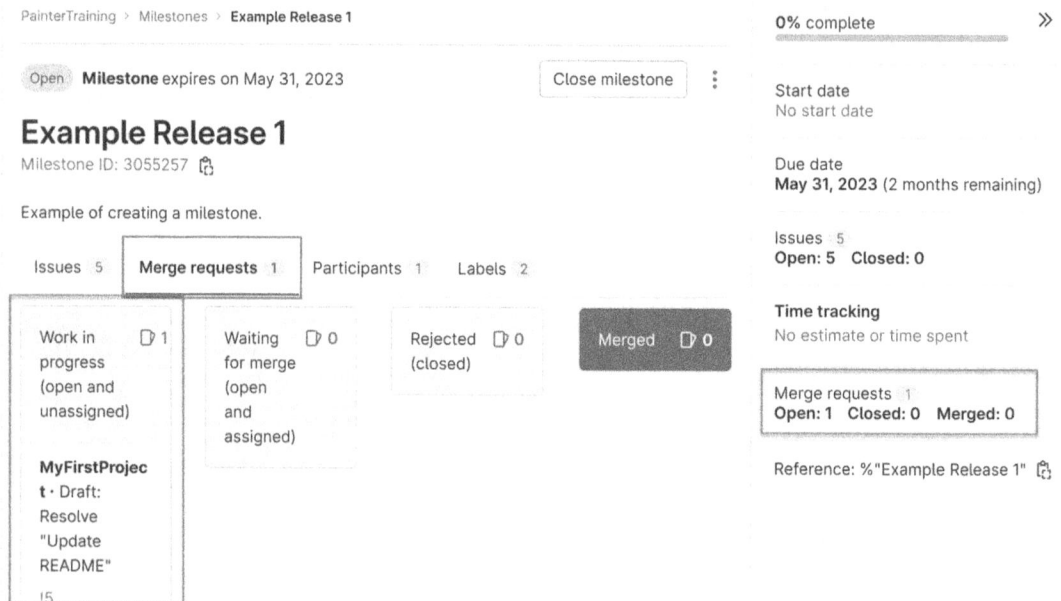

Figure 9-11. Milestone detail page merge request view

Viewing Milestones from the Top-Level Dashboard

You can also view milestones from the top-level dashboard as shown in Figure 9-12. This is handy to see milestones across all groups and projects to which you have access. As with the other milestone summary lists, you can see the number of issues and merge requests associated with each milestone along with the percentage completed.

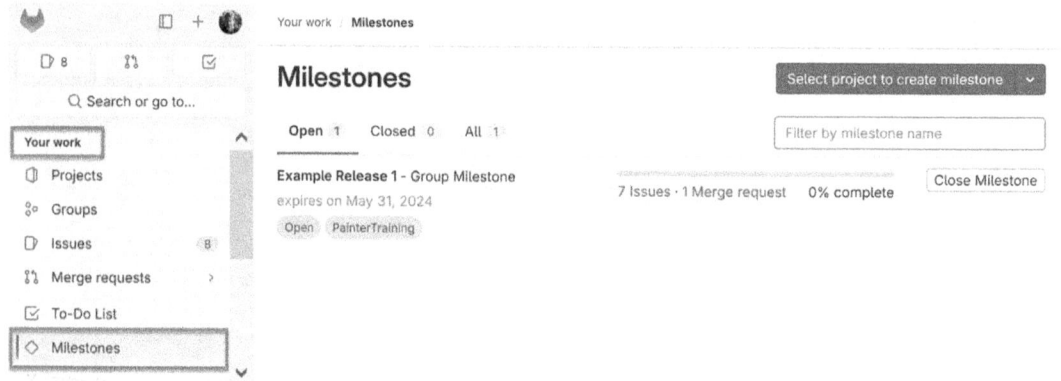

Figure 9-12. Top-level dashboard milestone list

Filtering Issues by Milestones

Clicking either the issues or milestones link takes you to a filtered view of the issues or merge requests as appropriate. In Figure 9-13, we see the issue list filtered by the "Example Release 1" milestone. The filter was automatically generated when clicking the "7 Issues" link in the previous figure. A similar filter would be generated for the merge requests summary list when selecting the "1 Merge request" link. Note that you can see from which group and project an issue came from.

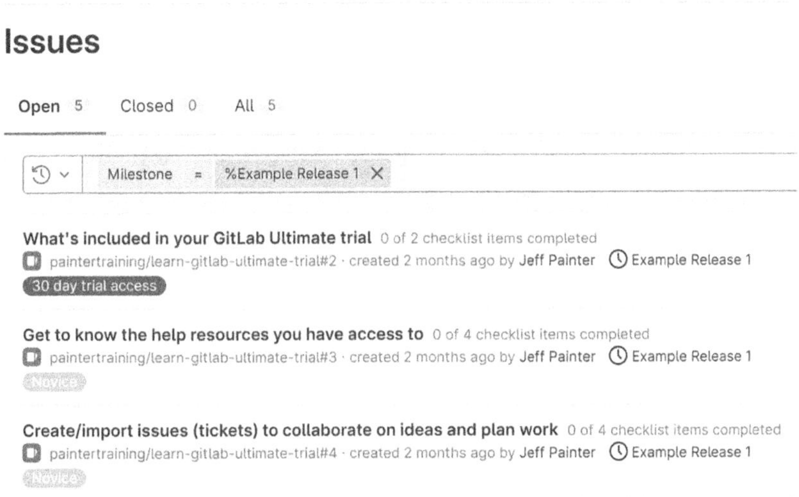

Figure 9-13. Issue list filtered by milestone

Special Considerations of Milestones

One final note about milestones: Although I said earlier that iterations are used for short-duration planning methodologies such as agile and kanban and that milestones are used for longer-term fixed-release methodologies, it is quite common to use milestones alongside iterations. GitLab does this for its own planning purposes. GitLab releases minor version updates on the third Thursday of every month with a major version update once a year; emergency and/or security patch updates may occur prior to the planned updates as needed. These version updates are managed using milestones.

It is important not to confuse milestones with epics; an epic is a feature used by agile methodologies, which, like iterations, is only available with a paid subscription. An epic is used for features that require multiple iterations to complete, which may span across milestones as well. Typically, an epic is aligned to a milestone when all work related to the epic is completed. You'll also see that epics play a role in GitLab planning. Since the epic feature is only available for paid subscriptions, I won't talk about them any further. If you have a paid subscription and are interested in epics, you can visit GitLab's documentation about it here: `https://docs.gitlab.com/ee/user/group/epics/`.

Having looked at how to group together issues into milestones, we'll next look at how to split issues into smaller, more manageable tasks.

Defining Tasks

Suppose you are assigned an issue that you know will take several days. Also, assume that you can break down that issue into multiple well-defined steps that taken together will resolve the issue. You could create issues for each step and relate it to the main issue, but that tends to skew things a bit; suddenly, it looks like you just doubled the work for a given iteration even though all you intended to do was split the workload up into more manageable pieces. This is where tasks come into play.

As of this writing, tasks are a relatively new feature introduced into GitLab.[2] It is part of a larger effort to refactor planning using work items. A description of this can be found in the GitLab epic `https://gitlab.com/groups/gitlab-org/-/epics/7103`. Defining tasks is a step toward that final vision. We'll take a look at how to create and manage tasks in this section. I expect there will be changes to tasks in the future (perhaps making them more first-class citizens), but I don't expect that what I describe in this section will have changed much.

Creating Tasks

You create tasks from within an issue; you cannot create tasks independently. To illustrate creating tasks, I created a new issue called "My spiffy new feature" in "MyFirstProject." To create a task, go to the "Tasks" section within the issue and select "New task" from the "Add" drop-down menu as shown in Figure 9-14. This will put you into edit mode where you can create one or more tasks associated with the issue.

---

[2] So new that I wasn't aware of them until I started writing this book. I could have made use of them as part of my previous employment.

CHAPTER 9   THE BEST LAID PLANS

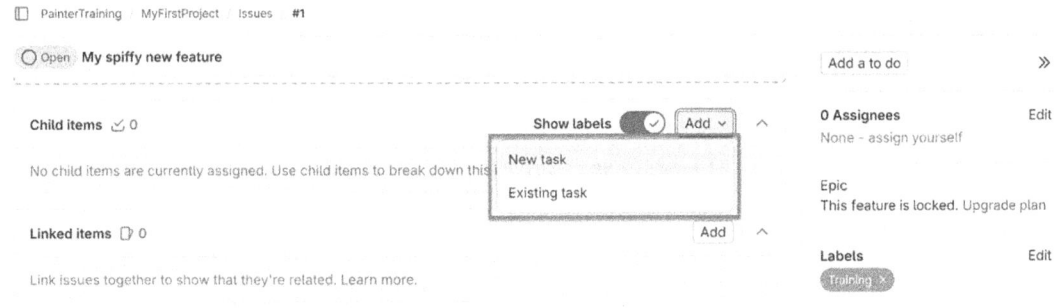

Figure 9-14. Issue add task menu

Selecting "New task" presents the create task form as shown in Figure 9-15. You use this form to create one or more tasks as needed. When creating a task, you only provide the title of the task; you can add details to a task by editing it later. Here, I've already added four tasks. The green circles indicate that the tasks are open. Note that the "X" next to a task enables removing it from the list.

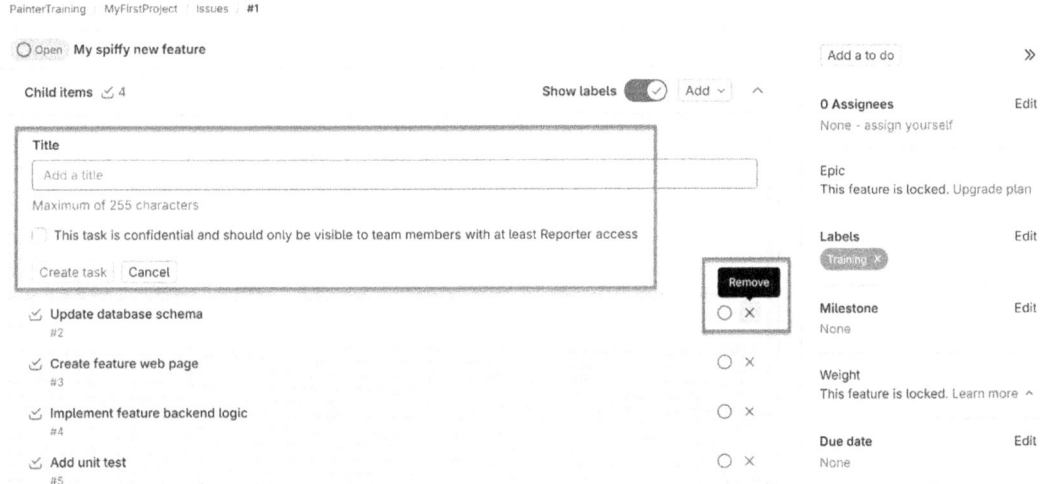

Figure 9-15. Task creation form

335

Editing a Task

Once you've created a task, you can edit it by selecting the task's title. This brings up the task's detail pop-up form as shown in Figure 9-16. From here, you can assign a task to a member of the project, set a label, associate the task to a milestone, and set the start and end dates for the task. In addition, you can set a description. Note that at the present time, the description is plain text only; it is not enabled to use markup language.[3] Like an issue, you can also add comments and threads to discuss the implementation.

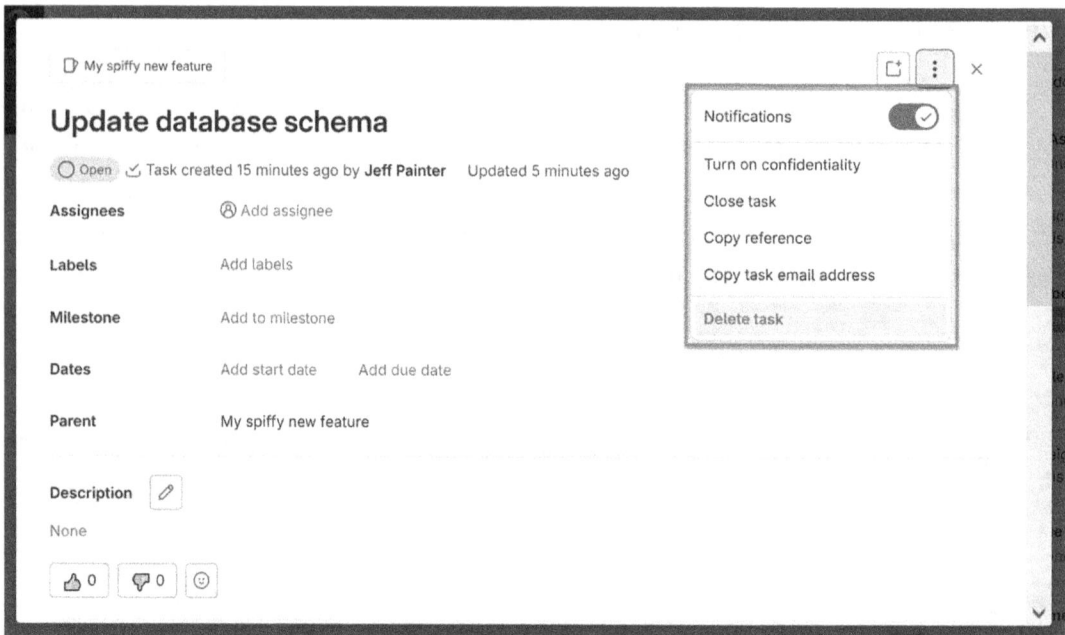

Figure 9-16. *Task edit pop-up form*

Completing a Task

Once you've completed a task, you close it by selecting the "Close task" option from the vertical ellipsis menu as shown in Figure 9-17. Once closed, you can simply reopen it by using the "Reopen task" that appears in the same menu. Figure 9-18 shows what the task list looks like after a task has been closed. Closed tasks are displayed with a dash inside the green circle.

---

[3] At the time of this writing, the task description markup is in beta. It is likely to be enabled by the time you read this.

CHAPTER 9   THE BEST LAID PLANS

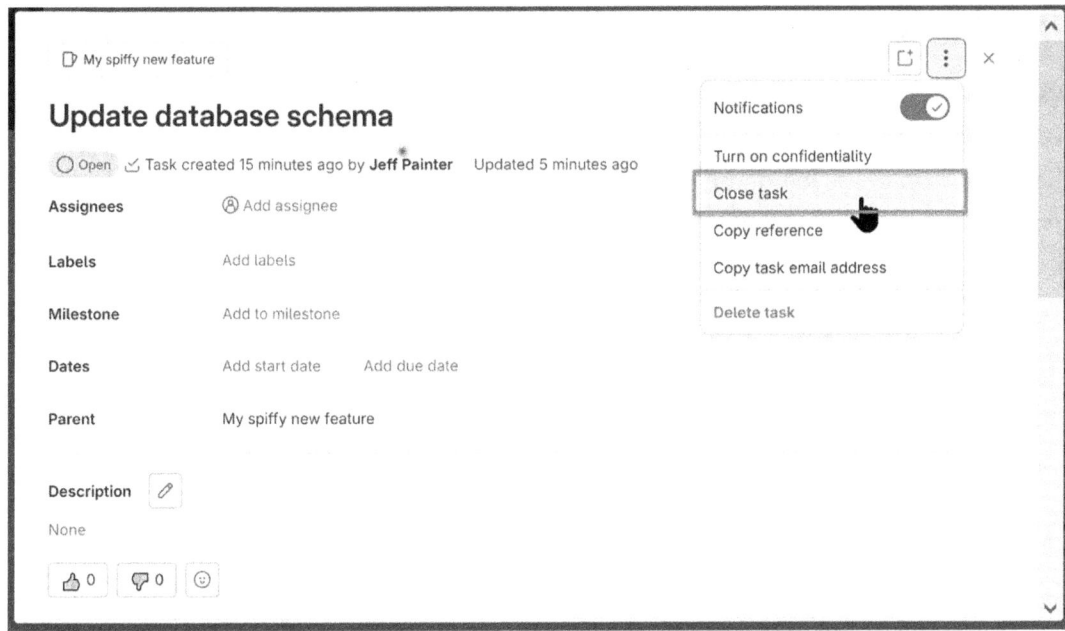

Figure 9-17. *Task status change to closed*

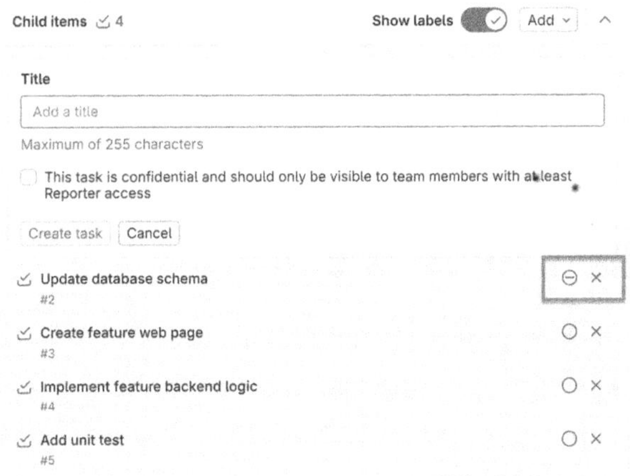

Figure 9-18. *Task list with closed tasks*

Viewing Tasks in the Issue List

A special feature of tasks is that they are displayed alongside issues in the issue summary list. Figure 9-19 shows the issue summary list for the "MyFirstProject" project. Tasks have their own icon to the left of the title; otherwise, they look like any other issue. The astute reader will notice that task identifiers actually use issue identifiers and that tasks are included in the issue counts for "Open," "Closed," and "All."

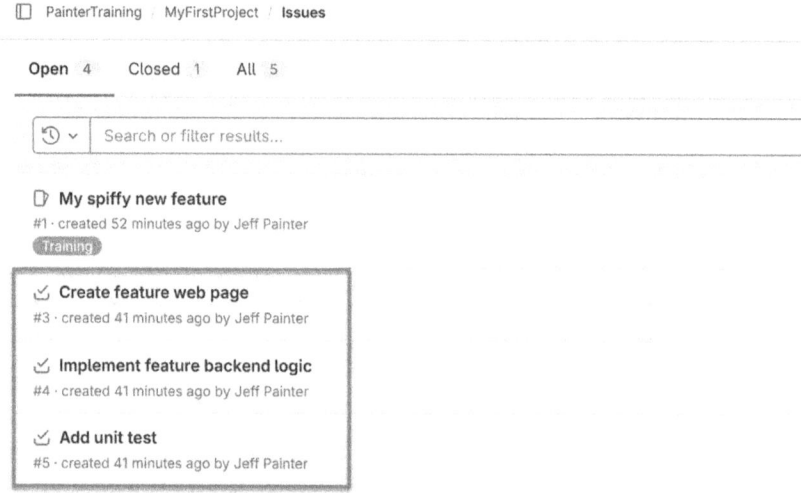

Figure 9-19. Issue summary list with tasks

Associating Tasks to Milestones

As mentioned earlier, tasks can be assigned to milestones. Figure 9-20 shows the "Create feature web page" task being associated with the "Example Release 1" milestone. Once associated with a milestone, the task appears on the milestone's detail page as shown in Figure 9-21. Note that within the milestone's issue list, there is no visible indication of what is a task and what is an issue.

CHAPTER 9   THE BEST LAID PLANS

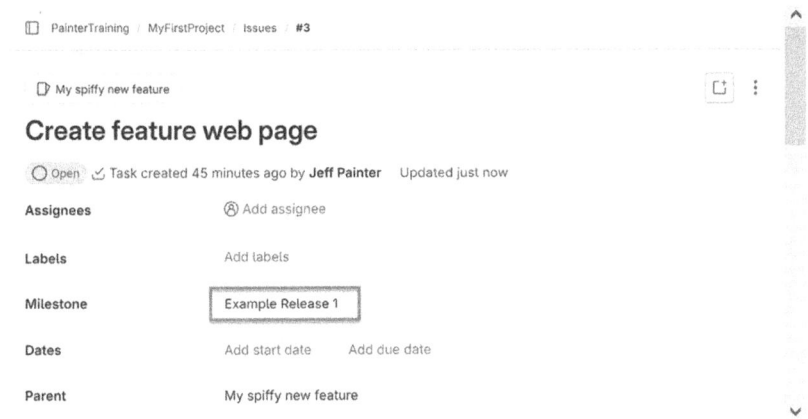

Figure 9-20. Milestone assignment for a task

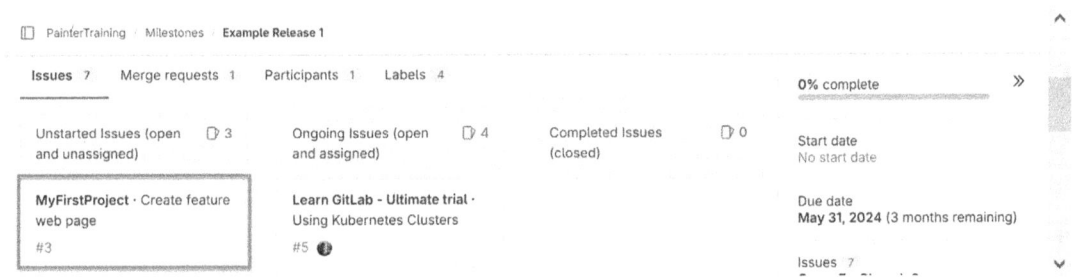

Figure 9-21. Milestone list with tasks

Filtering Tasks from an Issue List

From a project's issue list, it is possible to display just tasks by filtering on "Type is task" as shown in Figure 9-22. You can also filter tasks from the group's issue list in the same manner.[4]

---

[4] Interestingly, trying to filter by tasks from the dashboard's issue list results in an error. I assume this will be fixed by the time you read this.

339

CHAPTER 9   THE BEST LAID PLANS

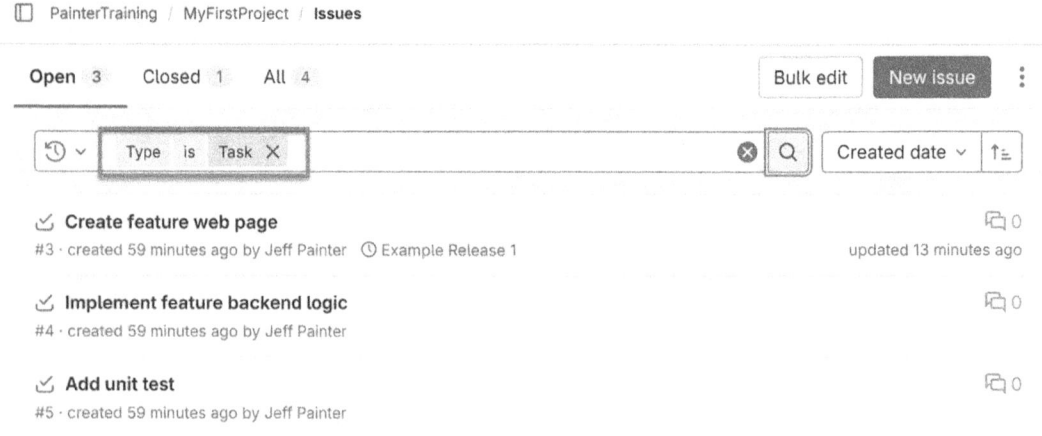

Figure 9-22. Issue list filtered to show only tasks

Converting Document List Items to Tasks

That's basically it for tasks. I assume their functionality will be enhanced in future versions. Before we leave the topic of tasks, there is one quirky task feature to be discussed. If you have a list of items in the description of an issue, you can convert a list item into a task as shown in Figure 9-23. In this example, I chose one of the issues from the "Learn GitLab" project that had such a list. For a given list item, you use the vertical ellipsis menu item and select "Convert to task." This will remove the item from the description's list and create a task from it.

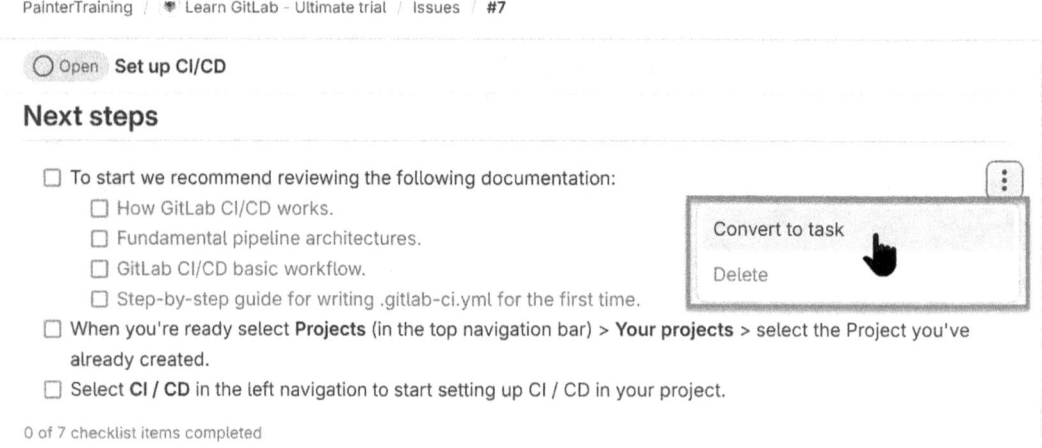

Figure 9-23. Issue item conversion to task

CHAPTER 9 THE BEST LAID PLANS

In the next section, we'll turn our attention to another way of managing issues and tasks: issue boards.

Planning with Boards

If you've had any experience with agile or kanban methodologies, you know that issue boards play an important role in planning, especially in visualizing work. As you may have guessed by now, using issue boards with the free tier is a bit limited, but with some effort issue boards are still useful. We'll take a look at the free tier version of issue boards in this section.

Exploring an Existing Issue Board

So rather than creating an issue board from scratch, let's look at a board already created for the "Learn GitLab" project. Figure 9-24 shows what that board looks like. You can find the board under the project's "Plan ➤ Issue Boards." The name of the board is "GitLab onboarding" and has columns named "Open," "To do," and "Closed." The "Open" and "Closed" columns are standard columns; the "To do" column contains open issues with the "To do" label. This board is known as a label-based issue board, which is the only type of issue board available under the free tier.

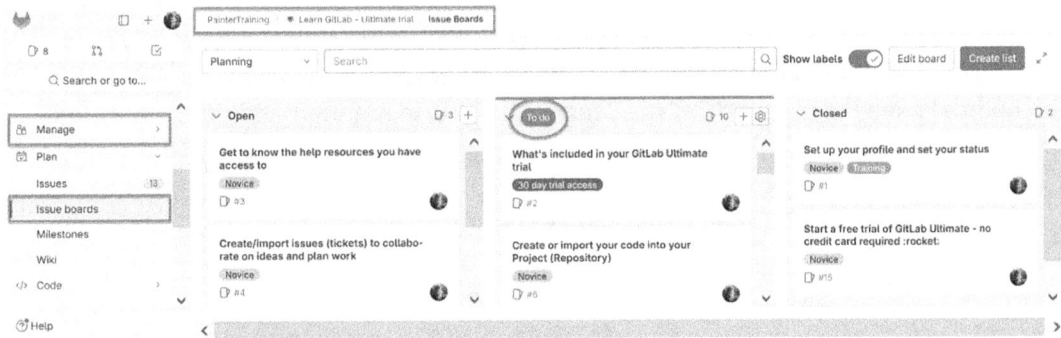

Figure 9-24. *Example issue board for a project*

341

CHAPTER 9   THE BEST LAID PLANS

Creating Additional Column Lists

You can add additional label columns using the "Create list" button as shown in Figure 9-25. When you select the "Create list" button, you get a list of labels to choose from. For this example, I created two new project labels: "In progress" and "Done." For the new list, I choose the "In progress" label. By default, this list appears after the last labeled list of "To do."

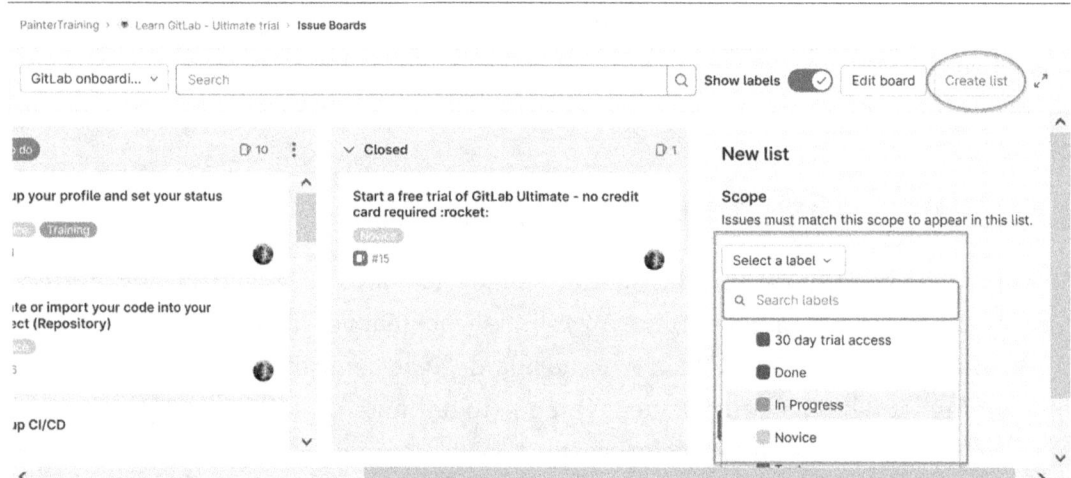

Figure 9-25. *Issue board list creation*

I also went ahead and created the "Done" list, which will follow the "In progress" list. The board after adding these two lists is shown in Figure 9-26. In order to display most of the board, I used the toggle view by selecting the button highlighted in the upper right. Since these labels are new, there are no issues in either of the two new label columns.

CHAPTER 9   THE BEST LAID PLANS

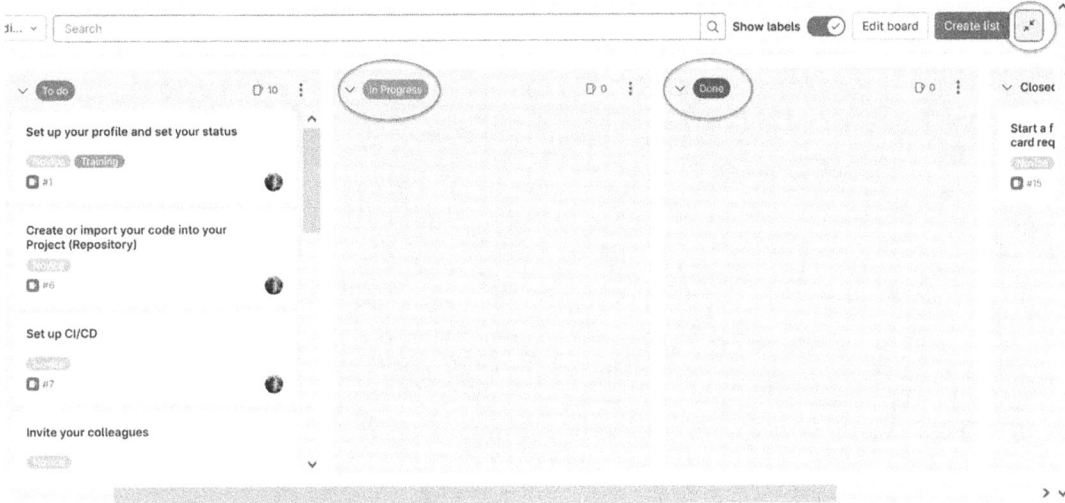

Figure 9-26. Issue board toggle view

Editing an Issue Board

Figure 9-27 shows the pop-up form that appears when selecting the "Edit board" button. From here, you can change the name of the board as well as choose whether to independently show the "Open" and "Closed" lists. In this example, I chose to not show the "Open" list. Figure 9-28 shows the board after changing this option.

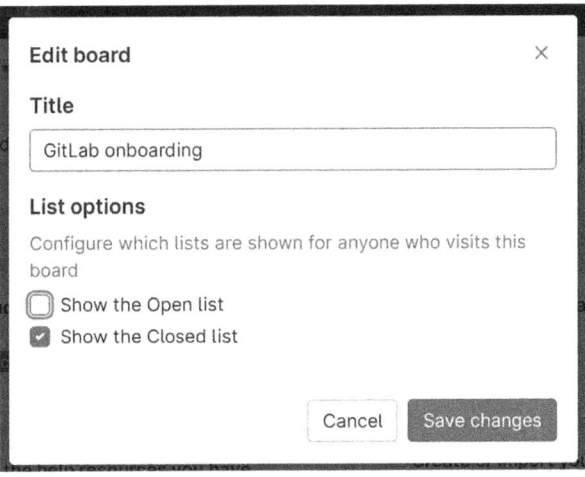

Figure 9-27. Issue board edit pop-up form

343

CHAPTER 9   THE BEST LAID PLANS

Figure 9-28.   Issue board with open list hidden

Moving Items Between Columns on an Issue Board

With the "In progress" and "Done" columns in place, it is a simple matter of clicking an issue in the "To do" column and dragging it to the "In progress" column. I did this for the first issue on the list; the resulting board is shown in Figure 9-29. Behind the scenes, the "To do" label was removed from this issue, and the "In progress" label was added. We can see this more clearly by looking at the issue's detail page as shown in Figure 9-30. If we were to move the issue back to the "To do" list, the reverse label changes would take place as expected.

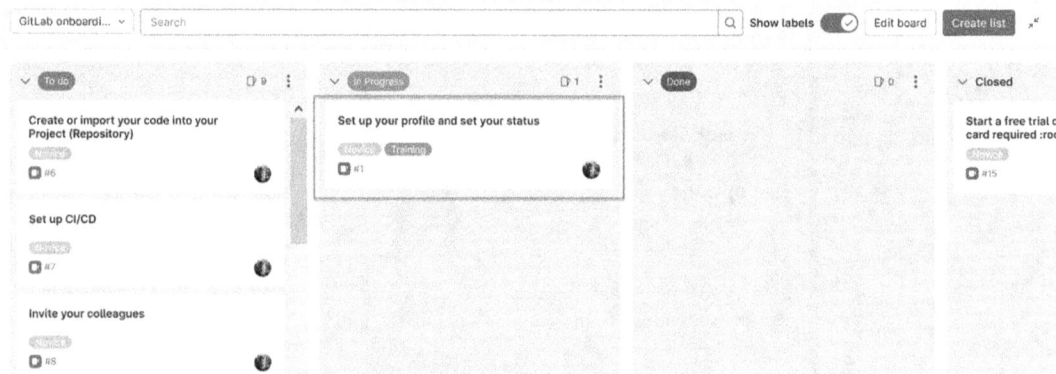

Figure 9-29.   Board issue move to progress

CHAPTER 9   THE BEST LAID PLANS

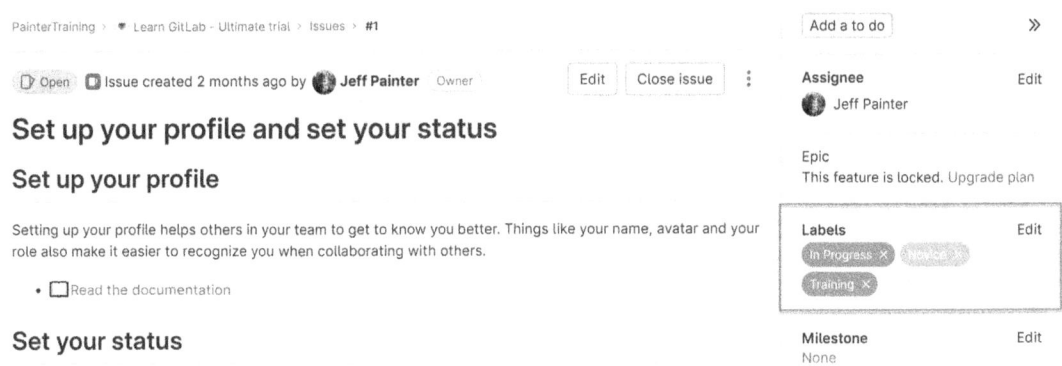

Figure 9-30. Issue labels after board move to in progress

Impact of Closing an Issue from the Board

So, what happens if we move the issue to the "Closed" column? Figure 9-31 illustrates that the "In progress" label is removed, and the issue is marked as closed. If we were to move the issue back to the "In progress" or "Done" columns, the appropriate label would be added to the issue and the issue would be marked as "Open." In case you are wondering, there are no restrictions on how to move issues around.[5] You can move a "To do" issue to "Done" or a "Closed" issue to "To do."

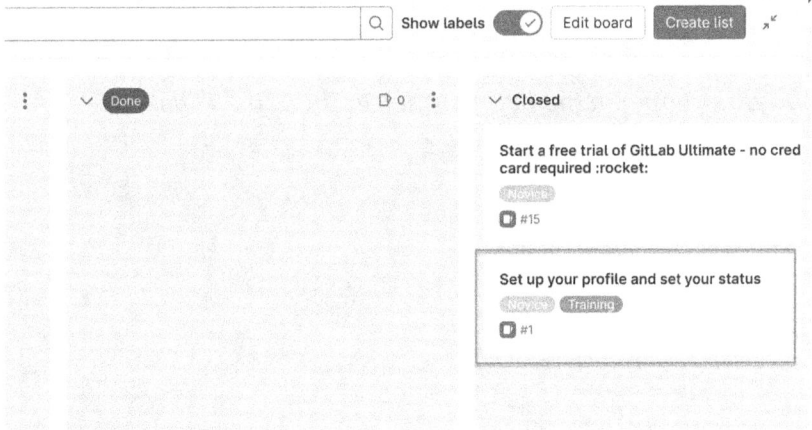

Figure 9-31. Board issue move to closed

---

[5] This is in contrast to Jira, for example, where you can establish rules that restrict how you can move an issue from one state to another in addition to who can make the move.

345

CHAPTER 9   THE BEST LAID PLANS

Moving Issues Within a Column

As expected, you can move an issue from the "Open" column to the "To do" column. In Figure 9-32, I've selected the first issue on the "Open" list. When moving it to the "To do" list, I can place it anywhere in that column. For this example, I placed the issue at the top of the list. Once done, I can easily move it to the bottom of the list using the drop-down menu as shown in Figure 9-33. I could also simply select the issue and drag it to where I want it displayed in the list. This is convenient if you want to prioritize issues by the order in which they appear in the list.

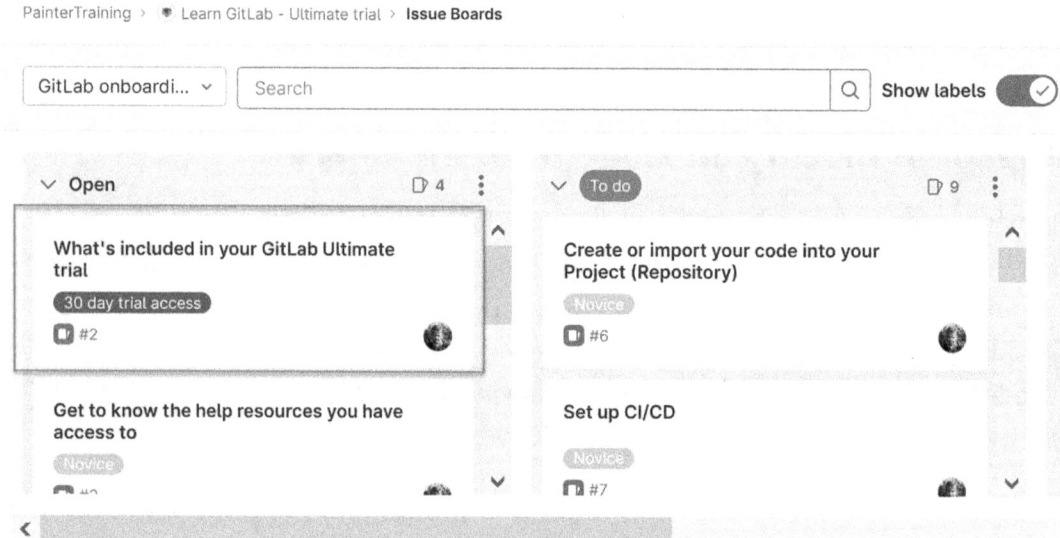

Figure 9-32.   Board open issue before move to the "To do" list

CHAPTER 9 THE BEST LAID PLANS

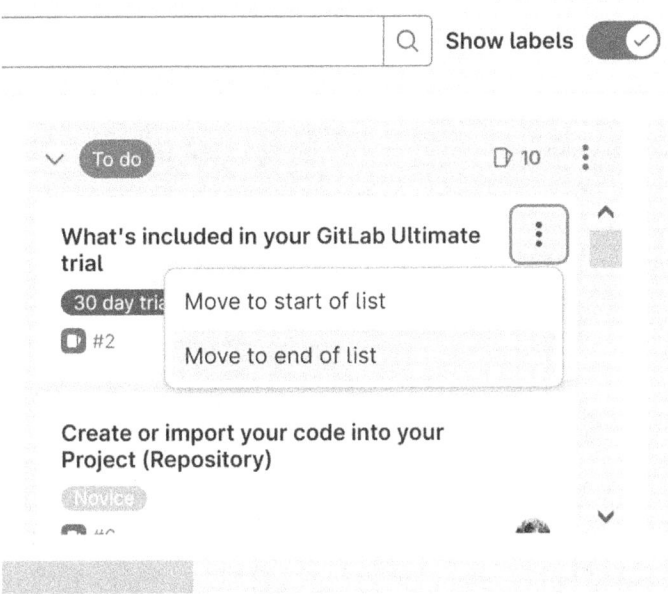

Figure 9-33. Board reorder issue within a list

Creating and Editing a Group-Level Issue Board

As you might expect, you can create an issue board at the group level. With the free tier, however, you can only create one; with a paid tier, you can create multiple boards if you wish. Figure 9-34 shows what the initial group board looks like. It is simply a board with the "Open" and "Closed" columns.

347

CHAPTER 9   THE BEST LAID PLANS

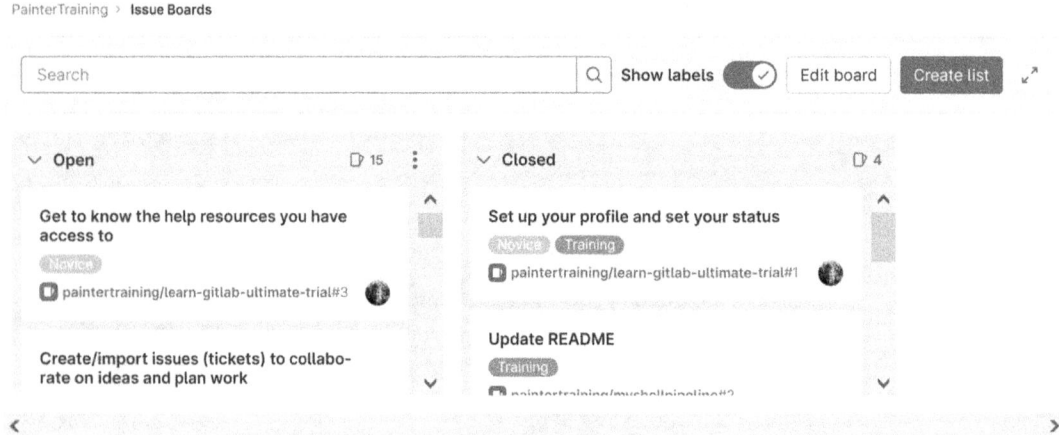

Figure 9-34. Initial group issue board

Like a project issue board, you can edit the group board by changing the name of the board and selecting whether to show the "Open" and "Closed" lists. You can also include lists based on the group labels. Figure 9-35 shows changes after adding the "In progress" list. Note that since there are no issues currently with the label "In Progress," nothing currently shows up in that list.

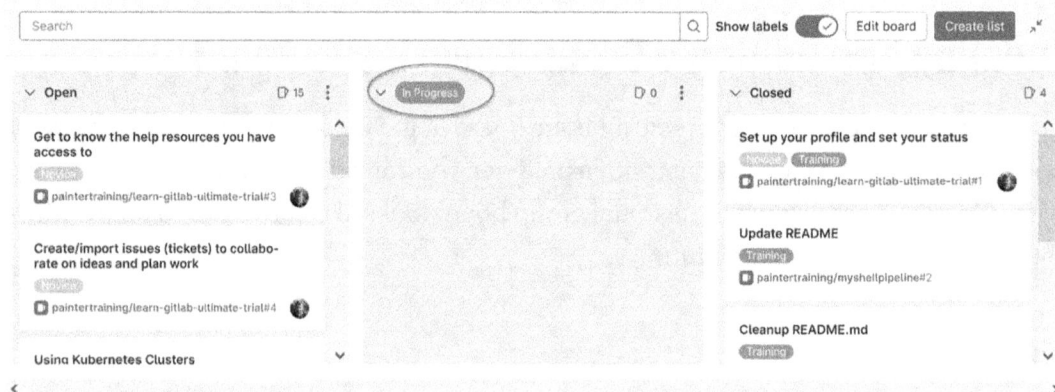

Figure 9-35. Group board with new "In Progress" list

CHAPTER 9   THE BEST LAID PLANS

Creating a New Project Issue Board

Figure 9-36 shows how to create a new board. You create a new board by using the "Create new board" option from the drop-down box associated with the board's name, which in this example is the default "Development" board. Selecting this option pops up the new board form as shown in Figure 9-37. With the free tier, you simply provide a name and select whether to include the "Open" and "Closed" lists. The paid tiers provide more options that you can explore further in the GitLab documentation here: https://docs.gitlab.com/ee/user/project/issue_board.html#gitlab-enterprise-features-for-issue-boards.

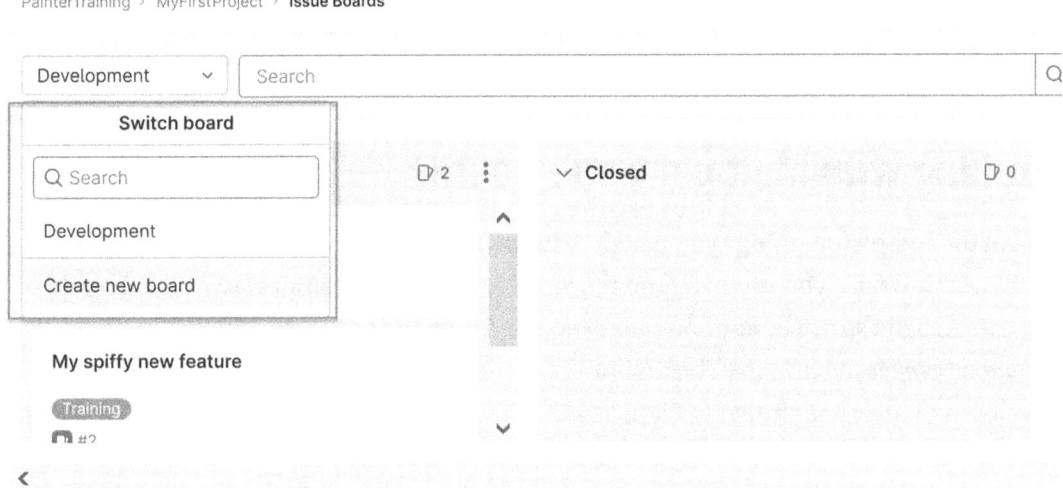

Figure 9-36. *Issue board creation option*

349

CHAPTER 9   THE BEST LAID PLANS

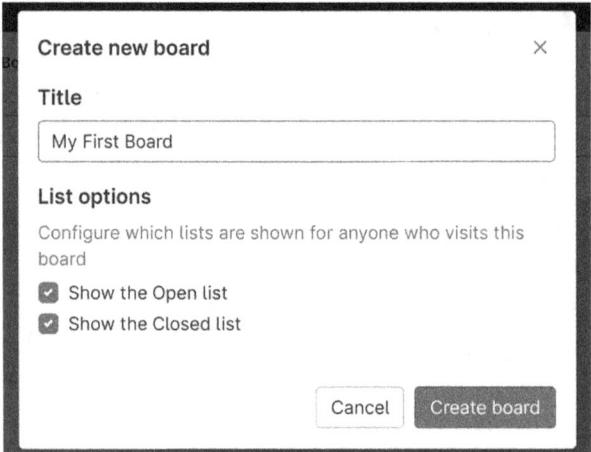

Figure 9-37. Issue board creation form

Working with Multiple Issue Boards

One of the interesting things you can do with project issue boards is create multiple boards. Why would you do this? One reason is to provide different views based on the stage in an agile sprint or kanban planning session. For the "Learn GitLab" project, I created three issue boards. The first board is the primary board used during a development cycle as shown in Figure 9-38. The "GitLab onboarding" board just has the "To do," "In Progress," and "Done" columns provided, which shows just the issues during an agile sprint or kanban session. You can then switch to the other two boards using the board's drop-down menu.

CHAPTER 9   THE BEST LAID PLANS

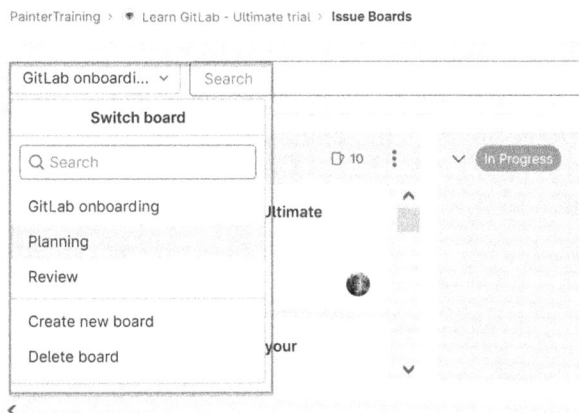

Figure 9-38. Issue board switch option

Figure 9-39 shows the board that would be used in a planning session. This board only shows the "Open" and "To do" issues so that at the beginning of a planning session, the team can move "Open" items to be worked on into the "To do" list or move "To do" items back into the "Open" list if it is decided to postpone that work for a later date.

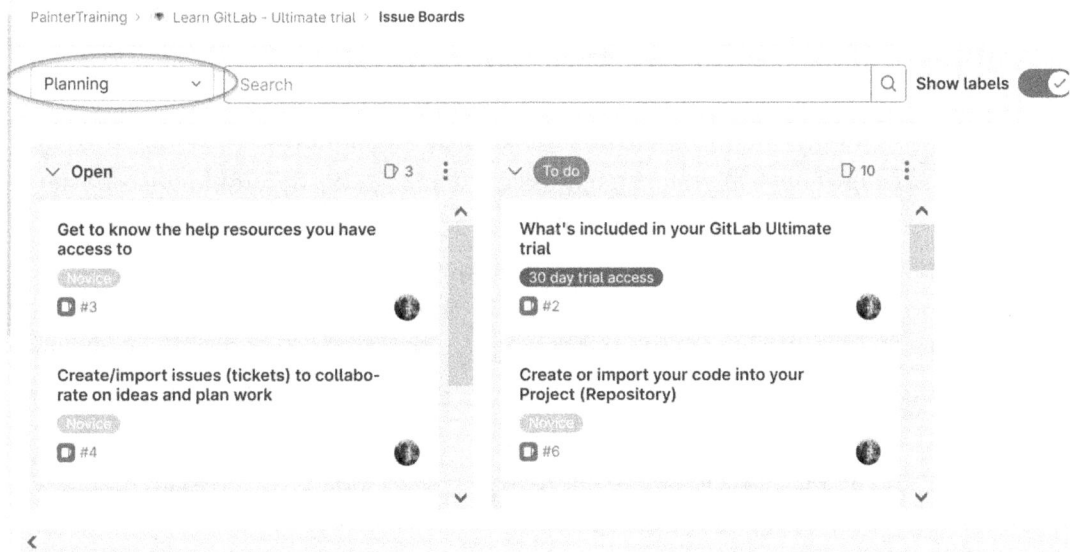

Figure 9-39. Issue board view for planning

Finally, Figure 9-40 shows the "Review" board that would be used to discuss what work has been completed during a development cycle. In this board, the "In Progress," "Done," and "Closed" items are displayed. The "In Progress" list is shown to see what

351

work was not completed or to inquire whether the issue was actually completed. The "Done" list shows what issues were completed during the development cycle so that they can be presented to leaders to indicate how much progress has been made. After a review session, the "Done" items can then be quickly moved to the "Closed" state.

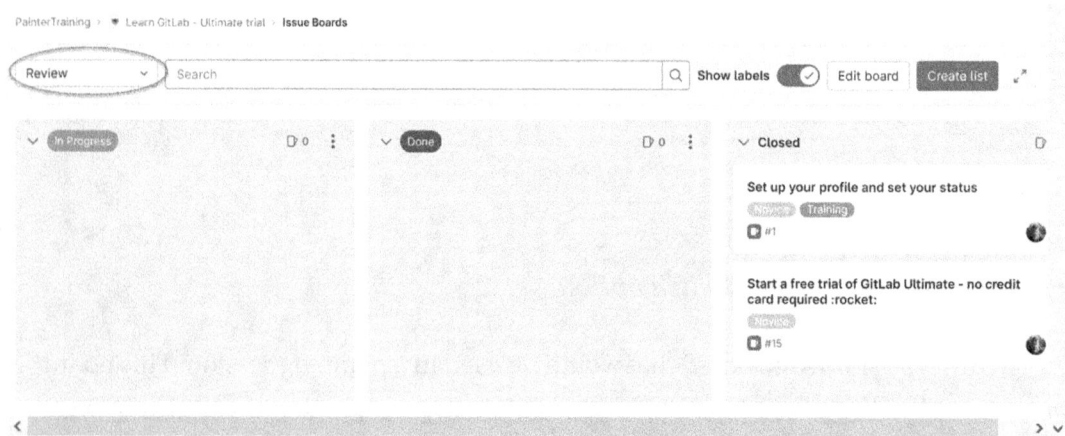

Figure 9-40. *Issue board view for review*

Additional Features with Paid Subscriptions

What additional things can be done with issue boards under paid subscriptions? Well, in addition to using label lists, you can use assignee, milestone, or iteration lists to view your issues; you can only select one type of list for a given board. These additional types of boards are useful to visualize loading across a team, across milestones, or across iterations. For kanban boards, you can set work in progress (WIP) limits for each list excluding the open and closed lists; this helps keep a balance across the board to keep things moving smoothly.[6] For agile boards, you can also assign weights to issues to help prevent work overload during a given iteration.

With the GitLab planning features out of the way, let's look at how we can integrate GitLab with the external planning tool Jira.

---

[6] If you are not familiar with kanban, you can think of the workflow lists as an assembly line where you move an issue from one stage to another. Like a real assembly line, you don't want work to pile up at a given stage as it can disrupt the overall flow later down the line.

CHAPTER 9   THE BEST LAID PLANS

Integrating with Jira

We end this chapter with a discussion on how to integrate GitLab with the popular Jira issue manager. If you are not using it or not interested in integrating with Jira, feel free to skip this section. Since Atlassian, the publisher of Jira, is moving companies toward the Jira Cloud product, we'll focus on integrating with that product in this section; instructions for other Jira installations can be found in GitLab's Jira integration documentation here: `https://docs.gitlab.com/ee/integration/jira/configure.html`.

Setting Up a Jira Cloud Account

If you don't have a Jira Cloud account, creating one is quite easy. It is free for the first ten users and does not require a credit card to set up. Simply go to the Atlassian site, search for Jira, and fill out the requested information including a username and email address. Figure 9-41 shows my setup with the "MyAgileProject" Jira project. I kept the stages at the default "To Do," "In Progress," and "Done" workflow and created an initial issue, MYAP-1, to get things started. At this point, there is no connectivity between GitLab and Jira.

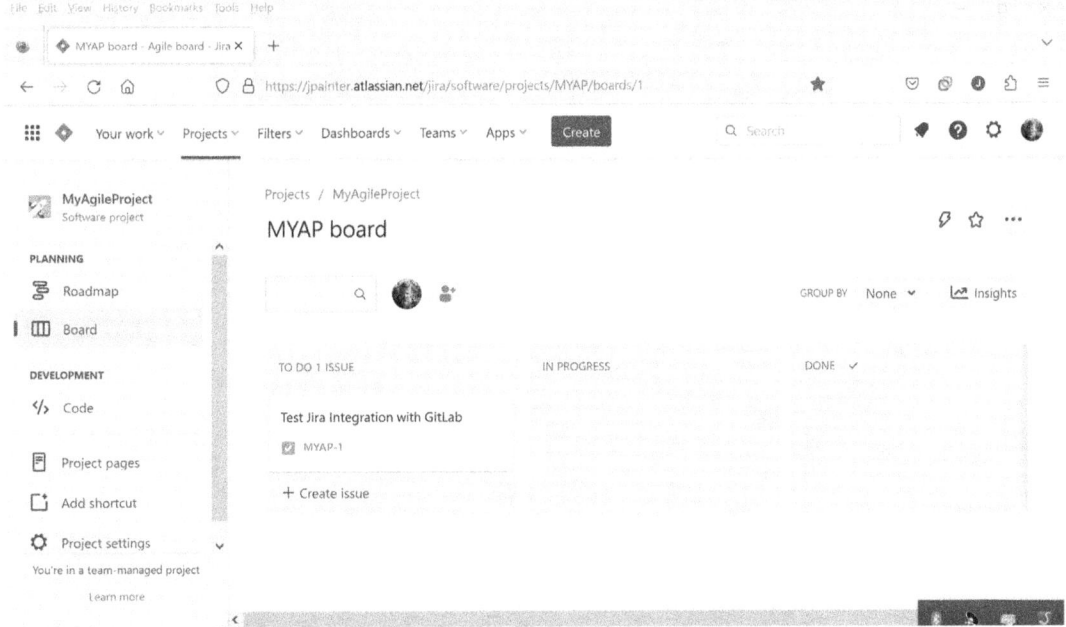

Figure 9-41. Jira MYAP board for Jira project MyAgileProject

353

CHAPTER 9   THE BEST LAID PLANS

Installing the GitLab for Jira Cloud App

The first step in integrating Jira with GitLab is to install an app from your Jira Cloud account. Figure 9-42 shows the "Explore more apps" option from the "Apps" drop-down menu. This takes you to a search box where you enter GitLab as shown in Figure 9-43. This will show a number of apps related to GitLab. Since we are integrating with our account on gitlab.com, we need to select the "GitLab for Jira Cloud" application.

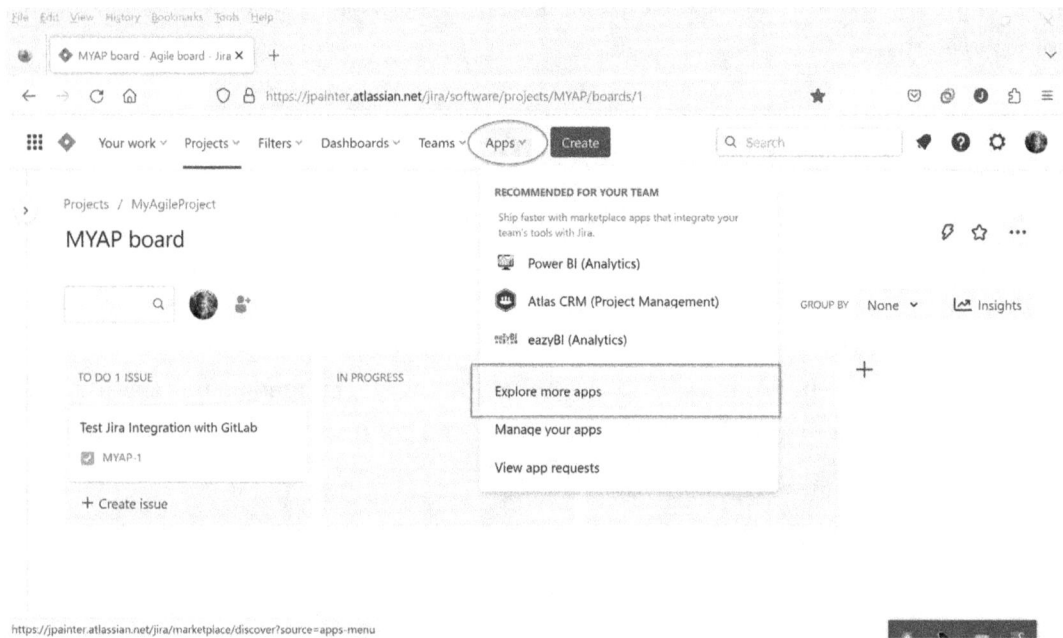

Figure 9-42. *Jira explore more apps selection*

CHAPTER 9   THE BEST LAID PLANS

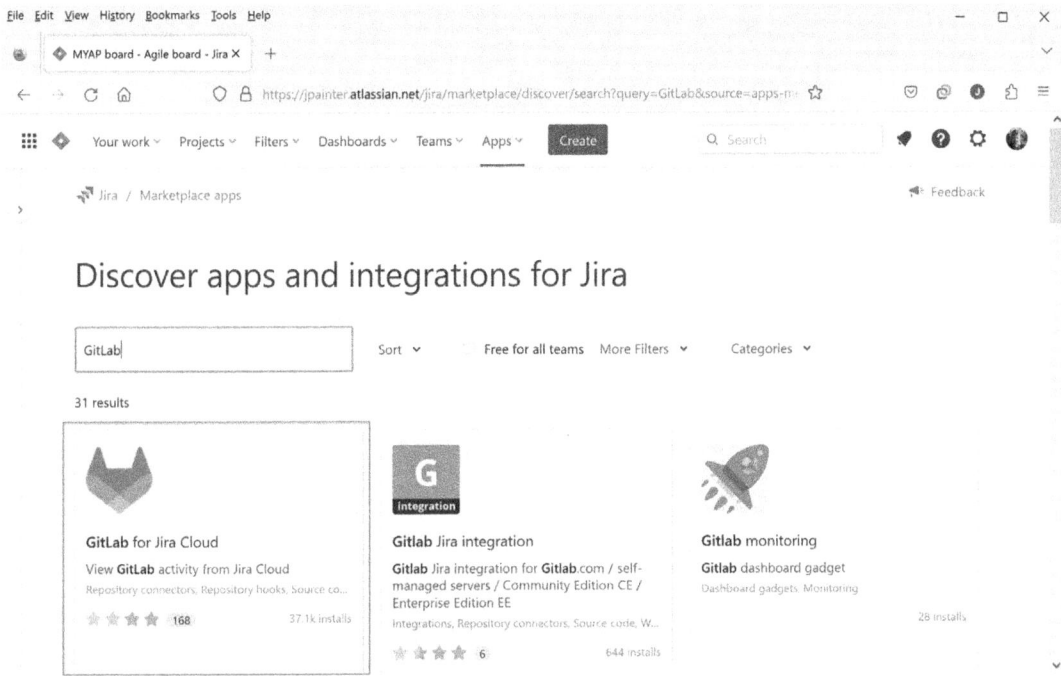

Figure 9-43. *Jira GitLab application selection*

Selecting the "GitLab for Jira Cloud" app takes you to the app's overview page as shown in Figure 9-44. Select the "Get app" button to install the app on your web browser. Once you've installed the app, you'll need to configure it for your GitLab account.

355

CHAPTER 9   THE BEST LAID PLANS

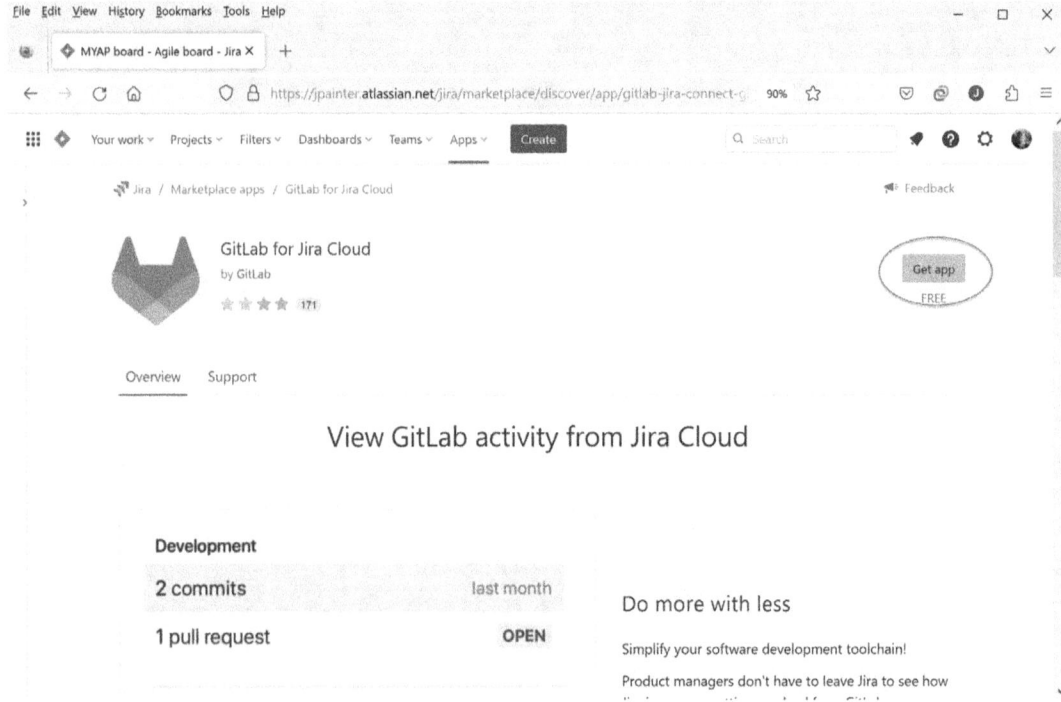

Figure 9-44. *Jira GitLab app browser installation*

Configuring the GitLab for Jira Cloud App

To configure the Jira app, select the "Manage your apps" option from the "Apps" drop-down menu as shown in Figure 9-45. From here, you should see "GitLab for Jira" under the "User-installed apps" section. Expanding that app exposes the "Get started" description as shown in Figure 9-46. Configuration begins when you select the "Get started" button.

CHAPTER 9   THE BEST LAID PLANS

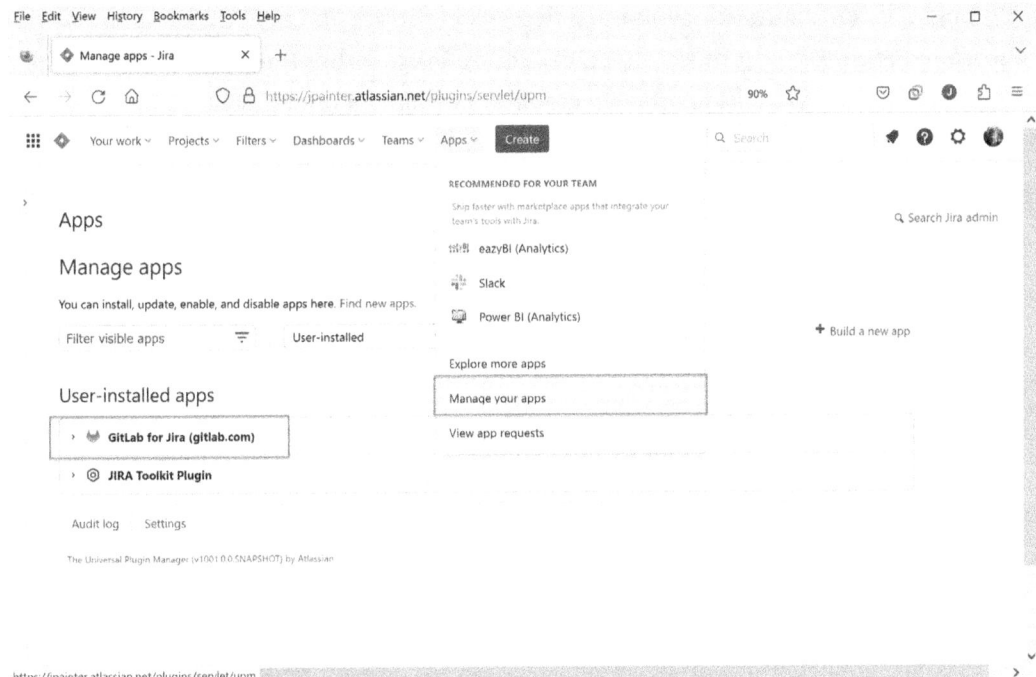

Figure 9-45. *Jira manage your apps selection*

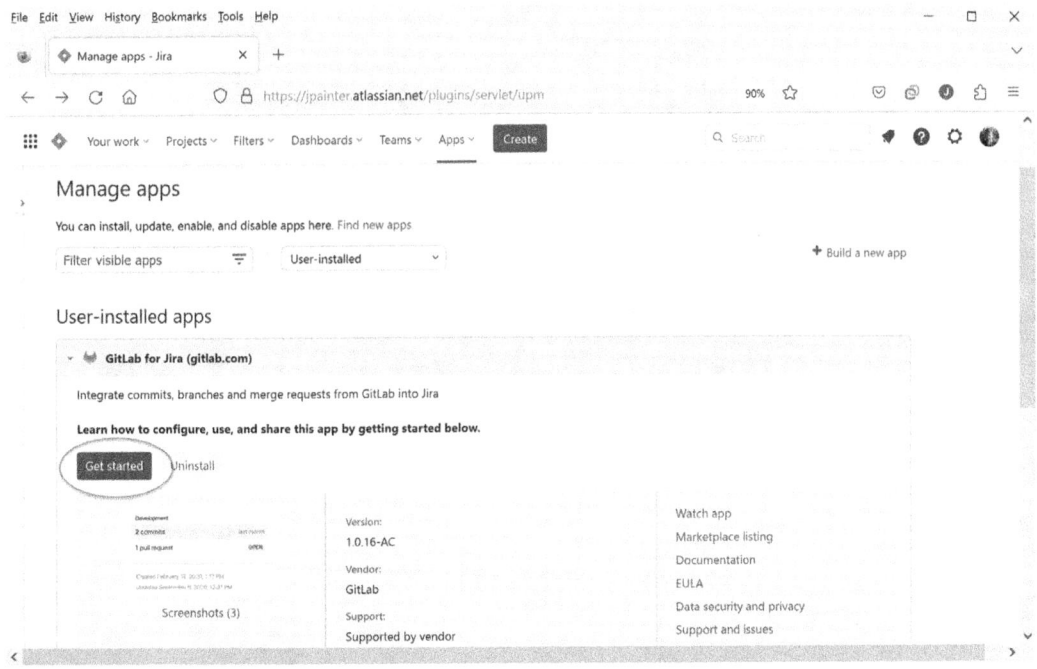

Figure 9-46. *Manage apps get started option*

357

CHAPTER 9   THE BEST LAID PLANS

To begin the configuration, you must first select the version of GitLab you are using as shown in Figure 9-47. In this context, version refers to either the SaaS version or the self-managed version of GitLab; the exact release version is not relevant here. Since we are using gitlab.com, keep the version at the default setting and select "Save."

Figure 9-47. App configuration of GitLab version

Authorizing the App to Connect to Your GitLab Account

You'll then be asked to sign in to your gitlab.com account as shown in Figure 9-48. Selecting the "Sign in to GitLab" button will automatically connect to your account on the `gitlab.com site`. At this point, you will be asked to authorize the GitLab for Jira app to connect to your GitLab account as shown in Figure 9-49.

CHAPTER 9   THE BEST LAID PLANS

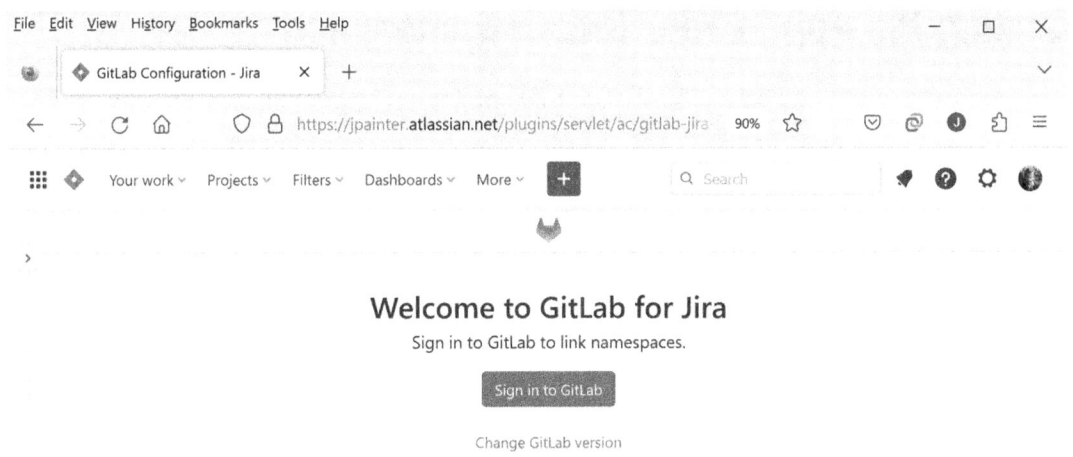

Figure 9-48. *App configuration sign-in to GitLab option*

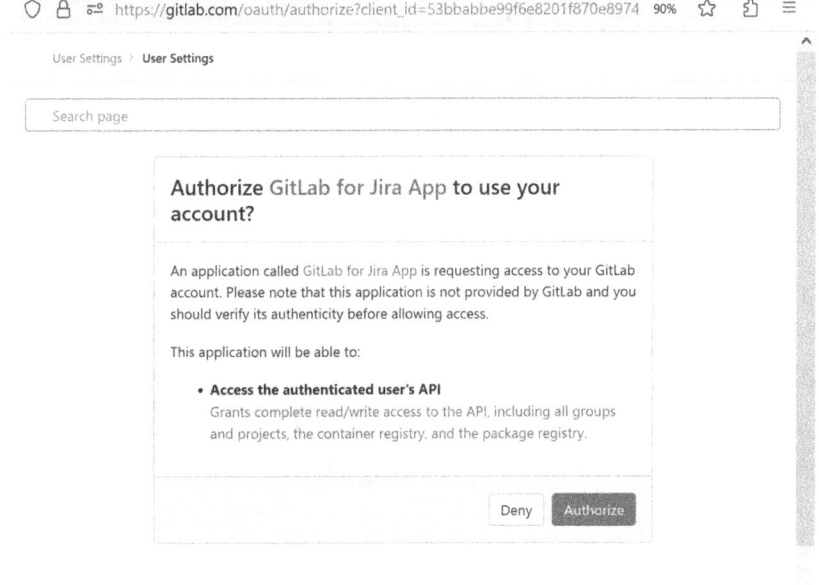

Figure 9-49. *GitLab app authorization request*

359

CHAPTER 9   THE BEST LAID PLANS

Linking the App to Your GitLab Namespace

If all goes well, you'll see a page similar to that shown in Figure 9-50. In the upper-right corner, you should see the message that you are signed in to GitLab with your GitLab username. You'll also see the message that there are no linked namespaces. The next step, as you might have guessed, is to link to a GitLab namespace, a.k.a. a GitLab group.

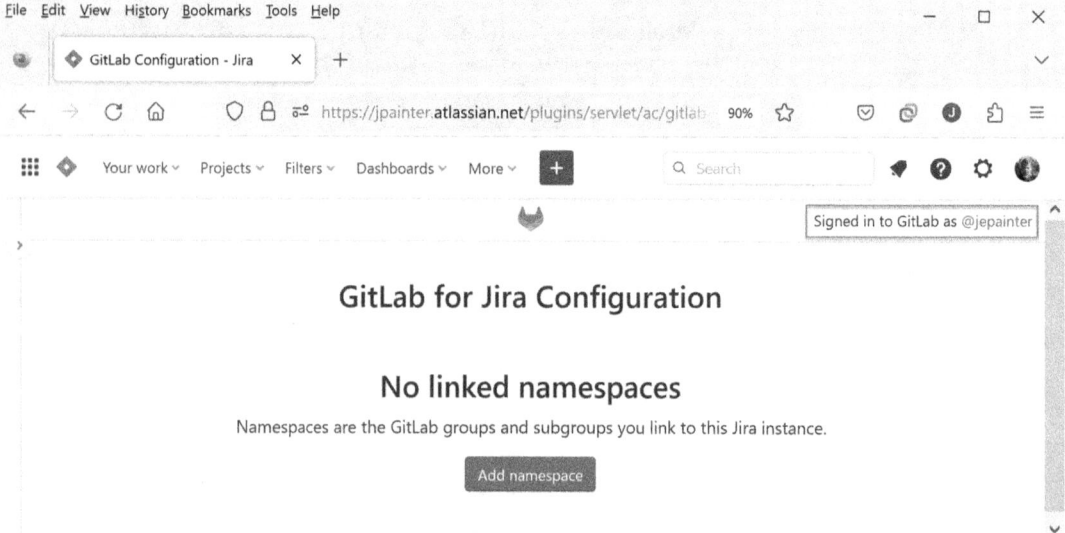

Figure 9-50. *Jira initial configuration for GitLab*

Clicking the "Add namespace" button should show you a list of GitLab groups that you control. Figure 9-51 shows that the GitLab for Jira app discovered my top-level group, "PainterTraining," and the subgroup under that, Special Projects. For this example, I selected to link with the "PainterTraining" top-level group. The result of linking to "PainterTraining" is shown in Figure 9-52.

CHAPTER 9   THE BEST LAID PLANS

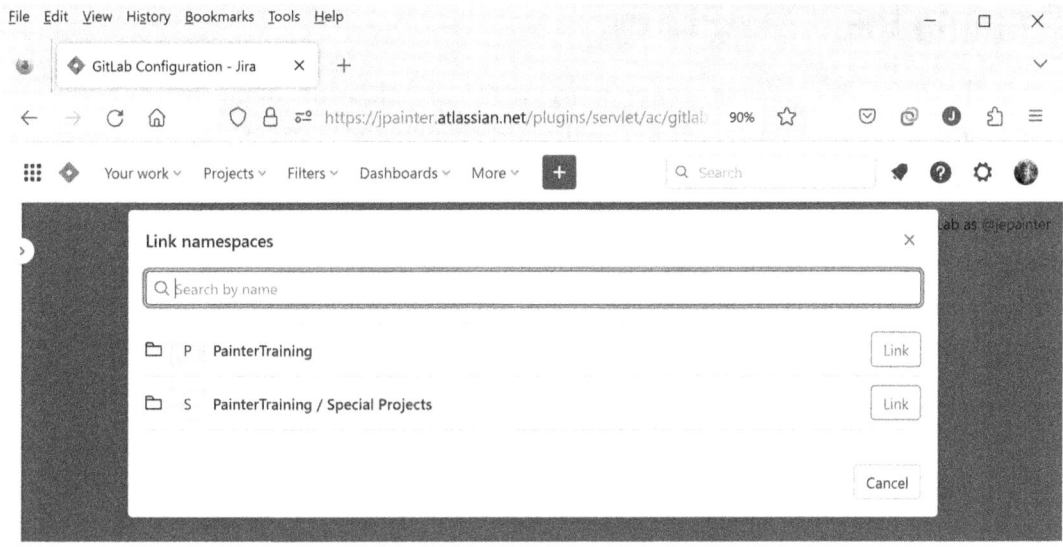

Figure 9-51. *Jira link to GitLab namespace (a.k.a. group)*

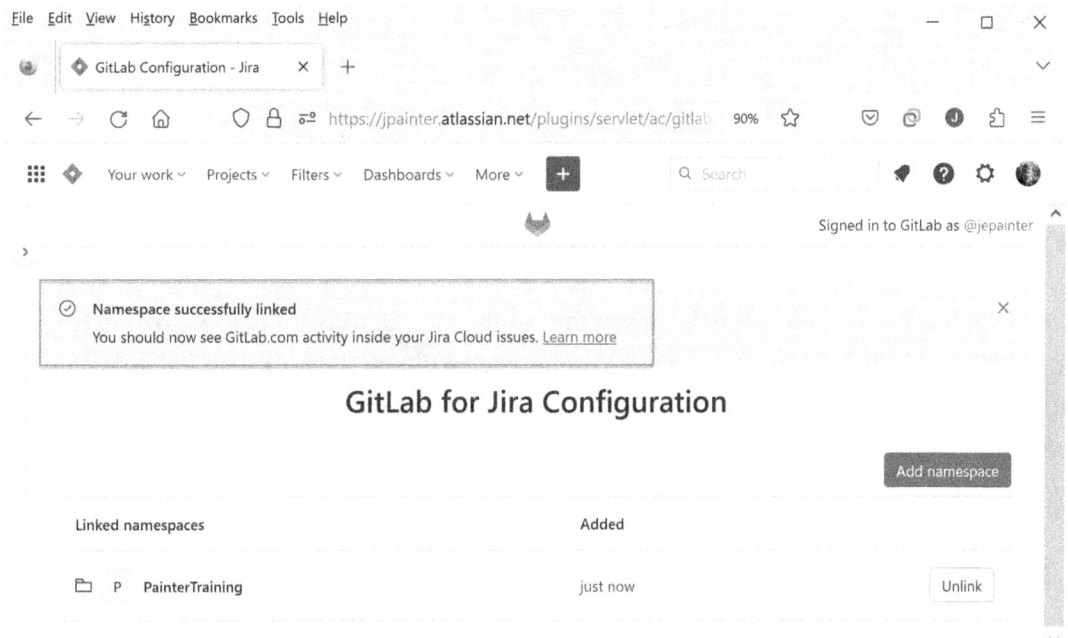

Figure 9-52. *Jira link to GitLab namespace confirmation*

361

CHAPTER 9   THE BEST LAID PLANS

Creating the Jira API Key

Although we've made the connection from the Jira Cloud to our GitLab account, there is still more configuration to be done on the GitLab side. Before we do that, however, we need to first create a Jira API key so that GitLab can authenticate against our Jira account. Jira's instructions seem to make this key creation straightforward, but it is actually a little tricky to discover. To create the API key, you need to switch to the "Administrator" page as shown in Figure 9-53. This is found via the leftmost drop-down menu.

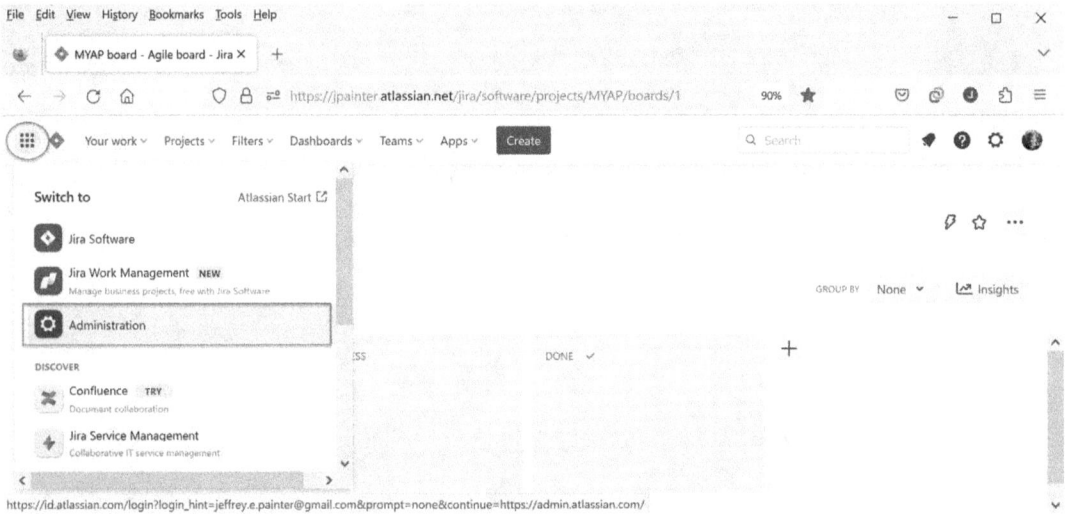

Figure 9-53. *Jira switch to administration page*

From there, select the "API keys" section under the "Settings" tab as shown in Figure 9-54. To create a new key, select the "Create API key" button. This will take you to the "Create an API key" page as shown in Figure 9-55. All you need to do is specify a name for the key to help you identify what it is for and an expiration date no more than a year from the current date.

CHAPTER 9   THE BEST LAID PLANS

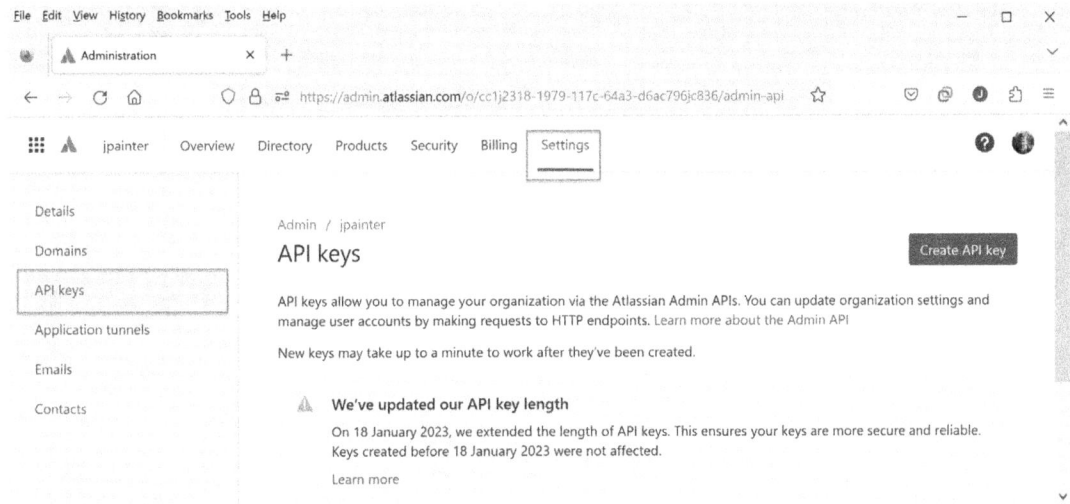

Figure 9-54. Jira administration API keys section

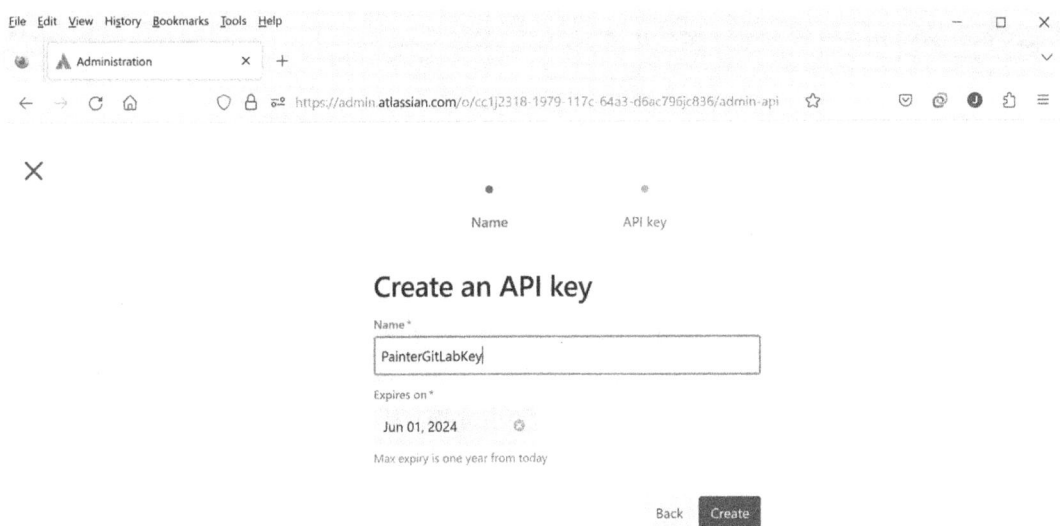

Figure 9-55. Jira administration API key creation form

Selecting the "Create" button will generate the key as shown in Figure 9-56. As with most key generators, you'll need to copy the key and save it in a safe place before leaving the page. You can also copy the Organization ID, although it isn't needed for the GitLab configuration. Be forewarned, the API key is huge (my key was roughly 200 characters long), so make sure to copy all of it.

363

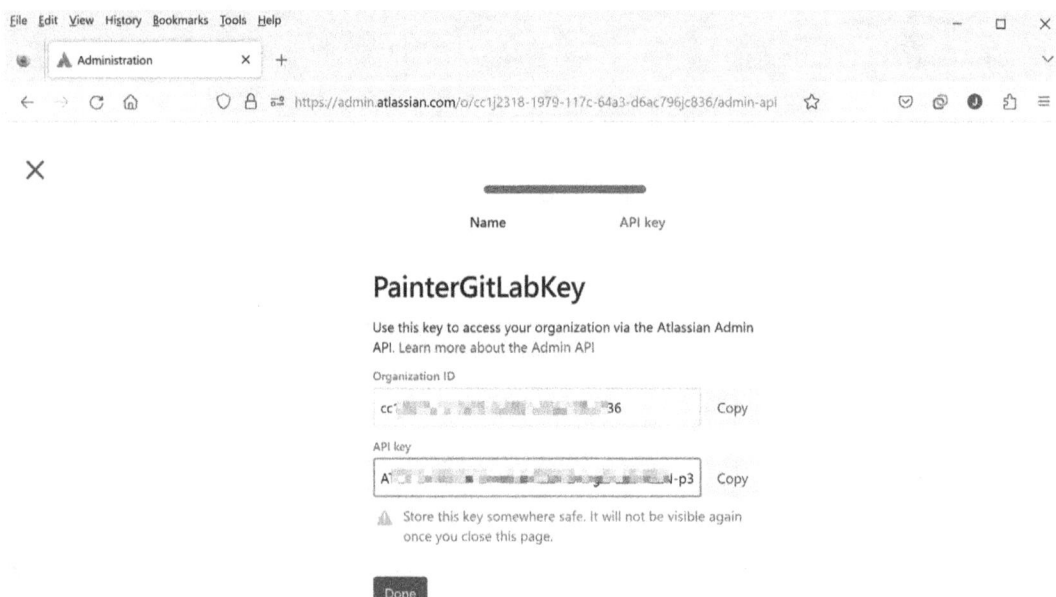

Figure 9-56. *Jira API key creation results*

Configuring a GitLab Project for Jira Integration

Now that we have a Jira API key, we can focus on configuring the GitLab Jira integration. For this example, we'll integrate the Jira "MyAgileProject" with the GitLab "MyShellPipeline" project. From the GitLab website, go to your project's settings and select the "Integrations" section as shown in Figure 9-57. In that section, you'll see a set of applications that you can integrate with. Scroll down until you see the Jira application and select that link.

CHAPTER 9   THE BEST LAID PLANS

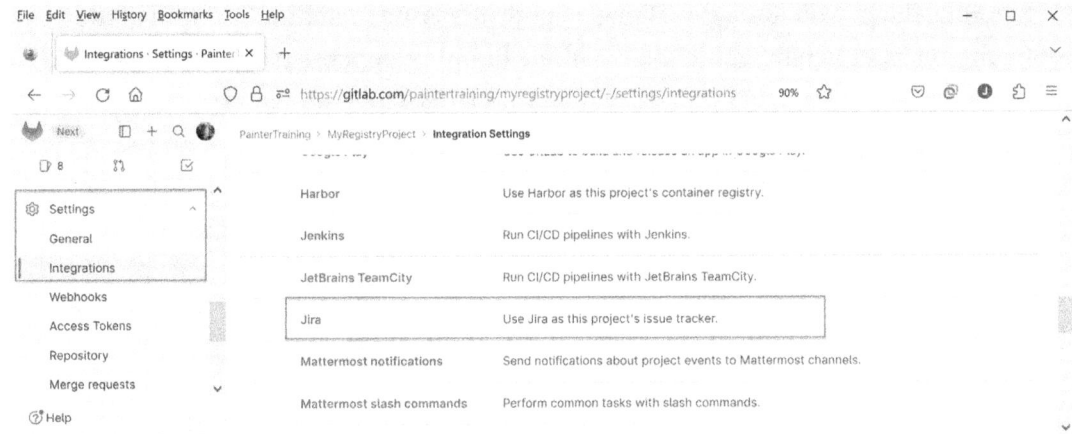

Figure 9-57. GitLab integration settings page with Jira highlighted

This will take you to the Jira configuration page as shown in Figure 9-58. This is a lengthy page, so we'll focus on different parts of it in turn. The first set of configurations is the connection details. Here, you need to set the web URL to your Jira account; the URL consists of your Jira username followed by ".atlassian.net". Since we are using the Jira Cloud, we need to keep the authentication set to "Basic" where you need enter your email address (the one used to sign up for Jira) and that huge API key created earlier.

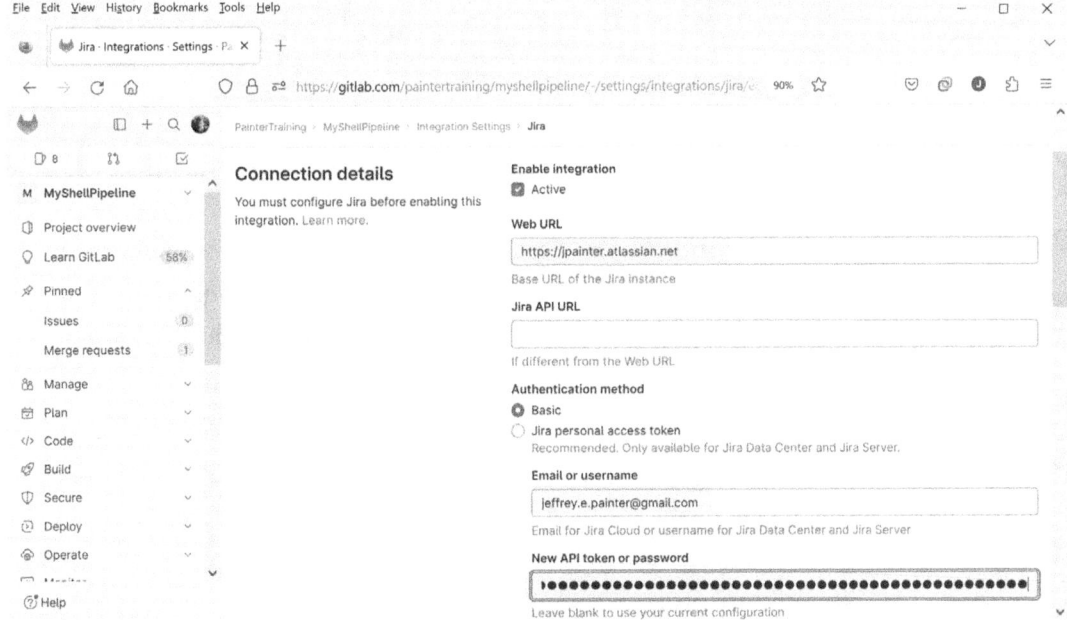

Figure 9-58. GitLab Jira configuration of connection details to Jira

365

CHAPTER 9   THE BEST LAID PLANS

Scrolling down, you'll see the "Trigger" and "Jira issue matching" portion of the configuration as shown in Figure 9-59. In this example, I kept the trigger configuration at the default settings. Since I want to connect "MyShellPipeline" issues to the "MyAgileProject" Jira set of issues, I set the Jira issue prefix to be MYAP. Using issue prefixes allows us to have multiple Jira issue boards that correlate to specific GitLab projects. If you go this route, make sure the prefixes for each Jira project are distinct to avoid confusion when correlating issues.

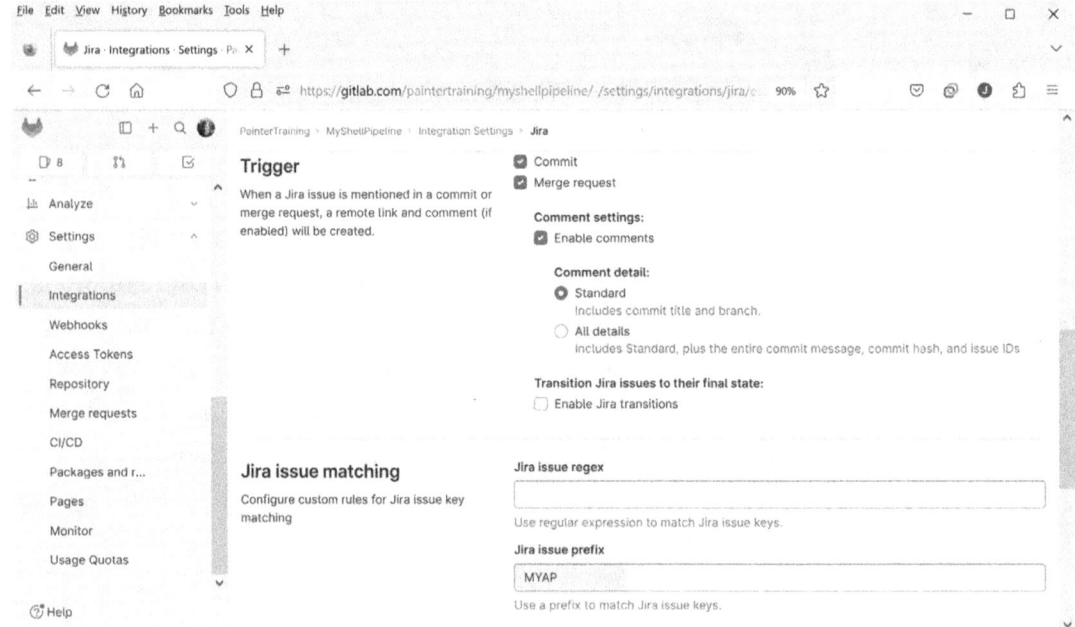

Figure 9-59. *GitLab configuration trigger and Jira issue matching sections*

For completeness, I show the last set of configurations under "Issues" as shown in Figure 9-60. As you can see, this is available only for paid licenses, so there is nothing for us to set here. If you did have a premium or higher license, you would be able to view and manipulate Jira issues directly from GitLab; as it stands, you need to go to the Jira Cloud to interact with issues directly. Selecting "Save changes" completes the integration process from the GitLab side of things.

CHAPTER 9 THE BEST LAID PLANS

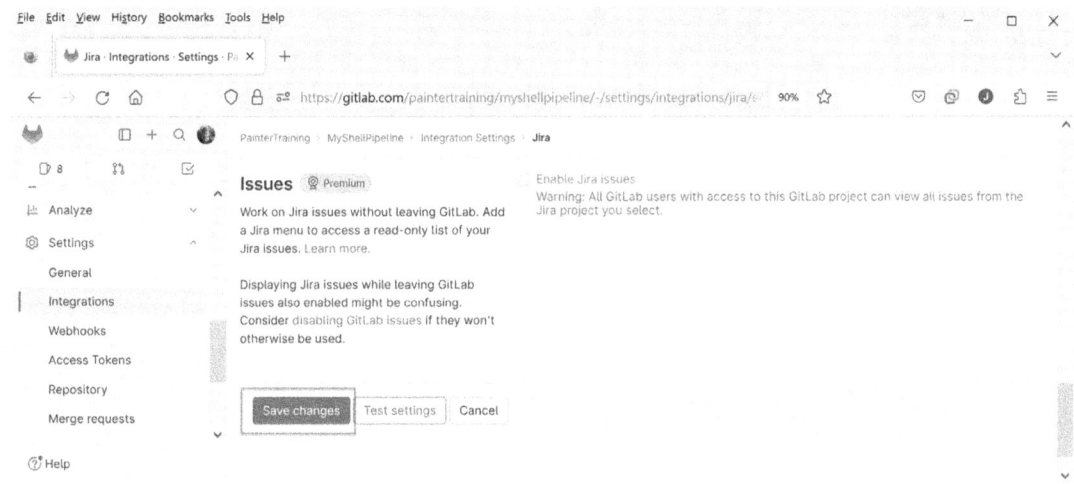

Figure 9-60. *GitLab configuration issues section*

Verifying the Project Is Integrated with Jira

Once saved, you'll see that for the given project, Jira is listed as an active integration as shown in Figure 9-61. You can set up additional integrations with other GitLab projects. You can also integrate Jira issues with a group, although this should be reserved for special circumstances where a team is managing multiple projects. Once an integration is active, you can change the settings by selecting the Jira link. You can also deactivate the integration; in this case, the configuration remains in case you need to reactivate things again.

367

CHAPTER 9   THE BEST LAID PLANS

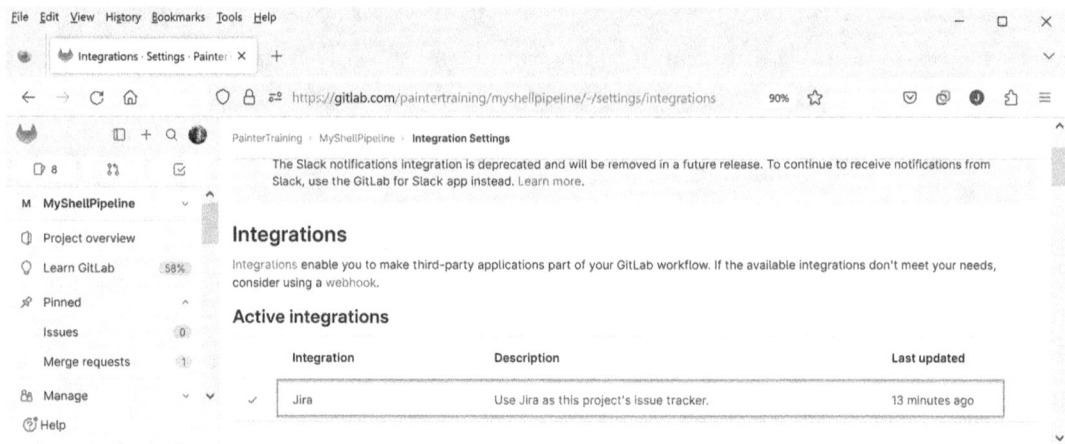

Figure 9-61. GitLab list of active Jira integrations

Viewing Integrated Issues from GitLab

Now that we've configured both Jira and GitLab for the "MyShellPipeline" project, let's take a look at the "Issues" page for "MyShellPipeline." Figure 9-62 shows the "Issues" page after setting up the Jira integration. Hmmm, we can see the old GitLab issues that have been closed but don't see the Jira MYAP-1 issue listed here. Why? It appears that you need to have a premium license or above to see Jira issues from GitLab.

Figure 9-62. GitLab issue list showing no associated Jira issues

CHAPTER 9   THE BEST LAID PLANS

Viewing Integrated Issues from Jira

So, what does the issue look like from the Jira point of view? Figure 9-63 shows the details of MYAP-1. Here, we see some interesting items that make the issue look like a GitLab issue. For instance, there is a "Description" section just like a GitLab issue as well as an "Activity" section. And under "Details," we see GitLab issue fields such as "Assignee" and "Labels" as well as links to create a branch or a commit. This gives us a warm fuzzy that Jira is indeed treating our issues as GitLab issues.

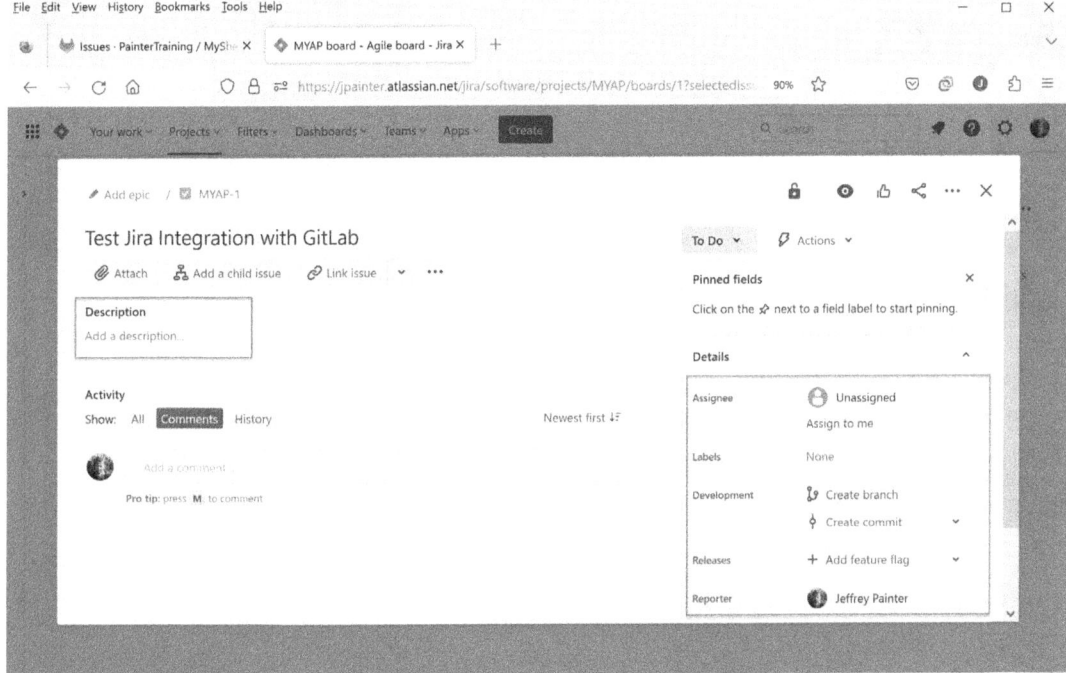

Figure 9-63. *Jira issue view*

Impact of Issue Changes Made from Jira

So, let's make some changes to the Jira issue and move it to the "To-Do" list. Figure 9-64 shows those changes. In this example, I added a description, assigned the issue to myself, and switched the status to "In Progress."

CHAPTER 9   THE BEST LAID PLANS

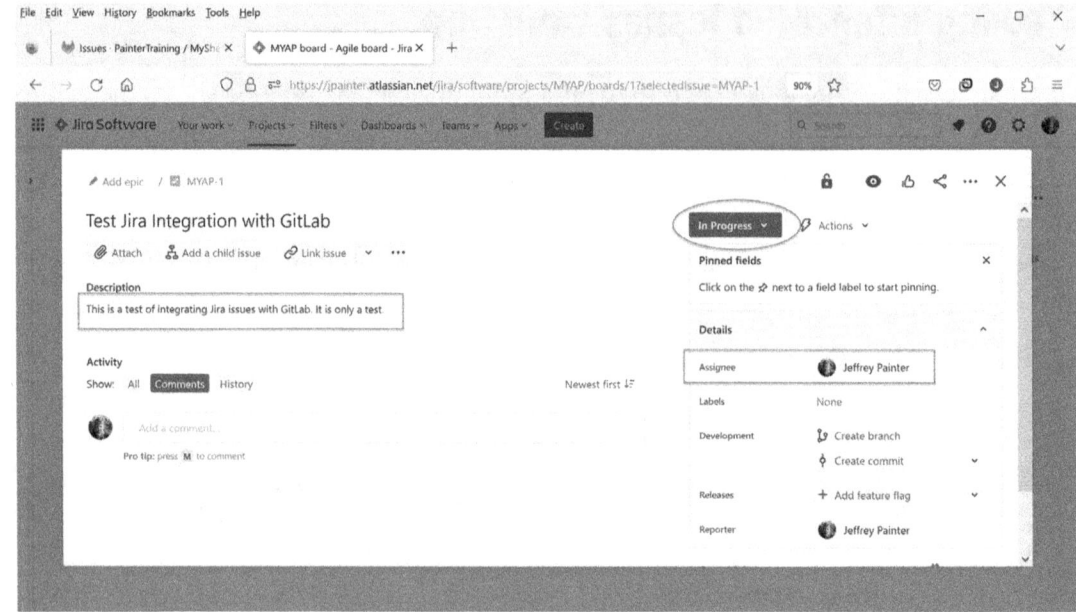

Figure 9-64. *Jira creation of "In Progress" issue*

From here, I clicked the "Create branch" link to create a GitLab branch as shown in Figure 9-65. Note that doing this opens up the "Create branch" page within GitLab. For the "Project" field, I selected "MyShellPipeline" and kept the branch name to the generated value of MYAP-1-test-Jira-integration-with-gitlab. Figure 9-66 shows that the branch was successfully created.

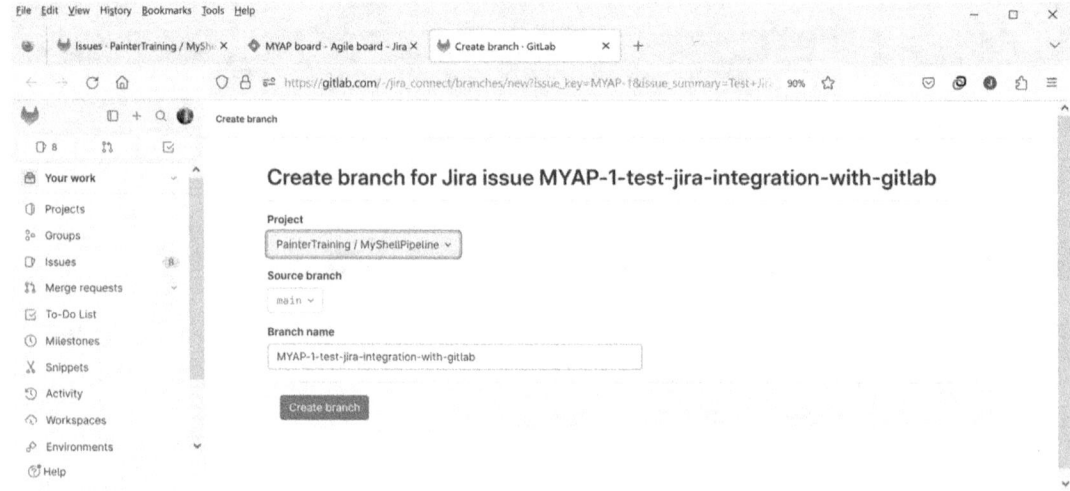

Figure 9-65. *GitLab branch creation for the newly created Jira issue*

CHAPTER 9   THE BEST LAID PLANS

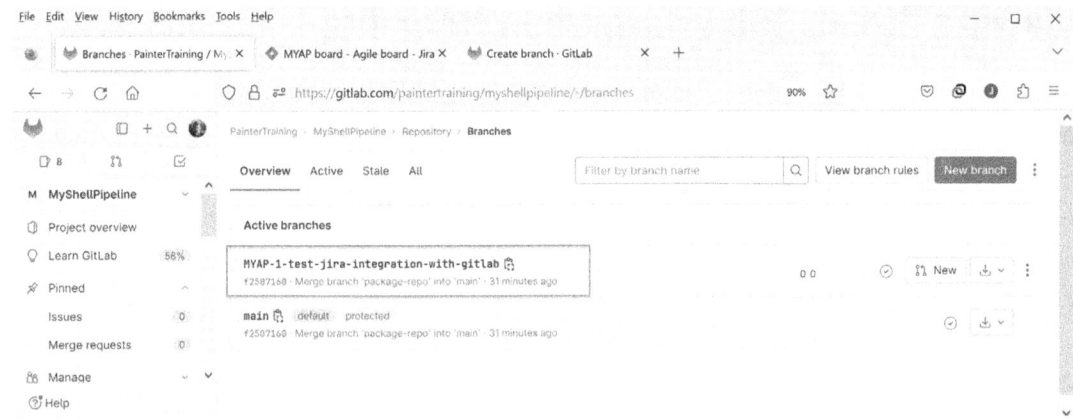

Figure 9-66. *GitLab branch list showing branch created by Jira*

Impact of Issue Changes Made from GitLab

From here, I followed the standard practice of making changes on the branch, committing them, and merging them back to main. Figure 9-67 shows what the Jira issue looks like after following that process. As you can see, it shows one commit and one pull request (a.k.a. merge request). It also shows that the build succeeded.

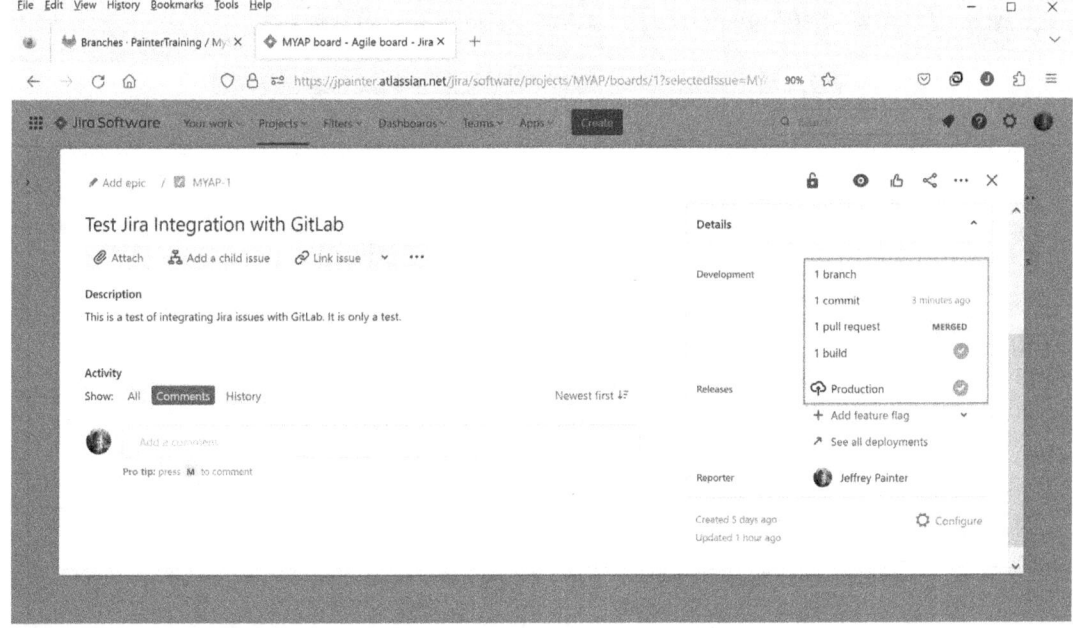

Figure 9-67. *Jira issue view after GitLab branch merge*

371

CHAPTER 9   THE BEST LAID PLANS

Viewing GitLab Job Information from Jira

Note that all the items in the highlighted box are clickable. So, selecting "1 build" pops up information about the build as shown in Figure 9-68. From here, you can drill down to the build details in GitLab. And Figure 9-69 pops up information about the merge pipeline where you can drill down to the pipeline details within GitLab.

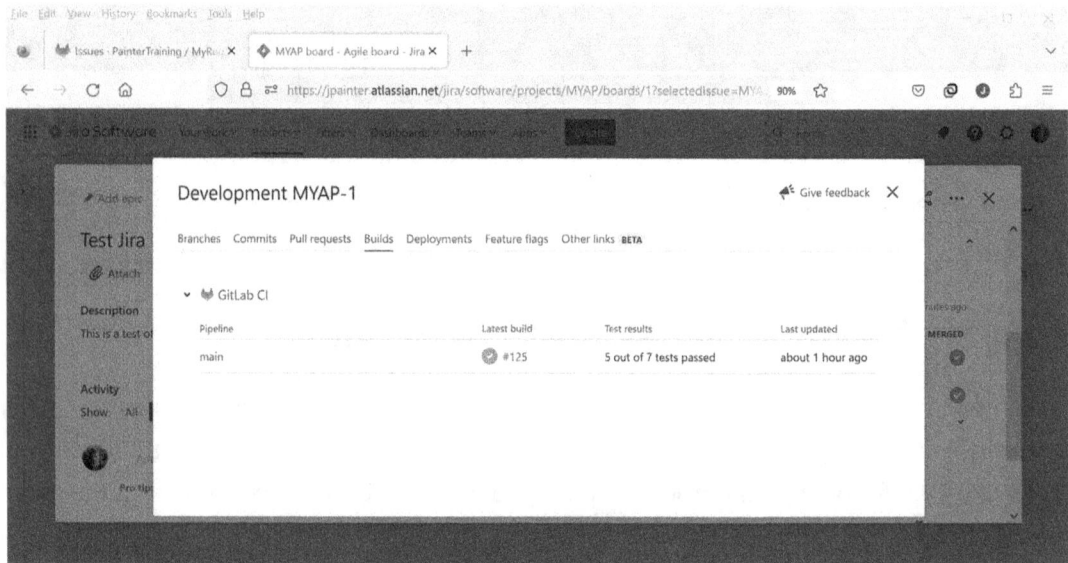

Figure 9-68. *Jira build overview for a Jira issue*

CHAPTER 9   THE BEST LAID PLANS

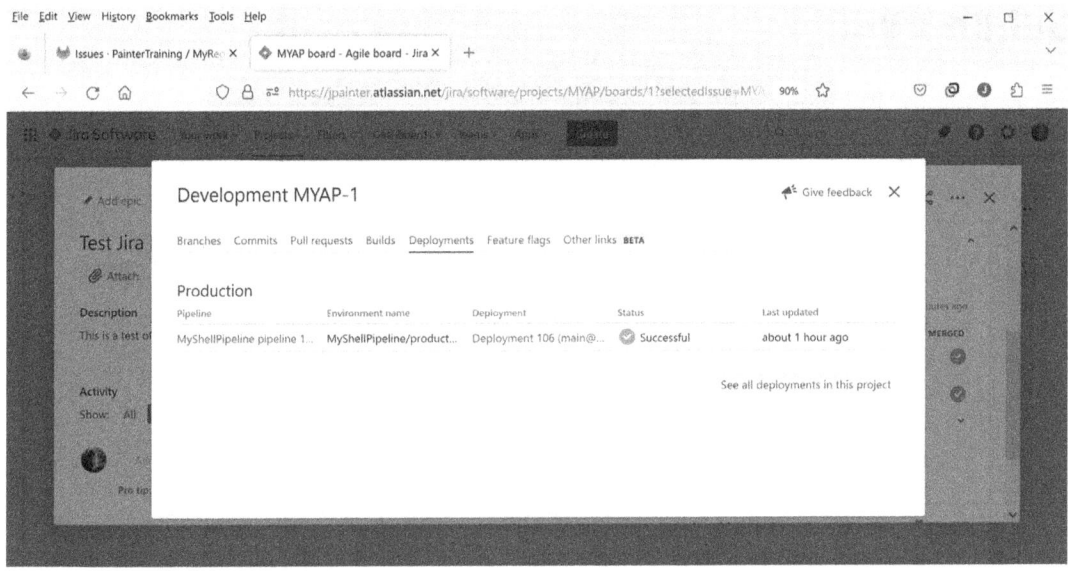

Figure 9-69. *Jira deployment overview for a Jira issue*

Additional Jira Integration Features with Paid Subscriptions

For the free version of GitLab, Jira integration is pretty one-sided in that it is heavily weighted toward Jira. Having used the premium integration, I can tell you that it is much more friendly on the GitLab side. You'll be able to see the Jira issues within a project's issues page and more intuitively manage them from within GitLab. The Jira integration documentation describes how to set this up if you have a licensed version of GitLab.

Summary

We covered the following topics in this chapter:

- Described how to use milestones to group issues into a long-term plan
- Introduced tasks as a way to break down short-term work for an issue
- Discussed how to use GitLab's issue boards to plan work over a regular cadence
- Reviewed how to integrate Jira with GitLab to better manage issues for a project

In the next chapter, we'll switch gears to look at how to make objects generated by a project available to other projects.

CHAPTER 10

It's Nice to Share

We have now covered the basic features of GitLab that should handle all your day-to-day software development needs. The time has come to look at some of GitLab's specialized features that you might miss, at least I did when I first started using GitLab. In this chapter, we are going to focus on GitLab's facilities for storing generated objects to be used by other developers. There are a number of them, but we'll focus on two in particular: the Docker container registry and the binary package registry.

Managing Docker Images

We've seen how shared runners use Docker images to run CI/CD jobs. So far, we've downloaded images created for us from Docker Hub. One of the consequences of that is the need to install any additional software packages, such as bash, each time we run a job needing that software. For small packages like bash, it isn't too much of a performance hit to do the install each and every time. But sometimes we need to use a more complicated installation process where doing it each and every time for all jobs becomes a performance burden. In these cases, we would like to create our own Docker images with the necessary software preinstalled so that all we have to do is pull the image down for a job and start using it straightaway.

Considerations When Creating Our Own Docker Images

To create our own Docker image, there are two main questions that need to be answered. First, how do we create a Docker image from a CI/CD job? This seems like a straightforward thing to do but is complicated by the need to have Docker run as a service, so how do we do that in a GitLab CI/CD job? Second, we need a place to put our image so that we can download it for use in other jobs. Although we could push the

CHAPTER 10 IT'S NICE TO SHARE

image to Docker Hub, assuming that we have an account there, that seems a bit much for an image that is specifically configured for our project. Plus, we need to make sure the image is not accessible by the public (unless, of course, that is the intent of the project).

Accessing the Project Container Registry

Let's answer the second question first. Every GitLab project has its own Docker container registry referred to as simply the container registry. This is a place where you can store your own Docker images for use within your project or by other projects. For this example, I created a new project called "MyRegistryProject." Figure 10-1 shows what the registry looks like before any images are stored there. You can get there by selecting "Container Registry" from the project's "Deploy" tab. The page provides hints as to how to build and push images to this repository (not shown here). Since this is the gitlab.com site, the registry path starts with registry.gitlab.com; if you are on a self-managed site, the registry path will be set by that site's administrator. The remainder of the registry path is the project's location, in this case, paintertraining/myregistrypipeline.

Figure 10-1. Initial container registry page

Process for Creating and Storing a Docker Image

Now that we have a place to put our image, let's look at how to update the CI/CD pipeline to create the image and store it in the project's registry. For project "MyRegistryProject," I created a development branch called docker-setup and added two files, Dockerfile and .gitlab-ci.yml, as shown in Figure 10-2. File Dockerfile contains instructions on how to generate a new image, and file .gitlab-ci.yml contains the pipeline needed to generate and use the new image.

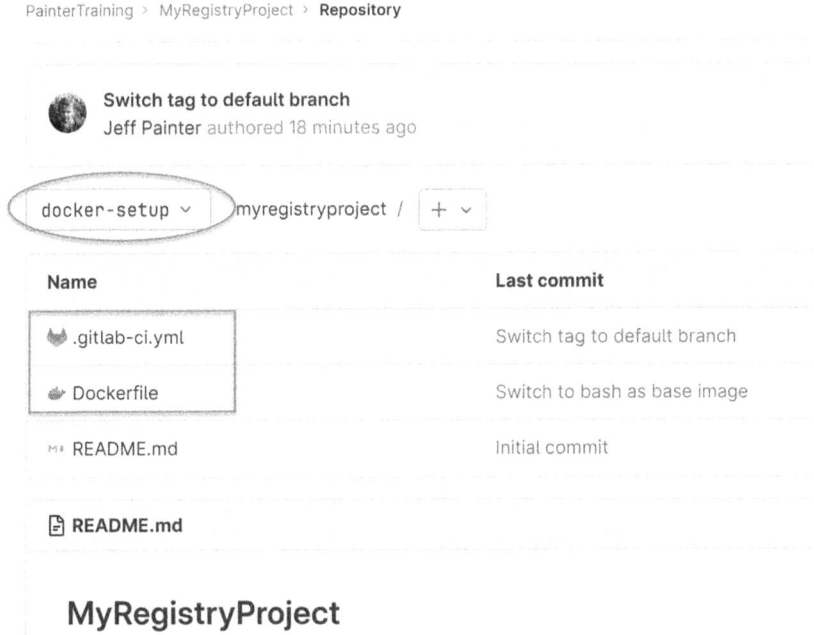

Figure 10-2. *New files to create a Docker image*

Exploring the Dockerfile

Let's first take a look at the Dockerfile. This is shown in Figure 10-3. Our goal is to create an image that has Bash, Java, and Maven installed based on the Alpine image. As you recall in the "MyShellPipeline" project, we used a Maven image downloaded from Docker Hub that is based on Ubuntu, which is a fairly large image. Using Alpine, we can create a smaller image that meets our needs. The first line of Dockerfile defines the base

CHAPTER 10   IT'S NICE TO SHARE

image from which we are deriving our image. In this case, I am using the Docker Hub bash image[1] that uses Alpine version 3.17. The bash version is 5.2, which is the latest version available when I created this example.

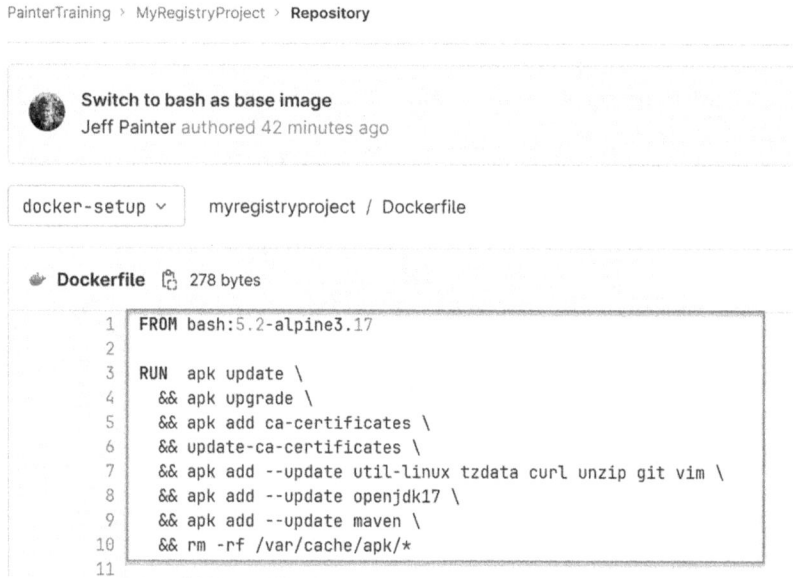

Figure 10-3.   Contents of Dockerfile

The RUN command in Dockerfile is used to install all the software needed for our build environment image. In addition to installing version 17 of Java and the latest version of Maven, it also installs some helpful utilities such as curl, unzip, and vim that we may need when debugging jobs. It also contains packages needed for Java, such as ca-certificates and tzdata. Note that the last rm command is used to clean up the apk cache, which helps keep the image small.

If you are wondering why there is only one RUN command with all the commands chained together to execute sequentially rather than have multiple RUN commands, it is because it creates a single layer in the generated image rather than multiple layers. Having one layer keeps the image smaller as well.

---

[1] Although I could have used the Alpine image directly and installed bash within that image, the default shell would still be /bin/sh. Using the bash Docker image ensures that /bin/bash is the default shell.

Pipeline Configuration for Creating, Storing, and Using a Docker Image

Figure 10-4 shows the contents of the .gitlab-ci.yml file. It consists of two stages: docker-build, which creates the Docker image, and build, which uses that image. The DOCKER_IMAGE variable contains the location of our image within the project's container registry. The predefined CI_REGISTRY_IMAGE variable is set to the location of the project's container registry, which in this case is registry.gitlab.com/paintertraining/myregistryproject. The DOCKER_TAG variable defines the image tag used when we create and run the image. It is set to the value of the CI_COMMIT_REF_SLUG variable so that each branch gets its own image version.

```yaml
include:
  - template: 'Workflows/Branch-Pipelines.gitlab-ci.yml'

stages:
  - docker-build
  - build

default:
  image: $DOCKER_IMAGE:$DOCKER_TAG

variables:
  DOCKER_IMAGE: "$CI_REGISTRY_IMAGE/my-build-env"
  DOCKER_TAG: "$CI_COMMIT_REF_SLUG"

docker-build:
  stage: docker-build
  image: docker:23.0.4
  services:
    - name: docker:23.0.4-dind
      alias: docker
  before_script:
    - echo -n $CI_REGISTRY_PASSWORD | docker login -u "$CI_REGISTRY_USER" --password-stdin $CI_REGISTRY
  script:
    - docker build --pull -t "$DOCKER_IMAGE:$DOCKER_TAG" .
    - docker push "$DOCKER_IMAGE:$DOCKER_TAG"
    - |
      if [ "$CI_COMMIT_BRANCH" == "$CI_DEFAULT_BRANCH" ]; then
        docker tag "$DOCKER_IMAGE:$DOCKER_TAG" "$DOCKER_IMAGE:latest"
        docker push "$DOCKER_IMAGE:latest"
      fi

build:
  stage: build
  script:
    - bash --version
    - java -version
    - mvn -version
```

Figure 10-4. Contents of .gitlab-ci.yml file

CHAPTER 10   IT'S NICE TO SHARE

Overview of the docker-build Job

Looking at the docker-build job, we see that it is using the Docker Hub docker image version 23.0.4. This image has Docker already installed on it so that we can build and run Docker images from within GitLab. Unfortunately, that isn't enough. We need to also run Docker as a service when we run the job so that we can pull images from Docker Hub and push images to our project's container repository. This is what the services keyword is for. Here, we ask GitLab to spin up the Docker service in the background so that our job can use those special commands. Note that in this example, we are running the 23.0.4-dind[2] version of Docker for the service. Since we are using a specific version of Docker rather than the latest version, we use the alias keyword so that the shared runner can locate the Docker service by using the name "docker."

The rest of the docker-build job defines the steps needed to build the new image. The before_script uses docker login to log in to the project's container registry. It uses the predefined variables CI_REGISTRY_USER and CI_REGISTRY_PASSWORD to log in to the registry contained in the CI_REGISTRY variable. Note that CI_REGISTRY_PASSWORD is different each time the job runs, so even if you were to display the value of it, it won't be of any use in other jobs. The script contains two main commands: docker build and docker push. By default, the docker build command uses the Dockerfile in the current directory. This creates an image in the service's local image repository. The docker push command then pushes that image to the project's container registry. The push is necessary because the image generated by the build is local to the docker image and disappears when the job is completed.

The final two commands are only run when pushing to the main branch. The docker tag command tags the image with the label "latest." This is just a label that links to the original image, which is tagged main in this example. The push is then used to push the tag to the project's container registry. Note that the tagged images are not duplicated in the container registry but are linked together. We'll see this shortly.

---

[2] In case you're wondering, dind stands for Docker-in-Docker. What that means is that you use the Docker software to run the Docker service. Yes, this is a weird quirk of Docker. Do a web search to learn more on this topic if you want to understand why.

Overview of the Build Job

Looking at the build job, it uses the image we just created (via the default: image keyword) and displays some information such as the versions of Bash, Java, and Maven. This job does not need the Docker service since GitLab is downloading the image as part of the job and using it like any other image downloaded from Docker Hub. It's important to note that we did not need to specify any credentials for the project's container registry; GitLab does not require explicit credentials for images downloaded from within the same project. If you can run the job, you have permission to download the image from that project's container registry.

Pipeline Results of Creating, Storing, and Using a Docker Image

Now let's take a look at the output from each of the jobs when we commit changes to the docker-setup branch. Figure 10-5 shows part of the output of the docker-build job. Here, we can see that it downloaded the dind version of Docker first since it needs to start the service before we run the build commands. This may generate a warning message that you can normally ignore. If the service fails to come up, you will get failures later on when the build commands run. Once the service is up, it then downloads the plain-vanilla Docker image without dind. The before_script and script commands are run in that image.[3] I don't show the rest of the docker-build output since it just shows feedback from running the docker commands.

---

[3] What this implies is that you can use any image that has Docker installed on it; you don't have to use the Docker Hub docker image to run those commands. It does help if the Docker version of the service matches the Docker version of the build image.

CHAPTER 10 IT'S NICE TO SHARE

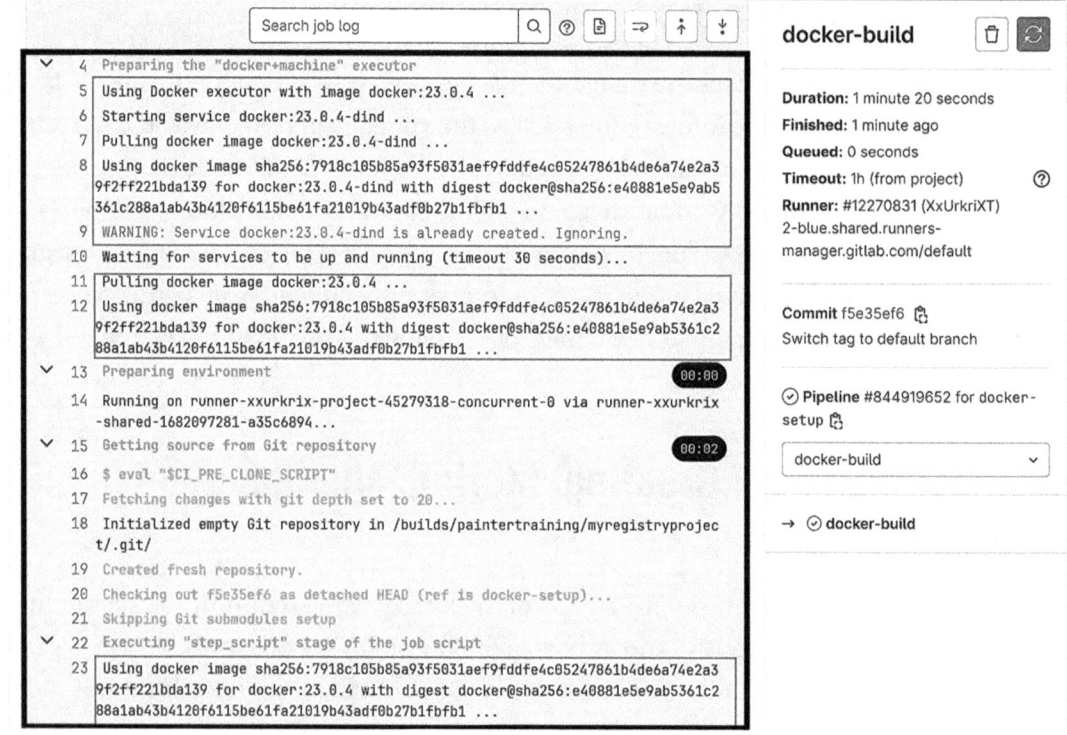

Figure 10-5. Output of docker-build job

Figure 10-6 shows the corresponding output of the build job. The key thing to note here is that the job downloaded the Docker image we generated from the docker-build job, which has the tag "docker-setup." The docker-setup tag came from the name of the branch, which happens to be the value of CI_COMMIT_REF_SLUG in this example. We can see that we are using bash version 5.2.15, Java version 17.0.6, and Maven version 3.8.6, which shows that the image has those packages installed.

CHAPTER 10 IT'S NICE TO SHARE

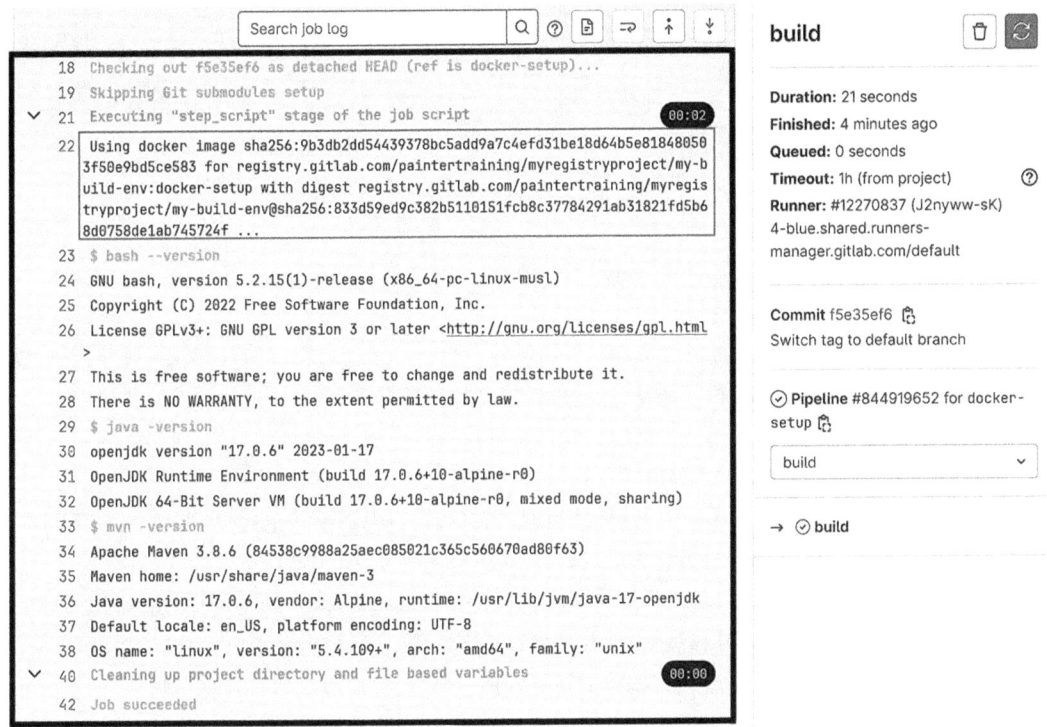

Figure 10-6. Output of build job

Viewing Container Registry Changes

Let's now switch over to the project's container registry to see what is there currently. Figure 10-7 shows the contents of the container registry for "MyRegistryProject." What we see is a link to the my-build-env image under myregistryproject and that it has one tag associated with it. Note that a container registry can have multiple Docker images. In addition, myregistryproject can itself be a Docker image; this can get confusing if you have both myregistryproject as a container registry and an image, so I tend to use one or the other. The trashcan icon associated with the link can be used to delete the container registry and all Docker images within it.

383

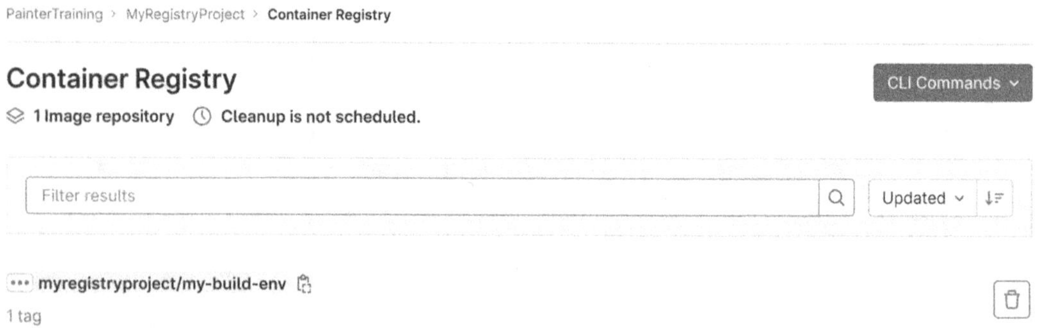

CHAPTER 10   IT'S NICE TO SHARE

Figure 10-7.   Contents of container registry after build

Clicking the link takes us to the my-build-env page as shown in Figure 10-8. Here, we see that the my-build-env Docker image has only one tag associated with it: docker-setup. Clicking the horizontal ellipsis icon next to the tag provides additional information about the "my-build-env:docker-setup" image. The vertical ellipsis icon is a drop-down menu that enables you to delete the tag. If that is the only tag associated with the image, the underlying image is also deleted.

Figure 10-8.   Listing of tags for my-build-env Docker image

CHAPTER 10   IT'S NICE TO SHARE

Merge Request Results of Creating and Storing a Docker Image

After performing a merge request for the docker-setup branch, Figure 10-9 shows the output of the build job. The key thing to note here is that the merge request created a new image with tag main, which you can see highlighted in the build output. Although the contents of my-build-env for tags docker-setup and main are the same, they are distinct images.

Figure 10-9. *Output of build job after merge of docker-setup branch to main*

Figure 10-10 shows the tag list for my-build-env image after the merge request is performed. Here, we see that there are now three tags: docker-setup, main, and latest. If you compare the digest of docker-setup to main, you can see that they are different. If you compare the digest of main and latest, you can see that they are the same; this tells you that the two tags refer to the same image. By the way, it is standard convention to tag an image as latest so that users of the image know which is the latest one to use.

385

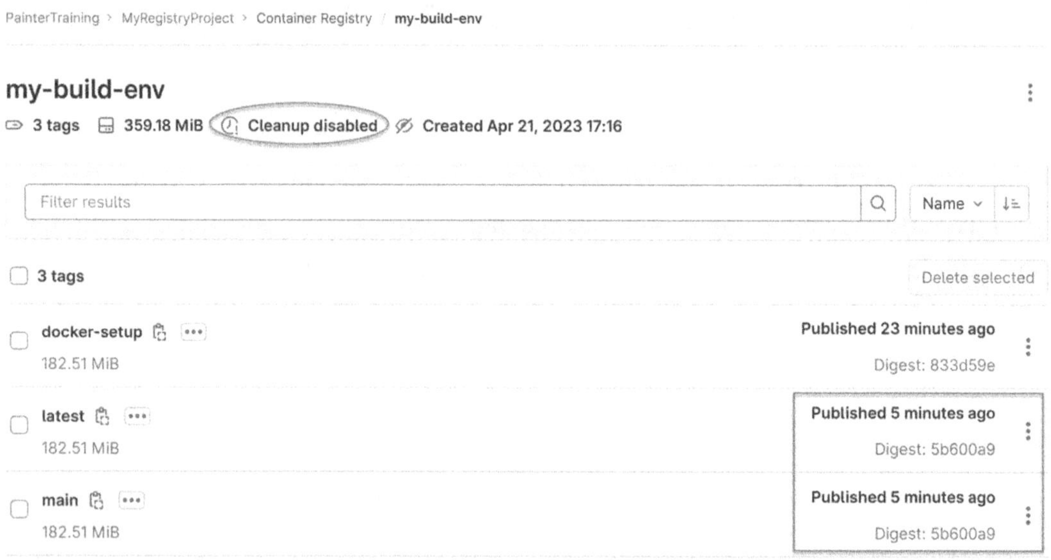

CHAPTER 10   IT'S NICE TO SHARE

Figure 10-10. Listing of tags for my-build-env after merge

The Problem of Unneeded Images

Note in the previous figure that the "my-build-env:docker-setup" image remains on the tag list even though I've deleted the docker-setup branch as part of the merge request. Essentially, I have an old image that is no longer needed. Also, note the highlighted message that cleanup is disabled. So how do you delete the unneeded image? You could, of course, go to the my-build-env page and manually delete it from there. But if lots of images are being created for different branches, it can become quite cumbersome to have to manually delete these images, not to mention error prone if you delete an image that is still being used. So, the question becomes, is there an automated way of cleaning up these unused images?

The first thought that usually occurs to solve this problem is to delete the image when the merge request is completed. However, this is not as easy as you may think. Although you could use the docker rm command, that command only applies to the Docker service's local repository, not the project's container repository.

CHAPTER 10 IT'S NICE TO SHARE

There is a GitLab API[4] that can be used to accomplish this task as described here: https://docs.gitlab.com/ee/user/packages/container_registry/delete_container_registry_images.html#use-the-gitlab-api. Although this approach works, it is not as clean as the "docker rm" command; it requires that you set up a private access token and retrieve both the project and repository ID, which makes the API command rather cryptic.

Setting an Image Cleanup Policy

It turns out that there is an indirect way of doing this as implied by the "Cleanup disabled" message shown in the earlier my-build-env page. You can set up a cleanup task that periodically prunes images based on some criteria. To do this, go to the project's "Packages and registries" tab under the Settings section as shown in Figure 10-11. From here, you access the cleanup policies using the "Edit cleanup rules" button.

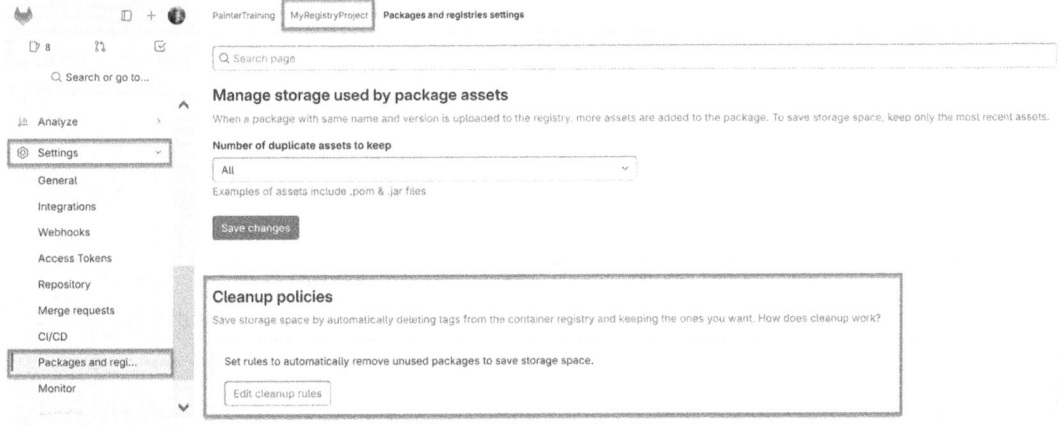

Figure 10-11. *Cleanup policies section in project settings for container registries*

Figure 10-12 shows the top of the "Cleanup policies" page. You enable the cleanup policy by selecting the "Enabled" button. In this example, I am selecting "Run cleanup" to be "Every week" (from the default "Every day"). Under the "Keep these tags" section, I kept the default setting for "Keep the most recent" to "10 tags per image name" and set

---

[4] The GitLab API (Application Programming Interface) is described in a later chapter.

the "Keep tags matching:" to main. If your project ends up creating a lot of images per week, you will probably want to run cleanup every day. Which tags you want to keep depends on your tagging strategy.

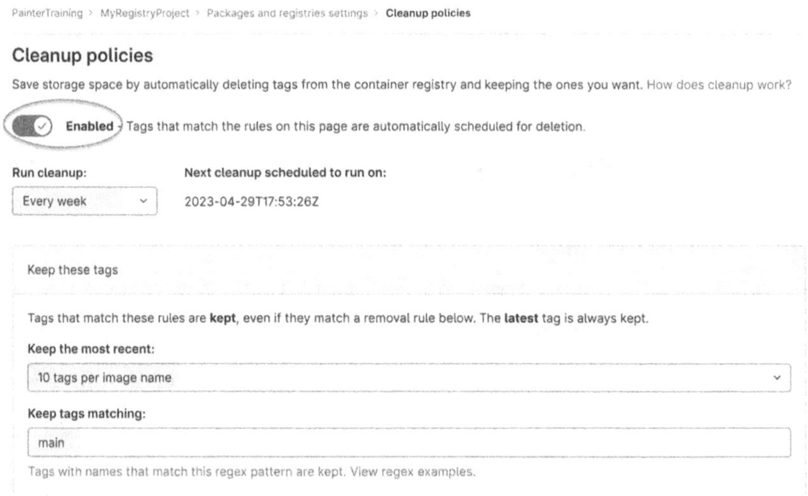

Figure 10-12. Cleanup policies page (top)

Figure 10-13 shows the remaining part of the "Cleanup policies" page. This contains the "Remove these tags" section where you can specify what tags to remove that are not explicitly kept. In this example, I set the "Remove tags older than" value to "7 days," which assumes that development branches are not kept for more than seven days. I kept the "Remove tags matching:" value to the default "*". With these settings, all images that are not latest and main will be deleted as soon as they become more than seven days old. Note that since the cleanup task is run once a week, it is possible that some images will stick around for more than 7 days but will not remain for more than 13 days.

Figure 10-13. Cleanup policies page (bottom)

Clearly, using cleanup policies will keep some images around for longer than needed (which tends to bug some people who like to see images cleaned up as soon as they are no longer relevant). You can keep tweaking the policies to get close to that ideal with the risk of removing images that are still in use. Note that if you do end up deleting an image that is still relevant, you can always recreate it. One of the things I like about using cleanup policies is that it runs in the background so that I don't have to continually pay attention to what is in the registry in order to remove unused images.

Now that we've seen how to create and store Docker images in a project's container registry, let's see how we can use them in other projects.

Sharing Docker Images

We've seen how to create and use Docker images within a project. Is there a way we can share a Docker image with another project? We would do this for cases where one project creates an image that can be used for building products in related projects for a group or perhaps an organization.

Chapter 10   IT'S NICE TO SHARE

First Attempt Accessing an Image from Another Project

So, let's see what happens when we try to use the my-build-env in the "MyShellPipeline" project. After all, my-build-env was designed to replace the Docker Hub maven image. Figure 10-14 shows the one-line change needed to the .gitlab-ci.yml file in the "MyShellPipeline" project.

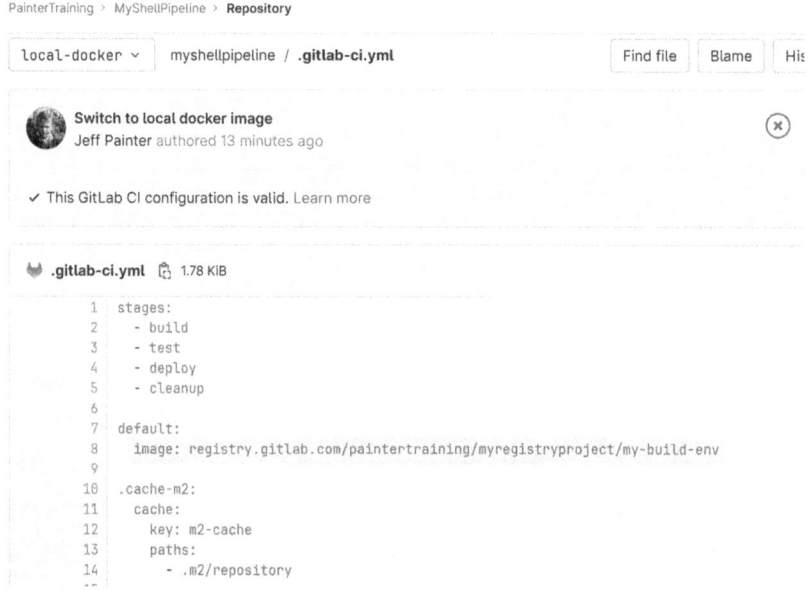

Figure 10-14. *Change to MyShellPipeline CI/CD configuration to use the my-build-env image*

When we make this change, we discover that the pipeline for "MyShellPipeline" project fails. The job error log is shown in Figure 10-15. We can see that the failure occurs as soon as we try to download the myregistryproject/my-build-env image. Reading the warning and error message, we see that downloading the image was denied. It states that either the image does not exist (which we know it does) or that we do not have permission to download it (which, by process of elimination, must be the issue).

CHAPTER 10   IT'S NICE TO SHARE

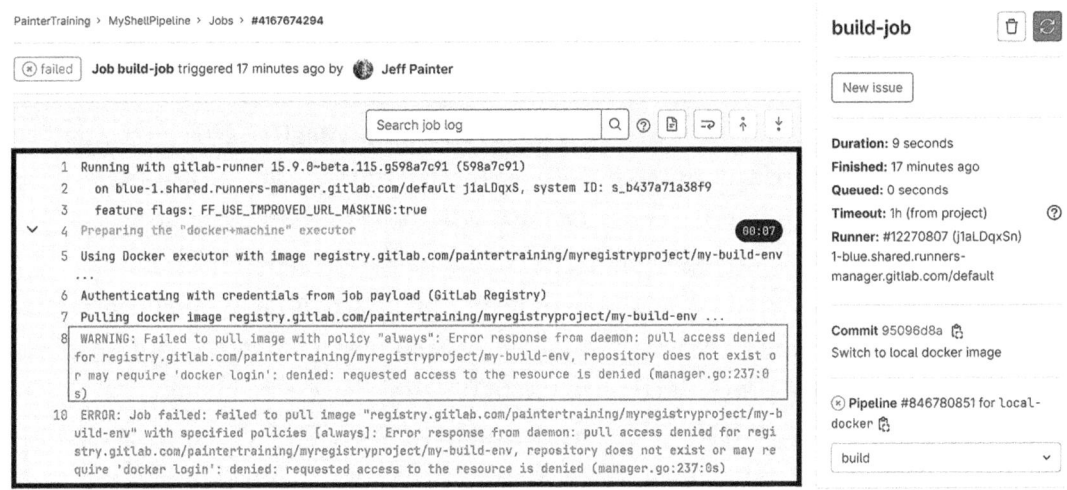

Figure 10-15.   Failure after image tag change

Investigating Why Access Was Denied

The first question that needs to be answered is why? Well, it turns out that the "MyRegistryProject" is private. Even though I have access to both the "MyShellPipeline" and "MyRegistryProject" projects, the runner process that attempts to download the image is not using my credentials. In fact, it doesn't know that I'm the one running the pipeline. The shared runner is external to GitLab and so requires some type of credentials to access the image.

The second question, then, is what credentials is it trying to use? It isn't totally obvious in the job log, but if you take a look at the previous log statement, it states that it is authenticating with credentials from the job payload. Well, that's clear, not. What it is trying to use is the job CI_REGISTRY_USER and CI_REGISTRY_PASSWORD (a.k.a. CI_JOB_TOKEN) variables that we used when we created the image using docker login. Unfortunately, the image keyword does not let us do an explicit docker login command. And installing Docker in the my-build-env image doesn't solve the problem either since the runner is downloading the image before we can even access the contents of the image.

391

CHAPTER 10   IT'S NICE TO SHARE

Enabling a Project to Access Another's Container Registry

There turns out to be a number of ways to provide the credentials to the shared runner so that it can download the private Docker image within "MyRegistryProject." Some of these methods require a premium license when used from the gitlab.com site, so I'll pass over those options for now. The most direct way to do this is to update the "MyRegistryProject" settings to allow "MyShellPipeline" to access the registry. Figure 10-16 shows how to do this. Within project "MyRegistryProject," you need to go to the "CI/CD" section under "Settings." From here, you will see a "Token Access" section where you can enter the project(s) that you want to enable access to. In this example, I entered paintertraining/MyShellPipeline and added it to the Project access list. With this setting in place, "MyShellPipeline" will be able to use the CI_REGISTRY_USER and CI_REGISTRY_PASSWORD variables as credentials to the "MyRegistryProject" container registry.

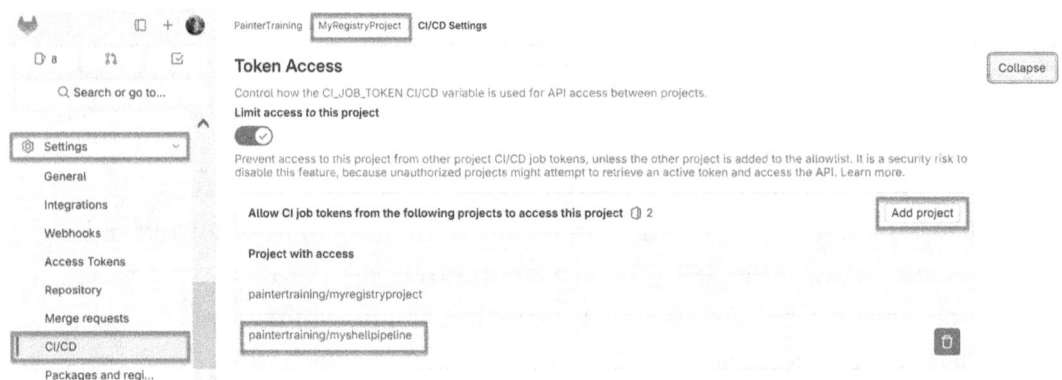

Figure 10-16. Setting to allow MyShellPipeline token access to MyRegistryProject

Running the "MyShellPipeline" pipeline again with this setting in place, we see the output as shown in Figure 10-17. From the log, we see that the download of the my-build-env image succeeds, and the job begins to execute. So that's a positive sign. However, the job still fails in the end as shown in Figure 10-18. After some investigation, it turns out that the scripts/build.sh file is requesting /bin/bash (via the #! /bin/bash statement at the start of the file). However, the bash image we used as the basis for my-build-env installs bash at /usr/local/bin/bash and not at /bin/bash.

CHAPTER 10   IT'S NICE TO SHARE

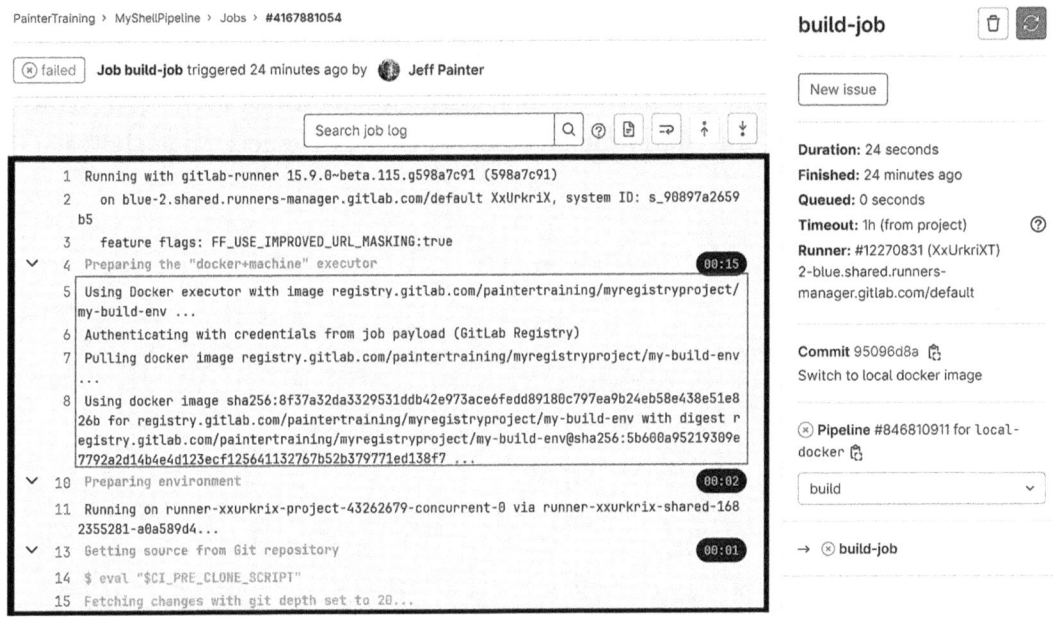

Figure 10-17. Output of build-job showing successful download of the my-build-env image

Figure 10-18. Output showing different failure after token access granted

CHAPTER 10 IT'S NICE TO SHARE

This turns out to be an easy fix. Figure 10-19 shows the one-line change needed to the Dockerfile in "MyRegistryProject." We simply add the soft link /bin/bash that points to /usr/local/bin/bash. With that fix, we rebuild the my-build-env image and rerun the pipeline in "MyShellPipeline." And with that, the pipeline finally succeeds as shown in Figure 10-20.

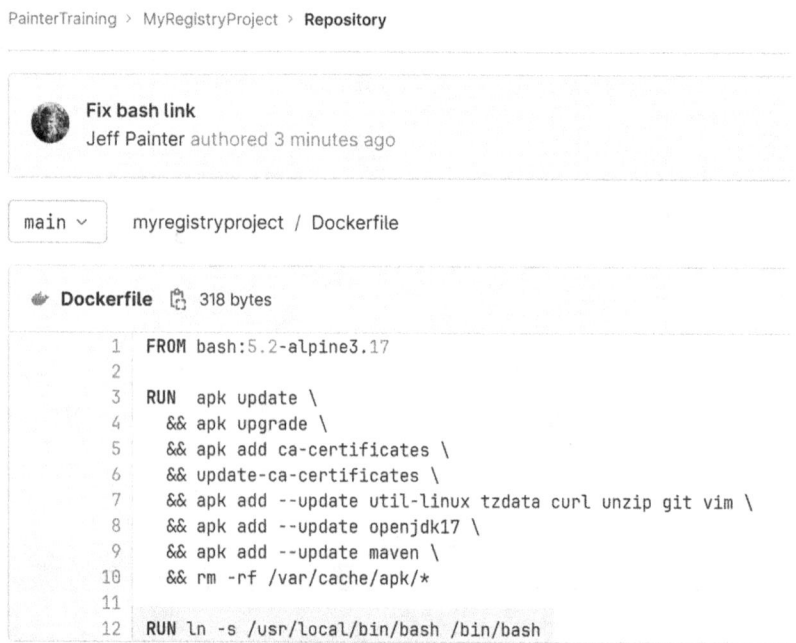

Figure 10-19. *Fix to Dockerfile defining /bin/bash link*

CHAPTER 10 IT'S NICE TO SHARE

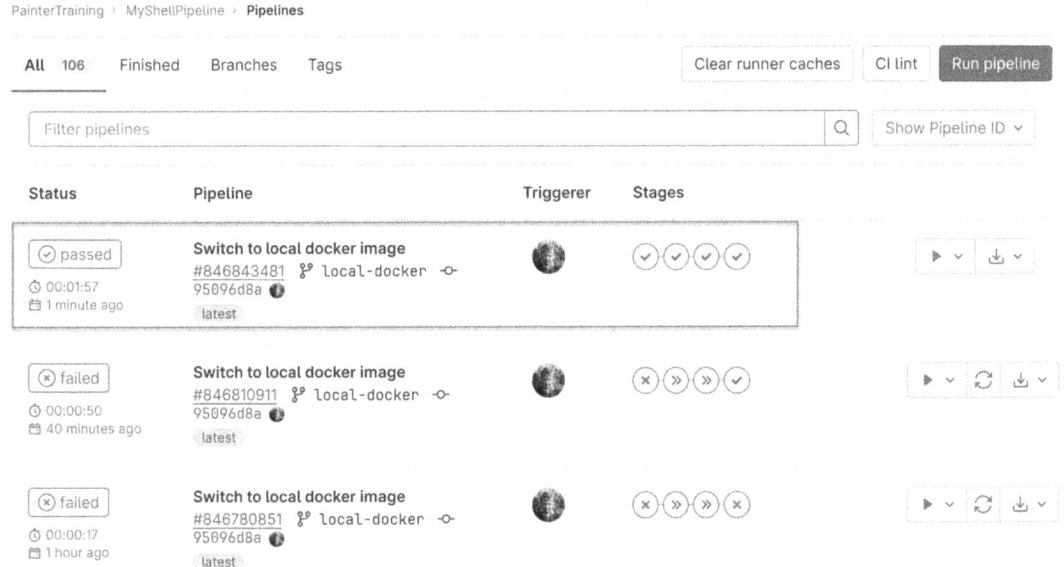

Figure 10-20. Pipeline summary showing successful run with fixes in place

Accessing Container Registry Images Outside of GitLab

Now that we know how to access images from a container repository from within a GitLab job, let's see how we can access those same images from outside of GitLab, in particular from your local machine. You could, of course, use your personal username/password credentials with docker login, but that comes at a risk of your credentials getting exposed should someone gain access to your machine. GitLab provides another way of providing credentials called personal access tokens. These tokens act as alternative passwords along with your username but provide fine-grain control on what you can access within GitLab. They are also revocable should they become compromised, which is easier than changing your password everywhere it is used.

395

CHAPTER 10   IT'S NICE TO SHARE

Creating Personal Access Tokens

Figure 10-21 shows how to create a personal access token from your user settings.[5] You can create different tokens for different purposes and with different permissions. In this example, I am creating an access token with the name jp-registry-token. Note that the name is not used anywhere; it's just a name you use to help remember what it is for. Personal access tokens require an expiry date; you can set it for a month, quarter, or year from now if you choose. Finally, you select the permission scopes for the token. In this example, I've selected read_repository, write_repository, read_registry, and write_registry. The repository scopes are for the Git repository, which you can use with HTTPS Git access. The registry scopes are for all the registry types, which include the container registry. When you first create the token, you'll be shown the token itself that you must copy; this is the only time you can see the token value.

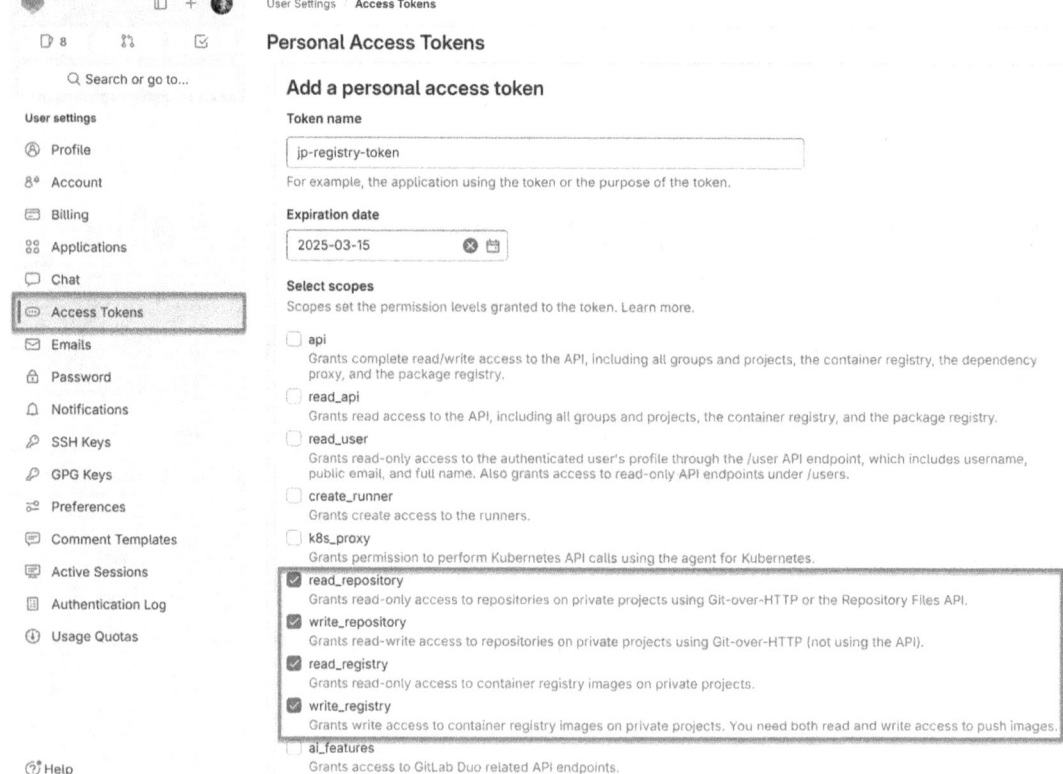

Figure 10-21. Personal access token creation

---

[5] If you forgot how to get to your user settings, select "Preferences" from your user profile picture in the upper-right corner of GitLab's left-hand panel.

CHAPTER 10   IT'S NICE TO SHARE

Once you've created your token, you can view it on the same page near the bottom as shown in Figure 10-22. In this example, it shows the newly created jp-registry-token with the repository and registry scopes it applies to along with when it was created and when it will expire. You can revoke the token by selecting the trash icon associated with the token. Note that you cannot edit the token to change its behavior or reset the expiration date. You will have to delete the token and recreate it, which will give you a different token value.

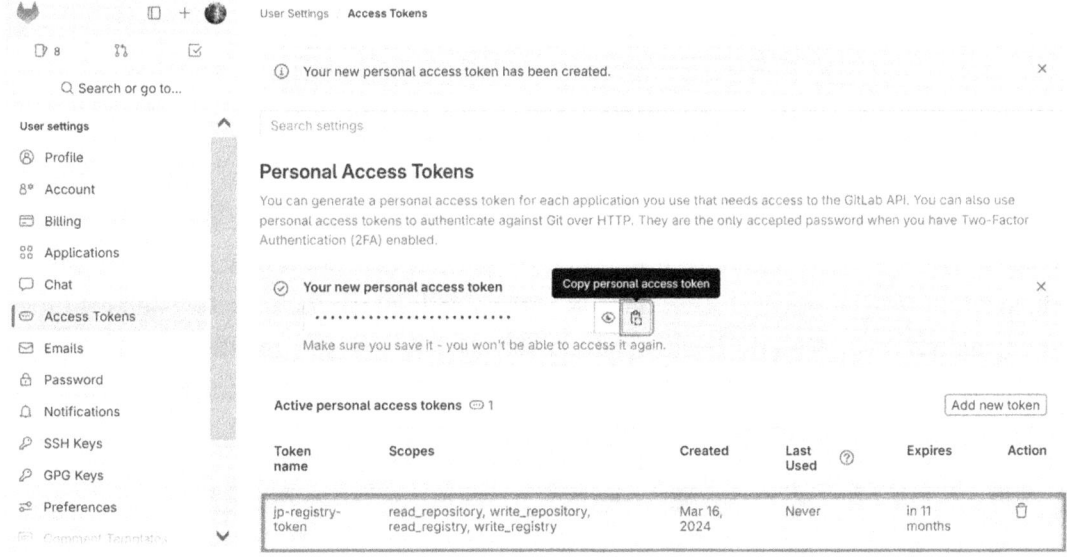

Figure 10-22. *Listing of personal active tokens*

Accessing Images Using Personal Access Tokens

Now that you have the token, you can use it with docker login to access your images from GitLab's container registry. Figure 10-23 shows running docker login with my username and access token, which is partially blurred out. Note that for container registries on the gitlab.com site, you simply use registry.gitlab.com as the registry to log in to; don't use the HTTPS URL or add the path to any given registry. If GitLab accepts the username/token combination, you will see the "Login succeeded" message. If you don't, you'll need to try again with the corrected credentials or create a new access token. Note that you only need to do this once for the life of the access token. Docker will save the credentials

397

CHAPTER 10   IT'S NICE TO SHARE

for you so that you can simply run docker pull and docker push without having to log in again. Docker will know what credentials to use based on the registry.gitlab.com portion of the Docker image path that you provide to docker push or pull.

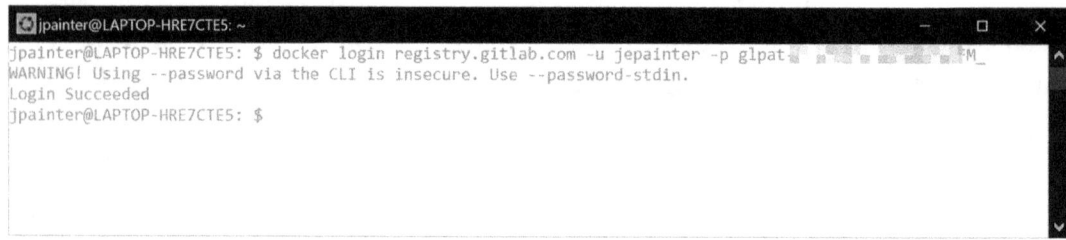

Figure 10-23. *Docker login using personal access token*

With the login part out of the way, Figure 10-24 shows the results of doing a docker pull on the my-build-env image. As you can see, it begins to download the latest my-build-env image from the paintertraining/myregistryproject container. Once complete, it will be stored in your local Docker registry with the full image path name. The next time you do a docker run with that image path, it will not check to see that the image is up to date and will use the image contained in your local registry; to download the latest image from GitLab, you should use –pull=always.

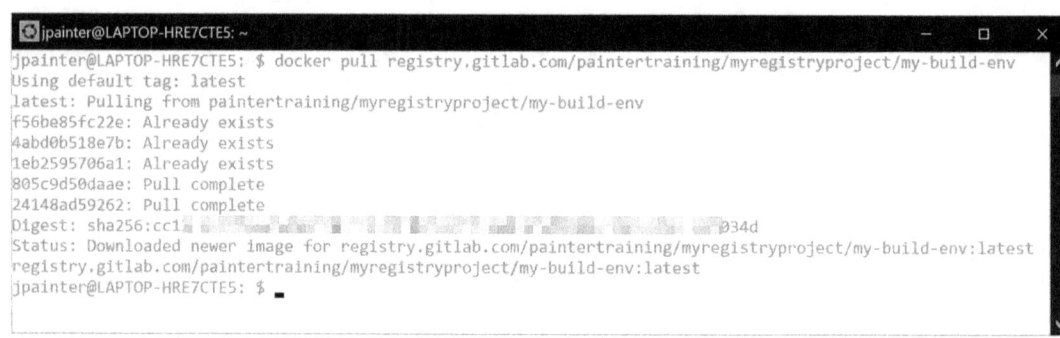

Figure 10-24. *Docker pull of my-build-env image*

Using DOCKER_AUTH_CONFIG to Access a Project's Container Registry

That's all there is to it. Let's circle back to accessing Docker images from within GitLab. We saw how we can set up a project's container registry to enable access using the CI_REGISTRY variables. This is fine if you have a small number of projects that need access to a given project's container registry but becomes unwieldy if we want a large number of projects to access it, say all projects within a common group. So, is there a way to use token credentials from within a GitLab project without having to explicitly enable permission through that project's token access settings?

Well, it turns out that there is a way, although it can be a bit tricky to find in GitLab's documentation. You can set up credentials similar to what docker login stores internally using the CI/CD variable DOCKER_AUTH_CONFIG. Figure 10-25 shows how to set this variable for a project or group. The value is a JSON value defined by Docker. It is a dictionary under the "auths" keyword with the registry name as a key and an authentication string as the value. Yes, it is a bit of a bizarre structure, but it does work.

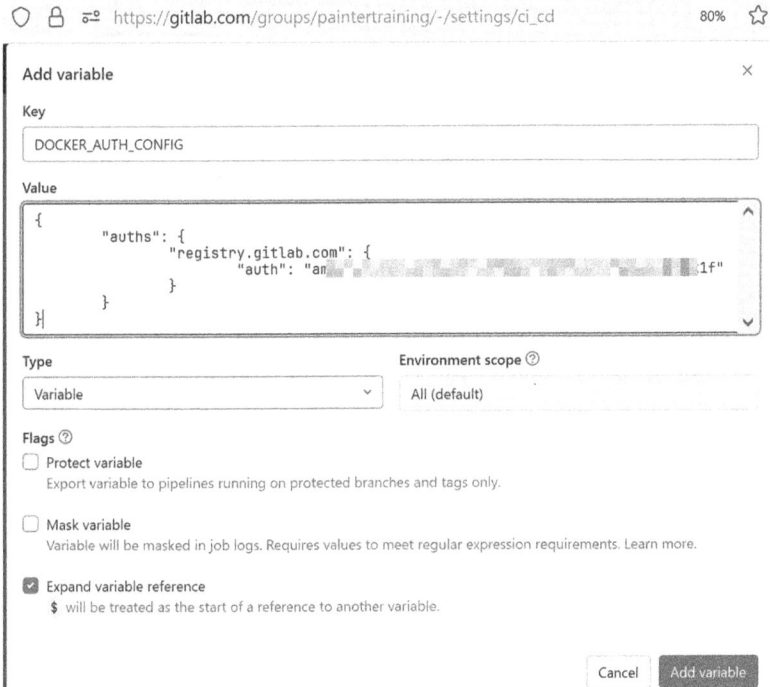

Figure 10-25. *Definition of the DOCKER_AUTH_CONFIG variable for a project or group*

Determining the DOCKER_AUTH_CONFIG Authentication String

In some older versions of Docker, you can access this JSON structure directly in your ~/.docker/config.json file. Newer versions store the authentication value in a secured place that you can't see. Looking at the preceding example, you can see that the auth value is a weird string of characters rather than a plain text version of your username and token value. So, if you can't see this value as generated by docker login, how can you generate it? Figure 10-26 shows how to generate this value using the openssl command. You pipe in the value as "username:token" to openssl base64 -A. This creates the value as a base64 value.[6] This is the value you use as the auth value in the DOCKER_AUTH_CONFIG variable.

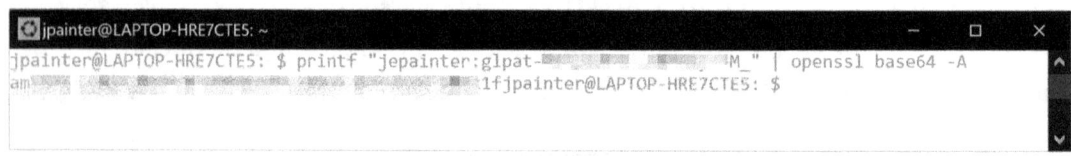

Figure 10-26. *Generation of base64 value of "auth" for the DOCKER_AUTH_CONFIG variable*

Setting DOCKER_AUTH_CONFIG As a Group CI/CD Variable

So, for this example, I added the DOCKER_AUTH_CONFIG variable as a group CI/CD variable so that it will be available to all projects within the group and removed the explicit token access setting for "MyShellPipeline" that I added earlier. Rerunning the pipeline for "MyShellPipeline" gives the build-job results as shown in Figure 10-27. As we can see, the job was able to download the my-build-env image as before. However, note the message about authenticating with credentials from $DOCKER_AUTH_CONFIG. This is how we know that the image was downloaded using our personal access token, just as we downloaded the image to our local registry on our local machine.

---

[6] It's important to note that base64 is an encoding, not an encryption as used in SSH. It simply obfuscates the actual value, which you can retrieve by simply decoding the value using openssl.

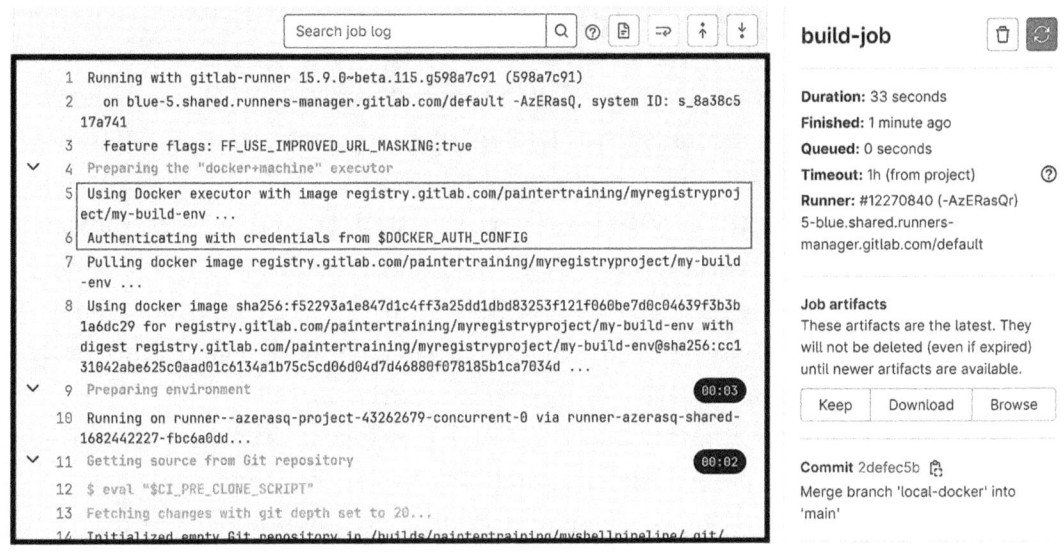

Figure 10-27. Build job run using DOCKER_AUTH_CONFIG

Security Concerns with DOCKER_AUTH_CONFIG

Now some of you might be concerned (and rightly so) that we are authenticating using the personal credentials of a team member, even if the password is a personal access token and not an actual password (which would be even worse). There are a couple of issues here. First, someone else could grab the DOCKER_AUTH_CONFIG value and use that to gain access to other projects or groups that I manage and/or decode the auth value to determine the value of the access token. This is somewhat mitigated by CI/CD variables being restricted to maintainers and owners, but still. The other issue is what happens if the team member leaves the team or the company. Those credentials will become invalid, and all jobs will begin to fail.[7]

---

[7] In case you are wondering, yes, I've seen this happen despite telling users not to use personal credentials in team environments.

CHAPTER 10   IT'S NICE TO SHARE

Creating Project Deploy Tokens

Enter deploy tokens. Deploy tokens were first introduced to solve the Git automation problem. With external build tools such as Jenkins attempting to build products from a Git repository such as GitHub, there needed to be a way to use credentials that was not tied to a particular user for the very same reasons discussed for personal access tokens. A deploy token represents a pseudo-user with a token as the password; however, unlike a personal access token, the deploy token is associated to a given Git repository rather than a user. For GitLab, this association is made to a GitLab project or group and involves not just Git repositories but package and container registries as well.

Figure 10-28 illustrates how to create a project deploy token. To create such a token, you need to go to the project's repository settings. Expanding the "Deploy tokens" section reveals a form where you can generate the token. In this example, I set the name to be my-registry-deploy; as with personal access tokens, this name is purely for identifying what the token is for. You specify the username in the username field, which if left empty will generate a name for you. As with the personal access token, you then specify the scopes you want the token to be valid for. Note that the scopes for a deploy token are somewhat different from those of a personal access token; in particular, the deploy token scopes do not include API scopes, and the container and package registry scopes are separated.

CHAPTER 10   IT'S NICE TO SHARE

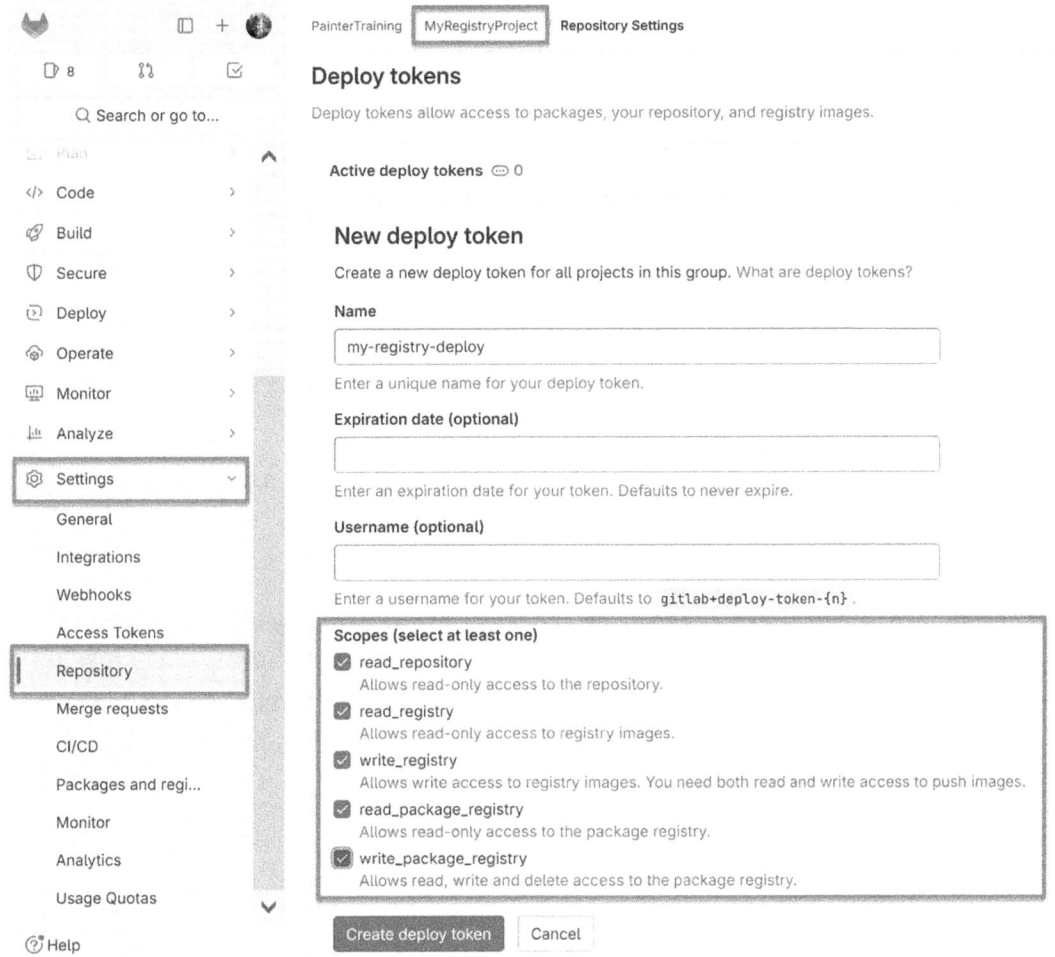

Figure 10-28. Project deploy token creation

When you create the token, the username and token value are displayed at the top of the same page as shown in Figure 10-29. I mention this because sometimes this part of the page remains hidden, and you might think that nothing happened. You'll need to scroll to the top of the page to see it. In this example, the username is set to gitlab+deploy-token-1994203, and the token itself is shown blurred. You need to copy both of these values in order to use them. Once you leave or refresh the page, this information disappears.

CHAPTER 10 IT'S NICE TO SHARE

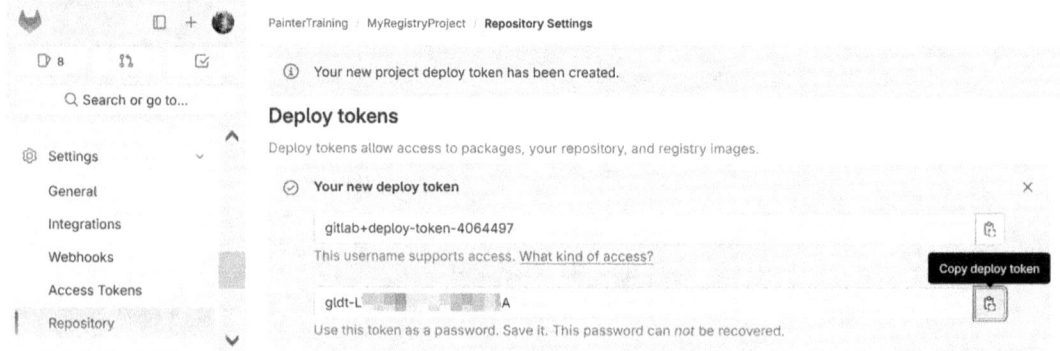

Figure 10-29. Creation result of the project deploy token

Refreshing the "Deploy token" page, you can see the active deploy tokens at the end of it as shown in Figure 10-30. This is similar to the active personal access token listing but includes the username as well. Note that unlike personal access tokens, deploy tokens can have an expiration date of "Never." This is by design since deploy tokens are expected to be used in automated scripts or build tools where having to change the token periodically can cause the automation to fail. As with personal access tokens, you can also use these tokens within GitLab to authorize access to the container registry via the DOCKER_AUTH_CONFIG value.

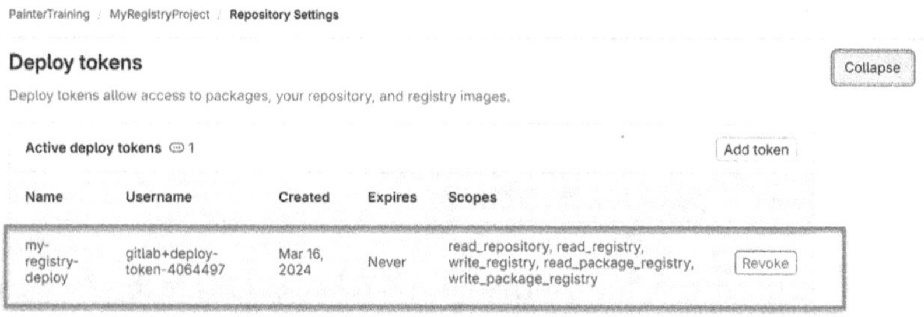

Figure 10-30. List of active project deploy tokens

Creating Group Deploy Tokens

You can also create group deploy tokens as shown in Figure 10-31. You can create a group deploy token by going to the group's repository settings and expanding the "Deploy tokens" section as you did for project deploy tokens. The form and output

CHAPTER 10   IT'S NICE TO SHARE

are the same. With the group deploy token, you can access any Git repository or container and package registry associated with projects within the group. This simplifies automation for projects across teams that use similar build automation scripts or tools.

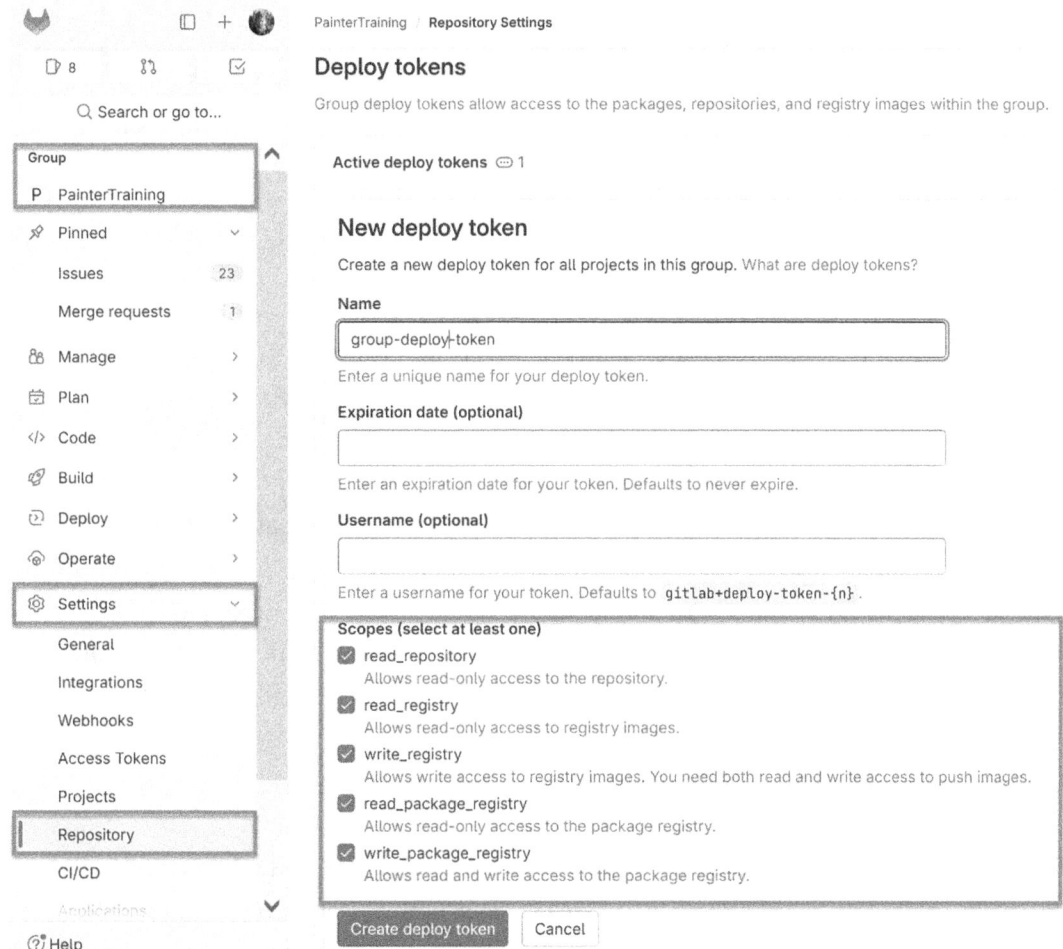

Figure 10-31.   Group deploy token creation

A Brief Mention of Project and Group Access Tokens

I'll mention here that for paid or self-managed versions of GitLab, there are two other alternatives to personal access and deploy tokens: project access tokens and group access tokens. These tokens are similar to personal access tokens but are specific to projects and groups, respectively. Project and group access tokens are not tied to an

405

actual user but to internally generated bot users.[8] Like personal access tokens, you can include API scopes. Like deploy tokens, the advantage of project and group access tokens is that they are tied to the project or group they were created from and cannot be used to access other projects or groups. Plus, you don't have to worry about bots leaving the team or company.

Now that we've covered how to store and retrieve Docker images in a project's container registry, let's turn our attention to storing binary objects in the package registry.

Working with the Package Registry

Docker images are one type of object that we can create and store in a project's container registry. But there are other types of binary objects such as jar, pypi, and Ruby gem files that a project can create. In order for them to be used by other projects, we need a place to store them. One of the most common products used to store binary objects in a corporate environment is the Artifactory by JFrog. It is a full-featured product that requires a paid license and, for a self-managed installation, significant resources and staff to support it. If you have it already, then uploading objects to it from a GitLab pipeline is pretty straightforward; there are many articles on the Internet about how to do this.

Accessing the Project Package Registry

If you don't already have access to a binary object repository like the Artifactory, you can use GitLab's package repository that is available with every project.[9] Figure 10-32 shows what the package registry looks like initially for the "MyShellPipeline" project. You access it from the "Package Registry" tab under the project's "Deploy" section. When there are no packages stored there, a link is provided to describe how to publish and share packages.

---

[8] In case you are worried about license costs, these bot users do not use a license seat, so you will not be charged for them.

[9] If you have a self-managed GitLab instance, it is possible the administrator has disabled this feature, so be aware.

CHAPTER 10 IT'S NICE TO SHARE

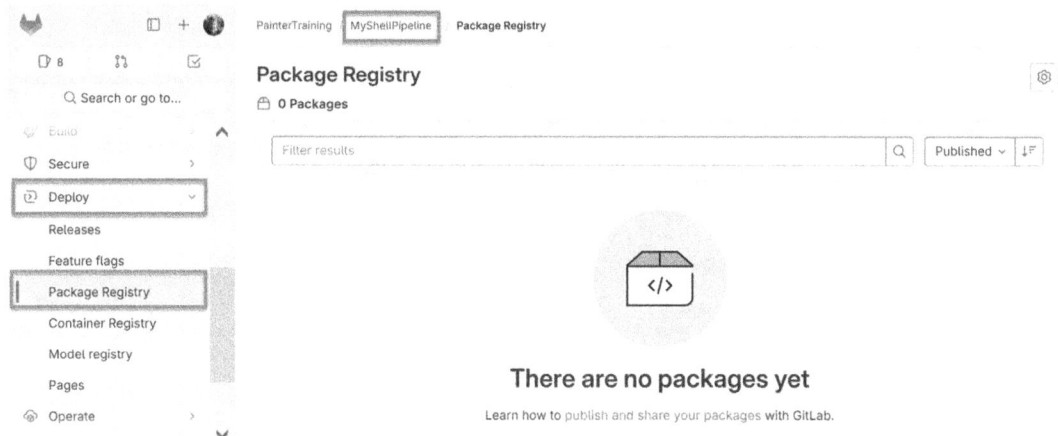

Figure 10-32. Initial package registry page

A Maven Example of Creating and Storing a Jar File

To illustrate how to store an object in a GitLab package registry, we are going to update the existing "MyShellPipeline" project to store a jar file using Maven. This project already uses Maven to compile a trivial Java program, so we are going to extend the example to create a jar file and store it in the project's package registry. There are a number of small changes needed to accomplish this, which we'll first describe before rerunning the pipeline.

Changes to pom.xml

Figure 10-33 shows the changes needed to the pom.xml file that describes the server where the jar file is to be published. There are two sections added: "repositories" and "distributionManagement." The "repositories" section defines the server that we will pull from, and the "distributionManagement" section describes the servers we will push to. In this example, we are specifying the URL to the project's GitLab package registry; the highlighted number is the project ID for "MyShellPipeline," which is how GitLab will know where to store the jar file. In this example, the ID gitlab-maven[10] is associated with each of the URLs.

---

[10] This ID is arbitrary but must match the ID provided in the settings.xml file. There is nothing special about the name gitlab-maven; we could just as well have used my-server as the ID.

407

```
16        <maven.compiler.source>1.7</maven.compiler.source>
17        <maven.compiler.target>1.7</maven.compiler.target>
18    </properties>
19
20    <repositories>
21      <repository>
22        <id>gitlab-maven</id>
23        <url>https://gitlab.com/api/v4/projects/43262679/packages/maven</url>
24      </repository>
25    </repositories>
26
27    <distributionManagement>
28      <repository>
29        <id>gitlab-maven</id>
30        <url>https://gitlab.com/api/v4/projects/43262679/packages/maven</url>
31      </repository>
32
33      <snapshotRepository>
34        <id>gitlab-maven</id>
35        <url>https://gitlab.com/api/v4/projects/43262679/packages/maven</url>
36      </snapshotRepository>
37    </distributionManagement>
38
39    <dependencies>
```

Figure 10-33. *Update to the pom.xml file defining the package registry location*

Changes to settings.xml

So how does Maven know what credentials to use for our GitLab package registry? This is where the settings.xml file comes in. Figure 10-34 shows the added "servers" section where the credentials are specified. In this example, it defines a server with ID gitlab-maven and some HTTP properties passed to GitLab as credentials; the properties of name and value are specific to GitLab that will be described shortly. Rather than hard coding the credentials into the settings.xml file, we'll be passing them through the environment variables REPO_TOKEN_NAME and REPO_TOKEN_VALUE.

CHAPTER 10 IT'S NICE TO SHARE

```
 1  <?xml version="1.0" encoding="UTF-8"?>
 2
 3  <settings xmlns="http://maven.apache.org/SETTINGS/1.0.0"
 4            xmlns:xsi="http://www.w3.org/2001/XMLSchema-instance"
 5            xsi:schemaLocation="http://maven.apache.org/SETTINGS
 6
 7    <localRepository>${env.CI_PROJECT_DIR}/.m2/repository</localRepository>
 8    <interactiveMode>false</interactiveMode>
 9    <offline>false</offline>
10
11    <servers>
12      <server>
13        <id>gitlab-maven</id>
14        <configuration>
15          <httpHeaders>
16            <property>
17              <name>${env.REPO_TOKEN_NAME}</name>
18              <value>${env.REPO_TOKEN_VALUE}</value>
19            </property>
20          </httpHeaders>
21        </configuration>
22      </server>
23    </servers>
24  </settings>
```

Figure 10-34. *Update to the settings.xml file specifying the package registry location*

Extracting Credentials with maven-env.sh Script

Now to update each of the script files to run the appropriate Maven commands. To avoid redundancy in specifying the credentials, I created a new maven-env.sh file as shown in Figure 10-35. This file sets the environment variables REPO_TOKEN_NAME and REPO_TOKEN_VALUE based on the environment in which the scripts are run. When the scripts are run as part of the project's pipeline, the CI_JOB_TOKEN variable will be defined; in this case, I set REPO_TOKEN_NAME to "Job-Token" and set REPO_TOKEN_VALUE to the value of CI_JOB_TOKEN. When the scripts are run manually from my machine, CI_JOB_TOKEN will not be defined, in which case I check to see if GITLAB_DEPLOY_TOKEN is defined. I set this variable in my .bashrc file to refer to the group deploy token I defined earlier for the container registry. If this variable is defined, I set REPO_TOKEN_NAME to "Deploy-Token" and REPO_TOKEN_VALUE to the value of GITLAB_DEPLOY_TOKEN. If GITLAB_DEPLOY_TOKEN is not defined, I set these variables to "None," which will cause Maven to fail.

```
    package-repo ∨    myshellpipeline / scripts / maven-env.sh

    maven-env.sh    326 bytes

    1  if [ -n "$CI_JOB_TOKEN" ]; then
    2      export REPO_TOKEN_NAME="Job-Token"
    3      export REPO_TOKEN_VALUE="$CI_JOB_TOKEN"
    4  elif [ -n "$GITLAB_DEPLOY_TOKEN" ]; then
    5      export REPO_TOKEN_NAME="Deploy-Token"
    6      export REPO_TOKEN_VALUE="$GITLAB_DEPLOY_TOKEN"
    7  else
    8      export REPO_TOKEN_NAME="None"
    9      export REPO_TOKEN_VALUE="None"
   10  fi
```

Figure 10-35. *Script that sets REPO_TOKEN_NAME and REPO_TOKEN_VALUE under different scenarios*

Changes to the Build Script

Figure 10-36 shows the simple change to the build.sh script. Here, I added the line that reads (a.k.a. "sources") the maven-env.sh file in order to define the environment variables. This ensures that Maven doesn't complain about undefined variables in the settings.xml file even though it doesn't need the server credentials to compile the Java files.

```
    build.sh    881 bytes

    1  #! /bin/bash
    2
    3  MY_RC=0
    4  MY_DIR=$( realpath $( dirname $0 ) )
    5  MY_PARENT_DIR=$( realpath $MY_DIR/.. )
    6  MY_OUTPUT_DIR=$( realpath $MY_PARENT_DIR/output )
    7
    8  [[ -n $CI_PROJECT_DIR ]] || export CI_PROJECT_DIR=$MY_PARENT_DIR
    9
   10  source $MY_DIR/maven-env.sh
   11
   12  create_html() {
   13      echo '<!DOCTYPE html>'
   14      echo '<html>'
   15      echo '<body>'
   16      echo '<h1>My GitLab Artifact</h1>'
```

Figure 10-36. *Update to build.sh to set REPO_TOKEN_NAME and REPO_TOKEN_VALUE*

CHAPTER 10   IT'S NICE TO SHARE

Changes to the Unit Test Script

Next are the changes to the unit-test.sh file as shown in Figure 10-37. The top set of highlighted changes mimic what is in the build.sh file to source the maven-env.sh file. The bottom set of highlighted changes adds the Maven command to compile and run the Java test files (a.k.a. the Maven test phase). Note that the build.sh file simply compiles the Java source files and leaves the test files alone.

```
 unit-test.sh    529 bytes
 1  #! /bin/bash
 2
 3  MY_RC=0
 4  MY_DIR=$( realpath $( dirname $0 ) )
 5  MY_PARENT_DIR=$( realpath $MY_DIR/.. )
 6
 7  [[ -n $CI_PROJECT_DIR ]] || export CI_PROJECT_DIR=$MY_PARENT_DIR
 8
 9  source $MY_DIR/maven-env.sh
10
11  echo '*** Start unit-test.sh'
12
13  if [ "$FAIL_UNIT_TEST" == "true" ]; then
14      echo "Unit test failed!"
15      MY_RC=1
16  else
17      pushd $MY_PARENT_DIR/maven-projects/my-app > /dev/null
18      mvn -s $CI_PROJECT_DIR/.m2/settings.xml test || MY_RC=1
19      popd > /dev/null
20      echo "Unit test succeeded!"
21  fi
```

Figure 10-37. *Update to the unit-test script to use the project package registry*

Changes to the Deploy Script

Finally, Figure 10-38 shows the changes to the deploy.sh file. Like the changes to the unit-test.sh file, the top set of changes is added to source the maven-env.sh file. The bottom set of changes adds the Maven command to create and deploy the Java jar file to the project's package registry (a.k.a. the Maven deploy phase). Note that maven.test.skip is added to keep Maven from compiling and running the Java test files; running the tests is not needed here since it was done as part of running unit-test.sh.

CHAPTER 10 IT'S NICE TO SHARE

```
 deploy.sh   534 bytes
 1  #! /bin/bash
 2
 3  MY_RC=0
 4  MY_DIR=$( realpath $( dirname $0 ) )
 5  MY_PARENT_DIR=$( realpath $MY_DIR/.. )
 6
 7  [[ -n $CI_PROJECT_DIR ]] || export CI_PROJECT_DIR=$MY_PARENT_DIR
 8
 9  source $MY_DIR/maven-env.sh
10
11  echo '*** Start deploy.sh'
12
13  if [ "$FAIL_DEPLOY" == "true" ]; then
14      echo "Deploy failed!"
15      MY_RC=1
16  else
17      pushd $MY_PARENT_DIR/maven-projects/my-app > /dev/null
18      mvn -s $CI_PROJECT_DIR/.m2/settings.xml -Dmaven.test.skip deploy || MY_RC=1
19      popd > /dev/null
20      echo "Deploy succeeded!"
21  fi
22
23  echo '*** End deploy.sh'
24
25  exit $MY_RC
```

Figure 10-38. Update to the deploy script to use the project package registry

Pipeline Results of Creating and Storing a Jar File

With these changes committed and pushed, the pipeline now runs both the Maven test and deploy phases. Figure 10-39 shows part of the deploy-dev-job output that verifies that files were uploaded to the package registry. If you are not familiar with Maven, multiple files including the pom.xml file and a generated maven-metadata.xml file are uploaded in addition to the jar file to provide context for the package registry.

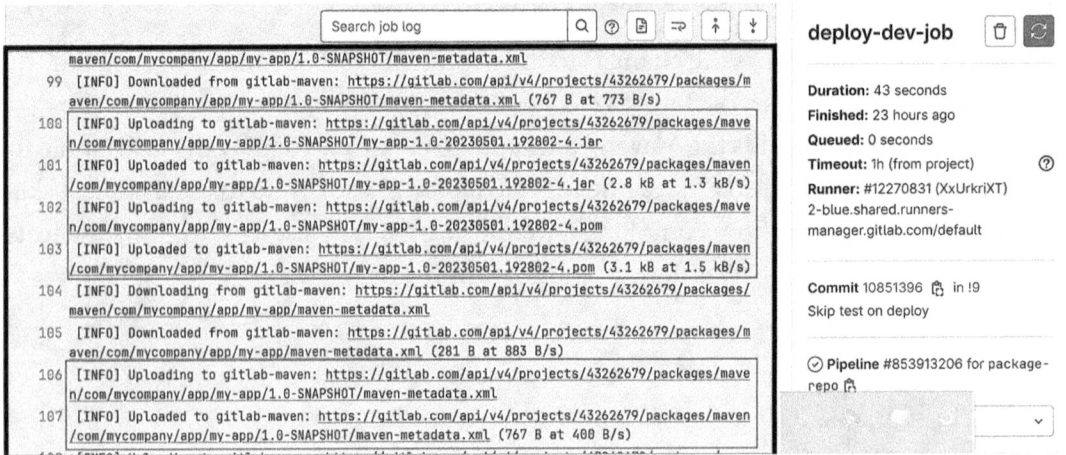

Figure 10-39. Output of deploy-dev-job showing the upload of files to the project's package registry

In case you are wondering, when the product version ends in "-SNAPSHOT" as it is here, the uploaded files are given distinct versions based on the date and time the files were uploaded. This helps when another project wants to download the jar file via a Maven dependency; in this case, it ensures that the latest 1.0-SNAPSHOT version is downloaded.

Viewing Package Registry Changes

Let's now switch back to see what is in the "MyShellPipeline" package registry. In Figure 10-40, we see that there is now one package with the link com/mycompany/app/my-app.[11] We also see feedback that this is a Maven package with version 1.0-SNAPSHOT. Different types of packages such as pypi would be listed here with different link paths appropriate to the type of package.

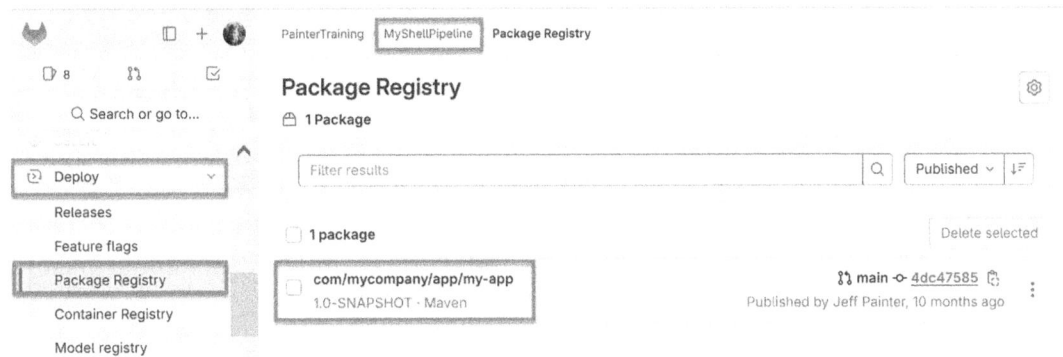

Figure 10-40. *List of Maven packages in the MyShellPipeline package registry*

Viewing Package Details in the Registry

Figure 10-41 shows the top of the page for the com/mycompany/app/my-app link. It provides feedback that this is a Maven package along with its storage size and when it was last downloaded. It also provides some helpful information about how to set up a dependency in a Maven pom.xml file that wants to use the jar file.

---

[11] This path is derived from the groupId and artifactId values in the pom.xml file, which in this example are com.mycompany.app and my-app, respectively.

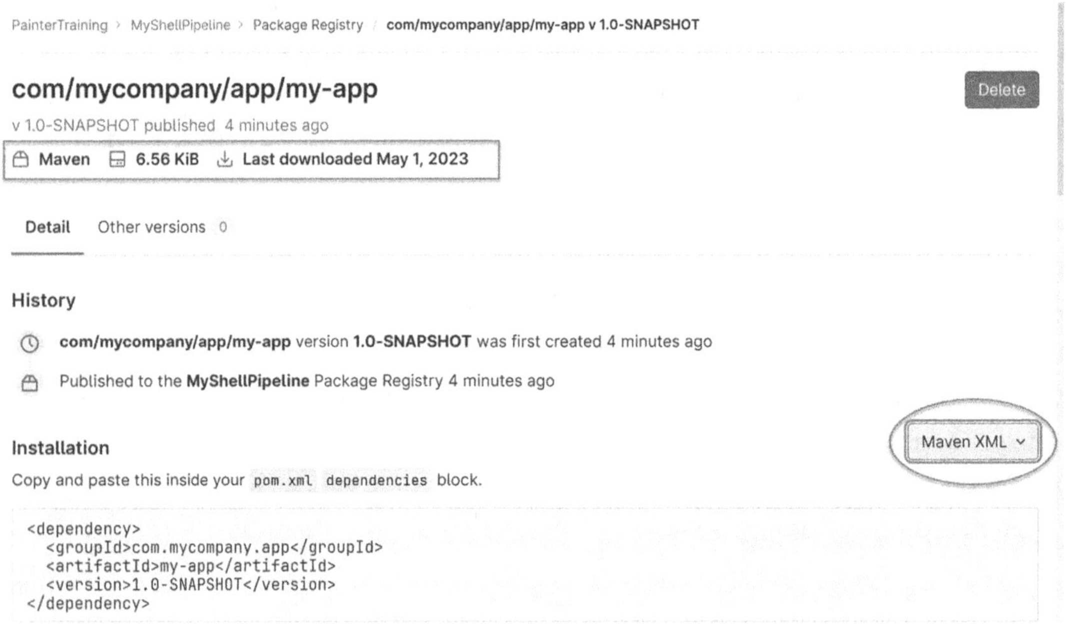

CHAPTER 10   IT'S NICE TO SHARE

PainterTraining > MyShellPipeline > Package Registry / **com/mycompany/app/my-app v 1.0-SNAPSHOT**

com/mycompany/app/my-app   [Delete]
v 1.0-SNAPSHOT published 4 minutes ago

🄼 Maven   🗔 6.56 KiB   ⤓ Last downloaded May 1, 2023

Detail   Other versions 0

History

⏱ **com/mycompany/app/my-app** version **1.0-SNAPSHOT** was first created 4 minutes ago

🄼 Published to the **MyShellPipeline** Package Registry 4 minutes ago

Installation   (Maven XML ⌄)
Copy and paste this inside your `pom.xml dependencies` block.

```
<dependency>
  <groupId>com.mycompany.app</groupId>
  <artifactId>my-app</artifactId>
  <version>1.0-SNAPSHOT</version>
</dependency>
```

***Figure 10-41.** Package detail view (part 1)*

Figure 10-42 shows more of that page describing how to set the "repositories" and "distributionManagement" sections in the pom.xml file. We've already set these sections in our pom.xml file; this information is mainly useful for developers who want to make use of our jar file.

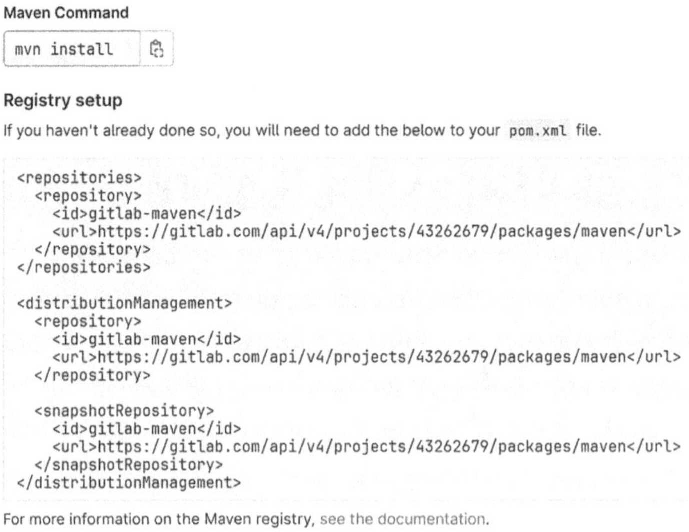

Maven Command

`mvn install` 📋

Registry setup

If you haven't already done so, you will need to add the below to your `pom.xml` file.

```
<repositories>
  <repository>
    <id>gitlab-maven</id>
    <url>https://gitlab.com/api/v4/projects/43262679/packages/maven</url>
  </repository>
</repositories>

<distributionManagement>
  <repository>
    <id>gitlab-maven</id>
    <url>https://gitlab.com/api/v4/projects/43262679/packages/maven</url>
  </repository>

  <snapshotRepository>
    <id>gitlab-maven</id>
    <url>https://gitlab.com/api/v4/projects/43262679/packages/maven</url>
  </snapshotRepository>
</distributionManagement>
```

For more information on the Maven registry, see the documentation.

***Figure 10-42.** Package detail view (part 2)*

CHAPTER 10   IT'S NICE TO SHARE

Finally, Figure 10-43 shows the "Assets" section found at the end of that page. This is where you will find the files uploaded to the registry as part of the Maven deploy step. Although you could download these files manually from this page, you would normally do this via Maven itself. You could also delete them if you wish, but unless you know what you are doing, it is best to keep them as is. Deleting packages that may be in use with other projects could create havoc within those projects.

For more information on the Maven registry, see the documentation.

Additional metadata

ⓘ App name: my-app

ⓘ App group: com.mycompany.app

Assets   Delete selected

	Name	Size	Created	
☐	⌄ 🗒 maven-metadata.xml	767 bytes	4 minutes ago	⋮
☐	⌄ 📄 my-app-1.0-20230501.181136-1.pom	3.05 KiB	4 minutes ago	⋮
☐	⌄ 🗃 my-app-1.0-20230501.181136-1.jar	2.75 KiB	4 minutes ago	⋮

Figure 10-43. *Package detail view (part 3)*

Effects of Multiple Pipeline Runs on the Package Registry

So, what happens when the project's pipeline is run multiple times? Figure 10-44 shows what the "Assets" section looks like when we deploy multiple snapshots of our jar file with Maven. As you can see, we get multiple copies of each file associated with each deploy. Note that this only happens with packages with snapshot versions; with specific release versions such as 1.0, only the first deployed set of files is saved. Multiple attempts to deploy the same release version will cause the deployment to fail.[12]

---

[12] This is part of the Maven contract regarding release versions. For projects that use a given release version, Maven knows to only download the product with that version if it hasn't already been downloaded. If it has, it won't redownload it again to save time. Because of this contract, Maven will not allow deployments of the same release version.

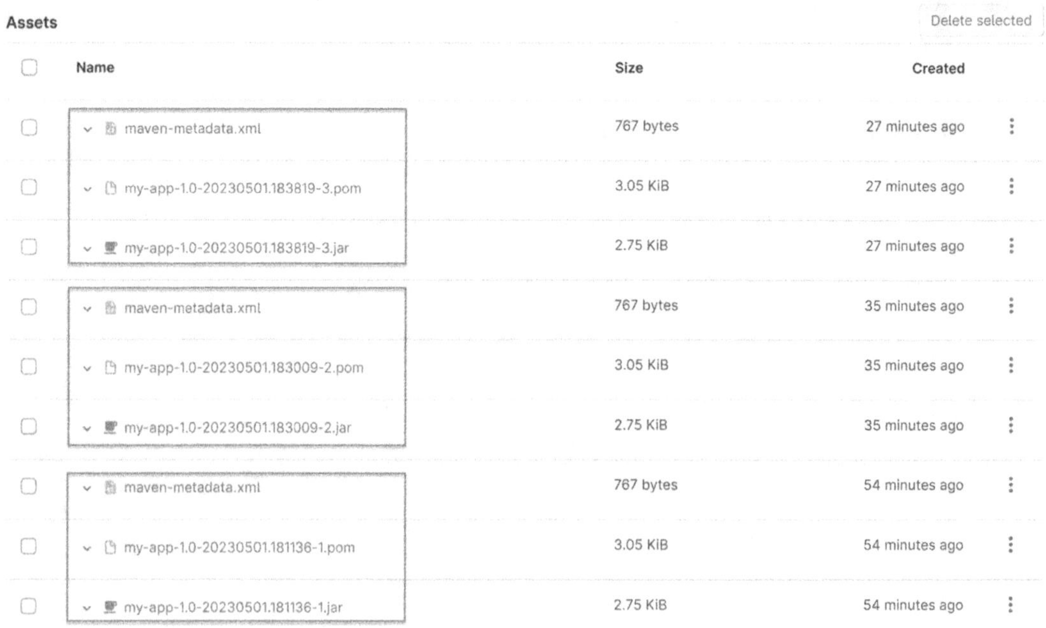

CHAPTER 10   IT'S NICE TO SHARE

Assets			
Name	Size	Created	
maven-metadata.xml	767 bytes	27 minutes ago	
my-app-1.0-20230501.183819-3.pom	3.05 KiB	27 minutes ago	
my-app-1.0-20230501.183819-3.jar	2.75 KiB	27 minutes ago	
maven-metadata.xml	767 bytes	35 minutes ago	
my-app-1.0-20230501.183009-2.pom	3.05 KiB	35 minutes ago	
my-app-1.0-20230501.183009-2.jar	2.75 KiB	35 minutes ago	
maven-metadata.xml	767 bytes	54 minutes ago	
my-app-1.0-20230501.181136-1.pom	3.05 KiB	54 minutes ago	
my-app-1.0-20230501.181136-1.jar	2.75 KiB	54 minutes ago	

Figure 10-44. *List of Maven snapshot assets after multiple pipeline runs*

Automating Cleanup of the Package Registry

As you might guess, this package registry could end up holding a lot of snapshot assets. So, is there a way to automate the cleanup of these assets as there is for container registry images? Figure 10-45 shows the "Manage storage used by package assets" section of the project's "Package and registries" settings. Here, you can specify how many duplicate assets to keep around. By default, it is all. In this example, I am setting it to 1. Note that if there is a lot of activity regarding this product, setting it to 10 might be more appropriate to avoid issues when a project is trying to download an earlier version just when a new snapshot version is being uploaded.

CHAPTER 10   IT'S NICE TO SHARE

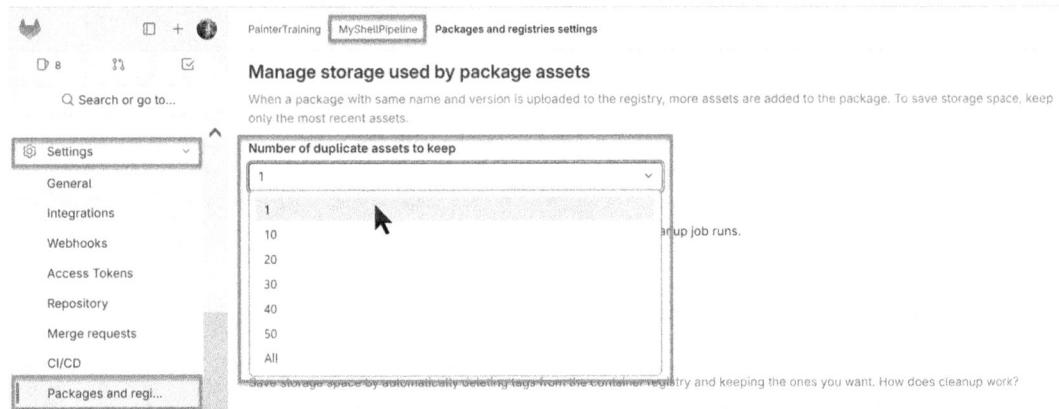

Figure 10-45. *Package registry storage settings to control space usage*

Different package types have their own way of storing them into the package repository and retrieving them from it. Since there are a large number of package types, I'll leave it to you to search the GitLab documentation on how to publish and share the package types you are interested in. The list of package types that GitLab supports will grow over time.

Summary

To summarize, we covered the following topics in this chapter:

- Described how to modify a pipeline to store Docker images in a container registry

- Discussed various ways to define and use security credentials known as tokens

- Showed how to download Docker images to other projects as well as outside of GitLab

- Demonstrated how to upload binary objects to a project's package registry

- Considered ways of cleaning items automatically from container and package registries

In the next chapter, we'll look at how to use GitLab's API features to automate maintenance tasks from scripts run outside of GitLab.

417

CHAPTER 11

There's an API for That

Up to now, almost everything we have done has been directly through the GitLab UI or remotely using Git commands. There are times, though, when you, as a developer or administrator, want to create automation scripts to do routine maintenance not provided by GitLab through its UI. For these situations, GitLab has provided an Application Programming Interface (API). In fact, there are two APIs provided by GitLab: the REST API and the GraphQL API.

In this chapter, we will describe the two APIs provided by GitLab and how to use them in scripts. We will also cover the interactive GraphiQL tool that you can use to formulate GraphQL queries. Finally, we will cover the structure of the GraphQL reference documentation since it can be a bit tricky at first to navigate.

Introducing the GitLab REST API

The GitLab REST API is one of two types of APIs provided by GitLab, the other being the GitLab GraphQL API. The REST API is the older of the two technologies and is the one we'll focus on first.

Differences Between GitLab UI and REST API URLs

When we set up the package manager for the "MyShellPipeline" project, you might have noticed the strange-looking URL used by Maven to access packages in our registry. For the "MyShellPipeline" registry, it looks like the following:

```
https://gitlab.com/api/v4/projects/43262679/packages/maven
```

This URL is different from the URLs you typically see when accessing pages from the GitLab UI. For example, the following URL displays the project overview page for the "MyShellPipeline" project:

CHAPTER 11   THERE'S AN API FOR THAT

> https://gitlab.com/paintertraining/myshellpipeline

The key difference between these two URLs is the presence of /api/v4 in the registry URL, which is not present in the project overview URL. The registry URL is an example of the GitLab REST API. Beside using /api in the URL, the /v4 indicates that this is the fourth version of the GitLab REST API. There were previous versions of the API that have evolved over time and are no longer available with the latest versions of GitLab. The /v4 remains in the URL in case there is a newer version of the API in the future.

Differences Between GitLab UI and REST API Responses

The other difference is what is returned to the web browser. Figure 11-1 shows the page source sent to the browser for the "MyShellPipeline" project page. Here, we see that the content returned for this project page is an HTML document, which your browser interprets to provide the visual elements you see.

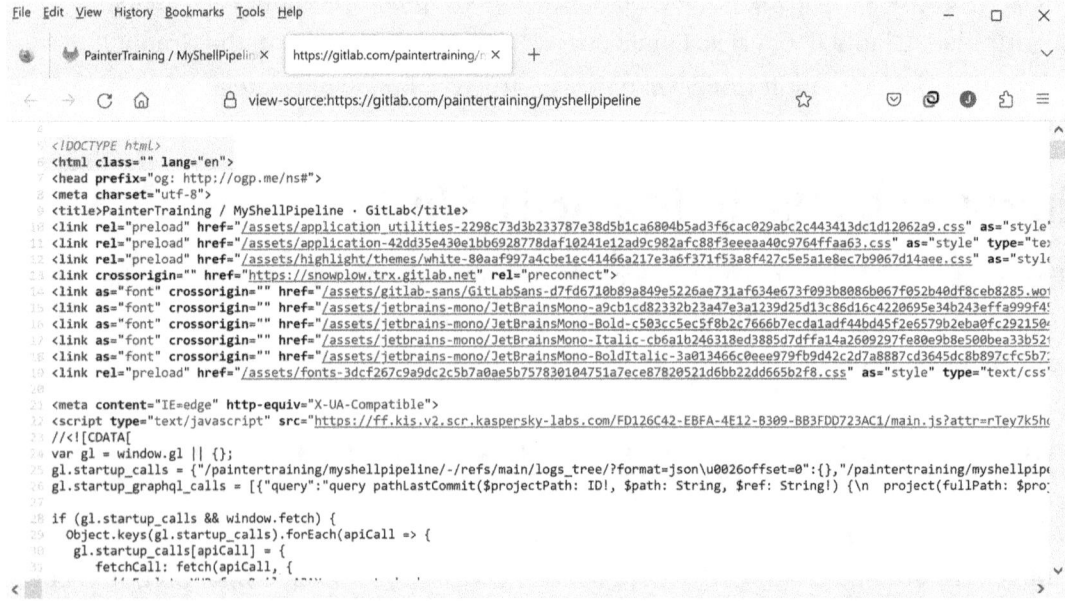

Figure 11-1. Browser page source for the MyShellPipeline project

The API URL returns something completely different, however. Figure 11-2 shows the result of using the API URL without the /maven piece. What you see in the browser is the JSON document returned by the API URL. Note that different browsers will show

420

CHAPTER 11 THERE'S AN API FOR THAT

this differently. What this JSON document tells us is that there is a package in the registry with id 14296434, name com/mycompany/app/my-app, and package type "maven," among other things.

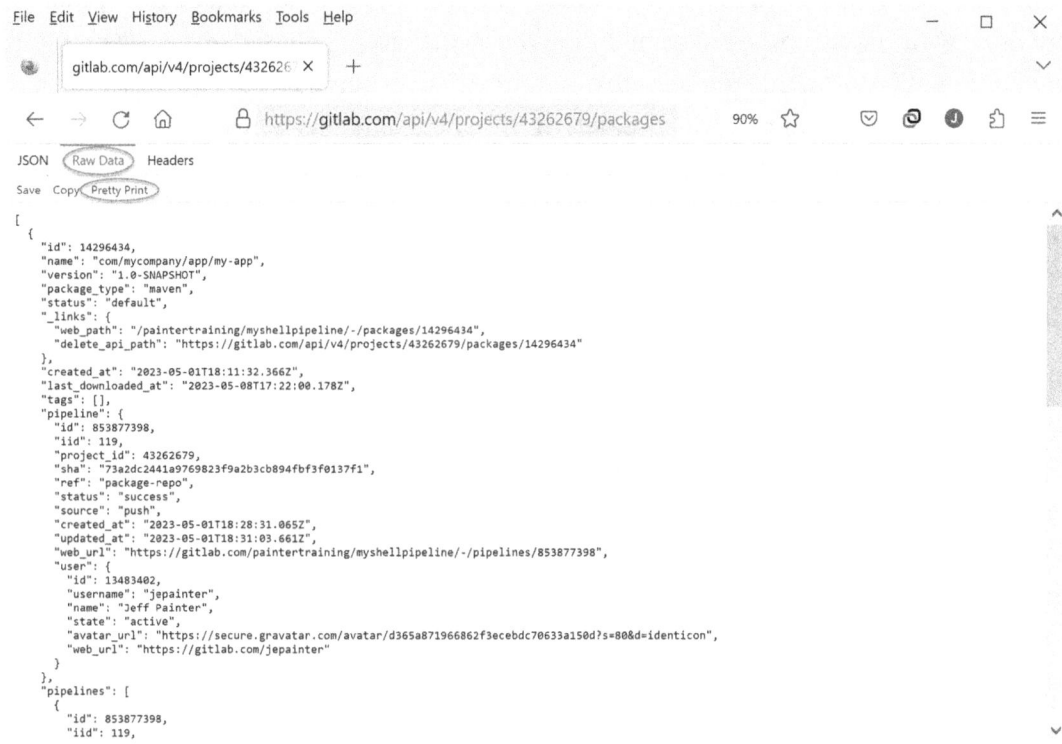

***Figure 11-2.** JSON document returned for the API URL*

REST API Basics

You can find the full documentation of the GitLab REST API at https://docs.gitlab.com/ee/api/rest/. There is a lot to digest there, so we'll go through some of the basics here to get you comfortable using it. Here is some history first. The REST API was developed to use the HTTP protocol to retrieve and push information using the standard HTTP methods of GET, PUT, POST, and DELETE. This is in contrast to other APIs such as the SOAP API that uses XML to request and retrieve data. REST is adopted by GitLab since it is easier to use than SOAP.

One of the nice features of using the REST API with GitLab is that you can use the web browser to explore resource retrieval via the HTTP GET method, which is the default mode when you enter a URL in the browser. It's also useful to use the browser since authentication is built in (assuming you've logged in to GitLab, of course). We'll use this feature of the web browser to test some basic queries; we'll explore how to use the REST API outside of the browser in a later section.

It's important to note that just like some features are based on the license tier you are using with GitLab, there are some API requests that are also based on the license tier. In addition, there are some requests that require Administrator access or are restricted based on your role. Your role will also determine what content is returned in the JSON document, so not everyone will see the same result. These restrictions are clearly noted in the GitLab API documentation.

GitLab REST API Resources

For the REST API, GitLab defines three types of resources: projects, groups, and standalone. You can tell what type of resource is being used based on what appears after the /api/v4 portion of the URL. Project resources start with /projects, and group resources start with /groups. Standalone resources are all other resources that do not start with /projects or /groups; for example, user resources start with /users. If you end the URL with just the resource type, you will typically get a list of all resources available to you. Figure 11-3 shows the list of groups that I can access from gitlab.com, which in my case are "PainterTraining" and "Special Projects."

CHAPTER 11   THERE'S AN API FOR THAT

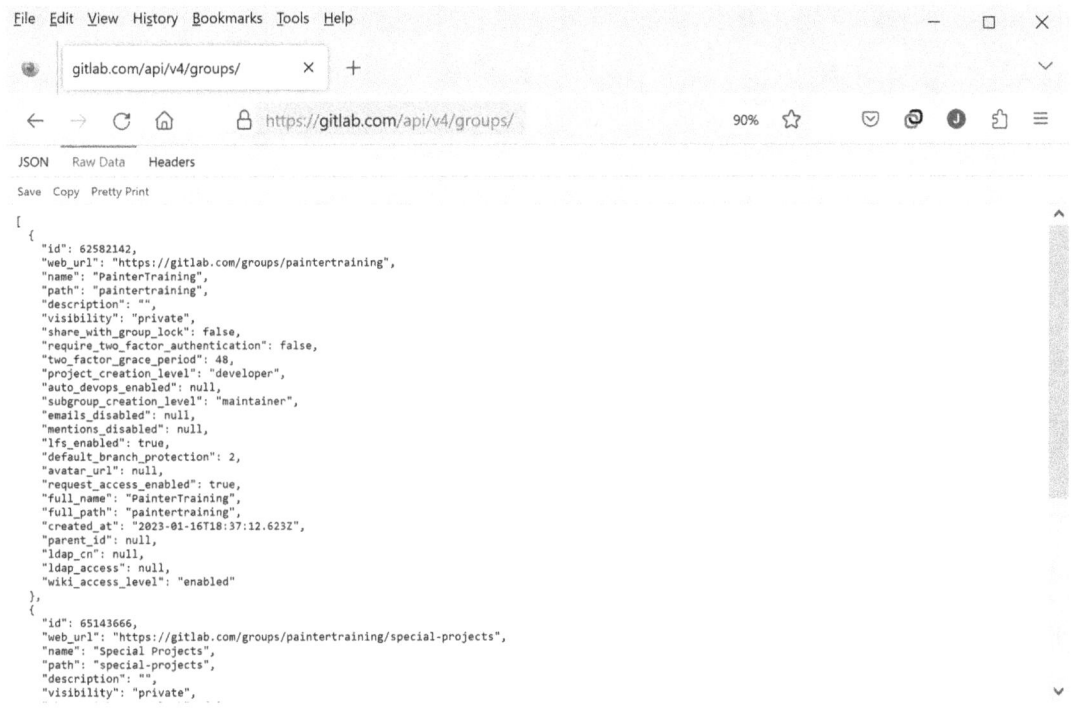

Figure 11-3. *Group listing API response*

Restricting Resources with URL Endpoints

You restrict the resource by adding the resource id following the resource type. For example, Figure 11-4 shows the results specific to the group with id 62582142. Note that more information is provided here than in the previous "all groups" request. This is done to reduce the amount of information returned by the "all groups" query. Imagine how large the JSON document would be if the all group query returned all projects for every group. Just enough information is returned by the all group query so that you can filter groups based on that information and then "drill down" to specific groups one by one to access their projects.

CHAPTER 11   THERE'S AN API FOR THAT

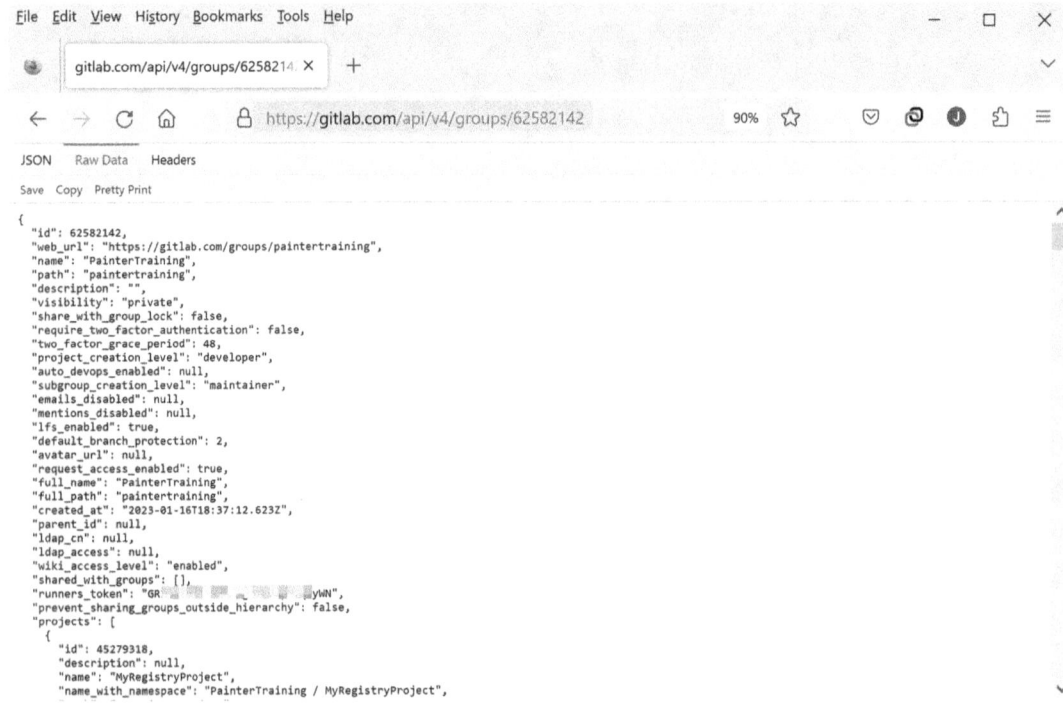

Figure 11-4.   Group detail API response

Restricting Results with URL Parameters

You can also restrict API results using URL parameters that are specific to the resource. For example, in the group listing shown earlier, you get all groups for which you have access including subgroups. If you have a lot of groups, you may only want to see the top-level groups. For this, you can add the top_level_only parameter as shown in Figure 11-5. Parameters follow the standard URL parameter convention with the question mark (?) marking the start of the parameters and the ampersand (&) separating each parameter when there is more than one.

CHAPTER 11 THERE'S AN API FOR THAT

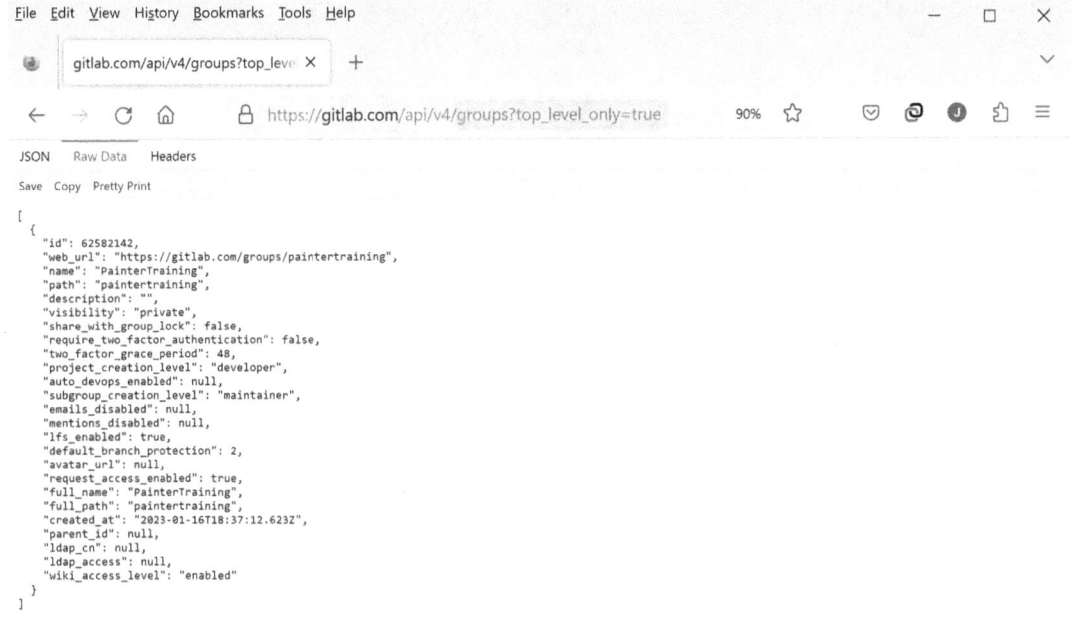

Figure 11-5. Group top-level only API response

Requesting Additional Information with URL Endpoints

Whereas parameters are used to filter results, some resources use additional endpoints to provide additional information. For example, Figure 11-6 shows how to list all subgroups for a given group by adding the "subgroups" endpoint. And Figure 11-7 shows how to list all deploy tokens for a given group using the "deploy_tokens" endpoint.

Chapter 11 THERE'S AN API FOR THAT

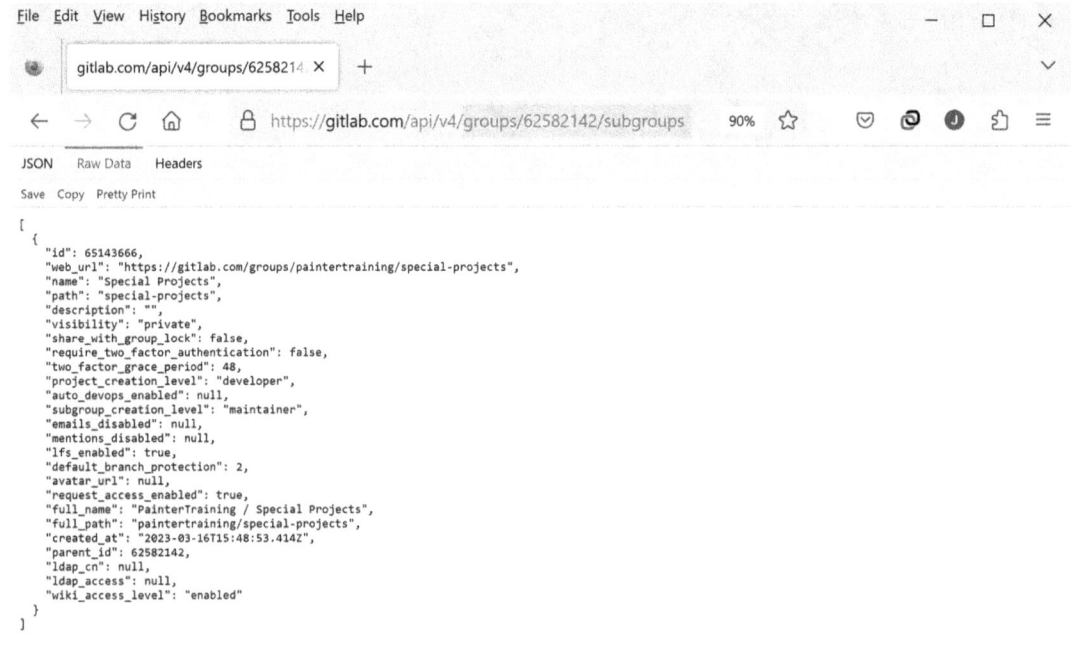

Figure 11-6. Subgroup listing from group API response

Figure 11-7. Deploy token listing from group API response

CHAPTER 11   THERE'S AN API FOR THAT

URL Endpoint Patterns

Note that the pattern of an endpoint that gives a list of items followed by an id to show the details of an item can continue. For example, Figure 11-8 shows how to list all the members of a particular group using the members endpoint. In this example, the "PainterTraining" group has two members, me and Heidi. Adding my id to the end of the members endpoint provides details about myself as shown in Figure 11-9.

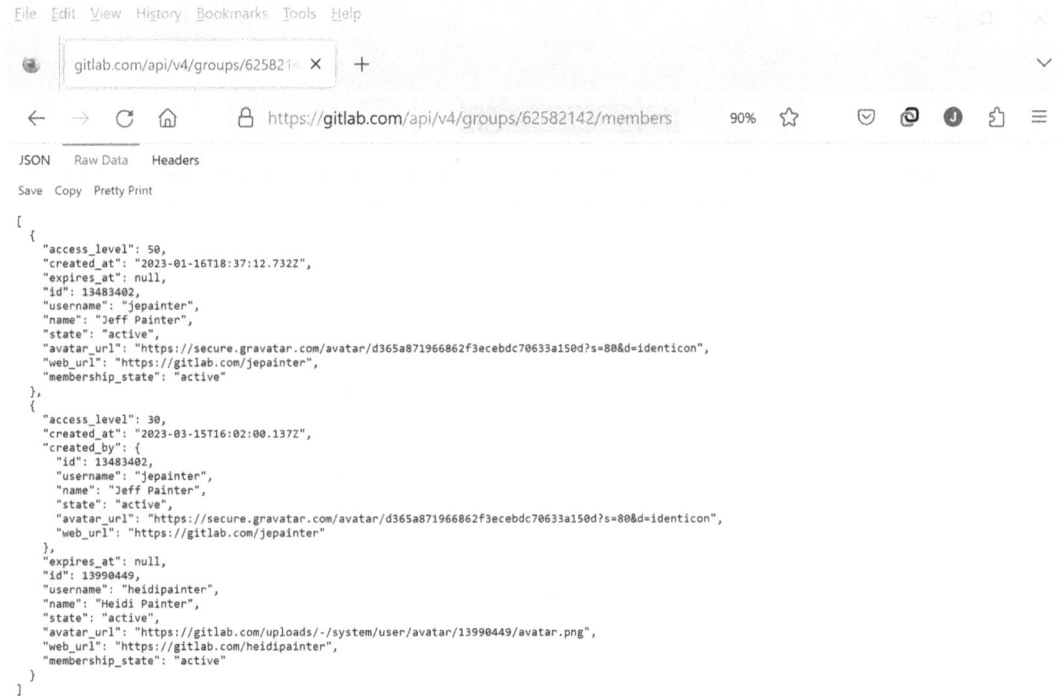

Figure 11-8. *Member listing for group API response*

427

CHAPTER 11   THERE'S AN API FOR THAT

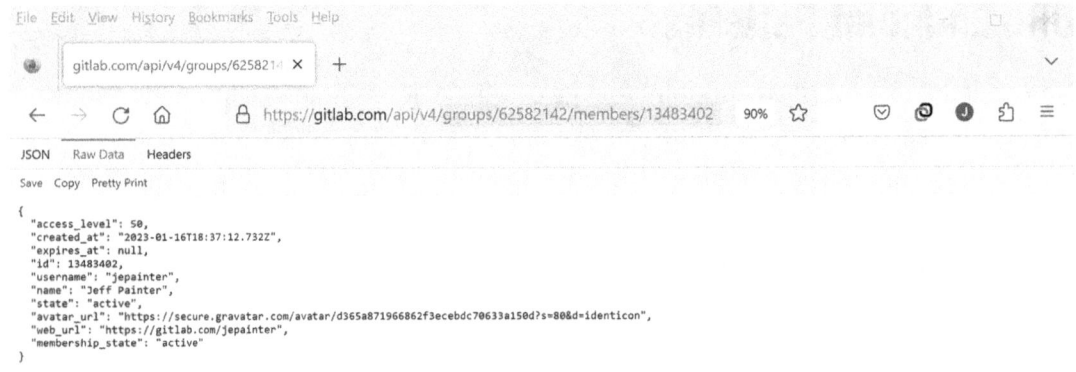

Figure 11-9. Group member detail API response

Paginating Responses

In the examples so far, there were only a small number of resources returned: two groups, two group members, one deploy token, etc. In these cases, the JSON document returned was a reasonable size. But what if a resource contains a large number of items, say 100 or more? You can imagine that the JSON document could get quite large as well as be slow to create and download for a given HTTPS request. For these cases, the GitLab API uses a pagination concept where a given request returns only a small portion of the overall results. Figure 11-10 shows what is returned for the "projects" resource.

CHAPTER 11   THERE'S AN API FOR THAT

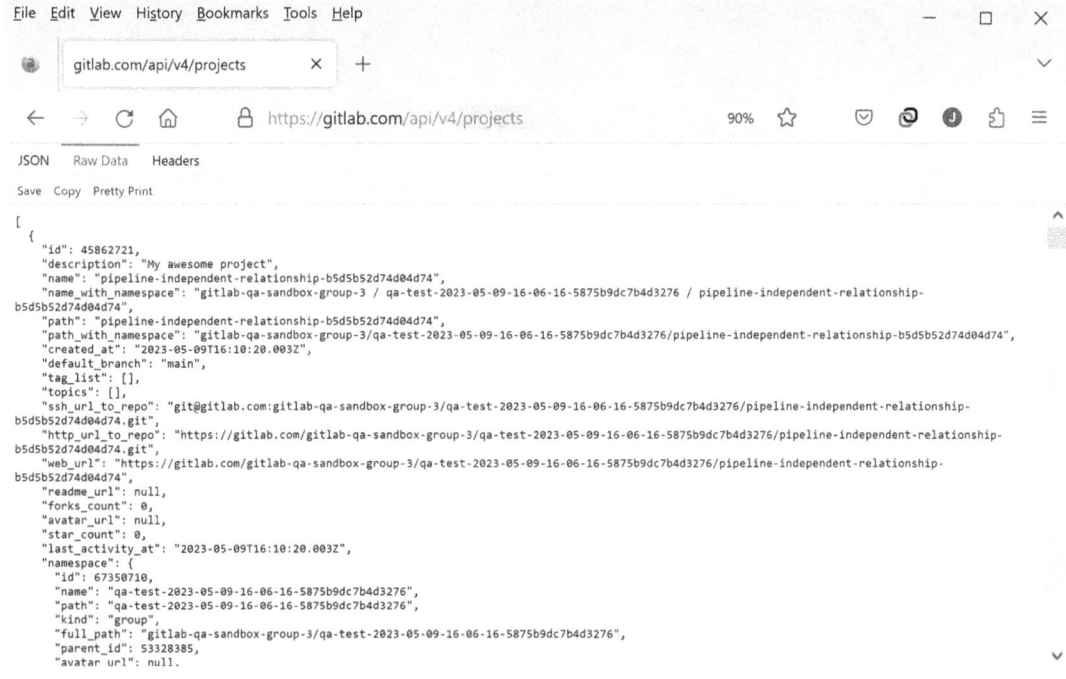

***Figure 11-10.** Projects listing API response*

First of all, note that the request is returning a lot more than what I was expecting; it is returning all public projects that I have access to but am not a member of. And there are a lot of them. You can't see this from this screenshot, but only 20 projects were returned, and none of them were ones that I created. This is the pagination feature in effect. How can we tell if this is the case? And how can we tell what page we are on? It turns out that this information is returned via the HTTP response header as shown in Figure 11-11. Here, we see various attributes that tell us how many items there are per page (x-per-page), what page we are on (x-page), and what the next and previous pages are (x-next-page and x-prev-page).

429

CHAPTER 11 THERE'S AN API FOR THAT

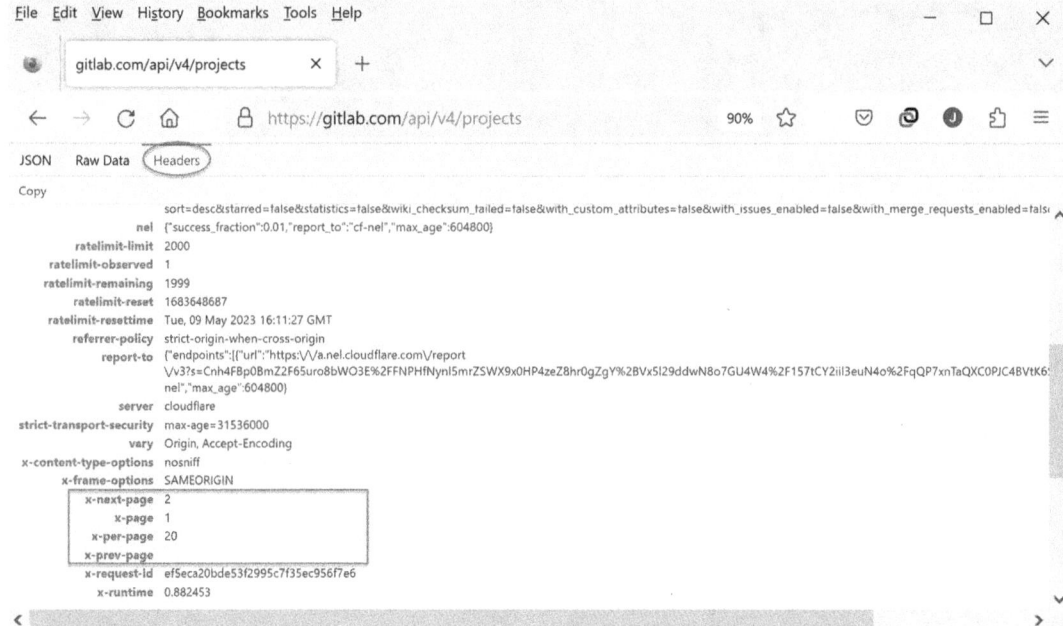

Figure 11-11. Projects listing API response header

Retrieving Additional Pages

Now that we know the results are being paginated, how do we see another page? For this we use the page parameter as shown in Figure 11-12. The JSON document returned with this query has the next 20 items. Figure 11-13 shows the values of the various page attributes for the page 2 request. You'll know when you are on the last page when x-next-page has no value just as we saw that x-prev-page had no value on the first page. Obviously, paging this way via the web browser is pretty painful. We'll talk about how to automate the paging process when we discuss how to use the GitLab REST API outside of the web browser using tools like curl.

CHAPTER 11 THERE'S AN API FOR THAT

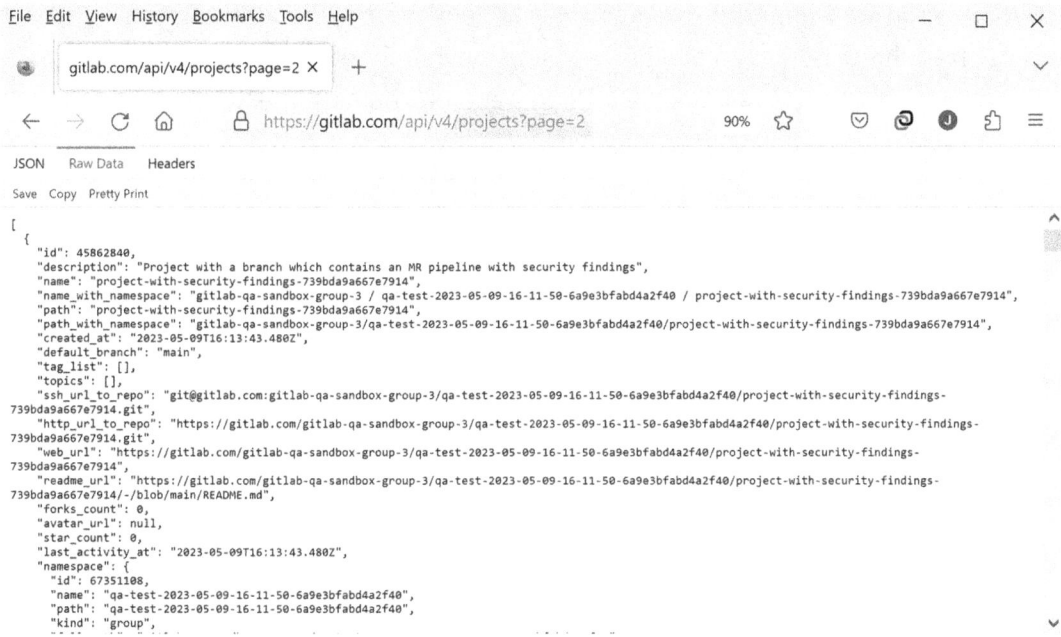

Figure 11-12. *Page 2 of projects listing API response*

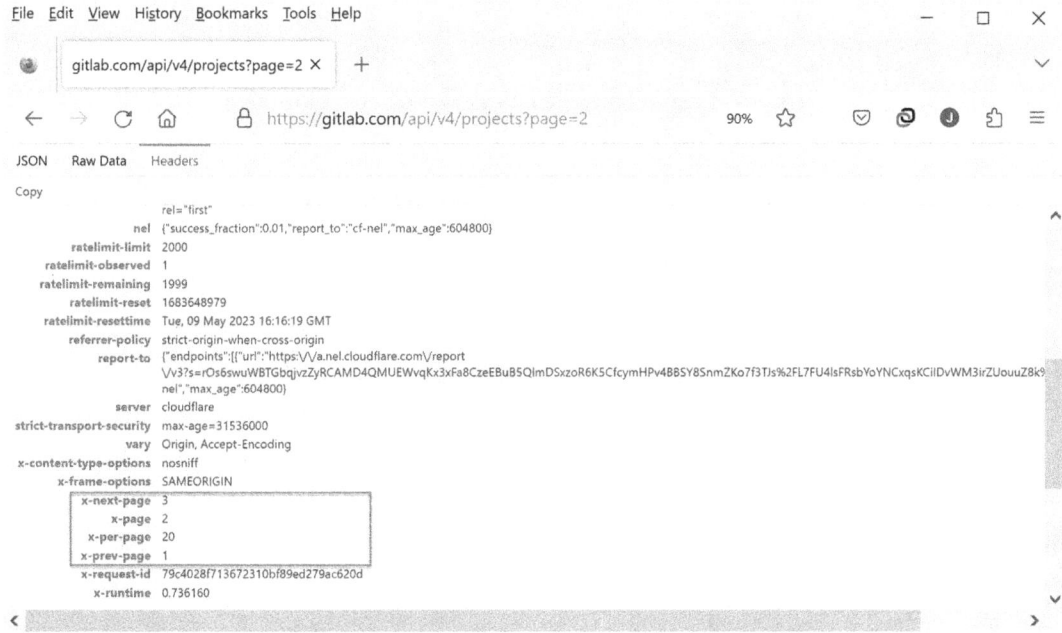

Figure 11-13. *Page 2 of projects listing API response header*

CHAPTER 11   THERE'S AN API FOR THAT

In case you are wondering, there is a way to filter out projects where I am a member. Figure 11-14 shows how to create this list using the membership parameter. Although not shown in this screenshot, the JSON document returned just the five projects that I've created so far without the need for pagination.

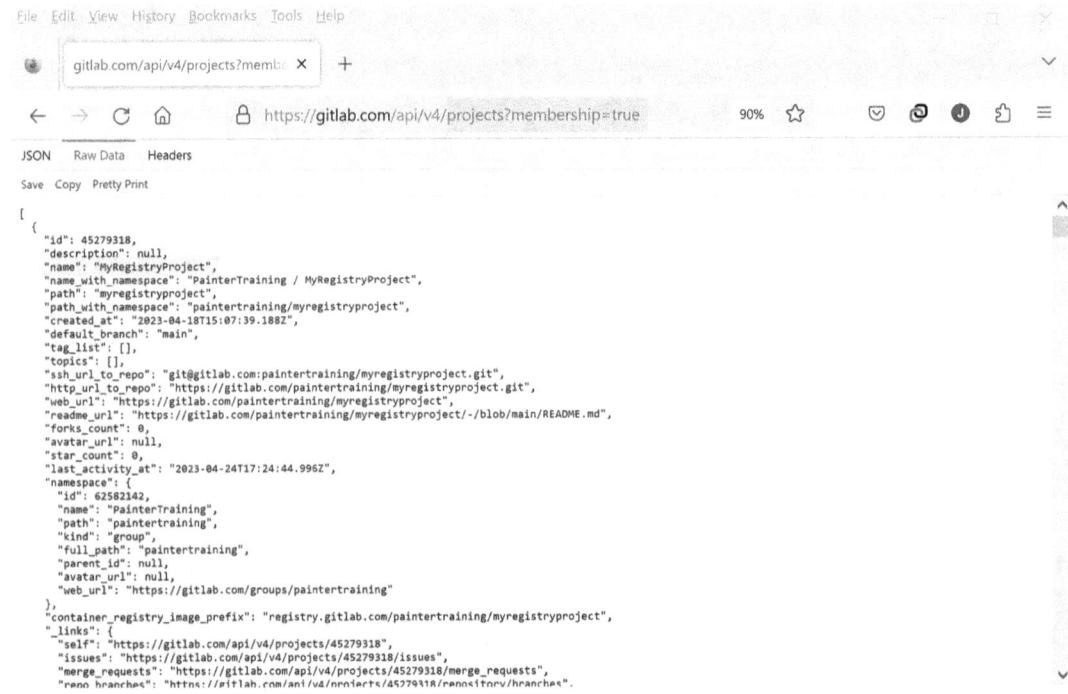

Figure 11-14. Projects listing for given member API response

Standalone Resource Examples

Now that we've explored some of the group and project resources, let's briefly look at the standalone category of resources. This category of resources includes all resources that are not directly tied to groups or projects. The "users" resource is one such resource. When you use just the /users endpoint, you end up listing all users on the gitlab.com or self-managed site. Like projects, it will return results using the pagination mechanism. Rather than show that, I'll instead filter the results by doing a search for my name.[1] The results are shown in Figure 11-15. Since spaces cannot be used directly in a URL, I had to

---

[1] You can search for just part of a name. I used my full name since searching for Painter returned a lot of users with that last name. Who knew?

CHAPTER 11   THERE'S AN API FOR THAT

use the special %20 code to represent the space. What may surprise you (as it did me) is that there are two of me registered as a user on the gitlab.com site. It turns out that both of them are indeed me. The jepainte username was my work username; the jepainter username is currently my personal user account.

Figure 11-15. *User search API response*

My final example using the API via the web browser is shown in Figure 11-16. Since I am not an administrator of the gitlab.com site, the query only returns my personal access tokens. Now you might think that access to these tokens would be via the user resource as in /users/6384121/personal_access_tokens. Oddly, it does not. However, creating a personal access token does go through that endpoint, although you have to be an admin to create the token. All other actions with respect to personal access tokens, such as retrieving or revoking a token, use the /personal_access_tokens resource.

433

CHAPTER 11 THERE'S AN API FOR THAT

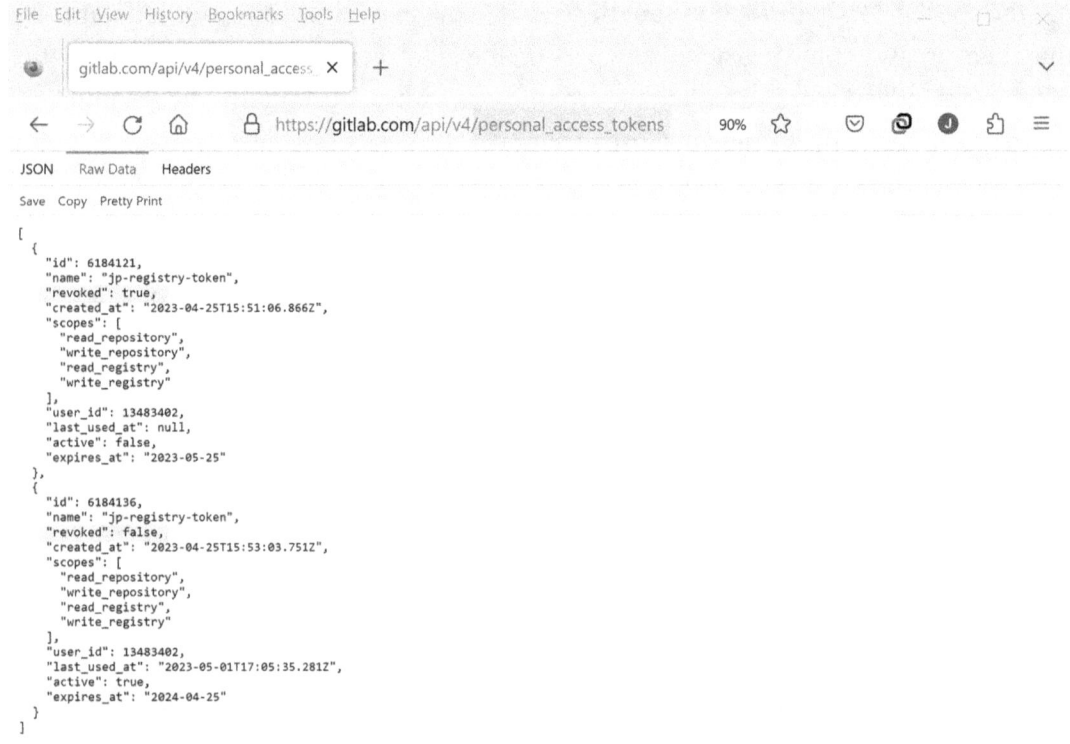

***Figure 11-16.** Personal access tokens API response*

We've seen how to make REST API requests through the browser. The next section describes how to make REST API requests using the Linux tool called curl.

RESTing with Curl

As useful as it is to run GitLab REST API queries from the web browser, it isn't how the API is used in practice. After all, the P in API stands for programming, so it makes sense to make queries from a programmatic context outside of the GitLab web interface. There are many ways to make queries, especially from programming languages such as Java or Python. Using these languages requires some in-depth understanding of the libraries or modules provided by them to make HTTP requests and process JSON documents. So rather than querying the GitLab API through these interfaces, we'll instead use the standard Unix/Linux curl command. This is the approach described in the GitLab API documentation.

Setting Up Authentication to Make API Requests

In order to make API requests via curl, we need to set up authentication to allow requests. We didn't need to do this via the web browser as it was handled behind the scenes via cookies when we logged in to gitlab.com. Looking at the documentation, there are a number of authentication mechanisms available for the API. The one that is available to us via the free version of GitLab is the personal access token. With paid versions of GitLab, we would also have group and project access tokens available; their usage isn't any different from the personal access token. Note that group and project deploy tokens, which we used for accessing the package and container registries, cannot be used in this context since their authorizations are limited to those registries and the Git repository.

In a previous chapter, I set up a personal access token to access the package and container registries. That token, however, can't be used to query the API since we limited it to just the Git repository and the various registries. Figure 11-17 shows how I created a personal access token just for API access. Here, I just selected the "api" option to enable read and write access via the REST API. Although it is tempting to just create a token that has full access to everything, it's generally a good practice to create separate tokens with different authorizations in case the token becomes compromised.

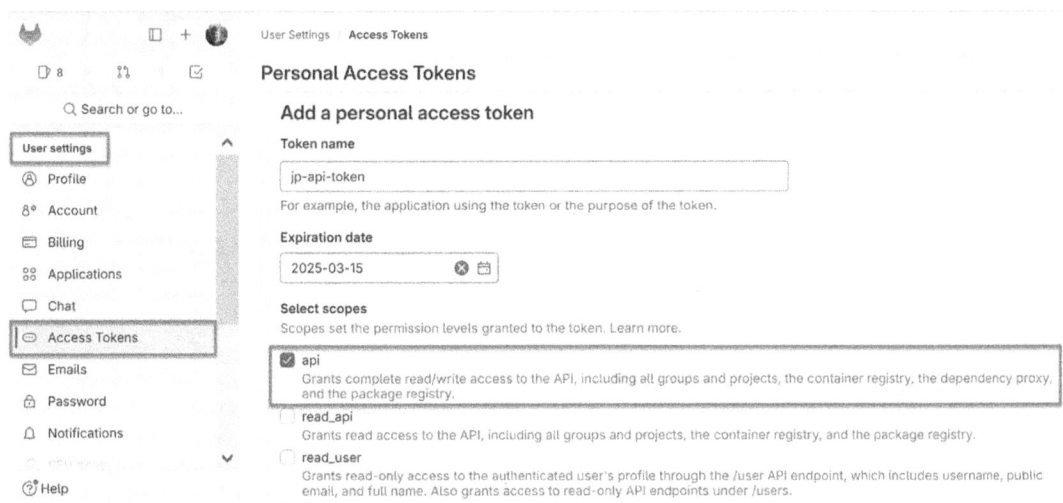

Figure 11-17. Personal access token for API creation

CHAPTER 11 THERE'S AN API FOR THAT

A Simple REST API Query with Curl

With the new access token created, let's make a simple query with curl to list groups that I have access to, just as we did in the first web browser query. Figure 11-18 shows the curl query and its results. I chose to use the header PRIVATE-TOKEN method of passing my personal access token rather than passing it as a parameter to the query as I prefer this method. Only the personal access token needs to be passed for authentication (which is partially blurred out in this example); the username is not specified since GitLab can determine that from the token.

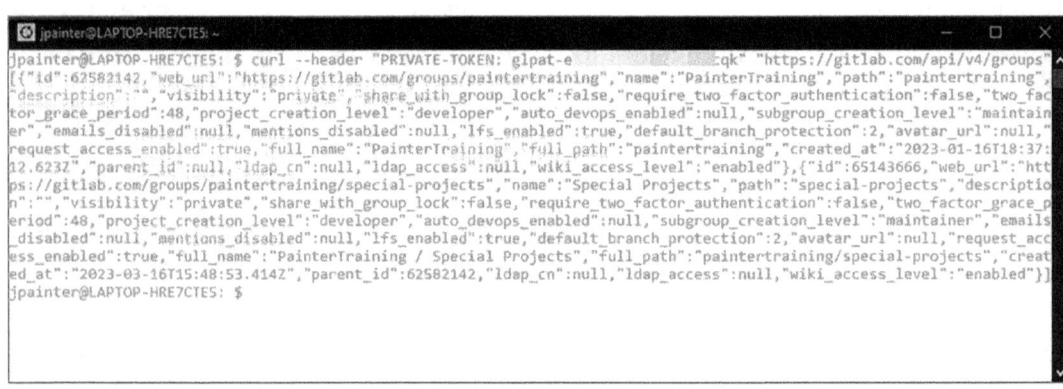

Figure 11-18. API request using curl (in Linux)

The result of the curl API request is a single line containing the JSON document. It is returned in this flattened form rather than in a pretty-printed form since it is expected to be used by a program rather than a user. Unfortunately, this flattened form isn't very useful to us in examining the results. So, is there a way to pretty-print the results so that we can better see the JSON document structure? Although curl has a lot of command-line options, pretty-printing JSON documents isn't one of them.[2]

---

[2] This makes sense since curl can be used to return all sorts of output formats such as html responses, not just JSON documents.

Using jq to Manipulate JSON Responses

In terms of processing JSON documents, there turns out to be another Unix/Linux command-line tool that is extremely useful: jq.[3] The jq tool is a general-purpose tool for querying JSON documents that also provides a way to pretty-print JSON documents. You install jq using the package manager that comes with your flavor of Linux. Figure 11-19 shows the steps used to install jq on an Ubuntu server. It involves doing a "sudo apt update" followed by "sudo apt -y install jq." Other package managers have a similar process for installing jq.

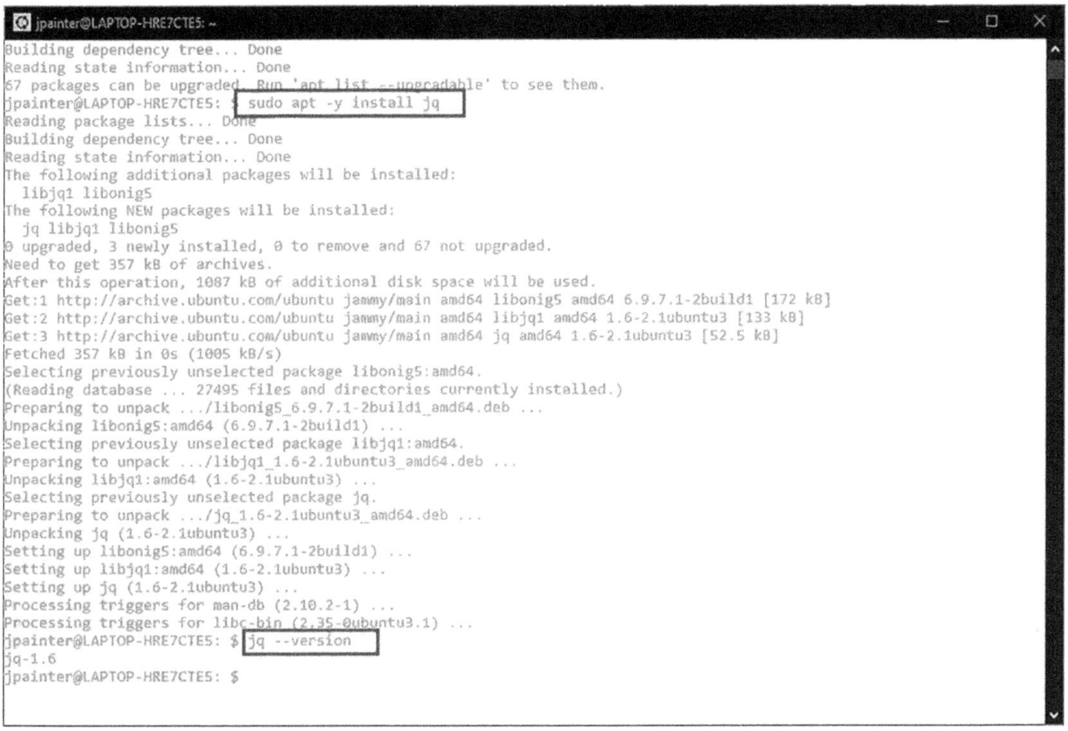

Figure 11-19. Installing jq in Linux

---

[3] The command jq stands for JSON Query Language. Yes, it probably should have been called jql, but in keeping with the Unix tradition of reducing the amount of typing, jq it is.

CHAPTER 11   THERE'S AN API FOR THAT

Using jq to Pretty-Print REST API Responses

One of the simplest uses of jq is to pretty-print a JSON document that is provided as the standard input to the command. Figure 11-20 shows how to do this with our "groups" API request. In this example, I set MY_API_TOKEN to the value of my personal access token, which I inserted into my .bashrc file; this simplifies future examples as I don't have to blur the token out every time. The -s with curl is to keep additional output silent.[4] Taken with no query statements, jq simply takes the standard input and pretty-prints it. By default, it will colorize the output, which doesn't work so well with some color schemes, so in this example, I use -M to "monochrome" the output. If you compare the results using curl with the results from the web browser, you'll see that it returns the same information.

Figure 11-20. Using jq to pretty-print JSON results from curl

---

[4] The curl command checks to see if the output is going to the terminal and only displays the JSON document. When piping it to other commands or redirecting it to an output file, curl provides status information on how the request is proceeding, which can get annoying sometimes when feeding the output to jq.

CHAPTER 11 THERE'S AN API FOR THAT

Since this is Linux, you can also redirect the pretty-printed output to a file, which is useful when dealing with large JSON documents. Figure 11-21 shows the same query redirected to the file result.json. Since the output is being redirected to a file, we don't need to use the -M option. With the results captured in a file, you can use your favorite editor to view it and do simple searches.

```
jpainter@LAPTOP-HRE7CTE5: $ curl -s --header "PRIVATE-TOKEN: $MY_API_TOKEN" "https://gitlab.com/api/v4/groups" | jq > result.json
jpainter@LAPTOP-HRE7CTE5: $ head result.json
[
  {
    "id": 62582142,
    "web_url": "https://gitlab.com/groups/paintertraining",
    "name": "PainterTraining",
    "path": "paintertraining",
    "description": "",
    "visibility": "private",
    "share_with_group_lock": false,
    "require_two_factor_authentication": false,
jpainter@LAPTOP-HRE7CTE5: $
```

Figure 11-21. *Redirecting JSON output of the curl request to a file*

Using curl and jq in this way, you can now go through all the different queries we made with the web browser in the previous section. Since the results will be the same, I'll forgo repeating those queries here; you can do this as an exercise if you so choose. But note that we can do more than just repeat queries we've done before. Remember that jq is a query tool, so we can use jq to do much more than pretty-print a JSON document. We can use jq to extract information from the JSON document that can be used in an automation task. Since the GitLab REST API doesn't provide a way to extract just the information we need, we have to rely on a tool such as jq to do that for us.[5]

Using jq to Extract Information from REST API Responses

Learning jq is beyond the scope of this book. I'll give a few examples of how to use jq to extract information from a JSON document. Figure 11-22 provides a few examples using the result.json file created in the previous example. The key operator is the dot (.)

---

[5] This is one of the downsides to using the REST API since it returns all of the information for a given request, which can result in a large document payload. It is similar to making a database query where all of the columns in a database table are returned. The GitLab GraphQL API was designed to extract just the information you are interested in at the cost of being more complex to use.

439

CHAPTER 11 THERE'S AN API FOR THAT

operator that separates each item to be extracted. Since the result.json file contains a top-level list of items, we use ".[]" to extract (i.e., drill down) each item from the list. The .name then extracts the name from each list item. If we were interested in just the first item's name, we could have done ".[0].name". The second example retrieves the "full_path" value from each list item.

```
jpainter@LAPTOP-HRE7CTE5:~$ jq ".[].name" result.json
"PainterTraining"
"Special Projects"
jpainter@LAPTOP-HRE7CTE5:~$ jq ".[].full_path" result.json
"paintertraining"
"paintertraining/special-projects"
jpainter@LAPTOP-HRE7CTE5:~$ jq ".[] | {id,full_path}" result.json
{
  : 62582142,
           : "paintertraining"
}
{
  : 65143666,
           : "paintertraining/special-projects"
}
jpainter@LAPTOP-HRE7CTE5:~$ jq ".[] | [.id,.full_path]" result.json
[
  62582142,
  "paintertraining"
]
[
  65143666,
  "paintertraining/special-projects"
]
jpainter@LAPTOP-HRE7CTE5:~$
```

Figure 11-22. *Examples of simple queries using jq*

In addition to the dot operator, there is the pipe operator (|) that takes the previous structure and applies additional operations on it similar to the pipe operator in Unix/Linux. In the third example, we use the pipe operator with the dictionary constructor to extract the id and full path items from each list item and create a set of key-value pairs (a.k.a. a dictionary). Note that the output is not a JSON document. The fourth example does the same but uses the list constructor to create a set of id and full_path value lists.

There is a lot to the jq query language, which I'll leave for you to explore. If you want to learn more about how to use jq, you can check out the jq manual at https://stedolan.github.io/jq/manual/. Like the Linux awk tool, it can take a bit of learning and experimenting to use it effectively.

CHAPTER 11   THERE'S AN API FOR THAT

Using Programming Languages to Manipulate REST API Responses

Using jq is great for one-off queries, but if you want to do some more serious transformations of the JSON document(s) returned from curl, I suggest looking at a programming language such as Python. It has a nice module called json that can read a JSON document and convert it into a Python data structure composed of lists and dictionaries. Once converted, you can use standard Python operators and functions to filter and extract the information you want in the form you want it. You can also combine the json module with the httplib2 or httpx modules to make the HTTP requests in lieu of curl. This is particularly useful for generating reports and handling multiple paging requests.

Using Curl to Manipulate Resources

Let's switch gears and look at how we can use curl to create and delete objects. This is done via the HTTP POST and DELETE methods. By default, when using curl, you create HTTP requests that use the GET method implicitly. To use a different method, you use curl's request parameter with the method in uppercase, for example, curl --request DELETE. To experiment with these methods, let's look at how we can create and delete a project deploy token.

Creating a Resource with the REST API

To create an object, you use the POST method (which, BTW, is what happens when you fill out a web form and submit it). Using the POST method requires passing web parameters for the fields specific to the object you are creating. Some parameters are required, and some are optional. For the project deploy token, you can see what parameters you need from the documentation at https://docs.gitlab.com/ee/api/deploy_tokens.html#create-a-project-deploy-token. From the documentation, you find that we need an id (which is sent as part of the request path), a name, and an array of scopes. Optionally, we can set the "expires_at" and "username" fields.

For this example, I'm going to create a read-only deploy token for "MyRegistryProject" whose project id is 45279318. Figure 11-23 shows the contents of the script create_deploy_token.sh I created to generate the deploy token and the results

CHAPTER 11   THERE'S AN API FOR THAT

of running it. I gave it an expiration date but not a username, letting GitLab generate one for me. The JSON result lists the contents of the new deploy token, including the secret token, which is the only time it shows up, so will need to be copied in order to use the deploy token.

```
jpainter@LAPTOP-HRE7CTE5:~$ cat create_deploy_token.sh
#!/bin/bash

curl --request POST --header "PRIVATE-TOKEN: $MY_API_TOKEN" --header "Content-Type: application/json" \
    --data '{"name": "my-read-token", "expires_at": "2024-01-01", "scopes": ["read_registry", "read_package_registry"]}' \
    "https://gitlab.com/api/v4/projects/45279318/deploy_tokens/"

jpainter@LAPTOP-HRE7CTE5:~$ ./create_deploy_token.sh
{"id":2050155,"name":"my-read-token","username":"gitlab+deploy-token-2050155","expires_at":"2024-01-01T00:00:00.000Z","scopes":["read_registry","read_package_registry"],"revoked":false,"expired":false,"token":"Ka████████VxL"}jpainter
jpainter@LAPTOP-HRE7CTE5:~$
```

Figure 11-23. *Script that creates a deploy token using the REST POST method*

Looking at the deploy token settings for "MyRegistryProject" via the web browser, we see that the deploy token does indeed show up as shown in Figure 11-24. Other than the id and the token value itself, the settings page shows the same values as returned from the curl creation command.

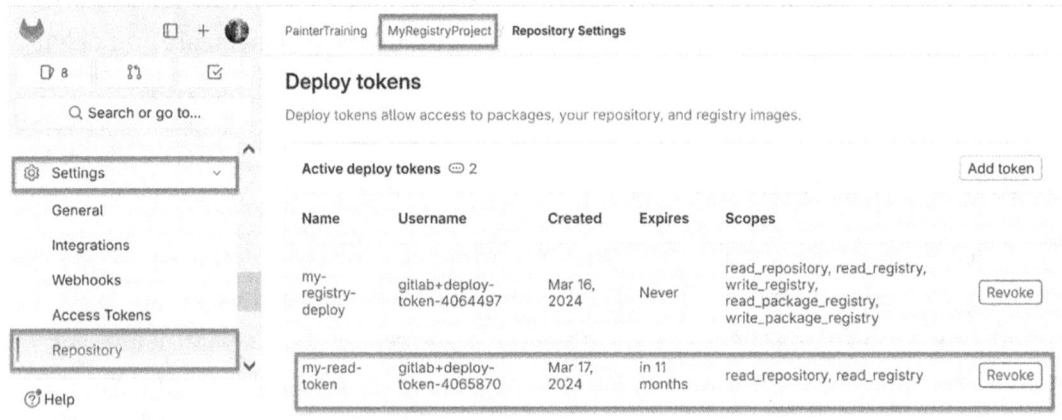

Figure 11-24. *Verifying API token creation in GitLab*

Listing the project's deploy tokens from curl gives us the results as shown in Figure 11-25. Since the GitLab web interface doesn't provide the ids for each of the deploy tokens, using the curl command is handy for seeing what the id is, especially if we want to delete it, as we'll see in the next example.

CHAPTER 11 THERE'S AN API FOR THAT

```
jpainter@LAPTOP-HRE7CTE5: ~                                              —    □    ×
jpainter@LAPTOP-HRE7CTE5: $ curl -s --header "PRIVATE-TOKEN: $MY_API_TOKEN" "https://gitlab.com/api/v4/projects/45279318
/deploy_tokens" | jq -M
[
  {
    "id": 1994203,
    "name": "my-registry-deploy",
    "username": "gitlab+deploy-token-1994203",
    "expires_at": null,
    "scopes": [
      "read_repository",
      "read_registry",
      "write_registry",
      "read_package_registry",
      "write_package_registry"
    ],
    "revoked": false,
    "expired": false
  },
  {
    "id": 2050155,
    "name": "my-read-token",
    "username": "gitlab+deploy-token-2050155",
    "expires_at": "2024-01-01T00:00:00.000Z",
    "scopes": [
      "read_registry",
      "read_package_registry"
    ],
    "revoked": false,
    "expired": false
  }
]
jpainter@LAPTOP-HRE7CTE5: $
```

Figure 11-25. Listing deploy tokens via the API to verify a new token was created

Deleting a Resource with the REST API

Deleting the new deploy token is pretty straightforward. Here, we use the DELETE method with the deploy token endpoint, as shown in Figure 11-26. For deletion, there are no web parameters to send, and no JSON response is provided. If successful, we get a return code of zero. Listing the deploy tokens after the deletion shows that we are back to one token again; the token we created earlier no longer exists.

CHAPTER 11   THERE'S AN API FOR THAT

```
jpainter@LAPTOP-HRE7CTE5: $ curl --request "DELETE" --header "PRIVATE-TOKEN: $MY_API_TOKEN" "https://gitlab.com/api/v4/p
rojects/45279318/deploy_tokens/2050155"
jpainter@LAPTOP-HRE7CTE5: $ echo $?
0
jpainter@LAPTOP-HRE7CTE5: $ curl -s --header "PRIVATE-TOKEN: $MY_API_TOKEN" "https://gitlab.com/api/v4/projects/45279318
/deploy_tokens" | jq -M
[
  {
    "id": 1994203,
    "name": "my-registry-deploy",
    "username": "gitlab+deploy-token-1994203",
    "expires_at": null,
    "scopes": [
      "read_repository",
      "read_registry",
      "write_registry",
      "read_package_registry",
      "write_package_registry"
    ],
    "revoked": false,
    "expired": false
  }
]
jpainter@LAPTOP-HRE7CTE5: $
```

Figure 11-26. *Deleting the deploy token using the REST DELETE method*

Modifying Resources with the REST API

The preceding examples show how easy it is to use the GitLab REST API to retrieve, create, and delete resources using the GET, POST, and DELETE HTTP methods. It was mentioned earlier that the PUT method is sometimes used, but for what purpose? As it turns out, some resources allow you to use the PUT method to modify an already existing resource.[6] In these scenarios, you use web parameters to specify which attributes of the resource to update. Issues are one resource that lets you do this. See `https://docs.gitlab.com/ee/api/issues.html#edit-issue` for an example of how to edit an Issue resource.

That's it for our REST API discussion. In the next section, we turn our attention to the more powerful API provided by GitLab: GraphQL.

---

[6] It is easy to confuse PUT with POST, but they are not the same. POST is used to create a new resource, whereas PUT is used to edit an already existing resource.

Exploring GraphQL

As easy as the GitLab REST API is to use, it does have some drawbacks. For one, the ability to filter queries is limited to the various parameter options made available for a given resource. In addition, there is no way to limit the output of a query to just the information you are interested in accessing. Because of these limitations, GitLab introduced the GraphQL API. According to their documentation, this is the primary API they now promote, although they still plan on supporting the REST API.

Like the REST API, the GitLab GraphQL API uses HTTP to make queries. Unlike the REST API, however, GraphQL only uses the POST method of HTTP rather than the full GET, PUT, POST, and DELETE methods. The contents of the GraphQL request determine what action is being requested. Because of the POST method, using URLs with the GitLab web browser is not directly supported as it is with the REST API. GitLab does provide an alternative way of making GraphQL queries via the web interface using a hidden tool called GraphiQL (pronounced as graphical), which I'll explain later in the next section. For now, we'll look at using curl to make GraphQL requests.

Making GraphQL Requests with Curl

To begin, GraphQL supports two types of requests: queries and mutations. As you would expect, queries are used to retrieve data. Mutations are used to perform all other actions of creating, editing, and deleting objects. Let's start with a simple GraphQL request that queries the name of the current user.[7] I'm including the text of the query in the following multiline form so that it is easier to read. I'm using the MY_API_TOKEN that I set up in the REST API examples.

```
curl -s "https://gitlab.com/api/graphql" \
    --header "Authorization: Bearer $MY_API_TOKEN" \
    --header "Content-Type: application/json" \
    --request POST \
    --data "{\"query\": \"query {currentUser {name}}\"}" | jq -M
```

---

[7] I'm starting with query examples given in the GitLab GraphQL documentation since, to be honest, I'm not an expert on GraphQL.

CHAPTER 11   THERE'S AN API FOR THAT

The first thing you should note is that I'm using the OAuth-compliant header for authentication rather than the PRIVATE-TOKEN header; both forms are acceptable for GraphQL. An additional header is provided to let HTTP know that the data content is in JSON format. The data section contains the actual request that uses "query:" as the top-level dictionary entry, the value of which is the query to retrieve the name of the current user. Since the result is JSON, I use jq to pretty-print it. Figure 11-27 shows the result of running the query from the Linux command line.

```
jpainter@LAPTOP-HRE7CTE5: $ curl -s "https://gitlab.com/api/graphql" --header "Authorization: Bearer $MY_API_TOKEN" --header "Content-Type: application/json" --request POST     --data "{\"query\": \"query {currentUser {name}}\"}" | jq -M
{
  "data": {
    "currentUser": {
      "name": "Jeff Painter"
    }
  }
}
jpainter@LAPTOP-HRE7CTE5: $
```

Figure 11-27. *Result of the GraphQL query run via curl*

Let's look at a more interesting example involving projects. The query is provided as follows. In this example, I provide authentication using PRIVATE-TOKEN in the header as was done with REST API examples. The query here is broken up into two parts. The first part consists of the filter fullPath, "paintertraining/myshellpipeline,"[8] that is contained in parentheses following the object being queried (project in this case). The second part bracketed in curly braces specifies what fields from the project should be returned. In this case, we are requesting each jobs id and duration that is associated with the project:

```
curl -s "https://gitlab.com/api/graphql" \
    --header "PRIVATE-TOKEN: $MY_API_TOKEN" \
    --header "Content-Type: application/json" \
    --request POST \
    --data '{"query": "query {project(fullPath: \"paintertraining/myshellpipeline\") {jobs {nodes {id duration}}}}"}' | jq -M
```

---

[8] Replace this with the full path of a project to which you have access.

CHAPTER 11   THERE'S AN API FOR THAT

Figure 11-28 shows the results of the query. Note how the nodes section under jobs is used to return the list of job objects. Using nodes in the query is how GraphQL knows to "traverse" the jobs objects for a given project. This pattern is used whenever there is a list of objects associated with a given resource.

Figure 11-28.   GraphQL query to list some job attributes for a given project

Reading GraphQL Queries from a File

One of the issues with using curl to make GraphQL queries is that the data parameter ends up flattening the query, making it difficult to read. This is especially true when queries get more complex. So how can we make our GraphQL request easier to read? Put it in a file and have curl read the contents of the file. To illustrate, let's create a new GraphQL request that queries a group and returns information about it including a list of projects. I created a group-query.json file with the following contents:

```
{
  "query": "
    query {
      group(fullPath: \"paintertraining\") {
        id
        name
        projects {
```

CHAPTER 11   THERE'S AN API FOR THAT

```
            nodes {
                name
            }
        }
      }
    }
  }
"
}
```

Note how much easier this is to read. It is a little quirky due to having to escape quoted values within the query itself, but at least the structure of what is being requested is easier to understand. In this example, we are querying the paintertraining group and returning the group's id, name, and list of project names. Figure 11-29 shows the results of this request. Note how the data parameter references the group-query.json file using the @ notation; this is how curl knows to get the data from that file rather than from the command line.

Figure 11-29. GraphQL query returning id, name, and list of project names for a given group

A Query to Retrieve Issues Associated with a Project

Let's do one more example querying issues associated with a project. We will first create a request to list all issues associated with "MyFirstProject," then make a request to show the details of a specific issue and then show how to sort the issues list. The first request to list all issues associated with "MyFirstProject," which I put into the file issues-query.json, is given as follows:

```
{
  "query": "
    query {
      project(fullPath: \"paintertraining/myfirstproject\") {
        name
        issues {
          nodes {
            iid
            id
            title
            state
          }
        }
      }
    }
  "
}
```

The results of running this query are shown in Figure 11-30. There are some things to take note of here. First, there are two ids: iid and id. The id value is the "global id" of the issue that is independent of the project. The iid value is an "internal id" that is an identifier relative to the project. We can see these internal ids displayed on the project's issue page as shown in Figure 11-31. The other thing to take note of is that the issues in the query result are listed in reverse order of their iid. We'll see how we can change that order in a bit.

CHAPTER 11   THERE'S AN API FOR THAT

```
jpainter@LAPTOP-HRE7CTE5: ~                                              -  □  ×
jpainter@LAPTOP-HRE7CTE5: $ curl -s "https://gitlab.com/api/graphql"    --header "PRIVATE-TOKEN: $MY_API_TOKEN"  --h
eader "Content-Type: application/json"    --request POST    --data "@issues-query.json" | jq -M
{
  "data": {
    "project": {
      "name": "MyFirstProject",
      "issues": {
        "nodes": [
          {
            "iid": "6",
            "id": "gid://gitlab/Issue/126302537",
            "title": "Add unit test",
            "state": "opened"
          },
          {
            "iid": "5",
            "id": "gid://gitlab/Issue/126302522",
            "title": "Implement feature backend logic",
            "state": "opened"
          },
          {
            "iid": "4",
            "id": "gid://gitlab/Issue/126302482",
            "title": "Create feature web page",
            "state": "opened"
          },
          {
            "iid": "3",
            "id": "gid://gitlab/Issue/126302391",
```

Figure 11-30. *GraphQL query returning name and select attributes of issues for a given project*

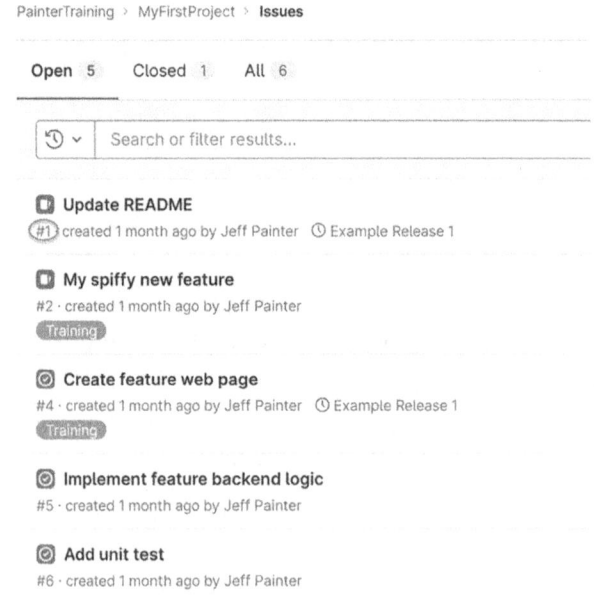

Figure 11-31. *GitLab issues listing to compare with the GraphQL query*

450

CHAPTER 11　THERE'S AN API FOR THAT

A Query to Retrieve One Issue Associated with a Project

So, what if we are only interested in one particular issue of the project rather than a listing of all issues? The contents of issue-query.json, which perform a query to select just the second issue of "MyFirstProject," are given as follows. Instead of using the issues-nodes combination made in the previous request, we use issue (the singular form of issues) with the filter iid: "2."[9] Figure 11-32 shows the result of the query. One reason for using iid is that it makes project-issue queries easier to form; it's easier to request the first issue of any project using iid, "1," than querying on the issue's global id.

```
{
  "query": "
    query {
      project(fullPath: \"paintertraining/myfirstproject\") {
        name
        issue(iid: \"2\") {
          id
          title
          state
        }
      }
    }
  "
}
```

---

[9] We put quotes around the value of iid since it is a string value, not an integer value. We can see this in the results returned from the issues request made earlier.

CHAPTER 11   THERE'S AN API FOR THAT

```
jpainter@LAPTOP-HRE7CTE5: $ curl -s "https://gitlab.com/api/graphql"   --header "PRIVATE-TOKEN: $MY_API_TOKEN"
eader "Content-Type: application/json"   --request POST   --data "@issue-query.json" | jq -M
{
  "data": {
    "project": {
      "name": "MyFirstProject",
      "issue": {
        "id": "gid://gitlab/Issue/126302264",
        "title": "My spiffy new feature",
        "state": "opened"
      }
    }
  }
}
jpainter@LAPTOP-HRE7CTE5: $
```

Figure 11-32. GraphQL query of a project returning name and select attributes for one issue

A Query to Return a Sorted List of Issues Associated with a Project

So, let's return to the sorting question: How can we sort the issues list ascending on the iid? Looking at the documentation that describes how to sort with GraphQL located at https://docs.gitlab.com/ee/api/graphql/getting_started.html#sorting, you might get the impression that you can simply use the name of the field to be sorted on followed by "_asc" or "_desc" (e.g., issue(sort: iid_asc)), but that is an incorrect assumption.[10] Let's first show the request and its result and then discuss how to determine what fields you can sort on. The contents of the sorted-issues-query.json that I used to request issues be sorted ascending on iid are given as follows. Figure 11-33 shows the results of running this query.

```
{
  "query": "
    query {
      project(fullPath: \"paintertraining/myfirstproject\") {
        name
        issues(sort: CREATED_ASC) {
          nodes {
            iid
            id
```

---

[10] I know this because that is what I tried. What you do get is a hint that directs you to the IssueSort object.

452

```
            title
            state
          }
        }
      }
    }
  "
}
```

Figure 11-33. GraphQL query returning a sorted list of issues in order of creation

How did I know to use (sort: CREATED_ASC) as the issues qualifier and what other fields can be sorted on? Through trial and error, I discovered that the sort qualifier uses the IssueSort enumeration object that is defined in the GraphQL reference here: https://docs.gitlab.com/ee/api/graphql/reference/#issuesort. This provides values such as CREATED_ASC[11] and TITLE_DESC that can be used to sort on those fields. Unlike the GitLab REST API reference, the GitLab GraphQL API reference is difficult to maneuver, so much so that I devote an entire section just on that.

---

[11] Note that the sorting example uses created_asc as the sort qualifier, but as mentioned in the IssueSort documentation, created_asc and created_desc are deprecated in favor of using all uppercase values.

CHAPTER 11   THERE'S AN API FOR THAT

Creating an Object with GraphQL

OK, so let's take a look at mutations. I'll continue using the "getting started" example in the GitLab documentation and create, update, and delete a note for "My spiffy new feature" issue listed earlier. Note that the documentation doesn't show how to use mutations with curl, so I had to do some web searching to find the answer. You would think that the top-level key would be mutation, but it turns out to be query; if you did use mutation, you would get an unhelpful error stating that an unexpected end of document occurred. In any case, the contents of the create-issue-note.json are given as follows:

```
{
  "query": "
    mutation {
       createNote(input: { noteableId: \"gid://gitlab/Issue/126302264\",
           body: \"*sips tea*\"
       }) {
         note {
           id
           body
           discussion {
             id
           }
         }
         errors
       }
    }
  "
}
```

Running this "query" with curl gives the results shown in Figure 11-34. The mutation used createNote to generate a note attached to the issue based on its global id. The body of the note consists of the emphasized text "sips tea." Like a query, we tell GraphQL what to return, which in this example consists of some fields related to the new note and a list of errors, if any. Figure 11-35 shows what the note looks like from the "My spiffy new feature" page.

CHAPTER 11   THERE'S AN API FOR THAT

```
jpainter@LAPTOP-HRE7CTE5: $ curl -s "https://gitlab.com/api/graphql"    --header "PRIVATE-TOKEN: $MY_API_TOKEN" --h
eader "Content-Type: application/json"    --request POST    --data "@create-issue-note.json" | jq -M
{
  "data": {
    "createNote": {
      "note": {
        "id": "gid://gitlab/Note/1400202203",
        "body": "*sips tea*",
        "discussion": {
          "id": "gid://gitlab/Discussion/b5a711d20ef0dc41f9c49a8cd65dd9370bbf4902"
        }
      },
      "errors": []
    }
  }
}
jpainter@LAPTOP-HRE7CTE5: $
```

Figure 11-34. *GraphQL request to attach a new note to an issue*

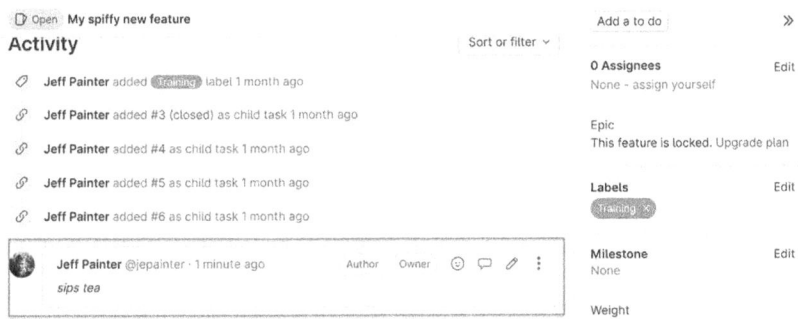

Figure 11-35. *View of issue in GitLab to show the note was created*

Updating an Object with GraphQL

Extracting the note id from the result of the previous creation query, we can make an update to the note. The contents of update-issue-note.json are given as follows. Here, we tell GraphQL to replace the contents of the note with "SIPS TEA." Again, we tell GraphQL to return the id and body of the updated note and a list of errors, if any.

```
{
  "query": "
    mutation {
      updateNote(input: { id: \"gid://gitlab/Note/1400202203\",
        body: \"*SIPS TEA*\"
      }) {
        note {
```

455

CHAPTER 11   THERE'S AN API FOR THAT

```
        id
        body
      }
      errors
    }
  }
"
}
```

Figure 11-36 shows the result of running the update mutation, and Figure 11-37 shows the updated note for the "My spiffy new feature" page. Note that the note creation time shows 17 minutes ago, whereas the edit time shows 2 minutes ago.

```
jpainter@LAPTOP-HRE7CTE5: $ curl -s "https://gitlab.com/api/graphql"     --header "PRIVATE-TOKEN: $MY_API_TOKEN"    --h
eader "Content-Type: application/json"    --request POST    --data "@update-issue-note.json" | jq -M
{
  "data": {
    "updateNote": {
      "note": {
        "id": "gid://gitlab/Note/1400202203",
        "body": "*SIPS TEA*"
      },
      "errors": []
    }
  }
}
jpainter@LAPTOP-HRE7CTE5: $
```

Figure 11-36. *GraphQL request to update an existing note for a given issue*

Figure 11-37. *View of the note in GitLab to show that the note was updated*

456

Deleting an Object with GraphQL

To finish the example, the contents of delete-issue-note.json are shown as follows. Figure 11-38 shows the result of running the mutation with curl. What is interesting to note here is that the query on "note" shows that it is null, which we expect after any deletion. Because of this, we could have removed the note section from the mutation input and just shown errors. BTW, I don't show the issue page after the deletion here since it will show just the actions without the note as expected.

```
{
  "query": "
    mutation {
      destroyNote(input: { id: \"gid://gitlab/Note/1400202203\" }) {
        note {
          id
          body
        }
        errors
      }
    }
  "
}
```

```
jpainter@LAPTOP-HRE7CTE5:~$ curl -s "https://gitlab.com/api/graphql"      --header "PRIVATE-TOKEN: $MY_API_TOKEN" --h
eader "Content-Type: application/json"     --request POST     --data "@delete-issue-note.json" | jq -M
{
  "data": {
    "destroyNote": {
      "note": null,
      "errors": []
    }
  }
}
jpainter@LAPTOP-HRE7CTE5:~$
```

Figure 11-38. GraphQL request to destroy the previously created note

Now that we've seen how to use curl to make GraphQL requests, let's see how we can form GraphQL requests using GitLab's graphical editor GraphiQL covered in the next section.

CHAPTER 11   THERE'S AN API FOR THAT

Interacting with GraphiQL

Having explored GraphQL using curl, let's look at how we can interactively try out GraphQL requests. Since we can't use web browser URLs to explore the GitLab GraphQL API like we can with the GitLab REST API, GitLab provides an interactive interface called GraphiQL to let us try out GraphQL requests. Getting to it requires knowing the "magical" URL since there is no way to get to it via GitLab menus. On the gitlab.com site, you access GraphiQL using `https://gitlab.com/-/graphql-explorer`. On self-managed sites, replace gitlab.com with your site's name.[12]

The GraphQL Explorer

The first time you go to the GraphQL explorer, you'll get a page similar to the one in Figure 11-39. On the left-hand side are comments that describe how to use the interface; this is where you put GraphQL requests to be executed. On the right-hand side is the area where the JSON results are displayed. The interface also provides various buttons to help with managing your request as well as a "Docs" section to guide you on what to do next.

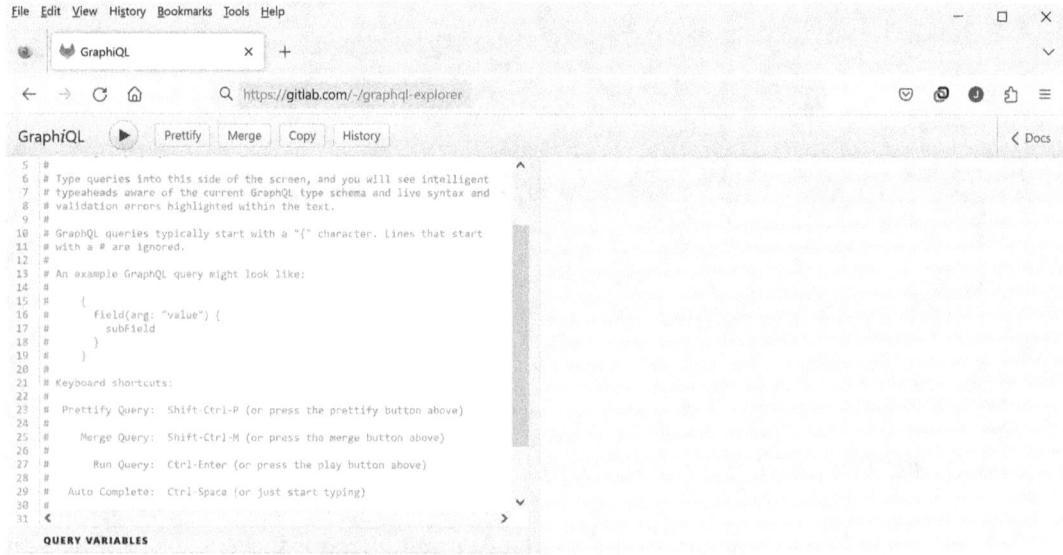

Figure 11-39. *Initial GraphQL explorer (a.k.a. GraphiQL) page*

---

[12] For self-managed sites, the GraphiQL interface might not be enabled, in which case contact your administrator about enabling it.

CHAPTER 11   THERE'S AN API FOR THAT

So, let's dig in and see how we can make queries using the GraphQL explorer. The following code shows how to query the issues for a given project, which is a query we did earlier using curl. Note that the input to GraphiQL is simpler in that we don't have to wrap it into a json document with a top-level element of "query:". And because of that, we don't have to add backslashes to the quotes within the request.

```
query {
  project(fullPath: "paintertraining/myfirstproject") {
    name
    issues {
      nodes {
        iid
        id
        title
        state
      }
    }
  }
}
```

Figure 11-40 shows the results of running this request within the GraphQL explorer. In this example, I entered the query on the right-hand side and then selected the highlighted play button to run the query. The JSON document result is shown in the right-hand-side pane. If you compare this document with the one returned via the earlier curl example, you can see that the output is the same, including the sort order of the issues.

459

CHAPTER 11 THERE'S AN API FOR THAT

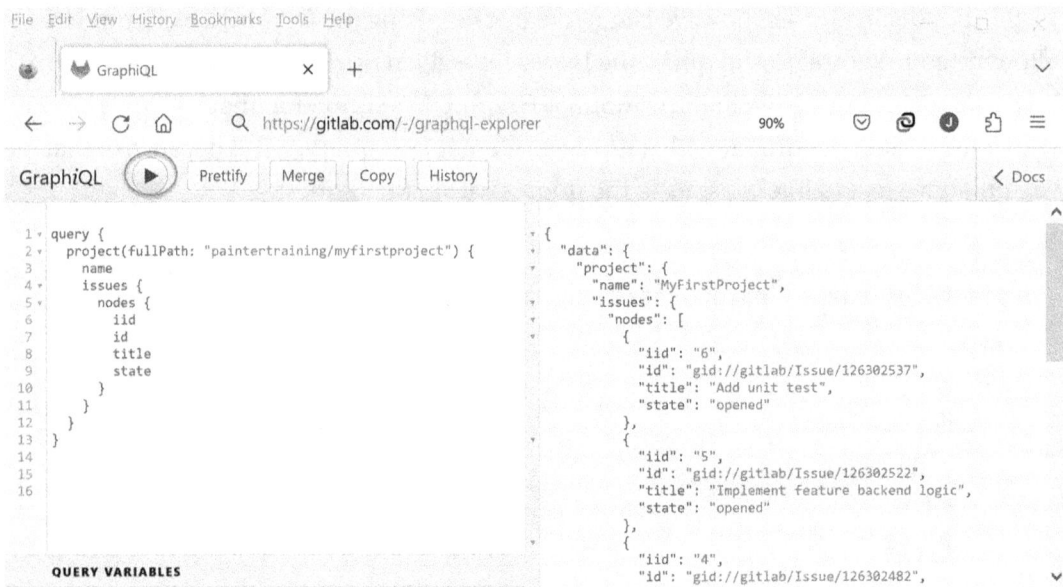

Figure 11-40. Issue query and result via GraphiQL

Getting Help Making GraphQL Requests

For the first-time user, figuring out how to create a GraphQL request from scratch can be a bit daunting. The first source of help with this is the "Docs" section that can be expanded via the "Docs" button on the upper right-hand side of the explorer. Figure 11-41 shows the initial "Docs" page when there is nothing entered in yet. It shows that there are three root types: query, mutation, and subscription.[13] The second source of help occurs when we start typing within the left-hand-side panel. In this case, when we start entering "qu," we get a context menu providing options that are valid in the given context. In this case, "query" shows up as an option that we can select.[14]

---

[13] A subscription is a special root type used within GitLab's Ruby code to notify it whenever a change is made and is beyond the scope of this book.

[14] So, what's up with the curly brace ({) option listed in the context menu? Well, since query is the most common request vs. mutation or subscription, entering query is optional; in other words, you can enter a query with just the starting curly brace.

CHAPTER 11   THERE'S AN API FOR THAT

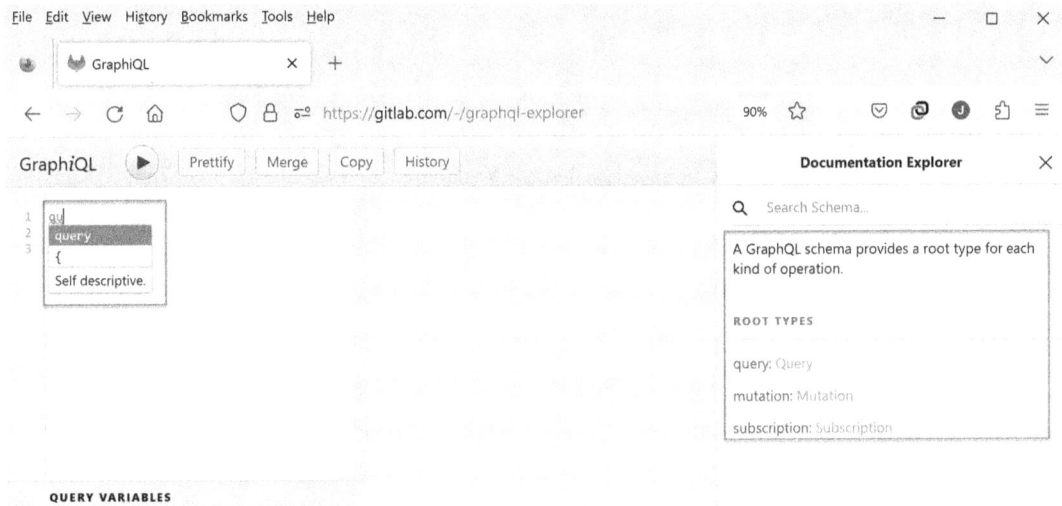

Figure 11-41. *Initial GraphiQL documentation section*

Starting a Project Query

After completing the query and adding the curly braces, selecting the "Query" link in the Documentation Explorer gives us a list of objects that we can query against, as shown in Figure 11-42. In this example, I scrolled down within the document to find both project and projects as viable options. With project, you discover that you need to enter the argument "fullPath" with the full path of the project to be queried. With projects, you discover a number of arguments you can use to select which projects to list.

CHAPTER 11   THERE'S AN API FOR THAT

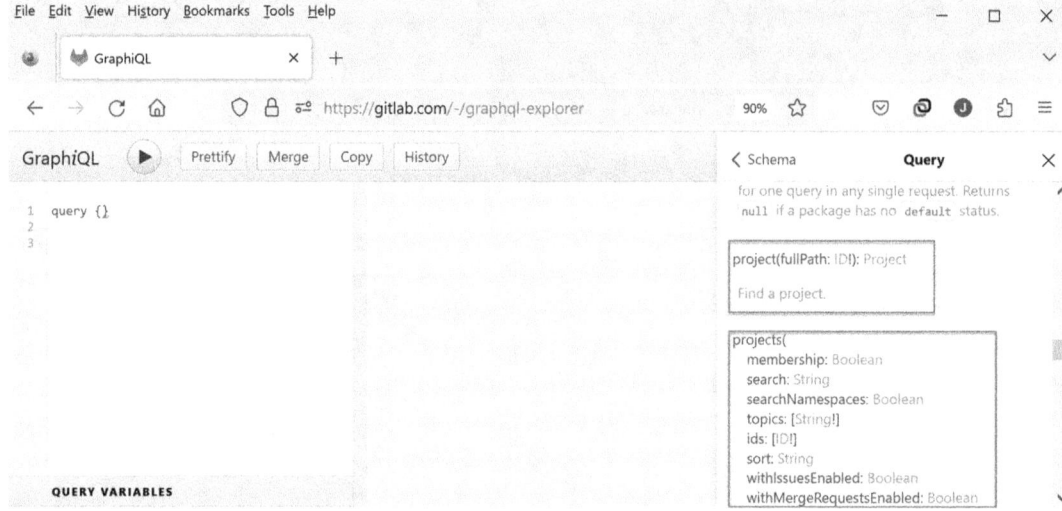

Figure 11-42. GraphiQL documentation for query schema

Setting the fullPath Option

Entering "project(" within the query curly braces provides the context help as shown in Figure 11-43. Here, we see just the one fullPath option along with a description of what value to use for that option. After selecting the fullPath option and entering a value for it, we can explore what fields we can use for a project by selecting the "Project" link as shown in Figure 11-44.

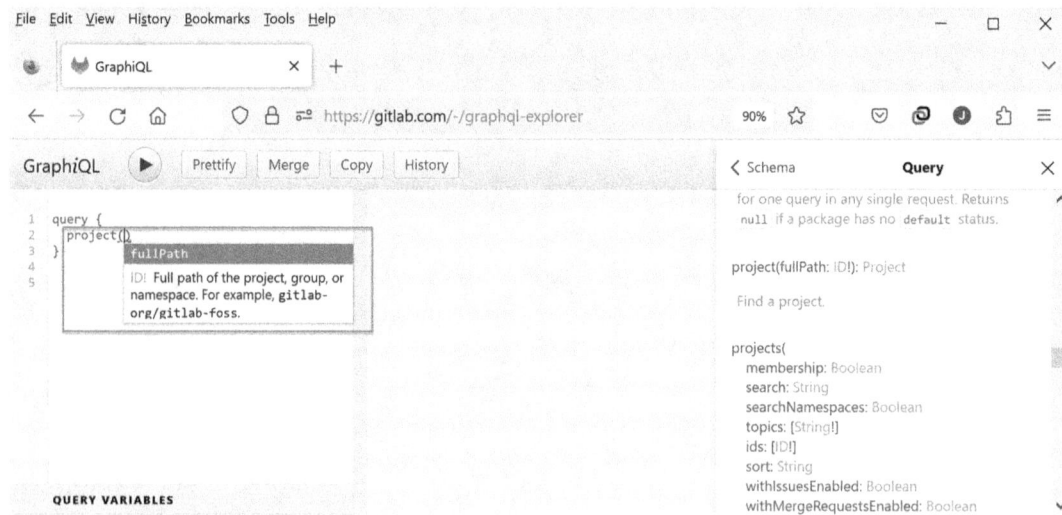

Figure 11-43. GraphiQL context help for project query

CHAPTER 11   THERE'S AN API FOR THAT

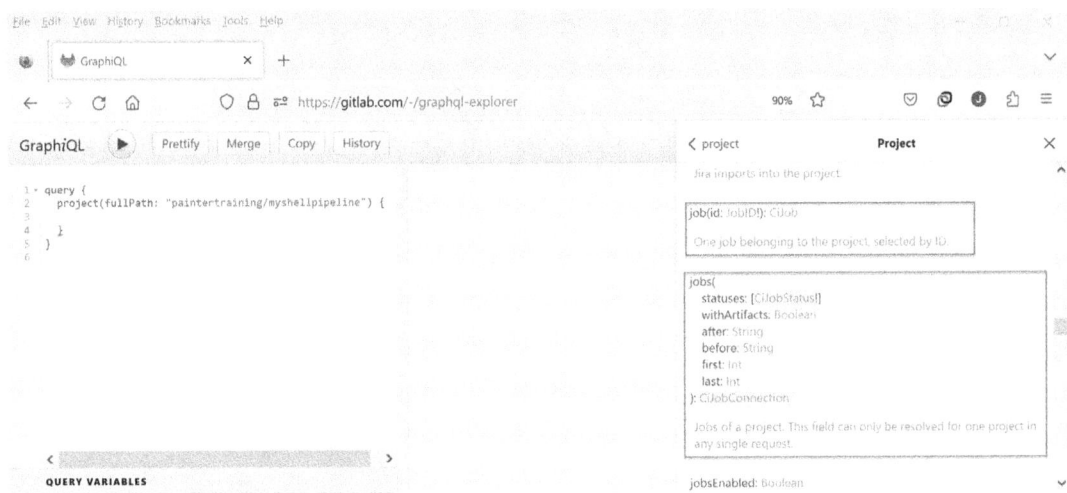

Figure 11-44. *GraphiQL field options for project query*

Requesting Successful and Failed Jobs for the Project

Within the "Project" documentation, I scrolled down to expose options for jobs. Here, we see two options: job and jobs. This matches the standard pattern of using the singular form of an object to select just one item (a job in this case) and the plural form of an object to select multiple items (jobs in this case) based on selection filters, if any. In this example, I want to display just successful and failed jobs associated with the "MyShellPipeline" project. The documentation help for jobs shows that I can filter on statuses. In case I don't know what statuses I can enter, the CiJobStatus link provides a list of the statuses as shown in Figure 11-45.

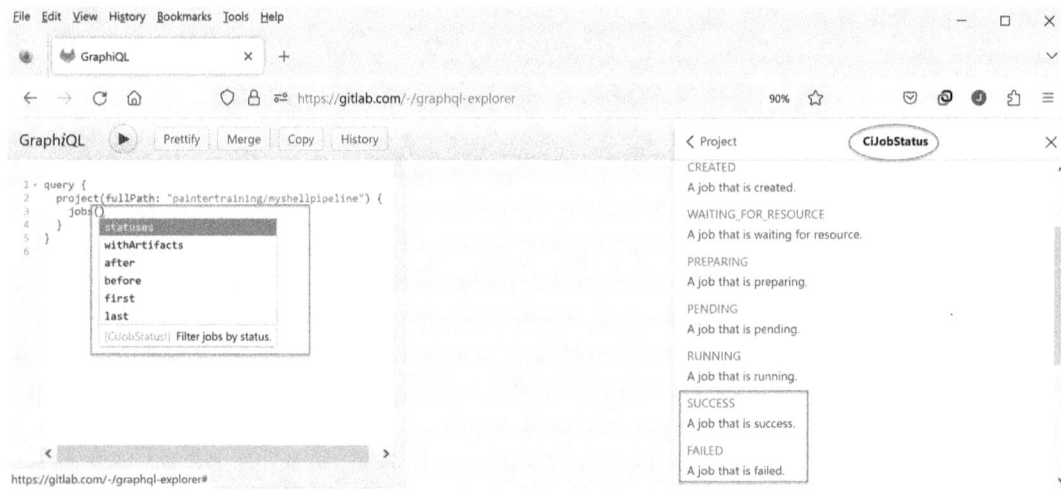

***Figure 11-45.** GraphiQL documentation for job status filter*

Restricting the Number of Jobs Returned

CiJobStatus is known as an enumeration type, which means that you use the values as is without bracketing them in quotes like you do with a string type. Figure 11-46 shows the status condition restricted to just SUCCESS and FAILED. Knowing that there are a lot of jobs associated with the "MyShellPipeline" project, it is best to restrict the number of jobs that are returned by the query. Looking at the menu options for jobs arguments, we see there is a "first" argument that might meet our needs. Highlighting the "first" option in the menu tells us that it "Returns the first n elements from the list." Looking at the jobs field description under "Project" in the documentation pane, we see that it takes an integer value.

CHAPTER 11   THERE'S AN API FOR THAT

Figure 11-46. GraphiQL help for job status restrictions

Selecting Job Fields to Be Returned by the Query

Selecting "first" and setting the value to 3, we move on to select the fields we want to show for each job. From the project jobs description shown in the documentation page, we see that the fields for jobs are defined using the CiJobConnection object. Figure 11-47 shows the fields associated with the CiJobConnection object. It is here that we see our old friend "nodes." As it turns out, "nodes" isn't the only field option for jobs; there is also "edges" and "pageInfo," which we'll explore momentarily.

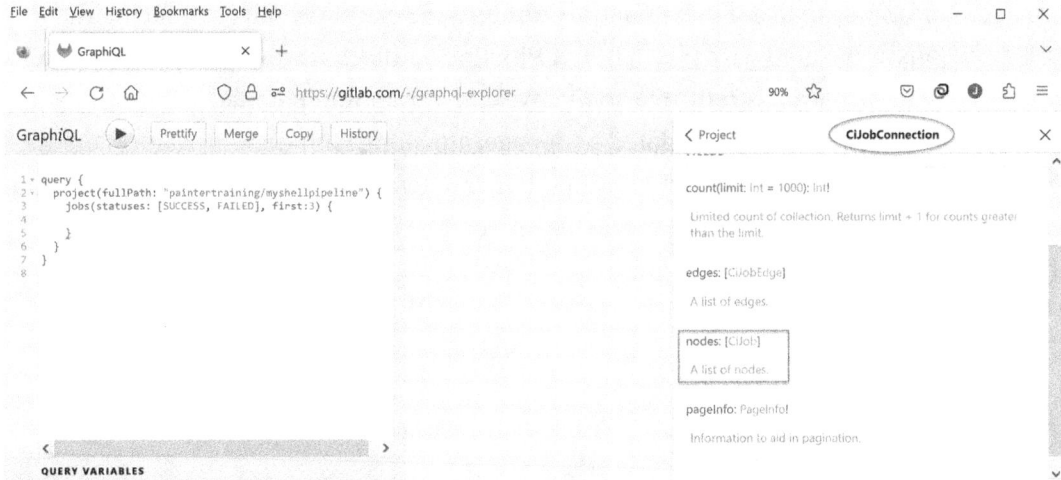

Figure 11-47. GraphiQL documentation of job connection fields

465

Continuing on with our example, we enter "nodes" along with the curly braces as shown in Figure 11-48. Clicking the "CiJob" link next to "nodes" in the documentation page gives us the set of fields for a job. In the example, I selected id, status, and startedAt as the fields to be returned for each job, which is a reasonable set of fields to start with.

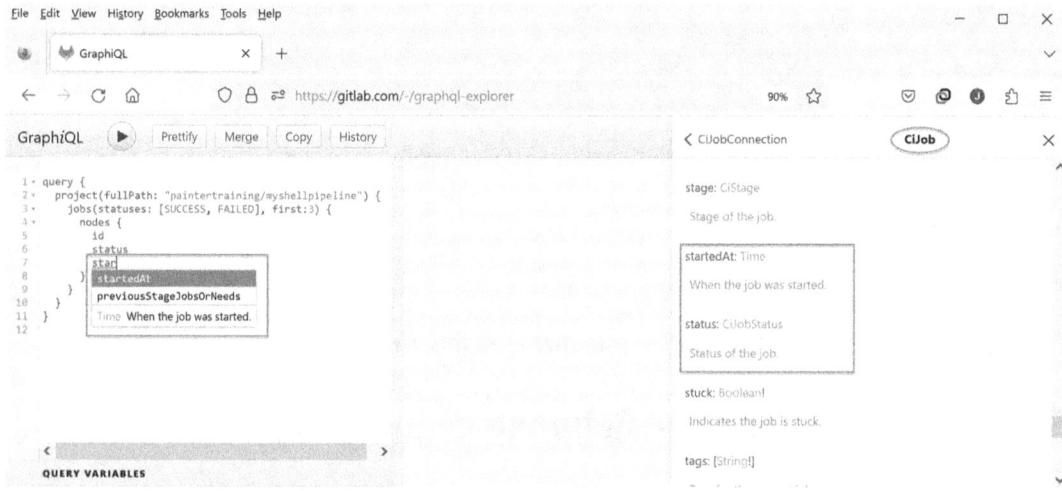

Figure 11-48. GraphiQL documentation of job fields

Requesting Paging Information

So, before we complete this query, let's cycle back to the pageInfo field from the CiJobConnection object. According to the documentation displayed earlier, pageInfo provides "Information to aid in pagination." Since we are initially only displaying the first three jobs associated with the "MyShellPipeline" project, it would be nice to know what kind of information is returned so that we can implement pagination for our jobs. Figure 11-49 shows our query updated with pageInfo along with documentation on the PageInfo object. From that documentation, there are two fields that are of interest for our example: hasNextPage and endCursor. This info can be used for us to page forward to the next set of jobs meeting our criteria.

CHAPTER 11   THERE'S AN API FOR THAT

Figure 11-49. *GraphiQL documentation of page info fields*

Running the Completed Query

With that change in place, let's go ahead and run the query. Figure 11-50 shows the results of our query. Under the nodes section, we see just three jobs as requested, which in this case are all successful. Under the pageInfo section, we see that hasNextPage is true, letting us know that there are more jobs to page through. In addition, the endCursor value provides a key (a.k.a. a cursor) to the last job in the nodes list. We use this value to let GraphQL know where to begin the next page of jobs.

CHAPTER 11   THERE'S AN API FOR THAT

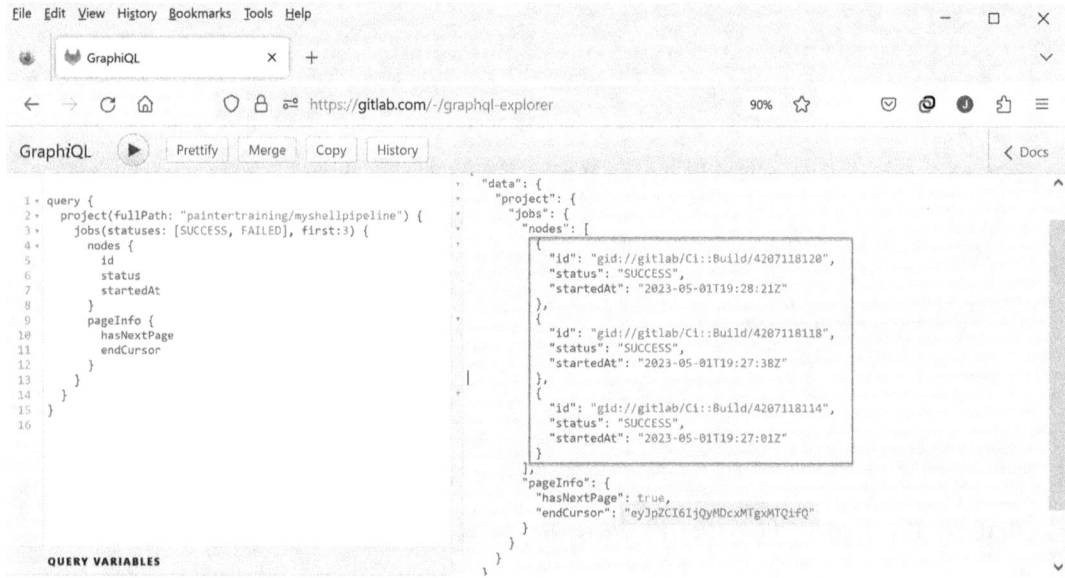

Figure 11-50. GraphiQL results of job query

Pagination with GraphQL

Since we are on the topic of pagination, let's see how we can use the value of endCursor to display the next three sets of jobs. In the process, we'll also take a moment to describe the edges field of CiJobConnection to see how it differs from the nodes field. Figure 11-51 shows the beginning of changes to the previous query. First, note that we add the "after" argument as a condition to "jobs" along with the endCursor value returned from the previous query. We could end things there and rerun the query to get the next set of jobs. However, I include an edges section for jobs and display documentation for the CiJobEdge object. Here, we see two possible fields: cursor and node. The cursor field returns a cursor for each job, and the node determines what fields of the CiJob object to retrieve.

CHAPTER 11   THERE'S AN API FOR THAT

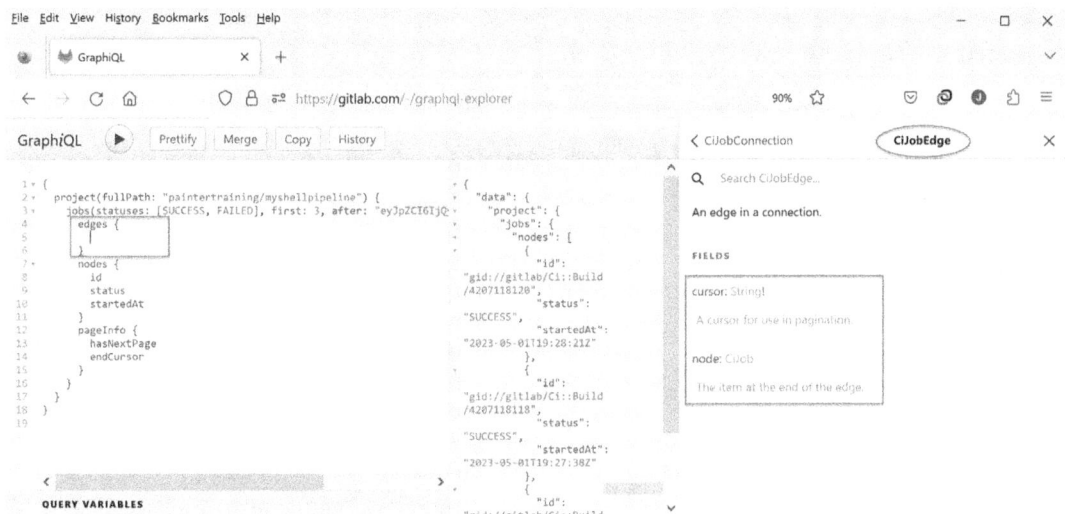

Figure 11-51. *GraphiQL documentation of edge fields for a job*

Adding cursor under edges and moving the nodes section under edges (renaming nodes to node) gives us the query in Figure 11-52. Running the query shows the next three jobs along with a cursor for each. If you look closely, you'll see that the cursor value of the last job matches the endCursor value under pageInfo. Using edges to display the cursor for each job is an alternative to paging that relies on the startCursor and endCursor fields of pageInfo. Most of the time, you'll probably use the nodes field along with the pageInfo field to support paging rather than using the edges field to access the cursors.

CHAPTER 11 THERE'S AN API FOR THAT

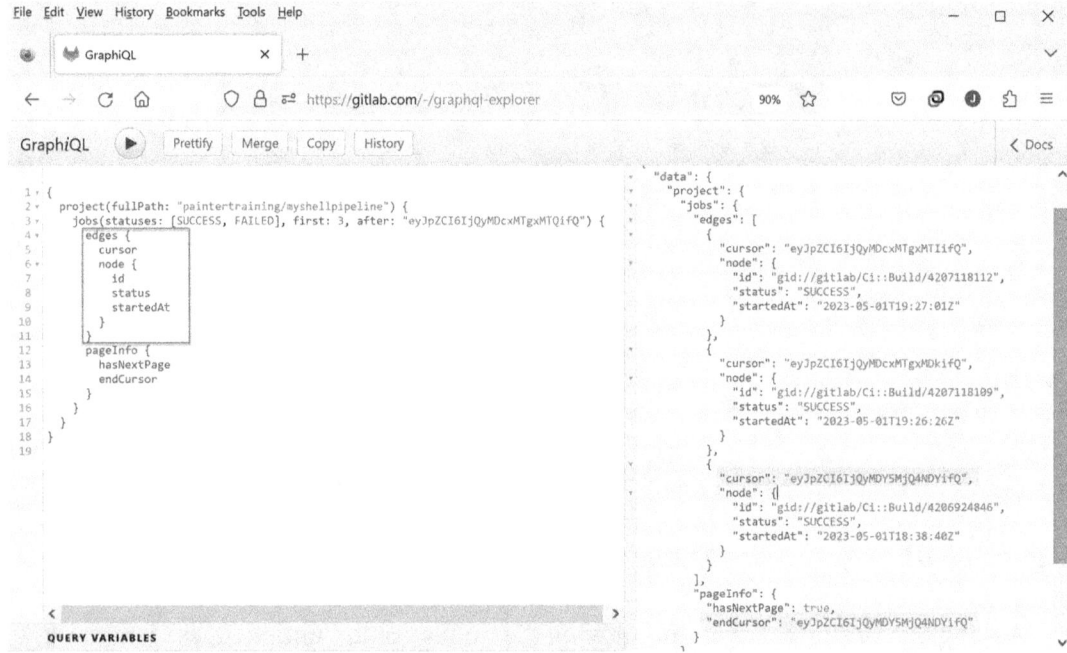

Figure 11-52. GraphiQL results of job query highlighting cursor and endCursor field values

In case you are wondering, it is possible to have multiple pages of information for different fields such as jobs and issues in the same query and manage the paging of each separately. The paging mechanism used by GraphQL supports this (unlike the paging mechanisms used in the GitLab HTTP API). In practice, however, you'll most likely use paging for just one set of objects (e.g., jobs or issues) unless you are trying to create a snapshot summary report of an object such as projects that doesn't involve paging associated objects such as jobs or issues.

Using GraphQL Introspection

So far, we've seen two ways to discover GraphQL: context help within the GraphiQL editor and the document pane of the GraphQL explorer. There is a third way of discovering the objects and types of GraphQL: introspection. An introspective query is used to query objects and types themselves. Figure 11-53 shows a query to return all the types available via the GitLab GraphQL API. Here, we use the special object __schema to return the name of all known types.

CHAPTER 11   THERE'S AN API FOR THAT

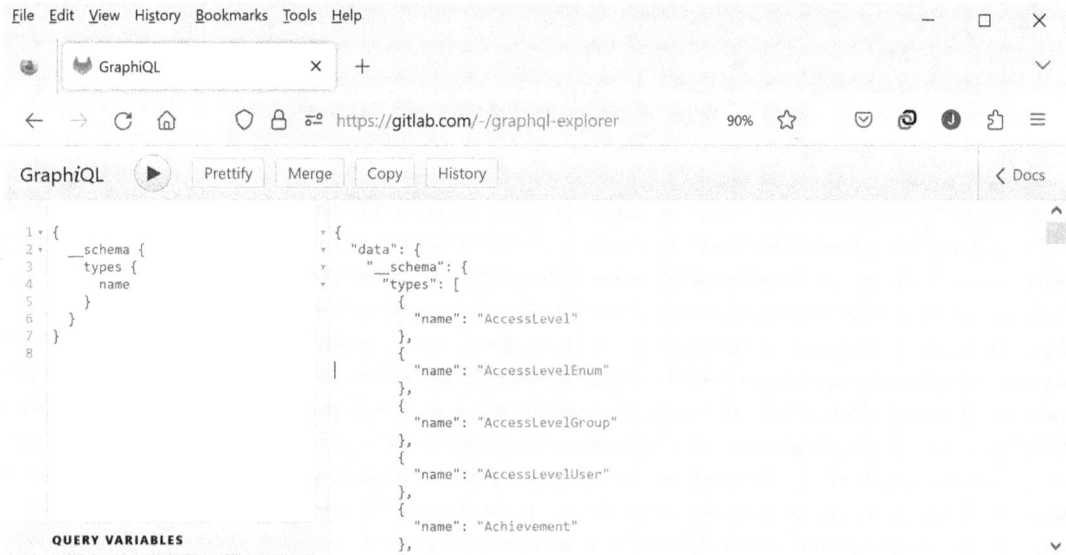

Figure 11-53. *GraphiQL documentation of introspective types*

You can also query object types such as "Project" as shown in Figure 11-54. In this example, we query the kind of type Project is (in this case, OBJECT) along with all the field names, descriptions, and types. You can use the context help to determine what fields and arguments are available for introspection queries; unfortunately, you won't find introspection queries defined in the "Docs" pane of the GraphQL explorer.

471

CHAPTER 11   THERE'S AN API FOR THAT

Figure 11-54.   GraphiQL query of project type

There are other features to the GraphiQL interface and the GraphQL specification that you can discover on your own through GitLab's documentation on the GitLab GraphQL API, which you can find at https://docs.gitlab.com/ee/api/graphql/. I covered the basic features in this section that you'll find useful in your day-to-day work should you decide that the GitLab GraphQL API is of interest to you. In the next section, we'll look at the organization of the GraphQL reference document.

Deciphering the GraphQL Reference

The GitLab documentation includes a GraphQL reference that can be found at https://docs.gitlab.com/ee/api/graphql/reference/. Whereas the REST API Resources manual, which explains the resources that can be queried using HTTPS, is relatively easy to navigate, the GraphQL reference can be mind-boggling to search through. Part of the issue is that it is generated using the introspection queries described in the previous section. This certainly makes it easy to keep the reference up to date, but it can be a bit

CHAPTER 11   THERE'S AN API FOR THAT

dry as well as confusing to navigate through.[15] This section will help you understand the structure of the GraphQL reference so that you can more easily understand how to navigate through it.

Main Sections of the GraphQL Reference

Let's first start off with the main sections of the reference, which isn't easily presented. To understand what I mean, Figure 11-55 shows the start of the GraphQL reference page. The rightmost pane entitled "On this page" is an index to all the GraphQL types and objects. The highlighted "Query type" is a top-level section under which all the query types are listed. To get to the next top-level section of "Mutation type," you have to keep scrolling down the "On this page" index to find it. This is true for all the top-level sections. This scrolling makes it tedious to discover what all the top-level sections are.[16]

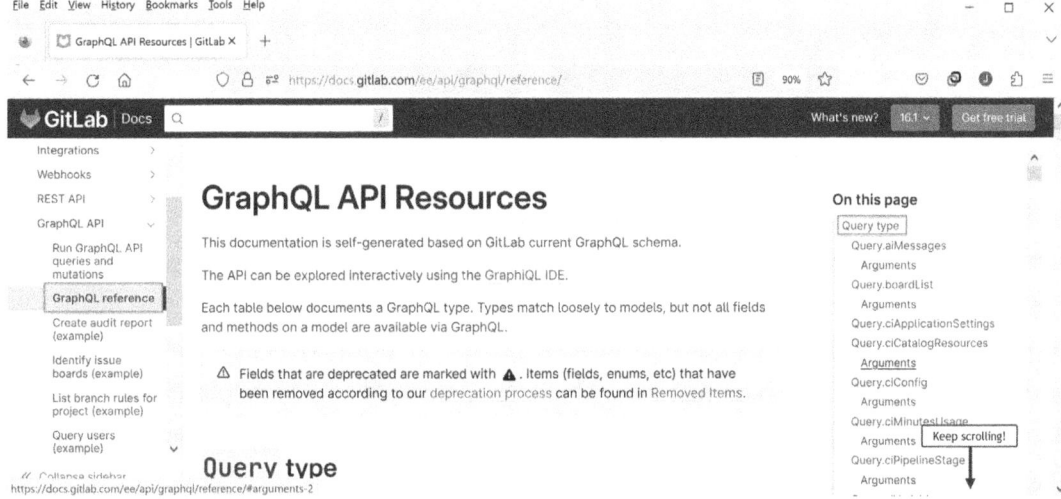

Figure 11-55. Beginning of GraphQL API reference including the reference section for query types

---

[15] Much like the old mainframe reference manuals of yore.

[16] Personally, given the size of this reference document, it would have been better to have these subsections listed under the GraphQL reference tab located in the leftmost pane or to make the top-level sections collapsible so that you can quickly navigate to them.

CHAPTER 11   THERE'S AN API FOR THAT

To help you navigate through this reference, I provide the top-level sections here so that you can better see how the document is organized. I'll also give examples that show how to navigate from one type to another within the manual. To start, there are eight top-level sections as follows:

- Query type
- Mutation type
- Connections
- Object types
- Enumeration types
- Scalar types
- Abstract types
- Input types

The Query Type Section

Let's start with the "Query type" section, which is located here: https://docs.gitlab.com/ee/api/graphql/reference/#query-type. The reason it is called a type and not types like the "Object types" section is because "query" is indeed a single type in GraphQL speak; the various queries associated with the query type are referred to as entry points. Take a look back at Figure 11-43. Note that in the "Docs" pane, the title at the top of the pane is "Query"; this is the type. The project and projects shown in the "Doc" pane are entry points that define what you are querying for.

Figure 11-56 shows what the entry point for project looks like from the GraphQL reference manual viewpoint. The index in the rightmost pane shows that we are at the Query.project entry point. An entry point typically defines a set of arguments that can be used to filter the query.[17] In this case, project only defines one argument: fullPath. Each argument specifies its type and a description. In this example, fullPath has type "ID!", which is a scalar type;[18] clicking the "ID!" link will take you to the place in the reference

---

[17] An entry point does not need to have arguments as can be seen in the index for Query.queryComplexity.

[18] In case you are wondering, the exclamation point in "ID!" indicates that it is a non-null value; this field will always return a value.

CHAPTER 11 THERE'S AN API FOR THAT

manual that describes this type. The highlighted "Returns Project" tells you that this query returns an object of type Project. Clicking the Project link will take you to the location in the reference manual that defines this object.

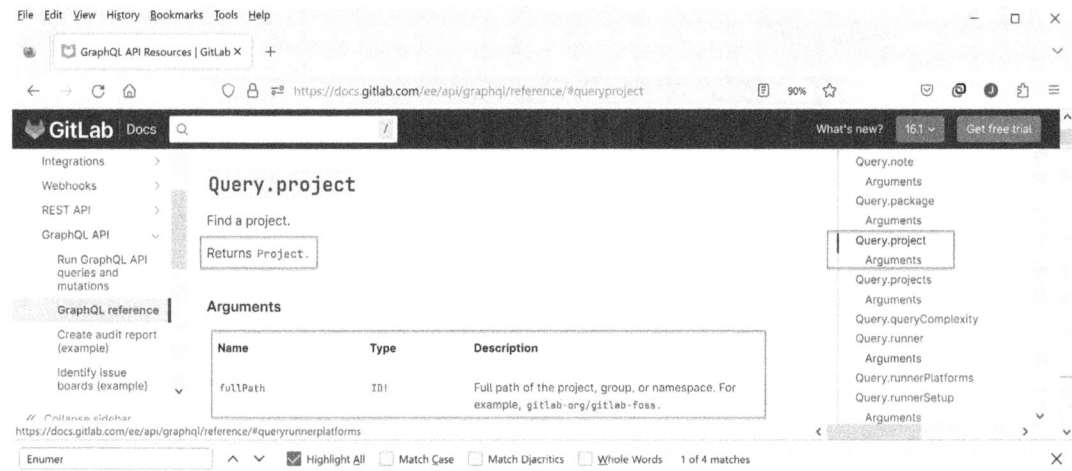

Figure 11-56. Description of project query type

The Scaler Types Section

Using the Query.project description as an example, let's skip down to the "Scalar types" section located at https://docs.gitlab.com/ee/api/graphql/reference/#scalar-types. This is where "ID!" is defined. Figure 11-57 shows the introduction to scalar types. As it states, a scalar type defines an object that cannot be divided any further (i.e., an atomic value). You may be most familiar with Int and String as scalar values; this section includes specially defined scalar values for GitLab's GraphQL API. Most of these are object identifiers (a.k.a. IDs).

475

CHAPTER 11   THERE'S AN API FOR THAT

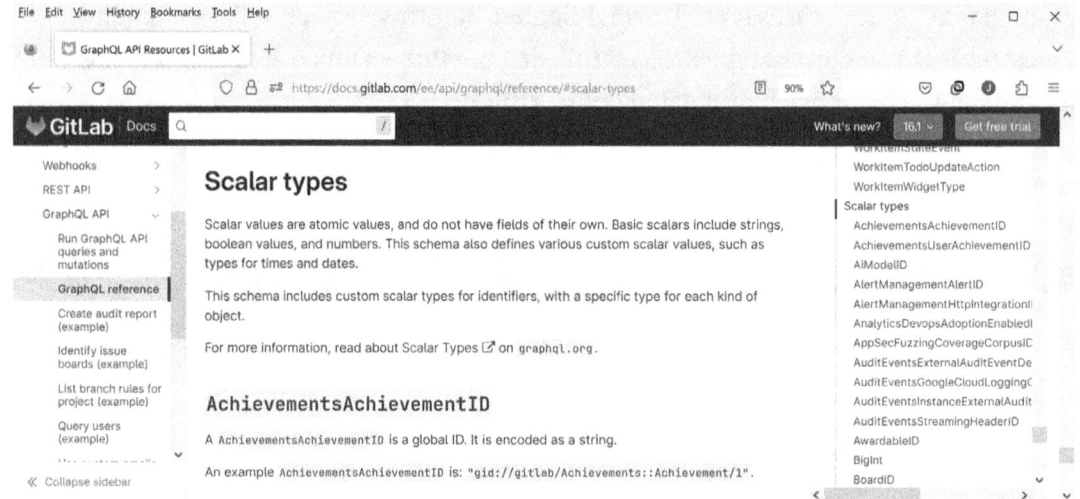

Figure 11-57. GraphQL reference section for scalar types

In our previous Query.project example, if you click "ID!", you'll be taken to the ID scalar type description as shown in Figure 11-58. This simply describes what the project ID value looks like. Note that when you click the "ID!" link, the index remains with the Query.project still visible. This allows you to go back to the Query.project definition if you want. You can, of course, use the web browser's back button to take you there as well.

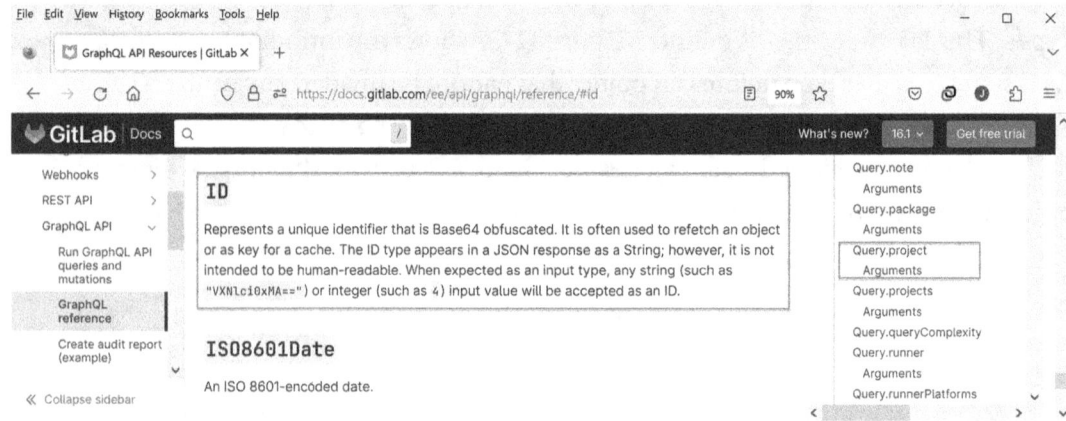

Figure 11-58. Description of ID scalar type

CHAPTER 11　THERE'S AN API FOR THAT

The Object Types Section

Let's now take a look at the Object types section. Figure 11-59 shows the definition of an object type. As stated in the description, an object type is what is returned from a query and hence is one of the most common types used in GraphQL. An object type defines the fields that can be returned in a query. Like attributes, each field specifies the field's type and descriptions. As the introduction states, some fields may also take arguments to filter which fields of that type are returned.

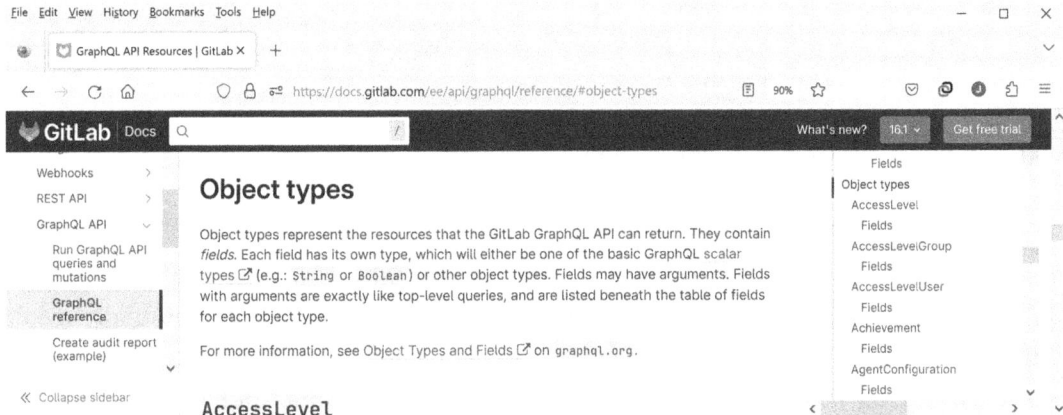

Figure 11-59. GraphQL reference section for object types

Let's swing back to our Query.project example. Figure 11-60 shows what we get when we click the Project link. The Project object has two subsections: "Fields" and "Fields with arguments." The "Fields" section defines those fields that do not require any qualification like fullPath, id, or namespace; these fields may be scalar, enumeration, object, or connection types. Also, some fields, such as languages, may return a list of values.

477

CHAPTER 11   THERE'S AN API FOR THAT

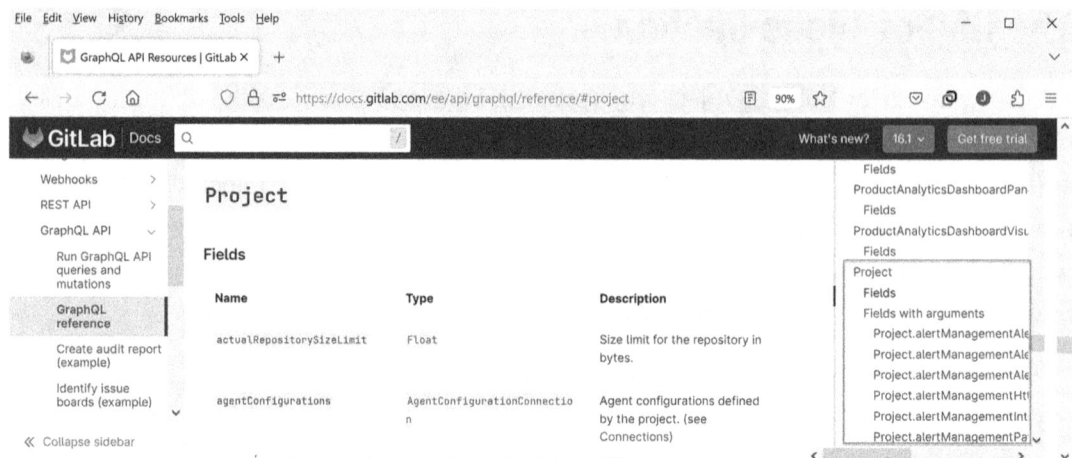

Figure 11-60. *Description of Project object type*

The "Fields with arguments" section defines fields that may be qualified to restrict what is returned by the query. These fields typically are object type fields such as "job" or connection type fields such as "issues." Figure 11-61 shows the documentation of the job field. In this case, there is only one argument, id, which restricts which job related to the project is to be retrieved. The fields returned are described by the CiJob object.

Figure 11-61. *Description of arguments for job field of Project object type*

Figure 11-62 shows the arguments available for the jobs field. In this case, there are two possible arguments: statuses and withArtifacts. The statuses argument takes a list of values (as indicated by the square brackets) from the CiJobStatus enumeration type. The withArtifacts takes a true/false value (that unlike a string is not quoted) from the Boolean

478

CHAPTER 11 THERE'S AN API FOR THAT

scalar type.

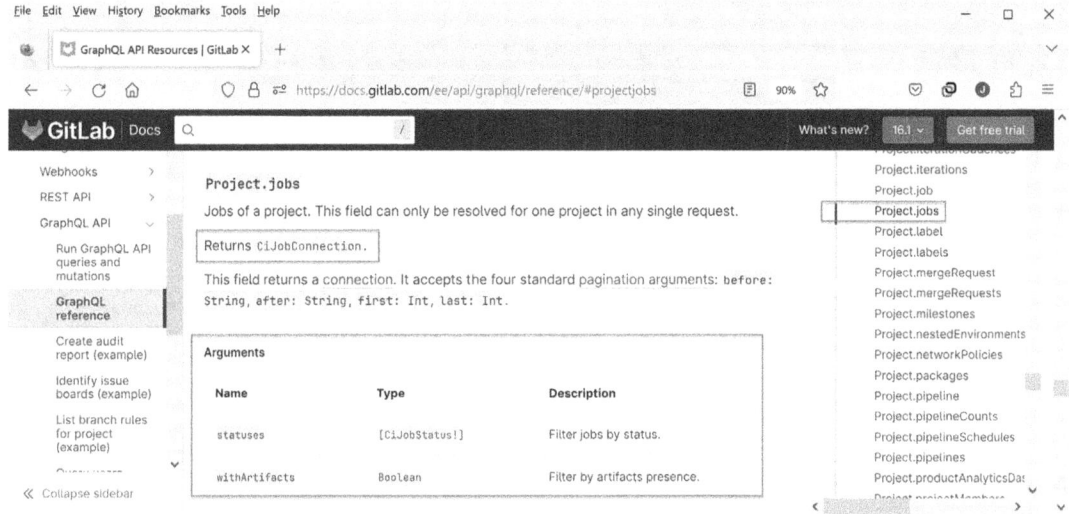

Figure 11-62. *Description of arguments for the jobs field of Project object type*

The Enumeration Types Section

Before we look at the definition of CiJobStatus, let's look at the description of enumeration types found at https://docs.gitlab.com/ee/api/graphql/reference/#enumeration-types as shown in Figure 11-63. Enumeration types are like scalar types in that they are atomic; that is, they cannot be broken down into smaller pieces. Unlike a scalar type, an enumeration type consists of a set of values that a field may take; these values typically follow the convention of being in all uppercase[19] and are not quoted like strings are.

---

[19] Some of the enumeration types that describe sort orders, such as ISSUE_SORT, have older lowercase values. These have been deprecated and turned into an equivalent uppercase value.

479

CHAPTER 11   THERE'S AN API FOR THAT

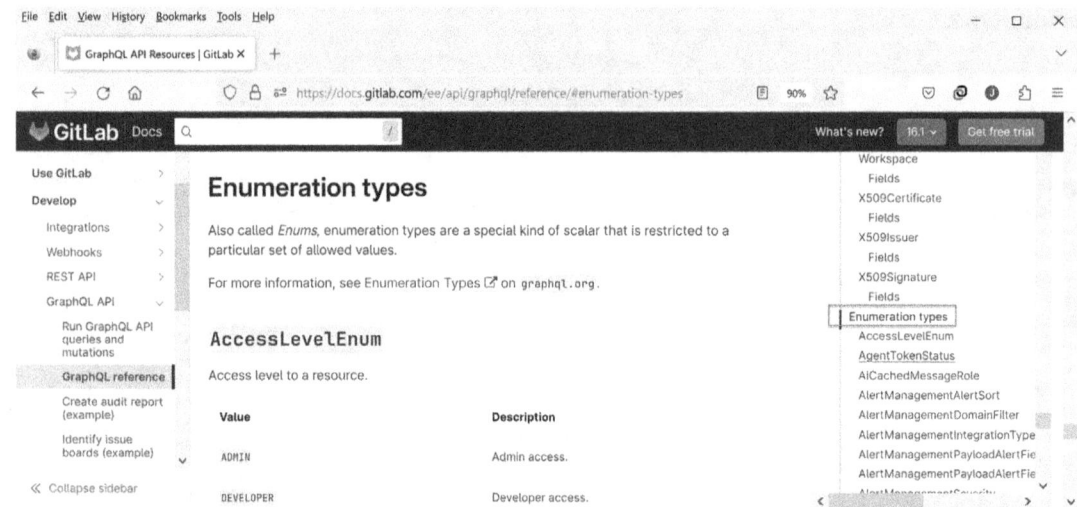

***Figure 11-63.** GraphQL reference section for enumeration types*

Clicking the CiJobStatus link in the jobs field description provided earlier takes us to the enumerated CiJobStatus type as shown in Figure 11-64. Because this is an atomic type, there are no arguments or fields defined for it.

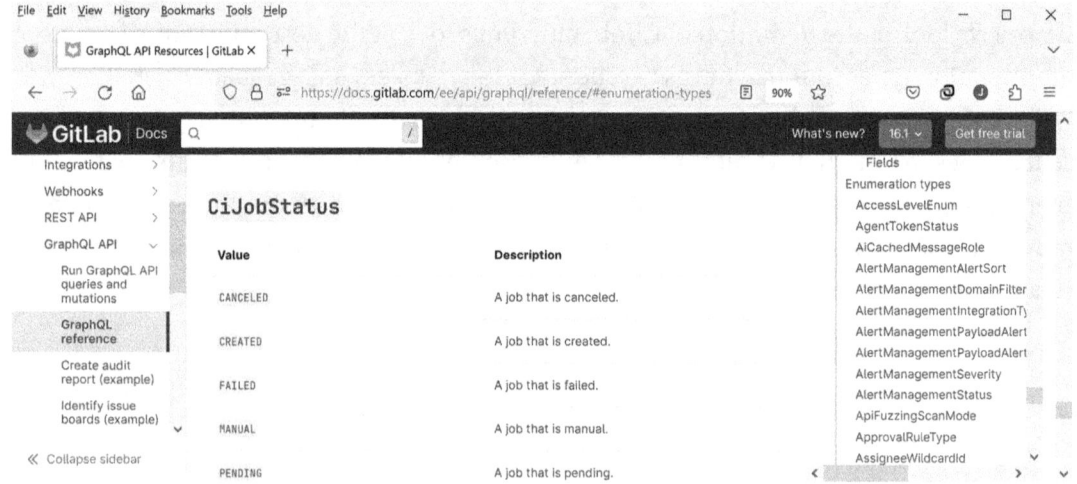

***Figure 11-64.** Values of CiJobStatus enumeration type*

CHAPTER 11 THERE'S AN API FOR THAT

The Connections Section

Continuing on the jobs description, we see that the jobs field returns a CiJobConnection type. This is distinct from the job field that returns the object type CiJob. So let's check out the description of Connections found at https://docs.gitlab.com/ee/api/graphql/reference/#connections as shown in Figure 11-65. As you may have gathered, a Connection type describes the association between two objects such as a Project object and its associated Job objects. The Connections section is broken up into three subsections: Pagination arguments, Connection fields, and Connection types. I'll describe each in turn.

Figure 11-65. GraphQL reference section for connections

Pagination Arguments

First off, let's look at the pagination arguments section shown in Figure 11-66. The reason for putting these arguments in its own section is that all Connection types use these arguments, so this avoids repeating them for each connection type. We've seen these arguments in practice from examples on pagination in the GraphiQL section.

481

CHAPTER 11   THERE'S AN API FOR THAT

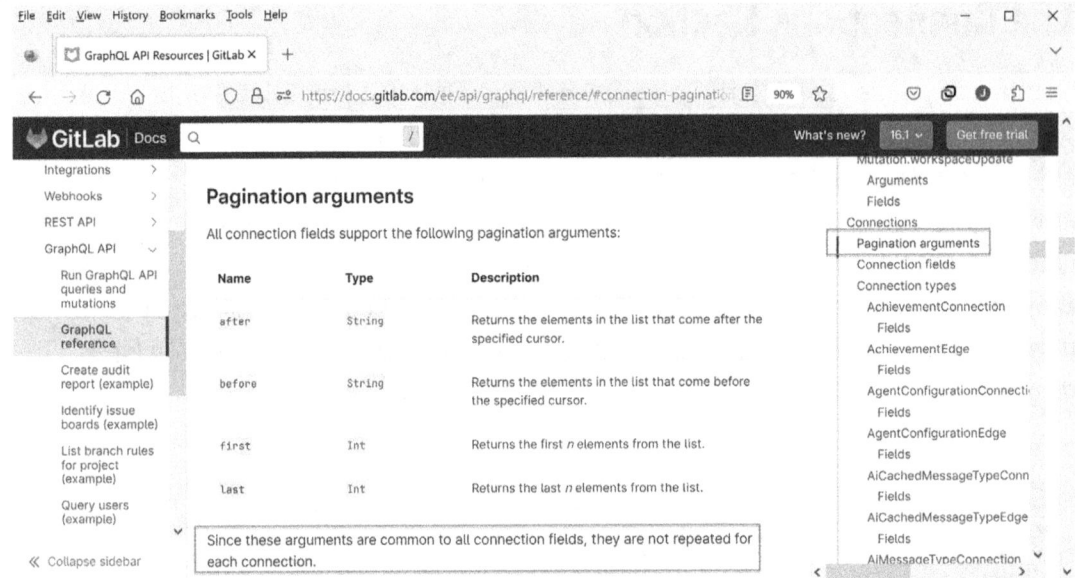

Figure 11-66. *Description of pagination arguments common to all connections*

Connection Fields

Next, Figure 11-67 shows the common fields returned by all Connection types. We've already seen these in use in earlier GraphQL examples. Note that this section describes the common names of the fields used by Connection types, but, except for the pageInfo field, the types of those fields are generic. Because of that, each of these fields is repeated for each connection type so as to expose their explicit type.

CHAPTER 11 THERE'S AN API FOR THAT

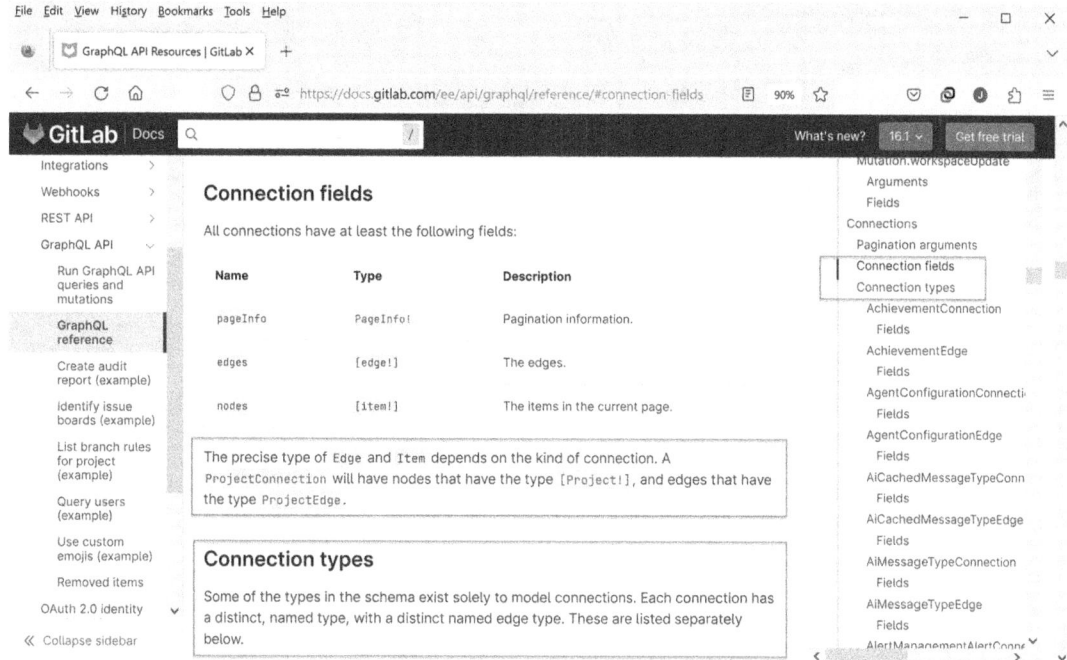

Figure 11-67. Description of fields common to all connections

Connection Types

Going back to our jobs field example, clicking the CiJobConnection takes you to the description shown in Figure 11-68. Here, we see the same fields as described in the Connection fields section but with explicit types for the edges and nodes fields. The edges field returns a list of CiJobEdge objects, and the nodes field returns a list of CiJob objects.

CHAPTER 11   THERE'S AN API FOR THAT

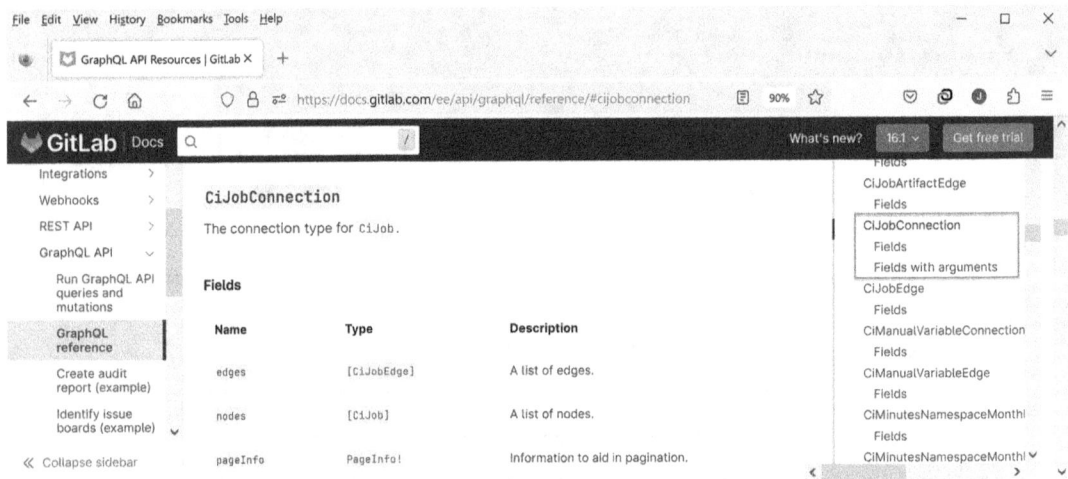

Figure 11-68.   Description of CiJobConnection

One interesting aspect of the CiJobConnection type is that it defines a field with arguments as shown in Figure 11-69. As you may guess, the reason for a special limit field for the CiJobConnection type and not for other connection types is that a project can have a large number of jobs associated with it. This field appears to restrict the number of jobs returned in the background process (similar to the COUNT field in a database query) so as to improve performance of the query overall.

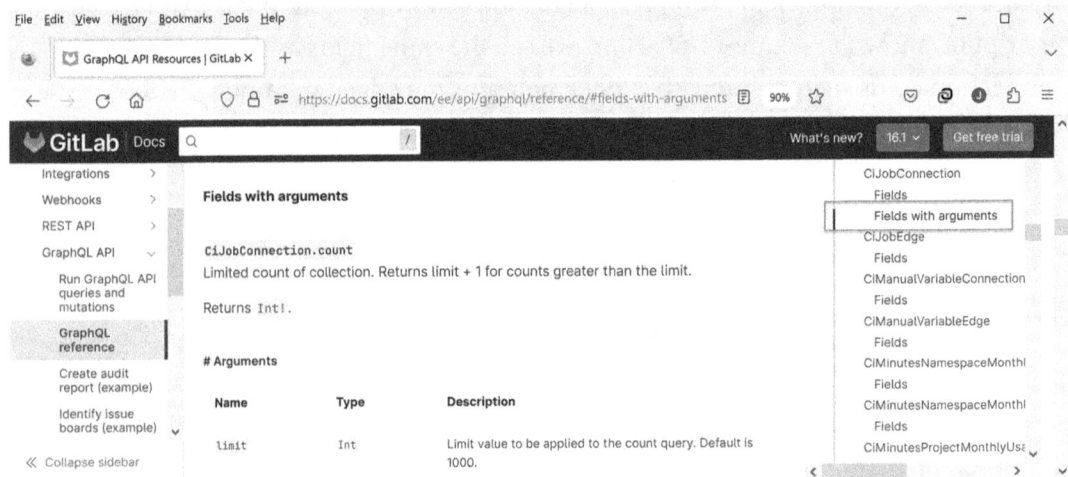

Figure 11-69.   Description of special limit field for CiJobConnection

CHAPTER 11 THERE'S AN API FOR THAT

The Mutation Type Section

Having considered the types related to queries, let's turn our attention to the Mutation type, whose description can be found here: https://docs.gitlab.com/ee/api/graphql/reference/#mutation-type. Like the Query type, the Mutation type is a single type with entry points that define the executable actions that may be made on various objects. Figure 11-70 shows the section describing the Mutation type. Like the Query type, each action has a set of fields to be returned by the action, but unlike the Query type, each action has a set of arguments that are defined under a single input key.

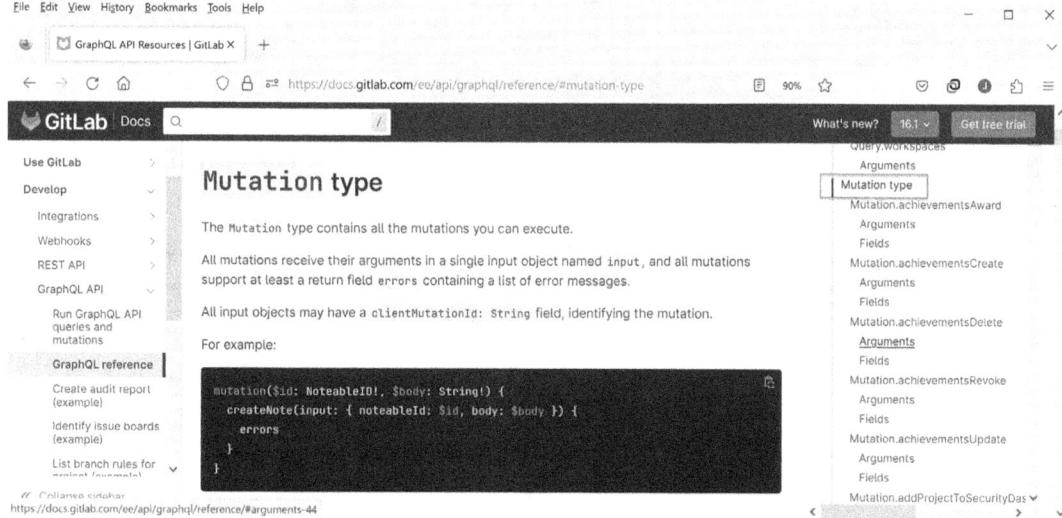

Figure 11-70. *GraphQL reference section for the Mutation type*

To illustrate, let's take a look at the createIssue action as shown in Figure 11-71. The createIssue mutation requires a lot of input arguments, as might be expected with an Issue. This collection of arguments makes up an input type, which in this case is CreateIssueInput. Note that the input type is not a link to another section of the document as is the return type of a query entry point. The reason for this is that an input type is unique to a given mutation unlike, say, a Project object that can be used in a number of contexts such as a return type or as an argument or field value.

485

CHAPTER 11   THERE'S AN API FOR THAT

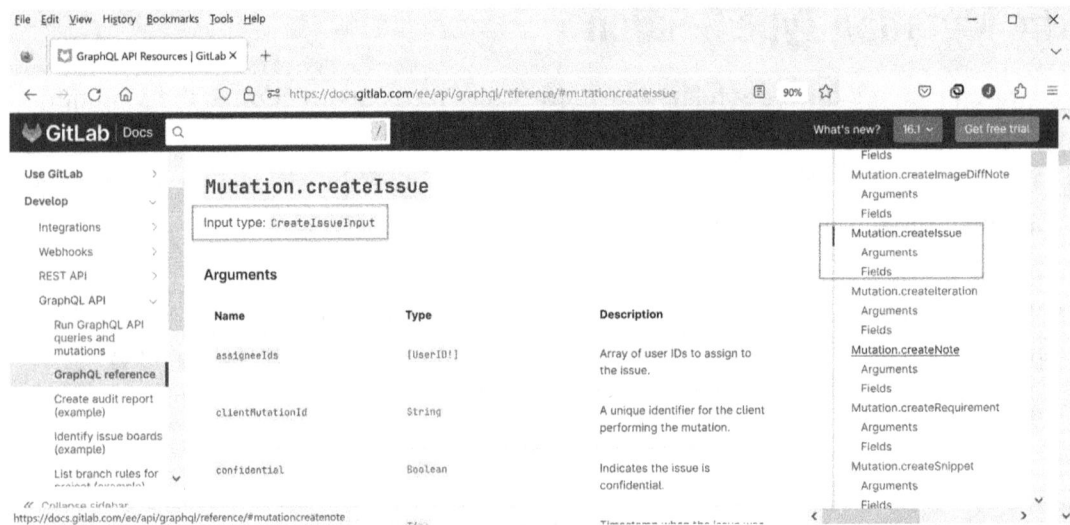

Figure 11-71. *Description of input arguments for a createIssue mutation*

Continuing the createIssue description, Figure 11-72 shows the fields returned after the mutation is completed. All mutation actions return an errors field that is simply a list of String messages, if any.[20] Typically, mutations return the object reflecting the changes made, which in this example is the Issue object created by the createIssue action.

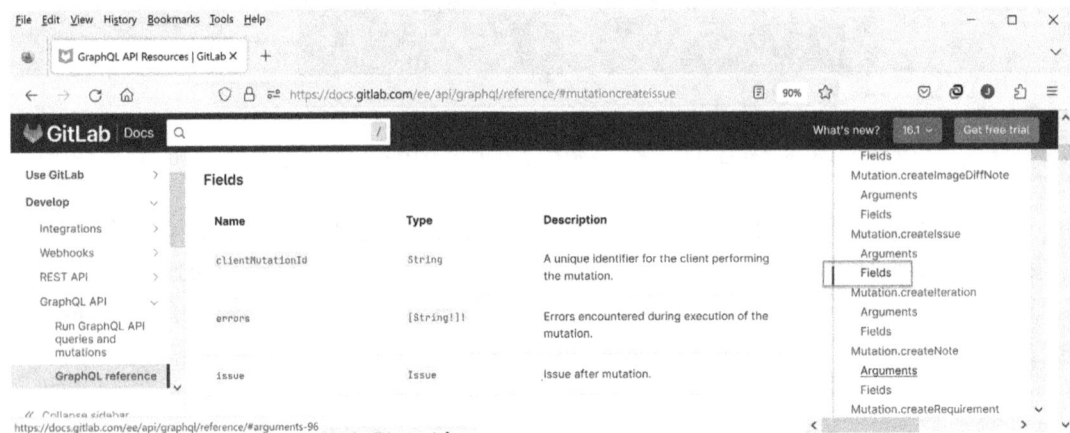

Figure 11-72. *Description of fields returned by a createIssue mutation*

---

[20] The exclamation mark outside the brackets means that if there are no errors, an empty list ([]) is returned rather than a null value. The exclamation after String means that every message in the list is a string of one or more characters.

CHAPTER 11 THERE'S AN API FOR THAT

The Input Types Section

With respect to mutation input types, most arguments fall into one of the already described types of scalars, enumerations, and objects. For example, the confidential argument in Figure 11-71 is the Boolean scalar type. However, there are some input arguments that don't fall into one of these categories. For these arguments, the Input types section is provided to describe them, which is located at https://docs.gitlab.com/ee/api/graphql/reference/#input-types. Figure 11-73 shows the initial description of input types.

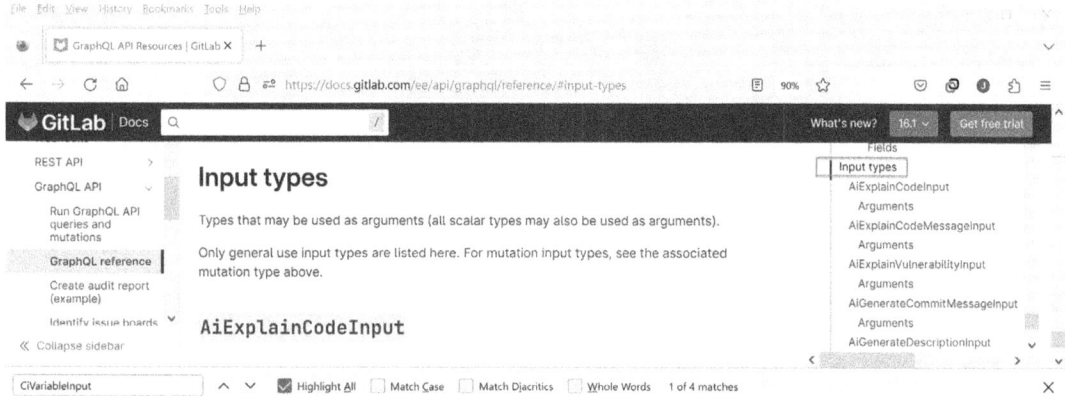

Figure 11-73. *GraphQL reference section for input types*

As an example of a general input type, Figure 11-74 shows the definition of the CiVariableInput type. It consists of two arguments: key and value. This input type is referenced in arguments by two mutation actions: jobPlay and jobRetry. Figure 11-75 shows the description of jobPlay with the variables argument referencing the CiVariableInput type.

CHAPTER 11 THERE'S AN API FOR THAT

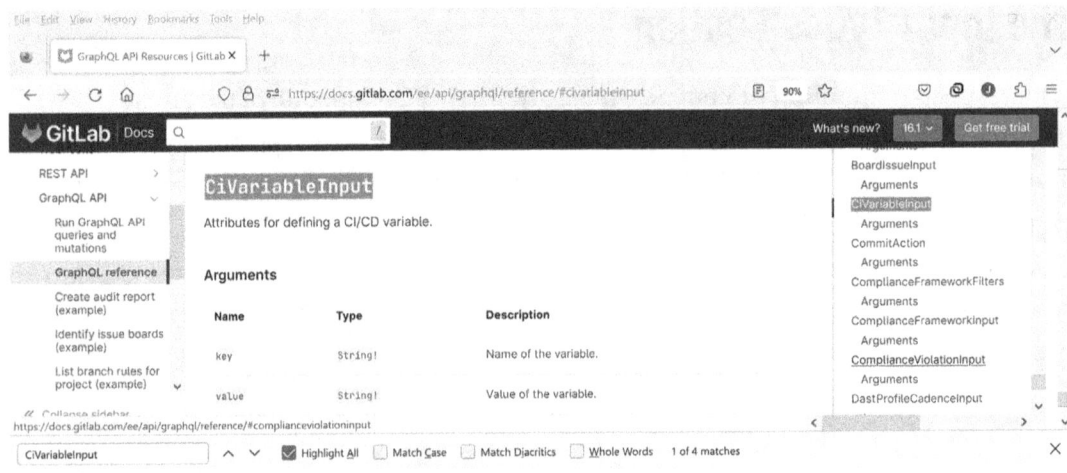

Figure 11-74. Description of input type CiVariableInput

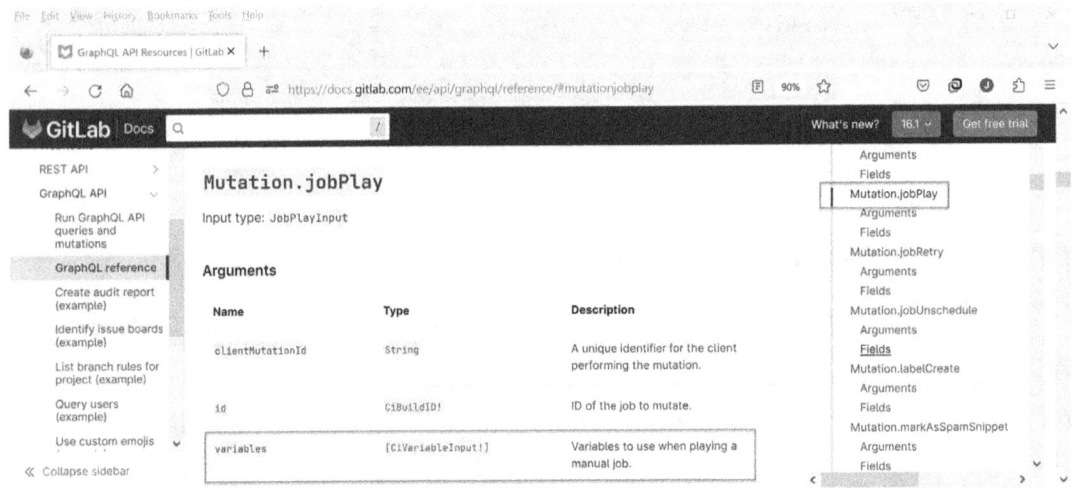

Figure 11-75. Description of jobPlay mutation highlighting the variables argument of type CiVariableInput

The Abstract Types Section

We end this section with a description of the final set of types: Abstract. These types are more for development purposes to simplify the definition of other types within GraphQL. This section can be found in the GraphQL reference here: https://docs.gitlab.com/ee/api/graphql/reference/#abstract-types. Figure 11-76 shows the description of abstract types. There are two categories of abstract types that we'll discuss in turn: union and interface.

488

CHAPTER 11 THERE'S AN API FOR THAT

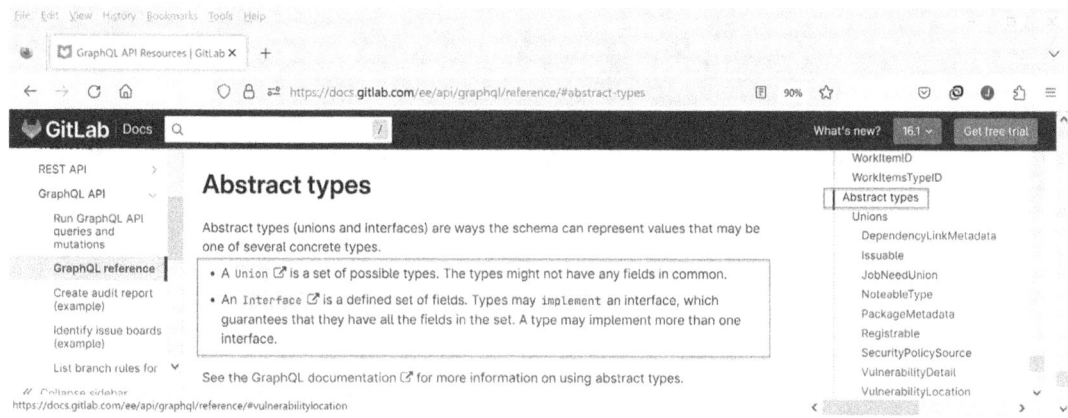

Figure 11-76. GraphQL reference section for abstract types

Union Abstract Types

A union abstract type is a type used for fields that can take on one of a number of other object types. A good example is provided in Figure 11-77. What this definition states is that an object of type NotableType can be a Design, Issue, or MergeRequest object. To see this in context, Figure 11-78 shows the description of the Discussion type, which defines the notable field of type NotableType. This seems a bit convoluted, so to help understand the connections between these objects better, recall that issues and merge requests can have a discussion section. A discussion is an independent object in its own right, so the notable field of a discussion simply defines the "belongs to" relationship to the design, issue, or merge request.

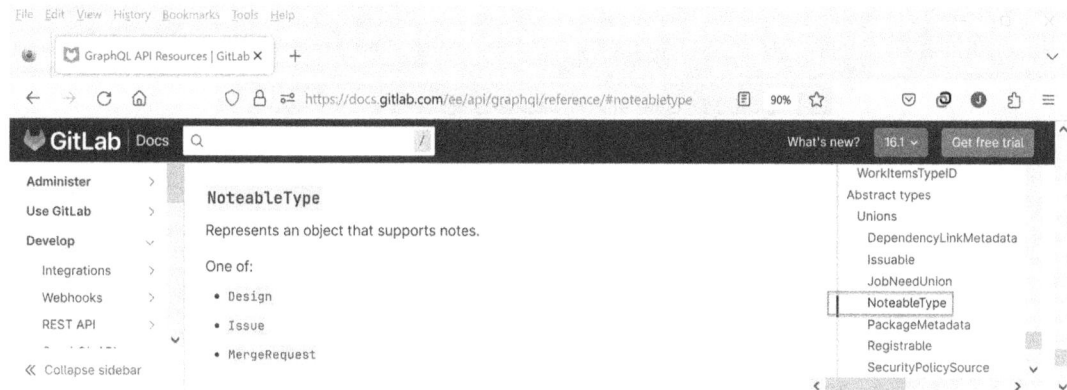

Figure 11-77. Description of union abstract type NotableType

489

CHAPTER 11   THERE'S AN API FOR THAT

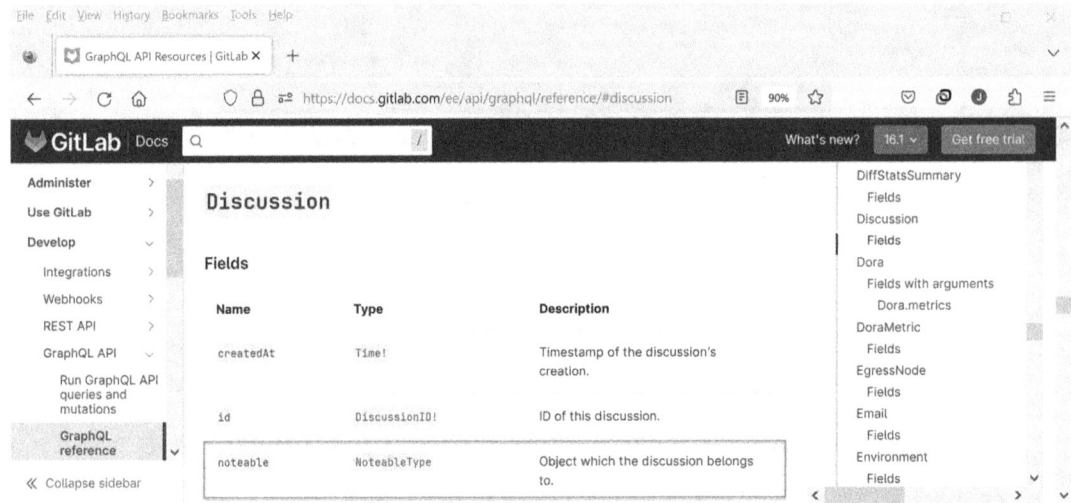

Figure 11-78. *Description of the Discussion type highlighting the notable field of type NotableType*

Interface Abstract Types

An interface abstract type is used to define common fields for a number of objects; those objects can have other distinct fields but will always have these common fields defined. Using CI/CD variables as an example, Figure 11-79 shows the description of the CiVariable interface. This interface defines four fields that all variable types must have: id, key, raw, and value. The "Implementations" section helpfully specifies the five variable types that include these four fields.

CHAPTER 11 THERE'S AN API FOR THAT

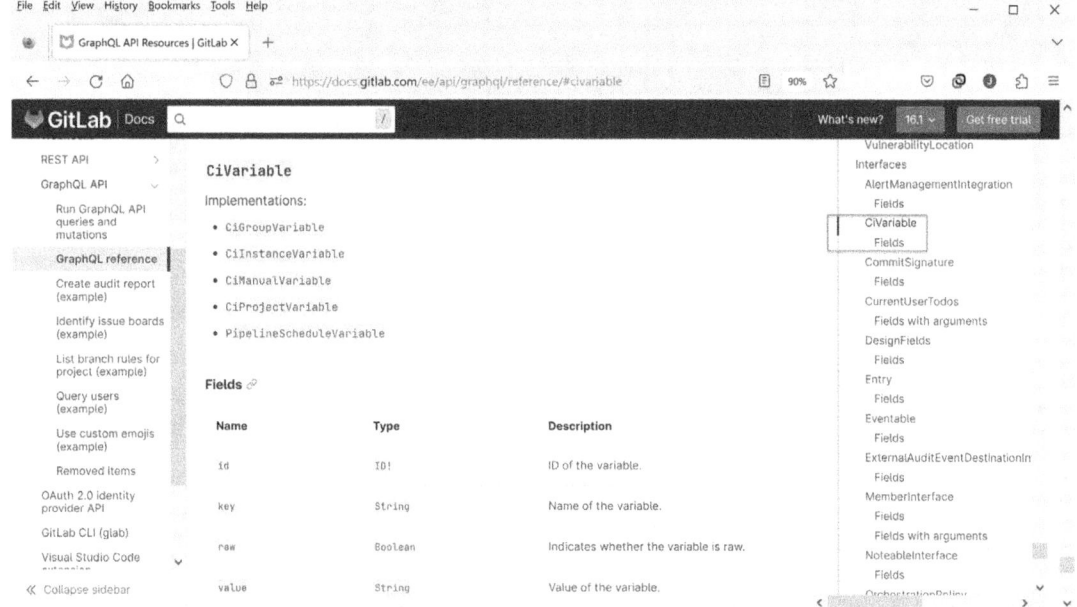

Figure 11-79. *Description of interface abstract type CiVariable*

Figure 11-80 shows the definition of the CiGroupVariable object. The highlighted areas show the fields defined by the CiVariable interface. The remaining fields, such as environmentScope, are specific to group variables.

CHAPTER 11   THERE'S AN API FOR THAT

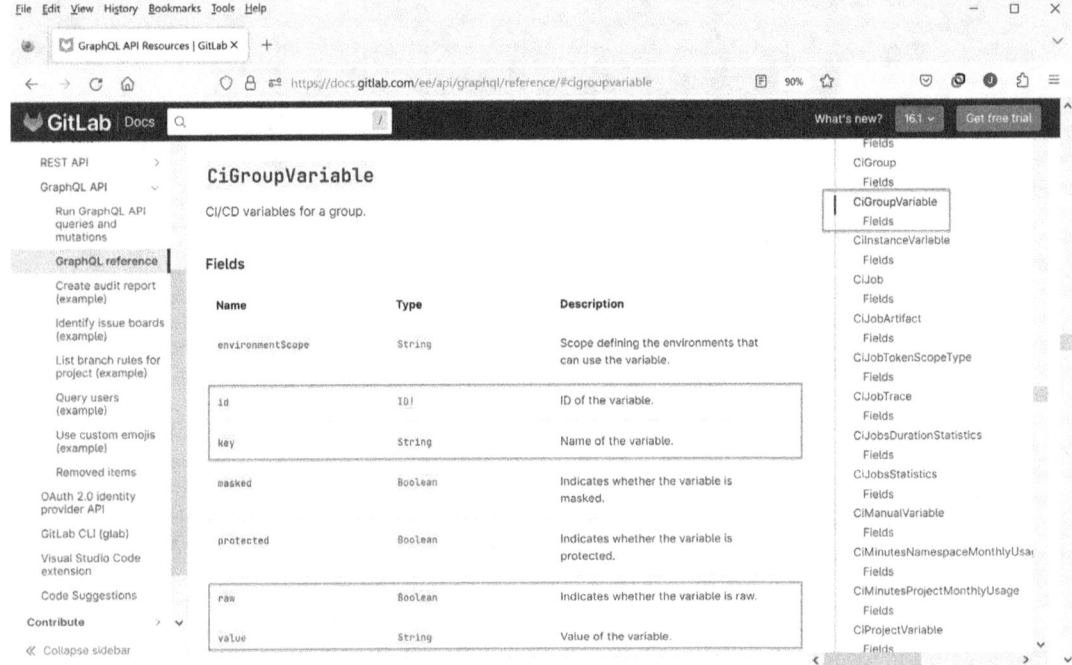

Figure 11-80. Description of the CiGroupVariable object highlighting fields defined by CiVariable interface type

And with that, we've covered the overall structure of the GitLab GraphQL API reference. It is a lot to digest, but once you've mastered navigating around, it becomes second nature to find the info you need to create a GraphQL query or mutation. And in case you do get totally lost, remember the web browser search capability can help you find the way.

Summary

In this chapter, we've covered the following topics:

- Described how to make REST API queries with the web browser
- Showed how to use curl with the REST API to create, read, update, and delete objects
- Introduced GitLab's more powerful GraphQL API

- Demonstrated how to use the GraphQL explorer, GraphiQL, to form queries and mutations
- Discussed how to navigate the GraphQL reference documentation.

For the next chapter, we'll look at two special features of GitLab: creating web documents for public consumption and storing binary objects in Git.

CHAPTER 12

Well, Isn't That Special

We are near the end of covering GitLab features. In this chapter, we will cover two features of GitLab that are often overlooked by developers but useful, nonetheless. We'll first cover the feature known as GitLab Pages where you can generate static web pages that provide an overview of a project for those outside of it. We'll then talk about how to handle the storage of binary files using the Git LFS feature.

Generating Web Pages

If you have any experience with open source software on a site such as GitHub, you know that in addition to the source code being available in a Git repository that you can fork and download, there is almost always a web page or two that describes the software, how to install it, how to make changes, what releases are defined, etc. GitLab enables a similar feature called GitLab Pages.

The GitLab Pages feature allows you to create web pages alongside your groups or projects that describe not only software but your team, your project architecture, links to supporting websites, etc. It should be noted that GitLab Pages is not a generic web service. It provides a way to generate web pages that can be presented via the GitLab UI, but those pages are static. You cannot, for instance, use GitLab pages to present a form to be filled out by the user and submitted to perform some action. For that type of thing, you can provide a link in your GitLab page to a fully functional website either internal or external to your corporate environment. As long as you understand these limitations, your experience in creating GitLab pages will be less frustrating.[1]

---

[1] Less frustrating? What I mean by this is that your web pages have to be generated programmatically or provided directly in HTML. You can't use a fancy web page designer for your web pages, so there will be some iterative development to get your pages looking the way you want.

CHAPTER 12 WELL, ISN'T THAT SPECIAL

Exploring Project Templates for GitLab Pages

Fortunately, GitLab makes it easy to explore how to use GitLab Pages. There are a wide variety of project templates that you can use based on different static web generators. Figure 12-1 shows a list of templates you can select from when creating a new project. Here, I'm going to create a project based on the Pages/Plain HTML template, which is the simplest Pages template available.

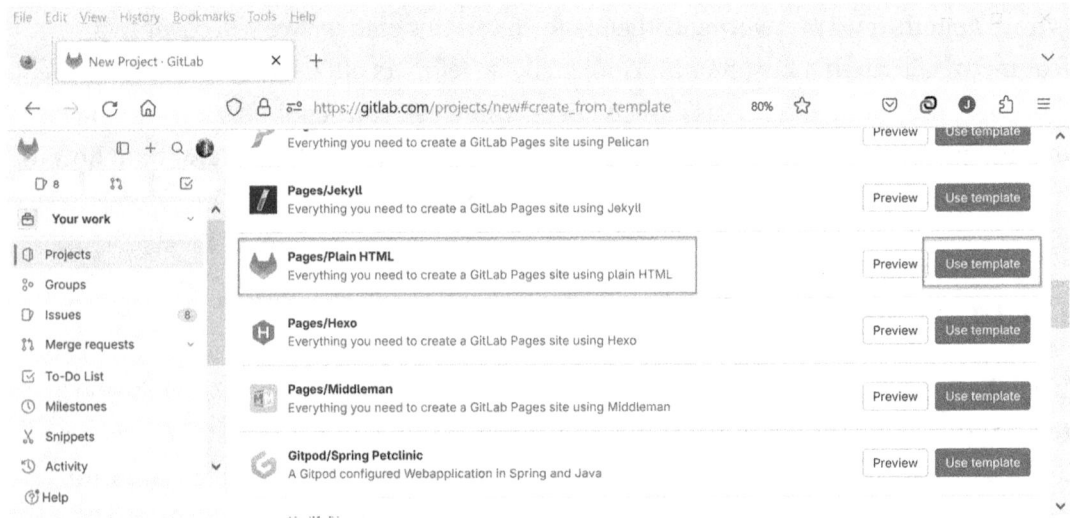

Figure 12-1. Listing of GitLab Pages templates

Creating a Project from a Template

Upon selecting the "Use template" button, you are taken to a project creation page as shown in Figure 12-2. Like any other project, you specify the name, group, and description for the project to be created. It is also important to select the private visibility level to keep any outsiders from messing with your web page. Use "Create project" to create the new GitLab pages project.

CHAPTER 12 WELL, ISN'T THAT SPECIAL

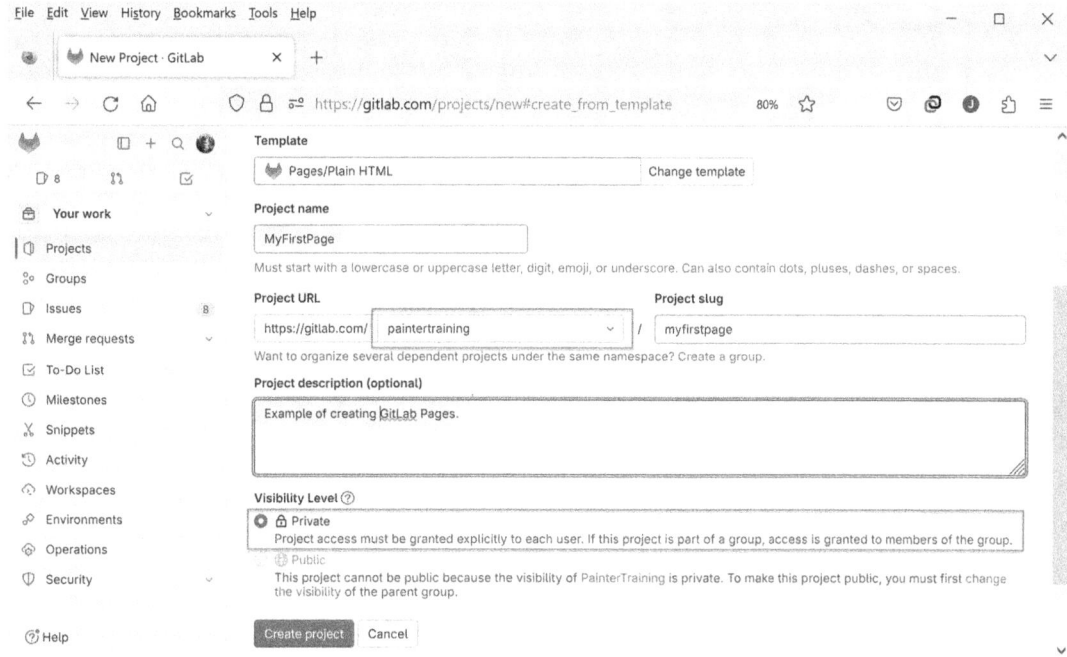

Figure 12-2. *Project creation form for Plain HTML template*

Overview of Files Generated by the Template

As you can see in Figure 12-3, the template has created some files and a public directory. The README.md file has some information regarding GitLab Pages that you will find useful in getting started; I'll ignore showing the contents of this file. You'll recognize the .gitlab-ci.yml file as the CI/CD file; here, it will be used to generate the pages for us. Since this is a project created from a template, you may notice that the pipeline was not run automatically; this is by design.

497

CHAPTER 12   WELL, ISN'T THAT SPECIAL

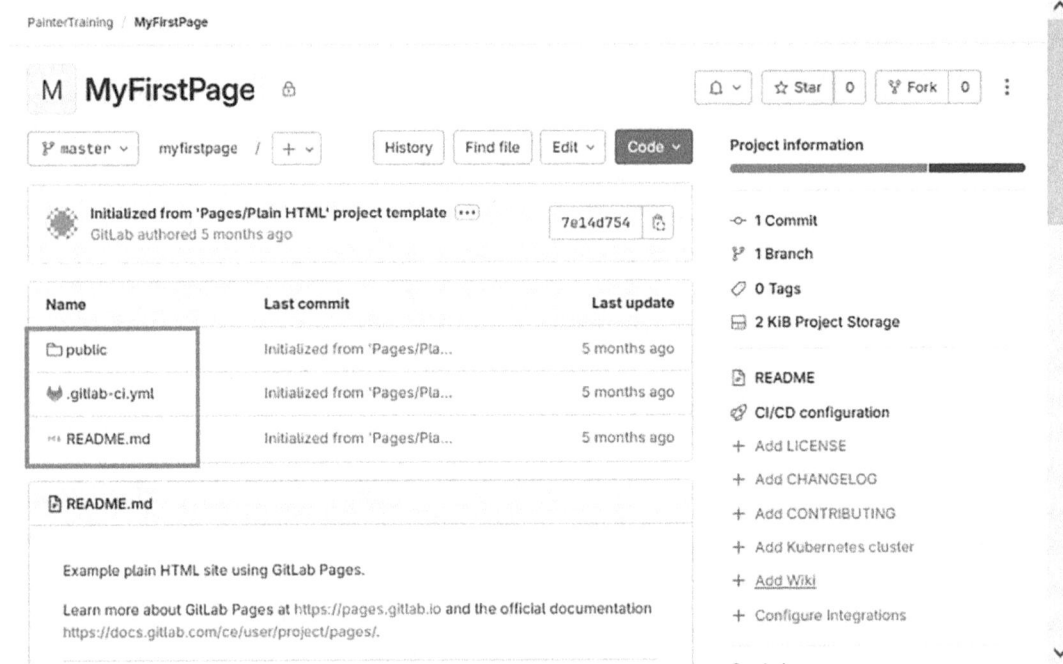

Figure 12-3. Project files generated by Plain HTML template

Before we explore the .gitlab-ci.yml file, let's take a look at what files are in the public directory. Figure 12-4 shows two files that were generated for us: an index.html file and an associated style.css file. If you know anything about web pages, this is the barest bones set up that you can have.[2] One thing to know about GitLab Pages is that it requires a public folder containing the web elements to be deployed; this directory could either be manually created as is done here or could be dynamically created by a static website generator.

---

[2] Well, technically, you could forgo the style.css file and just have an index.html, but this setup is the recommended approach for HTML.

498

CHAPTER 12 WELL, ISN'T THAT SPECIAL

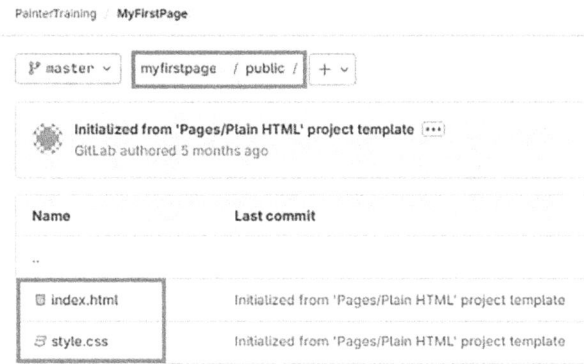

Figure 12-4. Public files generated by Plain HTML template

Contents of the Generated index.html File

Since we are here, let's take a look at the contents of the index.html file that was created for us. This is shown in Figure 12-5. It contains a head section with some metadata, the title of the page, and a link to the style.css file. There is also the required body of the page that defines a navigation bar (which we'll see when we deploy the site), a header, and a simple paragraph. Nothing too exciting here.

Figure 12-5. Contents of generated index.html file

499

CHAPTER 12   WELL, ISN'T THAT SPECIAL

Contents of the Generated style.css File

For reference, Figure 12-6 shows the contents of the style.css file. It contains style information about the page itself (such as the font family to use and max width in pixels) and the navigation bar. If you are not familiar with web style sheets, there are plenty of books on HTML 5 that go into the details of how they work.

Figure 12-6. Contents of generated style.css file

Contents of the Generated .gitlab-ci.yml File

Now let's circle back to the .gitlab-ci.yml file and see how the mechanics of GitLab Pages work. Figure 12-7 shows the content of this file as generated by the template. What is different about this .gitlab-ci.yml file from others we have seen before is the top-level keyword "pages."[3] It is this keyword that lets GitLab know that a web page is being created for this project; without this keyword, you'll just have some HTML files with no link to it. Since this template is for a plain-HTML website, the script is basically a no-op; other page templates will invoke the static generator to create the HTML files for us. The artifacts section describes what files are required for the website to function properly. Here, we only need the public directory and all files underneath it. I'll explain later why we are restricting the creation of the GitLab page to just the master branch.

---

[3] Because this is a top-level keyword, you cannot have a job named "pages."

CHAPTER 12   WELL, ISN'T THAT SPECIAL

```
.gitlab-ci.yml  339 B
 1   # This file is a template, and might need editing before it 
 2   # Full project: https://gitlab.com/pages/plain-html
 3
 4   image: busybox
 5
 6   pages:
 7     stage: deploy
 8     script:
 9       - echo "The site will be deployed to $CI_PAGES_URL"
10     artifacts:
11       paths:
12         - public
13     rules:
14       - if: $CI_COMMIT_BRANCH == $CI_DEFAULT_BRANCH
15
```

Figure 12-7.   Contents of generated .gitlab-ci.yml file

Running the GitLab Pages Pipeline

Since I haven't made any changes and checked them into master, I need to manually run the pipeline to see what is generated. Figure 12-8 shows the results of running the pipeline. As you can see, there is only one stage: deploy. The "pages" job is the standard job that runs; you can click it to see the output generated by the job. The "pages:deploy" is a pseudo job that lets us know that our GitLab web page was deployed. It isn't a real job, and clicking it does not do anything; it is simply a marker.

Figure 12-8.   First pipeline run of the generated project

CHAPTER 12 WELL, ISN'T THAT SPECIAL

Accessing the Generated Web Page

So how do we get to our GitLab page? This isn't intuitive. Within the project, you need to go to the "Deploy" section in the left-hand pane and select "Pages." This shows the "Pages" page as shown in Figure 12-9. Note that this isn't the generated GitLab page but rather a section that looks like a settings page. If you look under "Access pages," you'll see the link that will take you to the GitLab page generated by the job. Look closely at the link and you'll see that it uses a slightly different URL than the gitlab.com URL we are used to. Before we click that link, note the default option of forcing HTTPS; since we are using the URL provided for us to access our site, we don't need to worry about setting up TLS certificates; we are using GitLab's certificate here.

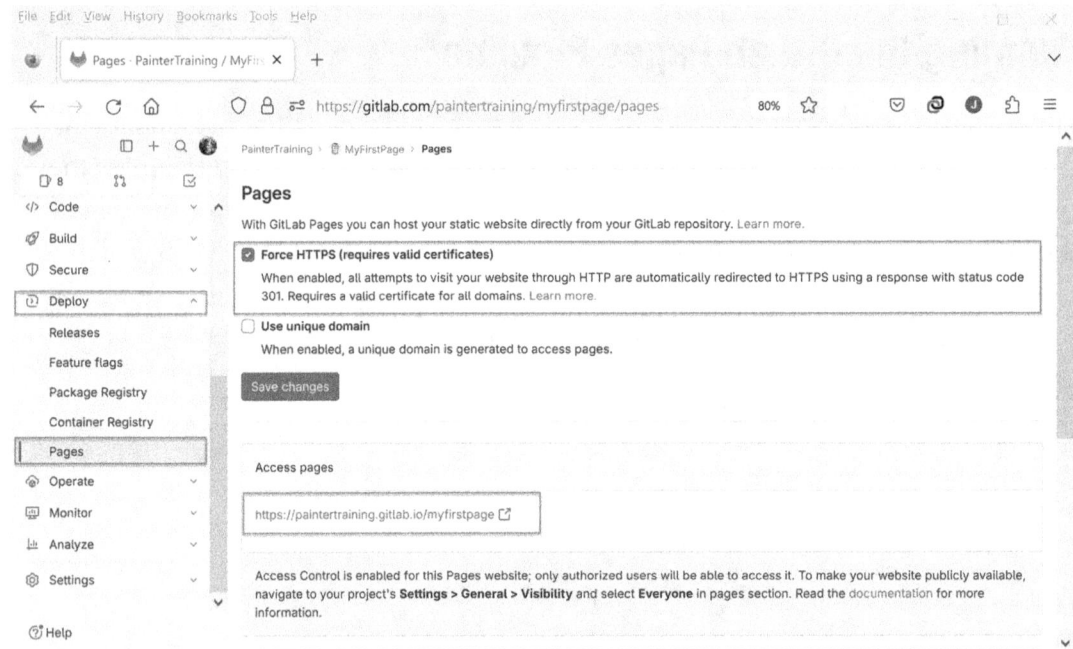

Figure 12-9. Deploy pages section for the project

CHAPTER 12   WELL, ISN'T THAT SPECIAL

Clicking our access link, we see the page shown in Figure 12-10. This is more like it. Here, we see the "Hello World!" heading and the simple text paragraph defined in the index.html file. At the top is the navigation bar that takes you to the current page, the repository code page, and an external link to other examples. Everything looks as we expected.

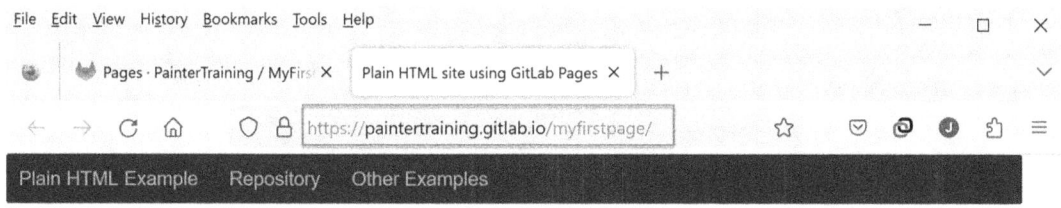

Figure 12-10.   *View of the generated web page*

Exploring the "Other Examples" Page

Since we are here, let's take a quick look at the "Other Examples" page. Figure 12-11 shows what this page looks like. Note that this page may change over time as new examples are added or removed. If you click one of the icons, it will take you to the source code for that example. More interesting is the link embedded within the text describing the example; this takes you to the GitLab page generated for that example.

CHAPTER 12   WELL, ISN'T THAT SPECIAL

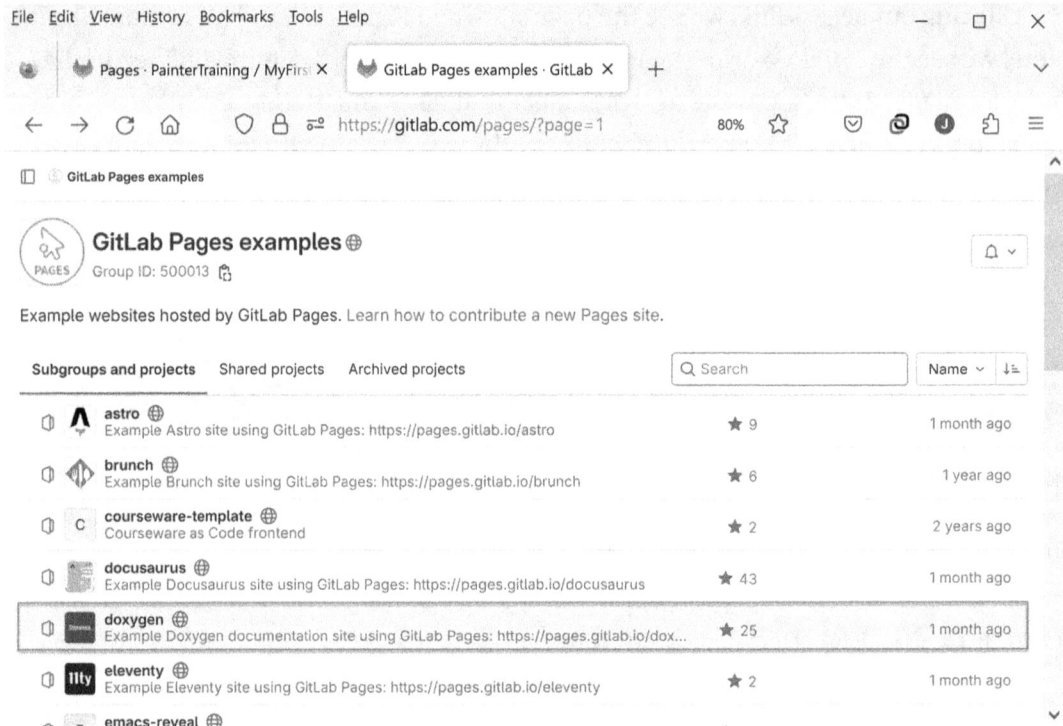

Figure 12-11. *Listing of other GitLab Pages examples*

Previewing Example Websites Generated by GitLab Pages

Figure 12-12 shows the GitLab page generated for the Doxygen example. Doxygen is one of many static web generators that you can use for your own GitLab page website. You can go through each example generator to see the types of sites they generate as well as the code used to create it. Each has their own learning curve.

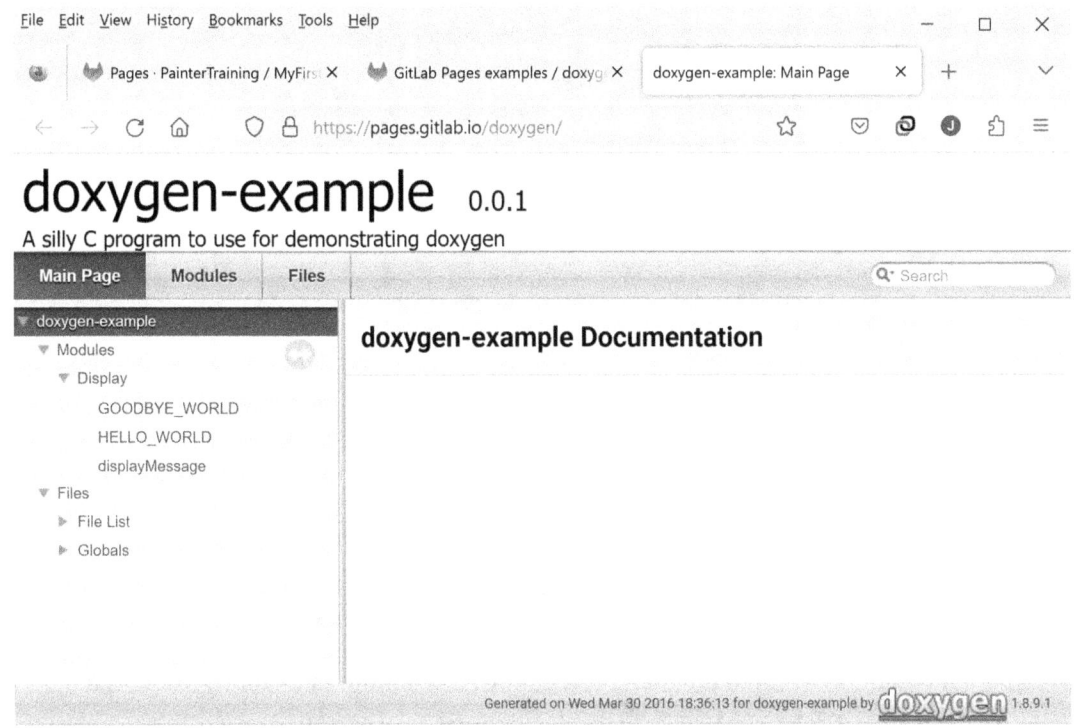

Figure 12-12. *GitLab Pages example of a page generated using Doxygen*

Enabling Access to the Generate GitLab Page

Let's look back at Figure 12-9. Under the "Access pages" section is a note about accessibility. By default, access to the GitLab page is based on project access; that is, only project members can access the GitLab page. So, what if you want to provide more access to other people in your account that are not project members? You could make the project itself public, but that is risky since it allows others to update your GitLab page and any other source code related to the project. Instead, you go to the project's "General Settings" section and look under "Visibility" as shown in Figure 12-13. From there, you'll see a "Pages" subsection where you can switch from "Only Project Members" to "Everyone." This provides access to the GitLab page website without exposing the project to others.

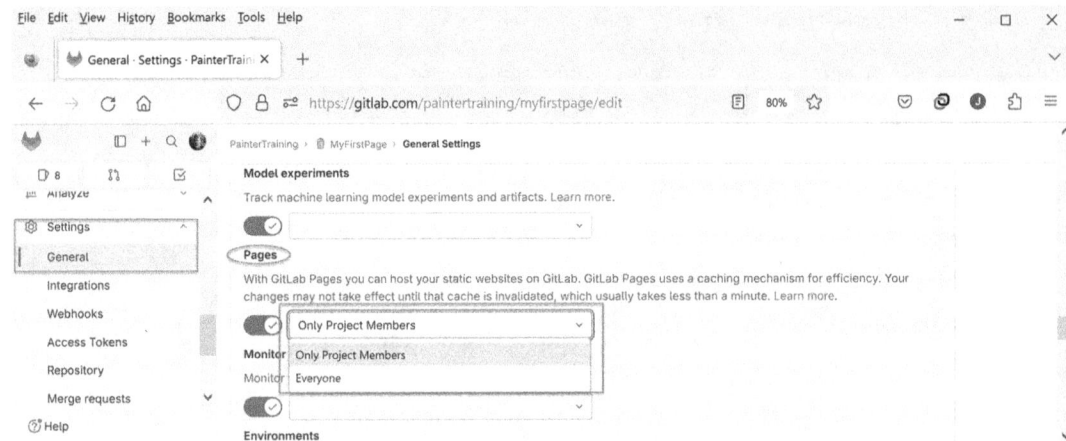

Figure 12-13. *GitLab Pages visibility settings*

Creating GitLab Pages Without Templates

By the way, you don't need to create a project with a template in order to use GitLab Pages. You can add the pages keyword to an existing CI/CD configuration file along with the supporting files. Templates are there to provide examples of how the different static generators work.

Caveat to Using GitLab Pages

There is a caveat to GitLab Pages that you should be aware of. In essence, there can only be one version of the website generated by GitLab Pages at any given time. The reason the previous HTML example restricted the pages keyword to only running on the master branch is because any branch that created a website using pages would override the existing website. If you want to test your website before deploying it, you can create a test job that performs the same operations as the page deployment, but you would have to view the artifacts package created by the test job explicitly. You cannot use the access link to view the test website.

Using Alternative URLs for GitLab Pages

Before we leave the topic of GitLab Pages, there is one aspect of GitLab Pages that I want to address: URLs. As you've seen in our "MyFirstPage" project, GitLab will use a default URL that can be used to access the generated website. The thing is, you might not want to expose that URL to the general public. With the gitlab.com site, there are a couple of alternative URLs that can be used.

Figure 12-14 shows the effect of selecting the "Use unique domain" option on the Deploy pages page and saving the changes. What you get is a unique domain URL. The advantage is that it doesn't require a path such as /myfirstproject to access the index. html page; this is useful for some site generators that expect everything to be under the root domain. The clear disadvantage of the unique domain is that it isn't very friendly to type in; to make it unique, the URL has to contain a generated sequence of alphanumeric characters.[4]

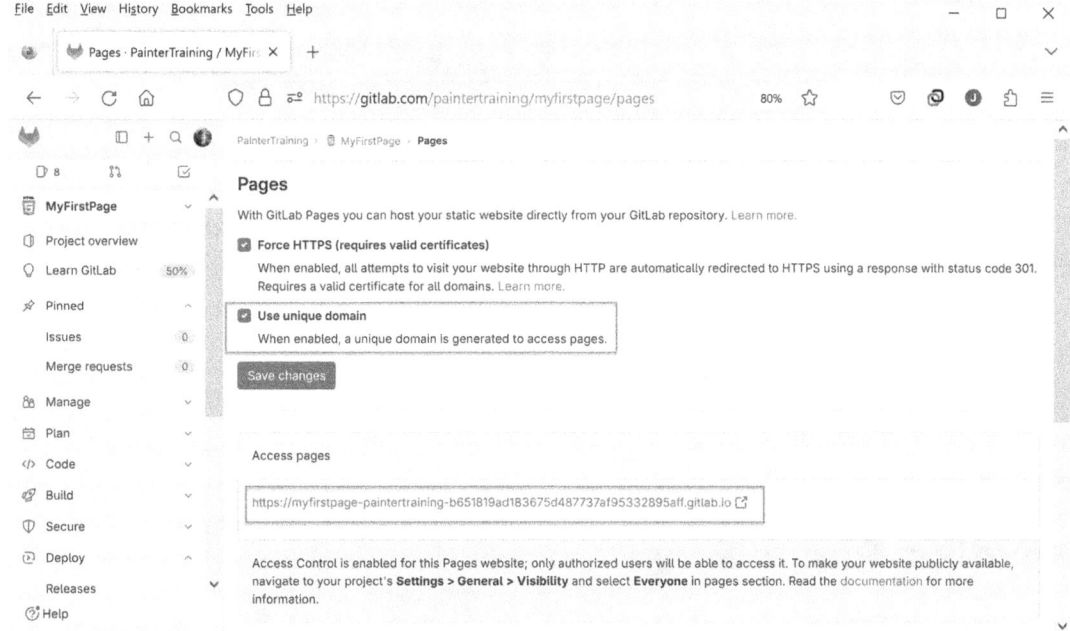

Figure 12-14. GitLab Pages unique domain option

---

[4] Actually, it appears that the string consists of hexadecimal characters since I only see numbers and the characters a to f.

The other option is to use a domain that you control along with TLS certificates for that domain. Figure 12-15 shows the options available at the end of the "Deploy Pages" page following the "Access pages" section. Here, you can add your own domain to be used for your GitLab pages site. Along with the domain, you can either use Let's Encrypt to create the TLS certificates for you or provide your own. You can check the documentation on how this works, if interested.

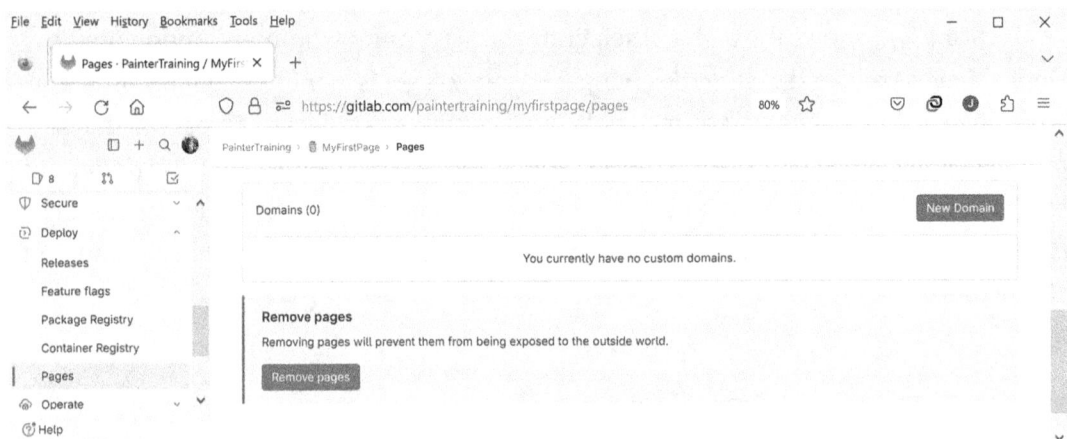

Figure 12-15. Other GitLab Pages options where you can add your own domain

For those using pages from a standalone GitLab service, there are other options you can do as well. Again, I won't go over these here as they are fairly well documented. The key thing to keep in mind is that with the self-managed service, you will need to manage the TLS certificates yourself.

We are now going to switch our attention in the next section to managing binary files, such as images that can be used in GitLab Pages, for example.

Handling Binary Files

There are times when some projects will need to handle binary files. Website projects, for instance, typically need to manage image, video, and/or audio files to be distributed with the web application. Git, unfortunately, isn't well designed for this. As you may recall, Git keeps track of text file differences rather than whole file snapshots, which works well with text files but not so much with binary files. In fact, for binary files such as images, Git will maintain whole file versions rather than deal with pixel differences.

The Problem of Storing Versioned Binary Files in Git

So, what is wrong with storing versioned binary files as snapshots? Well, recall that when a developer clones a Git repository to their local machine, they clone the entire repository. If there are a lot of binary files (which tend to be quite large, relatively speaking), a Git clone will end up downloading all versions of every binary file. This will end up using a lot of the developer's disk space not to mention the increased time to clone the repository to the developer's local filesystem.

Although a developer could restrict a clone to being "shallow," such a clone cannot be used to push changes back to the remote Git repository. Making changes requires that a developer have the entire Git repository present on their local filesystem. One possible workaround to storing binary files in a Git repository would be to manage those files using a separate file management tool (say S3 in AWS). The process that assembles the application would then have to figure out which binary files are needed for a given version of the product – not an ideal solution.

The Git LFS Feature

Enter Git LFS, where LFS stands for large file storage. As it turns out, Git LFS is not part of the normal Git distribution;[5] it is an add-on tool that works with Git to manage files stored in a filesystem separate from the main Git repository. The way LFS works is that it uses proxies in the Git repository that reference the actual binary files; these proxies are text based and typically take less space in the Git repository than the binary files would. LFS uses "lazy resolution" for the proxies; that is, the actual files are downloaded only when needed. In this way, you can clone an entire Git repository containing these references onto a local filesystem without having to download all the binary files, which saves considerable space and download time.

Since I'm talking about Git LFS, you probably gathered that GitLab supports it. It does indeed. GitLab administrators determine where the secondary file storage resides. You as the user don't have to worry about where those files live. For cloud-based implementations of GitLab, LFS storage is typically managed by the underlying cloud service; for example, in AWS, GitLab uses S3 to store these large files. For in-house implementations, a file service such as NFS (Network File Service) is typically used.

---

[5] Although it is part of the Git for Windows distribution.

CHAPTER 12   WELL, ISN'T THAT SPECIAL

Prerequisites to Git LFS

There are some prerequisites to using Git LFS with GitLab. First, the administrator of the GitLab installation needs to enable and configure LFS. It is the administrator that prepares the secondary storage for LFS objects and defines restrictions on the size of individual files that may be stored by LFS. You should know that standalone GitLab installations do not enable Git LFS out of the box; this makes sense since storage for binary objects can explode quite rapidly. Fortunately, gitlab.com has Git LFS enabled but with varying size restrictions on its use based on licensing. Note that there may be additional costs for LFS storage via gitlab.com.

Second, the GitLab project or group that you are using needs to enable Git LFS. If LFS is enabled by the GitLab administrator, then typically it is enabled by default for every group and project. An administrator could, however, disable LFS by default in order to contain costs. Even so, a project owner or maintainer or a group owner is able to enable or disable Git LFS as they choose. To enable it at the GitLab project level, go to the project's general settings, expand the "Visibility, project features, permissions" section, and select the "Git Large File Storage" option. To enable it at the GitLab group level, go to the group's general settings, expand the "Permissions and group features" section, and select the "Projects in this group can use Git LFS" option.

The third prerequisite to using Git LFS is that as a developer, you need to install the git-lfs client software on your local machine. If any of the projects you work on uses Git LFS, you should install it whether or not you plan on managing binary files. The good news is, like Git, you only need to install Git LFS once in your development environment. For the record, Git LFS software is maintained as a GitHub project. You can find details on how to install it onto your local environment at `https://github.com/git-lfs/git-lfs#readme`.

Marking Files to Be Managed by Git LFS

Once you've cloned a project repository onto your local development environment and have Git LFS installed, how do you let Git know what files are to be managed by Git LFS? You might think it would know which files are binary files (like .jpg or .mp4) and would automatically manage them via LFS. Unfortunately, no such magic happens. You need to let Git know what files you want managed by LFS. Fortunately, you can use filename wildcards such as "*.bmp" to indicate that all bmp files are to be stored by LFS. And, of course, you can be explicit about what files are to be managed, such as "superbigfile.doc".

As a developer, the first thing you have to do is "initialize" the project so that it knows that Git LFS is being used. Just enabling Git LFS for the project at the settings level is not enough. You have to run "git lfs install" within your cloned project on your local machine. Despite the name, it does not install Git LFS itself. What it does is make changes to the .gitconfig file located at the base of your project's source code and adds hooks so that LFS works properly. This only needs to be done once per project.

Once you've run git lfs install, you mark what files that LFS is to keep track of using the git track command. For example, "git track *.bmp" will tell Git that you want LFS to track all bmp files. The git track command will create the .gitattributes file (if it does not exist already) at the root of your project's source code and will add the tracking files within it. It is important to ensure that the .gitattributes file is managed by Git (via git add .gitattributes) so that all developers as well as GitLab know what files are being tracked.

Migrating Existing Files to Use Git LFS

The best time to track binary files is at the start of a project before any of those files are committed. Foresight is always better than hindsight in these things, but, of course, stuff happens. You may find that someone has committed a large number of binary files that are not being tracked by LFS, and you want to start tracking them. In this case, you can't just run the git track command and expect that all existing files to be tracked in the repository will be automatically switched to LFS. Instead, you have to run the "git lfs migrate" command to replace tracking files with their references.[6]

A word of warning about running git lfs migrate. This command ends up rewriting history in the Git repository, which is a very risky operation. Migrating tracking objects should be planned and performed by one person when no other work is going on. Once the migration is completed, all developers will need to re-clone their local Git repositories so that everyone is in sync. I've done this successfully many times, so don't let me talk you out of it. As long as you follow the preceding advice, you should be fine.

---

[6] In case you are wondering, you can run the process in reverse to "untrack" files, but this is a rarer case.

Cases When Git LFS Should Not Be Used

Before I leave this section, I want to talk about a use case where Git LFS should not be used: binary dependency files. Some projects depend on externally sourced library files to build a product such as those found in Maven projects. I get the temptation here. Someone high up wants to ensure that everything used to build a product is tightly controlled down to the exact versions of those objects. There are also those who are nervous about the idea of downloading files from an external package repository located somewhere on the Internet.

A primary problem with using Git LFS to maintain these files is that they are maintained per project. What happens if multiple projects want to use the same version of the same binary package? You end up with multiple copies of the same files stored in your secondary file storage, which can be costly. The better solution is to use GitLab's package repository to store these objects. Alternatively, set up a standalone Nexus or Artifactory service to manage all these objects for the company; both of these products provide for shadowing of library objects from external repositories. With such a setup, security scans can be performed, and performance improved when downloading packages.

So when should you use Git LFS and when to use a package repository? A rule of thumb that I use is to store objects in Git LFS such as images that will be delivered as part of the final product and to store objects in a package repository that are used to build a product.

Summary

In this chapter, we've covered the following topics:

- Explored how to browse through project templates when creating a new project
- Reviewed the components generated for GitLab Pages
- Discovered where to find the web pages generated for a project
- Discussed how to store binary files using Git LFS
- Considered conditions when Git LFS should not be used

This chapter ends our discussion of GitLab features. Starting with the next chapter, we are going to discuss how to spin up your own self-managed GitLab service.

CHAPTER 13

I Can Do This on My Own

I mentioned in Chapter 1 that in order to illustrate the various features of GitLab, which we've just now completed, it was easier to create an account on gitlab.com rather than install GitLab as a self-managed service. This is because installing GitLab on your own is much more involved than simply downloading a binary and installing it. There are a lot of moving pieces to a self-managed GitLab. The good news is, there is more than one way to install GitLab. The bad news is, there is more than one way to install GitLab.

How you install it depends on a number of factors that I'll explore in this chapter. We'll also set up some of the basic infrastructure in AWS needed to support both the back-end and front-end services.

Deciding on a Plan of Implementation

The first question to answer is why do you want to install a self-managed version of GitLab vs. using the gitlab.com website? If the reasoning is that you have a small development team of up to, let's say, 50 people and you want to save money by installing the free-tier self-management version rather than paying the per-seat cost of a premium license on gitlab.com, that certainly is a valid reason. Realize, though, that the free tier for the self-managed install still has the feature limitations of the free tier of gitlab.com; on the other hand, you won't have some of the physical limitations, such as storage, which comes with gitlab.com. Also, realize that you won't have the support that you would get with the paid subscriptions, so if something goes haywire, you may have to wait a long time (roughly days to weeks) to get a solution to your issue from the open source support website.

CHAPTER 13   I CAN DO THIS ON MY OWN

On-Premises vs. Cloud Considerations

For larger companies, I would gather that the primary reason for installing a self-managed version has to do with security. With the gitlab.com site, there is a certain amount of trust required of GitLab to ensure your data remains private to your company; after all, your source code most likely is the lifeblood of your company. By having that data in-house, you have a greater sense of security that your data will remain private than on a public website. But is it, though? If you plan on installing GitLab on servers that you physically own, then your privacy depends on your networking and security teams ensuring that all firewalls are set up properly and that your servers are physically secured in a data center. If not, your code could be open to a security breach.

However, if you are like most companies today, you will probably end up using a cloud service, such as that provided by Amazon, Google, or Azure, to install your self-managed GitLab software. And with that, you are back to the trust issue you had with gitlab.com. You need to consider how much you trust the cloud provider in protecting your data. Assuming you use VPN[1] access to your servers in the cloud and depending on how proficient you are with the cloud service, you may feel more comfortable with using the cloud service over using gitlab.com. That's understandable. Chances are you are already using a cloud service to deploy your services and/or products, so using it to maintain your code base isn't much of a stretch.

Administrative Considerations

Security isn't the only reason companies consider the self-managed GitLab service. Managing your own service gives you access to administrative features and settings, also commonly referred to as instance-wide settings. For instance, you can control user quotas such as storage and project limits. You can also create commonly used project templates that can be used by all users on your site, not just templates restricted by group or project. And, of course, you can set up your own shared runners that can be used across all groups and projects.

Having your own self-managed instance also gives you control over when release upgrades are performed. With gitlab.com, upgrades are performed automatically whether you are ready for them or not; on the plus side, sometimes you get access to features before self-managed services do. So why might this be an issue? For minor

---

[1] Virtual private network.

release upgrades, performing the upgrade every month isn't much of an issue.[2] With yearly major releases, however, certain deprecated features may be removed. Generally, these affect the back-end infrastructure such as what database versions are allowed. But sometimes these deprecated features affect users directly, such as when a pipeline keyword is removed or updated in such a way as to not be backward compatible. Although GitLab does its best in providing a list of deprecated features to be removed in a major release, not everyone is ready for the change. By controlling when you upgrade to a major release, you can provide users time to prepare for the changes.[3]

Architecture Considerations

Moving off of why you might want to install your own self-managed service, let's look at the considerations in installing your own. The biggest factor in the architecture of the GitLab service is the number of users you expect to support. As you might expect, the more users accessing your service, the more servers you will need. But it is a little more complicated than that. With a small number of users (generally less than 1000), you can get by with a single server that has multiple components running on it. But as soon as you get above that number, some components will need to be separated into running on their own servers. And the greater number of users, the more separation of components will be required.

To help administrators determine what is needed based on the number of expected users, GitLab provides reference architectures for various levels of usage. You can find this documented at `https://docs.gitlab.com/ee/administration/reference_architectures/`. It separates the architectures starting at "up to 1000 users" and ending at "up to 50,000 users." Since these are reference architectures, you don't need to follow them exactly, but the closer you are to the reference, the better, especially in terms of GitLab support.

---

[2] Note, however, that with each minor update, regression issues may occur; what this means is that sometimes features that used to work no longer do. This is normally fixed with a patch release, but not always.

[3] If you are wondering about security patches for prior releases, note that GitLab maintains three major releases simultaneously, so if there is a security patch needed on your current release, it will be made available so you can apply it before you perform the major upgrade.

CHAPTER 13   I CAN DO THIS ON MY OWN

High-Availability Considerations

In addition to the number of users, there are some other factors you need to consider before setting up your own GitLab service. One such factor is high availability (HA). Do you need to keep the service up and running 99.99% of the time despite the inevitable server failures? If so, you'll need to look at reference architectures that take high availability into account. For example, the reference architectures for up to 1000 and 2000 users do not take HA into consideration. If you have fewer than 2000 users and want to have high availability, then you should use the reference architecture for up to 3000 users downscaling some components as needed. The reference architecture guide gives you advice on how to do this.

One benefit of having high availability is that you can do zero-downtime upgrades. With single server setups, you will have to plan for downtime to upgrade your release, which can take up to an hour at times. Note that even with zero-downtime upgrades, there will be times when you will need to take your service down for maintenance. This typically occurs during major release upgrades when a database version also needs to be upgraded; this is especially true when an older database version is no longer supported.

Disaster Recovery Considerations

A related factor to HA is disaster recovery (DR). To be clear, they are not the same thing. With disaster recovery, you are concerned with how quickly you can recover when a massive failure occurs. For example, if you are on a cloud provider in a specific region and that region goes down for a period of time,[4] you need a disaster recovery plan to ensure that you can get back up and running as quickly as possible with little loss of data. This generally involves replicating the service across multiple regions that include other countries, especially if you support users across the globe. With replication, you also need to consider if you need automatic failover to kick in so that your service is minimally disrupted; alternatively, you can consider using a manual failover[5] approach where you switch to a new primary service region. In a worst-case scenario, you need to be able to recover a site from backups.

---

[4] Due to a natural disaster or denial-of-service attack, for example.

[5] You might be thinking that an automatic failover approach is desired over a manual failover approach. However, you need to take into consideration how long a regional service outage will last. If it is expected to recover within the hour, you might want to hold off doing a switchover.

Cost Considerations

Depending on the factors you need to support your self-managed service, you may be calculating the infrastructure costs required to support those factors and thinking, wow, this is going to be pricey. Let's add onto this the license costs, which, like the gitlab.com SaaS service, come in three flavors: free, premium, and ultimate. The license costs are actually the same between the GitLab SaaS and self-managed products. At least the free version supports up to 2000 users using the self-managed service as opposed to the 5-user limit with the SaaS service. However, you should know that the free tier does not support DR, so if this is a factor that you require, you will need to consider the premium tier at a minimum.

Since we are talking about costs, there are some other costs to take into consideration: personnel costs. If you are thinking that you could get by with a single user maintaining the self-managed service on a part-time basis, this isn't realistic. Realize that your staff is going to end up providing support to your developers whether they want to or not. Even with a smaller setup with up to 2000 users, you will need a full-time staff to support the service itself and the developers using it. The larger and more complex the setup, the more staff you will need. And if you have users across the globe, which many companies now have, you will need staff at different time zones to provide support. It's also possible that some of that staff will need to be on-call to provide support during off-hours or common holidays.

GitLab Support Considerations

Now one of the benefits of having a paid subscription is that you will get support from GitLab itself, but this is mostly to the administrators of the self-managed service. With the free tier, not so much. As you might expect, you get more support with the ultimate subscription than you do with the premium subscription. It is one of the reasons why the ultimate subscription is significantly pricier than the premium subscription; the costs of support are built-in. In case you are worried, I've personally had experience with both levels of support, and even though I really liked the ultimate support, the premium support is amazingly good. So, base your consideration of the ultimate tier on the additional features, not solely on the quality of the support.

Alternative Service Considerations

Before I look into how to install a self-managed GitLab service, there is a third option that I briefly mentioned in the first chapter: GitLab Dedicated. If you are thinking that running a self-managed GitLab service is too complicated, but you don't want to go with the GitLab SaaS service due to security concerns, GitLab Dedicated provides an alternative where GitLab hosts the service for you separate from the gitlab.com site. With this setup, your data is in an environment that is under your control, but you don't have to worry about managing the service directly. At the time of this writing, GitLab Dedicated is in limited release but may be available for you to use when you read this. Documentation on this service can be found here: https://about.gitlab.com/dedicated/.

Assuming you are going with the self-managed installation, we'll next consider how to set up your own AWS account to support it.

Instantiating the AWS Account

For the GitLab self-managed service, we will use the AWS Proof-of-Concept (POC) setup as described here: https://docs.gitlab.com/ee/install/aws/manual_install_aws.html. What I describe here is a slightly different set of directions since AWS has made some changes in how the networking piece is performed; the newer network setup is much easier to use than what is described in the GitLab documentation, which is good because it was one of the more difficult parts of the POC configuration. Note that there is a cost to setting up the POC, but I'll try to keep the costs down as much as possible. The goal is to get familiar with the various components of a basic GitLab self-managed installation.

Creating an AWS Account

If you don't already have an AWS account, setting one up is pretty easy. Just go to https://aws.amazon.com and follow the directions to set up your account. Note that you'll need to provide a valid credit card number as they will charge you for certain features. No worries, they will let you know when something will be charged and by how much. When you sign up, you will be given a root access account based on your email address. This account has full access (think super-user access in Linux). You don't want to use this account for your day-to-day work. Instead, you should set up a user account using the Identity and Access Management service (IAM).

Creating an Admin User Group with IAM

Figure 13-1 shows how to access IAM from the services menu. It can be found under the Security, Identity, & Compliance category. Alternatively, you can do a search for IAM using the Services search box.

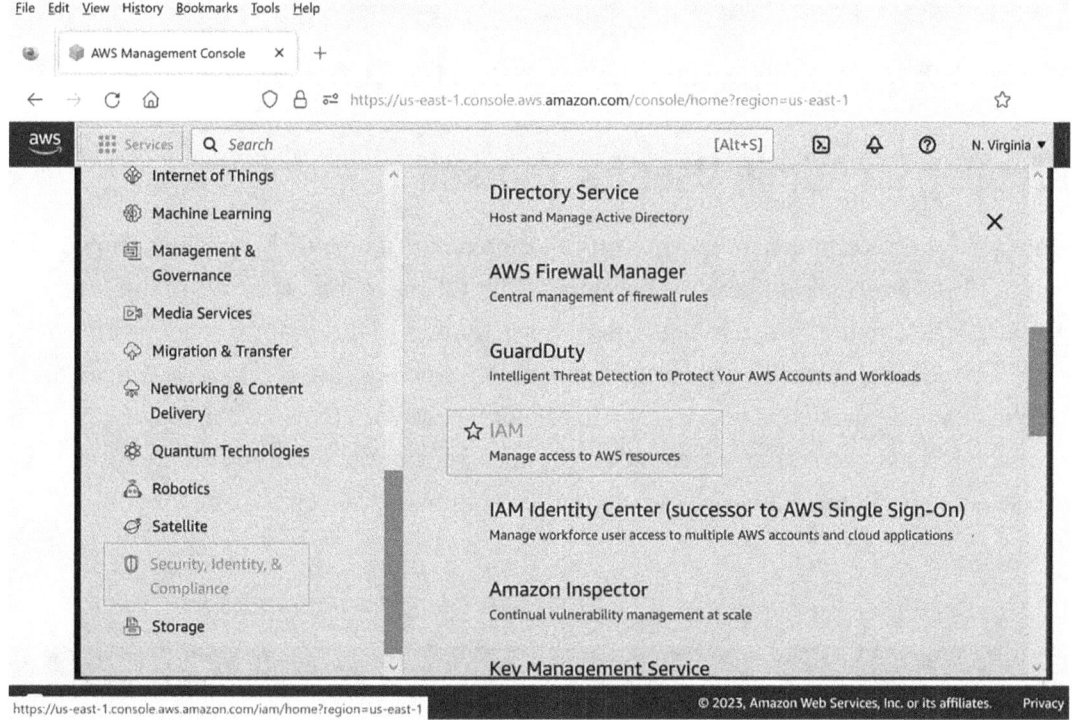

Figure 13-1. IAM selection from the services menu

From this IAM service page, you need to first create a user group as shown in Figure 13-2. In this example, I created the user group called "Admin" that has "Administrator Access" privileges. If you plan on having other users, you can set up different user groups that give them selected privileges to create, delete, and modify various services. For now, you'll want the "Admin" user group for your own user account, which we will create next.

CHAPTER 13   I CAN DO THIS ON MY OWN

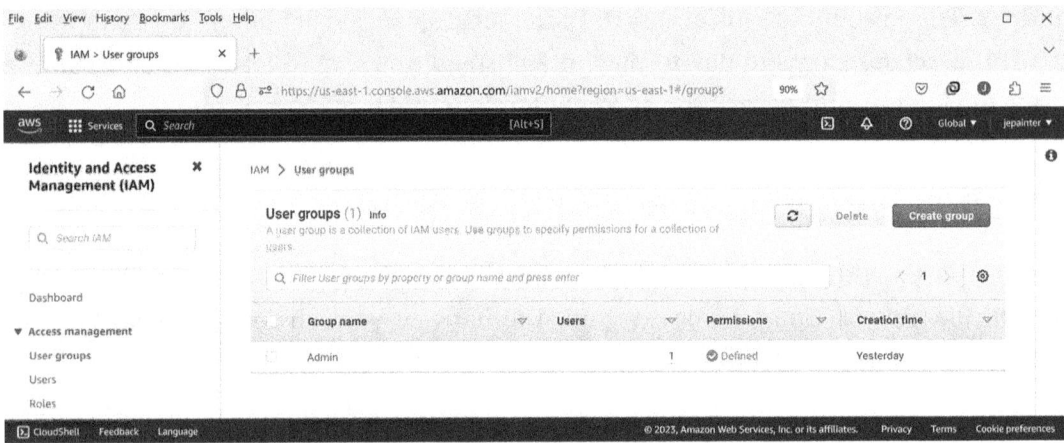

Figure 13-2. *Listing showing the newly created Admin user group*

Creating an Admin User for Yourself

Once you've created the user group, you can then create a user for yourself as shown in Figure 13-3. Here, I created the user jepainter that I'll use to log in to AWS in the future. As part of the creation process, I assigned user jepainter to the "Admin" user group so that I'll have administrative access to create, delete, and edit the services we'll need for GitLab. Also, as part of this process, it will ask for a password to use when logging in. This should be a password different from the root access account. Since you are the user, you can select to enter the password directly rather than have AWS create one for you.

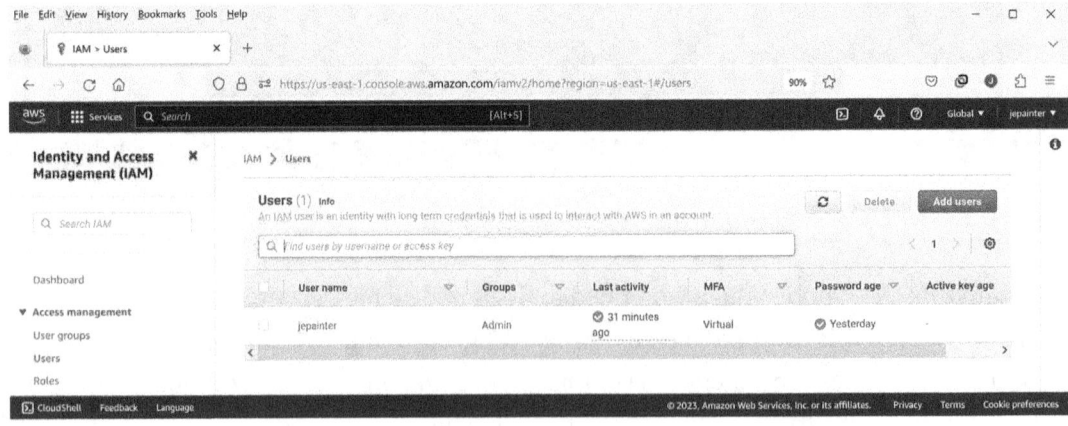

Figure 13-3. *Listing showing the newly created Admin user*

CHAPTER 13   I CAN DO THIS ON MY OWN

Setting Up Multifactor Authentication

Before you log out of the root access account and log in to your new user account, it is important to set up multifactor authentication (MFA) for the root access account (if you don't, you'll see a warning advising you to do so). This is similar to two-factor authentication (2FA) that you may have set up with other phone or web applications. Setting up MFA for the root access account or user is pretty straightforward. The most common method of establishing MFA is to use an authenticator app on your phone. Figure 13-4 provides a list of authenticator apps at the time of this writing that are accepted by AWS. Typically, these apps accept a QR code provided by AWS that you can use to synchronize with your account.

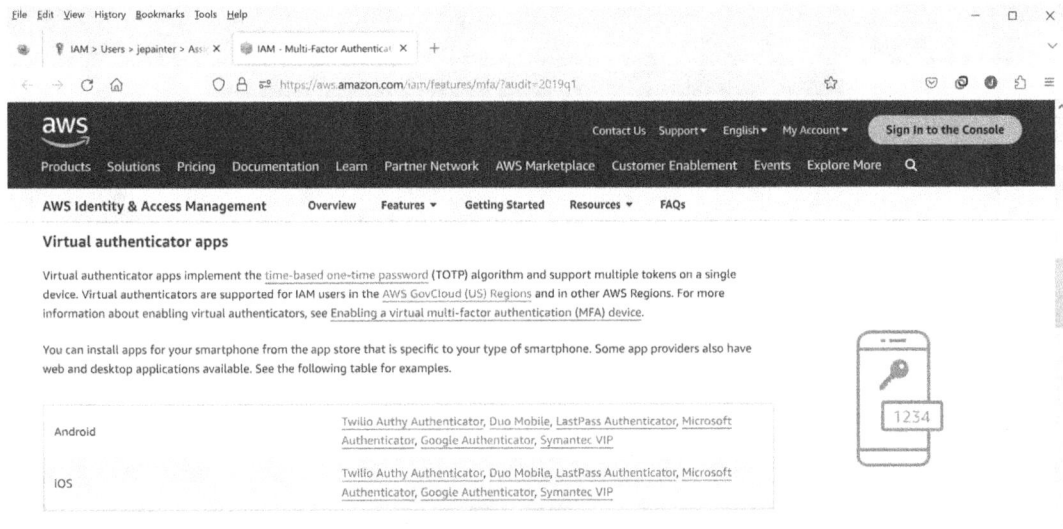

***Figure 13-4.** Listing of authenticator apps*

Once you've set up MFA for the root access account, you can log out and log back in as the admin user previously created. As with the root access account, you should set up MFA for that user as well. Note that the authenticator app will require you to create a new entry for your user account; you can't share MFA between two different accounts. Once the MFA is set up for your admin user, you are ready to begin setting up services for the GitLab POC.

Next up, we'll lay the groundwork for our GitLab POC by creating a virtual private network.

CHAPTER 13   I CAN DO THIS ON MY OWN

Preparing the VPC Network

We'll begin our journey by setting up what I believe is the trickiest service to configure: the Virtual Private Cloud (VPC). This service sets up the network environment under which the GitLab POC will run. You'll find the VPC service under the Networking & Content Delivery category as shown in Figure 13-5. As with IAM, you can also search for VPC using the Services search box.

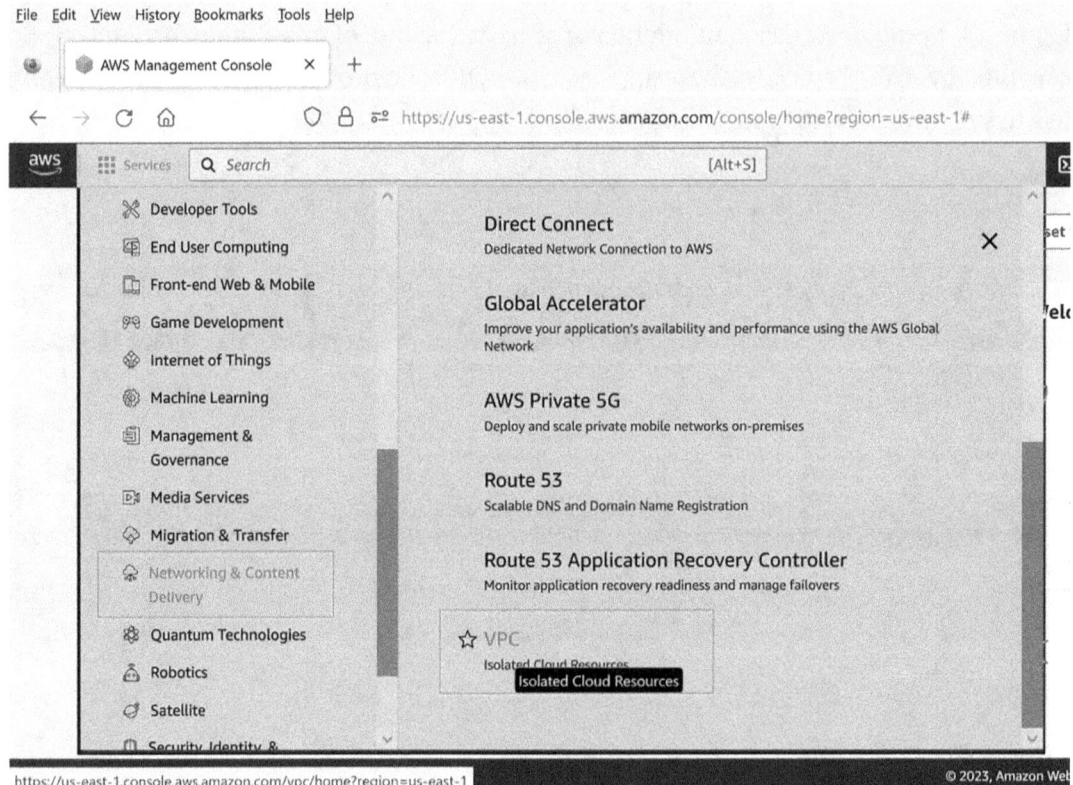

Figure 13-5.   *VPC selection from the services menu*

Determining the AWS Region for the GitLab POC

The first major decision to make involves what AWS region you want to use for your GitLab POC. An AWS region is a general location where the AWS data centers reside. Most likely, you will be in a default region chosen by AWS, for example, us-west-1. This may or may not be where you want to run the POC. You can change the region using the drop-down in the upper-right corner adjacent to your name. Selecting this

CHAPTER 13   I CAN DO THIS ON MY OWN

drop-down will give you a list of regions that have been enabled for you. I chose one of the most common regions, us-east-1, located in Northern Virginia. If you are on the US west coast, you may want to stick with us-west-1, which is in Northern California. If you are in Europe, you will most definitely want to pick a region in Europe such as eu-west-1 located in Ireland. Pick a region that is near to you as this will improve your overall web experience.

Creating a Private VPC

From the VPC main page, you'll probably see that a default VPC has been set up for you already as part of the account creation process. You do not want to use this VPC as it has full public IP access; we want to protect our GitLab services using private IP addresses. Figure 13-6 shows my VPC dashboard. Note that the second line is the default VPC created for me, which has IPs starting with 172.31.0.0. The fact that the IP starts with 172 tells me that it is a public IP range. The first VPC is the private VPC I created for my GitLab POC. Note that this IP range starts with 10. IPs that start with 10 are private IPs associated with my account. You can create a private VPC starting with 10.0.0.0 as well; there is no collision with my IP range since private IP ranges are relative to the user account.[6]

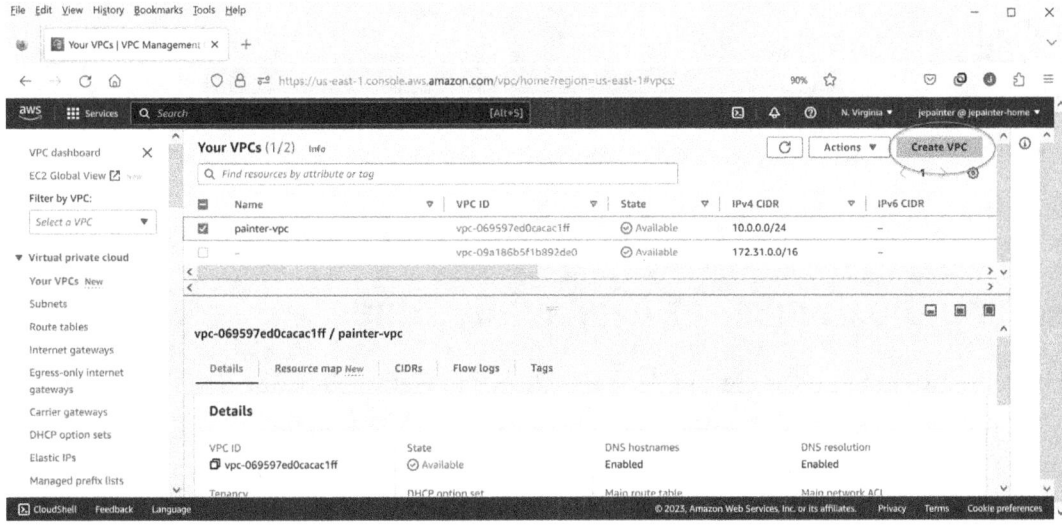

Figure 13-6. Initial VPC dashboard showing default VPC

---

[6] Although this seems confusing to the first-time user, it is what makes VPC "virtual."

523

CHAPTER 13   I CAN DO THIS ON MY OWN

I created the private VPC using the "Create VPC" button as highlighted in the previous figure. This takes you to the form shown in Figure 13-7. To make life easier for you, make sure to select the "VPC and more" option under "Resources to create." This will create all the components such as subnets, route tables, and Internet gateways that you'll need for the GitLab POC. Under auto-generate, I selected painter as the prefix to use for all the components; obviously, choose a name that makes sense for you. For the IPv4 CIDR block,[7] I chose to use 10.0.0.0/24 rather than the default of 10.0.0.0/16. This gives me 256 IP addresses to play with, which is more than enough for the POC.

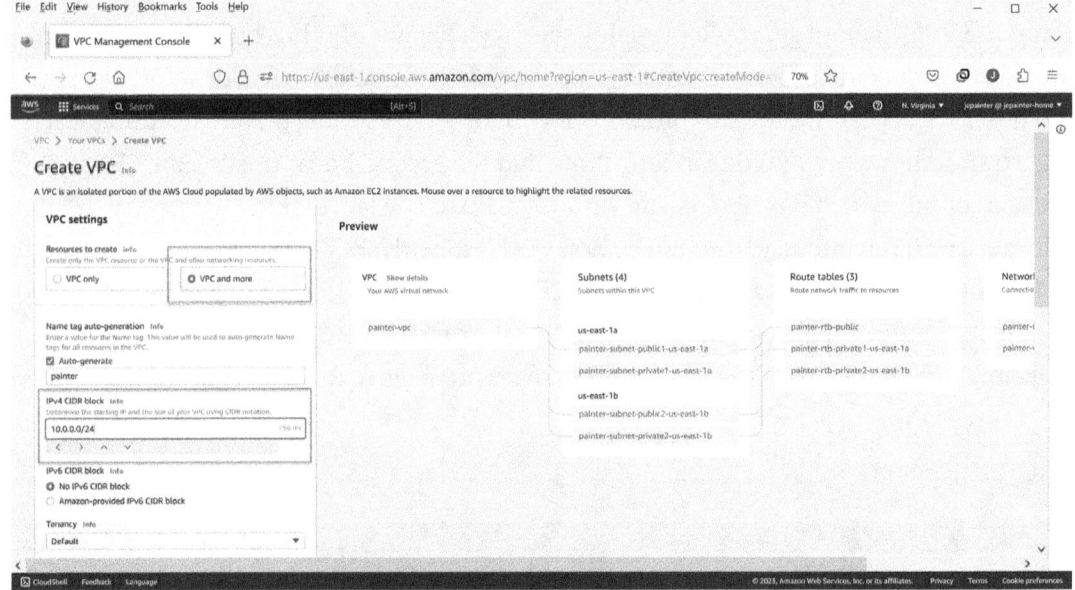

Figure 13-7. VPC creation form (part 1)

Setting the Number of Availability Zones

The remainder of the "Create VPC" form is shown in Figure 13-8. The first thing to select is the number of availability zones (known as AZs). Each region has at least two AZs that you can choose from (some, like us-east-1, have up to six). An AZ corresponds to a data

---

[7] CIDR stands for Classless Inter-Domain Routing. Intuitive, no? It's just a way of stipulating a range of IP addresses where you provide the initial IP address followed by the number of bits to use for the initial part of the IP that remains constant. The larger the number, the fewer the IPs associated with that CIDR. Look up "CIDR to IP" in a web browser to find tools that will translate CIDRs to explicit IP ranges.

CHAPTER 13   I CAN DO THIS ON MY OWN

center located within the region you've chosen. This is done to ensure reliability across the region. If communication with one data center goes down, you'll most likely still have access to another data center in the region. It is best to select at least two AZs for your VPC; for production purposes, you will probably want to go with at least three AZs. In this example, I selected two AZs.[8]

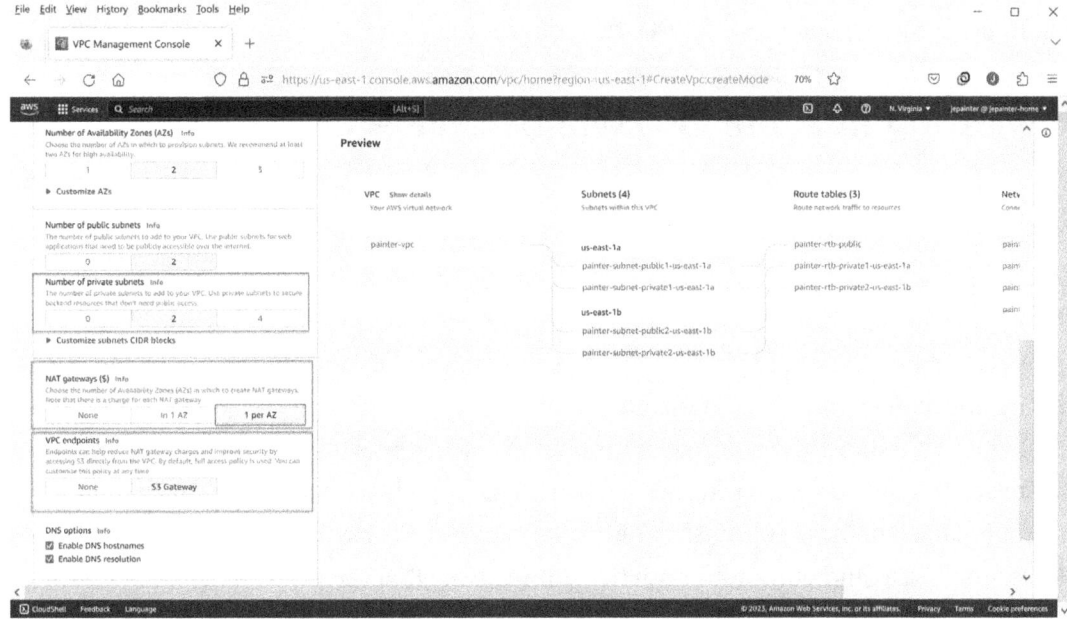

Figure 13-8. VPC creation form (part 2)

Setting Up Public and Private Subnets

Next comes the networking part. Your range of IPs will be split into subnets. There are two types of subnets available: public and private. The public subnet is where you'll put the load balancer that will have "public" access to your web service. The private subnet is where the back-end components, such as databases, web servers, and the like, will reside. In my case, I selected two public subnets and two private subnets. Each subnet will map to 64 of my 256 IP addresses. You can vary this so that you'll have fewer IP addresses in the public subnets and more IP addresses in the private subnets, but this current allocation is fine for the POC.

---

[8] Note that you won't be able to select which data centers in a region you'll have access to. This is determined randomly when you create your VPC.

CHAPTER 13   I CAN DO THIS ON MY OWN

Setting Up the NAT Gateway

Next on the VPC form is the selection of NAT gateways. By default, this is set to none, but I've selected to have one NAT gateway per AZ. A NAT gateway enables Internet access to servers running in a private subnet. This allows a server in the private subnet to access the Internet in order to download software and the like; however, it prevents access from the Internet to your server, which is what you want.

Reviewing How the VPC Will Be Created

For the rest of the form, I kept the default settings for "VPC Endpoints" and enabled "DNS options." What you'll see on the right-hand side is a relatively new feature of VPC that shows what components will get automatically created. This is handy as you change the VPC options on the left-hand side. Note that once the VPC is created, it will be difficult to make any major changes such as the number of AZs and the like as these will impact the allocation of IPs, for instance.

Figure 13-9 shows the graph of components associated with a public subnet. There are two public subnets in each of the two AZs (us-east-1a and us-east-1b in this example). Each of these subnets shares a common route table that controls how traffic flows inbound to and outbound from the subnet. Note that the route table connects to an Internet gateway that enables access to the Internet from within the public subnets. Unlike the NAT gateway, the Internet gateway allows access both to and from the Internet.

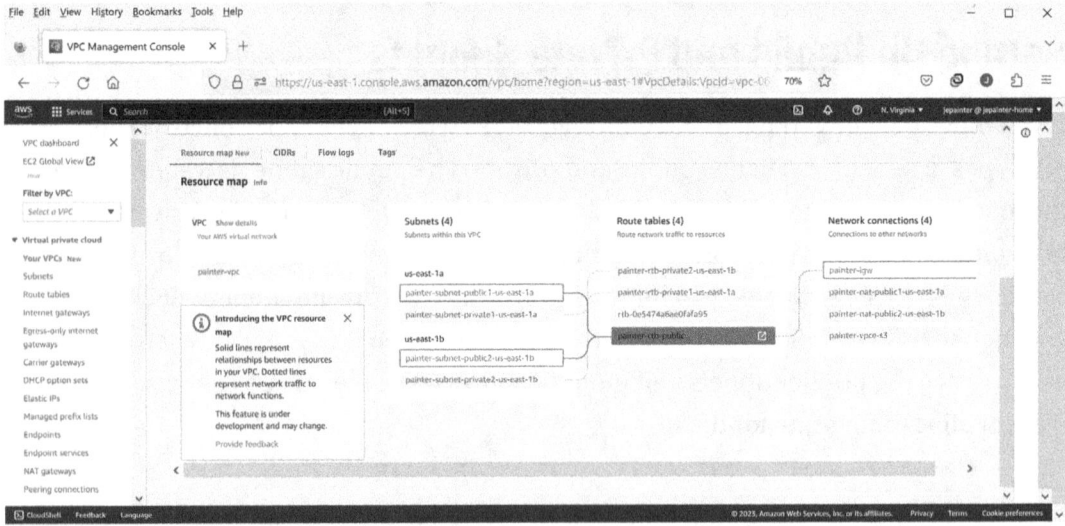

Figure 13-9. *VPC graph of public subnets*

526

CHAPTER 13 I CAN DO THIS ON MY OWN

Figure 13-10 shows the graph of components associated with a private subnet. Here, we see that each private subnet has its own routing table. The routing table in turn connects to the NAT gateway associated with the private subnet AZ as well as the VPC S3 endpoint. Note that it is possible for private subnets to share the same NAT gateway, but experience has taught me that having one NAT per AZ is prudent; otherwise, if the AZ containing the shared NAT gateway goes down, all AZs would be affected preventing access from all servers to the Internet.

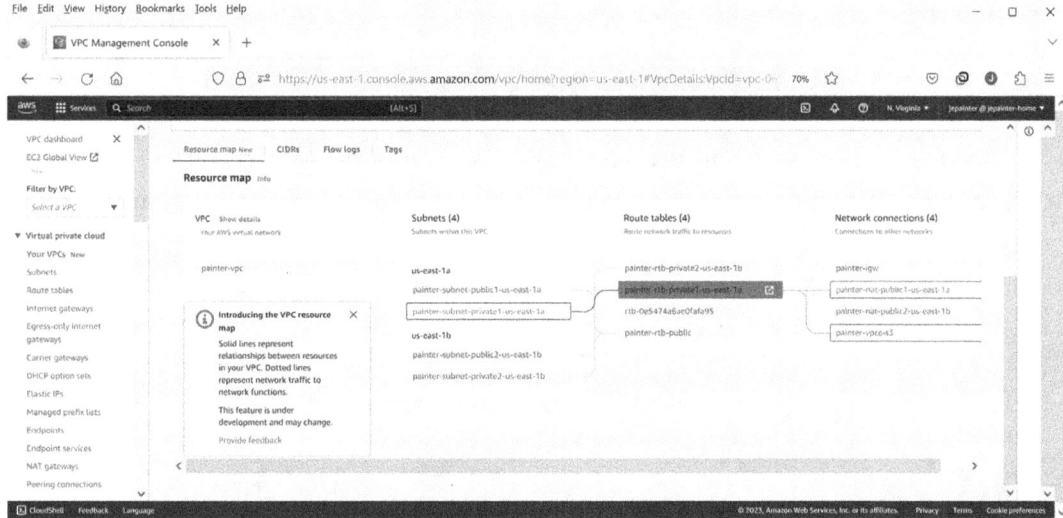

Figure 13-10. *VPC graph of private subnets*

Reviewing the Components of the VPC

If you've never worked with VPCs before or have not used the automated creation option, this would be a good time to take a moment and see what was created. Especially check out the routing tables to see how connections are being made. You'll also see some pleasant surprises such as Elastic IPs (EIPs) created automatically for you. An EIP is a public IP address that is used for servers in a private VPC to enable access to them. We'll see how these are used later on.

With the VPC set up, we are going to need an SSH key pair to eventually access our services, which we consider next.

CHAPTER 13   I CAN DO THIS ON MY OWN

Creating the SSH Key Pair

Before we implement the various components for our GitLab POC, there are some preliminary steps we need to take.[9] The first thing we need to do is create an SSH key pair with AWS. This will allow us to ssh into our servers once they have been created. We talked in the section of Git about creating your own SSH keys; you can create your SSH keys this way and upload them to AWS. An alternative is to let AWS create the keys for you, which is what I'll illustrate now.

Creating SSH Key Pairs in AWS

You'll find the SSH key pair feature under the Elastic Compute Cloud (EC2) service located in the Compute category as shown in Figure 13-11. From the EC2 dashboard, you'll see a wide range of resources available as shown in Figure 13-12. Select the "Key pairs" link on the dashboard or scroll down the left-hand panel to find the "Key pairs" link there.

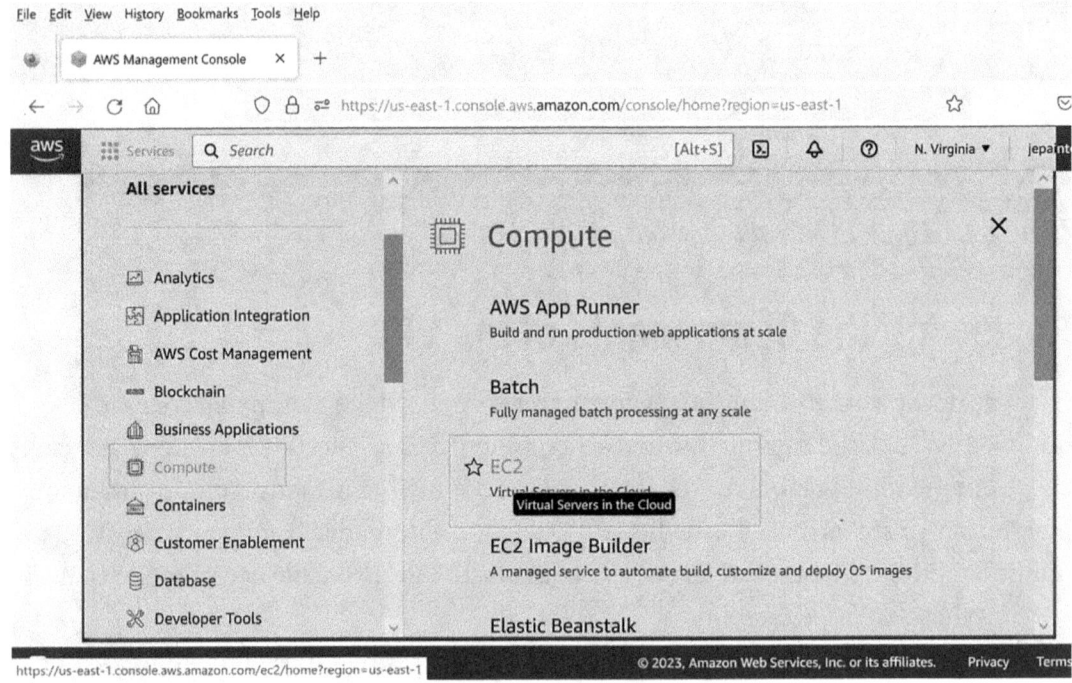

Figure 13-11. *EC2 selection from the services menu*

---

[9] These are listed under requirements in the GitLab POC documentation.

CHAPTER 13   I CAN DO THIS ON MY OWN

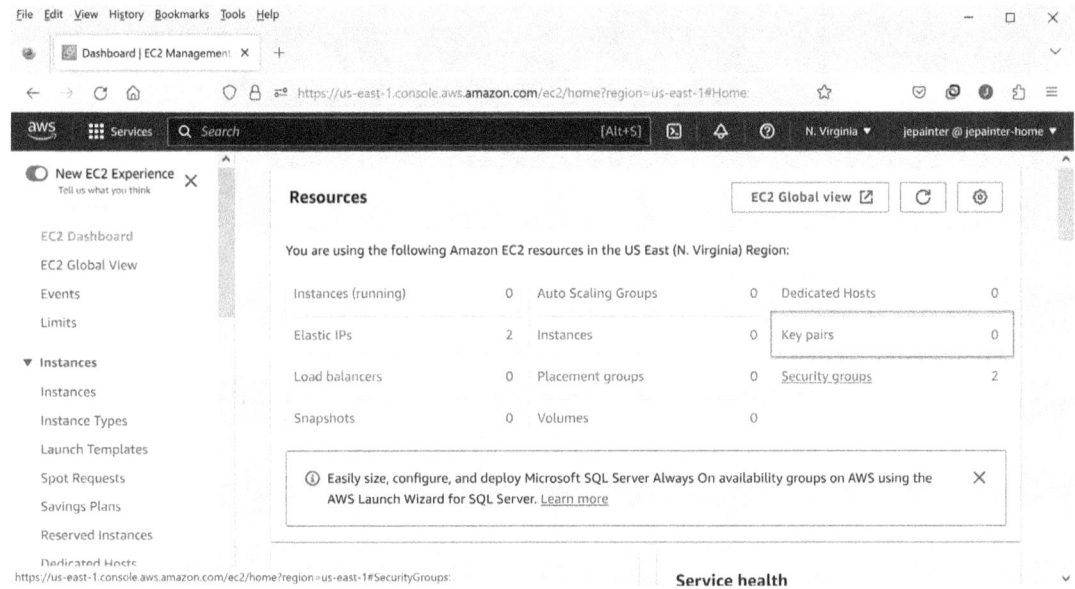

Figure 13-12. *Selection of "Key pairs" EC2 resource*

From the "Key pairs" page, select the "Create key pair" button as shown in Figure 13-13. This will take you to the form shown in Figure 13-14. Give the key pair a name; I recommend giving it a name that denotes the purpose of the key. For the key pair type, I recommend using the stronger ED25519 type. Finally, select the "pem" format corresponding to the OpenSSH-compatible key format. If you have PuTTY installed on your Windows laptop, you could alternatively select the ppk format.[10] Once you create the key pair, AWS will store the public SSH key for you and will automatically download the private key to your computer. Store the pem file in your home .ssh directory (if using Linux) and set the file permissions to read-write only for you.

---

[10] PuttyGen recognizes both the pem and ppk formats and enables converting between the two.

529

CHAPTER 13   I CAN DO THIS ON MY OWN

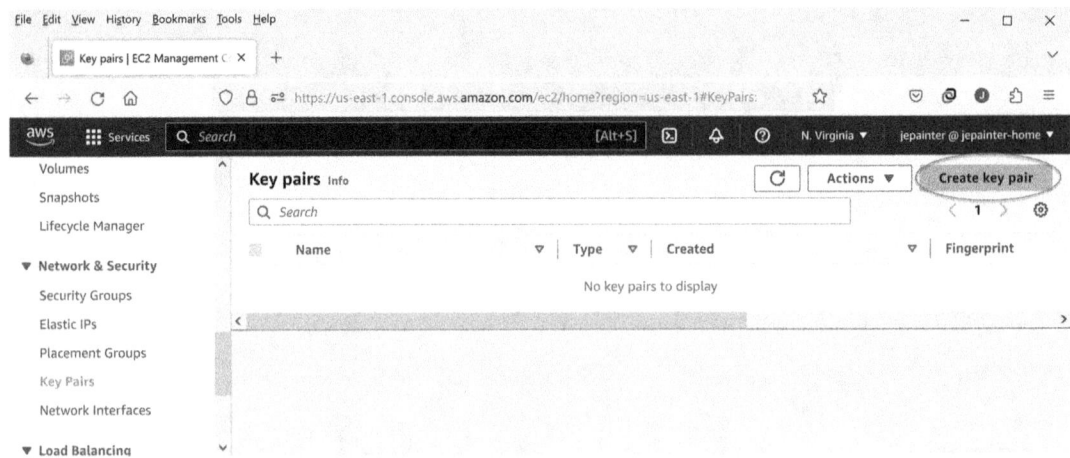

Figure 13-13. Option to create a key pair

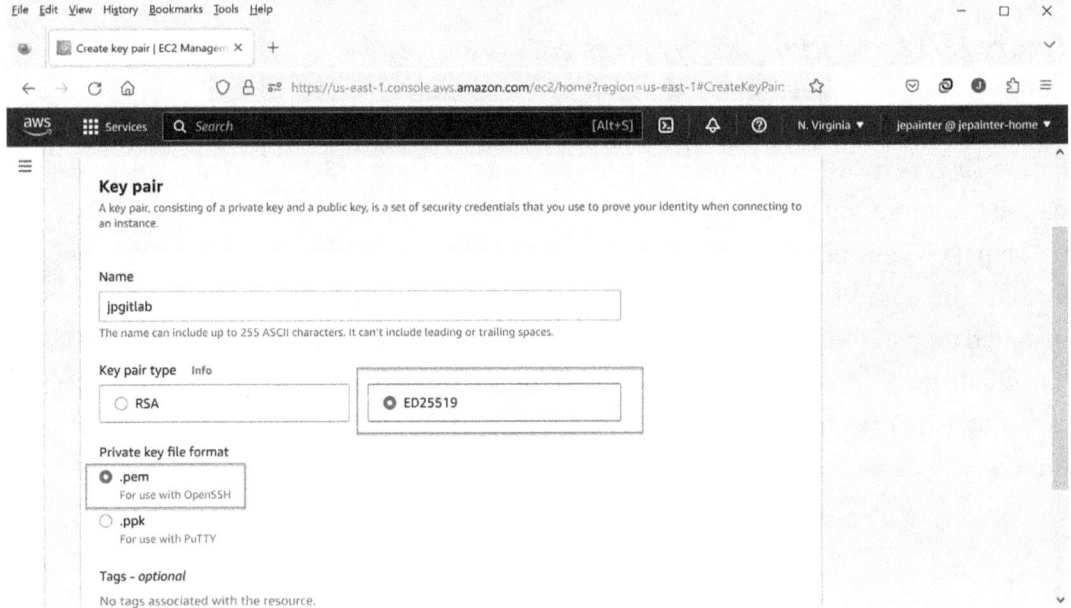

Figure 13-14. EC2 key pair creation form

With the SSH key pair created, we also need to set up a domain in order to connect to our service from the outside world. We take this up in the next section.

CHAPTER 13   I CAN DO THIS ON MY OWN

Establishing the Domain Name

The next thing to set up is the domain name for your GitLab POC web service. If you already have one, great; you can move on to setting up the TLS/SSL certificate. Otherwise, you could have AWS create and register a domain for you. To do this, select the Route 53 service under the Networking & Content Delivery category as shown in Figure 13-15.

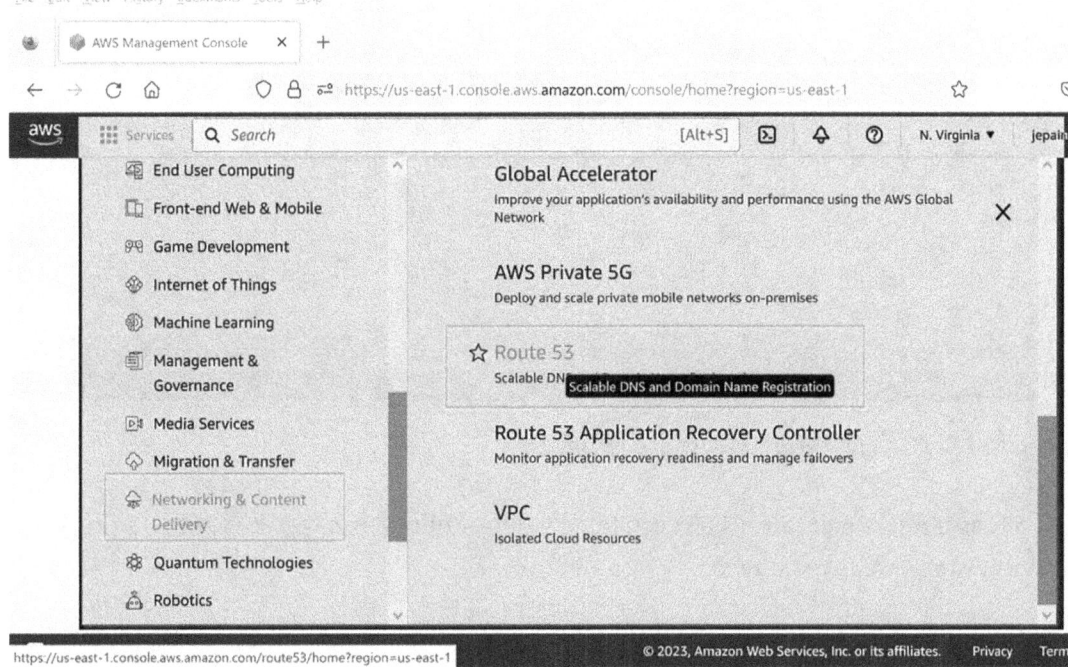

***Figure 13-15.** Route 53 selection from the services menu*

Registering a Domain Through AWS

From the Route 53 page, select the "Register domains" button to create and register your own top-level domain as shown in Figure 13-16. This will take you to a form (not shown here) where you can select a domain for your GitLab POC. I chose jpgitlab.com for my top-level domain. The domain search will verify that your choice of domain name is available and, if not, will give you possible alternatives. Note that once your domain name is registered, you will control all subdomains underneath the top-level domain.

CHAPTER 13   I CAN DO THIS ON MY OWN

For example, I can use test.jpgitlab.com as a name for a web service that I control. I should note that there is a yearly cost for setting up your own domain, which is pretty reasonable unless you go for a more exotic extension such as .guru instead of .com.

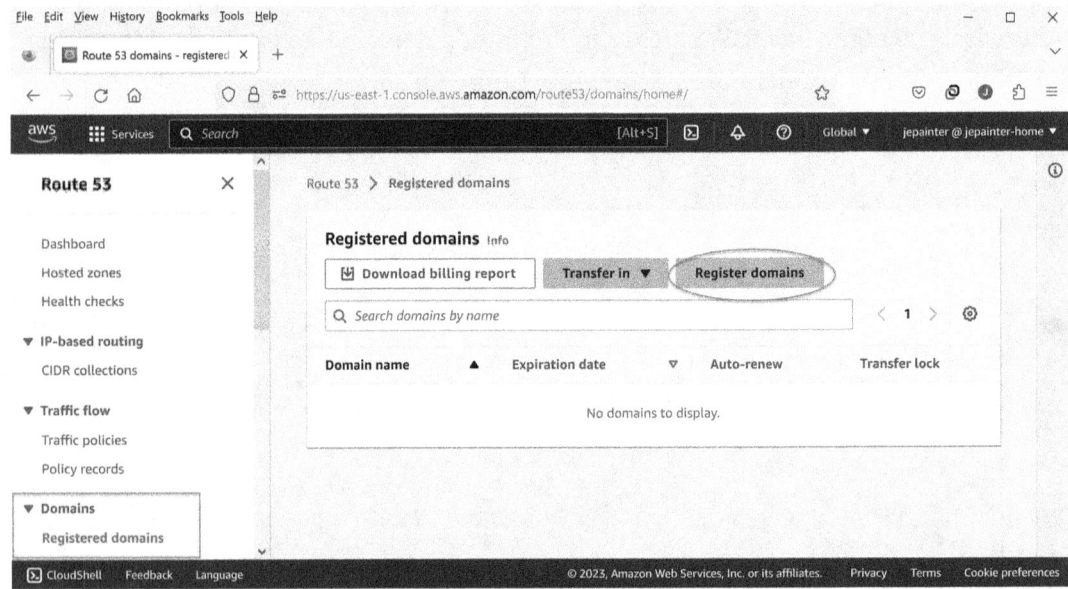

Figure 13-16. *Option to register a domain*

We also need to create a TLS certificate to allow outside users safe access to our service, which we take up next.

Generating the TLS Certificate

The final preliminary step is to create a TLS/SSL certificate for use with HTTPS. This step is a little bit trickier than registering your domain with Route 53, but AWS simplifies the process for you. For this, you go to the Certificate Manager service located under the Security, Identity, & Compliance category as shown in Figure 13-17.

CHAPTER 13   I CAN DO THIS ON MY OWN

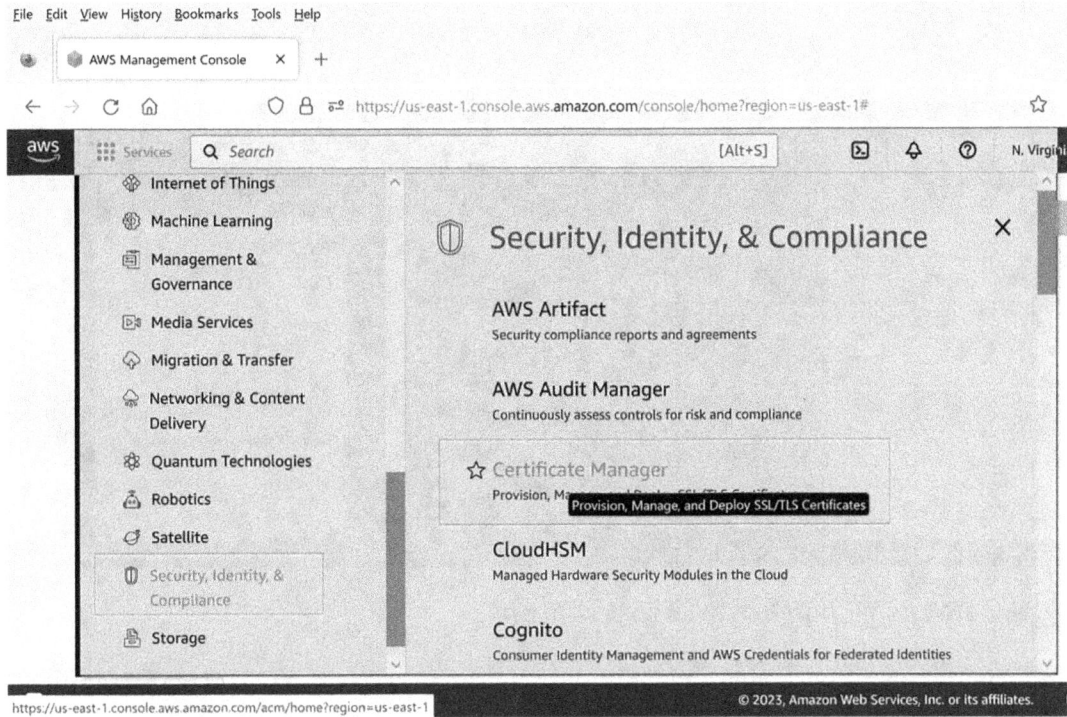

Figure 13-17.   Certificate Manager selection from the services menu

Requesting a TLS Certificate Through AWS

From the "AWS Certificate Manager" page, select the "Request a certificate" button to start the request process as shown in Figure 13-18. If you already have a certificate that you requested from an outside vendor, select the "Import a certificate" button instead to upload your certificate to AWS. Either way, AWS needs to know about the certificate in order to use it with your web service.

533

CHAPTER 13   I CAN DO THIS ON MY OWN

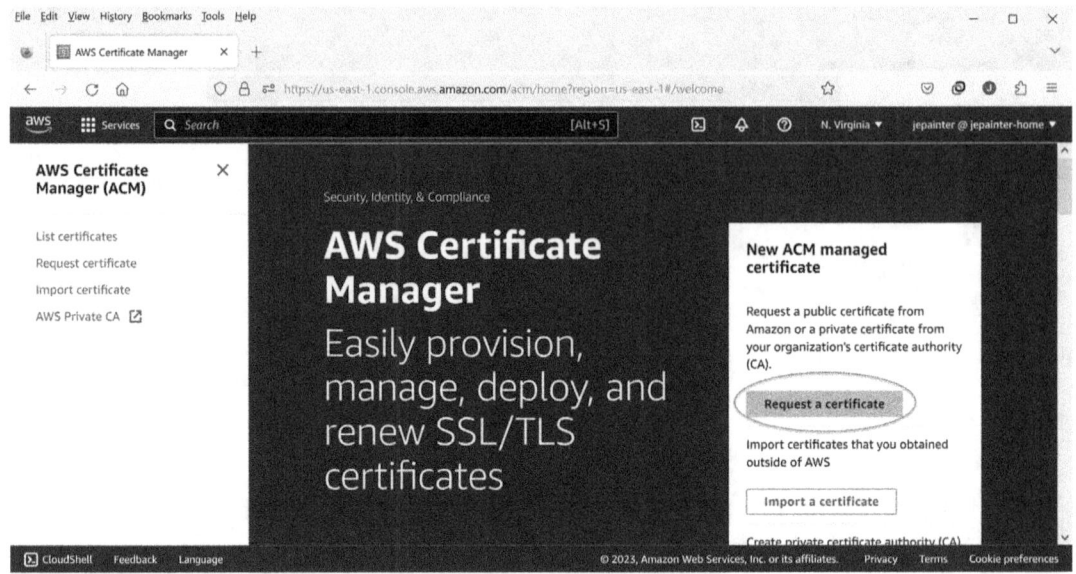

Figure 13-18. *Option to request a certificate*

From the "Request certificate" page, you should select the "Request a public certificate" option as shown in Figure 13-19. You'll need a public certificate since you will be accessing your GitLab POC from your computer, which AWS considers an outside entity. Yes, this means that other users will be able to access your website, but there are ways of controlling what they can do.

CHAPTER 13 I CAN DO THIS ON MY OWN

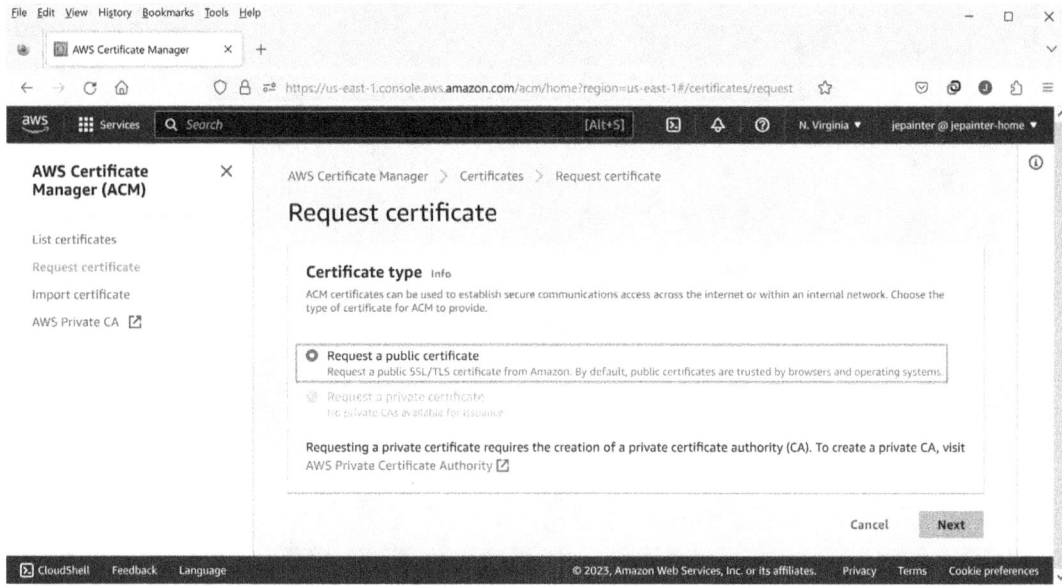

Figure 13-19. Selection to request a public certificate

Associating Your Domain with the Certificate

Next, you need to specify the domain tied to the certificate as shown in Figure 13-20. In this example, I am requesting what is called a "wildcard" certificate. By using "*.jpgitlab.com" as the fully qualified domain name (FQDN), I can use the certificate for any domain name I create just below the .jpgitlab.com domain. For example, I can use it for test.jpgitlab.com or stage.gitlab.com; however, I cannot use it for subdomains like special.test.jpgitlab.com. For that, I would need to create another certificate specifically for that case; it could either be for the explicit domain of special.test.jpgitlab.com or a wildcard domain of "*.test.jpgitlab.com".

CHAPTER 13   I CAN DO THIS ON MY OWN

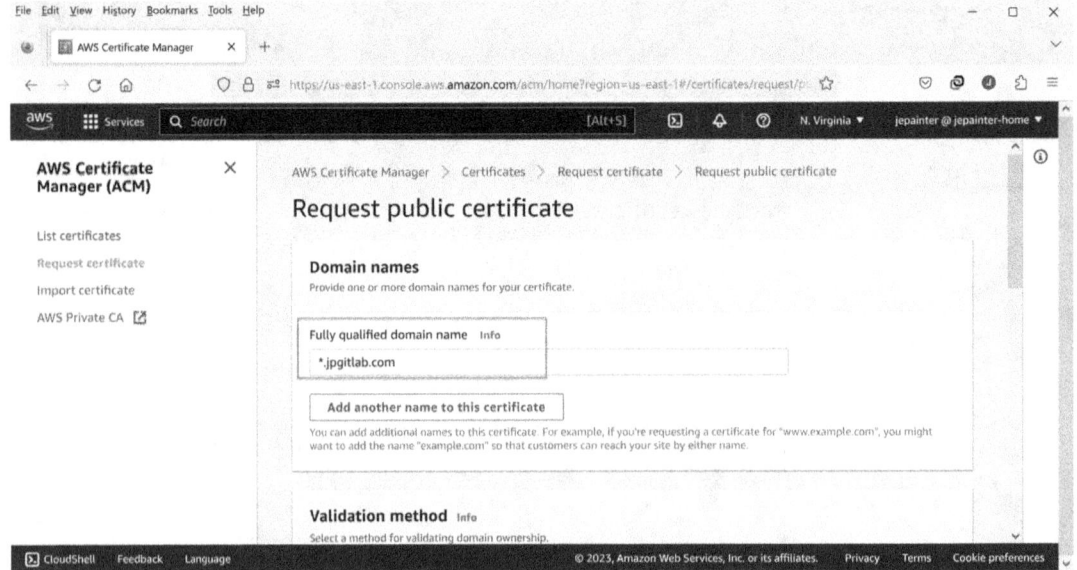

Figure 13-20. Defining fully qualified domain name in a public certificate request

Validating Domain Ownership

Figure 13-21 shows the remaining settings to set when requesting a public certificate. The first setting is the method for validating that you actually own or control that domain. Since I created the domain using Route 53, I chose the DNS validation method. If you created the domain outside of AWS, you could select this method if you are the registered owner of the certificate. The second setting is the key algorithm to use. Here, I selected the more generally accepted algorithm of RSA 2048.

CHAPTER 13   I CAN DO THIS ON MY OWN

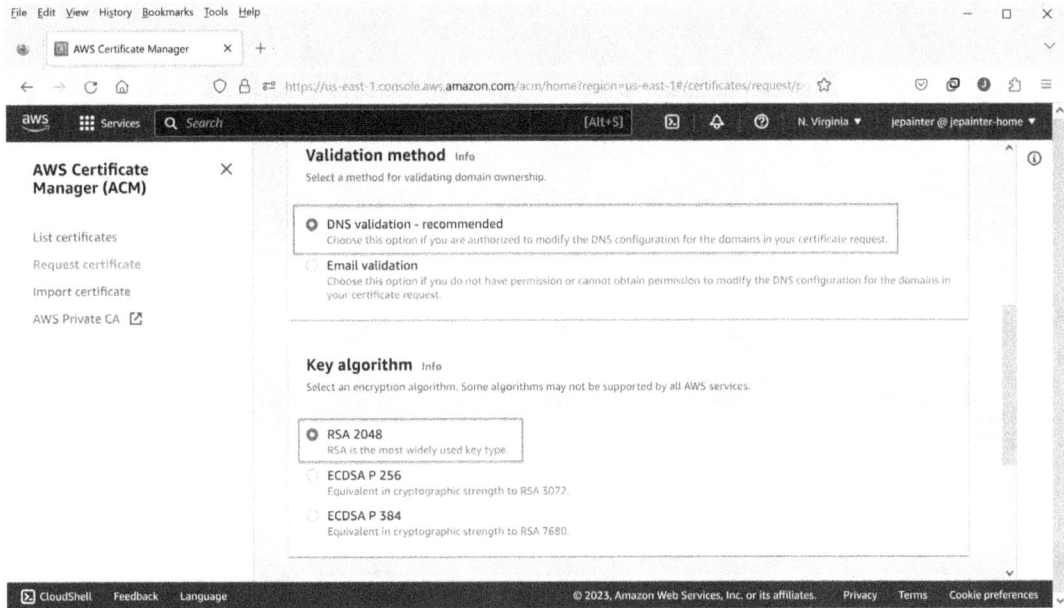

Figure 13-21.   Additional options in a public certificate request

Waiting for the Certificate to Be Approved

At this point, you make the request and wait for a response as shown in Figure 13-22. You'll need to wait for the request to be approved, which can take several hours. You can check the status of your request by clicking the link to your new certificate on the "List certificates" page. Note that if you created your domain using Route 53, check the Domains section associated with your certificate. If none are listed, select the "Create records in Route 53" button to create CNAME records for DNS. This is needed for the certificate verification process to eventually pass. Once the CNAME records are created, your certificate may still be in the pending status for up to 30 minutes.

CHAPTER 13   I CAN DO THIS ON MY OWN

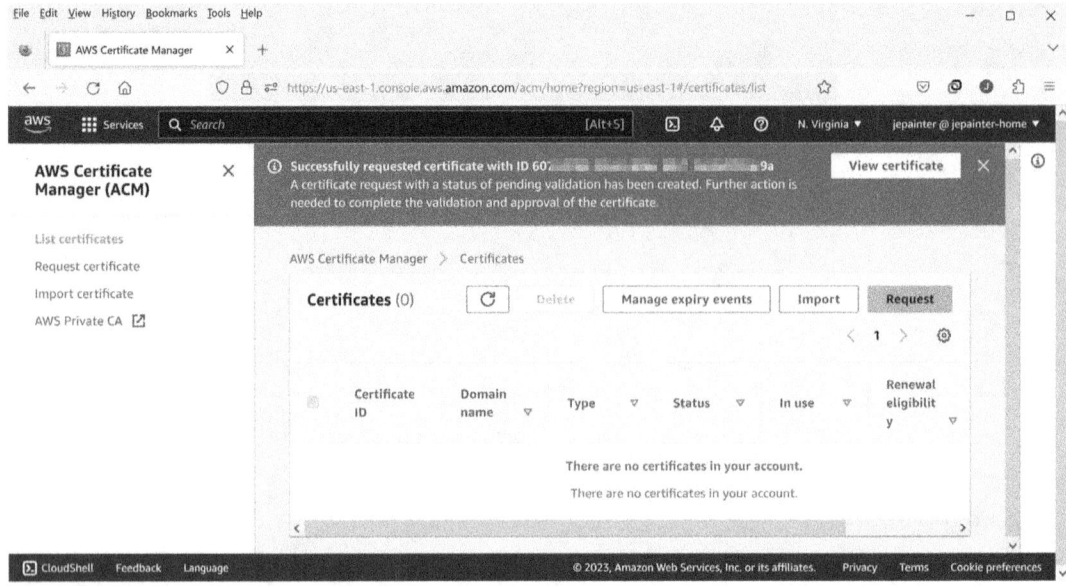

Figure 13-22. *Initial feedback from a public certificate request*

In the next section, we'll describe how to set up a role to enable access to S3 buckets that will be needed by the POC servers.

Preparing the IAM Role

The next thing to create is what is known as an IAM role. An IAM role defines permissions for a server that we spin up. In the case of the GitLab POC, the web servers that we spin up will need access to various S3 resources[11] to store things like artifacts and registry objects, among other things.

Creating an IAM Policy

As you may guess, an IAM role is created using the IAM service. What may not be obvious is that for custom resources, such as the GitLab S3 resources, we need to create an IAM policy first. Figure 13-23 shows the Policies page that lists existing policies; initially, these are defined by AWS to cover common scenarios. Although we could select

---

[11] S3 stands for Simple Storage Service. It was one of the first services provided by AWS to enable storage of image files and the like for web services.

CHAPTER 13   I CAN DO THIS ON MY OWN

a preexisting policy that allows a server to perform any action on any S3 resource, we want to be more selective in what S3 resources our GitLab servers can access as well as what actions we can perform on those resources.

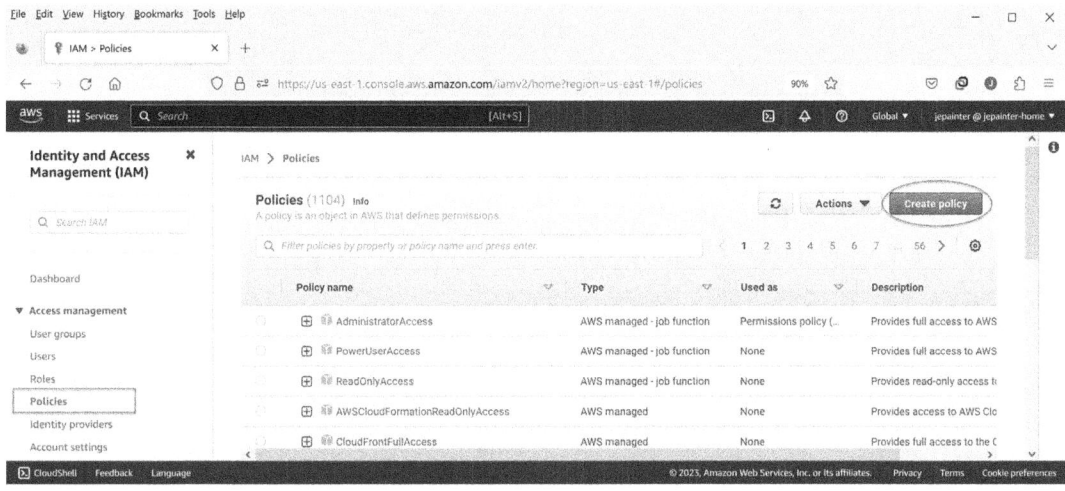

Figure 13-23. *Option to create an IAM policy*

Entering a JSON Policy with the Policy Editor

When selecting "Create policy," you are taken to the policy editor. You can either use the wizard to create a policy or enter the policy as a JSON document. Figure 13-24 shows the JSON policy editor that we'll use to create our new policy. To access it, you need to select the JSON tab as shown in the figure. From there, you can enter the JSON policy provided as follows. Make sure to replace jpgitlab-poc with the prefix for your S3 buckets.

```
{ "Version": "2012-10-17",
  "Statement": [
  {
  "Effect": "Allow",
  "Action": [
  "s3:PutObject",
  "s3:GetObject",
  "s3:DeleteObject",
  "s3:PutObjectAcl"
  ],
```

539

CHAPTER 13   I CAN DO THIS ON MY OWN

```
"Resource": "arn:aws:s3:::jpgitlab-poc-*/*"
},
{
"Effect": "Allow",
"Action": [
"s3:ListBucket",
"s3:AbortMultipartUpload",
"s3:ListMultipartUploadParts",
"s3:ListBucketMultipartUploads"
],
"Resource": "arn:aws:s3:::jpgitlab-poc-*"
}
]
}
```

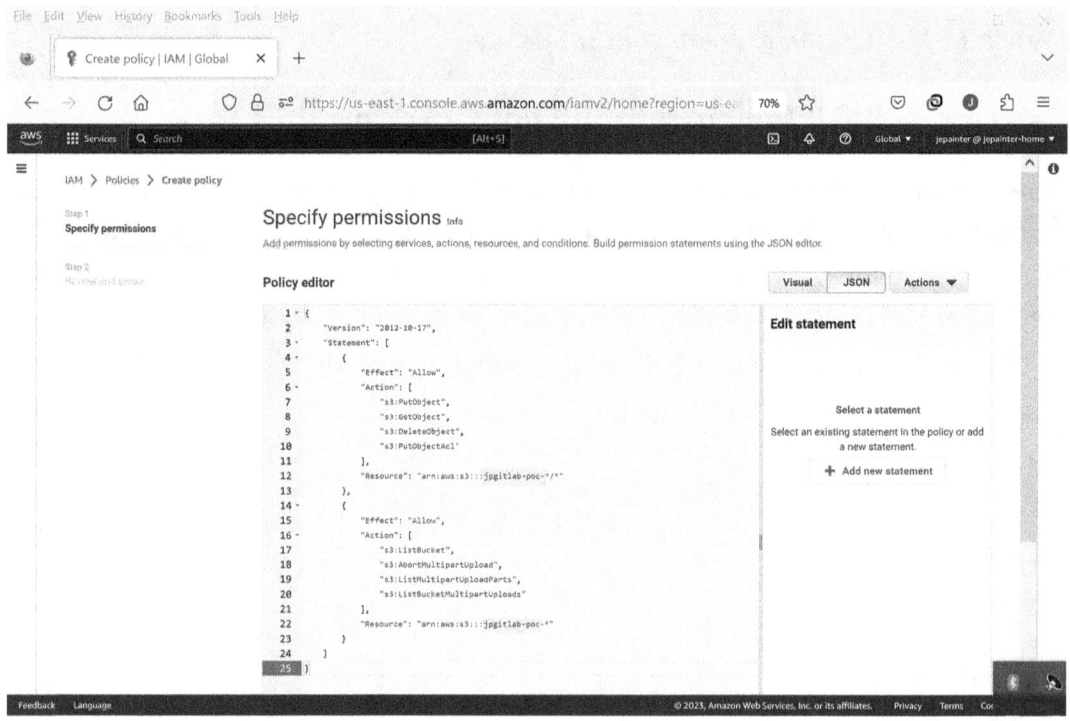

Figure 13-24. *JSON view of the IAM policy editor*

CHAPTER 13   I CAN DO THIS ON MY OWN

The first part of the policy applies to actions on objects within those buckets such as GetObject and PutObject. The second part of the policy applies to the buckets themselves. It allows certain actions such as ListBucket and ListBucketMultipartUploads.

Setting the Policy Name and Description

Once you've entered the JSON policy, selecting Next takes you to the policy details page as shown in Figure 13-25. This is where you enter the name of the policy along with an optional description of it. In this example, I've named the policy gl-s3-policy.

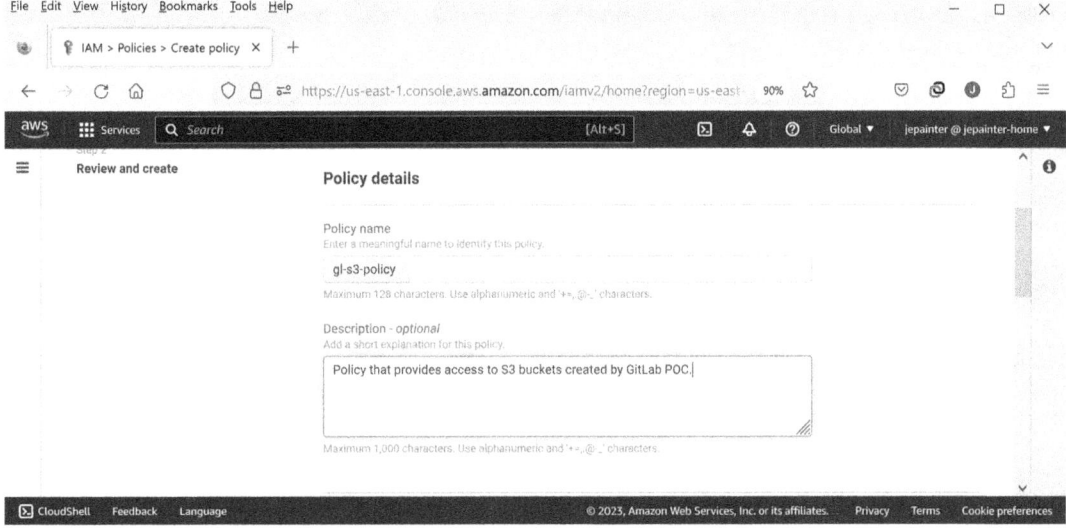

Figure 13-25. *IAM policy details*

541

CHAPTER 13   I CAN DO THIS ON MY OWN

Creating the IAM Role

With the IAM policy now created, we can proceed to creating the IAM role. Figure 13-26 shows the IAM roles page. This page lists the set of predefined AWS roles. Since we want to create our own custom role, we select the "Create role" button as highlighted in the figure.

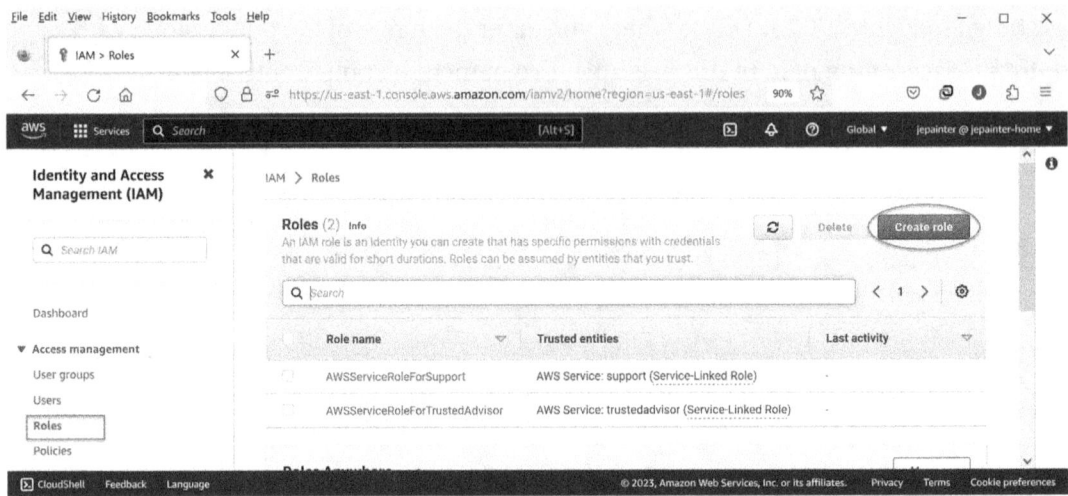

Figure 13-26. Option to create an IAM role

Defining the Trusted Entity for the Role

The first thing we need to define for our role is the trusted entity as shown in Figure 13-27. Since we are creating a role for a server generated by the EC2 service, we select the AWS service entity type. For "Use case," we select EC2; this allows an EC2 instance (a.k.a. server) to call AWS services on our behalf.

CHAPTER 13   I CAN DO THIS ON MY OWN

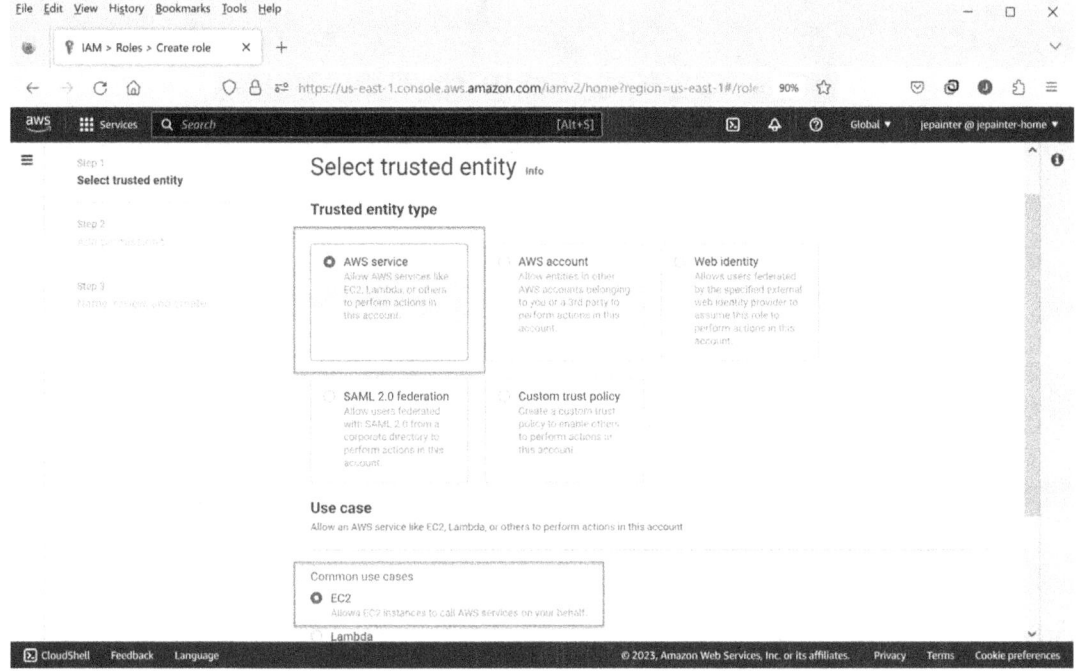

Figure 13-27. *Selection of IAM role trusted entity*

Setting the Role Permissions

Selecting Next takes us to the permissions page as shown in Figure 13-28. It is here that we select the gl-s3-policy permission created earlier. Although we could add additional permission policies to our role, we only need the gl-s3-policy for our GitLab POC.

CHAPTER 13　I CAN DO THIS ON MY OWN

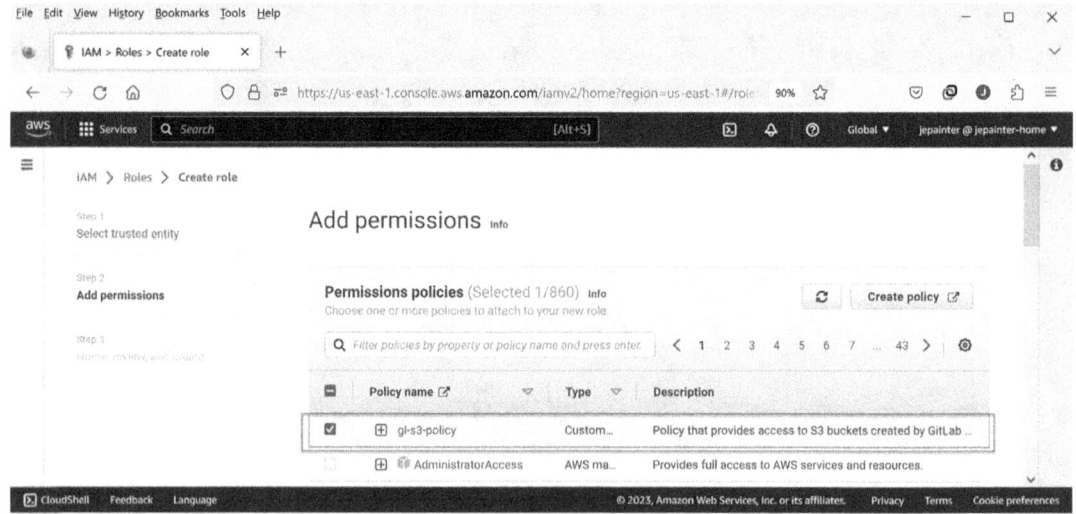

Figure 13-28. Selection of IAM policy for IAM role

Setting the Role Name and Description

Selecting Next takes us to the final step of setting details for our AWS role. This is shown in Figure 13-29. It is here that we set the name of the role as well as the required description of the role.[12] In this example, we set the name of the role to GitLabS3Access. Once defined, saving the role creates it.

---

[12] If you are wondering why the description of an AWS policy is optional but the description of an AWS role is required, I have to admit, I don't know the answer to that. It's just one of those inconsistencies that occur in AWS that we have to accept.

CHAPTER 13   I CAN DO THIS ON MY OWN

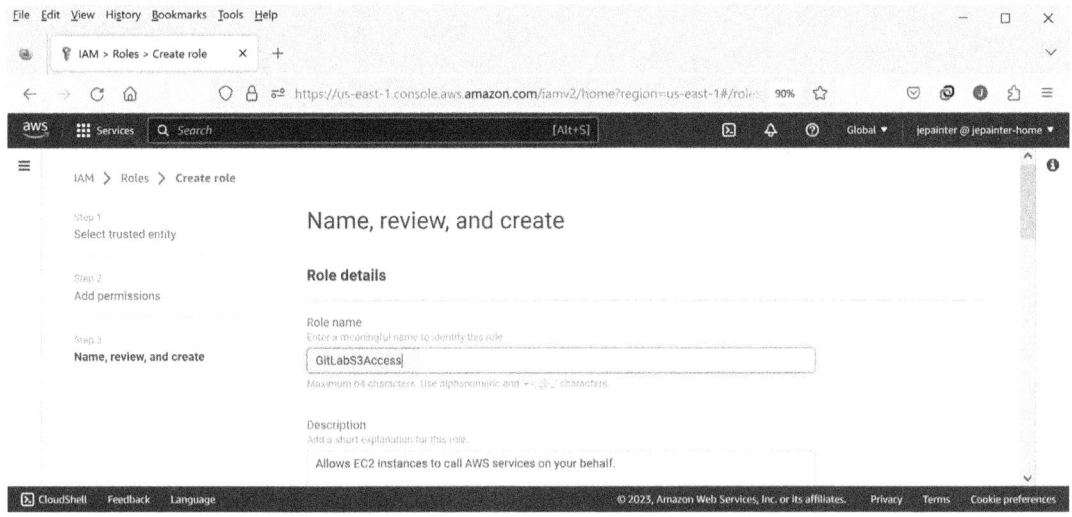

Figure 13-29. *IAM role details*

With all that prep work out of the way, we next describe how to spin up the load balancer that will enable access to our GitLab POC service.

Building the ELB

We are now ready to build out the various components for the GitLab POC. First up is the load balancer known as the ELB (Elastic Load Balancer) in AWS speak. Load balancers can be found under the EC2 category as shown in Figure 13-30. You should also be able to find this page by doing a search on ELB. It may seem odd to create the load balancer first, but we'll need the security group created in the following process for the database and elastic-cache components set up later on.

545

CHAPTER 13   I CAN DO THIS ON MY OWN

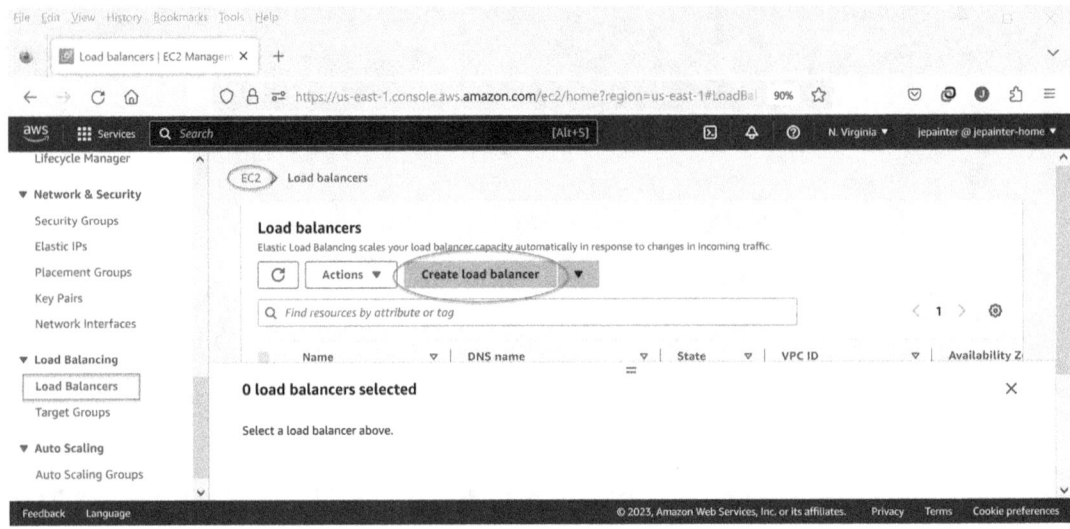

Figure 13-30.   EC2 option to create a load balancer

Creating a Classic Load Balancer

Selecting the "Create load balancer" button from the load balancer page, we need to first specify the type of load balancer. AWS defines a number of load balancer types optimized for certain scenarios. For example, there is the application load balancer type defined specifically for web services and a network load balancer for other types of services. It turns out that these two types of load balancers are mutually exclusive; for example, you can't use the network load balancer for a web service (not easily anyways), nor can you set up other network services with an application load balancer. For the GitLab POC, we need a load balancer that handles both web requests as well as SSH requests (for Git services) in one load balancer.

For this, we need to use the original load balancer provided by AWS, what they refer to as the classic load balancer (CLB). The CLB is a bit tricky to find as AWS tries to discourage the use of it, but for the GitLab POC, we need it. Figure 13-31 shows the Classic Load Balancer choice that appears at the end of the "type selection" page. It initially appears in collapsed form, so you need to expand it to expose the Create button as shown in the figure.

CHAPTER 13   I CAN DO THIS ON MY OWN

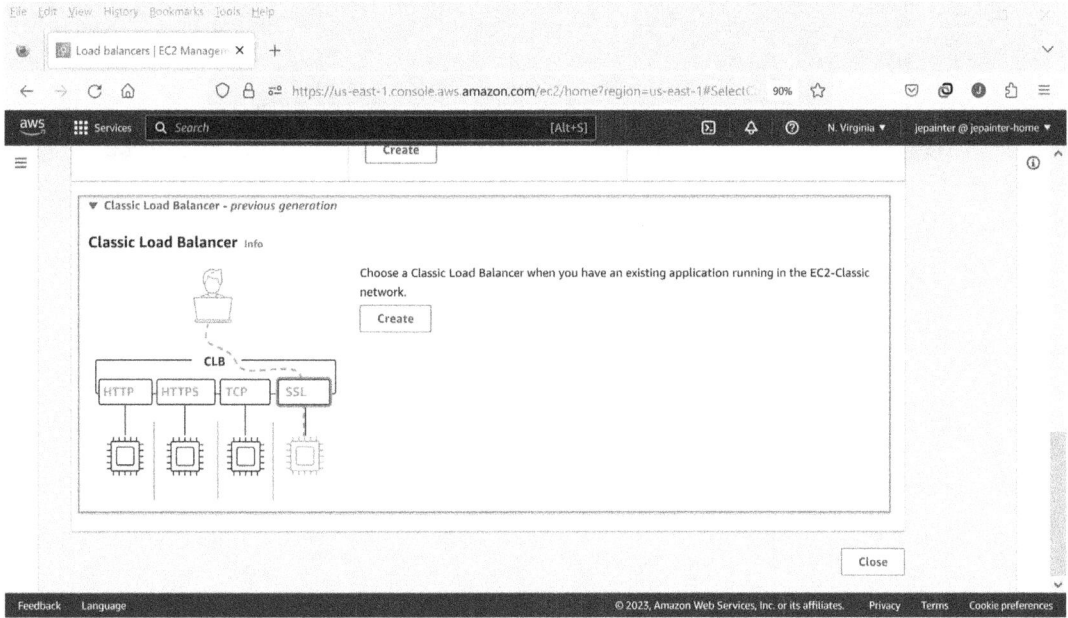

Figure 13-31. *Classic load balancer selection*

Setting the ELB Name and Scheme

Upon selecting the Create button associated with the CLB, the first item we need to configure is the name of the CLB and whether the CLB is an Internet-facing or internally facing load balance, what AWS refers to as the scheme. Figure 13-32 shows the settings for our GitLab POC load balancer. We set the name as gitlab-loadbalancer and the scheme to be Internet-facing.

CHAPTER 13   I CAN DO THIS ON MY OWN

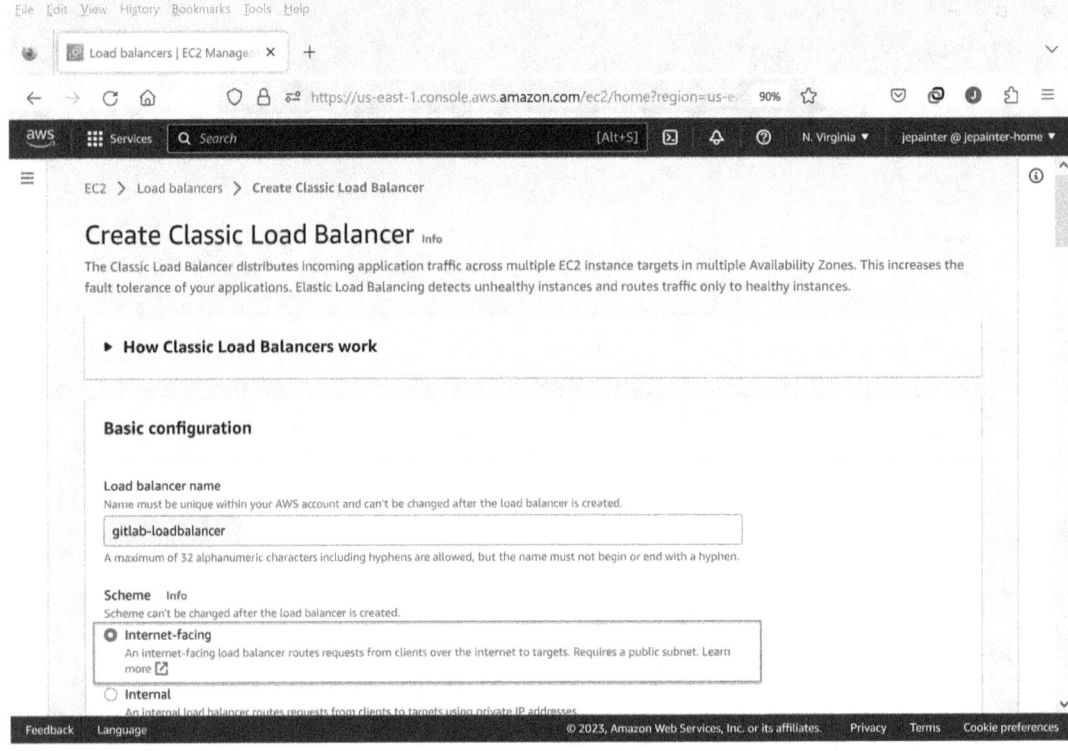

Figure 13-32.   ELB name and scheme configuration

Setting the ELB Network Mappings

Next, we need to set some network mappings as shown in Figure 13-33. Here, we select the private VPC created earlier. Once selected, we then determine what AZs and associated subnets to use. This is where the load balancer will find and/or place the web servers. In this example, we select both the us-east-1a and us-east-1b AZs and the public subnets associated with each. Make sure that the public subnets are chosen since the default mappings chosen by AWS may include the private subnets. If it does, you'll see a warning that the subnet chosen cannot be reached from the Internet, which is necessary for the ELB.

CHAPTER 13   I CAN DO THIS ON MY OWN

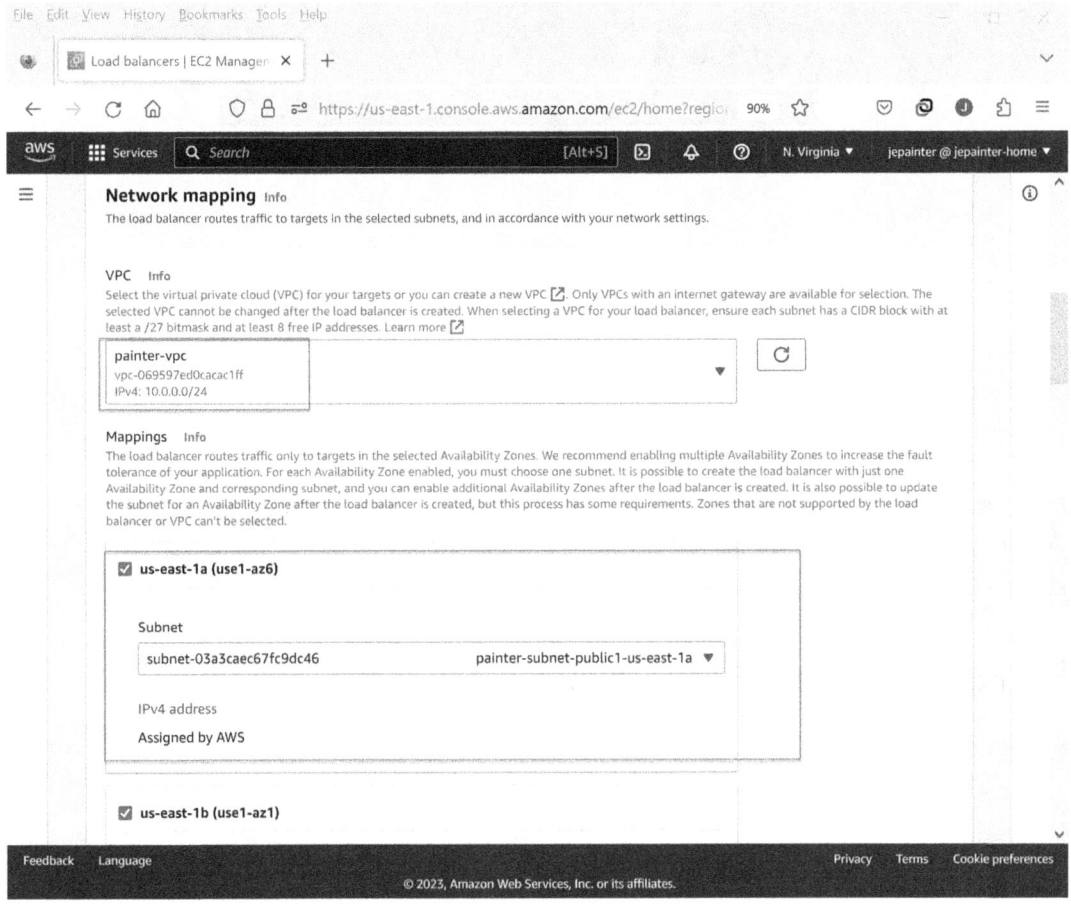

Figure 13-33. *ELB network mapping configuration*

Creating the ELB Security Group

Next, we take a side trip to creating the ELB security group (SG) as shown in Figure 13-34. A security group defines a set of firewall rules that controls the traffic to our ELB. We probably should have created the security group first, but since we are here, clicking the "create a new security group" link will pop up a new browser tab or window where we can create the security group.

CHAPTER 13   I CAN DO THIS ON MY OWN

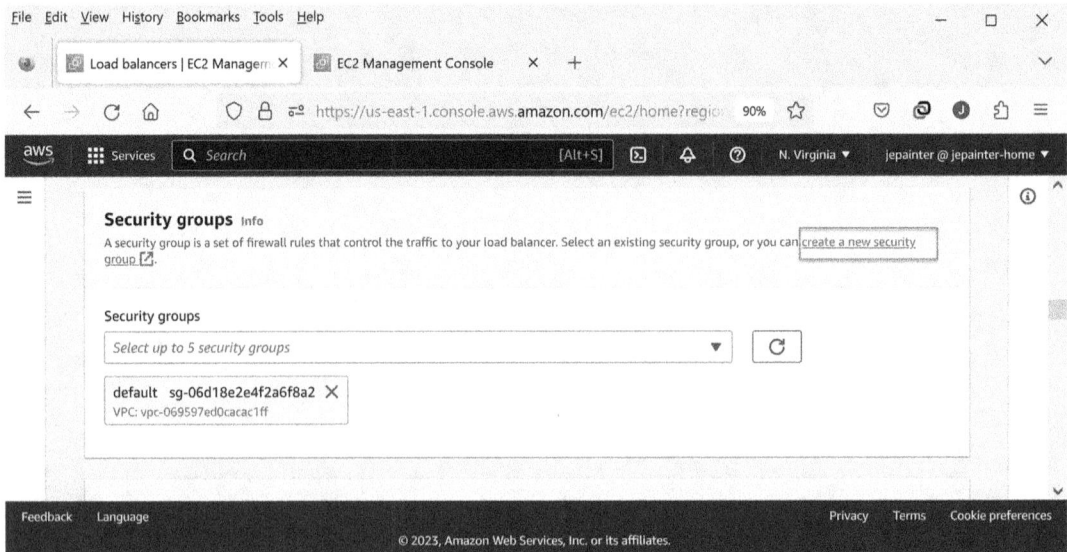

Figure 13-34. ELB option to create a new security group

Setting the Security Group Name, Description, and VPC

Figure 13-35 shows the basic settings for our new security group. Here, we set the name of the SG to gitlab-loadbalancer-sec-group. We also need to select the private VPC where the ELB resides. Note that to select it, you may need to backspace through the VPC that was selected automatically or start typing "vpc-" to get the pop-up as shown in Figure 13-35. I needed to do this since the VPC chosen by AWS was not the correct one. You'll also need to add a description as the SG requires it.

CHAPTER 13 I CAN DO THIS ON MY OWN

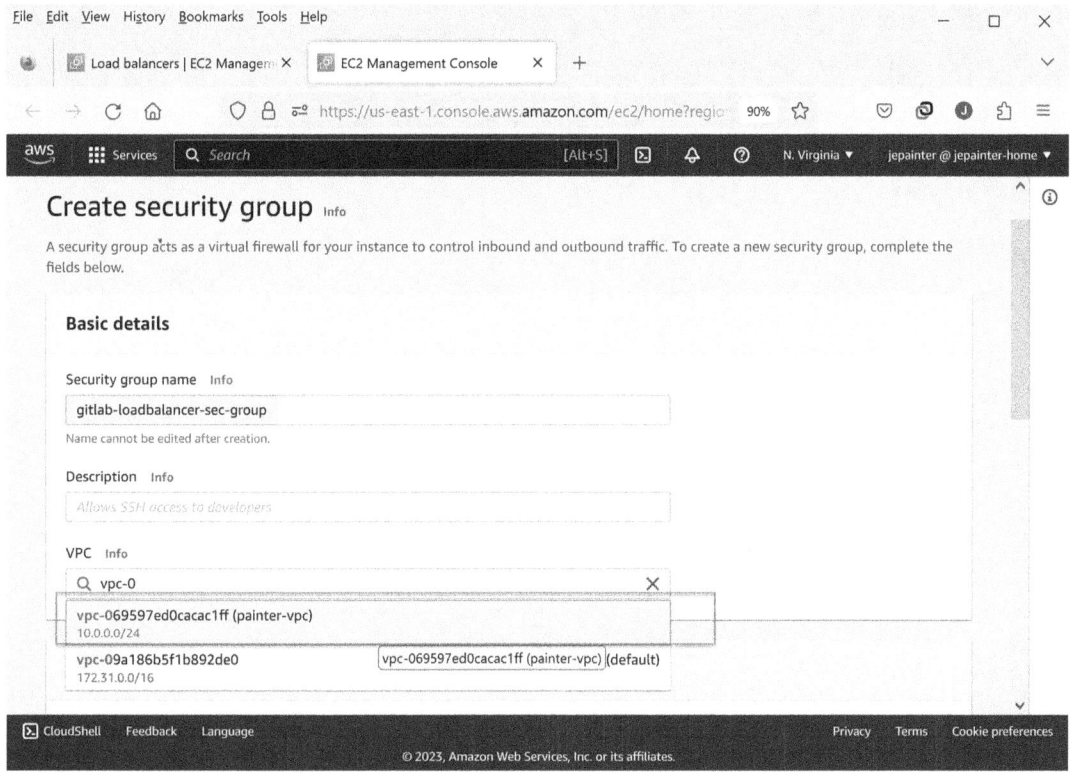

Figure 13-35. *Basic detail options for the ELB security group*

Setting Up the Security Group Inbound Rules

From here, we need to set up the SG inbound rules. The first set of rules is for HTTP/HTTPS as shown in Figure 13-36. For the rule, we specify the type of the rule (HTTP, HTTPS, TCP, etc.), the source type CIDR, and the port range. In this example, we use the standard port 80 for HTTP and port 443 for HTTPS. For both ports, we allow anyone from the Internet (shown as source type Anywhere-IPv4[13]) to access the ports.

---

[13] IPv4 refers to the original form of IP addresses known as version 4 (x.x.x.x). You could also select IPv6 to enable the newer version 6 form of IP addresses, but we'll stick with IPv4 for our POC.

CHAPTER 13   I CAN DO THIS ON MY OWN

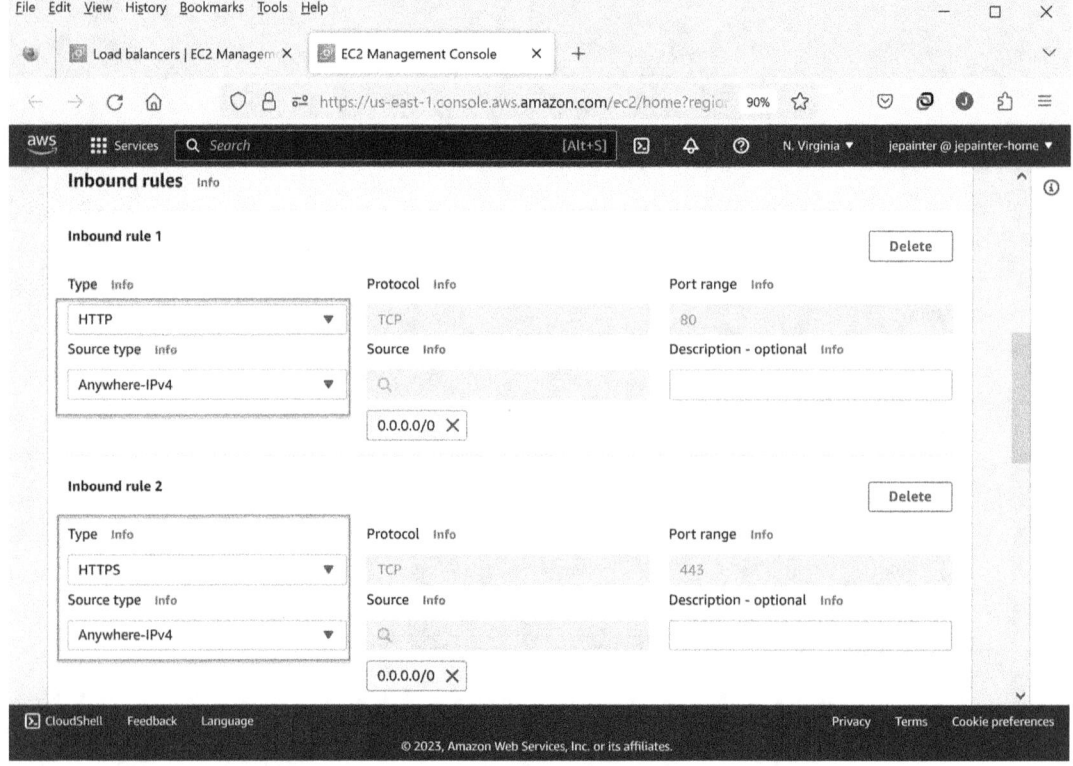

Figure 13-36. *HTTP inbound rules for the ELB security group*

Next, we set the inbound rule for SSH access as shown in Figure 13-37. Here, we select type SSH, which uses port 22, and source type Anywhere-IPv4, which sets the IP CIDR range to 0.0.0.0/0. In general, it is not a good idea to allow anyone to access SSH over the Internet, but without a corporate IP range to use here, we don't have much choice. Note that I show the Source type menu list that includes the choice of "My IP"; if you are security paranoid, you could select this to restrict the ELB to only allow SSH access from the current IP address; however, you most likely have a dynamic IP address chosen by your Internet service provider, so if you do go this route, you'll need to keep updating the SG to use the latest IP address assigned to you.

CHAPTER 13   I CAN DO THIS ON MY OWN

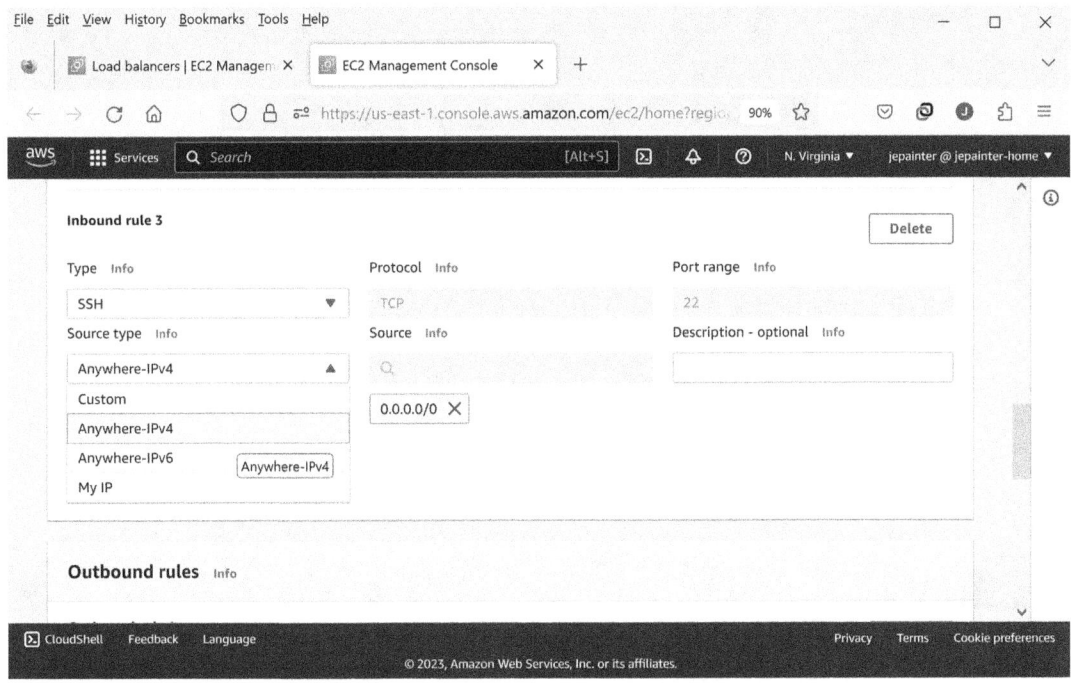

Figure 13-37. *SSH inbound rule for the ELB security group*

Associating the New Security Group to the ELB

We'll keep the outbound rules as is. Once you create the SG, you can select it for your ELB as shown in Figure 13-38. Note that you'll probably need to refresh the security group list using the refresh button highlighted in the figure. Once you see your newly created SG, select that from the drop-down list as shown in the figure. Also, make sure the default SG is not selected.

553

CHAPTER 13   I CAN DO THIS ON MY OWN

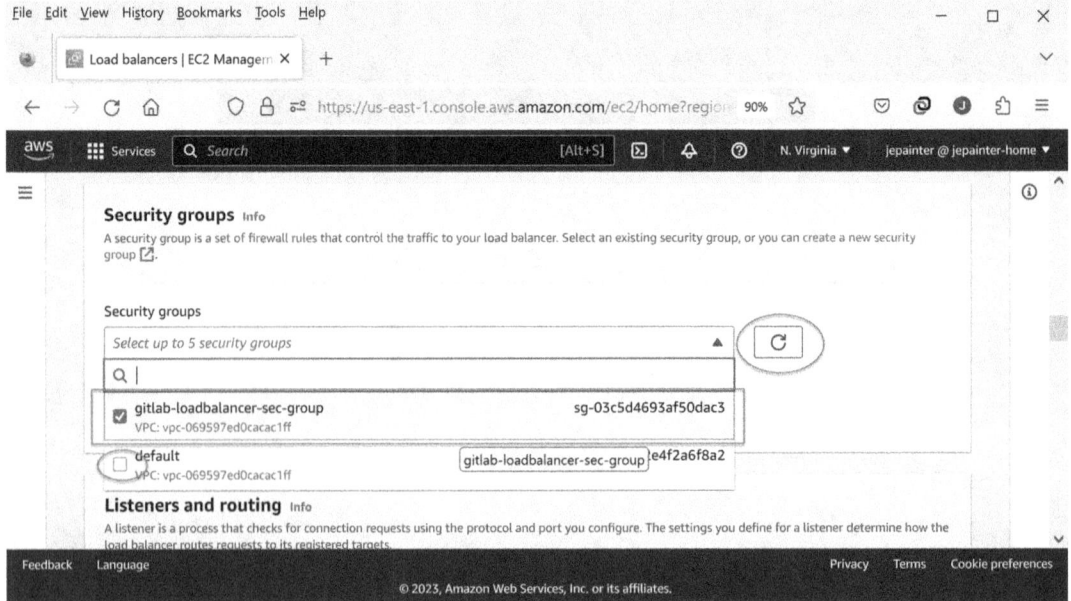

Figure 13-38.   ELB security group selection

Setting Up ELB Listeners

Now that we've set up the ELB security group to accept traffic from ports 80, 443, and 22 (and no other ports), we next need to set up listeners on our ELB that determine how we route these ports through the ELB to ports on our web server instances. Figure 13-39 shows the settings for each port. For HTTP port 80, the ELB will direct traffic to the instance port 80, and for the SSH port 22 (shown as TCP), we'll direct that traffic to instance port 22. For the HTTPS port 443, we will be doing something different here. We'll be directing traffic to the instance HTTP port 80. The reason for this is that we'll set up the ELB shortly to manage the TLS certificate for HTTPS that we created earlier rather than having the instance manage the certificate. Since the ELB will validate HTTPS requests using the certificate, it will only pass validated requests on to the instance's HTTP port 80.

CHAPTER 13 I CAN DO THIS ON MY OWN

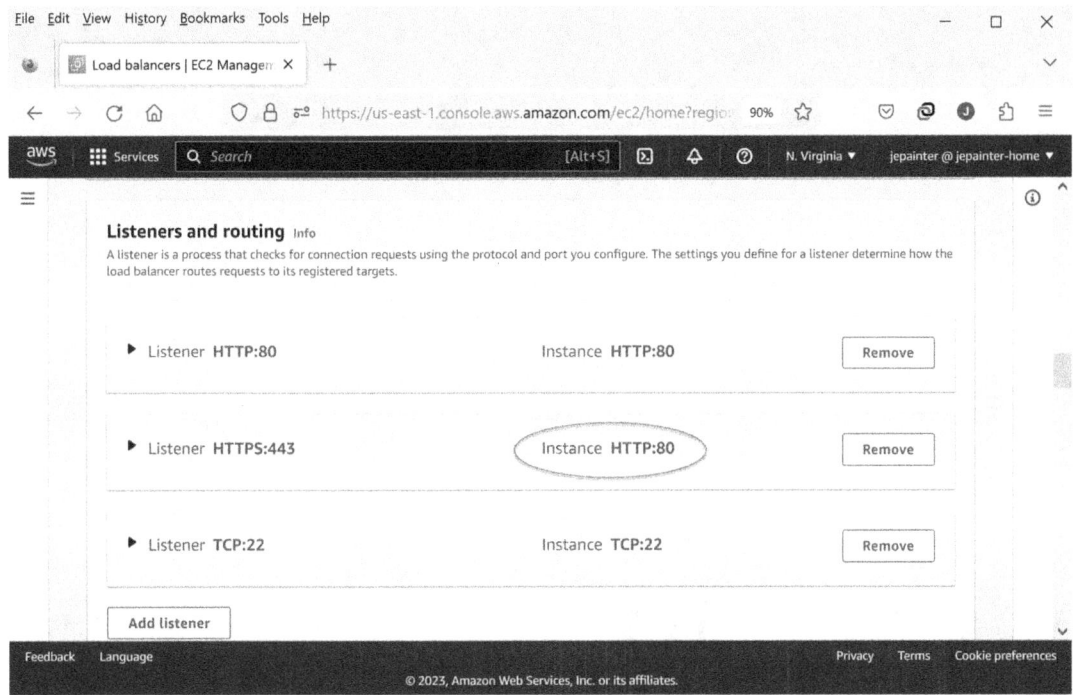

Figure 13-39. ELB listeners and routing configuration

Associating the TLS Certificate with the ELB

With the listeners set up, the next step is to configure the ELB to handle the TLS certificate as shown in Figure 13-40. Since the certificate is managed by the AWS Certificate Manager, we simply need to select the wildcard option provided in the pop-up menu for "Select a certificate." AWS knows how to apply this to the HTTPS listener. As for security policies, you can also select a more restrictive one than the 2016-08 one, but we'll stick with that default for our POC.

555

CHAPTER 13   I CAN DO THIS ON MY OWN

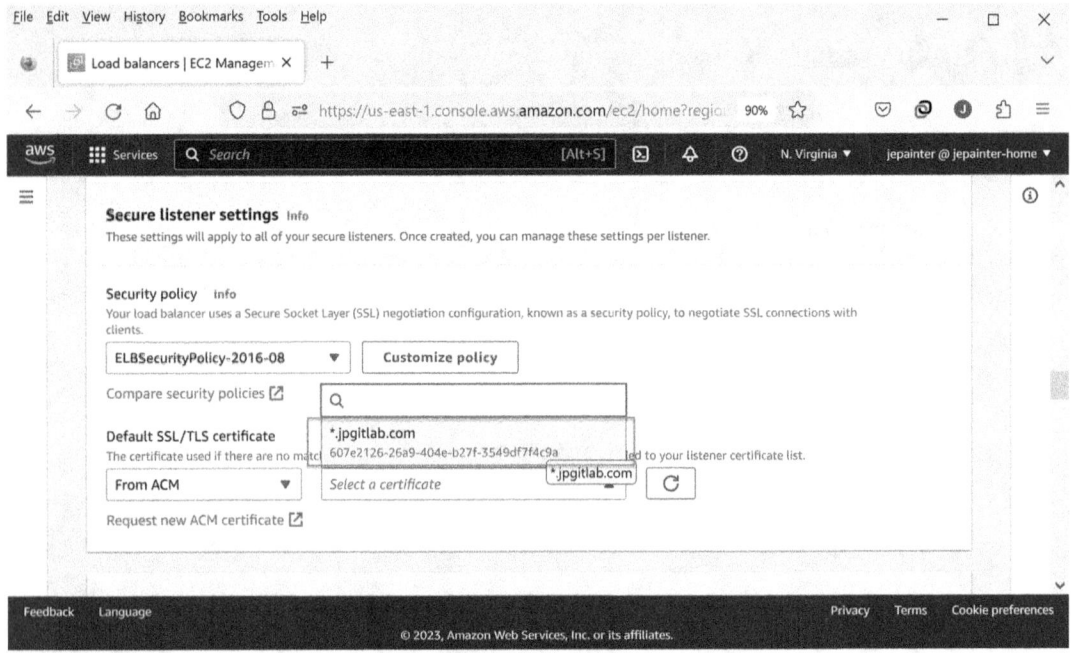

Figure 13-40. ELB secure listener settings

Setting Up the ELB Health Check

Almost done configuring the ELB. Yes, there are a lot of options to configure for an ELB. The next thing to set up is the health check as shown in Figure 13-41. A health check is a feature of an ELB that periodically checks the health of instances managed by the ELB. Here, we set up a ping to HTTP port 80 using GitLab's readiness check. For each instance, the ELB will form an HTTP request using the IP address of the instance appended with the readiness check provided (as opposed to the default /index that many websites accept). If GitLab is running properly on an instance, it will reply with an HTTP/OK to the health check; otherwise, it will return a failure letting the ELB know something is not running properly and hence not direct requests to that instance. There are advanced health check settings to determine how long to wait initially before starting to ping the instance as well as how often to make pings. We'll keep the advanced settings as they are for our POC.

CHAPTER 13 I CAN DO THIS ON MY OWN

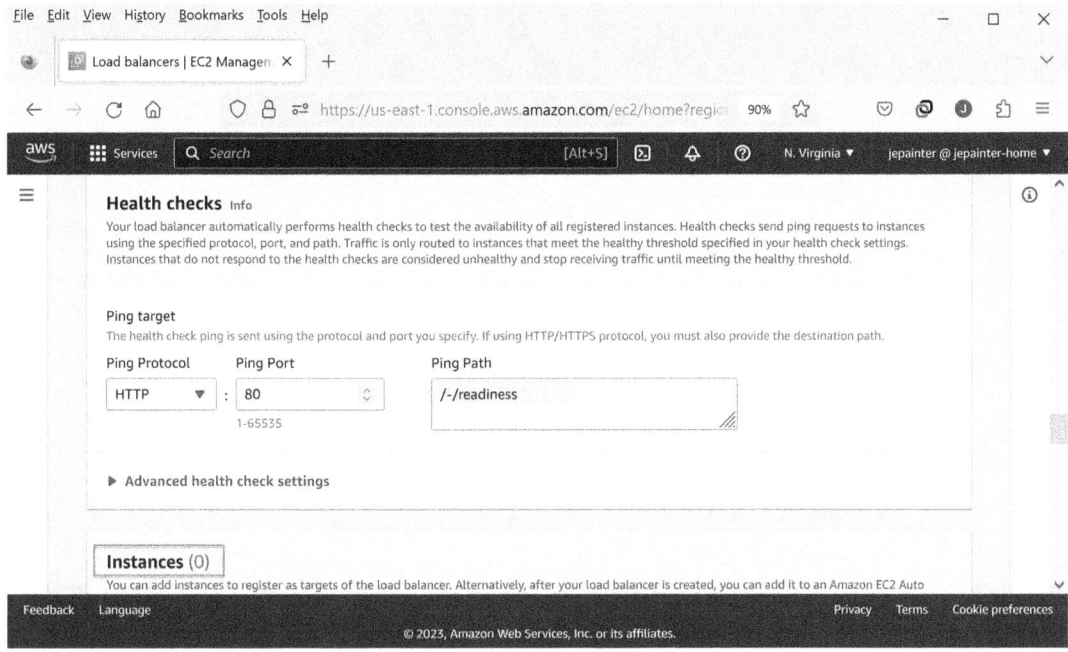

Figure 13-41. *Configuration of ELB health checks*

Setting ELB Special Attributes

Finally, there are a set of special attributes to configure as shown in Figure 13-42. The first attribute "Enable cross-zone load balancing" enables the load balancer to balance requests across all zones, which is what we want for our GitLab POC. The second attribute "Enable connection draining" provides an interval to wait before finally disconnecting an instance from the ELB. This allows any action being performed by the instance time to complete before it is disconnected from the ELB or deleted by the ELB.[14] During the connection drainage period, no new requests will be sent to that instance.

---

[14] We'll talk later about how instances are managed by the ELB when we look at AWS Auto-Scaling Groups.

CHAPTER 13   I CAN DO THIS ON MY OWN

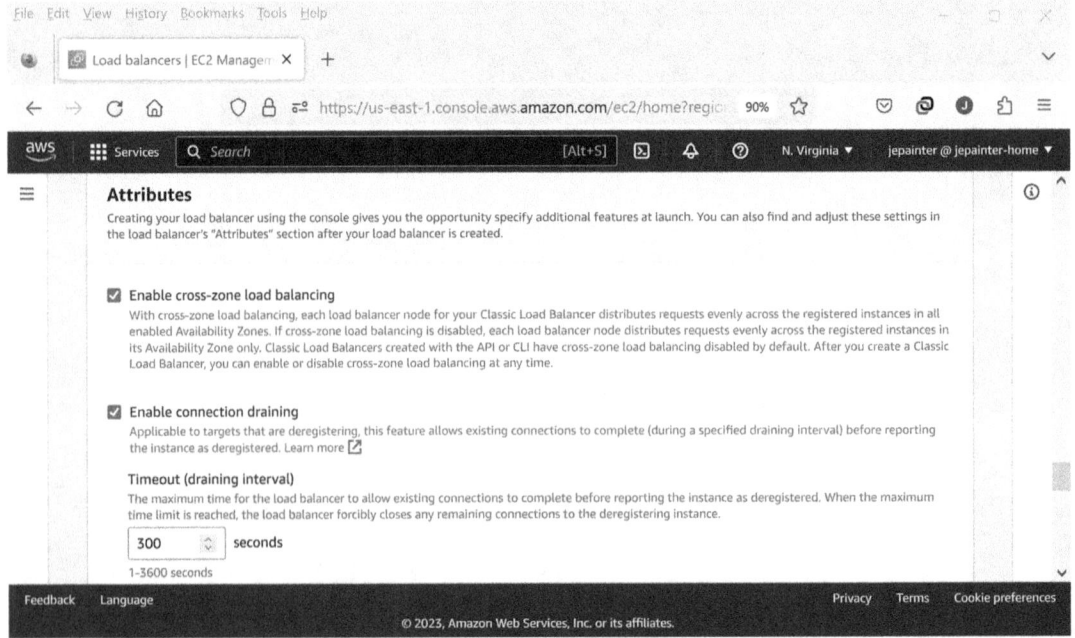

Figure 13-42. Configuration of ELB special attributes

Spinning Up the ELB

Note that we'll leave the final section of associating instances to the ELB as is. We will not be manually associating existing instances to the ELB but rather use an AWS auto-scaling group to dynamically spin up and spin down instances as needed. With that, you create the ELB. It will take a bit to come up, but you can view the progress by listing the ELBs as shown in Figure 13-43.

CHAPTER 13   I CAN DO THIS ON MY OWN

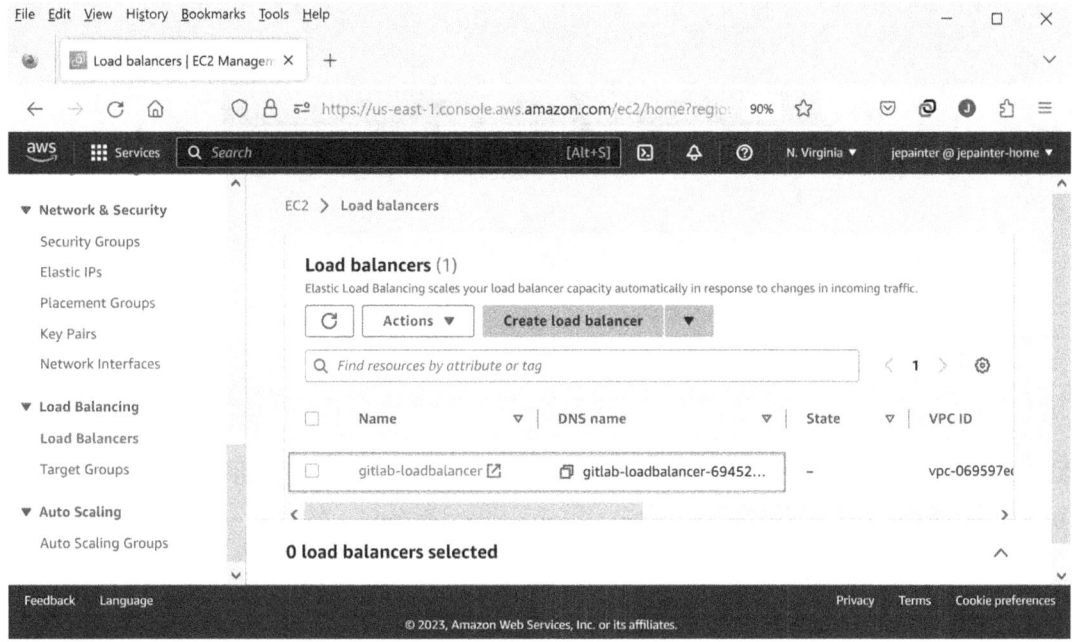

Figure 13-43. *Listing of newly created ELB*

Connecting Your Domain

So, we've seen how the ELB listeners manage traffic through the ELB to your instances, but how do we get to the ELB itself? This is where you need to define a domain to connect to your ELB. This is done using hosted zones as shown in Figure 13-44. Within the Route 53 service is the "Hosted zones" page where you tied your top-level domain (jpgitlab.com in this example) to a zone after registering that domain.

Creating a Hosted Zone Record

To get started, select the "Create record" button as shown in Figure 13-44. If you get a choice to use the wizard, select that to make the process of creating a record easier.

559

CHAPTER 13   I CAN DO THIS ON MY OWN

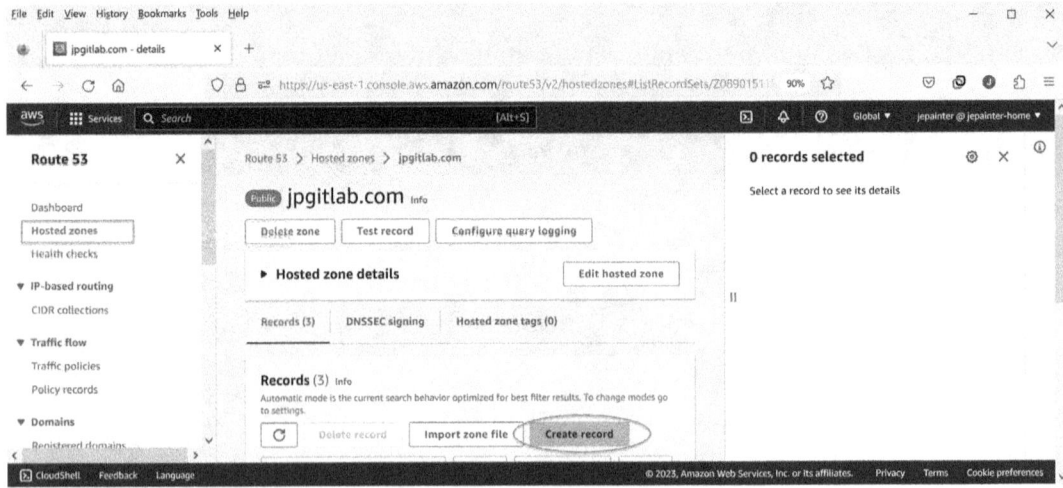

Figure 13-44. *Route 53 option to create a hosted zone record*

Setting the Routing Policy

The first thing to do is to select a routing policy as shown in Figure 13-45. For our GitLab POC, we want to select the "Simple routing" option. We use this policy since we want to associate a domain name directly to our ELB. The other options handle cases where there are multiple ELBs spread across regions.

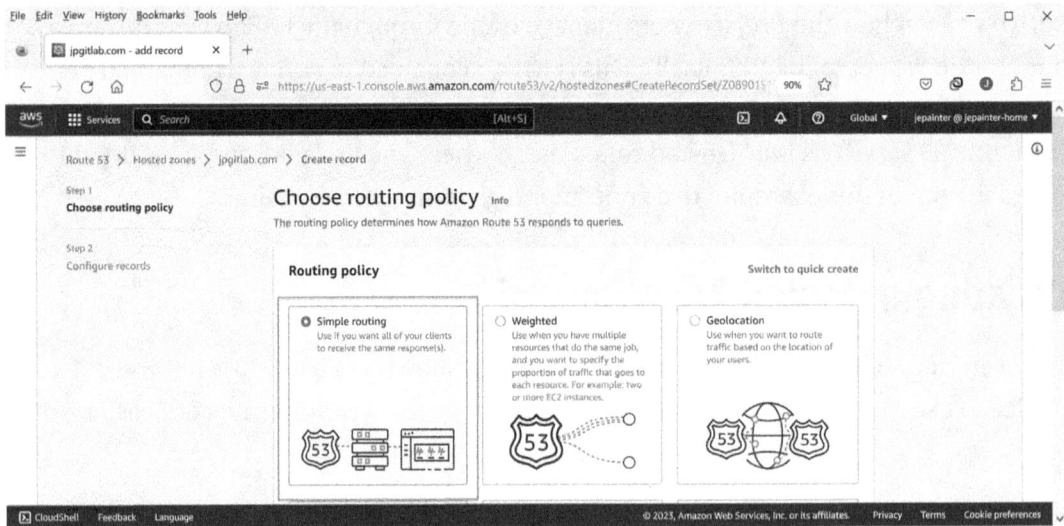

Figure 13-45. *Selection of routing policy*

CHAPTER 13   I CAN DO THIS ON MY OWN

Configuring Records for Simple Routing Policy

Selecting the simple routing policy takes you to the "Configure records" page as shown in Figure 13-46. This is where we create a DNS record that connects to the ELB.

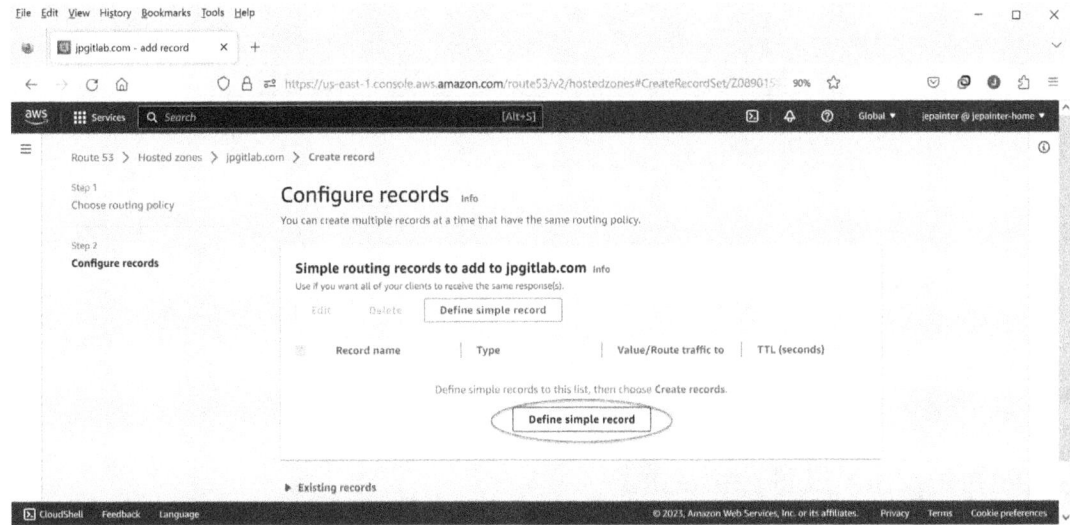

Figure 13-46. *Option to define simple record*

Creating an "A" Record for Routing DNS Traffic to Our Domain

Selecting the "Define simple record" button pops up a form where you define the record you want as shown in Figure 13-47. In this example, I'm creating an "A" record for the poc.jpgitlab.com domain. This is how we'll be able to access our GitLab POC from our web browser (e.g., `https://poc.jpgitlab.com`).

561

CHAPTER 13 I CAN DO THIS ON MY OWN

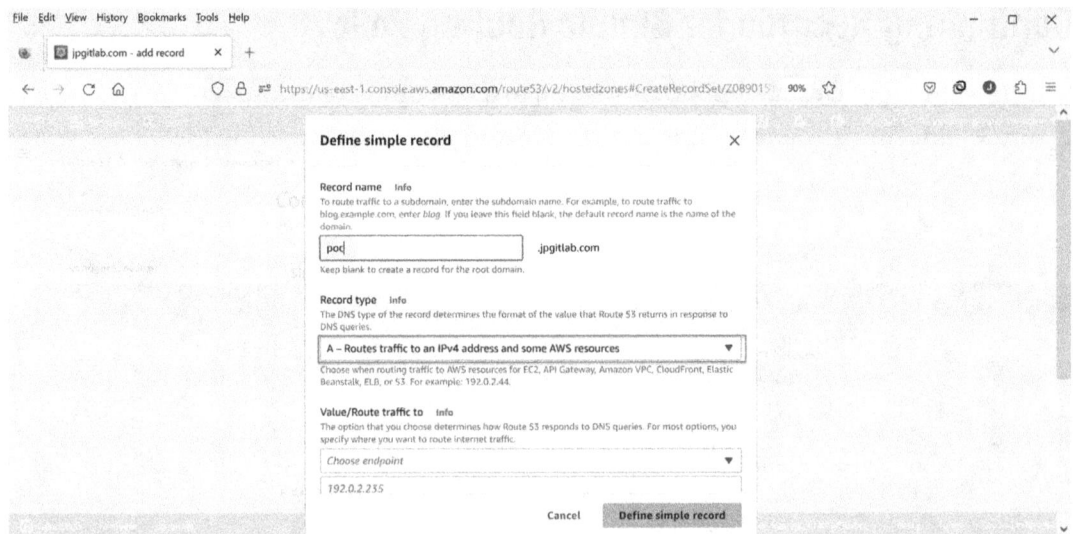

Figure 13-47. Simple record creation form (part 1)

Specifying the ELB Endpoint

Further down on the form, we specify the endpoint where traffic will be routed to as shown in Figure 13-48. For our POC, we select the "Alias to Application and Classic Load Balancer" option. Once that option is selected, additional fields appear on the form where we select the region and ELB to use as the endpoint. This is shown in Figure 13-49.

CHAPTER 13 I CAN DO THIS ON MY OWN

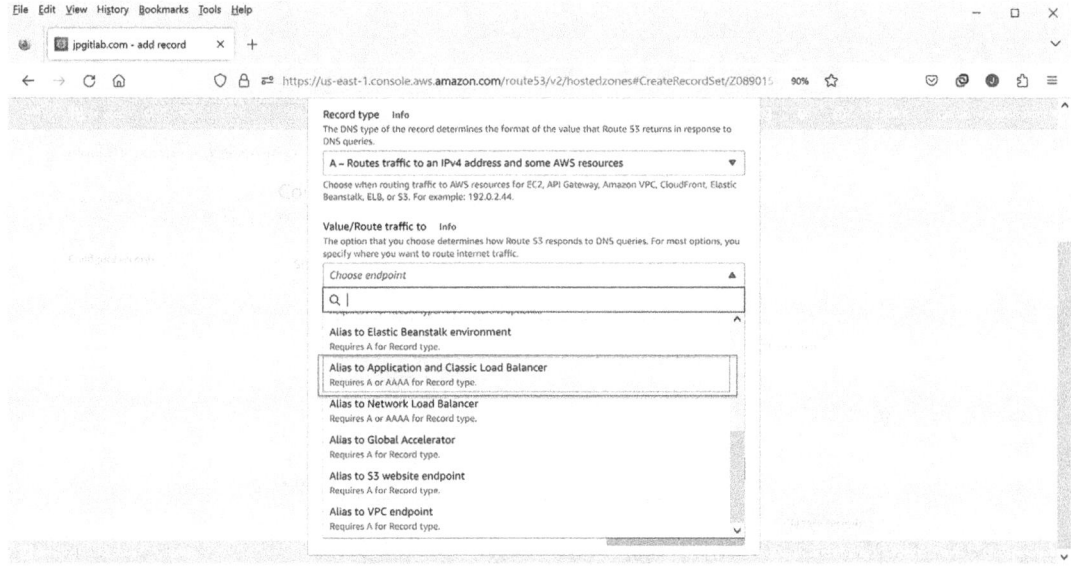

Figure 13-48. *Simple record creation form (part 2)*

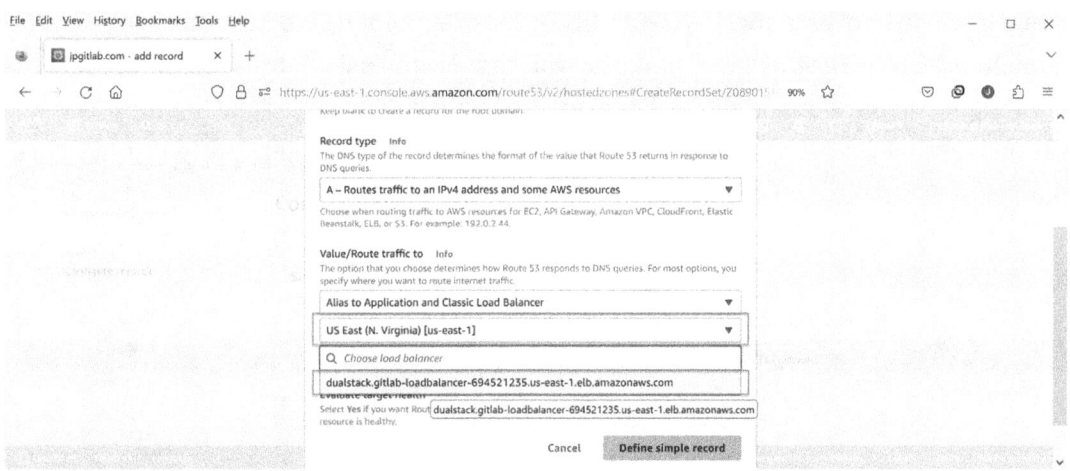

Figure 13-49. *Simple record creation form (part 3)*

Disabling the ELB Target Health Option

Once the ELB is selected, we configure the target health option as shown in Figure 13-50. For our GitLab POC, we turn this option off since the ELB itself will monitor the health of our instances. Selecting the "Define simple record" will add the new A record to the DNS service.

563

CHAPTER 13   I CAN DO THIS ON MY OWN

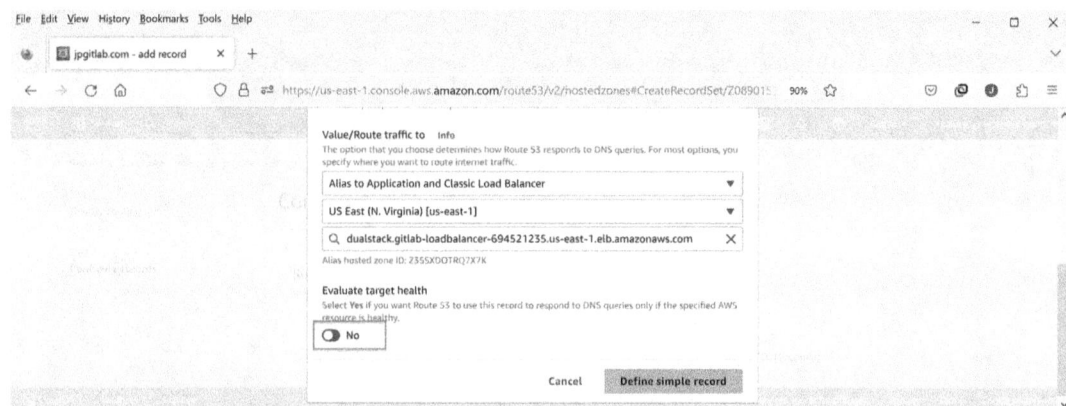

Figure 13-50. Simple record creation form (part 4)

Verifying Domain Connectivity to the ELB

We can verify that our A record is defined by listing the records as shown in Figure 13-51. Here, we see that our fully qualified domain name is routing traffic to our ELB. Although there are no instances associated with the ELB at the moment, we can still check that the domain has an IP assigned to it. In Linux, you can use the nslookup command to see the IPs assigned to our domain name. For example, nslookup poc.jpgitlab.com returns the various IPs that DNS returns for our ELB. If the nslookup fails, you know that something is incorrect with the zone configuration.

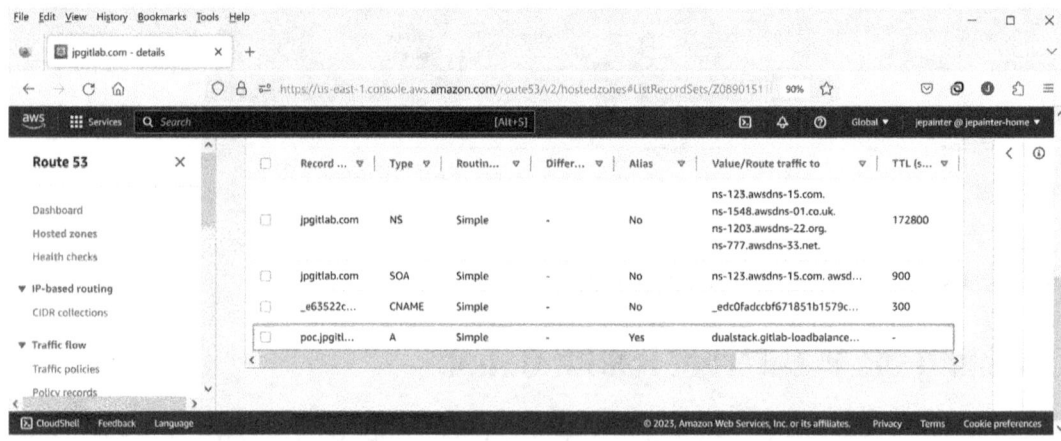

Figure 13-51. Hosted zone listing of the newly created record

Summary

In summary, we've covered the following topics in this chapter:

- Shown how to create your own AWS account
- Described how to create an Admin user group and add yourself as a user of that group
- Explained how to set up a VPC for our GitLab POC
- Introduced how to create an SSH key pair through AWS
- Learned how to register your own domain and create a TLS certificate through AWS
- Discussed how to create an IAM role for S3 accessibility from our back-end servers
- Reviewed how to create a classic load balancer for our GitLab POC
- Demonstrated how to connect your domain to the load balancer

In the next chapter, we'll look at how to set up the back-end services in AWS such as databases and the like.

CHAPTER 14

Things That Lurk in the Background

Now that the preliminary infrastructure for our GitLab POC is in place, we are ready to build up the key components of the POC back-end services. In this chapter, we will cover the creation of both the PostgreSQL database and the Redis database required for GitLab. We will also tackle the spinning up of bastion servers in our public subnets that we will need later to access servers in our private subnets.

Raising the RDS

The GitLab service uses a PostgreSQL database to store all sorts of information about your installation such as users, projects, groups, jobs, pipelines, etc. Although the GitLab installation process includes setting up a PostgreSQL database managed by the GitLab service, we won't be using that on the AWS cloud. The reason for this is that AWS provides a PostgreSQL service with many benefits, such as automatic failover, cross-region replication (which we won't be using for the GitLab POC), and backup capabilities that are difficult and/or more expensive to do on your own.

Creating the RDS Security Group

To manage databases, AWS provides the Relational Database Service (RDS). Before we go there, however, we need to create a security group that will be used by that service. Figure 14-1 shows the security groups page available from the EC2 service. From here, you should see the previous security group we created for the load balancer. We'll create a new one for RDS by selecting the "Create security group" button as highlighted in the figure.

CHAPTER 14   THINGS THAT LURK IN THE BACKGROUND

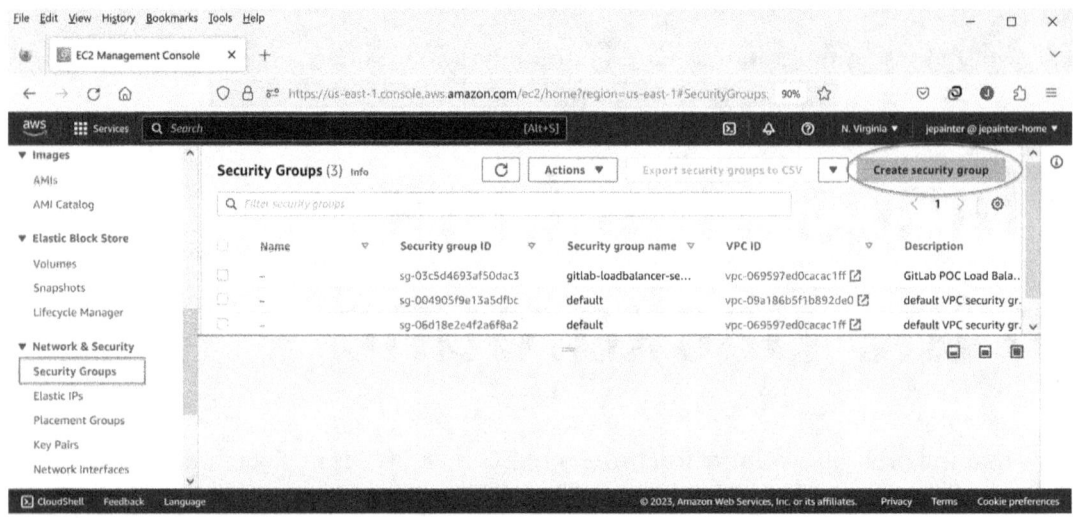

Figure 14-1. Option to create a security group for RDS

From here, we select the basic configuration as shown in Figure 14-2. Just as we did for the load balancer SG, we specify a name for our security group, which in this case will be gitlab-rds-sec-group. We also select our private VPC as we did for the load balancer, by entering "vpc-" and selecting the private VPC from the drop-down.

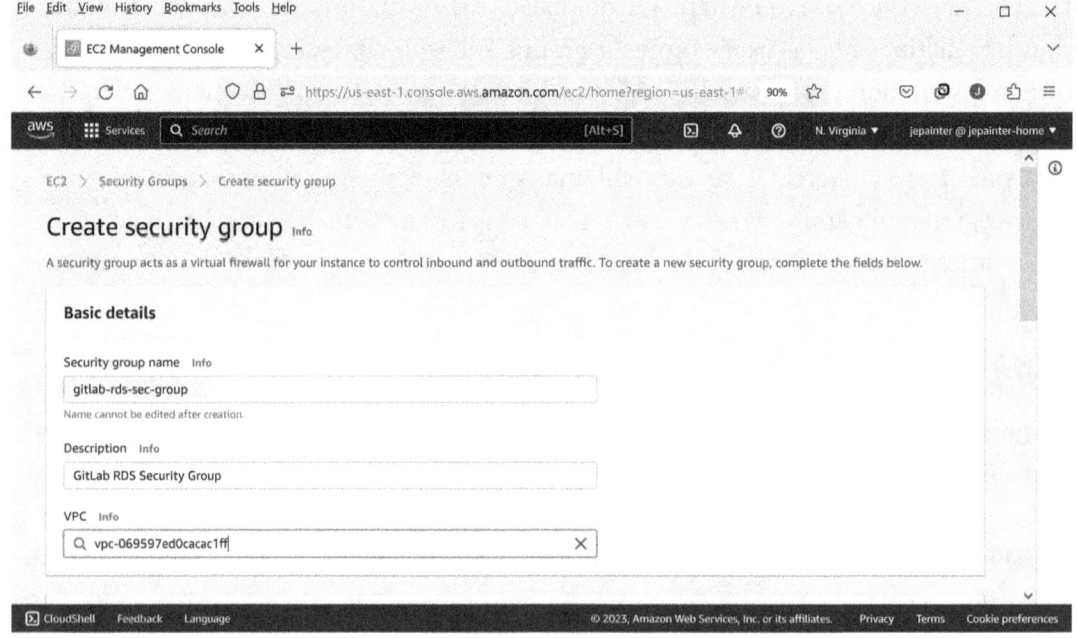

Figure 14-2. Basic detail options for the RDS security group

CHAPTER 14   THINGS THAT LURK IN THE BACKGROUND

Scrolling down, we set the inbound rule as shown in Figure 14-3. For the type, we select PostgreSQL, which automatically sets the Port range to the standard PostgreSQL port 5432. For the source, type in "git" to find the gitlab-loadbalancer SG. What this does is restrict input to our database from the load balancer and any other entities that use the gitlab-loadbalancer-sec-group SG. This provides a level of protection from anyone connecting via the Internet attempting to attack our database.

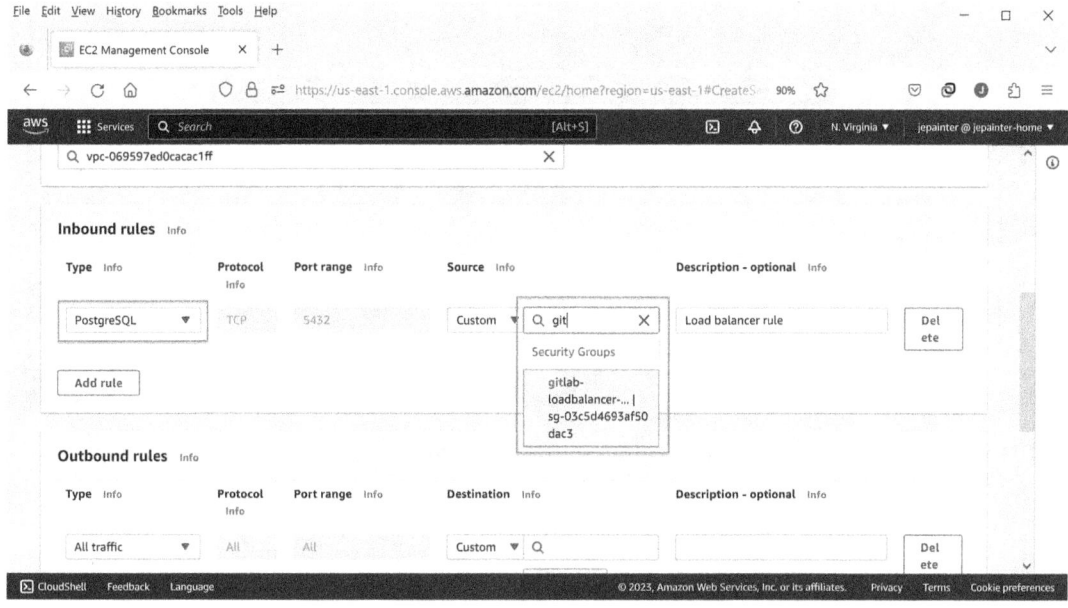

Figure 14-3. *PostgreSQL inbound rule for the RDS security group*

Accessing RDS

With the gitlab-rds-sec-group created, we can now proceed to creating our PostgreSQL database. We can find the RDS service under the Database category as shown in Figure 14-4. Alternatively, you can do a service search for RDS.

569

CHAPTER 14   THINGS THAT LURK IN THE BACKGROUND

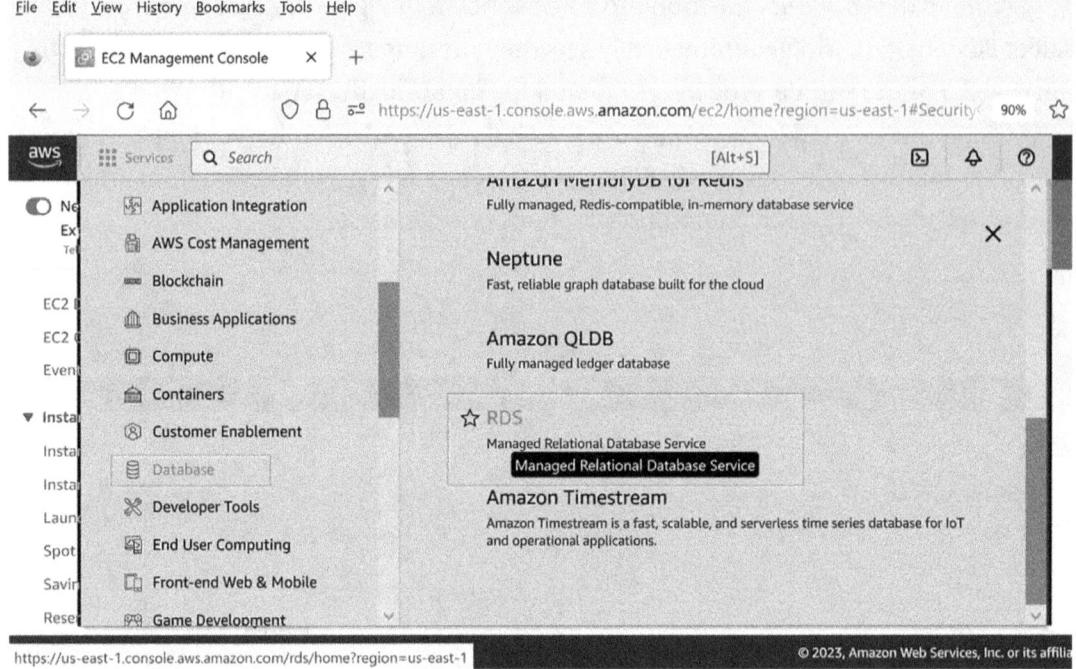

Figure 14-4. RDS selection from the services menu

Creating the DB Subnet Group

To use our database, we need to let the service know what the networking environment is. We do this by creating a subnet group. Figure 14-5 shows the "Subnet groups" page when the "Subnet groups" link is selected. Since no subnet groups exist, we create one by selecting the "Create DB subnet group" button as highlighted in the figure.

CHAPTER 14   THINGS THAT LURK IN THE BACKGROUND

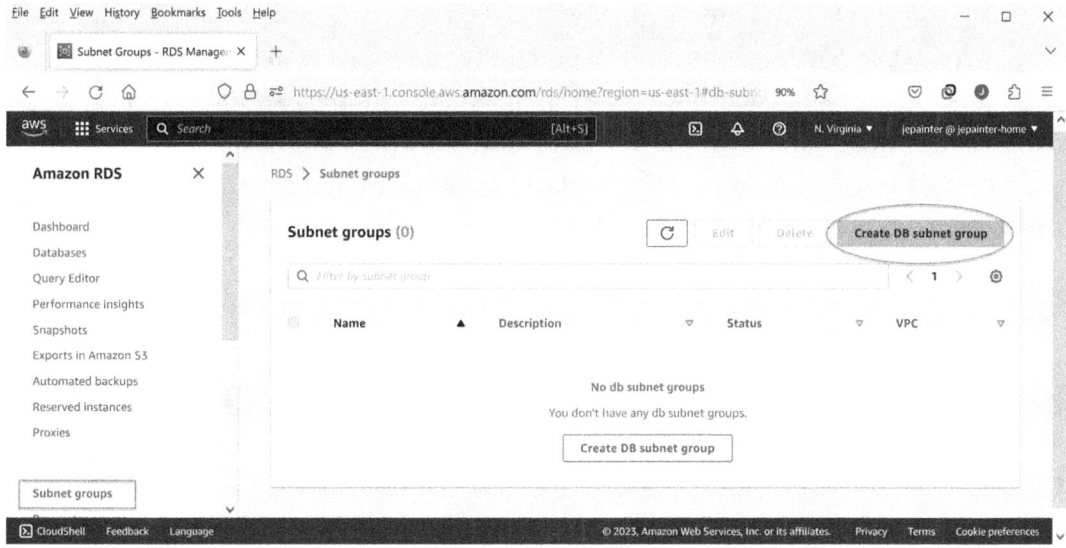

Figure 14-5. *Option to create a DB subnet group*

We first need to fill out the subnet group details as shown in Figure 14-6. Here, we set the name of the subnet group to gitlab-rds-group as well as add a description for the group. For the VPC, we select our private VPC from the drop-down list.

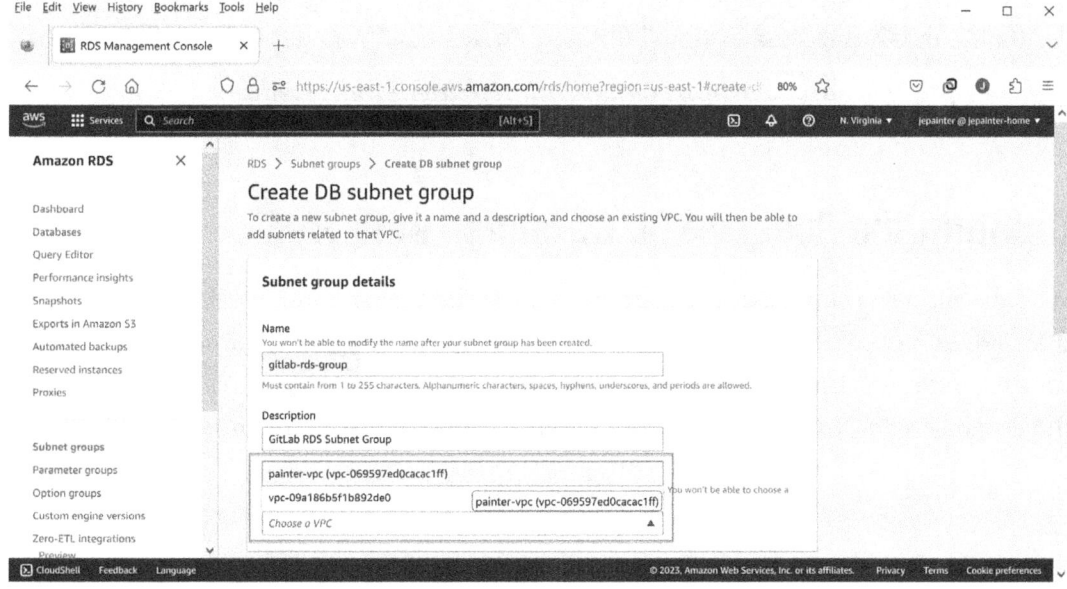

Figure 14-6. *DB subnet group details*

CHAPTER 14   THINGS THAT LURK IN THE BACKGROUND

Next, we select the availability zones and associated subnets as shown in Figure 14-7. Here, we select both of our zones and, within those zones, select the private subnets. Unfortunately, the listing doesn't show the names of the subnets, so you may need to go to the VPC subnet page to determine which subnets are private. It is important that you select the private subnets and not the public ones as you want the database to run in the isolated subnets.

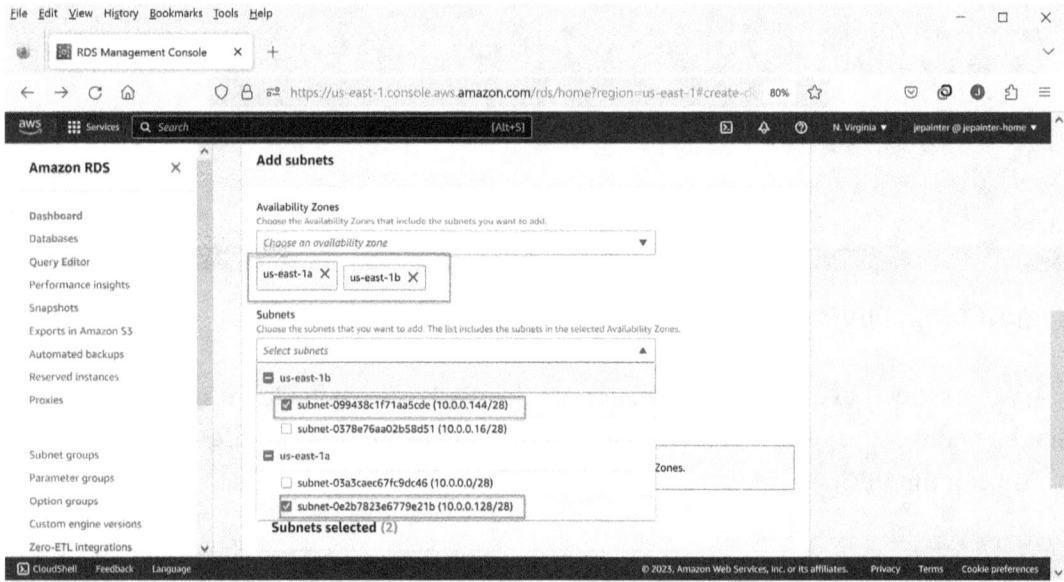

Figure 14-7. *DB subnet group configuration of availability zones and subnets*

Creating the PostgreSQL Database with RDS

With the subnet group created, we are ready to create the database itself. Be forewarned, there are a lot of configuration options to go through, so make sure you set aside enough time to go through them all. Figure 14-8 shows the databases page available by selecting the Databases link. Select the "Create database" button to begin the process.

CHAPTER 14 THINGS THAT LURK IN THE BACKGROUND

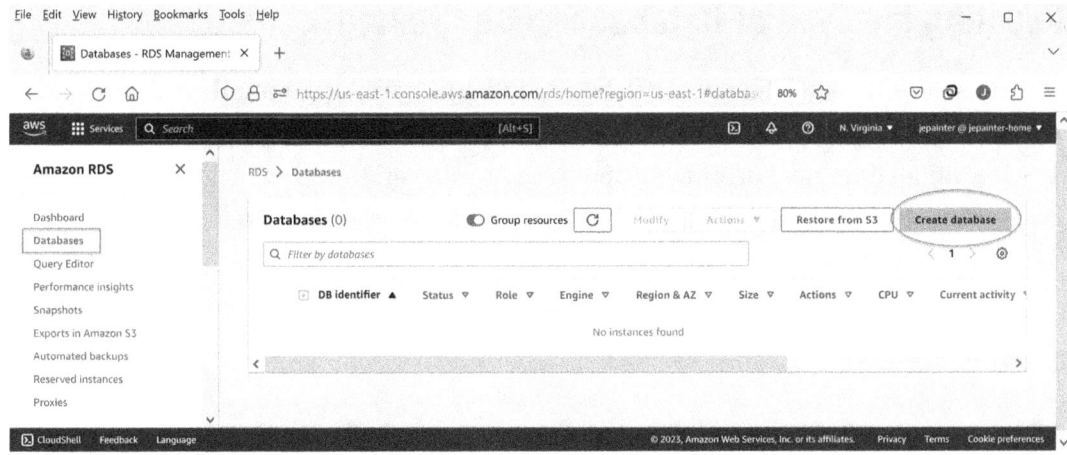

Figure 14-8. Option to create the RDS database

Selecting How to Create the Database

We begin by selecting the method of creating the database as shown in Figure 14-9. Here, we select the standard create method as opposed to the easy create method. Although it takes longer to create the database this way, it gives us full access to the configuration options.

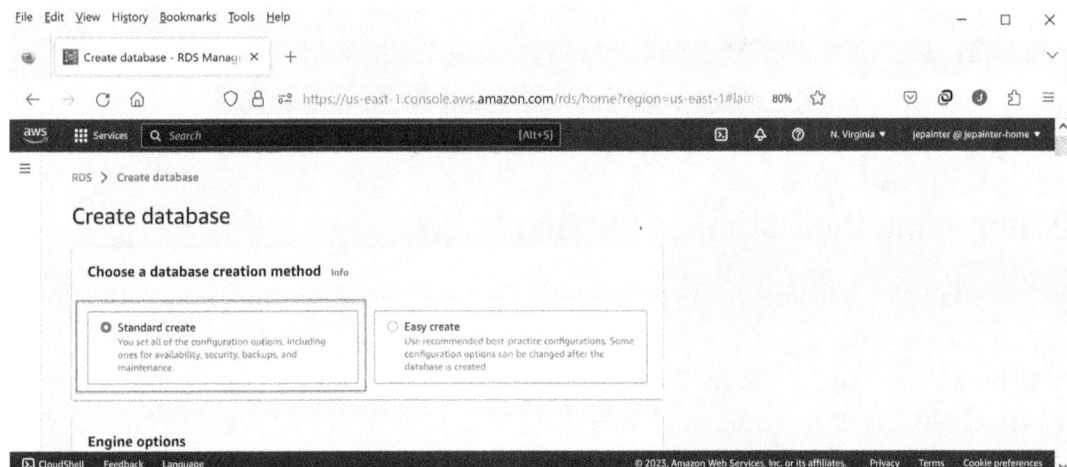

Figure 14-9. Selection of standard database creation method

573

CHAPTER 14   THINGS THAT LURK IN THE BACKGROUND

Selecting the Type of Database to Be Created

Next, we select the type of database to be created. AWS supports a number of database vendors including a variant called Aurora that simulates both PostgreSQL and MySQL. GitLab does not currently support the Aurora variant, so we'll need to select the PostgreSQL vendor as shown in Figure 14-10. Selecting this option updates the list of PostgreSQL versions supported by AWS.

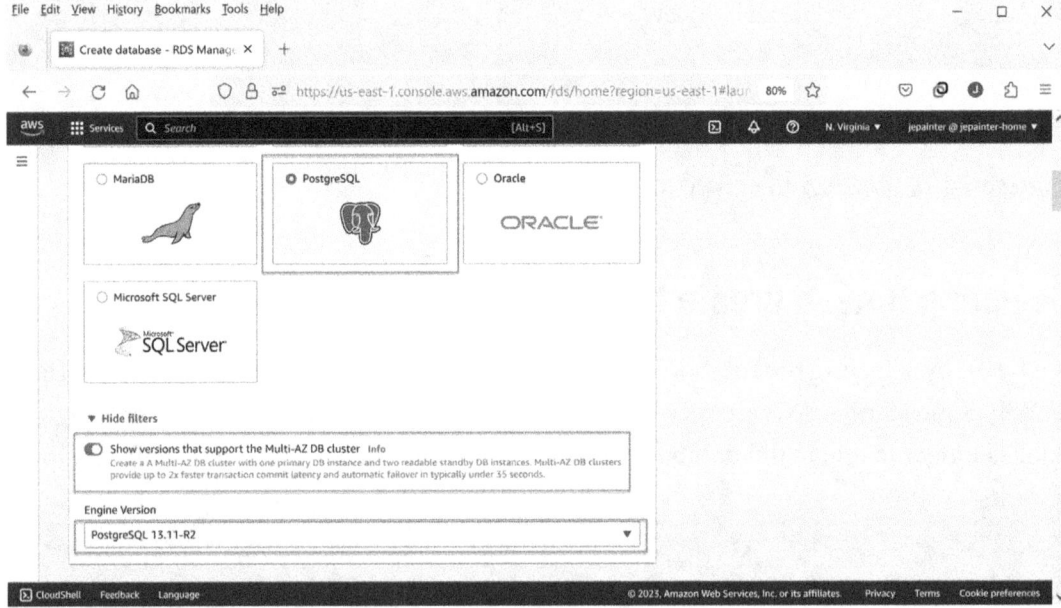

Figure 14-10.   RDS PostgreSQL type selection

Determining the Database Version to Use

As far as database versions go, it's important to choose a version compatible with the GitLab release you plan on installing. Later versions of databases might not work with earlier releases of GitLab. To find out what PostgreSQL versions are compatible with the latest GitLab releases, run a web search on "GitLab Postgres versions" to find the list as shown in Figure 14-11. Since I'll be installing the 16.0 version of GitLab, I chose the

CHAPTER 14   THINGS THAT LURK IN THE BACKGROUND

PostgreSQL 13.11 version as suggested in the search. Since you may be installing a later version of GitLab[1] when you read this, choose the database version appropriate for that version.

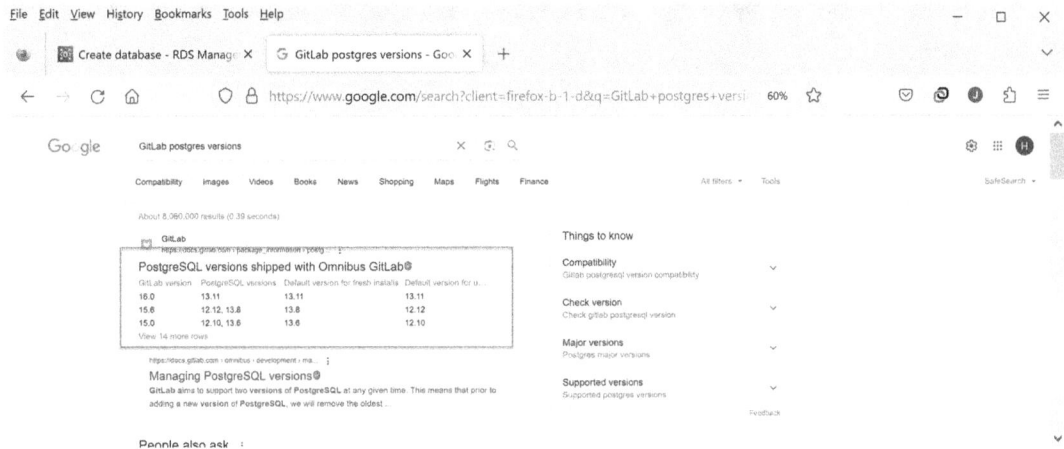

Figure 14-11. Web search of current PostgreSQL versions

Selecting the Database Template

Once you've selected the database type and version, select a template as shown in Figure 14-12. The GitLab documentation for the POC recommends using the Production template. This template supports high-availability and consistent performance. As we'll see later on, this is a costly solution, so you may want to deviate from this tutorial and select the Dev/Test template instead. I proceed with the Production template, so you'll see how the configuration works for that.

---

[1] GitLab generally maintains the latest three major versions (in this case, 14, 15, and 16). Every year around May, a new major release of GitLab is released (minor releases occur on the third Thursday of every month). With a new release, the oldest release is retired and no longer maintained, even for security patches, so keep that in mind.

575

CHAPTER 14　THINGS THAT LURK IN THE BACKGROUND

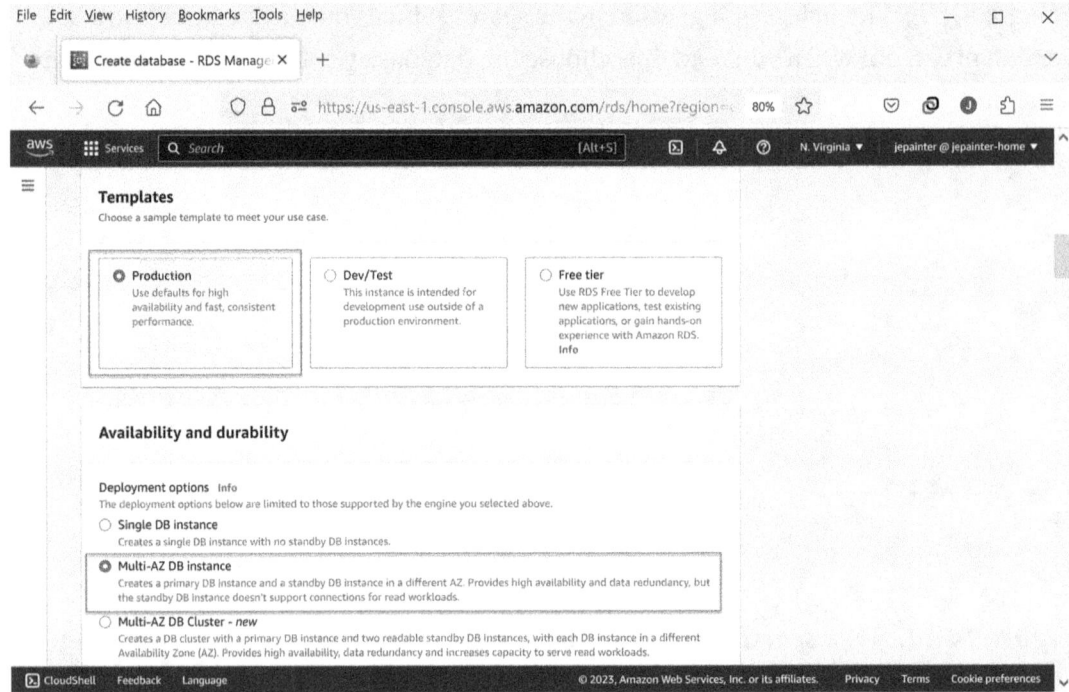

Figure 14-12. *RDS template and RDS availability and durability configuration*

Determining Whether to Use a Multi-AZ or Single DB Instance

Under the "Availability and durability" section, I'm going with the "Multi-AZ DB instance" option, which enables high availability. As recommended by GitLab, do not choose the "Multi-AZ DB Cluster" option as it is not supported by GitLab. Again, selecting the "Multi-AZ DB instance" comes with an increased cost since you will be using database server instances in each of your AZ zones. If you are just experimenting with the GitLab setup, feel free to choose the "Single DB instance" option, realizing that if the AZ under which the database is running goes down, your GitLab service will become unavailable.

Setting the Database Identifier and Credentials

Figure 14-13 shows the configurations for the AWS database identifier and the credentials to be used. Here, we set the DB instance identifier to gitlab-db-ha. If you are not going with the high-availability setup, feel free to select a name such as gitlab-db.

CHAPTER 14 THINGS THAT LURK IN THE BACKGROUND

As for credentials, I selected gitlab as the master username and chose to enter my own master password. Note that you should remember that password as you'll need it when configuring GitLab to use this PostgreSQL database.

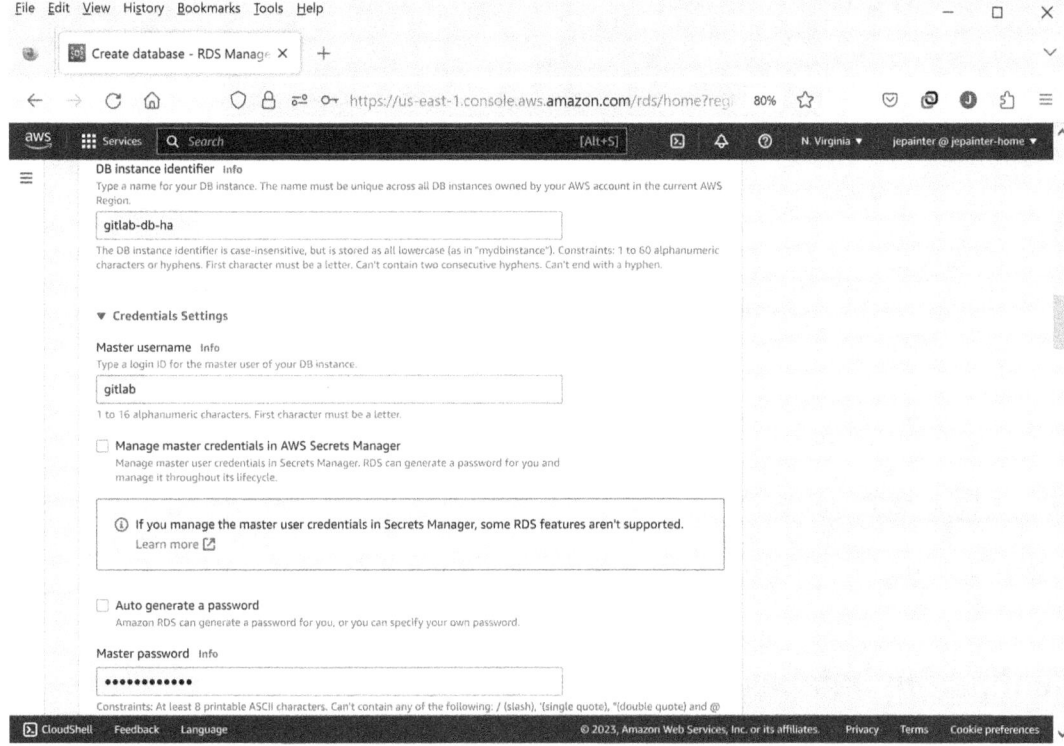

Figure 14-13. RDS DB instance identifier and credential configuration

Selecting the Instance Type for Database Server Instances

RDS will be spinning up database server instances on its behalf (you won't have direct access to these instances). You are able to configure the type of instance to use, however. AWS provides a wide range of server instance types with different characteristics with, of course, different cost footprints. The more CPUs or memory sizes, for example, the higher the per-hour costs of those servers. For the GitLab POC, I've selected the standard

CHAPTER 14   THINGS THAT LURK IN THE BACKGROUND

set of server classes known as the m-series as shown in Figure 14-14. For this example, I chose the db.m5.large[2] server type, which provides enough horsepower for the POC needs.

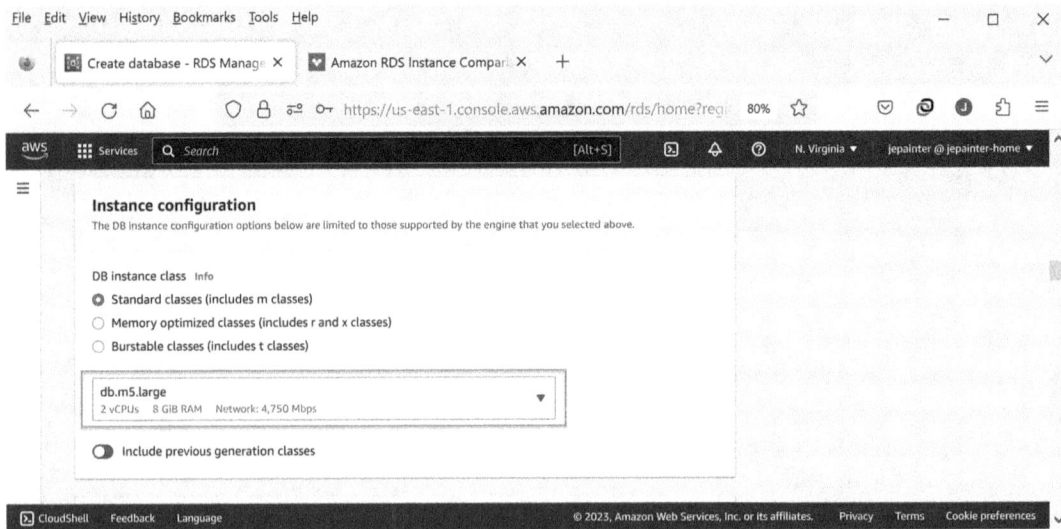

Figure 14-14. RDS server instance type configuration

Configuring Database Storage

Of course, databases need to store their data somewhere, so the next thing to configure is the type and amount of storage needed. Figure 14-15 shows the available storage configuration options. As recommended by the GitLab documentation for the POC, I select the "Provisioned IOPS SSD" option. SSD indicates that this is a solid-state drive as opposed to the older magnetic disks. IOPS stands for Input/Output Operations per Second. In this example, I am starting with the minimum allocated storage allowed (100GB) and using the minimum provisioned IOPS of 1000.

---

[2] Beware, AWS might suggest a higher power configuration such as the db.m5d.large type, which is about twice the cost of the db.m5.large type. You can do a web search on "RDS server classes" to see what the costs will be.

CHAPTER 14 THINGS THAT LURK IN THE BACKGROUND

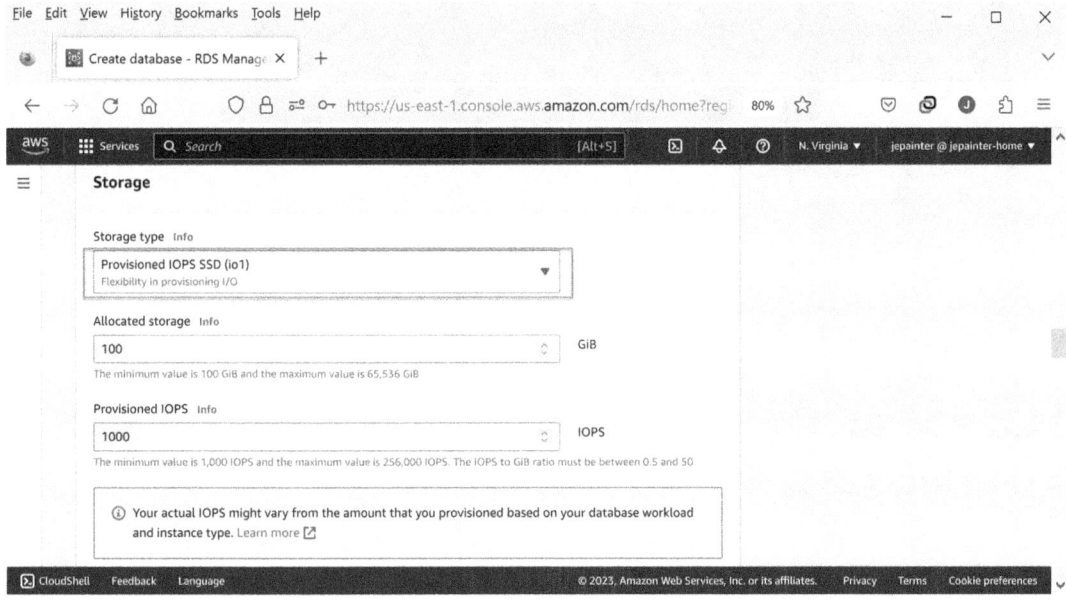

Figure 14-15. *RDS storage configurations*

In terms of storage, it's always difficult to judge how much you need, and there is always the possibility you might start filling it up. One feature of RDS is the ability to auto-scale the storage size when it begins to get close to filling up. Figure 14-16 shows the option to enable auto-scaling for your database storage. By enabling auto-scaling, RDS will automatically increase the storage for you; note that this will not stop the database from running although it might slow things down a bit while the expansion is occurring. When you enable auto-scaling, you need to specify the maximum storage threshold; this is a safety feature in the event that something goes awry, and the database begins to fill up unexpectedly.[3]

---

[3] Although rare, I've seen this happen. Not so much with the primary GitLab database, but rather with the Praefect database that keeps track of differences across a cluster of servers used to manage the Git repository or with the GitLab Geo database that keeps track of replication across different regions.

CHAPTER 14   THINGS THAT LURK IN THE BACKGROUND

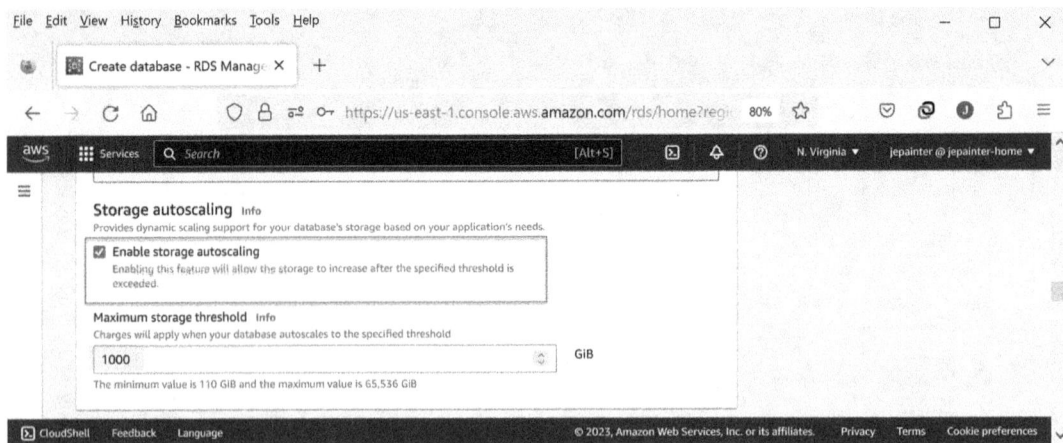

Figure 14-16. RDS storage auto-scaling configuration

Configuring Connectivity Options

The next set of options to be configured deals with connectivity as shown in Figure 14-17. There are a few options to be configured. The first involves setting up a connection to an EC2 compute resource; we'll leave this at the default of no connection since we don't have any EC2 servers defined yet. As for the network type, we'll keep it at the default of IPv4 since that is what our VPC networking setup uses. Finally, we set the VPC to use our private VPC created for the GitLab POC.

CHAPTER 14   THINGS THAT LURK IN THE BACKGROUND

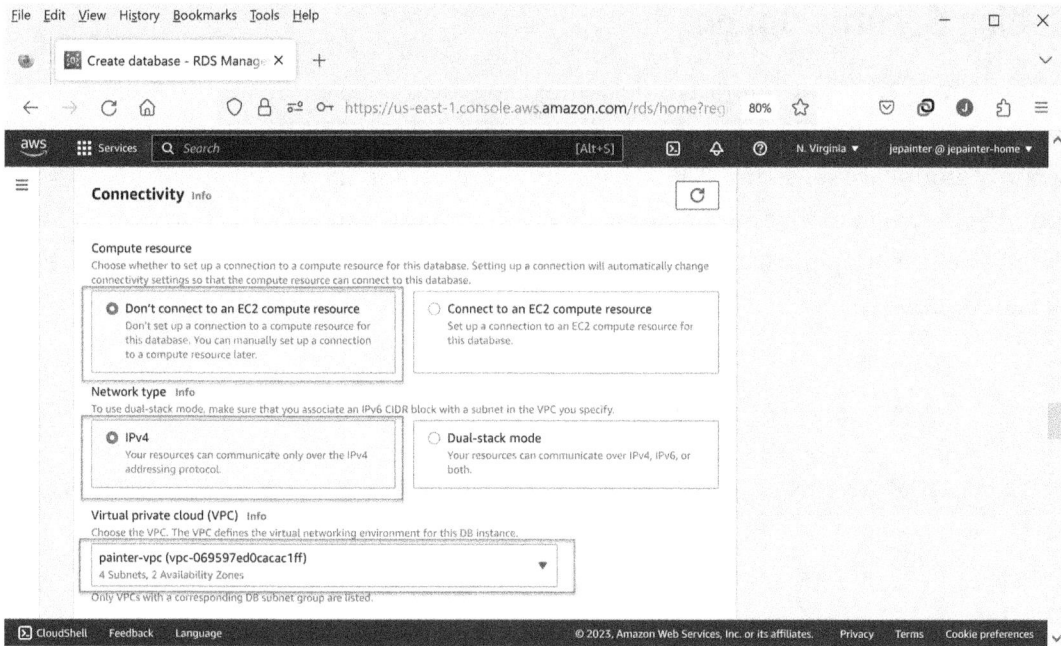

Figure 14-17. RDS connectivity configuration

Setting the DB Subnet Group and Disabling Public Access

Up next is the selection of the subnet group and whether public access is required. These options are shown in Figure 14-18. Here, we select gitlab-rds-group from the "DB Subnet group" drop-down. As for public access, we want to disable that by selecting No.

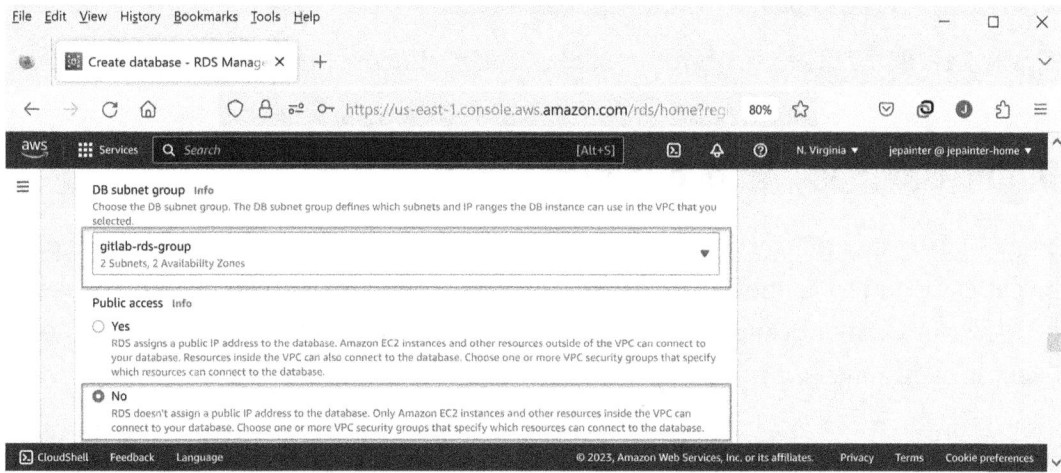

Figure 14-18. RDS DB subnet group and public access configuration

CHAPTER 14   THINGS THAT LURK IN THE BACKGROUND

Setting Security Options

Getting tired yet? We are almost done configuring the database. Figure 14-19 shows the various options related to security groups, proxies, and certificate authority. Under "VPC security group," we select the "Choose existing" option and then enter gitlab-rds-sec-group as the SG to use for our database. For RDS proxy, we keep this option disabled as it doesn't behave properly with GitLab. Finally, we keep the certificate authority set to the default value.

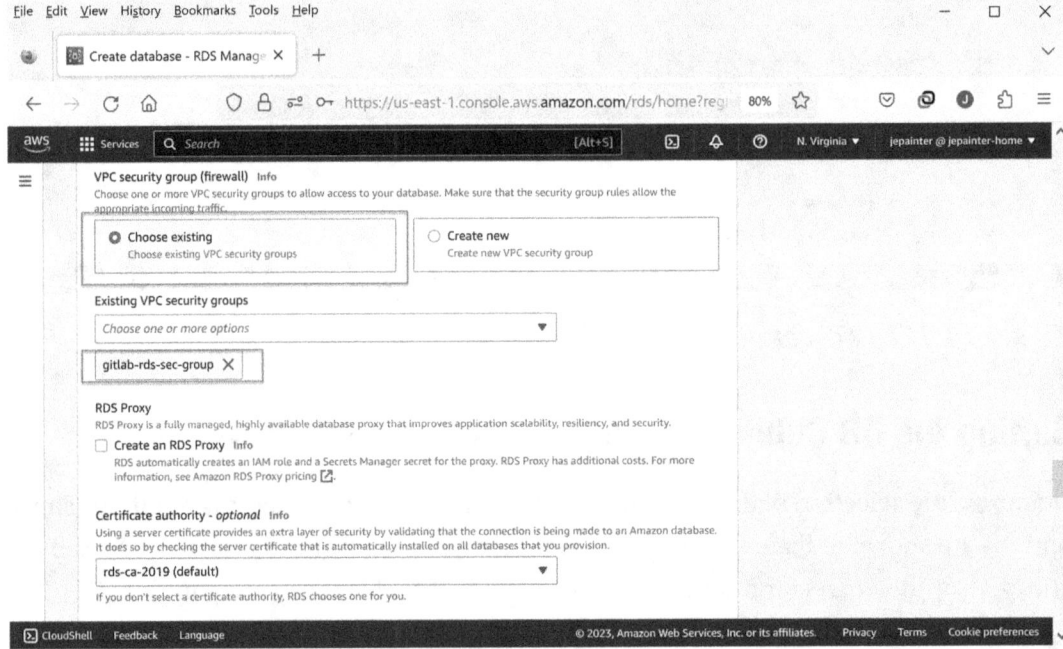

Figure 14-19. RDS security group, proxy, and certificate authority configurations

Setting Database Authentication Option

Figure 14-20 shows the next set of options. Under "Additional configuration," we keep the database port set to the default of 5432. And for "Database authentication," we use the "Password authentication" option as we'll be configuring GitLab to connect to the database using passwords.

CHAPTER 14   THINGS THAT LURK IN THE BACKGROUND

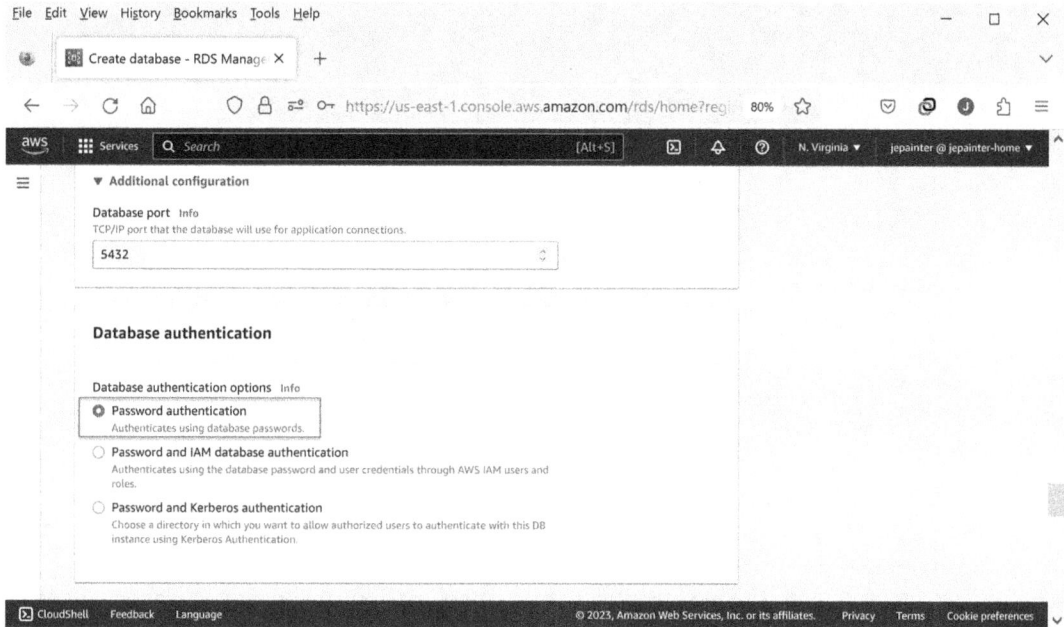

Figure 14-20. *RDS port and authentication configurations*

Overview of Monitoring Options

The Monitoring section of options, shown in Figure 14-21, controls how the database will be monitored. In a production environment, this is vitally important in order to catch anomalies in the performance of the database. The cost of doing this is minimal. I made sure the performance insights were enabled and kept the related options set to their defaults; these can be tweaked later, if necessary.

CHAPTER 14   THINGS THAT LURK IN THE BACKGROUND

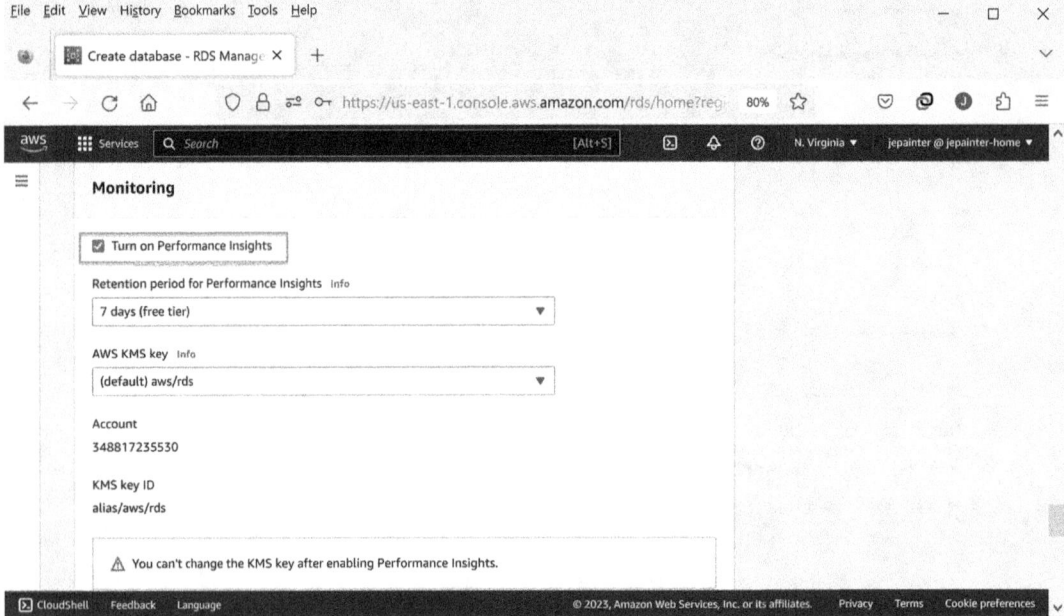

Figure 14-21. *RDS monitoring configuration*

There are also enhanced monitoring options as shown in Figure 14-22. In the example, I show both the "DevOps Guru" and "Enhanced monitoring" enabled. Note that there is an additional cost for these monitoring options. For my database, I went back and disabled both of these options since I don't plan on keeping the GitLab service up for very long.

CHAPTER 14   THINGS THAT LURK IN THE BACKGROUND

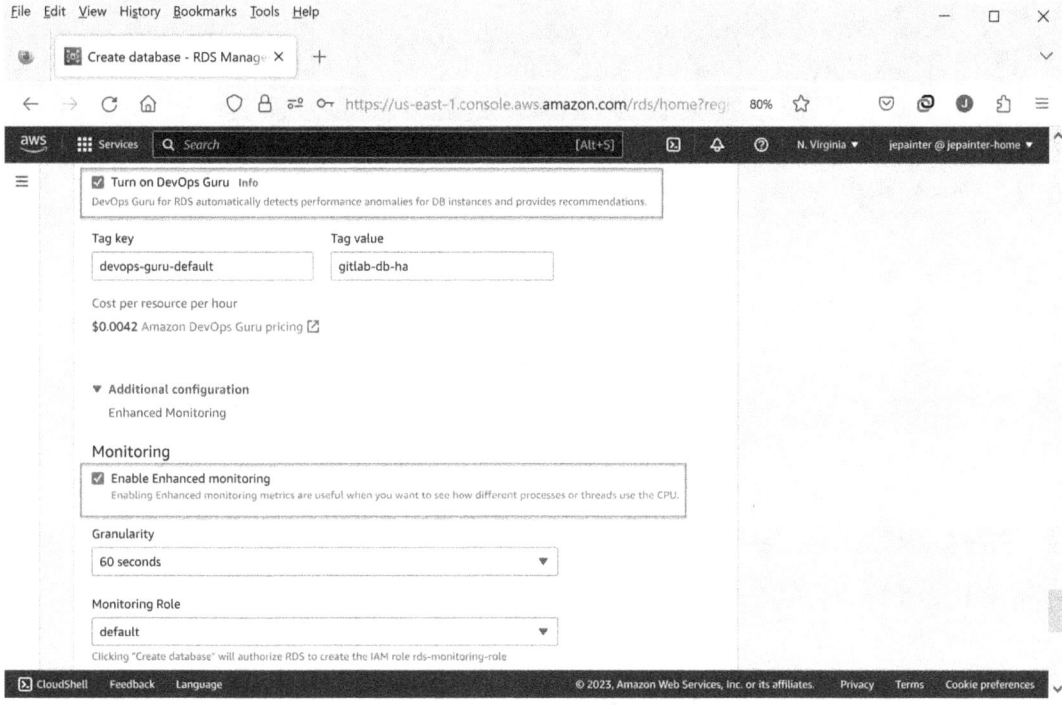

Figure 14-22. RDS enhanced monitoring configuration

Setting the Database Name and DB Parameter Group

As we near the end of the configuration, there are some miscellaneous options that need to be set as shown in Figure 14-23. The key option here is the initial database name that I've set to "gitlabhq_production." As the message indicates, the name must be specified in order for the database to be created; this is how GitLab will refer to it. I kept the DB parameter group at the default of default.postgres13, which is fine for the POC. However, I recommend creating your own parameter group using the default as a basis; there may be database options you will need to set, and you won't be able to set them with the default parameter group.[4]

---

[4] Although you can create a new parameter group later, changing it will require that the database be shut down in maintenance mode, a fact I learned the hard way.

585

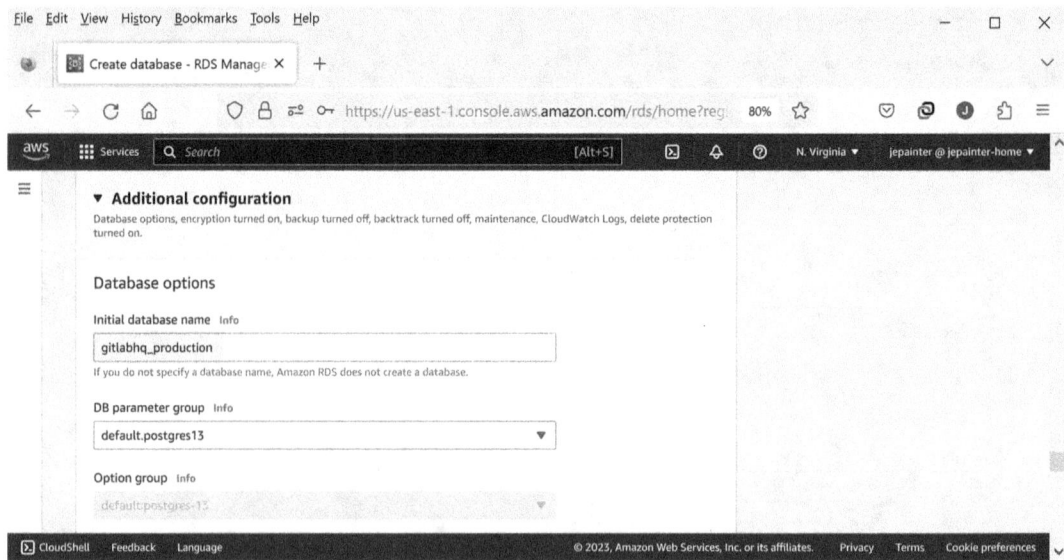

Figure 14-23. *RDS additional configuration options*

Overview of Backup Options

RDS provides a feature to automatically back up your databases, which is a handy feature for production and development GitLab implementations. In addition, RDS has a feature to encrypt the database "at rest," meaning that the filesystem used to store the database schema will be encrypted. Figure 14-24 shows how I set these options for the GitLab POC. I disabled automated backups for my POC since there is a cost involved in enabling backups. As for encryption, I enabled this feature, which is always a good idea whether or not you are running a production database.

CHAPTER 14   THINGS THAT LURK IN THE BACKGROUND

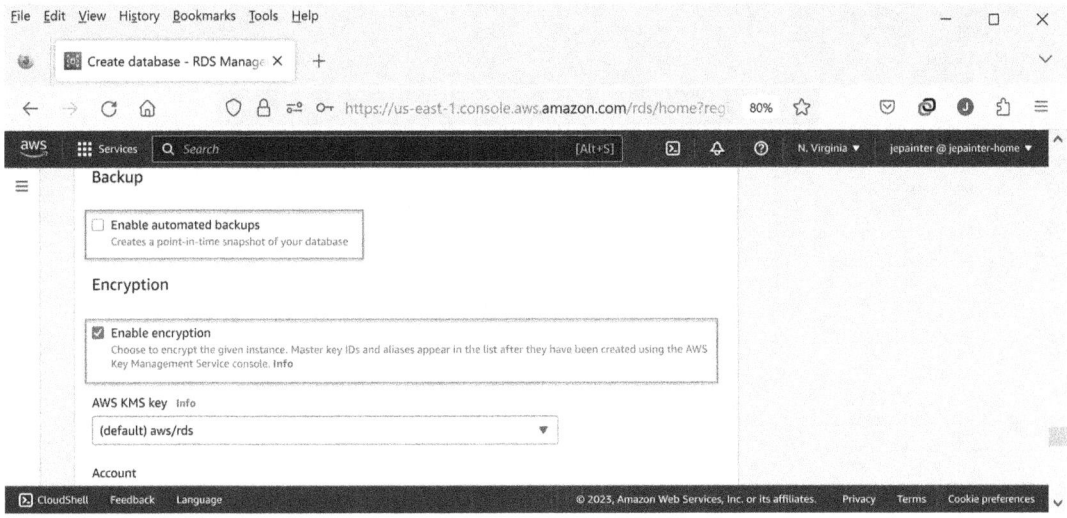

Figure 14-24. *RDS backup and encryption configurations*

Configuring Maintenance Options

The final configuration options involve maintenance as shown in Figure 14-25. As per GitLab guidelines, I disabled the "auto minor version upgrade" feature; this prevents any unforeseen issues that might arise with GitLab should RDS upgrade the minor version. As for setting a maintenance window, I kept it at the default "No preference" option; I don't plan on keeping this database around for long, so maintenance isn't something I plan on doing. The last option is the "Deletion protection" feature; I enabled this feature to prevent accidentally deleting the database.

587

CHAPTER 14   THINGS THAT LURK IN THE BACKGROUND

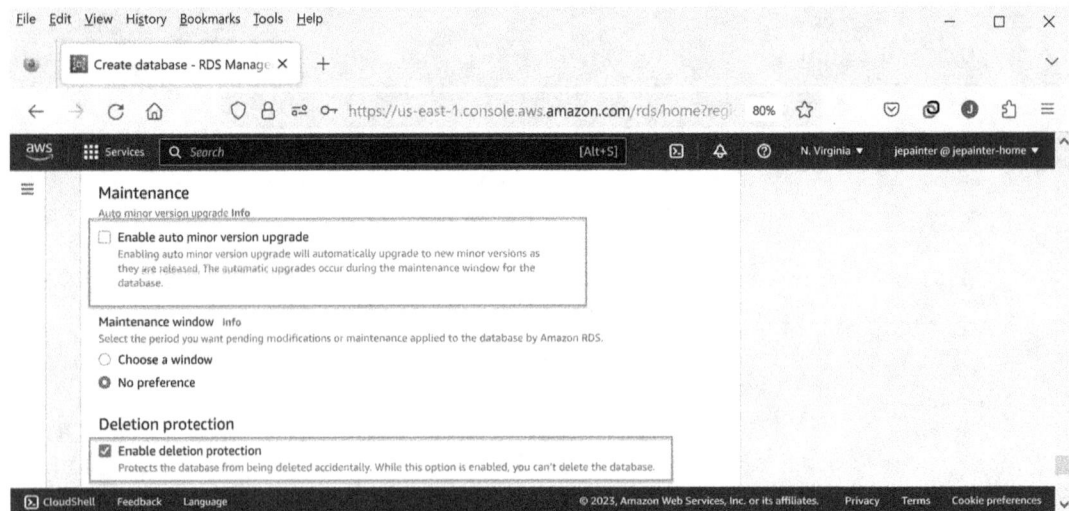

Figure 14-25. RDS maintenance configuration

Reviewing Database Costs

And with that, all the database configuration options have been set. After the deletion protection option and before the Create button, you'll see information about the costs. Normally, AWS doesn't do this for other services, but since databases are quite expensive, this is useful in determining whether you want to change any options. Figure 14-26 shows the costs for my setup. As you can see, the RDS service can be quite pricey compared to other services. Before you create your database, you can go back and change your configuration (as I did). As you make changes, the estimated costs are adjusted accordingly.

CHAPTER 14   THINGS THAT LURK IN THE BACKGROUND

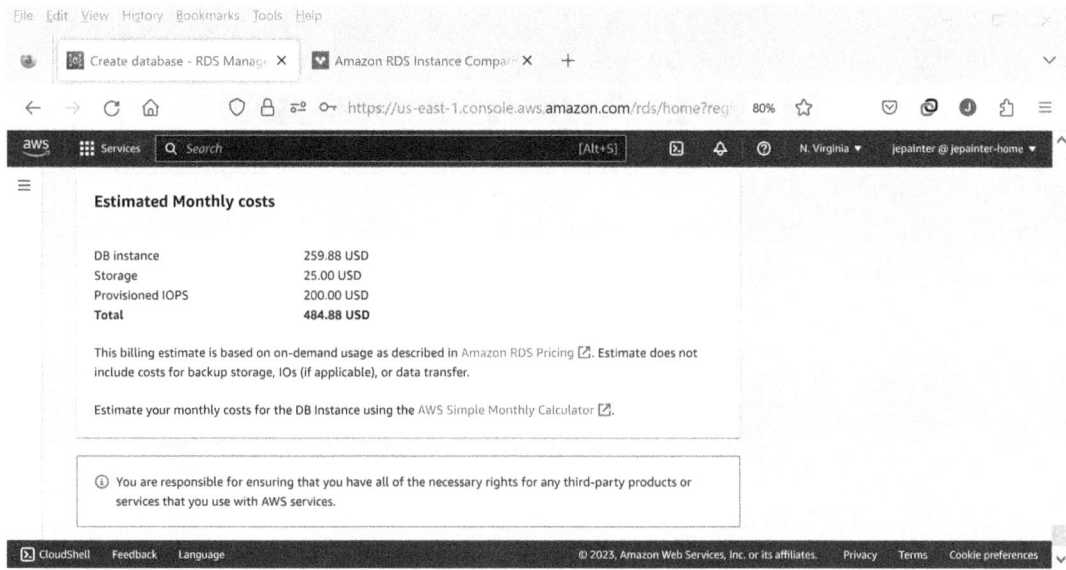

Figure 14-26. *Example of RDS estimated monthly costs based on previous configurations*

Stopping the Database Temporarily

Since you won't be using your database right away, there is the option to stop the database after it is created. Figure 14-27 shows how to stop the database temporarily for a week. To do this, select your database once it is up and running and select the "Stop temporarily" option on the drop-down Actions menu as highlighted.

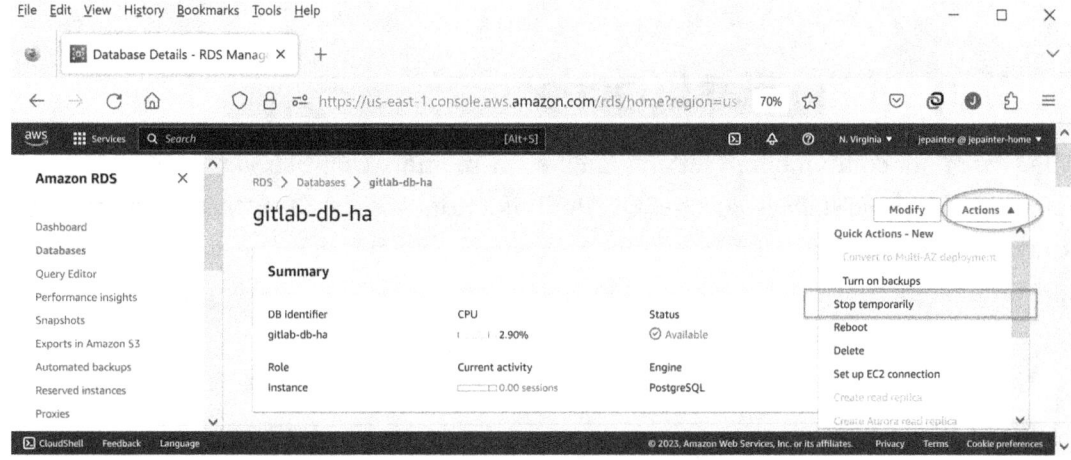

Figure 14-27. *Option to stop the database after creation to reduce costs*

589

CHAPTER 14 THINGS THAT LURK IN THE BACKGROUND

When you select the "Stop temporarily" action, you will see a pop-up message as shown in Figure 14-28. You will have to select the acknowledgment that lets you know the database will be down for seven days. You also have the option to perform a snapshot of the database as a safety measure. Since there is nothing in the database yet, I chose not to do a snapshot. If you are the only one experimenting with the GitLab POC, you can use the temporary stop option after you bring down the GitLab servers. If, however, there are other users experimenting with the POC, you'll need to coordinate with them before shutting things down, say on the weekends, for example.

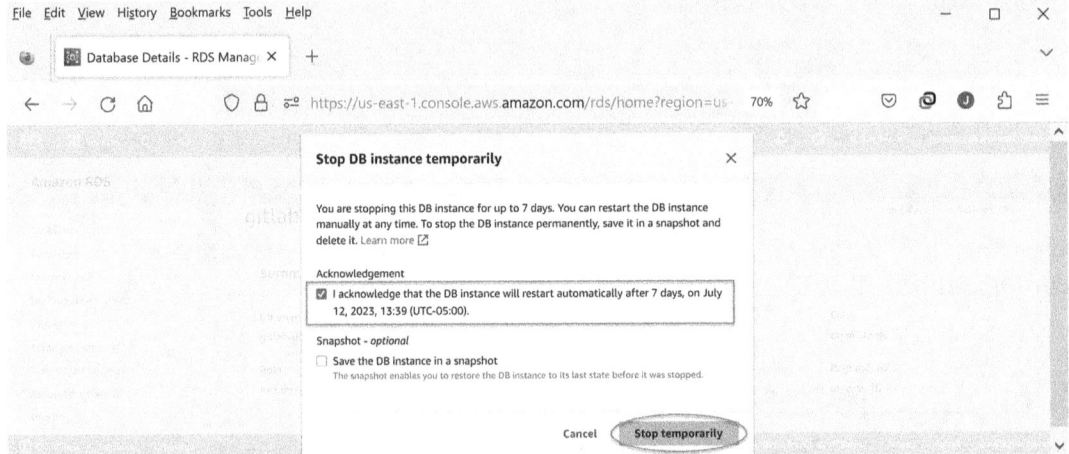

Figure 14-28. Pop-up notice when stopping the database temporarily

With the PostgreSQL database set up, we describe how to set up the Redis non-SQL database in the next section.

Setting Up the ElastiCache

The next major component to set up is a Redis in-memory cache server. Unlike a relational database such as PostgreSQL, Redis is a non-SQL database that stores data in a key-value format. Since it is in-memory, it responds quickly to requests and so is useful for storing temporary cache information as an example. Unlike the PostgreSQL database, the Redis database is easier and considerably cheaper to set up.

CHAPTER 14 THINGS THAT LURK IN THE BACKGROUND

Creating the Redis Security Group

Before we create the Redis cache, we need to create a security group much like we did for the PostgreSQL database. Figure 14-29 shows the details for that security group. As shown in the figure, we name it gitlab-redis-sec-group, give it an appropriate description, and make sure to select the private VPC we are using for the GitLab POC. In addition, we set up an inbound rule for port 6379 with the gitlab-loadbalancer-sec-group.

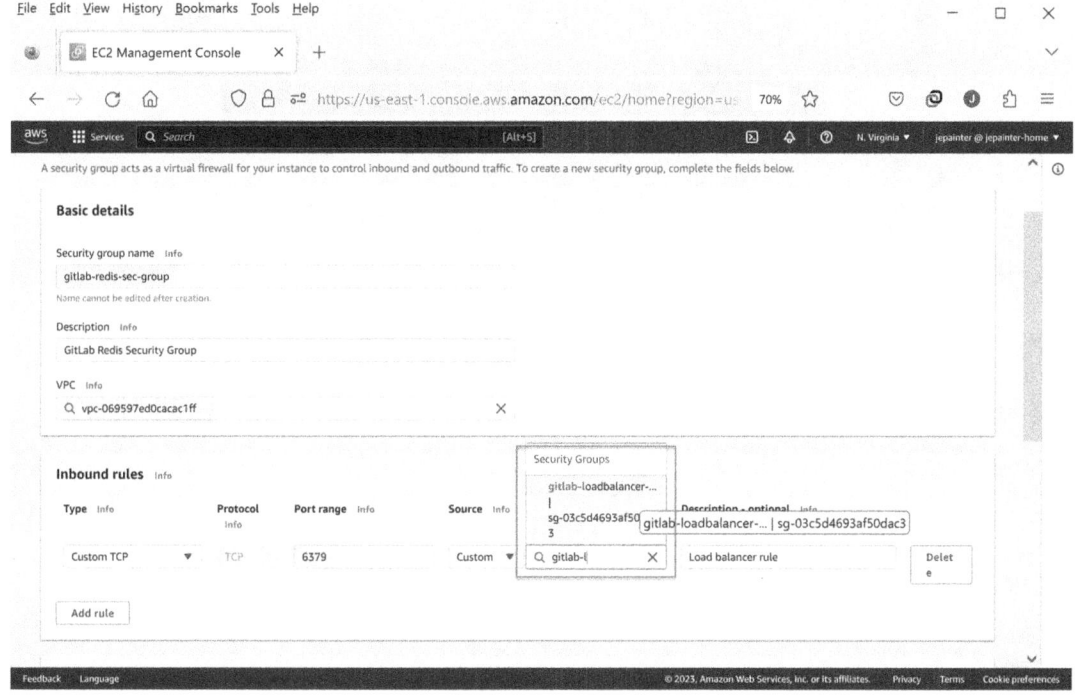

Figure 14-29. Redis security group creation

Accessing ElastiCache

With the security group in place, we can now create the Redis database. As shown in Figure 14-30, we select the ElastiCache option under the Database category. Redis is just one of a number of in-memory cache services enabled by AWS.

CHAPTER 14 THINGS THAT LURK IN THE BACKGROUND

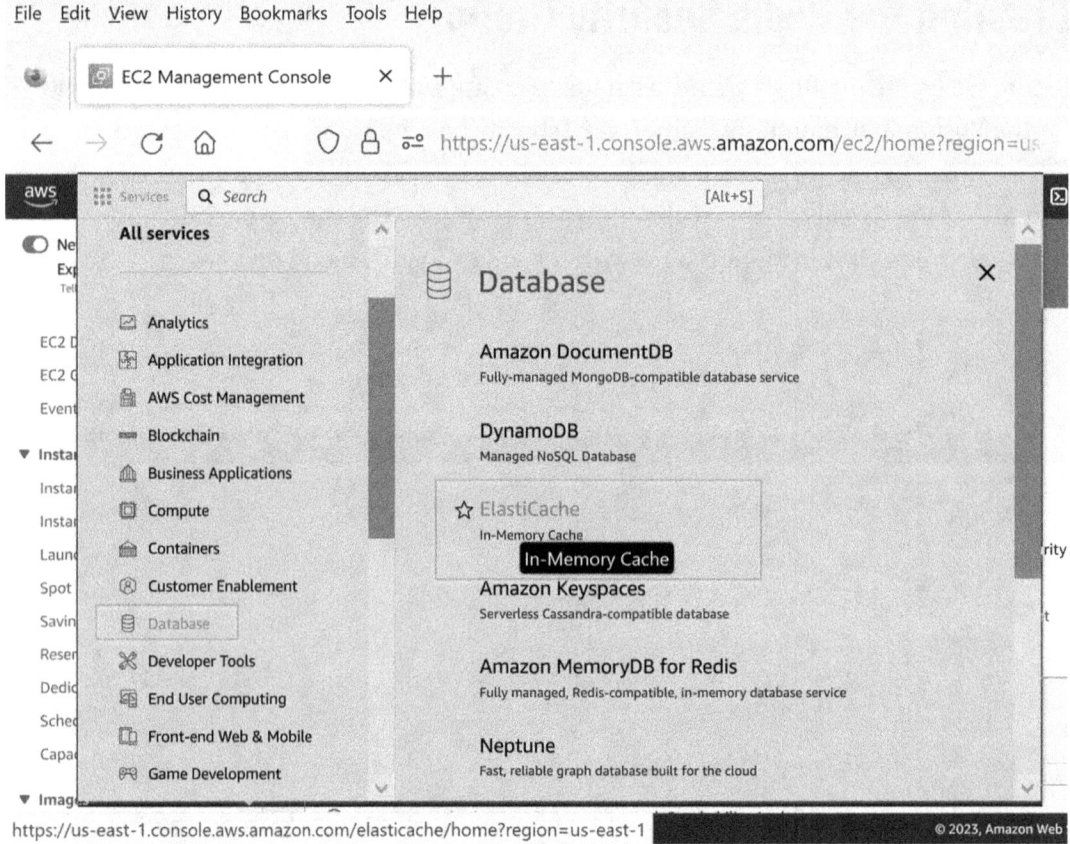

Figure 14-30. ElastiCache selection from the services menu

Creating the Redis Subnet Group

As with the RDS database services, we need to create a subnet group for our ElastiCache service. As shown in Figure 14-31, the subnet group is created by selecting the "Subnet groups" link that takes us to the list of existing subnet groups. From there, selecting the "Create subnet group" button will begin the process of creating an ElastiCache subnet group.

CHAPTER 14   THINGS THAT LURK IN THE BACKGROUND

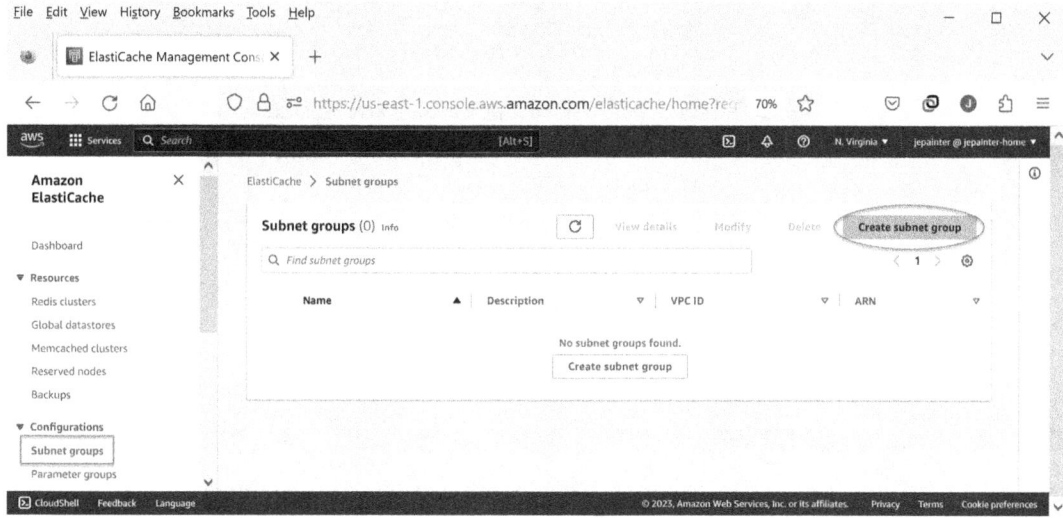

Figure 14-31. *Option to create a Redis subnet group*

Figure 14-32 shows the details for our subnet group. Here, we name the subnet group gitlab-redis-group and select our private VPC. We then select the availability zones and the private subnets in each of them as shown in Figure 14-33. This is the same setup we did for the RDS subnet group for our PostgreSQL database.

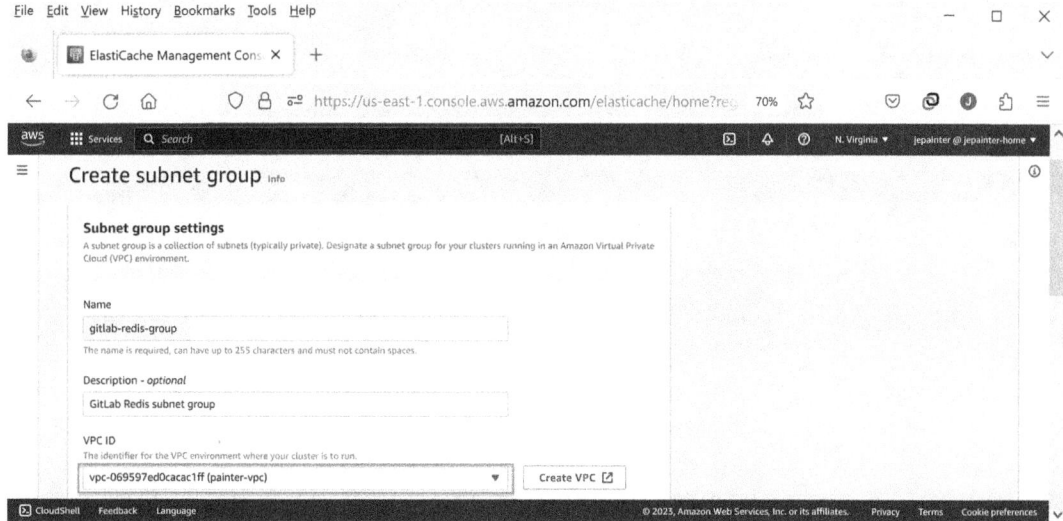

Figure 14-32. *Redis subnet group settings*

CHAPTER 14   THINGS THAT LURK IN THE BACKGROUND

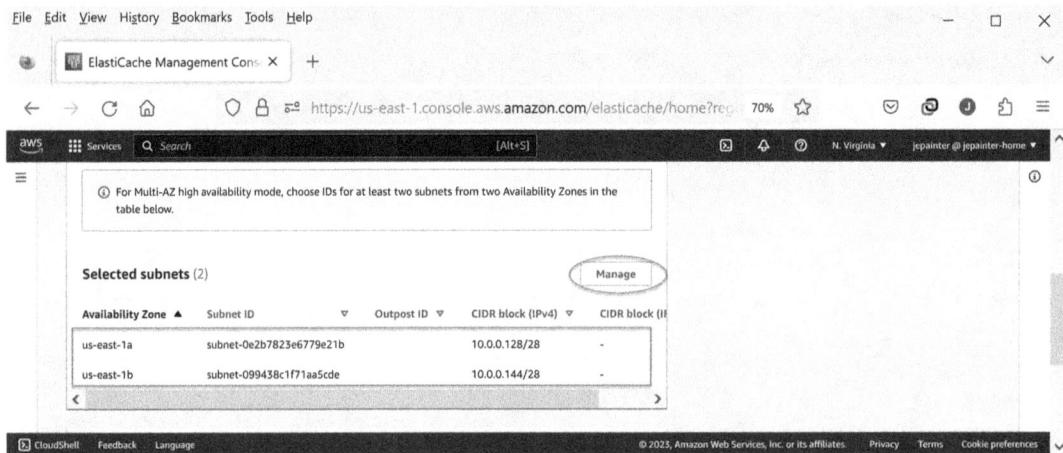

Figure 14-33. Redis subnet group configuration of availability zones and subnets

Creating the Redis Cluster

With the subnet group created, we next create the Redis service as shown in Figure 14-34. Selecting the "Redis clusters" link under Resources takes us to the list of existing Redis clusters. At this point, there are none. To create a new one, we select the "Create Redis cluster" button as highlighted in the figure.

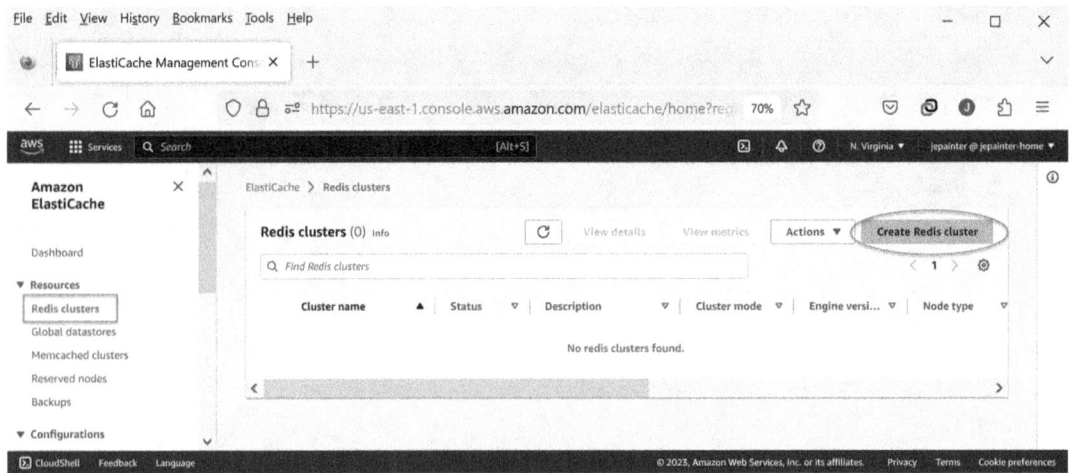

Figure 14-34. ElastiCache option to create the Redis cluster

CHAPTER 14   THINGS THAT LURK IN THE BACKGROUND

Selecting How to Create the Redis Cluster

Fortunately, there aren't as many configuration options for the Redis cluster as there are for the PostgreSQL database. The first thing to select is the method for creating the cluster as shown in Figure 14-35. We will use the "Configure and create a new cluster" option.

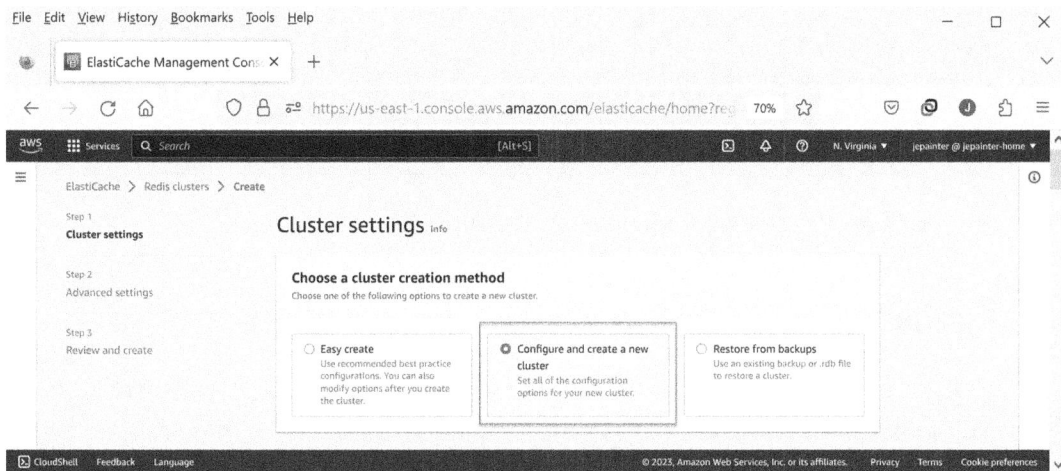

Figure 14-35. *Selection of method to create the Redis cluster*

Disabling Cluster Node

Next, we disable the cluster mode as shown in Figure 14-36.[5] The reason for this is that GitLab does not support this special mode. Note we'll still be able to run the cluster in multiple availability zones, so we'll still have high availability for our Redis service.

---

[5] Wait, what? Yes, I find disabling cluster mode for a Redis cluster confusing as well. It's like when I have to order chicken salad salad at a deli to get the salad instead of the sandwich. Probably would have been better to call this option multi-shard mode instead.

CHAPTER 14   THINGS THAT LURK IN THE BACKGROUND

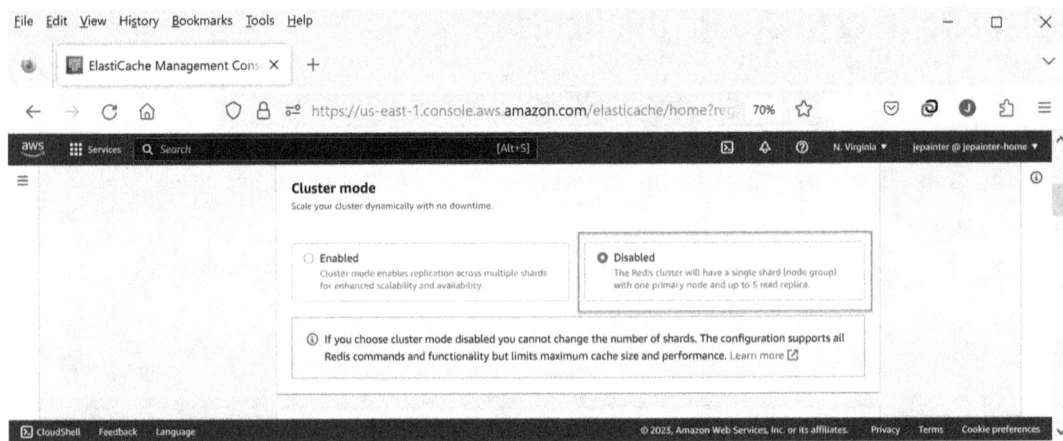

Figure 14-36. *Redis cluster mode configuration*

Setting the Redis Name, Description, and Location

The next thing to configure is the cluster info as shown in Figure 14-37. Here, we name the cluster gitlab-redis and provide an appropriate description. After that, we specify the cluster's location as shown in Figure 14-38. Here, we let AWS know that the cluster will be in the AWS cloud (as opposed to an on-premises location). In addition, we enable multi-AZ so that we'll have auto-failover enabled.

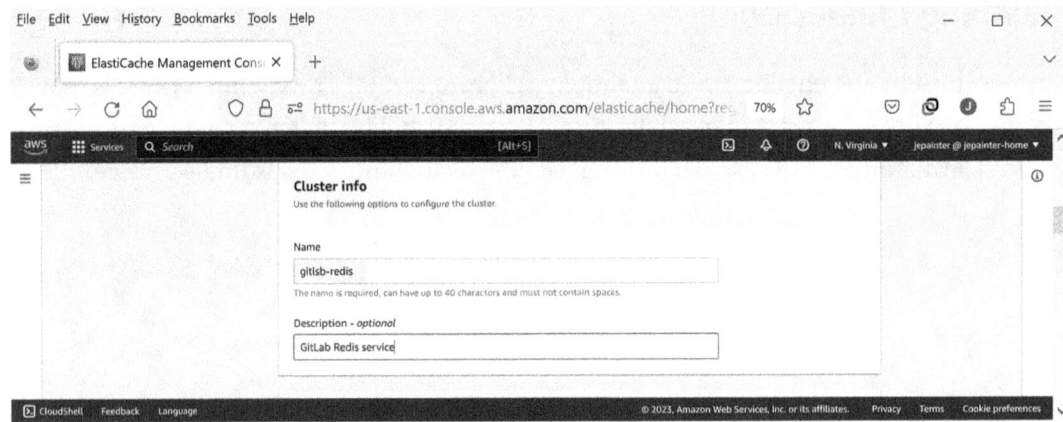

Figure 14-37. *Redis cluster info configuration*

CHAPTER 14   THINGS THAT LURK IN THE BACKGROUND

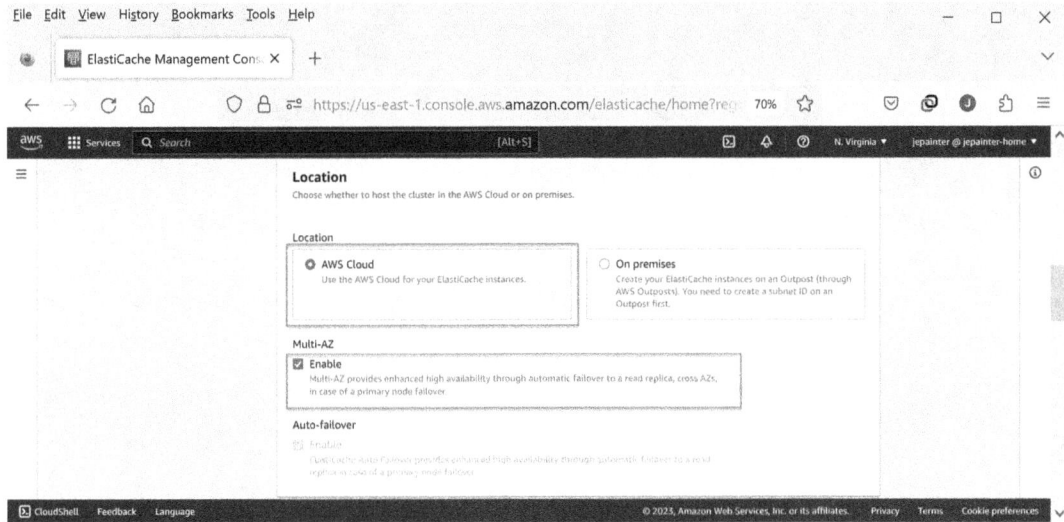

Figure 14-38.   Redis location and multi-AZ configurations

Configuring Various Cluster Settings

With the location defined, we specify some basic cluster settings as shown in Figure 14-39. Here, we select the latest version, which at the time of this writing is 7.0. We ensure that the port remains at the default of 6379. For our POC, I kept the parameter group at default.redis7. In a production environment, I recommend creating your own parameter group for the same reason I recommended creating a parameter group for the PostgreSQL database. For node type, I used the GitLab recommendation of cache. t3.medium, which is a pretty inexpensive server type. Finally, in order to reduce costs, I selected to have one replica in total rather than the one per zone as is recommended in a production environment.

597

CHAPTER 14   THINGS THAT LURK IN THE BACKGROUND

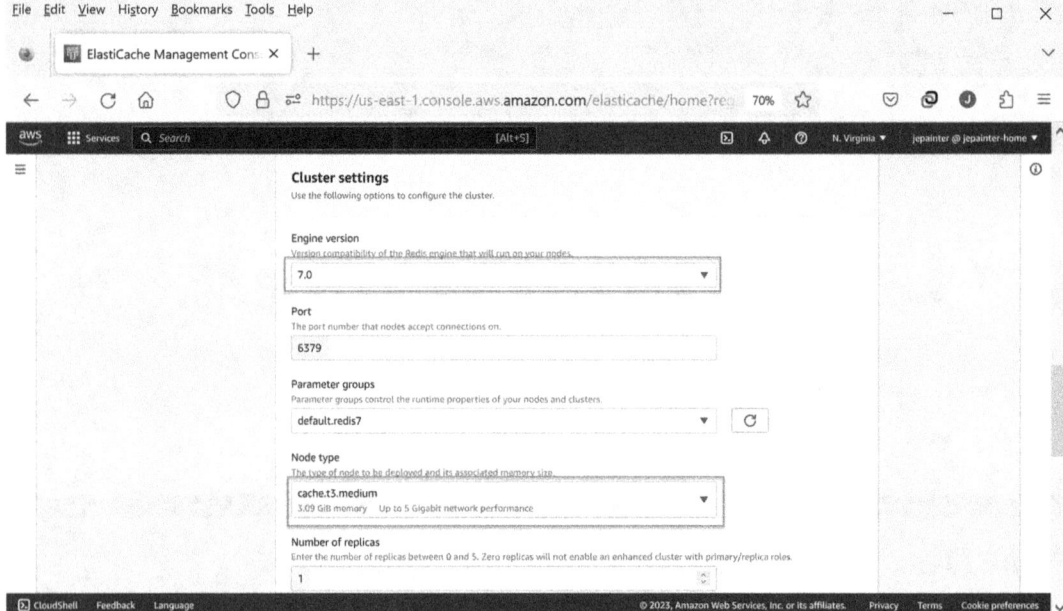

Figure 14-39. Configuration of various Redis cluster settings

Configuring Redis Connectivity and Subnets

Next, we configure the Redis connectivity. As shown in Figure 14-40, the connectivity configuration is similar to the database connectivity options. We keep the network type at IPv4 and select the "Choose an existing subnet group" option. With that option enabled, we then select the gitlab-redis-group created earlier. Finally, we select the private subnet in each availability zone.

CHAPTER 14 THINGS THAT LURK IN THE BACKGROUND

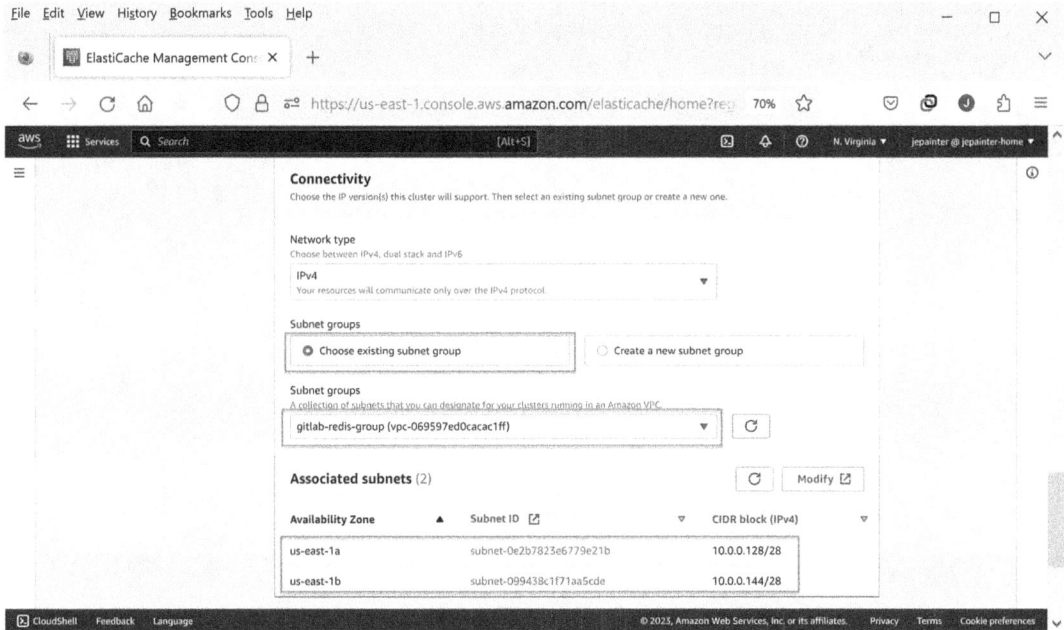

Figure 14-40. Redis connectivity and associated subnet configuration

Selecting Location of Primary and Replica Servers

With the zones configured, we need to select where the primary server and remaining replica servers will reside. This is shown in Figure 14-41. In this example, I've chosen the option to "Specify Availability Zones" rather than to let AWS randomly choose the placement. I chose the primary to be in us-east-1a and the replica in us-east-1b. There is no particular reason for this selection; I just made sure the one replica was in a different AZ from the primary.

599

CHAPTER 14   THINGS THAT LURK IN THE BACKGROUND

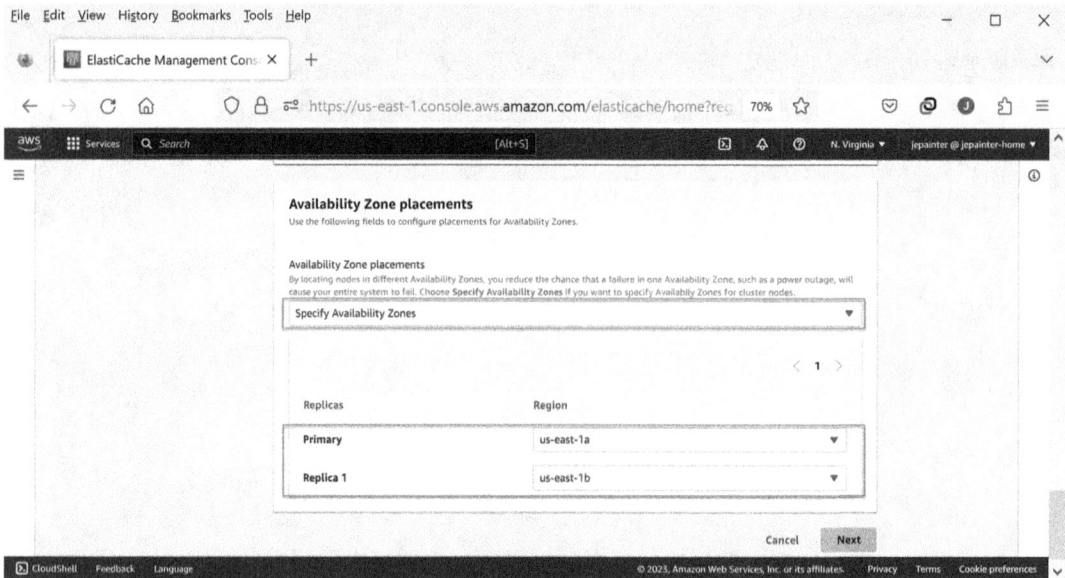

Figure 14-41. Redis availability zone placement configuration

Configuring Security Options

Security configuration is next. Figure 14-42 shows the "Encryption at rest" option enabled, which, like the database encryption at rest option, is always recommended even with a development setup. For the GitLab POC, I chose to disable the "Encryption in transit" option. This option is similar to using HTTPS for communicating with a website. In general, I recommend enabling this option in a production environment, but for our POC, disabling this option simplifies the GitLab configuration.[6] The final security option is the security group, which is set here to gitlab-redis-sec-group.

---

[6] Trust me, enabling encryption in transit is tricky to get right with GitLab. I recommend disabling it initially to get Redis working correctly with GitLab and then attempt to configure in-transit encryption afterward, if needed.

CHAPTER 14   THINGS THAT LURK IN THE BACKGROUND

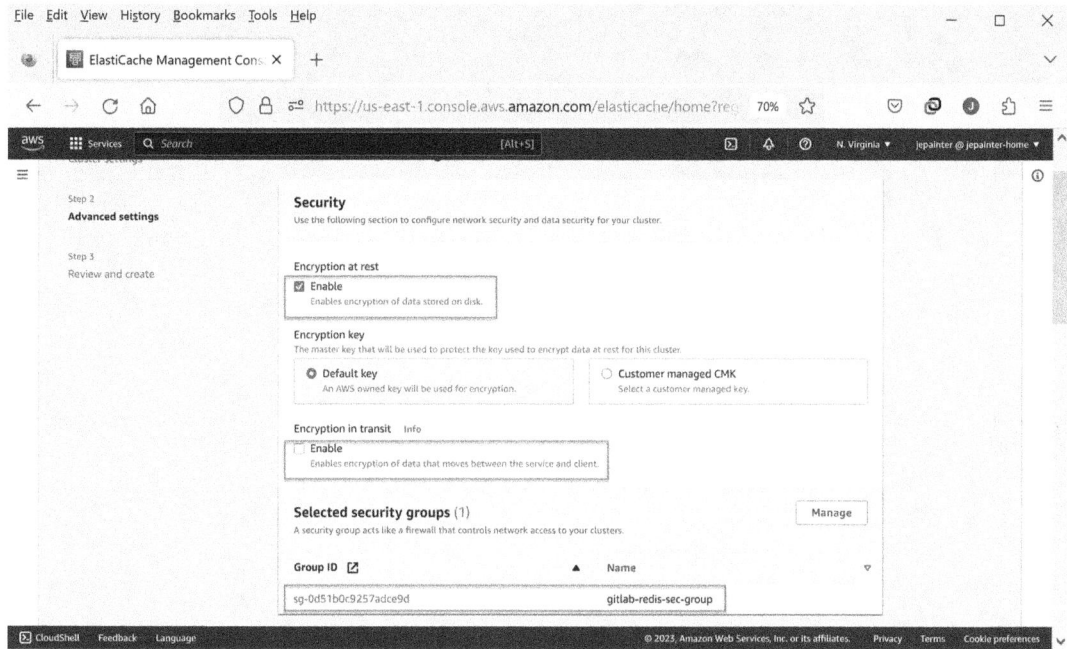

Figure 14-42. *Redis security configurations*

Configuring Backup and Maintenance Options

The last piece of configuration is setting up backups and maintenance as shown in Figure 14-43. This section is pretty self-explanatory. For the POC, I decided to disable the automatic backups, but for a staging and production environment, it is recommended to enable them. I selected "No preference" for the maintenance window, although in a production environment, I like to set up specific times to reduce disruption to the GitLab service. Unlike the PostgreSQL database, I selected to have minor version upgrades to be applied automatically during the maintenance window. GitLab is less sensitive to Redis version upgrades than to PostgreSQL version upgrades.

CHAPTER 14   THINGS THAT LURK IN THE BACKGROUND

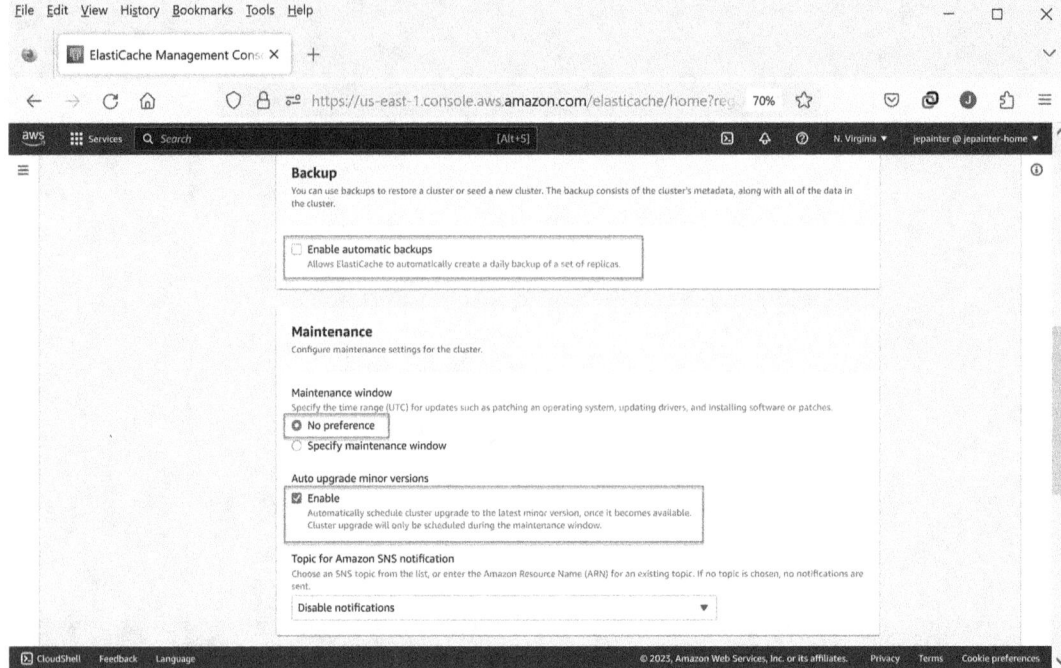

Figure 14-43. *Redis backup and maintenance configurations*

Starting the Redis Service

That's all that is needed for the Redis configuration. There is no cost estimate provided here as there was for the PostgreSQL configuration since the costs are pretty reasonable for a Redis service. Note that creating the Redis service takes a while (more than 5 minutes on average but less than 30 minutes in general), so refresh the Redis listing while the new Redis service is being built.

In the next section, we turn our attention to spinning up bastion servers in the public subnets to enable access to servers that will eventually be spun up in the private subnets.

Preparing the Bastion Hosts

The term bastion comes from medieval times. It refers to a defensive structure attached to a fortress or castle that makes it easy to protect against invaders. In the same vein, a bastion server is a protective server placed in the public subnet to protect access to servers in the private subnets. Its sole purpose is to provide SSH access to those private servers without having to expose them to the public-facing Internet.

CHAPTER 14   THINGS THAT LURK IN THE BACKGROUND

Launching the Bastion Servers

Since we have two AZs, we will set up two bastion servers. Fortunately, these servers don't have to do much, so we can use the least expensive server type, which is part of the free tier. Launching these servers is pretty easy. Figure 14-44 shows how to launch a server from the EC2 page. Selecting the Instances link takes you to the list of existing instances. The "Launch instances" button begins the process of creating a new server.

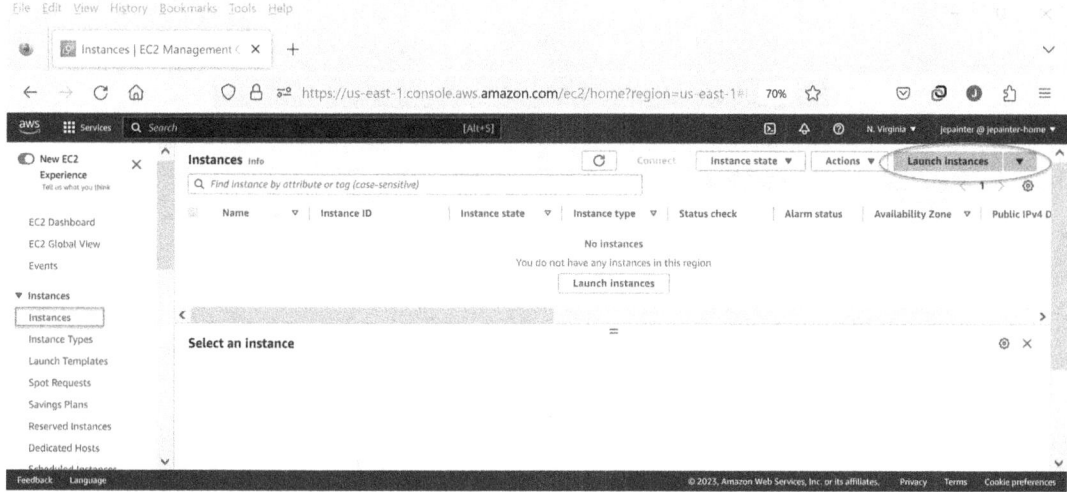

Figure 14-44. EC2 option to launch a new instance

Setting the Server Name and OS

The first thing to configure is the name of the server as shown in Figure 14-45. Since I'll be creating this server in the us-east-1a zone, I give it the name "Bastion Host A." Next, we select the server operating system as shown in Figure 14-46. In this example, I've chosen the Ubuntu OS and selected the latest version of 22.04.

603

CHAPTER 14　THINGS THAT LURK IN THE BACKGROUND

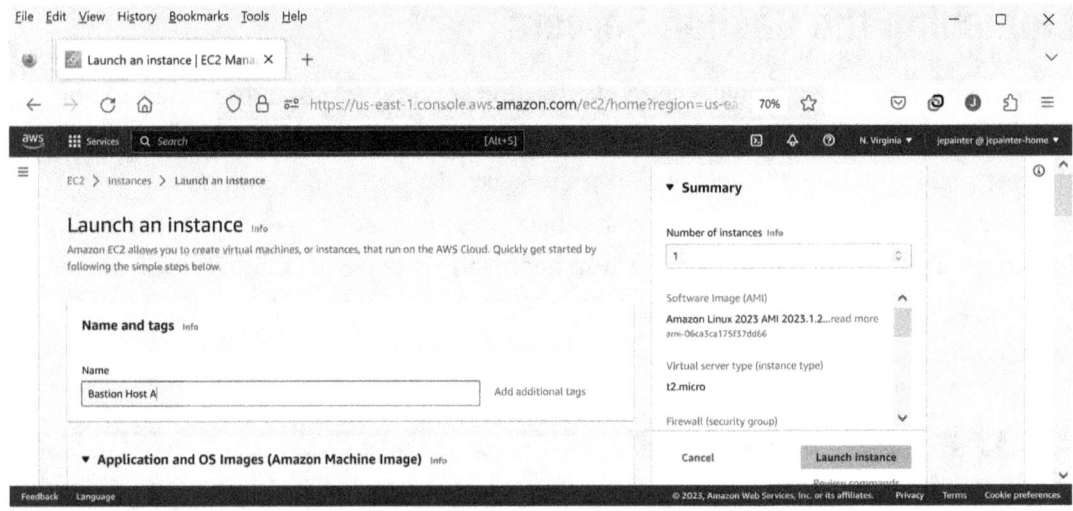

Figure 14-45. *Bastion instance name definition*

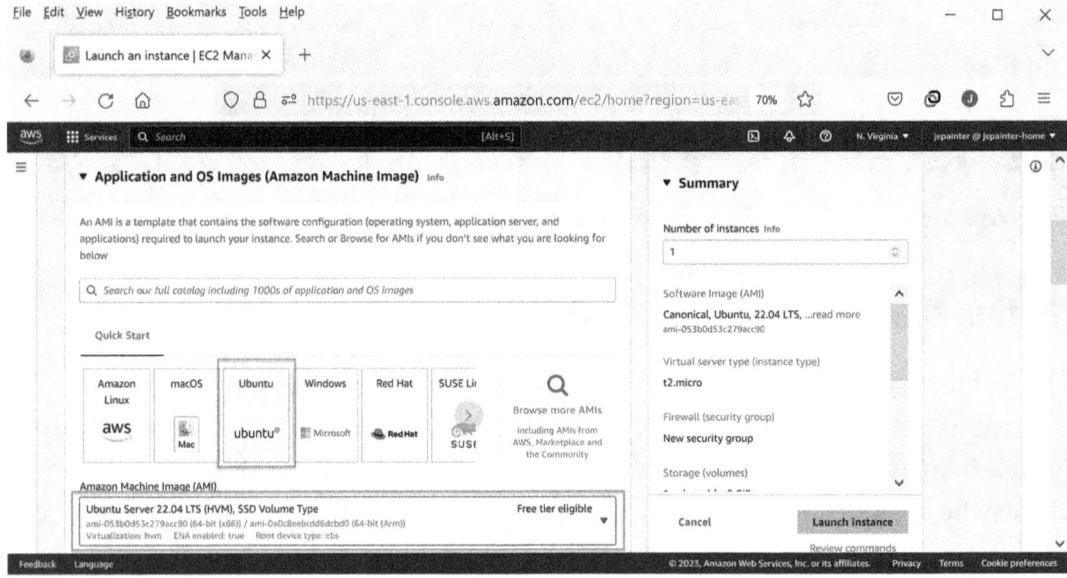

Figure 14-46. *Bastion AMI selection*

CHAPTER 14 THINGS THAT LURK IN THE BACKGROUND

Setting the Instance Type and SSH Key Pair

So far, so good. Next up is the instance type. Figure 14-47 shows that I selected the t2.micro instance type, which, as it notes, is free tier eligible. The free tier is eligible for new AWS users within 12 months of signing up, so if you are a new AWS user, there is no cost for using a server of this instance type. I also selected the key pair I created earlier; this will allow us to ssh into the server using the private SSH key associated with that key pair.

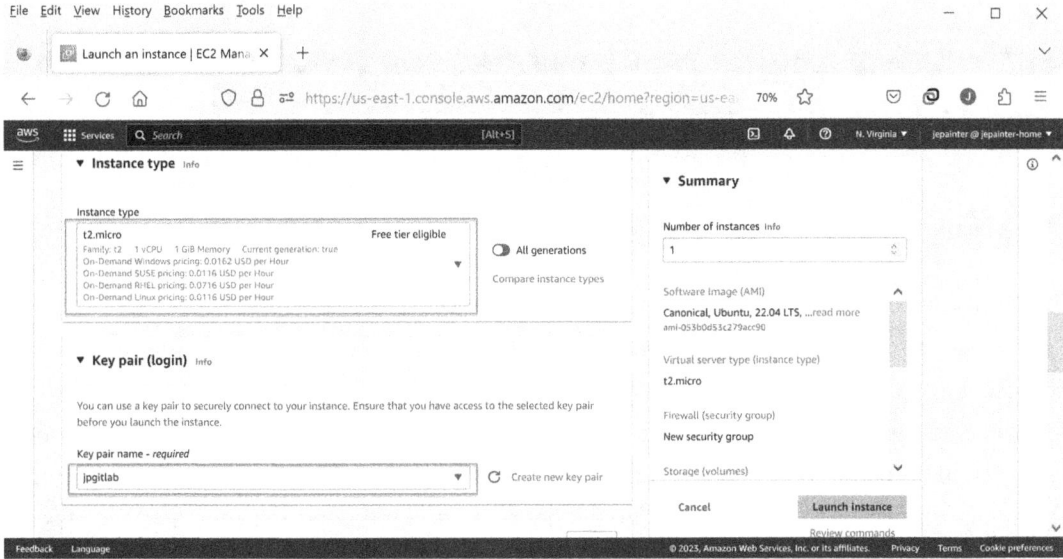

Figure 14-47. Bastion instance type and key pair selections

Configuring Network Settings

As with the RDS and ElastiCache services, we need to specify the subnet to use for our server; unlike those other services, we only need to select one subnet. This is illustrated in Figure 14-48. First, we need to select the private VPC we created for our GitLab POC. Once that is selected, we choose the public subnet for AZ us-east-1a. Finally, we enable the auto-assigning of a public IP address (a.k.a. the EIP); this is necessary in order for us to access the server from our local machine.

CHAPTER 14   THINGS THAT LURK IN THE BACKGROUND

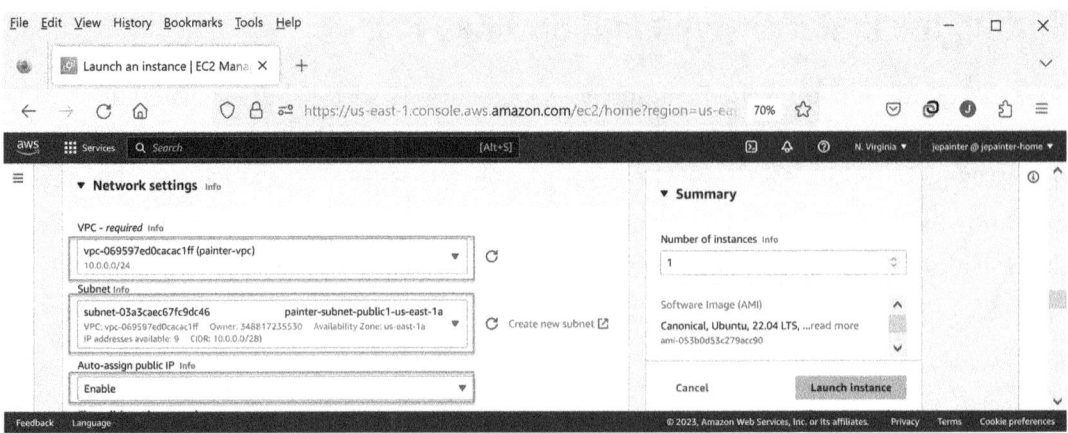

Figure 14-48. Bastion network settings

Creating the Security Group

Since this is a bastion server, we especially need to set up a firewall as shown in Figure 14-49. Since this is the first bastion server being created, I selected the "Create security group" option. Here, I've given it the name bastion-sec-group and added an appropriate description. The default inbound rule for SSH works for our bastion server. Note that if you are coming from a corporate network, you will want to restrict the source IP range; otherwise, as a regular home user, you'll need to keep the range at all access.

CHAPTER 14   THINGS THAT LURK IN THE BACKGROUND

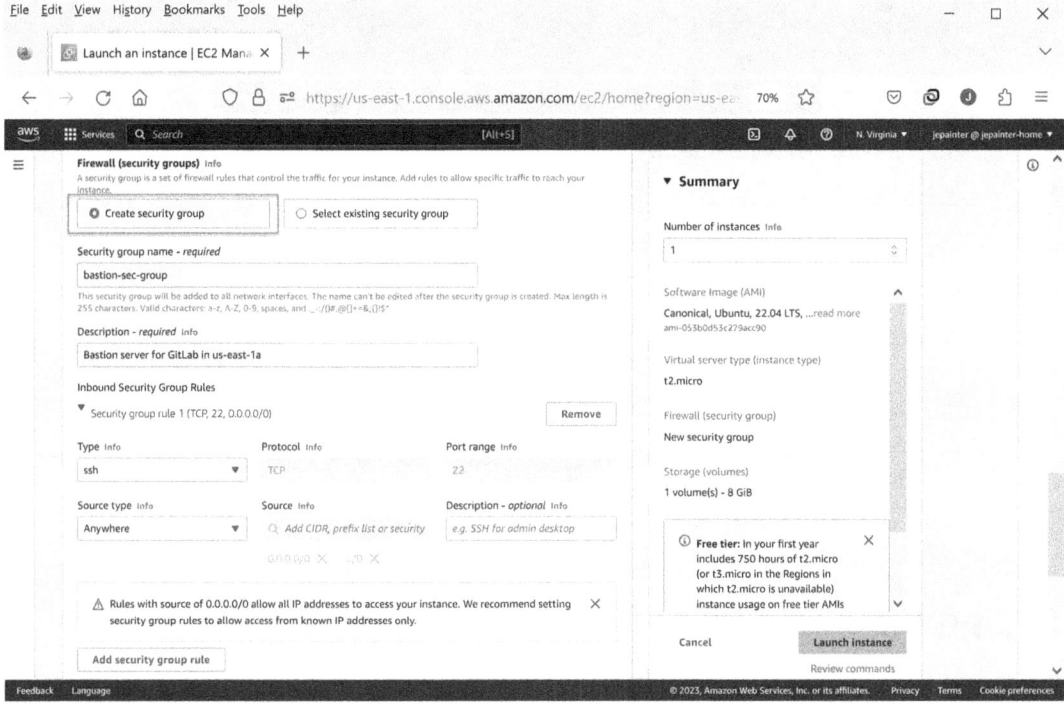

Figure 14-49. *Bastion firewall security group settings*

Configuring Bastion Storage and Launching the Instance

Every server needs storage, so the next configuration involves setting up the root volume storage as shown in Figure 14-50. As suggested by the GitLab documentation, we keep the root volume size set at 8GB. We won't be running any applications on this server, so the only thing that will suck up space will be the standard log files, which take a while to fill up the server storage. There is no need here to add any additional storage volumes (a.k.a. disks). With storage defined, we are ready to launch the server via the "Launch instance" button as highlighted in the figure; it usually takes a minute or so for the server to be up and running.

607

CHAPTER 14   THINGS THAT LURK IN THE BACKGROUND

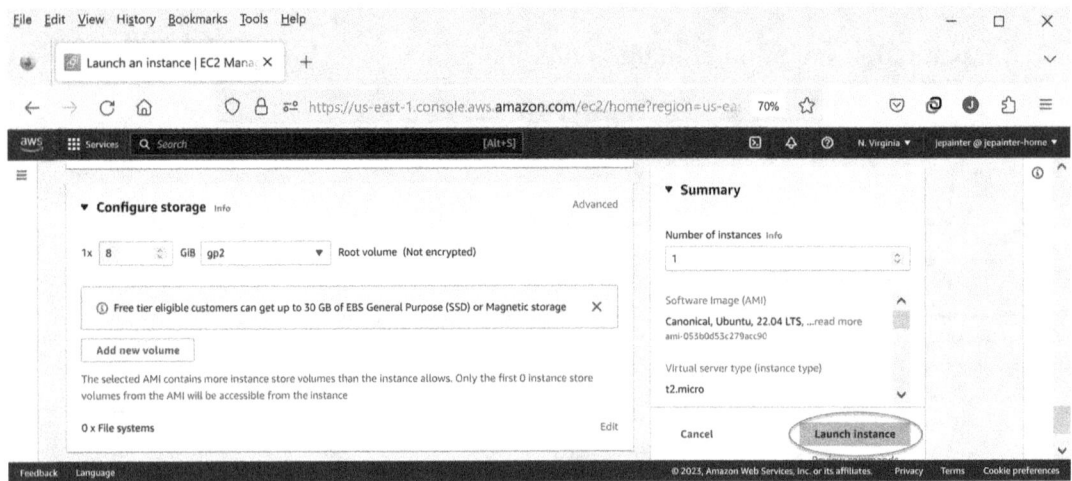

Figure 14-50. *Bastion storage configuration*

Testing Connectivity to the Bastion Server

Now the fun part. Before creating the second bastion server, we need to verify that we can connect to the newly created bastion host. AWS makes this easy to do. From the instance list shown in Figure 14-51, select the "Bastion Host A" server and use the Connect button at the top of the page. You need to make sure the server is in the "Running" state before doing this or your connection attempt may time out.

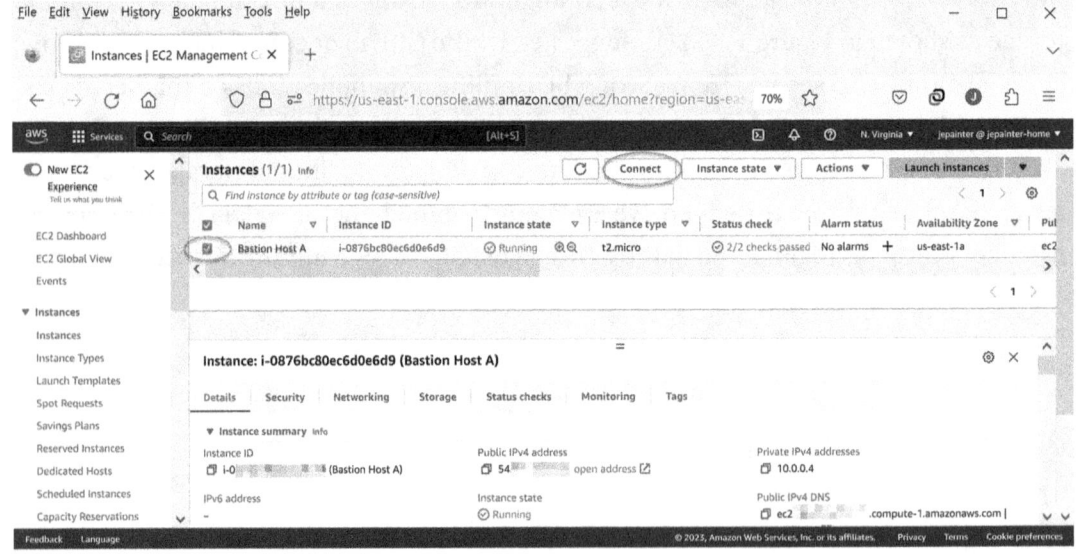

Figure 14-51. *EC2 option to test connection with running bastion instance*

CHAPTER 14 THINGS THAT LURK IN THE BACKGROUND

When you first connect, you'll get a request to verify the host. Since you are the one who created this host and you are connecting through the AWS console, it is safe to accept the host verification. If all is successful, you'll get a Linux console window as shown in Figure 14-52. Congratulations, you now have access within your bastion server. Feel free to look around and then enter exit to leave the Linux session; you'll also need to close the window.

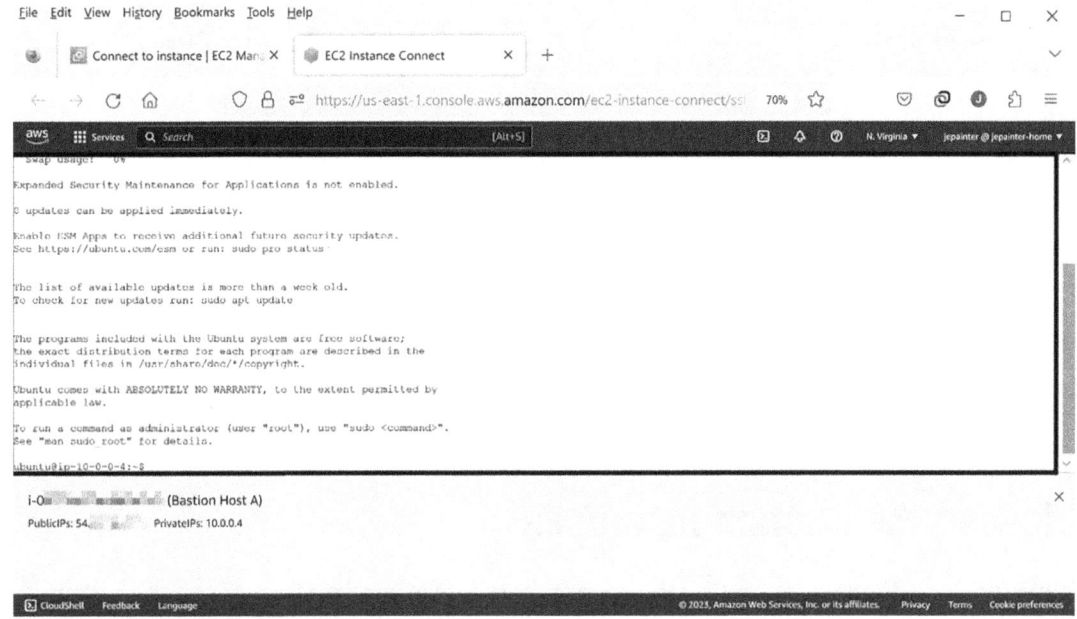

Figure 14-52. Bastion AWS console window

Creating the Second Bastion Server

Creating the second bastion server in us-east-1b is similar to creating the first bastion server.[7] The main difference is that you need to select the public subnet in the alternative AZ. For the security group, select the existing security group bastion-sec-group as shown in Figure 14-53. Once the server is up and running, check connectivity as you did for the first bastion server.

---

[7] So why create two bastion servers? In case one of the AZs goes down, you'll still be able to use the other one to connect to your private subnet servers.

CHAPTER 14   THINGS THAT LURK IN THE BACKGROUND

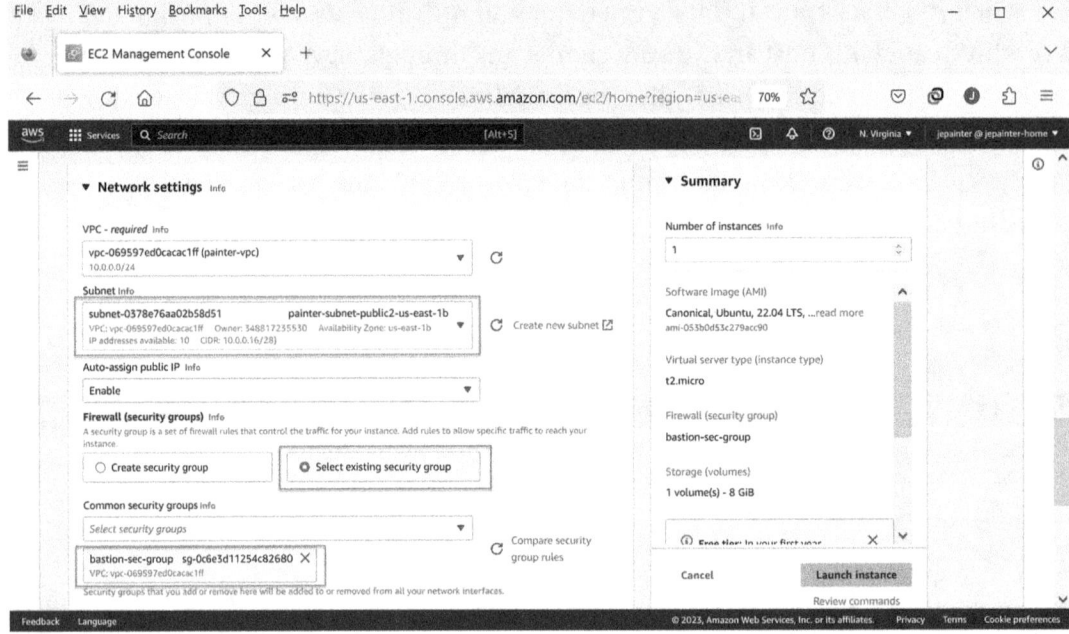

Figure 14-53. Network settings for second bastion instance

Viewing the Bastion Instances

When you are done with creating the second bastion server, you should see the instance listing as shown in Figure 14-54. Verify that each server is in a different AZ and that the status check shows "2/2 checks passed." Note that the status checks may take a few minutes to pass; this is normal. If one of them takes longer than ten minutes, there is an issue with connectivity. Verify that these servers are in the public subnet and the security group is applied correctly.

CHAPTER 14 THINGS THAT LURK IN THE BACKGROUND

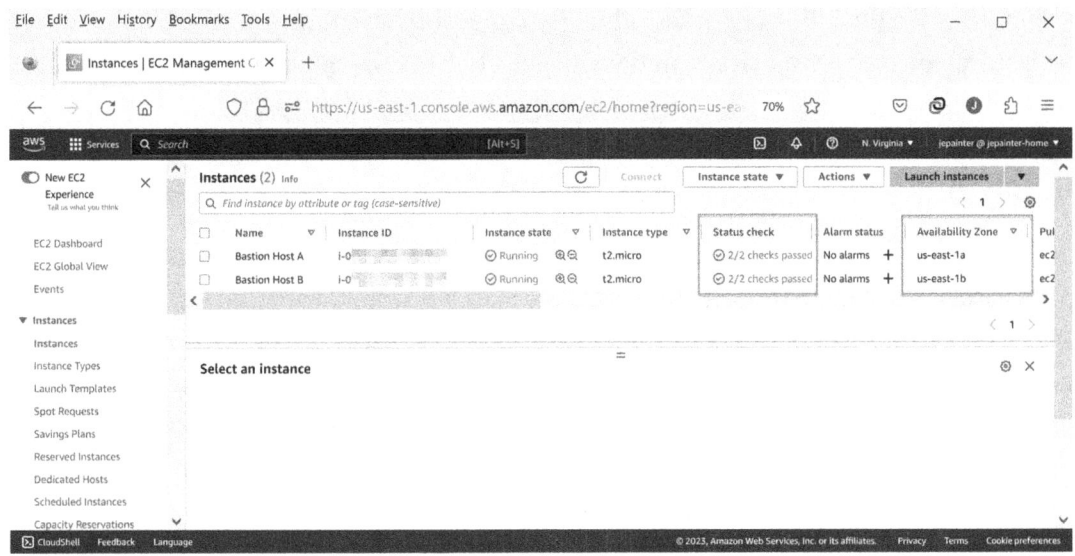

Figure 14-54. EC2 instances list showing bastion servers

Configuring SSH Forwarding

Now that you've verified connectivity to the bastion servers via the AWS console, you'll want to set things up so that you can ssh directly to these servers outside of the AWS console. The reason for this is that in order to connect to private servers from a bastion server using SSH, you should use what is known as "SSH forwarding." We've seen earlier when setting up SSH connectivity to our GitLab SaaS service that we stored the private SSH key in the user's home .ssh directory. We don't want to do this on the bastion server in case it becomes compromised. We don't want an attacker to gain access to our private SSH key.

Using PuTTY for SSH Forwarding

Setting up SSH forwarding seems like a complicated process, but it is actually quite straightforward. The AWS documentation shows how to set up forwarding if you are interested in following those directions. Since I assume many of you are using Windows-based machines, I'm going to show how to set up SSH forwarding using the Putty application.[8] In the following description, I assume you have Putty installed. If not, do a web search on Putty installation, and you'll get a link to download the installer that runs on your machine.

Importing Your OpenSSH Key into Putty

Since we've launched our bastion servers using the SSH key pair that we uploaded to AWS earlier, we need to import the private SSH key associated with that key pair into Putty. We do that using Puttygen.[9] It turns out that Putty uses a different format for SSH keys than OpenSSH. Fortunately, Puttygen knows how to convert the OpenSSH private key into the Putty-specific key. Figure 14-55 shows how to make the conversion using Puttygen. Under the Conversions menu, select "Import key" as shown in the figure. From there, use the Load button to load in the OpenSSH private key; you should find this in your home's .ssh directory.[10]

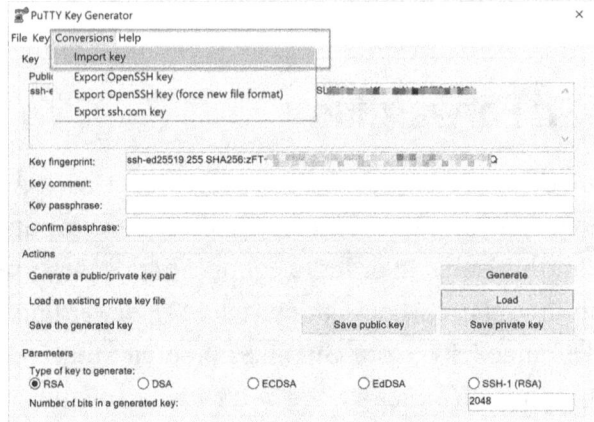

Figure 14-55. *Option to import key using the PuTTY Key Generator (for Microsoft Windows systems)*

---

[8] You'll see that this application is referred to as PuTTY by the creator. So, what's with the TTY capitalization? Us gray beards who worked in the 1970s know this stands for teletypewriter where communication between this device and the computer was via text only. Fun times! Nowadays, it simply refers to setting up a text-based session between two computers.

[9] Puttygen is automatically installed with Putty.

[10] For example, C:/Users/<you>/.ssh where <you> is your Window's username.

CHAPTER 14   THINGS THAT LURK IN THE BACKGROUND

Generating the Putty Private Key

Once loaded in, you create the Putty private key using the "Save private key" button. The Putty key will be generated with the .ppk extension as shown in Figure 14-56. In this example, I gave it the same base name as the private OpenSSH key. When you connect with Putty, it will know to look for .ppk files in this directory.

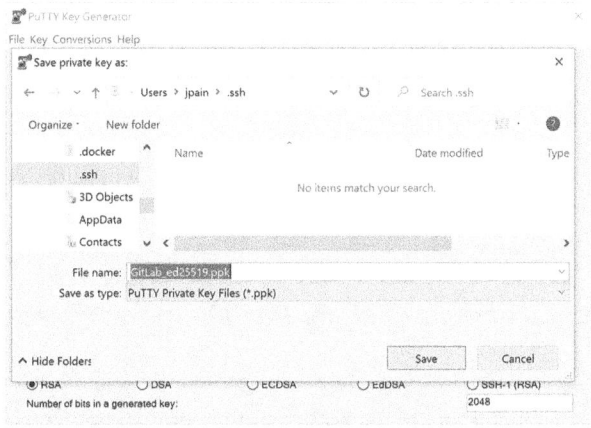

Figure 14-56. *Creation of the PuTTY private key file (with .ppk file extension)*

Creating the Putty Session Configuration

With the Putty key in place, the next step is to create a session configuration for our Bastion Host A server. The configuration page is the one that shows up when you open the Putty application. The first thing we need to do is let Putty know where the SSH key is. Figure 14-57 shows the Credentials section found under the Connection ➤ SSH ➤ Auth category. Here, we select the ppk file we generated earlier.

613

CHAPTER 14   THINGS THAT LURK IN THE BACKGROUND

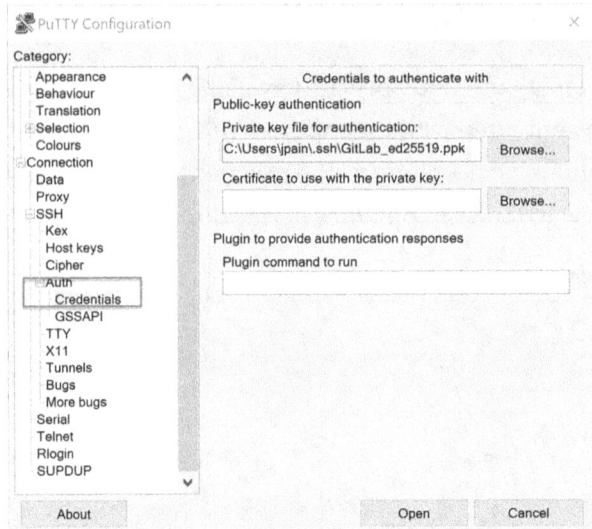

Figure 14-57. *Selection of credentials for PuTTY session configuration*

Enabling SSH Forwarding for the Putty Session Configuration

Next, we enable SSH forwarding as shown in Figure 14-58. This is located one level up from the Credentials section. By default, this option is unchecked, so we simply need to check it to enable the option.

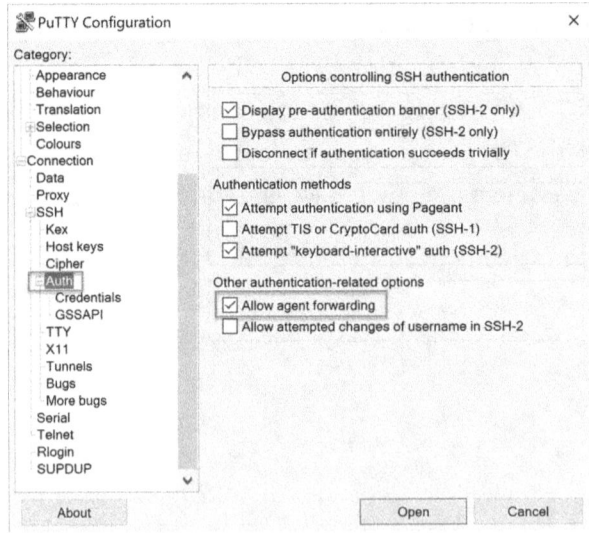

Figure 14-58. *Selection of agent forwarding for PuTTY session configuration*

CHAPTER 14   THINGS THAT LURK IN THE BACKGROUND

Setting the Host IP in Putty

Finally, we specify the host IP to connect to. This is illustrated in Figure 14-59. This is found by selecting the Session category. Enter the IP address in the Host Name field. Before we connect to the host, save the session configuration by entering a name in the "Saved Sessions" field and clicking Save. In this example, I used the name GitLab-Bastion-A. Note that the name is only used by Putty to identify the session; there is no correlation to the server name created in AWS. Once you've saved the session, you'll be able to double-click the name in the session list to open up a connection to that server.

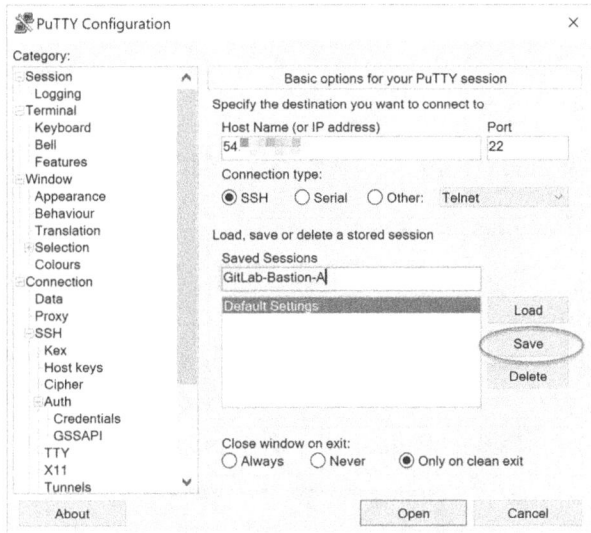

Figure 14-59. *Creation of PuTTY session configuration for the first bastion instance*

Testing Connectivity to the Bastion Host with Putty

To test the connection out, select the Open button in the previous figure (or if you see the session list, double-click the GitLab-Bastion-A name.) Like with the AWS connection, you will need to verify the host the first time you open it up with Putty. You will see an alert message similar to the one shown in Figure 14-60. Selecting Accept will take you to a Linux session window just like the one you saw with the AWS connection. If Putty asks for a user, use "ubuntu" as the username.

615

CHAPTER 14   THINGS THAT LURK IN THE BACKGROUND

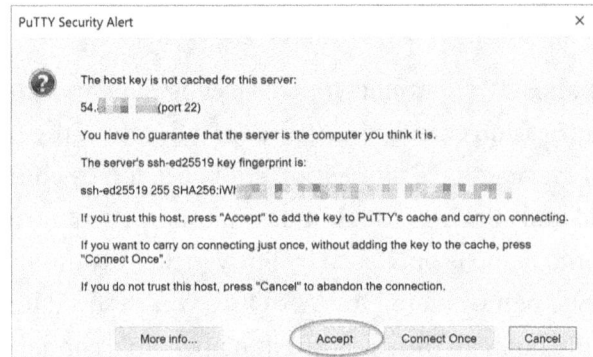

Figure 14-60. *PuTTY security alert when connecting to bastion instance for the first time*

Adding the Putty SSH Key to the Pageant Service

There's one more step we need to take. We need to add the SSH key to Pageant so that it will forward it to our bastion servers. This is a little tricky. First, you need to make sure that Pageant is running. You do this through the Start list and search for Pageant. Selecting that will start Pageant if it is not already running; if it is, it will give you a pop-up message that it is. Then, to add the key, you need to go to the notification bar at the bottom of your screen and select Pageant from there as shown in Figure 14-61.

Figure 14-61. *Selection of Pageant via the Windows start menu*

Selecting that will take you to the Pageant key list as shown in Figure 14-62. Select the "Add Key" button and select the .ppk file for the key you want to add. This will be the key that will be forwarded to the bastion host. I used the same key that I used to connect to the bastion host, but you can use a different key if you wish. If you do use a different key, make sure to add it as an AWS key pair.

CHAPTER 14   THINGS THAT LURK IN THE BACKGROUND

Figure 14-62. *Selection of key to be forwarded to the bastion host*

How SSH Forwarding Enables Accessing Private Servers from the Bastion Server

OK, so how is this different from accessing the Linux session window using AWS? Well, with the SSH forwarding option set with Putty, you will now be able to connect to servers in the private subnet from the bastion host by simply using "ssh ubuntu@<privateServerIP>." This will use one of the keys added to Pageant. The private key used to connect to the bastion server is used to connect to the private server without the private key being exposed on the bastion server itself. Nifty, eh? Of course we can't test this yet since we don't have any servers in the private subnet, but we'll remedy that in the next chapter.

Setting Up Pageant to Run When Your Computer Starts Up

Before we leave, you should know that adding the key to Pageant is temporary. If you log off your computer and log back in, you'll need to restart Pageant and re-add the private key. This can be a pain if you plan on using the SSH forwarding service a lot (which we will in the next chapter). Putty has instructions on how to create a Window's desktop shortcut that adds the key automatically.[11] To run Pageant every time you log in to your computer, you can add the shortcut to your startup folder usually found at C:\ProgramData\Microsoft\Windows\Start Menu\Programs\Startup. Otherwise, you can just click the desktop shortcut whenever you want to use SSH forwarding.

---

[11] Do a web search of "Putty Pageant startup with key."

Summary

In summary, we've covered the following topics in this chapter:

- Described how to create a PostgreSQL database using RDS
- Explained how to create a Redis database using ElastiCache
- Demonstrated how to spin up and configure bastion servers in our public subnets
- Investigated how to set up SSH forwarding with PuTTY

In the next chapter, we will complete the stand-up of the GitLab POC service.

CHAPTER 15

The Proof Is in the Cloud

We now have the key back-end components that we need to spin up a GitLab POC service. In this chapter, we will start by spinning up a single GitLab server that will connect to the PostgreSQL and Redis databases set up earlier. We will then look at how to split off the Gitaly service onto its own server so that we can use it with multiple GitLab servers. Toward that goal, we will also discuss how to set up SSH on our GitLab servers so that host keys used by Git SSH clients don't constantly change; in addition, we'll look at how to set up S3 storage for binary objects such as artifacts. Finally, we will show how to scale our GitLab service using the AWS feature known as auto-scaling groups.

Spinning Up a Standalone GitLab Service

We are now ready to spin up a GitLab server. What surprises most people is that this is a two-step process. First, we spin up a server with GitLab installed, configure it, make a snapshot of the server, and spin it down. Second, we create what AWS calls an auto-scaling group that uses that server image to spin up multiple servers. To understand why we go through this process, we need to step back and look at how AWS manages services via the EC2 service.

Introduction to AMIs

Recall that when we spun up our bastion servers, we had to select what operating system to use along with its version. Conceptually, that makes a lot of sense, but how exactly does that work? Well, AWS uses a machine image referred to as an AMI (Amazon Machine Image). These images are used in a virtual machine environment, typically of the HVM (Hardware Virtual Machine) type. For the standard operating systems, a vendor is responsible for creating the AMI for that OS. Most provide variants based not just on the OS release but on the hardware characteristics such as x64 or ARM instruction sets. These AMIs are certified and provided to AWS by those trusted vendors.

Thus, when you ask for an Ubuntu 22.04 OS based on the x64 architecture, you are actually requesting the AMI created by the Ubuntu vendor with those specifications. How that image is created is beyond the scope of this discussion. What is important for our discussion is that you can create your own AMI based on these vendor-provided AMIs. To do this, you spin up a server with the base AMI you want to use for your application, install the necessary software on it, and create a snapshot AMI that you can use to spin up other servers. This is especially useful for applications like GitLab that may take a while to install and configure.

Searching for the Official GitLab AMI

In case you are wondering, there is a marketplace where software vendors provide AMIs with their software preinstalled. As you might guess, some of those vendors charge a fee for using their AMIs, but some do not. GitLab provides AMIs that you can use that have GitLab preinstalled (no fee for the AMI itself). You still need to configure GitLab to let it know what PostgreSQL and Redis databases to use, so there is still a need to create an image with the configurations in place.

Finding the AMIs is a bit tricky as you are led through a wild goose chase through various links to find them. To save you the trouble, the easiest way to access them is directly through the EC2 AMIs page. From there, you need to select "Public images" from the upper-left menu and search for "GitLab CE" and Owner alias = 782774275127.[1] Figure 15-1 shows a sample listing of the GitLab CE AMIs available at the time of this writing. In this example, I selected the latest one at the time, 16.1.2 for the x86_64 architecture (also referred to as AMD).

---

[1] Searching just on GitLab CE will show images created by different companies in addition to GitLab, so you need to restrict the owner ID to GitLab's ID.

CHAPTER 15   THE PROOF IS IN THE CLOUD

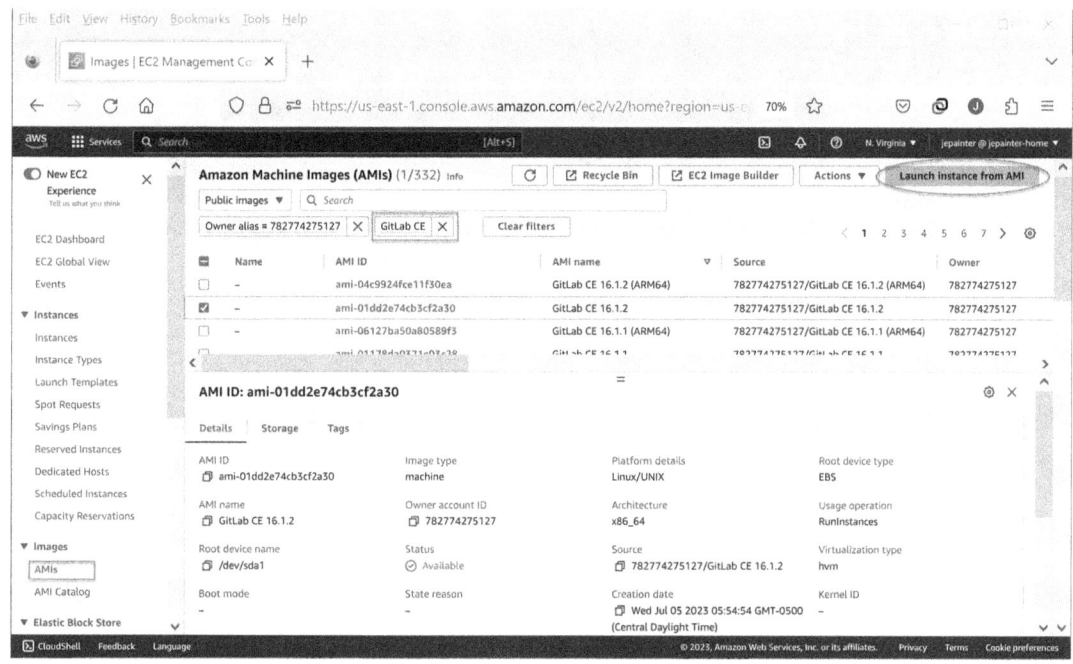

Figure 15-1. *EC2 selection of GitLab CE AMI*

Creating a GitLab Instance from an Image

Once you've selected an image, you can create an instance using that image via the "Launch instance from AMI" button as highlighted in the previous figure. This is similar to the Launch instance option from the EC2 Images page but without needing to select the OS.[2] Figure 15-2 shows the options to select the instance type. For the POC, I've selected the GitLab recommended c5.xlarge type. You can look around and choose a different type, but note that it should have four CPUs. Also, select the key pair created earlier.

---

[2] GitLab AMIs are based off of Ubuntu images.

CHAPTER 15   THE PROOF IS IN THE CLOUD

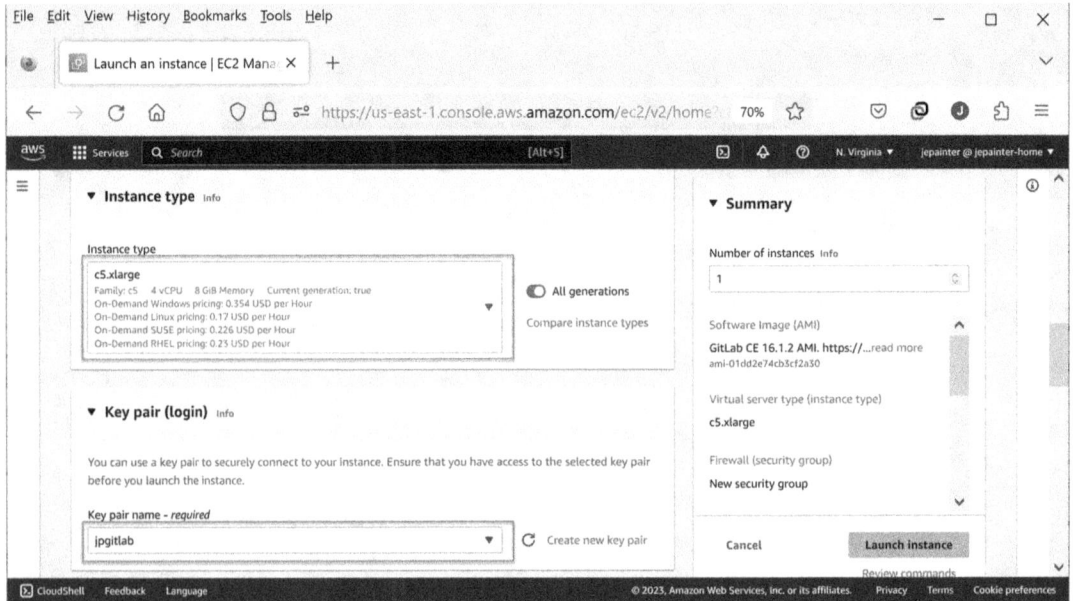

Figure 15-2. *Selection of instance type and key pair for the standalone GitLab server*

After selecting the instance type and key pair, you need to set up the network options as shown in Figure 15-3. Note that to set the options, you will need to select the Edit button (not shown) to enter edit mode. Set the VPC to the GitLab VPC as usual. For the subnet, I selected the private us-east-1b subnet just to be different. Since we want to protect this instance from the outside world, we keep the auto-assign public IP option at "Disable." Finally, for the security group, we select gitlab-loadbalancer-sec-group from the drop-down list.

CHAPTER 15   THE PROOF IS IN THE CLOUD

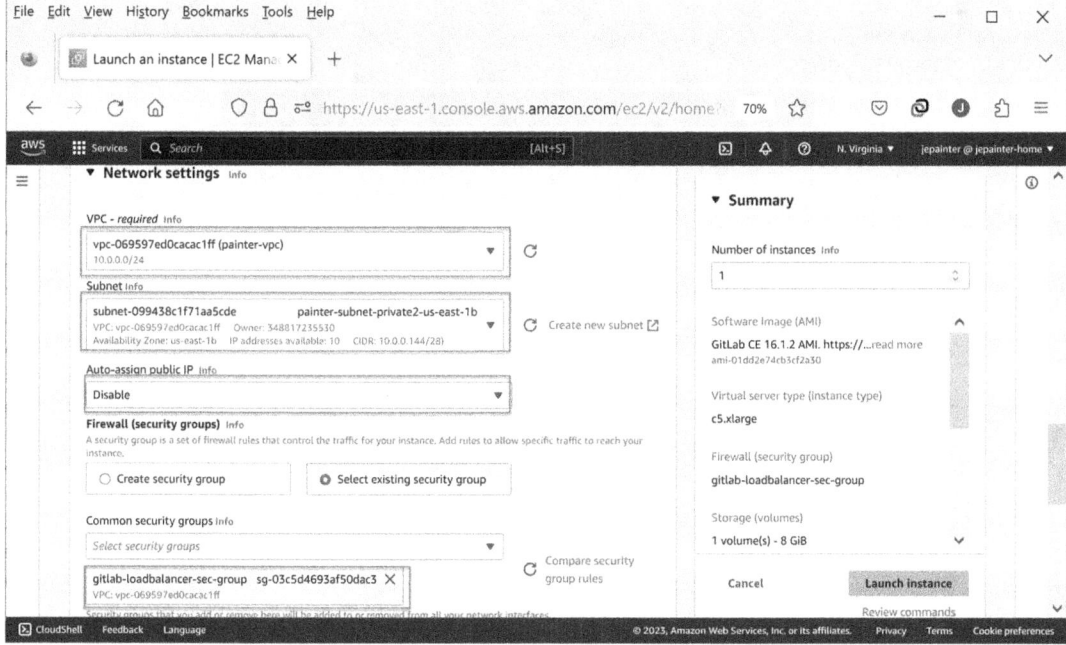

Figure 15-3. *Configuration of network settings and firewall security groups for the standalone GitLab server*

Next up is the storage option as shown in Figure 15-4. Here, I deviate from the GitLab POC documentation and select gp2 from the drop-down list rather than the io1 option. The reason for this is that I will be the only one accessing this service, so choosing the more expensive IOPs option is not required; however, if you do plan on having multiple developers testing the service out, feel free to go with the io1 option as suggested. As suggested by GitLab, the storage size is kept at the default of 8GB. That's all the configuration needed for the GitLab server instance. Selecting the "Launch instance" button will spin up the server in the usual manner.

623

CHAPTER 15   THE PROOF IS IN THE CLOUD

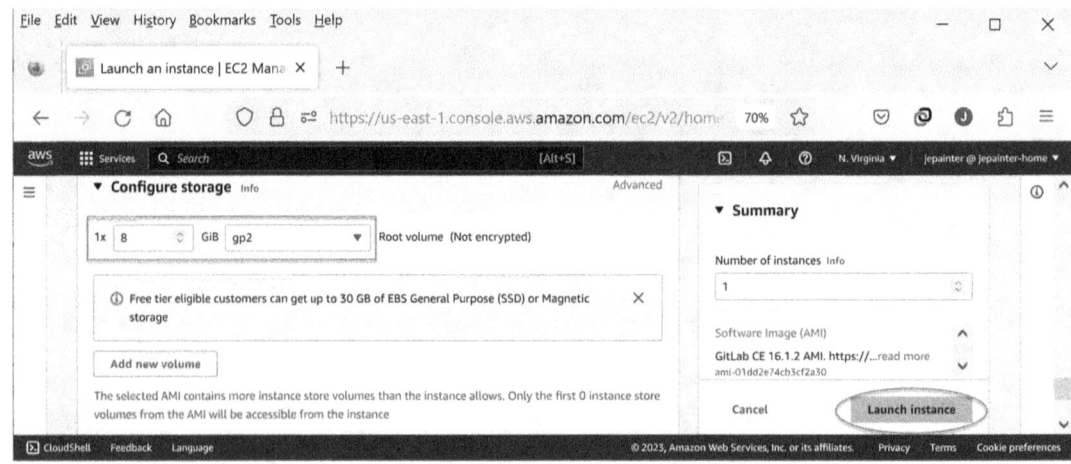

Figure 15-4. Configuration of storage for the standalone GitLab server

Accessing the GitLab Instance via SSH

Once our GitLab server is up and running, it's time to ssh into it and configure the GitLab service. This is where the SSH forwarding comes into play since we cannot connect to the GitLab server directly from our laptop (by design). If you are using Putty on Windows, make sure that Pageant is running and is using the private key; if you are using Mac or Linux, make sure to SSH in using the -A option. In this example, I am logging in to the Bastion B server first. From there, I log in to the GitLab server as ubuntu using its IP address (in my case, 10.0.0.155). Figure 15-5 shows the results of logging in to the GitLab server. As usual, the first time you do this you need to accept the host key.

CHAPTER 15   THE PROOF IS IN THE CLOUD

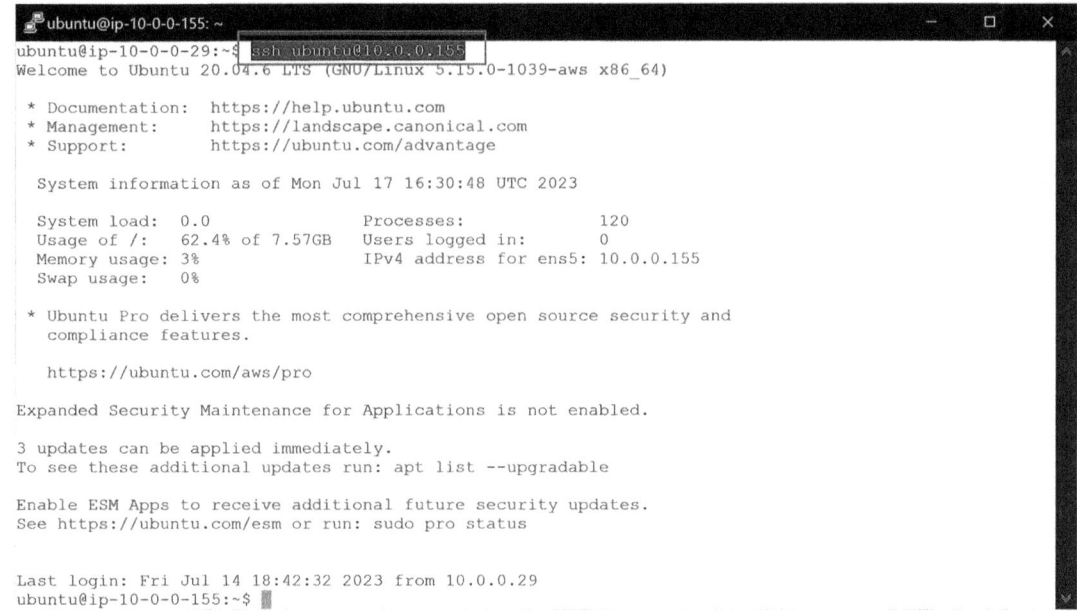

Figure 15-5. *Using ssh to log in to the standalone GitLab server from a bastion instance*

Adding PostgreSQL Extensions

Once inside the GitLab server, we are first going to add some extensions to our PostgreSQL database.[3] This only needs to be done once. To do that, we need to find the RDS endpoint of our GitLab database. You'll find this by selecting the database in the RDS Databases page. The endpoint will begin with "gitlab-db" and end with .rds. amazonaws.com". In our GitLab server, we'll be using the PostgreSQL client installed by GitLab located at /opt/gitlab/embedded/bin/psql. The command to run is shown in Figure 15-6. Note that we have to run psql as the root user using sudo. The first argument, -U gitlab, tells psql to run as user gitlab. The second -h argument is the RDS endpoint that tells psql where to find the database. And the last -d gitlabhq_production option is the DB Name of the database to connect to. You'll be prompted for the master password.

---

[3] If you are following along with the GitLab POC documentation, I'm doing some things out of order, which I feel makes more sense.

625

```
ubuntu@ip-10-0-0-155:~$ sudo /opt/gitlab/embedded/bin/psql -U gitlab -h gitlab-db.c       3.us-east
-1.rds.amazonaws.com -d gitlabhq_production
Password for user gitlab:
psql (13.11)
SSL connection (protocol: TLSv1.2, cipher: ECDHE-RSA-AES256-GCM-SHA384, bits: 256, compression: off)
Type "help" for help.

gitlabhq_production=> CREATE EXTENSION pg_trgm
gitlabhq_production-> ;
CREATE EXTENSION
gitlabhq_production=> CREATE EXTENSION btree_gist;
CREATE EXTENSION
gitlabhq_production=> \q
ubuntu@ip-10-0-0-155:~$
```

Figure 15-6. Setting of PostgreSQL extensions used by GitLab on the standalone GitLab server

If all goes well, you'll see the "gitlabhq_production=>" prompt. You are now in PostgreSQL mode. You need to add the extensions pg_trgm and btree_gist[4] using the CREATE EXTENSION database command. Make sure to end each command with a semicolon (;). If successful, you'll get the message CREATE EXTENSION returned; otherwise, you'll get an error message probably telling you that there was a typo of some sort or that the extension is not recognized. When done, exit the psql mode using "\q", at which point you'll be taken back to the Linux command line.

Disabling Let's Encrypt

We are ready to configure the service. The first thing we need to do is shut off the "Let's Encrypt" option since we are using the ELB to handle the SSL/TLS certificates. The GitLab configuration file is located in the /etc/gitlab directory and is named gitlab.rb.[5] You won't be able to read or edit this file as user ubuntu since it is a root-owned file with read-write permissions set only to root. No worries. We can edit the file using "sudo vi /etc/gitlab/gitlab.rb"; if you are not comfortable using vi, you can use a different editor such as emacs instead. Within the editor, do a search for "Let's Encrypt." Figure 15-7 shows the location of the Let's Encrypt section within the gitlab.rb file. To turn Let's

---

[4] Double-check with the GitLab POC documentation about the extensions to be added in case they have changed or new ones added.

[5] The .rb extension tells you that GitLab is a Ruby application.

Encrypt off, remove the "# " at the beginning of the line containing letsencrypt['enable'] and change the value from true to false. This change will take effect the next time we reconfigure the service,[6] which we'll get to shortly.

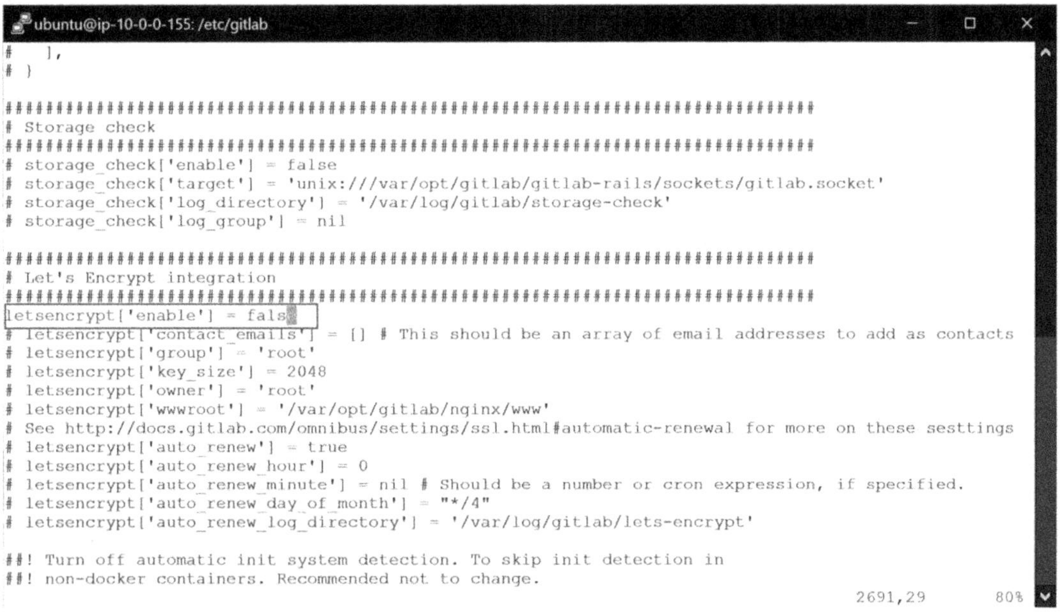

```
ubuntu@ip-10-0-0-155: /etc/gitlab
#    ],
# }

################################################################################
# Storage check
################################################################################
# storage_check['enable'] = false
# storage_check['target'] = 'unix:///var/opt/gitlab/gitlab-rails/sockets/gitlab.socket'
# storage_check['log_directory'] = '/var/log/gitlab/storage-check'
# storage_check['log_group'] = nil

################################################################################
# Let's Encrypt integration
################################################################################
letsencrypt['enable'] = false
# letsencrypt['contact_emails'] = [] # This should be an array of email addresses to add as contacts
# letsencrypt['group'] = 'root'
# letsencrypt['key_size'] = 2048
# letsencrypt['owner'] = 'root'
# letsencrypt['wwwroot'] = '/var/opt/gitlab/nginx/www'
# See http://docs.gitlab.com/omnibus/settings/ssl.html#automatic-renewal for more on these sesttings
# letsencrypt['auto_renew'] = true
# letsencrypt['auto_renew_hour'] = 0
# letsencrypt['auto_renew_minute'] = nil # Should be a number or cron expression, if specified.
# letsencrypt['auto_renew_day_of_month'] = "*/4"
# letsencrypt['auto_renew_log_directory'] = '/var/log/gitlab/lets-encrypt'

##! Turn off automatic init system detection. To skip init detection in
##! non-docker containers. Recommended not to change.
                                                        2691,29       80%
```

Figure 15-7. *Disabling "Let's Encrypt" in the GitLab configuration file*

A word about the structure of the gitlab.rb file: Many options are commented out using the "#" character at the start of the line. This not only helps with knowing what configuration options are available, it also communicates the default setting of that option. So, the original line "# letsencrypt['enable'] = true" tells you that Let's Encrypt is enabled by default; we don't have to uncomment the line to set this option.

Setting the External URL

The next important change to make is the external URL. You'll find this near the top of the file as "external url" as shown in Figure 15-8. The initial value is something like "example.gitlab.com"; this won't work since we don't own that domain. You'll need to replace it with your own URL. In my case, I set the external URL to poc.jpgitlab.com, which is the AWS Zone record set in the "Connecting Your Domain" section of Chapter 13.

[6] Note that the GitLab POC documentation tells you to reconfigure right after making this change. This will fail, however, since we need to set the URL first. We'll do this next.

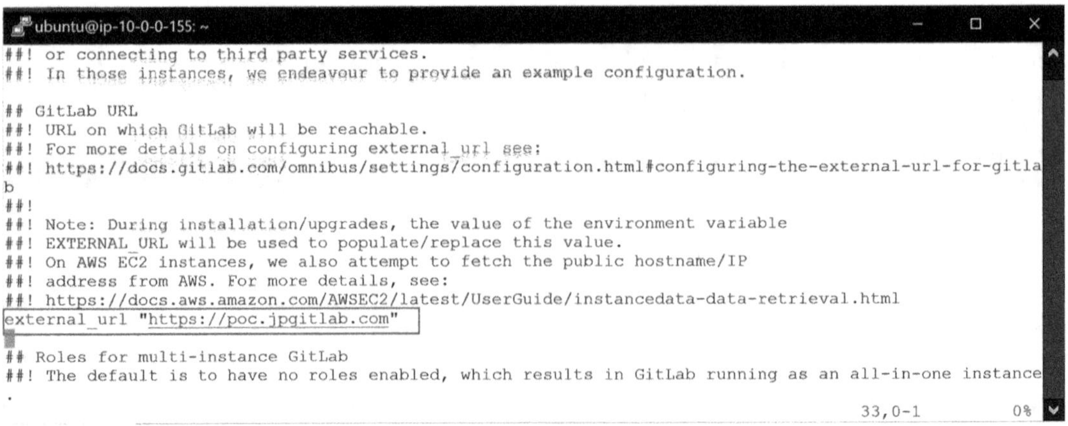

Figure 15-8. Setting external_url in the GitLab configuration file

Disabling the Internal PostgreSQL Database

We now need to let GitLab know to use our external PostgreSQL and Redis databases. By default, GitLab will use its own internal database; we need to disable that. Find the line containing "postgresql['enable']" as shown in Figure 15-9. Remove the "#" from the beginning of that line and change the value from true to false. This will tell the GitLab service not to use its internal PostgreSQL database. It's important to note that once we switch GitLab to use the external database, we cannot switch back to the internal database.

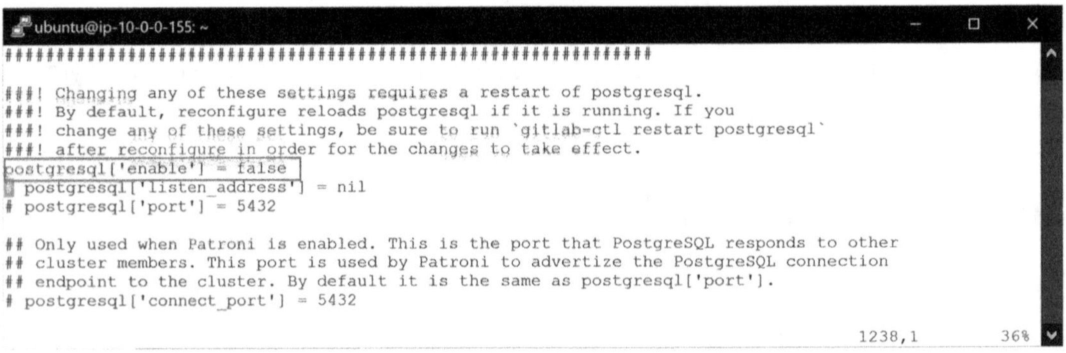

Figure 15-9. Disabling the use of GitLab internal PostgreSQL in the GitLab configuration file

Configuring the External PostgreSQL Database

Of course, we now need to tell GitLab where the external database is. The configuration is found elsewhere in the gitlab.rb file. A search on "GitLab database settings" should take you to that section. Figure 15-10 shows the changes to be made for our external database. In the example, I've commented out the first set of options even though we are keeping the defaults on many of them; it just makes it easier to see the configuration. The key changes to make are the db_password[7] and the db_host. The db_password is the master database password, and db_host is the RDS endpoint we used with the psql command earlier.

```
### GitLab database settings
###! Docs: https://docs.gitlab.com/omnibus/settings/database.html
###! **Only needed if you use an external database.**
gitlab_rails['db_adapter'] = "postgresql"
gitlab_rails['db_encoding'] = "unicode"
gitlab_rails['db_collation'] = nil
gitlab_rails['db_database'] = "gitlabhq_production"
gitlab_rails['db_username'] = "gitlab"
gitlab_rails['db_password'] = "          "
gitlab_rails['db_host'] = "gitlab-db.c       3.us-east-1.rds.amazonaws.com"
gitlab_rails['db_port'] = 5432
# gitlab_rails['db_socket'] = nil
# gitlab_rails['db_sslmode'] = nil
# gitlab_rails['db_sslcompression'] = 0
```

Figure 15-10. Updating the GitLab configuration file to use the RDS database

Disabling the Internal Redis Database

Next, we need to disable the internal Redis database. Doing a search for "GitLab Redis" should take you to the section shown in Figure 15-11. As with disabling the internal PostgreSQL database, uncomment the redis['enable'] line and set the value from true to false. This will tell GitLab to not use its internal Redis database.

---

[7] Yes, the database password is in clear text, which is one reason why the gitlab.rb file is readable to only the root user. Do not change the file permissions of gitlab.rb!

CHAPTER 15 THE PROOF IS IN THE CLOUD

```
## GitLab Redis
##! **Can be disabled if you are using your own Redis instance.**
##! Docs: https://docs.gitlab.com/omnibus/settings/redis.html

redis['enable'] = false
# redis['ha'] = false
# redis['start_down'] = false
# redis['set_replicaof'] = false
# redis['hz'] = 10
# redis['dir'] = "/var/opt/gitlab/redis"
# redis['log_directory'] = "/var/log/gitlab/redis"
# redis['log_group'] = nil
```

Figure 15-11. Disabling the use of the internal Redis database in the GitLab configuration file

Configuring the External Redis Database

Find the section "GitLab Redis settings" as shown in Figure 15-12. You'll need to locate the Redis endpoint in the ElastiCache Redis clusters page similar to how you found the RDS endpoint. It will begin with "gitlab-redis-" and end with ".cache.amazonaws.com". Uncomment out the first two lines and set the redis_host option to that Redis endpoint. Keep the redis_port at the default value of 6379.[8]

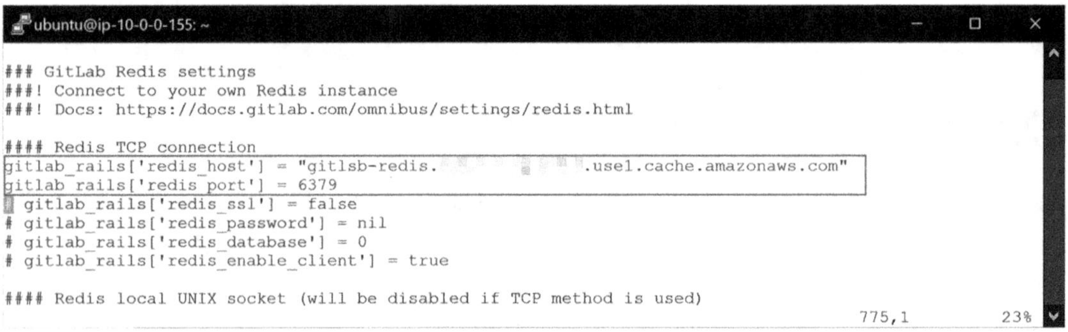

```
### GitLab Redis settings
###! Connect to your own Redis instance
###! Docs: https://docs.gitlab.com/omnibus/settings/redis.html

#### Redis TCP connection
gitlab_rails['redis_host'] = "gitlsb-redis.          .use1.cache.amazonaws.com"
gitlab_rails['redis_port'] = 6379
# gitlab_rails['redis_ssl'] = false
# gitlab_rails['redis_password'] = nil
# gitlab_rails['redis_database'] = 0
# gitlab_rails['redis_enable_client'] = true

#### Redis local UNIX socket (will be disabled if TCP method is used)
```

Figure 15-12. Updating the GitLab configuration file to use the Redis database

---

[8] Yes, I didn't need to uncomment the redis_port line, but I did it to make it explicitly clear.

CHAPTER 15   THE PROOF IS IN THE CLOUD

Applying Configuration Changes

With that, we are done making our initial set of configuration changes. At this point, save the changes and exit the editor. We are now ready to apply our changes. This is done using the command "sudo gitlab-ctl reconfigure." Without running this command, no changes are applied, so make sure that whenever you edit the gitlab.rb file, rerun this command to ensure the changes are applied. Note that the first time you run the reconfigure command, the GitLab services will also be started. Figure 15-13 shows the end of the output of the reconfigure command; there are a lot of output messages returned by this command, so I could not show all of them. If all is successful, you will see the "GitLab Reconfigured!" as the last message.[9]

```
ubuntu@ip-10-0-0-155: ~

Recipe: monitoring::alertmanager
  * runit_service[alertmanager] action restart (up to date)
[2023-07-17T17:13:03+00:00] INFO: Cinc Client Run complete in 128.537466028 seconds

Running handlers:
[2023-07-17T17:13:03+00:00] INFO: Running report handlers
Running handlers complete
[2023-07-17T17:13:03+00:00] INFO: Report handlers complete
Infra Phase complete, 429/1202 resources updated in 02 minutes 09 seconds

Notes:
Default admin account has been configured with following details:
Username: root
Password: You didn't opt-in to print initial root password to STDOUT.
Password stored to /etc/gitlab/initial_root_password. This file will be cleaned up in first reconfigur
e run after 24 hours.

NOTE: Because these credentials might be present in your log files in plain text, it is highly recomme
nded to reset the password following https://docs.gitlab.com/ee/security/reset_user_password.html#rese
t-your-root-password.

gitlab Reconfigured!
ubuntu@ip-10-0-0-155:~$
```

Figure 15-13. *Running gitlab-ctl reconfigure to apply configuration file changes*

Checking the Status of GitLab Services

Even though we got the "GitLab Reconfigured!" message telling us that the reconfiguration succeeded, it's always good to check the status of the GitLab services. You do this by running "sudo gitlab-ctl status" as shown in Figure 15-14. This command shows the status of each of the GitLab services. If all is well, the gitlab-ctl status command should show that all services are running. Oh oh! It looks like the nginx service

---

[9] If you don't get this message, search back through the output to find any error messages and double-check the configuration changes made earlier.

is down. If you are familiar with web service tools, you may know that nginx is a standard web service tool used to manage HTTP and HTTPS web services. So, let's try to figure out what could be going on.

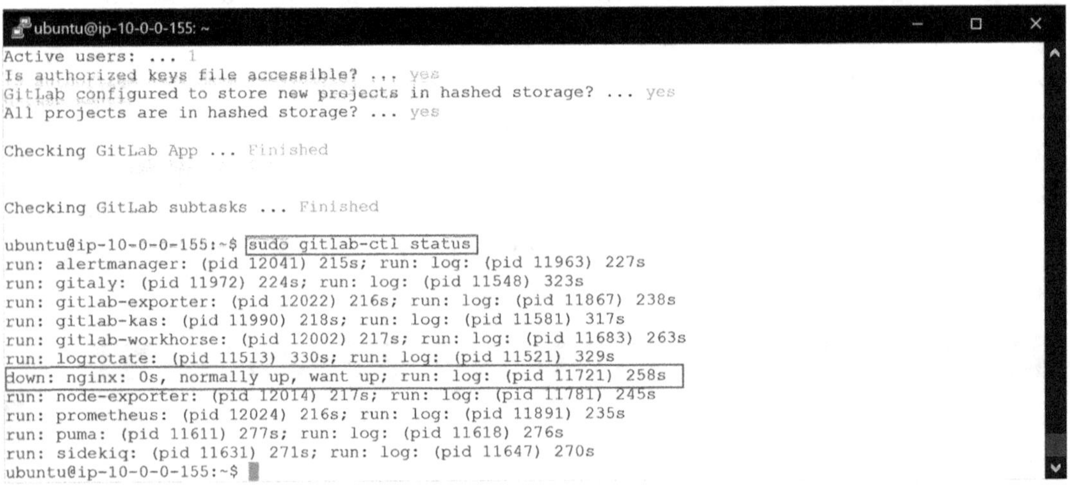

Figure 15-14. Running gitlab-ctl status to check if all GitLab services are running

Investigating Nginx Service Failure

OK, so we know that there is an issue with the web service, and our entry to the GitLab web service is via the load balancer we set up earlier. After all, we set the external URL in the gitlab.rb file to point to our ELB, so let's see what is going on from the ELB side of things. Figure 15-15 shows the Instances section of our ELB. Hmmm, there are no instances registered to our ELB; in other words, the ELB isn't connected to our GitLab instance. Well, that could be a problem. There is the "Edit Instances" button, so let's click that and see if we can add the GitLab instance to our ELB.

CHAPTER 15   THE PROOF IS IN THE CLOUD

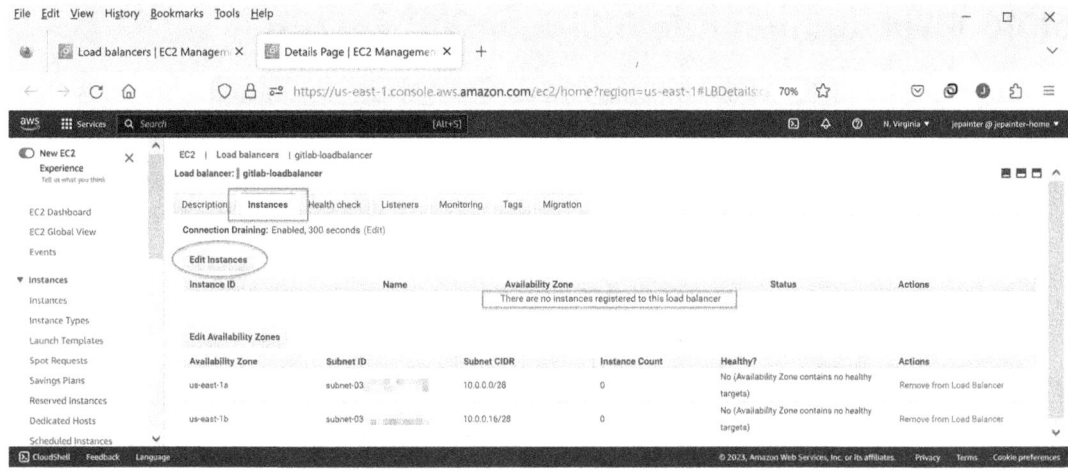

Figure 15-15. ELB option to connect instances to ELB

Connecting the GitLab Server to the ELB

Figure 15-16 shows the resulting screen after selecting "Edit Instances." Here, we see the set of instances we've created so far along with the ability to add or remove them from the ELB. Since we want to connect to the GitLab instance, we select that one from the list and save it. That should do the trick, eh?

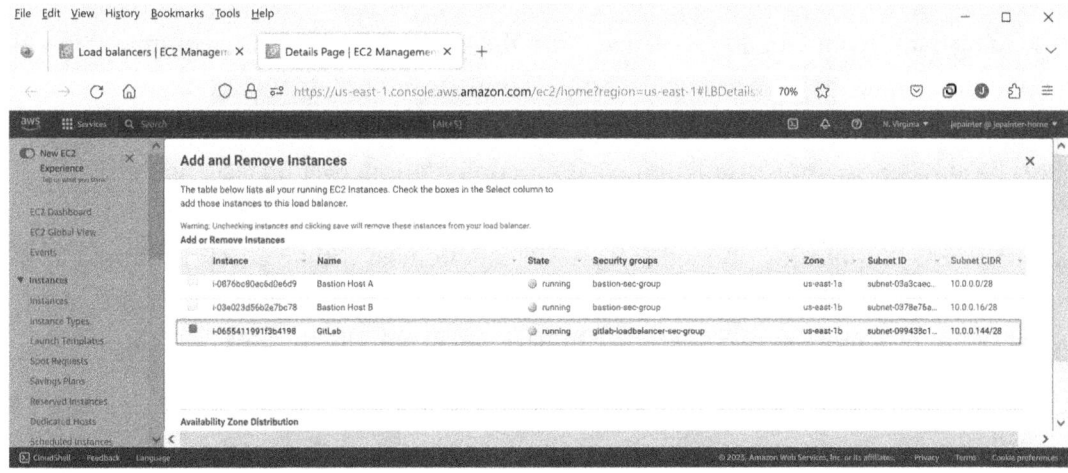

Figure 15-16. Adding the standalone GitLab server to the ELB instance list

633

CHAPTER 15   THE PROOF IS IN THE CLOUD

More Investigation into nginx Server Failure

Looking at Figure 15-17, we see that our GitLab server is now connected to the ELB. Note the status, however. It shows that the server is "out of service." So, let's think for a minute about why. We know that the GitLab nginx service is not running, so perhaps we need to do a reconfigure again to get things working.[10]

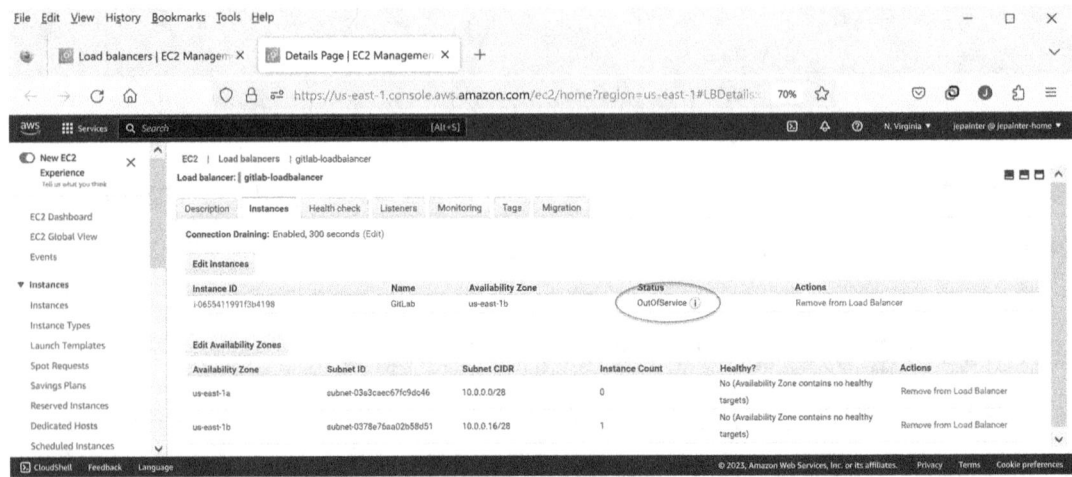

Figure 15-17. *ELB status of the standalone GitLab server showing that it is out of service*

Going back to our GitLab server, we rerun the gitlab-ctl reconfigure command to see if our nginx service now starts up. After the reconfigure completes, we run the gitlab-ctl status command to see if nginx is now running. To our chagrin, it is not. Something else must be amiss. Searching through the POC documentation, we find a section entitled "Add support for Proxied SSL," which in turn has a link to the GitLab documentation referenced as "Supporting proxied SSL." As an experienced GitLab administrator running GitLab on AWS, I can save you some debugging grief; we need to tell nginx that we are running a proxy server (a.k.a. the ELB) that will handle the SSL certificates.

---

[10] This is the equivalent of rebooting a machine to see if things clear themselves up. It doesn't always work, but it doesn't hurt either.

Configuring the nginx Reverse Proxy

To set up the reverse proxy, we edit the gitlab.rb file and make the changes as shown in Figure 15-18. The changes are pretty simple. We need to set the nginx listen port to 80 (rather than 443) and disable the listen_https option. Let's cross our fingers and hope that gets nginx started.

Figure 15-18. Updating GitLab configuration to use reverse proxy

Since we changed the gitlab.rb file, we do our magical "sudo gitlab-ctl reconfigure" and see what happens. As before, we get a "GitLab Reconfigured!" message, so at least GitLab liked the changes. But of course, we know that we need to run the "sudo gitlab-ctl status" command to see if nginx is running properly. Looking at Figure 15-19, we see that nginx is now up and running. Whew!

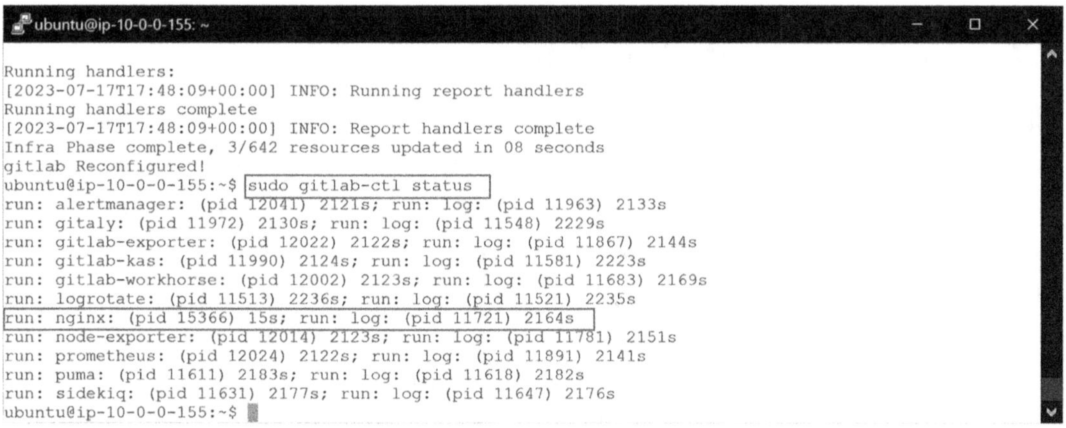

Figure 15-19. Running gitlab-ctl status to verify that nginx service is now up and running

Investigating ELB Out of Service Failure

With nginx up and running, let's circle back and take a look at the ELB instance status in AWS. Hmmm. Even after waiting ten minutes or so, we still see that the GitLab instance status remains at "out of service." Drats! Going back through the POC documentation, it looks like we did everything right, so what could the issue be?

At this point, I needed to do some Linux debugging work. First thing I did was check to see if I could connect to port 80 on the GitLab server. From the bastion server (either one), I used the nc command to check things out. Running "nc -zv 10.0.0.155[11] 80" returned "connection success," so I knew that nginx was responding to port 80 requests. I then logged back in to the GitLab server and ran a simple curl command to see if the health check used by the ELB was running: curl -o - -I http://localhost/-/readiness. This returned a status code of 200 and a JSON message showing that everything was OK.

I have to admit, it took me awhile to figure out the issue. After a good night's sleep, I tried running a curl command from the bastion server and got a 302 (redirect) status code. It was then, based on prior experience I had forgotten, that I realized what was happening. The first time you set up a GitLab service, you need to log in as root to change the password. Until then, any requests to HTTPS or HTTP from the ELB will give you a redirect to the sign-in page. This meant that the readiness health check that was set up on the ELB was always failing; it expected a 200 status code, not a 302 code, hence the out-of-service status. Changing the ELB health check to test the SSH port 22 cleared the problem. The GitLab instance was now showing as "In Service."

Learning Through Debugging

Some of you may be wondering why I bothered describing the debugging I had to do to get things working and not just go back and fix the problems in previous sections so that your install would work properly. There are two answers to that. First of all, it drives home the point that the GitLab POC documentation isn't always accurate. For example, it tells you to disable Let's Encrypt and then run the gitlab-ctl reconfigure command; that doesn't work until you set the external URL, which is described later in their documentation. Also, it fails to mention that you have to add the instance to the ELB in order for there to be connectivity to the GitLab server; unless you are familiar with AWS, readers might not be aware of that.

---

[11] Obviously, use the IP address assigned to your GitLab instance in place of 10.0.0.155.

Secondly, as a self-managed GitLab administrator, it is important to get used to debugging issues using various Linux and GitLab tools as I did earlier. Things don't always work "out of the box," and you need to figure out why. Sometimes, it is easy, but many times it is not. There are a lot of components to GitLab, and the AWS environment surrounding it makes it difficult at times to trace an issue. And as discussed earlier, there may be more than one issue causing problems. For example, to get the GitLab instance to the InService state in the ELB, I had to fix both the nginx reverse proxy and the ELB health check.

Logging In to Your GitLab Standalone Service

So now that we have the GitLab server configured properly and connected via the ELB, we can now log in to the GitLab service for the very first time. From your web browser, you should be able to enter the HTTPS URL for your service and get a sign-in page. You'll need to log in as root. To find the password, you need to ssh into the GitLab server and find the /etc/gitlab/initial_root_password.[12] If it exists, you can read the file as the root user. If it doesn't exist, you'll have to reset the password using the following command, which will prompt you to enter a new password:

```
sudo gitlab-rake "gitlab:password:reset[root]"
```

Congratulations, you now have access to your GitLab service as an administrator. You may see a message on the initial dashboard warning you that your service allows anyone who accesses your GitLab service to sign up. You don't want this, so follow the directions provided to turn this feature off. We'll explore other administrative features via the GitLab UI in a later chapter.

You may be tempted to experiment with your self-managed GitLab service but hold off on that for now. We will be making changes later on that impact where certain things go such as our Git data and binary data. Configuration options are fine to update since those are stored in the PostgreSQL database. Refrain from creating Git repositories for now.

In the next section, we'll explore how to split off the Gitaly service, which manages Git storage, onto its own server.

---

[12] BTW, the POC document states that for GitLab-provided AMIs, the password is the server's AWS instance ID. Nope, doesn't work.

CHAPTER 15   THE PROOF IS IN THE CLOUD

Splitting Off the Gitaly Service

So, we are now ready to create our own GitLab AMI, right? Well, not quite. There is one more component that we have to create separate from our GitLab instance: Gitaly. If you look back in the gitlab-ctl status results, you'll see that the gitaly service is running on our GitLab instance. That would work if we were only going to have the one GitLab instance. But since we eventually want to spin up several GitLab instances to spread the web service workload, we can't have gitaly running on all of those servers.

The Reason for Splitting Off the Gitaly Service

Why not? Because the gitaly service is what manages the storage of your Git repositories. That storage turns out to be in a filesystem on a disk, what AWS refers to as EBS (Elastic Block Store). With EBS, a disk can only be connected to one instance; it cannot be shared across multiple instances like an NFS (Network File Service) storage solution can. To enable sharing of the Git filesystem, GitLab originally used NFS to manage the Git data, but that turned out to be a performance nightmare, especially with lots of small file reads and writes. So GitLab switched to a different service called Gitaly.

Like NFS, Gitaly is a standalone service that accepts read and write requests from multiple servers. Unlike NFS, it is tuned specifically for git push and pull requests using the RPC (remote procedure call) protocol. Since we want to enable running multiple GitLab instances, we need to extract the Gitaly service onto its own server with its own disk. I know some of you might be thinking, "why didn't we create the Gitaly server first like we did with the PostgreSQL and Redis databases?" Good question. It has to do with the generation of GitLab secrets.

Locating the Generated GitLab Secrets File

When the GitLab service is first started, it creates a set of secrets unique to the new service. This way, no two GitLab services use the same set of secrets, which is a good thing. These secrets are stored in the file /etc/gitlab/gitlab-secrets.json, which is, as you may have guessed, only readable by the root user. Feel free to ssh into the GitLab server and take a look at the secrets file.

Now in order to function, all servers related to a given GitLab service must share the same set of secrets; it is how they trust each other. This includes the server running the Gitaly service. We can't install the Gitaly service without those secrets, and those secrets need the GitLab service to run. It's a chicken-and-egg type scenario.

To resolve the chicken-and-egg scenario, we create the GitLab service first using the internal Gitaly service as we've done already. We then create a new instance where Gitaly is installed; we'll see how to do this momentarily. Before we start the new Gitaly service, we copy the secrets from the GitLab server to the Gitaly server so that the two servers can trust each other. Once the new Gitaly service is up and running, we go back to the GitLab service and reconfigure it to use the new Gitaly service in place of its internal Gitaly service.[13] At that point, we will be able to create our own GitLab AMI configured to use the external PostgreSQL, Redis, and Gitaly services.

Creating the Gitaly Security Group

To start, we need to first create a security group specific to the Gitaly service. At this point, you should know how to create a security group, so I won't go through the details of how to do this. Figure 15-20 shows the resulting gitlab-gitaly-sec-group SG. It has two inbound rules. The first rule is the SSH rule whose source is the bastion-sec-group; this enables us to ssh into the Gitaly server from the bastion servers. The second rule is for port 8075 used by Gitaly to communicate with the GitLab servers. For this inbound rule, we use gitlab-loadbalancer-sec-group as the source; this ensures that only the GitLab servers can use the Gitaly service running on this server.

---

[13] In other words, we do a bait and switch.

CHAPTER 15   THE PROOF IS IN THE CLOUD

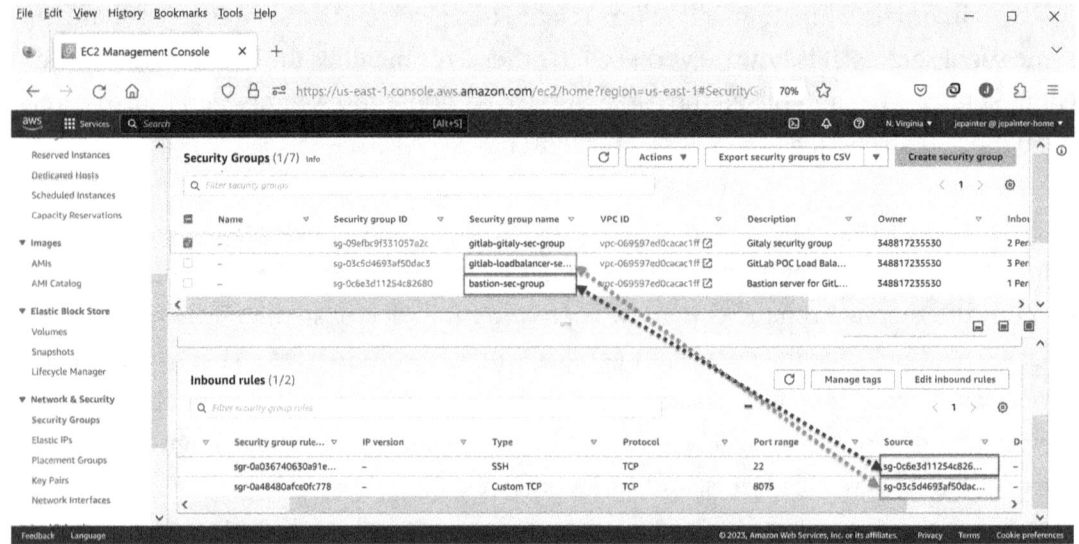

Figure 15-20. *Definition of the Gitaly security group*

Spinning Up the Gitaly Server

Next, we create the Gitaly server as shown in Figure 15-21. In this example, I've created a server that is similar to the GitLab server except it is based on the Ubuntu image rather than the GitLab image; we'll install GitLab manually on the Gitaly server. I placed the server in the us-east-1a private subnet just to balance things out a bit; it isn't required to be in a different AZ than the GitLab server. For storage, I used the POC recommendation of 20G, since I don't plan on doing much Git work with this server.[14] For the security group, I used the gitlab-gitaly-sec-group that we just created.

---

[14] In a production or development environment, I strongly suggest attaching an additional disk separate from the root volume. This will allow you to replace the server by detaching the disk from the old server and attaching it to the replacement server.

CHAPTER 15   THE PROOF IS IN THE CLOUD

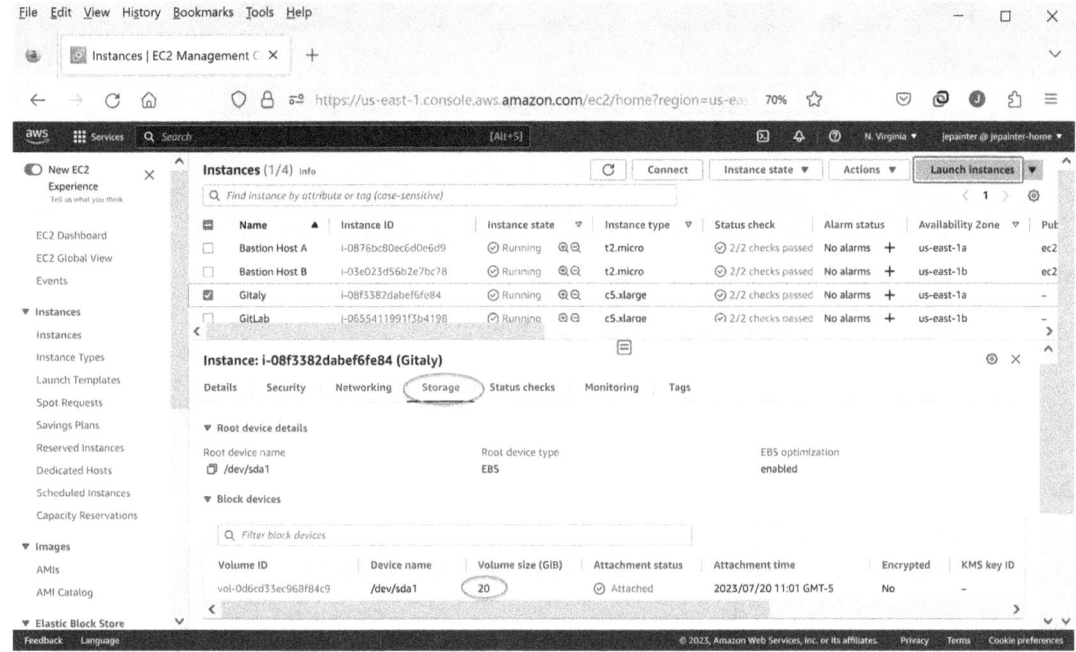

Figure 15-21. *Instance storage options for the Gitaly server*

Installing the GitLab Package on the Gitaly Server

As soon as the Gitaly instance is up and running, we can ssh into it via one of the bastion servers and install the GitLab[15] software. Installation is a two-step process. First, we need to set up the apt repository that references the location of GitLab packages, and second, we use that repository to download and install the specific version of GitLab that we are interested in. Figure 15-22 shows the commands used in the two-step process.

---

[15] Gitaly is a component of GitLab, so there is no separate software package needed to install it.

641

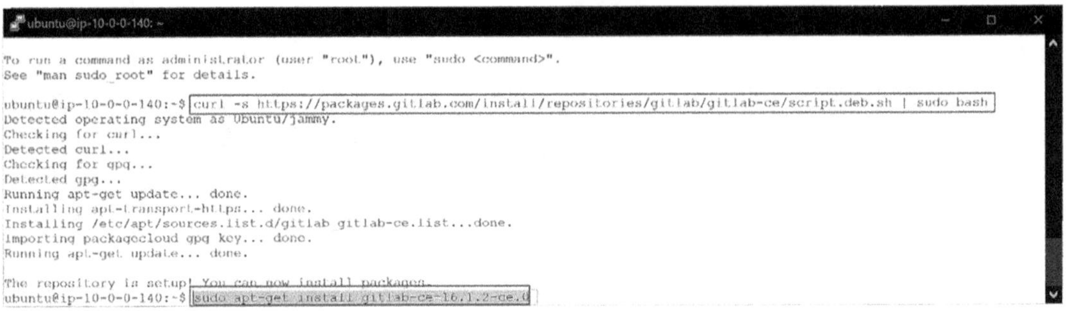

![Figure 15-22 screenshot showing terminal output of GitLab installation commands]

Figure 15-22. *Installation of the GitLab Ubuntu package on the Gitaly server*

For reference, the two commands are provided as follows:

```
curl -s https://packages.gitlab.com/install/repositories/gitlab/gitlab-ce/script.deb.sh | sudo bash
sudo apt-get install gitlab-ce=16.1.2-ce.0 # Replace 16.1.2 with the GitLab version installed
```

In the first command, note the use of gitlab-ce. The -ce suffix indicates that we want the community edition (a.k.a. free version) of GitLab. Also, note that what is downloaded is a bash script that when run detects the specific OS you are using and sets up the proper apt repository. Yes, it is safe to run this script, but if you are skittish, feel free to download the script first, view it, and then run it explicitly.

Make sure that the version of GitLab you install on the Gitaly server matches the version on the GitLab server. If you are not sure what version is installed on the GitLab server, ssh into it and run the command "apt list --installed | grep gitlab".

Copying the GitLab Secrets File to the Gitaly Server

Before we configure and start the gitaly service, we must first copy the gitlab-secrets.json from the GitLab server to the Gitaly server. This is a bit tricky since the SSH port of those servers is only open to the bastion servers, not between them; in other words, you cannot ssh into the GitLab server from the Gitaly server (by design). Another issue is that the secrets file is readable by the root user, and transfers will need to be made by the ubuntu user. So here goes.

First, ssh into the GitLab server as user ubuntu and run the following commands:

```
sudo cp /etc/gitlab/gitlab-secrets.json .
sudo chmod 0644 gitlab-secrets.json
```

CHAPTER 15 THE PROOF IS IN THE CLOUD

Then ssh into one of the bastion servers and run the following commands replacing gitlab-ip and gitaly-ip with their respective IP addresses:

sftp ubuntu@gitlab-ip
get gitlab-secrets.json
exit
sftp ubuntu@gitaly-ip
put gitlab-secrets.json
exit
rm gitlab-secrets.json

Next, ssh into the Gitaly server as user ubuntu and run the following commands:

sudo cp gitlab-secrets.json /etc/gitlab
sudo chmod 0600 /etc/gitlab/gitlab-secrets.json
rm gitlab-secrets.json

Finally, ssh back into the GitLab server as user ubuntu and remove the gitlab-secrets.json file from the ubuntu user's home directory. When done, the gitlab-secrets.json file should only exist in the /etc/gitlab directory of the GitLab and Gitaly servers and should be readable only to root; all copies of the gitlab-secrets.json file in the ubuntu user's directory on all three servers should no longer exist.

Configuring the Standalone Gitaly Service

OK, so now that the GitLab and Gitaly servers share the same secrets file, we can start with the configuration of the Gitaly service. As with the GitLab service, we edit the /etc/gitlab/gitlab.rb file as the root user. Figure 15-23 shows the initial set of changes to be made to this file. Note that I like to put all of these near the start of the file so that it is clearer that this is a Gitaly-specific configuration. We set the external url just as we did for the GitLab service. We then disable all services except gitaly since they are not needed by the gitaly service. We also need to disable the database auto-migrate feature since we don't want to update the database when the gitaly service is updated in the

643

future; otherwise, we would mess up the gitlab services. Since gitaly doesn't use the database, this is not an issue. Finally, we set the internal_api_url[16] to the same value as the external url.

```
##! address from AWS. For more details, see:
##! https://docs.aws.amazon.com/AWSEC2/latest/UserGuide/instancedata-data-retrieval.html
external_url 'https://poc.jpgitlab.com'

# Avoid running unnecessary services on the Gitaly server
postgresql['enable'] = false
redis['enable'] = false
nginx['enable'] = false
puma['enable'] = false
sidekiq['enable'] = false
gitlab_workhorse['enable'] = false
grafana['enable'] = false
gitlab_exporter['enable'] = false
gitlab_kas['enable'] = false

# If you run a separate monitoring node you can disable these services
prometheus['enable'] = false
alertmanager['enable'] = false

# Prevent database connections during 'gitlab-ctl reconfigure'
gitlab_rails['auto_migrate'] = false

# Configure the gitlab-shell API callback URL. Without this, `git push` will
# fail. This can be your 'front door' GitLab URL or an internal load
# balancer.
# Don't forget to copy `/etc/gitlab/gitlab-secrets.json` from Gitaly client to Gitaly server.
gitlab_rails['internal_api_url'] = 'https://poc.jpgitlab.com'

## Roles for multi-instance GitLab
```

Figure 15-23. GitLab configuration file settings to disable services not used by Gitaly

Next, we need to configure the Gitaly service itself as shown in Figure 15-24. Note that there already is a gitaly['configuration'] section with all sorts of options; because of the large number of options, I find it best just to create the section with just the options we need so that it is clearer what is being set. In this section, we set up the listen address to use the default Gitaly port of 8075, which matches the port defined in the gitlab-gitaly-sec-group SG. We also need to set up an authorization token that will be used by the GitLab service to verify that it has access to the Gitaly service. You'll need to define one here since this won't be in the gitlab-secrets.json file; we'll update the GitLab configuration to use this token later on.

---

[16] To be honest, I don't know if the internal_api_url setting is still necessary since I don't see this defaulted anywhere else in the gitlab.rb file. If it isn't used anymore, it doesn't hurt to set it since it would be ignored.

CHAPTER 15   THE PROOF IS IN THE CLOUD

```
##########################################################################
## Gitaly
##! Docs: https://docs.gitlab.com/ee/administration/gitaly/configure_gitaly.html
##########################################################################
gitaly['configuration'] = {
  # ...
  #
  # Make Gitaly accept connections on all network interfaces. You must use
  # firewalls to restrict access to this address/port.
  # Comment out following line if you only want to support TLS connections
  listen_addr: '0.0.0.0:8075',
  auth: {
    # ...
    #
    # Authentication token to ensure only authorized servers can communicate with
    # Gitaly server
    token: '          ',
  },
  storage: [
    {
      name: 'default',
      path: '/var/opt/gitlab/git-data',
    },
    {
      name: 'storage1',
      path: '/mnt/gitlab/git-data',
    },
  ],
}
```

Figure 15-24.   Configuration of Gitaly service

Configuring Gitaly Storage

The last part of the gitaly configuration defines where the storage of the Git data will be. At a minimum, a gitaly service needs to define storage with the name "default"; otherwise, the service won't run properly even if you don't use it. In this example, I kept the location set to the default directory /var/opt/gitlab/git-data. I don't plan on using this directory; I'll show you how we disable GitLab from using it later on.

For the second storage, I've given it the name "storage1." There isn't anything magical about the name; I could just have called it myspecialplace. What is important is that if you have another standalone gitaly server, you cannot use the same storage name there. In this example, I've used the path /mnt/gitlab/git-data as suggested in the GitLab documentation. Since this path does not currently exist, we need to create it and change the ownership to git. You can do that with the following commands:

```
sudo mkdir -p /mnt/gitlab/git-data
sudo chown git.git /mnt/gitlab
sudo chown git.git /mnt/gitlab/git-data
```

CHAPTER 15   THE PROOF IS IN THE CLOUD

Note that the /mnt directory is normally used for mounting additional server disks. So, if you did create an additional disk when you spun up the Gitaly server, you can mount that disk to /mnt/gitlab/git-data so that the data for storage "storage1" will reside on that disk. The AWS documentation clearly shows how to do that, so I won't discuss it here. In my throwaway setup, I kept things simple and left that storage to be on the root disk.

Spinning Up the Standalone Gitaly Service

With those gitlab.rb changes in place, we can now spin up the gitaly service by using the same command we used for the gitlab services: sudo gitlab-ctl reconfigure. If all goes well, you should see the familiar "GitLab Reconfigured!" message. Just as we did with the gitlab services, we still need to verify everything is up and running by running the sudo gitlab-ctl status command. The result of this will be similar to that shown in Figure 15-25.

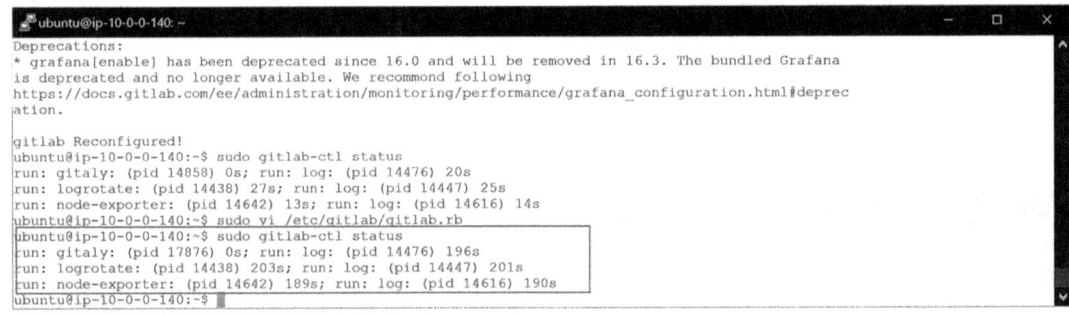

Figure 15-25. *Running of gitlab-ctl reconfigure and gitlab-ctl status on the Gitaly server*

As you can see, we now have a few services running: gitaly, logrotate, and node-exporter. These should be the only services running.[17] If you see another service running, update the gitlab.rb file, disable it, and run the gitlab-ctl reconfigure again. The logrotate service is a standard service that, as its name suggests, rotates and prunes the various GitLab logs on a regular basis. The node-exporter is a service used by external monitoring services to ensure that the gitaly service is running properly. Technically, you could disable these last two services, but I recommend that you keep these enabled.

---

[17] I assume there are no additional services added in a future release that is required by gitaly. Just in case, check the GitLab documentation regarding Gitaly to see if there are any changes in the gitaly configuration.

646

CHAPTER 15   THE PROOF IS IN THE CLOUD

Running the Gitaly Check Command

With Gitaly, there is an additional check specific to it that you should perform to ensure that it is running as expected. The results of this command are shown in Figure 15-26. If all is well, you should see "OK" as the final output. If you don't, you should double-check that the security group is set up correctly. Also, make sure that you logged in to your GitLab service as root; otherwise, access to the GitLab API will fail.[18]

```
ubuntu@ip-10-0-0-140:~$ sudo /opt/gitlab/embedded/bin/gitaly check /var/opt/gitlab/gitaly/config.toml
Checking GitLab API access: OK
GitLab version: 16.1.2
GitLab revision:
GitLab Api version: v4
Redis reachable for GitLab: true
OK
ubuntu@ip-10-0-0-140:~$
```

Figure 15-26. *Running gitaly service check on the Gitaly server*

Checking Gitaly Connectivity from the GitLab Server

Now that we know the Gitaly service is running correctly, it's time to focus on the GitLab side of things. First, however, we need to check that the GitLab service can connect properly to the new Gitaly service **before** we switch to using it. Fortunately, there is a special command we can use from the GitLab server to test that out. First, ssh into the GitLab server as user ubuntu and run the command "sudo gitlab-rake gitlab:tcp_check[*gitaly-ip*,8075]" where gitaly-ip is the IP of the Gitaly server. The results of this for my Gitaly server are shown in Figure 15-27. A succeeded response means that the GitLab server can connect to the Gitaly service via the 8075 port. If it fails, double-check the gitlab-gitaly-sec-group SG.

---

[18] Another one of those things that the POC documentation does not tell you. In fact, it tells you to log in after setting up Gitaly, which, as I found, does not work. This is because of the HTTP 302 redirection issue mentioned earlier.

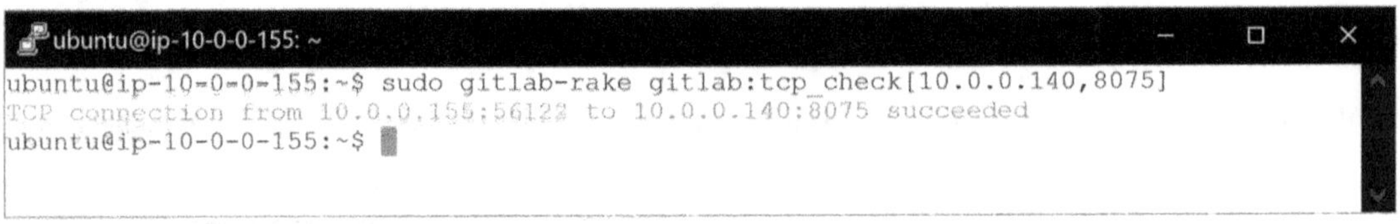

CHAPTER 15   THE PROOF IS IN THE CLOUD

```
ubuntu@ip-10-0-0-155:~$ sudo gitlab-rake gitlab:tcp_check[10.0.0.140,8075]
TCP connection from 10.0.0.155:56122 to 10.0.0.140:8075 succeeded
ubuntu@ip-10-0-0-155:~$
```

Figure 15-27. Test of connection to Gitaly service from the standalone GitLab server

Configuring GitLab to Use the New Standalone Gitaly Service

Good, we can now update the GitLab configuration to use the standalone Gitaly service. Figure 15-28 shows the set of changes to the gitlab.rb file on the GitLab server. Here, we need to set the gitaly_token to match the one we defined in the Gitaly server configuration. It is important that the token values match between the two servers, or Gitaly will reject any attempts to connect to its service. In addition, we set the git_data_dirs section to point to the default and storage1 storage defined in the Gitaly server. Of course, you'll need to replace 10.0.0.140 with the IP address of your Gitaly server. Save the changes and do a sudo gitlab-ctl reconfigure as usual. By the way, it is fine to keep the internal gitaly service running while we switch to using the standalone gitaly service; the changes we just made will ignore that internal service.

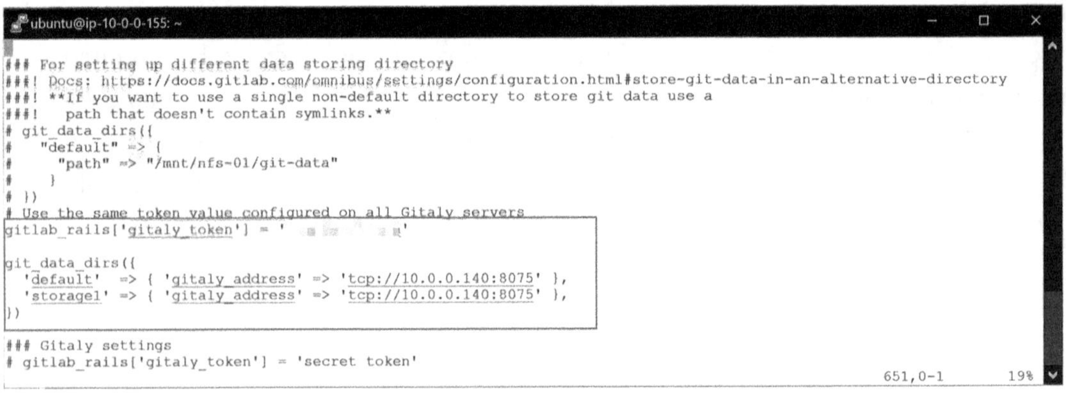

```
### For setting up different data storing directory
###! Docs: https://docs.gitlab.com/omnibus/settings/configuration.html#store-git-data-in-an-alternative-directory
###! **If you want to use a single non-default directory to store git data use a
###!   path that doesn't contain symlinks.**
# git_data_dirs({
#   "default" => {
#     "path" => "/mnt/nfs-01/git-data"
#   }
# })
# Use the same token value configured on all Gitaly servers
gitlab_rails['gitaly_token'] = '            '

git_data_dirs({
  'default' => { 'gitaly_address' => 'tcp://10.0.0.140:8075' },
  'storage1' => { 'gitaly_address' => 'tcp://10.0.0.140:8075' },
})

### Gitaly settings
# gitlab_rails['gitaly_token'] = 'secret token'
```

Figure 15-28. Configuration file changes on the standalone GitLab server to use the new Gitaly service

Verifying GitLab Is Using the New Gitaly Service

Once the GitLab service is back up and running (check with gitlab-ctl status), we can now run one more specialized test to see that GitLab is using the new Gitaly service. This time, we run "sudo gitlab-rake gitlab:gitaly:check" from within the Gitlab server. The results should look like Figure 15-29. If all is working as expected, you should see both default and storage1 return with an OK; otherwise, you may get an error saying that the storage was not found.[19]

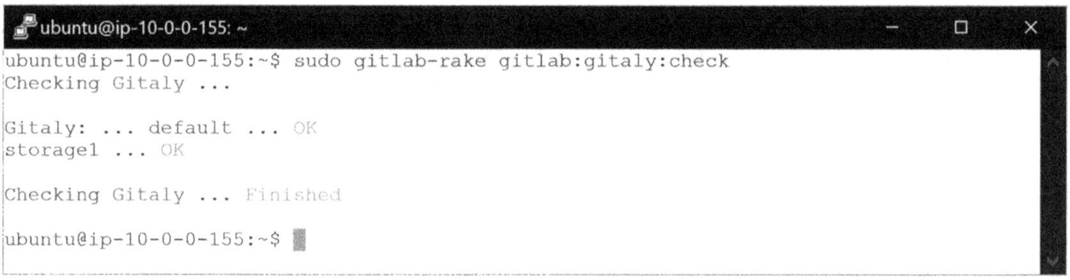

```
ubuntu@ip-10-0-0-155:~$ sudo gitlab-rake gitlab:gitaly:check
Checking Gitaly ...

Gitaly: ... default ... OK
storage1 ... OK

Checking Gitaly ... Finished

ubuntu@ip-10-0-0-155:~$
```

Figure 15-29. *Running gitlab-rake test of connection to Gitaly service from the standalone GitLab server*

Disabling the Internal Gitaly Service

The last step is to disable the internal gitaly service in the GitLab server. This is pretty easy to do as shown in Figure 15-30. Simply find the line with gitaly['enable'], remove the "#", and change the value from true to false. Save and reconfigure. Now when you do a gitlab-ctl status from the GitLab server, you should see that the gitaly service is no longer running. Just for peace of mind, rerun the previous gitlab:gitaly:check rake command to verify that we are still using the standalone Gitaly service.

---

[19] If you get this message, try restarting Gitaly followed by restarting GitLab. You can do this using either the gitlab-ctl reconfigure or gitlab-ctl restart commands.

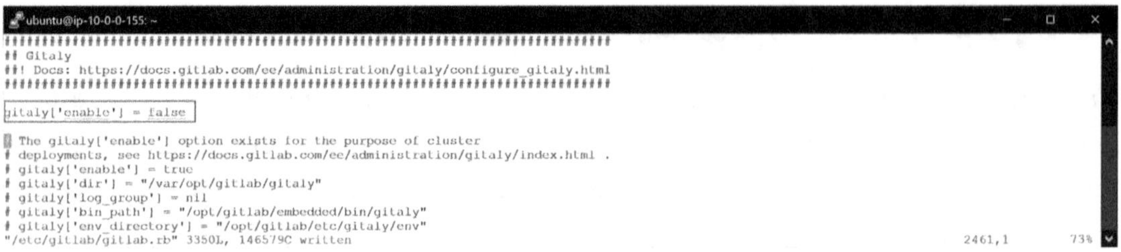

```
# Gitaly
##! Docs: https://docs.gitlab.com/ee/administration/gitaly/configure_gitaly.html
gitaly['enable'] = false
```

Figure 15-30. Configuration file update to disable running of Gitaly service on the standalone GitLab server

Changing Storage Allocations Through the Administrative UI

At this point, I'm going to diverge from the POC documentation and describe how to disable the default storage and enable the storage1 storage. This may seem strange, but control of where data goes is managed via the GitLab administrative UI, not the gitlab.rb configuration file. By default, all Git data will go to the default directory and no data will go anywhere else. We could, of course, have some data go to default and some go to storage1, but current convention is that we disable the default storage. I won't get into why; just trust me on this one.

Let's log in to the GitLab service as root and see how we can change the storage allocations. Figure 15-31 shows the dashboard page for an administrator (which root is) and where we can access the system configuration. On that page, you'll see a "Configure GitLab" area as highlighted in the figure.[20] Click anywhere in that box to get to the configuration page. Alternatively, add /admin to the end of your GitLab URL.

---

[20] Note that the layout of things can change over time as well as the mechanism to access the configuration.

CHAPTER 15   THE PROOF IS IN THE CLOUD

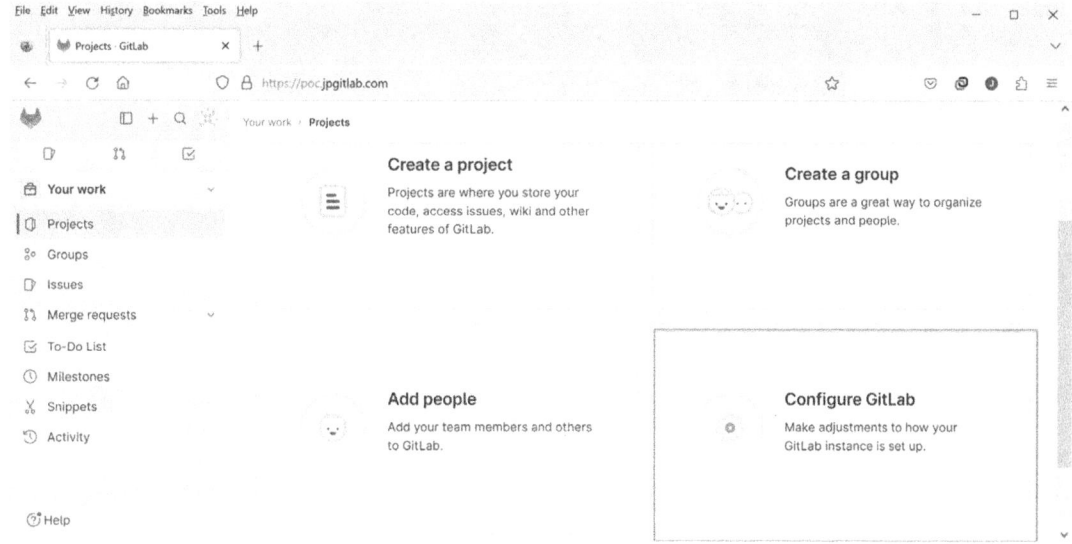

Figure 15-31. *Configure GitLab selection from the standalone GitLab administrative dashboard*

Viewing Gitaly Server Status

Figure 15-32 shows how to view the current set of Gitaly servers. From the "Admin Area" menu on the left-hand side, look for the "Gitaly Servers" link and click that. This is useful for an administrator to verify that the Gitaly servers are accessible and up to date version-wise. As expected, we see the default and storage1 storage names, both of which refer to the same Gitaly server. That gives us a warm fuzzy, but it doesn't tell us how Git data is allocated between them.

651

CHAPTER 15 THE PROOF IS IN THE CLOUD

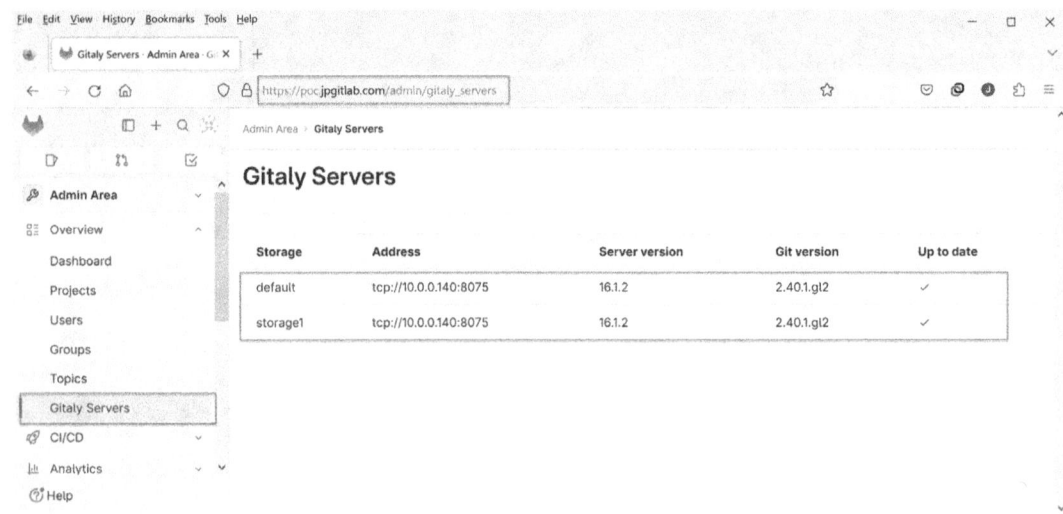

Figure 15-32. Admin Area listing of Gitaly servers

Locating Repository Storage Settings

For that, we need to go into the Settings section and look for Repository as shown in Figure 15-33. You can find this in the Admin Area menu on the left-hand side by expanding the "Settings" submenu and selecting the Repository link as highlighted in the figure. On the right-hand side, you scroll down to find the "Repository storage" section, which by default is collapsed. Select the Expand button to view the configuration settings.

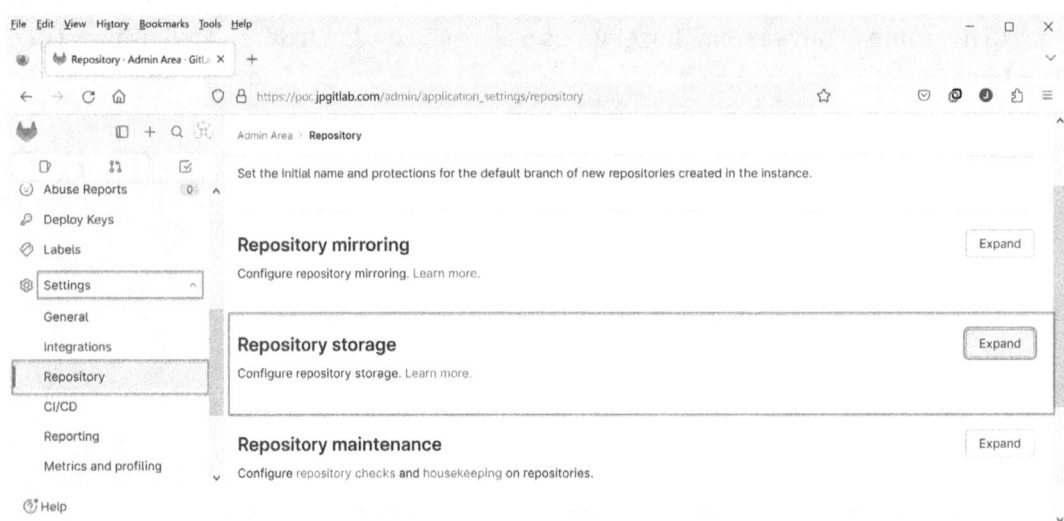

Figure 15-33. Selecting the repository storage section of Admin Area repository settings

CHAPTER 15   THE PROOF IS IN THE CLOUD

Changing Storage Weights for New Repositories

Within the "Repository storage" section, you'll see a section entitled "Storage nodes for new repositories" as shown in Figure 15-34. The settings are initially set with default set at 100 and all other storages such as storage1 set to 0. As the name of this section implies, any new Git repositories will always go to the default storage area. We want to change these settings to 0 for default and 100 for storage1. For these changes to take effect, you need to use the "Save changes" button just below this section (not shown in the figure).

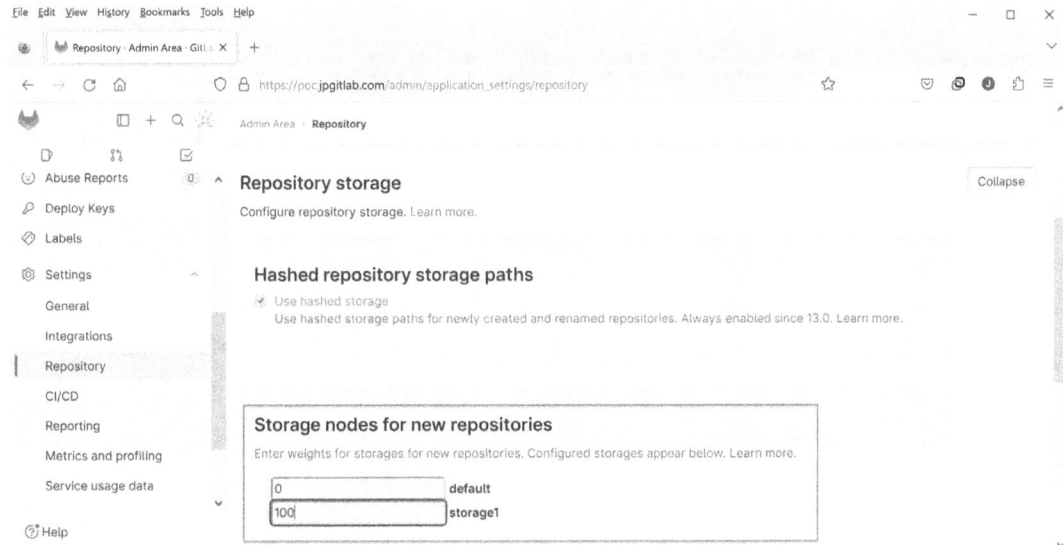

Figure 15-34. Disabling default repository storage by changing storage node weights

A Note About Gitaly Storage Weights

Since no Git repositories have been created yet, this change will essentially disable the default storage. What is important to note here is that nothing changes for any existing repositories; any repository that was stored in the default storage will remain there. So, these weights don't affect the distribution of repositories already in a storage area, only how new repositories will be distributed. If you notice that a storage area is getting filled up, you can either increase the disk space used by that storage area or create a new storage space and redirect new repositories to that one.

Before we consider how to spin up a cluster of GitLab servers, there is another problem regarding SSH host keys that we tackle in the next section.

653

CHAPTER 15   THE PROOF IS IN THE CLOUD

Configuring Server-Side SSH

Because our GitLab service will be accepting SSH requests for Git operations, the GitLab server relies on a server-side SSH service separate from the gitlab service. This is a standard Linux service typically referred to as sshd;[21] it is not something the GitLab team created, so you won't see this service displayed via the gitlab-ctl status command. We will need to make some configuration changes for sshd due to the way AWS prepares the service when a new server is spun up.

A Description of SSH Server Host Keys

The SSH service uses what are called host keys. These keys are used the first time an SSH client connects to the SSH service on the GitLab server. You've seen this in action when you first connected to a server via ssh. You will get prompted to accept the host key. When you accept, this key is stored in the home directory's .ssh/known_hosts file. Thereafter, any time you connect to the GitLab server, SSH will verify that the host key returned by the GitLab server matches the host key in the known_hosts file. If it does, SSH trusts that the server is legitimate and will connect with you. If not, you will get a "man-in-the-middle" warning, and SSH will prevent you from connecting to the GitLab server.

The Need for Consistent Host Keys Across Multiple GitLab Servers

In practice, every server that you connect to will have a unique host key.[22] This is a standard practice to ensure security across multiple servers. If there is a breach to one remote server with a given host key, you won't be able to use the same host key to gain access to another remote server. AWS enables this behavior by generating a unique host key whenever a new EC2 instance is created. This is a good thing security-wise.

---

[21] The term sshd is shorthand for ssh daemon. In the Linux/Unix world, a daemon is a background process that starts up automatically when the server is booted up and remains running all the time unless explicitly stopped.

[22] Actually, there is a set of host keys differentiated by encryption algorithms such as rsa, ed25519, etc.

Here's the problem. If we want to scale our GitLab service by using multiple GitLab servers to handle the load, those servers will have to use the same host key. Otherwise, when you first connect to a GitLab server chosen via the load balancer, you'll accept that server's host key. The next time you use Git, however, the load balancer might take you to a different GitLab server. If it doesn't use the same host key as the first one, GitLab will fail doing a Git operation via SSH.

Bad Approaches to Man-in-the-Middle Messages

There are a number of ways to handle this, some of which are bad practices. If we allow each server to have their own host keys, one of two things will happen from each user's client side. One approach that users use is to simply delete the GitLab host entry in the known_hosts file and reconfirm the host key when making the connection. This gets annoying (because the man-in-the-middle message will eventually occur again) and sometimes leads to panic. To avoid these messages, what some users end up doing is disable host key checking for the GitLab service. This is really not a good idea even in a private corporate environment but especially with a public-facing GitLab service; perhaps there really is a man-in-the-middle attack made against your GitLab service.

The SSH-Approved Approach Using Host Certificates

From the server side of things, there are a couple of approaches to take. The SSH-approved way of dealing with multiple servers is to use host certificates. I've used this approach myself in a corporate environment. I won't go over the process here since it involves a number of steps to get it set up properly. If you are interested in this approach, check out the web article at https://smallstep.com/blog/use-ssh-certificates/ entitled "If you are not using SSH certificates, you're doing SSH wrong."[23] This approach works well except that you need to tell your users how to configure the known_hosts file in order to use the host certificate; otherwise, you will end up with users falling back to the "bad" approaches because they'll get the man-in-the-middle message if they don't update their known_hosts file correctly.

---

[23] Yes, it's an opinionated article, but it clearly goes through the steps of how and why to configure a host certificate.

CHAPTER 15 THE PROOF IS IN THE CLOUD

GitLab's Approach Using Static Host Keys

The approach I describe here is the same as the one described in the POC documentation and is one used by GitLab itself for its SaaS offering.[24] What we are going to do is make a copy of the host keys in our standalone GitLab server and update the SSH configuration file to use those copied keys. AWS will still generate new host keys as usual, but we will be ignoring them. So here goes.

First, ssh into the GitLab server as user ubuntu via a bastion host as usual. You'll then create the /etc/ssh_static directory and copy all the files from /etc/ssh into that directory. Figure 15-35 shows the results. I threw in the ls command to list the contents of the new /etc/ssh_static directory to verify the files were copied. Technically, we only need the ssh_host* files.

```
ubuntu@ip-10-0-0-155:~$ sudo mkdir /etc/ssh_static
ubuntu@ip-10-0-0-155:~$ sudo cp -R /etc/ssh/* /etc/ssh_static
ubuntu@ip-10-0-0-155:~$ ls -l /etc/ssh_static
total 576
-rw-r--r-- 1 root root 535195 Jul 26 17:53 moduli
-rw-r--r-- 1 root root   1603 Jul 26 17:53 ssh_config
drwxr-xr-x 2 root root   4096 Jul 26 17:53 ssh_config.d
-rw------- 1 root root   1393 Jul 26 17:53 ssh_host_dsa_key
-rw-r--r-- 1 root root    608 Jul 26 17:53 ssh_host_dsa_key.pub
-rw------- 1 root root    513 Jul 26 17:53 ssh_host_ecdsa_key
-rw-r--r-- 1 root root    180 Jul 26 17:53 ssh_host_ecdsa_key.pub
-rw------- 1 root root    411 Jul 26 17:53 ssh_host_ed25519_key
-rw-r--r-- 1 root root    100 Jul 26 17:53 ssh_host_ed25519_key.pub
-rw------- 1 root root   2602 Jul 26 17:53 ssh_host_rsa_key
-rw-r--r-- 1 root root    572 Jul 26 17:53 ssh_host_rsa_key.pub
-rw-r--r-- 1 root root    342 Jul 26 17:53 ssh_import_id
-rw-r--r-- 1 root root   3287 Jul 26 17:53 sshd_config
drwxr-xr-x 2 root root   4096 Jul 26 17:53 sshd_config.d
ubuntu@ip-10-0-0-155:~$
```

Figure 15-35. Creation of /etc/ssh_static directory on the standalone GitLab server

Next, we need to update the /etc/ssh/sshd_config file (**not** the ssh_config file). Figure 15-36 shows the changes to be made. In this file, we uncomment the HostKey lines and change /etc/ssh to /etc/ssh_static. Note that later versions of openssh no longer use the ssh_host_dsa_key, so that is left off the HostKey list. In case you are wondering, we don't need to restart the SSH service, although you can by running "sudo service sshd reload."

---

[24] I mean, you didn't have to set up a host certificate to use gitlab.com, now did you?

CHAPTER 15   THE PROOF IS IN THE CLOUD

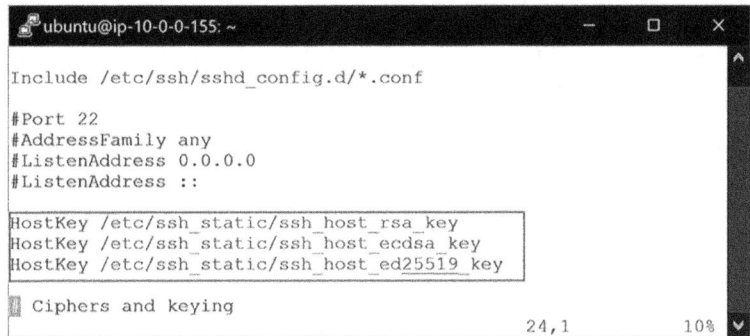

Figure 15-36. *Update to host keys in the /etc/ssh/sshd_config file on the standalone GitLab server*

Enabling Fast Lookup of Authorized SSH Keys

Since we are on the topic of SSH, there is one more thing we need to configure: fast lookup of authorized SSH keys. As you may recall, users can register their keys for use with Git over SSH. GitLab needs to be able to look up these keys whenever a user invokes Git with SSH. By default, these keys are stored in an authorized keys file on the GitLab server. Not only does this slow access down significantly when there are a lot of users, this file is not shared across multiple GitLab servers, which is what we want to achieve. Fortunately, GitLab provides a way to store these user keys in the PostgreSQL database instead of a single authorized_keys file.

To enable this feature, we have to first update the /etc/ssh/sshd_config file on the GitLab server. Figure 15-37 shows the lines to add to the sshd_config file. You can find the exact lines to copy in the GitLab documentation by doing a web search on "GitLab fast ssh key lookup." The lines tell SSH to run a script provided by GitLab to perform the search.

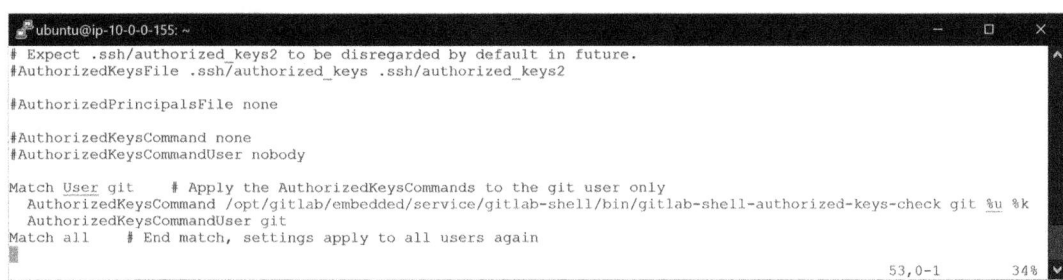

Figure 15-37. *Updating /etc/ssh/sshd_config to enable GitLab fast ssh key lookup*

CHAPTER 15   THE PROOF IS IN THE CLOUD

Once the fast key lookup is enabled on the sshd side, we need to disable lookups using the authorized_keys file. For this, you need to log in to your GitLab service and go to the Admin Area menu as described in the previous section. From there, you need to expand the Settings section in the left-hand pane[25] and select Network as shown in Figure 15-38. As part of the Network settings, you should find a "Performance optimization" section. Expand that and the first option you see should be the "Use authorized_keys file to authenticate SSH keys." This will be checked by default. Uncheck this option as shown in the figure and save the changes using the "Save changes" button just below this section. You may need to scroll down to find the button. At this point, the database will always be used to authenticate the user's SSH keys.

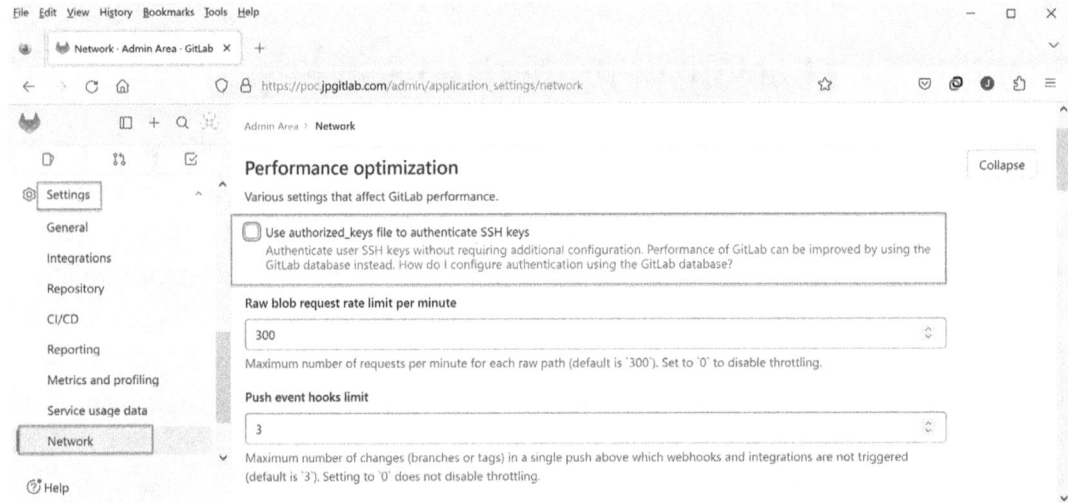

Figure 15-38. *Disable the use of the authorized keys file via Admin Area network settings*

There is one more thing to tackle before we can scale up our GitLab servers, which we'll discuss in the next section: S3 object storage.

---

[25] If you don't see a left-hand pane, stretch the web page horizontally until it shows up.

Enabling S3 Object Storage

There are binary objects such as artifacts and registry packages that need to be stored somewhere. The PostgreSQL database doesn't handle varying-sized binary objects very well, and neither the Redis nor Gitaly services are designed for long-term storage of these types of objects. By default, GitLab stores these in the filesystem under the /var/opt/gitlab/gitlab-rails/shared directory. Of course, this doesn't work in a horizontally scaled environment, so we need to deal with these objects specially.

A Possible Storage Approach Using NFS

One approach is to use an NFS service that mounts the /var/opt/gitlab/gitlab-rails/shared directory. This is certainly doable and is something I've done early on in my managing of GitLab services. In AWS, there is the Elastic File Service (EFS) that can handle this without you having to spin up a new server and installing NFS software on it. EFS has some benefits in that it can replicate its services across multiple availability zones and can be used with its backup service. A disadvantage is that it can be slow at times and is not recommended by the GitLab team.[26]

Another Approach Using S3 Object Storage

For some cloud services such as AWS, GitLab has provided a way to store these objects in their cloud-provided file storage such as S3. This is the approach I describe for our GitLab POC. I should warn you that configuring GitLab object store can be a tad tricky to get right. One issue is that starting in 2023, AWS requires that S3 storage be encrypted; the GitLab POC assumes that encryption is optional. It took me a couple of days to get this right; to save you the grief, I'll describe the process that worked for me.

Creating the KMS Encryption Key

To use S3 encryption, we need to first create a key using the Key Management Service (KMS). This is easy to find by doing a service search for KMS. It can also be found under the Security, Identity, and Compliance services category. Under "Customer managed

---

[26] With that said, I've used it successfully in small- to medium-sized environments.

CHAPTER 15   THE PROOF IS IN THE CLOUD

keys," there is a "Create key" button that takes you to the "Configure key" page as shown in Figure 15-39. Here, we keep the key type as Symmetric and key usage as "Encrypt and decrypt."

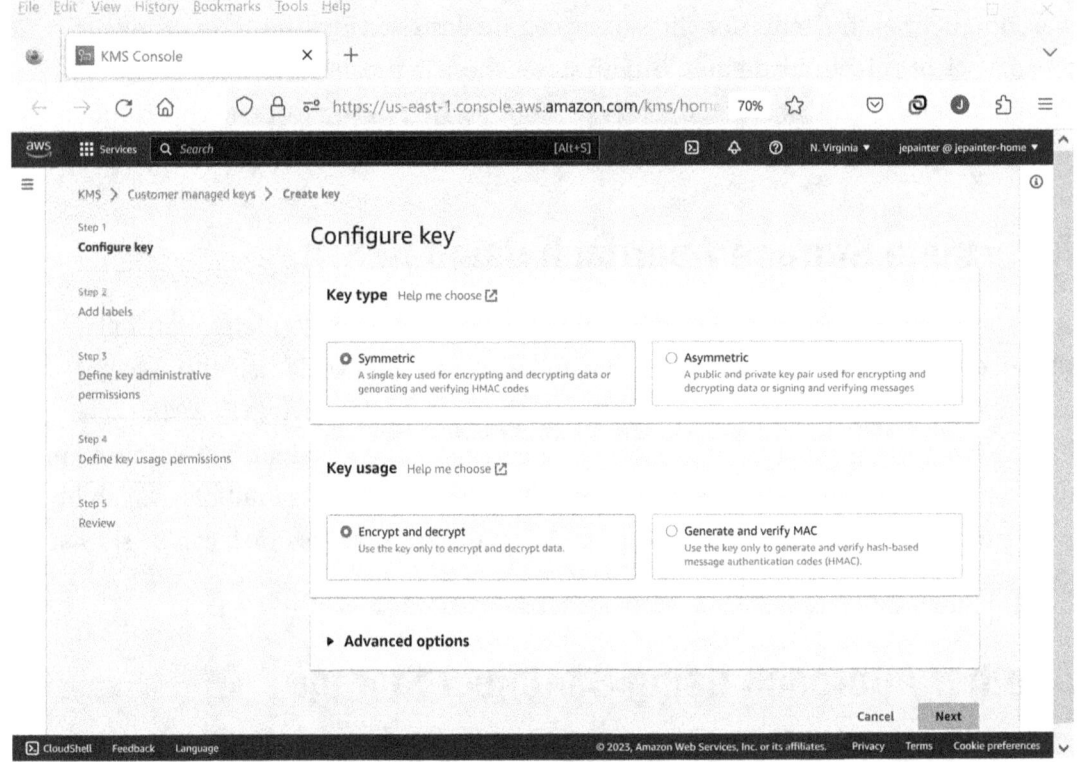

Figure 15-39.   *Configuring the KMS key via the Key Management Service*

Selecting Next takes us to the "Add labels" page as shown in Figure 15-40. In this example, I set the alias to gitlab-s3-key and added an appropriate comment.

CHAPTER 15 THE PROOF IS IN THE CLOUD

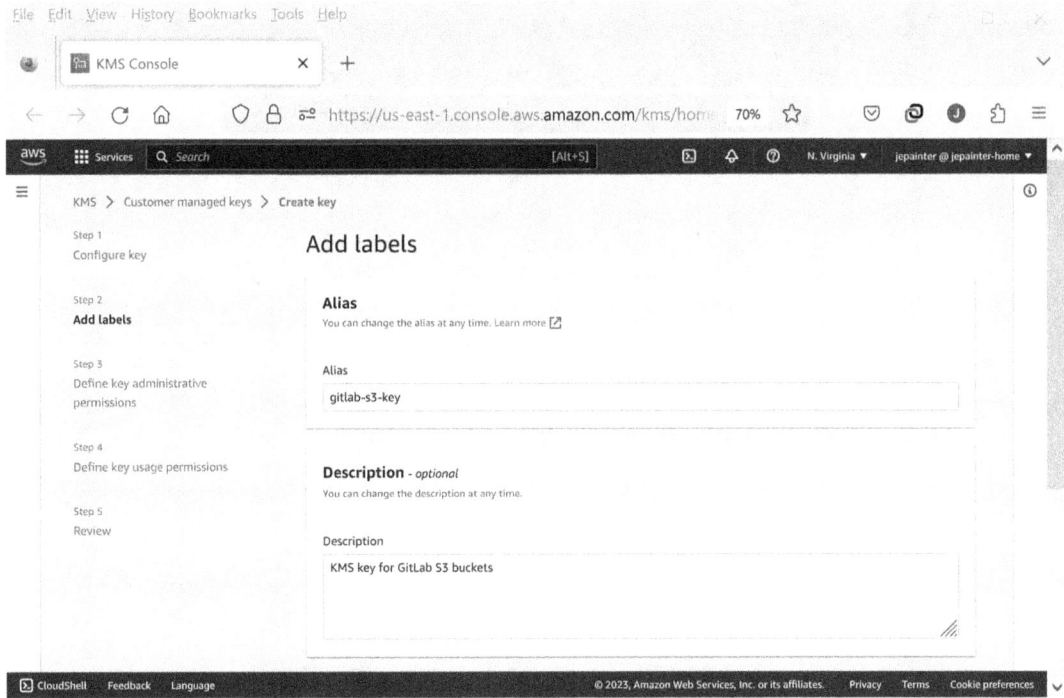

Figure 15-40. Adding labels to the KMS key

Specifying Who Can View and Make Changes to the KMS Key

The next page shown in Figure 15-41 allows us to specify who can view and make changes to the key. In this example, I chose myself and the GitLabS3Access IAM role we created earlier. If there are other administrative users, you can add them here as well or add them in the future. Note that I didn't need to add the GitLabS3Access role, but it was important to add at least one person as an administrator.

CHAPTER 15   THE PROOF IS IN THE CLOUD

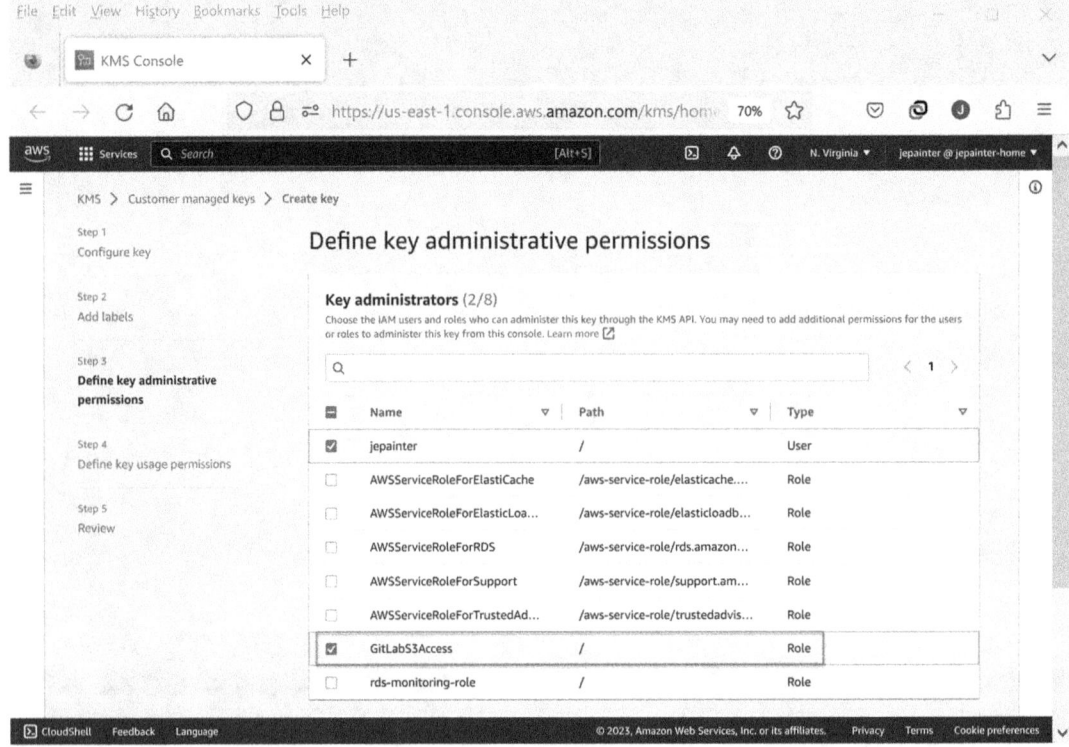

Figure 15-41. Selecting administrative permissions to the KMS key

Specifying Who Can Use the KMS Key

In addition to who can administer the key, we need to specify who can use the key as shown in Figure 15-42. As with the previous page, I selected myself and the GitLabS3Access IAM role. Note that I didn't need to add myself, but it was important to add the GitLabS3Access role as GitLab will need to access the key.

CHAPTER 15   THE PROOF IS IN THE CLOUD

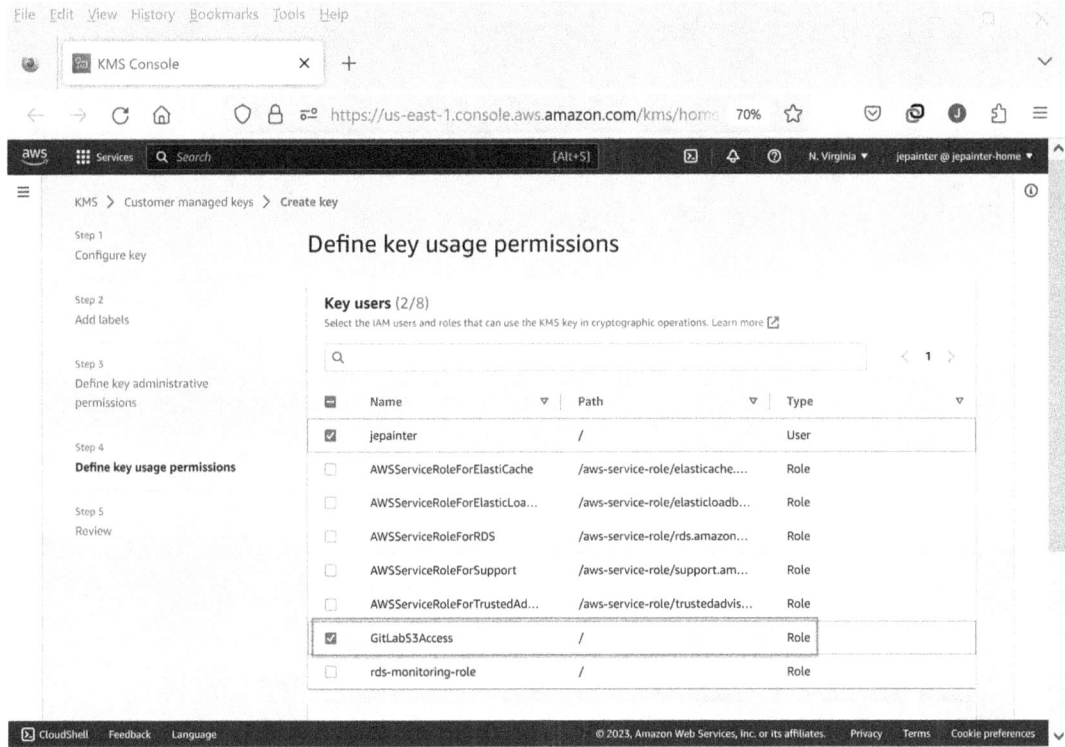

Figure 15-42.   Selecting usage permissions to the KMS key

Reviewing and Creating the KMS Key

The last step in the key definition is to review and create the key (not shown here). Once created, you should see the key in the customer managed key list. Selecting the key, you should see details of the key as shown in Figure 15-43. The important piece of information is the key's Amazon Resource Name (ARN), which you'll need in the GitLab configuration.

CHAPTER 15   THE PROOF IS IN THE CLOUD

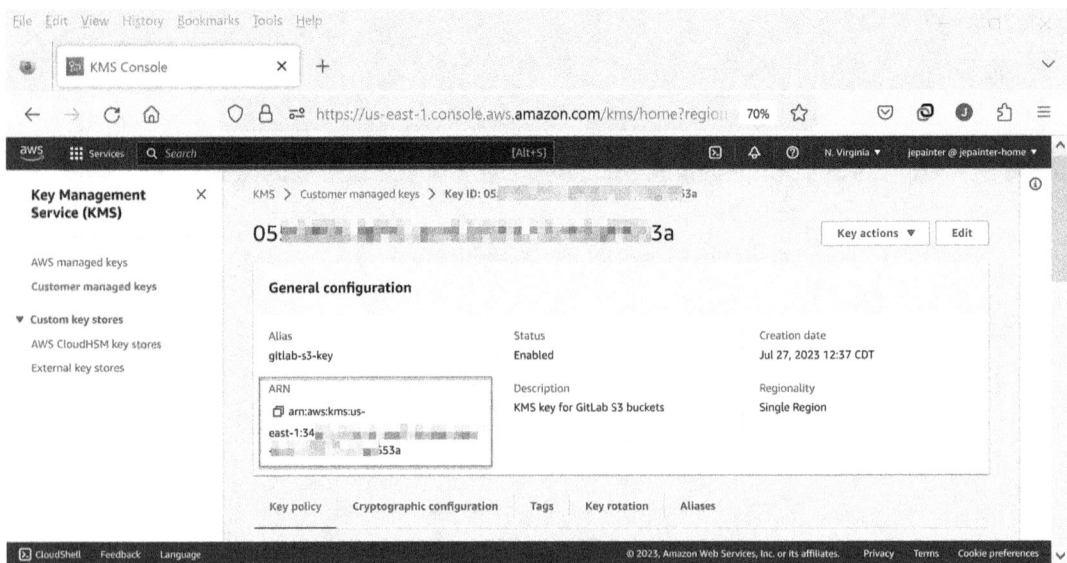

Figure 15-43. *Detail view of the KMS key after creation*

Creating the S3 Buckets

Now that our KMS key is created, we can now proceed to creating the S3 object store buckets.[27] If you go to the S3 service, you'll see the "Create bucket" button as shown in Figure 15-44. Note that I already created the jpgitlab-poc-uploads bucket already.

---

[27] Note that it is unclear from the GitLab documentation whether we are supposed to create the buckets or not. It doesn't say either way. Given that the IAM role does not have the CreateBucket permission set, I'm of the opinion that we need to create them manually. In any case, it is what I used to do as part of automation scripts, so it doesn't hurt.

CHAPTER 15   THE PROOF IS IN THE CLOUD

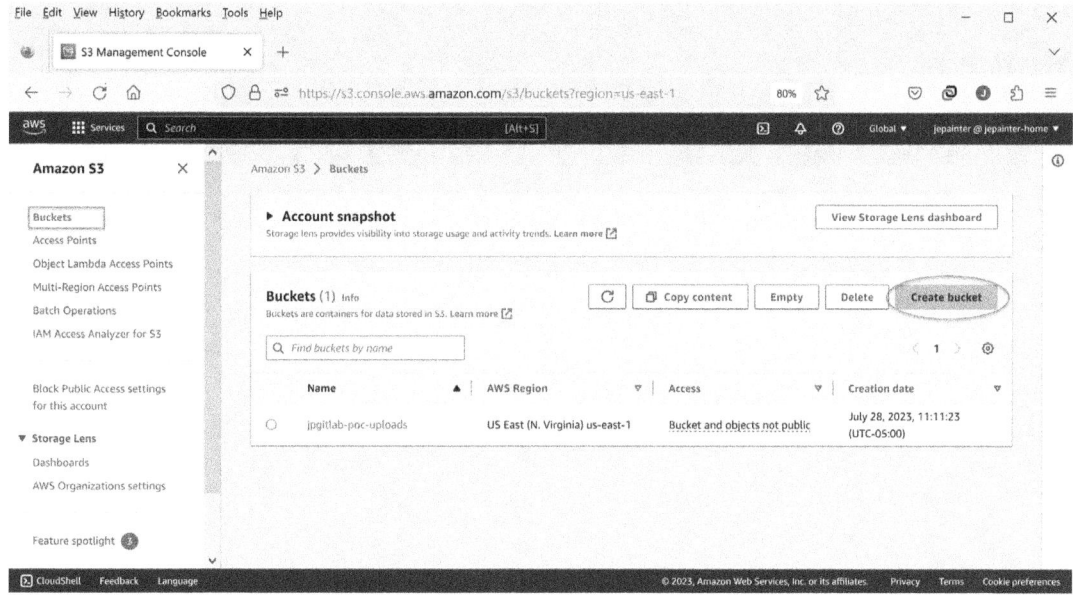

Figure 15-44. *S3 option to create a bucket*

Setting General Configuration Options

Figure 15-45 shows the top of the "Create bucket" page. Here, we specify the name of the bucket to be created, which in this example is jpgitlab-poc-artifacts. Note that S3 bucket names have to be unique across all AWS accounts, so you won't be able to use the same name as presented here. You also select the region where the bucket will reside; note that you won't need to (nor can you) specify an availability zone. For the first bucket, you'll need to scroll down and set the other configurations as we'll do shortly. Thereafter, you can create the remaining buckets using the "Choose bucket" button.

665

CHAPTER 15   THE PROOF IS IN THE CLOUD

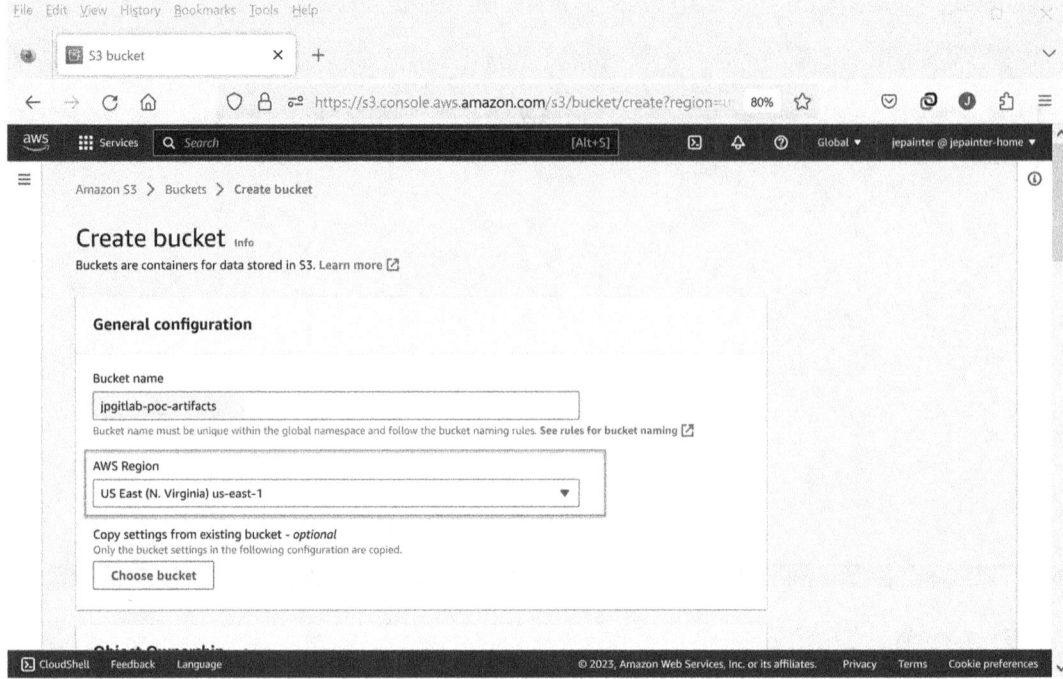

Figure 15-45.   S3 bucket general configuration

Configuring Object Ownership Settings

Next up is the Ownership configuration, which we keep set to the defaults shown in Figure 15-46. We don't plan on sharing this bucket outside of our environment, so we don't need to set any Access Control Lists (ACLs). And since this bucket will not be exposed to the public, we keep the "Block all public access" checked as shown.

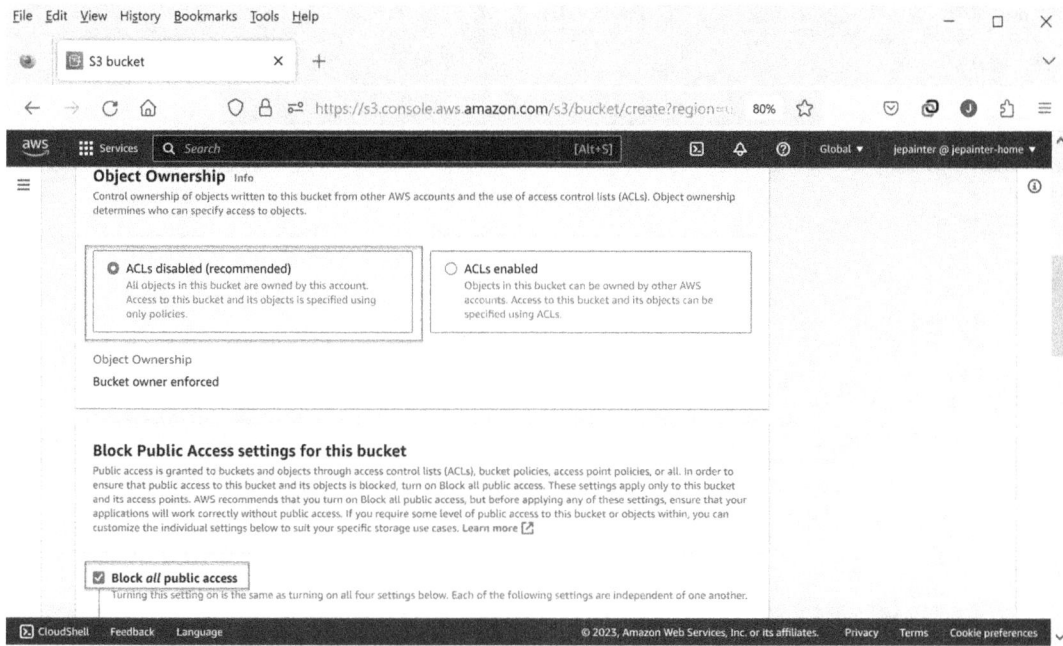

Figure 15-46. *S3 bucket object ownership configuration*

Disabling Bucket Versioning

Likewise, we keep the Bucket Versioning options set to their defaults as shown in Figure 15-47. In other words, we don't want versioning to be applied. GitLab will handle all of that for us, if needed. As for tags, I didn't create any in this example. You can always add them later on if you need to.

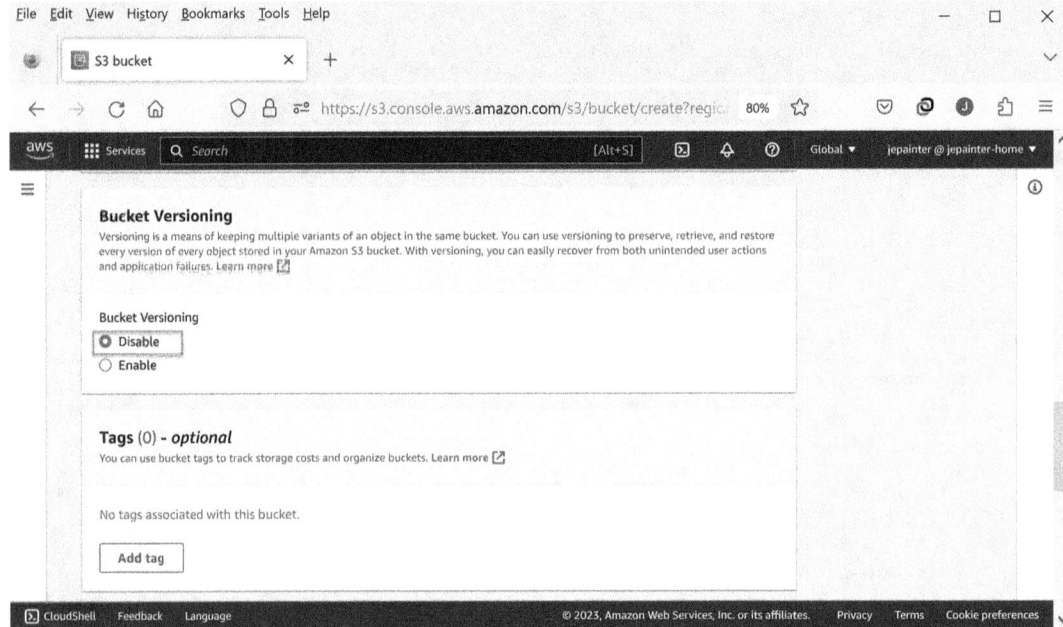

***Figure 15-47.** S3 bucket versioning configuration*

Setting Encryption Options

So far, it's been pretty easy since we've stuck with defaults and only had to specify the bucket name and region. We won't be so lucky with the encryption settings as shown in Figure 15-48. For encryption type, we don't want to use the default setting of Amazon S3 managed keys; we want to select the AWS KMS keys instead. This is what GitLab will need to use in its configuration settings. When you select the SSE-KMS option, you'll see additional items regarding the AWS KMS key show up in the form. Since we already created the key, we'll select the "Choose from your AWS KMS keys" option and then pick the KMS key we just created earlier. I kept the Bucket Key option enabled.[28]

---

[28] To be honest, I don't know what this does exactly, but it doesn't appear to effect GitLab operations, so why not.

CHAPTER 15   THE PROOF IS IN THE CLOUD

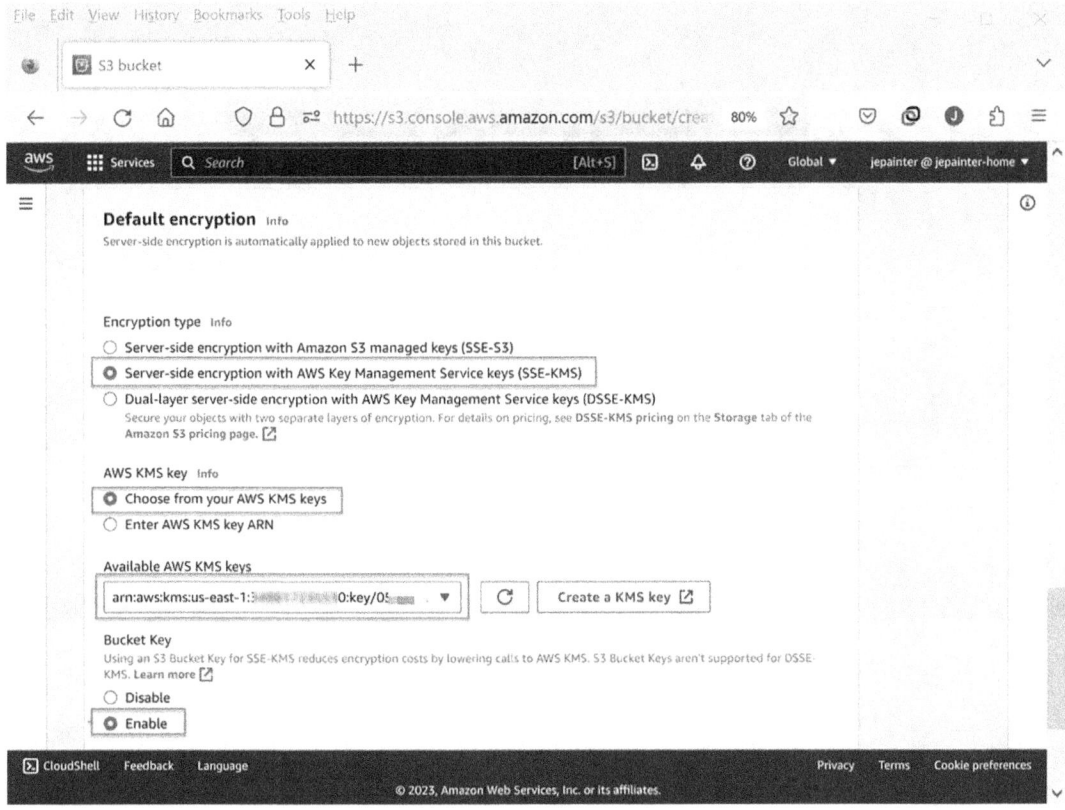

Figure 15-48. S3 bucket encryption configuration

Creating the Object Store Buckets

At this point, you can create the bucket. When done, it should show up in the S3 list of buckets. You'll need to create a total of nine buckets as shown in Figure 15-49. To simplify the creation of the remaining buckets, use the "Choose bucket" button as shown in Figure 15-45. Use the prefix you have selected and make sure the suffixes after the jpgitlab-poc prefix match exactly the suffixes in the diagram. The names of these buckets will be used in the GitLab configuration.

669

CHAPTER 15   THE PROOF IS IN THE CLOUD

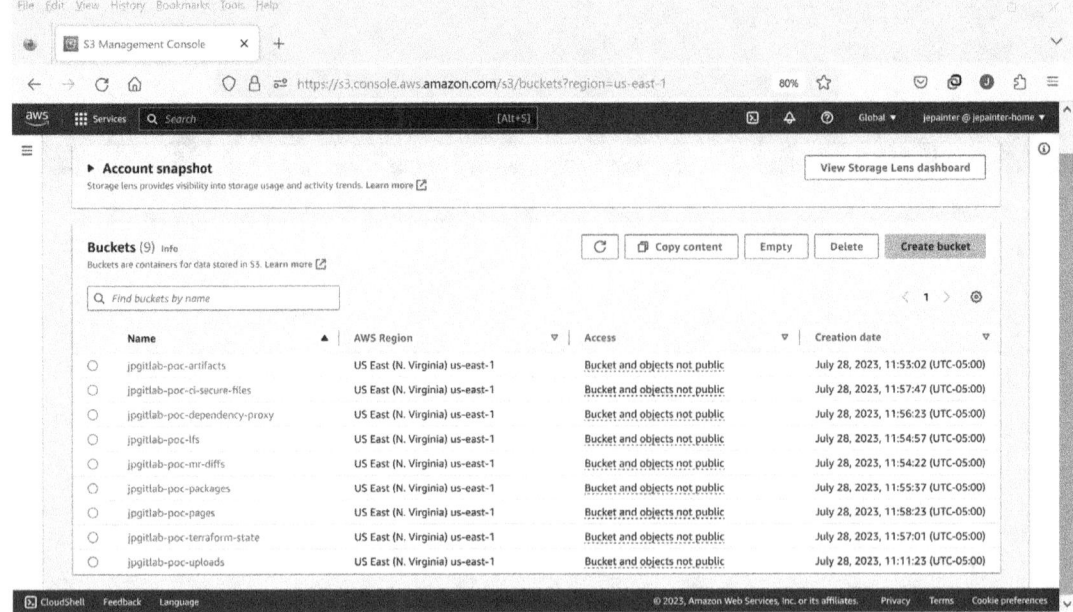

Figure 15-49. S3 listing of GitLab-specific buckets

Setting the Server IAM Role to Allow Access to the S3 Object Store

With the S3 buckets in place, we are now ready to configure the GitLab server to use them. First, we need to set the server's IAM role. Figure 15-50 shows how to do this. From the EC2 server list, select the GitLab server. Then from the Action drop-down menu, select Security ➤ Modify IAM role.

CHAPTER 15   THE PROOF IS IN THE CLOUD

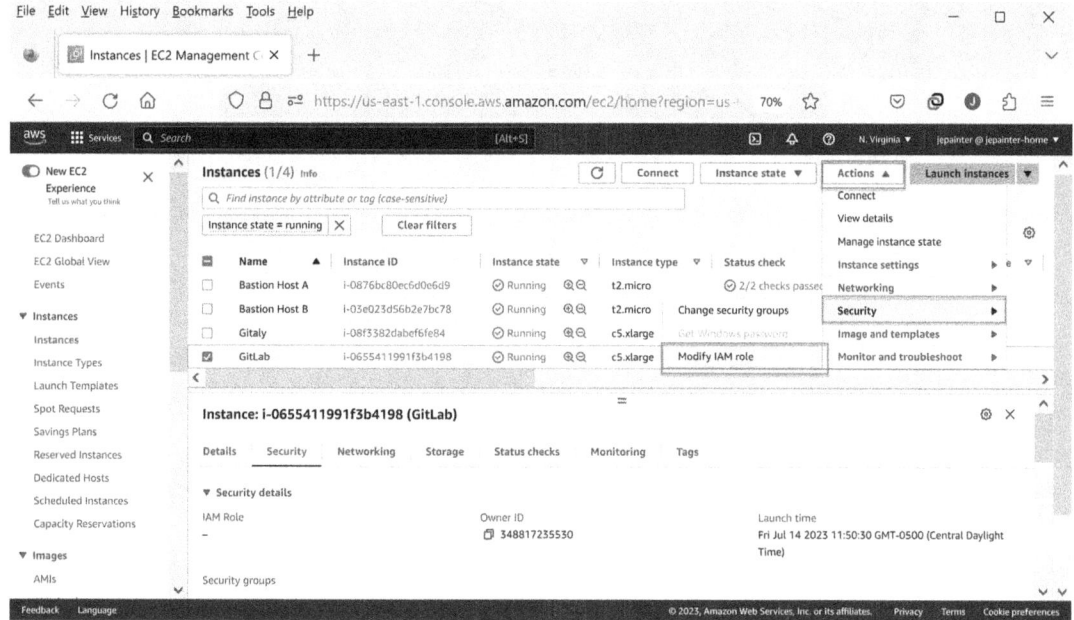

Figure 15-50. *EC2 instance option to modify the IAM role for the standalone GitLab server*

This takes you to the "Modify IAM role" page as shown in Figure 15-51. Simply select the GitLabS3Access role from the drop-down list and use the "Update IAM role" button to save the change. Note that unlike security groups, a server can have no more than one IAM role attached.

671

CHAPTER 15   THE PROOF IS IN THE CLOUD

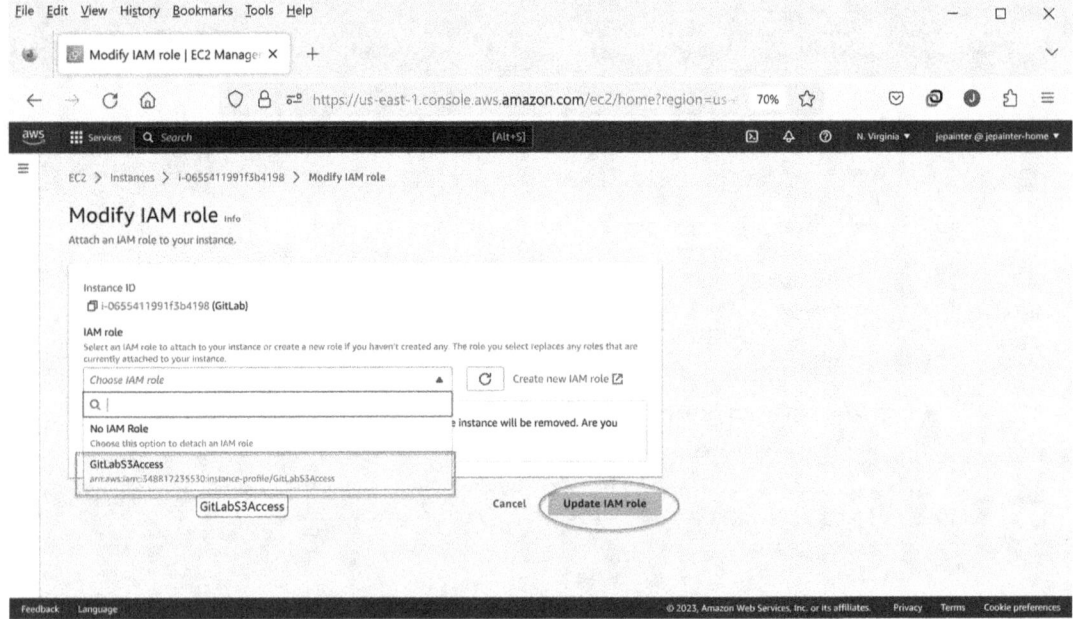

Figure 15-51. Selection of the IAM role to use for the standalone GitLab server

Verifying the IAM Role Is Attached to the Standalone GitLab Server

You can verify that the GitLabS3Access role is attached to the GitLab server by selecting it from the instance list and looking under the Security tab. Figure 15-52 shows where the IAM role is located under the security details. Note that we don't need to set the IAM role for the Gitaly server since it will not be accessing the S3 object store buckets.

CHAPTER 15   THE PROOF IS IN THE CLOUD

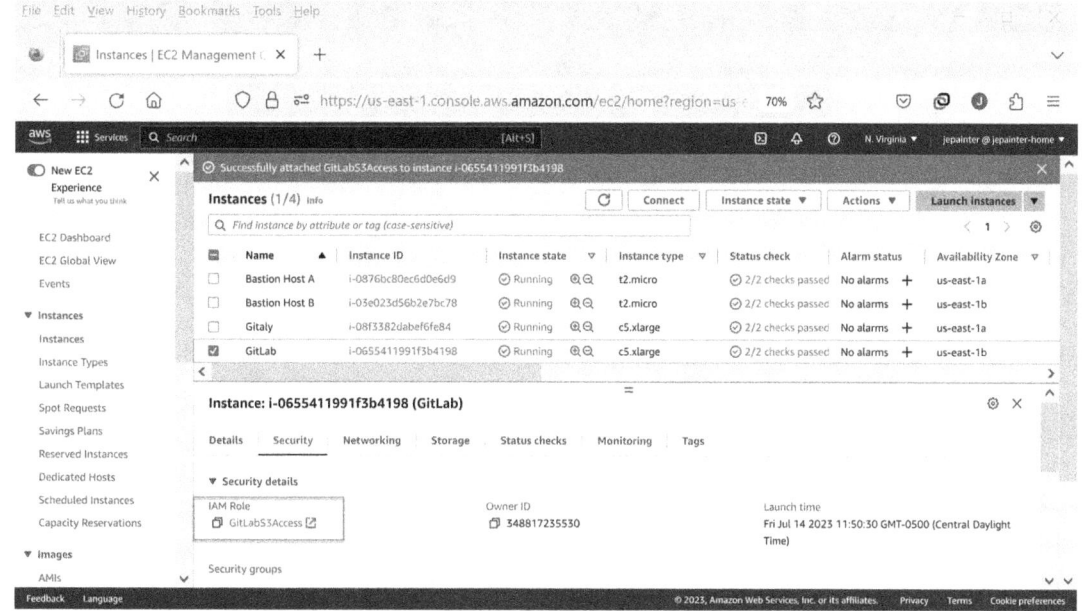

Figure 15-52. EC2 security settings view of the GitLab server to verify the S3 IAM role

Configuring GitLab to Use the S3 Object Storage

The final step is to ssh into the GitLab server and update the gitlab.rb file. The changes to be made are shown in Figure 15-53. In this example, I am using the consolidated form as described in the GitLab documentation found at https://docs.gitlab.com/ee/administration/object_storage.html. Since we have the IAM role attached to the GitLab server, I am using the use_iam_profile option set to true. For the object_store storage_options, I am using server_side_encryption set to "aws:kms" and the key ID set to the ARN of the KMS key we defined earlier. For the bucket names, I am using my prefix of jpgitlab-poc; the suffixes were obtained from the list of commented out bucket names.[29]

---

[29] There is one additional suffix for ci_secure_files that was not listed in the GitLab documentation. The commented section in gitlab.rb takes precedence over the documentation. Note that you may find new object stores defined for your version, so create those buckets as needed.

673

```
# Consolidated object storage configuration
gitlab_rails['object_store']['enabled'] = true
gitlab_rails['object_store']['proxy_download'] = true
gitlab_rails['object_store']['connection'] = {
  'provider' => 'AWS',
  'region' => 'us-east-1',
  'use_iam_profile' => true
}
gitlab_rails['object_store']['storage_options'] = {
  'server_side_encryption' => 'aws:kms',
  'server_side_encryption_kms_key_id' => 'arn:aws:kms:us-east-1:34                              3a'
}
gitlab_rails['object_store']['objects']['artifacts']['bucket'] = 'jpgitlab-poc-artifacts'
gitlab_rails['object_store']['objects']['external_diffs']['bucket'] = 'jpgitlab-poc-mr-diffs'
gitlab_rails['object_store']['objects']['lfs']['bucket'] = 'jpgitlab-poc-lfs'
gitlab_rails['object_store']['objects']['uploads']['bucket'] = 'jpgitlab-poc-uploads'
gitlab_rails['object_store']['objects']['packages']['bucket'] = 'jpgitlab-poc-packages'
gitlab_rails['object_store']['objects']['dependency_proxy']['bucket'] = 'jpgitlab-poc-dependency-proxy'
gitlab_rails['object_store']['objects']['terraform_state']['bucket'] = 'jpgitlab-poc-terraform-state'
gitlab_rails['object_store']['objects']['ci_secure_files']['bucket'] = 'jpgitlab-poc-ci-secure-files'
gitlab_rails['object_store']['objects']['pages']['bucket'] = 'jpgitlab-poc-pages'
```

Figure 15-53. GitLab configuration updates to use S3 buckets

As usual, with the gitlab.rb file changes saved, rerun the sudo gitlab-ctl reconfigure command for them to take effect. If you want to test that the object storage refers to the S3 buckets, log in to your GitLab service via your web browser and upload a new photo for your avatar. If all went correctly, you should see the avatar.png file in the S3 uploads bucket under user/avatar/1 (assuming you set the avatar for user root). If you don't see this file, try running sudo gitlab-rake "gitlab:uploads:migrate:all" while logged in to the GitLab server and wait a few minutes to see if the file shows up. If not, make sure the IAM profile is attached, that the use_iam_profile option is set in the gitlab.rb file, and that the name of the uploads bucket matches the S3 uploads bucket name; also, check that the IAM policy uses the prefix for your S3 buckets.

And with the S3 object storage out of the way, we are ready to scale our GitLab service, which we tackle in the next section.

Scaling the GitLab Service

We are now ready to horizontally scale our GitLab service. As you've seen, there was a lot to do in preparation of this moment. Some of the steps involved setting up AWS services that only needed to be done once, such as the RDS database, the Gitaly server, and the S3 object store buckets. The remaining steps involved configuring the gitlab.rb file to use those services. To enable horizontal scaling, we need a way to create duplicate GitLab servers that are configured similarly to use those AWS services.

CHAPTER 15   THE PROOF IS IN THE CLOUD

Although we can set up a system that spins up an EC2 instance and configures it "on the fly," the recommended approach is to create our own AMI with the configuration already in place. This allows us to spin up our GitLab servers quickly without waiting on the configuration process to finish. This is done by creating an AMI based on our already existing standalone GitLab server.

Creating Our Own GitLab Server AMI

Generating the AMI turns out to be a simple process. As shown in Figure 15-54, you simply select the instance from which to create the image, and from the Action menu, select "Image and templates ➤ Create image." This will bring up a form as shown in Figure 15-55. All you really need to do is specify a name for the AMI and a description for it. In this example, I include the date the AMI is created so that I can differentiate it from future GitLab AMIs. Note that the "No reboot" Enable option is left unchecked. This is a confusing double negative setting that simply means that the server will be temporarily stopped while the image is taking place and then be rebooted afterward. We keep all other settings at their default and select the "Create instance" button (not shown) to start the creation process.

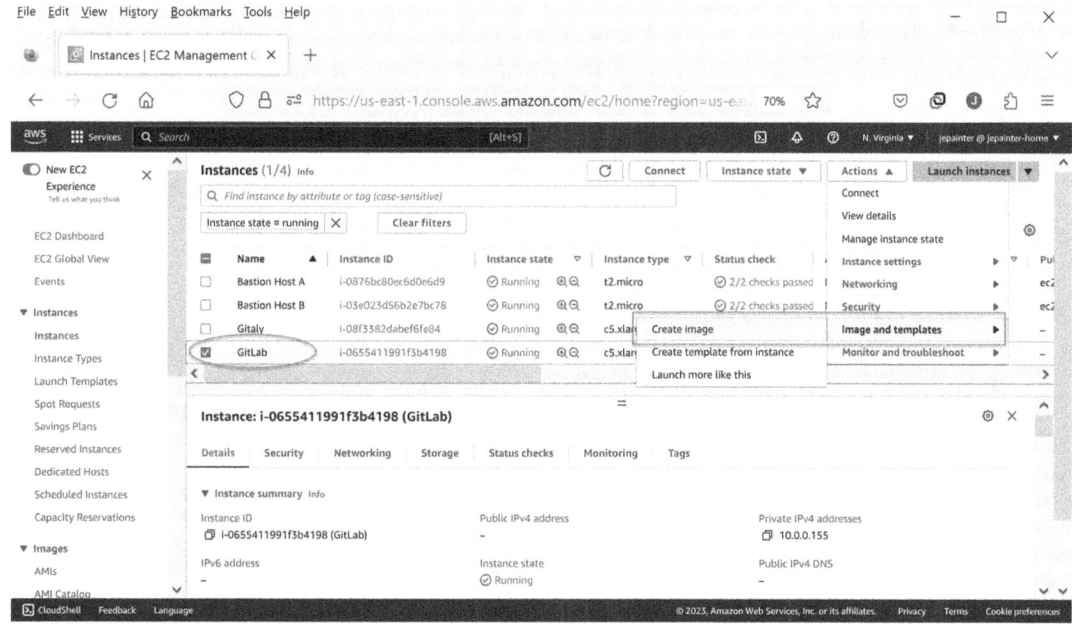

Figure 15-54. *EC2 creation of AMI from the standalone GitLab server*

CHAPTER 15   THE PROOF IS IN THE CLOUD

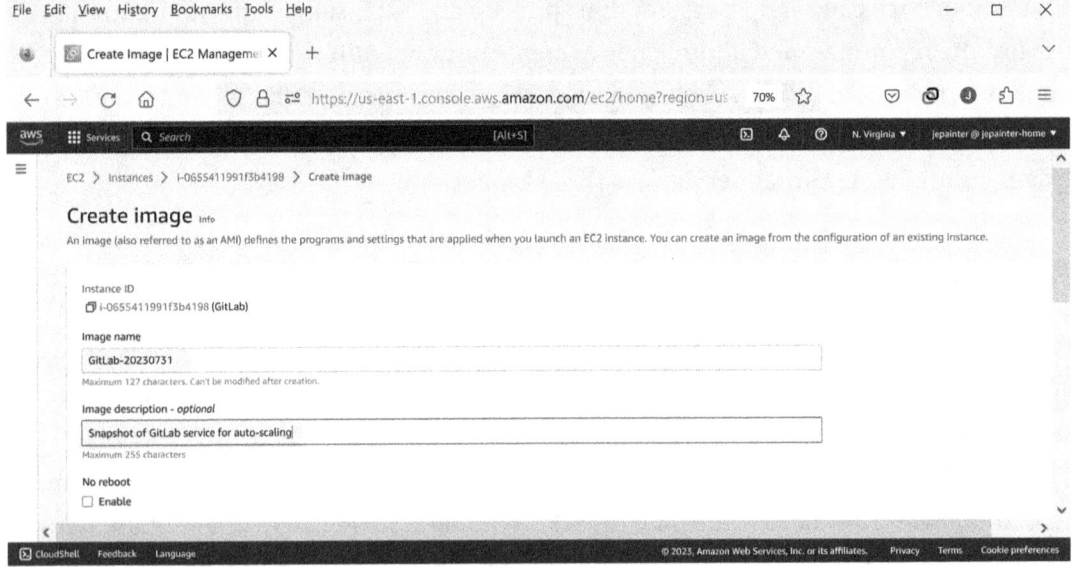

Figure 15-55. *Create AMI details*

It can take a while (several minutes typically) for the AMI to finish being completed. Note that during that time, your GitLab service will be out of commission; if you want your service to be available while the image is being created, you can check the Enable box on the "No reboot" option before creating the AMI. Once completed, your AMI will be in the "Available" status as shown in Figure 15-56. At this point, you are ready to use the AMI.

CHAPTER 15   THE PROOF IS IN THE CLOUD

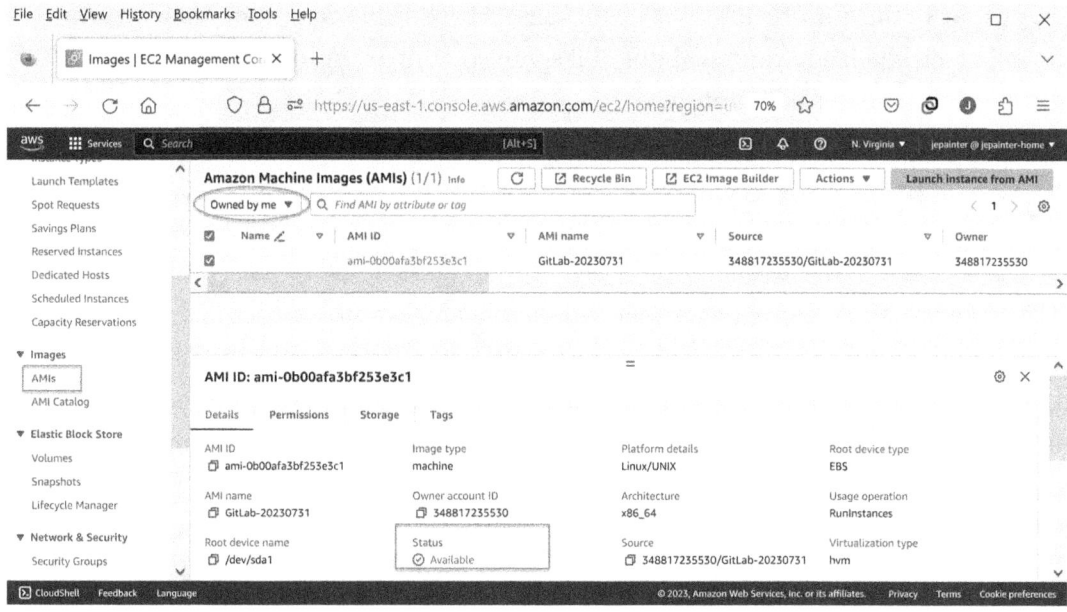

Figure 15-56. *Check of AMI creation status*

Testing the ELB Health Check

Before we set up the AWS Auto-Scaling Group to automatically manage our GitLab services for us, there is one order of business we need to resolve: the ELB health check. Recall in Figure 13-41, we originally set the health check to send an HTTP request of /-/readiness at port 80. Because this failed, we temporarily set the health check to simply test whether port 22 was open. This isn't a very good test since the ssh service normally comes up before the GitLab service, and if the GitLab service goes down, the health check won't catch it. We could simply change the health check to test port 80 in place of port 22, which is better but not great. If the Gitaly service goes down, for instance, the GitLab service can still be running at port 80, but all requests to it will fail.

We need to get back to using the readiness health check provided by GitLab to verify the service is running properly on a given server and, if not, have the auto-scaler replace the server with a new one. So now that we've previously logged in to the standalone GitLab service as the root user, let's try resetting the ELB health check to send the HTTP readiness request as originally set. It turns out that if you do this, the health check begins to fail again, and our standalone GitLab server appears to be out of service. We can't have this with the auto-scaler since it will cause a cycling of servers spinning up and down (which you'll get warned about). I'll spare you the details of how I debugged this and show you the final solution.[30]

Determining the Readiness Check Access Token

First, reset the ELB health check to simply test port 80 as a TCP request rather than an HTTP request. Your standalone server should quickly show to be back in service again. Once it does, log in to your GitLab service from the web browser as user root. We are then going to the Health Check page available under the Monitoring subsection from the Admin Area as shown in Figure 15-57. On this page, you'll notice something unexpected. The readiness check requires an access token in order to work correctly. Why? Because in order to use our GitLab service, we changed the settings to only let known users access our service. This means that using an anonymous readiness health check is no longer allowed. To get around this, GitLab provides an access token that we can send with the request to prove that we have the authorization to run the readiness health check.

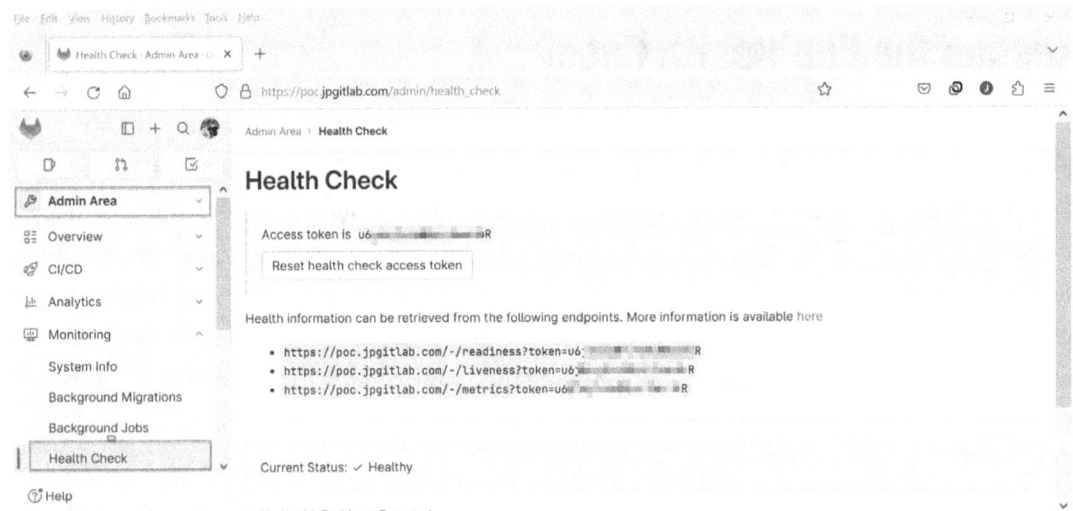

Figure 15-57. Discovering health check URLs via Admin Area

---

[30] Don't worry. You'll have plenty of opportunities to debug things as an administrator.

CHAPTER 15 THE PROOF IS IN THE CLOUD

Resetting the ELB Health Check to Use Readiness Check with Access Token

So, let's test that out. Go back to the ELB, select the "Health check" tab, and set the readiness check as shown in Figure 15-58. You'll need to use the "Edit Health Check" button to reset it. Here, we go back to the HTTP check using /-/readiness with the access token appended to the request using the token parameter. Make sure to use the access token provided on the UI health check page.

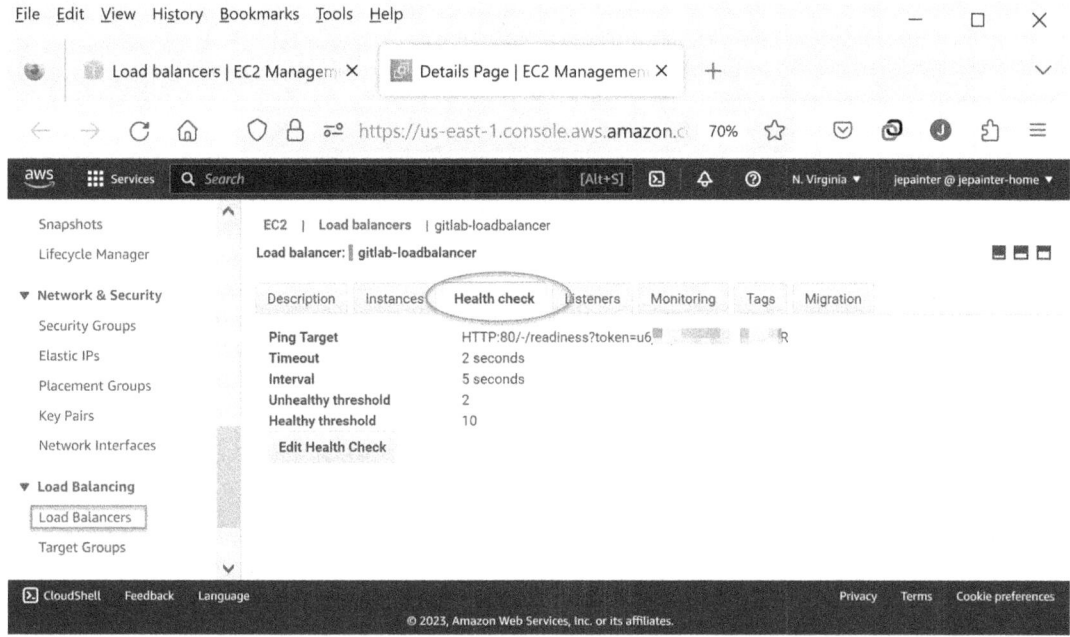

Figure 15-58. *ELB update to health check*

With that ELB health check in place, go to the ELB instances page and verify that the standalone GitLab instance still shows as in service as shown in Figure 15-59. You should probably refresh the page a few times just to be sure, but if the health check is incorrect, your server will go into out-of-service status quickly. Once you feel confident that the health check with the given access token is working properly, you could remove the instance from the ELB before setting up the auto-scaler if you want, but note that it will disrupt users. To remove the instance from the ELB, simply use the link highlighted in the figure to remove it. Keep the server running for now until we get the auto-scaler configured properly.

679

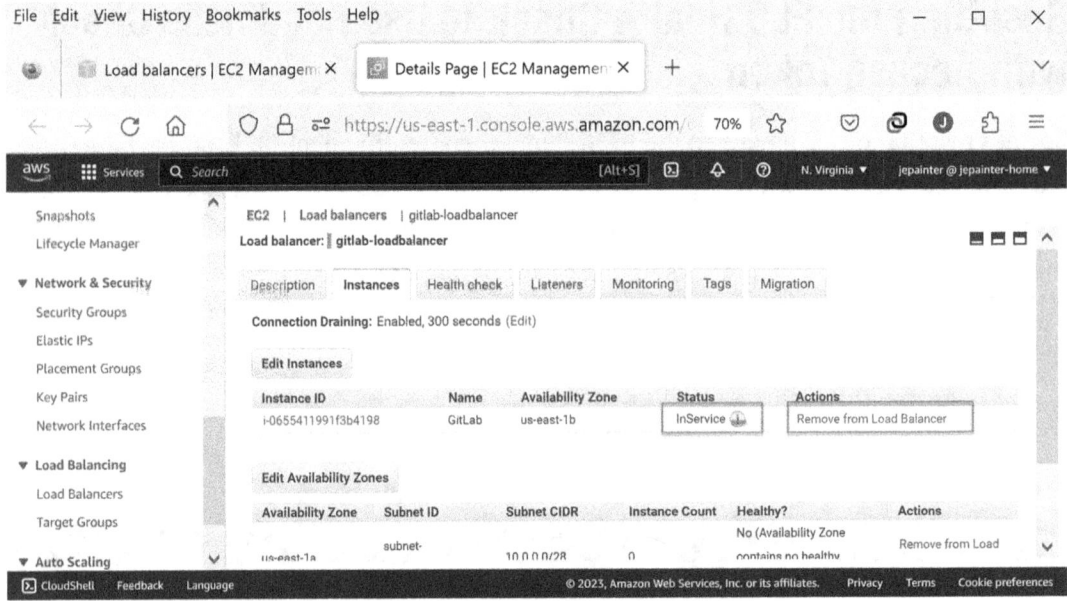

Figure 15-59. ELB check of GitLab instance status

Creating the Launch Template

In AWS, scaling servers consists of two parts. The first part to be set up is known as a "launch template," formerly known as a "launch configuration." To understand the need for a launch template, recall that an AMI is simply a machine image that consists of the OS (in our case, Ubuntu), software packages (in our case, GitLab), and the configuration of those services. An AMI, however, does not specify what type of virtual machines the software will run on. This is the job of the launch template. It enables us to spin up instances of the same type with our auto-scaler.

Accessing the Launch Template Service

Creating a launch template is performed under the EC2 category of services. Figure 15-60 shows the initial page displayed when creating a launch template. Here, we specify the launch template name, which I've set to gitlab-template, and a description of the version. I also selected the "Auto scaling guidance" option since we will indeed be using the template with an auto-scaler.

CHAPTER 15   THE PROOF IS IN THE CLOUD

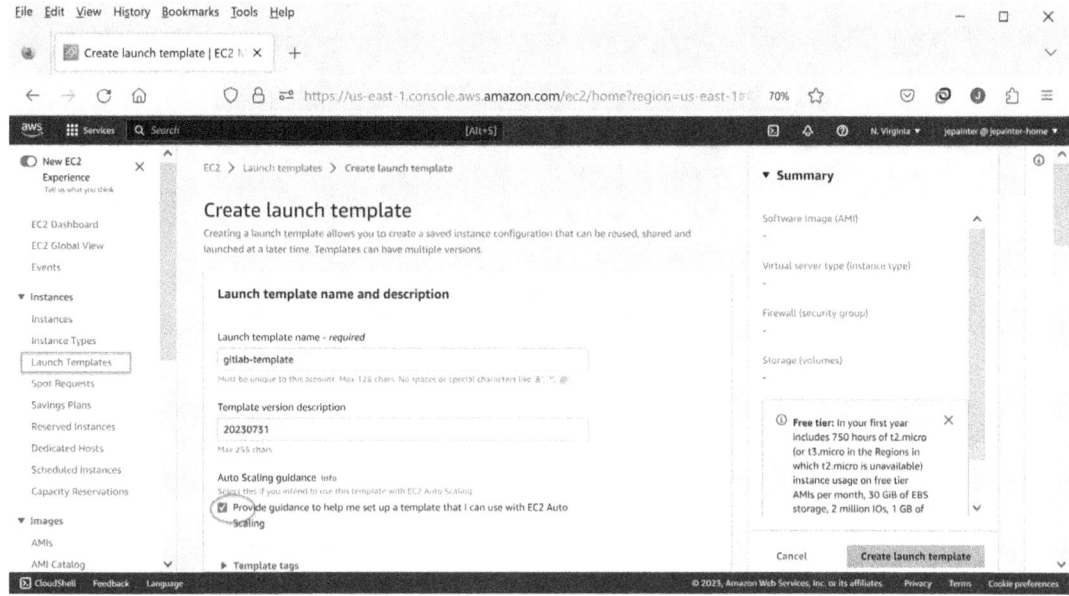

Figure 15-60. *Launch template name and version settings*

Setting the Launch AMI

Next, we select the AMI to be used with our launch configuration as shown in Figure 15-61. Under the "My AMIs" tab, select the "Owned by me" option to only display AMIs that we've created. This will provide a list of AMIs to choose from; in this case, I've selected the AMI created earlier. This section also provides some additional information about the AMI to help us remember how we created it.

681

CHAPTER 15 THE PROOF IS IN THE CLOUD

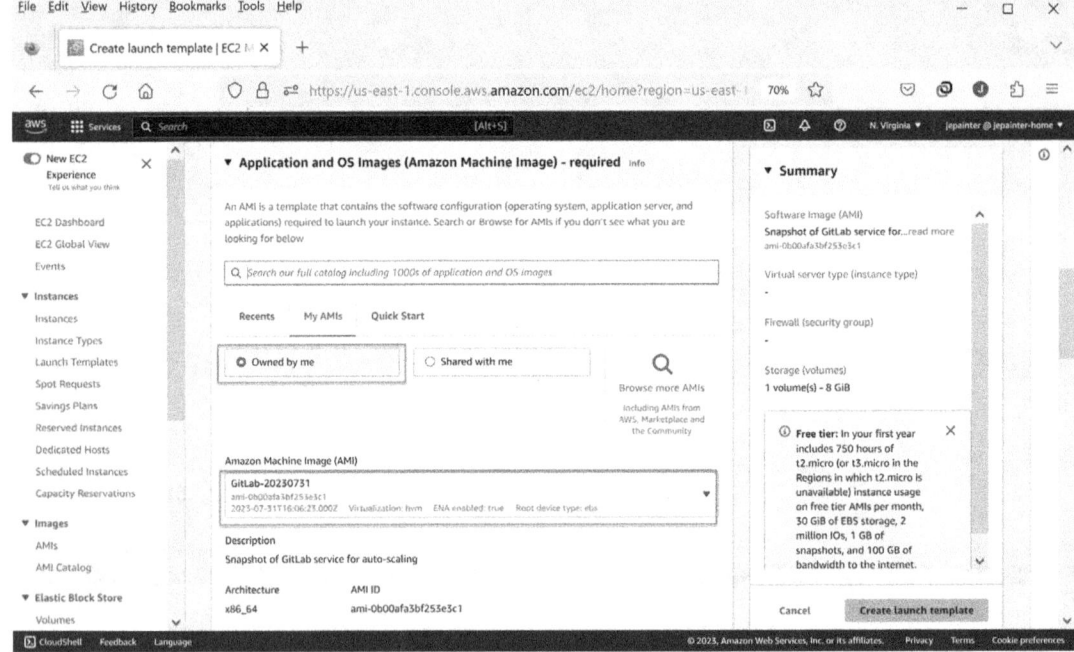

Figure 15-61. Launch template AMI settings

Setting the Instance Type and Key Pair

Next, we specify the instance type and the key pair. This is illustrated in Figure 15-62. Here, I've selected the c5.xlarge instance type, which is the same one I used for the standalone GitLab server; you can obviously choose a different type, but note that it should have at least four CPUs associated with it. I also selected the key pair used with the standalone server. It is critical that we use the same key pair here since that is the one that allows us to ssh into the server from the bastion servers.

CHAPTER 15   THE PROOF IS IN THE CLOUD

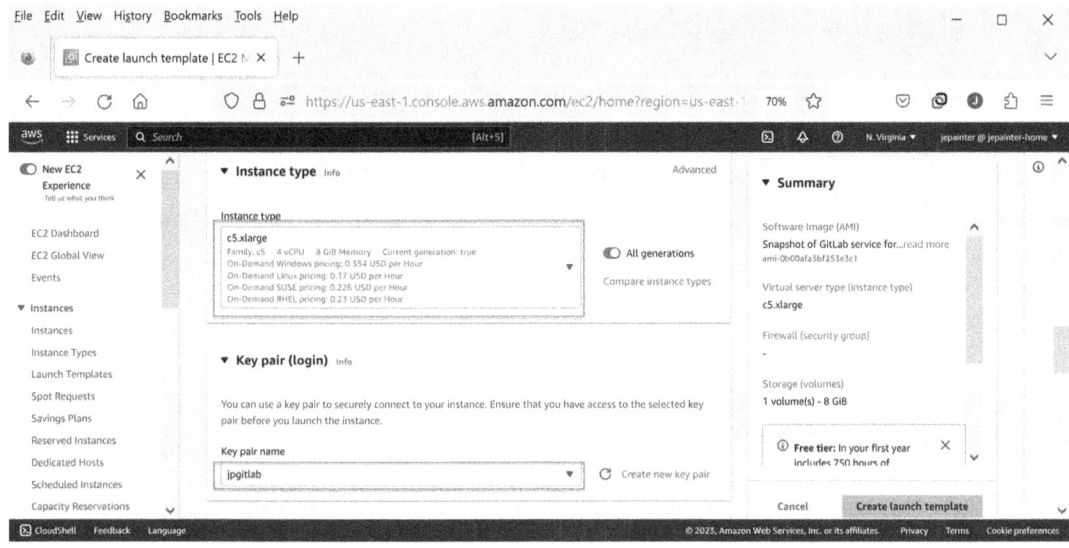

Figure 15-62.   Launch template instance type and key pair settings

Configuring the Network Settings

Figure 15-63 shows the network settings for our template. For the subnet option, we keep this at the default option of not including it in our template as the auto-scaling group will handle this for us. We use the gitlab-loadbalancer-sec-group as the security group to attach automatically to our scaling instances.

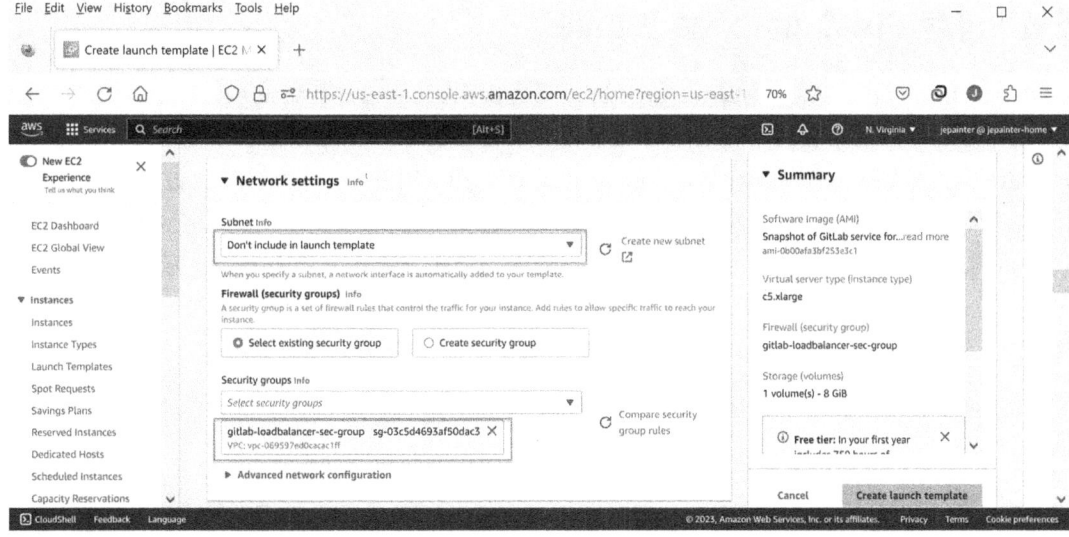

Figure 15-63.   Launch template network settings

CHAPTER 15   THE PROOF IS IN THE CLOUD

Configuring the Storage Settings

Under the storage settings as shown in Figure 15-64, we are keeping those settings as is. You could, of course, switch to a provisioned IOPS disk type if performance is a concern, but for the POC, we'll stick to the gp2 disk type defined in the AMI. As for additional storage volumes, there is no need to add any others since we won't be able to use them with our AMI configuration.

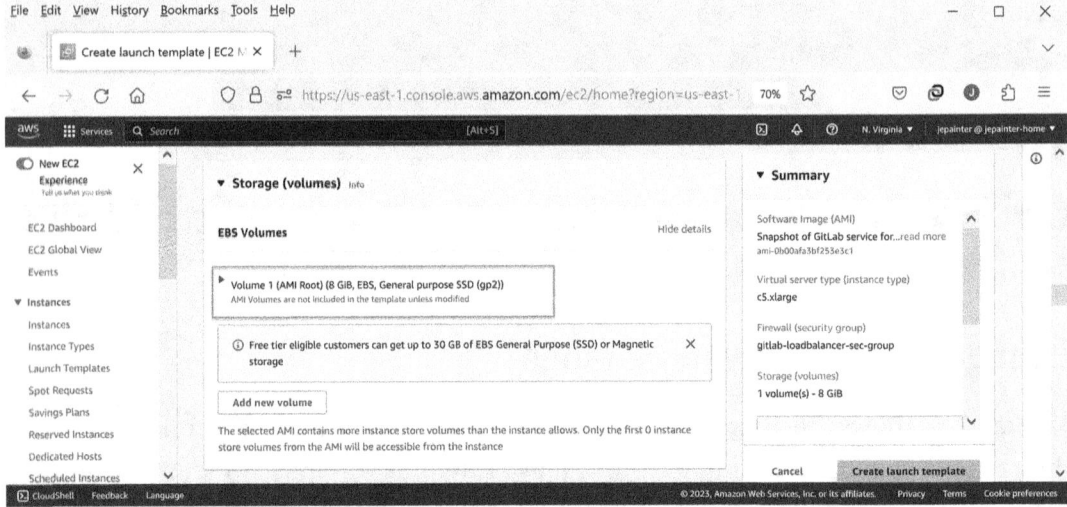

Figure 15-64.   Launch template storage settings

Setting the IAM Instance Profile

Last, we specify the IAM instance profile under the Advanced settings as shown in Figure 15-65. This is necessary since the GitLab servers to be spun up by the auto-scaler require access to the S3 object storage as configured within our AMI. All other template options will remain at their default settings. We create the new template by selecting the "Create launch template" button in the right-hand Summary section.

CHAPTER 15   THE PROOF IS IN THE CLOUD

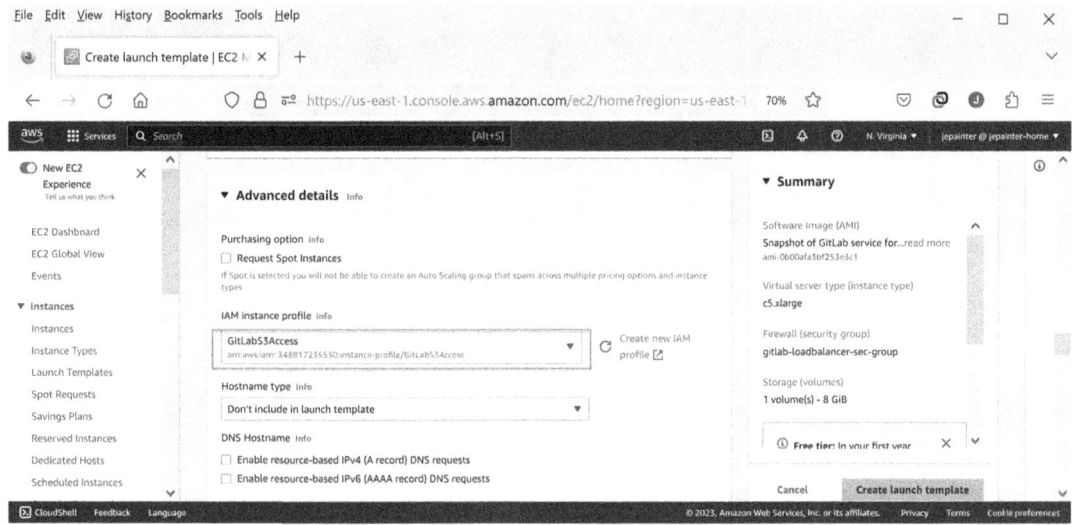

Figure 15-65. *Launch template advanced details*

Creating and Verifying the Launch Template

The creation of the template is quick. Once created, we'll be able to see it show up in the "Launch templates" list as shown in Figure 15-66. A key feature to note about our launch template is that it is versioned. We see in the list that the default version is set to 1 and that the latest version is also set to 1. What this implies is that we can go back and edit our template and change some of the settings while keeping the name of the template the same. We can also set what the default version is should there be an issue with the latest version.

685

CHAPTER 15   THE PROOF IS IN THE CLOUD

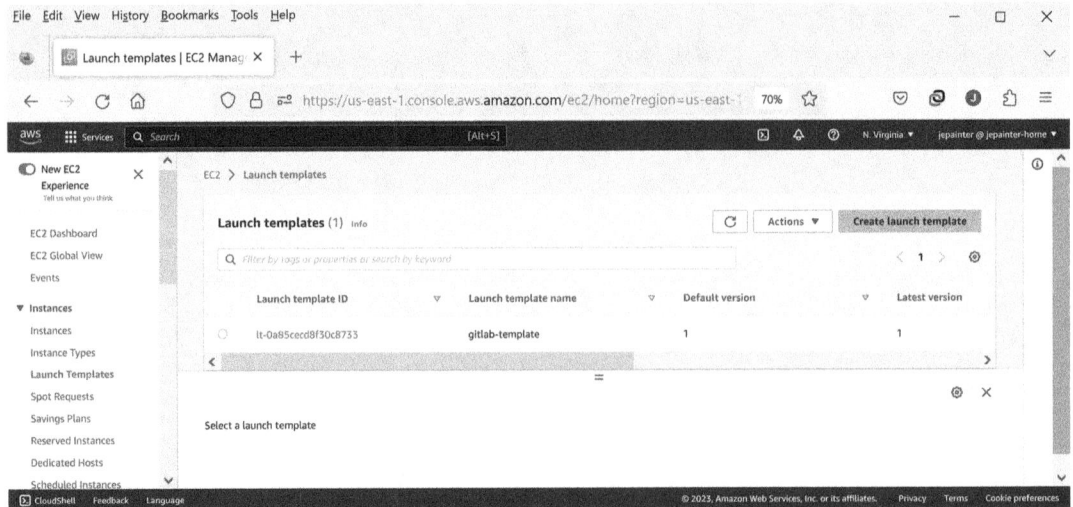

Figure 15-66. *EC2 launch template listing showing newly created GitLab template*

Creating the Auto-Scaling Group

The second part of auto-scaling is the creation of the auto-scaling group (ASG). It is the auto-scaling group that controls what subnets the instances can reside in and how many instances are created. It also defines rules that determine when to scale up or scale down servers based on CPU loading, for instance. From the Launch templates page, select the launch template and then from the Actions menu, select "Create Auto Scaling group" as shown in Figure 15-67. You could also go to the Auto Scaling Groups section in the left-hand pane and create the auto-scaling group from there.

CHAPTER 15   THE PROOF IS IN THE CLOUD

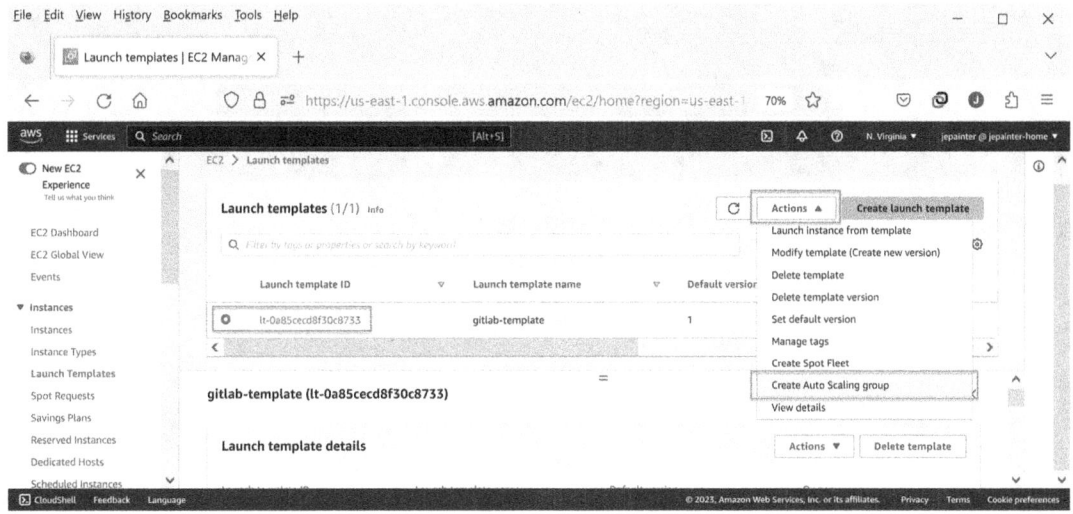

Figure 15-67. *Option to create an auto-scaling group from the GitLab template*

Specifying the ASG Name and Launch Template

In either case, you'll be taken to the auto-scaling wizard, the first page of which is shown in Figure 15-68. On this page, you specify the name of the auto-scaling group. In this example, I used the name gitlab-auto-scaling-group. You also choose the launch template to use with the group. If the launch template that you just created does not show up from the drop-down list, use the recycle button next to the drop-down menu to refresh the list. Note that you can also select a version of the template if there is more than one defined. After the launch template is selected, the remainder of the page will provide feedback information about the template chosen.

CHAPTER 15   THE PROOF IS IN THE CLOUD

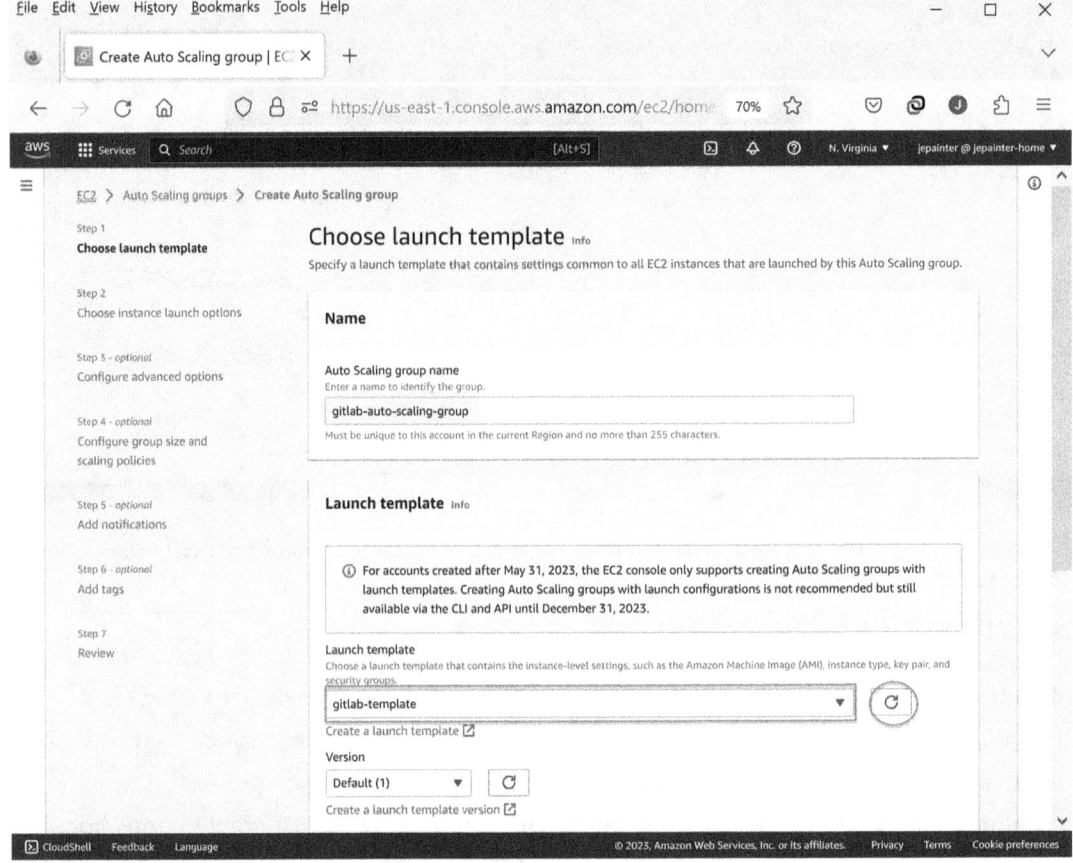

Figure 15-68.   *Choosing launch template*

Selecting the Instance Launch Options

In step two of the wizard, you select the instance launch options. The main options to set involve the network under which the auto-scaling group will run. These options are displayed in Figure 15-69. You first need to select the GitLab VPC. Once selected, you then need to pick the two private subnets for our GitLab POC. There is also a section on this page (not shown) where you can override some of the launch template options; for our POC, we won't make any changes here.

CHAPTER 15   THE PROOF IS IN THE CLOUD

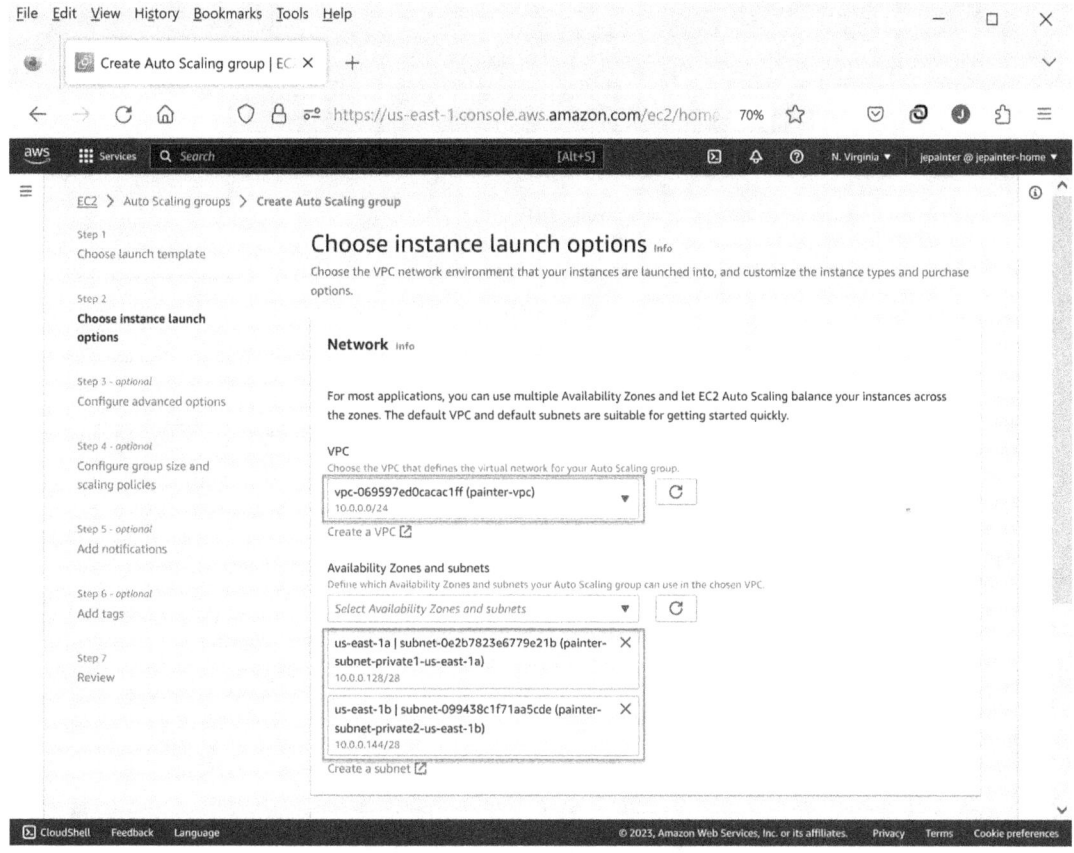

Figure 15-69.   *Choosing launch options*

Connecting the ASG to the ELB

Step three of the auto-scaling group wizard is where you connect the auto-scaling group to the ELB. This is shown in Figure 15-70. Under "Load balancing," select the "Attach to an existing load balancer" option. This will change the remaining options on that page. Since we are using a classic load balancer, select that option under "Attach to an existing load balancer." This will give you a list of load balancers to choose from. Select the GitLab load balancer here.

689

CHAPTER 15　THE PROOF IS IN THE CLOUD

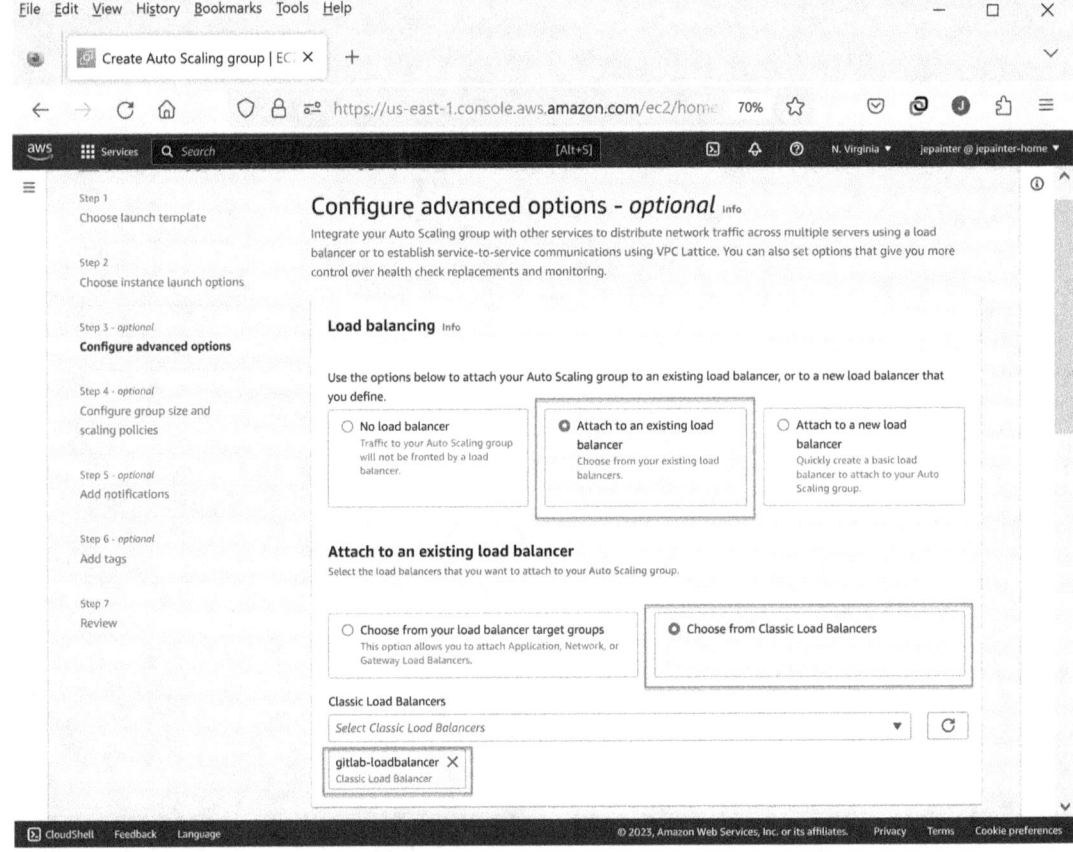

Figure 15-70.　*Configuring ELB settings*

Setting the ASG Health Check Options

Following the ELB section, there is a section on the VPC Lattice integration options, which we'll ignore. After that section is the "Health checks" section, which is displayed in Figure 15-71. Here, we need to select the "Turn on Elastic Load Balancing health checks" option. This will enable the ELB to communicate with the auto-scaling group whenever the ELB detects an issue with one or more instances. Without this option, the auto-scaling group will only check the health of the server and its network connectivity, not the GitLab service, which the ELB monitors. We'll keep the health grace check period at 5 minutes (300 seconds); this is the amount of time we give a server to come up and start the GitLab service.

CHAPTER 15   THE PROOF IS IN THE CLOUD

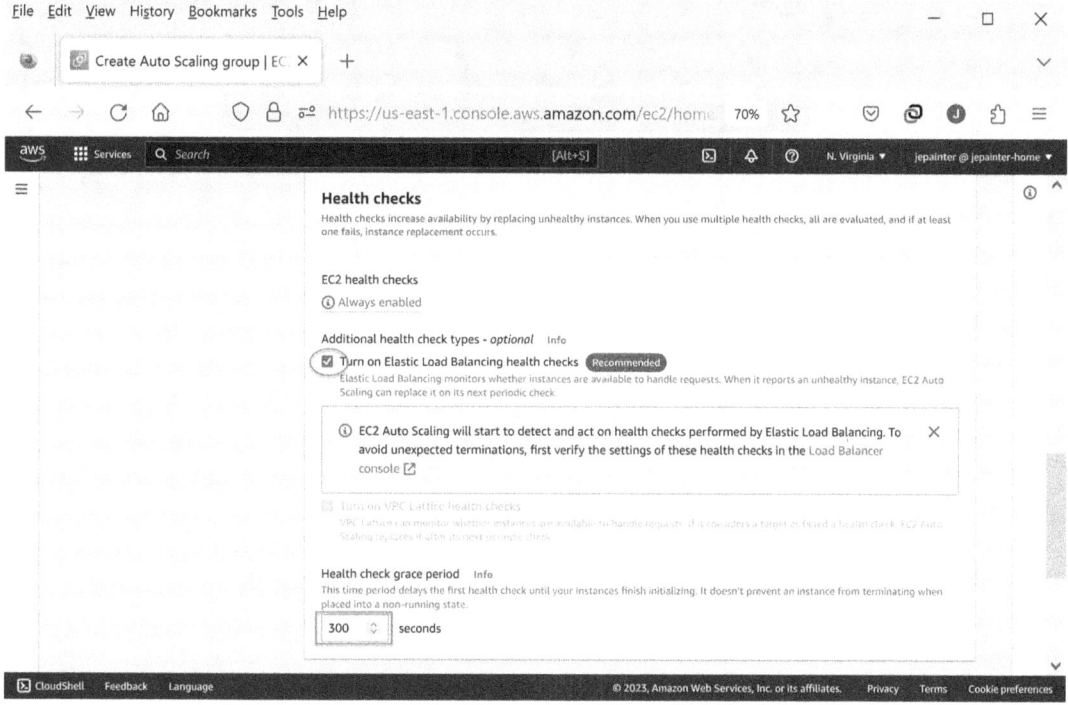

Figure 15-71. *Configuring ELB health check options*

Setting Minimum, Maximum, and Desired Capacity Requirements

Now we get to the interesting part, step four. This is where we tell the auto-scaling group how many servers we want to manage and the rules for scaling out and scaling in the GitLab servers. The first set of options are shown in Figure 15-72. Here, we set three values: the desired capacity, the minimum capacity, and the maximum capacity. The desired capacity is the number of servers we want running at normal loading. The minimum and maximum capacities set, as expected, the minimum and maximum number of servers we allow. The maximum is important as it keeps the auto-scaling group from spinning up too many servers when things go crazy. In case you are wondering why we don't set the minimum and desired capacities to 1, it is to handle the case when one of the availability zones goes down; we'll at least have another server to immediately take the slack without having to wait five minutes for a new server to come up.

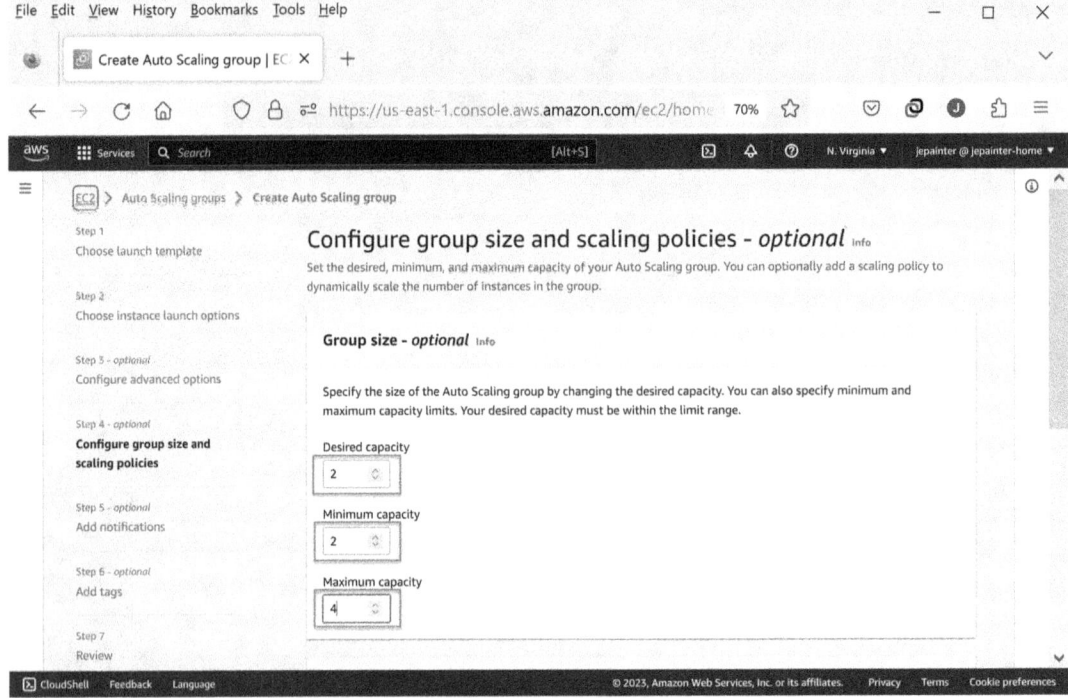

Figure 15-72. *Configuring ASG group size settings*

Setting Scaling Policies

Scrolling down, you'll see the options that control automatic scaling in and out of servers. This is shown in Figure 15-73. Here, we want the "Target tracking scaling policy" option to be selected. You can change the scaling policy name if you want; I kept it at the default name. For the GitLab POC, we use the "Average CPU utilization" metric as the statistic to monitor. In this example, I changed the target value from 50 to 60, but you can use a different value if you want. What this setting means is that if the average CPU utilization across all servers in the auto-scaling group exceeds 60%, a new server will be spun up unless the maximum capacity has been reached.

CHAPTER 15   THE PROOF IS IN THE CLOUD

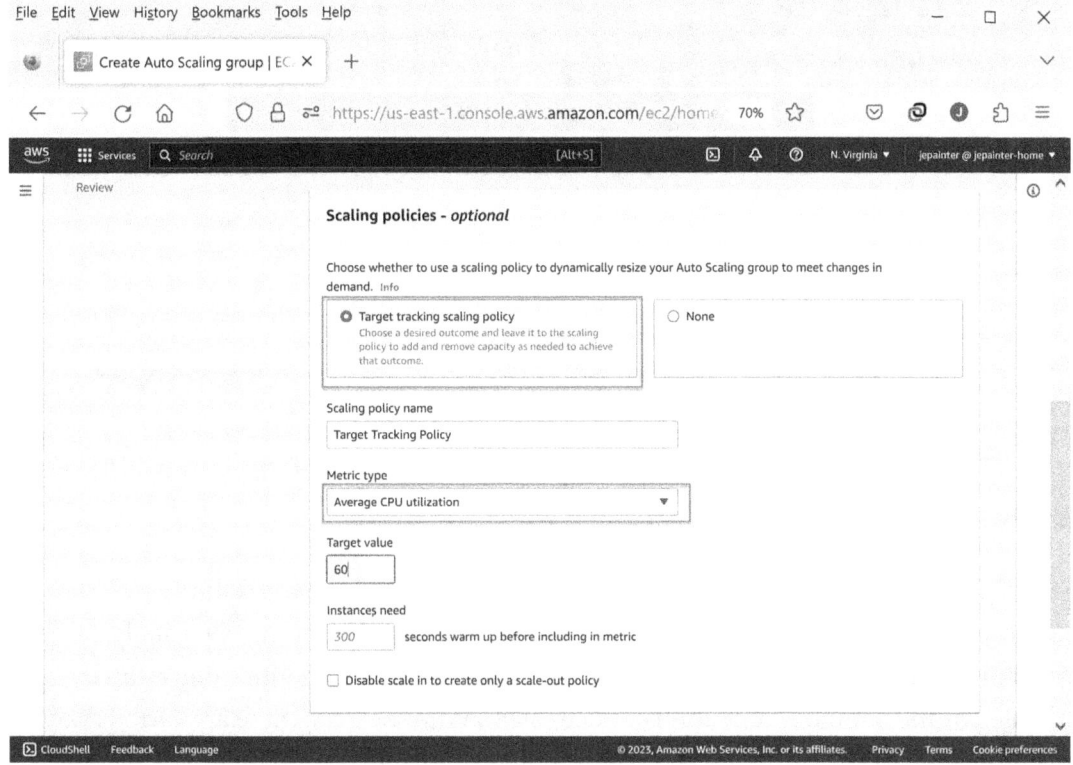

Figure 15-73. *Configuring ASG scaling policies*

So, what about the scale-in policy? Clearly, it can't be based on the 60% value since once you've raised a new server, the average CPU utilization will likely go below 60%. If the scale-in was based on being less than 60%, you would end up with a cycling of servers being brought in and out of service, not what you want. What you are not told is that the scale-in target value is computed from the scale-out target value. As I'll show you later, the scale-in value here is computed at 42%. So, if the average CPU utilization falls below 42%, one of the servers will be brought out of the auto-scaling group and terminated.

Disabling Instance Scale-In Protection

The final section in step four is the scale protection section as shown in Figure 15-74. We'll keep the instance scale-in protection disabled for our POC. If we enabled the scale-in protection, it would prevent that server from being removed from the auto-scaling group and terminated, which would add to our overall costs.

CHAPTER 15   THE PROOF IS IN THE CLOUD

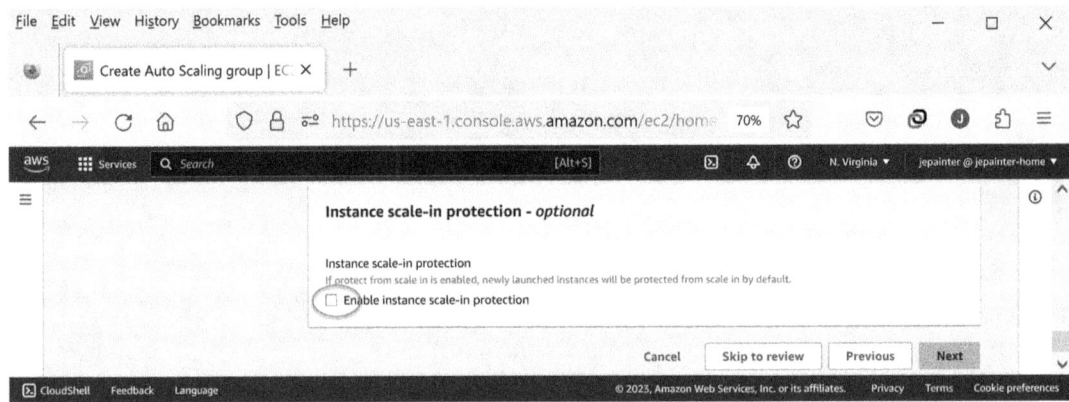

Figure 15-74. Disabling scale-in protection option

Adding Notification Options

Step five of the auto-scaling wizard, shown in Figure 15-75, involves setting up notifications for various events that occur with the auto-scaling group. Normally, I recommend setting this up, especially in a production environment. Notification is handled by the Simple Notification Service (SNS). With the SNS, there are various ways of sending notifications, but the most common one is to send messages to your email address. It is easy to set one up, and it will verify that the email address you provide is a valid one. You can also opt out later if you wish. In this example, I did not set up any notifications. But you can add them after the auto-scaling group is created.

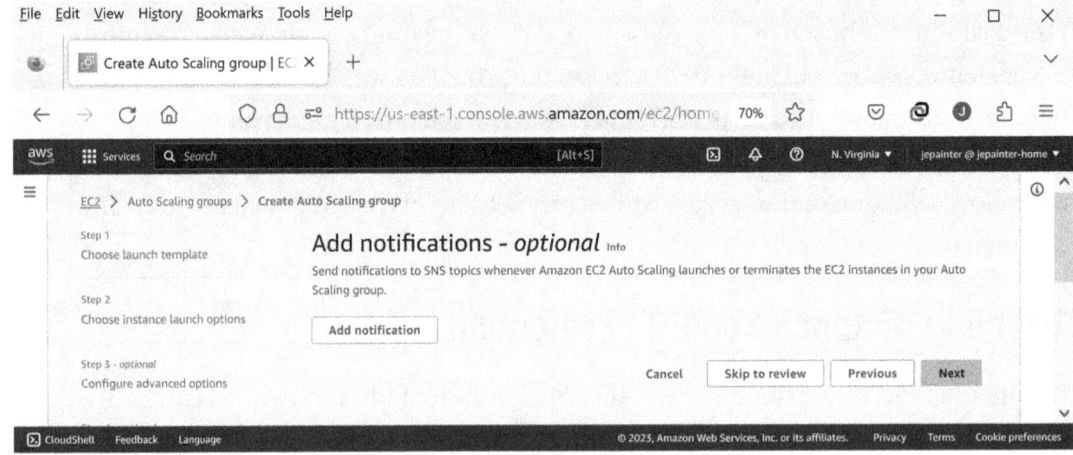

Figure 15-75. Setting notifications (none added here)

CHAPTER 15   THE PROOF IS IN THE CLOUD

Reviewing ASG Settings and Creating the ASG

You can skip the remaining wizard steps and proceed to review all the settings before creating the auto-scaling group. As soon as you create the auto-scaling group, you'll see that it starts creating instances right away. From Figure 15-76, you can see that the status of the group shows as "Updating capacity." This is how you know that it works to spin up instances.

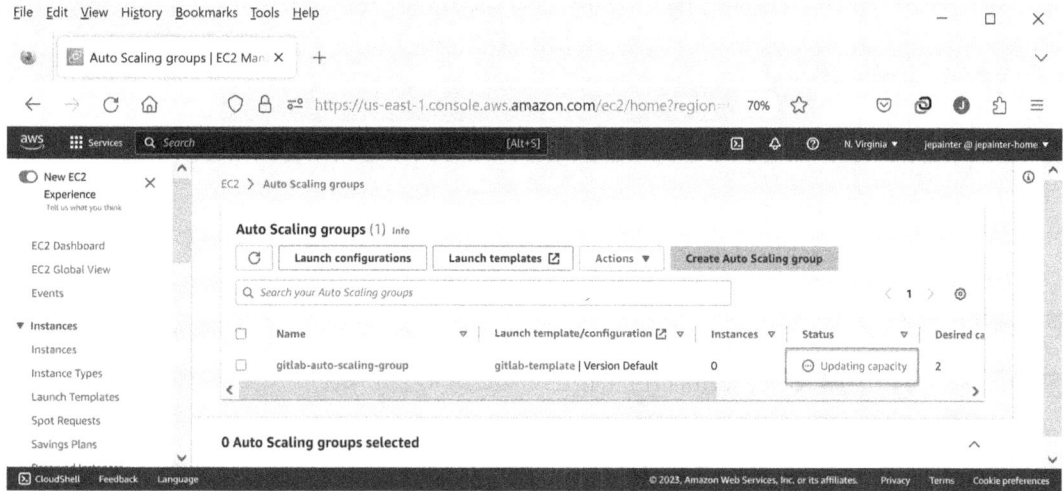

Figure 15-76. *EC2 listing of GitLab auto-scaling group*

Viewing EC2 List of Instances Created by the ASG

Now is a good time to check out the list of instances. Figure 15-77 shows the list of instances in my account after the ASG is initially created. As you can see, there are two additional servers, one in each availability zone. This is a characteristic of an ASG; it tends to spread servers across multiple zones. Also, note that the standalone GitLab server I created manually is not counted as part of the ASG. The dashes that appear in the Name column for the two new servers indicate that they do not have a name defined; this is because I did not define tags as part of the ASG. I'll show how to fix this later, but for now, let's continue to see what effect the ASG has had on the ELB.

695

CHAPTER 15   THE PROOF IS IN THE CLOUD

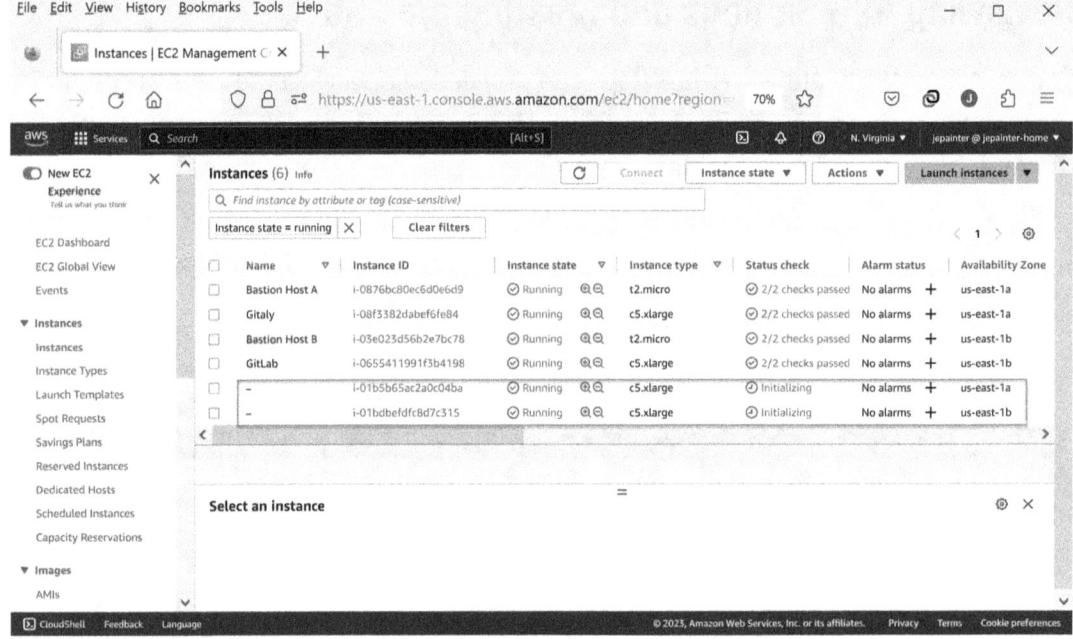

Figure 15-77. *EC2 listing showing auto-scaled GitLab instances*

Viewing ELB List of Instances Created by the ASG

Figure 15-78 shows the instances from the point of view of the GitLab ELB. Here, we see that in addition to the standalone GitLab server, the ELB has connected to the two servers brought up by the ASG. Also, note that they now show as being in service. This shows that the ELB health check on the readiness HTTP request to those servers is passing; the GitLab service on those services is up and ready to take on requests. Given that, we can safely remove the standalone GitLab server from the ELB (if you haven't already) without disrupting the GitLab service available through the URL. Users will not notice anything different.

CHAPTER 15 THE PROOF IS IN THE CLOUD

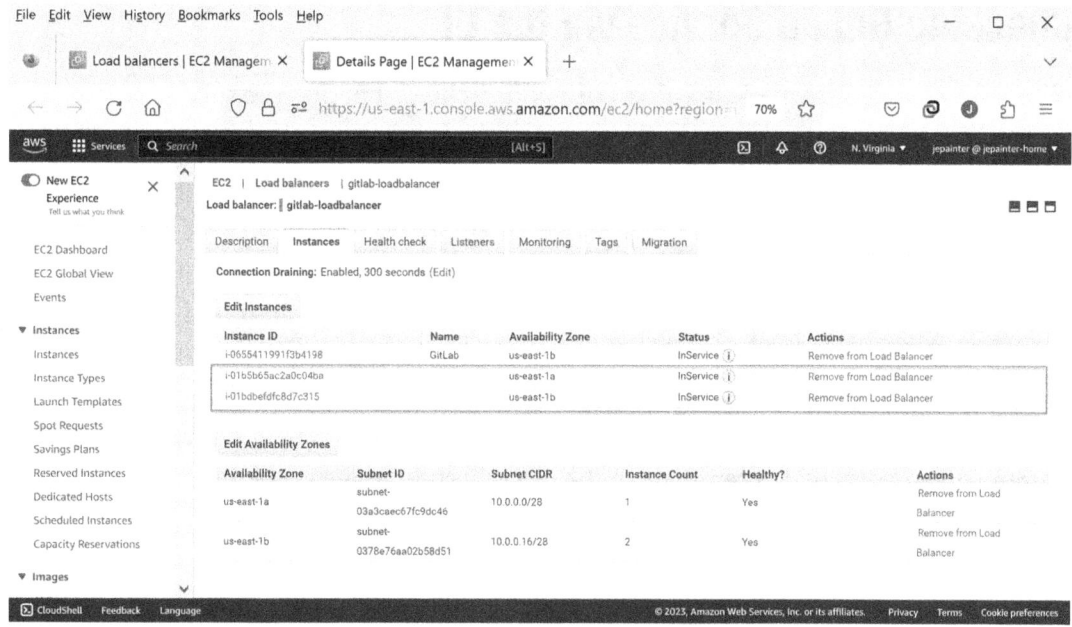

Figure 15-78. ELB listing of auto-scaled GitLab instances

Testing SSH Connectivity to the Newly Spun-Up Servers

We can now ssh into either of the new GitLab servers and check on the status of the GitLab service. Figure 15-79 shows the results of running gitlab-ctl status on my new GitLab server running in us-east-1a. As expected, everything is up and running, which boosts our confidence level that the ASG was set up properly.

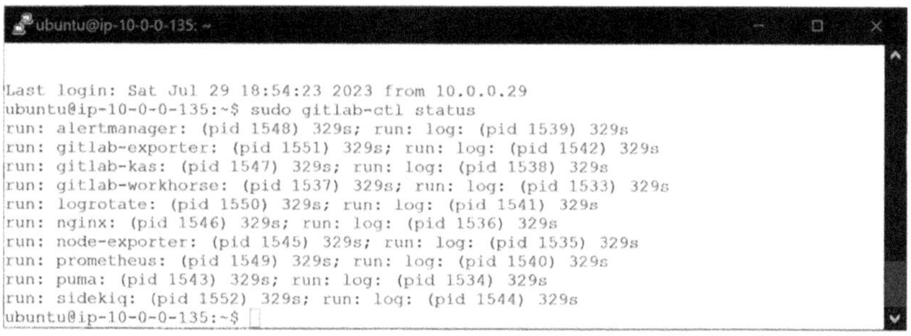

Figure 15-79. Running gitlab-ctl status on an auto-scaled GitLab server

697

CHAPTER 15   THE PROOF IS IN THE CLOUD

Checking GitLab Service via the UI

Whenever changes are made like this, it is good to check that the web service is responding correctly. If you access the GitLab service from your browser, you should see that it responds as it did before. If you were logged in, you should still be logged in after the switch to the ASG. As an administrator, there is a way to check the status of the GitLab server the ELB has routed you to.[31] Figure 15-80 shows an example of the System Info page available under the Admin Area menu in the left-hand pane. In this example, it shows that the server managing the web request is a four-core CPU, is using a small amount of memory, and is using a large portion of the root disk space.[32] Especially note the "System started" time; here, it shows nine minutes ago, which tells me that I'm running on one of the ASG servers, not the original standalone server.

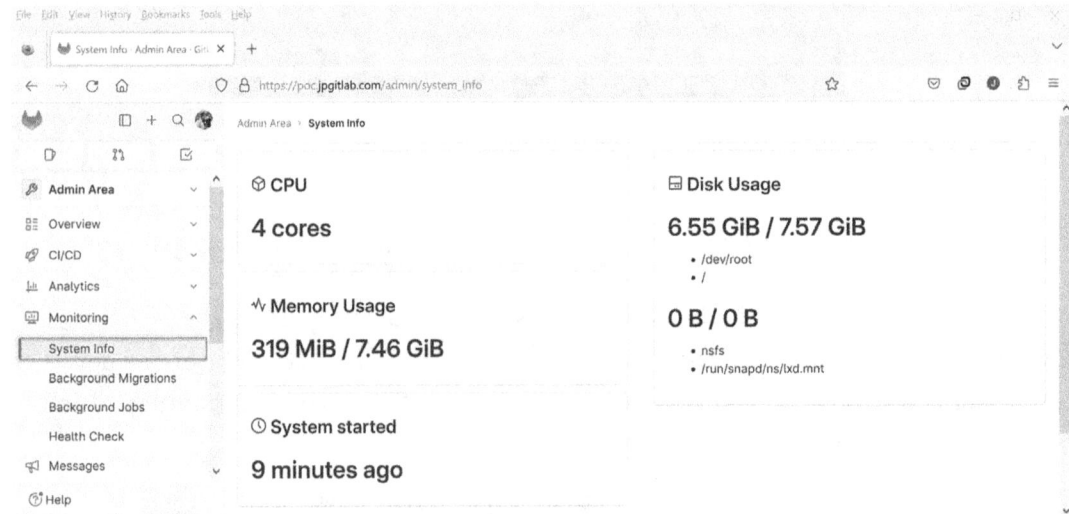

Figure 15-80. Admin Area system info page

---

[31] Unfortunately, this page does not show the system info for all servers, just the one you managed to land on.

[32] The admin in me tells me that I should probably increase the disk space a tad. 10GB should give a little breathing room for ever-growing log files.

698

Stopping the Standalone GitLab Server

So now that things are working properly with the ASG in place, there are some cleanups we can do. First, since I've removed the standalone GitLab server from the ELB, there is no point in keeping it running. Rather than terminate it, it is best to stop it so that we can restart it later in case we need to make changes to our custom AMI. Note that while a server is in a stopped state, there are no costs incurred from AWS, in case you are worried about that. Stopping the server is simple. Select the server from the instance list[33] and select "Manage instance state" from the Actions drop-down menu. You'll be taken to the form as shown in Figure 15-81. Select the Stop option followed by the "Change state" button. You'll be shown a warning message where you can confirm or cancel the change.

If you accidentally terminated the standalone GitLab server, no worries. You can always recreate it with the GitLab AMI created earlier.

---

[33] Make sure to only select the standalone GitLab server and NOT one of the auto-scaling servers. Stopping an auto-scaling server will cause the ASG to terminate the server and replace it with a new one.

CHAPTER 15   THE PROOF IS IN THE CLOUD

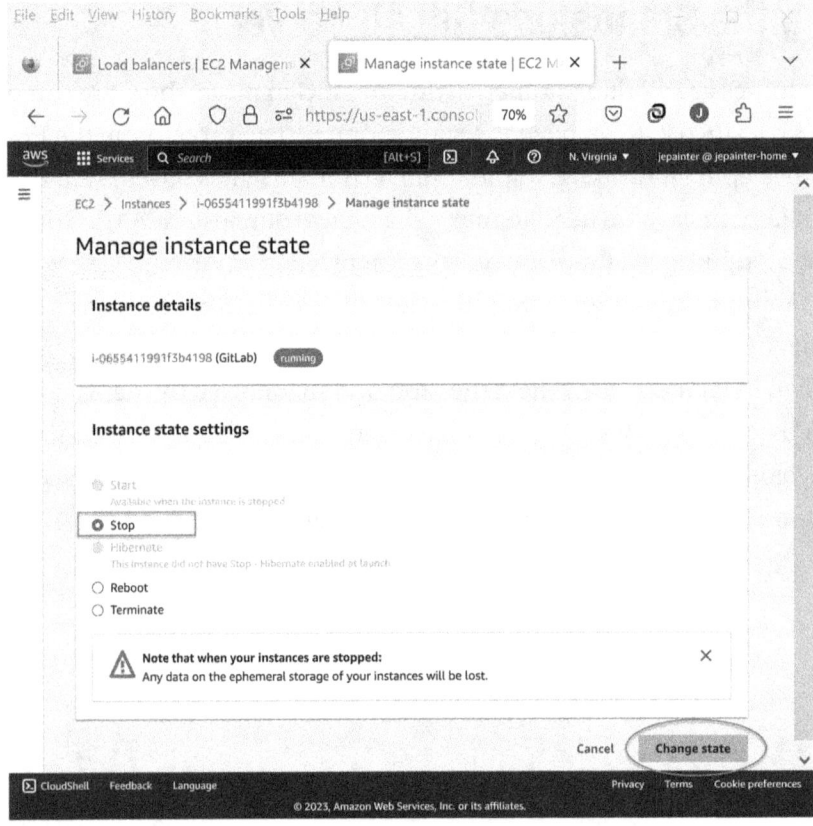

Figure 15-81. *Using manage instance state to stop the standalone GitLab server*

Tagging the ASG Instances

Now let's take care of the naming of our auto-scaling servers. It is best to provide names for them to differentiate them from other servers; this is especially true when we implement GitLab runner servers. We first need to update the tags of the ASG so that instances spun up by the ASG will have a given Name tag. Select the ASG from the auto-scaling list and scroll down to the Tags section. From there, select the "Edit" button. Figure 15-82 shows the page where you can add, remove, or change the values of tags. Here, I've added the Name tag with the value "GitLab-Auto" so as to differentiate it from the standalone GitLab server. Feel free to choose a different name if you wish.

700

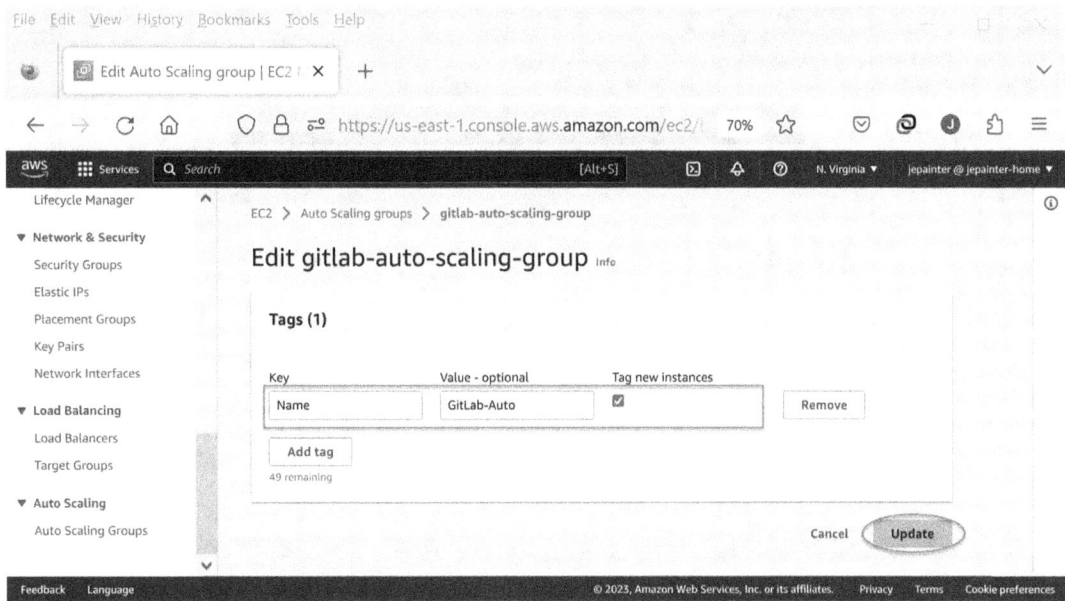

Figure 15-82. *Adding the Name tag to the auto-scaling group to mark auto-scaled GitLab instances*

This change only affects new servers created by the ASG, so we should go to the instances and set their names explicitly. Figure 15-83 shows how to do this easily. Select the instance in the EC2 instance list, and within the Name column, select the little pencil icon that shows up there. This will allow you to enter the name directly as shown in the example. Do this for both of the unnamed servers, and you'll be all set. From here on out, any new servers spun up from the ASG will use the GitLab-Auto name.

CHAPTER 15   THE PROOF IS IN THE CLOUD

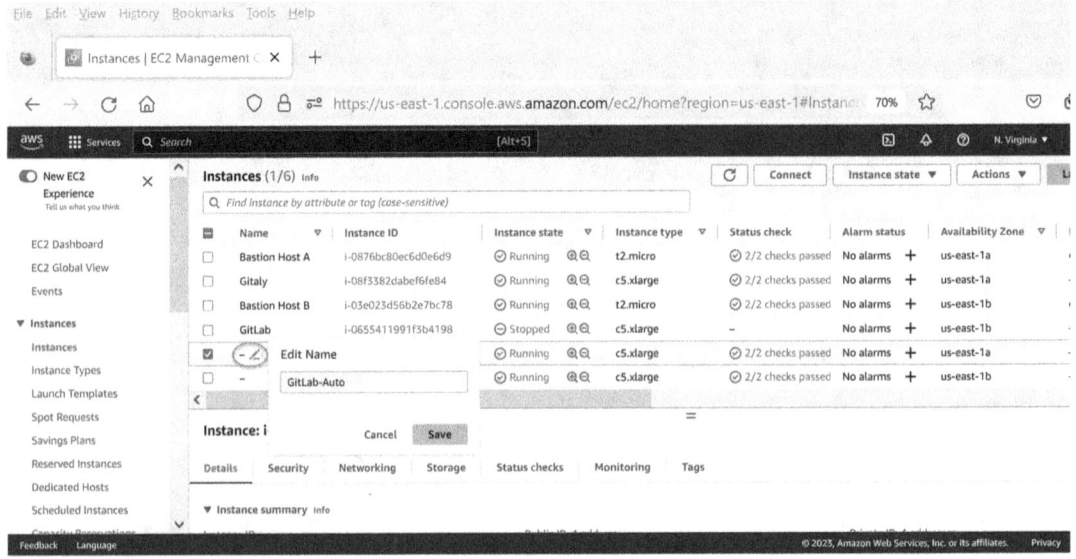

Figure 15-83. Updating name of existing auto-scaled instances

Reviewing the Behind-the-Scenes Scaling Rules

So as promised, I'll show you where the scaling rules for the ASG are stored. It isn't obvious; you would think they would be part of the auto-scaling group definition, but they are not. AWS provides a generic monitoring service called CloudWatch that you can find under the "Management and Governance" category of services. This service is used for many different types of AWS entities, not just auto-scaling groups, and it contains a number of sub-services such as alarms, logs, and metrics. Figure 15-84 shows the alarms defined by the ASG for scaling.

CHAPTER 15   THE PROOF IS IN THE CLOUD

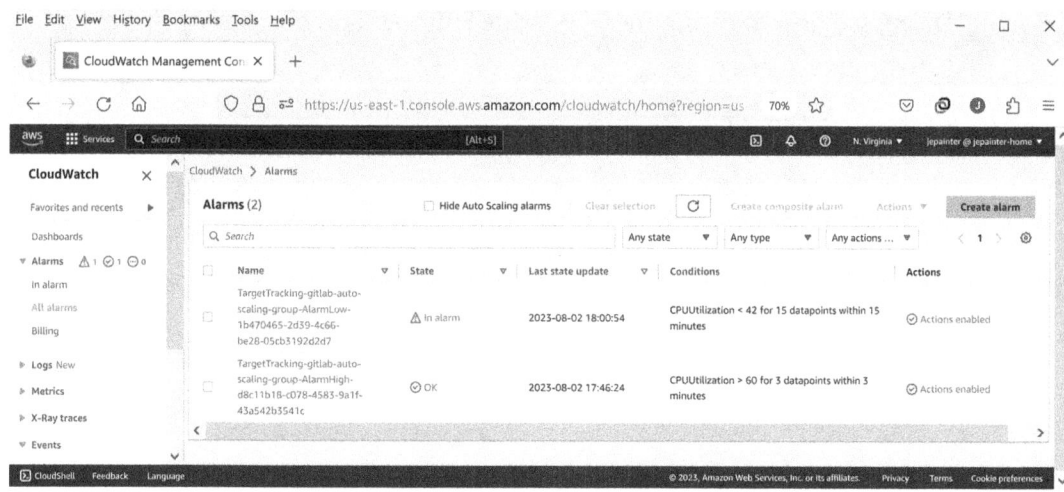

Figure 15-84. *CloudWatch alarms created by ASG scaling policies*

It may seem odd at first that these are classified as alarms, but in AWS, an alarm is simply a mechanism for monitoring one or more metrics and performing an action should the metric go beyond some thresholds set by the alarm. For the ASG, there are two alarms defined, one for scaling out and one for scaling in. In the preceding example, the second alarm is for scaling out. It shows a status of OK since the CPUUtilization metric is NOT above 60.[34] The first alarm is for scaling in. It shows a status of "In alarm" since the CPUUtlilization metric is below 42.[35] Normally, this tells the ASG to scale down, but since the desired capacity is set to two, the ASG will ignore this alarm. If there were three or more servers, one of those servers would be brought out of service.

Summary

In summary, we've covered the following topics in this chapter:

- Described how to create and configure a standalone GitLab server
- Investigated how to split off the Gitaly service onto its own server

---

[34] Alarms can be confusing at first since they determine the criteria in which the alarm is triggered. A status of OK means that the criteria is NOT met and hence the alarm is NOT triggered.

[35] The "In alarm" state here causes some people to freak out, which in certain circumstances would be warranted. In this case, however, the In Alarm state is expected.

703

- Discussed how to configure server-side SSH to retain host keys across servers
- Learned how to set up S3 object storage for GitLab
- Shown how to scale the GitLab service using auto-scaling groups

At this point, we now have a working GitLab POC service that we can experiment with. There is still some more configuration to do to make things ready for developers. In the next chapter, we will describe how to set up our own shared runners.

CHAPTER 16

Working the Never-Ending Queue

With your self-managed GitLab service up and running, it's now time to focus on administrative tasks related to managing that service. The first order of business involves setting up runners so that users can run jobs for their CI/CD pipelines.

Managing Shared Runners

There are a number of approaches to managing shared runners, which we consider in this section.

The Do-Nothing Approach

One approach is to do nothing. That's right, nothing. With this approach, you force users to set up their own runners, which they can do at either the group or project level. After all, users know what their build and deploy needs are, so why not let them deal with their own runners? GitLab makes this relatively easy to do by providing the GitLab runner software that they can install on a server and configure to use the GitLab service you've provided. You can just sit back and not be bothered managing those pesky runners. Except that you'll probably be asked to help those users in the setting up of their own runners, so you are not entirely off the hook.

Managing a Farm of GitLab Runners

Another approach is to set up a farm of GitLab runners or even a farm of farms of GitLab runners depending on various server characteristics such as CPU/memory power and OS types. For example, if you are supporting developers creating products for Windows or Macs, your best approach would be to set up a farm of Windows and/or Mac servers that they can use. You'll have to haggle with them about the CPU/memory power of those servers, but hopefully you'll be able to come to a happy middle ground with them and require them to manage their own servers for tasks that require high-powered servers.

A disadvantage of using farms of GitLab runners is that they must be up and running 24/7, which can be costly given that there will be times when they won't be used. Now I know some of you might be thinking that you could simply schedule servers to shut down during off-peak times, such as in the late evenings or on weekends, which is easy to set up with AWS. But what happens when a job is still running on a runner when it is scheduled to shut down or during certain weekends before a release of software comes out? You'll need to take these things into consideration.

Managing Auto-Scaling GitLab Runners

This leads us to the approach of using auto-scaling shared runners that can be spun up or down on demand. You've seen auto-scaling shared runners in action when you use gitlab.com to run your jobs via a Docker container; you just haven't seen how they work in the background. In this chapter, I'm going to reveal the magic behind how these runners work so that you can set up your own. As usual, I'm going to do this in AWS, but you can also apply this to other common cloud services.

First, a word on terminology since I'm likely to slip and say shared runners when I actually mean auto-scaling shared runners.[1] Technically, a shared runner, also known as an instance-level runner, is one that is available to any developer that can run jobs no matter what group or project they belong to. This is opposed to group-level or project-level runners that are only available to developers who are members of a given group or project. An auto-scaling runner is one that can be spun up or down based on demand. These runners are managed as a pool, so a runner that is spun up may be used to handle many jobs in sequence; it should be noted that a runner can only run one job at a time. As demand for jobs ramps down, say in the evening or weekends, a runner is removed from the pool and spun down as long as a job is not currently running on.

---

[1] It's a habit since those were the only kind of shared runners I managed in my corporate environment.

Now it is possible for a group or project to set up their own auto-scaling runners, but it is not likely since it is tricky to set these up, as you'll soon see. Most often, they set up a farm of standalone runners that are up 24/7 since this is the easiest path to managing runners on their own. I'll note that I have helped teams set up their own auto-scaling runners, but it is not something I promoted as it still required significant time on my part to manage.

On the other side of the coin, I refused to manage farms of shared runners, only auto-scaling shared runners. The reason for this is that it leads to a slippery slope toward madness on behalf of the GitLab service administrators. Once you do special runner setups for one group, others will follow. Over time, it becomes difficult to keep track of them all and upgrade them when needed. If a team has special needs, they can manage their own runner setup using group-level and/or project-level runners. As a consequence of all this, when I say shared runners, I really mean auto-scaling shared runners.

Enough politics. Let's get into how to set up auto-scaling shared runners in AWS.

Setting Up Auto-Scaling Shared Runners in AWS

The first secret behind auto-scaling runners is that they use a now outdated Docker tool called docker-machine.[2] This tool runs on a controlling server referred to as the runner manager that, when requested, spins up a server (an EC2 server in the case of AWS), installs Docker Engine on it, and manages Docker containers on that server; the controlling server never runs a job directly. Now on its own, docker-machine does not manage the auto-scaling of servers; that's the job of the GitLab software. The GitLab runner software works in conjunction with docker-machine to manage the scaling of servers and running Docker jobs on them.

Preliminary AWS Setup

As we did with the GitLab service itself, there are some preliminary items that need to be set up in AWS before we create the runner manager server.

---

[2] The Docker developers no longer support docker-machine, so GitLab had to take over and provide updates to docker-machine themselves.

CHAPTER 16 WORKING THE NEVER-ENDING QUEUE

Creating the Security Group for Spun-Up Runners

First, we need to set up a security group for the runners that will be spun up by the runner manager. Figure 16-1 shows the inbound rules of gitlab-runner-sec-group that I created. I modeled this after the gitlab-gitaly-sec-group but with port 2367 in place of the Gitaly port of 8075. This security group enables port 22 from within the VPC as well as from the bastion hosts so that we can debug the scaled-up runners if needed.

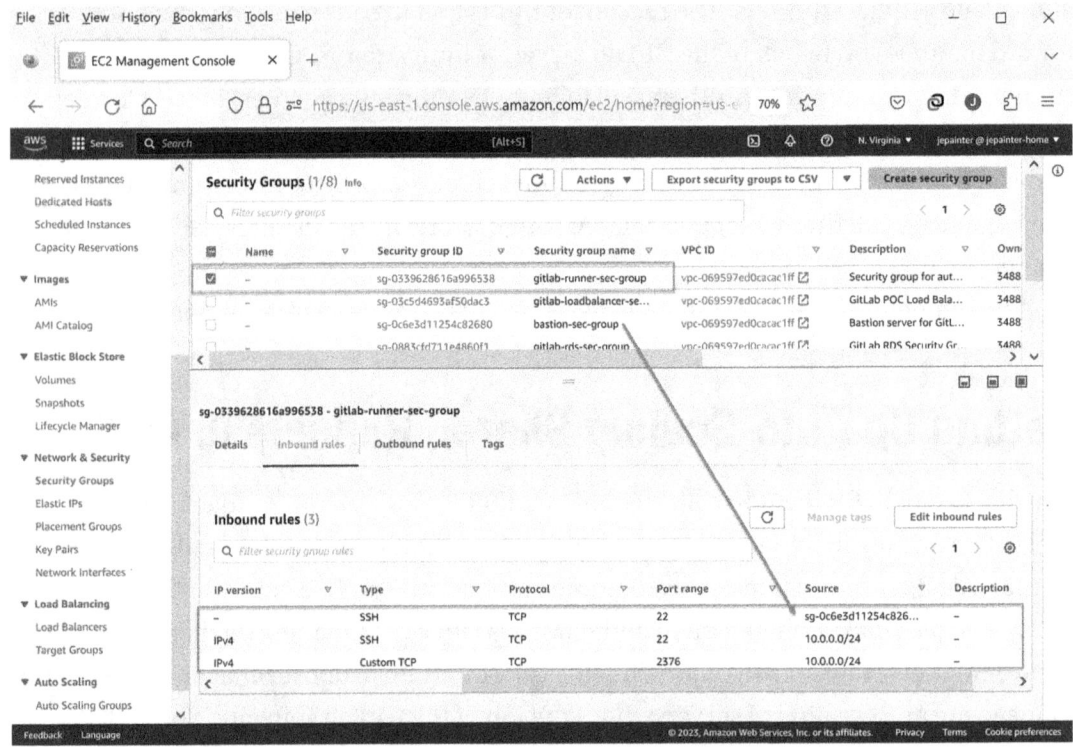

Figure 16-1. Inbound rules of gitlab-runner-sec-group

Creating IAM Policies for the Runner Manager

For the runner manager, I created the IAM Policy gl-kms-policy as shown in Figure 16-2. This will enable the runner manager to use the KMS key we created specifically for our S3 buckets. Note that I restricted the policy to all keys within my account; you may require a more restrictive policy that specifies specific KMS keys.

CHAPTER 16   WORKING THE NEVER-ENDING QUEUE

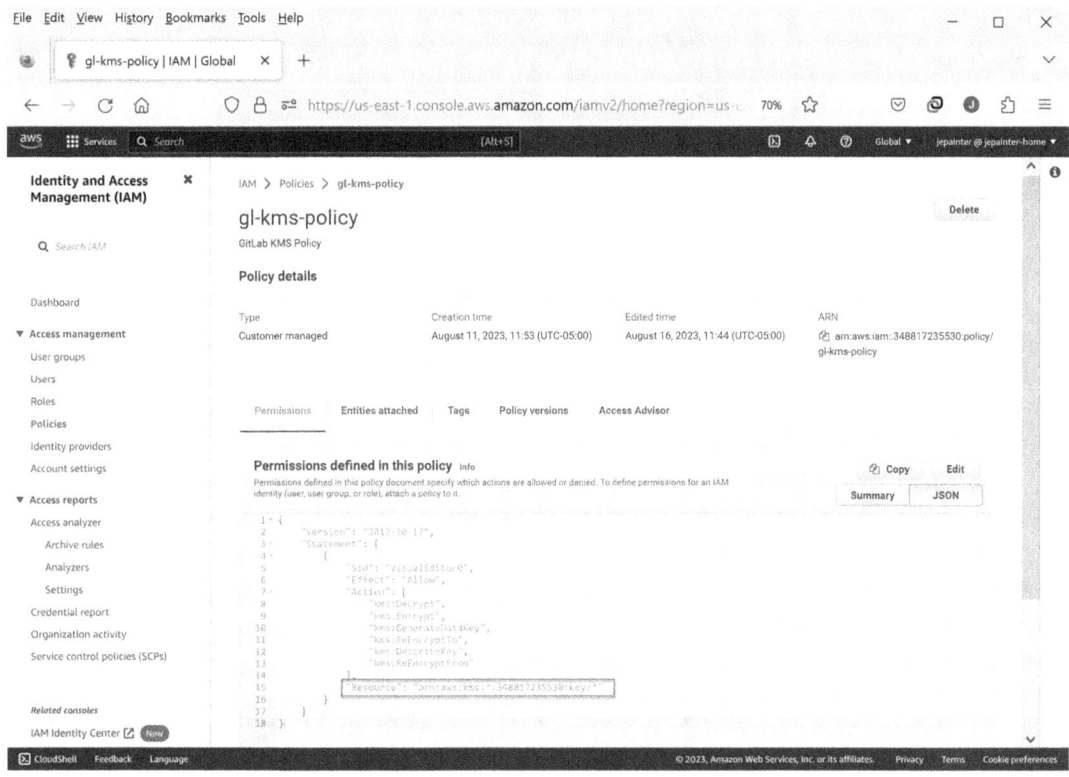

Figure 16-2. *Runner manager gl-kms-policy IAM policy*

Also, for the runner manager, I created the gl-iam-policy as shown in Figure 16-3. You won't see this policy mentioned in the GitLab Runner documentation since they use explicit AWS access keys in their runner configuration. This isn't a good idea since those keys tend to have full administrative rights. The better approach is to use IAM roles for authorization. However, this requires the special permission iam:PassRole that allows the runner manager instance to pass that role onto the runner instances. Note that I restricted this policy to all roles in my account that start with GitLab. For extra security, you may need to restrict the policy to explicit roles.

CHAPTER 16   WORKING THE NEVER-ENDING QUEUE

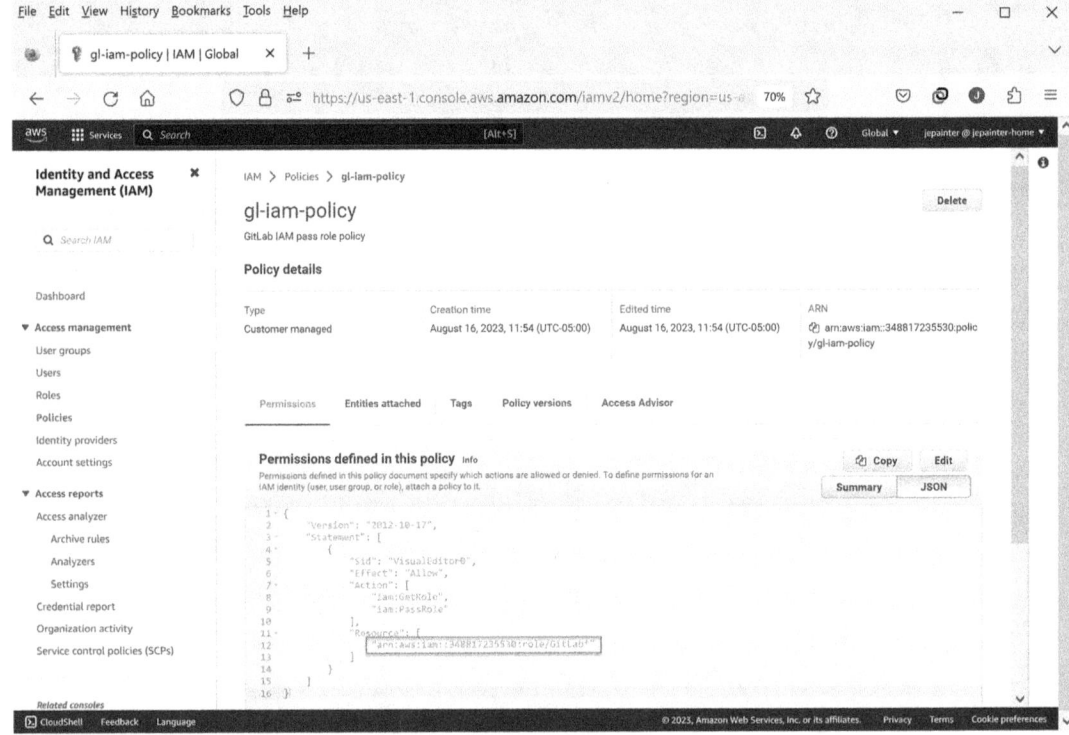

Figure 16-3. Runner manager gl-iam-policy IAM policy

Updating the S3 Policy

One more thing on policies: According to the documentation on the docker-machine S3 requirements, I modified the existing gl-s3-policy to include the GetObjectVersion permission. The change is shown in Figure 16-4. Note that this change will apply to existing S3 buckets but will not be used for them. I felt it was better to have a single S3 policy rather than create a new one that only had one permission difference.

CHAPTER 16 WORKING THE NEVER-ENDING QUEUE

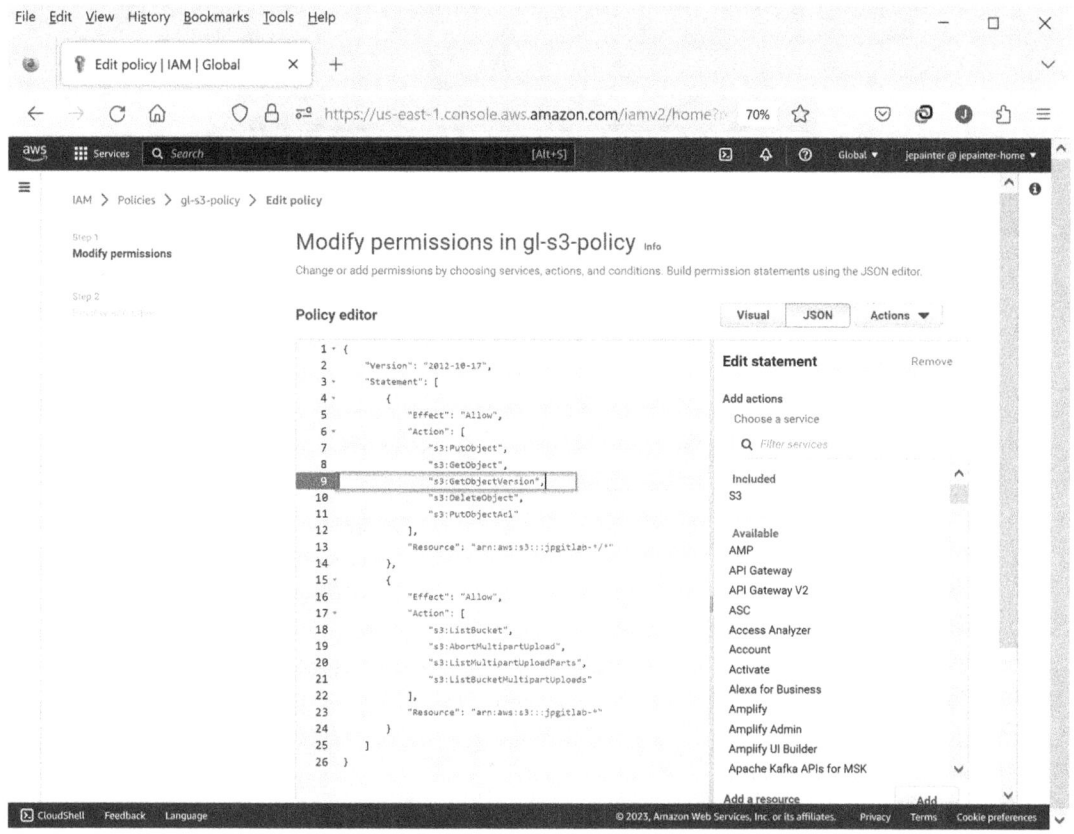

Figure 16-4. *Update to gl-s3-policy for runner managers*

Creating the IAM Role for the Runner Manager

With the gl-kms-policy and gl-iam-policy created and with the gl-s3-policy updated, we can now create a role specific for the runner manager. This new role, GitLabRunnerManagerRole, is shown in Figure 16-5. Four policies are used for this role: gl-iam-policy, gl-kms-policy, gl-s3-policy, and AmazonEC2FullAccess.[3] The reason for these policies is to enable the runner manager to spin up and down EC2 instances and to manage the runner cache in S3.

---

[3] I'm not too keen on using the EC2 full access role in this context for security reasons. However, I had a hard time finding documentation on what permissions are actually needed.

711

CHAPTER 16   WORKING THE NEVER-ENDING QUEUE

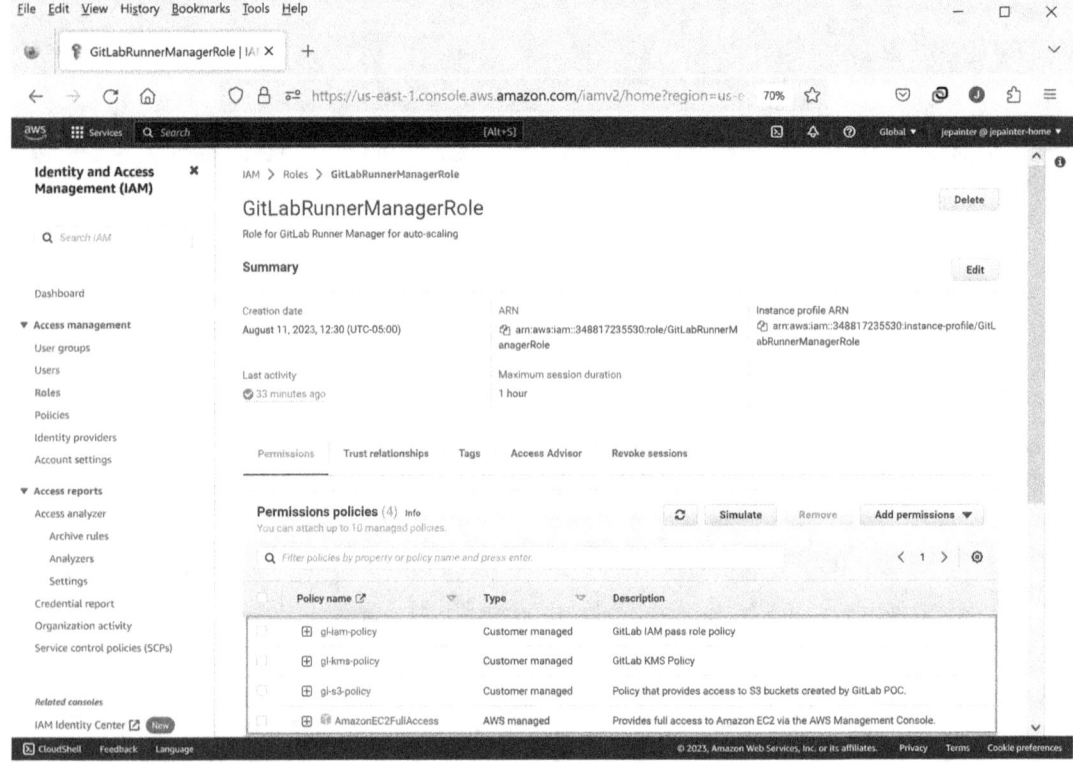

Figure 16-5. *Policies assigned to GitLabRunnerManagerRole*

Setting Up the S3 Cache Bucket

We also need to set up the S3 cache bucket. This is used to preserve cache files between job runs. Since jobs can run on different runner servers, there needs to be a shared location for the job cache. This could be done using NFS, but since we are in AWS, using S3 buckets is the preferred approach. Figure 16-6 shows the new cache bucket, jpgitlab-poc-cache, created based on the uploads bucket.

CHAPTER 16   WORKING THE NEVER-ENDING QUEUE

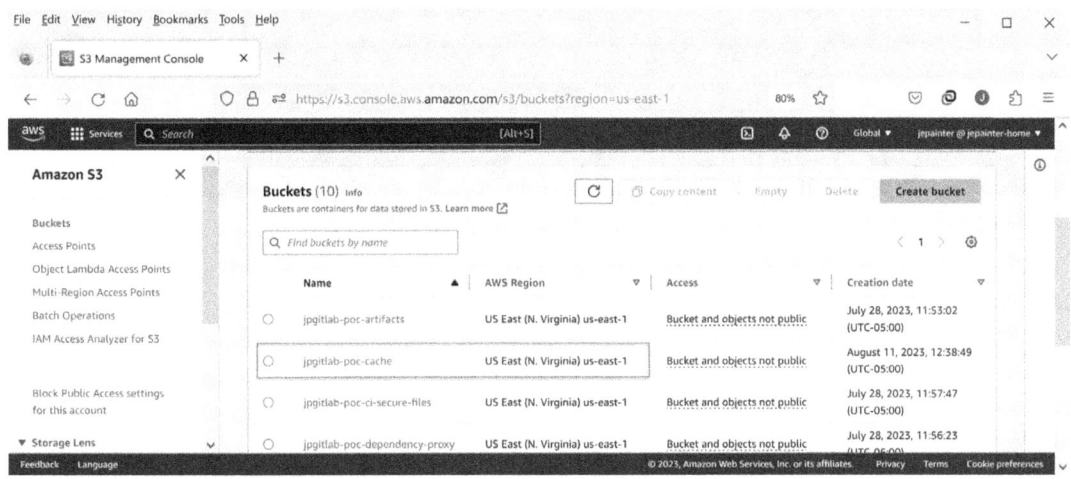

Figure 16-6. *Creation of S3 bucket for the runner job cache*

Creating an SSH Key Pair Specific to Runners

One last thing before we spin up the runner manager server. Since the runner manager will be communicating with the spun-up runner servers via SSH, we need to create an SSH key pair specific for that purpose. We don't want to use any other keys that are used to connect to our GitLab servers as we will have to store both the private and public keys in clear text on the runner manager. For this, I used openssh to generate the key pairs[4] for the runner like so: ssh-keygen -t ed25519 -f ~/.ssh/runner. In Linux, this generated both the private key named runner and the public key named runner.pub in my home .ssh directory. Using the contents of runner.pub, I was able to import the key pair into AWS as shown in Figure 16-7. Since I plan on using SSH to debug the spun-up runner server, I also created a corresponding runner.ppk file using PuttyGen.

---

[4] The reason for using ssh-keygen to generate the key pairs is because we need both the private and public key files. Creating the key pair via AWS would give access to the private key but not expose the public key.

713

CHAPTER 16   WORKING THE NEVER-ENDING QUEUE

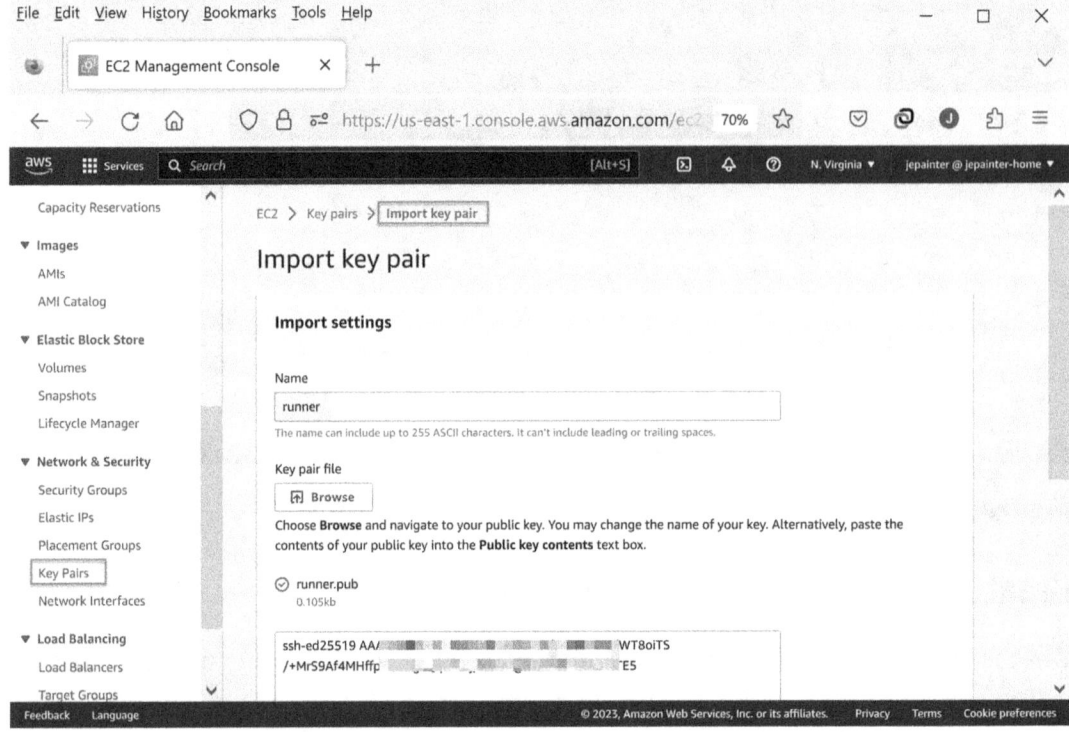

Figure 16-7. *Import of key pair to be used by spun-up runners*

Creating the Runner Manager Server

We are now ready to create the runner manager server. As an admin, you should, by now, have enough experience in spinning up an EC2 server, so I will forgo doing the step-by-step instructions here. Since the runner manager is simply a job coordinator, we only need to spin up a relatively small EC2 instance; in my case, I used a t3.large instance type with an Ubuntu 22.04 AMI. I placed the server in the private subnet within the us-east-1b availability zone. For the disk size, I used a slightly larger 10GB. As shown in Figure 16-8, I added the security group gitlab-loadbalancer-sec-group and set the IAM role to GitLabManagerRunnerRole. For the key pair, I used the same key pair, jpgitlab, that I use for the other GitLab servers.

CHAPTER 16   WORKING THE NEVER-ENDING QUEUE

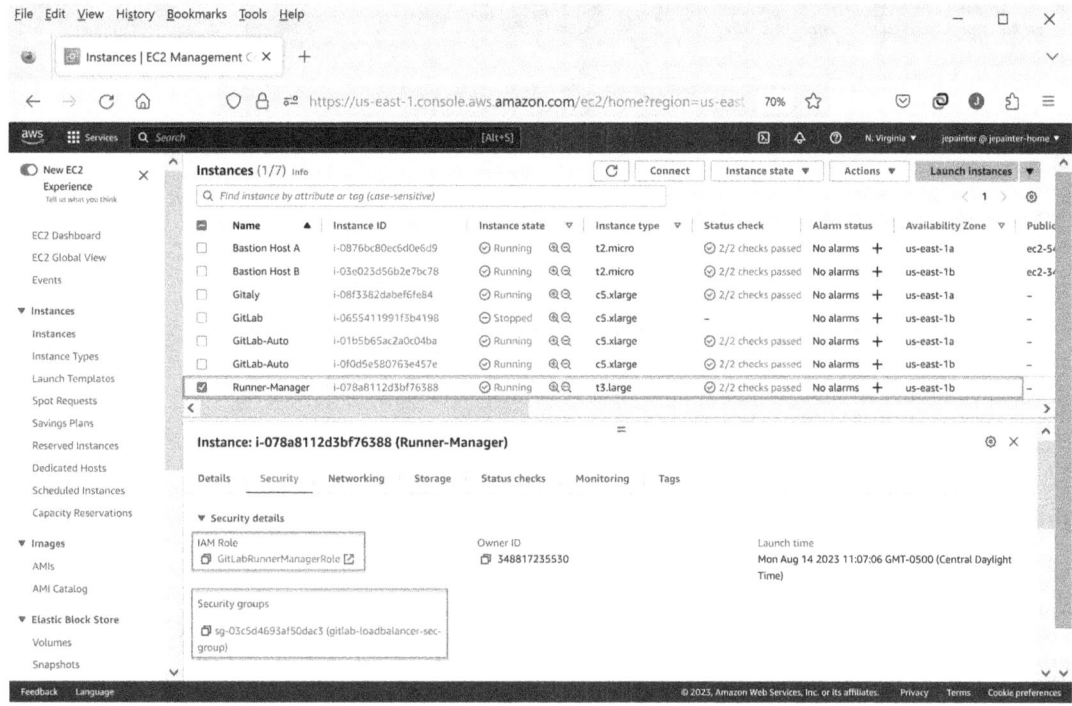

Figure 16-8. *Creation of runner manager instance*

Installing the GitLab Runner Software on the Runner Manager

Once the server is up and running correctly, ssh into it and install the gitlab-runner software as described at `https://docs.gitlab.com/runner/install/linux-repository.html#installing-gitlab-runner`. This involves downloading and running a script that prepares the Linux package repository. The results of doing this for Ubuntu are shown in Figure 16-9. It is important to make sure the runner version is compatible with the GitLab version. For Ubuntu, this involves running the "apt-cache madison gitlab-runner" command as shown in the figure. Since I am currently running the 16.1.2 version of GitLab, I find the latest runner version in the 16.1.x series,[5] which in this case is 16.1.1.

---

[5] Runner software is patched separately from the GitLab software. So here, the patch version of GitLab was 16.1.2, but the latest patch version of the runner was 16.1.1. In other words, the major and minor versions have to match, but the patch version does not.

CHAPTER 16   WORKING THE NEVER-ENDING QUEUE

```
ubuntu@ip-10-0-0-152:~$ curl -L "https://packages.gitlab.com/install/repositories/runner/gitlab-runner/script.deb.sh" | su
do bash
  % Total    % Received % Xferd  Average Speed   Time    Time     Time  Current
                                 Dload  Upload   Total   Spent    Left  Speed
100  6885  100  6885    0     0  32340      0 --:--:-- --:--:-- --:--:-- 32323
Detected operating system as Ubuntu/jammy.
Checking for curl...
Detected curl...
Checking for gpg...
Detected gpg...
Running apt-get update... done.
Installing apt-transport-https... done.
Installing /etc/apt/sources.list.d/runner_gitlab-runner.list...done.
Importing packagecloud gpg key... done.
Running apt-get update... done.

The repository is setup! You can now install packages.
ubuntu@ip-10-0-0-152:~$ apt-cache madison gitlab-runner
 gitlab-runner |     16.2.1 | https://packages.gitlab.com/runner/gitlab-runner/ubuntu jammy/main amd64 Packages
 gitlab-runner |     16.2.0 | https://packages.gitlab.com/runner/gitlab-runner/ubuntu jammy/main amd64 Packages
 gitlab-runner |     16.1.1 | https://packages.gitlab.com/runner/gitlab-runner/ubuntu jammy/main amd64 Packages
 gitlab-runner |     16.1.0 | https://packages.gitlab.com/runner/gitlab-runner/ubuntu jammy/main amd64 Packages
 gitlab-runner |     16.0.3 | https://packages.gitlab.com/runner/gitlab-runner/ubuntu jammy/main amd64 Packages
 gitlab-runner |     16.0.2 | https://packages.gitlab.com/runner/gitlab-runner/ubuntu jammy/main amd64 Packages
 gitlab-runner |     16.0.1 | https://packages.gitlab.com/runner/gitlab-runner/ubuntu jammy/main amd64 Packages
 gitlab-runner |     16.0.0 | https://packages.gitlab.com/runner/gitlab-runner/ubuntu jammy/main amd64 Packages
 gitlab-runner |    15.11.1 | https://packages.gitlab.com/runner/gitlab-runner/ubuntu jammy/main amd64 Packages
 gitlab-runner |    15.11.0 | https://packages.gitlab.com/runner/gitlab-runner/ubuntu jammy/main amd64 Packages
```

Figure 16-9. *Installation of the gitlab-runner package repository on the runner manager*

Once we know the correct version of the GitLab runner software, we can install that explicit version. Figure 16-10 shows the result of installing version 16.1.1 of the runner package in Ubuntu. Note that there are a lot of messages returned during the install process. Since this is the first time installing the package, there are messages noting that Docker has not yet been installed and that there is no existing version of the software. This is to be expected. These messages will change when the GitLab runner software is updated in the future.

CHAPTER 16   WORKING THE NEVER-ENDING QUEUE

```
ubuntu@ip-10-0-0-152:~$ sudo apt-get install gitlab-runner=16.1.1
Reading package lists... Done
Building dependency tree... Done
Reading state information... Done
Suggested packages:
  docker-engine
The following NEW packages will be installed:
  gitlab-runner
0 upgraded, 1 newly installed, 0 to remove and 106 not upgraded.
Need to get 460 MB of archives.
After this operation, 502 MB of additional disk space will be used.
Get:1 https://packages.gitlab.com/runner/gitlab-runner/ubuntu jammy/main amd64 gitlab-runner amd64 16.1.1 [460 MB]
Fetched 460 MB in 13s (36.6 MB/s)
Selecting previously unselected package gitlab-runner.
(Reading database ... 64299 files and directories currently installed.)
Preparing to unpack .../gitlab-runner_16.1.1_amd64.deb ...
Unpacking gitlab-runner (16.1.1) ...
Setting up gitlab-runner (16.1.1) ...
GitLab Runner: creating gitlab-runner...
Home directory skeleton not used
Runtime platform                                    arch=amd64 os=linux pid=2528 revision=51ecdcff version=16.1.1
gitlab-runner: the service is not installed
Runtime platform                                    arch=amd64 os=linux pid=2536 revision=51ecdcff version=16.1.1
gitlab-ci-multi-runner: the service is not installed
Runtime platform                                    arch=amd64 os=linux pid=2556 revision=51ecdcff version=16.1.1
Runtime platform                                    arch=amd64 os=linux pid=2620 revision=51ecdcff version=16.1.1
INFO: Docker installation not found, skipping clear-docker-cache
Scanning processes...
Scanning linux images...

Running kernel seems to be up-to-date.

No services need to be restarted.

No containers need to be restarted.

No user sessions are running outdated binaries.

No VM guests are running outdated hypervisor (qemu) binaries on this host.
ubuntu@ip-10-0-0-152:~$
```

Figure 16-10. Installation of gitlab-runner software on the runner manager

Installing Docker Engine on the Runner Manager

Speaking of Docker, we need to install the Docker Engine on the runner manager. Note that installing Docker Engine on the runner manager is solely needed to run docker-machine, not to run Docker containers for GitLab jobs. The servers spun up by docker-machine will have their own Docker Engine software installed; it is that Docker software that will run GitLab jobs in Docker containers. Since the install of Docker Engine differs by operating system and there are quite a number of steps involved, I'll simply refer you to the page that describes how to install it: https://docs.docker.com/engine/install/#server. When done, you can test your install by running "sudo docker run hello-world". If all goes well, you should see the messages highlighted in Figure 16-11.

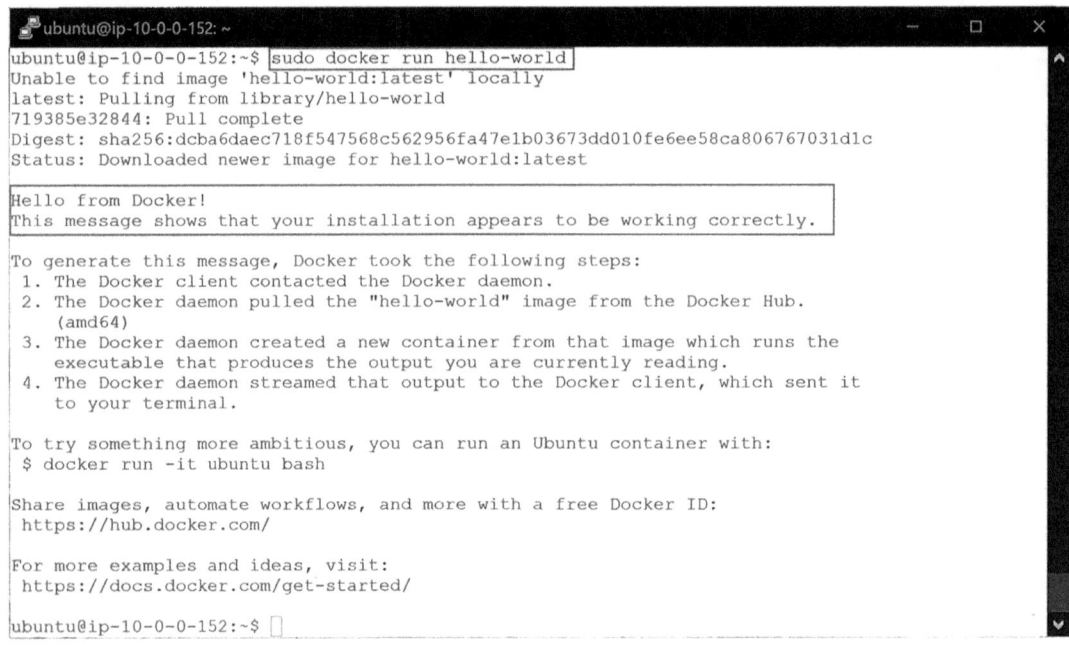

Figure 16-11. Test of Docker Engine installation on the runner manager

Installing the docker-manager Package on the Runner Manager

The final package to be installed on the runner manager server is the docker-manager package. As mentioned earlier, GitLab now maintains a fork of the docker-manager project; you'll need to install the latest version of GitLab's docker-manager software. You can find the GitLab project here: https://gitlab.com/gitlab-org/ci-cd/docker-machine. In the README section of that project, you'll find a link on "Installation and documentation." At the time of this writing, the latest version was v0.16.2-gitlab.11.[6] Figure 16-12 shows the commands and their results used to install this version. Note the use of sudo[7] to copy and change the execution status of docker-machine.

---

[6] Version 0.16.2 was the last official version of docker-machine released by the Docker team. The -gitlab.11 suffix indicates the version maintained by GitLab after the Docker official release.

[7] I mention this since the documented instructions failed to show this.

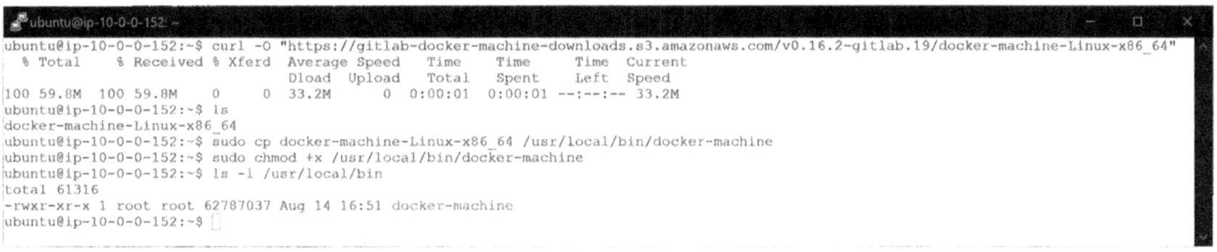

CHAPTER 16 WORKING THE NEVER-ENDING QUEUE

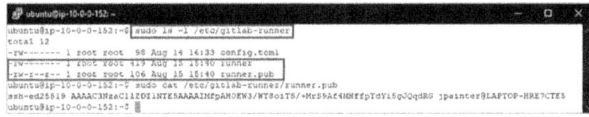

Figure 16-12. Installation of the docker-machine package on the runner manager

Spinning Up a Test Runner with docker-machine

We can now turn our attention to configuring the gitlab-runner. When the gitlab-runner package is installed, it creates the directory /etc/gitlab-runner that is owned by root and is only accessible by the root user. The reason for this is to keep secrets within the configuration file private; we will also be storing SSH keys there. While logged in to the runner manager server, become the super user by running "sudo su" and cd to the /etc/gitlab-runner directory. Here, create the runner private key file and the runner.pub public key file by copying and pasting the contents from your local SSH key files created earlier. Make sure the runner file is readable only to root (chmod 0600 runner). Figure 16-13 shows what the directory will look like after the SSH key files are created there.

Figure 16-13. Preparation of runner SSH key files on the runner manager

You'll see a generated config.toml file in the /etc/gitlab-runner directory. This is the configuration file for gitlab-runner. By default, it does nothing. We'll update this momentarily, but before we do that, this is a good time to test docker-machine to ensure that it can spin servers up and down. The reason for testing this separately from the GitLab runner configuration is that it helps isolate any issues with the runner configuration; if we can't get docker-machine to create and destroy EC2 servers, neither will gitlab-runner be able to.

719

CHAPTER 16   WORKING THE NEVER-ENDING QUEUE

Creating and Running a Test Script for docker-machine

Since testing docker-machine is something I frequently do when debugging issues with the GitLab runner, I add a shell script in /etc/gitlab-runner directory called testme.sh that runs the docker-machine create command. The contents of this file are shown as follows. Feel free to copy the contents for your own script file, making sure to update REPLACEME with the specifics of your AWS environment. Note that you'll need to be root (via sudo su) to create this file. Also, make sure the testme.sh is executable (chmod +x testme.sh).

```bash
#!/bin/bash
docker-machine create -d amazonec2 \
  --amazonec2-iam-instance-profile GitLabRunnerManagerRole \
  --amazonec2-region us-east-1 \
  --amazonec2-vpc-id vpc-REPLACEME \
  --amazonec2-subnet-id subnet-REPLACEME \
  --amazonec2-zone b \
  --amazonec2-private-address-only \
  --amazonec2-security-group gitlab-runner-sec-group \
  --amazonec2-instance-type "t2.micro" \
  --amazonec2-keypair-name runner \
  --amazonec2-ssh-keypath /etc/gitlab-runner/runner \
  --amazonec2-tags "runner-manager-name,gitlab-aws-autoscaler,gitlab,true,gitlab-runner-autoscale,true" \
  runner-test
```

A special thing to note here is that docker-machine can only create servers in a specific availability zone. In the preceding script, it creates servers in zone b of us-east-1. Your subnet-id needs to refer to the private subnet associated with that zone within your GitLab private VPC. If you need to manage GitLab runners in another zone, you'll need to create another runner manager server for that zone; that runner manager is typically in the same zone as the runner servers that it will spin up. Because of the dependencies between the region, vpc-id, subnet-id, and zone options earlier, using a testme.sh script helps to ensure that they all work correctly together.

Figure 16-14 shows the results of running the testme.sh script as user root. If all goes well, you'll see the "Docker is up and running!" message when docker-machine create is done. Along the way, you'll see the various steps it takes to set up the runner-test server. You may notice when you run this that one of the longer steps is the installation of Docker. If you want to optimize this, you could create your own AMI with Docker preinstalled; I won't go through that here, but at this point, you should be able to figure this out on your own.

```
root@ip-10-0-0-152:/etc/gitlab-runner# ls -l
total 16
-rw-------  1 root root  98 Aug 14 16:33 config.toml
-rw-------  1 root root 419 Aug 15 15:40 runner
-rw-r--r--  1 root root 106 Aug 15 15:40 runner.pub
-rwxr-xr-x  1 root root 606 Aug 15 17:01 testme.sh
root@ip-10-0-0-152:/etc/gitlab-runner# ./testme.sh
Running pre-create checks...
Creating machine...
(runner-test) Launching instance...
Waiting for machine to be running, this may take a few minutes...
Detecting operating system of created instance...
Waiting for SSH to be available...
Detecting the provisioner...
Provisioning with ubuntu(systemd)...
Installing Docker...
Copying certs to the local machine directory...
Copying certs to the remote machine...
Setting Docker configuration on the remote daemon...
Checking connection to Docker...
Docker is up and running!
To see how to connect your Docker Client to the Docker Engine running on this virtual machine, run: docker-machine env runner-test
root@ip-10-0-0-152:/etc/gitlab-runner#
```

Figure 16-14. Sample results of running the testme.sh script

Debugging Failures of the Test Script

If the testme.sh script fails, it usually means something isn't aligned properly. In this case, you'll need to go through and double-check the "docker-machine create" options as well as the roles and policies. There are times, though, when the docker-machine create option successfully creates the EC2 instance but fails to initialize it. One example of this is shown in Figure 16-15. In this case, the EC2 instance was created and SSH connectivity was established; however, a failure occurred when running "sudo apt-get update." The apt-get update command does tend to be a bit flaky at times. It isn't docker-machine's fault, although it could work to better detect this situation. If this becomes a problem for you, I recommend creating an AMI with Docker already installed so that the docker-machine command does not try to install it.

CHAPTER 16   WORKING THE NEVER-ENDING QUEUE

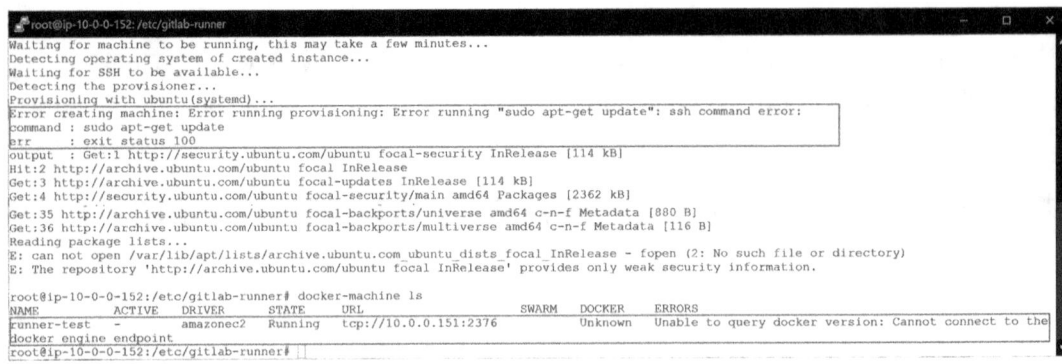

Figure 16-15. Example testme.sh error

Verifying the Test Runner Server Is Running

When the testme.sh script completes successfully, you'll be able to see the new runner in your list of EC2 instances as shown in Figure 16-16. As you can see, the name of the new instance is runner-test, which is the name passed within the testme.sh script. Also shown are the tags that were defined in the script; there isn't anything special about them, in case you were wondering. This just illustrates how you can create tags using the docker-machine create command. In case you are wondering about the t2.micro type, it's fine to use for debugging since the runner-test server won't be used to run any GitLab jobs.

CHAPTER 16 WORKING THE NEVER-ENDING QUEUE

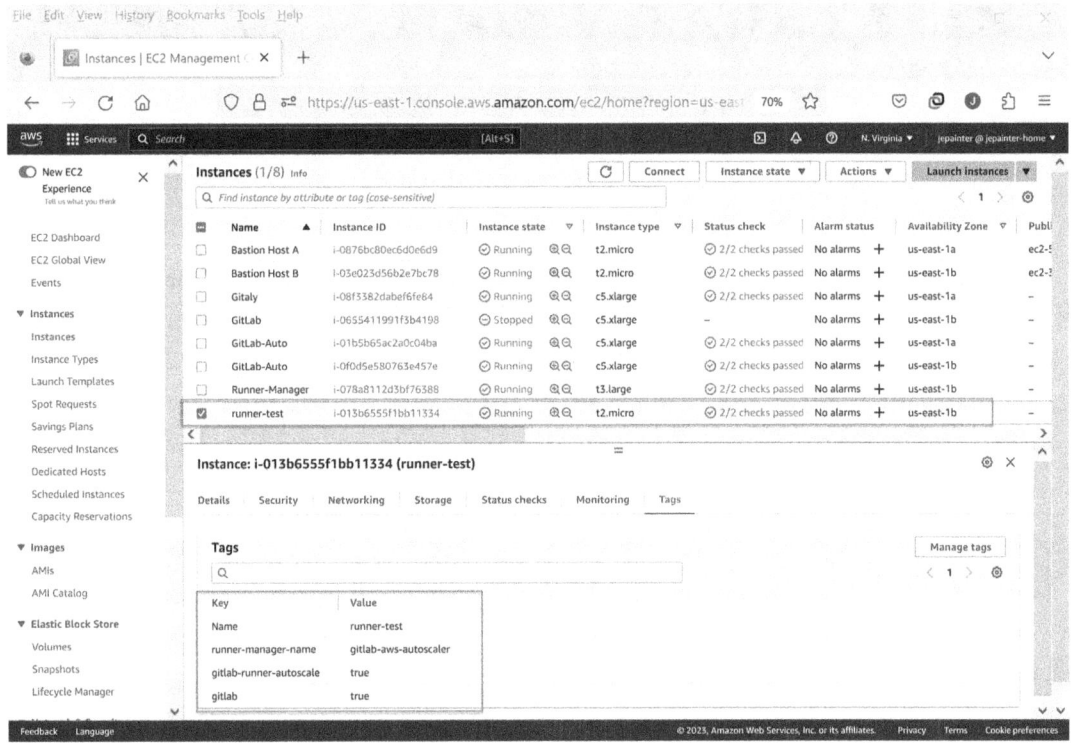

Figure 16-16. *EC2 instance list showing runner-test instance*

Terminating the Test Runner Server with docker-machine

At this point, you might be tempted to stop or terminate the runner-test instance via the AWS console. It is important to realize that docker-machine is managing this server; stopping or terminating the runner-test server will interfere with the proper operation of docker-machine. So, while we are here, let's look at other docker-machine commands that are useful to know.

The most useful docker-machine command is ls. This lists all the runner servers managed by docker-machine on this runner manager. Figure 16-17 shows an example of running docker-machine ls. In this example, you see that the runner-test server is running. It also shows what version of Docker was installed and what the Docker URL is. When other servers are being created, you'll also see the status of those servers. In case of failure, you'll see those listed here as well.

723

CHAPTER 16   WORKING THE NEVER-ENDING QUEUE

```
root@ip-10-0-0-152:/etc/gitlab-runner# docker-machine ls
NAME          ACTIVE   DRIVER      STATE     URL                      SWARM   DOCKER    ERRORS
runner-test   -        amazonec2   Running   tcp://10.0.0.148:2376            v24.0.5
root@ip-10-0-0-152:/etc/gitlab-runner#
```

Figure 16-17. *Listing of runners via the docker-machine ls command*

Another useful command is rm. This removes the runner server managed by docker-machine. Figure 16-18 shows the results of running "docker-machine rm runner-test." Note that when you run this command, you'll get a notification reminding you that continuing with this command will terminate the EC2 runner instance, if any. You'll need to run this command even when the docker-machine create command fails to create an EC2 instance.

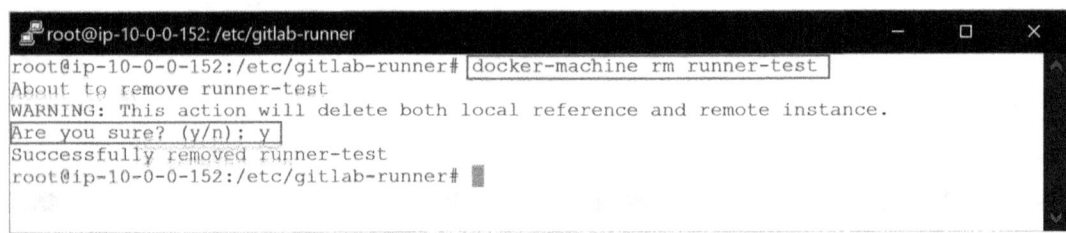

Figure 16-18. *Removal of runner via the docker-machine rm command*

You should know that you can only have one runner server with a given name. So, if you run the testme.sh script twice, the second run will fail since docker-machine already has a server named runner-test. You must use docker-machine rm to remove it before running the script again. It is also important to know, when gitlab-runner uses docker-machine to create runners on its behalf, you should not use the docker-machine rm command to delete that server as it will interfere with any GitLab jobs running on that server. However, there may be times when docker-machine fails when managed by gitlab-runner; in those cases, you will need to use docker-machine rm to remove those "orphaned" servers.

Logging In to the Runner Server via SSH

Before we switch to configuring gitlab-runner, let's take a minute to see how to ssh into the spun-up runner instance. First, if you are using Pageant to manage the ssh-agent keys, make sure to add the runner.ppk key to Pageant as shown in Figure 16-19. You may need to stop Pageant and restart it again with the key or manually add the key.

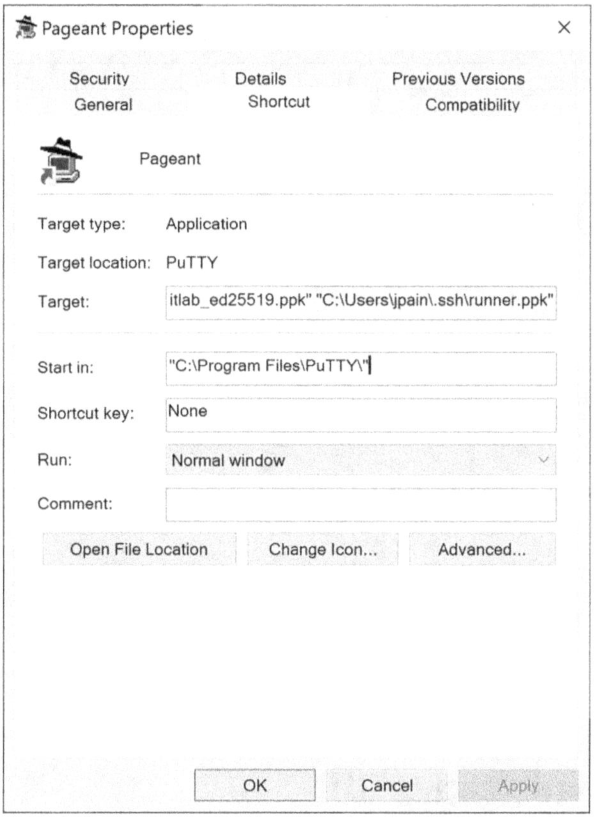

CHAPTER 16   WORKING THE NEVER-ENDING QUEUE

Figure 16-19. Adding the runner.ppk key to Putty's Pageant startup configuration

With the new ssh-agent keys set up, re-log in to one of the bastion servers so that those keys take effect. Now, if you terminated runner-test, run testme.sh again to spin a new server up and then note the new IP address. In order to ssh into the spun-up server, you need to exit back to the bastion server; you cannot ssh from the runner manager server to the spun-up runner instance, at least not using ssh-agent. From the bastion server, you can then ssh into the runner-test instance as shown in Figure 16-20. In this example, 10.0.0.152 is my runner manager server, and 10.0.0.29 is my bastion server. The spun-up runner instance in this example is 10.0.0.150. Once logged in to the runner-test instance, note the Linux prompt uses runner-test rather than the IP address; this is one way I can tell that I'm on the runner-test instance. Running "sudo docker info" confirms that the Docker version installed on the runner instance matches the version returned by the "docker-machine ls" command.

725

CHAPTER 16   WORKING THE NEVER-ENDING QUEUE

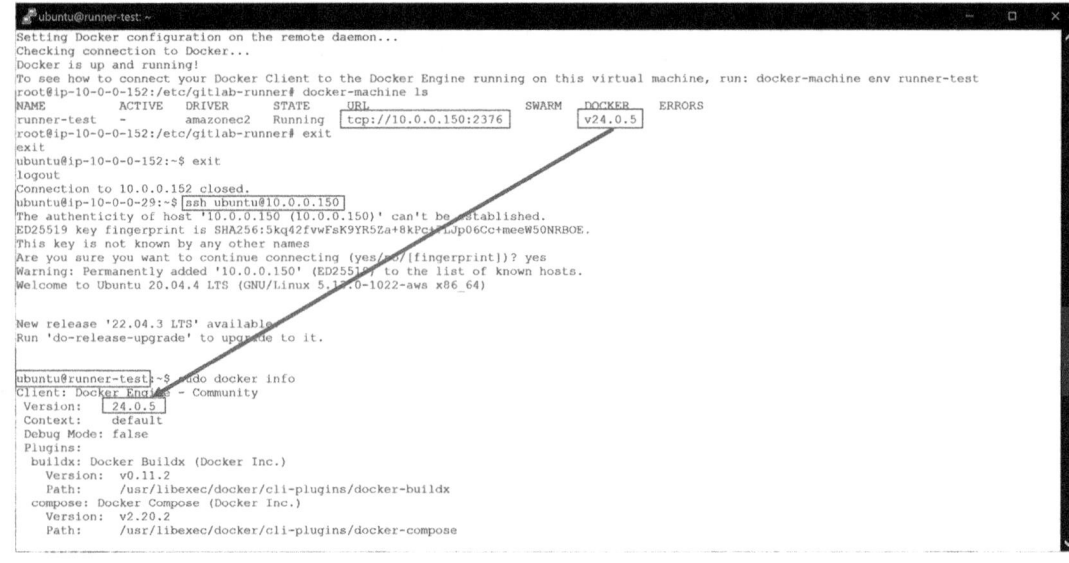

Figure 16-20. *Using SSH to log in to the spun-up runner instance from the bastion server*

Creating an Instance Runner Entry from the Administrative GUI

With the docker-machine stuff out of the way, we can now begin to look at the gitlab-runner configuration. Since gitlab-runner is a service separate from the GitLab service, we need a way to register the gitlab-runner service with GitLab to ensure it has the authority to run jobs on GitLab's behalf. Starting with version 15.0 of gitlab-runner, there has been a change in how the registration process is started. The process that I used in my admin days is now deprecated, so I'll focus on the new process here. I must say, it is an improvement on how registration was performed in earlier versions of gitlab-runner.

Registering the Runner Manager

Registration begins with the GitLab administrative UI. Figure 16-21 shows how to set up shared runners, also known as instance runners. From the Admin Area menu, select Runners under the CI/CD submenu. Here, you'll see the list of runners currently available; in this example, none have been set up yet. Selecting the "New instance runners" button begins the registration process. Note that we are not actually creating the runner from here, just creating an entry for it.

CHAPTER 16 WORKING THE NEVER-ENDING QUEUE

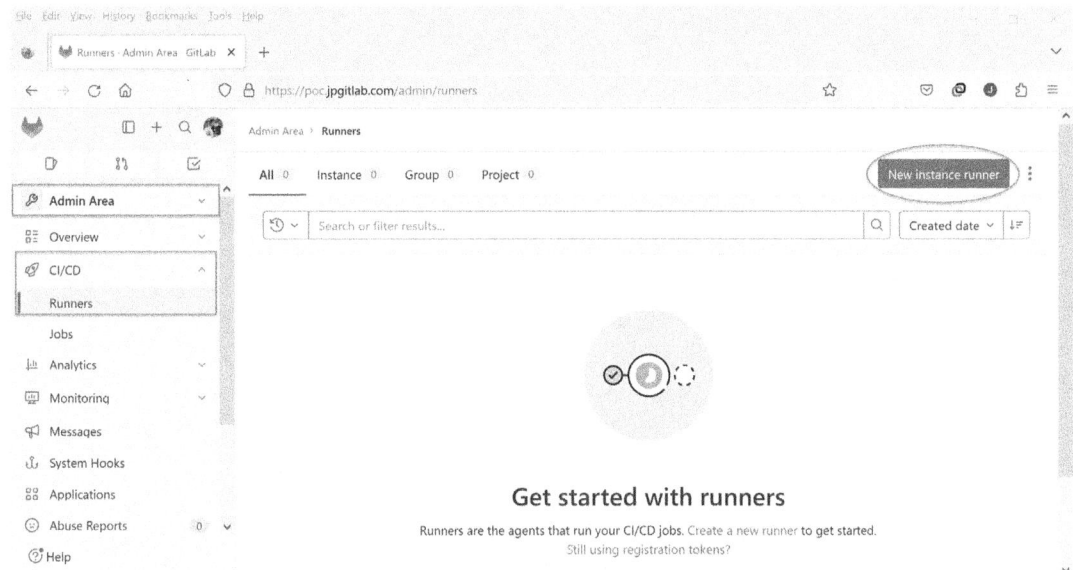

Figure 16-21. *Initial shared runner administration page*

Figure 16-22 shows the top of the "New instance runner" form. Here, we select what type of operating system or Docker container service we are using for the actual runner. Since we are implementing the auto-scaling runner service via EC2, we select the Linux operating system as the platform.[8]

---

[8] This can get confusing. Although we are spinning up Docker servers via the runner manager, we need to select Linux since that is the OS used by the runner manager. The Containers section is used when gitlab-runner itself is run in a Docker container either standalone or as part of Kubernetes.

CHAPTER 16   WORKING THE NEVER-ENDING QUEUE

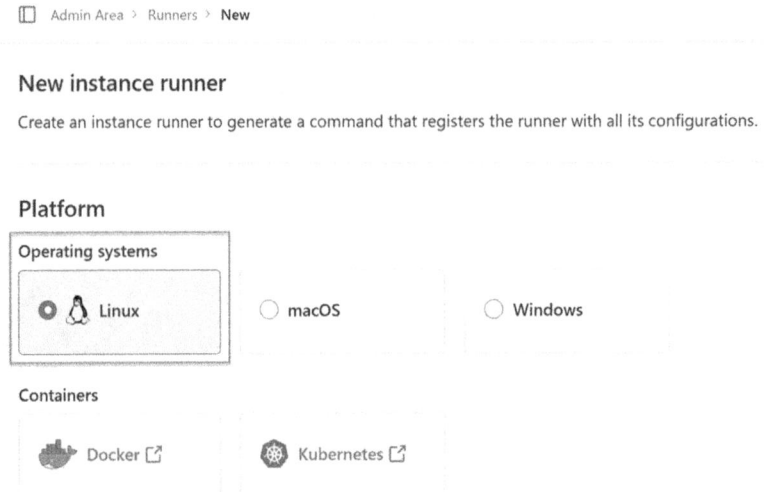

Figure 16-22. Selection of operating system for spun-up runners

Setting GitLab Runner Tags

Further down on the "New instance runner" form is the section on tags as shown in Figure 16-23. It is important to note that these are not AWS tags but rather GitLab job tags within a CI/CD script to filter what runners are allowed to execute the job. In this example, I've added the two tags "shared" and "us-east-1b"; you can use whatever tags make sense in your development environment. I've also selected the "Run untagged jobs" option that allows these runners to execute any GitLab jobs that are not tagged; this is a common option with shared instance runners.

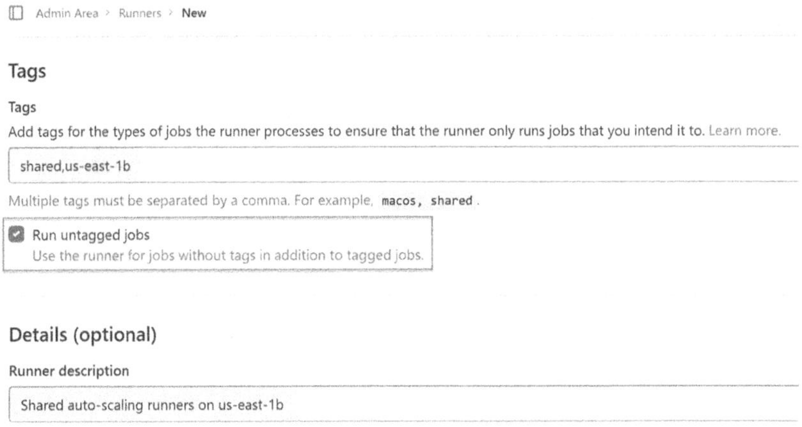

CHAPTER 16   WORKING THE NEVER-ENDING QUEUE

```
Admin Area > Runners > New
```

Tags

Tags
Add tags for the types of jobs the runner processes to ensure that the runner only runs jobs that you intend it to. Learn more.

```
shared,us-east-1b
```

Multiple tags must be separated by a comma. For example, `macos, shared`.

☑ Run untagged jobs
   Use the runner for jobs without tags in addition to tagged jobs.

Details (optional)

Runner description

```
Shared auto-scaling runners on us-east-1b
```

Figure 16-23. Definition of runner tags and runner description

Preventing the Runner Manager from Taking Jobs

Next on the form are some additional runner configuration options. This is shown in Figure 16-24. Since we are using a runner manager, I selected the "Paused" option so that jobs don't get assigned to this runner when we register it from the runner manager server. The reason for this is due to the complexity of the runner configuration for auto-scaling runners. We'll see this later. Once the configuration is completed, we can come back to the Admin UI and unpause the runner so that it can start taking new job requests. I left the "Protected" option unchecked and did not specify a maximum job timeout.

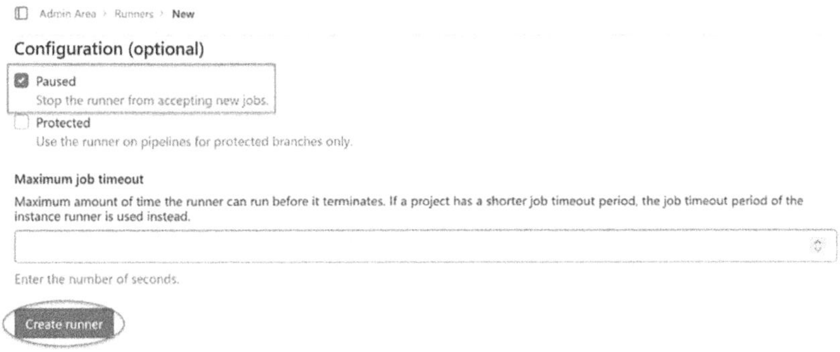

```
Admin Area > Runners > New
```

Configuration (optional)

☑ Paused
   Stop the runner from accepting new jobs.

☐ Protected
   Use the runner on pipelines for protected branches only.

Maximum job timeout
Maximum amount of time the runner can run before it terminates. If a project has a shorter job timeout period, the job timeout period of the instance runner is used instead.

```
                                                                    ◊
```

Enter the number of seconds.

(**Create runner**)

Figure 16-24. Additional runner configuration options

Retrieving the Runner Authentication Token

Selecting "Create runner" displays the runner created page as shown in Figure 16-25. This page gives a set of steps to be performed on the runner server side. The important piece of information is the runner authentication token provided in step one; it starts with the prefix "glrt-" that lets the gitlab-runner software know this is part of the new registration process. Make sure to copy this token including the "glrt-" prefix since you won't be able to access it once you leave this web page. You can ignore the steps provided here as they are slightly different for auto-scaling runners.

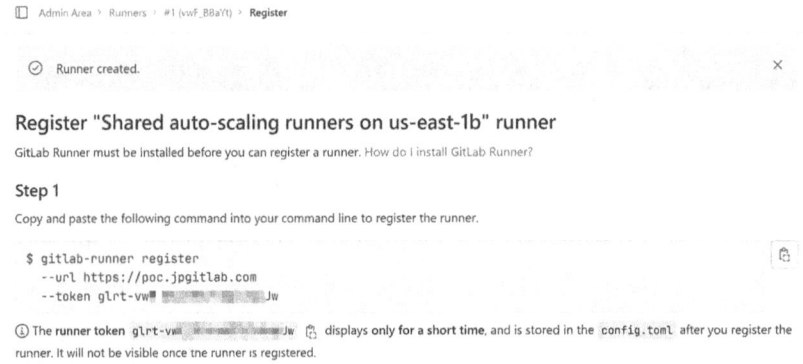

Figure 16-25. Instructions containing the generated runner authentication token

Reviewing the Instance Runner Entry from the Administrative UI

Before we configure gitlab-runner on the runner manager server, let's take a look at the runner entry created by the form just filled out. Figure 16-26 shows the entry for our instance runner. Note that it is marked as an instance runner as opposed to a group or project runner. Also, note the GitLab tags underneath the runner description matches what we entered in the form. By the way, if you want to change these tags, you can do so by editing the runner in the UI. We also can see that the runner is in the Paused state by the label underneath the Status column. Once the configuration is completed on the runner manager, we can select the play button on the right-hand side to unpause it.

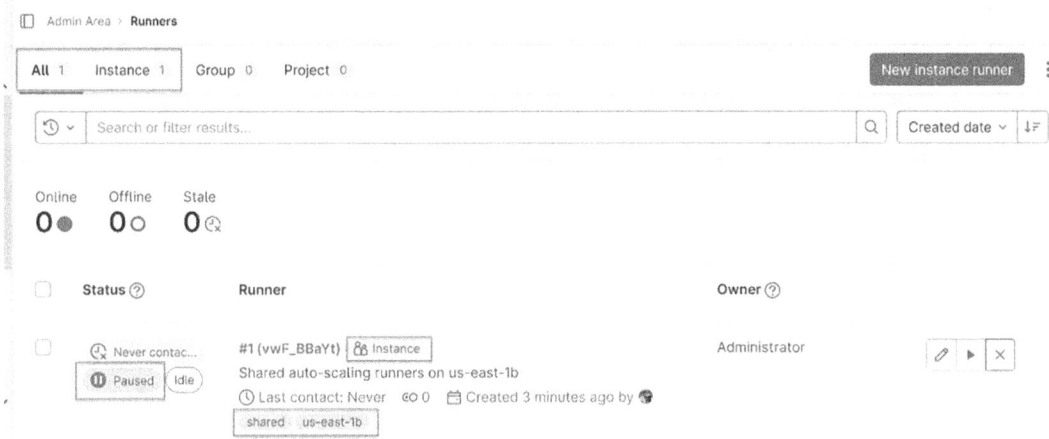

Figure 16-26. Listing of system-wide instance runners

Creating the register-me Script on the Runner Manager

With the runner entry created on the UI side, we now switch to the runner manager server. Like I did with the testme.sh script, I created a register-me.sh script in /etc/gitlab-runner to make life easier. A copy of this script with secrets redacted is given as follows. Note that the script is owned by root and is marked as executable (chmod 0755). If you use this script, make sure to change the URL and the name accordingly as well as copy your runner authentication token:

```
#!/bin/bash
# The register-config.toml file contains the initial config.toml settings
generated by gitlab-runner register.register-me.sh
# If the file does not exist, the gitlab-runner will register with the
GitLab server and create the register-config.toml file.
# If the file does exist, this script skips the registration process.
# In either case, the script returns all settings with the word
token in it.
#
if [ ! -f /etc/gitlab-runner/register-config.toml ]; then
 gitlab-runner register \
 --non-interactive \
 --config /etc/gitlab-runner/register-config.toml \
 --url "https://poc.jpgitlab.com" \
```

```
  --token "glrt-REDACTED" \
  --executor "docker+machine" \
  --docker-image alpine:latest \
  --name "aws-autoscaler-1b" \
  &> /etc/gitlab-runner/register-me.log
fi
grep "token" /etc/gitlab-runner/register-config.toml
```

Results of Running the register-me Script

Figure 16-27 shows the results of running the register-me.sh script from my runner manager server. Running the script created two files: register-config.toml and register-me.log. The log file just shows the output generated by the gitlab-runner register command and is useful for debugging issues. The register-config.toml file is the configuration file generated by the register command; the original config.toml file remains untouched. The reason the register-me.sh script creates the register-config.toml file rather than replaces the config.toml file is because the generated toml file does not work for our auto-scaling setup. Instead, we'll explicitly create the config.toml file using information extracted from the register-config.toml file.

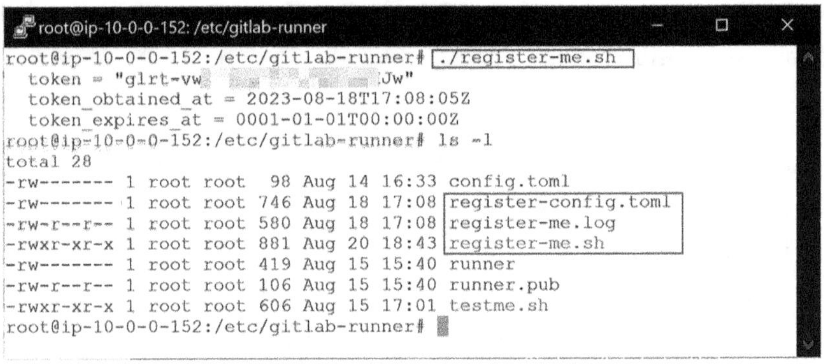

Figure 16-27. Results of running the register-me.sh script on the runner manager

Creating the config.toml File

The final step on the runner manager is to set up the config.toml file. With auto-scaling, this gets a bit complicated, so we'll work through the different sections in turn. A copy of my config.toml file with secrets redacted is given as follows:

```
#
# Useful links:
#
# https://docs.gitlab.com/runner/configuration/advanced-configuration.html
# https://docs.gitlab.com/runner/configuration/runner_autoscale_aws/
# https://docs.gitlab.com/runner/executors/docker_machine.html
# https://docs.docker.com/machine/drivers/aws/
#
concurrent = 3
check_interval = 0
#log_level = "debug"
[[runners]]
 name = "runner-manager-1b"
 url = "https://poc.jpgitlab.com"
 clone_url = "https://poc.jpgitlab.com"
 token = "glrt-REDACTED"
 token_obtained_at = 2023-08-18T17:08:05Z
 token_expires_at = 0001-01-01T00:00:00Z
 executor = "docker+machine"
 limit = 3
 output_limit = 204800
 environment = ["DOCKER_TLS_CERTDIR="]
 [runners.docker]
 image = "alpine:latest"
 tls_verify = false
 privileged = true
 disable_cache = true
 shm_size = 0
 volumes = ["/cache"]
 [runners.cache]
 Type = "s3"
 Shared = true
 [runners.cache.s3]
 ServerAddress = "s3.amazonaws.com"
 BucketName = "jpgitlab-poc-cache"
```

```
BucketLocation = "us-east-1"
ServerSideEncryption = "KMS"
ServerSideEncryptionKeyID = "alias/gitlab-s3-key"
[runners.machine]
IdleCount = 1
IdleTime = 1800
MaxBuilds = 50
MachineDriver = "amazonec2"
MachineName = "jpgitlab-poc-1b-%s"
MachineOptions = [
"engine-label=my-name=jpgitlab-poc-1b",
"amazonec2-region=us-east-1",
"amazonec2-vpc-id=vpc-REPLACEME",
"amazonec2-subnet-id=subnet-REPLACEME",
"amazonec2-zone=b",
"amazonec2-private-address-only=true",
"amazonec2-tags=runner-manager-name,runner-manager-1b,gitlab,true,gitlab-runner-autoscale,true",
"amazonec2-security-group=gitlab-runner-sec-group",
"amazonec2-iam-instance-profile=GitLabRunnerManagerRole",
"amazonec2-instance-type=m6a.large",
"amazonec2-keypair-name=runner",
"amazonec2-ssh-keypath=/etc/gitlab-runner/runner",
"amazonec2-root-size=50",
]
[[runners.machine.autoscaling]]
Periods = ["* * 9-17 * * mon-fri *"]
IdleCount = 1
IdleTime = 1800
Timezone = "America/Chicago"
[[runners.machine.autoscaling]]
Periods = ["* * * * * sat,sun *"]
IdleCount = 0
IdleTime = 1200
Timezone = "America/Chicago"
```

An Overview of the config.toml File

Looking at the contents of the config.toml file, your first impression is that it is like an INI configuration file. In fact, TOML, which stands for "Tom's Obvious, Minimal Language," was written as a replacement for INI. Its use is as a format for configurations (hence the name config.toml). There are some subtleties to the format such as the difference between items enclosed in single brackets, such as "[runners.docker]," and items enclosed in double brackets, such as "[[runners]]." The former denotes the beginning of a dictionary, and the latter denotes items related to an array.[9] The good news is, you won't have to create this by hand; you can simply copy and edit the file contents.

The Global Options Section

As an admin, I like to put useful links at the top of the file so that maintainers can find relevant information about the content.[10] These are entered as comments using the pound (#) character. The first set of lines represent global options applicable to everything else within the file. The concurrent option determines the maximum number of jobs managed by this runner manager that can run concurrently. Here, I've set the value to three since this is a poc environment where I don't expect a lot of jobs to run. Remember that with an auto-scaler runner, one job equals one spun-up runner server, so this value also determines the number of runner servers that may be spun up. The check_interval option determines the time interval in seconds for checking new jobs; the value of zero here indicates that the default time interval of three seconds should be used. I commented out the debug log_level option since this generates a lot of data in /var/log/syslog; I leave it here in case things don't work properly, and we need to do some debugging.

The Runners Section

After the global options section is the runners section. The double brackets mean that this is an array. In other words, we can have multiple "runners" sections with their own configurations. Here, we only define one such configuration for runner servers in the us-east-1b availability zone. We could have additional sections to control runners in different availability zones or with different instance types if we wanted to.

---

[9] If you think this is not very "obvious," there are many who agree.
[10] Not only maintainers but myself as well since I tire of having to continually search the Web for this information.

Within the runners section, the name option is simply a description that isn't used.[11] Following the name option are the url and clone_url options both set to the standalone GitLab server. In my experience, setting both options to the same URL reduces issues with the spun-up runner servers. The token, token_obtained_at, and token_expired_at options are the same ones retrieved from the register-config.toml file. In the old days, the token was a value different from the runner authentication token generated by the gitlab-runner register command; with the latest changes, token is the same as the runner authentication token.

The most important option here is the executor option. Setting it to "docker+machine" tells gitlab-runner that docker-machine is used to spin up the actual runners. The limit option is similar to the global concurrent option in that it sets the maximum number of jobs that can be run for this runner configuration. Since we only have one "runners" section, the limit value should match the global concurrency value. The output_limit option controls the maximum size of the job log. The default is, IMHO, set pretty low at 4Mb, so I've set it here to around 200Mb.

Using the environment option, we can set system variables in the spun-up runner server. Here, I am setting the DOCKER_TLS_CERTDIR system variable to be null (a.k.a. unset). I am doing this to disable TLS checking when the runner manager connects to the Docker daemon on the runner server. An explanation of this can be found here: https://about.gitlab.com/blog/2019/07/31/docker-in-docker-with-docker-19-dot-03/. In short, this workaround is being done so that users can run jobs that need Docker-in-Docker (a.k.a. dind).

Subsections of the Runners Section

Underneath the runners section are three subsections: runners.docker, runners.cache, and runners.machine. At a high level, the runners.docker subsection contains configuration options specific to Docker. The runners.cache subsection contains options specific to the runner cache environment, and the runners.machine subsection contains options for docker-machine. We'll look at each subsection in turn.

---

[11] Perhaps the option would have been better named "description" rather than "name," but I digress.

The runners.docker Subsection

Within the runners.docker subsection, we set the default Docker image to the latest version of alpine; this applies only when an image is not specified in the CI/CD job configuration. We disable TLS by setting the tls_verify option to false. In order to enable dind services for jobs, we set the privileged option to true; note that running Docker in privileged mode is a security risk, but within a corporate environment should be OK. Setting disable_cache to true disables the use of local caches on the runner's filesystem; it does not impact the global S3 cache. I included the shm_size option to show that you can set aside some memory on the runner that can be shared across containers on that runner; this is useful for test environments where you need to set up coordinating containers. Finally, I set up a Docker volume for /cache using the volumes option.

The runners.cache Subsection

Options for S3 caching are defined in the runners.cache subsection. Here, we set the "type" option to be "s3" and set "shared" to true to indicate that the s3 bucket will be shared across all runners managed by this runner configuration. Within the runners.cache subsection is the runners.cache.s3 subsection that defines the options specific to AWS S3. These include options that specify the name and location of the S3 bucket to use for caching (in this case, the jpgitlab-poc-cache bucket in the us-east-1 region). Also included are the encryption options pointing to the KMS key we created with alias gitlab-s3-key.

The runners.machine Subsection

The final subsection, runners.machine, includes options specific to docker-machine. It is here that we let docker-machine know we are using the MachineDriver amazonec2. The MachineName option determines the names of runners associated with this configuration. Note that this name must include "%s" in order for each spun-up runner to receive a unique name. The IdleCount of zero is the default minimum number of servers to have up and ready to receive jobs; a value of zero means that no runners will be spun up prior to accepting jobs. IdleTime represents the time in seconds a server needs to remain idle before taken down. Here, I've set the idle time to 30 minutes. The MaxBuilds option sets the maximum number of jobs a runner may execute; once this number is reached, the runner is terminated to be replaced by another.[12]

Looking at MachineOptions, you'll recognize the same types of options we used in the testme.sh script. In place of Linux options such as "--amazonec2-region us-east-1," we have key-value pairs in the form "amazonec2-region=us-east-1." The values used in the testme.sh script should be used here with a couple of differences. Under MachineOptions, I set amazonec2-instance-type to m6a.large, which should be adequate for most Docker jobs run by the shared runners. I also set amazonec2-root-size to 50 so that there will be enough disk size (50Gb) for generated artifacts and the like. You may need to tweak these for your own development environment.

The one odd option under MachineOptions is engine-label. It is not well described in the docker-machine documentation, but it can be useful when doing metrics. The "engine" part of engine-label refers to the Docker engine, and the "label" part refers to Docker object labels. An object label is a key-value pair added as metadata to Docker objects. In this example, I am setting the key "my-name" to the value "jpgitlab-poc-1b." I'll show how this manifests itself later once a runner is spun up.

The runners.machine.autoscaling Subsections

Finally, there are two subsections titled runners.machine.autoscaling. Each of these sections sets up overriding options based on specific time periods. For example, the first set of autoscaling options defines options to use during normal operating business hours. The second set defines options for weekends. You may recognize the values for Periods as being cron specifications. The most common options used with autoscaling are IdleCount and IdleTime. The trade-off here is between improving performance during busy times and reducing costs during off-peak times. In a production environment, you'll find yourself tweaking these values initially to get the right balance for your needs.

Other Configuration Options

There are a lot of other configuration options you can set in the config.toml file. I've only included ones that I found useful in my development environments and that you can use as a starting point in yours. You can find a comprehensive list of options in the first

---

[12] This seems like an odd thing to require, but it turns out that runner servers tend to "get crusty" over time with leftover images and the like.

CHAPTER 16 WORKING THE NEVER-ENDING QUEUE

advanced-configuration html link at the top of the config.toml file earlier. I find it best to start with a configuration that works and tweak the options iteratively to get to the configuration that works best for you.[13]

Applying the New Gitlab-Runner Configuration

Well, that was a lot to go through, but now you should be able to copy and edit the preceding config.toml file in your runner manager's /etc/gitlab-runner directory. Once the changes are checked in, it usually doesn't take long for gitlab-runner to apply them (usually within three minutes). If you get impatient like me, you can simply run "gitlab-runner restart" to get things going. Once you do, the first thing to do is check out the /var/log/syslog file. Figure 16-28 shows a sample output of running "tail -f /var/log/syslog | grep gitlab-runner." If all goes well, you should see messages similar to when you ran testme.sh. If not, you will likely see error messages pointing to what gitlab-runner is complaining about, typically a syntax error or unrecognized option in the config.toml file.

Figure 16-28. Example system log output on the runner manager

---

[13] I say this from experience as it is hard to get configurations working properly. I've seen people ignore my advice and take two to three days trying to get runners to spin up as expected. Experience matters here.

739

CHAPTER 16   WORKING THE NEVER-ENDING QUEUE

Checking the Gitlab-Runner Status

The next step is to check the gitlab-runner status and do a docker-machine ls as shown in Figure 16-29. For gitlab-runner status, you should see that it is up and running; if not, do a gitlab-runner start to kick things into gear. For docker-machine ls, you should see the runner server up and running as shown in the figure. If you run ls while the server is being spun up, you may see error messages about not being able to connect, etc. These are expected. Give it a minute or so for the server to be fully prepped.

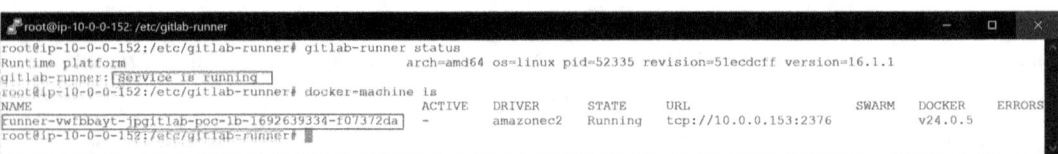

Figure 16-29. Check of gitlab-runner status

Viewing Spun-Up Runner EC2 Instances

From here, check out the EC2 list from the AWS console as shown in Figure 16-30. Here, we can see the spun-up runner server whose name starts with "runner-". Assuming everything went well with gitlab-runner, the instance should be up and running with instance type m6a.large in availability zone us-east-1b. Also, note how the tags match the values specified under MachineOptions in config.toml.

CHAPTER 16   WORKING THE NEVER-ENDING QUEUE

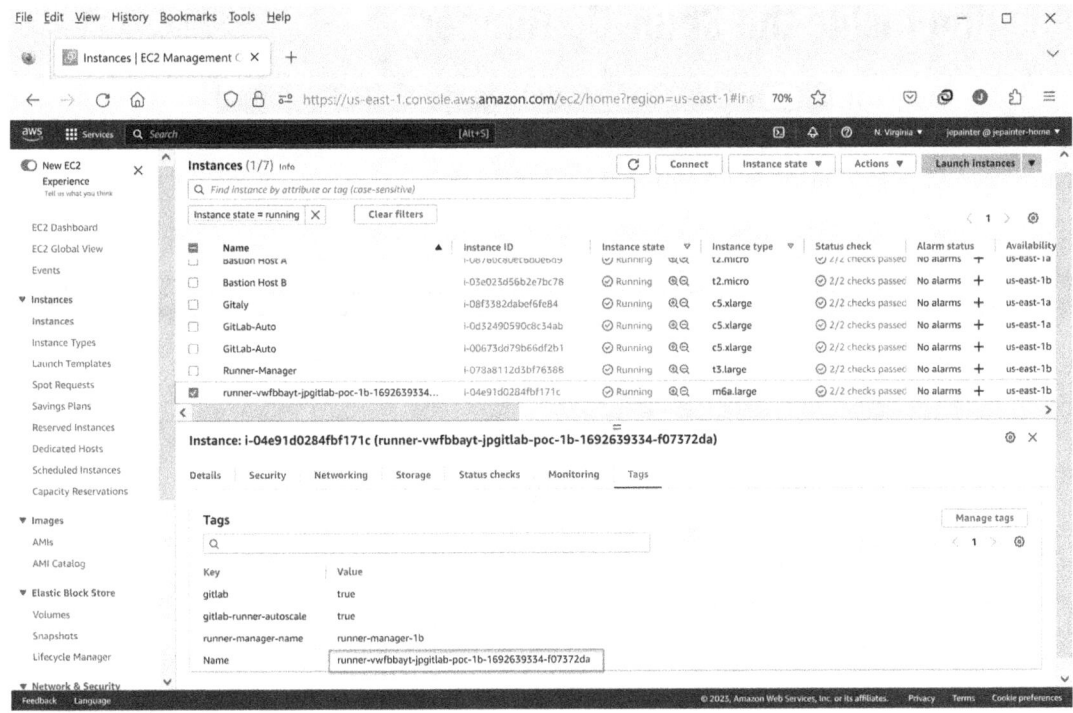

***Figure 16-30.** EC2 instance list showing spun-up runner instances*

Take special note on how the runner's name is formed. The suffix "-jpgitlab-poc-1b-169…" is based on the MachineName option under runners.machine; the hexadecimal number following the "1b-" is generated by gitlab-runner. The prefix is a combination of "runner-" and a transformation of the authentication token. In this example, my runner token started out as "vwF_BBaYt"; this got transformed into "vwfbbayt."[14] This prefix enables multiple runners from different runner managers to coexist in the same instance name space without colliding with each other. This is important since docker-machine identifies specific servers by that name; if there were two servers with the same name, docker-machine would get confused as to which server was under its control.

---

[14] You can surmise that the algorithm is to remove special characters such as underscores from the token value, convert all letters into lowercase, and use the first eight characters as the prefix value.

741

Peeking Inside the Spun-Up Runner

Let's take a quick peek inside the spun-up runner. Figure 16-31 shows the results of running docker info inside the newly spun-up runner. We can see the name of the runner and the my-name object label. You'll also see the provider object label set to amazonec2 that was set by gitlab-runner.

Figure 16-31. Example output of docker info command

Viewing Runner Instance List from the Administrative UI

Taking a look at the runner instance list from the administrative UI, we see the status of our runner manager as shown in Figure 16-32. Now when we look at our shared runner, we can see the "Online" icon displayed. This tells us that the runner manager is now in contact with the GitLab server. Also, notice the "Last contact" message that tells you when the GitLab server was in last contact with the runner server. At this point, it is safe to unpause the runner so that it can start taking jobs. You can do that either by clicking the pencil icon to enter edit mode and deselecting the Pause option or by clicking the play icon.

CHAPTER 16   WORKING THE NEVER-ENDING QUEUE

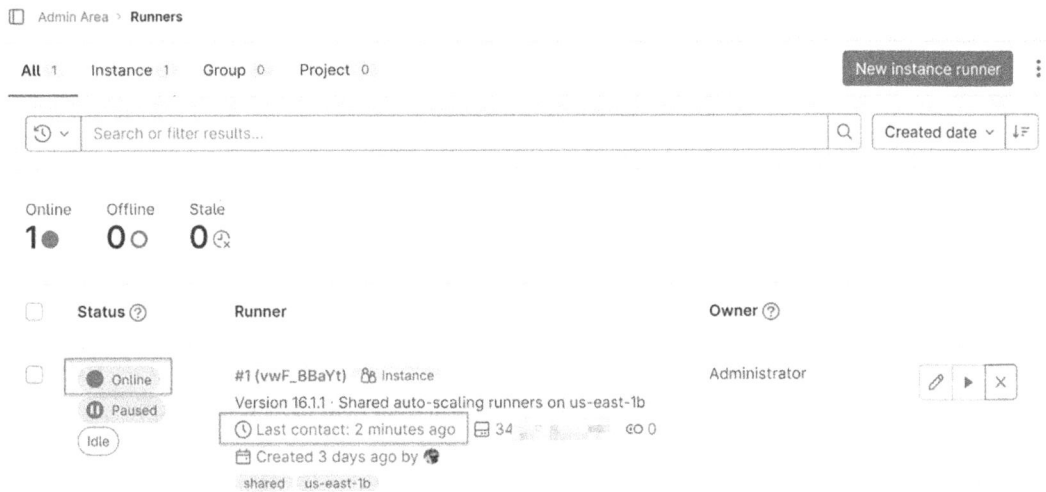

Figure 16-32. *Status of the runner manager after connecting successfully with the GitLab server*

Testing Running Jobs with Our Shared Runner Service

At this point, you might think your job as an admin is done. We verified that the runner manager is spinning up a runner server and that the GitLab server shows the runner manager is online and able to accept jobs. Nothing more to do, right? Well actually, we still need to verify that our runner manager can actually run jobs.[15] This is especially true if this is the first auto-scaling runner service you have set up. So, let's go about testing our setup.

Creating a Test Project

The first thing to do is to create a simple test project. On my server, I first created a new GitLab group called AdminTestProjects and a new project underneath called TestRunners. I created the TestRunners project as a blank project with a simple README file. I then added a .gitlab-ci.yml file with the following contents:

```
build-job:
 stage: build
 script:
 - echo "Building something"
```

---

[15] Or you could just wait and let your users start screaming that jobs aren't running properly. Best to be proactive.

CHAPTER 16   WORKING THE NEVER-ENDING QUEUE

```
test-job:
 stage: test
 script:
 - echo "Testing something"
deploy-prod:
 stage: deploy
 script:
 - echo "Deploying something"
```

After checking the .gitlab-ci.yml file into the master branch, I got a pipeline run as shown in Figure 16-33. So that's good news. All three pipeline jobs ran successfully and only took a total of 15 seconds to do so, which indicates that it ran the jobs using the idle runner server. If you run this pipeline yourself, feel free to check out each of the jobs to see that the echo statements are showing up as expected. Also, check out how the runner server is identified in each job.[16]

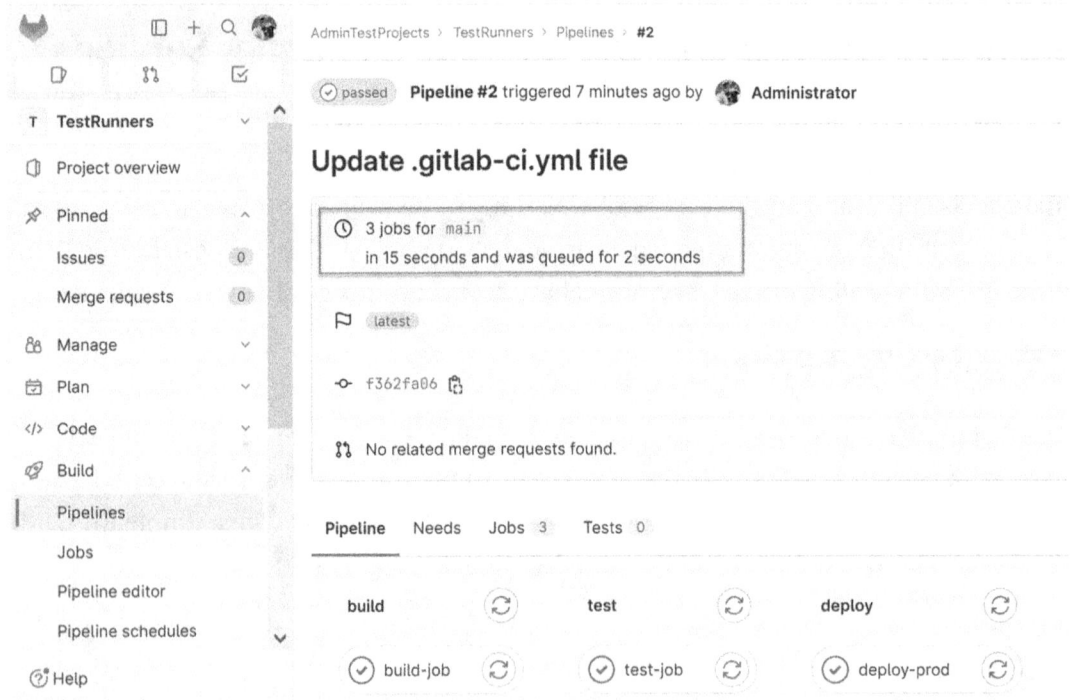

Figure 16-33. Test pipeline run successfully using a shared runner

---

[16] Hint: It uses the runner server's name so that you know which server ran the job. This is useful when debugging issues.

CHAPTER 16　WORKING THE NEVER-ENDING QUEUE

Viewing Runner Details from the Administrative UI

Let's take a look at the runner details from the administrative point of view. Figure 16-34 shows the runner details after selecting the vwF_BBaYt link from the runner list. This provides an overview of the runner manager. Most of the information here, such as Version, Executor, and Platform, is what you would expect. One oddity here is the IP address. It actually refers to the public IP address of the bastion server in us-east-1b.[17]

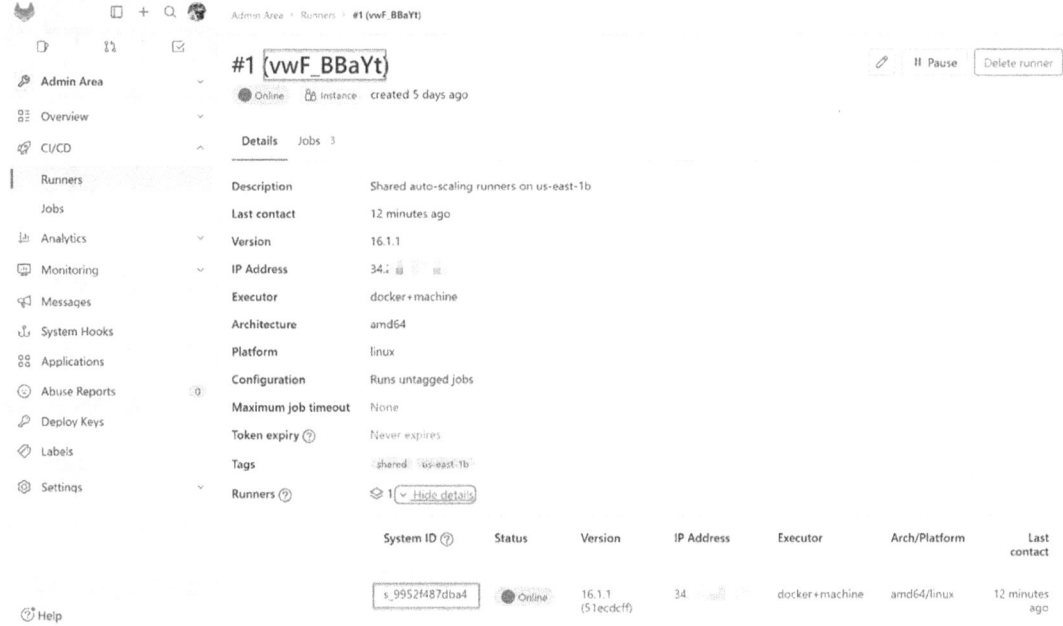

Figure 16-34. Details page of the shared runner

More interesting is the contents of the Job tab as shown in Figure 16-35. Here, you get to see all the jobs that were run by the given runner manager. In this example, there are three jobs each corresponding to the build, test, and deploy jobs of the pipeline we just ran. Note that only administrators can see this information; developers who ran the jobs cannot. As an administrator, this information is useful to identify problems with the runner. If you notice a large number of failures that are not due to normal pipeline failures, you'll need to investigate the runner manager configuration and the syslog to see if something is misconfigured.

---

[17] To be honest, I don't know why it shows this IP address. As far as I know, the runner manager does not communicate with the bastion server.

CHAPTER 16   WORKING THE NEVER-ENDING QUEUE

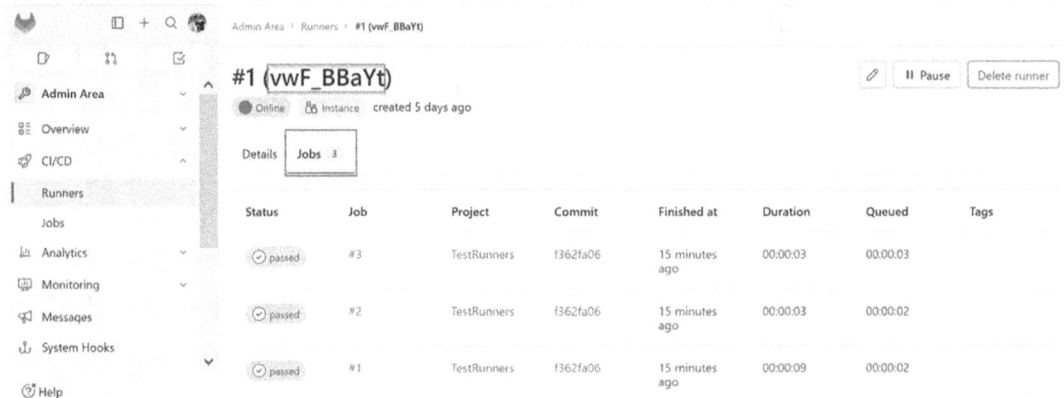

Figure 16-35. Status of jobs run by the shared runner

Showing Status of docker-machine After a Job Run

Now that the pipeline jobs have run, let's take a look at what docker-machine shows on the runner manager. Figure 16-36 shows the results of running docker-machine ls. Notice there are now two runner servers managed by docker-machine. The gitlab-runner spun up a new server as soon as the pipeline jobs started running. Why? Well, we configured the runner manager to keep a server idle. As soon as a job started running on the idle server that was up, it needed to spin up another server to be the idle server. Remember that the GitLab runner doesn't know how long a job will run on a given server. It could be a few seconds as it was here, or it could be an hour. So, in order to prepare for new jobs entering the queue, the GitLab runner spins up a new idle server to handle those jobs.[18]

```
ubuntu@ip-10-0-0-152: ~
ubuntu@ip-10-0-0-152:~$ sudo docker-machine ls
NAME                                              ACTIVE   DRIVER      STATE     URL                       SWARM   DOCKER
ERRORS
runner-vwfbbayt-jpgitlab-poc-1b-1692807452-f7ec3bcc   -     amazonec2   Running   tcp://10.0.0.153:2376             v24.0.5
runner-vwfbbayt-jpgitlab-poc-1b-1692811550-50863fe0   -     amazonec2   Running   tcp://10.0.0.150:2376             v24.0.5
ubuntu@ip-10-0-0-152:~$
```

Figure 16-36. Output of docker-machine ls after pipeline jobs executed

---

[18] So, what happens when the limit has been reached? In this case, you'll have two servers running jobs and one idle server. As it turns out, the idle server will remain idle; jobs will remain waiting in the queue until one of the two running jobs complete.

CHAPTER 16 WORKING THE NEVER-ENDING QUEUE

From the AWS point of view, we can see the two instances in the EC2 list as shown in Figure 16-37. Not shown here is the time when the instances were launched. If you look at your own setup, you will see that the original idle server was spun up in the morning as requested in the config.toml file and the new server was just spun up.

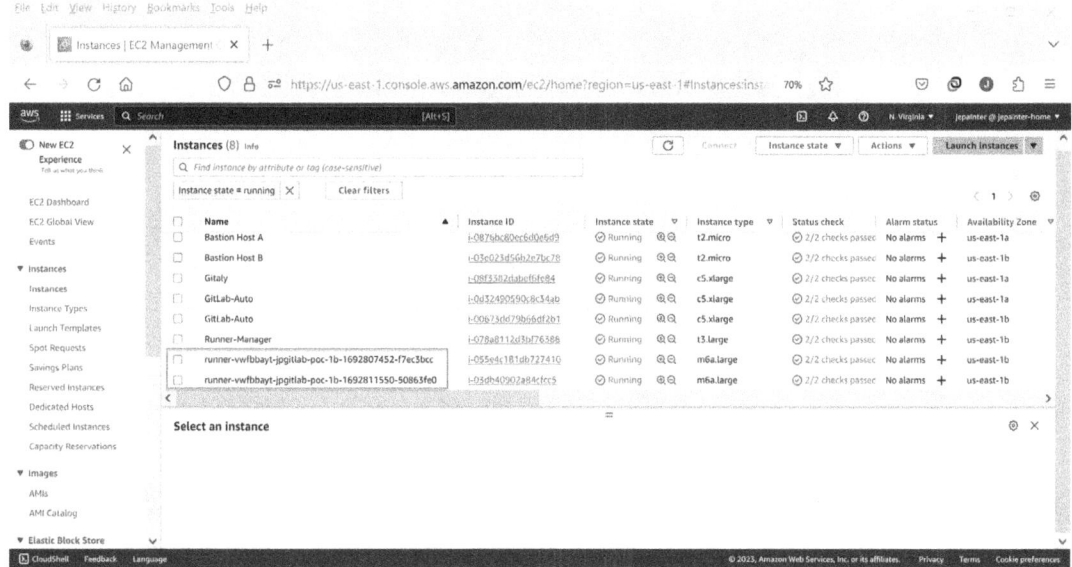

Figure 16-37. EC2 instance list of spun-up runners used to execute pipeline jobs

Verifying the S3 Object Cache

So far, so good. We validated that the jobs are running on our auto-scaling setup. We are not quite done, though. We should verify that jobs store their cache in the S3 cache bucket setup in the config.toml file. So let's update our TestRunner job to include caching. Figure 16-38 shows the changes to the .gitlab-ci.yml file to test caching. In this project, I created a mycache directory with a .gitignore file to ignore everything but the .gitignore file itself. I then added a cache of the mycache directory and updated the build, test, and deploy jobs to store and retrieve data from the testcache.txt file.

747

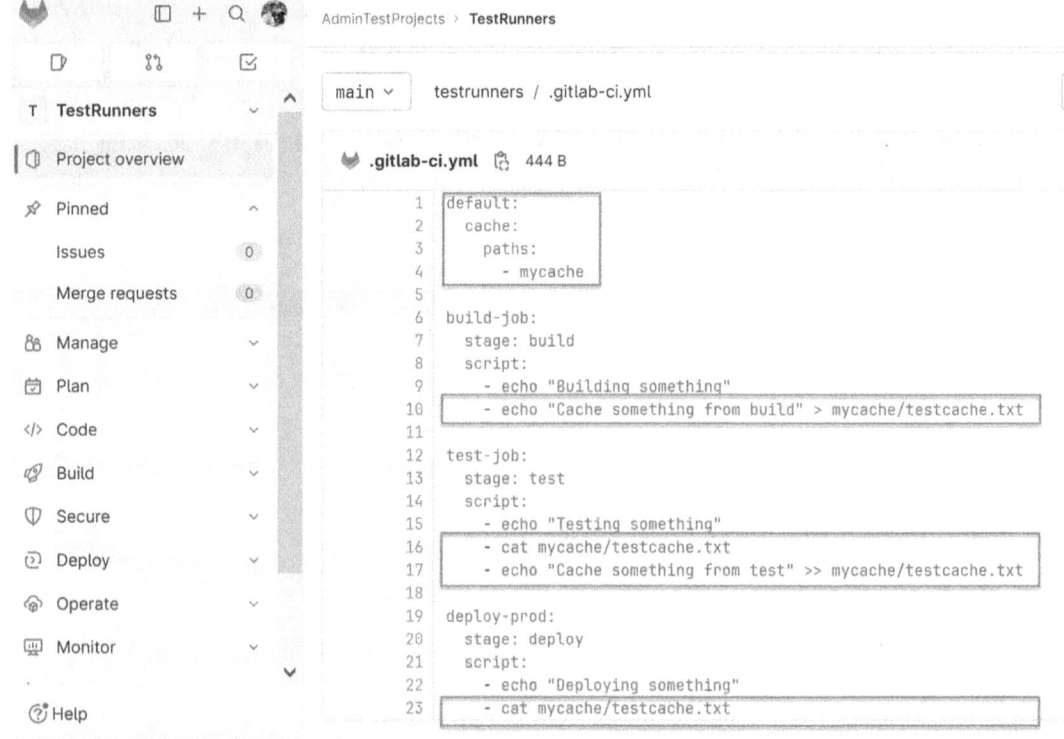

Figure 16-38. Updated test job with caching

Checking Out the S3 Cache Bucket

Once the changes are checked in and a new pipeline runs, let's take a look at the S3 cache bucket in AWS to see what is there. Figure 16-39 shows a drill down into project 1 on the jpgitlab-poc-cache bucket. Here, we see an S3 object named default-protected, which is based on the GitLab cache key project/1/default-protected. What this all shows is that our runner manager is indeed caching data in our S3 cache bucket. Note that if you download the default-protected object and try to view it directly, you'll see a bunch of binary glyphs. This is because that object is actually a zip file. If you want to see what is inside default-protected (or any other cache), use zip to access the contents.[19]

---

[19] An easy way to do this from Windows is to simply rename the downloaded file as default-protected.zip and then double-click it to view it with the zip utility.

CHAPTER 16   WORKING THE NEVER-ENDING QUEUE

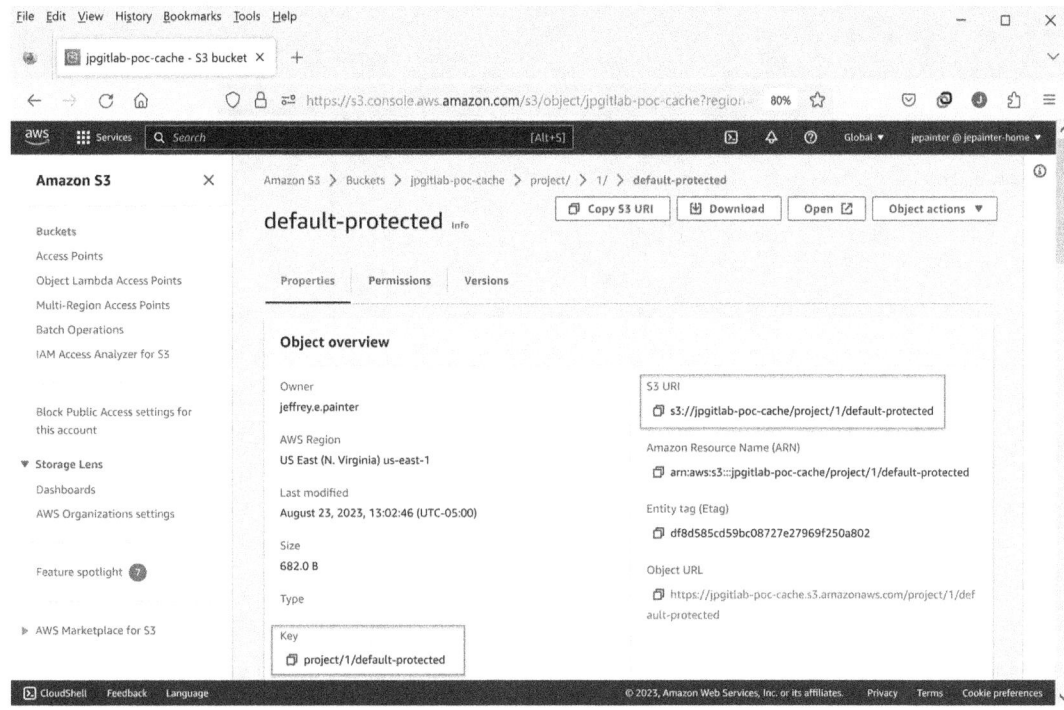

Figure 16-39. *Drill down into S3 job-cache bucket*

Viewing Cache Details in the Deploy Log

Now let's take a look inside the deploy job's log via GitLab as shown in Figure 16-40. Here, you can see that the deploy job is restoring the cache from the S3 cache bucket. Note that it gives you the full URL you can use to display it. You should note that only those given access to the S3 bucket can view it; normal users will not be able to via the URL. The cat command verifies that the testcache.txt file contains the messages added to it via the build and test jobs. And with that, we know that our S3 caching setup is working as expected.

749

CHAPTER 16 WORKING THE NEVER-ENDING QUEUE

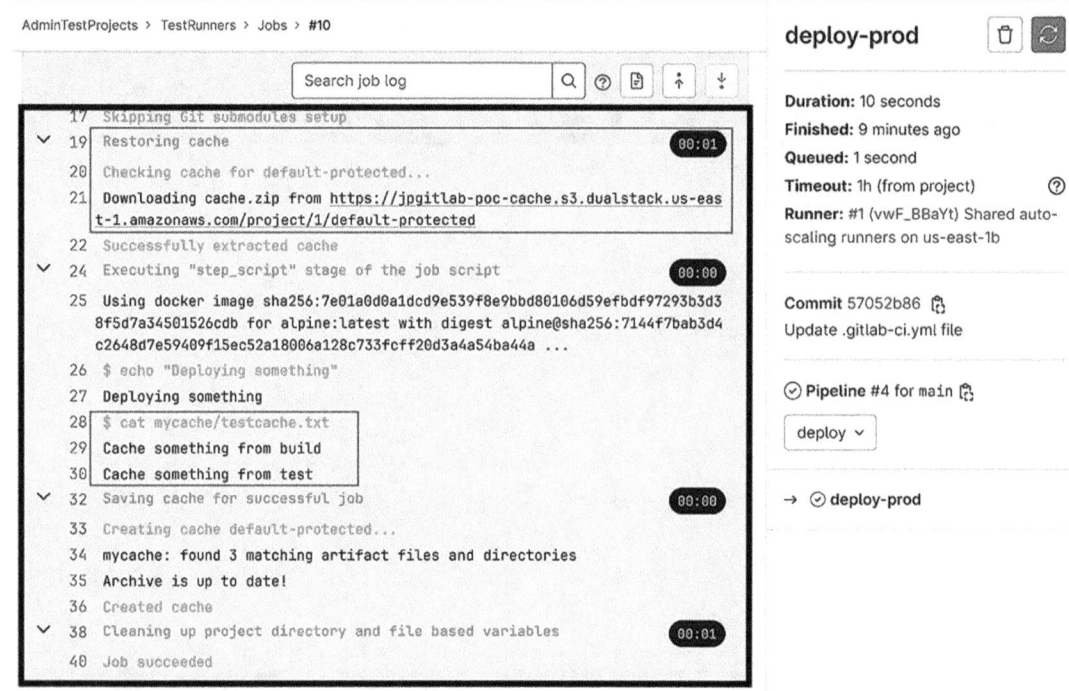

Figure 16-40. Output of deploy job showing location of job cache

Checking Out the S3 Artifacts Bucket

By the way, since we are looking at S3 buckets, let's take a quick look at the S3 artifacts bucket to see what is there. You might think that since we did not explicitly create artifacts in the pipeline job, there wouldn't be anything in the S3 artifacts bucket for this project. So, let's see. Figure 16-41 shows the contents of the jpgitlab-poc-artifacts bucket drilled down to the latest set of objects. As it turns out, there is something there: a job.log file. GitLab considers a job's log as an implicit artifact. It is always uploaded assuming a job actually ends up running. Since the job.log is a text file, you can simply click the link to view it directly. By the way, if you don't see anything in the S3 artifacts bucket, you'll need to double-check the /etc/gitlab/gitlab.rb file on the GitLab host server.

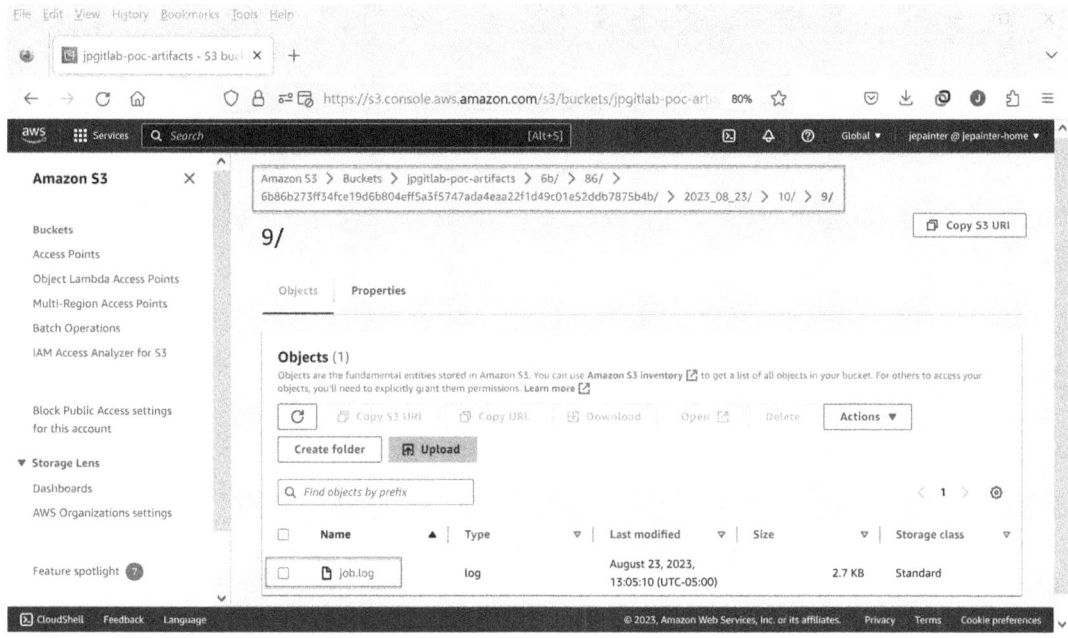

Figure 16-41. *Drill down into S3 job-artifacts bucket*

Checking Docker State in the Spun-Up Runner Server

Finally, before we end this chapter, let's take a quick look inside the runner server itself. Figure 16-42 shows the results of running "sudo docker images" in the runner server where the GitLab jobs ran. Interestingly enough, there are two images sticking around after all jobs have run. One image is the alpine:latest image, which is the default image we configured in the config.toml file, so this makes sense. The other image is the gitlab-runner-helper image. So, what is that? It is an image automatically downloaded by the gitlab-runner to help manage the job environment in Docker. It contains the Git utility, needed to download the project's Git repository into the job's Docker container, and the docker-runner-helper binary, needed to manage GitLab artifacts, caches, and the like for the job. By the way, this holding onto images is one reason for setting a maximum limit of jobs that can run on a runner server; these images can start sucking up disk space possibly interfering with future jobs executed on that runner.

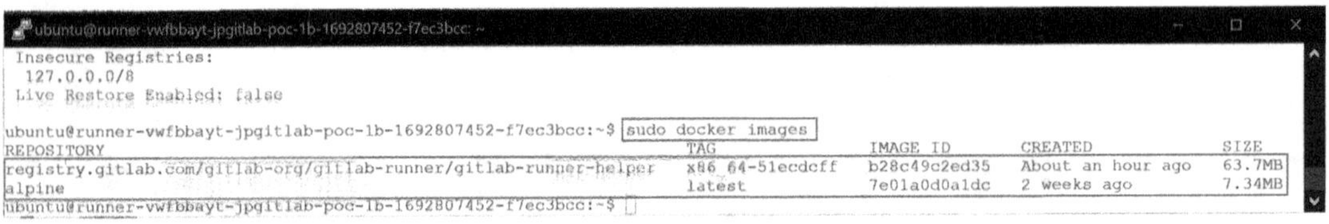

CHAPTER 16   WORKING THE NEVER-ENDING QUEUE

Figure 16-42. Listing of Docker images on the spun-up runner server after a job run

Summary

In summary, we've covered the following topics in this chapter:

- Discussed the need for setting up a shared runner service
- Described how to prepare the AWS environment for our shared runner service
- Reviewed how docker-machine is used to manage AWS runner instances
- Learned how to set up a runner manager service and register it with GitLab
- Shown how to test the running of jobs with our new shared runner service

With the shared runner service out of the way, you may think we are done configuring services. But alas, there are some additional services not configured automatically with our self-managed setup. We'll consider these in the next chapter.

CHAPTER 17

But Wait, There's More

In addition to setting up shared hosted runners that your developers can run their CI/CD builds on, there are other services that you will probably want to set up. An important service that should be configured is connectivity to an external email service. This will allow GitLab to send email notifications to your users regarding build results and the like. There are also secondary services, such as GitLab pages and GitLab container registries, that you may want to enable; these services are not provided automatically. We'll consider how to configure these services in this chapter.

Establishing Email Connectivity

One of the key things that needs to be configured for a standalone GitLab service is email connectivity. By default, this is not enabled since there are many ways to configure email depending on your circumstances. For example, if you are in a corporate environment, there will already be an email service setup to which you can easily connect. Otherwise, you will have to set up your own SMTP[1] service.

Setting Up SMTP with Amazon's Simple Email Service

Given that we've established a standalone GitLab service in AWS, I'm going to describe how to set up an SMTP service using Amazon's Simple Email Service (SES).[2] This isn't the only way to do this; GitLab integrates with a wide variety of third-party email services from Google, Outlook, Mailgun, etc. You can find the complete list of instructions for each at `https://docs.gitlab.com/omnibus/settings/smtp.html`.

---

[1] SMTP stands for simple mail transfer protocol.
[2] Just to be clear, I am not promoting this service as the best solution. I chose it since it was something I was familiar with.

CHAPTER 17   BUT WAIT, THERE'S MORE

Creating an Identity with SES

Figure 17-1 shows the initial start page for SES. As is typical with many AWS services, this page introduces the service with videos and links to documentation that describe how the service works and how to get started. We are going straight to creating an identity, which is the first step in setting up the SES service. Simply use the "Create identity" button to get started.

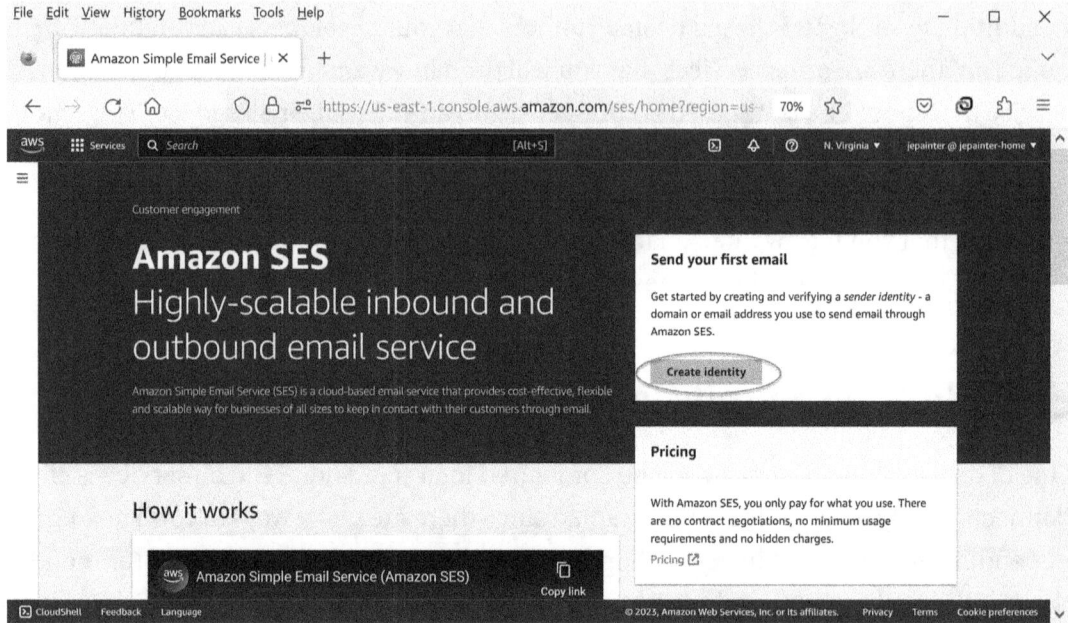

Figure 17-1. *Initial start page for SES*

An identity is required to verify that you are who you say you are with respect to sending and receiving emails. In terms of domains, this step verifies that you have control of the domain. In terms of email addresses, it verifies that you have access to the email address; we'll see the use case for this later on. For now, we need to verify our domain as shown in Figure 17-2. To do this, select domain as the identity type and enter the domain name. In this example, I am using jpgitlab.com as the domain, since this is the domain that I created for my GitLab service.

CHAPTER 17   BUT WAIT, THERE'S MORE

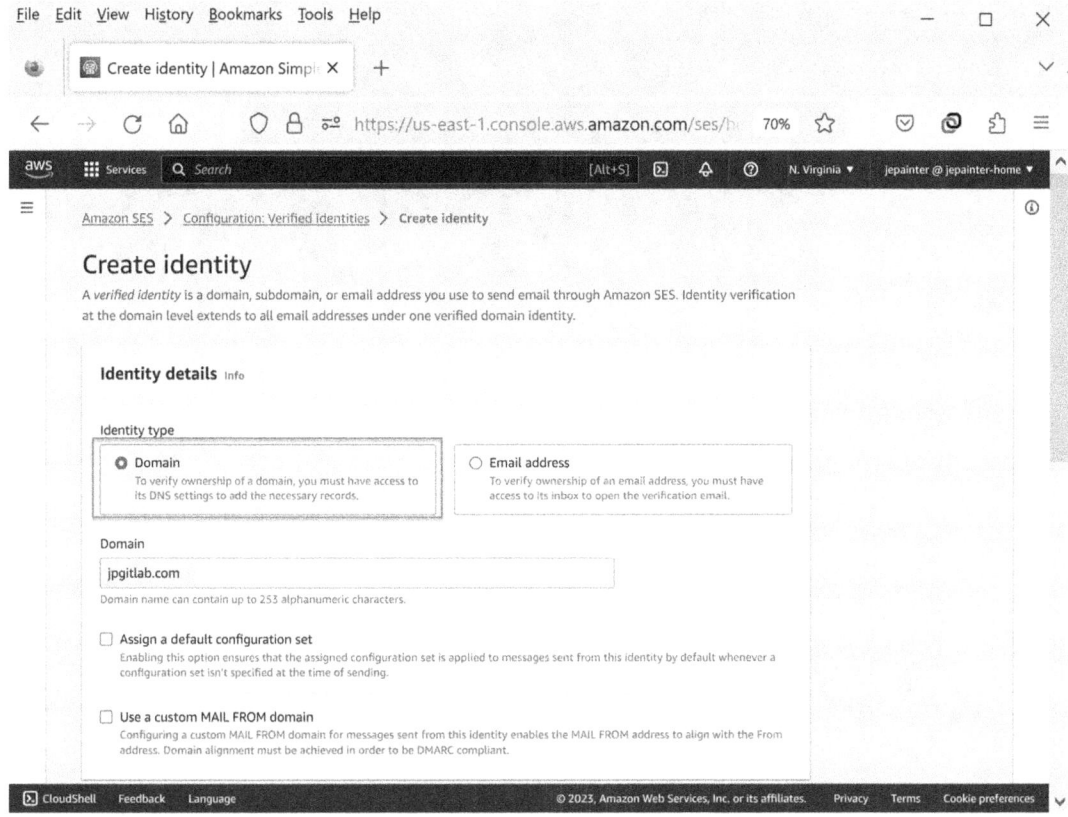

Figure 17-2. Creating an SES verified entity for a domain

Verifying Your Domain Identity

Once you create the identity, an email will be sent to the owner(s) of the domain in order to verify control of that domain. In addition, you'll be taken to the "Verified identities" page that shows the status for the given domain as pending. This is demonstrated in Figure 17-3. Here, you'll see an informational message about using DomainKeys Identified Mail (DKIM) as the means to verify the domain. Since this domain was created using AWS, there is nothing further that we need to do as this is the standard method of verification in AWS. However, if you created the domain elsewhere, you'll need to check if it uses DKIM.

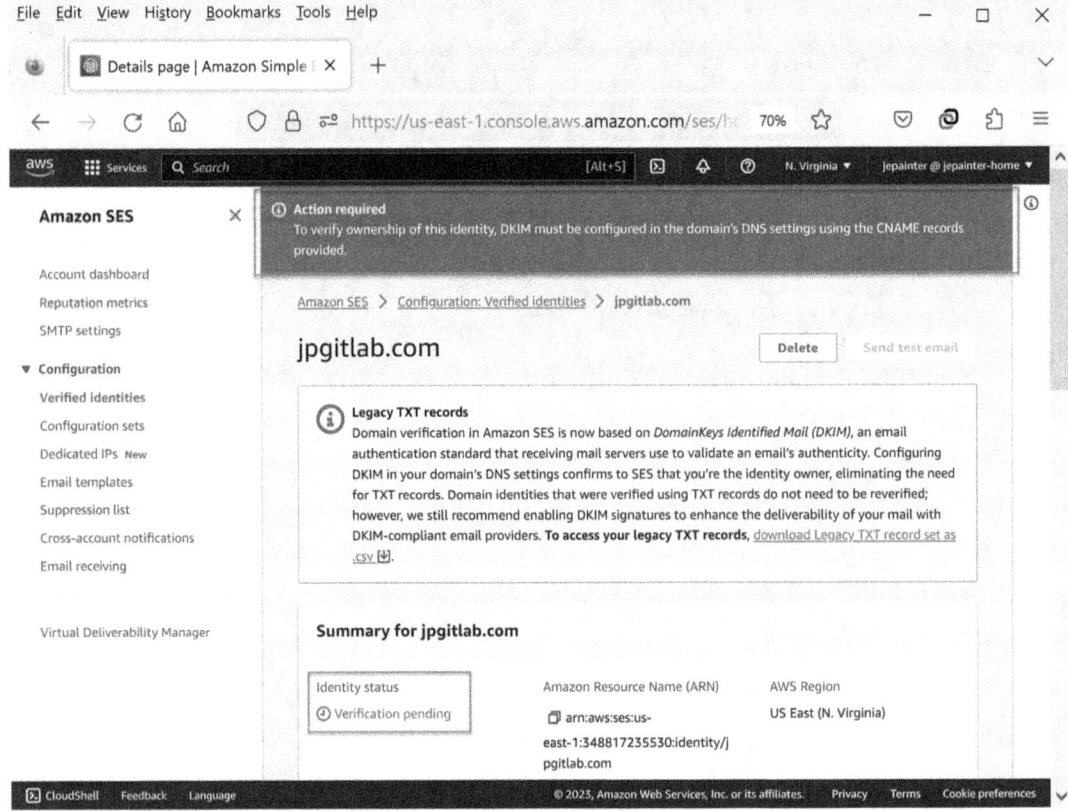

Figure 17-3. *SES verified identities page showing verification is pending*

As soon as you verify the identity via the email sent to you by AWS, the verified identities page will show that your domain is now verified as shown in Figure 17-4. You may need to refresh the page in order to see that your domain has been verified. Once verified, the SES service is ready to use for our domain.

CHAPTER 17 BUT WAIT, THERE'S MORE

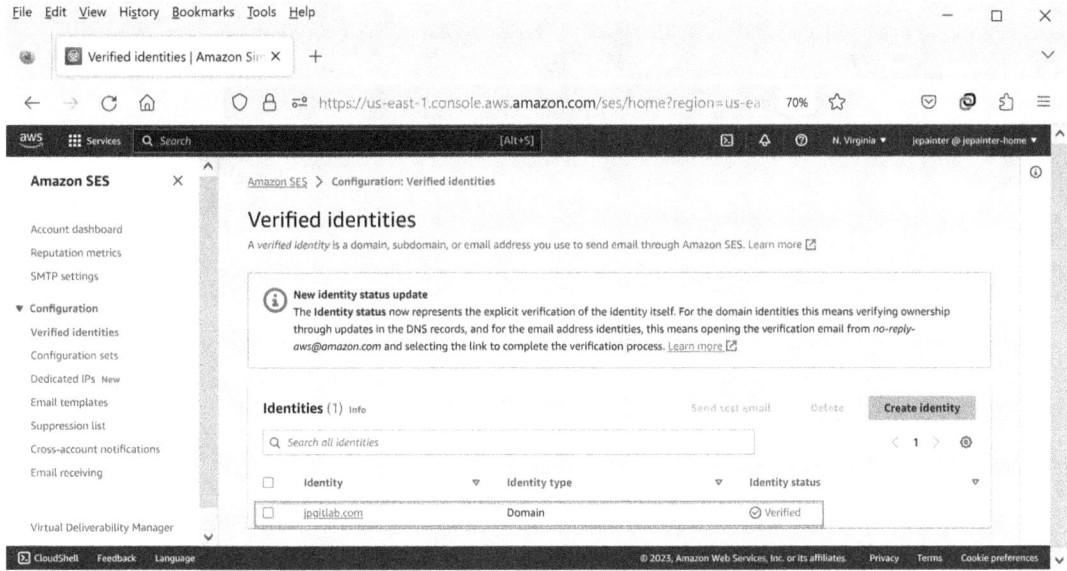

Figure 17-4. SES verified identities page showing verification succeeded

Reviewing the SES Dashboard

In order to configure GitLab to use our new SES service, we need to get some settings that GitLab will need. Before we do that, let's first go to the SES dashboard page as shown in Figure 17-5. Here, we see a message that lets us know that the SES for our account is in "sandbox" mode. This mode has some restrictions on how many emails we can send in a 24-hour period, in this case 200. It also shows that we are restricted to sending one email per second. This is done to prevent misuse of the SES service, for example, a user who tries to set up a spam email service. There is the option to request production access that requires a person on the AWS team to allow the restrictions to be removed; we'll look at this later, but for now, we'll keep the sandbox in place.

CHAPTER 17   BUT WAIT, THERE'S MORE

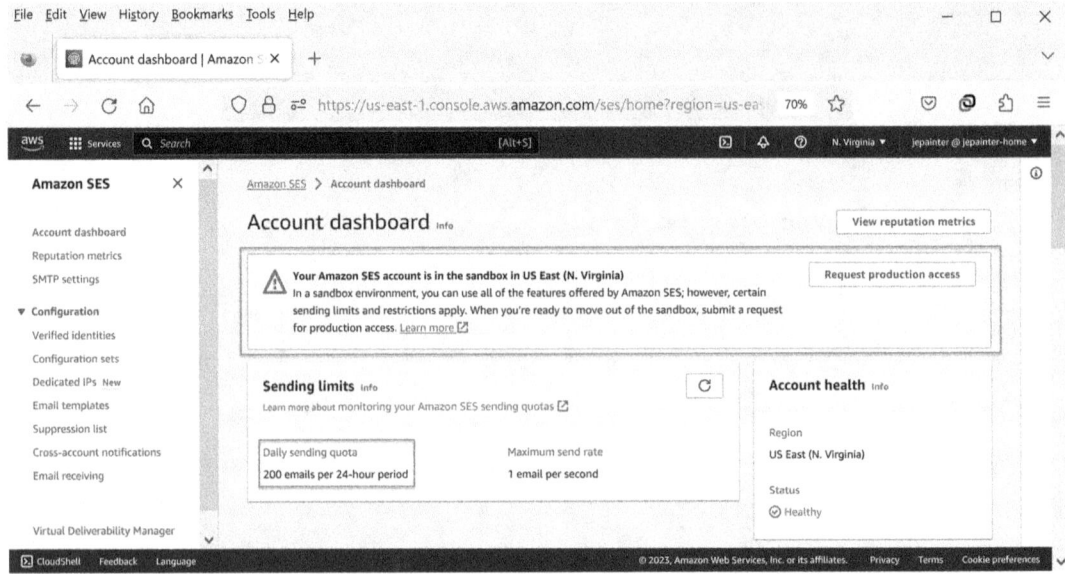

Figure 17-5. *SES account dashboard*

Creating SMTP Credentials

Figure 17-6 shows the settings page accessible via the "SMTP settings" link in the left-hand panel. Here, we see details of our SES service that we need in order to configure SMTP. We'll need the SMTP endpoint as well as one of the STARTTLS[3] ports, the most common of which is port 587. As is typical with AWS services, we also need to create credentials in order for our GitLab application to authenticate with SES.

---

[3] STARTTLS is the most recent TLS connectivity option. TLS Wrapper is an earlier option that is provided for SMTP configurations that don't currently support STARTTLS. GitLab does support STARTTLS, so that is the option we use.

CHAPTER 17   BUT WAIT, THERE'S MORE

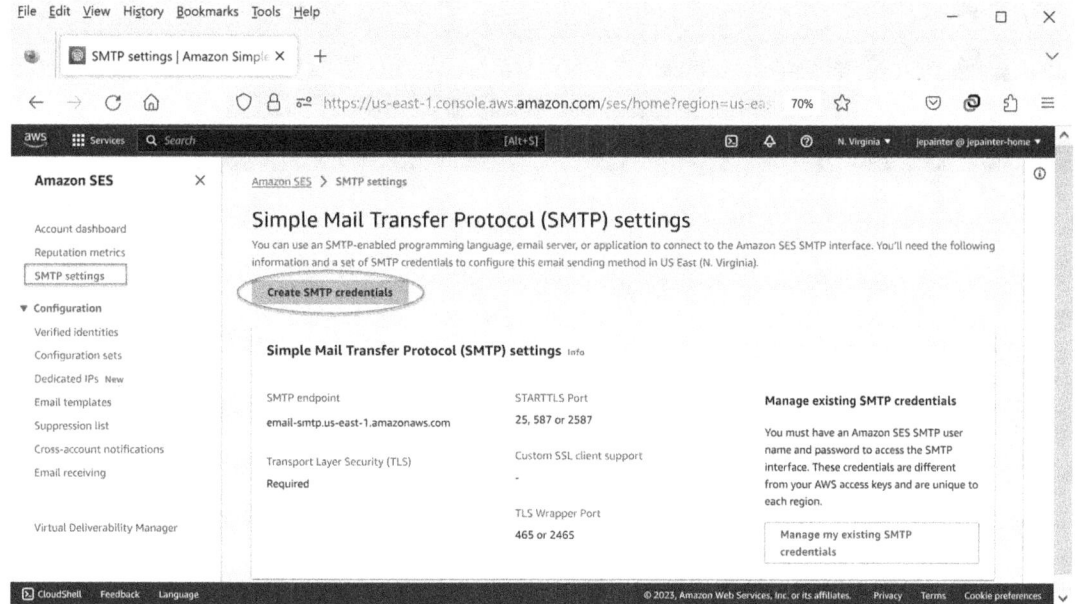

Figure 17-6.   SMTP settings page

Selecting "Create SMTP credentials" takes us to the first step in creating credentials specific to SMTP. It is important to note that SMTP credentials are not the same as the more generic AWS credentials used for IAM users and roles. To use SES from your application, you need to create these special credentials. Figure 17-7 shows the first step of the process where we enter details on the SMTP user. In this example, I use the default values for the username and permissions policy.

CHAPTER 17   BUT WAIT, THERE'S MORE

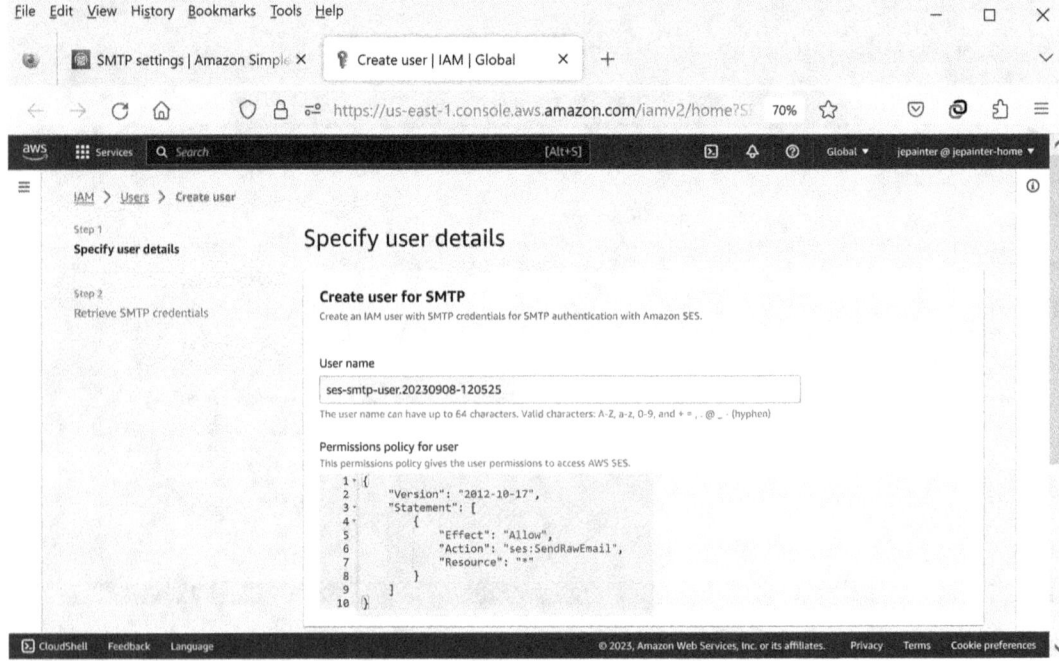

Figure 17-7.   *User details for SMTP credential creation*

Accepting these options from the first step, the second step provides the actual credentials as shown in Figure 17-8. As you might expect with AWS, this is the only time you'll be able to retrieve those credentials. Once you leave this page, there is no way to access them. An easy way to save them is to download a CSV file containing the IAM username, SMTP username, and SMTP password. With those credentials downloaded, we are now ready to configure GitLab.

CHAPTER 17   BUT WAIT, THERE'S MORE

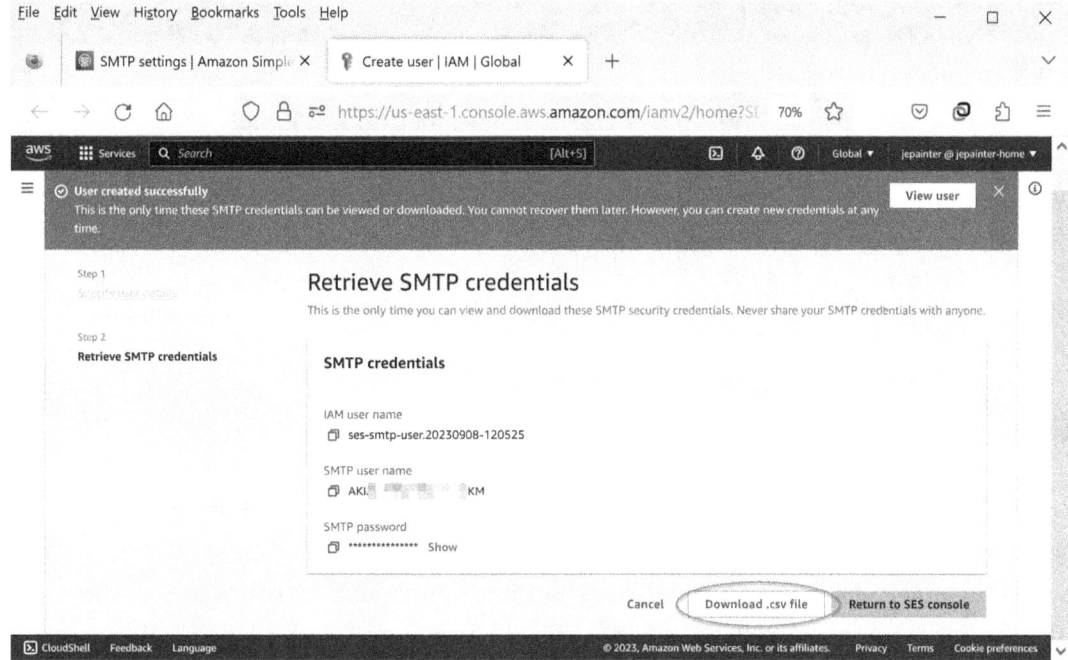

Figure 17-8. Generated SMTP credentials page

Configuring SMTP Settings in GitLab

Within the gitlab.rb file is a section starting with "GitLab email server settings" as shown in Figure 17-9. This section defines the SMTP configuration for GitLab. Update the settings in this section by removing the "#" comment prefix for all the settings but the last two. The smtp_enable should be set to true to enable using SMTP for sending emails. The smtp_address and smtp_port should be set to the address and STARTTLS port provided in the SES settings. We use the SMTP credentials for smtp_user_name and smtp_password (not the IAM user_name). Finally, set the smtp_domain to your DNS domain.

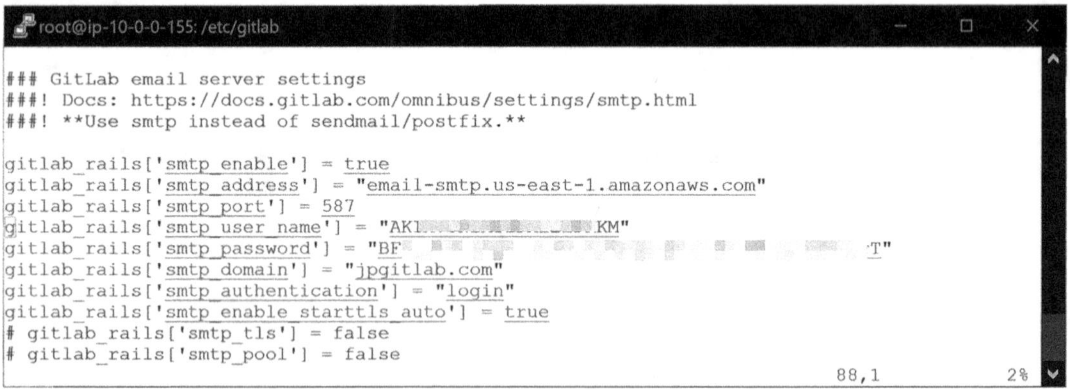

CHAPTER 17 BUT WAIT, THERE'S MORE

```
### GitLab email server settings
###! Docs: https://docs.gitlab.com/omnibus/settings/smtp.html
###! **Use smtp instead of sendmail/postfix.**

gitlab_rails['smtp_enable'] = true
gitlab_rails['smtp_address'] = "email-smtp.us-east-1.amazonaws.com"
gitlab_rails['smtp_port'] = 587
gitlab_rails['smtp_user_name'] = "AK1███████████████KM"
gitlab_rails['smtp_password'] = "BF████████████████████T"
gitlab_rails['smtp_domain'] = "jpgitlab.com"
gitlab_rails['smtp_authentication'] = "login"
gitlab_rails['smtp_enable_starttls_auto'] = true
# gitlab_rails['smtp_tls'] = false
# gitlab_rails['smtp_pool'] = false
                                                         88,1           2%
```

Figure 17-9. SMTP email server settings in GitLab configuration file

There is another section further down in the gitlab.rb file that should be set. This section begins with "Email Settings" as shown in Figure 17-10. Here, you need to change the gitlab_email_from, gitlab_email_display_name, and gitlab_email_reply_to values to match your domain rather than example.com. I chose to use admin@poc.jpgitlab.com as the value for gitlab_email_from and noreply@poc.jpgitlab.com as the value of gitlab_email_reply_to.

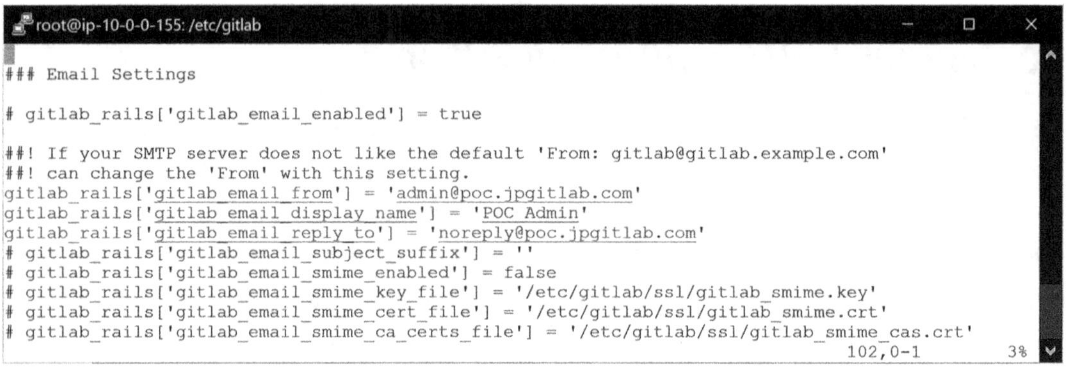

```
### Email Settings

# gitlab_rails['gitlab_email_enabled'] = true

##! If your SMTP server does not like the default 'From: gitlab@gitlab.example.com'
##! can change the 'From' with this setting.
gitlab_rails['gitlab_email_from'] = 'admin@poc.jpgitlab.com'
gitlab_rails['gitlab_email_display_name'] = 'POC Admin'
gitlab_rails['gitlab_email_reply_to'] = 'noreply@poc.jpgitlab.com'
# gitlab_rails['gitlab_email_subject_suffix'] = ''
# gitlab_rails['gitlab_email_smime_enabled'] = false
# gitlab_rails['gitlab_email_smime_key_file'] = '/etc/gitlab/ssl/gitlab_smime.key'
# gitlab_rails['gitlab_email_smime_cert_file'] = '/etc/gitlab/ssl/gitlab_smime.crt'
# gitlab_rails['gitlab_email_smime_ca_certs_file'] = '/etc/gitlab/ssl/gitlab_smime_cas.crt'
                                                         102,0-1         3%
```

Figure 17-10. Email Settings section in the GitLab configuration file

Testing GitLab Email Settings Programmatically

After applying the changes via sudo gitlab-ctl reconfigure, we can test the new settings programmatically. Before we do that, however, we need to verify the email address that we plan on sending to. The reason for this is that SES is still in the sandbox mode, and as such we need to add any email addresses we test against. If this is not done, any email we

CHAPTER 17 BUT WAIT, THERE'S MORE

send to outside of our domain will get bounced. Just like we added our domain as an SES identity, we do the same for email addresses as shown in Figure 17-11. In this example, I added my own Gmail address, which I know will get verified correctly by AWS.

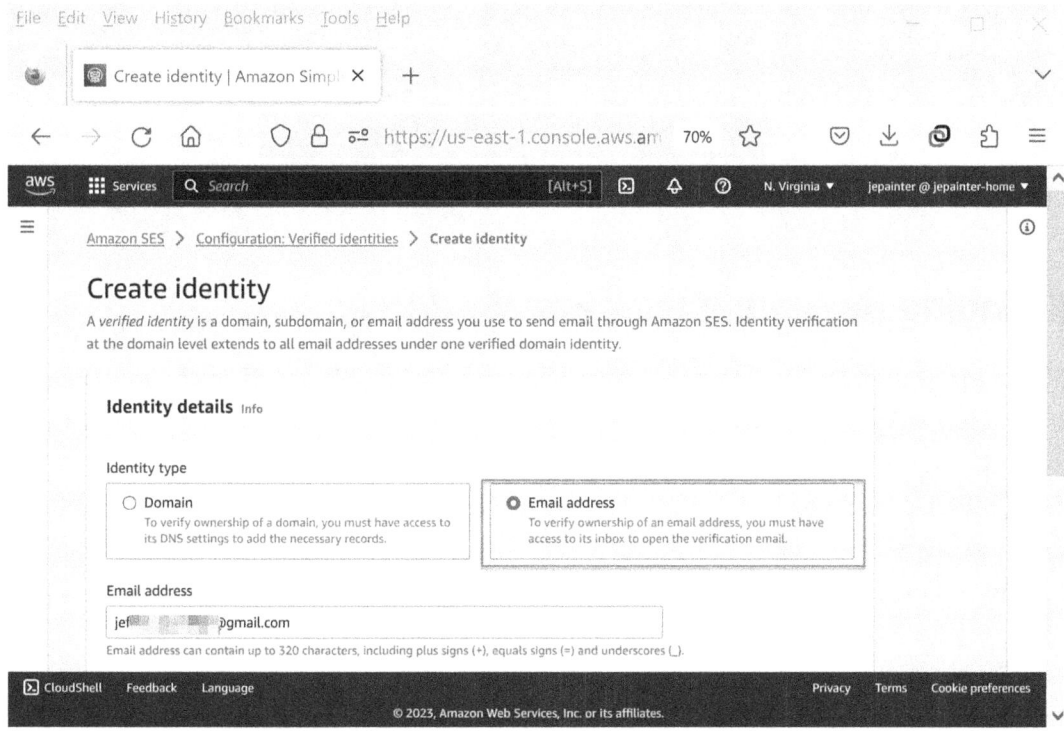

Figure 17-11. *SES request to verify email address for sandbox*

With that done, we can now send a test email from our GitLab instance. This is done by running "sudo gitlab-rails console." Once in the console, we send a test email using a command in the form "Notify.test_email('email-address','subject','body').deliver_now". You can find this command in the GitLab SMTP documentation under "Testing the SMTP configuration." Figure 17-12 shows the results of sending an email to my personal account using the Notify.test_email function. If all goes well, you'll see an echo of the email headers in green as well as an email in your inbox. If you get a red failure message, double-check your SMTP configuration and ensure that the email address you sent to has been verified by SES.

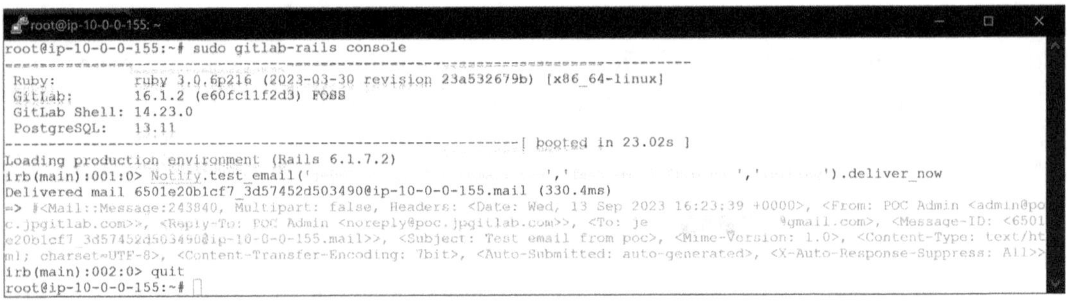

CHAPTER 17   BUT WAIT, THERE'S MORE

Figure 17-12. Test of sending email from the GitLab server

Changing the Admin User Email Address

Although we changed the email settings within the config.rb file, it doesn't affect the email address for the admin user. You can see this when you go to the admin user in the GitLab UI. So, for completeness, we should change the address associated with the admin user to match what was set in the config.rb file. As an admin, edit the Administrator user as shown in Figure 17-13, change the email address to reflect the new address, and save the changes.

Figure 17-13. Update of administrator email address

You can verify that the email address has been successfully changed by selecting the Administrator user from the list of users as shown in Figure 17-14. You will also see a secondary email address that shows the original email address before the change; this address can be safely deleted.

Figure 17-14. Verification of email change for the Administrator user

Setting Up Email Routing with AWS

Now that we have configured GitLab to successfully send emails to our SES service, a related question you might have is what happens to emails that are sent to our admin email address. With SES, it turns out nothing at the moment; they are simply ignored. To handle receiving emails with our SES service, we have to do some additional configuration on the AWS side of things; there is nothing more to be done from the GitLab perspective.

Creating a Hosted Zone for Receiving Emails

Using SES to receive emails is a bit trickier than setting SES up to send emails. There are a few steps that need to be completed in order for SES to successfully handle incoming emails. The first, not so obvious, step is to create a special record for our DNS service to accept email requests. For this, we start by going to our Route 53 hosted zone as shown in Figure 17-15. Once we pick our GitLab domain (which in this example is jpgitlab.com), we select the "Create record" button to create the record.

CHAPTER 17   BUT WAIT, THERE'S MORE

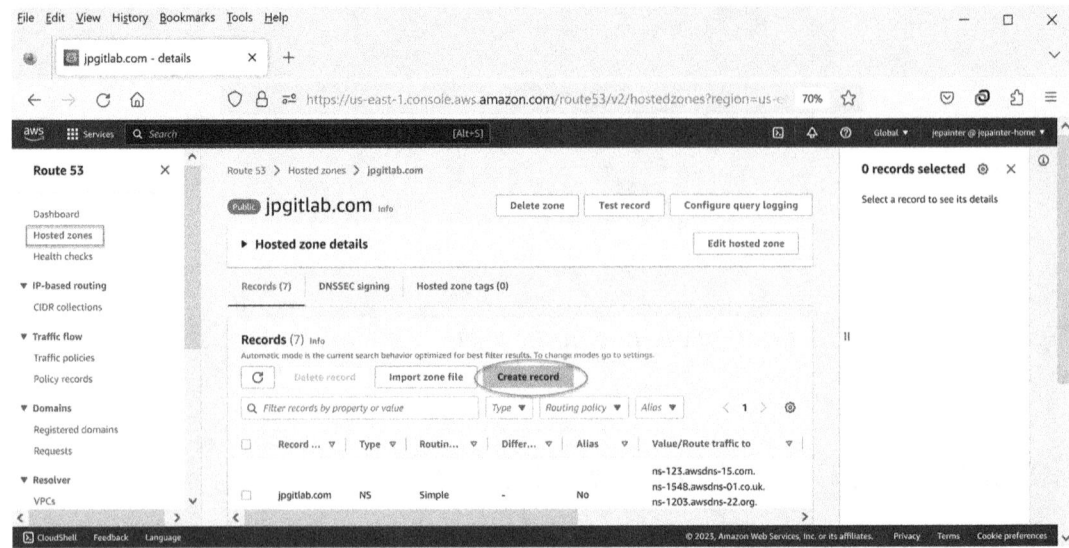

Figure 17-15. *Option to create a hosted zone record for receiving emails*

Setting the Routing Policy

From the list of available routing policy options, we select the "Simple routing" option. This is shown in Figure 17-16.

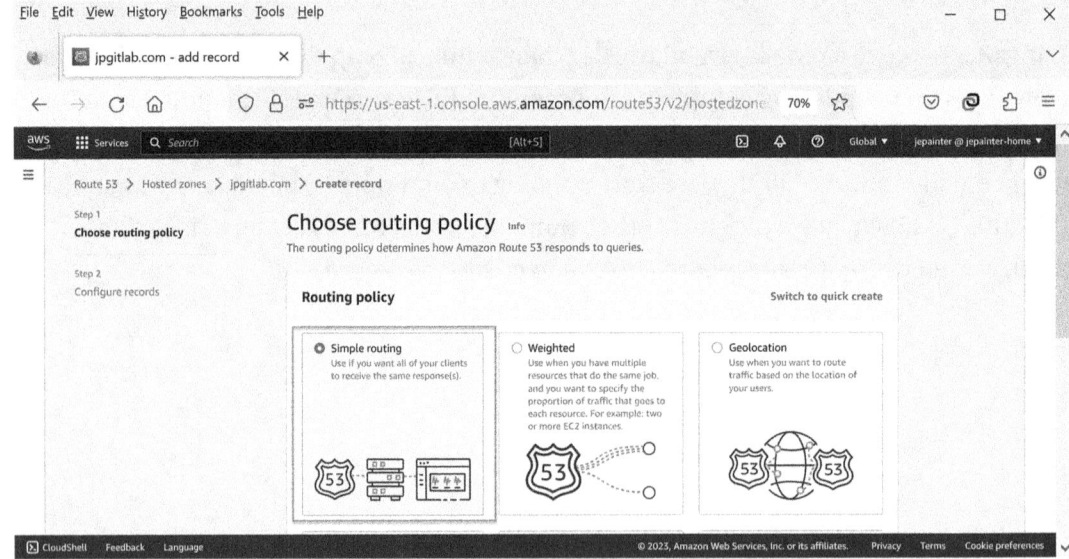

Figure 17-16. *Selection of simple routing policy*

CHAPTER 17 BUT WAIT, THERE'S MORE

Defining a Simple Record for Incoming Emails

After selecting the routing policy, we next select "Define simple record" that displays the pop-up form as shown in Figure 17-17. In this example, I leave the subdomain field as blank; this will create a record for the full jpgitlab.com domain. The important part of this form is the record type. For mail servers, the MX record type is selected. To direct traffic to our SES server, we use a modified name for the service that uses inbound in place of email; the number 10 at the start of the line is required.

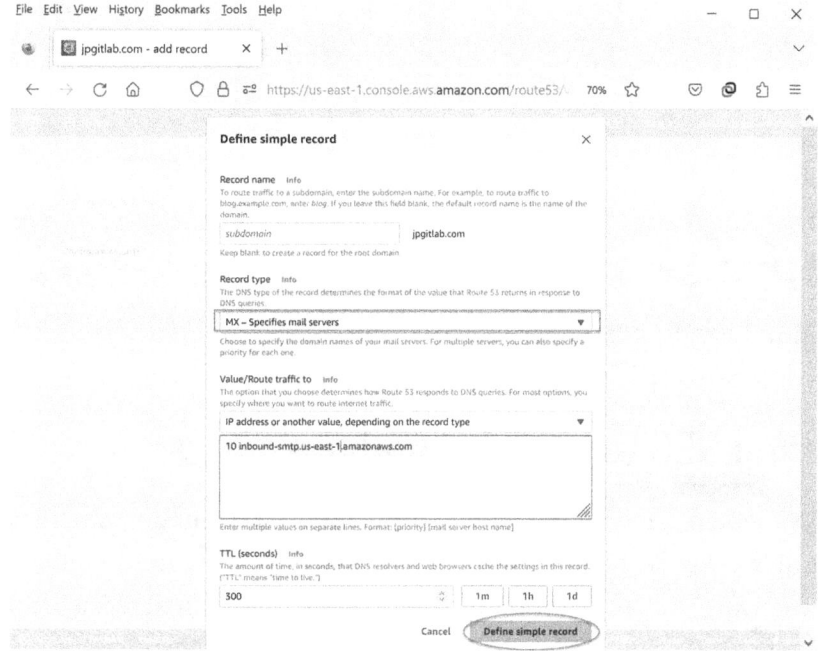

Figure 17-17. *Definition of simple record for email*

Once you've defined the simple record, you'll be taken to the configure records page as shown in Figure 17-18. Selecting the "Create records" button adds the record for the GitLab domain. Note that with this process of defining records first, you can create multiple records that are added all at once. This is important since it takes time to propagate changes to all underlying DNS servers, so best to create a single batch of changes to be pushed to all DNS servers rather than multiple single changes.

CHAPTER 17   BUT WAIT, THERE'S MORE

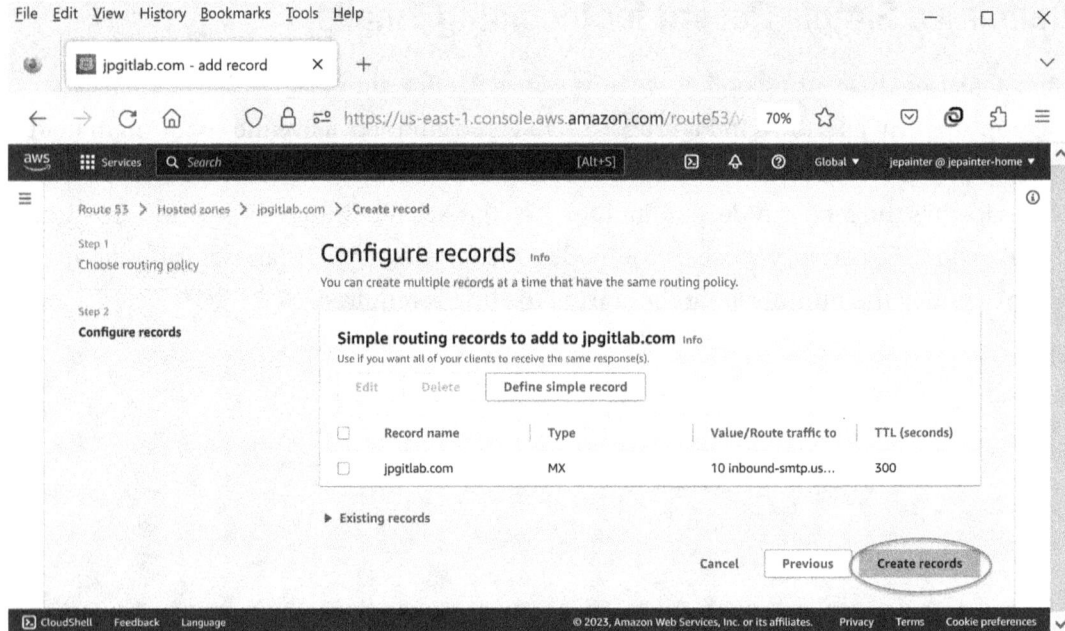

Figure 17-18. Creation of routing records for GitLab domain

Configuring SES to Handle Email Requests

Now that DNS servers know where to send email requests to our domain, the next step is to update SES to handle those email requests. Going back to the SES service, selecting the "Email receiving" link in the left-hand panel displays the email receiving page as shown in Figure 17-19. Notice the informational message that instructs you to create a domain identity and define an MX record. Since we've already done this, we can proceed with the next step of creating a rule set.

CHAPTER 17   BUT WAIT, THERE'S MORE

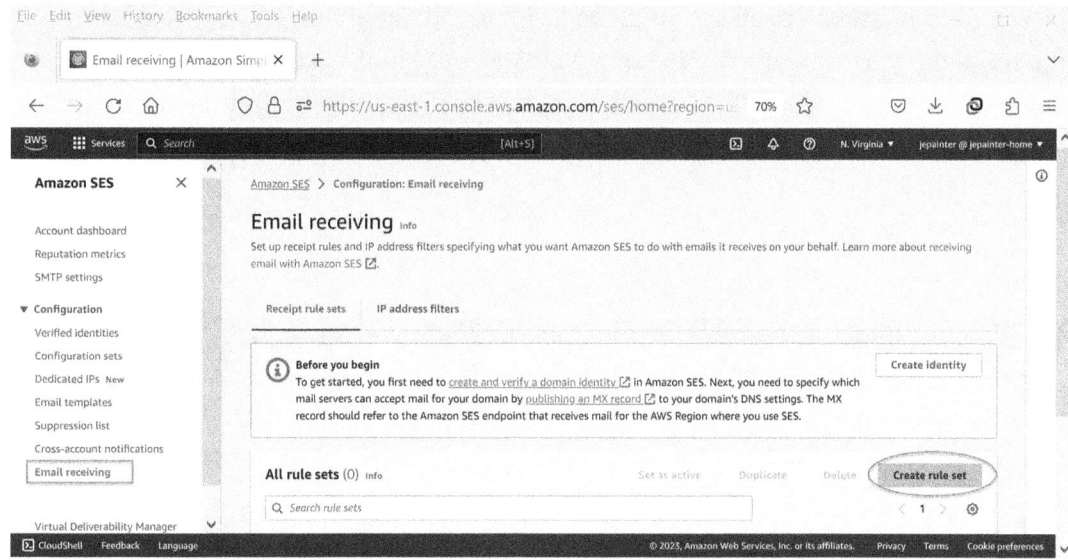

Figure 17-19. *SES email receiving option to create a rule set*

Creating an Email Rule Set

Selecting the "Create rule set" button takes you to the page shown in Figure 17-20. Here, you enter a name for the rule set. In this example, I chose the name pocadmin. Choose a name that makes sense for your GitLab configuration.

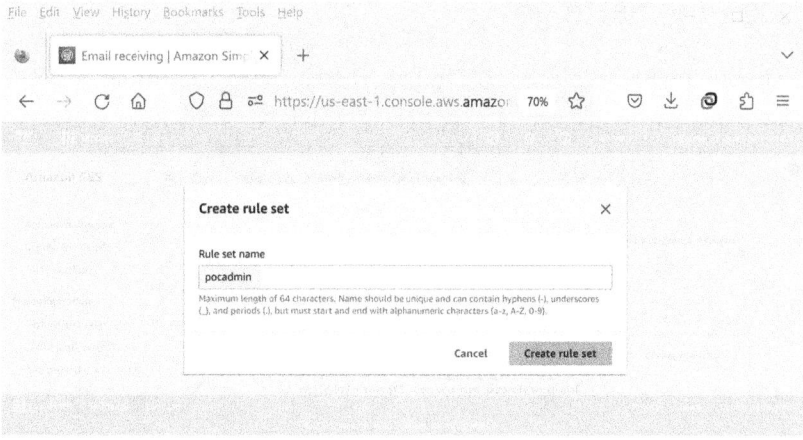

Figure 17-20. *Setting the rule set name*

CHAPTER 17   BUT WAIT, THERE'S MORE

Once the name has been set, you'll be taken to the initial rule set page that has no rule sets defined yet. Figure 17-21 shows what this page looks like. At this point, the only option is to create a rule via the "Create rule" button. Selecting this button takes you to a multistep process for defining the rule.

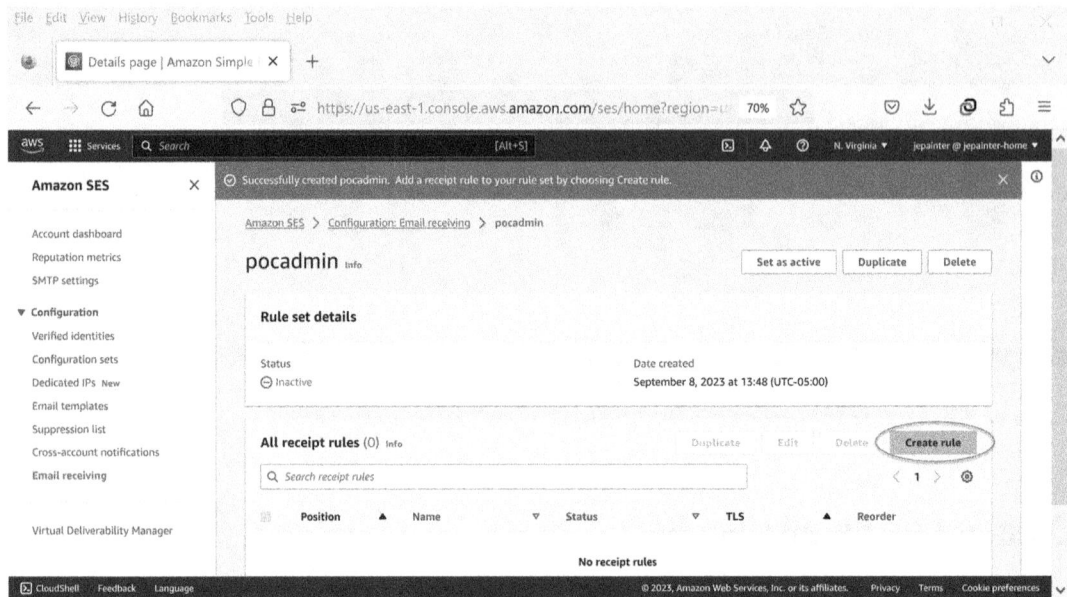

Figure 17-21. Option to create a rule for the given rule set

Defining the Rule Settings

Figure 17-22 shows the first step titled "Define rule settings." In this step, you define a rule name and select some options. Here, I've set the rule name to pocadmin-incoming. I left the other options set to their default values.

CHAPTER 17 BUT WAIT, THERE'S MORE

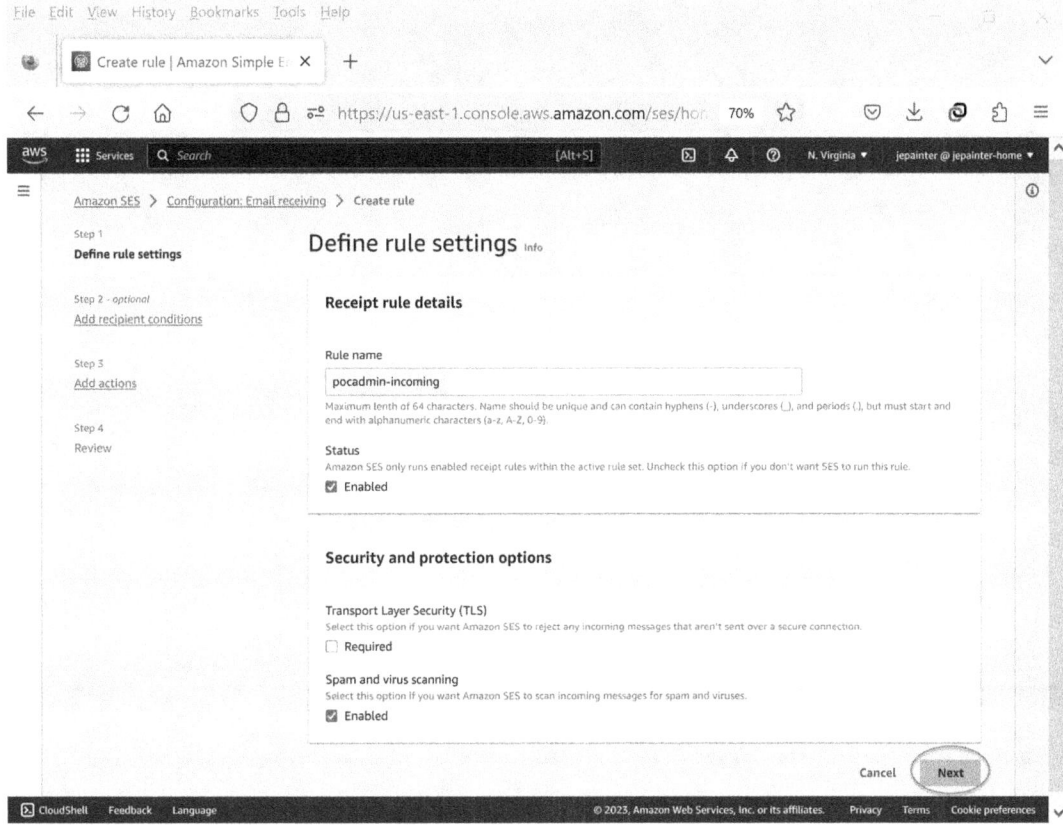

Figure 17-22. *Step to define the rule settings*

Adding a Recipient Condition

Next up is to add a recipient condition. As shown in Figure 17-23, I entered a condition that applies to all of the jpgitlab.com domain. If I wanted, I could have made the condition on the subdomain poc.jpgitlab.com, but my intention here is to handle emails to any address in the jpgitlab.com domain.

771

CHAPTER 17   BUT WAIT, THERE'S MORE

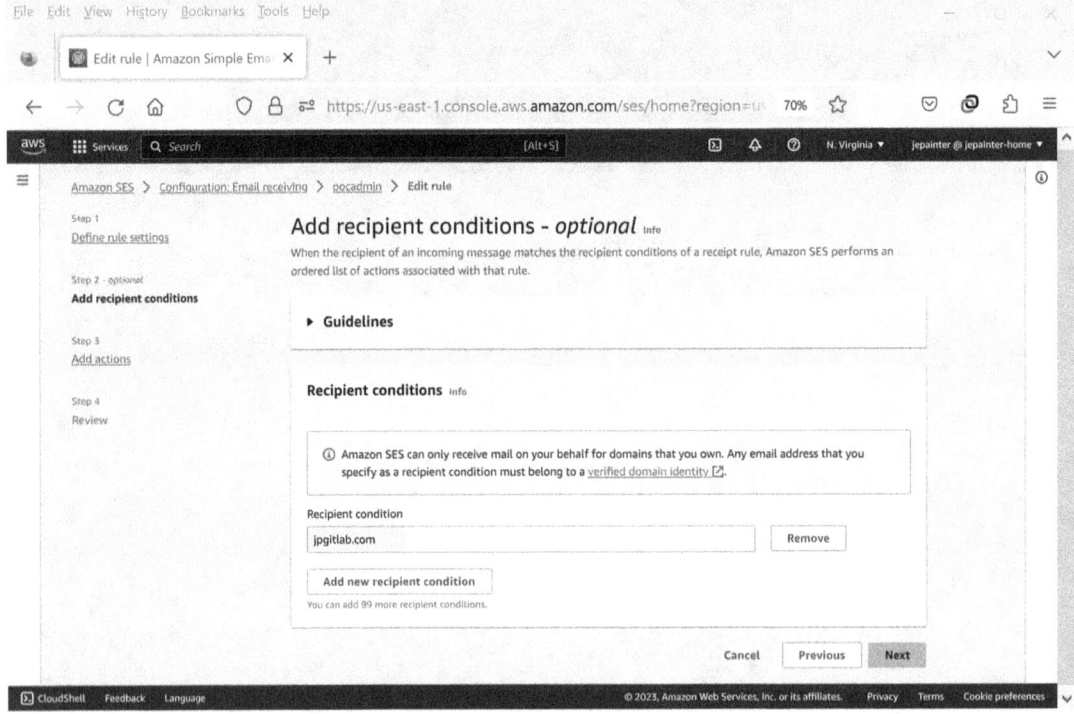

Figure 17-23. *Step to add recipient conditions*

Adding an Action to Forward to the SNS Service

The third step, "Add actions," is the most interesting one. This step determines what to do when an email to the given recipient is received. The "Add new action" drop-down provides a number of options as demonstrated in Figure 17-24. You can go through the SES documentation to learn what each action does. In this example, I chose to publish to an SNS[4] topic. The reason for choosing this action is that I want to redirect the incoming email to an external email address, in this case my personal Gmail account.

---

[4] SNS stands for Simple Notification Service.

CHAPTER 17   BUT WAIT, THERE'S MORE

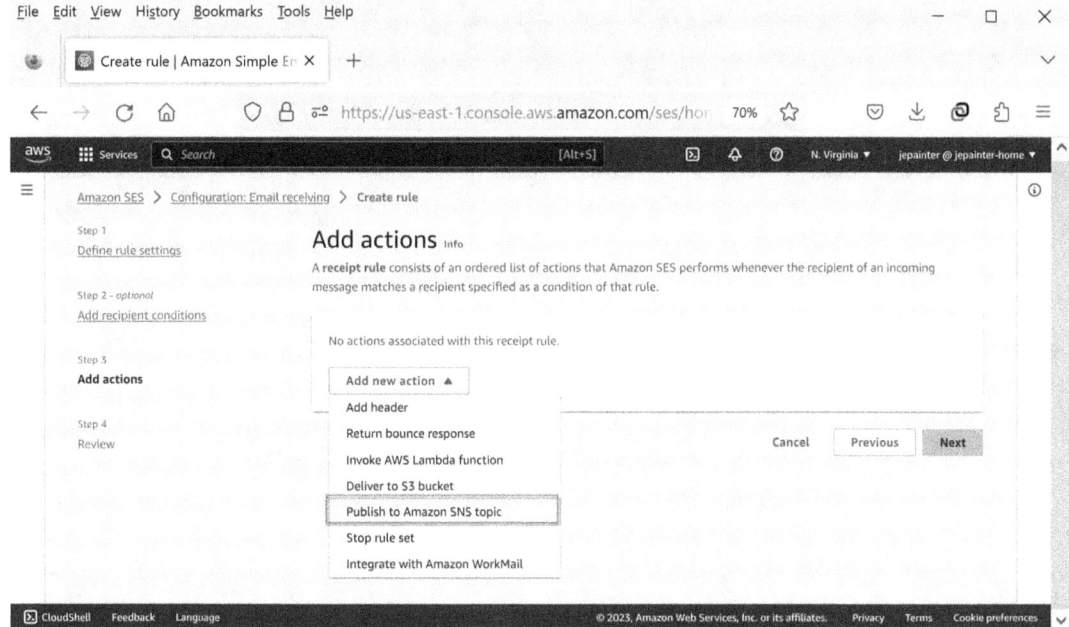

Figure 17-24. Step to add actions

Figure 17-25 shows the change to the Add actions page when the publish to SNS topic option is chosen. The simple notification service is composed of topics where messages are sent to. For each topic, one or more subscriptions can be created that specifies where messages go. In this example, I could have created a topic directly using the SNS service and chosen that topic here. Since I didn't do that, a new topic can be created from this page by selecting the "Create SNS topic" button.

CHAPTER 17 BUT WAIT, THERE'S MORE

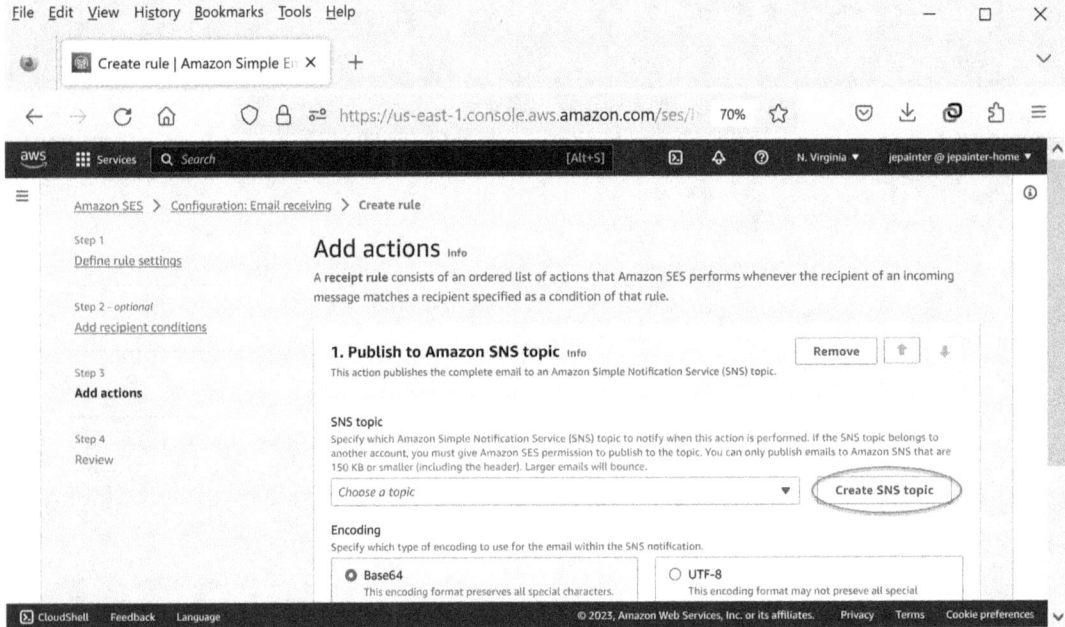

Figure 17-25. Options to publish to an SNS topic

Creating the SNS Topic

Selecting the create button takes you directly into SNS where you can create the topic. Figure 17-26 shows the form that pops up when you do that. All you really need to define is the topic name and an optional display name. I chose pocadmin-email for the name and POCAdminEmail for the display name.

CHAPTER 17 BUT WAIT, THERE'S MORE

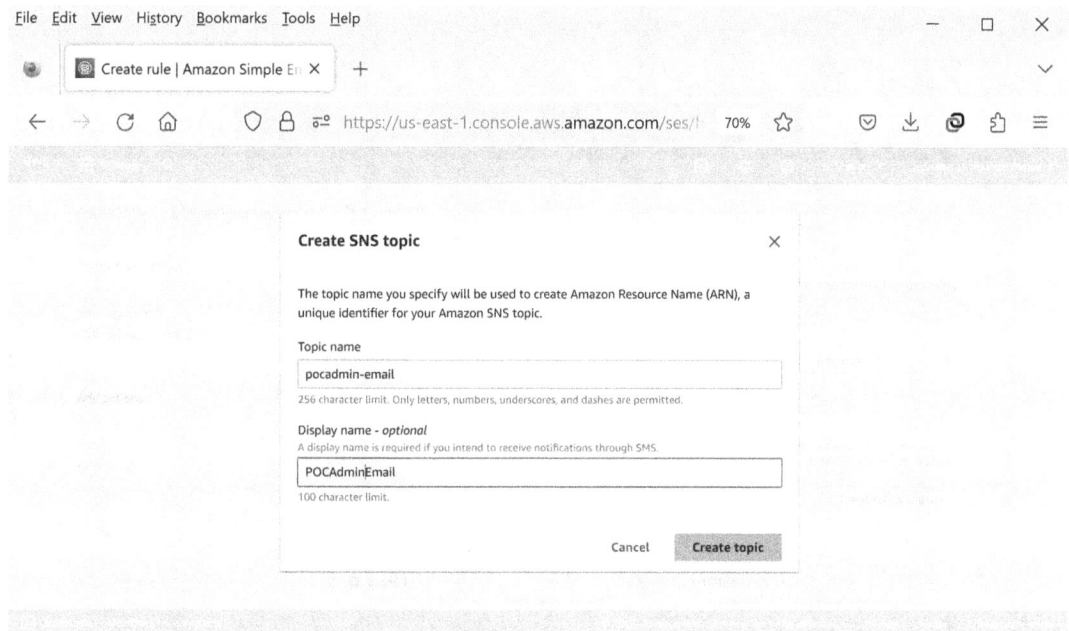

Figure 17-26. *SNS topic creation form*

Selecting the "Create topic" button creates the topic and takes you back to the SES "Add actions" page. Here, you select the topic just created and move on to review the rule options. Once you've approved the rule settings, you save the changes as a new rule. From the SES perspective, you are done.

Creating an SNS Subscription

However, you still need to create a subscription to the topic; otherwise, any message sent to the topic will be ignored. To add a subscription, you first go to the topics list under SNS and select the topic just created. As shown in Figure 17-27, you create a new subscription using the "Create new subscription" button.

775

CHAPTER 17   BUT WAIT, THERE'S MORE

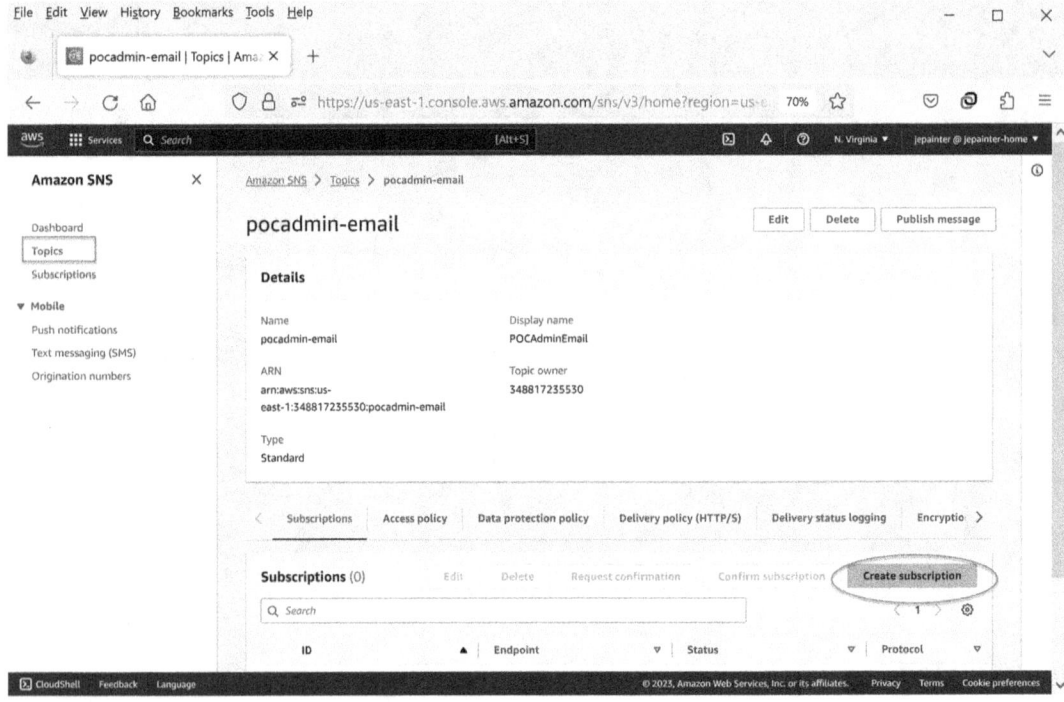

Figure 17-27. *Option to create a subscription to the given SNS topic*

As with the various actions provided with SES rules, there are a number of options you can choose when creating a subscription such as sending a text message to a phone or forwarding the message to an email address. In this example, I chose the email protocol as demonstrated in Figure 17-28. For the email protocol, the email address you want to forward to is entered in the Endpoint field. When the subscription is saved, an email is sent to the address requesting a confirmation.[5] The user (or one of the users for a group email) must acknowledge the request before any messages can be sent to it.

---

[5] Confirming an email subscription is different from validating an email address. Validating an email simply tells AWS that the address is legitimate. Confirming an email subscription verifies that the email sender is willing to accept the request or cancel it.

CHAPTER 17 BUT WAIT, THERE'S MORE

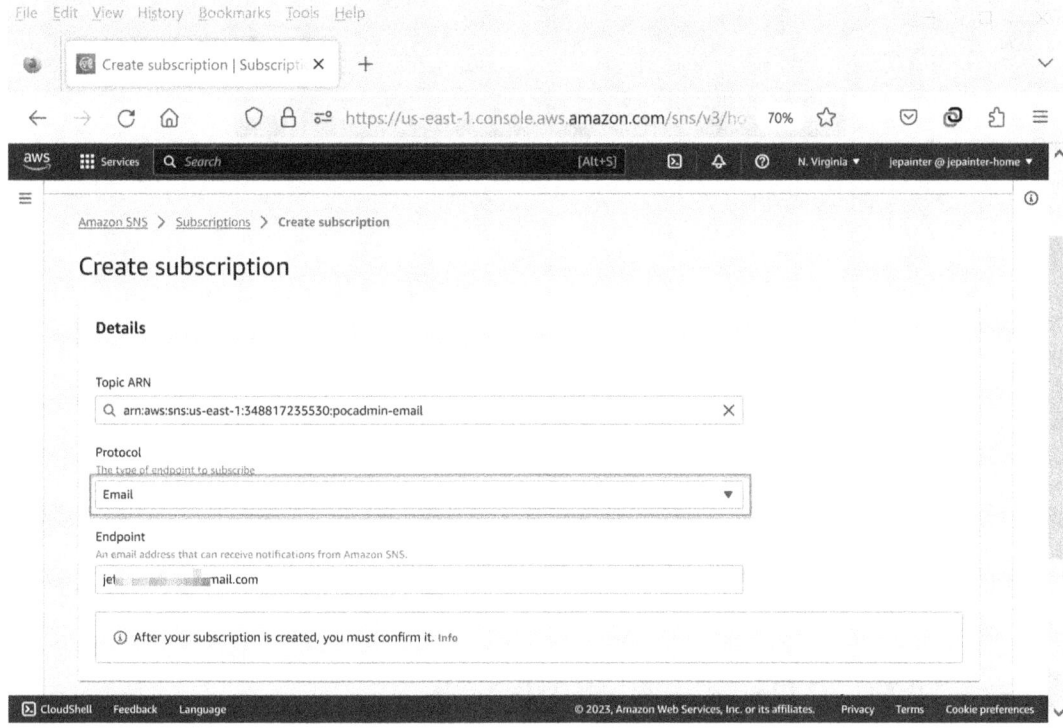

Figure 17-28. *SNS subscription creation form*

Activating the SES Rule

Once the rule is in place, you should go back into SES and check that the rule is active. It is possible that it is not as can be seen in Figure 17-29. If the rule status is inactive, you can select the rule and mark it as active using the "Set as active" button. If all is good, the rule's status should show as "Active." At this point, any email sent to a jpgitlab.com email address will be routed through SNS back out to the email addresses subscribed to. You can test this out by sending an email from your personal email account to the GitLab poc admin address.

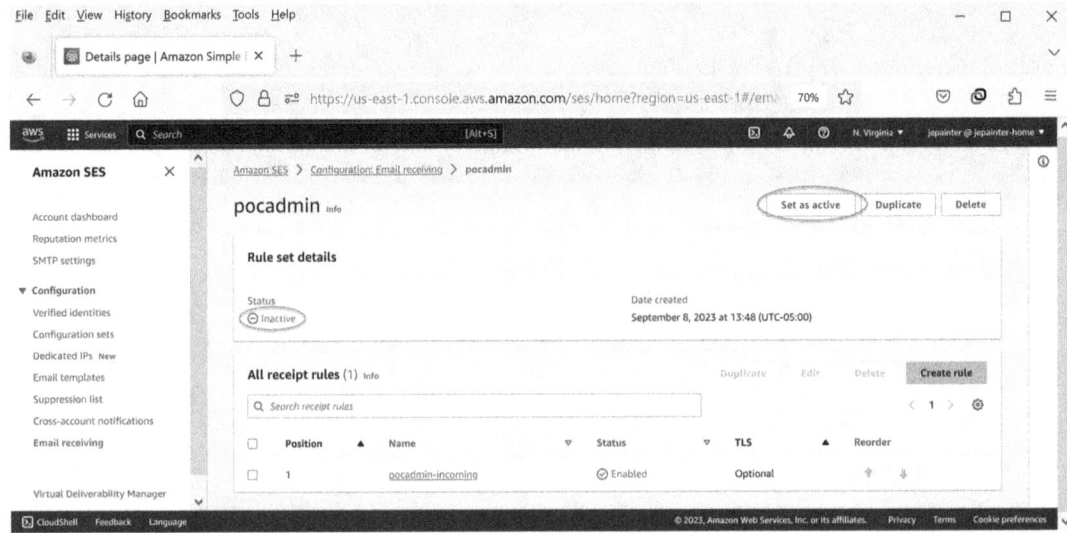

Figure 17-29. Option to make an inactive rule active

Alternatives to Using SNS with SES

A word of warning: Using SNS like this to redirect email to an outside email account will publish a json document rather than the email format you might be expecting. If you look within that json document via your email browser, you can find the email subject and body embedded within it, but it won't be easy to read. This is a quirk of SNS, not SES.

If you decide to use SES as your email server, a better email forwarding solution can be found here: https://aws.amazon.com/blogs/messaging-and-targeting/forward-incoming-email-to-an-external-destination/. You can also access this link by doing a web search on "aws ses forward email." This solution uses SES to store the message in an S3 bucket. It then uses AWS Lambda to retrieve the message from S3, create a new email message, and send it to the external email address.

In the next section, we'll consider how to enable various secondary services.

Enabling Secondary Services

As you've seen in earlier chapters, GitLab stores more than Git repositories and CI/CD job information. There are also secondary services such as the GitLab registry for Docker files, GitLab Pages for static web content, and Terraform state data, to name a few. What may surprise you is that not all of these secondary services are enabled with the out-of-the-box GitLab self-managed service. Part of the reasoning for this is that some of these features, when enabled, can take up a lot of storage space and/or web server loading. So, in this section, we are going to look at which secondary services are enabled by default (and can be shut off if desired) and which are disabled. For those disabled services, we'll describe how to enable them.

Overview of Secondary Services

To get an idea of the secondary services discussed in this section, recall the S3 object storage settings that were enabled for our poc. Figure 17-30 shows the list of S3 buckets that were set for each of the secondary services. Even though we set up the object store for all of these services, it doesn't mean those services are enabled. That is done through options such as gitlab_rails['artifacts_enabled'] that are set to either true or false.

```
gitlab_rails['object_store']['objects']['artifacts']['bucket'] = 'jpgitlab-poc-artifacts'
gitlab_rails['object_store']['objects']['external_diffs']['bucket'] = 'jpgitlab-poc-mr-diffs'
gitlab_rails['object_store']['objects']['lfs']['bucket'] = 'jpgitlab-poc-lfs'
gitlab_rails['object_store']['objects']['uploads']['bucket'] = 'jpgitlab-poc-uploads'
gitlab_rails['object_store']['objects']['packages']['bucket'] = 'jpgitlab-poc-packages'
gitlab_rails['object_store']['objects']['dependency_proxy']['bucket'] = 'jpgitlab-poc-dependency-proxy'
gitlab_rails['object_store']['objects']['terraform_state']['bucket'] = 'jpgitlab-poc-terraform-state'
gitlab_rails['object_store']['objects']['ci_secure_files']['bucket'] = 'jpgitlab-poc-ci-secure-files'
gitlab_rails['object_store']['objects']['pages']['bucket'] = 'jpgitlab-poc-pages'
```

Figure 17-30. Review of object store settings of S3 buckets

The following object services are enabled by default: artifacts, lfs, uploads, packages, dependency_proxy and terraform_state. Except for uploads, these services can be disabled, although I don't recommend it. The remaining services of external_diffs, ci_secure_files and pages are off by default. One service not listed here is registry. It relies on the packages service but is toggled separately via gitlab_rails['registry_enabled']. Although the gitlab.rb file shows that the registry is enabled by default, in our poc it is not since we disabled the Let's Encrypt feature. We'll talk about how to enable each of these services in turn.

Enabling the External Diffs Service

Let's talk about external_diffs first. The name external_diffs is a little misleading but makes sense once you understand what the gitlab_rails['external_diffs_enabled'] does. This actually controls where merge request differences are stored as described here: https://docs.gitlab.com/ee/administration/merge_request_diffs.html.

By default, merge request differences are stored in the database. As the documentation states, large installations might overload the database table that stores these differences. For those cases, you can set gitlab_rails['external_diffs_enabled'] to store merge request differences "external" to the database. Whether those differences go to the file or object store depends on the object store settings, which for our poc setup will go to the object store. Unless you have 10,000 users or more, I suggest you keep this option disabled.

Enabling the ci_secure_files Service

The gitlab_rails['ci_secure_files_enabled'] option controls whether secure files may be stored for CI/CD pipelines. This relatively new feature is described in https://docs.gitlab.com/ee/ci/secure_files/. Since our poc service will store these objects in an encrypted S3 bucket, it is safe to switch this option on. Your security team, if you have one, might have a different opinion on the matter, so check with them before enabling this service. If you have an external security service such as HashiCorp Vault (which is supported by GitLab), you may want to require developers to use that service instead.

Enabling the Container Registry Service

This leaves two remaining services to discuss: registry and pages. Each requires changes above simply enabling the service, so we will go through those changes in more detail in the remainder of this section. First up is the registry since that is the simpler of the two services to set up.

With respect to the registry, there are two basic configuration options. The first option is to use the same domain name as the GitLab service (poc.jpgitlab.com in my case) listening on a specific port other than 443. The second is to create a registry-specific domain name such as poc-registry.jpgitlab.com that listens on the standard 443 port. Since we implemented the poc using AWS with an ELB in front of the GitLab servers, the simplest approach is to use the first option.

Updating the GitLab Configuration File for the Registry Service

I'm first going to show the changes to the config.rb file in order to see what ports need to be opened. Figure 17-31 shows the changes required to set the URL for the registry. Here, we set the registry_external_url to reference our existing GitLab service HTTPS URL but with 5050 as the port. Next are some settings for GitLab itself. We explicitly enable the

CHAPTER 17 BUT WAIT, THERE'S MORE

registry, set the registry_host to match our external domain (minus the https and 5050 components), and set the registry_port to 5005. Note that we set registry_port to 5005 since that will be the HTTP-equivalent port for the registry.

```
root@ip-10-0-0-155: /etc/gitlab
################################################################################
## Container Registry settings
##! Docs: https://docs.gitlab.com/ee/administration/packages/container_registry.html
################################################################################

registry_external_url 'https://poc.jpgitlab.com:5050'

### Settings used by GitLab application
gitlab_rails['registry_enabled'] = true
gitlab_rails['registry_host'] = "poc.jpgitlab.com"
gitlab_rails['registry_port'] = "5005"
# gitlab_rails['registry_path'] = "/var/opt/gitlab/gitlab-rails/shared/registry"
                                                              895,1           26%
```

Figure 17-31. *Settings to enable container registry in the GitLab configuration file*

Further down in the config.rb file are settings for nginx that are specific to the registry. These settings are shown in Figure 17-32. First, we enable nginx for the registry by setting registry_nginx['enable'] to true; by default, it is set to false. We then set the registry_nginx listen_port to 5005 and set listen_https to false. The reason for these settings is to let nginx know that it will not need to handle the TLS certificates; these will be handled by the ELB as we'll see in a moment.

```
root@ip-10-0-0-155: /etc/gitlab
################################################################################
## Registry NGINX
################################################################################

# All the settings defined in the "GitLab Nginx" section are also available in
# this "Registry NGINX" section, using the key `registry_nginx`. However, those
# settings should be explicitly set. That is, settings given as
# `nginx['some_setting']` WILL NOT be automatically replicated as
# `registry_nginx['some_setting']` and should be set separately.

# Below you can find settings that are exclusive to "Registry NGINX"
registry_nginx['enable'] = true

# registry_nginx['proxy_set_headers'] = {
#   "Host" => "$http_host",
#   "X-Real-IP" => "$remote_addr",
#   "X-Forwarded-For" => "$proxy_add_x_forwarded_for",
#   "X-Forwarded-Proto" => "https",
#   "X-Forwarded-Ssl" => "on"
# }

# When the registry is automatically enabled using the same domain as `external_url`,
# it listens on this port
registry_nginx['listen_port'] = 5005
registry_nginx['listen_https'] = false
                                                              2122,1          63%
```

Figure 17-32. *Settings to enable nginx for the container registry*

CHAPTER 17   BUT WAIT, THERE'S MORE

Updating the ELB Security Group

Before we run "sudo gitlab-ctl reconfigure," there are a couple changes we need to make with respect to the ELB. First, we need to update the security group gitlab-loadbalancer-sec-group to accept ports 5050 and 5005. These changes are reflected in Figure 17-33. Note that the rule types are set to Custom TCP since the HTTPS and HTTP rule types are tied to 443 and 80, respectively, and cannot be changed for rules. This is fine for our needs as the ELB listener changes that will be made shortly handle HTTPS and HTTP protocols.

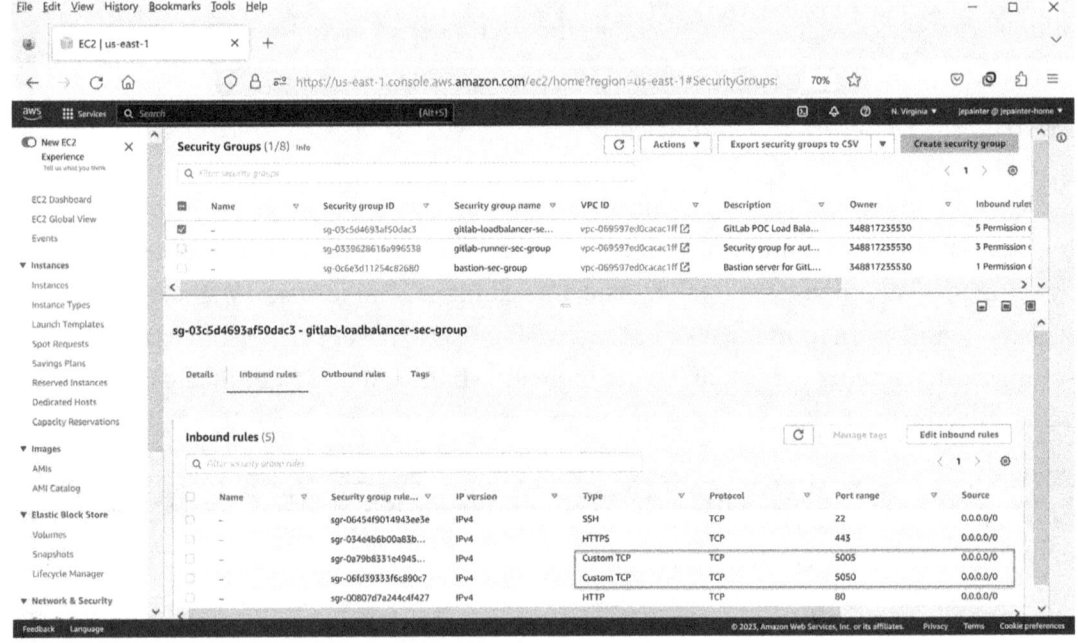

Figure 17-33.   ELB updates for the container registry

Updating the ELB Listener Settings

Figure 17-34 shows the ELB listener changes that are needed to handle the new registry ports. For port 5050, we set the protocol to HTTPS and set the instance port to 5005 with protocol set to HTTP. We use the same SSL certificate that was used for the 443 port since the registry uses the same domain name. For completeness, we set the protocol for port 5005 to HTTP and set the instance port to 5005 using the HTTP protocol as well.

CHAPTER 17 BUT WAIT, THERE'S MORE

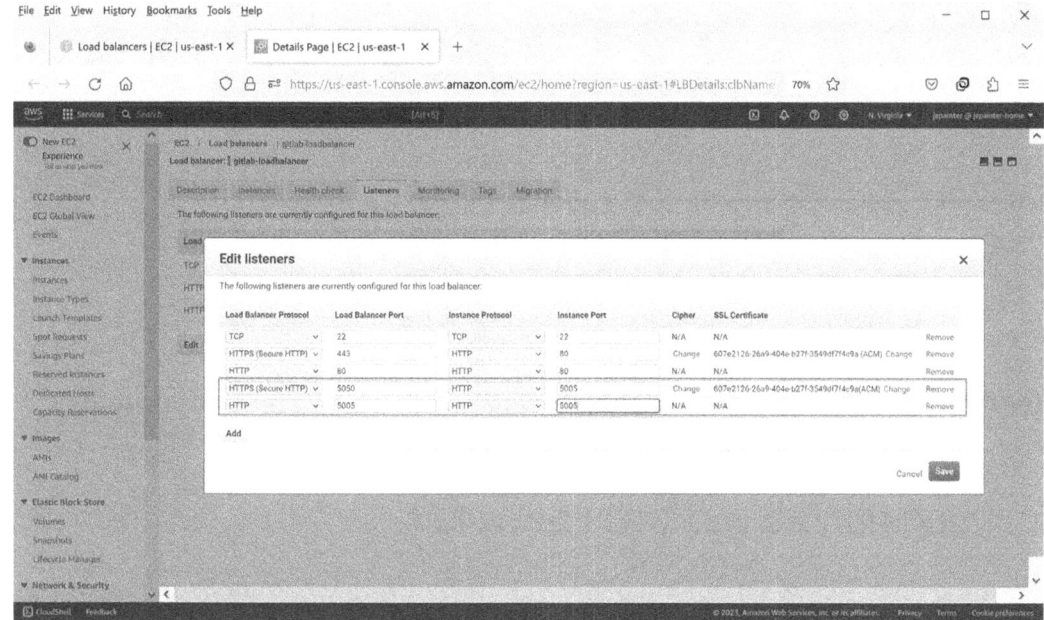

Figure 17-34. *ELB listener changes for the container registry*

Those are the only changes we need to make. At this point, we run the "sudo gitlab-ctl reconfigure" command to apply the changes. To test that we can now log in to the container repository, we run "docker login poc.jpgitlab.com:5050" from our local Linux OS. As shown in Figure 17-35, we get the "Login Succeeded" message.

Figure 17-35. *Test of access to container registry from the local Linux OS*

Verifying Container Registry Is Enabled

As a final check, we need to look at a project's Deploy ➤ Container Registry page. An example is shown in Figure 17-36. The fact that "Container Registry" shows up under the project's Deploy section tells us that the registry is enabled; if it doesn't, we need to double-check all the settings made earlier. As shown in the figure, we see that the docker login command is the same as used in our previous test. We've successfully enabled the container registry for our poc GitLab service.

783

Figure 17-36. Project container registry page verifying the registry is enabled

Enabling the GitLab Pages Service

With the GitLab registry service out of the way, we now turn to the configuration of GitLab Pages. What makes configuring GitLab Pages trickier than GitLab registry is that Pages require its own domain name separate from the GitLab service; what this means is that we cannot use poc.jpgitlab.com directly or any subdomain of it like pages.poc.jpgitlab.com. Hence, the trick we used for registry to use the same domain name with a different port won't work for Pages. In addition, if we wish to use HTTPS with Pages (and we do), we will need to create a wildcard TLS certificate specific to our Pages domain; we can't use the wildcard certificate that we created for our GitLab service.[6]

Defining the Pages Domain

For my Pages domain to be used with the poc, I chose to use poc-pages.jpgitlab.com. Note the dash between poc and pages. Once the Pages domain is decided on, the first step is to create the TLS certificate with the wildcard *.poc-pages.jpgitlab.com. Recall from the poc installation, certificates take a while to create, so best to create it early before we need to use it.

---

[6] You should also know that TLS certificates can only have one wildcard, so you won't be able to combine the wildcards under the same certificate.

Creating the TLS Certificate for the Pages Domain

The next complication for GitLab pages is that since it requires ports 80 and 443 for HTTP and HTTPS, respectively, and since the TLS certificate for our 443 port is different from the certificate used for port 443 with our existing ELB, we will need to create a new ELB specific to GitLab Pages. And with that, we'll need to create an additional standalone server for our GitLab Pages service.[7] Figure 17-37 shows the new certificate I created for the poc-pages domain. As part of creating the certificate, I used the certificate manager to create the Route 53 records for it.

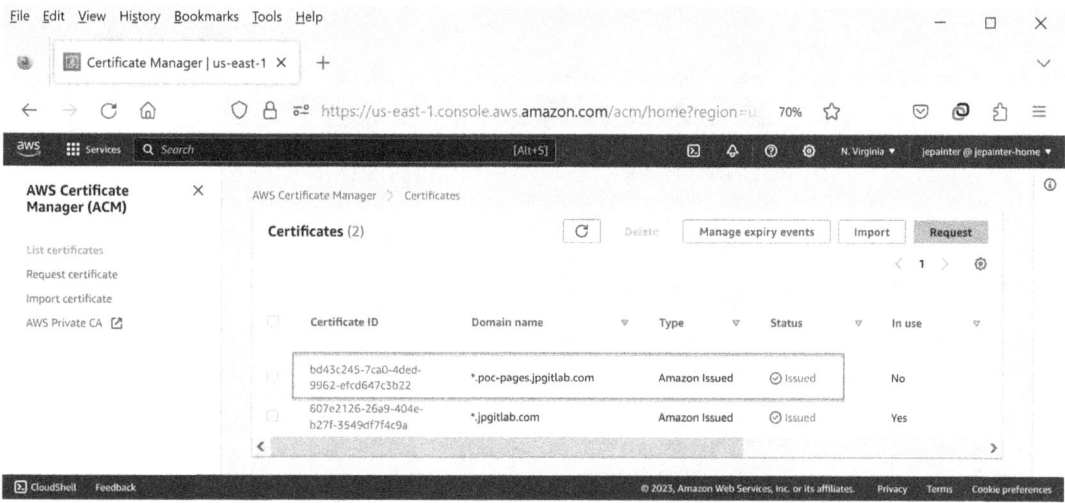

Figure 17-37. *Creation of TLS certificate for GitLab pages domain*

Creating the ELB for the Pages Service

Once the certificate is ready, creating the ELB for the pages service is next. For my setup, I created the poc-pages-loadbalancer as shown in Figure 17-38. Like the ELB created for the poc GitLab service, I used a classic load balancer using the same security group. I also created listeners for ports 22, 80, and 443 as highlighted in the figure, and for port 443, I included the certificate just created. In addition, the health check was set to

---

[7] Technically, if we were only going to have static servers rather than auto-scaled ones, we could get by with pointing both ELBs to the same standalone server. But with auto-scaling servers, we cannot share them across ELBs.

match the health check on the primary ELB. Since the primary ELB is pointing to the standalone GitLab server, I also added that server as an instance to the Pages ELB. Doing this makes updating the GitLab configuration simpler.

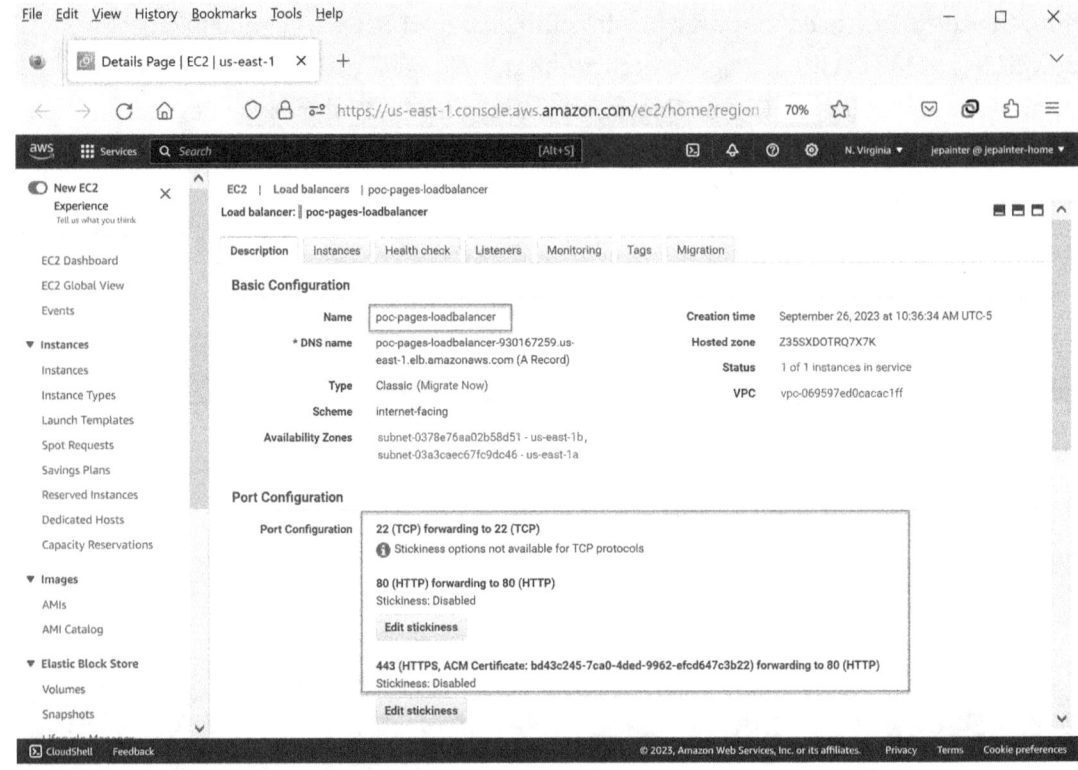

Figure 17-38. Configuration of GitLab pages ELB

Creating the DNS Record for the Pages Service

The next step after creating the ELB is to create the DNS record for the pages service. Using the Route 53 hosted zone defined for the GitLab poc service, I defined a wildcard A record, *.poc-pages.jpgitlab.com, as highlighted in Figure 17-39. I associated this A record to route traffic to the ELB just created. With that change, all requests to the poc-pages.jpgitlab.com will be sent to the poc-pages ELB.

CHAPTER 17 BUT WAIT, THERE'S MORE

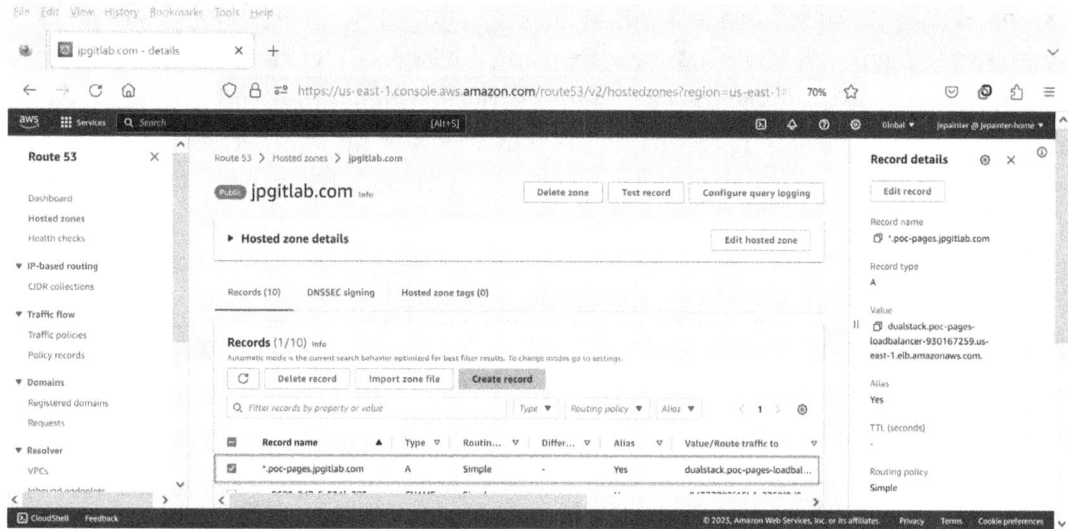

Figure 17-39. *Definition of wildcard DNS record for GitLab pages service*

Updating the GitLab Configuration for the Pages Service

With the AWS changes in place, it is now time to update the gitlab.rb configuration to enable the pages service. By default, it is disabled. There are two sets of changes to be made in the gitlab.rb file. The first involves enabling the pages service and setting the pages_external_url value as shown in Figure 17-40. Note that the external URL uses HTTPS rather than the default HTTP; this is important since we want to direct pages requests to port 443 where the TLS certificate is managed by the ELB. Also, note that we don't use the wildcard with the external URL, just the poc-pages.jpgitlab.com domain name.

```
################################################################################
## GitLab Pages
##! Docs: https://docs.gitlab.com/ee/administration/pages/
################################################################################

##! Define to enable GitLab Pages
pages_external_url "https://poc-pages.jpgitlab.com/"
gitlab_pages['enable'] = true

##! Configure to expose GitLab Pages on external IP address, serving the HTTP
# gitlab_pages['external_http'] = []
                                                              1772,0-1      52%
```

Figure 17-40. *GitLab configuration updates to enable GitLab pages service*

787

The second set of settings involves the Pages nginx service. The changes for this are shown in Figure 17-41. Because we are using the Pages ELB to manage the TLS certificate, we have to enable the Pages nginx service, which is disabled by default. We also need to tell the Pages nginx service to listen at port 80 rather than 443 (since the ELB will redirect traffic from port 443 to 80). Similarly, to what was done with the primary nginx service, we need to set listen_https to false so that nginx knows not to handle the TLS certificates.

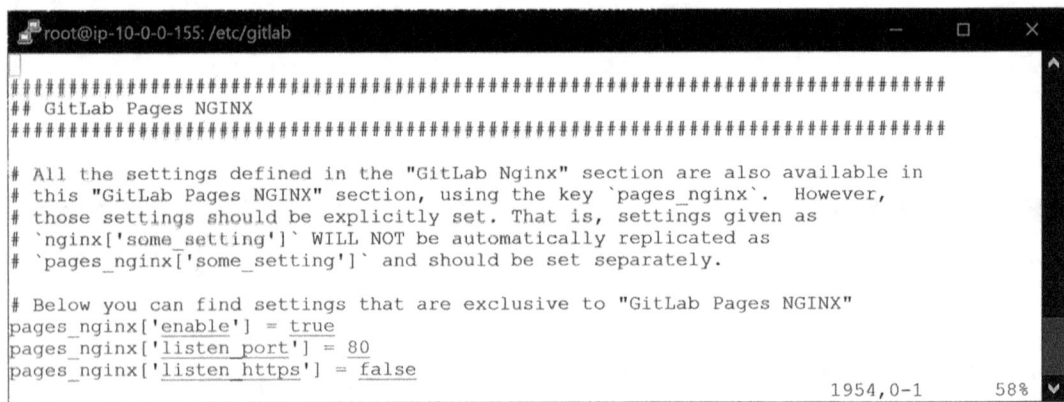

Figure 17-41. *GitLab configuration changes to enable nginx for the GitLab pages service*

Verifying Pages Service Is Running

With those changes in place, it is time to run the "sudo gitlab-ctl reconfigure" command as usual. If all went well, the reconfiguration should have succeeded; if not, it will tell you that there was an issue that you will need to debug. To verify that the Pages service is running, run the "sudo gitlab-ctl status" command to verify that gitlab-pages is in the run state as shown in Figure 17-42. If "gitlab-pages" does not show up or its status is stopped, retrace the preceding steps to make sure connectivity and configuration are set up properly.

CHAPTER 17   BUT WAIT, THERE'S MORE

```
root@ip-10-0-0-155:/etc/gitlab
Infra Phase complete, 32/732 resources updated in 17 seconds
gitlab Reconfigured!
root@ip-10-0-0-155:/etc/gitlab# gitlab-ctl status
run: alertmanager: (pid 225394) 1285496s; run: log: (pid 1513) 2061097s
run: gitlab-exporter: (pid 1516) 2061097s; run: log: (pid 1508) 2061097s
run: gitlab-kas: (pid 1519) 2061097s; run: log: (pid 1512) 2061097s
run: gitlab-pages: (pid 113922) 12s; run: log: (pid 113902) 16s
run: gitlab-workhorse: (pid 1506) 2061097s; run: log: (pid 1504) 2061097s
run: logrotate: (pid 113016) 1874s; run: log: (pid 1505) 2061097s
run: nginx: (pid 113914) 12s; run: log: (pid 1507) 2061097s
run: node-exporter: (pid 1534) 2061097s; run: log: (pid 1533) 2061097s
run: prometheus: (pid 4019918) 1122379s; run: log: (pid 1531) 2061097s
run: puma: (pid 113950) 6s; run: log: (pid 1509) 2061097s
run: registry: (pid 4180906) 514862s; run: log: (pid 4180888) 514866s
run: sidekiq: (pid 113907) 12s; run: log: (pid 1511) 2061097s
root@ip-10-0-0-155:/etc/gitlab#
```

Figure 17-42. Output of gitlab-ctl status verifying gitlab-pages service is running

As a final check, log in to the poc service as an admin and go to the Admin Area dashboard as shown in Figure 17-43. Under the Components section, you should see "GitLab Pages" appear with the same release value as the GitLab service. If it doesn't appear, it means that the Pages service is not running for the poc. Assuming that it does appear under the Components section, you could do a further check (not shown here) by going into a project's settings and validating that Pages show up there.

Statistics		Features		Components	
Forks	0	Sign up	⏻	GitLab	v16.1.2
Issues	0	LDAP	⏻	GitLab Shell	14.23.0
Merge requests	0	Gravatar	✓	GitLab Workhorse	v16.1.2
Notes	0	OmniAuth	✓	GitLab API	v4
Snippets	0	Reply by email	⏻	GitLab Pages	16.1.2
SSH Keys	0	Container Registry	✓	GitLab KAS	v16.1.3
Milestones	0	GitLab Pages	✓	Ruby	3.0.6p216
Active Users	2	Shared Runners	✓	Rails	6.1.7.2

Figure 17-43. Admin Area dashboard showing that GitLab pages is running

Creating a New AMI with Services Enabled

At this point, we've successfully enabled the registry and pages services as well as set up the external_diffs and ci_secure_files to use the S3 object store. With everything working, it is time to create a new AMI from the standalone GitLab server to capture the configuration changes. Once the AMI is completed, you can then switch the primary ELB to use the auto-scaling group and disconnect the standalone GitLab server from it.

Scaling Considerations for the Pages Service

So, what about the pages ELB? You have two choices here. You can either keep it connected to the standalone GitLab instance, or you can create a new auto-scaling group for the Pages service that references the new AMI and connect that ASG to the pages ELB. If you go with the latter, you'll have two ELBs with their own ASGs automatically managing the instances for each service.[8] Most likely, the loading for Pages servers will be lower than the loading for the primary GitLab services. If you do create an ASG for the Pages service, you can disconnect the standalone GitLab server from the Pages ELB and set it to the stopped state until you need to make further configuration or release changes.

Summary

In summary, we've covered the following topics in this chapter:

- Described how to connect to an external email service using Amazon's SES as an example

- Covered how to enable the GitLab container registry using the existing ELB

- Learned how to enable the GitLab Pages service that requires its own ELB

With these special one-time configurations in place, we next delve into the periodic tasks required of a self-managed GitLab administrator.

---

[8] You might be tempted to do some optimization by disabling the Pages service for instances spun up for the primary GitLab service. Don't do that. It's important that those instances know that Pages are enabled and what the external URL for the Pages service is so that traffic can be rerouted to the Pages ELB.

CHAPTER 18

It's an Admin's Life

In addition to one-time tasks such as setting up connectivity to an external email service and enabling secondary services, there will be tasks you will need to do periodically as an administrator to keep things running smoothly. In this chapter, we'll talk about three such tasks.

First, we'll look at how to manage users of your self-managed service. This is especially important if you are using a per-seat license. Second, we'll look at how to update GitLab's configuration, something you'll probably need to do on a regular basis. And third, we'll look at how to upgrade to a new release, which is a bit trickier than simply updating a configuration.

Dealing with Users

When you use the SaaS gitlab.com service, life with respect to users is easy. If you want someone to join your project or group, you simply have them sign up on gitlab.com just as you did in the first chapter of this book and have them give you their username in order for you to add them explicitly. Life gets more complicated when you run your own self-managed GitLab service. There are many options available for managing users depending on your circumstances and your licensing model.

Managing Users via the Administrative UI

We will start by looking at the most direct way of managing users: through the administrative UI. You of course need to be an administrator of your self-managed service to get to the Admin Area section. Figure 18-1 shows the initial Users page accessible under the expanded Overview subsection. Three users are created automatically when you set up a self-managed instance: Administrator, GitLab Alert Bot, and GitLab Support Bot. The Administrator is the "root" user that you logged in

CHAPTER 18 IT'S AN ADMIN'S LIFE

as initially. The other two "users" are bot users created by GitLab that are used by the application for alerts and support tasks. You cannot log in to GitLab as these bots, nor can you get rid of them. The good news is these bots do not count toward your user license count.

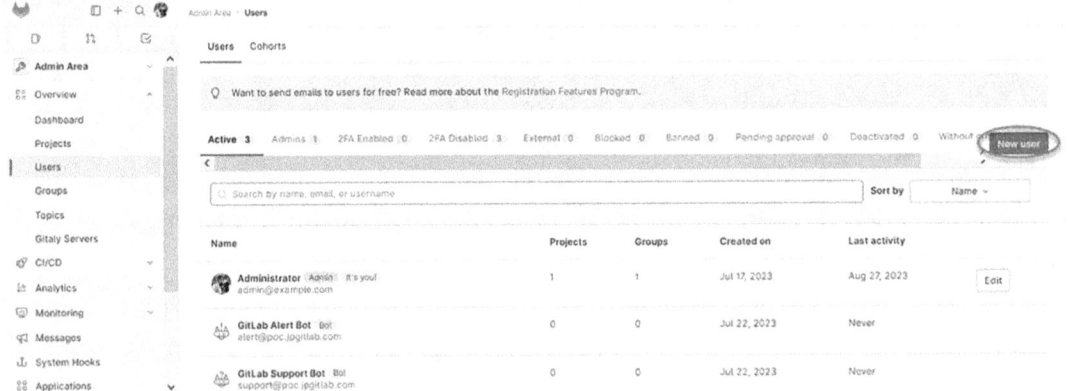

Figure 18-1. Initial Admin Area user list

Adding a New User

To add a new user, simply select the "New user" button in the upper right of the Users page. This will take you to a form to enter information about the new user. The first part of the form is shown in Figure 18-2. Here, you enter basic information about the user such as the user's email address, full name, and username. In this example, I am creating a user just for myself so that there is accounting for things I do as an administrator. If you plan on having multiple administrators on this GitLab service, it is highly recommended that you create accounts for each of those users and keep the root password private. Note the message about the password being sent via email; you do not set it with this form.

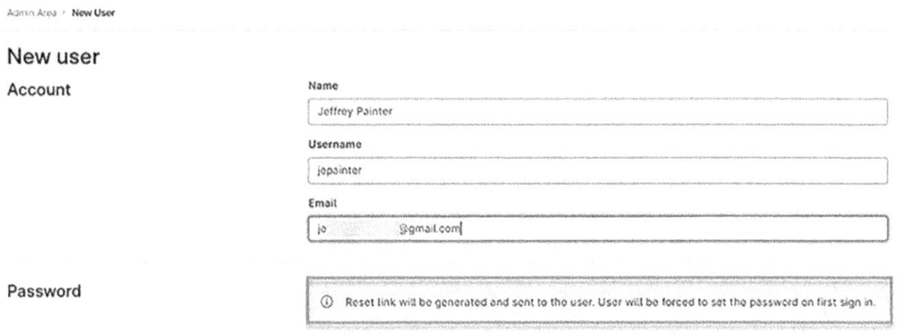

CHAPTER 18 IT'S AN ADMIN'S LIFE

Figure 18-2. New user form (part 1)

Scrolling down, you'll see some access settings for the user as shown in Figure 18-3. Since the user I am creating is myself, I give myself administrator access. For most users, you would use the regular access level that gives those users at last read access to their private groups and projects on your site in addition to any groups and projects they have been invited to. If you want something more restrictive, there is a special access mode for external users; these users will not have access to private groups or projects unless explicitly added to them. They will, however, have read access to public groups and projects. The last checkbox option to validate by credit card is useful if you plan on having a public-facing self-managed site. I left it unchecked because I want to keep this just to the people I invite.

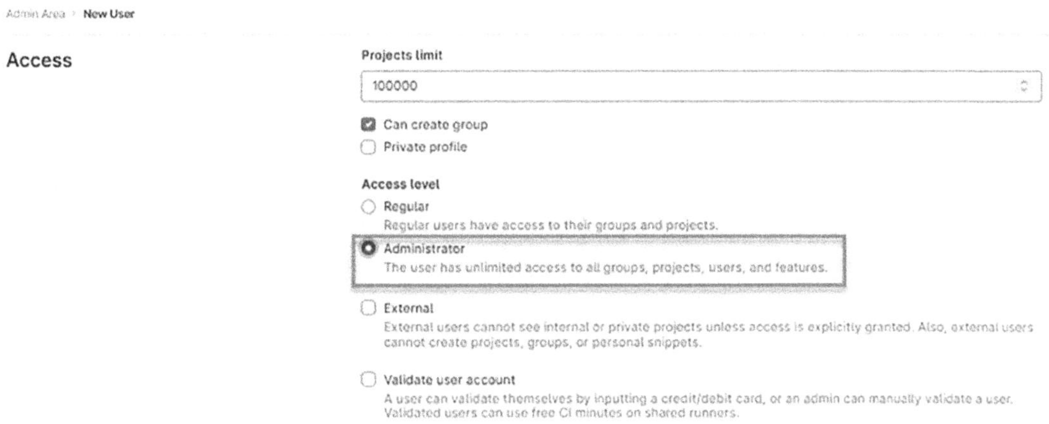

Figure 18-3. New user form (part 2)

CHAPTER 18   IT'S AN ADMIN'S LIFE

The final part of the new user form is shown in Figure 18-4. Most likely, you'll keep this section blank when adding users other than yourself. Here, I've added an Avatar for myself and left the rest of the profile information blank. Users can add their own profile information if they choose. The last part is an optional admin note that only administrators can see. This is useful to communicate among administrators about who the person is, who they work for, etc.

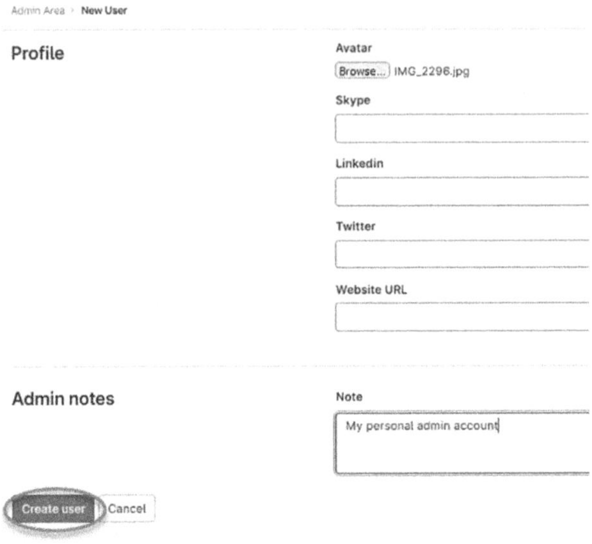

Figure 18-4. New user form (part 3)

With the form filled out, you create the user using the "Create user" button. When you do, you'll be taken to the user's page as shown in Figure 18-5. You should see the message that the user was successfully created. You should also see the "Verified" message next to the user's email address that confirms the email has been verified. If it hasn't, check that you entered the email correctly; otherwise, block that user and attempt to contact the person to find out what the valid email is.

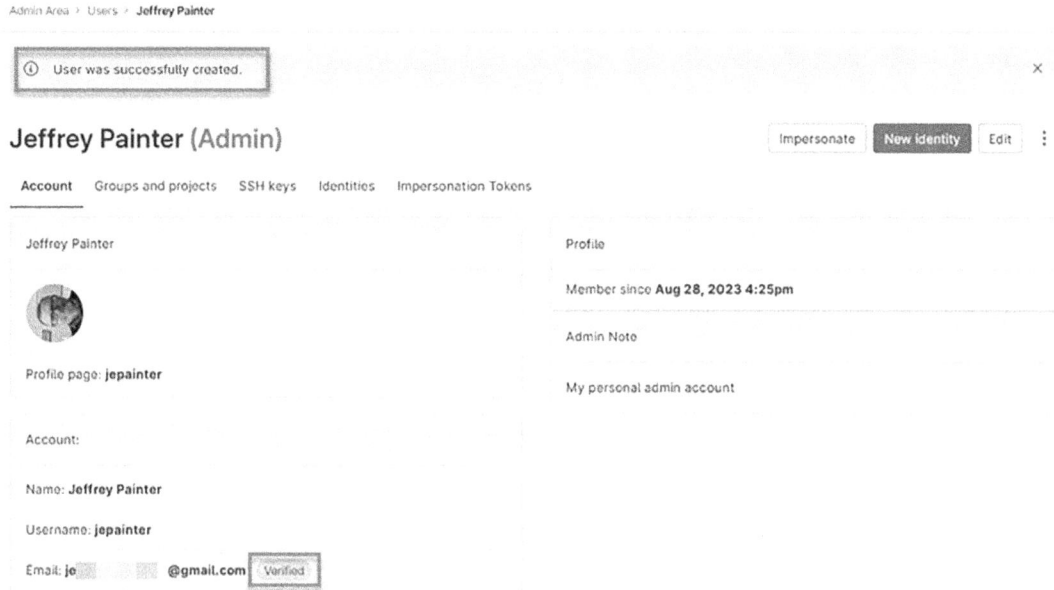

Figure 18-5. *New user's page*

Now if you created a user for yourself as I did, you are probably now waiting for that email promised on the new user form in order to set your password. Note that if you haven't configured GitLab to connect to an external email service as described in the previous chapter, you'll be waiting a long time as that email will not come through. In that case, you'll need to set the password manually through the administrative UI as described next.

Resetting a User's Password

To set a password for a user, go to the user's information page (like that shown earlier) and select the Edit button. You'll get a page like the one shown in Figure 18-6. Simply enter the password twice in the Password section; as typical with password changes, the password confirmation must match the password entered. When done, make sure to scroll down to the bottom of the page and select "Save changes." If the email service hasn't been configured yet, no email will be sent with this change; in that case, you'll need to contact the person to let them know what the password is (assuming it isn't yourself, of course) along with the username you set up. When that user logs in with the provided password, they will be prompted to change their password; hence the password you provide is a one-time temporary password.

CHAPTER 18   IT'S AN ADMIN'S LIFE

Figure 18-6. User password change via administrator

Configuring Site-Wide Settings for Users

Let's now switch focus to administrative settings that impact users signing up and signing in. Figure 18-7 shows the General Settings page. Here, you'll see two collapsed categories titled "Sign-up restrictions" and "Sign-in restrictions." Both of these categories define restrictions on users. We'll take each category in turn.

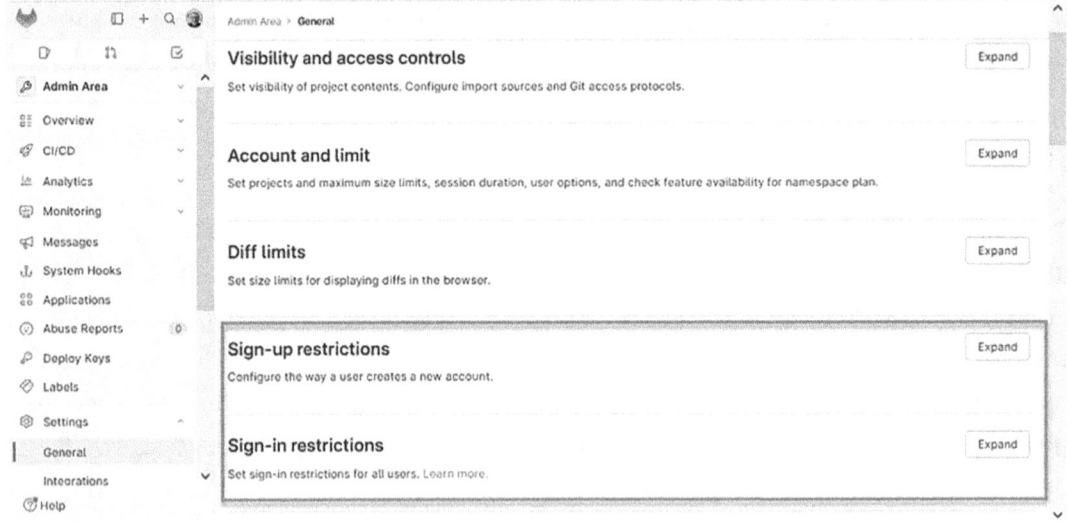

Figure 18-7. Administrative section in general settings for restricting users

Configuring Sign-Up Restrictions

The "Sign-up restrictions" category of settings shown in Figure 18-8 controls how new users can sign up for your service. We already saw the first option earlier when we initially spun up the service. This controls whether users can sign up to join the GitLab service on their own or not. I disabled it initially to keep anyone from joining while GitLab was being configured. If you really want people to sign up on their own, feel free to select this option. If you do enable this, the second option requires that an administrator approve the request before allowing them to log in.[1] You can also control how email confirmations are handled. In this example, I chose the soft option, but if you want to be fully restrictive, choose the hard option. The final option is the minimum password length, which in this example is set to 8 characters; increase this limit to something like 12 for more security.[2]

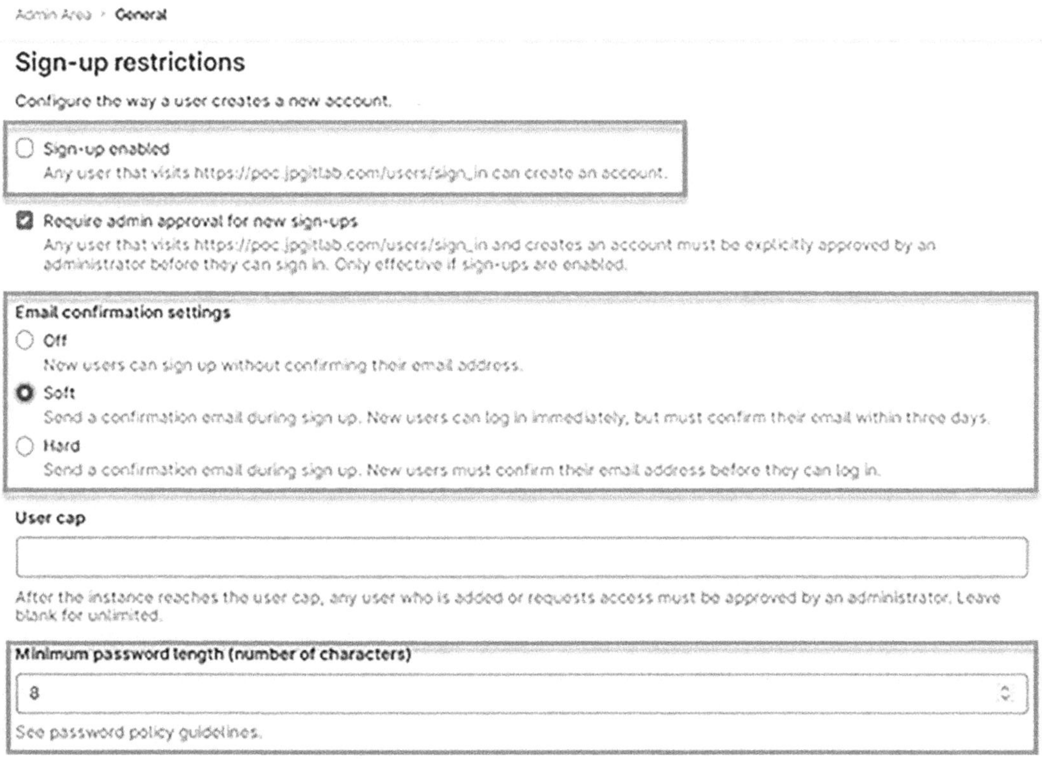

Figure 18-8. User sign-up restrictions page

---

[1] I highly recommend enabling this option, especially if your service is open to the Internet.

[2] Don't go too crazy, though. I managed a server in China that had a minimum requirement of 21 characters. That was a bit much, IMHO.

CHAPTER 18   IT'S AN ADMIN'S LIFE

Setting Sign-In Restrictions

For existing users, the "Sign-in restrictions" category imposes restrictions on authentication. Figure 18-9 shows the more important options for sign-in. The first option determines whether GitLab will perform the password authentication (the default) or an external third-party provider. The second option allows passwords with Git over HTTPS; if not selected, users will have to use personal access tokens instead. If you really want to tighten security, the third and fourth options, if selected, will require that all users use two-factor authentication.[3] The last option in this figure is recommended to let users know if someone else is possibly attempting to log in as them. As for the admin mode, I haven't used it myself, but it looks like a reasonable option to set as a way to prevent accidental mistakes using the UI.[4]

Figure 18-9. User sign-in restrictions page

---

[3] I personally don't recommend requiring this for ALL users; they can set up 2FA for themselves if they want.

[4] This is sort of like using sudo to perform administrative functions in Linux/Unix.

798

Integrating with External Authentication Services

So, if you only plan on having a small number of users signing in to your GitLab service, then managing those users via the administrative UI should suffice. However, if the number of users grows to 100 or more, managing those users via the UI will become cumbersome. GitLab provides a number of authentication integrations that you can use depending on your developer environment. For example, if you are in a corporate environment, there may already be an LDAP or Active Directory service available that you can tap into. This way, users can use the same usernames and passwords to log in to GitLab as they do to log in to their personal machines. Alternatively, there may be an identity provider external to your corporate environment that they use in place of LDAP. If you are providing an open source platform, you may end up using a third-party identification service to manage your users.

You can find a description of all the authentication and authorization options supported by GitLab at `https://docs.gitlab.com/ee/administration/auth/`. The list is pretty extensive, but can be captured into a few basic categories as follows:

- LDAP-compatible services including Active Directory
- OmniAuth providers such as Google, AWS Cognito, etc.
- SAML SSO providers such as Okta and Google Workspace
- OAuth 2.0 services via gitlab.com

Integrating with one of these authentication services requires updating the gitlab.rb configuration file. If you already have an active GitLab service with a number of users managing their projects on it, you should plan some downtime while you configure and test your authentication setup. If not, you can integrate with the identity provider prior to any users officially signing in to your GitLab service.

Integrating with LDAP/Active Directory Authentication Service

Since LDAP/Active Directory is a common authentication service used in many companies, I'll discuss the setup for that here. Figure 18-10 shows the section within the gitlab.rb that deals with LDAP settings. Fortunately, the starting comments point you to the documentation for configuring LDAP, so I won't repeat that link here.

CHAPTER 18 IT'S AN ADMIN'S LIFE

```
## LDAP Settings
###! Docs: https://docs.gitlab.com/ee/administration/auth/ldap/index.html
###! **Be careful not to break the indentation in the ldap_servers block. It is
###!   in yaml format and the spaces must be retained. Using tabs will not work.**

# gitlab_rails['ldap_enabled'] = false
# gitlab_rails['prevent_ldap_sign_in'] = false

###! **remember to close this block with 'EOS' below**
# gitlab_rails['ldap_servers'] = YAML.load <<-'EOS'
#   main: # 'main' is the GitLab 'provider ID' of this LDAP server
#     label: 'LDAP'
#     host: '_your_ldap_server'
#     port: 389
#     uid: 'sAMAccountName'
#     bind_dn: '_the_full_dn_of_the_user_you_will_bind_with'
#     password: '_the_password_of_the_bind_user'
#     encryption: 'plain' # "start_tls" or "simple_tls" or "plain"
#     verify_certificates: true
#     smartcard_auth: false
#     active_directory: true
#     allow_username_or_email_login: false
#     lowercase_usernames: false
#     block_auto_created_users: false
#     base: ''
#     user_filter: ''
#     ## EE only
#     group_base: ''
#     admin_group: ''
#     sync_ssh_keys: false
#
#   secondary: # 'secondary' is the GitLab 'provider ID' of second LDAP server
```

Figure 18-10. LDAP settings within the GitLab configuration file

To enable LDAP, uncomment the first gitlab_rails line with ldap_enabled set to true. You'll want to keep the prevent_ldap_sign_in option set to the default of false in order to allow users to sign in with their LDAP credentials; otherwise, setting it to true would enable LDAP only for Git authentication.

The ldap_servers section is used to let GitLab know how to connect to your LDAP or Active Directory service. This section uses a Ruby "here document" to denote the end of the section; this is similar to the Linux/Unix here document mechanism where input is grabbed from within the configuration itself rather than from an external file. As mentioned in the comments, you'll need to make sure the end of string (EDS) at the bottom of the LDAP section is uncommented.

The ldap_servers section shows two subsections, one labeled main and the other labeled secondary. You need to at least specify settings under main, which represents the primary LDAP service to which you will be connecting. Note that if you have an unlicensed version of GitLab, you can only specify one LDAP service; for licensed GitLab versions, you can have more than one LDAP service defined. Those settings would be defined under the secondary or tertiary subsections as needed.

You can find a description of possible options via the documents link described earlier. The most common options are provided in the gitlab.rb file, but there are other special options not shown in gitlab.rb. The label option is used on the sign-in page; you'll be able to log in either using LDAP or what GitLab calls the "standard" login that you've been using up to now. If you are not the one who set up the LDAP or Active Directory service, you'll need to get the details for the remaining options from the administrator who set up the service.[5]

Two options are of special note: bind_dn and password. These two options are used to authenticate with the LDAP/Active Directory service, which is necessary in order to look up both users and groups associated with the service. The "dn" part of bind_dn stands for "distinguished name" and should refer to a service user that has rights to perform lookups; you should never use your own username for this. For security reasons, you should request a service user specifically for GitLab just in case the password for that user is exposed; it's easier to change the password for GitLab than it is to change passwords for all other applications that require access to LDAP/Active Directory.

If you are concerned that the LDAP bind_dn and password are exposed in plain text within the gitlab.rb file, there is a way to encrypt both of these values in a file that GitLab will detect and use. This involves running a gitlab-rake command that spins up a text editor of your choice (typically vim) where you can enter both the bind_dn and password values. When you finish editing, the gitlab-rake command will encrypt the information and store it in the GitLab database. You can then remove the two entries in the gitlab.rb file.

Additional LDAP Options Available for Licensed Sites

If you look closely at the gitlab.rb file, you'll notice the comment "## EE Only." In GitLab speak, "EE" stands for Enterprise Edition. In other words, it is a licensed version of GitLab. The three options of group_base, admin_group, and sync_ssh_keys are used to enhance the LDAP integration. The group_base is used to enable LDAP groups; with this option, you can use LDAP groups for permissions of GitLab projects and groups. So, for example, if you have a development team in LDAP, you can mark that LDAP group with Developer permissions for a project or GitLab group. The admin_group option is handy

---

[5] In many corporate environments, this is easier said than done. Most likely, you'll need to get special director approval, and even then, you might have to go back and forth with the administrator to get the info you need.

to control who are administrators of your GitLab service; using this option, if a person leaves the company or is moved to a different department, the LDAP group will handle this for you. Finally, the sync_ssh_keys is an option that enables users to use SSH keys already maintained in LDAP.

Impact of Authentication Service on License Costs

There's one thing to be aware of when using LDAP or any other identity service. Users in the identity service are not added as a licensed GitLab user until that user has logged in to GitLab. This is a good thing since it prevents all users in a company from being automatically added as a licensed user in GitLab. The downside of this is that any user can sign in and become a licensed user, which will increase your license costs. You can control this to some extent by using the "Require admin approval for new sign-ups" option in the sign-up settings described earlier. As an administrator, you can also "block" users after the fact to keep them from using a license seat. With the most expensive ultimate license model, you can also mark users as "Guests" that gives them read-only access to portions of your GitLab service but does not take a license seat.[6]

Blocking Users

Since we are on the topic of blocking users, let's take a look at how you block a user. For this example, I added Heidi as a regular user to my poc service. Figure 18-11 shows Heidi in the user list. Selecting the vertical ellipsis button shows a menu of actions that we can apply to Heidi as an administrator. We can block Heidi by simply selecting the Block option. Once blocked, we can unblock using the same technique (the menu will show Unblock in place of the Block option). A blocked user won't be notified but will realize they have been blocked when they are denied access when logging in to GitLab or attempting to do a Git operation. Other users will still see the contributions to a project of that user.

---

[6] As you may have gathered, this leads to a tug-of-war between those who want to use your GitLab service and those who pay for it. As an administrator, you will be stuck in the middle of this feud.

CHAPTER 18   IT'S AN ADMIN'S LIFE

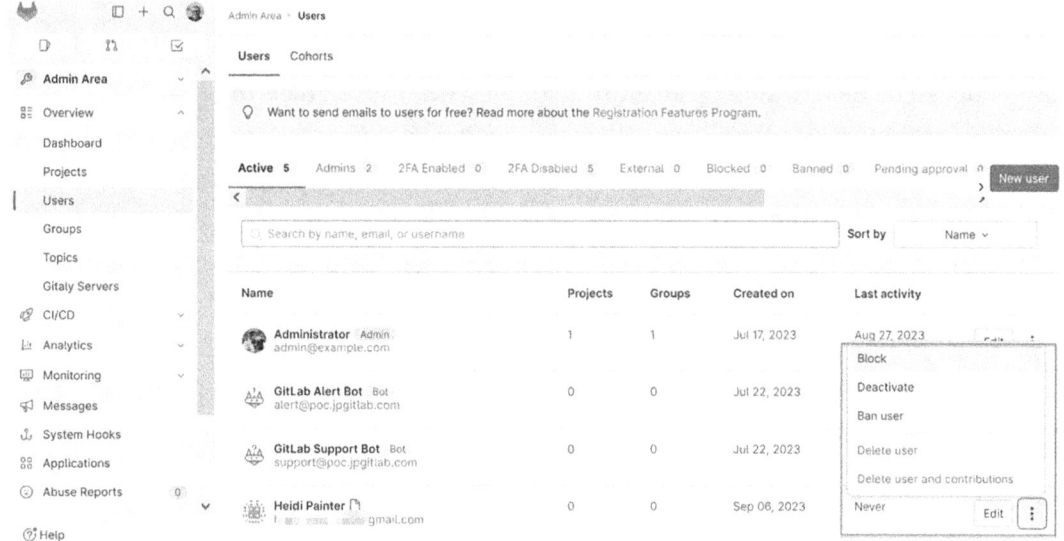

Figure 18-11. Option to block a given user

Banning Users

The "Ban user" option is a bit more severe. Not only does it block the user but will hide that user from any contributions (such as issues and comments) and will hide any projects solely owned by that user. Banning a user is usually done in response to an "abuse" report made by another user. In this case, a user is acting as a "bad actor" with respect to other users; marking that user as banned as opposed to blocked lets administrators know that the user should be handled specially.[7]

Deactivating Users

Notice that there is a Deactivate option for Heidi. This option does not always show up for users. Deactivating a user is similar to blocking a user. When deactivated, that user does not take up a license seat; however, unlike a blocked user, a deactivated user can still log in. As soon as they do, they become automatically active. Like a blocked user,

---

[7] It is not unusual for an administrator to get a request to unblock a user, which is typically done without much consideration. Unbanning a user will give an admin some pause before allowing the request.

a deactivated user cannot perform Git operations; they have to explicitly log in to reactivate themselves. There are two cases when a user becomes deactivated. New users like Heidi can be deactivated by an administrator within seven days of being created; new users are active by default, so you have to act quick to deactivate a new user. Once a user is active, they cannot be deactivated until after 90 days of inactivity.

There is a special option to automatically deactivate dormant users after 90 days or more of inactivity. Figure 18-12 shows the section under "General Settings ➤ Account and limit" where this option can be enabled (it is disabled by default). Check the "Deactivate dormant users after a period of inactivity" option to enable automatic disabling of users. By default, the minimum of 90 days is specified; you can increase this value if you prefer.

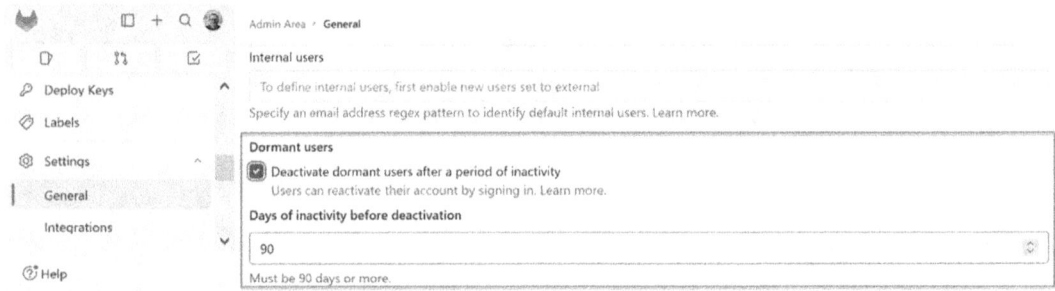

Figure 18-12. Setting to deactivate users who are inactive for specified number of days

Status of GitLab Users When Removed or Disabled from Authentication Service

So, what happens when a user is disabled, deactivated, or removed from the LDAP/Active Directory service? They are automatically blocked by GitLab usually within the hour of detecting the change in LDAP status. Thus, you don't need to manually block users who have left the company or an identity provider service. By blocking the user, it prevents that user from logging in to the GitLab service and removing them from a license seat. That user will still remain in the GitLab user database allowing any past work to be attributed to them.

Deleting Users

This brings us to the topic of deleting users. As you saw in Figure 18-11, there are the options "Delete user" and "Delete user and contributions." So, what does deleting a user do? It converts that user into a "ghost" user. Their username will remain, but their profile and other identifying information are removed. The "Delete user" option will simply convert that user into a ghost user unless there are groups or projects that are solely owned by that user; if there are groups or projects solely owned by a user, GitLab will refuse to delete that user using the "Delete user" option.

The second option of "Delete user and contributions" will not only mark the user as a ghost user but will remove any associated records (such as issues, comments, etc.) and remove all groups and projects solely owned by that user. That last part is the most dangerous aspect of deleting user contributions, especially deleting groups solely owned by that user. Although not recommended, there are times when other users rely on projects or groups solely owned by a user. Deleting a user's contributions will impact those other users.[8] What is worse, those projects may not be retrievable later when they are eventually deleted from GitLab.[9]

Importance of Establishing User Management Policies

Bottom line when dealing with users in a formal setting: Establish policies early on. Determine when users are blocked or banned as well as establish a policy of how to unblock or unban them. For the more severe banning of a user, you may want to require a manager's approval before unbanning the user or perhaps a more formal disciplinary committee. Also, determine when to delete users and possibly their contributions, if at all. A policy that worked for me in the past is to change a project's ownership to another user or move the project to a common group owned by other users before deleting the owning user. Whatever policies you decide to use, make sure they are published for all users of your GitLab service.

---

[8] As typical in this situation, it tends to take a while before those users realize what has happened. By the time the impact is detected, it may be too late to undo the project deletion.

[9] As an admin, you can specify that project deletions be delayed by a period of days, typically seven days. But once that "soft" deletion period ends, the project is physically deleted and cannot be retrieved.

Next, we'll take a look at the common task of updating GitLab's configuration in an auto-scaled environment.

Updating GitLab's Configuration

There will be times when you'll need to update the GitLab's server configuration file, gitlab.rb. Although you might be tempted to update the gitlab.rb file directly on the GitLab servers, this won't work unless you are using a single standalone server. Remember that the GitLab servers are part of an AWS auto-scaling group[10] that use a launch template to spin up new servers either when they fail or when additional servers are needed to handle high-demand situations. In those cases, the ASG will spin up an AMI that was created prior to any changes made manually to the running GitLab servers.

Hence, to make any changes to the gitlab.rb configuration file, you're going to have to create a new AMI with those changes applied. In this section, I'll introduce a process you can use to make configuration changes. Note that I'm not going to talk about GitLab release updates here as those changes impact a number of components including Gitaly and the GitLab runner; I'll talk about those changes in the next section.

Remember that with the AWS auto-scaling solution introduced in the last chapter, we kept the standalone server around but removed it from the auto-scaling group and put it into a stopped state. The process for updating the AMI with a new configuration involves reversing those steps. Note that if the standalone GitLab server has been terminated for some reason, you'll be able to recreate it using the latest AMI used by the ASG.

Restarting the Standalone GitLab Server

So, the first step of the update process is to restart the standalone GitLab server. Figure 18-13 shows how to start that server. From the EC2 instances list, select the standalone GitLab server and right-click it to bring up the pop-up menu as shown. From that pop-up menu, select "Start instance" to restart the instance. Note that it may take a few minutes for the server to get back up and running. When the status check shows the 2/2 checks have passed, you are ready for the next step.

---

[10] This discussion assumes that AWS is used to manage your GitLab service. If you've gone a different route using a different cloud service provider or using Kubernetes, you'll need to translate this process to what works best for your setup.

CHAPTER 18 IT'S AN ADMIN'S LIFE

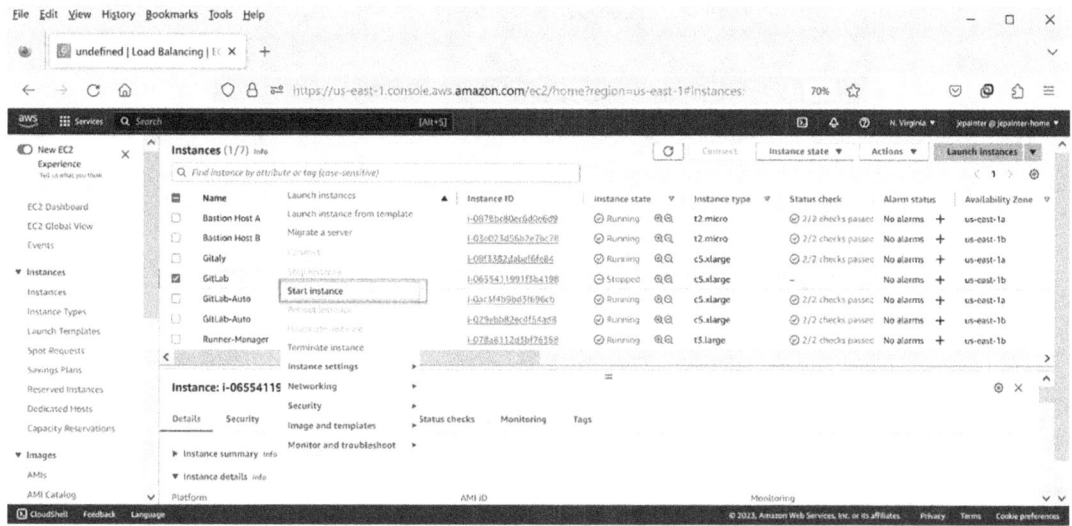

Figure 18-13. *Starting standalone GitLab server via EC2*

Adding the Standalone GitLab Server to the ELB

Next, we need to add the standalone server back into the ELB so that we can access it from the service's URL. Figure 18-14 shows the load balancer associated with our service. Once the load balancer is selected from the list, we can use "Manage instances" from the Action drop-down list to show the list of instances currently associated with the ELB. If you are wondering what prevents the ASG from spinning down a server while we are working with the standalone GitLab server, remember that the alarm triggers that control spinning up and spinning down servers only apply to the ASG-specific servers; the standalone GitLab server is not part of that triggering mechanism.

807

CHAPTER 18   IT'S AN ADMIN'S LIFE

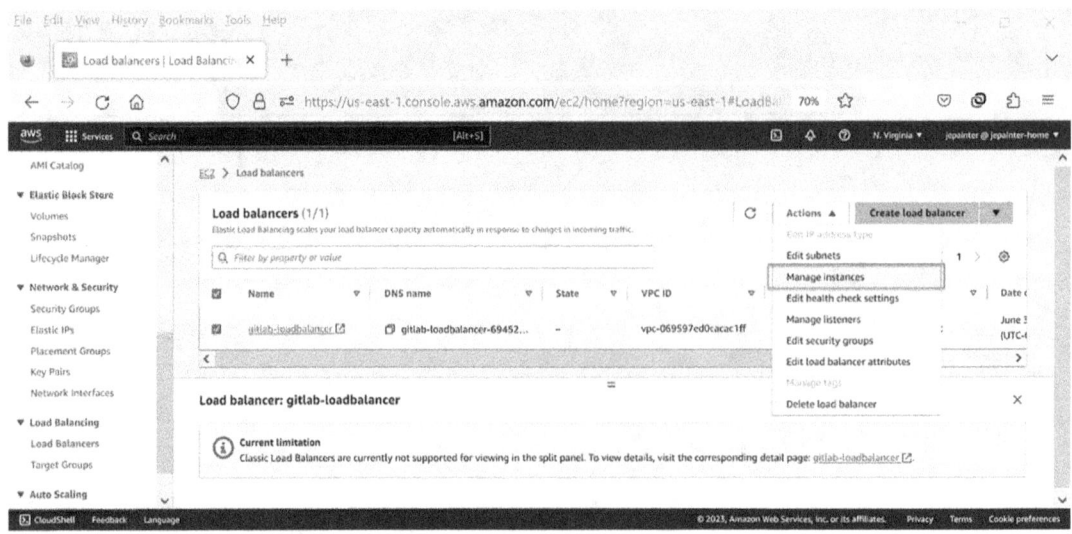

Figure 18-14. *Selecting to manage instances from the ELB*

At this point, we select the standalone server from the list of instances as shown in Figure 18-15. It is important to keep the GitLab-Auto servers selected since they are controlled by the ASG; deselecting them will cause confusion to the ASG that will likely end up terminating those servers. With the standalone GitLab server selected, use the Save button to connect it with the ELB.

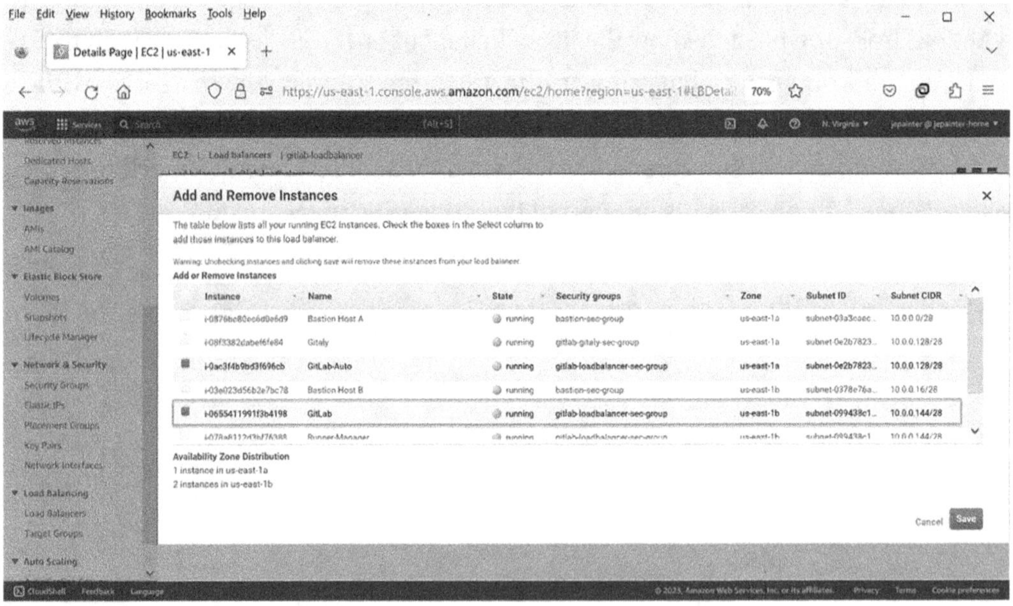

Figure 18-15. *Adding standalone GitLab instance to ELB*

CHAPTER 18　IT'S AN ADMIN'S LIFE

Before we move on, verify that the instance is in service as illustrated in Figure 18-16. Note that this may take a minute or so for the health check to indicate that the service is reachable. If, after a few minutes, the service is not in service, ssh into the server to verify via "sudo gitlab-ctl status" that all the components of the GitLab service are properly running.

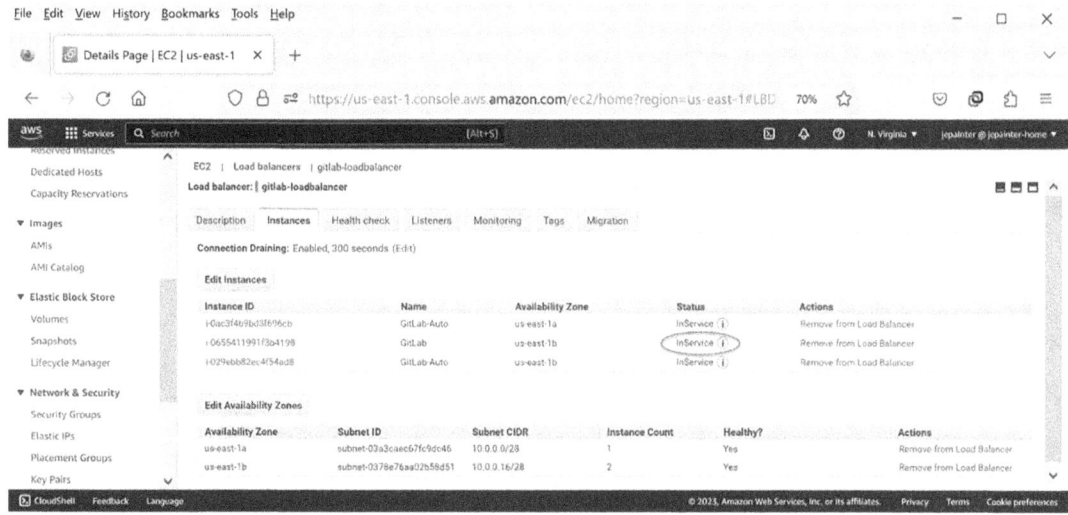

Figure 18-16. *Verifying standalone GitLab instance is in service for ELB*

Optionally Spinning Down Existing ASG Servers

With the standalone GitLab server in service, it is time to spin down the servers created by the auto-scaling group. We do this for major configuration updates such as setting email connectivity or configuring GitLab pages as discussed in the previous chapter. The reason for spinning down the ASG servers for major changes is the need to test those changes through the UI. Note that this will have a performance impact on the service if there are developers actively using it, so you may want to perform those types of changes when the system is less active, such as late at night or during the weekends. For minor changes, see the "Using the last refresh feature to replace ASG servers" at the end of this section that describes an alternative method of updating ASG servers with a new configuration.

CHAPTER 18   IT'S AN ADMIN'S LIFE

Remember that we cannot directly terminate or stop these servers as the ASG will detect that they are no longer responding and end up spinning up new servers to take their place. So how do we get around this ASG behavior? For this, we need to edit the auto-scaling group and manually set both the minimum and desired capacities to zero. Figure 18-17 shows the group size changes that accomplish that. It's important to set both the minimum and desired capacities to zero, not just one of them.

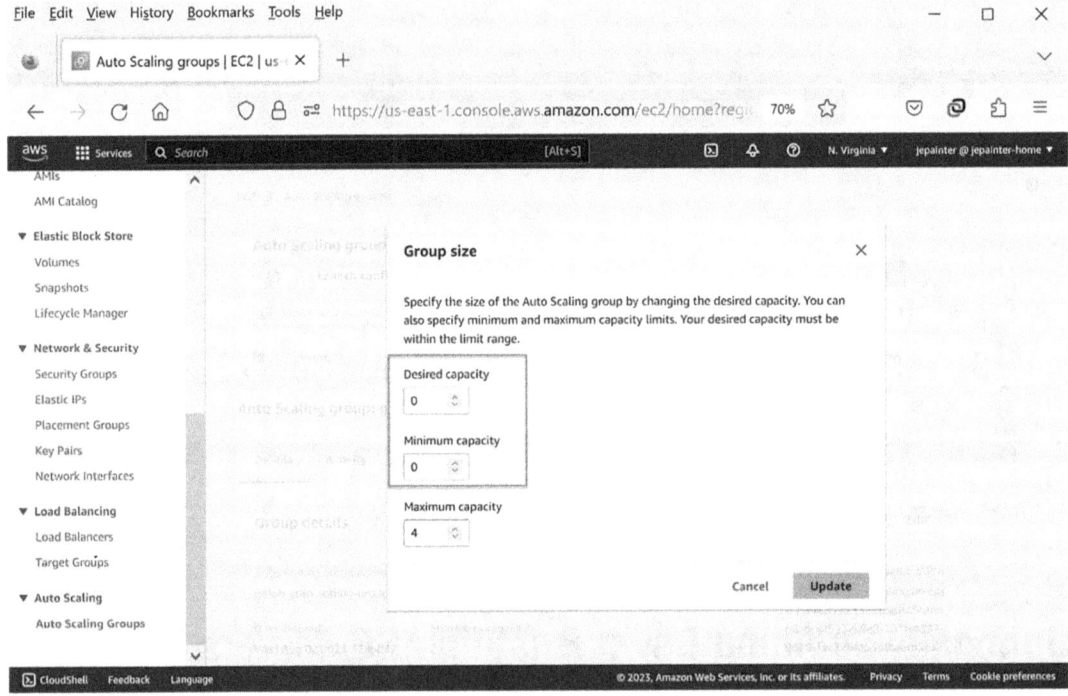

Figure 18-17. *Spinning down automated GitLab instances via auto-scaling group*

With that change in place, you should be able to see the ASG-controlled servers eventually terminated. Note that this may not happen in parallel; one server may start terminating before the other one. Rest assured that all ASG-controlled servers will end up terminated as shown in Figure 18-18. How do we know that the ASG won't spin up any new servers once we set the desired capacity to zero? Remember that the CloudWatch alarm triggers used to control the spinning up of servers only apply to the ASG-controlled servers, not the standalone GitLab server. With no ASG servers running, there is no way that the CPU average load will exceed the specified limit and hence no additional servers will be raised.

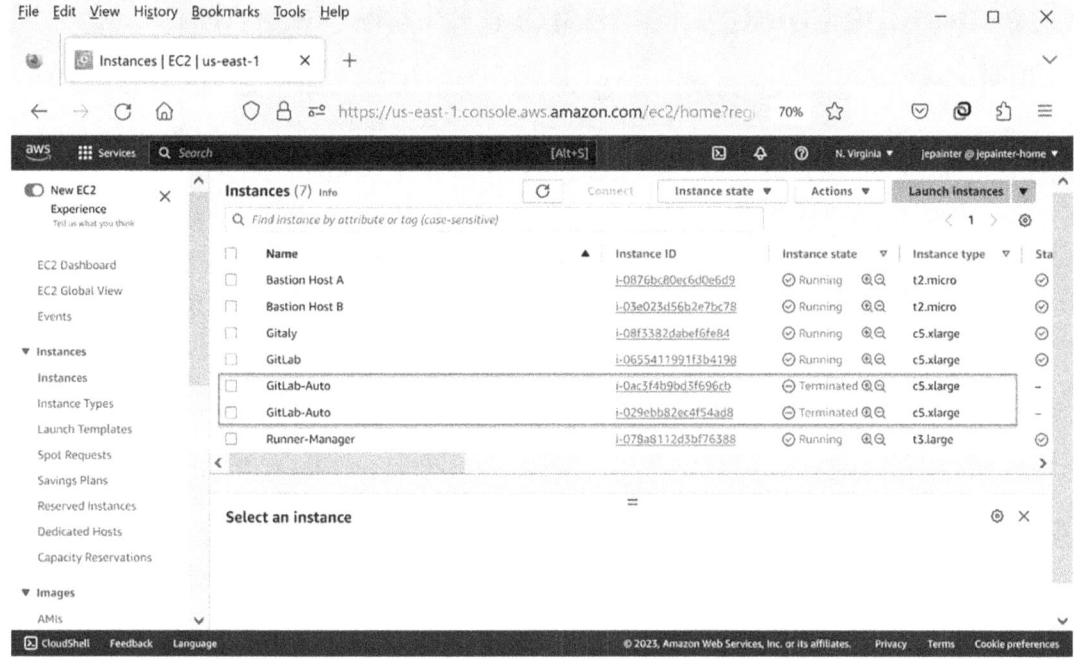

Figure 18-18. *Verifying automated instances have been terminated via EC2 instances list*

Updating the GitLab Configuration File and Creating a New AMI

At this point, you can make changes to the gitlab.rb file, apply them via "sudo gitlab-ctl reconfigure," and test them out. Note that while the configuration is being updated, there may be momentary blips in service from the user's point of view. Once you have made all the configuration changes, you are ready to create a new AMI off the standalone GitLab service. As a reminder of how to do this, simply select the standalone GitLab server from the EC2 instances list and choose "Image and templates ➤ Create image" from the Action menu.

CHAPTER 18   IT'S AN ADMIN'S LIFE

Updating the Launch Template with the New AMI

Once the new image becomes available, we need to update the launch template to use the new AMI. This involves selecting the launch template and choosing "Modify template" from the Action menu as shown in Figure 18-19. The reason for modifying the launch template rather than creating a new one is because the template is already tied to our auto-scaling group. Otherwise, we will have to remove the auto-scaling group from the ELB and add a new auto-scaling group with the new launch template, which is doable but more work than needed.

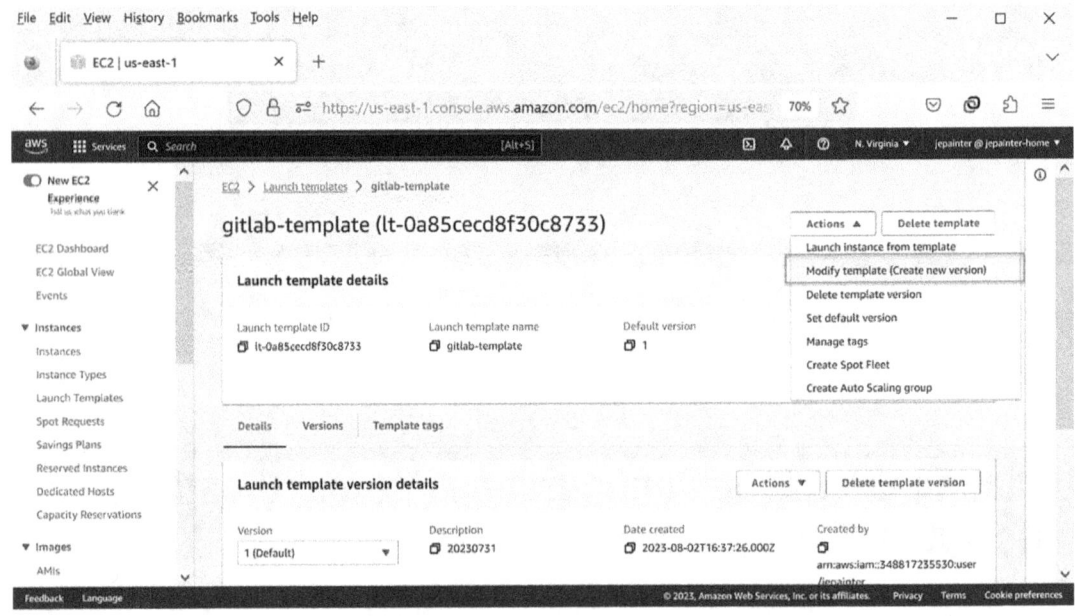

Figure 18-19. *Selecting to modify the GitLab launch template*

For the launch template, the only change to be made is the AMI; all other template options will remain the same.[11] Figure 18-20 shows the change I made to switch to the AMI I just created from the standalone GitLab server. This involved selecting the "Browse more AMIs" link and choosing the AMI from "My AMIs" list. Selecting the "Create template version" button will complete the template modification.

---

[11] Unless, of course, you want to change the instance type or disk size, for example.

CHAPTER 18   IT'S AN ADMIN'S LIFE

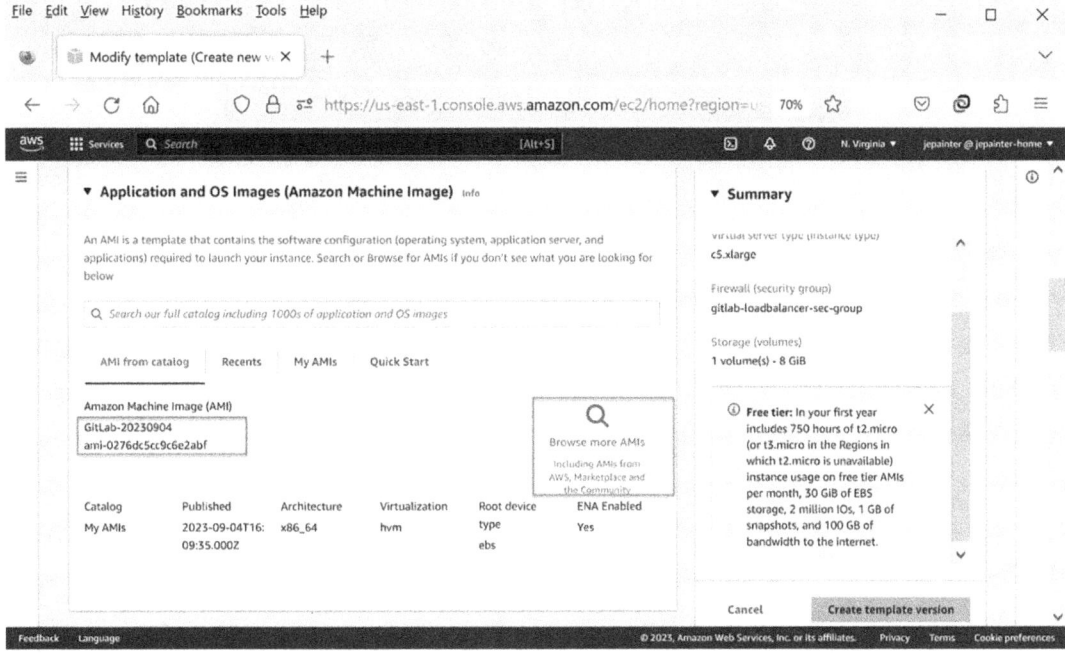

Figure 18-20. *Updating launch template to use newly created AMI*

We are not quite done yet with the launch template. We still need to set the default version to the one just created. This is done by selecting the "Set default version" option from the Action menu as shown in Figure 18-21. This will bring a pop-up dialog where you can select the latest version as the default version. It is important to do this as the default version will remain as before and none of the configuration changes will be used when new servers are spun up by the ASG.

813

CHAPTER 18 IT'S AN ADMIN'S LIFE

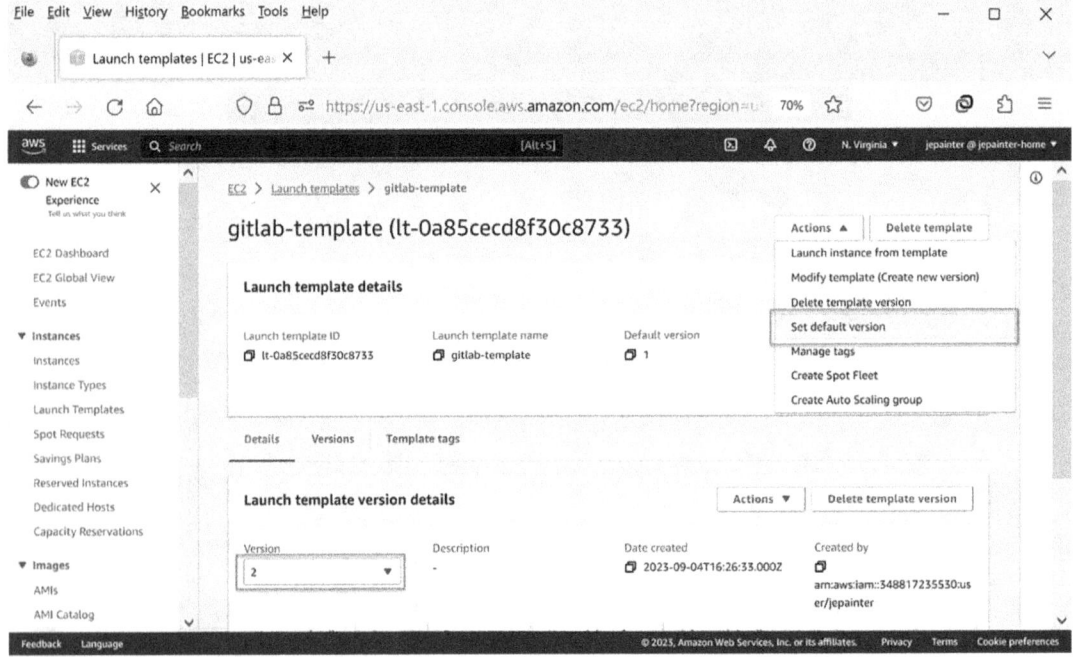

Figure 18-21. *Setting default AMI version for launch template*

Spinning Up New ASG Servers

With the new default AMI in place on our launch template, we can now go back to the ASG and reset the desired and minimum capacities to their previous values assuming the ASG servers were spun down earlier. Before we do that, double-check that the AMI is the one expected. Figure 18-22 shows the details of our ASG. Under "Launch template/configuration," you should see the name of the template along with "Version Default" as highlighted in the figure. Also, if you scroll down on the ASG details section, you should see that the AMI ID is set to the one we just created. With that confirmation, edit the ASG and reset the desired and minimum capacities back to two (or whatever values you had before). You should then see new GitLab-Auto instances being raised in the EC2 instances list.

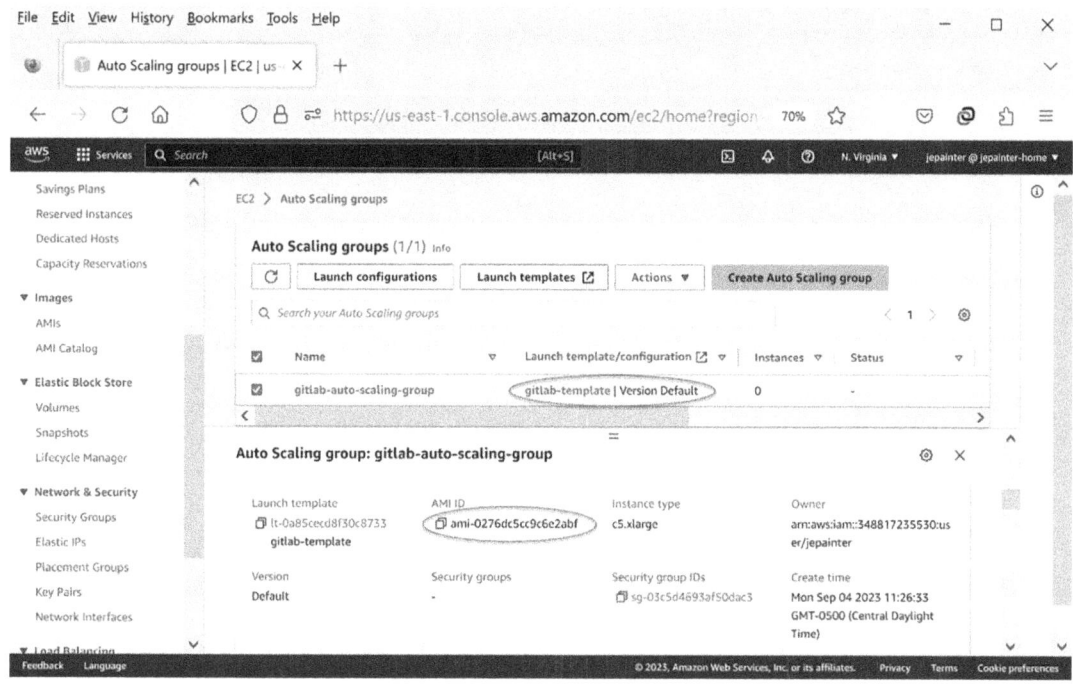

Figure 18-22. *Verifying ASG is using latest AMI from launch template*

Detaching and Shutting Down the GitLab Standalone Server

Once the new ASG-controlled instances are back up and running, you can then go to the ELB, remove the standalone GitLab server from the ELB instances list, and stop the standalone server until the next time a new configuration change is required. If you discover that there are issues with the new configuration, you can go back to the launch template and set the default version back to the previously working version. Note that changing the default version has no effect on existing instances. Fortunately, AWS has provided a way to replace instances in an ASG using the "Instance Refresh" feature.[12] This is shown in Figure 18-23.

---

[12] This is a relatively new feature for auto-scaling groups, which I wished existed when I was administering my previous corporate GitLab setup.

815

CHAPTER 18   IT'S AN ADMIN'S LIFE

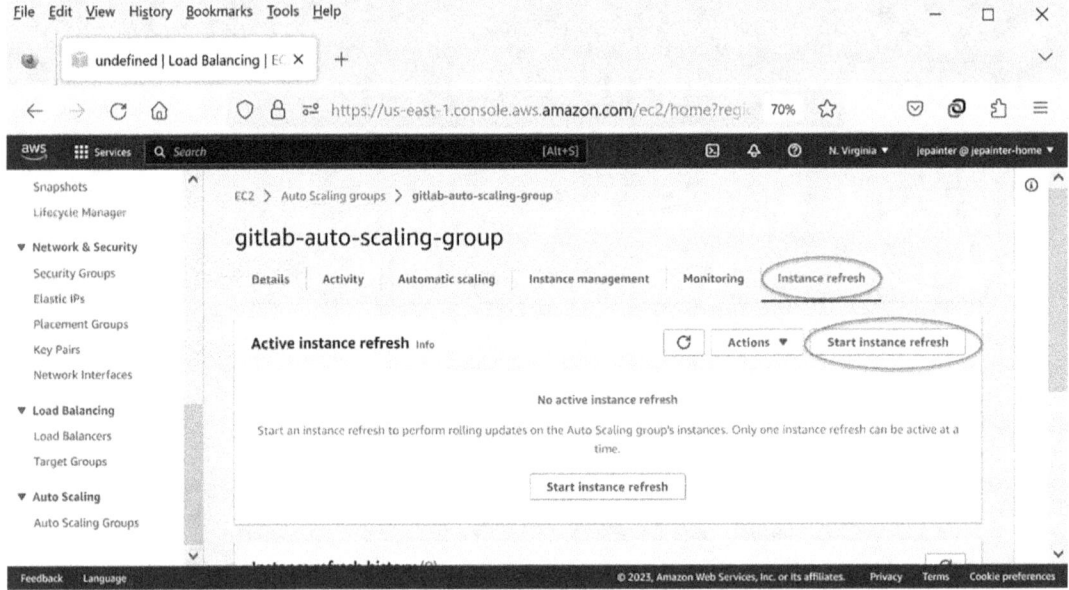

Figure 18-23. *Replacing running instances using ASG instance refresh feature*

Using the Instance Refresh Feature to Replace ASG Servers

Given the ASG instance refresh option, there is an alternative to the preceding process for cases when configuration changes are minor. In those cases, you would still spin up the standalone GitLab server. However, you would not need to add it to the ELB and set the ASG desired and minimum capacities to zero. Instead, you would make the configuration changes to the standalone server, create an AMI from it, and make the AMI the default for the launch template. Once that is done, simply use the ASG instance refresh feature to replace the existing servers with new ones.

In the final section of this chapter, we'll look at the more involved process of upgrading the GitLab service to a new release.

Upgrading to a New Release

Earlier, we saw how to update a GitLab configuration for our GitLab poc service. In this section, we are going to look at the steps needed to upgrade GitLab to a later release version. Upgrading to a new release is similar to updating the GitLab configuration but involves updates not just to the application servers but the Gitaly and runner manager servers as well.

Overview of the Release Upgrade Process

The upgrade process requires that components be upgraded in a particular sequence in order for the overall GitLab service to behave properly. In this section, we will focus on upgrading the poc that is assumed to have application and page servers behind auto-scaling groups, a standalone Gitaly server (as opposed to a Gitaly cluster) and at least one runner manager. In the next chapter, we'll consider a more complex scenario for a production service that uses a Gitaly cluster and potentially a secondary GitLab mirror setup via GitLab Geo.

An overview of the poc release upgrade process is as follows:

1. Pause shared runners.
2. Spin down all application and page servers tied to an ASG.
3. Spin up the standalone GitLab server without connecting to the ELB.
4. Create backups of the standalone GitLab server and the Gitaly server.
5. Create a backup of the RDS database.
6. Upgrade the Gitaly server.
7. Upgrade the standalone GitLab server.
8. Upgrade the runner manager.
9. Create a new AMI from the standalone GitLab server.
10. Update the launch templates with the new AMI.
11. Spin up all application and page servers tied to an ASG.
12. Spin down the standalone GitLab server.

As you can see, that is quite a list just to upgrade the service. Plan on taking a while the first few times you perform the procedure. The good news is, with practice, you'll be able to perform an upgrade within an hour.[13] Still, plan for at least a two-hour downtime with your users to handle any unexpected situations during the upgrade process.

The Need for Doing a GitLab Service Shutdown

Based on the list, you probably noticed that the upgrade process requires that the service be taken down for a period of time. There are two main reasons for this. One is the need for making backups of different components; the system needs to be in an inactive state in order for the backups to be in sync. The second reason is that upgrading the single Gitaly service impacts the overall service; performing a Linux package upgrade will disable the Gitaly service temporarily.

Since this is a proof-of-concept service, this shouldn't be a big deal with the users. However, you will need to plan for when the upgrade takes place (typically on the weekend when things are not so busy) and to let users know about the planned interruption ahead of time. You could, of course, notify users via email or some other communication system, but GitLab provides a way to notify users via the GitLab service itself.

Broadcasting System-Wide Messages

Figure 18-24 shows the top of the form for broadcasting a system-wide message. As an admin, you can locate the Messages page under the Admin Area. Here, you enter the message in the Message field where you will see the message as it will appear in the banner. Although not necessary, it is nice to enable the "Allow users to dismiss the broadcast message" so that users can select to remove the banner after they've read it.

---

[13] It's hard to get under an hour since the RDS backup takes a while as well as creating a new AMI.

CHAPTER 18   IT'S AN ADMIN'S LIFE

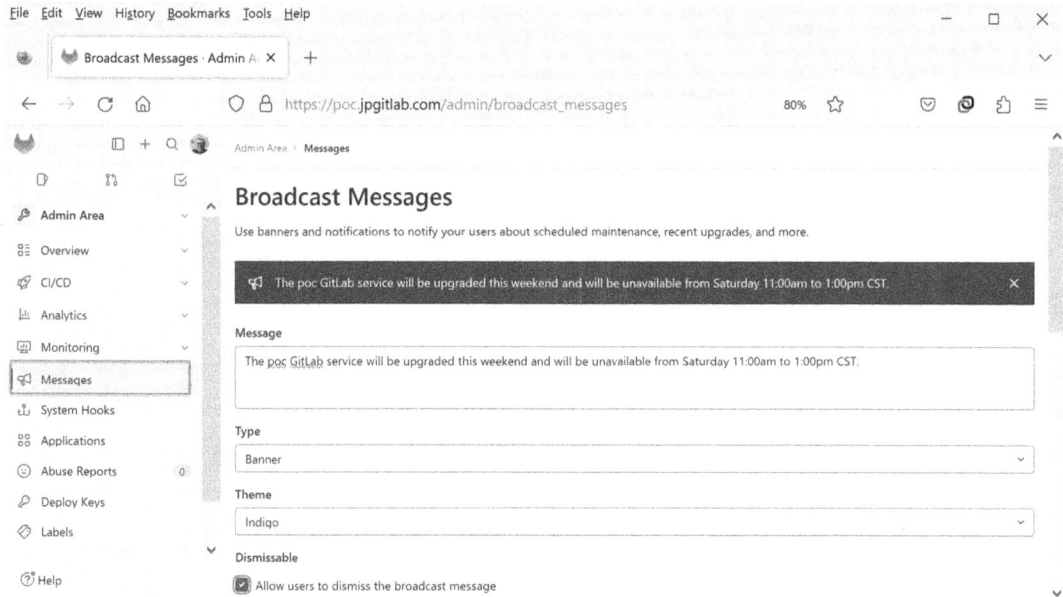

Figure 18-24. *Setting of broadcast message about poc update (part 1)*

The bottom part of the form is shown in Figure 18-25. Here, you can select whether the message appears with Git responses, which is useful since not all users access the GitLab UI for their work. The main part of the form is the dates when the message should be displayed. You can choose to have the message displayed immediately or set a time in the future for when it will be broadcast. You also need to select a time when the message will no longer be displayed.

819

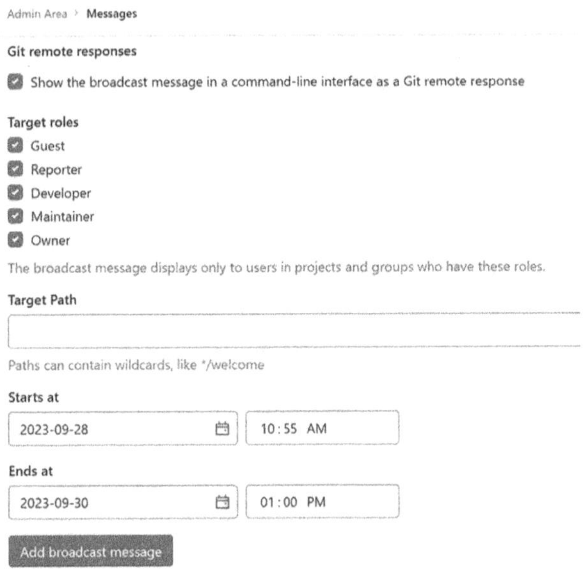

Figure 18-25. Setting of broadcast message about poc update (part 2)

Pausing Shared Runners Under Your Control

So, let's go through the process step by step. The first step is to pause any shared runners that you control[14] so that no future jobs are started. You want to avoid having jobs running when you start the upgrade process. As such, you should probably do this step some time before you shut the service down, say an hour before the upgrade.[15] Figure 18-26 shows how easy it is to pause your shared runners by simply clicking the pause button as highlighted in the figure. You can then drill down into the runner to see what jobs, if any, are currently running.

---

[14] I focus on shared runners that are under the admin's control since it is nearly impossible to go through all runners owned by groups and projects and pause them.

[15] This really depends on how busy your shared runners are. If there are a lot of jobs running prior to the upgrade, you want to give them time to complete before you begin. You should be aware based on my experience that some users rush to start jobs when they know the service is about to go down.

CHAPTER 18   IT'S AN ADMIN'S LIFE

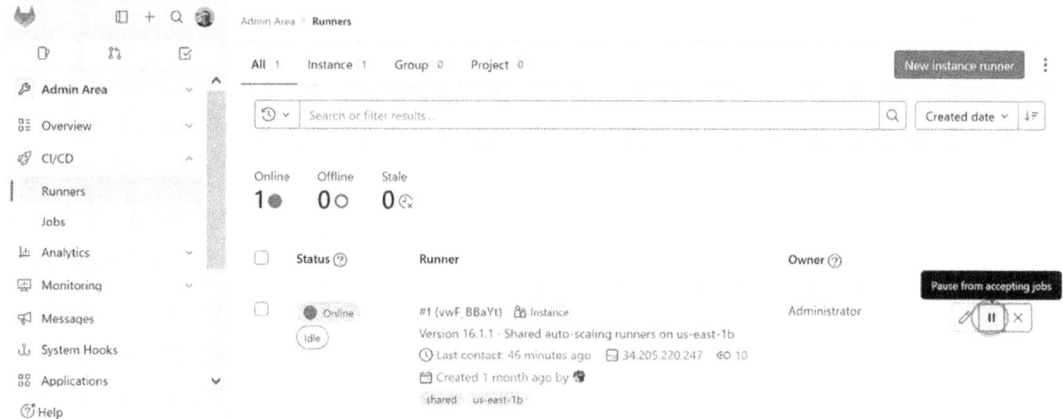

Figure 18-26.   Pausing shared runners

Special Maintenance Mode for Licensed Sites

I'll mention here that with the licensed version of GitLab, there is an option to put the service into "maintenance mode." This settles the system down by refusing write operations (via git push, for example) to be performed; read operations (such as git clone) are still available in this mode. An admin can put the system into maintenance mode by going to the General Settings section under the Admin Area and searching for Maintenance Mode. This reduces any potential corruption of data being written while the application services are spinning down.

Spinning Down ASG Servers

The next step of spinning down all application and page servers controlled by an ASG is the same process as described earlier in the "Updating GitLab's Configuration" section. Essentially, you set the minimum and desired capacity values of the ASG to zero and wait for the instances to be terminated. Note that the effect of spinning down a server is not immediate; there is a built-in wait time (typically 30 seconds) to allow any ongoing operations to complete before the instance is brought down. In the meantime, the ELB is notified of the shutdown request to prevent any new requests to go to that instance.

Spinning Up the Standalone GitLab Server

Once the auto-scaling application and page servers are spun down, it's time to spin up the standalone GitLab server. However, unlike with a configuration update, the standalone GitLab server should remain disconnected from any ELB. The reason for this is to keep anyone from performing activities while the server is being upgraded. If the standalone server was already connected to an ELB, it should be disconnected now.

Creating Backups of the Standalone Servers

At this point, it is recommended to create backups of the standalone GitLab server as well as the standalone Gitaly server. Backups of servers are done by creating AMIs of those instances. When creating the AMI, it is OK to let the image creation process reboot the instance in order to get a stable backup.

Backing Up the RDS Database

After the backup AMIs are completed, it is time to make a backup of the RDS database. This is done by taking a "snapshot" as shown in Figure 18-27. Simply select the database from the RDS list and choose "Take snapshot" from the Actions drop-down menu. This will pop up a dialog box as shown in Figure 18-28 where you simply enter a name for the snapshot and select "Take snapshot." Note that this will take around 20 to 30 minutes to complete; you'll need to wait for it to complete before you can do the release upgrade since the upgrade is likely to make schema changes.

CHAPTER 18 IT'S AN ADMIN'S LIFE

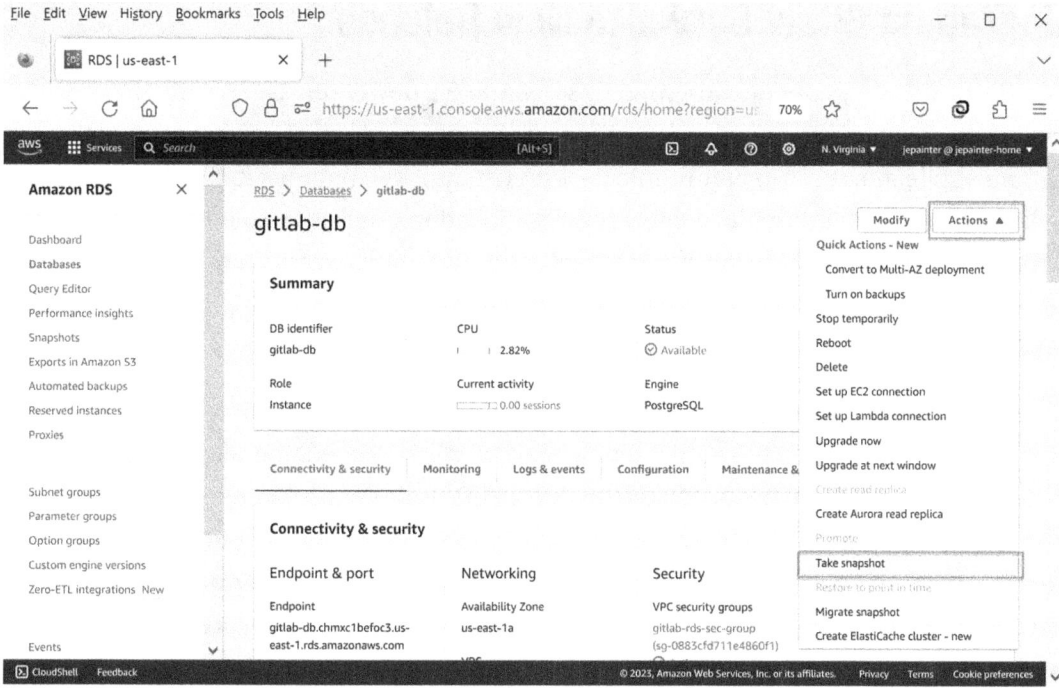

Figure 18-27. *Selecting option to create RDS database snapshot*

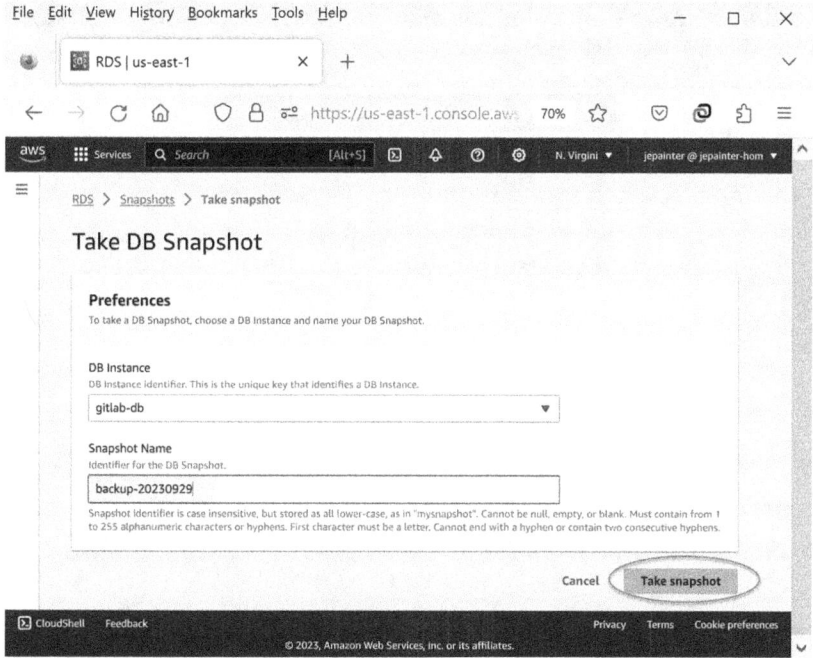

Figure 18-28. *Setting snapshot name for backup*

823

Upgrading Gitaly Server to New Release

We are now ready to upgrade the GitLab software to a newer release. We need to start with the Gitaly server first since there may be changes to the RPC interface that the GitLab application uses to communicate with Gitaly. Any upgrades to the RPC interface will be backward compatible to earlier communication interfaces, so it is safe to upgrade Gitaly first; the older GitLab release will still work with the newer Gitaly release.

Syncing with Latest apt Package Versions

Since we are using Linux on AWS, upgrading the instance involves more than just upgrading the GitLab software to the new release. We also need to make upgrades of other Linux packages installed on the instance. This is done to ensure that important security updates are taken care of. First, we need to ssh into the Gitaly server and do some preparatory work. We first need to become the root user by doing a "sudo su." Then we need to run "apt-get update" in order for apt to sync with the latest versions of all packages it manages. To discover what packages are in need of an upgrade, we run "apt list --upgradable" to get the full list as shown in Figure 18-29. Note that gitlab-ce shows up in that list.

Figure 18-29. Getting the list of Linux packages that require upgrades

Upgrading Non-GitLab Packages

Now we could just run "apt-get upgrade" to upgrade all packages to their latest version, but I prefer to do this in two steps since I want to upgrade the gitlab-ce separately. So, in the first step, we "hold" the gitlab-ce package from being upgraded by running "apt-mark hold gitlab-ce" as shown in Figure 18-30. Once gitlab-ce is marked as held, running "apt-get upgrade" will upgrade all other packages that need to be upgraded. Note the feedback about excluding gitlab-ce from the upgrade. A list of the packages to be upgraded is then shown before being prompted to continue.

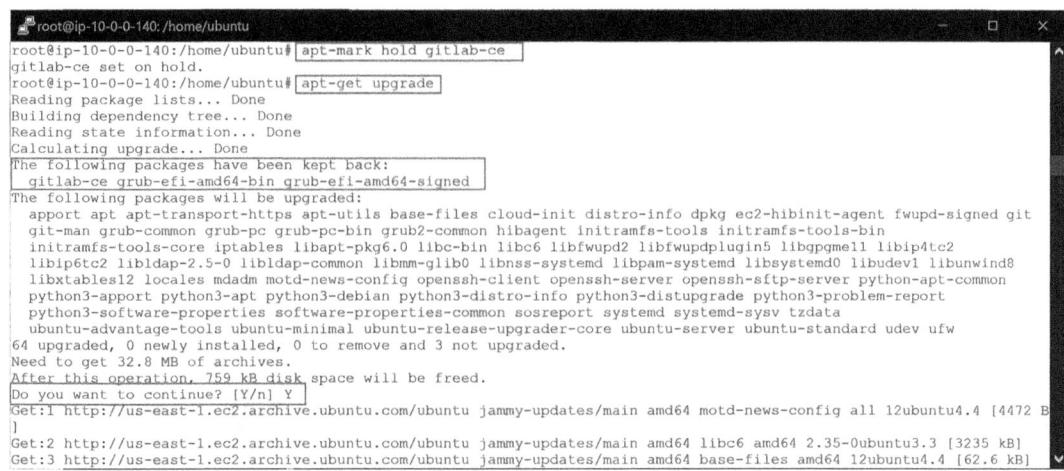

Figure 18-30. *Upgrading all packages other than gitlab-ce*

Note that when the package upgrade is complete, you will probably get some messages about the server needing to be restarted (usually necessary for security updates relating to Ubuntu itself) and about services being restarted. Just accept the prompts; we'll restart the server after we upgrade gitlab-ce.

Removing the Hold on the GitLab Package

After the first package upgrade step, it helps to view what packages need to be upgraded and to take the hold off the gitlab-ce package. The results of running "apt list — upgradable" and "apt-mark unhold gitlab-ce" are shown in Figure 18-31. Note that there may be more packages other than gitlab-ce shown to be upgradable. In this example, some grub packages are shown as requiring an upgrade; these are part of the Ubuntu upgrade and will be taken care of after we restart the server.

CHAPTER 18　IT'S AN ADMIN'S LIFE

Figure 18-31. Removing hold on gitlab-ce upgrade

Impact of Potential Upgrade Stops

Figure 18-32 shows an interesting message when I tried to upgrade from 16.1 to the latest 16.4 release. It lets me know that I have to upgrade to 16.3 first. This typically happens when there are database changes in a particular version before moving further; it usually happens between major release versions such as between 14.x and 15.x, but it can occasionally happen between minor versions as well.

Figure 18-32. Upgrade of gitlab-ce that results in error

CHAPTER 18 IT'S AN ADMIN'S LIFE

Taking the URL provided in the error message takes us to the "Upgrade Stops" documentation as shown in Figure 18-33. This is a relatively new feature that I find quite useful (it didn't exist when I was an administrator). In this example, the documentation refers to background migrations that need to be completed before moving on to a later version.

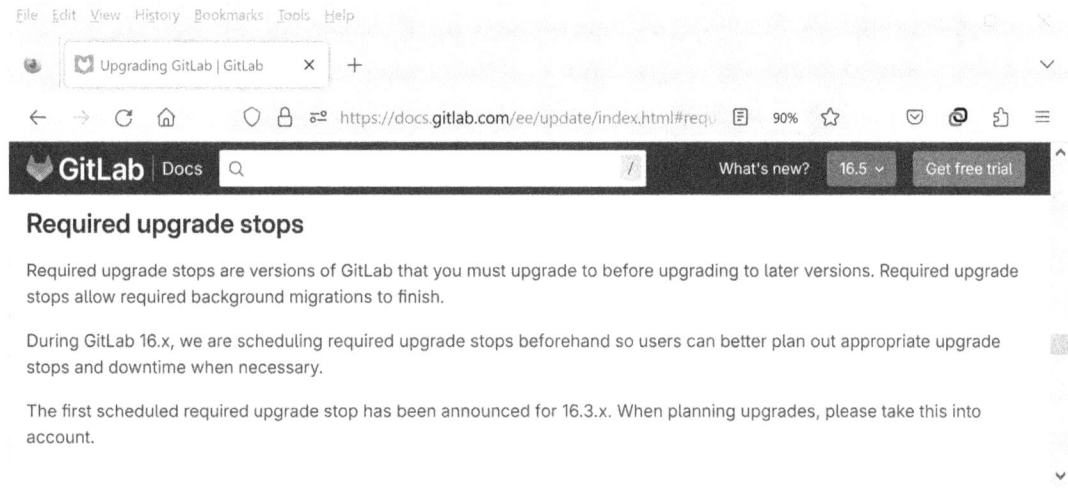

Figure 18-33. Reviewing GitLab's required upgrade stops documentation

At this point, we could try searching through the GitLab documentation to discover what the latest 16.3.x version is, but there is an easier way to discover the version. Running the rather obscure "apt-cache madison gitlab-ce" command gives us a list of all versions of gitlab-ce that are available. The results of running this command are shown in Figure 18-34. From this listing, we can see that 16.3.5 is the latest patch release of 16.3, so that will be the version we upgrade to in this example.

```
root@ip-10-0-0-140:/home/ubuntu# apt-cache madison gitlab-ce
 gitlab-ce |  16.4.1-ce.0 | https://packages.gitlab.com/gitlab/gitlab-ce/ubuntu jammy/main amd64 Packages
 gitlab-ce |  16.4.0-ce.0 | https://packages.gitlab.com/gitlab/gitlab-ce/ubuntu jammy/main amd64 Packages
 gitlab-ce |  16.3.5-ce.0 | https://packages.gitlab.com/gitlab/gitlab-ce/ubuntu jammy/main amd64 Packages
 gitlab-ce |  16.3.4-ce.0 | https://packages.gitlab.com/gitlab/gitlab-ce/ubuntu jammy/main amd64 Packages
 gitlab-ce |  16.3.3-ce.0 | https://packages.gitlab.com/gitlab/gitlab-ce/ubuntu jammy/main amd64 Packages
 gitlab-ce |  16.3.2-ce.0 | https://packages.gitlab.com/gitlab/gitlab-ce/ubuntu jammy/main amd64 Packages
 gitlab-ce |  16.3.1-ce.0 | https://packages.gitlab.com/gitlab/gitlab-ce/ubuntu jammy/main amd64 Packages
 gitlab-ce |  16.3.0-ce.0 | https://packages.gitlab.com/gitlab/gitlab-ce/ubuntu jammy/main amd64 Packages
 gitlab-ce |  16.2.8-ce.0 | https://packages.gitlab.com/gitlab/gitlab-ce/ubuntu jammy/main amd64 Packages
 gitlab-ce |  16.2.7-ce.0 | https://packages.gitlab.com/gitlab/gitlab-ce/ubuntu jammy/main amd64 Packages
 gitlab-ce |  16.2.6-ce.0 | https://packages.gitlab.com/gitlab/gitlab-ce/ubuntu jammy/main amd64 Packages
 gitlab-ce |  16.2.5-ce.0 | https://packages.gitlab.com/gitlab/gitlab-ce/ubuntu jammy/main amd64 Packages
 gitlab-ce |  16.2.4-ce.0 | https://packages.gitlab.com/gitlab/gitlab-ce/ubuntu jammy/main amd64 Packages
 gitlab-ce |  16.2.3-ce.0 | https://packages.gitlab.com/gitlab/gitlab-ce/ubuntu jammy/main amd64 Packages
 gitlab-ce |  16.2.2-ce.0 | https://packages.gitlab.com/gitlab/gitlab-ce/ubuntu jammy/main amd64 Packages
 gitlab-ce |  16.2.1-ce.0 | https://packages.gitlab.com/gitlab/gitlab-ce/ubuntu jammy/main amd64 Packages
 gitlab-ce |  16.2.0-ce.0 | https://packages.gitlab.com/gitlab/gitlab-ce/ubuntu jammy/main amd64 Packages
```

Figure 18-34. Listing available package versions of gitlab-ce

Chapter 18 It's an Admin's Life

Upgrading to a Specific Version of the GitLab Package

To install a specific version of gitlab-ce, we use the "apt install" command as shown in Figure 18-35. In this example, I ran "apt install gitlab-ce=16.3.5-ce.0". Note that the version follows the name of the package using the equals symbol and that the full version as shown in the version list is required (you can't just use 16.3.5 as the version, for example). Since you are doing a single package install to a particular version, you won't be prompted to proceed as you were with the apt-get upgrade command. Also, take note of the messages during the install process about missing a database and not running puma. This is expected since this is the Gitaly instance that does not use those components, so don't fret about those warnings.

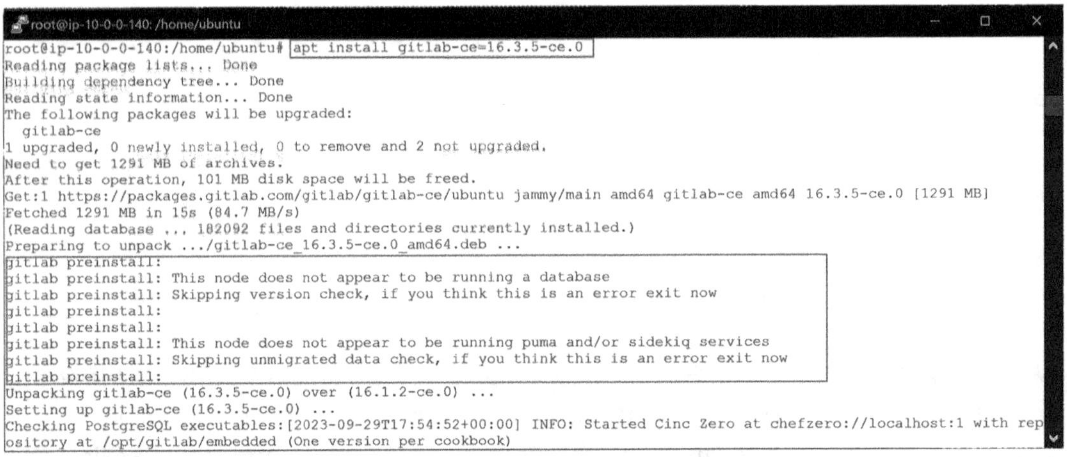

Figure 18-35. Installing a specific version of gitlab-ce on the Gitaly server

Rebooting the Gitaly Server

Now that the GitLab software has been upgraded, we need to reboot the server in order for the security updates to take place. The easiest way to do this is via the AWS EC2 interface. Simply select the Gitaly server in the instances list and choose "Reboot instance" from the "Instance state" drop-down as illustrated in Figure 18-36. This will cause the instance to be rebooted, during which time the server will lose connectivity with all other servers. It will take a minute or so before all services including ssh will become available. You know when everything is back up and running when you can ssh back into the server again.

CHAPTER 18 IT'S AN ADMIN'S LIFE

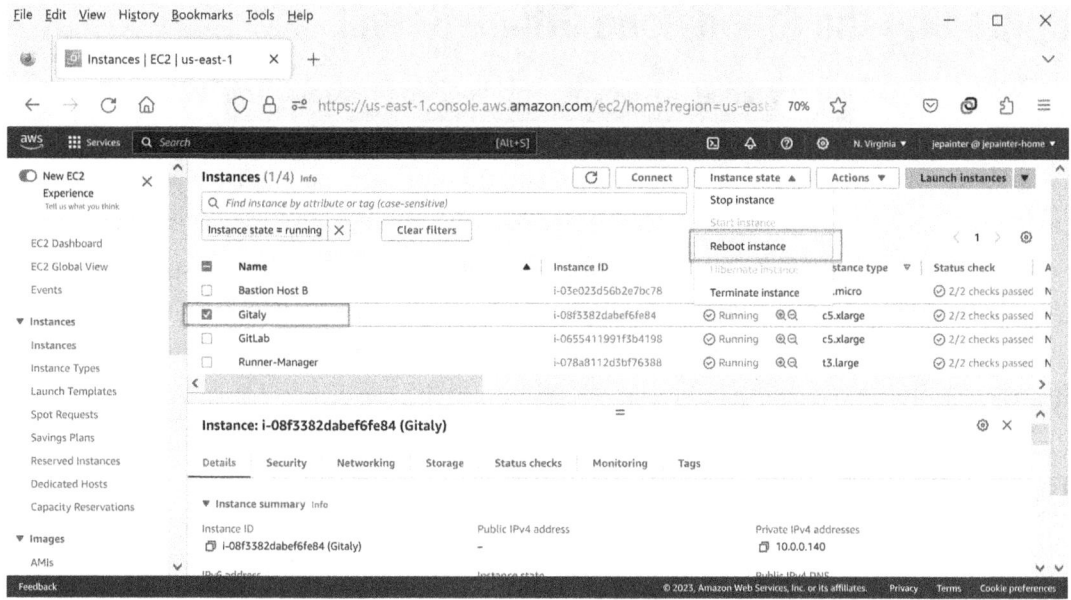

Figure 18-36. Rebooting Gitaly service via the EC2 instances list

Checking the Gitaly Service

As a check that all went OK, ssh into the Gitaly server and run some commands as shown in Figure 18-37. Running "sudo gitlab-ctl status" shows that the gitaly service is running as expected. Running "apt list | grep gitlab-ce" in this example shows that the gitlab-ce version is set to 16.3.5. Note that I don't upgrade to the later 16.4 version at this time since the application service should be upgraded to the 16.3.5 version first. Best to keep all components in sync on upgrades.

```
ubuntu@ip-10-0-0-140:~$ sudo gitlab-ctl status
run: gitaly: (pid 754) 482s; run: log: (pid 751) 482s
run: logrotate: (pid 752) 482s; run: log: (pid 749) 482s
run: node-exporter: (pid 753) 482s; run: log: (pid 750) 482s
ubuntu@ip-10-0-0-140:~$ apt list | grep gitlab-ce

WARNING: apt does not have a stable CLI interface. Use with caution in scripts.

gitlab-ce/jammy 16.4.1-ce.0 amd64 [upgradable from: 16.3.5-ce.0]
ubuntu@ip-10-0-0-140:~$
```

Figure 18-37. Running various checks on the Gitaly server

829

Upgrading the Standalone GitLab Server

Once Gitaly has been upgraded, we can now proceed to upgrading the standalone GitLab server. Here, we follow the same process that was used for upgrading Gitaly. We update all packages except for gitlab-ce and then update the gitlab-ce package. We need to make sure to use the exact same release used to upgrade Gitaly. Note that unlike Gitaly, the upgrade for GitLab will update the database. This doesn't cause any issues since database upgrades are backward compatible with earlier releases. In case you are wondering, the package install runs gitlab-ctl reconfigure automatically; there is nothing more to do unless you need to do a server reboot.

Upgrading the GitLab Runner Manager

The remaining component to be upgraded is the GitLab runner manager. The upgrade process of the runner manager is similar to the upgrade process of GitLab. The main difference is that the software package to be updated is gitlab-runner, not gitlab-ce. Hence, you are going to run "apt-mark hold gitlab-runner" before doing the "apt-get upgrade command." Ditto for the unhold command. You still need to run the "apt-cache madison gitlab-runner" command to get the available versions of gitlab-runner since patch releases of gitlab-runner are independent of patch releases of gitlab-ce.

Figure 18-38 shows the results of apt-cache madison for gitlab-runner. Since in this example, I upgraded Gitaly and GitLab to 16.3.5, the relevant release for gitlab-runner is 16.3.1, which is the latest patch release for gitlab-runner. Running "apt install gitlab-runner=16.3.1" not only installs the new version but also restarts the gitlab-runner service.

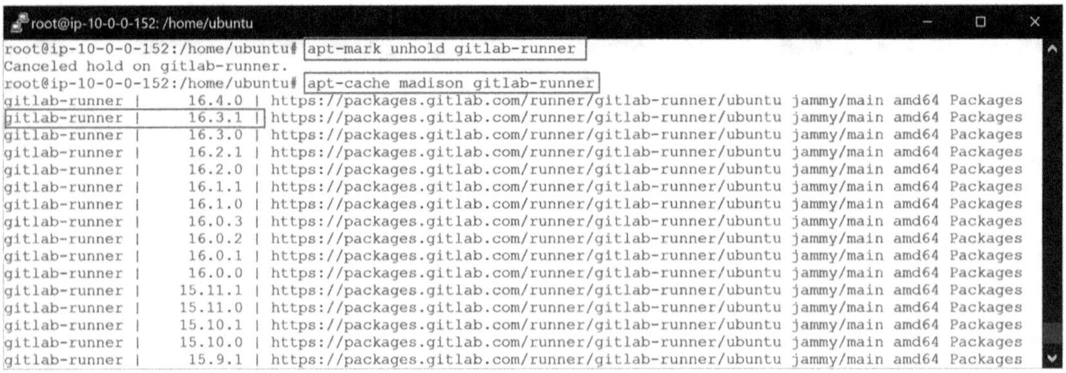

Figure 18-38. Listing available package versions of gitlab-runner

CHAPTER 18   IT'S AN ADMIN'S LIFE

From the GitLab admin interface (after the service has been reconnected to the ELB), we can verify that the runner version has been upgraded. Figure 18-39 shows that the version of the shared runner is now 16.3.1. Also, note that installing the new version of the runner took it out of the paused state. At this point, all GitLab components for the poc have been upgraded.

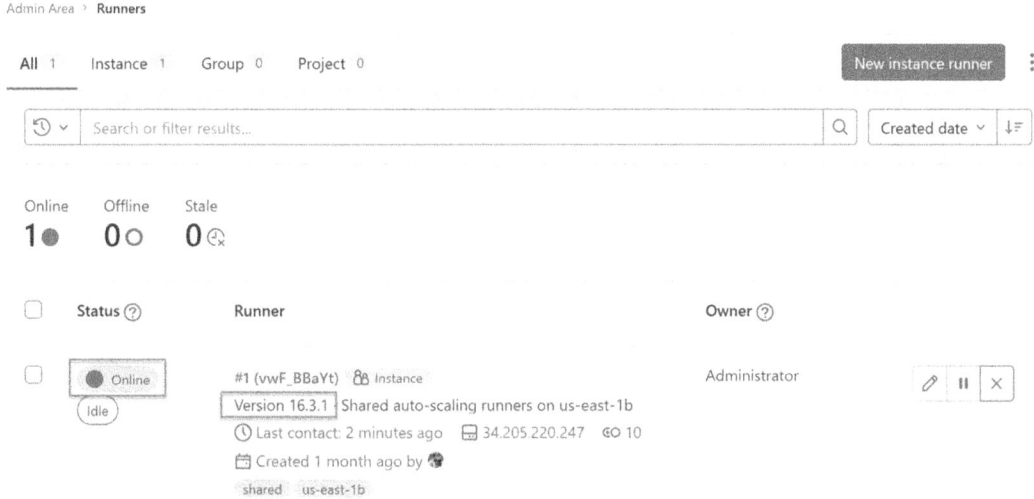

Figure 18-39. *Verifying version of the updated shared runner*

Completing the Release Upgrade Process

The remaining steps are the same as for a configuration update. We create an AMI image off the standalone GitLab server, update the launch templates, spin up new application and page servers from their respective auto-scaling groups, and spin down the standalone GitLab server. Note that we don't have to disconnect the standalone server from any of the ELBs since it was not connected to them for the upgrade process. You can now check and verify that the poc GitLab service is back up and running with the new release.

Summary

In summary, we've covered the following topics in this chapter:

- Described how to add, edit, and block users on a self-managed service
- Showed how to restrict what users can sign up and how they can sign in
- Discussed how to update the GitLab configuration for a multiple host configuration
- Learned how to perform a release upgrade for the proof-of-concept service

Having covered setting up a proof-of-concept service, the time has come to discuss what is needed to set up a production-level service, which we'll cover in the next chapter.

CHAPTER 19

Lights, Camera, Action!

In high school, I had an astronomer friend who liked to make his own telescopes. He learned how to make a telescope through a local planetarium, which included the skill of grinding and polishing mirrors. For beginners, the planetarium had a saying that the quickest way to make a 4-inch mirror is to make a 3-inch mirror first. The reasoning was based on two things. First, it takes a long time to grind and polish glass to make a mirror, and the larger the mirror, the longer it takes to grind. Second, the likelihood of making a mistake is higher the first time you go through the process. Since it is likely you are going to mess up the first mirror, it is better to learn from the failure by making a smaller one.

The same lesson applies to setting up your own standalone GitLab service. It is better to set up a proof-of-concept service first and learn from the mistakes in doing so than it is to go directly to setting up a production-level service. If you make a mistake with the poc service, no serious harm is done. Not so with a production-level service where hundreds or thousands of users depend on ensuring their code base is safe. No one wants to go through losing a week's, a month's, or even a year's worth of work because your GitLab service failed. So, if you haven't already gone through the exercise of spinning up your own poc GitLab service as was done in a previous chapter, now would be the time to do it.

Planning Your Production Setup

Assuming you've successfully stood up a poc GitLab service, you will have a sense of the costs of running it on the cloud provider of your choice. For me on AWS, my monthly costs at the time of this writing were around $700. This was for a poc service with the minimum number of servers and the smallest database size that I could reasonably get by with. No bells and whistles added here.

CHAPTER 19   LIGHTS, CAMERA, ACTION!

Considering Monthly Production Costs

For a production service, the monthly costs will be significantly higher. We'll get into the reasons for this shortly, but let's do a quick "back of the envelope" calculation. To go from a poc standalone service to a high-availability production service, double the costs. So, for me, that takes me to $1400. For testing purposes, you should also have a staging service where changes such as release upgrades can be made and tested without affecting the primary production service. That doubles the cost again, so for me that takes it to $2800/month. To handle disaster recovery, you'll need a replicated service running somewhere else in the world. Assuming only one replicated service that matches both the production and testing services, that doubles the price yet again. For me, that takes me to $5600/month or roughly $68K/year.

Inflationary Cloud Provider Costs

You should note that the calculated price is not static. For one, there are inflationary costs as the cloud provider services will likely go up over time. But that isn't all. As time goes by, the amount of storage for the databases, Git repositories, and object repositories will increase faster than the inflationary costs. In a few years, you could be easily talking about $200K/year for a moderate number of users.[1] And of course, there are operational costs for a full-time staff to support the production and testing services. So, for a rough overall calculation, let's settle on $500K/year.

License Costs Related to High-Availability and Disaster Recovery Solutions

But wait, there's more. I didn't include the license costs that would be required to support a high-availability, disaster recovery proof standalone service. Assuming you went with a premium license, which is the least expensive option,[2] you are talking about $350K/year to support 1000 users. So yes, it can cost close to a million dollars per year to support 1000 users. Have I gotten your attention yet?

---

[1] For the purposes of this discussion, I'm assuming a moderate number of users are roughly 1000.
[2] At the time of this writing, the premium license cost was $29/user/month.

Comparing Self-Managed Costs to Using SaaS

Compare this to using the GitLab SaaS option. For 1000 users, you still have the $350K/year license cost to deal with. In addition, there are extra costs for storage and job services that come with GitLab SaaS. However, you no longer have the cloud provider and staff operational costs to deal with, so you are likely able to reduce your costs by $300K/year depending on how much storage and runner resources your company uses. By the way, your company could work with a sales associate to get those costs down. Another consideration is the GitLab Dedicated option[3] available for companies with over 1000 users.

GitLab User Audits

By the way, if you are wondering how GitLab knows how many licenses are used for your standalone GitLab service, you should know that there is a three-month audit taken by GitLab, what is sometimes referred to as a true-up. Your GitLab service creates metrics that you upload to GitLab so that they can determine the license costs for your setup. Note that this is done for your primary production service; it is assumed that any staging service you have will have a significantly small number of users running on it limited to admin staff and developers interested in testing new GitLab features.

Other Operational Costs

I realize this is a lot to take in. I can't recommend which path for you to take here. There are pros and cons to each option that you'll need to consider. Besides costs, there is a stress concern with respect to an operational staff. Having been a member of such an operational staff tasked with ensuring the integrity of the corporate source code, it is indeed quite stressful. You'll need to factor in the peace of mind you would have in letting experts maintain the GitLab service as well as your corporate assets.

---

[3] I don't have insight into the costs involved with the dedicated option as it is relatively new to me. It is worth looking into if your company wants to maintain greater control over your GitLab service.

Additional Needs of a Production-Level Self-Managed Service

With that said, let's at least look into what it takes to set up a production-level standalone GitLab service, assuming, of course, I haven't scared you away from it. As I mentioned earlier in this section, there are two requirements for a production-level service: high availability and disaster recovery. These two requirements are related but different. With high availability, we are concerned with keeping a service up and running as much as possible in the face of a server and/or database failure or a version upgrade. With disaster recovery, we are concerned with recovering a service in the face of overall failure, such as a data center going offline due to a natural disaster or denial-of-service attack. Both need to be considered to reduce both loss of productivity and loss of data.

High-Availability Needs

To maintain high availability, the goal is to implement redundancy for all components in order to handle failure of any given component with little to no impact to the service. For the poc, we've already taken redundancy into account for many of the key components. In our poc we set up earlier, we already enabled redundant GitLab servers spread across various availability zones to handle the load; in addition, we set up an auto-scaling group for the GitLab servers to handle failover for any server that starts behaving unexpectedly or loses connectivity because of a zone failure. We also used redundancy for the RDS database by enabling multi-AZ support; here, AWS will handle automatic failover should the primary database become unavailable. The same holds true for the Redis service; we chose to implement the multi-AZ option so that AWS will handle automatic failure for us. And since we store artifacts and other binary objects in S3 storage, which is agnostic to zones, we are fine there as well.

GitLab Runner High-Availability Needs

So far, so good. It looks like the poc already has some high-availability support built into it. However, there are still some weak points in the poc that need to be addressed. The GitLab runner manager, which operates in a single zone, is easily addressed by adding more runner managers in different availability zones. In this way, if one zone goes down, GitLab can still run jobs in the other availability zones, although in a diminished capacity.

Gitaly Service High-Availability Needs

This leaves the most glaring weak point of our poc: the Gitaly server. This is of concern since it stores what some would call the most important data: Git repositories. Without access to the Git repositories, nothing much useful can happen with respect to GitLab services. As it stands, the Gitaly server in the poc is a single server running in a single availability zone. There is no redundancy for that server, so if an issue arises with that zone, we lose access to our Git repository data. Granted that it is rare for a zone to go down, but when it does, it can take hours to a day for it to recover.

As it turns out, enabling redundancy for the Gitaly service is not an easy task. In the early days before Gitaly was used to store Git repositories, NFS (Network File Service) was the go-to implementation. Like our poc Gitaly solution, NFS is also a single point of failure. However, there are solutions out there that enable replication of an NFS server with and without automatic failover.[4] AWS itself provides a replicated NFS service with its EFS[5] (Elastic File Service). For performance reasons, GitLab moved away from an NFS implementation toward Gitaly.

The solution that GitLab came up with regarding high availability of the Gitaly service is the Gitaly cluster. As you can guess, this involves replicating Gitaly servers. The main complication with this solution involves keeping those Gitaly servers in sync. Because of that complexity, I will discuss this topic in its own section later on.

Disaster Recovery Needs

Now let's turn our attention to disaster recovery. When you think of disaster recovery, your first thought may be "backups." Now I'm not saying that you shouldn't do backups; you should. But you should be aware that backups (of databases, Git filesystems, object storage, etc.) are not enough. The main issue for GitLab has to do with synchronization. Let's say you do backups of your databases (which include both RDS and Redis) once

---

[4] I was involved in developing a replicated NFS service for GitLab that required manual failover in case of a failure. Not a pleasant experience when zone failures occurred.

[5] This replication feature of EFS, however, comes with an unacceptable performance cost with respect to Git data, which is why GitLab does not recommend it. Trust me. I've gone down this path with EFS and came across many issues when using it with GitLab including, but not limited to, total service shutdown for hours at a time when certain AWS limits were reached.

a day and your more precious Git filesystems once an hour. In the event of a failure, those backups will not be "in sync." Your database backup will not align with your Git filesystem backups or your S3 object backups, for example.

Issues with Restoring Service from Backups

If you try to restore your GitLab service simply from those backups, you will lose something. This is true even if you synchronize your backups to be at the same time for everything. A database backup will take a certain amount of time to complete than a filesystem backup, so there will always be something lost in the recovery. You could ensure synchronization by shutting everything down (on the weekend, say) and taking a backup of everything all at the same time. But this, of course, impacts your high availability. It also means that if a disaster occurs in the middle of the week, all the work accomplished since the last backup will be gone.

Dealing with Regional Failures

There is another issue to take into consideration. If the disaster is due to a regional failure (say a hurricane in the eastern US coast), you may want to recover in a different region (say in the western US coast) until the original data centers are back online. This requires that your backups be replicated to that other region (AWS, by the way, doesn't do this for you automatically). It also requires that your AMIs be copied over to another region so that they can be used to restart your GitLab services. But realize that restarting a service in a different region will also require changes to your GitLab configurations since there will be settings specific to a given region.

Introducing GitLab Geo

At this point, experienced administrators will be thinking "what if we mirrored the service in a different region?" After all, this is a natural extension of replicating components in a high-availability scenario but across regions rather than within a single region. This is the concept behind GitLab Geo. With GitLab Geo, you start with a primary service in one region and set up one or more secondary services that mirror the primary service. Changes made on the primary service are replicated to each of the secondary services.

Using GitLab Geo, you can implement a disaster recovery plan wherein if anything happens to the primary service, you can failover to one of the secondary services. An added benefit to Geo is that users in an area close to a secondary service can use that service to speed up read operations; write operations forward to the primary service. The only caveat to using Geo is that you have to have a licensed version of GitLab; it doesn't work with the community edition of GitLab.

As you might expect, setting up GitLab Geo is a bit complicated. Like creating a telescope mirror for the very first time, you are likely to make mistakes; I did the first time I set up Geo. It's more complicated than setting up a high-availability service. And if you are using AWS, there are some features of AWS you should be aware of that reduce the overall cost. Because of the complexity in setting up Geo, I will describe its setup in a separate section later on in this chapter.

Release Upgrade Complications

Creating a highly available, disaster recovery resistant production service has a side effect (other than the increased cost) that you should be made aware of. With all these moving parts, upgrading all of them to a new release version requires some coordination. Certain components need to be upgraded before others in order for things to work smoothly. This is especially important to enable the holy grail of releases: zero-downtime upgrades. Yes, it is doable even with the many components. Because of the coordination involved and the many steps needed to make such an upgrade, it is highly recommended to automate the overall upgrade process. I will discuss this topic in its own section later on in the chapter.

Reasons for a Staging Service

Before I close this section, you might be wondering why I advocate for having a staging service. Yes, you can cut costs significantly by not maintaining such a service, but it saves you when testing release upgrades. There have been times in my experience when a release introduced unexpected issues. Better to find these out with a staging service first than impact all users running on the production service.

As such, it is important that the staging setup matches the production setup as much as possible (absent all the users and Git data, of course). So, if the production service uses a Gitaly cluster, the staging service should have one as well. And if you use Geo for the production service, you should use it for the staging service, too. You don't need to have as many GitLab servers running on the staging server, but they should be under an auto-scaling group like the production service is. In other words, the architecture between the production and staging service should be the same. You can reduce costs of the staging service by using less powerful servers and smaller disk space, when possible.

Monitoring Needs

For a production-level setup, you will need a service to monitor the various components of your self-managed GitLab service. This is done to not only alert you to problems but to gather performance metrics on your GitLab service. GitLab enables the Prometheus service by default as described at `https://docs.gitlab.com/ee/administration/monitoring/prometheus/`; however, in a production system, you should consider setting up a separate Prometheus server to perform the monitoring. In addition, you should also consider importing performance metrics into a tool such as Grafana to get some spiffy time-series graphs.

If you are hosting your GitLab service in AWS, you could also use AWS monitoring services as well. This could be in place of Prometheus or in conjunction with it. In any case, you will need to use AWS CloudWatch services for AWS-specific components such as RDS and Redis.

Since Prometheus and Grafana are third-party products, their installation and configuration is beyond the scope of this book – likewise for the AWS CloudWatch service. No worries. There are plenty of online and book resources you can reference to get you started.

Creating Your Production Setup

Since we created the proof-of-concept service using AWS, this section assumes that you will create the staging and production services in AWS as well. Of course, you can use a different cloud provider or an in-house data center for this. If that is the case, you should be able to infer from this section how to set up your production-level services in those environments. At the very least, the concept of isolation to enhance security, testing, and maintainability should be adhered to in your own implementation.

Deciding Where the Primary Service Should Reside

Your first decision is where you want your primary service to reside.[6] AWS provides a number of regions that you can choose from. You can find this information on their website here: https://aws.amazon.com/about-aws/global-infrastructure/regions_az/. You should choose a region that is close to you to reduce latency issues. In North America, the two most common regions are us-east-1 (Northern Virginia) and us-west-1 (Northern California). In Europe, a common region is eu-west-1 (Ireland). There are other regions that might be closer to you, but you should verify that they have all the services you require since not all regions support all services.

There are two special region classes that you should be aware of. The first is known as the AWS GovCloud in the United States. This has special security requirements for US government work. Unless you are a government contractor or worker who has a need for using the GovCloud, avoid using these regions. Also, if your primary GitLab service is in the GovCloud, any secondary GitLab services must also be in the GovCloud.

The second class of regions are the China regions. The China AWS services are managed by China-owned providers and require their own account credentials separate from those used in other regions. The types of services available are more limited and tend to be behind in features from other regions. You should also be aware that network connectivity is throttled at times making certain download operations extremely slow. In addition, GitLab uses JiHu (pronounced G-Who) to manage licensing and services in China, so if you need to install GitLab in China, contact GitLab for more details on their restrictions. You can't obtain a license in the United States and apply it in China. And if you need to set up secondary GitLab services, they must be located in China.

Considering AWS Direct Connect

If you are a corporation, you should also look into using the AWS Direct Connect service to directly connect your computing infrastructure to AWS's infrastructure. This is done to reduce latency to AWS's infrastructure and to provide more security when connecting with your internal infrastructure. If you are close to an AWS region, you can directly connect to that. There are also "local zones" located in major cities such as Chicago,

---

[6] We'll talk about secondary sites in the chapter on disaster recovery.

CHAPTER 19   LIGHTS, CAMERA, ACTION!

New York City, and Los Angeles to which you can connect your infrastructure. Setting this up is beyond the scope of this book. Contact AWS services for more details on how to set up Direct Connect.

Establishing a Naming Convention for Your GitLab Services

This is a good time to lay out the naming of your services. If you set up the poc service described earlier, you have already established a high-level domain[7] (for me, it was jpgitlab.com). Hereafter, I'll refer to that high-level domain as your-gitlab-domain. If you plan on only setting up a primary service, you could name your staging GitLab service as stage.your-gitlab-domain and your production GitLab service as main.your-gitlab-domain.[8] If you also plan on enabling GitLab Pages with your primary service, you'll need to choose the domain names for those as well. For example, you could use stage-pages.your-gitlab-domain and main-pages.your-gitlab-domain as the domain names of your staging and production Page services, respectively.

Now if you plan on setting up secondary services via GitLab Geo, you'll need to consider carefully how to name them, especially if, in a disaster recovery situation, a secondary service becomes a primary service. This may also impact the name of your primary services. For example, if you have your primary service in North America and your secondary service in Europe, you could use prefixes such as na- and eu- to distinguish them, so, for example, na-stage.your-gitlab-domain for your primary staging service and eu-stage.your-gitlab-domain for your secondary staging service. On the other hand, if you have your primary service on the east coast of the United States and the secondary on the west coast of the United States, you could use prefixes such as us-east- and us-west- (e.g., us-east-main.your-gitlab-domain). I suggest avoiding using AWS region codes (e.g., us-east-1-main) as they have little meaning to users.

---

[7] If you changed your mind and don't like that high-level domain name, now is the time to choose a new one realizing that you'll be stuck with it from here on out.

[8] I recommend not using prod as the specific domain name of your production service. Although it makes sense, your users will hate it, trust me.

CHAPTER 19   LIGHTS, CAMERA, ACTION!

Preparing Production-Level VPC Environments

Let's now turn to setting up your production-level services.[9] First up are the AWS VPC environments. You should establish two separate VPCs: one for your staging service and one for your production service. These VPCs must also be separate from your proof-of-concept service. You are going to need a larger range of IP addresses than was used for the poc service as well as a larger number of availability zones. At a minimum, I suggest using a CIDR range of /21, which provides for 2048 IP addresses that will be spread across four availability zones. So, for example, you can set up a staging VPC with a CIDR of 10.1.0.0/21 and a production VPC with a CIDR of 10.2.0.0/21. With four availability zones, you will then have 256 IP addresses for each of your public and private subnets. Using CIDR ranges of /24 will divide up the IP addresses evenly across each subnet ensuring that all IP addresses are accounted for.

Unfortunately, not all AWS regions have four or more availability zones. In North America, there is us-east-1 in Northern Virginia that has six AZs and us-west-2 in Oregon that has four AZs. Most other regions at the time of this writing have three AZs. So, if you plan on having your service in Europe or Asia Pacific, you will need to settle with three AZs.

There are a couple of ways to deal with regions with only three availability zones. You could set up one availability zone with four subnets, two private and two public, so that each subnet still has 256 IPs available. Alternatively, you can set up your VPC to use three CIDR ranges. So rather than defining your VPC using a single CIDR range of 10.1.0.0/21, you could define it using three CIDR ranges of 10.1.0.0/23, 10.1.2.0/23, and 10.1.4.0/23. In this case, you'll have three availability zones each with 512 IP addresses (256 for a private subnet and 256 for a public subnet) that give you a total of 1536 IP addresses. If you find that you are running low on IP addresses, you can always add additional ranges in 512 IP increments to your existing VPC.

Other than the larger size of the VPC, you set up everything else as you did for the poc service. You create private and public subnets in each of the availability zones and set up both Internet and NAT gateways along with routing tables. Fortunately, all of this is pretty simple to set up using the "Create VPC" wizard. Make sure to name your VPCs accordingly, for example, stage-gitlab-poc and main-gitlab-poc.

---

[9] I use the term production-level to refer to both staging and production environments.

CHAPTER 19　LIGHTS, CAMERA, ACTION!

Establishing AWS Component Naming Conventions

Speaking of naming, this is a good time to set up some naming conventions. Assuming you will maintain your staging and production services in the same AWS region, you need to be mindful that most objects, such as security groups, share the same regional namespace. To keep things manageable, you should adopt a policy of using prefixes (or similar device) to denote which objects are used by the staging service and which are used by the production service. So, for example, rather than using a name such as gitlab-loadbalancer-sg for the production security group, use a name such as main-loadbalancer-sg; and for the staging security group, use a name such as stage-loadbalancer-sg.

Preparing TLS Certificates

Next up are the TLS certificates to use with your services. Since you already established a top-level domain for the poc (jpgitlab.com in my case), you can reuse[10] the wildcard TLS certificate for both your staging and production services. However, if you plan on enabling GitLab Pages with your service, you will need to create specific TLS certificates for them. These will be distinct wildcard certificates such as "*.stage-pages.your-gitlab-domain" and "*.main-pages.your-gitlab-domain". Since creating TLS certificates takes a while, now is a good time to order them either through AWS Certificate Manager or your own certificate provider.

If you plan on having a secondary GitLab service, you should be aware that TLS certificates managed by AWS Certificate Manager are regionally based. In this case, you'll end up having to create your top-level wildcard TLS certificate in both the primary service region and the secondary service region. It isn't a high cost, but if you want to avoid that, now might be the time to switch to a third-party TLS certificate provider such as GlobalSign.

Defining Service-Specific AWS Key Pairs

Next, you should create the key pairs for your production-level services. Since key pairs are AWS resources that are not limited to a particular VPC, you could, in practice, share a key pair between the staging and production services; however, you should refrain

---

[10] This is a case where reuse of resources is acceptable and, because of costs, desirable.

from doing this. For security reasons, create two different key pairs, one for the staging environment and one for the production environment. In this way, if you have a new administrator coming onboard, you could restrict their access to the staging servers initially until they become trusted enough to gain access to the production servers. The same advice holds true for secondary services; create key pairs that are distinct from the primary service key pairs.

Creating Independent IAM Roles and Policies per Service and Region

Whereas AWS key pairs are resources that are regionally based, IAM roles and policies are resources that are globally based, meaning that they are accessible within any standard region.[11] So, an IAM role that is available in us-east-1 is also available in eu-west-1. Although it may be tempting to share these IAM resources across staging and production services in both primary and secondary regions, I highly advise against this. Use the naming conventions established earlier to create independent[12] IAM roles and policies for each service in each region. This way, if you need to make updates to a given service's IAM role or policy, you can do so without impacting other services.

Database Production-Level Requirements

For the most part, setting up production-level GitLab services is the same as setting up the poc GitLab service. There are some variations to that setup that I'll explain here. First off, in terms of the RDS databases, you should enable automated daily backups. It also helps to enable more performance monitoring and email notifications to your admin staff when issues arise. For the production-level RDS databases, I highly recommend creating RDS parameter groups rather than using the default parameter group; using a specific parameter group will allow you to make performance tweaks without having to bring the database down. These features obviously add to the RDS costs but are worth it when maintaining a production-level service. The same holds true for the Redis service.

---

[11] By standard region, I mean any region that is not China or GovCloud based.
[12] Although this violates the DRY (Don't Repeat Yourself) principle, it is warranted here to ensure isolation and security.

Bastion Server Considerations

As for bastion servers, you should be able to get by with two of them each in a separate availability zone. Even though you might have three or four AZs, running bastion servers in two of them should be enough since the likelihood of two zones going down simultaneously is very rare. Just in case, you should create an AMI of one of your bastion servers so that you could quickly spin one up in a working AZ should the need arise. If you really want to be prepared, you could create a launch template for bastion servers.

Creating a Provisioning Server

For production-level services, I'm going to add an additional type of server that I'll call the provisioning server. This isn't documented by GitLab but is something I've found useful, especially when setting up Gitaly clusters and automating upgrades. A provisioning server is similar to a bastion server except that it exists in a private subnet rather than a public subnet. Since it is in a private subnet, the provisioning server has access to all other servers and the RDS databases. As such, it should not be assigned a public elastic IP address; access to the provisioning server is provided through the bastion servers like all other servers in the private subnet.

For the provisioning server, you should create a security group that allows SSH access to port 22 from only the bastion servers.[13] In terms of software, the one additional package you should install is the PostgreSQL client; this will allow you to access the RDS databases using the psql command-line tool provided by the PostgreSQL client package. To gain access to the RDS databases, you'll need to include the load balancer security group as you do for GitLab application servers.[14] You only need one provisioning server, but like the bastion server you can set up multiple ones in different AZs and/or create a launch template for it so that you can create a new one should there be a zone failure.

---

[13] Check out how the Gitaly security group restricts source access to the bastion servers.

[14] Recall in Chapter 14 that the RDS security group defines an inbound rule for the load balancer security group to enable any servers using the load balancer SG access to the database. For tightened security, you could create a special security group for the provisioning server and give that group access to the RDS database as well.

Gitaly Cluster Considerations

Before exposing your production-level server to users, you need to decide whether you will be using a standalone Gitaly server or a Gitaly cluster. If you plan on using a Gitaly cluster, now is the best time to set it up since you can reset the "default" storage to point to the cluster rather than a single server storage option. If you start with a standalone Gitaly server and later decide to switch to a Gitaly cluster, you won't be able to set the default storage to point to your cluster even if you migrate all your data from the standalone Gitaly server to the Gitaly cluster.[15] In the migration case, you'll have to set up a "dummy" default storage where no Git data will be stored.

If you want your new production-level service to use a Gitaly cluster, then do not set up a standalone Gitaly server as you did with the poc; use the built-in Gitaly service initially and then set up the cluster as described in the next section. If, however, you want to set up a standalone Gitaly server, then make sure that the server uses a secondary storage volume to store the Git data repository; do not use the root volume for storing this data as we did for the poc Gitaly server. The reason for this is that sometime in the future you will need to replace the Gitaly server with an updated operating system AMI; having the Git repository on a separate volume will allow you to detach the volume from the old server and attach it to the new server.

GitLab Application Server Considerations

This brings us to the topic of GitLab application servers. Just like we will need to replace Gitaly servers using newer operating system AMIs, we will need to do the same for the GitLab application servers. This means that periodically we will need to reinstall the GitLab software and reconfigure it from scratch. In the section on automating upgrades, we'll talk about how to do this, but in preparation for that, I'm going to suggest one change on how GitLab is configured: minimize the changes made directly to the /etc/gitlab/gitlab.rb file. The reason for this is that new installations of GitLab will add, remove, or otherwise modify the configuration options included in the gitlab.rb file. If you keep reusing the gitlab.rb file from an earlier release, you will miss those changes.

---

[15] Let's just say I discovered this the hard way.

Preparing for Automated Configuration File Changes

The approach to minimizing changes to the gitlab.rb file is to put those changes into separate files and then "including" those files in the gitlab.rb file. For example, you can place your email smtp options in a /etc/gitlab/gitlab-smtp.rb file and then add the line "from_file /etc/gitlab/gitlab-smtp.rb" at the end of gitlab.rb. Ditto for pages and registry configurations. Note that those specific configuration files need to have the same file permissions as the gitlab.rb file. The one change that you will have to explicitly include in the gitlab.rb file is the external_url setting; you can't maintain that option in a separate file.

Now this may seem like more work than simply updating the configurations directly in the gitlab.rb file, but as we'll see in the automating upgrades section, it is a simple matter of automating (via the Linux sed command) the setting of the external_url option and appending the from_file lines in the gitlab.rb file. As you may have guessed, part of automating the upgrade process will rely on managing those special configuration files in source code control.[16] So, to make our lives easier later on, we might as well start using the technique now, even if it is done manually for now.

Instance-Level Shared Runner Considerations

As for the instance-level shared runners, the setup described for the poc remains the same. The main difference is the increased number of availability zones where runner managers will reside along with the increase in spun-up instances they'll manage. As for runner key pairs, you should create specific key pairs for each production-level service in each region to enhance security.

Planning for the Gitaly Cluster

One word of note: If you plan on setting up the Gitaly cluster as part of your initial production-level service, just create the standalone GitLab application server. You can hold off creating the auto-scaling groups until after the Gitaly cluster configuration is complete. You won't be enabling access to users during this initial setup, so no need to bother with the dynamic server management until you're ready.

---

[16] Yes, we will end up managing our GitLab services using GitLab itself.

The next section looks at how to switch up from a standalone Gitaly server to a Gitaly cluster.

Switching to Gitaly Clusters

When talking about creating a production-level GitLab service, we need to address the elephant in the room: Gitaly. In the poc self-managed service, we set up a single Gitaly server to store our Git repository data. Given that this data is one of the most, if not the most, important data to maintain, storing it on a single server is risky. If the availability zone containing the Gitaly server goes down, even temporarily, we lose access to that data right away. Users can't clone or push data until the Gitaly server comes back up.

The Gitaly Sharding Option

Now you could reduce the loss of data access by creating multiple standalone Gitaly servers. These servers can be placed in different availability zones. The caveat, though, is that you need to tell GitLab what percentage of new data goes to each Gitaly server. This does not replicate data across servers but simply splits the data up so that a given Git repository is placed on one and only one Gitaly server. This is known as sharding. It is a technique used when there is a large number of Git repositories, and you need to reduce the loading on any given Gitaly server. In case you are wondering, the location of any given Git repository is maintained in the RDS database, so when a request is made to clone or push updates to a Git repository, GitLab knows where to access that data. The placement of that data is controlled by GitLab.

Of course, this doesn't fully solve our problem when an availability zone goes down. Some users will still have access to any repositories stored on a Gitaly server that is still up and running, but other users will lose access to their Git repositories for those Gitaly servers in the downed availability zone. It is a degradation in service but not a full outage of the service. In this case, we say that the service degrades "gracefully."[17]

---

[17] Although one can argue that for those users impacted, the service degradation isn't terribly graceful.

CHAPTER 19   LIGHTS, CAMERA, ACTION!

The Gitaly Cluster Option

The high-availability solution provided by GitLab, the corporation, is to set up a Gitaly cluster. As you might expect, this creates copies of the Git repository data spread across multiple availability zones. As you might expect, this is a more complicated solution. I also need to tell you that this is a much more expensive option,[18] as we will soon see.

The Concept Behind the Gitaly Cluster

To understand the solution, let's first look at the end game. We want to have multiple Gitaly servers in different availability zones, each with a copy of all Git repositories. So, if we have three availability zones at our disposal, we would have at least three[19] Gitaly servers, one per zone. This part of the Gitaly cluster architecture is not hard to understand.

OK, so let's say we now have multiple Gitaly servers. That certainly makes our architecture more robust against zone failures. But the question now is, how are Git repository data replicated across each of those Gitaly servers? To solve this, we need a monitoring service that keeps track of the replicated data. When a new Git repository is created or updated, it is not possible to ensure immediate synchronization across these Gitaly servers. Some servers will have older versions (or no versions in the case of a new repository) than others. The monitoring service then needs to keep track of what versions of data are on each of the servers and, for those servers that have out-of-date information, queue changes to them so that the Gitaly servers will "eventually" be in sync.

The Need for a Gitaly Cluster Database

You might, then, envision that a database is used to keep track of all Gitaly servers along with the versions of every Git repository that are on them. Although GitLab already has a database for storing group, project, and job information, you might think we could use that database for the Gitaly cluster information. It turns out that the amount of data needed to keep track of all Gitaly clusters along with the versions of every Git repository is a lot of data that would end up impacting the performance of the GitLab database.

---

[18] So expensive, in fact, that I won't be setting up a Gitaly cluster in AWS.
[19] You could also use sharding with the Gitaly cluster, but I won't go there. It's for very large installations.

After all, the monitoring service will need to continually access this information in a way to minimize the amount of time any given Git repository is out of sync. Because of this, the Gitaly cluster architecture uses its own database separate from the GitLab database.

The Need for Multiple Gitaly Monitoring Servers

There is another issue, though. The monitoring service itself can't be run on a single server for the same reason we shouldn't run Gitaly on its own server. If the monitoring service is run on a server in an availability zone that goes down, we are back to our original high-availability issue: we lose access to our Git repository data. So, the monitoring service needs to run on multiple servers spread across different availability zones. This is simple to understand conceptually, but not so easy to implement in reality.

To better understand the implementation complexity, let's first look at the single monitoring server case. With one monitor, implementation is pretty straightforward. At a high level, the monitor checks the repository status database to determine what Gitaly servers need to be updated for a given Git repository. When an update needs to be made, the monitor service marks the status for a given Gitaly server within the status database and proceeds to update that Git repository to match the latest version. Once complete, the status database is updated to record the new version of the Git repository on that Gitaly server, and the process continues for other out-of-sync Git repositories.[20]

Now let's look at what happens when we add multiple monitor servers to the mix. Although the status database is referenced by each monitoring server, there needs to be a way to decide which server will perform any given update. Otherwise, a race condition can form when two or more monitors attempt to update the same Git repository on a given Gitaly server, which could lead to a potential deadlock or corruption of the repository.

---

[20] In reality, updates are performed in parallel up to some limit.

CHAPTER 19   LIGHTS, CAMERA, ACTION!

Deciding Which Monitoring Servers Synchronize a Git Repository Change

In the early days of the Gitaly cluster, the primary solution was to use an election strategy among the monitoring servers. That is, each monitor "elects" which monitor server is in charge; this server is then used to keep track of changes on the repository status database and then to delegate to itself or another monitor service the task of updating a given Git repository on a Gitaly server that is out of sync.

This election strategy works fine when all monitors are up and running and communication between them is intact. But what happens if either a monitor goes down or network communication between some monitors is lost? From a given monitor's point of view (one that is running, of course), it is hard to distinguish between the two cases. This leads to what is known as the split-brain syndrome. If indeed the issue is loss of network communication with one of the servers, you have a scenario where all monitors are up and running but some are unaware of monitors on the other side of the network failure. One of the monitors on each side of the network failure, via the election strategy, could decide that it is in charge; in this case, we are back to our original problem of two servers attempting to make uncoordinated updates[21] to a given Gitaly server.

With the latest releases of GitLab, the election strategy has been replaced with a different strategy. In the new strategy, Git repository updates are "assigned" across the monitors so that one monitor would be responsible for making the update for a given Git repository on a particular Gitaly server. If a monitor goes down or network connectivity is split, the monitors continue making their assigned updates. In the case where a server has gone down, this could be detected by noting that the queue of updates for a given monitor are piling up (an indication that the server is down), at which point those outstanding updates can be "reassigned" to monitors that are still running.[22]

---

[21] A possible solution to this dilemma is to always use an odd number of monitors. So, if you have three monitors, for example, should there be a network failure, the side that has two servers could elect one to be in charge and the side with one server could simply do nothing.

[22] This is an oversimplification of what happens. Reality is a bit more complex especially when there is a network disconnect. Remember that the database is in a given availability zone, so it is possible that connectivity to the database from some servers is also impacted.

Introducing Praefect

Enough theory. The monitoring system used by a Gitaly cluster is referred to as Praefect.[23] The status database is called the Praefect tracking database, and the monitoring servers are referred to as Praefect servers. In a Gitaly cluster, you need to create a separate RDS database for the Praefect tracking database, which in a high-availability setup should be a multi-AZ PostgreSQL database. In addition, the gitaly cluster requires at least three Praefect servers. You don't need to have the same number of Praefect servers as you do Gitaly servers. For instance, you can have three Praefect servers monitoring five Gitaly servers. However, you do have to have an odd number of Praefect servers, so you can have three or five but not four.

If you are creating a production and/or staging GitLab service from scratch, make sure to start with a Gitaly cluster. It's more complicated to set up but will be easier than trying to migrate from a standalone Gitaly server to a Gitaly cluster. If you already have a standalone Gitaly server, don't worry. You can still migrate your Git repositories from that standalone server to the Gitaly cluster. It just takes some time and patience to complete, especially if you have a large number of Git repositories to migrate.[24]

The Praefect Load Balancer

You can find the architecture of a Gitaly cluster in the GitLab documentation here: `https://docs.gitlab.com/ee/administration/gitaly/#architecture`. Looking at the architecture, you should note that there is a separate load balancer standing in front of the Praefect servers. The GitLab application servers communicate to the Praefect servers via this load balancer. Note that the Praefect load balancer must be private to the GitLab service; you cannot use the same load balancer as the GitLab service since that is a publicly available service.[25]

---

[23] Yes, the spelling is weird. I guarantee you will misspell it at least once in your time as an admin.
[24] I speak from experience here. It took me days babysitting this migration process.
[25] Even if you've restricted access to the GitLab service to your corporate Intranet, you need to prevent access to the Praefect servers from your corporate users.

CHAPTER 19   LIGHTS, CAMERA, ACTION!

The Case for Moving to a Licensed Version of GitLab

Before we dive into the configuration of a Gitaly cluster, here's some advice. Although you can configure a Gitaly cluster for the community edition of GitLab, I highly advise against it, especially for a production service. The unlicensed version of GitLab does not include support, so if anything goes wrong with your Gitaly cluster (and it will), you are, as the saying goes, up the creek without a paddle. Sure, you could rely on searching the Web for any problem that might pop up, but with a production service, time is of the essence, and there is no guarantee that you'll find the issue in your web search. Either proceed with at least a premium license to get the support you need or consider an alternative to using a Gitaly cluster.[26]

Establishing a Gitaly Cluster in AWS

The remaining description assumes that the production and staging services are managed using AWS. If you are using a different cloud provider or an in-house data center, you should be able to follow https://docs.gitlab.com/ee/administration/gitaly/praefect.html for instructions on installing the Gitaly cluster. The description I provide here pretty much follows those instructions with some variations specific to AWS. In other words, I'm going to fill in the gaps for an AWS implementation that are, for some reason, not described in the official GitLab documentation.

Gitaly Cluster VPC and Availability Zone Assumptions

Let's start with some assumptions. Because we need at least three Gitaly servers and three Praefect servers, the assumption here is that you have at least three availability zones with their associated public and private subnets. It is also assumed that the staging and production services are maintained in their own VPC[27] and that neither VPC shares the VPC used for the proof-of-concept service.

---

[26] Although GitLab advises against using NFS for performance reasons, there is nothing stopping you from setting up a Gitaly server where your Git repository data is stored on an NFS server. You'll have to consider ways to ensure high availability by mirroring the NFS service, which is challenging but doable. There are also third-party NFS solutions that provide backup and mirroring out of the box.

[27] Two reasons for this. First is for security. Should anyone break into any one of these VPCs, the others are protected from that intrusion. Second, it minimizes change impacts from one service

Defining Gitaly Security Groups

The first thing we need to do (which is not described in the cluster documentation) is to create three interrelated security groups. First, we need to create a security group for the Praefect load balancer that will be created later. Use a name with a suffix such as praefect-balancer-sg (e.g., stage-praefect-balancer-sg). The Praefect balancer security group should have an inbound rule that accepts TCP traffic at port 2305 from the private subnets.[28]

The second security group is modeled after the Gitaly security group. Use a name with a suffix such as praefect-sg (e.g., stage-praefect-sg). The Praefect security group should have inbound rules that accept SSH traffic at port 22 from the bastion security group, accept TCP traffic at port 2305 from the Praefect balancer security group, and accept TCP traffic at port 9652[29] from the private subnets.

The third security group is the Praefect RDS security group. Use a suffix such as praefect-rds-sg (e.g. stage-praefect-rds-sg). The Praefect RDS security group should have inbound rules that accept port 5432 from both the Praefect security group and the provisioning security group.

Creating the Praefect Tracking Database

The first component of the cluster to be implemented is the Praefect tracking database. Like the primary GitLab database, this database should be a multi-AZ PostgreSQL database managed by the AWS RDS service. I recommend, although it is not required, that the version of PostgreSQL used by the Praefect tracking database matches the version of the GitLab database. Use the Praefect RDS security group created earlier. Create an RDS subnet group that is specific to the tracking database rather than reuse the one from the GitLab database. I would also advise creating an RDS parameter group specific to the Praefect database.

---

to another. So, if the staging service environment is upgraded in such a way that brings it down, the production service remains up and running.

[28] The Praefect load balancer will only be accessible to servers within the private subnets associated with a given server and region. No outside connectivity to the Praefect load balancer will be allowed.

[29] The 9652 port is the port used by Prometheus for monitoring the Praefect nodes.

The Undocumented Chicken-and-Egg Scenario

Now if you are following along with the "Configure Gitaly Cluster" documentation, you may start getting confused. This is because there is a chicken-and-egg scenario that isn't very well documented. First off, the Praefect database instructions state that you need a Praefect host to set up the database, yet the Praefect configuration comes later in the instructions. Second of all, the Praefect configuration states that you need the Gitaly node IP addresses, which means you need to spin those up before configuring the Praefect nodes. But, of course, instructions on configuring the Gitaly nodes are described after the Praefect nodes.

Using the Provisioning Server to Configure the Praefect Tracking Database

So how do we handle this dilemma? Let's first deal with the Praefect database configuration first. The reason the instructions have a Praefect node as a prerequisite to preparing the Praefect database is that it wants you to use the PostgreSQL client built into the GitLab package. This client is located at /opt/gitlab/embedded/bin/psql. There are a couple of choices here. You could spin up a server that will act as one of the Praefect nodes and install the GitLab software on it without configuring and starting any services. You can then use the psql client provided by GitLab. Alternatively, you can use the provisioning server that I mentioned in the previous section. This server already has the PostgreSQL client installed on it; you can use that psql tool to configure the tracking databases. Using the provisioning server to connect to the tracking database is the preferred option.[30]

Using psql, you connect to the Praefect database using the master user and password you set when creating the RDS tracking database and invoke the following two database commands replacing PRAEFECT_SQL_PASSWORD with a password specific to the praefect user. Note that the praefect user password must not be the same as the database's master password.

```
CREATE ROLE praefect WITH LOGIN PASSWORD 'PRAEFECT_SQL_PASSWORD';
CREATE DATABASE praefect_production WITH OWNER praefect ENCODING UTF8;
```

---

[30] This makes automating the Gitaly cluster upgrade process easier as we'll see in a later section.

Seriously, those two database commands are the only things you need to prepare the tracking database. The GitLab software will create and populate the tables automatically once you've configured the Praefect nodes. There isn't anything magical about using the GitLab embedded psql command.

The Case for NOT Using PgBouncer

As part of the Praefect tracking database setup, the configuration instructions make mention of a tool called the PgBouncer. The PgBouncer instructions are mainly for installations where the PostgreSQL database is installed on its own node as opposed to using an RDS database. Do not set up the PgBouncer when using the RDS service from AWS. It just complicates the cluster implementation and is not really needed when using RDS. In addition, don't bother using the AWS RDS Proxy feature (which is a service similar to PgBouncer). It doesn't work properly with the Gitaly cluster.

Creating an Initial Praefect Server and Three Gitaly Servers

With the Praefect tracking database set up, we now need to tackle the second chicken-and-egg scenario regarding Praefect configuration needing the Gitaly node IPs. This is how we are going to handle this with AWS. Take the latest AMI used for the GitLab application services and spin up four servers: one for the initial Praefect node and three for the Gitaly nodes. The reason for using the GitLab application AMI is that all of these servers need to use the same copy of the /etc/gitlab/gitlab.secrets.json file used with the application servers. I recommend naming the Praefect server as Praefect-1 and the Gitaly servers as Gitaly-1, Gitaly-2, and Gitaly-3.

An Overview of the Gitaly Cluster Configuration Process

The overall approach to configuration here is to first configure the Praefect-1 node, create an AMI from that, and use that to create the Praefect-2 and Praefect-3 nodes. We will then modify each of the Gitaly nodes to include a secondary volume to hold the Git repository data and then configure each of the Gitaly servers to run the gitaly service. Following that, we will set up the Praefect load balancer and then configure the standalone GitLab server to use the Gitaly cluster. Using that updated standalone GitLab server, we can then create a new GitLab application AMI to be used with the auto-scaling groups.

Whew, that's a lot of work (and rework) to get to the final Gitaly cluster configuration! Fortunately, it is a process that you only have to do once (well, once per production-level service and region). As you'll see with the upgrade automation process, things are much easier when all the components are already in place.

Configuring the Initial Praefect Instance

At this point, make sure to set the Praefect-1 instance to use the Praefect security group; no other security groups are required. You should be able to easily follow the Praefect configuration instructions for configuring Praefect-1 at https://docs.gitlab.com/ee/administration/gitaly/praefect.html#praefect. As described in those instructions, you are going to need two distinct tokens: an external Praefect token and an internal Praefect token. These must be different to prevent inadvertent data corruption. For security reasons, you should also use different tokens across the production-level services.[31] For the initial Praefect configuration, I suggest disabling the database TLS mode by setting the "database:sslmode" option to false as directed in the instructions; you can enable TLS mode if you desire at a later point after you have the Gitaly cluster working properly.[32]

If you already have a standalone Gitaly server that has been running with a virtual storage name of "default" for a while, you will need to change the Praefect configuration's virtual_storage name from default to a different one such as cluster1. Otherwise, you can keep the virtual_storage name as default. Just remember the name used when you configure the GitLab application nodes; they need to match.

Testing Connectivity Between the Initial Praefect Server and the Tracking Database

Make sure that when the Praefect-1 server configuration is completed, you run the special sql-ping command described in the last step. This ensures that the Praefect node can access the Praefect tracking database. If it doesn't, go through each step again and verify that everything was configured properly with the database options and security groups. You can always use the embedded psql command to verify that you can manually connect to the tracking database.

---

[31] As you may have guessed by now, I've had several run-ins with corporate security teams.

[32] This is a common philosophy that I follow as an admin: keep things simple at first to get something working before adding more advanced features.

Creating the Praefect Server AMI and Remaining Praefect Servers

Before you create the remaining two Praefect nodes, go into the Praefect-1 node configuration and temporarily set the praefect['auto_migrate'] option to false. Also, make sure that the /etc/gitlab/skip-auto-configuration file exists. With those changes in place, create an AMI from the Praefect-1 node. Using that AMI, create the Praefect-2 and Praefect-3 nodes. Make sure to run the special sql-ping command from the Praefect-2 and Praefect-3 nodes; this may seem unnecessary, but it verifies that there is connectivity to the Praefect tracking database from each of the availability zones. Finally, go back into the Praefect-1 node and set the praefect['auto_migrate'] option to true; this ensures that on any version upgrade of the Praefect nodes, only the Praefect-1 node updates the tracking database schema.[33]

In the instructions for Praefect, you will see sections on enabling TLS support and setting up service discovery. Ignore those sections for now. You can go back and enable TLS support once you have the Gitaly cluster working properly. As for service discovery, I haven't tried setting that up for AWS. It looks like it might be doable using Route 53, but I'm not certain if it would work. Stick with explicit IP address for now and experiment with service discovery when you have some time to experiment.

Prepping the Gitaly Servers

For the Gitaly nodes, you should first go into the Gitaly security group and add an inbound rule to accept TCP traffic at port 9236 from your private subnets. This will enable Prometheus monitoring of your Gitaly nodes. Make sure each of the Gitaly nodes uses this security group; it should be the only one required.

In addition to the security group change, you should add secondary volumes for each of the Gitaly nodes. You do this by creating a volume in the same AZ as the instance, attach the new volume on a device such as /dev/sdf, format the volume, and create a mount point for it. All of these steps are explained in AWS documents that you can find by doing a web search on "Create an Amazon EBS volume." For Gitaly, I suggest creating

---

[33] It's not that updating the database schema multiple times is an issue since GitLab keeps track of the latest schema versions. The issue we are trying to prevent is upgrading the database from multiple nodes at the same time.

a mount point such as /mnt/gitlab/git-data/repositories. You'll need this mount point in the Gitaly storage configuration. Make sure that the volume mounts automatically after a server reboot as described in AWS's documentation.

Configuring the Gitaly Servers

Once you've prepped the three Gitaly servers, configure them as described by GitLab here: https://docs.gitlab.com/ee/administration/gitaly/praefect.html#gitaly. The configuration is pretty straightforward. Stick with the same naming conventions and use the mount points created previously; you should be fine. Once you've completed the configuration, make sure to run the special dial-mode command (provided at the end of the Gitaly section) from each of the Praefect nodes to ensure that the Praefect nodes can communicate properly with the Gitaly nodes. Do not proceed further until the test works correctly.

Creating the Praefect Load Balancer

Things get easier from here. The next component of the cluster to create is the Praefect load balancer. Since it won't be handling any HTTP or HTTPS applications, you should create an AWS network load balancer. Make sure that this load balancer is internal as opposed to Internet-facing. Use the private VPC created for the given service and include mappings to all availability zones (even ones that may not have a Praefect node in it). You will only need to add one listener with a TCP protocol on port 2305. Once the load balancer has been created, manually attach each of the Praefect node servers to it. Although you might be tempted, do not create an auto-scaling group for the Praefect ELB.

Updating the GitLab Configuration to Use the New Cluster

For the standalone GitLab node, update the configuration as described here: https://docs.gitlab.com/ee/administration/gitaly/praefect.html#gitlab. I would initially skip setting up the Prometheus scrape_configs section; in a high-availability configuration, the Prometheus service should be run on its own node. The only complication to the configuration occurs if you have a working standalone Gitaly server. In that case, you'll need to make sure that in the git_data_dirs section default points to the standard Gitaly server as it did before and then add an entry for cluster1 (or whatever name you gave it in the Praefect configuration) to point to the Praefect load balancer. Use the DNS name of the Praefect load balancer provided in the AWS balancer's detail section; it should end with amazonaws.com.

Testing the GitLab Configuration Changes

With the GitLab configuration changes applied, make sure to run the various checks included at the end of the GitLab configuration section. Each of these checks is important. If any one of them fails, double-check the GitLab configuration. Once all checks have passed, you now have a functioning Gitaly cluster.

Completing the GitLab ASG and ELB Configuration

At this point, create a new AMI from the standalone GitLab node, update (or create if not done so earlier) the launch template, create the auto-scaling groups for the application and page servers, and update their respective ELBs.

Optionally Migrating Existing Git Repositories to the Gitaly Cluster

One final cleanup to discuss: If you already have a standalone Gitaly cluster, migrate any existing Git repositories from it to the cluster. First, make sure to disable creating new Git repositories on the "default" storage as described in the poc Gitaly section. You can find out how to do the migration by doing a web search on "gitaly cluster migration." It isn't hard to do but could take a long time with many iterations depending on how many repositories are stored there.

After you've migrated the Git repositories onto the cluster, you can go back and update the GitLab git_data_dirs configuration so that the default storage points to a local gitaly service. You do this in a roundabout way by enabling the gitaly service on the application nodes, updating the gitaly storage configurations on those nodes to point to an empty directory, and updating git_data_dirs configuration for default to refer to the GitLab load balancer instead of the Praefect load balancer. Of course, you'll have to open the port to 8075 on the GitLab load balancer as well. Otherwise, you can keep the standalone Gitaly server up and running in a diminished state (i.e., smaller instance type) and use that Gitaly server as your provisioning server.

CHAPTER 19   LIGHTS, CAMERA, ACTION!

Reviewing the Gitaly Troubleshooting Guide

As a final note, you should take the time to read the Gitaly troubleshooting guide available at https://docs.gitlab.com/ee/administration/gitaly/troubleshooting.html. It has a lot of information about what can go wrong with Gitaly along with ways to diagnose and fix well-known problems. For not-so-well-known problems, keep the contact information of your GitLab service representative handy. If you do not know who that is, now is the time to find out before you need it, because you probably will at some point.

With the Gitaly cluster in place, we now turn our attention in the next section to disaster recovery.

Preparing for Disaster

In 1988, I was working at an office park off the Illinois Tollway in the city of Hinsdale, a western suburb of Chicago. Not far from that complex was a nondescript two-story brick building owned by Illinois Bell, the regional phone company at the time. Most people, including myself, didn't realize at the time how important that building was to the western suburban phone network. In early May, we were soon to find out.

On Sunday, May 8 (Mother's Day in the United States), a late afternoon thunderstorm came through the area, not unusual for that time of year. Shortly before 4 pm that day, an alarm was sent from that unmanned building to a central dispatch center indicating that there was a fire. Since false alarms were typical during thunderstorms, there was no urgency in checking it out. It was Mother's Day after all, so why disturb someone's afternoon to check it out.

A half an hour later, a second alarm was sent. That was not a usual glitch event, so someone was dispatched to check things out. When that person arrived, he discovered that there was indeed a fire. Ironically, he couldn't call the fire department because the phone service was down. He had to drive to the fire station to let them know about the fire. By the time the fire trucks arrived (an hour after the first alarm), it was too late. The damage was significant. Reports at the time stated that from 250,000 to 500,000 customers in the western suburbs had lost their phone service. Note that this was a time before cell phones were common, so the impact was serious.

What made matters worse, it turned out that communications between the regional air traffic control center in Aurora just west of Hinsdale and the major Chicago airports of O'Hare and Midway had been severed because of that fire. Flights into and out of those airports were immediately stopped. People couldn't believe that there were no redundant communication lines between the air traffic control center and the airports.[34]

The fire also impacted emergency services since no one could call the fire, police, or ambulance services to report a problem. Fortunately, those services used a separate radio network to communicate with each other, so police cars were distributed in key locations throughout the area so that residents could at least walk to them and request help. Not ideal, but it worked.

It took four weeks for phone service to be restored to all impacted customers. Contractors worked round the clock to replace switching equipment and tediously restore phone lines one by one. Priority, of course, was given to the air traffic communications and emergency services.

Questions arose from this incident. How could Illinois Bell not anticipate this event? Well, they did in that alerts were set up, but because false alarms were more prevalent than true events, they were meaningless. And how come there wasn't an automated fire suppression system in place to squelch the fire when it first appeared? And most importantly, why wasn't there redundancy in place for critical services such as air traffic control communications?

AWS Disaster Recovery Considerations

When it comes to disaster recovery, it is impossible to plan for every contingency. It is possible, however, to prepare for the unexpected by following certain principles such as redundancy and planning. Had the phone company followed these principles, the impact of a fire at that phone center would have been minimized. Some customers might have been impacted, but not an entire region. You can't ensure 100% availability of services, but you can get pretty darn close.

We've seen how cloud providers use redundancy to reduce the impact of computing resource outages. With AWS, we've seen how Amazon has set up multiple data centers within a region to reduce outages to their customers. Other cloud providers do the same. The GitLab high-availability solution that we've implemented using AWS availability

---

[34] In fact, people outside the impacted area couldn't believe that an entire area in the western suburbs had no phone service. After all, the phone company was known for how reliable it was.

zones is based on that redundancy. It is quite something to see this in action when we lose communication with an AZ. Using auto-scaling groups, for example, I've watched as application servers automatically spun up in other availability zones to take up the slack. Users might feel a momentary degradation in the level of service, but things continue working, nonetheless.

In terms of disaster recovery of our GitLab production-level services, we need to answer the question of how likely it is to lose connectivity to an entire AWS region. With the redundancy built into a region, the answer is quite low. Not impossible, but highly unlikely. With that in mind, we need to weigh the possibility of such an outage occurring against the cost of losing valuable data. If your source code and data are a key asset to you or your company, such a loss of service for an extended amount of time would be unacceptable.

In this case, you need to extend the concept of redundancy from multiple data centers within a region to multiple data centers across regions. You still don't have a 100% guarantee that you'll have access across multiple regions, but your odds are significantly better that your source code and related data are safe. Unfortunately, with a multiregional cloud provider like AWS, you just can't simply spin up servers in one region and have them communicate directly with servers in another region. Things don't work that way.

Mirroring Services with GitLab Geo

Instead, you will need to implement mirror services to your primary service in one or more distinct regions via GitLab Geo. Changes made to the primary service are propagated via the Internet to the secondary mirror services to ensure that everything is in sync. If the primary service goes down, you can failover to a secondary service to take the place of the primary service. It's important to know that the secondary services implemented via GitLab Geo deal with read-only operations directly but forward all write operations to the primary service. In other words, synchronization for data is one way from the primary to the secondary services.

If you do implement secondary service sites, I suggest that you consider using at least two secondary sites. Here is my reasoning. Suppose you just have one primary and one secondary site. If you lose connectivity to either site, you lose redundancy altogether. You'll be back to a one-regional solution. Although you can set up a new secondary site after a regional failure, it takes time to implement that site and synchronize all the primary data to it. During that time, you'll be vulnerable to losing access to your new primary site. You need to calculate whether that is an acceptable risk or not.

High-Level Steps to Setting Up GitLab Geo

So, let's look at what it takes to use GitLab Geo to manage your mirrored services. Conceptually, setting up a secondary site using GitLab Geo is easier than setting up a Gitaly cluster. You are essentially implementing your secondary service the same way as you do your primary service with some differences that we'll get to in a bit. Once your secondary site is implemented, you have to tell your primary service that you are using GitLab Geo and that it is the primary site. Likewise, you need to tell the secondary service that you are using GitLab Geo and connect it to the primary service. If you go to https://docs.gitlab.com/ee/administration/geo/replication/multiple_servers.html, you will find a set of instructions on how to configure Geo. I'm not going to go through those instructions since they are pretty straightforward.[35]

Considerations When Using GitLab Geo to Perform All Replications

The complicating factor in setting up GitLab Geo sites is in the way replication from the primary service to the secondary services is handled. The simplest case is to implement your secondary site like you do your primary site. In this case, a secondary site will use a database and object storage solution independent of the primary site. In this setup, all replication is handled by the GitLab software; the underlying cloud service will view each site as two independent applications running independently of the other.

Implementing your secondary sites in this way makes switching a secondary site to a primary site quick and easy. You'll have to make a conscious effort to make the switch, however. The reason for requiring a manual switch is that only an administrator can determine whether the primary site is under a disaster scenario and for how long as opposed to downtime due to maintenance. Unfortunately, relying on GitLab to replicate

---

[35] Well, they are now at least. They weren't when I was configuring Geo.

all data from the primary to the secondary site requires that the replicating data be sent externally across the Internet. Services such as AWS set higher costs for data sent via the Internet rather than across their own internal networks.

Using RDS and Redis Cross-Region Read Replication

To reduce costs, you could rely on the cloud provider to perform some of the replication for you. For example, Amazon's RDS service has a feature called cross-region read replication. Using this feature, you set up a read replica database in your secondary site, and AWS will ensure that your GitLab application database in the secondary site is replicated with data from the primary site. As the name implies, this database is a read-only copy of your primary database. A similar cross-region read replication feature exists for Redis data stores.

Using S3 Cross-Region Replication

Likewise, for S3 object storage, Amazon has a cross-region replication feature as well. Like with database cross-region replication, Amazon copies the data from the primary site to the secondary site via its own internal network, avoiding the premium cost of sending data over the Internet. This is especially important when dealing with large binary objects. Using this feature with S3 requires that you enable object versioning so that AWS can keep track of changes. Unlike database replication, S3 cross-region replication is bidirectional, which is useful when a secondary site becomes a primary site. It is important to note that the GitLab software will not make changes directly to the secondary S3 buckets when a site is designated as a secondary Geo site.

Synchronizing Git Repository Changes via the Geo Tracking Database

Note that in either implementation, the secondary site will have its own Geo tracking database to keep track of synchronization of Git repositories between the sites; this is similar to the Praefect tracking database that monitors synchronization across Gitaly nodes but is independent of it. What this implies is that replication of Git repositories must be done across the Internet; there is no special AWS feature that will perform the replication via its internal network for you.

Complications with Disaster Recovery When Using AWS Replication

The downside of relying on the cloud provider to perform replication instead of the GitLab software is that switching a secondary Geo node (as it is referred to in the Geo documentation) to a primary Geo node requires more manual changes. You'll need to convert your RDS database to a standard read-write database, which severs the read replication relationship. And if you have other secondary sites, you'll have to set up read replication of your newly liberated database to those sites – likewise for the Redis data stores. These conversions are not instantaneous; the switchover of a secondary to a primary node will disrupt your service for an hour or so.[36]

Switching from a primary service to a secondary service brings up another concern: DNS naming. The secondary service will have a load balancer referenced by a different DNS name than the primary service's load balancer. Will you require all your users to make changes to refer to the new DNS name of your service? Or will you change the name of the secondary load balancer to the name of the old primary load balancer? This will cause a lot of confusion if you use regionally based names such as na-main.mygitlab.com and eu-main.mygitlab.com.

One possible approach to this would be to keep the regionally based names and define a more generic DNS name such as main.mygitlab.com that always points to the primary load balancer wherever it may be. This way, anyone using the generic name would remain unaffected by the switchover; users that use the name of the service that went down (for instance, na-main.mygitlab.com) would have to switch names.

Establishing a Disaster Recovery Plan

By the way, implementing Geo by itself is not enough to avert disaster. You need to document a disaster recovery plan and make sure that all of your GitLab administrators have access to it. I also recommend creating paper copies of it since you might also lose access to centrally stored electronic documents during a disaster. It's old school, but it works.

---

[36] This is based on my own experience performing a disaster recovery drill using the AWS replicated services solution.

In addition to a disaster recovery plan, I recommend going through a disaster recovery drill once every three to six months. This is where your staging service becomes useful. You want to avoid practicing on your production service since there is the possibility of losing data during the drill. Performing a drill also interferes with normal 24/7 operation. Since your staging service is less critical and not as frequently used, any outages to it will be more tolerated.

With all these new production-level components, you can imagine the impacts to performing a GitLab release upgrade. We discuss these impacts in the next section.

Automating Upgrades

Upgrading a production-level service is more involved than upgrading the proof-of-concept service. Most likely, you'll have a Gitaly cluster to deal with and perhaps one or more secondary Geo sites to manage. Even without these additional components, you will have a large number of users who depend on your production service, and these users don't like interruptions in service even if it is for planned maintenance. The goal of upgrading to a production-level service, therefore, is to perform zero-downtime upgrades whenever possible.

The Concept of Zero-Downtime Upgrades

A zero-downtime upgrade is one in which the GitLab components are upgraded to a release while maintaining service to users. Zero-downtime upgrades are tricky to do and require some planning on how to achieve it. Fortunately, zero-downtime upgrades of GitLab are possible with some limitations. A primary limitation is that you have to perform upgrades from one minor release to the next minor release; you can't skip across minor releases.[37] Note that patch releases are not required to follow this pattern in that you can skip past the last set of patches when going to the next release. Most importantly, you can upgrade directly to a later patch release of the next minor release; you don't have to upgrade to the major.minor.0 release first.

---

[37] See https://docs.gitlab.com/ee/update/zero_downtime.html#requirements-and-considerations for more details.

CHAPTER 19   LIGHTS, CAMERA, ACTION!

This may not seem like a big restriction, but realize that minor releases come out on the third Thursday of the month. In between, there are usually several patch releases, some that are not critical and some that include important security patches that require immediate attention. Major releases come around May, which might require a downtime upgrade, but not always.

Given this release schedule, you'll be updating GitLab frequently in order to maintain zero-downtime upgrades. The good news is, you don't have to upgrade to minor releases right when they first come out. In fact, you might want to wait a week or two after a minor release comes out; this way, you can wait for patch releases to come out that fix an unexpected problem with the initial minor release. If you are worried about critical security patches appearing during that lag time, note that security patches are back ported to earlier releases. You won't be forced to upgrade to the next minor release in order to apply a security patch.

Order of Upgrading Components

The bad news about these frequent releases is that production-level services have many components that need to be upgraded, more so than a poc-level service. These components need to be upgraded in a particular order in order for zero-downtime upgrades to work properly. You can find out about the specific order in the GitLab documentation here: https://docs.gitlab.com/ee/update/zero_downtime.html. In general, the following rules apply:

- Gitaly nodes need to be upgraded before Praefect nodes.
- Praefect nodes need to be upgraded before GitLab application nodes.
- The Geo primary site needs to be upgraded before Geo secondary sites.
- Runner and other supporting services are updated after the application.

It's not hard to follow this process manually,[38] but it is tedious and error prone, especially with new administrators coming onboard. As such, you will want to invest in automating the upgrade process to speed up upgrades and reduce errors that might

---

[38] I suggest that you attempt the upgrade process manually at least once, so you get an idea of how it works.

occur. The GitLab documentation doesn't provide any details on this as the topic of automating GitLab upgrades is highly dependent on the skill of the administrators. Each team will need to decide among the various tools and programming languages that they are comfortable using. It might also require some learning curve time to become acquainted with new tools and/or languages. In any case, automating the upgrade process will take time.[39]

Tools to Automate the Upgrade Process

In this section, I'm going to suggest different tools and programming languages that you can use to automate your upgrade process. I won't go into a detailed example here as automation is an opinionated topic; some of you would love my example automation setup, and others will hate it.[40] I suggest that you go with the philosophy that some automation is better than no automation even if it isn't complete. Start by documenting your manual upgrade process in a way that new administrators can immediately use it and then iterate by automating different parts of the process.

Choosing a Source Control Management Solution for Automating Upgrades

Since you will be iterating the automation process and undoubtedly making changes to the process over time as GitLab evolves, you'll need a way to manage this across your team. So, the first thing you'll need to decide on is a source code management solution to maintain the process. Hmmm, I wonder what tool we could possibly use to do that. Clearly, I recommend using GitLab for this. And as a bonus, you could use GitLab to run the upgrade process as well.

Using GitLab as the source code manager is pretty much a no-brainer, but the question then arises as to which GitLab service you use. You could use your standalone production service to manage your process, but what happens when that service goes down? If you use GitLab to run the process, you are out of luck. You could use your

---

[39] Think months, not days.

[40] Don't be surprised when this occurs within a team. Many administrators come with different levels of expertise and philosophies. If you are a lead administrator as I was, learn to let some things go. If the majority of your team wants to go one way and you want to go another, accept it and move on. Your team needs to feel comfortable running the process.

standalone staging service, but the same issue arises when upgrading the staging service itself. Perhaps use a bootstrapping GitLab service such as your poc service? It's a possibility but not ideal.[41]

One approach that our team took was to create an automation project in the production service where the process was maintained. We then created a mirror of that project on the staging service so that any changes made to the production project were automatically pushed to the staging project. This way, we always had a copy of the source code whether the production or staging service was running or not. With this setup, the staging service performed the upgrade process on the production service and vice versa.

Another approach that looks promising but one that I haven't tried is to use the GitLab SaaS service to maintain and run the automation process. This works well when using a cloud provider such as Amazon or Google. However, some corporate managers (as well as corporate security teams) might have issues with this approach as you will have to manage secrets such as SMTP passwords off-site. Fortunately, many of the GitLab configuration secrets can now be encoded by GitLab tools so that they are not stored in plain text, which was a problem with earlier GitLab releases. For the other secrets, you'll have to investigate ways of using tools such as HashiCorp Vault to manage them. If you do go the SaaS route, I suggest talking to GitLab support engineering to explore your options regarding secrets.

An Example of Automating GitLab AMI Creation

Rather than simply listing all the possible tools and languages that can be used in automating a process, let's take a look at one step in the automation process and use that to discuss the options available. One such step is automating the creation of the AMI used for the GitLab application servers. The approach I am going to describe here is a bit different from the upgrade process for the poc. Rather than updating the GitLab application on the standalone server via yum install, I'm going to look at how to install and configure a new release of GitLab from scratch. Doing a fresh install will allow us to start with an up-to-date base Ubuntu AMI.[42]

---

[41] This is one of those lead administrator decisions that I fought for and lost, BTW.
[42] Alternatively, you could start with a public GitLab AMI in order to skip having to install GitLab software on the base AMI.

CHAPTER 19   LIGHTS, CAMERA, ACTION!

To automate the creation of a new application server AMI, let's look at the manual steps needed to accomplish this. These high-level steps are as follows:

1. Establish a connection to AWS.
2. Spin up an EC2 instance.
3. Install GitLab and other supporting software on the instance.
4. Configure the GitLab application.
5. Stop the EC2 instance.
6. Create the application server AMI from that instance.
7. Terminate the EC2 instance.

Looking at this list, we can see that there are two aspects to the automation task: managing AWS resources and managing the software configuration. As we will soon see, there are a lot of tools that can be used to automate either one of these aspects. Resource management tools are used to handle the former, and configuration management tools are used to handle the latter.

Resource Management Tools

For this automation task, there are two AWS resources that need to be managed: an EC2 instance and the resulting AMI. So what tools are available to manage AWS resources? The good news is, Amazon has provided a number of ways to manage their resources. The bad news is, Amazon has provided a number of ways that you are going to have to choose from and learn about.

Using the AWS Command Line Interface

One way of managing AWS resources is via the AWS Command Line Interface (a.k.a. the CLI). As the name implies, it uses an operating system's command line (e.g., bash or Window's shell) to establish a connection to AWS and manage its resources. You can find out more about the AWS CLI here: https://aws.amazon.com/cli/. To use it, you need to first install it for your particular OS. You'll also need to set up authentication credentials[43]

---

[43] The CLI provides a number of ways to specify those credentials, including command-line options, credential files, and environment variables.

to a user that has the permissions needed for the resources you plan to manage. Once the CLI is in place, you simply run commands such as "aws run-instances --image-id blah-blah." CLI commands return output in JSON format that you will need to parse with a tool such as jq to extract information such as the instance-id. As you can guess, it is not the easiest method of managing resources but is great for system administrators to make ad hoc queries of resources.

Using the AWS Software Development Kit

A second way of managing AWS resources is via an AWS Software Development Kit (a.k.a. SDK). If you are a developer, you'll realize that this is a programming-level interface to managing AWS resources. What programming languages, you might ask? There are about a dozen of them supported by AWS ranging from Java, Python, Ruby, Go, and even JavaScript. You can find more information here: https://aws.amazon.com/developer/tools/.

Python is a common language that is used by many AWS developers (and is the underlying language used by the AWS CLI). The Python SDK is in the form of the boto3 module that you download via pip. At the time of this writing, Python version 3 is the preferred version to use with the SDK. Like the CLI, the SDK authenticates with AWS in a variety of ways.[44] As you might expect, Python uses an object model to manage AWS resources such as an EC2 instance. This makes it easier to use than the CLI. Also, you can use Python json modules to directly access elements of the JSON results without having to parse the results first. Other programming languages have the same kind of features that make manipulating resources easier.

If you look at the reference manuals for the AWS CLI and SDK, your head is likely to swirl with all the options provided to manage AWS resources. Using the resource manuals alone won't give you a clue as to how all these resources interact, which is why Amazon provides "Getting Started" guides to get you going. To help you get further proficient in using the CLI or SDK, there are also a myriad number of books available.[45] If you are thinking that mastering either the CLI or an SDK requires a high learning curve, you are correct.

---

[44] Unfortunately, some of the SDK authentication methods conflict with the CLI authentication methods, so beware if you use both the SDK and the CLI.

[45] Many of which tend to be sorely out of date.

CHAPTER 19 LIGHTS, CAMERA, ACTION!

Using AWS CloudFormation

This brings us to a third, higher-level way of managing AWS resources: AWS CloudFormation. CloudFormation uses templates to define resources either in the form of JSON documents or the more preferred YAML documents. With templates, you specify what you want the resources to look like, and CloudFormation determines the order in which objects should be created. You can find out more information here: https://docs.aws.amazon.com/AWSCloudFormation/latest/UserGuide/Welcome.html.

What is interesting about CloudFormation is that once a template is applied to create an initial set of resources, it maintains a state of those resources. If you make changes to the template, you can reapply it to update those managed objects, delete them, or create new ones accordingly. To aid with this, CloudFormation has an interactive design tool to generate the template for you. Although there is a learning curve for CloudFormation, it is lower than the learning curves for the CLI and SDK.

Using Third-Party Resource Management Tools

More experienced developers will realize that this is similar to resource management tools such as Puppet, Chef, Terraform, or Ansible that are used to manage a set of resources by tracking their state. And indeed, it is so. Tools such as CloudFormation, Puppet, Chef, and Terraform are good for managing a set of resources that will exist for long periods of time, such as databases, application servers, web servers, and the like. System administrators like these tools since they can apply changes and enforce them across a large number of resources.

The Short-Term Resource Management Problem

Unfortunately, tools like CloudFormation, Puppet, Chef, and Terraform aren't good for short-term resources such as the EC2 instance that we need to spin up and configure in order to create an AMI before terminating it. This is where Ansible comes in. Ansible is a tool that uses playbooks composed of tasks that may be encapsulated into roles to perform administrative tasks. As it turns out, like Puppet, Chef, and Terraform, Ansible has modules for managing AWS resources. You can find out more about the Ansible AWS modules here: www.ansible.com/integrations/cloud/amazon-web-services.

A Brief Overview of Ansible

Ansible playbooks and roles are YAML-formatted files. Like the other resource management tools, you define what you want and Ansible figures out how to create and/or update it. For example, you can specify an EC2 instance as a task in a playbook like the following:

```
- name: start an instance and Add EBS
  amazon.aws.ec2_instance:
    name: "public-withebs-instance"
    vpc_subnet_id: subnet-5ca1ab1e
    instance_type: t2.micro
    key_name: "prod-ssh-key"
    security_group: default
    volumes:
      - device_name: /dev/sda1
        ebs:
          volume_size: 16
          delete_on_termination: true
```

Each time the playbook is run, it looks to see if the given object exists. If not, it creates it. If it does, it compares the instance's attributes to the Ansible description and makes changes to the instance if needed. If no changes are needed, Ansible simply continues with the rest of the playbook. Ansible adheres to a principle called idempotent, meaning that if a playbook is run more than once, a task is ignored if it meets the given conditions; you don't end up with a duplicate instance. This makes rerunning playbooks easy whenever an error is encountered.

Later on in the playbook, if you want to delete that instance, you simply add a task as follows:

```
- name: terminate the given instance
  amazon.aws.ec2_instance:
    instance_id: i-xxxxxx
    state: absent
```

You could, of course, do all this using the AWS CLI or SDK. However, you will have to add code that performs all the underlying checks that Ansible makes with the single task. It is doable, but tedious to do. In case you are wondering, the Ansible AWS modules use the Python SDK to implement the specific AWS tasks. The hard work is done for you. By the way, there is a task that creates AMIs. It looks like the following:

```
- name: Basic AMI Creation
  amazon.aws.ec2_ami:
    instance_id: i-xxxxxx
    wait: true
    name: newtest
    tags:
      Name: newtest
      Service: TestService
```

Configuration Management Tools

Enough about resource management tools. Let's switch gears and look at various configuration management tools that will allow us to install and configure software packages on a given server. We'll first look at how Amazon handles configuration management since that is how we started with the resource management tools.

Using AWS User Data

The primary way AWS handles configuration is through the use of "user data." User data comes into play when an instance resource first comes up. With user data, you can specify a list of commands to be executed, such as yum install, to prepare your server before it is put into use. You can also update metadata about the EC2 instance by changing the server's hostname, for example. In addition to a shell script, you can also use a Linux feature known as cloud-init, which consists of directives. You can find out more about cloud-init at https://cloud-init.io/. You can find out more about AWS user data at https://docs.aws.amazon.com/AWSEC2/latest/UserGuide/ec2-instance-metadata.html.

User data is injected into a server when it is created using any of the AWS resource management tools discussed so far. This includes the AWS CLI, an AWS SDK, and CloudFormation templates. Note that cloud-init is used by AWS behind the scenes to set up the .ssh/authorized_keys file so that you can log in via ssh once the server is up and running. A disadvantage of using AWS user data to install and configure your server is that it increases the time needed to boot up your server. It also doesn't handle errors well. In addition, you can't use user data to enforce a configuration. Once software is installed and configured on a server at boot time, it can be modified manually later, which leads to "snow-flake" configurations.

Using Puppet, Chef, or Ansible

Fortunately, some of the resource management tools we've talked about so far, such as Puppet, Chef, and Ansible, can also be used for configuration management. In fact, these tools are primarily designed for configuration management; they enable resource management as a secondary service. Of those tools, Terraform, is purely a resource management tool. Like the AWS tools, you can define AWS user data with Terraform to prepare a newly created server.

Using Puppet, Chef, or Ansible, you can configure your server after the fact (i.e., after it has been spun up and running). In addition, you use these tools to enforce a server's configuration to ensure that the software installed on the system is the correct version and is configured properly. These tools also enable making changes to a server's software configuration either by upgrading the version of a package or by changing a specific attribute in a configuration file.

One thing to note about Puppet and Chef is that they require special agents to be installed on the server being managed in order for these tools to communicate with it. You might think, no problem, we can bake the agent into an AMI. Remember, though, we are trying to automate the installation process on an AMI with a basic operating system such as Ubuntu or CentOS. In order to install software using these tools, you first have to install their agents. This is where user data typically comes in. When you create a server using a resource management tool, you can install the agent via user data.

Ansible, on the other hand, is a bit different. All it needs is an SSH connection, which we've already seen is enabled via cloud-init by AWS automatically. It's one of the advantages of using Ansible over Puppet and Chef. In addition, you can make quick ad hoc queries and changes using Ansible that you can't do using the other tools. Purists tend to not like this feature, but system administrators love it.

How Configuration Management Tools Install and Configure Software

All of these third-party tools allow you to easily install a software package with a specific version using a single resource description or task. And configuring software such as GitLab can be done by copying files from your source code repository to the server replacing variables within them as necessary. They also allow you to reapply manifests, recipes, or playbooks to ensure the correct version of software and configuration options on a given server are in conformity with them.

The beauty of these tools is that you can mix and match them as needed. You are not stuck having to use one tool. For example, you can use CloudFormation to set up the AWS resources, use Ansible to install and configure the GitLab software, and use the AWS CLI to create the resulting AMI. You'll just have to figure out how to orchestrate all these tools to automate the process.

A Word About Packer

Since we are discussing how to automate the AMI creation process, I would be remiss if I didn't mention an orchestration tool that is well adept at automating the entire process: HCP[46] Packer. You can find out more about Packer here: www.packer.io/. This is a multipurpose tool that you can use to create not just AWS AMIs, but Docker images, VMware images, VirtualBox images, and the like. At a high level, the tool uses builders (such as AWS) and provisioners (such as Ansible) to perform the creation of one or more images. For a given task, you pick the builders and provisioners that you need to create the image. It performs all of the steps described at the start of this section. For this process, I highly recommend looking into this tool.

Automating Upgrades to the Gitaly Cluster

The next component upgrade to automate is the Gitaly cluster (or the standalone Gitaly server, if that is what you use). In some ways, this is easier to automate than the creation of the application AMI. Note, however, that there are two scenarios that you need to automate. The first is the simple upgrade where you go to each Gitaly server and

---

[46] HCP is shorthand for HashiCorp Cloud Platform. If you plan on doing a web search, use HCP Packer as the search term as packer by itself will give you results on meat packing plants and the like.

upgrade the package; likewise for the Praefect servers. It is important to upgrade these in sequence rather than in parallel since you want part of the cluster to remain in operation during the upgrade process. What makes this tricky is that you have to wait for each upgrade to complete, which could be based on going to sleep for a period of time to give the upgrade time to complete and/or monitoring the gitlab-ctl status.

The second scenario you need to automate is the clean replacement of each of the Gitaly and Praefect servers. A good time to do this is during a major release upgrade where you will most likely have to do a shutdown of the entire system. Alternatively, you can do a server replacement every three to six months. Replacement would consist of using the GitLab AMI created for the application servers and updating the gitlab.rb file to run as a Gitaly or Praefect service accordingly. For the Gitaly server, you'll also have to bring up a new server with a dummy secondary volume and then switch the secondary volumes between the old and new Gitaly servers.

What makes the replacement scenario tricky is that the Gitaly and Praefect server IP addresses will change, so you'll need to update the data storage configurations accordingly and update the Praefect ELB to swap out the old Praefect servers with the new ones. Although you could do the replacement scenario while the GitLab service is running, it is best to do this when there is little to no activity on the servers. Unlike a simple package upgrade that completes relatively quickly, replacing servers takes a longer time and could impact data integrity.

Automating Upgrades to Shared Runner Managers

As for the shared runner managers, it is best to create new ones from scratch each time and pause existing runners. The reason for pausing existing runners rather than deleting them outright is that there may be long-running jobs that need to be completed before destroying the runner manager. You can then wait a day or so for all jobs on older runner managers to complete before deleting the manager. Of course, you could decide on doing a simple package upgrade on the runner managers, but you risk interfering with ongoing jobs, especially if something goes wrong.[47]

---

[47] In my experience, there have been times when an upgrade of a runner manager has an issue that fails jobs due to the manager. By keeping the older runner managers around, it is easy to pause the new runner managers and unpause the old ones. This will buy you time to figure out what the issue is.

CHAPTER 19   LIGHTS, CAMERA, ACTION!

Orchestrating the Upgrade Process

Let's now cycle back to the topic of orchestrating the upgrade process. I mentioned at the start of this section that GitLab CI/CD pipelines are a good solution for this. I say pipelines plural since there will be times when you want to run or rerun just one part of the upgrade process rather than the entire process in one giant pipeline. This is especially true when a failure occurs somewhere in the middle of the process. In these cases, you don't want to have to redo work that was already completed successfully. Child pipelines are the easier solution in that they keep everything under one project; however, there might be cases where a multi-project pipeline will work.[48]

Creating a Docker Image to Support the Automation Process

In any case, you'll need to automate the build Dockerfile(s) used for the upgrade automation process. Whatever tools and programming languages you decide to use for your upgrade automation, you will need to create at least one Docker image with those tools and languages installed. It is highly unlikely that you'll find a Docker image on Docker Hub with everything installed on it; however, you can start with an image that already has some of the tools installed (for instance, Ansible that also has Python installed with it).

Creating the build Docker image is a prime example of using a multi-project pipeline. In this scenario, you have a project with the sole purpose of creating the build Docker image and storing it in the GitLab repositories (both the staging and production GitLab services). The downstream projects would then use the image from the respective GitLab repository to perform the upgrade processes. In addition to a build Docker image, you might also consider creating a test Docker image (used to test your automation process) in the same project or in its own project.

---

[48] I realize I didn't discuss child or multi-project pipelines in this book, but they are well described in the GitLab documentation, so you should be able to figure out how to use them on your own.

Testing the Automation Process

Speaking of testing, let's end this section with some ideas on how to test your automation. You may think testing your automation framework is either unnecessary or impossible, but I assure you, testing your automation framework is doable and worth the effort. After all, your framework will evolve over time as your GitLab services add new services or change the way some components work.

If you used a tool like Ansible with all of its ever-changing modules, you probably expect that there already are ways of testing Ansible. And so there are. The most common tool you should be aware of is ansible-test. As it turns out, ansible-test is built into the Ansible core, so it is readily available. You can find out more about ansible-test here: `www.ansible.com/blog/introduction-to-ansible-test`.

If you have some Python code and are using the boto3 module to interact with AWS, you can use the standard Python testing tool, pytest, along with a module specific to mocking AWS objects called moto. With this combination, you can mock AWS entities and perform tests on them to ensure that your scripts and/or tools (including Ansible) are behaving as you expect. This combination enables testing without the high overhead and costs of spinning up real AWS objects.

There are other testing frameworks that you might find useful. Even if you don't use Ruby in your automation infrastructure, it has an intuitive framework called RSpec that can be used to test your automation code. In particular, there is a testing framework built on top of RSpec called ServerSpec that is useful for testing the structure of an AMI or a Dockerfile. You can find out more about RSpec at `https://rspec.info/` and ServerSpec at `https://serverspec.org/`.

Chef has a testing framework called Chef InSpec that can also be used to test AWS (and other) cloud infrastructure. You don't need to use Chef in your automation when using Chef InSpec (although if you do use Chef to manage your cloud infrastructure, Chef InSpec is a natural testing tool for that). You can find more information about how to use Chef InSpec to test your cloud infrastructure at `https://docs.chef.io/inspec/platforms/`.

As you can see, there are a number of frameworks available to test your automation process. It is worth trying some of these out before committing to a specific set. A good place to start experimenting is to test your AMI structure after it is built. Your tests should include checking that the correct version of GitLab is installed on your AMI and that it is configured as you expect. By the way, if you use HCP Packer, check their documentation to see what testing options they integrate with. Happy exploring!

Summary

In summary, we've covered the following topics in this chapter:

- Discussed the costs and options of setting up a production-level service
- Described the steps for creating a production-level service in AWS
- Showed how to switch from a standalone Gitaly server to a Gitaly cluster
- Learned how to prepare for disaster recovery using GitLab Geo
- Investigated various ways to automate the upgrade process
- Considered ways to test the automation process

And with that, we have come to the end of the book. Thank you for taking the time to read it. Whether you are a developer using GitLab for your development work or an administrator needing to maintain a self-managed service, I hope you found the information in this book useful.

Index

A

Access Control Lists (ACLs), 666
Administrative settings, 796
Administrative UI, 650–653, 726, 730, 742, 745, 791–792, 795, 799
Administrators, 271, 282, 791, 794
AdminTestProjects, 743
Agile methodology, 323, 333, 341
Alpine Docker Hub description, 111
Alpine Docker Hub how-to page, 112
Alpine Docker Hub page, 110
Alpine Docker Hub tags, 113
Alpine Linux Docker image, 109
Alpine package manager apk, 114
AmazonEC2FullAccess, 711
Amazon Machine Image (AMI), 619
Ansible, 874–878, 881
App.java, 221, 225
Application Programming Interface (API), 419
    Jira (*see* Jira)
    REST (*see* REST)
    GraphQL (*see* GraphQL)
Application servers, 846–848, 853, 857, 864, 871, 879
"apt-cache madison gitlab-runner" command, 715
Artifactory, 406, 512
Artifacts
    access, 209, 210
    additional artifacts options, 220
    build.sh script, 206
    vs. caches, 221
    creation, 209, 210
    directory creation, 207
    download artifacts, GitLab, 213, 214
    generated objects, 205–208
    .gitignore file, 207
    jobs, follow-on stages, 211, 212
    merge request, 216–220
    output, build job, 209
    output directory, 210
    redirect warning, html artifact, 211
    rename artifacts zip file, 215, 216
    unit test
        build job, 211, 212
        result, 212, 213
    update scripts/build.sh file, 207, 208
    web page, 211
ASG-controlled servers, 810
Associated MR, 314–316
    after the merge, 316
    issue was closed, 315, 316
    Mark as ready, 314
    README file, 314
    workflow, 316
Auditor role, 271
Aurora, 574, 863
Authentication, 422, 435, 436, 446
Authentication methods, 873
Auto DevOps, 17
Auto-scaling application, 822
Auto-scaling group (ASG), 619, 686, 687
    capacity requirements, 691

INDEX

Auto-scaling group (ASG) (*cont.*)
    create, 686, 687
    EC2 listing, 696
    ELB, 689, 690
    ELB list, 696, 697
    gitlab-ctl status, 697
    group size, 692
    health checks, 690, 691
    instance launch options, 688, 689
    launch template, 687, 688
    notifications, 694
    review, 695
    scale-in protection, 693
    scaling policy, 692, 693
    scaling rules, 702, 703
    standalone GitLab server, 699, 700
    tagging instances, 700, 701
    UI, 698
    updating name, 702
Auto-scaling shared runners, 706, 707
Auto-scaling shared runners setup, AWS
    config.toml file (*see* config.toml file creation)
    docker info command output, 742
    docker-machine, 707
    docker status checking, 751
    gitlab-runner configuration, 719–725
    gitlab-runner restart, 739
    gitlab-runner status checkup, 740
    instance runner entry creation, 726–730
    preliminary, 707–713
    register-me.sh script, 731
    results, register-me.sh script, 732
    runner instance list, administrative UI, 742, 743
    runner manager server, 714–718
    S3 object cache verification, 747–750
    spun-up runner EC2 instances viewing, 740, 741
    testing running jobs, 743–747
AWS
    auto-scaling group, 806
    CLI, 872, 873, 876, 878
    cloud, 3, 596
    CloudFormation, 874
    Direct Connect service, 841, 842
    domain name, 531
    domain registration, 531, 532
    DR, 863, 864
    Gitaly cluster, 854
    key pairs, 845
    network load balancer, 860
    RDS, 855, 857
    regions, 841
    resources, 872, 873
    SSH key pair
        creation, 529, 530
        creation form, 529, 530
        EC2 dashboard, 528
        formats, 529
        selection, 528, 529
    user data, 876, 877
    VPC environments, 843
AWS account
    Admin user, 520
    Admin user group, 519, 520
    creation, 518
    IAM, 519
    MFA, 521

B

Ban user, 803
Bash, 375, 377, 381
Bash scripts, 153, 155, 642

Bastion firewall security group, 607
Bastion servers, 602, 603, 846
    Bastion AWS console window, 609
    configure ssh forwarding, 611
        access private servers from Bastion server, 617
        add ssh key to Pageant, 616
        create session configuration, 613, 614
        enable ssh forwarding, 614
        generate Putty private key, 613
        import OpenSSH key into Putty, 612
        Putty, 611, 612
        PuTTY session configuration, 615
        restart Pageant and re-add private key, 617
        set host IP, 615
        test connectivity, 615, 616
    create second bastion server, 609, 610
    launch server, 603
        AMI selection, 604
        configure network settings, 605, 606
        create security group, 606
        instance type and ssh key pair, 605
        set server name and OS, 603, 604
        storage configuration, 607, 608
    test connectivity, 608, 609
    view Bastion instances, 610, 611
before_script keyword, 116
Binary files
    Git LFS
        cases, 512
        feature, 509
        marking files to be managed, 510, 511
        migrating existing files, 511
        prerequisites to, 510
    storing versioned, 509
    text file, 508

bind_dn and password, 801
Blocking users, 802
Branches
    cache, 237
    committing changes, 32, 33
    committing multiple changes, 34–36
    merge request pipelines, 172
    new branch creation, 26–29
    pipelines, 166
    reviewing project changes, 29–31
    visualizing branch changes, 33, 34
Branching strategies, 63, 64
Build-artifacts, 217, 218
Build job, 381–383, 385, 401
build.sh script, 410
Bulk edit, 302

C

Caches
    vs. artifacts, 221
    build job rerun result, 234–236
    build job results, 230–232
    build job updates, Maven, 224–226
    cache keys
        build job, 239
        build job result, 240–242
        unit test, 240
    clear caches, 246, 247
    create multiple caches, pipeline
        branch cache, 237
        cache key, 237
        issue, 236
        parallel job, 236
        separate caches, 237, 238
        target files, 236
    directories, build job, 228

INDEX

Caches (*cont.*)
    git ignore file, Maven target
        directories, 226
    Maven, 221–223
    Maven build script, 224
    Maven pom.xml file, 222
    Maven settings.xml file, 223
    pipeline updates, cache maven
        objects, 227–231
    policy, 243
    read-only caches
        deploy jobs, 243, 245
        deploy jobs results, 245, 246
        hidden job, 243, 244
    unit test, cache directories, 229
    unit-test-job results, 232–234
Chef, 874, 877, 881
Chicken-and-egg scenario, 856
CI/CD configuration file
    CI/CD editor, 139
    CI/CD variables defining at project
        level, 128, 129
    defining, 121
    defining, manually running pipelines,
        124, 125
    defining rules, 121
    echo commands, 122
    .gitlab-ci.yml file, 135
    global *vs.* local job variable
        settings, 122
    include types, 140
    masking secret values (*see* Masking
        secret values, /CD variables)CI
    multiple files, 135–138
    predifined variables usage, 123
    reusing jobs, 140–143
    reusing jobs,
        reference tags, 144–149
    setting descriptions and default
        values, 125–127
    shell variable syntax, 121
    string value, 121
CI/CD variable expressions
    CI_PIPELINE_SOURCE, 161, 163
        (*see also* CI_PIPELINE_SOURCE)
    compound expressions, 161
    GitLab predefined variables, 161
    programming languages, 159
    regular expression matches, 160, 161
    string comparisons, 159, 160
    variable status tests, 160
CI_COMMIT_BRANCH, 165, 167
CI_COMMIT_REF_SLUG variable, 379
CiJobStatus, 463, 464, 478–480
CI_MERGE_REQUEST_SOURCE_
    BRANCH, 165
CI_MERGE_REQUEST_TARGET_
    BRANCH, 165
CI_PIPELINE_SOURCE
    deploy-dev-job
        merge request event, result, 165, 166
        non-main branches, 163
        pipeline run summary, 163, 164
        result, push event, 164
        variable, 161
        web event, pipeline run
            summary, 165
CI_REGISTRY_IMAGE variable, 379
Classic load balancer (CLB), 546, 547
Classless Inter-Domain Routing (CIDR),
    524, 551, 843
Cleanup-failure job, 189, 190
Cleanup policies, 387–389
Cloning, 65, 67
Cloning with https
    Git Credential Manager, 69–71

INDEX

preparing local environment, 67
remote environment, 67
URL determination, 68, 69
username and password
   credentials, 71, 72
Cloning with ssh
   cloning project with ssh, 79, 80
   debugging common connecting
      issues, 78
   key pair creation, local
      environment, 72–74
   registering ssh public key, 74–76
   security, 72
   testing ssh connectivity, 77, 78
   URL determination, 79
Cloud-based implementations, 509
Cloud providers, 514, 516, 833–835, 840, 854, 863, 864, 866, 867, 871
Cloud provider services, 834
Cloud service, 509, 514, 659, 706, 806, 865
CloudWatch, 702, 703, 810, 840
Cointainer Registry Service
   ELB listener settings, 782, 783
   ELB security group, 782
   GitLab configuration, 780, 781
   nginx, 781
   verify, 783
Colleague sign-up page, 7, 8
Color-coded labels, 303
Command Line Interface (CLI), 872–874, 876, 878
Commit hash, 30, 35
Commit message text box, 23
Commit "My first commit", 31
"Common setup before test" message, 147
Compound expressions, 161
config.toml file creation
   brackets, 735

global options section, 735
runners.cache subsection, 737
runners.docker subsection, 737
runners.machine.autoscaling
   subsection, 738
runners.machine.other configuration
   options, 738
runners.machine subsection, 737, 738
runners section, 735, 736
subsections, runners section, 736
Continuous delivery, definition, 193
Continuous integration and continuous
   delivery/deployment (CI/CD), 42
editor, 139, 148
pipeline configuration file, 94
variables, 271
CPUUtlilization metric, 703
Create MRs
   associated branch, 311
   associated MR, 314–316
   development life cycle, 311
   generated, 312, 313
   label-example, 311
   list with issue labels, 314
   MyShellPipeline, 311
Curl
   authentication, 435
   jq tool
      extract information, 439, 440
      JSON document, 438, 439
      JSON responses, 437
   programming languages, 441
   query, 436
   resource
      creation, 441–443
      deletion, 443, 444
      manipulation, 441
      modification, 444

INDEX

D

DB subnet group, 570–572, 581
Deactivate user, 803
Debugging, 636, 637
Deleting users, 805
demoLocalEdits, 83, 87
Dependency proxy, 272
deploy.sh file, 411, 412
devBranchA, 47, 48, 50, 57
Disaster recovery (DR), 516, 837, 838
    alarms, 862, 863
    AWS replication, 867
    communications, 863
    considerations, 863, 864
    emergency services, 863
    plan, 867
    RDS service, 866
    Redis service, 866
    S3 cross-region replication, 866
Docker
    agents, 108
    case, 108, 109
    default image overriding, 118–120
    defining tasks, 116, 117
    exploring docker hub, 109–112
    GitLab, 108
    Jenkins, 106–108
    machine, 103
    specifying new default image, 113–115
DOCKER_AUTH_CONFIG, 399, 400
Docker-build job, 380–382
Docker Engine installation, 717, 718
Docker Engine software, 717
Dockerfiles, 109, 111, 377–378, 380, 394, 880, 881
Docker Hub, 375–378, 380, 381
Docker images, 106, 108, 109, 120
    access container registry, 376
    bash, 375
    cleanup policies, 387–389
    create, 375
    delete unneeded image, 386
    Docker Hub, 375
    with package registry
        access binary object repository, 406
        automate cleanup, 416, 417
        deploy-dev-job output, 412
        Maven packages in MyShellPipeline, 413
        multiple pipeline runs, 415, 416
        view package details in registry, 413–415
    process for create and store
        build job, 381
        contents, Dockerfile, 378
        contents, .gitlab-ci.yml file, 379
        docker-build job, 380
        Dockerfile, 377
        docker-setup, 377
        explore Dockerfile, 377, 378
        .gitlab-ci.yml, 377
        output, build job, 383
        output, docker-build job, 382
    share Docker images
        access container registry images outside of GitLab, 395
        access image from another project, 390
        create personal access token, 396–398
        DOCKER_AUTH_CONFIG authentication string, 399, 400
        enable access another's container registry, 392–394
        investigate denied access, 391

INDEX

project deploy token creation, 402–404
roup deploy token creation, 404, 405
security concerns with DOCKER_AUTH_CONFIG, 401
set DOCKER_AUTH_CONFIG as group CI/CD variable, 400
store jar file using Maven
    changes to pom.xml, 407, 408
    changes to settings.xml, 408, 409
    change to build.sh script, 410
    deploy.sh, 411, 412
    extract credentials with maven-env.sh script, 409
    unit-test.sh, 411
view container registry changes, 383, 384
DOCKER_IMAGE variable, 379
Docker-in-Docker, 380, 736
Docker-manager package installation, 718, 719
docker rm command, 386, 387
DOCKER_TLS_CERTDIR system, 736
Domain
    configure records, 561
    connectivity, 564
    ELB endpoint, 562, 563
    hosted zone record, 559, 560
    routing policy, 560
    simple record creation form, 561, 562
    target health option, 563, 564
Don't Repeat Yourself (DRY) principle, 140, 845
Doxygen, 504, 505
Dynamic Application Software Testing (DAST), 140

E

ElastiCache option, 591, 594
ElastiCache services, 592, 605
Elastic Block Store (EBS), 638, 859
Elastic Compute Cloud (EC2) service, 528, 542, 567, 619
Elastic File Service (EFS), 659, 837
Elastic IPs (EIPs), 527
Elastic Load Balancer (ELB), 545
    health check, 556, 557
    listeners, 554, 555
    name/scheme configuration, 547
    network mappings, 548, 549
    SG (*see* Security group (SG))
    special attributes, 557, 558
    spin up and spin down, 558, 559
    TLS certificate, 555
Export project, 288, 289
External database, 629
external_diffs service, 779
External Redis database, 630

F

FAIL_UNIT_TEST variable, 182
Failures
    cleanup-deploy job, 191, 192
    cleanup-failure job, 189
    cleanup jobs, definition, 189
    cleanup stage, 188
    conditional ignore job failure, 182, 183
    deploy-dev-job failure, 190
    exit codes
        FAIL_LINT_TEST, 188
        lint-test-job, 185, 186
        lint test result, 187
        lint tools, 184

INDEX

Failures (*cont.*)
    pipeline result,lint test, 187
    scripts/lint-test.sh script, 184, 185
  ignore job failure, 180–182
  lint test failure
    pipeline result, 180
    pipeline run, 179
  lint-test-job, 178, 179
  pipeline process, 178
  rerun failed job, external events, 192
File-based conditions, 171–173, 204
File-based rule conditions, 168, 171, 172
Files generation
  generated .gitlab-ci.yml file, 500, 501
  generated index.html File, 499
  generated style.css file, 500
  .gitlab-ci.yml file, 498
  Plain HTML template, 498
  and public directory, 497
  web elements, 496
First GitLab project page, 7
Free-tier self-management, 513

G

Generated .gitlab-ci.yml file, 500, 501
Generated index.html File, 499
Generated style.css file, 500
GetObjectVersion permission, 710
GFML, 300
Gitaly cluster, 847
  AMI, 859
  ASG/ELB configuration, 861
  availability zones, 854
  AWS, 854
  chicken-and-egg scenario, 856
  concept, 850
  configuration process, 857
  connectivity, 858
  database, 850
  election strategy, 852
  migration, 861
  monitoring service, 851
  PgBouncer, 857
  Praefect, 853
  Praefect-1 instance, 858
  Praefect load balancer, 853, 860
  Praefect nodes, 859
  Praefect tracking database
    creation, 855
    provisioning server, 856, 857
  SG, 855
  testing, 861
  update, 860
  upgrade, 878, 879
  VPC, 854
Gitaly server, 837, 849
  checks, 829
  configuration, 860
  hold off gitlab-ce package, 825, 826
  install specific version, gitlab-ce, 828
  latest apt package versions, 824
  non-gitlab packages, 825
  potential upgrade stops impact,
    826, 827
  and Praefect server, 857
  prepping, 859, 860
  reboot, 828, 829
  RPC interface, 824
  sharding option, 849
  troubleshooting guide, 862
Gitaly service, split off
  admin area, 652
  administrative UI, 650, 651
  changing storage weights, 653
  check command, 647

configuration, 645
configuring standalone, 643
connectivity, 647, 648
copy GitLab secrets file, 642, 643
disable services, 644
disable the internal, 649, 650
EBS, 638
GitLab configuration, 648
GitLab service, 639
install GitLab package, 641, 642
NFS, 638
note about storage weights, 653
repository storage, 652
security group, 639
spinning Standalone, 646
spin up, 640, 641
storage, 645, 646
verify GitLab, 649
view server status, 651
Git configuration
    locating global configuration file, 81
    username and email address, 81
Git Credential Manager, 69–72
GitHub, 1, 2, 290, 402, 495, 510
Git installation, 65, 66
Git install instructions, 66
GitLab, 799
    capabilities, 2
    CI/CD pipelines, 248
    Dedicated service, 518
    definition, 1
    documentation, 66, 78, 853
    free sign-up page, 4
    Git manager, 2
    image repository, 120
    installation process, 567
    Jenkins, 2
    licensed version, 854
    permission model, 268
    runner manager, 830, 831
    runtime environment, 94
    single DevOps platform, 1
    source code management tool, 1
GitLab Account setup
    cloud environment, 3
    main interface, 8, 9
    MyFirstProject creation, 6–8
    SaaS account creation, 4–6
    SaaS option, 3
    VirtualBox, 3
    Windows or Mac installations, 3
GitLab-Auto servers, 808
.gitlab-ci.yml file, 93–95, 120, 135, 377, 379, 498, 744
.gitlab-ci.yml keyword, 220
gitlab.com, 513, 514, 517, 518, 535
GitLab configuration file
    account validation, first pipeline execution, 97, 98
    advantage, 93
    associating jobs, 96
    .CI/CD pipeline configuration, 94, 95
    .gitlab-ci.yml file, 94
    pipeline job execution, stages, 99–101
    project's status impacts, 105, 106
    restarting pipeline, 98
    viewinig job's output, 102, 103
    viewinig project's pipeline status page, 104
GitLab Flavored Markdown Language (GMFL), 297
GitLab Geo, 838, 839
    considerations, 865
    mirror services, 864
    setting up, 865
    tracking database, 866

INDEX

GitLab interface
    accessing dashboard home page, 13-15
    setting user preferences, 12, 13
    user profile updation, 10, 11
gitlab-loadbalancer-sec-group, 550, 569, 591, 622, 639, 683, 714, 782
GitLab pages
    access pages, 505, 508
    alternative URLs, 507, 508
    caveat, 506
    certificate, 502
    creation, 495
    creation without templates, 506
    deploy pages, 508
    Doxygen, 504, 505
    examples, 503, 504
    feature, 495
    project templates
        creation, 496, 497
        files generation, 497-501
        listing, 496
    running the pipeline, 501
    standalone service, 508
    UI, 495
    unique domain option, 507
    view, 503
    visibility, 505, 506
GitLab registry service
    auto-scaling, 790
    create new AMI, 790
    define page domain, 784
    DNS record, 786, 787
    ELB pages service, 785, 786
    nginx, 788
    TLS certificate, 785
    update, 787
    verify running process, 788, 789
GitLabRunnerManagerRole, 711, 712
GitLab server, spin up
    AMI, 619, 620
    CE AMI, 621
    check services, 631, 632
    configuration changes, 631
    debugging, 636, 637
    EC2 AMI, 620
    ELB instance status, 636
    ELB option, 632, 633
    external PostgreSQL, 629
    external Redis database, 630
    external URL, 627, 628
    gitlab-ctl status, 632
    instance from image, 621, 622
    instance via ssh, 624, 625
    internal PostgreSQL, 628
    internal Redis database, 629, 630
    Let's Encrypt section, 626, 627
    log in, 637
    network settings, 623
    nginx service, 634
    official AMI, 620
    PostgreSQL database, 625, 626
    RDS database, 629
    reverse proxy, 635
    storage, 624
Git LFS
    cases, 512
    feature, 509
    marking files to be managed, 510, 511
    migrating existing files, 511
    prerequisites to, 510
git lfs migrate command, 511
Git repository, 72, 80, 495, 509, 637, 751, 849-854, 857, 861, 866
Google Compute Engine (GCE), 108, 231
GraphQL API

INDEX

abstract types section
    description, 488, 489
    interface abstract type, 490–492
    union abstract type, 489, 490
connections section
    connection fields, 482, 483
    connection types, 483, 484
    description, 481
    pagination arguments, 481, 482
    subsections, 481
enumeration types section
    CiJobStatus, 480
    description, 479, 480
    sort orders, 479
explorer, 458–460
header, 446
HTTP methods, 445
input types section
    CiVariableInput type, 487, 488
    description, 487
    jobPlay mutation, 487, 488
introspection, 470–472
mutation section
    createIssue action, 485, 486
    description, 485
    returned fields, 486
MY_API_TOKEN, 445
object
    creation, 454, 455
    deletion, 457
    updation, 455, 456
object types section
    definition, 477
    description, 477, 478
    job field arguments, 478, 479
    job field documentation, 478
pagination, 468–470
PRIVATE-TOKEN, 446

queries
    parts, 446
    reading, 447, 448
    results, 447
    retrieving issues, project, 449–451
    sorted issues list, project, 452, 453
    type section, 474, 475
reference
    documentation, 472
    sections, 473
requests, 445, 460, 461
    fullPath option, 462
    job fields, 465, 466
    job query results, 467, 468
    number of jobs, 464, 465
    paging information, 466, 467
    project query, 461, 462
    successful/failed jobs, 463
run, curl, 446
scalar types section, 475, 476
web browser URLs, 458
Group-and project-specific resources management
    CI/CD variables, 271
    packages and registries, 272, 273
    product/team based, 271
    runners, 272
Groups
    activity, 251
    add members, 252, 253
    deploy tokens, 404, 405
    developer-specific views, 262, 263
    group member change role options, 257
    group-specific projects, 250
    group *vs.* project change role lists, 256–258
    invite member form, 252

Groups (cont.)
   maintainer-specific views, 263, 264
   members, 251, 252
   new members, 253
   project impacts, add group
       member, 254
   project invite members form, role
       selection, 255
   project member change role
       options, 257
   project members after role promotion,
       255, 256
   project members and roles, 254
   roles allowed to create projects,
       264, 265
   roles allowed to create subgroups,
       265, 266
   Subgroups (*see* Subgroups)

H

Hardware Virtual Machine (HVM), 619
HashiCorp Cloud Platform (HCP),
   878, 881
HashiCorp Vault, 780, 871
High availability (HA), 516, 836, 837
Host keys, 654–657
HTTP methods, 421, 444, 445

I

Identity and Access Management
   service (IAM)
   IAM role
      creation, 542
      permissions page, 543, 544
      role name/description, 544, 545

      trusted entity, 542, 543
   policy
      creation, 538, 539
      JSON policy editor, 539, 540
      policy name/description, 541
Import failures, 291
Import project, 289–291
Instance-level user, 271
Instance runner entry creation
   gitlab runner tags setting up, 728, 729
   preventing, job requests, 729
   registering runner manager, 726, 727
   retrieving runner authentication
       token, 730
   reviewing, administrative UI, 730
Instance runners, 706, 726, 730
Internal database, 628
Internal Redis database, 629, 630
Issue boards, 341
   adding features, paid
       subscriptions, 352
   closing issue, 345
   editing, 343
   exploring, 341
   group level, 347, 348
   list creation, 342
   moving issue, 346, 347
   moving items, 344, 345
   multiple boards
      agile sprint/kanban planning
         session, 350
      planning session, 351
      review, 351, 352
      switch option, 350, 351
   new project, 349
   toggle view, 342, 343
Iterations, 323, 333

INDEX

J

Jenkins, 2, 93, 94, 106–108, 267, 268, 402
Jenkins as a Service (JaaS), 106–108
Jenkins configurations, 108
Jenkins plug-ins, 2, 107
Jira
    active integration, 367, 368
    API key, 362–364
    Cloud account, 353
    GitLab
        apps selection, 354, 355
        authorization, 358, 359
        configuration, 356, 358
        connection details, 365
        installation, 355, 356
        integrated issues, 368
        integration settings, 364, 365
        issue changes, 371
        issue section, 366, 367
        job information, 372, 373
        namespaces, 360, 361
        trigger/issue matching section, 366
    integrated issues, 369
    integration documentation, 353
    integration features, paid subscriptions, 373
    issue changes, 369–371
    project, 294
Jobs, 94, 96

K

Kanban methodology, 323, 333, 341
Key Management Service (KMS), 659–664, 668, 673, 708, 737
Key-value pairs, 121, 143, 144, 440, 738

Keyword referencing, 143
known_hosts file, 77, 655

L

Labeling issues
    color-coded labels, 303
    editing, 305
    filtering, 304, 305
    issues list, 303, 304
    manage, 306
    and MRs (*see* Merge requests (MRs))
    new label creation, 308, 309
    prioritizing, 306, 307
    promote label to group labels, 309, 310
Launch template, 812–814, 816
LDAP-compatible services, 799
ldap_servers section, 800
Lightweight Directory Access Protocol (LDAP), 268, 269, 801, 802
    active directory authentication service, 799–801
    LDAP-enabled sites, 271
    self-managed GitLab sites, 268
Linking issues
    "blocking", 317
    deleting, 320
    "depends on", 317
    "duplicates", 317
    in GitLab, 317
    linked items, 318–320
    one issue to another, 317–319
    paid subscription, 320
    "relates to", 317
    types, 320
lint tools, 178, 184
Linux-based Git tool, 65

INDEX

Linux shells, 121
Load balancers, 545, 546

M

Mac-and Linux-based filesystems, 78
Making Changes with Git
    branch creation, 83
    branch synchronization, 83
    cleaning local repository, 89, 90
    committing changes, local repository, 86
    GitLab project repository, pushing changes, 87
    git remote-v command, 82
    local repository, 84
    MR creation, 88, 89
    pushing changes, confirming project repository, 87
    staging changes, local repository, 85, 86
Managing issues
    activity, 300, 301
    creating an new issue, 295, 296
    details, 297
    edit, 297, 298
    filtering, 301, 302
    import issues option, 294
    "Learning GitLab" project, 295
    multiple edits, 302, 303
    project-specific issues, 294, 295
    reaction, 298, 299
    top-level dashboard, 293, 294
Man-in-the-middle message, 655
Manual run job, 198
    cancel manual job, 203
    continuous delivery, 193

deploy-dev-job, 194–197
FAIL_PERF_TEST, run perf-test-job, 201
GitLab, 193
perf-test-job, 198–201
perf-test-job fail, 202, 203
pipeline results, cancel deploy job, 203
Masking secret values, CI/CD variables
    CI/CD settings summary, 131
    GitLab, 134
    job build-job, 132
    job unit-test-job, 133
    "Mask variable" flag, 130, 131
    MY_DB_PASSWORD, 134
    MY_DB_PASSWORD variable, 132
    "Protect variable" flag, 130
Maven, 221–231, 233–237, 377, 378, 381, 382, 407–413, 415, 419, 421, 512
Maven Docker image, 227
maven-env.sh file, 409–411
Maven .m2/repository cache, 237, 246
maven-projects directory, 221, 225
"Merge blocked" message, 50
Merge conflicts
    committing conflict resolution change, 53–56
    generation, 49–51
    performing MR merge, 56–59
    resolving methods, 51–53
    reviewing project status, 59–63
    setting up conditions, 47–49
Merge_request_event, 161, 162, 165, 166, 172
Merge requests (MRs)
    creation, 37–39, 311 (see also Create MRs)
    definition, 37

INDEX

merging changing, 43, 44
multiple MRs, 313
reviewing project changes, 44, 45
tracking open MR, 41, 42
viewing details, 39–41
and labeling (*see* Labeling issues)
Merging, 26, 39, 43, 45, 58, 59, 64, 88, 143, 144, 314–316, 371
Milestones
considerations, 333
creation, 324, 325
detail page, 325
issues
adding, 326–328
filtering, 333
project's list, 328, 329
removing, 329
merge requests (MRs), 331, 332
project's summary list, 330
promotion, project to group, 330, 331
top-level dashboard, 332
Multifactor authentication (MFA), 521
my-build-env Docker image, 384
"my-build-env:docker-setup" image, 384, 386
MyFirstBranch, 30–36, 38, 43–45, 57, 58, 80
"MyFirstProject/.git/config" file, 81
"MyFirstProject/.git" directory, 79
MY_PIPELINE_CHOICE, 125–127
MyRegistryProject, 376, 377, 383, 392
MySandboxProject, 274, 276–279
"MyShellPipeline" project, 94, 105, 135, 254, 255, 258
Myspecialplace, 645
MY_TEST_VAR1, 143
MY_TEST_VAR2, 143
MY_VAR2 value, 122

N

Network File Service (NFS), 509, 638, 712, 837, 854
Network mappings, 548, 549
Non-gitlab packages, 825
NOT_DEFINED_VAR reference, 121
"Null" project, 291

O

OmniAuth providers, 799
OpenSSH's ssh-keygen, 73

P, Q

Package registry, 272, 281, 283, 375, 402, 405–409, 411–413, 415–417
Packer, 878, 881
Pageant, 616, 617, 624, 724, 725
Pagination, 428–430, 432, 466, 468–470
PainterTraining group, 249, 251, 254, 262, 276, 311
group overview page, 250
group summary page, 250
See also Groups
Permissions via roles
assignment, 267
CI/CD pipelines, 267
comparision GitLab's permission model with other models, 267, 268
developers, 267
guest role, 266
import members from another project, 270
invite GitLab groups as members, other groups/projects, 269
invite group form, 270
member, group/project, 266

897

INDEX

Permissions via roles (*cont.*)
    reporter role, 266
    special roles, self-managed sites, 271
Personal access tokens, 395, 396, 398, 400–402, 404, 405
Personal projects
    creation, 273–276
    GitLab, 273
    project summary, 276
    special caveats, 277
pom.xml file, 407, 408
PostgreSQL database, 567, 569, 625, 626
    create RDS database, 572, 573
    with RDS
        backup and encryption configurations, 586, 587
        configure database storage, 578, 579
        configure for database identifier and credentials, 576, 577
        connectivity configuration, 580, 581
        database authentication option, 582, 583
        determine database version, 574, 575
        enable auto-scaling, 579, 580
        maintenance configuration, 587, 588
        monitoring section of options, 583–585
        RDS PostgreSQL type selection, 574
        review database costs, 588, 589
        select database template, 575, 576
        select instance type, 577, 578
        selection, standard database creation method, 573
        select type of database, 574
        set database name and DB parameter group, 585, 586
        set security options, 582
        subnet group and public access, 581
        use multi-AZ/single DB instance, 576
PostgreSQL service, 567
Praefect servers, 853, 854, 857, 879
Preliminary AWS setup
    creating ssh key pair, 713, 714
    gitlab-runner-sec-group, 708
    IAM Policy creation, 708, 709
    IAM role creation, 711
    S3 cache bucket setting up, 712, 713
    S3 policy updation, 710, 711
Prioritizing labels, 306, 307
Production-level service, 833
    AMI, automating, 871, 872
    application servers, 847
    automated configuration file, 848
    automation tools, 870
    AWS Direct Connect service, 841
    bastion servers, 846
    configuration management tools
        Ansible, 877
        Chef, 877
        configuring software, 878
        Packer, 878
        Puppet, 877
        User data, 876, 877
    Docker image, 880
    DR
        backups, 838
        regional failure, 838
        requirements, 837
    Gitaly cluster, 847
    HA, 836
        Gitaly server, 837
        GitLab runner manager, 836
    IAM roles and policies, 845

instance-level shared runners, 848
key pairs, 845
monitoring, 840
monthly production costs, 834
    GitLab user audits, 835
    inflationary costs, 834
    license costs, 834
    operational costs, 835
    self-mamaged costs, 835
naming conventions, 842, 844
orchestration, 880
primary service to reside, 841
provisioning server, 846
requirements, 836, 845
resource management tools
    CLI, 872, 873
    CloudFormation, 874
    SDK, 873
    short-term, 874
    third-party, 874
source code management solution, 870, 871
staging service, 839, 840
testing, automation process, 881
TLS certificates, 844
upgrade, 839, 868
upgrade components, 869, 870
VPCs, 843
zero-downtime upgrade, 868, 869
Programming languages, 107, 120, 159, 178, 205, 434, 441, 870, 873, 880
Project deploy tokens, 402–404
Prometheus service, 840, 860
Proof-of-concept (POC), 518, 818, 833, 840, 843, 854, 868
Provisioning server, 846, 856, 861
Pull policy, 243
Puppet, 874, 877
Putty private key, 613
Python, 106–109, 143, 159, 228, 237, 434, 441, 873, 876, 881

R

RDS security group, 567–569, 582
README.md command, 84
README.md file, 18–20, 31, 32, 34, 47, 59, 84, 85, 87, 95, 151, 497
README.md File4.txt, 85
Read-only caches, 244–246
Redis database, 590, 836, 837, 840, 845, 866, 867
    access ElastiCache, 591, 592
    create Redis cluster, 594
        cluster mode configuration, 596
        configuration options, 595
        configure backup and maintenance options, 601, 602
        configure cluster settings, 597, 598
        disable cluster mode, 595
        Redis availability zone placement configuration, 600
        Redis connectivity and associated subnet configuration, 598, 599
        security configuration, 600, 601
        selection of method, 595
        select primary server and replica servers, 599
        set Redis name, description and location, 596
    create Redis security group, 591
    create Redis subnet group, 592–594
    in-memory cache server, 590
    security group, 591
    start Redis service, 602
    subnet group, 593

INDEX

Reference tags, 144–146, 149
Regular expression matches, 159–161
Relational Database Service (RDS)
    create DB subnet group, 570–572
    create PostgreSQL database with RDS (*see* PostgreSQL database)
    create security group, 567–569
    gitlab-rds-sec-group, 568
    service search, 569, 570
    "stop temporarily" option, 589, 590
Release upgrade process
    backup RDS database, 822, 823
    broadcast a system-wide message, 818–820
    create backups, 822
    Gitaly server to new release (*see* Gitaly server)
    gitlab-ce package, 830
    GitLab runner manager, 830, 831
    launch templates, 831
    maintenance mode, licensed sites, 821
    overview, 817, 818
    pause shared runners, 820, 821
    shutdown, 818
    spinning down ASG servers, 821
    spinning up, 822
Remote procedure call (RPC), 638, 824
Reorganization projects and groups
    advanced section, project's settings, 279
    archive project, 281
    change group's URL, 285
    change project's path impacts, 280, 281
    change project's URL path name, 279, 280
    delete group, 286
    delete project, 282
    filesystems, 277
    GitLab groups and projects, 277
    group name change, 285
    projects pending deletion, 283
    rename, 277–279
    transfer project to another group, 283, 284, 287
Repository graph, 33–34, 36, 45, 46, 48, 49, 54, 58, 64, 89
"Resolve conflicts", 50, 64
REST API, 419
    additional pages, retrieving, 430, 432
    curl (*see* Curl)
    documentation, 421
    features, 421
    HTTP methods, 421
    pagination, 428–430
    queries, 434
    requests, 422
    resources, 422, 423
    responses *vs.* GitLab UI, 420, 421
    standalone resources, 432–434
    URL endpoints
        additional information, 425, 426
        patterns, 427
        restricting resource, 423, 424
    URL parameters, restricting results, 424, 425
    URLs *vs.* GitLab UI, 419
Rules
    branch pipelines *vs.* merge request pipelines, 166–168
    build.sh script, 153, 154
    CI/CD variable expressions, 159–161
    CI_PIPELINE_SOURCE, 163–165
    conditions, 152
    effect, 155
    environment variable, 154
    example, 157, 158

file-based conditions,
consideration, 172
file-based rule changes, unit test, 174
file-based rules
conditions, 171, 172
manual run results, 174, 175
pipeline results, 174
key predefined variables values
push event, 162
web event, 162
override variables, 175–178
pipeline view, deploy rule impact, 159
rule-based variable override result
push, 176, 177
run job manual, 177
run build job, build script, 155, 156
run job build-job output, 156
script directory, 153, 154
"when" keyword, 152, 153
vs. workflow rules, 171
workflows, 152
branch pipeline/merge request, 168
GitLab, 169
specific jobs, 168
template, 169
use branch pipeline
workflow, 169–171
Runner manager gl-kms-policy IAM
policy, 709, 710
Runner manager server creation
Docker Engine installation, 717, 718
docker-manager package installation,
718, 719
EC2 server, 714
gitlab-runner software
installation, 715–717
security group gitlab-loadbalancer-
sec-group, 714

S

S3 object cache verification
bucket setup, 747
jpgitlab-poc-cache bucket, 748, 749
S3 artifacts bucket, 750
test jobs, 748
viewing cache details, 749
S3 object storage
ASG (*see* Auto-scaling group (ASG))
IAM role
configure, GitLab server, 673, 674
EC2 instance, 671
GitLab server, verify, 673
selection, GitLab server, 672
KMS
adding labels, 661
administrative permissions, 662
configure, 660
detail view, 664
review and create, 663
service search, 659
usage permissions, 663
view and make changes, 661
launch template
accessing, 680
advanced details, 685
AMI settings, 681, 682
create, 680
creation, 685, 686
IAM instance profile, 684
instance type, 682, 683
key pair, 682, 683
name and version settings, 681
network settings, 683
storage settings, 684
NFS, 659
scaling GitLab service

INDEX

S3 object storage (*cont.*)
    AMI, 675–677
    AWS services, 674, 675
    ELB health check, 677, 679, 680
    readiness health check, 678
    store buckets
        Bucket Versioning, 667, 668
        create, 664, 665, 669
        encryption settings, 668, 669
        general configuration, 665, 666
        GitLab-specific buckets, 670
        ownership configuration, 666, 667
SAML SSO providers, 799
Sandbox mode, 757
SCM managers, 90
Security group (SG)
    basic settings, 550, 551
    creation, 549, 550
    Gitaly cluster, 855
    inbound rules, 551–553
    selection, 553, 554
Self-explanatory, 295
Self-managed GitLab administrator, 64
Self-managed GitLab site, 290
Self-managed service
    achitecture considerations, 515
    administrative considerations, 514, 515
    cost considerations, 517
    disaster recovery (DR)
        considerations, 516
    GitLab support considerations, 517
    high availability (HA)
        considerations, 516
    on-premises *vs.* cloud
        considerations, 514
Self-managed sites, 271
Server-side ssh service
    fast lookup, 657, 658

    host certificates, 655
    host keys, 654
    man-in-the-middle message, 655
    multiple GitLab servers, 654, 655
    static host keys, 656, 657
settings.xml file, 408, 409
Shared runner managers, 879
Shared runners, 820
Shared runners management
    auto-scaling shared runners, 706, 707
    GitLab runners farm setup, 705, 706
    The Do-Nothing Approach, 705
Shell pipeline, 96
Simple Email Service (SES)
    account dashboard, 758
    adding action to SNS, 772–774
    admin user, 764
    create identity, 754, 755
    create rule set, 769, 770
    define rule settings, 770, 771
    define simple record, 767
    email requests, 768, 769
    GitLab server, 764
    hosted zone, 766
    json document, 778
    recipient condition, 771, 772
    routing policy, 766
    rule active, 778
    sandbox mode, 762, 763
    secondary services
        ci secure files, 780
        Container Registry Service
            (*see* Container Registry Service)
        external_diffs, 779
        GitLab registry service (*see* GitLab
            registry service)
        S3 object, 779
    SMTP

create credentials, 758, 760
generated credentials, 761
GitLab, 761, 762
settings page, 759
SNS subscription, 775–777
SNS topic creation, 775
start page, 754
verified identities, 755–757
Simple Notification Service (SNS), 694, 772–778
Software as a Service (SaaS), 3, 4, 15, 358, 517, 518, 611, 656, 791, 835, 871
Software Developer, 5
Software Development Kit (SDK), 873, 874, 876
Source code management (SCM), 65, 66, 90
ssh forwarding, 611, 614, 617, 618, 624
ssh-keygen command, 74
SSH keys, 74–76, 78
Static Application Software Testing (SAST), 140
Static pipelines, 151
String comparisons, 159–161
Subgroups
    add additional members, 261
    creation, 258, 259
    developer-specific views, 262, 263
    developer's view
        top-level group members, 263
        top-level group view, 262
    group members, special projects subgroup, 260, 261
    maintainer-specific views
        special projects members, 264
        special projects subgroup, 263
    roles allowed to create projects, 264, 265

special projects, 260

T

Target object cache, 237
Tasks, 334
    completion, 336, 337
    convertion, list item into task, 340
    creation, 334, 335
    editing, 336
    filtering, 339, 340
    issue summary list, 338
    milestone assignment, 338, 339
    milestone list, 338, 339
Testing frameworks, 881
Testing running jobs, shared runner service
    docker-machine status, 746, 747
    runner details, administrative UI, 745, 746
    test project creation, 743, 744
testme.sh script, 720–722, 724, 731, 738
Test runner with docker-machine
    directory /etc/gitlab-runner, 719
    logging, ssh-agent keys, 724–726
    runner ssh key files, 719
    termination, 723, 724
    testme.sh test script, 720, 721
    test script debugging failures, 721
    verification, 722, 723
The Do-Nothing Approach, 705
Third-party tools, 220, 878
TLS/SSL certificate, 502, 508
    approval, 537
    Certificate Manager service, 532, 533
    domain name, 535, 536
    domain ownership, 536, 537
    Request certificate page, 533–535

INDEX

"To do" label, 304, 305
To-do list, 293
Training label, 308–311
Two-factor authentication (2FA), 521

U

Ubuntu image, 119, 621, 640
Unit test Docker image override, 119
unit-test.sh file, 411
Update GitLab's server configuration
   AMI, 806
   ASG-controlled instances, 815
   ASG instance refresh feature, 816
   AWS auto-scaling group, 806
   create new AMI, 811
   ELB, 807–809
   gitlab.rb file, 806
   instance refresh feature to replace ASG servers, 816
   launch template with new AMI, 812–814
   restart, 806, 807
   spin down ASG servers, 809, 810
   spinning up new ASG servers, 814, 815
Users
   additional LDAP options, licensed sites, 801, 802
   add new user, 792–795
   administrative UI, 791
   authentication service impact, license costs, 802
   ban user, 803
   block, 802, 803
   configure sign-up restrictions, 797
   configure site-wide settings, 796
   deactivation, 803, 804
   deletion, 805
   disabled, deactivated/removed, authentication service, 804
   establish user management policies, 805
   external authentication services, 799
   general settings, restricting users, 796
   initial admin area user list, 792
   LDAP/active directory authentication service, 799–801
   new user form, 793, 794
   new user's page, 795
   password change via administrator, 796
   reset user's password, 795
   SaaS gitlab.com service, 791
   setting sign-in restrictions, 798

V

Variable status tests, 159, 160
Virtual machines (VMs), 108, 109, 619, 680
Virtual Private Cloud (VPC)
   availability zones (AZs), 524, 525
   AWS region, GitLab POC, 522, 523
   components, 527
   creation, 523, 524
   NAT gateway, 526
   options, 526
   security group, 582
   selection, 522
   subnets
      private, 525, 527
      public, 525, 526

W

Web IDE
   committing changes, 23–25
   editing, 18, 19

previewing markdown files, 21
README.md file, 20, 21
reviewing project summary page, 25, 26
viewing changes, source control panel, 22

Web pages
access pages, 502
deploy section, 502
GitLab Pages (*see* GitLab Pages)

Windows-based filesystems, 78

Windows binary, 66
Windows Subsystem for Linux (WSL), 3, 66, 67

X, Y

x64 architecture, 620

Z

Zero-downtime upgrade, 516, 839, 868–869

GPSR Compliance

The European Union's (EU) General Product Safety Regulation (GPSR) is a set of rules that requires consumer products to be safe and our obligations to ensure this.

If you have any concerns about our products, you can contact us on

ProductSafety@springernature.com

In case Publisher is established outside the EU, the EU authorized representative is:

Springer Nature Customer Service Center GmbH
Europaplatz 3
69115 Heidelberg, Germany

www.ingramcontent.com/pod-product-compliance
Lightning Source LLC
LaVergne TN
LVHW080308260326
834688LV00038B/1009